Ethiopia

the Bradt Travel Guide

Philip Briggs
Updated by Kim Wildman

edition
6

www.bradtguides.com

Bradt Travel Guides Ltd, UK
The Globe Pequot Press Inc, USA

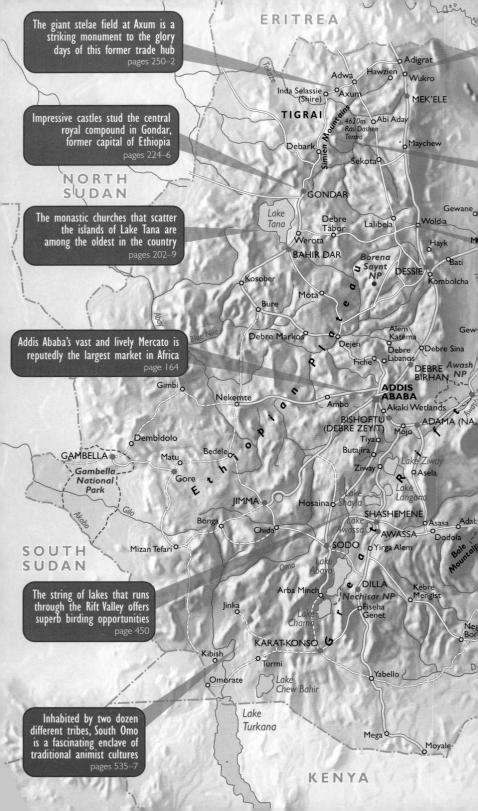

The giant stelae field at Axum is a striking monument to the glory days of this former trade hub
pages 250–2

Impressive castles stud the central royal compound in Gondar, former capital of Ethiopia
pages 224–6

The monastic churches that scatter the islands of Lake Tana are among the oldest in the country
pages 202–9

Addis Ababa's vast and lively Mercato is reputedly the largest market in Africa
page 164

The string of lakes that runs through the Rift Valley offers superb birding opportunities
page 450

Inhabited by two dozen different tribes, South Omo is a fascinating enclave of traditional animist cultures
pages 535–7

ERITREA

NORTH SUDAN

SOUTH SUDAN

KENYA

Adwa
Hawzien
Adigrat
Wukro
Inda Selassie (Shire)
Axum
MEK'ELE
TIGRAI
4620m Ras Dashen Terara
Abi Aday
Simien Mountains
Debark
Maychew
Sekota
GONDAR
Lake Tana
Debre Tabor
Lalibela
Woldia
Gewane
Werota
Hayk
BAHIR DAR
Borena Saynt NP
DESSIE
Bati
Kombolcha
Kosober
Mota
Gew
Bure
Blue Nile
Debre Markos
Dejen
Alem Katema
Debre Sina
Debre Libanos
Debre Birhan
Gimbi
Fiche
DEBRE BIRHAN
Awash NP
Abay
Nekemte
Ambo
ADDIS ABABA
Awash
Akaki Wetlands
ADAMA (NA.
BISHOFTU (DEBRE ZEYIT)
Dembidolo
Bedele
Tiya
Mojo
GAMBELLA
Matu
Butajira
Lake Ziway
Gambella National Park
Gore
Ziway
Asela
Lake Langana
Ethiopian Plateau
JIMMA
Hosaina
Lake Shayla
Akobo
Gilo
Bonga
Chida
SHASHEMENE
Asasa
Adab
Mizan Tefari
Lake Awassa
AWASSA
Dodola
SODO
Yirga Alem
Bale Mountains
Lake Abaya
DILLA
Omo
Arba Minch
Nechisar NP
Kebre Mengist
Jinka
Fiseha Genet
Lake Chamo
Neg Bor
Great Rift Valley
KARAT-KONSO
Kibish
Turmi
Yabello
D
Omorate
Lake Chew Bahir
Mega
Moyale
Lake Turkana

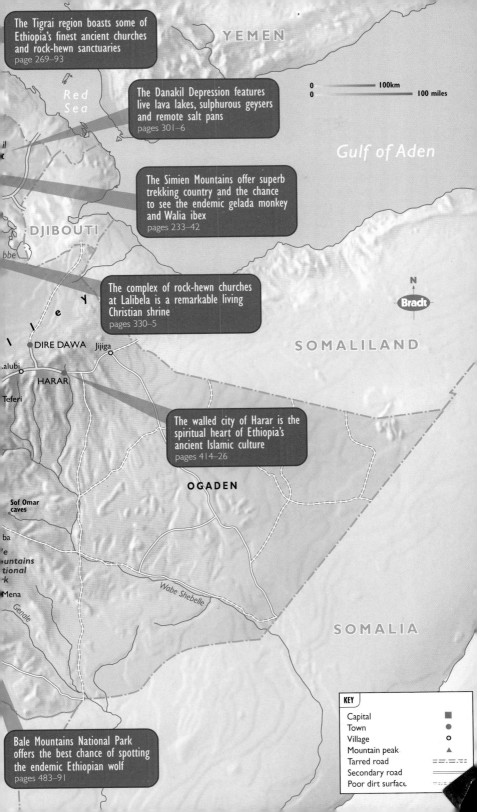

The Tigrai region boasts some of Ethiopia's finest ancient churches and rock-hewn sanctuaries
page 269–93

The Danakil Depression features live lava lakes, sulphurous geysers and remote salt pans
pages 301–6

The Simien Mountains offer superb trekking country and the chance to see the endemic gelada monkey and Walia ibex
pages 233–42

The complex of rock-hewn churches at Lalibela is a remarkable living Christian shrine
pages 330–5

The walled city of Harar is the spiritual heart of Ethiopia's ancient Islamic culture
pages 414–26

Bale Mountains National Park offers the best chance of spotting the endemic Ethiopian wolf
pages 483–91

YEMEN

Red Sea

Gulf of Aden

DJIBOUTI

bbe

SOMALILAND

N

Bradt

DIRE DAWA   Jijiga

alubi

HARAR

Teferi

OGADEN

Sof Omar caves

ba

untains tional k

Mena

Wabe Shebelle

Genale

SOMALIA

0 _____ 100km
0 _____ 100 miles

KEY

Capital	■
Town	●
Village	○
Mountain peak	▲
Tarred road	▬▬▬
Secondary road	▬ ▬ ▬
Poor dirt surface	▬ ▬ ▬

Ethiopia
Don't
miss...

The stelae at Axum
This 23m-high block
of granite is accredited
to King Ezana
(AVZ) page 251

Rock-hewn churches
at Lalibela
Early morning Mass at Bet
Giyorgis, which stands alone
from the two main sites
(AVZ) page 335

Blue Nile Falls
The 45-metre high waterfall is known locally as *Tis Abay* ('Smoke of the Nile')
(KW) page 199

Tribes of the South Omo Valley
Karo people are known for their elaborate body painting
(AVZ) page 552

The Danakil Depression
Afar Well in the Depression sits 116m below sea level
(AVZ) page 301

left A traditional Harari home decorated with baskets and bowls, some of them hundreds of years old (AVZ) page 414

below *Injera*, a large pancake made from the *tef* grain and served with a variety of sauces, is the staple dish in Ethiopia (KW) page 98

bottom The Sof Omar Caves, reputedly the largest in Africa, are an important site of pilgrimage for Ethiopian Muslims (AVZ) page 492

above   Hamer women applying ochre to their hair, Turmi; the Hamer are nomadic pastoralists (AVZ) page 545

right   Visitors to Mecheke, a traditional Konso town, may be greeted by children playing the *kechaita* (AVZ) page 531

below   Afar camel caravan carrying salt from the Danakil Depression to Mekele (AVZ) page 303

bottom   Karo men playing a traditional game at the Omo River, Kolcho (AVZ) page 552

above left   Hamer women tend to roll their hair in ochre and fat; the copper-coloured strands are known as *goscha*, and are a sign of health (AVZ) page 545

above middle   The clay hair buns worn by some Hamer men indicate that they have killed a person or a dangerous animal within the last year (AVZ) page 548

above right   Karo women often sport striking hairstyles (AVZ) page 552

above left   Mursi woman with lip plate. These are put in when the girls are around 16 years old, prior to marriage (AVZ) page 554

above centre   Young Afar woman. Her teeth have been filed into a V shape as a sign of beauty (EL) page 398

above right   Tsemai warrior; the feathers on his head indicate he has successfully jumped over a range of cows and is now looking for a wife (EL) page 541

right   The path to marriage can be rough for Mursi men: rival suitors traditionally participate in a violent stick fight (EL) page 554

AUTHOR

Philip Briggs (e *philari@hixnet.co.za*) has been exploring the highways, byways and backwaters of Africa since 1986, when he spent several months backpacking on a shoestring from Nairobi to Cape Town. In 1991, he wrote the Bradt guide to South Africa, the first such guidebook to be published internationally after the release of Nelson Mandela. Over the next decade, Philip wrote a series of pioneering Bradt guides to destinations that were then – and in some cases still are – otherwise practically uncharted by the travel publishing  industry. These included the first dedicated guidebooks to Tanzania, Uganda, Ethiopia, Malawi, Mozambique, Ghana and Rwanda, all of which have been updated for several subsequent editions. More recently, Philip wrote the first guidebook to Somaliland, published by Bradt in 2012. He still spends at least four months on the road every year, usually accompanied by his wife, the travel photographer Ariadne Van Zandbergen, and spends his rest of the time battering away at a keyboard in the sleepy village of Bergville, in the uKhahlamba-Drakensberg region of South Africa.

UPDATER

Kim Wildman (*www.wildwriting.com.au*) has spent the better part of the last ten years exploring the African continent from end to end as a guidebook author, travel writer and wannabe *National Geographic* photographer. She has authored and updated 15 guidebooks including the fifth editions of Lonely Planet's *South Africa* and *West Africa*, Bradt Travel Guides' *Tanzania* and *Ghana*, and Struik-New Holland's *Offbeat South Africa*. Kim has a Masters degree in African studies, attained from the University of Cape Town, and her travel articles have appeared in *Planet Africa*, *Travel Africa*, *AbouTime* and *Voyageur*. She was recently voted one of Tripbase's 100 Favourite Travel Writers in the world.

PUBLISHER'S FOREWORD — *Hilary Bradt*

When people ask me which is my favourite Bradt guide, I answer unhesitatingly: *Ethiopia* by Philip Briggs. Even if they don't ask I tell them, because this is an exceptional book. It receives more fan letters than any other, and one reader who was robbed of the contents of his tent spent two adventurous days retrieving the only possession he couldn't manage without – Philip's guide. Here is an extract from a recent letter:

> I left the safety of my overland tour in Kenya to travel Ethiopia independently. I found myself being shot at by bandits with AK47s in northern Kenya about 50km south of the border with Ethiopia. We were treated OK but all I was left with was the clothes I was wearing and my invaluable Bradt guide to Ethiopia. Due to my determination not to let the bandits win I then spent seven weeks travelling around Ethiopia. Your guide is the best I have used as it really does tell you how to get from tiny villages, to ancient sites, to cities, and to meet the ordinary people. Despite such a stressful start to my adventure, and the difficulties with bus travel in Ethiopia, I will never forget what wonderful people Ethiopians are. Without your guide I would have turned back.

Sixth edition September 2012   First published 1995

Bradt Travel Guides Ltd, IDC House, The Vale, Chalfont St Peter, Bucks SL9 9RZ, England; www.bradtguides.com
Published in the USA by The Globe Pequot Press Inc,
PO Box 480, Guilford, Connecticut 06437-0480

Text copyright © 2012 Philip Briggs
Maps copyright © 2012 Bradt Travel Guides Ltd
Illustrations copyright © 2012 Individual photographers and artists (see below)
Project manager: Maisie Fitzpatrick

ISBN-13: 978 1 84162 414 3

British Library Cataloguing in Publication Data
A catalogue record for this book is available from the British Library

Photographers FLPA: Neil Bowman (NB/FLPA), David Hosking (DH/FLPA), Ignacio Yufera (IY/FLPA); Eric Lafforgue (EL); Shutterstock: Galina Andrushko (GA/SS); Ariadne Van Zandbergen (AVZ); Kim Wildman (KW)
Front cover Meskel ceremony, Addis Ababa (AVZ)
Back cover South Omo tribesman (EL), Church of St George, Lalibela (GA/SS)
Title page Red hot pokers, Bale Mountains National Park (AVZ), Painting in the Narga Selassie Monastery, Lake Tana (AVZ), Hamer man, South Omo Valley, Turmi (AVZ)
Illustrations Annabel Milne, Carol Vincer, Mike Unwin, Roger Barnes
Maps David McCutcheon

Typeset from the author's disk by Wakewing, High Wycombe
Production managed by Jellyfish Print Solutions; printed in India

CONTRIBUTORS

Frank Rispin first went to Ethiopia in 1970, with his wife Ann and two small sons, to work at Sandford School. They returned to the UK with an Ethiopian daughter. In 1981 he became a headteacher in Southampton. Returning to Addis in 2002 he was soon involved in tourism. Meanwhile Ann set about starting new international schools such as BIS Addis. Today he writes regularly for Ethiopian Airlines' *Selamta* magazine. This is his first major venture into guidebook updating. He would like to thank Abram Makonnen and Behailu Fedlu, and Genet Mengistu, for their invaluable help with the Addis Ababa chapter.

John Graham, whose lively writings about Ethiopia for the *Addis Tribune* form the basis of several textboxes in this guide, grew up in Canada and obtained his BA in African history at the University of Calgary. Since volunteering with Oxfam for the 1984 famine in Ethiopia, John has lived in and visited much of Africa, working with Oxfam and Save the Children. A resident of Ethiopia since 1997, he has travelled throughout the country, and also regularly contributes travel articles to the *Entrepreneur* newspaper and the Ethiopian Airlines' *Selamta* magazine. His first book of travel essays, *Ethiopia off the Beaten Trail*, was published by Shama Books.

Ariadne Van Zandbergen (*ariadne@hixnet.co.za; www.africaimagelibrary.co.za*) is the main photographic contributor to this book, and she also supplied all update information for sections on the Simien Mountains, Arba Minch, the Konso Highlands, South Omo and the Danakil Desert. A freelance photographer and tour guide, Ariadne was born and raised in Belgium, before travelling through Africa from Morocco to South Africa in 1994–95. Now married to Philip Briggs and resident in South Africa, she has visited more than 25 African countries and her photographs have appeared in numerous books, maps, periodicals and pamphlets. Her first photographic book, *Africa: Continent of Contrasts*, a collaboration with Philip Briggs and photographer Martin Harvey, was published in 2005.

Acknowledgements

My deepest debt of gratitude goes to my three drivers: Ephrem Zegeye, Birehanu Andarge and Teshome Worku for their knowledge, skills and unending patience – not to mention their dogged determination to make sure I visited every last new hotel and tourist sight in Ethiopia! Hand-in-hand with their efforts are those of their respective companies: Mekonnen Mengesha, Margaret Woldetensae, Tesfaye Mideksa and everyone at Galaxy Express, Yared Belete and the staff at GETTS, and Nebait Yessuwork and Ephrem Merid at NTO. In Addis Ababa I'd like to thank Hewi Elias (Addis Regency Hotel), in Bahir Dar Bisrat Weldu (Ghion Hotel), in Lalibela Getachew Tekeba (Mountain View Hotel), Messay Mekonnen (Tukul Village) and Habte Yitbarek, in Gondar Sisay Asefa, and Anne-Marie Stewart (EWCP), Zegeye Kibrel (EWCP), Biniyam Admassu (FZS), Eliza Richman (FZS) and everyone in beautiful Bale. Special thanks also to Frank and Ann Rispin for showing me the ins and outs of Addis, Aiste Jakobsen (Simien Lodge) for helping me hit Harar, Sue Guthrie for the fun, laughs and expert advice, Rowena Luk for inadvertently taking part in my adventure, Mark Chapman (Tesfa), Nansi Gidiess (Ethiopian Airlines), Assefa Azene (Kibran Tours), and Tony Hickey (Ethiopian Quadrants) and the Friday night crew at Road Runners. Finally, to Philip Briggs for his guidance and faith and as always the team at Bradt for putting together another terrific guide.

Contents

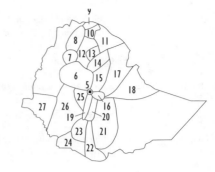

LIST OF MAPS

KEY TO SYMBOLS

—·—·—	International boundary
- - - - -	Province boundary
	National park/protected area
	National forest park/reserve
✈ ✈	Airport (international/domestic)
⛴	Ferry route (major/small boat)
	Paved roads (regional) main/other
===----	Unpaved roads other/4x4 track/footpath
	Paved roads (town plans) main/other
	Unpaved roads (town plans) main/other
------	Unpaved minor road/footpath
‖‖‖‖‖‖	Steps
	Railway
·············	Hike/trek/footpath featured in the text
⛽	Filling station/service garage
🚌	Bus station etc
⌂	Hotel/inn etc
☆	Night club/casino
✕	Restaurant/café etc
⌾	Bar
⌷	Café
E	Embassy
i	Tourist information office/kiosk

✉	Post office
e	Internet access
✚	Hospital/clinic etc
⬥	Museum/art gallery
☺	Theatre/cinema
⊞	Important/historic building
⌣	City wall
ᛘ	City gate
ᛘ	Castle/fort/fortification
†	Church/cathedral
✝	Cemetery (Christian)
⌡	Mosque
$	Bank/bureau de change
⚲	Statue/monument
∴	Archaeological/historic site
大	Stadium
▲	Summit (height in metres)
❊	Viewpoint
✿	Garden
Ä	Camp site
	Escarpment/cliff
	Marsh/swamp
	Urban park
	Urban Market

NOTE ABOUT MAPS

Several maps use grid lines to allow easy location of sites. Map grid references are listed in square brackets after listings in the text, with page number followed by grid number, eg: [136 A1].

ETHIOPIA UPDATES WEBSITE

For the latest travel news about Ethiopia, please visit the new interactive Bradt Ethiopia update website: http://bradtethiopiaupdate.wordpress.com.

Administered by *Ethiopia* author, Philip Briggs, this website will supplement the printed Bradt guidebook, providing a forum whereby the latest travel news can be publicised online with immediate effect.

This update website is a free service for readers of Bradt's *Ethiopia* – and for anybody else who cares to drop by and browse – but its success will depend greatly on the input of those selfsame readers, whose collective experience of Ethiopia's tourist attractions and facilities will always be more broad and divergent than those of any individual author.

So if you have any comments, queries, grumbles, insights, news or other feedback, you're invited to post them directly on the website, or to email them to Philip at e philari@hixnet.co.za.

Introduction

My first contact with things Ethiopian came by chance, when a friend suggested a meal at a Nairobi restaurant run by Ethiopian refugees. The food alone was extraordinary – a delicious fiery orange stew called *kai wat*, splattered on what looked like a piece of foam rubber with the lateral dimensions of a bicycle tyre, and was apparently called *injera* – but even that didn't prepare me for what was to follow.

A troupe of white-robed musicians approached our table and erupted into smirking discord. Then, signalled by an alarming vibrato shriek, all hell burst loose in the form of a solitary Ethiopian dancer. Her mouth was contorted into the sort of psychotically rapturous grimace you'd expect from Jack Nicholson at his most hammy. Her eyes glowed. Her shoulders jerked and twitched to build up a manic, dislocating rhythm. Beneath her robe – driven, presumably, by her metronomic shoulders – a pair of diminutive breasts somehow contrived to flap up and down with an agitated regularity suggestive of a sparrow trapped behind a closed window. I left that room with one overwhelming impression: Ethiopians are completely bonkers. I knew, too, that I had to visit their country.

A year later, back in July 1994, I found myself flying to Addis Ababa to research the first edition of this guide. In the months that followed, I discovered Ethiopia to be every bit as fantastic as I had hoped: culturally, historically and scenically, it is the most extraordinary country I have ever visited. Over subsequent years, however, I have learned that it is difficult to talk about Ethiopia without first saying what it is not.

To the world at large, Ethiopia is practically synonymous with famine and desert, to the extent that the Ethiopian Airlines' Johannesburg office regularly receives tactful enquiries about what, if any, food is served on their flights. This widespread misconception, regarding a country set in a continent plagued by drought and erratic rainfall, says much about the workings of the mass media. It says rather less about Ethiopia.

Contrary to Western myth, the elevated central plateau that covers half of Ethiopia's surface area, and supports the vast majority of its population, is the most extensive contiguous area of fertile land in the eastern side of Africa. The deserts do exist, stretching from the base of the plateau to the Kenyan border and the Red Sea and Somali coast, but they are, as you might expect, thinly populated; they have little impact on the life of most Ethiopians – and they are most unlikely to be visited by tourists. To all intents and purposes, the fertile highland plateau is Ethiopia.

Ethiopia's fledgling tourist industry revolves around the richest historical heritage in sub-Saharan Africa. The town of Axum was, from the 1st to the 7th century AD, the centre of an empire that stretched from the Nile River across the Red Sea to Yemen. The medieval capital of Lalibela boasts a cluster of monolithic rock-hewn churches regarded by many as the unofficial eighth wonder of the world. There is also Gondar, the site of five 17th-century castles built by King Fasil and his successors. And all around the country are little-visited monasteries and other rock-hewn churches, many of them over 1,000 years old and still in active use.

Although historical sites are the focal point of tourism in Ethiopia, they threaten at times to be swamped by the breathtaking scenery. Every bus trip in the Ethiopian Highlands is a visual treat, whether you are snaking into the 1km-deep Blue Nile Gorge, rolling past the sculpted sandstone cliffs and valleys of Tigrai, undulating over the grassy moorland and cultivated fields of the central highlands, winding through the lush forests of the west and south, or belting across the Rift Valley floor, its acacia scrub dotted by extinct volcanoes, crumbling lava flows and beautiful lakes, and hemmed in by the sheer walls of the Rift Escarpment. Mere words cannot do justice to Ethiopia's scenery.

Isolated from similar habitats by the fringing deserts, the Ethiopian Highlands have a remarkably high level of biological endemicity. Large mammals such as the Simien fox, mountain nyala, Walia ibex and gelada baboon are found nowhere but the highlands, as are 30 of the 800-plus species of birds which have been recorded in the country. This makes national parks like Bale and Simien a paradise for natural history enthusiasts, as well as for the hikers and mule trekkers who visit them for their scenery. Over a period of time, Ethiopia's recognised tourist attractions become incidental to the thrill of just being in this most extraordinary country. The people of the highlands have assimilated a variety of African, Judaic and even Egyptian influences to form one of the most unusual and self-contained cultures on this planet. Dervla Murphy said in 1968 that 'travelling in Ethiopia gives one the Orlando-like illusion of living through different centuries'. This remains the case: the independence of spirit which made Ethiopia the one country to emerge uncolonised from the 19th-century Scramble for Africa is still its most compelling attraction; even today, there is a sense of otherness to Ethiopia that is as intoxicating as it is elusive. Practically every tangible facet of Ethiopian culture is unique. Obscured by the media-refracted glare of the surrounding deserts, Ethiopia feels like the archetypal forgotten land.

Ethiopia confounds every expectation. Many people arrive expecting a vast featureless desert and human degradation, and instead find themselves overwhelmed by the country's majestic landscapes and climatic abundance, and immersed in a culture infectiously besotted with itself and its history. While the rest of the world taps its feet, Ethiopia, I suspect, will always breakdance with its shoulders. And, in case you're wondering, there's really no need to pack sandwiches for the flight.

Part One

GENERAL INFORMATION

ETHIOPIA AT A GLANCE

Location Northeast Africa; it shares borders with Somalia, Sudan, Eritrea, Kenya and Djibouti

Size 1,104,300km²; the tenth-largest country in Africa

Climate Varies by region, from temperate highlands to hot lowland desert

Status Federal republic

Population 90.8 million (July 2011 estimate, *CIA World Factbook*)

Life expectancy 56 years (2011 estimate, *CIA World Factbook*)

Capital Addis Ababa, population 2.8 million (2009, *CIA World Factbook*)

Other main towns Dire Dawa, Adama (Nazret), Gondar, Dessie, Mekele, Bahir Dar, Jimma, Bishoftu (Debre Zeyit), Awassa, Harar

Economy Subsistence agriculture, coffee, chat, mining, tourism

GDP US$1,000 per capita (*CIA World Factbook*, 2010 purchase power parity (PPP) estimate)

Languages Official language Amarigna (Amharic); Oromifa and English are most widely spoken

Religion Main religions are Ethiopian Orthodox Christianity, Islam and Protestant Christianity

Currency Birr

Rate of exchange US$1 = birr 18, €1 = birr 22 and £1 = birr 27 (June 2012)

National airline/airport Ethiopian Airlines/Bole International Airport

International telephone code +251

Time GMT +3

Electric voltage 220V current alternating at 50Hz. Plug standards vary; most common are the Type C (European two-pin) and Type L (Italian three-pin).

Weights and measures Metric

Flag Vertical bands of green at the top, yellow in the centre and red at the base. In the middle of this is a symbol representing the sun – a yellow pentagram from which emanate several yellow rays.

National anthem 'March Forward, Dear Mother Ethiopia'

National holiday 28 May, Downfall of the Derg

TRANSCRIPTION OF ETHIOPIAN NAMES

Ethiopians use a unique script to transcribe Amarigna and several other languages. This has led to a wide divergence in English transcriptions of Ethiopian place names and other Amarigna words, and also inconsistent use of double characters. Even a straightforward place name like Matu is spelt variously as Metu, Mattuu, etc, while names like Zikwala can become virtually unrecognisable (Zouquela). When consulting different books and maps, it's advisable to keep an eye open for varied spellings and to use your imagination. My policy in this book has been to go for the simplest spelling, or the one that to me sounds closest to the local pronunciation. I have stuck with Ethiopian versions of names: for instance, Tewodros (Theodore), Yohannis (John), Maryam (Mary) and Giyorgis (George). The exception is that if hotels or restaurants are signposted in English, then I have normally (but not infallibly) followed the signposted spelling exactly.

1

Background Information

GEOGRAPHY

LOCATION The Federal Republic of Ethiopia, formerly known as Abyssinia, is a land-locked republic in northeast Africa, or the Horn of Africa, lying between 3.5 and 15°N and 33 and 48°E. Ethiopia shares its longest border, of more than 1,600km, with Somalia to the east (this border includes part of the as yet unrecognised state of Somaliland). Ethiopia is bounded to the northeast by Eritrea for 910km, and by Djibouti for 340km. It shares a southern border of 830km with Kenya, and a western border of 1,600km with Sudan.

LANDSCAPE The Ethiopian landscape is dominated by the volcanically formed Ethiopian or Abyssinian Highlands, a region often but somewhat misleadingly referred to as a plateau, since it is in fact dramatically mountainous. The central plateau, isolated on three sides by low-lying semi-desert or desert, has an average altitude of above 2,000m and includes 20 peaks of 4,000m or higher. The Ethiopian Highlands are bisected by the Rift Valley, which starts at the Red Sea, then continues through the Danakil Depression (a desert area that contains one of the lowest points on the earth's surface) and through southern Ethiopia to Mozambique in southern Africa. The part of the Rift Valley south of Addis Ababa is notable for its string of eight lakes.

The most extensive mountain ranges on the highlands are the Simiens, which lie directly north of Gondar and rise to the fourth-highest peak in Africa, Ras Dejen (also spelt Ras Dashen), whose height is normally given as 4,533m. Another significant range is the Bale Mountains, which lie in the southern highlands to the east of the Rift Valley.

The Ethiopian Highlands form the source of four major river systems. The best known of these is the Blue Nile, or Abay, which rises near Lake Tana in the northwest, and supplies most of the water that flows into Egypt's Nile Valley. The Baro and Tekaze (or Shire) rivers feed the White Nile, the river that flows out of Lake Victoria in Uganda to join the Blue Nile at Khartoum in Sudan. Within Ethiopia, the Blue Nile arcs through the highlands south of Lake Tana to form a vast gorge comparable in size and depth to Namibia's Fish River Canyon and the Grand Canyon in the USA.

Several other major river systems run through Ethiopia. The Wabe Shebelle rises in the Bale area and courses through the southeast of the country into Somalia. The Omo River rises in the western highlands around Kaffa to drain into Lake Turkana on the Kenyan border. The Awash rises in Showa and then follows the course of the Rift Valley northwards before disappearing into a series of desert lakes near the Djiboutian border.

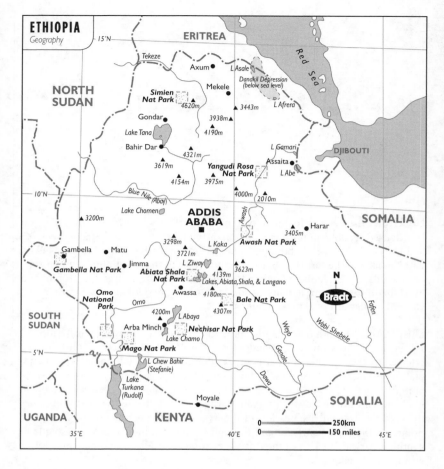

ETHIOPIA
Geography

15°N

ERITREA

Red Sea

NORTH SUDAN

Tekeze

Axum ●

L Asale

Danakil Depression (below sea level)

Mekele ●

▲ 3443m

L Afrera

Simien Nat Park ▲ 4620m

3938m ▲

Gondar ●

4190m

Lake Tana

Bahir Dar ●

▲ 4321m

L Gamari

DJIBOUTI

3619m ▲

Yangudi Rosa Nat Park ▲ 3975m

Assaita ●

L Abe

▲ 4154m

10°N

Blue Nile (Abay)

4000m ▲

2010m ▲

Lake Chomen

ADDIS ABABA ■

Awash

SOMALIA

▲ 3200m

3298m ▲

L Koka

3405m ▲ Harar ●

3721m ▲

Awash Nat Park

Gambella ●

Matu ●

L Ziway

Jimma ●

Abiata Shala Nat Park

4139m ▲

3623m ▲

Gambella Nat Park

Lakes, Abiata, Shala, & Langano

Omo National Park

Awassa ●

4180m ▲

Bale Nat Park

N

Bradt

Fafen

Omo

4200m ▲

4307m ▲

SOUTH SUDAN

L Abaya

Arba Minch ●

Nechisar Nat Park

Wejb

Wabi Shebele

Lake Chamo

Genale

5°N

Mago Nat Park

L Chew Bahir (Stefanie)

Dowa

Lake Turkana (Rudolf)

Moyale ●

SOMALIA

UGANDA

KENYA

250km

150 miles

35°E

40°E

45°E

CLIMATE

Ethiopia shows a wide climatic variation, ranging from the peaks of Bale, which receive periodic snowfall, to regular daytime temperatures of over 50°C in the Danakil Desert (see *Climate chart* box, pages 6–7). As a rule, the central highlands have a temperate climate and average daytime temperature of 16°C, belying their proximity to the Equator. The eastern lowlands and the far south are dry and hot. The western lowlands are moist and hot, making them the one part of the country that feels truly tropical. The southern Rift Valley, much of which lies at the relatively high altitude of 1,500m, is temperate to hot and seasonally moist.

The precipitation pattern in the northern and central highlands is that the bulk of the rain falls between mid June and early October. This pattern changes as you head further south: the rainy season in the Rift Valley generally starts and ends a few weeks earlier than in the highlands, while in South Omo most of the rain falls in March, April and May, and other parts of the south have two rainy seasons, falling either side of the highlands' rainy season of July to September. Contrary to popular perceptions, most highland parts of Ethiopia receive a healthy average annual rainfall figure, with the far west being

ETHIOPIAN CLIMATIC ZONES

Ethiopians traditionally recognise five climatic zones, each of which has distinctive features linked to altitude, rainfall and temperature. These are as follows:

BEREHA Hot and arid desert lowlands that typically lie below 500m and receive significantly less than 500mm of precipitation annually. Not generally cultivatable so mostly inhabited by pastoralists, eg: most of the Somali border area and the Rift Valley north of Addis Ababa.

KOLLA Warm to hot mid-altitude locations that receive sufficient rainfall for cultivation without relying on irrigation, eg: the Rift Valley between Addis Ababa and Awassa, or the Gambella region.

WEYNA DEGA Warm to cool medium- to high-altitude locations typically receiving more than 1,500mm of rainfall annually, often naturally forested though much of this has been cleared over the centuries. Excellent for cultivation of grains (especially *tef*) and coffee, eg: Addis Ababa, Gondar, Asela, Goba, Jimma, Matu and most other highlands below the 2,600m contour.

DEGA Cool to cold, medium-to-high rainfall, high-altitude locations that would naturally support grassland or coniferous forest and now are mostly used to cultivate grains such as barley and wheat, eg: Dinsho, Debre Birhan, Mehal Meda, Ankober and other highland areas with an altitude in the range 2,600–3,200m.

WORCH Chilly, medium-to-low rainfall Afro-alpine regions supporting a cover of heath-like vegetation that isn't generally conducive to cultivation, eg: Sanetti Plateau (Bale National Park), the eastern peaks of the Simiens, Guassa Plateau and other plateaux or peaks above 3,200–3,500m.

particularly moist – indeed much of the southwest receives an average annual rainfall in excess of 2,000mm.

The northeast highlands are much drier, and have a less reliable rainy season, than other highland parts of Ethiopia. Tigrai and parts of Amhara are prone to complete rainfall failure; this tends to happen about once every decade. It was such a rainfall failure that, exacerbated by tactics of the Mengistu government, led to the notorious famine of 1985. In normal years, however, the highlands become something of a mudbath during the rains, with an average of 1,000mm falling over two or three months. Fortunately, from a tourist's point of view, rain tends to fall in dramatic storms that end as suddenly as they start, a situation that is infinitely more conducive to travel than days of protracted drizzle.

HISTORY

Much of Ethiopia's fascination lies in its myriad historical sites. This is the only country in sub-Saharan Africa with tangible historical remnants stretching back to the ancient Mediterranean civilisations. One might reasonably expect there to be a

CLIMATE CHART

The local climate charts listed below have been selected to reflect the enormous regional variation in temperature, rainfall and seasons noted throughout the country.

ADDIS ABABA (2,400M)	Jan	Feb	Mar	Apr	May	Jun	Jul	Aug	Sep	Oct	Nov	Dec
Ave temp (°C)	16	17	18	18	18	17	16	16	15	15	15	15
Rainfall (mm)	30	40	45	70	90	110	210	280	160	30	10	15

ADAMA (1,130M)	Jan	Feb	Mar	Apr	May	Jun	Jul	Aug	Sep	Oct	Nov	Dec
Ave temp (°C)	19	21	22	23	22	21	20	20	19	19	18	18
Rainfall (mm)	10	15	60	55	45	60	180	220	100	30	10	20

DIRE DAWA (1,200M)	Jan	Feb	Mar	Apr	May	Jun	Jul	Aug	Sep	Oct	Nov	Dec
Ave temp (°C)	21	23	25	27	28	27	25	25	25	23	22	21
Rainfall (mm)	0	30	45	60	40	30	100	130	60	30	5	5

GAMBELLA (400M)	Jan	Feb	Mar	Apr	May	Jun	Jul	Aug	Sep	Oct	Nov	Dec
Ave temp (°C)	28	30	31	29	27	25	25	26	26	26	27	27
Rainfall (mm)	5	10	25	50	160	175	220	230	180	100	50	10

GOBA (2,750M)	Jan	Feb	Mar	Apr	May	Jun	Jul	Aug	Sep	Oct	Nov	Dec
Ave temp (°C)	12	13	14	14	14	15	14	13	13	12	11	12
Rainfall (mm)	25	30	75	125	100	50	90	115	120	130	60	15

GONDAR (2,120M)	Jan	Feb	Mar	Apr	May	Jun	Jul	Aug	Sep	Oct	Nov	Dec
Ave temp (°C)	19	20	21	22	21	19	18	18	19	19	18	18
Rainfall (mm)	10	10	25	40	90	170	310	300	160	30	20	15

HARAR (1,850M)	Jan	Feb	Mar	Apr	May	Jun	Jul	Aug	Sep	Oct	Nov	Dec
Ave temp (°C)	18	20	20	20	19	18	18	18	18	19	18	18
Rainfall (mm)	10	20	30	100	50	50	80	150	75	30	10	10

huge body of writing on Ethiopian history and its relationship to other civilisations. There isn't. To quote Philip Marsden-Smedley's *A Far Country*: 'Ethiopia crept up on me ... Often, where I'd expected a chapter, in general histories of the Christian Church, books of African art, there was a single reference – or nothing at all. And soon I found the same facts recurring and realised that Ethiopian scholarship was, like its subject, cut off from the mainstream. The only general history of the country I could find was published in 1935.'

In 1994, when I tried to get a general grasp of Ethiopian history before visiting the country, I had a similar experience. I was startled to discover that Oliver and Fage's *Short History of Africa* contains not one reference to Axum. In the end, my limited knowledge stemmed from a French history translated into English in 1959, unearthed for me by a friend who works in South Africa's largest library, and a 1992 book by Graham Hancock called *The Sign and the Seal* which attempts to substantiate the Ethiopian claim that the Ark of the Covenant resides in Axum. The situation improved when I arrived in Ethiopia to find a fair number of locally published books of a historical nature. But, even then, armed with all I could find on Ethiopian

JIMMA (2,300M)	Jan	Feb	Mar	Apr	May	Jun	Jul	Aug	Sep	Oct	Nov	Dec
Ave temp (°C)	18	19	20	20	19	19	18	18	19	18	18	17
Rainfall (mm)	40	50	85	160	150	210	195	175	160	90	20	30

KELAFO* (400M)*	Jan	Feb	Mar	Apr	May	Jun	Jul	Aug	Sep	Oct	Nov	Dec
Ave temp (°C)	28	30	32	33	30	28	28	29	30	30	29	30
Rainfall (mm)	0	0	25	50	40	0	0	5	10	30	40	5

*typical eastern desert 'Bereha' climate

MATU (1,800M)	Jan	Feb	Mar	Apr	May	Jun	Jul	Aug	Sep	Oct	Nov	Dec
Ave temp (°C)	18	20	21	21	20	18	18	19	19	18	17	17
Rainfall (mm)	40	45	90	80	210	240	300	290	285	140	45	50

MEKELE (2,500M)	Jan	Feb	Mar	Apr	May	Jun	Jul	Aug	Sep	Oct	Nov	Dec
Ave temp (°C)	17	18	18	19	20	18	18	18	18	17	17	16
Rainfall (mm)	0	10	25	30	25	35	200	210	60	10	10	5

MOYALE (1,200M)	Jan	Feb	Mar	Apr	May	Jun	Jul	Aug	Sep	Oct	Nov	Dec
Ave temp (°C)	24	24	23	22	21	20	20	21	21	22	23	23
Rainfall (mm)	10	15	50	210	90	20	15	20	20	200	110	50

NEGELE BORENA (1,450M)	Jan	Feb	Mar	Apr	May	Jun	Jul	Aug	Sep	Oct	Nov	Dec
Ave temp (°C)	19	21	20	19	18	18	17	18	19	18	18	19
Rainfall (mm)	15	30	40	185	155	15	10	10	30	180	30	15

NEKEMTE (2,000M)	Jan	Feb	Mar	Apr	May	Jun	Jul	Aug	Sep	Oct	Nov	Dec
Ave temp (°C)	19	20	21	20	18	17	16	18	18	19	19	18
Rainfall (mm)	15	20	50	80	260	380	400	375	260	90	75	30

SODO (2,000M)	Jan	Feb	Mar	Apr	May	Jun	Jul	Aug	Sep	Oct	Nov	Dec
Ave temp (°C)	23	23	22	21	20	18	16	18	20	23	23	22
Rainfall (mm)	25	20	90	130	140	130	210	260	120	130	45	30

history, I felt a strong sense of dissatisfaction with my booty. What was lacking was a centre from which a layperson could explore more esoteric or specific writings. This situation has improved since 1994, with the publication of a couple of useful and concise general histories (see *Appendix 5*, *Further information*, page 613), though both of these are primarily concerned with modern rather than ancient Ethiopia.

A basic grasp of ancient Ethiopian history is integral to getting the most from the country. Tourism to Ethiopia revolves around historical sites; no less important, Ethiopians identify strongly with their history, and they generally enjoy speaking to visitors who share their enthusiasm. I only wish there was a balanced general history I could recommend to readers. To produce something that will suffice, I have to work from a plethora of sources that are consistent only in their divergence. The traditional beliefs held by most Ethiopians and the orthodoxies of Western historians might as well be parallel universes. Even 'proper' historical writing is riddled with contradictory dates and ideas, and many of the oft-repeated orthodoxies are refuted by more recent and mostly unpublished archaeological research taking place in the country right now.

Fortunately, it is not my job to resolve the apparent contradictions of Ethiopian history, but to attempt to transmit its fascination and my enthusiasm to tourists. Bearing this in mind, what follows draws equally on the fantastic speculation of folklore and the necessarily conservative speculation of historians; in order to provide some balance, I have not been averse to a little speculation myself. Ethiopian history is too absorbing to be treated as blandly as sticking to the 'facts' would require. Determining the facts before about AD1600 is in any case full of open questions. To me, it matters less that the Queen of Sheba was really Ethiopian or Haile Selassie was really descended from the Jewish King Solomon than it does that most Ethiopians believe it to be true. It is such beliefs that have shaped Ethiopian culture; through repetition, they have attained a vicarious truth.

In the section on pre-Christian history, I am indebted to Graham Hancock's *The Sign and the Seal*, a book that is certainly not without flaws, but which does have the virtues of ignoring the orthodoxies where the evidence points elsewhere, and of probing the past with enthusiasm, imagination and an apparent lack of preconceptions. I also owe a great debt to Bahru Zewde's excellent and commendably plainly written *A History of Modern Ethiopia 1855–1974*; were it not for this book, the relevant period in this section would be considerably less cohesive than it is.

THE CRADLE OF HUMANKIND? The East African Rift Valley is almost certainly where modern human beings and their hominid ancestors evolved, and Ethiopia has as strong a claim as any African country in this respect. Hominids are generally divided into two genera, *Australopithecus* and *Homo*, the former extinct for at least a million years, and the latter now represented by only one species – *Homo sapiens* (modern humans). The paucity of hominid fossils collected before the 1960s meant that for many years it was assumed the most common australopithecine fossil, *A. africanus*, had evolved directly into the genus *Homo* and was thus man's oldest identifiable ancestor.

This linear theory of human evolution blurred when the Leakeys' discoveries at Olduvai Gorge in Tanzania suggested that at least two types of australopithecine had existed, and that the later species *A. robustus* had less in common with modern man than its more lightly built ancestor *A. africanus*. Then, in 1972, the discovery of a two-million-year-old skull of a previously undescribed species, *Homo habilis*, at Lake Turkana in Kenya, provided the first conclusive evidence that some *Australopithecus* and *Homo* species had lived alongside each other for at least one million years. As more fossils came to light, including older examples of *Homo erectus* (the direct ancestor of modern humans), it became clear that several different hominid species had existed alongside each other in the Rift Valley until perhaps half a million years ago. Increasingly, it looked as if all known members of *Australopithecus* and *Homo* belonged to two discrete evolutionary lines, presumably with a yet-to-be-discovered common ancestor. The only flaw in this theory was the timescale involved: it didn't seem possible that there had been adequate time for the oldest-known australopithecine to evolve into *Homo habilis*.

In 1974, an almost complete hominid skeleton was discovered by Donald Johanson in Hadar, in the Danakil region of northern Ethiopia. The skeleton, named Lucy (the song 'Lucy in the Sky with Diamonds' was playing in camp shortly after the discovery), turned out to be that of a 3.5-million-year-old australopithecine of an entirely new species dubbed *A. afarensis*. The discovery of Lucy not only demonstrated that bipedal (or semi-bipedal – the length of *afarensis*'s arms suggest it was as comfortable swinging through the trees as it was on its morning jog) hominids had evolved much earlier than previously assumed, but it also created a likely candidate for the common ancestry of later australopithecine species and the human chain of evolution. As more *A. afarensis* fragments came to light in the Danakil, many palaeontologists argued that the wide divergence in their skull and body sizes indicated that not one but several australopithecine species lived in the Danakil at this time, and that any one of them – or none of them, for that matter – might be ancestral to modern humans. This discrepancy was clarified in 1994, when the first complete male *afarensis* skull was uncovered less than 10km from where Lucy had lain. It is now clear that the difference in size is because *afarensis* males were almost twice the weight of females. And if all the Danakil australopithecine fossils are of one species, then that species was remarkably successful, as the known specimens span a period of almost one million years. The history of palaeontology is littered with fossils that rewrote the human evolutionary tree overnight but, until another such fossil is unearthed, it is difficult to escape the conclusion that Lucy and her kin were the common ancestor of the genus *Homo* and later australopithecine species. Incidentally, Lucy is now on display in the National Museum in Addis Ababa.

In the 1960s it was widely thought that humans and apes diverged around 20 million years ago, but recent DNA evidence has shown modern man and chimpanzees to be far more closely related than previously assumed – in fact, many biologists feel that less biased observers would place us in the same genus as chimpanzees, who are more closely related to humans than they are to any other living creature. It is now thought that the hominid and chimpanzee evolutionary lines diverged from a common ancestor between four and six million years ago. A recent fossil discovery in the Danakil is being mooted widely as the so-called missing link, the most recent common ancestor of modern African apes and modern humans. The fossils consist of the incomplete bones and the dentition of 17 hominids that lived in a forested habitat about 4.4 million years ago. The few bones discovered to date don't include specimens of legs or hips, which makes precise classification impossible, but the dentition is closer to that of chimpanzees than to any known hominid species, yet it has several hominid features. The species has been classified provisionally as a form of australopithecine, dubbed *A. ramidus*, but it may well belong to an entirely new genus that provides the final link in tracing the broad sweep of human evolution.

BEFORE LUCY

In 2001 it was announced that the northern Ethiopian Rift Valley had yielded yet another hominid fossil find of shattering significance. The jawbone and other parts of a 5.8-million-year-old hominid were unearthed in 1997 by Yohannis Haile Selassie, an Ethiopian graduate student. The fossils have been assigned to a new genus *Ardipithecus*, which shows clear affiliations with both chimpanzees and humans, and almost certainly forms the so-called missing link between hominids and their ape-like ancestors. Furthermore, while it remains the case that tracing the line of human ancestry based on the existing fossil evidence is akin to guessing the subject of a 1,000-piece jigsaw based on a random 20 pieces, this new finding, in an area that was densely forested six million years ago, does cast some doubt on the accepted notion that the first hominids started to walk upright as an evolutionary adaptation to a savanna environment.

So, is Ethiopia the cradle of humankind? Well, the specifics of human evolution remain controversial, and are likely to do so for some time, largely because it is impossible to gauge how complete or representative the known fossil record is. The discovery of large numbers of hominid fossils in one area may indicate simply that conditions at the time were suitable for fossilisation, that current conditions are suitable for recovering those fossils and, crucially, that palaeontologists are looking there. If a vital link in the evolutionary chain was once distributed in an area not yet explored by palaeontologists, it will remain unknown to science.

What does seem certain is that the entire history of human evolution was played out in Africa, including the evolution of *Homo sapiens* from *Homo erectus*. The fact that most crucial discoveries have taken place in the Rift Valley makes Kenya, Tanzania and Ethiopia the most likely candidates for the cradle of humankind, but it should be noted that the Rift is where palaeontologists have tended to focus their attentions in the search for our ancestry.

PREHISTORY The first known inhabitants of the Ethiopian Highlands were Stone Age hunter-gatherers who were closely related to the Khoisan of southern Africa. Stone Age rock paintings have survived in places like Dire Dawa and Cascase in Eritrea, and tools have been unearthed at several sites, most notably Melka Kunture near Addis Ababa.

The most researched part of Ethiopia in prehistoric terms is what is now the northern province of Tigrai and the newly independent country of Eritrea. The nature of the society in this region prior to about 1000BC is open to speculation. It can be assumed that pastoralism was practised before 4000BC. Conclusive evidence of millet cultivation dating from around 3000BC has been found at Gobedra near Axum, as has indigenous pottery of a similar vintage.

There is reason to think that the northern Ethiopian society of this time had links with ancient Egypt. The ethnic origin of the ancient Egyptians is an unsettled question, but some academics think they came to the area from elsewhere in Africa. Several Greek historians of the 1st millennium BC considered the Egyptians and Ethiopians to be of the same race, and one goes so far as to claim it was Ethiopians, led to the country by the Greek god Osiris in around 3000BC, who founded the Egyptian civilisation. Rather less questionable is that the ancient Egyptians, from around 2500BC, made some naval explorations south to a land they called Punt, which they believed to be their ancestral home. That Punt lay somewhere along the African coast is beyond dispute, but precisely where it lay is anybody's guess. Most current thinking places Punt in modern-day Somalia, while other sources suggest the Axumite port of Adulis in Eritrea or even somewhere on the Tanzanian coast. It is worth noting, as well, that the so-called Ethiopian dynasty founded in Egypt in 720BC was definitely of Nubian origin. There is, at present, no conclusive evidence one way or the other on links between Egypt and any part of Africa south of Meroe (in Nubia) prior to the 1st millennium BC.

Archaeological and written sources leave no room for doubt that, by 1000BC, northern Ethiopia supported an agricultural and probably quite urbanised civilisation of some magnitude. It was this so-called pre-Axumite society as much as any external influence which laid the foundation for the Axumite Empire that was to follow. The pre-Axumite period is commonly divided into two phases: the South Arabian or Sabaean period between 1000BC and 400BC, and an intermediary period that preceded the founding of Axum in around the 1st century AD. Several archaeologists currently working in Ethiopia feel these divisions are rather arbitrary, especially now it has been ascertained that Axum was occupied as early as 500BC.

One of the major pre-Axumite sites in northern Ethiopia is Yeha, where there is a large, well-preserved stone temple estimated to be at least 2,500 years old. There are also the remains of stone dwellings and catacomb-like tombs. Smaller temples have been found at other sites, as have large and impressive sculptures (many of which are on display in the Addis Ababa National Museum) and a variety of different free-standing altars. Strong religious and cultural links with the Sabaean Kingdom in modern-day Yemen have been noted at Yeha and sites of a similar vintage. It is clear from isolated discoveries of Egyptian and other foreign artefacts that this civilisation was in contact and probably traded with the other major civilisations of the time. Much of the indigenous pottery suggests Greek influences. At this stage, a mere handful of pre-Axumite sites have undergone more than cursory investigation; a 1988 paper by J W Michels lists at least 40 yet-to-be-excavated sites in Tigrai and Eritrea. It is likely that a great deal more will emerge about pre-Axumite society in the course of time.

TRADITIONAL HISTORY Ethiopians themselves are in little doubt about their early history. According to oral tradition, Ethiopia was settled by Ethiopic, the great-grandson of Noah. Ethiopic's son, Aksumai, founded the capital of Axum and also a dynasty of rulers that lasted for between 52 and 97 generations. The last, and many say the greatest, of these monarchs was Queen Makeda who, in the 11th and 10th centuries BC, owned a fleet of 73 ships and a caravan of 520 camels which traded with places as far afield as Palestine and India. Makeda ruled Ethiopia and Yemen for 31 years from her capital a few kilometres outside modern-day Axum, which, according to Ethiopians, was known as Sabea.

Early in her rule, it is claimed, the Queen of Sabea (better known to Westerners as the Queen of Sheba) travelled to Jerusalem to visit King Solomon. She brought with her gifts of gold, ivory and spices, and in return she was invited to stay in the royal palace. The two monarchs apparently developed a healthy friendship, the result of which was that Makeda returned home not only converted to Judaism but also carrying the foetal Ibn-al-Malik (Son of the King), whose name later became bastardised to Menelik. At the age of 22, Menelik returned to Jerusalem to visit his father. He was greeted by a joyous reception and stayed in Jerusalem for three years, learning the Law of Moses. When he decided to return home, he was, as Solomon's eldest son, offered heirship of the throne, which he declined. Solomon allowed Menelik to return to Ethiopia, but he also ordered all his high commissioners to send their eldest sons with Menelik and each of the 12 tribes of Israel to send along 1,000 of their people.

Accompanying Menelik on his journey home was Azariah, the first-born son of the high priest of the temple of Jerusalem. Azariah was told in a dream that he should take with him the holiest of all Judaic artefacts, the Ark of the Covenant. When Menelik was first told about this he was angry, but then he dreamt that it was God's will. King Solomon discovered the Ark's absence and led his soldiers after Menelik's enormous entourage, but he too dreamt that it was right for his son to have the Ark, though he insisted on keeping its disappearance a secret. The Ark has remained in Ethiopia ever since, and is now locked away in the Church of St Mary Zion in Axum. On Menelik's return, his mother abdicated in his favour. The Solomonic dynasty founded by Menelik ruled Ethiopia almost unbroken until 1974, when the 237th Solomonic monarch, Haile Selassie, was overthrown in the revolution.

Most Ethiopians accept this version of events unquestioningly, but it has never been taken very seriously by Western historians. The oldest written version of the Makeda legend is found in a highly fanciful 14th-century Ge'ez volume known as the *Kebre Negest*. This book claims to be a translation of a lost Coptic document dating to the 4th century or earlier; an unlikely claim, especially as the book was written at a time when the so-called Solomonic dynasty had reasserted its power after several centuries of Zagwe rule. Much of the *Kebre Negest* is undoubtedly medieval fabrication and royal myth-making woven from Sabaean legends around holes in the relevant biblical passages. Nevertheless, there is a significant grain of

THE ARK OF THE COVENANT

In Axum's Maryam Tsion Church lies an artefact which, were it proved to be genuine, would add immense substance to Ethiopian legendeering. Unfortunately only one person alive has ever seen this artefact. The Ark of the Covenant is, according to Ethiopian Christians, kept under lock and key in Maryam Tsion, and only the official guardian is allowed to enter. There is no doubting the importance the legend of the Ark plays in Ethiopian Christianity and few people would question the sincerity of the Ethiopian claim. But, superficially at least, its presence in Axum does seem rather far-fetched.

For those unfamiliar with the Old Testament, the Ark of the Covenant was built by the Children of Israel to hold the Tablets of Law given to Moses by God on Mount Sinai. According to the Bible, God gave Moses precise instructions on its design and embellishments. It was thus vested with a deadly power that was particularly devastating in time of battle. After the Jews settled in Jerusalem, the Ark was enshrined in a temple built by Solomon in the 10th century BC, where it remained until the temple was destroyed by the Babylonians in 587BC. While it resided in Jerusalem, the Ark was the most treasured artefact of the Jewish faith, virtually the personification of God, and in many biblical passages it is referred to simply as Jehovah. After the destruction of Solomon's temple, it disappeared. Despite several attempts over the centuries, the Ark has never been recovered.

Graham Hancock, in his book *The Sign and the Seal*, investigated the Ethiopian claim to the Ark and constructed a plausible sequence of events to support it. Hancock points out, and he is not the first person to have done so, that there is strong reason to believe the Ark vanished from Jerusalem long before 587BC. Nowhere in the Bible is it stated that the Ark was taken by the Babylonians, which seems decidedly strange, considering its religious importance; books written during the reign of Josiah (640BC) hint that it had probably disappeared by then. Hancock suggests the Ark was removed during the reign of Manasseh (687–642BC), a king who horrified religious leaders by desecrating Solomon's temple with an idol they considered to be sacrilegious. He suggests that the Ark was removed from the temple by angry priests and taken out of the kingdom, and that the loss of the Ark, when it was discovered by Josiah, was kept a secret from the laity.

Hancock circumvents the major historical loophole in the Ethiopian Ark theory, namely that the evidence currently available suggests that Axum was founded several centuries after Solomon's time, by dating the Ark's arrival in Axum to King Ezana's well-documented conversion to Christianity in the 4th century. He discovered that the priests at the Lake Tana island monastery of Tana Kirkos claim to have records stating that the Ark was kept on the island for 800 years prior to its removal to Axum. This claim is given some admittedly rather scant support by the presence of several sacrificial stones of probable Jewish origin on Tana Kirkos.

truth behind the elaboration. To disregard the *Kebre Negest* entirely is to ignore not just the many biblical references to Ethiopia, but also the considerable Jewish influences that permeate Ethiopian culture.

There are more than 30 Old Testament references to Ethiopia (or Cush, as it was known to the Hebrews). Moses, the most prominent early Hebrew prophet, is known to have married an Ethiopian woman (Numbers 12:1), while Genesis

Hancock then discovered that a large Jewish settlement and a temple modelled on Solomon's original had been built on Elephantine Island near Aswan on the Nile River. It is generally accepted this temple was founded in or around the reign of Manasseh, and the fact that the priests at the Elephantine corresponded with priests in Jerusalem is well documented. It appears that the priests here retained sacrificial rites similar to those of the Falasha, confirming that they diverged from the Jewish mainstream before the rule of Josiah. What's more, the temple was destroyed by the Egyptians around 410BC. The Jewish community on Elephantine is thought to have escaped from the island, but nobody knows where they fled. To all intents and purposes, they vanished. Hancock, naturally enough, suggests they went to Ethiopia. He also claims that this theory accords closely with the legend told to him by an old Falasha priest he met in Israel, who rejected the Makeda story, but claimed that his ancestors had lived in Egypt for several centuries *en route* from Israel, and that the Ark which they brought with them resided in the Lake Tana region for even longer before being stolen by the Axumite Christians.

As a non-historian, I am unsure how seriously to take Hancock's book, but I do find it difficult not to cock an eyebrow at any theory that contrives to incorporate both the Freemasons and the lost city of Atlantis. That said, the central thrust of the book – the ideas summarised and simplified above – seems soundly plausible, even if, by Hancock's own admission, it is purely circumstantial. My conclusion is that, if his facts are correct, Hancock has certainly proved it possible that the Ark is in Axum. He has also provided a strong case for the Falasha having arrived in Ethiopia from the northwest, and he has put a slant on Ethiopian history that makes sense of traditional accounts while explaining many of their more implausible aspects – the reasons why I have devoted so much space to his ideas here. But I am no better equipped than the average layperson to judge the accuracy of his facts. I hope the Ark is in Ethiopia; come to the crunch, I don't think I'd put money on it, but I'd rather never know than have my suspicions confirmed. If nothing else, *The Sign and the Seal* is a wonderful exercise in 'windmill-tilting'. It is also a most readable book, and its subject matter is fascinating. I suggest you locate a copy and decide for yourself.

Persuasive as Hancock's arguments might be, Stuart Munro-Hay points out that the story about the Ark of the Covenant is mentioned in none of the tales about Ezana's conversion, in none of the stories about the Nine Saints or about King Kaleb's conquest of Yemen (against a Jewish king, moreover), or even in the Ethiopian accounts of the end of the monarchy when Queen Gudit attacked the country, or when the Zagwe rose to power. In fact, the first reference to the Ark being in Ethiopia is by Abu Salib, during the reign of Lalibela around 1210. I can only agree with Munro-Hay that this is 'odd, to say the least', if the Ethiopians then believed that the most powerful symbol of God was in their capital city'. Certainly, I look forward to reading his book on the subject (see *Appendix 5, Further information*, page 613), which was published in 2005.

13

contains a reference to the Ghion River which, it claims, 'compasseth the whole land of Ethiopia'. Even if you take into account the fact that Ethiopia and Cush were once vague geographical terms referring to Africa south of the Sahara, the parts of Africa that are most likely to have been visited by Hebrews are those which were the most accessible. Moreover, the Ghion River is plainly what we now call the Blue Nile, which forms a sweeping arc beneath the part of Ethiopia most influenced by Judaism and the source of which is still referred to in Ethiopia as Ghion.

In the Book of Isaiah, we hear of the 'country ... beyond the rivers of Cush, who send ambassadors by sea, in papyrus skiffs over the waters ... a people tall and bronzed', while in the 7th-century BC Book of Zephaniah, the Lord speaks the following words: 'from beyond the rivers of Ethiopia my suppliants, even the daughter of my dispersed, shall bring mine offering', which surely suggests some sort of Jewish dispersal to Ethiopia.

As has been noted elsewhere, the Ethiopian Orthodox Church is unique in its Jewish influence and the emphasis placed on the Book of Jubilees (Genesis and the first part of Exodus). But the purest Jewish influence in Ethiopia is found among the Falasha people, whose tradition relating to Makeda and Solomon is broadly similar to the Christian version. Current Western opinion tends to favour the view that the Falasha are relatively recent arrivals to the area, descendants of a Jewish community established in Yemen in around AD70, but this theory disregards the archaic nature of Falasha rituals, which appear to date from before Josiah's reforms of around 640BC. There is no evidence to oppose the possibility that the Falasha's ancestors couldn't have arrived in Ethiopia directly from Jerusalem via the Nile and Tekaze rivers; in fact, this seems rather likely, as the Falasha homeland, as far as it can be established, has always been the area between the Tekaze and Lake Tana.

One reason why the Falasha may have been disregarded in the calculations of modern historians is that their numbers and importance have dwindled greatly in the last few centuries (the last few thousand individuals were airlifted to Israel in 1991) and there have been few modern studies on their traditions. But early travellers such as James Bruce, who spent a long time among the Falasha at a time when they had far more numerical and political importance, recorded their traditions clearly, and it has to be significant that, in 1973, the Chief Rabbi of Jerusalem recognised the Falasha as true Jews, excusing many of their outdated practices on the basis that they must have been severed from the main body of Jewry at a time when these practices were current.

Another serious objection to the traditional account is that pre-Axumite civilisations in Tigrai appear to have been predominantly pagan, worshipping the sun and moon, with later traces of Hellenistic (Greek) influences. Carvings of ibex suggest these animals had a special significance to pre-Axumites, as they did to Sabaeans, and the large statues of women found at many sites suggest a female fertility cult at odds with monotheistic Judaic traditions. But if the Falasha arrived from the west, and their homeland was roughly the same as in historical times (southwest of Tigrai), an absence of Jewish artefacts in Tigrai doesn't preclude the possibility of Jewish and pagan cultures existing side by side in Ethiopia prior to the arrival of Christianity. Perhaps the Jewish faith spread into Tigrai long after it had been established around Lake Tana. Possibly the Axumites were not Jewish at all, but their version of Christianity was influenced by neighbouring Jewish practices, or by Jews who converted at the same time. Either way, most objections to the traditional beliefs rest on the assumption that they originated in Axum. If the traditional account *does* relate to a real event, then the arrival of the Falasha seems the most likely candidate. I find it strange that I have nowhere encountered the suggestion that the *Kebre Negest* account is a Falasha tradition which was later adopted by the Axumites, who would in all probability have distorted it and merged it with their own legends.

The identity of the biblical Queen of Sheba is central to the Ethiopian legends. Although her origin is an open question, most scholars believe that she was Queen Bilkis of Sabea (in modern-day Yemen), on which basis they disregard the Ethiopian legend about Queen Makeda of Axum and suggest that the account in the *Kebre Negest* has borrowed cleverly from Arabian legends about Queen Bilkis. It strikes me, however, that a Sabaean origin for the Queen of Sheba does not preclude the possibility that one of her sons may have formed a dynasty in Ethiopia, especially as some pre-Axumite inscriptions from Ethiopia mention a ruler of Sabea, confirming that there was a place called Saba (Sheba) in Ethiopia in 500BC. In fact, given that the Sabaean civilisation appears to have had close links with pre-Axumite Ethiopia, and that the Ethiopian legends claim that Queen Makeda ruled over Yemen as well as Ethiopia, it seems rather likely. Ignore the more obvious mythologising around the Makeda legend (it does seem a little unlikely that her feet turned into asses' hooves when she stepped in the blood of a dragon as a child, a disfigurement which only Solomon was able to cure) and the traditional account is difficult to disregard entirely, if only as an allegory of a real Sabaean or Jewish migration to Ethiopia.

THE AXUMITE EMPIRE The roots of modern Ethiopia lie in the Axumite Empire. The origins of this empire and the age of the town of Axum remain obscure, and much of the information I have seems contradictory, but there are few who would query that Axum was one of the most important and technologically advanced civilisations of its time, or that it was a major force in world trade between the 1st and 7th centuries AD.

Most written sources will tell you the Axumite Kingdom became a trade centre of note in the 1st century AD. This assertion is based on the rather negative evidence that Axum is first mentioned by name in a 1st-century Greek document *The Periplus of the Ancient Sea*, and by the absence of any concrete evidence to date the city from an earlier period. In fact, Adulis, the main port of Axum, is probably older than Axum town. Furthermore, the Axumite Empire as described in the *Periplus* stretched along the coast from modern-day Port Sudan south to Berbera, and into the interior almost as far as the Nile. It seems unlikely such a vast kingdom sprang up in a matter of a few years. The long absence of any archaeological evidence dating Axum to before the 1st century AD is mainly because, prior to Neville Chittick's 1972–74 excavations, a minute percentage of Axum had been excavated, and no major archaeological work on Axum had been published since 1913! As it happens, Munro-Hay's full report on Chittick's excavations, published in 1989, pushes the date of foundation back to the 1st century BC. Furthermore, an archaeologist who worked on a 1992 excavation of a hill outside the modern town told me the team had found rock-hewn catacombs dating to around the 5th century BC. At the time of writing, only a fraction of Axum has been excavated and dozens of other sites in Tigrai await exploration. The simple truth is that nobody knows when Axum and its empire were founded; any date that is based only on formative excavations must in its very nature be conservative.

Adulis lay 50km from modern-day Massawa in Eritrea. According to the *Periplus*, it took three days to travel from Adulis to the main trading centre of Koloe and a further five days to the capital, Axum. The Axumites traded with India, Arabia, Persia and Rome, and the King of Axum was familiar with Greek literature. From other written sources, it is clear that in the 2nd century AD, under King Gadarat, Axum expanded its empire to include parts of modern-day Yemen. Some idea of Axum's contemporary importance is given by the 3rd-century Persian writer, Manni, who listed it as one of the four great kingdoms in the world, along with Persia, China and Rome.

The Axumites were a literate people who developed a unique language called Ge'ez and used a unique script that was based on the Sabaean alphabet. That they were skilled masons is apparent from the impressive free-masonry of the subterranean tombs in Axum town. But the most impressive technological achievement of the Axumites was the erection of several solid granite stelae, the largest of which, now collapsed, was 33m high, taller even than the similar granite obelisks of Egypt. Nobody knows how such heavy slabs of rock were erected; the tradition in Axum is that it was with the aid of the Ark of the Covenant.

The most powerful and influential of the Axumite kings was Ezana, who ruled in the early part of the 4th century along with his twin brother Saizana. Ezana was influenced by two Syrian Christians, Frumentius and Aedissius, and in AD337–40 he made Christianity the official religion of his empire. For once, scholars and Ethiopians are in agreement on this point, though some Ethiopians insist on the slightly earlier date of AD320. Ezana's conversion is documented by the Roman writer Rufinus, and on Axumite coins minted after AD341 the older sun and moon symbols are replaced by a cross. Ezana was a good military leader who led the campaign to conquer Yemen, and also led an expedition to secure control of the territory as far west as the confluence of the Nile and Atbara rivers, where he left a stele. Many inscribed stelae listing Ezana's exploits and recording his gratitude to God have been unearthed around Axum, most of them carved in Ge'ez, Greek and Sabaean.

The most influential of Ezana's actions was undoubtedly his conversion to Christianity. There is a traditional belief that an Ethiopian emissary brought news of the Christian faith to Axum in the time of Queen Candice (around AD50) but there is no suggestion that this led to any changes in Axumite beliefs. Ezana is reliably credited with building the first church in Axum, in which the artefact believed by Ethiopians to be the Ark of the Covenant was later placed. His mentor, Frumentius, was consecrated as the first bishop of Axum, Abba Salama. Ezana and his brother, who for many years ruled Ethiopia together, were almost certainly the Abreha and Atsbeha who are, rather optimistically, claimed locally to have initiated the carving of many rock-hewn churches throughout Tigrai and as far afield as modern-day Addis Ababa.

It is probable that Christianity only made serious inroads into the Axumite Empire in the mid 5th century, when nine so-called Syrian monks (the monks were in fact from a variety of parts of the Roman Empire) fled to Ethiopia. The nine monks preached widely throughout the empire, and they built many churches including the one still in use at Debre Damo Monastery. They have been canonised by the Ethiopian Church and each of them has a special holy day dedicated to his memory. Many churches bear one or other of their names – Abba (saint) Aregawi or Mikael, Abba Alef, Abba Tsama, Abba Aftse, Abba Gerima, Abba Liqanos, Abba Guba, Abba Yemata and Abba Panteleon.

Another important Axumite king was Kaleb, who took the throne in the early 6th century and ruled for at least 30 years. It is probable that the empire's prosperity peaked under Kaleb, who campaigned against a Jewish leader who had usurped

Yemen and won the territory back for Axum, albeit at a heavy cost. Kaleb's palace, on a hill above the town, was reportedly most beautiful; a Byzantine traveller called Cosmos who visited Axum in AD525 marvelled at the statues of unicorns on its corners, and the tame elephant and giraffe enclosed in the palace grounds. Kaleb's son, Gebre Meskel, appears to have ruled from the same palace. Gebre Meskel is remembered not so much for his military prowess as for his contribution to Ethiopian Christianity. He was the patron of St Yared, who is credited with inventing the notation and form of Ethiopian religious music, and also with writing many songs, poems and chants that are still in use today.

Axum has to this day retained its position as the centre of Ethiopian Christianity. In every other sense, it appears to have fallen into decline soon after Kaleb's rule ended. Many reasons for this have been put forward – local environmental factors such as deforestation and erosion, internal unrest, and the increasing wealth in the east of the empire – but the main factors were almost certainly those linked to a more general decline in Axumite fortunes: the rise of Islam and consequent Arab usurpation of Axum's Red Sea trade routes in AD640, and the increasing importance of Persian-founded routes between the Persian Gulf and the Swahili coast south of Mogadishu. By AD750, Adulis had become a ghost town, and the Kingdom of Axum sank thereafter into global obscurity. From that time on, the country was known as Abyssinia, until the 20th century when it became Ethiopia.

ETHIOPIA'S DARK AGE It is arguably only from a Western perspective that the collapse of Axum's maritime trade routes signalled the end of Axumite importance. More accurate to say that Axum turned its attention elsewhere by expanding its influence over the Jewish communities of Lasta (near Lalibela) and the Lake Tana region and further south into modern-day Showa. The period between AD750 and 1270 thus saw the Axumite Kingdom (based in what are now Tigrai and Ethiopia) transformed into the precursor of the Ethiopia we know: a Christian empire which covers most of the Ethiopian Highlands. It is also probably true that this extended period of isolation allowed the Ethiopian Church to become the cohesive and idiosyncratic institution it is today. Indicative of a renewed religious energy is the fact that most of Ethiopia's 300 rock-hewn churches date from this period.

Nevertheless, Ethiopia's increasing isolation during this period means that little detail is known of its internal politics, a situation paralleling that of, say, Britain for several centuries after the withdrawal and collapse of the Roman Empire. It is uncertain, for instance, whether the Axumite kings continued to rule from Axum after AD750, or whether they adopted a series of floating capitals. Arab writings suggest that a permanent capital called Kubar was used in the 9th and 10th centuries. The site of this capital has never been found, and it is likely that it was abandoned in the late 10th century, but it was probably south of Axum.

Ethiopian traditions relating to the end of the 1st millennium AD are dominated by the memory of one Queen Yodit (Judith), also known by the alternative names of Esat or Gudit, both of which mean 'the monster'. Yodit is said to have been born in Lasta, the daughter of a Falasha king called Gideon. She was born at a time of great religious tension. The Christian expansion southwards led to the repression of the Falasha Jews, who refused to pay taxes to the Axumite monarchy and suffered regular punitive raids as a result. Yodit is credited with uniting the Falasha into a cohesive unit, and with leading a march on Axum with the intention of removing Christianity from Ethiopia altogether. The holy city was reduced to rubble and dozens of other churches and Christian settlements were burnt to the ground. Yodit is reputed to have ruled Ethiopia until her death 40 years later, during which time she destroyed many of the finest achievements of the Axumite civilisation and had thousands of Christians put to death.

I have not encountered serious suggestion that Yodit was anything but a genuine historical figure. Exactly when she lived is another matter. Ethiopian tradition dates her rise to AD852, and claims that her onslaught precipitated the move of the Axumite monarchy to Showa. This seems unlikely. Arab writings suggest that Yemenic and Axumite rulers kept sporadic contact well into the 10th century. Furthermore, correspondence between the Nubian and Ethiopian monarchs in around AD980 states unambiguously that the area was plagued by a hostile queen at this time. It seems more likely, then, that Yodit's reign of terror was in the late 10th century which, given her legendary destructiveness, might explain why the site of the capital of Kubar (if it ever existed) has never been found.

THE ZAGWE DYNASTY Tradition has it that Yodit died in AD892 when a whirlwind swept her up near Wukro, and that she was buried at nearby Adi Kaweh, her grave marked by a pile of stones. Once news of her death filtered to Showa, the Solomonic heir Anbessa Wudim returned to Axum and defeated the Falasha in battle to reclaim his right to the throne. Axum remained unstable, however, and in AD922, King D'il Nead was overthrown by one of his generals, Tekle Haymanot, who took the regal name of Zagwe and founded the dynasty of the same name. This tradition doesn't tally with the most likely dates of Yodit's rule. It has been suggested that the Zagwe dynasty followed directly from Yodit, and was founded by Jews who later converted to Christianity. This idea is circumstantially supported by the fact that the Zagwe based themselves in Lasta, which at the time was a strongly Jewish region and was almost certainly the birthplace of Yodit.

However, the dating of the Zagwe dynasty is itself rather obscure. Various sources date their usurpation of the throne from as far apart as AD922 and 1150, with the latter date favoured by more credible sources. Several traditional lists of Zagwe rulers are in existence, but only seven kings appear on all versions and, rather improbably, all but the last are said to have ruled for exactly 40 years. Despite the uncertainty surrounding dates, the Zagwe leaders appear to have introduced a new stability and unity in Ethiopia. It was under the most renowned Zagwe king, Lalibela, that Ethiopian Christianity reached the pinnacle of its physical expression in the form of the cluster of rock-hewn churches carved at the Zagwe capital of Roha (which later became known as Lalibela in honour of the king). It is widely agreed that the Zagwe period of rule ended when a Solomonic descendant called Yakuno Amlak took the throne in 1270. Even here, however, some sources claim that the last Zagwe monarch abdicated of his own free will, others that he was killed in battle by the supporters of his Solomonic successor. Either way, the new king granted land and various other hereditary concessions to the Zagwe line, and these have been upheld into modern times.

It was almost certainly under the Solomonic rulers of the 13th to 15th centuries that much of the mythologising that surrounds Ethiopian history took place. The *Kebre Negest*, the book containing the first record of the Sheba legend and Solomonic claims, was written shortly after the line was reinstated, probably to lend credibility to the new rulers by responding to Zagwe claims of descent from Moses. In many respects, the period after 1270 can be seen as the Ethiopian renaissance. Ethiopian history after 1270 can be discussed on much firmer ground than anything that preceded it; writing and religious art apparently flourished, most particularly under Zara Yaqob (1434–68), who is regarded as having been one of Ethiopia's greatest and most influential kings. The empire continued to expand southward into Showa, and it was ruled from a succession of floating capitals in Showa and later the Lake Tana area. This slow expansion and relative stasis was accompanied by growing tension between the Christian empire and the Muslims who lived beyond its eastern fringes, and it was rocked by spasmodic conflict, including several generally unsuccessful incursions to capture the Red Sea ports which had once formed a part of Axum.

THE LAND OF PRESTER JOHN It was probably during Zagwe rule that the legend of Prester John took root in Europe. The origin of this legend is now rather obscure, but it seems to have taken hold in the 12th century and impressed the European clergy to such an extent that in 1177 Pope Alexander III sent a message to Prester John (the messenger apparently never returned). The essence of the legend, elaborated on by explorers such as Marco Polo, was that a vast and wealthy Christian kingdom existed somewhere in the 'Indies' (at the time a vague term which covered practically anywhere in the world that was unknown to Europeans) and that it was ruled over by Prester John, who was both king and high priest, and a descendant of the Magi (a group of Persian magicians, three of whom were probably the wise men who attended Jesus shortly after his birth).

As with so many aspects of Ethiopian history, the substance behind the Prester John legend is rather elusive. It is widely thought that the legend originated in Ethiopia, but precisely how knowledge of a Christian kingdom in Africa reached Europe is an open question. One Ethiopian legend is that Lalibela visited Jerusalem prior to becoming the King of Ethiopia. A few modern sources suggest that the Prester John story was founded on a letter sent to Europe by an Ethiopian king called Yohannis, and it was this letter to which the Pope responded. And as far as I am aware, the Ethiopian Church has maintained links with Alexandria throughout its history, so news could have infiltrated Europe through Egypt. Or perhaps the legend of Prester John and the reality of a Christian kingdom in Ethiopia is mere coincidence. Whatever truth lay behind the legend, Prester John was a shadowy fringe presence in medieval lore. References to him are scattered through religious and other mystical writing of the period, and it seems probable that the lure of his wealthy kingdom and desire to communicate with a fellow Christian empire was part of the reason behind the Portuguese explorations of Africa which resulted in their arrival in Ethiopia in 1520.

THE MUSLIM–CHRISTIAN WAR (1528–60)

Islamic presence in Ethiopia dates back to the time of Muhammad. In AD615, several of Muhammad's followers, his wife among them, fled to Axum where they were offered protection by the king and allowed to settle at Negash. Muhammad himself held Ethiopians in great esteem and warned his followers never to harm them. For several centuries, an uneasy peace existed between Christian Ethiopia and the Islamic world, even as an increasing amount of Islamic settlement took place along the eastern fringes of the Christian kingdom. By the end of the Zagwe era, the Muslim faith had spread throughout Somali and Afar territories and to the southern highlands around Harar, Bale and Arsi, while small bands of Muslims had dispersed into areas that were traditionally part of the Christian empire. Sensing a threat to their sovereignty, and to trade routes to the Red Sea, the Ethiopian Christians launched an attack against the Muslims of Adal in around 1290, which led to a series of skirmishes and wars, and, ultimately, in the mid 14th century, to the expansion of the Christian empire deep into southern Ethiopia. In its attempts to retain its sovereignty, Ethiopia made great efforts to convert pagan highlanders and Falasha to the Christian faith, and also sent abroad envoys to strengthen its links with Christian communities in the Sudan, Egypt, Alexandria and Armenia.

In 1528 a Muslim leader known as Ahmed Gragn (Ahmed the left-handed) took control of the Muslim city of Harar in the eastern highlands. From Harar, Gragn led his army of Afar and Somali Muslims on an annual raid on the Christian highlands, timed every year to exploit the weakness of Christians during the Lent fast. Gragn's destructiveness can be compared to that of Yodit several centuries before. Many rock-hewn churches throughout Ethiopia still bear the scars of his campaign; of less permanent structures, such as the church at Axum, which was rebuilt after Yodit's reign, no trace remains. The Ethiopian emperor of the time, Lebna Dengal, was chased around his kingdom by Gragn, eventually to die a fugitive in 1540. By 1535, Gragn held Showa, Lasta, Amhara and Tigrai – in other words most of Christian Ethiopia.

Gragn's campaign more or less coincided with the first contact between Europe and Ethiopia, which occurred in 1493, the second-last year of the reign of the youthful Emperor Iskinder, with the arrival – via Egypt, India and the Persian Gulf – of Pero de Covilhão, a 'spy' sent by the Portuguese King John in search of the legendary Land of Prester John. Instead of fulfilling the second part of his mission by returning home, however, Covilhão stayed on in Ethiopia to serve as an adviser to a succession of emperors and regents. He was still there in 1520, when the first full Portuguese expedition to Ethiopia, as documented by the priest Francisco Alvarez in the classic book *Prester John of the Indies*, was received at the monastery of Debre

Libanos by Emperor Lebna Dengal. Shortly before his death in exile, Lebna Dengal wrote to Portugal asking for help in restoring his kingdom. Were it not for the intervention of the Portuguese, it is quite likely that Ethiopian Christianity would have been buried under the Muslim onslaught.

In 1543, Emperor Galawdewos's army, propped up by the Portuguese, killed Gragn and defeated his army in a battle near Lake Tana. Galawdewos's attempts to rebuild the shattered Christian empire were frequently frustrated by raids led by Gragn's wife and nephew. In 1559 the emperor was killed and his severed head displayed in Harar. But the long years of war had drained the resources of Christians and Muslims alike; the real winners were the pagan Galla (now known as the Oromo) who expanded out of the Rift Valley into areas laid waste by the fighting. By 1560, the Galla had virtually surrounded Harar and had overrun much of Showa, providing not only a buffer zone between the exhausted Christians and Muslims, but also a new threat to both of the established groups.

THE GONDAR PERIOD (1635–1855) The Christians were faced with a new disaster as Portuguese ex-soldiers settled around the temporary capital on Lake Tana. In 1622, Emperor Susneyos made a full conversion to Catholicism under the influence of his close friend and regular travelling companion, the Spanish-born Jesuit priest Pedro Páez, and he outlawed the Orthodox Church and suspended traditional Church officials. This move was naturally very unpopular with Ethiopian Christians, thousands upon thousands of whom were persecuted to death for pursuing their centuries-old faith. Increasingly isolated from his subjects, the emperor was forced to abdicate in favour of his son Fasil in 1632. The new emperor reinstated the Orthodox Church and banned foreigners from his empire. From the 1640s until James Bruce's journey in 1770, only one European, a French doctor, was permitted to enter Ethiopia.

Ethiopia had lacked a permanent capital since 1270. In order to help reunite Church and state, Fasil broke with this tradition by settling at the small town of Gondar, north of Lake Tana. Gondar was named the permanent capital of Ethiopia in 1636, a title it kept for more than 200 years. This move to Gondar signalled an era of relative peace under a succession of strong, popular emperors, most notably Fasil himself and Iyasu I. Then, under Iyasu II (1730–55), the throne was gradually undermined by Ras (Prince) Mikael of Tigrai, who assumed an increasing backstage importance, twice assassinating emperors and replacing them with others of his choice. For much of the Gondar period, the war between Christians and Galla had been a problem, as had priestly fears about contact between the court and exotic Christian denominations. King Ioas (1755–69) lost almost all support by marrying a Galla woman and insisting on Galla being spoken in court. By 1779, when Takla Giyorgis took power, the king's role was little more than ornamental. The period between 1784 and 1855 is generally referred to as the 'era of the princes'; the Gondar-based rulers of this period are remembered as the shadow emperors.

ETHIOPIA UNDER EMPEROR TEWODROS II (1855–69) In 1855, Ethiopia was not so much a unified state as a loose alliance of squabbling fiefdoms run by wealthy local dynasties, which were in turn reigned over by an ineffectual emperor. The empire was threatened not merely by internal power struggles, but also by the external threat posed by Egypt, which wanted to control the Nile from its source in Lake Tana. Were it not for the vision of one Kasa Hayla, Ethiopia could well have collapsed altogether.

Kasa Hayla grew up in the home of Kenfu Haylu, a man who played a major role in campaigns against Egypt and who ruled a minor fief in western Ethiopia. When Kenfu died in 1839, Kasa was denied the heirdom of the fief he had hoped for, and instead became a *shifta* (bandit), though reportedly not an ignoble one, as he developed a Robin Hood-like obsession with wealth redistribution, and also led several private campaigns against Egyptian intruders. By 1850, he ruled the fiefdom he believed to be his by default. He then led a series of campaigns against other princes. In 1855 he defeated the heir to the throne outside Gondar, and had himself crowned Emperor Tewodros II.

History has cast Tewodros as the instigator of Ethiopian unity, and he is now among the country's most revered historical figures. That he never achieved sustained popularity in his lifetime is due to the brutality and ruthless fanaticism with which he pursued his goals of Ethiopian unity and independence. He attempted, with a fair degree of success, to reunite the fiefdoms under a strong central government, and, less successfully, to modernise the national army. He established an arms factory near his capital of Debre Tabor and gradually accumulated a large arsenal on Makdala Hill near Dessie. Tewodros had strong anti-feudal instincts that led to his abolition of the slave trade and his expropriation of large tracts of fallow Church-owned land for the use of peasant farmers. These socialist efforts won him few friends among the clergy and the nobility and, at any given time during his reign, one or other of the old fiefdoms was in rebellion. The strict discipline he imposed on his army led to a high rate of desertion and the continual internal strife cost many of his soldiers their lives: by 1866, his army had dwindled from 60,000 men to 10,000.

Amid growing unpopularity at home, Tewodros's sense of frustration was cemented by his failure to enlist European, and more specifically British, support for his modernising efforts and quest for absolute Ethiopian sovereignty. In 1867, Tewodros retreated embittered to the top of Makdala Hill. With him, he took several British prisoners in a final desperate bid to lever European support: a fatal misjudgement. In 1869, Britain sent a force of 32,000 men led by Sir Robert Napier to capture Tewodros. Makdala was encircled. Instead of fighting, Tewodros wrote a long letter to Napier listing his failed ambitions and castigating his countrymen for their backwardness. Then he took his own life.

ETHIOPIA UNDER EMPEROR YOHANNIS IV (1872–89) The struggle for succession after Tewodros's suicide took a military form, culminating in the Battle of Assam in 1871, wherein the incumbent emperor Takla Giyorgis was defeated by his brother-in-law and the ruler of Tigrai, Kasa Mercha, whose superior weaponry had been acquired in exchange for supporting Britain in the march to Makdala. Kasa crowned himself Emperor Yohannis IV and ruled from 1872 to 1889. Yohannis was a deeply religious man, a proud nationalist, and a skilled military tactician who nevertheless initiated a more diplomatic form of rule than had Tewodros.

Yohannis's ambition of creating national unity through diplomatic rather than military means was undermined by British duplicity, Egyptian ambitions to control the source of the Nile at Lake Tana, and, not least, the actions of his main rival for the throne, the Showan Prince Menelik, who consistently played internal politics while Yohannis fought external powers. Yohannis returned Menelik to his regional seat after ten years of imprisonment under Tewodros. Menelik repaid the favour by seizing Wolo and inserting his ally, Mohammed Ali, as governor while Yohannis was employed in leading successful campaigns against Egypt at Gundat and Gura in 1875–76. When Yohannis returned from his campaigning, Menelik was unwilling to take on the emperor's superior and more experienced army, and Yohannis preferred to settle things diplomatically: a compromise was reached under the Leche Agreement of 1878, which formalised the relationship between the emperor and regional leaders.

Yohannis then turned his attention to negotiating with Europe and Egypt for official recognition of Ethiopian sovereignty. His cause was helped greatly when the Mahdist War broke out in Sudan in 1882, and Britain, which that very year had unilaterally occupied Egypt, realised it needed Ethiopia's assistance to rescue its troops from Sudan. The Treaty of Adwa, signed by Yohannis and a British negotiator in 1884, met most of Yohannis's demands: most significantly the return of Bogos, a part of Ethiopia occupied by Egypt, and the right to the free import of goods including arms and ammunition. The treaty also allowed Britain dominion over the port of Massawa. While Yohannis faithfully kept his part of the bargain by rescuing British troops from Mahdist Sudan, and eventually gave his life in this cause, Britain broke the spirit of the agreement barely a year after it was signed by handing Massawa to Italy.

Italy was a newcomer to Africa. Nevertheless, with the tacit support of Britain, who had little interest in Ethiopia other than ensuring the source of the Nile was kept out of French hands, Italy proved a major threat to Ethiopian sovereignty. The Italian army occupied several Red Sea ports in 1886. Anticipating a march inland, Yohannis attacked their fort at the port at Saati in January 1887. The Ethiopians were repulsed at Saati, but the next day they attacked and destroyed a force of 500 Italians at Dogali. In March 1888, Yohannis led 80,000 men in an attack on Saati, but the Italians refused to leave their fort and fight, and the news of a successful Mahdist attack on Gondar, still the official capital of Ethiopia, and also of Menelik's plans to rise against the emperor, forced Yohannis to turn his troops on these more immediate problems. On 9 March 1889, Yohannis led his troops against the Mahdist stronghold at Matema. Ethiopia won the battle, effectively ending the Mahdist threat, but not before Yohannis was fatally wounded. Menelik was crowned Emperor of Ethiopia.

EMPEROR MENELIK II (1889–1913) From his base in Showa, Menelik had done much to unite Ethiopia during Yohannis's reign, even if his major motives were entirely cynical: the expansion of Showan territory, the opening up of trade routes blocked by hostile fiefdoms, and a demonstration of his own leadership and military prowess. Between 1882 and 1888, Harar, Arsi, most of the fiefdoms of the southwest, and large tracts of Galla land were captured by Menelik. It was also while Yohannis was in power that Menelik moved the Showan capital to the Intoto Hills, a range that was rich in Solomonic associations and which boasted two ancient rock-hewn churches. In 1886, Menelik moved his capital into the valley below Intoto, to the site of what was to become Addis Ababa.

Menelik came to national power during the most severe famine in Ethiopia's recorded history. The Kefu Qan (Evil Days) of 1888–92 was a direct result of a rinderpest epidemic triggered by the importation of cattle by the Italians, and the crisis was exacerbated by drought and locust plagues. This famine cannot be seen in isolation from the ongoing wars of the 19th century, nor can it be dissociated from the greed of the feuding princes. Peasant resources had been stretched to the limit long before the advent of rinderpest.

During Yohannis's time, Menelik had been in friendly contact with the Italians at Massawa, trading promises of peace for weapons to expand his own empire and to challenge the emperor. In May 1889, he signed the Treaty of Wechale, granting Italy the part of Ethiopia that was to become Eritrea in exchange for recognition of Ethiopian sovereignty over the rest of the country. What Menelik didn't realise was that the Italians had inserted a clause in the Italian version of the document, but not in the Amharigna equivalent, which demanded that Ethiopia make all its foreign contacts through Italy, in effect reducing Ethiopia to an Italian protectorate. Italy further undermined the spirit of the treaty when, in 1891, it successfully courted several Tigraian princes into alliance with Eritrea. When the princes revolted against the prospective colonisers in 1894, Italy was left with one course open to attain its goal of colonising Ethiopia: military confrontation.

In October 1895, Italy occupied Adigrat on the Tigraian side of the border, and also established a fort at the Tigraian capital of Mekele. Menelik led a force of 100,000 men to Tigrai and, after a couple of inconsequential skirmishes, the two armies met in the hills around Adwa. The memory of the Battle of Adwa, which took place on 1 March 1896, remains one of the proudest moments in Ethiopian history. Through their own faulty map reading as much as anything, the Italian troops were humiliatingly routed, the first time ever that a European power had been defeated by Africans in a battle of consequence. In Rome, nearly 100,000 people signed a petition demanding Italian withdrawal from Ethiopia and, although Italy retained Eritrea, the borders of which were formalised in 1900, it was to be almost 40 years before they again crossed the Ethiopian border in anger. Ethiopia was the only part of Africa to survive as an independent state following the European scramble.

In many senses, Menelik completed the process of unification and modernisation that had been started by Tewodros and Yohannis. His period of rule saw the introduction of electricity, telephones, schools and hospitals, and also the building of the Addis Ababa–Djibouti railway. It also saw a re-intensification of the slave trade which, although it had been present in Ethiopia since time immemorial, had been curbed if not halted by Tewodros. Slavery was the pretext used by Europe to block Ethiopia's entry to the League of Nations and to sanction against the import of arms and ammunition to Ethiopia. The slave raids, in which many thousands of Ethiopians died, were the major blemish on a period of rule that was one of the longest periods of sustained peace Ethiopia had known for a long time.

THE RISE OF HAILE SELASSIE (1913–36) Menelik died of old age in 1913. His chosen successor, Iyasu, is remembered as much for his good looks and raffish lifestyle as anything he achieved. In fact, had he ever been given the chance, Iyasu could well have been the relatively progressive leader that Ethiopia needed to drag it out of feudalism. Iyasu tried to curb the slave trade; he did much to incorporate Ethiopia's often neglected Muslim population (several of his wives were Muslim and he financed the building of many mosques); and he showed little regard for the ageing and self-serving Showan government which he inherited from Menelik. Or to put it another way, Iyasu succeeded in annoying the slave-owning nobility, the clergy of the Orthodox Church, and the political status quo. In 1916, while visiting Jijiga in an attempt to improve relations with Ethiopia's Somali population, Iyasu was overthrown. He was eventually captured in 1921 and imprisoned in Fiche in north Showa.

The two main rivals to succeed Iyasu were Zawditu Menelik, the sheltered daughter of the dead emperor, and Ras Tefari Mekonnen, the ambitious son of the Harari governor Ras Mekonnen and grandson of an earlier Showan monarch. The Showan nobility, who had called most of the shots as the ailing Menelik reached the end of his reign, favoured Zawditu for her political naivety and evident potential for ineffectuality. A compromise was reached wherein Zawditu became empress, and Tefari the official heir to the throne. In actuality, the younger, more worldly and better-educated Ras Tefari assumed a regent-like role and the two governed in tandem, a situation that became increasingly tense as Tefari's dominance grew. This ambiguous relationship was resolved in 1930, when the empress's husband was killed in rather murky circumstances in a civil battle. Two days later, Zawditu herself succumbed, apparently to that most Victorian of maladies, heartbreak. Ras Tefari was crowned under the name Haile Selassie (meaning 'Power of the Trinity') in November 1930.

Haile Selassie set to work on drafting a new constitution with the claimed intent of doing away with feudalism and limiting the powers of the regional princes. Consciously or not, the effect of the constitution was further to entrench the regional nobility in a ministerial system based more on heredity than on merit. The first parliament, which assembled in November 1931, consisted of a senate whose members were appointed directly by the emperor, and a chamber of deputies whose members were elected by the landed gentry. The only regional leader to challenge the constitution was Ras Haylu of Gojjam. After attempting to free Iyasu from his confinement in Fiche, Haylu was sentenced to life imprisonment in 1932 and Gojjam was placed under the administration of one of the emperor's allies. Haile Selassie can be credited with creating the first unambiguously unified Ethiopian state. Equally unambiguous was the fact that this state gave no meaningful constitutional protection or power to the overwhelming majority of its citizens.

THE ITALIAN OCCUPATION (1936–41) The first serious challenge to Haile Selassie's rule came not from within the country but from Italy. The immediate effect of the Battle of Adwa had been the abandonment of Italian colonial aspirations south of the Eritrean border, but the humiliation afforded to the Italian army at Adwa still rankled, particularly in the nationalistic fervour that accompanied the rise to power of Mussolini's fascists in 1922. Mussolini's initial attempts to gain economic control of Ethiopia were disguised behind diplomacy but, by the time Haile Selassie had gained absolute power over Ethiopia, the Italians had more or less abandoned this approach in favour of subterfuge and force. The former tactic was most effective in Tigrai, an outlying region of northern Ethiopia with close historical and cultural links to neighbouring Eritrea. Italy charmed the Tigraian nobility, whose response when war broke out in 1935 varied from lukewarm resistance to taking the Italian side against Ethiopia.

The first harbinger of war was the Walwal Incident of December 1934, wherein a remote Ethiopian military post on the disputed Italian Somaliland border region was attacked by Italian troops. The skirmish was initiated by Italy, and Italy suffered considerably less loss of life than did Ethiopia. Nevertheless, the political climate in Europe was such that countries like Britain and France were more than willing to sacrifice Ethiopian interests to the cause of frustrating an alliance between Mussolini and Hitler. Italy made absurd demands for reparations. Ethiopia took these to the League of Nations (it had become a member state in 1925) for arbitration, but its perfectly valid arguments were ignored; Italy was in effect given a free hand in Ethiopia.

The Italian army crossed from Eritrea to Tigrai in October 1935. By 8 November, Italy had occupied Adigrat, Mekele and, to its immense satisfaction, Adwa. The Ethiopian army entered Tigrai in January 1936. After a couple of minor Ethiopian victories, most notably at the first Battle of Tembien, Italy's superior air power and its use of prohibited mustard gas proved decisive. The Battle of Maichew, which took place on 31 March 1936, is generally regarded as the last concerted Ethiopian resistance to Italian occupation. Although several minor skirmishes distracted the Italians as they marched from Maichew to Addis Ababa, it was when news of Italy's victory at Maichew reached the capital that the emperor went into exile and the streets erupted into anarchic and unfocused mass violence.

Italy incorporated Ethiopia, Eritrea and Italian Somaliland into one large territory which they named Italian East Africa. Addis Ababa was made the colonial capital, while Jimma, Gondar, Harar, Asmara and Mogadishu became regional administrative centres. The Italian influence on all these cities is still evident today, as it is on several smaller towns. More lasting was the Italian influence on the internal transport infrastructure, particularly in the north, where they cut roads through seemingly impossible territory. This positive legacy must, however, be set against their successful bid to cripple indigenous businesses and replace them with parastatal organisations. This state interventionism proved to be particularly damaging in the agricultural sector: the importation of grain, almost unknown before 1935, became a feature of the Italian and post-Italian eras. Ultimately, though, the high level of internal resistance to the exotic regime, and its eventual collapse in 1941 meant that it was too ineffectual and short-lived to have many lasting effects on Ethiopia.

Throughout the Italian occupation, the Ethiopian nobility combined time-buying diplomacy and well-organised guerrilla warfare to undermine the regime. The fascists' response was characteristically brutal. When, in 1937, an unsuccessful attempt was made on the life of the Italian viceroy, the Italian Blackshirts ran riot in the capital, burning down houses and decapitating and disembowelling Ethiopians, mostly at random, though the intelligentsia was particularly targeted and few survived the rampage. The Ethiopian resistance won few battles of note, but its role in demoralising the occupiers laid the foundation for the easy British victory over the Italian troops in the Allied liberation campaign of January 1941.

POST-WAR ETHIOPIA UNDER HAILE SELASSIE (1941–74) Haile Selassie was returned to his throne immediately when the Allied troops drove Italy back into Eritrea. Eritrea and Italian Somaliland were placed under the rule of the British Military Administration. When war ended, the UN was left to determine the status of the three countries that had been co-administrated under Italy. Haile Selassie naturally wanted all the territories to be integrated under his imperial government. When it was decided that Italian Somaliland should be governed under a ten-year trusteeship then granted full independence, Ethiopia's demands for Eritrea and the access to the Red Sea it offered became more concerted. To its aid came the USA and Britain, both of which had a good relationship with Haile Selassie and a vested interest in keeping at least one Red Sea territory in friendly hands. With more than a touch of cynicism on the part of certain of its member states, and after no meaningful consultation with the Eritreans, the UN forced Eritrea into a highly ambiguous federation with Ethiopia.

The US intervention over Eritrea led to a decreasing European role in determining Ethiopian affairs and much stronger links being forged with the other side of the Atlantic. As the oil-rich Middle East came to play an increasingly important role in international affairs, so too did Ethiopia and its Red Sea harbours in US foreign policy. In exchange for using Asmara as their Red Sea base, the US developed a military training and armoury programme for Ethiopia which, by 1970, absorbed more than half the US budget for military aid to Africa. Little wonder, then, that the world barely noticed when, using the pretext of a minor skirmish the preceding year, Eritrean federation became colonisation. In 1962, Ethiopia formally annexed

Eritrea, dissolved the Eritrean Assembly, and placed the federated territory under what was practically military rule. The terms of federation gave Eritrea no recourse to argue its case before the UN. So began a war for self-determination that lasted almost 30 years, cost the lives of more than 100,000 Eritreans, and never once figured on the UN's agenda.

Few modern leaders have become so deeply associated with a country's image for so long a time as did Emperor Haile Selassie. As Ras Tefari, he wielded much of the power behind the throne between 1916 and 1930; as emperor he ruled almost unchallenged, except for the brief Italian interlude, between 1930 and 1974. Despite the mystique that surrounded him, however, Haile Selassie did very little to develop his country. The 1931 constitution created a united empire by entrenching the rights of the nobility; it had done little to improve the lot of ordinary Ethiopians. The revised constitution of 1955 introduced universal suffrage, but the absence of any cohesive political parties and the high salaries offered to parliamentarians attracted self-seeking careerists rather than politicians of substance. The low turnouts at elections suggest that political education was non-existent and most Ethiopians saw the constitutional revision for the window dressing it undoubtedly was. In essence, the Ethiopia of 1960 or 1970 was no less feudal than had been the Ethiopia of 1930. The economy remained as subsistence-based as ever, with trade and industry accounting for a mere 10% of the GDP. In many respects, and despite its proud independence, Ethiopia lacked an infrastructure comparable even to those of the underdeveloped colonies that surrounded it.

Little wonder, then, that the wave of colonial resistance that swept through Africa after World War II, and which resulted in the independence of most of the former African colonies in the early 1960s, was mirrored by a rising tide of imperial resistance in post-occupation Ethiopia. Underground opposition to the emperor started almost immediately the Italian occupation ended. The most persistent of the dissidents, Takala Walda-Hawaryat, had supported the emperor before the occupation but, like many ex-resistance leaders, he strongly opposed Haile Selassie's return to power after having sat out the occupation in exile. Takala attempted to install one of Iyasu's sons in place of Haile Selassie and was detained. In 1946 he became involved in another anti-imperial plot, and was detained for another eight years. Takala was killed in a police shoot-out in 1969. By this time, however, a more concerted anti-imperialist movement had emerged, its objections not so much to Haile Selassie himself as to the outmoded feudal system he represented.

The first serious threat to imperial power came in the form of an attempted military coup initiated by the left-wing intellectual Garmame Naway and implemented by his brother Brigadier-General Mengistu Naway, leader of the Imperial Bodyguard. On 14 December 1960, while Haile Selassie was away in Brazil, the Imperial Bodyguard effectively imprisoned his cabinet at the Imperial Palace, having lured them there by claiming that the empress was terminally ill, then announced that a new government would be formed to combat the country's backwardness and poverty. Haile Selassie flew back to Asmara and from there instructed the military – whose tottering loyalty was secured by the promise of a substantial pay rise – to storm the palace. Garmame Naway was killed in the shoot-out, along with several cabinet members, while his brother Mengistu was captured in the act of fleeing and hanged for treason.

Haile Selassie returned to his palace, but it wasn't quite business as usual from thereon, although the last person to recognise this was arguably the emperor himself. Indeed, on the pan-African front, as a spate of former European colonial possessions were transformed into independent self-governing nations during the early 1960s, the figurehead status of Ethiopia's septuagenarian head of state was entrenched by the selection of Addis Ababa as capital of the newly formed Organisation of African Unity (OAU) in 1963. On the domestic front, by contrast, the attempted coup sparked a more widespread cry for reform and greater recognition that imperial rule was open to challenge. Between 1963 and 1970, Bale was in a permanent state of revolt, while a successful local coup was staged in Gojjam in 1968. There were also revolts in parts of Sidamo (1960) and Wolo (1970), while Addis Ababa witnessed regular student demonstrations from 1965 onwards, and the military became increasingly divided into imperial loyalist and liberationist factions. From 1967 onwards, the Eritrean Liberation Front (ELF) and Eritrean People's Liberation Front (EPLF) became highly militarised in their bid to achieve full independence for their province.

The ageing Haile Selassie responded to the atmosphere of dissent and loud cries for land reform – most Ethiopian peasants were still subject to the whims of local landlords – with increasingly repressive measures. Matters came to a head over the tragic 1973 famine in Wolo and Tigrai. As the BBC aired heartbreaking footage of starving Ethiopians, the imperial government first refused to acknowledge the famine's existence, and then – having retracted its initial denials – failed to respond to the crisis with any action meaningful enough to prevent the estimated 200,000 deaths that ensued. The disgraced cabinet resigned in February 1974 and a new prime minister was appointed shortly thereafter. Too little, too late: at around the same time the armed forces and police had established a co-ordinating committee called the Derg, which – guided by the slogan *Ethiopia Tidkem* (Ethiopia First) – gradually insinuated itself into a position of effective power by arresting officials it regarded to be incompetent and/or self-serving, and replacing the recently installed prime minister with a stooge in July of the same year.

On 12 September 1974, following seven months of ceaseless strikes, demonstrations, local peasant revolts and military mutinies, what little power the octogenarian (and possibly semi-senile) Haile Selassie still wielded was finally curtailed. The military arrested the emperor in his palace, and – in mockery of a grandiose imperial motorcade – drove him to a prison cell in the back of a Volkswagen Beetle, while his embittered subjects yelled out '*Leba!*' (Thief!). Details of the imperial imprisonment are unclear and only started to emerge many years later. Certainly, Haile Selassie was still alive when the Derg officially abolished the monarchy in March 1975, and he even made one last (unofficial) public appearance three months later prior to being hospitalised for an operation. It would appear, however, that 3,000 years of supposed Solomonic rule ended in the imperial palace on 27 August 1975, with the ailing and deposed emperor succumbing not to a heart attack, as the official line had it at the time, but to a smothering pillow held in place by his effective successor Colonel Mengistu Haile Maryam. Ethiopia's last emperor was buried next to a latrine outside the palace, only for his remains to be exhumed in the early 1990s and stored for several years in the Menelik Mausoleum in Addis Ababa. Haile Selassie was finally accorded a formal burial at Trinity Cathedral in November 2000.

THE DERG (1974–91) Immediately after the arrest of the emperor, power was handed to the socialist-inspired Military Co-ordinating Committee known as the Derg. Lofty socialist ideals or not, the Derg soon proved to be even more ruthless and duplicitous in achieving its goals than was its predecessor. Despite the ELF and EPLF having helped them get to power, the Derg wanted to retain Eritrea and determined that this should be done through force. In September 1974, they asked the prominent General Aman to lead them and to be their spokesperson; when Aman resigned two months later in protest at the Derg policy on Eritrea, he was placed under house arrest and killed. Fifty-seven important officials were executed without trial, including two previous prime ministers.

A provisional military government was formed by the Derg in November under the leadership of General Tefari Benti. A series of radical policies was implemented, most crucially the Land Reform Bill of March 1975, which outlawed private land ownership and allowed for the formation of collective land use under local *kebele* councils. Disenchantment with US support for the previous government and the persistence of a feudalistic economy into the 1970s made Ethiopia a fertile ground for socialism. Most of the Derg's attempts at collectivisation, villagisation and resettlement were met neither with popular support nor with significant success. Agricultural productivity showed less growth than population figures throughout Derg rule.

The number of local and national opposition groups mushroomed in 1975–76. One of the most important was the Tigraian People's Liberation Front (TPLF), which received training from the EPLF and allied itself to the cause of Eritrean self-determination while demanding a truly democratic Ethiopian government rather than a ruthless military dictatorship. The Derg responded to this outbreak of dissent with mass arrests and executions. The situation was exploited mercilessly by Vice-Chairman Mengistu Haile Maryam, who used it to justify an internal purge of the Derg, a self-serving process that culminated in February 1977 with the execution of seven party leaders including General Tefari. Mengistu thus became the unopposed leader of the provisional government; those who opposed him didn't do so for long.

By 1977, large parts of Eritrea were under rebel rule. There were rumblings from the newly founded Oromo Liberation Front (OLF), the organisation that represented Ethiopia's largest ethnic group. Somali-populated parts of eastern Ethiopia rose against the government army, aided by troops from Somalia, precipitating Russian and Cuban withdrawal from Somalia and support for Ethiopia. The result was a low-scale but occasionally very bloody war (10,000 troops died on each side in 1978) between Somalia and Ethiopia which closed the Djibouti railway line for several years and was only fully resolved in 1988. The unrest spread to the capital, where street conflict resulted in several hundreds of deaths. Furthermore, in early 1979, an estimated one million Ethiopians were affected by a famine in Tigrai, Wolo and Eritrea, and at least 10,000 people died.

Mengistu contrived to pull the country back into some sort of order in 1980, as much as anything by arresting and killing opposition leaders, and driving those who survived his purges into exile. Thousands upon thousands of Ethiopians were killed by the army; it is evidence of the cruelty of his regime that when a family wanted to collect a body for burial, it was required to pay the cost of the fatal bullet. Despite the semblance of peace, much of Somali-populated Ethiopia was practically autonomous, and the EPLF and TPLF continued to engage the regime in sporadic conflict.

Ethiopia leapt into the world spotlight in 1985. The latest famine was the worst in living memory. Its roots lay in three successive rainfall failures in Tigrai, Wolo, the eastern lowlands and even parts of Gondar and Gojjam, but it was exacerbated by politics: at first a Western refusal to send aid to a socialist country, and then, when aid finally arrived, by Mengistu's unwillingness to help food get to the troublesome province of Tigrai. One in five Ethiopians was affected by the famine; one million died, most of them in the northeast. It was a natural phenomenon, but the tragic scale it reached was entirely preventable.

Ethiopians have a different system of naming from most Western countries, one that resembles the Islamic system. As is customary in the West, the first name of any Ethiopian is their given name. The difference is that the second name of any Ethiopian is not an inherited family name, but simply the father's given name. In other words, an Ethiopian man called Belai Tadese is not Belai of the Tadese family, but Belai the son of Tadese, and he would be addressed as Belai. It is polite to address people older than you, or whom you respect, as Ato (Mister) or Waziro (Mrs). Again, you would use the person's own name, not their father's name – Belai Tadese would be addressed not as Ato Tadese but as Ato Belai. If Ato Belai has a daughter who is named Guenet, she will be known as Guenet Belai. If she marries somebody called Bekele Haile, her name won't change to Guenet Haile but will stay Guenet Belai. She would be addressed as Waziro Guenet and her husband as Ato Bekele. If they have a child they name Yohannis, he will be known as Yohannis Bekele.

It is worth noting that Ethiopians will not ask for your surname but for your father's name. When dealing with officials, you should obviously give the parental name on your passport – your surname. You will also find that, even in the most formal of situations, Ethiopians address Westerners according to their custom rather than ours – I am often addressed as Ato or Mister Philip, never by my surname.

In September 1987, Ethiopia was proclaimed a 'People's Democratic Republic' and technically returned to civilian rule, on the basis of a contrived election in which all candidates were nominated by the Derg. Mengistu was returned to power. In the same year, the Ethiopian People's Revolutionary Democratic Movement (EPRDM), allied to the TPLF and apparently supported by the EPLF, was formed with the major aim of initiating a true national democracy as opposed to regional secession. In May 1988, the government declared a state of emergency in Tigrai and Eritrea as an increasing number of major towns, even some as far south as Wolo, fell under rebel rule. Attempted peace talks in April 1989 met with dismal failure. By the turn of the decade, Mengistu remained in control of most of Ethiopia, but his regime's days were numbered.

ETHIOPIA POST-1990 The final nail was driven into the Derg by the collapse of European socialism in 1990. This resulted in a cutback in military aid to Mengistu, and his weakened army was finally driven completely from Tigrai and Eritrea. In May 1991, the EPRDM captured Addis Ababa and Mengistu jetted to safety in Zimbabwe. The new transitional government established by the EPRDM and headed by President Meles Zenawi abandoned Mengistu's failed socialist policies, and allowed the EPLF to set up a transitional government in Eritrea. After a referendum in which Eritreans voted overwhelmingly in favour of secession, Eritrea was granted full independence in April 1993.

Ethiopia may have been the only African country that avoided long-term colonialism, but equally it was also one of the last to enjoy any semblance of democratic rule. The first move to correct this was taken in December 1994, when the transitional government implemented a federal constitution that divided the country into 11 electoral regions, each of which was guaranteed political autonomy on regional matters and proportional representation in a central government. This move paved the way for the country's first democratic election in May 1995, which saw Zenawi voted in as prime minster alongside President Nagasso Gidada (a coupling that was returned to power in the election of 2000). Ethiopia, in late 1995, seemed set to put its troubled past behind it, under a democratically elected government that is by far the most egalitarian and least repressive the country has ever known.

Ethiopia's first years of democratic rule were tainted, however, by a gradual deterioration in its relationship with neighbouring Eritrea. The first outward sign of the two countries' growing economic antagonism was the relatively innocuous Eritrean decision, in November 1997, to replace the common currency of the birr with a new currency called the nacfa. The growing estrangement between the two governments – which only ten years earlier had been fighting alongside each other against the Derg – took more concrete expression in May 1998. Up until this point, the EPLF and EPRDM had tacitly agreed that the international boundary between Eritrea and Ethiopia would adhere to the regional border under the Derg. On 6 May, however, Eritrean soldiers approached Badme, the principal town of Ethiopia's 400km² Yirga Triangle, provoking a police shoot-out in which both sides suffered fatalities. The joint Ethiopian–Eritrean commission that met in Addis Ababa two days later was unable to defuse the situation, and a second military skirmish followed on 12 May. Ethiopia demanded the immediate withdrawal of Eritrean troops from the Yirga Triangle. Eritrea responded by claiming that the Yirga Triangle historically belonged to Eritrea and had been effectively occupied by Ethiopia prior to the Eritrean attack.

The abrupt transformation from free border to open hostility – which surprised most outside observers and locals alike – seemed initially to be unlikely to amount to more than a few border skirmishes over what was, and remains, a relatively insignificant patch of barely arable earth. On 5 June, however, the stakes were raised when Eritrean planes cluster-bombed residential parts of Mekele, including an elementary school, leaving 55 civilians dead and 136 wounded. Ethiopia retaliated swiftly by launching two air strikes on Eritrean military installations outside Asmara. In the following week, Eritrea launched a second cluster-bomb attack on Ethiopian civilians, targeting the border town of Adigrat, and expelled an estimated 30,000 Ethiopian residents from Eritrea. Despite growing international pressure for a negotiated settlement, both parties set about amassing troops at the border – some estimates place the number as high as 200,000 on each side. Border tension erupted into a full-scale military conflict in the first week of February 1999. By the end of that month, it is estimated that at least 20,000 Eritreans had been killed in the conflict, with a similar number of casualties on the Ethiopian side. The total tally of dead and wounded over the ensuing months remains a matter for conjecture; the humanitarian and economic costs of the enforced conscription, mass expulsions of each other's citizens and displacement of thousands of civilians on both sides are impossible to measure.

In part due to Ethiopia's superior diplomacy, and in part because the disputed territory had clearly been under Ethiopian jurisdiction since Eritrean independence, the OAU called for Eritrea to withdraw from all occupied Ethiopian territories on 21 June. Eritrea refused, and another bout of fighting broke out over the next week, leaving thousands more dead on both sides. Eritrea did little to help its increasingly indefensible position when its president refused to attend an OAU peace summit in Libya on 10 July. The pattern of failed attempts at diplomacy, generally initiated by Ethiopia, followed by a fresh outburst of border fighting, persisted for the remainder of 1999. One of the most pointless wars in living memory had by now taken on a significance that extended far beyond the patch of land that had provoked it, and many observers queried whether either side would ever be prepared to back down. By early 2000, a tense virtual ceasefire hung over the border, but the Eritrean government publicly announced that it would not withdraw, and was ready for further conflict. The first diplomatic breakthrough occurred in late February 2000, when the US envoy Anthony Lake and OAU special envoy Ahmed Ouyahia shuttled between Asmara and Addis Ababa in an attempt to secure a negotiated solution. Renewed conflict broke out over May and June, but by this time the Yirga Triangle was firmly back under Ethiopian control, and this final Eritrean attack resulted in an outright victory for Ethiopia, presumably the spur that drove Eritrea to the negotiating table. The ensuing Algiers conference resulted in an immediate ceasefire under the supervision of a UN peacekeeping force. On 12 December 2000 a peace agreement was signed, and the Yirga Triangle was formally restored to Ethiopian territory.

Cliché it might be, but it is difficult to see either side as a victor of an episode that resulted in such large-scale loss of life, and in the wholesale economic and social disruption of two closely affiliated countries that must rank as among the poorest in the world. As this book goes to print, it remains the case that many thousands of Ethiopians formerly resident in Eritrea, or Eritreans formerly resident in Ethiopia, remain in 'exile' in their nominal 'home country'. The financial toll – money that could so easily have been pumped into the road infrastructure, education, you name it really – is immeasurable, as was the loss of economic momentum and growing international confidence that characterised Ethiopia's immediate post-Derg years.

That momentum has been regained since the war ended, though the continued closure of the border with Eritrea and occasional warmongering outburst from the Ethiopian government is cause for long-term unease. And, partially because of this, Ethiopia's third general election, held in May 2005, demonstrated a mass retraction of urban support for Zenawi and the EPRDF.

DANGER: TOURISTS

Tourism need not be a destructive force for tribal people, but unfortunately it frequently is. We at Bradt Travel Guides Ltd totally support the initiative of the charity Survival International in protecting the rights of tribal peoples:

RECOGNISE LAND RIGHTS
- Obtain permission to enter
- Pay properly
- Behave as if on private property

RESPECT TRIBAL PEOPLES
- Don't demean, degrade, insult or patronise

DON'T BRING IN DISEASE
- Diseases such as colds can kill tribal peoples
- AIDS is a killer

Survival International (*6 Charterhouse Bldgs, London EC1M 7ET, UK;* +44 020 7687 8700; f +44 020 7687 8701; e *info@survivalinternational.org; www.survival-international.org*) is a worldwide organisation supporting tribal peoples. It stands for their right to decide their own future and helps them protect their lives, lands and human rights.

IF IT'S 2005, WE MUST BE IN ETHIOPIA

In September of 2007 Ethiopia began a year-long millennium celebration, which probably had the rest of the world scratching its head. According to the Ethiopian calendar, 11 September marked the start of the year 2000. Why such a difference? For the answer you have to go back some 400 years.

In 1582, the Christian world as a whole dropped the established Julian calendar in favour of the revised Gregorian calendar. Ethiopia did not, and it never has! As a consequence, Ethiopia is seven years and eight months 'behind' the rest of the Christian world. The calendar consists of 13 months (hence the old Ethiopian Tourist Authority slogan '13 months of Sunshine'), of which 12 endure for 30 days each, while the remaining month is just five days in duration (six days in leap years).

The first month of the Ethiopian year, Meskerem, coincides with the last 20 days of the Gregorian month of September and the first ten days of October. The months that follow are Tekemt, Hidar, Tahsas (during which the Gregorian New Year falls), Tir, Yekatit, Megabit, Miyazya, Genbot, Sene, Hamle, Nahase and the short month of Pagumen. Key dates in the Ethiopian calendar include Gena (Christmas, celebrated on 29 Tahsas/7 January), Timkat (Epiphany, celebrated 11 Tir/19 January), Kiddist Mikael (St Michael's Day, celebrated 12 Tir/29 January), Good Friday and Easter (moveable, though calculated slightly differently from other countries, and usually a fortnight later), Assumption Day (16 Nahase/22 August) and Meskel (The Finding of the True Cross, celebrated 17 Meskerem/27 September).

Ethiopian New Year falls on 11 September, which means that Ethiopia is seven or eight years behind Western time, depending on whether the date is before or after 11 September. For instance, the year that we consider to be 2013 will be 2005 in Ethiopia from 1 January to 10 September, and 2006 from 11 September to 31 December. Fortunately, most institutions that are likely to be used by tourists – banks, airline reservation offices, etc – run on the Western calendar, but you can get caught out from time to time.

The final poll results, which were announced almost four months later following repeat elections in 32 controversial constituencies, saw the EPRDF win the third term it sought with 327 of the possible 547 seats as compared with the opposition Coalition for Unity and Democracy's 170. But this represented a dramatic swing from the 2000 election, when all but 12 seats had been held by the EPRDF. Furthermore, the opposition took all 23 seats in Addis Ababa, leaving the government without much credibility in the country's most sophisticated voting bloc. Where this left Ethiopia was unclear at the time, but – despite the violent clashes between protesters and armed forces that left 38 civilians dead in June 2005, and an EU report questioning how free and fair the election actually was – it felt like an exciting and positive development, one with few precedents anywhere in Africa.

In 2007, in the midst of increasing tension between its citizenry and government, Ethiopia scaled back its millennium celebration, yet the still-planned festivities went on without major incidents. In 2010, Ethiopia went back to the polls, but the dramatic swing noted five years earlier was reversed as the ruling EPRDF claimed a landslide victory, winning 23 of the 24 parliamentary seats in Addis. While government officials hailed the election as 'free, fair and peaceful', Human Rights Watch and opposition party members claimed otherwise, claiming Meles Zenawi's ruling party had harassed and intimidated voters. Unlike 2005, tensions didn't boil over and the country moved on. Of greater concern was the new threat of famine on Ethiopia's doorstep. In early 2011 some 900,000 Somali refugees fled across the border into Ethiopia and Kenya to escape famine in the war-torn country. According to the UNHCR, some 143,000 Somalis are currently sheltered in five Ethiopian camps in Dollo Ado, which is now the second-largest refugee settlement in the Horn of Africa. Having learned hard lessons from the past, fortunately the Ethiopian government is now more open about its food-aid needs, and distribution channels are in place to minimise the impact.

As of 2012 the Eritrean conflict still simmers on, with Eritrea getting involved in additional border disputes with Djibouti. A new development has been Ethiopia's conflict in the eastern Ogaden region, where the government has been battling Somali separatists organised as the Ogaden National Liberation Front (ONLF). In April 2007 the ONLF attacked a Chinese oil operation in the town of Abole, killing 74. Since then both sides have been accused of atrocities. In addition, Ethiopia has accused both Eritrea and Somalia of running a proxy war in the region to weaken the Ethiopian government. These tensions have taken their toll on the Ethiopian economy, and while they pose a limited threat to travellers except in remote border areas, the killing of five foreign tourists near Erta Ale volcano in northern Afar in January 2012 has led to a renewed war of words, with Ethiopia blaming Eritrean gunmen for the attack and calling it 'an act of open terrorism'.

GOVERNMENT AND POLITICS

Prior to 1974, Ethiopia was an empire with a feudal system of government, headed from 1930 onwards by His Imperial Majesty Haile Selassie. The emperor was deposed and killed in the 1974 revolution, after which a 'provisional' military dictatorship, known as the Derg (literally 'Committee'), was installed. In 1984, Mengistu Haile Maryam, leader of the Derg, established the so-called Workers' Party as the sole legal party in Ethiopia. A new constitution, making Ethiopia a one-party republic with a formal president, was enacted in 1987. President Mengistu was ousted in 1991 by two rebel movements, the Ethiopian People's Revolutionary Democratic Front (EPRDF) and Eritrean People's Liberation Front (EPLF).

In 1991, a transitional government was installed by the EPRDF, which was a coalition party comprising the Tigraian People's Liberation Front (TPLF), the Ethiopian People's Democratic Movement (EPDM) and the Oromo People's Democratic Organisation (OPDO). The transitional government, made up of an 87-seat Council of Representatives led by TPLF chairman Meles Zenawi, was charged with drawing up a new constitution to replace the dictatorial systems of the past with a more democratic and federal form of government.

In December 1994, Ethiopia adopted a new federal constitution that decentralised many aspects of government. The country has subsequently been divided into a revised set of eight regions and three city-states, with borders delineated along ethno-linguistic lines. The regions are constitutionally guaranteed political autonomy in most aspects of internal government, although central government remains responsible for national and international affairs and policies.

The new constitution also enforced for the first time in Ethiopian history a democratic parliamentarian government, based around two representative bodies: the Council of the People's Representatives and the Federal Council.

The head of state is the State President, currently Girmay Wolde Giyorgis, who is elected by a two-thirds majority in a joint session of both councils and can sit for a maximum of two terms. Executive power is vested in the Prime Minister and Council of Ministers, who are elected from members of the Council of the People's Representatives. Ethiopia's first democratic election was held in May 1995. On 22 August of that year, the newly elected federal government embarked on its first five-year term under the EPRDF and Prime Minister Meles Zenawi and President Nagasso Gidada. A second democratic election held in May 2000 returned Zenawi and the EPRDF to power, as did the May 2005 and October 2007 elections, albeit with a vastly reduced majority.

FEDERAL REGIONS Ethiopia has been subject to several regional reshuffles in recent decades. It was divided into 15 regions prior to 1987, reorganised into 29 regions in the 1987 constitution, and then returned to more or less where it had started in 1991, when the transitional government divided the country into 14 administrative regions. These were based precisely on 13 of the original regions, with Addis Ababa administered separately, and Assab and Eritrea by then part of independent Eritrea. In 1994, Ethiopia became a federal republic and the regional map was redrawn from scratch, this time along widely accepted ethno-linguistic lines. The result was eight regional states (*astedader akabibi*) and three city-states, all of which had far stronger federal powers than the old regions. Each region is divided into a few zones and a larger number of districts or *woredas*. On the whole, these district names are of no interest to tourists, but a few are of historical significance, or are regularly referred to in casual use, or function as 'Special *woredas*' devoted to a particular small ethnic group and with a higher degree of autonomy than normal *woredas*.

The modern regions of Ethiopia are described below in alphabetical order.

Addis Ababa Located more or less at the dead centre of Ethiopia, and surrounded by the state of Oromia, the capital city of Ethiopia is governed as a 540km² city-state of which less than 5% is rural. According to July 2011 estimates of the Central Statistical Agency of Ethiopia, the population of Addis Ababa is 2.9 million of which 51.6% are female. Almost half of Addis Ababa's cosmopolitan population is Amhara, with Oromo, Gurage and Tigraian residents respectively making up 19%, 17% and 7.6% of the remainder. More than 80% of its residents are Orthodox Christians. The capital city is subdivided into six zones and 28 *woredas*. Amharic is the working language, but English is widely spoken.

Afar Although it covers a vast area of 270,000km² running up the border with Djibouti and Eritrea, Afar region is arid, thinly populated and almost bereft of large towns. According to July 2011 estimates of the Central Statistical Agency of Ethiopia, the total population of Afar is 1.5 million, of which less than 10% live in urban areas. The tiny capital of Assaita will be replaced by the purpose-built capital of Semere in the near future. Afar region is named for the pastoral people who comprise roughly 92% of its population (the remainder consists mostly of people from elsewhere in Ethiopia who have settled in the region). Geographically, Afar forms the most northerly part of the Rift Valley, and it is characterised by low-lying plains that receive less than 200mm of rainfall annually. The Awash River runs through Afar from south to north, draining into a set of desert lakes south of Assaita on the Djiboutian border. Salt and various minerals are mined in the region.

Amhara Governed from its large modern capital city of Bahir Dar, on the southern tip of Lake Tana, Amhara covers an area of 170,752km² and supports a population estimated at 18.5 million in 2011. Although the substantial cities of Bahir Dar,

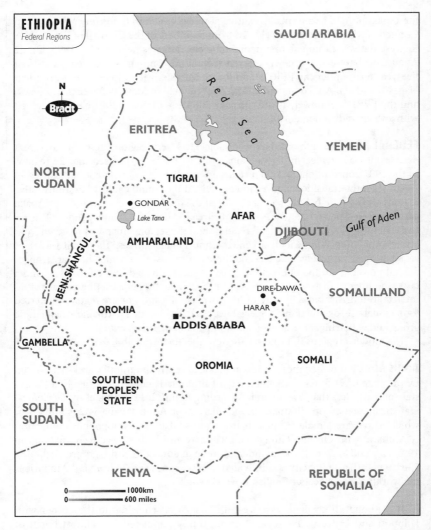

ETHIOPIA
Federal Regions

SAUDI ARABIA

Red Sea

ERITREA

YEMEN

NORTH
SUDAN

TIGRAI

● GONDAR
Lake Tana

AFAR

DJIBOUTI

Gulf of Aden

AMHARALAND

BENI-SHANGUL

SOMALILAND

DIRE-DAWA ●

OROMIA

HARAR ●

■ ADDIS ABABA

GAMBELLA

OROMIA

SOMALI

SOUTHERN
PEOPLE'S
STATE

SOUTH
SUDAN

KENYA

REPUBLIC OF
SOMALIA

0 ━━ 1000km
0 ━━ 600 miles

Gondar and Dessie all lie within Amhara, roughly 90% of the region's population is rural. The Amhara people for whom the state is named comprise more than 90% of the population, and Orthodox Christians outnumber Muslims by a ratio of 4:1. Several of Ethiopia's most popular tourist sites lie in Amhara, most notably the former imperial capitals of Lalibela and Gondar. The Simien Mountains to the north of Gondar include Ethiopia's highest peak, the 4,620m Mount Ras Dejen, and harbour the country's main concentrations of the endemic gelada baboon and Walia ibex. Lake Tana, Ethiopia's largest body of water and source of the Blue Nile, also falls within Amhara, as does the Blue Nile Falls.

Benishangul-Gumuz The most obscure of Ethiopia's regions, practically never visited by tourists, is Benishangul-Gumuz, which runs for about 2,000km along the Sudanese border to the east of Amhara, but is on average no more than 200km wide. Relatively low-lying but with an annual rainfall in excess of 1,000mm, this remote and poorly developed area is characterised by a hot, humid climate. The regional population of about 939,000 is governed from the small capital town of Asosa in the south.

Dire Dawa Dire Dawa is Ethiopia's second-largest city, with a population exceeding 377,000, but the administrative boundaries of the city-state cover an area of around 130km², boosting the total to 430,000. Surrounded on all sides by the region of Oromia, the dominant ethnic group of this cosmopolitan city is the Oromo (48%), but there are also substantial Amhara, Somali and Gurage populations. Amhara is the official language of Dire Dawa, and Muslims outnumber Christians by a ratio of 2:1.

Gambella The small state, which covers an area of 25,274km² along the southern Sudanese border, essentially comprises lush, humid lowland draining into the Baro River, an important tributary of the Nile. Relatively remote and undeveloped, Gambella region supports a predominantly rural population of roughly 369,000 ethnically varied people. The main nationalities represented in the vicinity of the regional capital, the small river port of Gambella, are the Nuer and Anuwak, who respectively account for 40% and 27% of the regional population. Minority

ETHIOPIAN TIME

Ethiopians, like the Swahili of neighbouring Kenya and Tanzania, measure time in 12-hour cycles starting at 06.00 and 18.00. In other words, their seven o'clock is our one o'clock, and vice versa. To ask the time in Amharigna, you say *sa'at sintno*? Times are *and sa'at* (hour one) through to *asir hulet sa'at* (hour 12). When talking Amharigna, you can be confident all times will be Ethiopian. When talking English, people may or may not give you European time, so check. If they say am or pm, it will definitely be European time. Otherwise, ask if it is Europe (pronounced like *Orop*) time or *habbishat* time; or else convert to Ethiopian time – for instance, if someone says a bus leaves at one, ask if they mean *and sa'at* or *sabat sa'at*. After a month in the country, I decided it was simplest to change my watch to Ethiopian time.

With typical Ethiopian perversity, kids who speak no other English love asking you the time. Of course, they don't understand the answer. It is worth getting to know how to give times in Amharigna purely for the astonishment of kids' faces when you whammy them with the reply they're not expecting. This is quite simple because Ethiopians only worry about gradations of five minutes – so four minutes past five becomes five minutes past five, etc. However, I was once quite sternly ticked off for giving seven minutes past as five minutes past – seven minutes past is, or so I was informed, ten minutes past!

So here, assuming you've pushed your watch six hours forward, is the full list of times from *and sa'at* to *hulet sa'at*:

13.00	*and*	13.35	*lehulet hamist guda*
13.05	*and kemist*	13.40	*lehulet haya guda*
13.10	*and kesir*	13.45	*lehulet rub guda*
13.15	*and kerub*	13.50	*lehulet asir guda*
13.20	*and kehaya*	13.55	*lehulet amist guda*
13.25	*and kahayamst*	14.00	*hulet*
13.30	*and tekul*		

groups include the Mezhenger, Apana, Komo and various recent migrants from the highlands. Although the state is predominantly Christian, more than half the population subscribes to recently introduced protestant and evangelical denominations, with the remainder adhering to Orthodox Christianity, Islam or traditional animism. A fair amount of wildlife – lion, elephant and buffalo as well as various monkeys and antelope – persists in Gambella region.

Harari Consisting of the walled city of Harar and its immediate environs, Harari is essentially a modern revival of the autonomous city-state of Harar, which was one of the most powerful regional political entities from the 16th until the late 19th century, when it was co-opted into Abyssinia by Menelik II. The state covers an area of roughly 350km² and supports a population estimated at 205,000, of which some 131,000 are city dwellers. Roughly half of the population is Oromo, with the Amhara accounting for another 33% and the Harari only 7%. Despite Harar's reputation as the home of Islamic Ethiopia, roughly 40% of its population is Christian. The lush farmland around Harar is known for its chat and coffee plantations, but other major crops include sorghum, maize and oranges.

Oromia The vast region of Oromia covers an area of more than 350,000km² (almost one-third of the country) and supports a correspondingly large population of over 30 million people. Roughly 85% of the regional population is Oromo, and another 10% Amhara. Aside from the 5% who still practise animist or other traditional religions, the regional split between Christian and Muslim is as good as even. The official language of Oromifa is inscribed with Latin script rather than the Arabic characters used elsewhere in the country. With its mostly fertile soils, Oromia is the breadbasket of Ethiopia, producing more than half of the nation's agricultural crop, and it is also home to almost half of its large livestock. Geographically and climatically diverse, Oromia hosts many of Ethiopia's more alluring natural attractions, notably Bale and Awash national parks and the lakes of the Rift Valley and Bishoftu. It is rich in minerals, ranging from gold and platinum to iron ore and limestone. Oromia encircles and is currently governed from Addis Ababa (known as Finfine in Oromifa and sometimes signposted as such within the state). In the year 2000, the administration was officially moved to Adama (Nazret), but 2005 protests by the Oromo Peoples' Democratic Organization succeeded in moving the offices back to Addis.

Somalia Named for the distinctive Somali people, who comprise 95% of its population, this is the second largest of Ethiopia's regions, covering an area of 250,000km² along the Somali border. Much of the region is desert or semi-desert, and despite its vast area, the total population is around 4.9 million. The capital is Jijiga, to the east of Harar. Almost 99% of the population is Muslim, and most of its residents are pastoralists. The important Wabe Shebelle River runs through the region.

Southern Nations, Nationalities and Peoples' State Although it smells like the handiwork of an uninspired committee, the name of this 112,323km² region does provide an accurate reflection of its incredible cultural diversity. The regional population of roughly 16.8 million represents some 45 different ethno-linguistic groups, of which none comprises 20% of the regional population, and only the Sidamo, Gurage and Walaita make up more than 10% each. The regional capital is the modern city of Awassa, set on the shore of the eponymous lake, and much of the region lies in the relatively low-lying Rift Valley and Kenyan border area. The most important crop is coffee. Aside from the Rift Valley lakes, the most popular tourist attraction is the remote cultural tribes of South Omo zone.

Tigrai Ethiopia's most northerly region is Tigrai, which covers 80,000km² and is administered from its capital city of Mekele. The population totals more than 4.8 million, of which 95% are Orthodox Christian and the remainder Muslim. The Tigraian people, the dominant ethnic group, are agriculturists who also herd cattle and other livestock. Tigrai is drier than other parts of highland Ethiopia, and prone to periodic droughts, but the region is intensively cultivated and in some areas terraced. Tigrai has been central to many of the more important events in Ethiopian history, from the adoption of Christianity by the Axumite emperor in the 4th century, to the defeat of Italy outside Adwa 1,500 years later. The city of Axum and associated archaeological sites are the main tourist attractions, but the 120 rock-hewn churches scattered throughout the east of the country are also well worth exploring.

ECONOMY

Ethiopia is one of the world's poorest nations. In the late 1980s, the per capita income was US$120 per annum, and it remained at that level until recently. Due to rapid growth over the past ten years, current per capita estimates have doubled to more than US$240 per annum. (This is the nominal figure. In terms of purchasing power parity (PPP), GDP per capita is US$1,000.) This rise, however, largely represents the emergence of a wealthy middle class and does not reflect an improved quality of life for all. The average life expectancy previously dropped from 47 to 45, primarily due to AIDS-related deaths (roughly three million Ethiopians are estimated to be HIV positive) but has recently rebounded to 56 years. The birth rate is 77 per 1,000 people, with an infant mortality rate of 9%. Adult literacy stands at 42.7%.

The Ethiopian economy is dominated by subsistence agriculture, accounting for almost 50% of GDP. The Ethiopian Highlands are very fertile, and are criss-crossed by large rivers with enormous untapped potential for irrigation projects, but many parts of the country, particularly in the east and northeast, are prone to periodic rain failures and locust plagues, so there is a constant threat of local famines. The growing of coffee occupies much of the population with coffee accounting for 60% of Ethiopia's exports. Ethiopia earned a record US$841.6 million from the export of nearly 200,000 tonnes of coffee in 2010/11, representing a 59% increase earned in 2009/10 and a 124% increase from 2008/09. The main crop grown for local consumption is *tef*, the grain used to make *injera* (a kind of pancake widely available throughout the country).

Ethiopia is rich in mineral deposits, and ores such as gold and iron have been mined since ancient times. There has been little commercial exploitation of Ethiopia's minerals, largely due to inaccessibility, but a new network of Chinese-built roads may change this in the near future. The main product mined is salt. Manufacture in Ethiopia is limited almost entirely to the processing of agricultural products, although Ethiopia did celebrate its first domestically built automobile courtesy of a joint Dutch venture in 2005.

The war with Eritrea forced the government to throw a large proportion of their scarce reserves at military investment, and to increase taxes. Development of services and the infrastructure suffered as a result of the war, which also precipitated a sharp decline in foreign investment. Both foreign investment and large, foreign-backed infrastructure projects have rebounded, but government services continue to suffer, with water and power shortages becoming increasingly common.

PEOPLE AND CULTURE

Ethiopia has a cultural, historical and linguistic identity quite distinct from that of the rest of Africa, largely because it has spent long periods of its history in virtual isolation. It is fair, if rather simplistic, to say that Ethiopia is where the ancient world and Africa meet. Northern Ethiopia, or more specifically the ancient Axumite Kingdom, which centred on the modern province of Tigrai, had strong links with ancient Egypt, the Judaic civilisations of the Middle East, and Greece, evidenced by much of the ancient art and architecture that has been unearthed in the region. Pre-Christian civilisation in Tigrai is divided by historians into several eras, but stripping away the technicalities it can be said that Axum was an urbanised culture of blended classical and African influences from at least 600BC and quite possibly earlier.

Modern Ethiopia is heavily influenced by Judaism. The Ethiopian Orthodox Church, founded in Axum in the 4th century AD, has multifarious Jewish influences, which – along with the presence of an ancient Jewish community in the former provinces of Gojjam and Wolo – suggests a large pre-Christian Judaic influence in Ethiopia. Islam, too, arrived in Ethiopia in its formative years, and it is the dominant religious group in eastern Ethiopia south of Tigrai. In this torrent of well-attested Judaic influences, it is often forgotten that much of what is now southern Ethiopia has few ancient links to the Judaic world. The Oromo (referred to as the Galla prior to the 20th century) are Ethiopia's largest linguistic group. They were pagan when they first swept up the Rift Valley into Ethiopia in the 15th century, but are now predominantly Christian, with imported Catholic and Protestant denominations more influential than they are in northern Ethiopia. The society and culture of southern Ethiopia are more typically African in nature than those of the north. In the Omo Valley and the far western lowlands near Sudan is a variety of peoples whose modern lifestyle is still deeply African in every sense – in fact, you would struggle to find people anywhere in east Africa so cut off from the mainstream of modern life.

Before plunging into further religious and historical discussion, it should be noted that the term Ethiopia, as used historically, need not refer to Ethiopia as we know it now. The term Ethiopic arose in ancient Greece (it means burnt-faced) and was one of two used to describe the dark-skinned people of sub-Saharan Africa. The other term, Nubian, referred to the almost black-skinned people of the Nile Valley in what is now Sudan. Ethiopians, in biblical or classical terms, are in essence Axumites, or more broadly the people who lived in the Ethiopian Highlands roughly north of the Blue Nile. In medieval times and during the Renaissance, nobody in Europe knew quite where Africa began or ended – medieval literature often uses the terms India and Ethiopia interchangeably – but there was a strong association of Ethiopia with the wealthy and isolated Christian kingdom of a person who Europeans called Prester John (see page 19). Once again, then, medieval Ethiopia is best thought of as the Christian empire of the highlands which, judging by the distribution of churches from this time, extended from Tigrai to Showa province just south of modern-day Addis Ababa. As Europeans gradually came to explore Ethiopia, the terms Ethiopia and Abyssinia (the latter deriving from the Arabic word *habbishat,* meaning 'mongrels') became interchangeable.

Again, the Abyssinians or Ethiopians would generally be seen as the subjects of the Christian empire, who were often at war with the Muslim empires of the eastern highlands and the Galla. Modern Ethiopia is a by-product of the 19th-century Scramble for Africa, and it incorporates the old Muslim empire based around Harar, vast tracts of thinly inhabited Somali, Afar and Borena territory, the lands occupied by the Oromo and, in the far west, areas that the Greeks would have considered to be Nubian. In my opinion – and in the context of what follows – Ethiopia, Abyssinia and *habbishat* are approximately synonymous terms relating to the Christian empire of the highlands, at least until the great unifying leaders of the late 19th century – Tewodros, Yohannis IV and Menelik II – laid the groundwork for the modern Ethiopian state. None of which means for a moment that, in a modern sense, a Muslim from Harar is any less Ethiopian than a Christian from Axum.

The previous *History* section dwells mainly on the old Christian cultures of the highlands, and their Muslim counterparts. Background details for other Ethiopian cultures are to be found in the appropriate chapters of Parts Two to Six.

POPULATION Ethiopia currently (July 2011) has a population of over 90.8 million people. This gives Ethiopia the second-highest population of any country in Africa, surpassing Egypt, and exceeded only by Nigeria. The major ethnic/linguistic groups are the Oromo (34.5%), Amhara (26.9%), Tigrai (6.1%), Sidamo (4%) and Somali (6.2%).

The 1987 population of Addis Ababa was approximately 1.6 million, but by 1994 it had swelled to 2.3 million and today it stands at around 3.1 million, though some estimates are significantly higher. Reliable population figures for other large towns do not exist, and the available estimates are evidently not entirely reliable (different sources place the population of Gambella, for instance, as far apart as 24,000 and 72,000) but other towns whose population probably exceeds the 100,000 mark are Dire Dawa (307,000), Adama (251,000), Gondar (214,000), Dessie (185,000), Mekele (185,000), Bahir Dar (184,000), Jimma (175,000), Bishoftu (144,000), Awassa (138,000), Harar (131,000), Jijiga (107,000) and Shashemene (102,000). Other towns with a population of greater than 50,000, in approximate descending order of size, are Kombolcha, Adigrat, Arba Minch, Nekemte, Debre Markos, Asela, Hosaina, Sodo, Debre Birhan, Gambella, Ziway and Dilla.

More than half of the population of Ethiopia is aged 17 or under, and the population growth rate stands at roughly 3.2% per annum. As some measure of the effect of this rapid growth, the population was estimated at 24.2 million (excluding Eritrea) as recently as 1968. Then, only 19 towns outside of Eritrea harboured more than 10,000 people, as opposed to approximately 125 such towns today. As a point of reference, the ten largest towns in Ethiopia back in 1968 were Addis Ababa (645,000), Dire Dawa (50,700), Harar (42,700), Dessie (40,600), Gondar (30,700), Jimma (30,580), Adama (27,800), Mekele (23,100), Bishoftu (22,000) and Debre Markos (21,500). Other towns whose populations then stood at greater than 10,000 were Axum, Adwa, Asela, Nekemte, Bahir Dar, Dilla, Akaki, Sodo and Yirga Alem.

MUSIC

Practically unknown to the rest of the world, the music of Ethiopia, in common with so many other aspects of this insular highland country, sounds like nothing you've ever heard before. True enough, many outsiders find the trademark lurching three-four signature, twitchy cross-rhythms, brassy instrumentation, taut pentatonic melodies and nail-on-blackboard vocal affectations somewhat impenetrable on initial contact, I daresay even a little irritating. But, while repeated exposure won't make converts of us all, Ethiopia's diverse blend of the traditional and the contemporary, of exotic and indigenous styles must rank as one of Africa's greatest undiscovered musical legacies, reaching its apex with the ceaselessly inventive and hypnotically funky horn-splattered sides of 'Ethiopian swing' recorded for a handful of independent labels in Addis Ababa between 1969 and 1978.

The roots of the music scene that blossomed in Addis Ababa during the dying years of the imperial era are predictably peculiar. It all started in April 1924, when Ras Tefari, then acting as regent for the Empress Zawditu, made a state visit to Jerusalem and was received by a brass band consisting of Armenian orphans. Who knows whether it was the actual music that caught the future emperor's attention, or simply the plight of his fellow Orthodox Christians, who had fled their homeland to escape the genocide perpetrated by their Islamic Turkish neighbours in 1915? Either way, the Arba Lijotch (Forty Children), as they came to be known affectionately by their hosts, arrived in Addis Ababa in September of that year to form the first imperial brass band under the tutelage of the long-time Armenian-born Ethiopian-resident music professor Kevork Nalbandian.

The underpaid Arba Lijotch disbanded of its own accord in July 1928. But the foundation stone had been laid for the permanent Imperial Bodyguard Band formed in 1929 under the leadership of the Swiss orchestra leader Andre Nicod. Comprising a few dozen arbitrarily chosen slaves from Wolega, the original Imperial Bodyguard Band was by all accounts more notable for its noisiness than its aptitude, but its limited repertoire of stuffy marches nevertheless became something of a fixture at important imperial occasions, and some genuine talent

ETHIOPIQUES

Compiled by Ethiopian music expert Francis Falceto, the ever-expanding series of *Ethiopiques* CDs released by the French label Buda is of particular significance for making available a vast number of old vinyl recordings that had been out of print since the 1970s. Available in specialist CD shops, the full series can also be ordered online through the label's website (*www.budamusique.com*) or other online retailers such as www.amazon.com or www.amazon.co.uk. Better still, the full series can be downloaded cheaply and legally from www.emusic.com, a superb site that charges as little as US$0.22 per track if you take out a contract.

Highlights of the series – there aren't really any lowlights – include *Ethiopiques 1* and *Ethiopiques 3*, which anthologise some of the most popular tracks released by Amha Records between 1969 and 1975, providing an excellent overall introduction to the era's leading artists such as Mahmoud Ahmed, Girma Beyene, Muluqen Mellesse, Hirut Bekele, Alemayehu Eshete and Tlahoun Gessesse. Either set is a great starting point.

Better still in my opinion, not least for its greater focus on female artists such as the sublime Bizunesh Bekele (the uncrowned 'First Lady' of Swinging Addis) and her unrelated namesake Hirut Bekele, is *Ethiopiques 13: Ethiopian Groove*. This is a re-release of an early 1990s collection of Kaifa's 1976–78 output, also compiled by Francis Falceto, and its present format is marred only by the criminal absence of the trio of early Aster Aweke recordings that ranked as highlights of the original.

Ethiopiques 5 performs a similar round-up of some of the best Tigrigna recordings made by prominent Eritrean artists of the same era, such as Tewelde Redda, Tekli Tesfa-Ezghi and the irresistibly nicknamed Tebereh 'Doris Day' Tesfa-Hunegn. Aside from the linguistic difference, much of this music has a more traditional, drum-based sound than its Amharigna equivalent, and the melodies,

soon started to emerge from the ranks prior to the Italian occupation of 1935. The occupation formed something of a low watermark for the fortunes of Ethiopian musicians, many of whom were imprisoned, in particular the traditional *azmari* minstrels whose subversive lyrics used the time-honoured *sem ena werk* (wax over gold) technique of using love songs as a vehicle for stinging political innuendo.

The reinstatement of Haile Selassie after six years in exile was soon followed by the creation of a new Imperial Bodyguard Band under Kevork Nalbandian, who handed over the reins to his equally influential nephew Nerses in 1949. From the mid 1940s to the late 1950s, a succession of foreign music teachers such as Alexander Kontorowicz and Franz Zelwecker were hired to run academies whose graduates went on to play in an ever-growing number of brass-oriented orchestras, all of which – oddly enough – were effectively on the payroll of one or other imperial institution, be it the police, the military or even Addis Ababa municipality. Despite this, the musical vocabulary of these brass bands gradually expanded by exposure to exotic new styles such as jazz, R&B and soul, which were broadcast around the country from the American military radio station in Asmara.

So the scene was set for the explosion of musical fecundity that peaked during the edgy, uncertain, exciting years that separated the failed coup of 1960 from its more consequential 1974 sequel. As was the case elsewhere in the world, the 1960s witnessed immense social changes in Addis Ababa, underlain by the growing sense of the imperial regime as an illiberal, outmoded and ultimately doomed institution. This realisation, initially confined to the educated classes in major urban centres

based on the same pentatonic scale, are often punctuated by yelps, chants and the wild ululation characteristic of African tribal music from the Cape to the Horn.

The 1970s recordings of Mahmoud Ahmed feature exclusively on *Ethiopiques* 6 and 7. The latter disc, subtitled *Ere Mela Mela*, is an expanded version of the eponymous release by the Belgian label Crammed Disc in 1986 and includes one full KLP as well as several 45s recorded in 1975. *Ere Mela Mela* is something of a legend as the first Western release by any Ethiopian artist, and it earned rave reviews in the likes of the *NME* and the *New York Times*. Other dedicated single-artist releases in the series include *Ethiopiques 9* (funky 'Abyssinian Elvis' Alemayehu Eshete) and *Ethiopiques 14* (the revered jazz-influenced saxophonist Getachew Mekurya).

For those with an ear for the more traditional forms, a highly recommended starting point is *Ethiopiques 2*, an anthology of *azmari* and *bolel* singers working the *tej* bets and bars of Addis Ababa. Very different but equally engaging is *Ethiopiques 18: The Lady With The Krar*, a collection of beautiful traditional azmari renditions on a lyre-like instrument called a *krar* by former actress Asnaqech Werku – as a bonus, English and French translations of the pithy lyrics are provided with the CD.

If you're looking to cherry-pick a few *Ethiopiques* tracks to download from www.emusic.com, here's my selection: 'Ete Endenesh Gedawo' by Muluqen Mellesse (vol 1), 'Yeqer Memekatesh' by Mahmoud Ahmed (vol 1), 'Tezeta' by Seyfu Yohannis (vol 1), 'Bolel' by Zawditu & Yohannis (vol 2), 'Temeles' by Alemayehu Eshete & Hirut Bekele (vol 3), 'Ab Teqay Qerebi' by Tewelde Redda (vol 5), the rocksteady-tinged 'Ewnetegna Feger' by Hirut Bekele (vol 13), the wonderfully haunting 'Ateqegn' by Bizunesh Bekele (vol 13), 'Yegenet Muziqa' by Getachew Mekurya (vol 14) and 'Fegrie Denna Hun' by Asnaqech Werku (vol 17).

such as Addis Ababa, Asmara and Dire Dawa, though it would spread into rural areas by the early 1970s, stemmed partly from the challenge that the failed coup of 1960 had presented to the notion of imperial immortality. But it was also doubtless associated with the increased exposure to an outside world that was itself changing rapidly, as more and more outsiders affiliated to broadly left-of-centre institutions such as the Organisation of African Unity, Non-Alignment Pact and American Peace Corps, which made Ethiopia their temporary home.

Sadly, the evocative monochrome photographs collected in Francis Falceto's recently published book *Abyssinie Swing* are practically all that remain of the wild R&B-influenced sounds and hedonistic nightclubs that partied until the early morning during the heady early years of the so-called Golden Age of Ethiopian Music. In 1948, the emperor had passed legislation that effectively granted the state-run Hagere Fiker Maheber an exclusive licence to import and produce gramophone records, and this no doubt worthy institution (literally, 'The Love of Country Association') concentrated its best efforts on recording dull state events and the like for posterity. As a result, those of us who weren't there can only guess what the music of this era actually sounded like, but mid 1960s photographs of rows of future recording stars such as Mahmoud Ahmed and Tlahoun Gessesse harmonising in finger-clicking unison suggest a greater dependence on vocal harmonies than is evident on the recorded material that would eventually emerge from 'Swinging Addis'.

For the modern audiophile, Ethiopia's musical golden age effectively began in 1969, when Amha Eshete, manager of the country's first non-institutional band the Soul Echoes, decided to risk imperial wrath and form his own independent label Amha Records. Despite some initial rumblings from Hagere Fiker Maheber, Amha was allowed to operate freely and it positively thrived, releasing an average of 20 45rpm singles and two LPs annually, and launching the recording careers of the likes of Mahmoud Ahmed, Muluqen Mellesse, Hirut Bekele, Alemayehu Eshete, Getachew Kassa and Tlahoun Gessesse prior to its closure in 1975. By that time, however, two other labels inspired by Amha were also thriving, Philips Ethiopia and Kaifa Records, the latter formed by the highly influential and long-serving Ali Abdullah Kaifa, better known as Ali Tango. The 500-odd two-track recordings produced by these independent labels collectively form practically the only aural record of the Ethiopian music scene during the last two decades of the imperial era, and it also constitutes the bulk of the music re-released on the *Ethiopiques* CDs since the late 1990s by the French label Buda.

So what did it sound like? Well, on one level, it was strongly derivative of contemporary Western music, as hinted at by the nicknames of popular artists such as the Asmara-based singers Tebereh 'Doris Day' Tesfa-Hunegn and Tukabo 'Mario Lanza' Welde-Maryam. Even the most cursory listen to a few tracks by Alemayehu Eshete, the so-called 'Abyssinian Elvis', suggests a more than passing familiarity with the extended funk workouts beloved of James Brown's backing band, while jazz buffs liken the blazing saxophone work of Getachew Mekurya to Albert Ayler and Ornette Coleman. Elsewhere, you'll hear hints of Stax, Motown, early rock 'n' roll, pop, fusion jazz, blues-rock bands such as Santana and Chicken Shack, and even – in the late 1970s – ska and reggae. But such influences are superficial, as almost every track recorded during this period also displays that distinctively Ethiopic combination of a lopsided rat-a-tat shuffle, uneasy Arabic-sounding pentatonic shifts and strained, quavering, rather nasal vocals. The result, in most instances, is at once edgy and hypnotic, mournful yet danceable, propulsive yet jerky – above all, perhaps, very, very strange. The recordings of Alemayehu Eshete, for instance,

ASTER AND GIGI

The most consistently popular Ethiopian recording artist since she first appeared on the scene in the late 1970s is Gondar-born, California-based Aster Aweke, who still enjoys such a high profile among her compatriots that it would be remarkable to go a full day in any Ethiopian city without hearing what the *Rough Guide to World Music* describes as 'a voice that kills'. It is certainly one of the most thrilling vocal instruments ever to have emerged from Africa, pitched somewhere amongst Aretha Franklin (a stated influence), Kate Bush and Björk, with a fractured but raunchy quality that can be utterly heartbreaking.

The closest thing Ethiopia has produced to a genuine crossover artist, Aster has 20 albums, though her earliest – and some say best – material for Kaifa is available only on hard-to-track-down cassettes in Addis Ababa (and long overdue the attention of those nice people at *Ethiopiques*). Seven albums are available on CD, of which *Aster* is frequently recommended as the best starting point, for reasons that elude me – aside from the standout acoustic rendition of the chestnut 'Tizita', one of her most compelling recordings ever, it is typified by bland mid-tempo backings and unusually muted vocal performances. My first choice would be the 1993 CD *Ebo*, which is distinguished by the propulsive growling opening blast of 'Minu Tenekana', the twitchy, wide-eyed 'Esti Inurbet', and a trio of fine ballads: the wracked 'Yene Konjo', the hauntingly melodic 'Yale Sime' and the pretty but overlong 'Yewah Libane'.

Heir apparent to Aster's long-standing international status as Ethiopia's best-known singer is the 31-year-old Ejigayehu Shibabaw, who embarked on a solo career under her more concise nickname of Gigi after stints singing and performing in Kenya, France and South Africa. Gigi is an acknowledged disciple of Aster (in a 2004 interview with *Afripop*, she states, 'If it wasn't for [Aster] I wouldn't be a singer. I was so much in love with her music and I still love her'), and she possesses a similarly haunting voice, though admittedly it's not quite so strung out or fractured.

Gigi's first album *One Ethiopia* (downloadable from www.emusic.com) is likeable enough without being hugely distinguished, but her second eponymous CD, which features contributions from the likes of jazz musicians Herbie Hancock, Wayne Shorter, Bill Laswell, Pharoah Sanders and various traditional Ethiopian musicians, is a stunner. Released in 2001, *Gigi*'s appeal lies in its organic, eclectic sound, which sets typical Amharigna vocal inflections against a rich fusion of jazz, reggae and other African styles – had I heard standout track 'Bale Washintu' blind, for instance, I would have assumed it originated from Mali rather than Ethiopia. The follow-up *Zion Roots*, released in 2004, is reputedly just as good.

The release of *Gigi* inspired *Afripop* to proclaim its namesake as 'the most important new African singer on the scene today', while the *New York Times* rated it number one in a year-end round-up of the Best Obscure Albums of 2001. Meanwhile, its bold experimentation across genres and the use of a song traditionally reserved for male singers has drawn criticism from conservative elements in Ethiopian society. But one person who evidently listened favourably is Aster, whose sublime 2004 release *Aster's Ballads* (re-recordings of 12 self-penned classics, many otherwise unavailable except on cassette) has a strikingly fresh and intimate sound, with the tinny keyboard fills that characterise her other CD releases replaced by a warmer, earthier ambience.

don't really sound like James Brown so much as they evoke the improbable notion of the Godfather of Soul in his funky late-'60s pomp being asked to perform an Islamic prayer call!

Over 1974–75, the imperial era came to its final, bloody conclusion, and Swinging Addis collapsed with it, to be replaced by the joyless socialist dictates of the Derg. The live music scene in particular was muted, thanks to an overnight curfew that endured for a full 16 years. The pioneering Amha Records closed in 1975, and its owner left Addis Ababa for the USA. All the same, Ethiopia in the late 1970s wasn't quite the musical wasteland it is sometimes portrayed to have been. Kaifa Records thrived on the demand for fresh recordings to accompany the surreptitious lock-in parties that replaced the nightclub scene of years earlier. Indeed, some of the label's finest vinyl releases date to 1976–78, as anthologised on the out-of-print 16-track CD *Ethiopian Groove: The Golden 70s* (recently reissued with an altered track listing as *Ethiopiques 13*). Furthermore, from 1978 onwards, Kaifa switched its attention from vinyl to the cheaper medium of cassettes, resulting in sales of greater than 10,000 copies for a popular release, as opposed to around 3,000 vinyl copies. It was in 1978, too, that a Gonderine teenage prodigy named Aster Aweke (see box, *Aster and Gigi*, page 45) – destined to become arguably the greatest recorded female vocalist ever produced by Africa – cut a pair of debut 45rpm singles for Kaifa, followed by five full-length cassettes, before relocating to the USA in 1981.

All the same, the dawn of the cassette era does seem to have coincided with a slump in innovative musicianship. Music was still recorded prolifically under the Derg, it still sold well, and the likes of Aster Aweke and Mahmoud Ahmed produced some superb vocal performances. But, linked perhaps to the demise of the live music scene and emigration of many of the country's finest musicians, the punch and elasticity that characterised the backing bands captured on Amha and Kaifa's vinyl releases gradually gave way to a more stodgy and synthetic will-that-do style of backing that detracted from even the most evocative singing. All-plodding mid-tempo dreariness punctuated by pointless tinkling frills, this genre of musical backing still persists on some recordings made in the post-Derg era, many of which also drag on for far too long – if the greats could say it in three minutes, why do mediocre modern session musicians require six, seven or eight minutes to plink-plonk their way to a tepid conclusion? More encouragingly, the potential breakthrough artist Gigi (see box, *Aster and Gigi*, page 45) has reverted to a warmer, more organic live sound on her recent recordings, and other newcomers such as the female duo Abro Adeg (literally 'Two Friends') and American-based warbler Hana Shenkute do at least attempt to use synthesised backings creatively. Recent years have also seen a resurgence of traditional music in the form of Addis Ababa's *bolel* singers, who mix the pithy sarcasm and grumbling bluesiness of the ancient azmari minstrels with more contemporary cultural and political observations.

Since the new millennium, Ethiopian music has continued to evolve with the emergence of a number of new artists who have garnered attention both locally and internationally. Stepping out in 2001 Teddy Afro (real name Tewodros Kassahun) has quickly become of one of the most successful, and controversial, Ethiopian singers and songwriters in recent times. Born to artistic parents – his mother was a well-known professional dancer and his late father a highly regarded Ethiopian songwriter – Teddy's politically and socially motivated songs from his third album *Yasteseryal* (2005) became the anthem for anti-government protests in 2005. That same year Ethiopia's first home-grown reggae artist Jonny Ragga (Yohannes Bekele) released his first solo album *Give Me the Key*. The singer who hails from Addis

Ababa has collaborated with several international artists including American R&B artist, K'alyn, and South African rapper Zola and has won several awards, including first place at the Fes'Horn Music Festival in Djibouti in 2006. Ethiopia's latest rising star is pop singer Helen Berhe (aka the Ethiopian Beyoncé) who is best known for her cover of Nada Algesa's 'Uzaza Allina' and in 2010 released her new album *Tasfelegnaleh* (I Need You).

In addition to the CDs mentioned in the textboxes *Ethiopiques* and *Aster and Gigi*, a good entry-level compilation of Ethiopian sounds is the *Rough Guide to Ethiopian Music*, which was released in 2004 and includes tracks by artists including Aster Aweke, Mahmoud Ahmed and Alemayehu Eshete.

LANGUAGE

Ethiopia supports a diverse mix of linguistic groups. Some 70 languages are spoken in Ethiopia, most of them belonging to the Semetic or Cushitic branches of the Afro-Asiatic family. The most important Semetic languages are Amharigna (Amharic) and Tigrigna of northern Ethiopia, both of which descend from Ge'ez, the language of ancient Axum, which is still used by the Ethiopian Orthodox Church. The Gurage and Zay of southern Ethiopia also speak Semetic languages, as do the people of Harar in the east. Amharigna was the official language of Ethiopia under Mengistu and it remains the lingua franca in most parts of the country that are likely to be visited by tourists. Ethiopia's Semetic languages are transcribed in a script that is unique to the country. This consists of over 200 characters, each of which denotes a syllable as opposed to a letter.

Cushitic languages are dominant in southern and eastern Ethiopia. The most significant of these is Oromifa (Oromigna), the language of the Oromo (or Galla), Ethiopia's largest ethnic group. The Somali language also belongs to the Cushitic group. Cushitic-speakers transcribe their language using the same Roman alphabet that we do: you may well be told that the Oromo 'speak' Roman. In the Omo river valley, a localised group of languages of Afro-Asiatic origin are spoken. These are known as Omotic languages, and are quite closely affiliated to the Cushitic group. Along the western border with Sudan, languages are mostly of the unrelated Nilotic group.

It should be noted that linguistic terms need not imply anything about ethnicity. Many British people with a purely Celtic genealogy, or Afro-Americans for that matter, speak only English, which is a language of the west Germanic branch of the Indo-European group. Linguistic patterns are the best means available to scientists for tracing the broad sweep of prehistoric population movements, and in some instances – for instance the Oromifa-speaking Oromo – there is a strong association between language and a cohesive ethnic identity. Nevertheless, the exclusive use of a Semetic language in Tigrai need not mean that all Tigraian people are of Semetic origin. Just as one would not refer to an English-speaking American as English, it is more accurate to speak of Cushitic- or Semetic-speakers, rather than Cushites or Semites. It's a semantic point, but one which is often misunderstood, particularly in the African context, and which has fuelled (I use the past tense optimistically) more than its share of racist pontificating.

English is the most widely spoken European language as it is used for secondary education. French is heard on occasion in some parts of the country, particularly in the southeastern highlands near Djibouti. Some elderly Ethiopians speak Italian, most commonly in Tigrai and around Addis Ababa. (See also *Appendix 1, Language*, page 597.)

RELIGION

The main religions in Ethiopia are Christianity and Islam. Until recently, a population of indigenous Ethiopian Jews, known as the Bet Israel (House of Israel) or Falasha, was concentrated in the part of Amhara region formerly administered as Gojjam and Wolo provinces. In medieval times, the Falasha were a major force in Ethiopia's internal politics, but several centuries of warfare and persecution had reduced their numbers greatly by the late 20th century, and the 30,000 individuals who survived were airlifted to Israel in the last decade of the Derg's rule. A few isolated Falasha communities reputedly inhabit the remote mountains of Lasta district in eastern Amhara.

It is difficult to find reliable figures for the relative distribution and proportion of Muslims and Christians in Ethiopia. Some sources suggest that 50–60% of Ethiopia is Muslim. Geographically, this could well be the case, as the thinly populated eastern lowlands are strongly Muslim, but I find this an incredible figure in population terms. The 2007 census suggests that 33.9% of Ethiopians are Muslim, which is at least plausible, though it still sounds a little high. The main concentrations of Muslims are in the eastern part of the country, especially in the regions of Harari, Somali and Afar, as well as in the far east of Tigrai, Amhara and Oromia. Whatever the statistics say, Ethiopia feels like a predominantly Christian country.

The majority of Ethiopian Christians belong to the Ethiopian Orthodox Church, which is often, but erroneously, referred to by outsiders as the Coptic Church. The Coptic Church is an Egyptian Church (*Coptic* is an Ancient Greek word meaning Egyptian), which took shape in Alexandria in the 2nd and 3rd centuries AD, and broke away from Rome and Constantinople in AD451 following its adoption of the Monophysitic doctrine. (This contentious doctrine, which asserts the single and primarily divine nature of Christ, was considered heretical by Rome and Constantinople, whose Dualistic philosophy held that Christ had discrete human and divine personalities.) The Ethiopian Orthodox Church was founded in Axum in the 4th century AD and its first bishop, Frumentius, was consecrated in Alexandria. Strong ties have always existed between the churches of Ethiopia and Alexandria, and until 1955 the Ethiopian Church *technically* fell under Alexandria's governance. Within Ethiopia, however, it was the Abbot of Debre Libanos and not the archbishop sent from Alexandria who assumed the role of Church primate. Since 1955, the Ethiopian Orthodox Church has been self-governing, with its own seat on the World Council of Churches. Not once have I heard an Ethiopian Christian call his church Coptic, nor did the word meet with any recognition when I used it in Ethiopia. The Church of Ethiopia is, like the much less numerically significant Coptic Church, a Monophysitic Church; more importantly, to Ethiopians it is *the* Ethiopian Orthodox Church, and bracketing it with the Coptic Church is a typical example of a Western refusal to recognise any institution that is unique to sub-Saharan Africa.

Am I being too harsh? I recently laid my hands on a history of religion (in its favour, almost the only source which confirmed my growing suspicion that the Coptic Church of Ethiopia was a Western label) which describes Ethiopian Christians as 'ignorant', their religious notions as 'almost entirely superstitious' and the Church itself as 'one of the most degraded forms into which Christianity has degenerated'.

Even the most casual familiarity with the customs of the Ethiopian Orthodox Church offers proof that it is a most singular institution, further removed from the Coptic Church than most Western denominations are from each other.

Apart from the odd emissary from Alexandria, Ethiopian Christianity developed in virtual isolation until the arrival of the Portuguese Jesuits in the 15th century and, although its fundamentals are indisputably Christian, the rituals are infused with all sorts of archaic Jewish influences, acquired, one imagines, from the Falasha and other ancient Jewish sects that lived in pre-Christian Ethiopia. Orthodox Ethiopians practise male circumcision a few days after birth, they hold regular fasting days and the women are governed by a variety of menstruation taboos. They recognise both the Christian Sabbath of Sunday *and* the Jewish Sabbath of Saturday, and they indulge in celebratory religious dances that would be considered blasphemous by other Christian denominations.

At the heart of Ethiopian mysticism lies an unfathomable, and I think rather fascinating, relationship between Christianity and the Ark of the Covenant, the very core of Judaism until its apparent disappearance from Jerusalem led to the reforms of Josiah in around 650BC. Ethiopians believe that the original Ark was brought to Axum in the 1st millennium BC, and that it rests there to this day. What's more, the most holy item in every Ethiopian church is the *tabot* – a replica of the Ark (or, more accurately, a replica of one of the Tablets of the Law which were placed in the Ark by Moses). The *tabot* is only removed from the Holy of Holies on important religious days, and it is at all times obscured from view by a cover of draped sheets.

While the north of Ethiopia is predominantly Orthodox, other exotic denominations such as Catholicism and Protestantism have found their way to the country, and they are practised widely in the south, most numerously among Oromifa-speakers, whose conversion to Christianity is a relatively recent thing.

GETTS

Grant Express Travel and Tours Services p.l.co

LOOKING FOR
THE BEST-EQUIPPED TOUR OPERATOR IN ETHIOPIA, WITH EFFICIENT AND RESPONSIVE MANAGEMENT, A LARGE FLEET OF WELL-MAINTAINED VEHICLES AND ARTICULATE, ENERGETIC, PROFESSIONAL GUIDES?

MAKE GETTS YOUR FIRST CHOICE

Services

Carefully-crafted tours to top destinations, including:
- The Northern Historic Route
- Simien Mountains National Park
- Omo Valley and the Southern tribes
- Bale NP, the walled city of Harar, and much more

Tailor-made tours for group and individuals:
- Special-interest programs and religious tours
- Day tours of Addis Ababa and surrounding sites
- Congresses, conferences and special events
- Chauffeured car and van rentals

The GETTS Difference

Competitive pricing, with flexible payment options
Meticulous attention to all of the details:
- Airline ticketing and reservations
- All bookings and hotel reservations
- Well-trained, multilingual guides
- State-of-the-art camping gear
- Friendly and knowledgeable staff
- Reliable, speedy, and secure communications

With GETTS, nothing comes between you and the best.......

P.O.Box 42662, Addis Ababa, Ethiopia Tel: +251-115-534379 / 534678
Mobile: +251-911-233289 Fax: +251-115-534395

2

Natural History

Ethiopia is a land of dramatic natural contrasts. Altitudes span the lowest point on the African continent as well as the fourth-highest peak, while climatic conditions range from the scorching arid badlands of the Somali–Kenyan border region to the drenched slopes of the fertile southwest. The vegetation is no less diverse than the topography and climate, embracing parched desert, drenched rainforest, brittle heath-like Afro-alpine moorland, and pretty much everything in between.

Far from being the monotonous thirstland of Western myth, the southern and western highlands of Ethiopia boast the most extensive indigenous rainforest anywhere in the eastern half of Africa. The central highlands, though more openly vegetated, are fertile and densely cultivated. Towards the end of the rains, in September and early October, the wild flowers that blanket the highlands are second only to those of Namaqualand in South Africa. The northeast highlands of Tigrai are drier and generally thinly vegetated except during the rains. The Rift Valley south of Addis Ababa has a characteristically African appearance, with vegetation dominated by grasses and flat-topped acacia trees. The western lowlands around Gambella have lushly tropical vegetation. Only the vast but rarely visited eastern and southern lowlands conform to the image of Ethiopia as a featureless desert.

It is probably fair to say that Ethiopia's greatest natural attraction to the average tourist will be the wonderful and ever-changing scenery. Wildlife, though once prolific, has been hunted out in most areas, and even those savanna national parks – Nechisar, Mago, Omo and Awash – which do protect typical African savanna environments support low volumes of game by comparison with their counterparts in most eastern and southern African countries. Balanced against this, Ethiopia's fauna and flora, though essentially typical of sub-Saharan Africa, also display some strong links to lands north of the Sahara, ie: north Africa, Europe and the Middle East. One manifestation of this is the presence of several species that are endemic (unique) to Ethiopia because of their isolation from similar habitats, including the Ethiopian wolf, gelada monkey, mountain nyala, Walia ibex and Somali wild ass.

Whatever it may lack in terms of mammalian abundance, Ethiopia is one of Africa's key birdwatching destinations. A rapidly growing national checklist of more than 800 bird species includes 16 endemics, as well as a similar number of near-endemics whose range extends into a small part of neighbouring Eritrea or into Somalia. For birdwatchers based in Africa, Ethiopia is also of great interest for a number of Palaearctic migrants and residents that are rare or absent further south. For birdwatchers based elsewhere, Ethiopia offers as good an introduction to African birds as any country. True enough, Kenya, Uganda and Tanzania all have significantly longer checklists, but specialist ornithological tours to Ethiopia often pick up in excess of 450 species over two weeks, a total that would be difficult to beat anywhere in Africa.

MAMMALS

The number of large mammal species present in Ethiopia is comparable to countries like Kenya and Tanzania, but populations are generally low and many species' distributions are restricted to remnant pockets in remote areas. Because game viewing is not a major feature of tourism in Ethiopia, detailed descriptions of appearance and behaviour here are restricted to those species that are of special interest to visitors to Ethiopia. For species seen more readily in other parts of Africa, coverage is limited to details of known or probable distribution and status within Ethiopia. This section should thus be seen as an Ethiopia-specific supplement to any of the continental field guides recommended at the end of this book.

OVERVIEW OF ETHIOPIA'S PROTECTED AREAS

There are 15 national parks in Ethiopia, including several newly designated parks, and two sanctuaries. In the highlands, the Simien Mountains National Park (page 233) and Bale Mountains National Park (page 483) protect Ethiopia's two highest mountain ranges. The primary attractions of these parks are scenic and they are most popular with hikers, though Bale is accessible to non-hikers by the highest all-weather road in Africa. Neither park protects large volumes of game, but they do form the last remaining strongholds of Ethiopia's endemic large mammals. Bale is the better park for wildlife viewing: the endemic Ethiopian wolf and mountain nyala are common, as is a variety of more widespread mammal species and 16 endemic birds. Simien is the more scenic reserve and the best for trekking. Three endemic mammals – Walia ibex, Ethiopian wolf and gelada monkey – are present in the Simien range, but only the baboon is common enough to be seen by most hikers. About halfway between Simien and Bale, the newly designated Borena Sayint National Park (page 320) lies on the plateau in the heart of South Wolo. Its dense forests harbours some 23 large mammals including klipspringer, caracal, black-and-white colobus, jackal and bushbuck as well as 57 bird species, while endemic Ethiopian wolf and gelada can be spied in the higher-altitude moorlands.

Four national parks lie in the Rift Valley. The northernmost of these is Yangudi Rassa National Park (page 399), set in the very dry Somali border region. The park has been set aside to protect the Somali wild ass, the ancestor of the domestic donkey. It is reasonably accessible, as the main Assab road runs right through it, but is of marginal interest to most tourists, especially as the odds of seeing the ass are negligible. The more accessible Awash National Park (page 389), which lies a few hours' drive east of Addis Ababa and protects a varied though somewhat depleted mammalian fauna, is a dry-country reserve abutting the Awash River below the impressive Fantelle Volcano. In the southern Rift, Abiata-Shala National Park (page 458) and Nechisar National Park (page 521) protect, respectively, lakes Abiata and Shala, and lakes Chamo and Abaya. Both parks are scenically attractive and provide wonderful birding, but only Nechisar supports significant herds of game, most visibly common zebra and various antelope.

The most important reserves for large game are Omo National Park (page 551) and Mago National Park (page 552), which adjoin each other in the Omo Valley near the Kenyan border. These national parks still support thin but substantial populations of elephant, buffalo, lion and a large variety of antelopes and primates. Finally, Gambella National Park (page 589) lies in the remote, marshy west close to the town of Gambella, and as with Mago and Omo it still supports

PREDATORS The most common large predator is the **spotted hyena**, which is present in the most thinly populated parts of the country, especially at lower altitudes, and is reasonably visible in most national parks and reserves. Scavenging hyenas commonly frequent the outskirts of towns. The most reliable place to see them is Harar, where a so-called hyena man lures them every evening with raw meat. The striped hyena also occurs in Ethiopia but it is very unlikely to be seen.

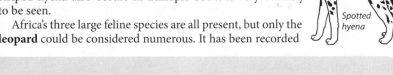

Spotted hyena

Africa's three large feline species are all present, but only the **leopard** could be considered numerous. It has been recorded

significant though diminishing herds of elephant and buffalo, as well as the localised white-eared kob and Nile lechwe, and predators such as lion and leopard.

Several important sanctuaries have not yet been awarded national park status. The most accessible of these is Senkele Game Sanctuary (page 466) near Shashemene, which despite its small size forms the main stronghold of the endemic Swayne's hartebeest. Yabello Wildlife Sanctuary near the town of the same name supports a variety of dry-country antelope, large herds of Burchell's zebra, and endemic Stresemann's bush crow and white-tailed swallow. The Babile Elephant Sanctuary (page 428) near Harar is home to a small but seasonally accessible population of small-tusked desert elephants. The Entoto Natural Park (page 165) on the outskirts of Addis Ababa supports some large game, but is mainly of interest to birders, as is the underrated Menegasha National Forest (page 568) to its west. A well-developed area of great interest to hikers, trekkers and wildlife enthusiasts is the trail through the Dodola–Adaba Forest Reserve (page 478), where five cabins offer access to highland species similar to those in Bale National Park. Then there is the little-known Guassa Community Conservation Area (page 363) near Debre Sina, a 300-year-old community reserve protecting the country's third-largest population of Ethiopian wolves, as well as most of the endemic highland birds.

Many unprotected parts of Ethiopia offer good but limited wildlife viewing; the following overview is far from comprehensive, and several other interesting spots are covered in the main body of this guide. The forests of the western highlands still support a high density of monkeys, often to be seen from the roadside, as well as a rich selection of forest birds. The Rift Valley lakes all offer superb birding, particularly the unprotected Ziway and Hawassa, the latter also home to troops of guereza monkey. Also in the Rift Valley, the forests around Wondo Genet are known for their excellent forest birding and prolific monkeys. Hippos and crocodiles survive in many unprotected areas, of which Lake Boyo outside Jimma and the Koko Dam near Adama are very accessible. Gelada monkeys are often seen outside national parks in certain parts of the northern highlands, notably Ankober and Mugar Gorge. Another great birding spot in the north is Lake Tana, and the nearby Blue Nile Falls. Due to the conservationist ethics of the Ethiopian Orthodox Church, many old monasteries and churches lie in isolated patches of indigenous woodland, which often support a few monkeys and forest bird species.

For further information, see the Ethiopian Wildlife Conservation Authority's website: http://www.ewca.gov.et.

Leopard

in most national parks and can be assumed to inhabit the forests of the south and west, but it is also notoriously secretive and you would be lucky to see one. Ethiopians often refer to it as a tiger, since the Amharigna word *nebir* is used to describe both cat species. The slighter **cheetah** is strongly associated with open country,

Cheetah

but it is now very rare in Ethiopia, with small numbers occurring in the dry plains of the southeast and in thinly populated parts of the Rift Valley.

The Abyssinian race of **lion**, distinguished by the male's impressive black mane, is still present in very small numbers in the savanna and dry thorn bush of the Rift Valley (for instance Awash, Nechisar, Omo and Mago national parks) and the Somali and Kenyan border regions. It has also been recorded in such unlikely habitats as the Afro-alpine moorland of Bale National Park. The one place you can be certain of seeing an Abyssinian lion is in the zoo at Siddist Kilo in Addis Ababa!

THE ETHIOPIAN WOLF

The one predator that every wildlife enthusiast will want to see is the Ethiopian wolf *Canis simensis*, the most rare of the world's 37 canid species, and listed as critically endangered on the 2000 IUCN Red List. The genetic affinities of this unusual predator puzzled scientists for several decades, as reflected in several misleading common names – until recently, outsiders most often called it the Simien fox, while Ethiopians still know it as the red jackal (*kai kebero* in Amharigna). But recent DNA tests have determined that despite appearances to the contrary, it is neither fox nor jackal, but a closer genetic ally of the European grey wolf than any other African canid. It probably evolved from an extinct wolf species that colonised the area in the late Pleistocene era. Two distinct races are recognised, distinguished by slight differences in coloration and skull shape, with the Rift Valley forming the natural divide between these populations.

The Ethiopian wolf stands about 60cm high, making it significantly larger than any jackal, and has a long muzzle similar to that of a coyote. It has a predominantly rufous coat, broken up by white throat and flank markings, and a black tail. It is a diurnal hunter of Afro-alpine moorland and short grassland, where it feeds mostly on rodents, including the endemic giant mole rat. Unlike most canids, it is essentially a courser rather than a hunter, though packs have been observed to bring down small antelope, and it will often eat carrion.

As recently as the mid 19th century, the Ethiopian wolf was widespread and common in the Ethiopian Highlands. Its numbers have since dwindled dramatically, for reasons that are not understood precisely but which are probably more related to introduced diseases such as canine distemper and rabies (the culprits, incidentally, for the drastic reduction in continent-wide African hunting dog populations in the last few decades) than to deliberate hunting. The wolf is now practically confined to high-altitude moorland in national parks and on other high mountains.

Ethiopia's best-known canid is the **Ethiopian wolf** (see box below) but it also supports all three African **jackal** species, with the black-backed jackal commonest in the south and Eurasian jackal in the north. The endangered **African hunting dog** has been recorded in southern Ethiopia but is probably now verging on extinction there. The **bat-eared fox** is common in parts of South Omo, while widespread but very rarely seen nocturnal predators include **civet**, **genet**, **serval**, **caracal** and **aardvark**.

Black-backed jackal

African wild dog

PRIMATES It is somewhat ironic, given Ethiopia's international image, that the large mammal most frequently seen from the roadside in the south and west is the forest-dwelling **guereza** or **black-and-white colobus monkey**. This beautiful monkey is easily distinguished from other primates by its white beard and flowing white tail and is commonly

Guereza monkey

Fewer than 600 Ethiopian wolves are left in the wild, spread across about ten isolated populations, of which only four are thought to number more than 20 individuals, and can be considered viable breeding populations. The southern race is by far the more numerous and more concentrated of the two. Its main stronghold is Bale National Park, where an estimated population of perhaps 200 represents a major decline from Chris Hillman's estimate of 700 in 1976. Another 80–150 Ethiopian wolves live in scattered pockets in the Arsi Highlands, which lie to the immediate east of Bale. It is not known to what extent the different populations in Arsi and Bale interbreed with each other, and thus whether they form one reasonably large gene pool or several smaller ones.

The northern race of Ethiopian wolf may number fewer than 100 in the wild. Its long-term prospects are forlorn indeed. The wolf population in the Simien Mountains has never recovered from a rabies epidemic several years ago, and it now stands at no more than 40 individuals, and probably fewer. A more important stronghold for the northern race is the Guassa Plateau, where at least 50 individuals are thought to remain. One or two packs probably survive in a few other remote moorland localities, such as Mount Guna and Mount Abuna Yoseph, but in such small numbers, and so far from other populations, that even their short-term prospects are bleak. Rare they might be, but Ethiopian wolves are not difficult to see, at least not in Bale National Park. On the road through the open Sanetti Plateau, sightings are virtually guaranteed, even from public transport. Hikers, or people who drive up for the day, might encounter wolves a dozen times!

The IUCN-published *The Ethiopian Wolf: Status Survey and Conservation Action Plan* compiled by Claudio Sillero-Zuburi and David Macdonald is highly recommended to those with a special interest in this unique canid and its conservation. See also the Ethiopian Wolf Conservation Programme (EWCP) website (*www.ethiopianwolf.org*).

The striking and unmistakable gelada monkey (sometimes referred to as the gelada baboon) *Thercopithecus gelada* is the most common of Ethiopia's endemic large mammal species, with the population estimated by some to be as high as 500,000. The male gelada is a spectacularly handsome and distinctive beast, possessed of an imposing golden mane and heart-shaped red chest patch. This patch is thought to serve the same purpose as the colourful buttocks or testicles found on those African monkeys that don't spend most of their lives sitting on their bums!

The gelada is the only mammal endemic to Ethiopia that cannot to some extent be regarded as endangered. This singular primate is unique in that it feeds predominantly on grasses, and it is probably the most sociable of African monkeys, with conglomerations of 500 or more regularly recorded in one field. It has a harem-based social structure that is regarded to be the most complex of any animal other than humans.

In evolutionary terms, the gelada is something of a relic, the only surviving representative of a genus of grazing monkeys that once ranged far more broadly across Africa. The gelada stock is ancestral not only to the modern baboons that have largely displaced them in savanna and other open habitats, but also to the baboon-like drills of west Africa, and to the smaller and more arboreal mangabeys, both of which have re-adapted to rainforest habitats.

The gelada is distributed throughout the northern highlands, where it is generally associated with cliffs and ravines. You're bound to see them if you visit the Simien Mountains, which form the species' main stronghold, and they are also numerous on the Guassa Plateau. They are often seen in the vicinity of Ankober, Debre Sina and Debre Libanos, and at the Muger River Gorge near Addis Ababa.

seen in family groups. Its major habitat is forest canopies so it is abundant in the western and southeastern highlands, but it is also found in smaller stands of moist woodland throughout the south, most notably on the shore of Lake Awasa, in the forests of Nechisar, at Wondo Genet and on Mount Zikwala.

Also common, the **grivet monkey**, sometimes considered to be conspecific with the east African vervet monkey, is generally associated with wooded savanna more than true forest, though in Ethiopia it is likely to be seen wherever there are indigenous trees. The Ethiopian form is quite distinct from other east African races; it is a darker grey in general colour and has white cheek-marks that could lead to it being mistaken at a glance for a form of blue monkey (which appears to be absent from Ethiopia's forests). The very localised and secretive **Bale vervet monkey**, thought by some authorities to be a race of vervet and by others a distinct species, is an Ethiopian endemic confined to bamboo stands in the Harenna forests and Bale Massif.

Common baboon

Two true **baboon** species are found in Ethiopia. The most common is the olive or **Anubis baboon** – regarded by some to be a race of the common or savanna baboon, Africa's most widespread primate. This dark olive-brown baboon has a wide habitat tolerance and is common in most of the national parks, as well as in rocky areas and cliffs throughout the south and west of the country. The more lightly built – and lightly coloured – **Hamadryas baboon** is found in Awash National Park and more northerly parts of the Rift Valley and its escarpment.

ANTELOPES A large number of antelope species are present in Ethiopia, many of them with limited distribution, largely because so many different habitats converge around the Ethiopian Highlands.

Bushbuck

The *Tragelaphus* family, a group of antelopes that is notable for its spiralled horns and striking markings, is the best represented antelope genus in Ethiopia, comprising six of the nine species present, including the endemic **mountain nyala** (see box, page 61). The most widespread of these is the **bushbuck**, a slightly hunchbacked inhabitant of all types of forest and riverine woodland, including exotic eucalyptus stands. Of particular interest is the handsome **Menelik's bushbuck**, an endemic highland race, commonly seen in Bale National Park and in forests near Addis Ababa, notable for the male being almost black in colour, but with white throat and leg markings, and light spotting on its flanks. The widespread **Powell's bushbuck** has more typical bushbuck coloration: the male is chestnut-brown with white striping or spotting and relatively small horns, and the female is reddish-brown with white spotting reminiscent of certain northern hemisphere deer.

Greater and lesser kudu

The **greater** and **lesser kudu** are both widespread in southern Ethiopia. Both species are dark grey in general colour and have white vertical stripes on their sides (the lesser kudu normally has ten or more stripes, the greater kudu fewer than ten). The greater kudu is the second tallest of all African antelopes and the male, when fully grown, has magnificent spiralling horns up

AFRICAN WILD ASS

Yangudi Rassa National Park, bisected by the Assaita road to the north of Awash National Park, is the home of the African wild ass, the ancestor of the domestic donkey. The wild ass is not a true Ethiopian endemic; it still occurs in parts of India, and was once a lot more widespread in Africa, where Nubian, Somali and Algerian races were recognised. The Nubian and Algerian races are probably extinct now – occasional reports of wild asses are thought to be misidentified feral donkeys. Neither is any wild ass left in Somalia, which had a population of 10,000 at the turn of the 20th century. The 300 to 500 wild asses that live in Yangudi Rassa are therefore the only confirmed population left in Africa.

I haven't seen a wild ass – few people have – but a former warden of Yangudi Rassa told me they are very beautiful in their wild state. They are seen with reasonable frequency in the park, but are difficult to distinguish from the more common feral donkeys with which they co-inhabit. Reportedly, you can tell the wild ass from the donkey by its sleeker, plainer coat – a rather subtle difference in the field, I would imagine.

to 1.5m in length. Both species live in woodland; they are often found alongside each other, though the lesser kudu has a greater tolerance of dry conditions. The greater kudu is very common in Nechisar National Park and a viable population is present in Abiata-Shala. Both kudu species are found in Awash National Park, and they may be seen outside reserves in the dry acacia woodland of the far south and east.

The only African antelope larger than the greater kudu is the **eland**, which has a rather bovine appearance, with twisted horns that seem small for an animal of its size. It is seasonally abundant in the parks of South Omo but absent elsewhere.

The **gazelle** family comprises a dozen similar-looking species, most of which inhabit arid habitats and half of which are thought to occur somewhere in Ethiopia.

Eland

Gazelles are medium-sized antelopes with gently curved small to medium-sized horns, a tan coat with white underparts and in some species a black side-stripe. **Grant's gazelle**, a long-horned species without a side-stripe, will be familiar to anybody who has visited east Africa's reserves. It reaches the northern extent of its range in the southern Rift Valley of Ethiopia, and is often seen in Nechisar National Park and along the Moyale road south of Dilla. The total Ethiopian population is estimated at about 6,000.

The gazelle most likely to be seen by tourists to Ethiopia is **Soemmerring's gazelle**, which like Grant's gazelle has no side-stripe, but is easily distinguished by its black face with white cheek-stripes and relatively small, backward-facing horns. Both species have a white rump, but that of Grant's is less extensive and is bordered by black stripes. Soemmerring's gazelle is quite common on the plains around Awash National Park and is often seen along the roads to Harar and Assab. This gazelle, though listed as present in six countries, is now extirpated or very rare in most of them. The nucleus population of about 6,500 in the northern Ethiopian Rift Valley is by far the most significant one left.

Thomson's gazelle is the most common east African species, easily recognised by its heavy black side-stripe and, in the case of the Ethiopian and Sudanese race (called the **Mongalla**), a white eye-circle. In Ethiopia, the 'Tommy' is historically restricted to the far southwest, where it might well be extirpated. Similar in size and general appearance to Thomson's gazelle, but darker and with a less defined side-stripe, **Speke's gazelle** is endemic to Somalia, bar one old record for the Ogaden area of southeast Ethiopia. The much paler and very plain **Dorcas gazelle** is a Saharan species that occurs in the Djibouti border area of Ethiopia, where it is quite common. **Heuglin's gazelle**, red in colour with a thin black side-stripe, is a race of the Sahelian red-fronted gazelle that occurs locally in the Sudanese–Ethiopian border area to the east of the Nile River.

Thomson's gazelle

The **gerenuk** is an atypical and unmistakable gazelle with a red-brown coat and a very long neck. Its range extends from east Africa into the drier parts of southern Ethiopia, where it may be seen stretched up on its hind legs browsing on the higher branches of acacia trees. The gerenuk is the most commonly seen large antelope in the South Omo region. Similar in appearance, the **dibatag** is a very rare antelope whose range has always been confined to a specific type of evergreen bush in Somalia and the Ogaden region of southeast Ethiopia. The population has decreased dramatically in recent years, and protection is complicated by the ongoing instability of the Somali border area. Should you happen to come across a dibatag, the combination of white eye-ring extending down the nose and elongated neck will be diagnostic.

Two virtually indistinguishable **reedbuck** species are found in Ethiopia. These are medium-sized antelopes with a plain light tan coat, generally found in high grass and moorland. The **Bohor reedbuck** is common in Bale National Park. The **mountain reedbuck** occurs throughout the country and is regularly seen at Fantelle Volcano in Awash National Park. Related to the reedbuck is the **waterbuck**, a large antelope with a shaggy brown coat and sizeable lyre-shaped horns; the Defassa race of waterbuck has a pale rump while the common race has an upside-down white on its rump. Waterbuck are most often seen grazing in relatively open vegetation near water; they are found at a few scattered localities in southern Ethiopia.

Reedbuck

The related **Nile lechwe** is an exceptionally handsome antelope associated with marshy ground and floodplains in the border area of Sudan and Ethiopia. Its main range is in Sudan, where it is still thought to be present in herds of 1,000 or more. In Ethiopia, it is practically restricted to Gambella National Park, where it is increasingly scarce and vulnerable – recent estimates suggest the Ethiopian population may be fewer than 100. Also restricted to the Gambella area, the **white-eared kob** is a localised and possibly endangered race of the widespread kob antelope. Its current status in Ethiopia is uncertain, but numbers are thought to be very low.

Lechwe

WALIA IBEX

Ethiopia's rarest endemic is the Walia ibex, formerly widespread in the mountains of the north, but now restricted to the Simien Mountains, where it is uncommon but quite often seen by hikers. The Walia ibex is a type of goat that lives on narrow mountain ledges, and can easily be recognised by the large decurved horns of adults of both sexes. The males' horns are larger than the females', and may measure in excess of 1m. The presence of carved ibex on many pre-Christian religious shrines in Axum indicates that it was once considerably more widespread than it is today.

By the 19th century, the Walia ibex's range was restricted to the Simiens, but the population is thought to have numbered several thousand before the Italian occupation. By 1963, it had dropped to below 200, largely as a result of hunting. The population is currently estimated at slightly more than 500, thanks to stringent enforcement of the ban on hunting. The ibex has no natural enemies, and the park could probably support 2,000–3,000 individuals.

Hartebeest

The **common hartebeest** is a large, tan, and rather awkward-looking plains antelope, related to the famous wildebeest or gnu (which, despite its abundance in east Africa, doesn't occur in Ethiopia). Several races of hartebeest are recognised, of which three occur in Ethiopia. The **Lelwel hartebeest** is quite common in parts of South Omo, the **tora hartebeest** is present in unknown numbers in the northwest lowlands, and the endangered **Swayne's hartebeest**, effectively endemic to Ethiopia following extinction in Somalia, is thinly distributed in the southern Rift Valley. The largest population of Swayne's hartebeest is protected in Senkele Game Reserve, where the civil war caused numbers to plummet from 2,400 in 1989 to fewer than 200 in 1991. The Senkele population has increased slightly since then, but even together with the small population found in Nechisar National Park, it is probable that fewer than 500 individuals remain in the wild. The closely related **tiang**, a race of the east African topi, is similar in gait and shape to the hartebeest, but the much darker coat precludes confusion. The tiang occurs widely in the Omo Valley and the Gambella region.

The unmistakable **Beisa oryx** is a large, handsome dry-country antelope, easily recognised by its distinctive scimitar-like horns. It occurs in dwindling numbers in and around Awash National Park, where small herds are often observed from the main road to Harar. Large herds also migrate seasonally within the South Omo region.

Dik-diks are small, brown antelopes with tan legs and distinctive extended snouts. Four species are recognised, two of which are found in Ethiopia. All dik-dik species are browsers that live independently of water, and they are generally seen singly or in pairs in dry acacia scrub. **Guenther's dik-dik** is found throughout the lowlands of southern Ethiopia and is often seen from the roadside, particularly in South Omo and Nechisar National Park. **Salt's dik-dik**, endemic to the Horn of Africa, is widespread in the dry east, and frequently seen from the Harar road. Some field guides indicate incorrectly the occurrence in eastern Ethiopia of a Somali endemic, the silver dik-dik.

Klipspringer

The **klipspringer** is a slightly built antelope with a stiff-looking grey-brown coat. It is associated with rocky hills and cliffs and may be seen in suitable habitats anywhere in Ethiopia. It is common in Bale National Park.

The **duiker** family is a group of over 15 small antelope species, most of which live in forest undergrowth. Until recently, it was assumed that the **common duiker**, the only member of the family to inhabit open country, was also the only duiker found in Ethiopia. In 1986, however, a small red duiker was reliably observed in the Harenna Forest within Bale National Park, while in 1996 a similar duiker was observed in Omo National Park. The geographical probability is that the former is **Harvey's red duiker** and the latter **Weyn's red duiker**, but this is far from certain, and an endemic race or species is not out of the question.

Common duiker

Ethiopia's one fully endemic antelope species is the mountain nyala *Tragelaphus buxtoni* – not, as its name might suggest, a particularly close relative of the nyala of southern Africa, but more probably evolved from a race of greater kudu. The mountain nyala is similar in size and shape to the greater kudu but it has smaller (though by no means insignificant) horns with only one twist as opposed to the greater kudu's two or three. The shaggy coat of the mountain nyala is brownish rather than plain grey, and the striping is indistinct. Mountain nyala live in herds of five to ten animals in juniper and hagenia forests in the southeast highlands.

The mountain nyala has the distinction of being the last discovered of all African antelopes; the first documented specimen was shot by one Major Buxton in 1908, and described formally two years later. The extent to which mountain nyala numbers declined in the 20th century is undocumented. The antelope probably has always had a somewhat restricted range, but numbers outside of national parks appear to be in decline, and the species is listed as endangered on the IUCN Red List.

The main protected population is found in the north of Bale National Park, around Dinsho and Mount Gaysay. Numbers here soared from about 1,000 in the 1960s to 4,000 in the late 1980s, but plummeted back to 150 in 1991 as the antelope were shot in revenge for forced removals undertaken by the Mengistu regime. Fortunately, the population quickly recovered to about 1,000, according to transect counts undertaken in 1997. Outside of Bale, a small population of mountain nyala is protected in the Kuni Muktar Sanctuary, which lies in the highlands southeast of Awash National Park. Substantial populations still cling on in forested parts of the Arsi Highlands such as Dodola, though numbers are unknown. The global population is estimated at around 2,500 individuals.

OTHER LARGE MAMMALS Within Ethiopia, many of Africa's most distinctive large mammals are practically restricted to South Omo, among them **elephant**, **giraffe**, **buffalo** and **black rhinoceros**, the last almost certainly now exterminated. Another small elephant population occurs in Babile Elephant Sanctuary to the south of Harar, and small numbers of giraffe and buffalo occur elsewhere in the little-visited Kenyan and Sudanese border areas.

African buffalo

The **hippopotamus** is widely distributed in the lakes and larger rivers of Ethiopia. It is common in Lake Tana and in most of the Rift Valley lakes, though current details of status are not available. The best places to see hippos are Nechisar National Park, at the source of the Nile near Bahir Dar on Lake Tana, at Lake Boye near Jimma, and at Koko Dam near Adama.

Two swine species are found in Ethiopia. The **desert warthog**, a species more or less endemic to the Horn of Africa, occurs in wooded savanna and is frequently

Warthog

seen near water. It is found in most national parks and is especially common around Dinsho in Bale. The **bushpig** is a larger, darker and hairier beast found in forests or dense woodland. It is probably common in all Ethiopian forests but its nocturnal habits and chosen habitats make it difficult to see. I was very lucky to see a pair in the Harenna Forest in Bale.

Burchell's zebra – also called the common or plains zebra – is the common equine of sub-Saharan Africa. It is found throughout the south of Ethiopia and is the most numerous large mammal species in Nechisar National Park. The larger and more densely striped **Grevy's zebra** is restricted to southern Ethiopia and northern Kenya. In Ethiopia, it is thinly distributed in the Kenyan border area east of the Omo Valley, and in the Rift Valley north of Awash National Park.

REPTILES

NILE CROCODILE The order Crocodilia dates back at least 150 million years, and fossil forms that lived contemporaneously with dinosaurs are remarkably unchanged from their modern descendants, of which the Nile crocodile is the largest living reptile, regularly growing to lengths of up to 6m. Once common in most large rivers and lakes, it has been exterminated in many areas since the early 20th century, hunted professionally for its skin as well as by vengeful local villagers. Today, large specimens are mostly confined to protected areas. The gargantuan specimens that lurk around the so-called Crocodile Market in Nechisar National Park are a truly primeval sight. Other possible sites for croc sightings are the southern Omo River, the Baro River downstream of Gambella, the Awash River near Awash National Park and Nazret, and other large bodies of water at lower to medium altitudes.

SNAKES A wide variety of snakes is found in Ethiopia, though – fortunately, most would agree – they are typically very shy and unlikely to be seen unless actively sought. One of the snakes most likely to be seen on safari is Africa's largest, the **rock python**, which has a gold-on-black mottled skin and regularly grows to lengths exceeding 5m. Non-venomous, pythons kill their prey by strangulation, wrapping their muscular bodies around it until it cannot breathe, then swallowing it whole and dozing off for a couple of months while it is digested. Pythons feed mainly on small antelopes, large rodents and similar. They are harmless to adult humans, but could conceivably kill a small child, and might be encountered almost anywhere when slumbering.

Of the venomous snakes, one of the most commonly encountered is the **puff adder**, a large, thick resident of savanna and rocky habitats. Although it feeds mainly on rodents, the puff adder will strike when threatened, and it is rightly considered the most dangerous of African snakes, not because it is especially venomous or aggressive, but because its notoriously sluggish disposition means it is more often disturbed than other snakes.

Several **cobra** species, including the spitting cobra, are present in Ethiopia, most with characteristic hoods that they raise when about to strike, though they are all very seldom seen. Another widespread family is the **mambas**, of which the black mamba – which will only attack when cornered, despite an unfounded reputation for unprovoked aggression – is the largest venomous snake in Africa, measuring up to 3.5m long. Theoretically, the most toxic of Africa's snakes is said to be the **boomslang**, a variably coloured and, as its name – literally 'tree snake' – suggests,

CHAMELEONS

Common and widespread in parts of Ethiopia, but not easily seen unless they are actively searched for, chameleons are arguably the most intriguing of African reptiles. True chameleons of the family Chamaeleontidae are confined to the Old World, with the most important centre of speciation being Madagascar, to which about half of the world's 120 recognised species are endemic. Aside from two species of chameleon apiece in Asia and Europe, the remainder are distributed across mainland Africa. Several species are present in Ethiopia, including at least two recently described endemics from the Harenna Forest in Bale National Park, and it is highly likely that other endemics await discovery in forests elsewhere in the country.

Chameleons are best known for their capacity to change colour, a trait often exaggerated in popular literature, and one influenced by mood more than environmental background. A more remarkable physiological feature common to all true chameleons is their protuberant round eyes, which offer a potential 180° vision on both sides and swivel independently of each other. Only when one eye isolates a suitably juicy-looking insect will both focus in the same direction. Another unique weapon in the chameleon armoury is a sticky-tipped body-length tongue that is uncoiled in a blink-and-you'll-miss-it lunge to zap a selected item of prey. Many chameleons are adorned with an array of facial casques, flaps, horns and crests that enhance their already somewhat fearsome prehistoric appearance.

In Ethiopia, you're most likely to come across a chameleon by chance when it is crossing a road, in which case it should be easy to take a closer look, since most move slowly and deliberately. The 15cm-long flap-necked chameleon *Chamaeleo delepis* is probably the most regularly observed species of savanna and woodland habitats. The closely related and similarly sized graceful chameleon *Chamaeleo gracilis* is generally yellow-green in colour with a white horizontal stripe along its flanks.

largely arboreal snake that is reputed not to have accounted for one known human fatality, as it is back-fanged and very non-aggressive.

Most snakes are in fact non-venomous and not even potentially harmful to any other living creature much bigger than a rat. One of the more non-venomous snakes in the region is the **green tree snake** (sometimes mistaken for a boomslang, though the latter is never as green and more often brown), which feeds mostly on amphibians. The **mole snake** is a common and widespread grey-brown savanna resident that grows up to 2m long, and feeds on moles and other rodents. The remarkable **egg-eating snakes** live exclusively on bird eggs, dislocating their jaws to swallow the egg whole, then eventually regurgitating the crushed shell in a neat little package. Many snakes will take eggs opportunistically, for which reason large-scale agitation among birds in a tree is often a good indication that a snake (or small bird of prey) is around.

LIZARDS All African lizards are harmless to humans, with the arguable exception of the **giant monitor lizards**, which grow up to 2.2m long and could theoretically inflict a nasty bite if cornered. They are sometimes mistaken for a small crocodile, but yellow-dappled skin precludes sustained confusion. Both species present in Ethiopia are predators, feeding on anything from bird eggs to smaller reptiles and mammals.

Visitors to tropical Africa soon become familiar with the **common house gecko**, an endearing bug-eyed, translucent white lizard, which as its name suggests reliably inhabits most houses as well as lodge rooms, scampering up walls and upside down on the ceiling in pursuit of pesky insects attracted to the lights. Also very common in some lodge grounds are various **agama** species, distinguished from other common lizards by their relatively large size of around 20–25cm, basking habits, and almost plastic-looking scaling – depending on the species, a combination of blue, purple, orange or red, with the flattened head generally a different colour from the torso. Another common family is the **skinks**: small, long-tailed lizards, most of which are quite dark and have a few thin black stripes running from head to tail.

TORTOISES AND TERRAPINS These peculiar reptiles are unique in being protected by a prototypal suit of armour formed by their heavy exoskeleton. The most common of the terrestrial tortoises in the region is the **leopard tortoise**, which is named after its gold-and-black mottled shell, and has been known to live for more than 50 years in captivity. The form present in Somaliland is the giant leopard tortoise (often designated as the race *Stigmochelys pardalis somalica*), which can weigh over 50kg. Four species of terrapin – essentially the freshwater equivalent of turtles – are resident. The largest is the **Nile soft-shelled terrapin**, which has a wide, flat shell and in rare instances might reach a length of almost 1m.

BIRDS

Ethiopia's proximity to the Equator and great habitat diversity mean its avifauna is one of the richest in Africa, with around 850 species recorded including a high proportion of eagerly sought endemics whose range is restricted to Ethiopia or to the Horn of Africa. It is also very possible that further species await discovery in the little-known forests of the south and west, or elsewhere (the wing of an apparently endemic species of nightjar was discovered as recently as 1992 in Nechisar National Park, and the live bird was first seen in 2009). Until recently, this rich avifauna was rather poorly covered in non-scientific literature, but that has changed drastically with a glut of superb new publications – including a field guide to the birds of the Horn of Africa, an ornithological atlas to Ethiopia and Eritrea, and two other birding handbooks since mid 2009 (see *Appendix 5, Further information*, page 613). This development can only further Ethiopia's burgeoning reputation as a top birding destination, one where a dedicated visit might easily amass a list of 400 species over a normal-length holiday, and see most of the country's endemics.

It is always difficult to know where to pitch the birding section in a general travel guide. This is because the birds most likely to capture the interest of the casual visitor are not generally those most significant to a serious ornithologist. For a first-time visitor to Africa with a passing interest in birds – an interest that often tends to develop as one travels amidst its avian abundance – it will be the most colourful and largest birds that tend to capture the eye: rollers, bee-eaters, cranes, storks, hornbills and such. The truly dedicated, by contrast, will be more than willing to make a two-day side trip to tick a range-restricted endemic lark which, when all's said and done, looks and behaves pretty much like any of a dozen other drab lark species found in Ethiopia. And there will be many visitors who fall between these poles. This section is directly primarily towards reasonably serious birders. The first heading below focuses on endemic and other species that are likely to be of high interest to all visiting birders. The second heading outlines the established itinerary used by most birding tours.

ENDEMICS AND OTHER 'SPECIALS' For any dedicated birdwatcher planning a once-in-a-lifetime trip to Ethiopia, particularly those with experience of birding elsewhere in Africa, a primary goal will be to identify those species whose range is actually – or practically – confined to Ethiopia. Indeed, many ornithological tours are structured almost entirely around this consideration, forsaking time in more generally rewarding and accessible birding areas for trips to remote parts of the country that host one particular endemic.

Ethiopia's 'must-see' birds fall into several categories, the most important of which are the true endemics, species not known to occur outside of Ethiopia. The taxonomic status of some such birds awaits clarification, and new species have been discovered with remarkable regularity in recent decades, making it impossible to say precisely how many birds fall into this category. The most conservative estimate is 16 species, but the spate of recent (and in some cases controversial) splits of what were formerly considered races into full species might boost that figure closer to 25.

A similar number of bird species might be described as former Ethiopian endemics, since their range extends into Eritrea, which became an independent state in 1993. For a variety of reasons – not least the practical consideration that very few visiting birders would be likely to undertake a separate trip to Eritrea at a later stage – these former endemics are treated as full endemics in the main body of this guide.

A third category of birds that any dedicated birder to Ethiopia would hope to encounter constitutes about half-a-dozen species that are more or less confined to Ethiopia and war-torn Somalia. There are, too, a considerable number of bird species whose range extends throughout the contiguous arid country of northern Kenya, Somalia and southern Ethiopia. In many instances, such birds are easily seen in parts of Ethiopia that are routinely visited by birders for their endemics, whereas their range within Kenya falls into areas infrequently included in birding itineraries.

Finally, there is a miscellaneous group of birds that fit into none of the above categories, but which for one or other reason are likely to be sought eagerly by any visiting birder.

An annotated list covering most of the endemics, near-endemics and other 'key' bird species follows. Names and sequence follow the plates in Redman, Stevenson and Fanshawe's *Birds of the Horn of Africa*, the most useful single-volume field guide for Ethiopia. A single asterisk (*) indicates a species endemic to Ethiopia, a double asterisk (**) one endemic to Ethiopia and Eritrea, a triple asterisk (***) a near-endemic or a 'Horn of Africa endemic' whose range might extend into Somalia, Sudan, Eritrea and/or the far north of Kenya, but which for all practical purposes is likely to be seen only in Ethiopia. A question mark indicates a controversial or tentative status.

**Wattled ibis *Bostrychia carunculata* Common, widespread and vociferous highland resident. Might be confused with the superficially similar hadeda ibis.

Northern bald ibis (waldrapp) *Gerontimus eremita* North African endemic. Formerly bred on cliffs in northern Ethiopian Highlands. Thought to be exterminated until three birds were recorded overwintering in central Ethiopia in 2006.

*Blue-winged goose *Cyanochen cyanopterus* Associated with water in the highlands. Reliable sites include Gefersa Reservoir near Addis Ababa, and Sanetti Plateau, Bale Mountains.

WEAVERS

Placed by some authorities in the same family as the closely related sparrows, the weavers of the family Ploceidae are a quintessential part of Africa's natural landscape, common and highly visible in virtually every habitat from rainforest to desert. The name of the family derives from the intricate and elaborate nests – typically (but not always) a roughly oval ball of dried grass, reeds and twigs – that are built by the dextrous males of most species.

It can be fascinating to watch a male weaver at work. First, a nest site is chosen, usually at the end of a thin hanging branch or frond, which is immediately stripped of leaves to protect against snakes. The weaver then flies back and forth to the site, carrying the building material blade by blade in its heavy beak, first using a few thick strands to hang a skeletal nest from the end of a branch, then gradually completing the structure by interweaving numerous thinner blades of grass into the main frame. Once completed, the nest is subjected to the attention of his chosen partner, who will tear it apart if the result is less than satisfactory, and so the process starts all over again.

All but 12 of the 113 described weaver species are resident on the African mainland or associated islands, with some 26 represented within Ethiopia alone. About 20 of the Ethiopian species are placed in the genus *Ploceus* (true weavers), which is surely the most characteristic of all African bird genera. Most of the *Ploceus* weavers are slightly larger than a sparrow, and display a strong sexual dimorphism. Females are with few exceptions drab buff- or olive-brown birds, with some streaking on the back, and perhaps a hint of yellow on the belly.

Most male *Ploceus* weavers conform to the basic colour pattern of the 'masked weaver' – predominantly yellow, with streaky back and wings, and a distinct black facial mask, often bordered orange. Eight Ethiopian weaver species fit this masked weaver prototype more or less absolutely, and another five approximate to it rather less exactly, for instance by having a chestnut-brown mask, or a full black head, or a black back, or being more chestnut than yellow on the belly. Identification of the masked weavers can be tricky without experience – useful clues are the exact shape of the mask, the presence and extent of the fringing orange, and the colour of the eye and the back.

The most extensive weaver colonies are often found in reed beds and waterside vegetation, generally with several species present. Most weavers don't

Ruddy shelduck *Tadorna ferruginea* Only sub-Saharan breeding population on Sanetti Plateau, where commonly observed near water.

Lammergeyer (bearded vulture) *Gypaetus barbatus* Associated with cliffs and mountains, this magnificent vulture is widespread in suitable Old World habitats, but increasingly rare except in Ethiopian Highlands, which form its major global stronghold.

Golden eagle *Aquila chrysaetos* The only population in sub-Saharan Africa was first identified at Bale Mountains in 1988 and confirmed to breed there in 1993. May occur elsewhere in Ethiopia. Requires experience to distinguish from other, more numerous brown *Aquila* eagles.

Vulturine guineafowl *Acryllium vulturinum* Large, distinctive fowl with brilliant

have a distinctive song, but they compensate with a rowdy jumble of harsh swizzles, rattles and nasal notes that can reach deafening proportions near large colonies. One more cohesive song you will often hear seasonally around weaver colonies is a cyclic 'dee-dee-dee-diederik', often accelerating to a hysterical crescendo when several birds call at once. This is the call of the diederik cuckoo, a handsome green-and-white cuckoo that lays its eggs in weaver nests.

Oddly, while most east African *Ploceus* weavers are common, even abundant, in suitable habitats, seven species are listed as range-restricted, and three of these are of global conservation concern. The only highly localised weaver whose territory nudges onto Ethiopian soil is the Juba weaver, a Somali-biome species that can be seen in a few specific locations in the southeast. Another species whose range centres on Ethiopia is Ruppell's weaver, which occurs throughout the highlands.

Most of the colonial weavers, perhaps relying on safety in numbers, build relatively plain nests with a roughly oval shape and an unadorned entrance hole. The nests of certain more solitary weavers, by contrast, are far more elaborate. Several weavers, for instance, protect their nests from egg-eating invaders by attaching tubular entrance tunnels to the base – in the case of the spectacled weaver, sometimes twice as long as the nest itself. The grosbeak weaver (a peculiar larger-than-average brown-and-white weaver of reed beds, distinguished by its outsized bill and placed in the monospecific genus *Amblyospiza*) constructs a large and distinctive domed nest, which is supported by a pair of reeds, and woven as precisely as the finest basketwork, with a neat raised entrance hole at the front. By contrast, the scruffiest nests are built by the various species of sparrow- and buffalo-weaver, relatively drab but highly gregarious dry-country birds that are common in the acacia scrub of the Ethiopian Rift Valley.

cobalt chest. Confined to arid parts of east Africa and the Horn. Very common in suitable habitats in southern Ethiopia.

***Harwood's francolin** *Pternistes harwoodi* Range practically restricted to Jemma Valley north of Addis Ababa, where it is quite common. Requires special visit to Jemma Valley to see it.

*****Erckell's francolin** *Pternistes erckelii* Large, dark-faced game bird restricted to northern highlands of Ethiopia, but nudging into Eritrea, with another isolated population in eastern Sudan.

*****Chestnut-naped francolin** *Francolinus castaneicollis* Near-endemic forest-fringe species common in Bale Mountains and other relatively moist highland areas. The only other confirmed population is northern Somalia.

***Orange River francolin** *Scleroptila gutturalis* A strong case exists for splitting Archer's francolin (*S. l. gutturalis*) as a near-endemic whose main range, centred on Ethiopia's Rift Valley, extends into Somalia and northern Kenya, with a second sub-population confined to the far northwest of Ethiopia.

Moorland francolin *Scleroptila psilolaemus* Highland fowl, very common in Bale and some other Ethiopian moorland habitats, elsewhere occurs only on four less accessible moorland areas in Kenya, where it is relatively uncommon.

White-winged flufftail *Sarothrura ayresii* Rare and elusive marsh bird, global population fewer than 1,000, restricted to a few specific localities in South Africa, Zimbabwe and Ethiopia. The main stronghold is Ethiopia's Sultata Plain, 100km north of Addis Ababa. Unlikely to be seen by casual visitors.

**Rouget's rail *Rougetius rougetii* Associated with marshes and vegetation fringing water. Widespread in the highlands, but most easily seen in Bale Mountains, where it is common and confiding.

Wattled crane *Bugeranus carunculatus* Endangered and localised resident of grassy or marshy highlands with discontinuous distribution from South Africa to Ethiopia. Sanetti Plateau in Bale Mountains is one of a handful of African sites where it is reliably observed.

***Heuglin's bustard** *Neotis heuglinii* Dry-country species likely to be seen only in Somali border region and South Omo.

Arabian bustard *Ardeotis arabs* Localised dry-country bird of north Africa and Arabia; resident in Awash National Park and northern Rift Valley.

*Spot-breasted plover** *Vanellus melanocephalus* Locally common in highlands, particularly Bale area, and usually associated with water.

**White-collared pigeon *Columba albitorques* Common to abundant in most highland habitats, including Addis Ababa.

***African white-winged dove** *Streptopelia semitorquata* Restricted-range species of Somalia, Ethiopia and Kenyan border region. Associated with riverine woodland, regularly observed near the Dawa River Bridge between Negele Borena and Yabello.

*Yellow-fronted parrot** *Poicephalus flavifrons* Localised forest inhabitant, often seen flying quickly and noisily between tree canopies at Wondo Genet, Menegasha Forest, Dinsho (Bale) and similar habitats.

**Black-winged lovebird *Agapornis swinderiana* Common in most wooded highland habitats. Often observed in the isolated forest patches that tend to surround churches.

***White-cheeked turaco** *Tauraco leucolophus* Striking and vociferous woodland near-endemic often seen in suitable highland habitats, including hotel gardens. Range otherwise extends to a small inaccessible part of Sudan.

***Prince Ruspoli's turaco** *Tauraco ruspolii* Eagerly sought but elusive endemic of southern forests, known from only a handful of localities, of which the most accessible is Genale near Negele Borena.

*****(Abyssinian) long-eared owl** *Asio abyssinicus* Formerly classified as a race of African long-eared owl, this would be regarded as an Ethiopian endemic were it not for a solitary specimen captured on Mount Kenya in 1961. Uncommon, shy and seldom seen unless the location of its daytime roost is known.

***Nechisar nightjar** *Caprimulgus solala* Probable endemic known only from one wing found in Nechisar National Park prior to it being observed on an ornithological expedition led by Ian Sinclair in 2009.

Hemprich's hornbill *Tockus hemprichii* Large, striking, cliff-associated hornbill whose range centres on Ethiopia, extending into portions of Somalia and Eritrea, and down the Kenyan Rift as far as Baringo.

****Banded barbet** *Lybius undatus* Widespread and quite common resident of woodland. Often seen in southern Rift Valley, but might be seen almost anywhere.

****Abyssinian (golden-backed) woodpecker** *Dendropicus abyssinicus* Widespread resident of woodland and forest, but nowhere common.

*(?)**Gillett's Lark** *Mirafra gilletti* First described in 1975, the Degodi lark *M. degodiensis*, only known from the Bogol Manyo area, was regarded as a rare endemic prior to being lumped with the more common Gillett's lark in 2009.

*(?)**Sidamo lark** *Heteromirafra sidamoensis* First collected in 1968 near Arero junction, 15km from Negele Borena, which remains the best locality. Recent studies indicate it may be conspecific with Archer's lark, an even rarer Somali endemic, and one or other bird was recently recorded in the vicinity of Jijiga.

*(?)**Erlanger's lark** *Calandrella erlangeri* A controversial recent split from *C. cinerea*, which it strongly resembles, this is among the more common and conspicuous larks of the Ethiopian Highlands.

*(?)**Brown saw-wing** *Psalidoprocne antinorii* Confined to forests in the southern highlands and Rift Valley, where it is the only saw-wing present, and reasonably common. Generally regarded as a race of *P. pristoptera*, but may warrant specific status.

***(?)**Ethiopian saw-wing** *Psalidoprocne oleagina* Confined to southwest Ethiopia and southern Sudan, where it is the only saw-wing present and quite likely to be seen around Yabello. Generally regarded as a race of *P. pristoptera*, but may warrant specific status.

***White-tailed swallow** *Hirundo megaensis* Endemic to Ethiopia. Restricted to arid acacia woodland around Yabello and Mega. Small parties often seen flying in the vicinity of termite hills. Distinguished from other swallows by conspicuous white tail.

*(?)**Ethiopian cliff swallow** *Hirundo* Uncollected and undescribed bird recorded by several observers in the vicinity of the Awash River Gorge and Lake Langano.

May be more widespread than current knowledge suggests, possibly synonymous with Red Sea cliff swallow, known from one specimen collected near Port Sudan.

*__Abyssinian longclaw__ *Macronyx flavicollis* Widespread resident of high-altitude grassland, particularly common in the Bale area.

***__Somali bulbul__ *Pycnonotus somaliensis* Recent split from common bulbul ranging between northern Somalia and eastern Ethiopia.

***__Somali wheatear__ *Oenanthe phillipsi* Rare and localised Somali species with range extended into southeast Ethiopia. Not known from any Ethiopian locality regularly visited by birders. Note that the black-eared wheatear, desert wheatear and red-tailed wheatear all regularly overwinter in Ethiopia but not further south.

***__Sombre rock chat__ *Cercomela dubia* Excluded from Ethiopian endemic status on the basis of records from one forest in northern Somalia, this is broadly confined to arid, rocky habitats in the northern Rift Valley, for instance Mount Fantelle in Awash National Park.

**__Rüppell's (black) chat__ *Myrmecocichla melaena* Common resident of rocky highlands north of Addis Ababa. Often tame around churches in Tigrai and Lalibela.

**__White-winged cliff-chat__ *Myrmecocichla semirufa* Occupies similar habitats to *M. melaena*, and also most common in the north. Could be mistaken for the very similar mocking cliff-chat, which often occurs alongside it in similar habitats.

*(?)__Bale parisoma__ *Parisoma griseaventris* Usually lumped with the practically indistinguishable brown parisoma, but confined to juniper and hagenia woodland and bracken thickets above 3,500m on the northern slopes of Bale Mountains.

*(?)__Winding cisticola__ *Cistocola marginatus* A nondescript but vocal and conspicuous resident of moist areas and rank grass in the Ethiopian Highlands. Some authorities split the local race *C. lugubris* as a good species.

**__Abyssinian slaty flycatcher__ *Melaenornis chocolatina* Common resident of highland wood and forest both sides of the Rift.

***__White-rumped babbler__ *Turdoides leucopygia* Common and conspicuous resident of wooded highlands and rivers, with range extending into small portions of Eritrea and Somalia.

*__Abyssinian catbird__ *Parophasma galinieri* Unusual species of undetermined affiliations, notable for its striking, melodic call. Common but elusive resident of juniper and other indigenous highland forest. Often observed at Dinsho (Bale) and in developed hotel grounds in Addis Ababa.

**__White-backed (black) tit__ *Parus leuconotus* Widespread but uncommon resident of forested habitats on both sides of the Rift. Often seen moving restlessly through mid stratum in Dinsho (Bale), Wondo Genet, and developed hotel gardens in Addis Ababa.

***Shining sunbird** Cinnyrus hebessinica* Brilliantly coloured sunbird common in Ethiopian Rift Valley but with range extending into parts of northern Kenya, Somalia and Eritrea.

***Ethiopian boubou** Laniarius aethiopicus* Common highland bird with distinctive call, sometimes given as a race of tropical boubou *L. major*.

****Abyssinian oriole** Oriolus monacha* Similar to black-headed oriole, but inhabits true forest rather than woodland, and has an equally distinct but different call. Fairly common and active in forested habitats.

(Red-billed) chough *Pyrrhocorax pyrrhocorax* Eurasian species with isolated Ethiopian population of perhaps 1,200 birds centred on Bale Mountains and northern highlands.

***Streseman's (Abyssinian/Ethiopian) bush crow** Zavattariornis stresemanni* The proverbial odd bird, loosely affiliated to the crow family, but quite unlike most crows in behaviour and appearance. Confined to a small area of dry thorn bush centred on Yabello, where parties of five or so birds are regularly seen from the roadside.

***Dwarf raven** Corvus edithae* Recent, controversial split from larger *C. ruficollis*, range more or less confined to Somalia and the eastern half of Ethiopia.

****Thick-billed raven** Corvus crassirostris* Common and widespread throughout the highlands.

***Somali starling** Onychognathus blythii* Within Ethiopia, formerly thought to be restricted to arid northeast, but has recently been recorded by reliable observers at sites as diverse as Ankober, Bale Mountains and Mount Fantelle. Could be confused with other chestnut-winged starlings, though the long, tapering tail is unique.

****White-billed starling** Onychognathus albirostris* Only chestnut-winged starling with white bill. Associated with cliffs and dwellings. Often seen around churches at Lalibela.

***Swainson's sparrow** Passer swainsonii* Recent split from grey-headed sparrow, range centred on Ethiopia, where it is common throughout, but extending into Eritrea, Somalia and far northeast of Sudan.

***Rüppell's weaver** Ploceus galbula* Restricted to the Horn of Africa and Yemen. Common, sociable resident of savanna and light woodland.

***Juba weaver** Ploceus dischrocephalus* Endemic to Horn of Africa. In Ethiopia, restricted to southeast, regular at Dawa River Bridge between Negele Borena and Yabello.

***Red-billed pytilia** Pytilia lineata* Pretty but little-known finch, recently split from the extralimital red-winged pytilia, and near-endemic with a small range extension into Sudan. Recorded a few times in the southern Rift Valley, but more common in the western lowlands, for instance around Gambella.

***African citril** *Serinus citrinelloides* Recently split from western and southern specific forms, of which the former nominate race is essentially a bird of the Ethiopian Highlands, with a discrete population confined to southern Sudan.

***Black-headed siskin** *Serinus nigriceps* Common, widespread and distinctive species of high-altitude grassland and heather. Abundant around Bale Highlands.

White-throated seedeater *Serinus xanthopygius* Confined to northern highlands, where it is uncommon to rare, and most likely to be seen at Tis Isat or the Ankober area.

*Yellow-throated seedeater** *Serinus flavigula* Uncommon and localised dry-country species that went unrecorded for more than a century after three specimens were collected in the 1880s, and formerly regarded by some authorities to be a hybrid rather than a discrete genetic form. Confined to northern Rift, it is now regularly seen on Mount Fantelle and at Aliyu Amba near Ankober.

*Salvadori's serin** *Serinus xantholaemus* Distinctive and very localised dry-country serin discovered in 1980, and until recently known only from a handful of locations, the best known being Arero and Sof Omar.

***Brown-rumped seedeater (serin)** *Serinus tristriatis* Endemic to Horn of Africa. Common and confiding in Addis Ababa and other highland towns, where it seems to occupy a house sparrow-like niche.

*Ankober serin** *Serinus ankobernis* Endemic to Ethiopia. Discovered in 1976 and until recently thought to be confined to a small area of steep escarpment near Ankober, but recent sightings in the Simien Mountains and elsewhere suggest it is actually quite widespread in the highlands.

ORNITHOLOGICAL ITINERARIES

While any ornithological itinerary will depend greatly on available time, level of interest and budget, Ethiopia does boast a defined birding itinerary which, with minor variations, is followed by most organised tours. Unlike the standard 'historical circuit', this itinerary is focused on areas south of Addis Ababa, which is where most of the more localised endemics are to be found, and it can only be covered thoroughly in a private vehicle. Most of the sites mentioned below are covered in detail in the main body of this guide, so what follows are outline itineraries only.

Southern circuit

The main birding circuit through the south requires an absolute minimum of ten days, though two weeks would be more realistic, and the extra four days would effectively double your birding time. With reasonable levels of dedication, luck and skill – or a skilled local bird guide – a total bird list of 350–400 species should be achievable over two weeks on this circuit. About 20 of the Ethiopia–Eritrea endemics are all but certain if you follow this route in its entirety over two weeks, though there are a few (Salvadori's serin, Degodi lark, Abyssinian woodpecker) that are occasionally missed by visiting birders – and you'd be extraordinarily lucky to see a Nechisar nightjar. If possible, there would be much to be said for keeping the day-to-day itinerary reasonably flexible, particularly with regard to sites associated with one specific endemic, so that you can stay on or push ahead depending on how quickly you locate the desired bird. Six Ethiopia–Eritrea endemics are predominantly found to the north of Addis Ababa, and are thus unlikely to be seen on this southern circuit (see *Northern excursions* on page 74).

Addis Ababa and Rift Valley (2+ nights) A typical birding itinerary might start with a night in Addis Ababa, visiting the Entoto Natural Park or Menegasha Forest (for highland forest endemics) or the Gefersa Reservoir (for water-associated and grassland endemics). This can be followed by a night or two in the Rift Valley, where one should stop at as many of the lakes as possible. Ziway is probably the best of the lakes for birds associated with open water and marsh, the Abiata-Shala complex for shorebirds, and Hawassa for a mix of good water and acacia woodland species. Another important site in the Rift Valley is Wondo Genet, which is excellent for forest birds including several endemics. Depending on your time limitations, anything from one night to a week could be spent in the Rift Valley at various lakes and at Wondo Genet.

Bale Highlands (2–3 nights) Leaving the Rift Valley, cut up the escarpment from Shashemene towards Bale National Park. The forested park headquarters at Dinsho is the most reliable place in Ethiopia for several localised and endemic forest birds. Allow a full day for the Sanetti Plateau, the best place in Ethiopia to see endemics associated with grassland as well as a number of other notable species. With reasonable levels of luck, dedication and skill (or at least a skilled guide), a list of well over 200 species, including about half of the birds endemic to Ethiopia (or to Ethiopia and Eritrea), could be expected after two nights each in the Rift Valley and Bale areas. With a third night at Bale, it would be possible to head out for a day trip to the Sof Omar Caves, which is the best place to seek out Salvadori's serin.

Negele Borena and surrounds (2–3 nights) From Bale, head south to Negele Borena through the Sanetti Plateau, Harenna Forest and Dola Mena. This road may be impassable after heavy rain, when the Genale River presents an insurmountable obstacle, so check road conditions first. This is a long drive, so there won't be too much birding time along the way, especially if you want to stop at Genale, the best place to seek out the endemic Prince Ruspoli's turaco. The junction of the Bogol Manyo and Arero roads, 15km from Negele Borena, is the only known site for the endemic Sidamo lark.

Yabello and surrounds (1–3 nights) The road from Negele Borena to Yabello offers good dry-country birding in general, and is home to several species associated with the arid Somali and Kenyan border areas. Three specific sites along this road warrant a stop. The first is the aforementioned junction with the Bogol Manyo road. The next is the Dawa River Bridge, a reliable place to pick up Juba weaver and white-winged turtle dove. Finally, the forests around Arero are home to Prince Ruspoli's turaco, and the surrounding area is also one of the few known localities for Salvadori's serin. Also at Arero, you should start looking out for Streseman's bush crow and white-tailed swallow, the two endemics whose restricted range is centred on Yabello. Both of these birds are generally easy to locate and identify, and the odds are you'll have seen them even before you arrive at Yabello. From Yabello, it is possible to drive to Addis Ababa or Awash National Park over a long day, provided you don't stop more often than is necessary. Less frenetic would be to break up the drive with a night at Wondo Genet or at one of the Rift Valley lakes – you could choose where to stay depending on the gaps in your list of birds identified to date. A third option (see below) would be to cut through via Konso to Arba Minch and Nechisar National Park.

Nechisar National Park (2–3 nights) Arguably something of a fool's errand, the diversion through Arba Minch allows you to spend time in Nechisar National Park, the only known locality for the Nechisar nightjar. This elusive bird aside, Nechisar's most interesting birding habitat is the groundwater forest near the entrance gate. From Nechisar, you can drive directly to Addis Ababa or Awash National Park in a day.

Awash National Park (2–3 nights) The two most important specials here are sombre rock chat and yellow-throated serin, both regular on Mount Fantelle. Allocate most of a day to seeking out these birds. The undescribed Ethiopian cliff swallow is most easily seen in the Awash Gorge at the southern end of the park. Awash is also one of the best general bird sites in Ethiopia, for which reason a second full day is strongly recommended.

Northern excursions On the whole, northern Ethiopia is of less interest to birders than the south, though any birdwatcher hoping to see all of Ethiopia's endemics would need to undertake two specific trips north, both of which are covered in detail in the regional part of this guide. The first trip is to Ankober, the best place to see the localised Ankober serin and the springboard for a short side trip to Aliyu Amba, a recently discovered site for the yellow-throated serin. This trip could be extended to include the Guassa Plateau near Mehal Meda, a moorland area supporting similar species to the Sanetti Plateau. The second trip leads to the Jemma Valley, the only reliable spot for the endemic Harwood's francolin. On either trip, one would stand a good chance of encountering some of the other four endemics whose range is more or less restricted to the north, ie: white-winged cliff-chat, Rüppell's black chat, white-billed starling and white-throated serin. At a serious push, either trip would form a viable day excursion from the capital, though in both cases it would be better to allow for two days and a full night.

3

Practical Information

This chapter covers most practical aspects of preparing for a trip to Ethiopia, from planning an itinerary to visas and other paperwork. Health-related preparation is covered in *Chapter 4*.

WHEN TO VISIT

Ethiopia can be visited at any time of year. People are sometimes advised against travelling during the rainy season, from June until early October, but with Lalibela now being accessible all year through this is less of an issue than it used to be. Indeed, the rainy season has several advantages, among them that there are fewer tourists at popular sites such as Lalibela, and that the scenery is so much more impressive when the countryside is green and well watered. A lovely time of year is September through to early October, when the whole country is a riot of wild meskel flowers.

The most popular time to visit Ethiopia is between October and January, when the rains are over but the countryside is still quite green. Many travellers try to schedule their trip to coincide with important festivals such as Ethiopian New Year, Ethiopian Christmas, Timkat or Meskel. The European winter is also the best time for birds, as resident species are supplemented by large numbers of Palaearctic migrants.

One area where travel options are restricted during the rains is South Omo. The rains here typically fall in April and May, but they may run earlier or later, for which reason March and June are also probably best avoided, as are the short rains in October.

SUGGESTED ITINERARIES

Itineraries are subjective things, dependent on how much time you have, your chosen or enforced style of travel, and your interests. So rather than prescribe a few specific itineraries, this section attempts to itemise what is and isn't possible within the confines of a normal vacation period. Perhaps the most important single item of advice when it comes to travel in Ethiopia is to allocate your time realistically. You can, for instance, easily cover the four main attractions of the historical circuit by air in eight to ten days. You could also do it in five to seven days at a push, but if you were constrained to that sort of period, it would be more realistic and enjoyable to cut one of the four main sites from your itinerary. Much the same can be said for visitors bussing around the historical circuit. If you really wanted to, you could cover the main attractions in under two weeks, but only if you are prepared to have at least half your days consumed by long and often uncomfortable bus trips.

THE HISTORICAL CIRCUIT Ethiopia's main tourist focus is the well-defined historical circuit in the north. This is covered in chapters 6–15 as a clockwise loop from Addis Ababa, passing through the four established tourist centres of Bahir Dar (the base for visiting Lake Tana's monasteries and Tis Abay Waterfall on the Blue Nile), Gondar, Axum and Lalibela. In this book, coverage of these major centres is supplemented by information on other towns and tourist attractions along the loop; this may be distracting to tourists who are flying. Basically, if you only want to read up on the 'big four', Bahir Dar is in *Chapter 7*, Gondar in *Chapter 8*, Axum in *Chapter 9* and Lalibela in *Chapter 13*.

By road, this loop covers a distance of more than 2,500km. Roads in the region have improved greatly in recent years, but many are still in poor repair, and pass through mountainous terrain that isn't conducive to speed. In other words, travelling by bus or private vehicle is not realistic if you want to rush between sites. Fortunately, Ethiopian Airlines covers all the main towns on the historical circuit. Although internal flights are reasonably efficient, they will not necessarily run at times that allow you to do any significant sightseeing on the day you fly, and delays are commonplace. On this basis, it's best to allow yourself a clear day between flights in every place you visit. This means that to visit all four major centres you need eight nights out of Addis. If you don't have this sort of time, you could think about cutting Bahir Dar or Axum from the itinerary. On the other hand, with more time available, you could easily devote a second day to Axum or Bahir Dar, and any number of days to visiting rock-hewn churches in the Lalibela region (by mule or on foot from town).

Two other attractions on the historical loop that might be of interest to short-stay visitors are Simien Mountains National Park and the rock-hewn churches of Tigrai. The Simiens (covered in *Chapter 8*) are visited from Gondar – you can reach the park headquarters at Debark in a morning by bus or taxi. The prime attractions here are spectacular scenery and the opportunity to see three of Ethiopia's four endemic large mammal species. Travelling by car, allow at least two nights to see the Simiens properly. Hikers would need to set aside at least four days (including travel to or from Gondar), but six days – or even longer – would be better. The rock-hewn churches of Tigrai lie north of the regional capital of Mekele. The possibilities in this area are practically endless, ranging from visiting some of the more accessible churches over a day or two on public transport through to seven-day hikes or driving trips in the Gheralta area (see *Chapter 10*). All that need be said here is that Ethiopian Airlines fly to Mekele, though visiting from Axum is another viable option.

Touring the historical circuit by public transport is relatively straightforward. If you have more time than money, travelling by bus is much cheaper than flying on a day-by-day basis. But, because it will take much longer, the overall cost will be much the same. The advantages of bus travel are that it allows you to soak up the magnificent scenery and to visit more obscure places of interest. To do a full tour of the historical circuit would use up the best part of ten days on buses alone (two days less if you bypassed Lalibela at Woldia). Allowing for at least one full day at each of the major tourist attractions, and a few days' rest here and there, anything much less than three weeks – four weeks if you have thoughts of hiking in the Simiens or exploring Tigrai in depth – would be heavy going.

If you don't have this sort of time, two compromise options exist. One is to skip Axum and cut across from Gondar to Woldia which, if you wanted to see Lalibela, would still require almost a week of pure travel and a very tight minimum of ten days overall. A more sensible compromise might be to go as far as Axum by bus, then to fly back to Addis via Lalibela.

THE SOUTH AND EAST The southern Rift Valley lake region is the most popular in Ethiopia after the historical circuit. There is, however, no single obvious circuit through the region – but there is no desperate need to think through your timing. Shashemene, the transport hub of the south, is only five or six hours from Addis by bus, and even from more dispersed spots like Harar, Arba Minch, Negele Borena or Goba, you are within a comfortable two days' reach of the capital. In other words, travel in most of this region can be as organised or as whimsical as your temperament dictates.

If you veer towards organised travel, the best way to see a fair amount of the south is to join a tour or hire a vehicle and driver (in Ethiopia, tours and car hire generally amount to the same thing) through an Addis Ababa operator. Tours can be arranged to cater for most tastes, but generally you would be looking at two or three days to see a few Rift Valley lakes, and you could extend this by a day or two by appending either Awash or Nechisar National Park to your itinerary. To see South Omo properly, eight days is the absolute minimum duration for a round road trip from Addis Ababa.

A more whimsical approach is just that. You could spend weeks exploring the south and east and it would be silly to try to suggest a specific public transport itinerary. The one place in the south that should be singled out here is Bale National Park. Not only is this the one place in southern Ethiopia geared towards hiking, but it also offers the most important concentration of Ethiopia's endemic animals. Unlike at Simien, you can see Bale's endemic mammals easily without having to hike. Bale is also home to about half of Ethiopia's endemic bird species, and most of these are easy to see in the area. Independent travellers should allow two days in each direction between Addis and Bale.

OFF-THE-BEATEN-TRACK TRAVEL If you have only a short time in Ethiopia, common sense dictates that you should focus your attention on the places you really want to see. But if you have the luxury of a longer period of time, it is worth exploring some of Ethiopia's less visited areas. You need not actually head 'off the beaten track' to do this – stopping along the beaten track can amount to the same thing. Ideas of this sort are scattered throughout this guide, but Tigrai and its rock-hewn churches offer particularly rich pickings for travellers who want to take things slowly.

A couple of relatively quick off-the-beaten-track trips suggest themselves. One, if you are visiting Bale, is to return to Shashemene via Dola Mena and Negele Borena. A good overnight trip from Addis is to the wonderful but little-visited cluster of historical sites around Melka Awash. And then there is the mother of off-the-beaten-track routes, the loop west through the forested mountains around Nekemte and Jimma to the remote river port at Gambella, a ten–14-day round bus trip, which fills an entire chapter of this guide (see *Chapter 26*).

TOUR OPERATORS

IN ETHIOPIA All of Ethiopia's better tour operators are based in Addis Ababa, though many also have satellite operations at the major tourist centres of the north. The following list is selective rather than exhaustive.

Abeba Tours ☎+251 115 15 9530/31; m +251 911 65 2294; e info@abebatoursethiopia.com; www.abebatoursethiopia.com. Tour operator based in Addis Ababa serving individual, group & business travellers.

Adonay Ethiopia Travel ☎+251 11 618 0844; m 091 161 3012/168 8007; e adonaytour@ ethionet.et or adonaytours@yahoo.com; www. adonaytour.com. With an office on Bole Rd, this operator is notable for its dynamic & responsive management & high service levels. In addition to the usual northern circuit tours, it has a good selection of hiking, trekking & birdwatching programmes, & it is flexible when it comes to individualised itineraries. Well-trained guides speak English, Italian & German.

Africa Riding Adventure Tours
\+251 11 551 3249; f +251 11 551 6366; e info@africaridingadventures.com; www.africaridingadventures.com

Amazing Ethiopia Tours \+251 911 427 728; m +251 912 481 022; e info@amazingethiopia.com; www.amazingethiopia.com. Serves individual, group & business travellers with a range of custom & package tours.

Awaze Tours \+251 91 162 3376 or USA toll free \+1 977 717 0939; e info@awazetours.com; www.awazetours.com. Operates exclusively in Ethiopia & offers both custom & scheduled tours.

B J Tours & Trekking \+251 58 111 5073; e bjtours@ethionet.et; www.bjtoursandtrekking.com. A wide variety of tours appealing to all interests.

Dinknesh Ethiopia Tour \+251 11 156 7837/2242; e mulugenet@ethionet.et; www.dinkneshethiopiatour.com or www.ethiopiatravel.com. A wide range of quality tours with an emphasis on excellent service.

Ethio Travel & Tours \+251 911 331138; f 251 111 567151; e ethiopiatravel@gmail.com, info@ethiopiatravelandtours.com; www.ethiotravelandtours.com. This joint Danish–Ethiopian venture offers a good range of tours around Ethiopia, & has its own base at the Ghion Hotel in Bahir Dar.

Ethiopia Community Tourism m +251 911 657768, USA \+202 518 6192; e info@rootsofethiopia.com; www.rootsofethiopia.com. This new community-based organisation works together with several leading NGOs including USAID, TESFA & the Frankfurt Zoological Society to encourage sustainable forms of tourism that allow visitors to connect closely with the communities they visit. They offer a hand-picked collection of authentic, cultural tours operated by small villages across Ethiopia.

Ethiopian Quadrants \+251 11 554 7529; e ethiopianquadrants@ethionet.et; www.ethiopianquadrants.com. Owned & managed by long-time resident Tony Hickey, this small company offers reasonable rates & reliable travel advice

based on years of travel experience in Ethiopia. In addition to the usual historical circuit packages, it specialises in the Awash & Afar regions, the rock-hewn churches of Tigrai, & trekking, ornithological & adventure tours. It also deals regularly with film crews & other specialist requirement groups.

Ethiopian Rift Valley Safaris \+251 11 155 2128/8591/1127; f +251 11 155 0298; e ervs@ethionet.et; www.ethiopianriftvalleysafaris.com. This highly regarded company owns the only permanent lodge in South Omo, & specialises in upmarket safaris to this region, inclusive of game drives, game walks & river rafting. Not for the impecunious, but otherwise highly recommended.

Experience Ethiopia Travel \+251 11 551 9291/515 2336; f +251 11 551 9982; e eet@ethionet.et; www.experienceethiopia.com. One of the leading tour operators in the country offering a wide variety of tailor-made tours from historic sightseeing in the north to birdwatching in the Rift Valley & Bale Mountains.

Galaxy Express Travel \+251 11 551 0355/7678; f +251 11 551 1236; e galaxyexpress@ethionet.et; www.galaxyexpress-ethiopia.com. One of the best-equipped tour operators in Ethiopia, with efficient & responsive management, a large fleet of well-maintained vehicles, & branch offices in Gondar, Axum & Bahir Dar staffed by articulate, energetic & flexible young guides. Rates are competitive & service is excellent – a recommended first contact. The office is next to the Ras Hotel in Addis Ababa.

Grant Express Travel & Tours Services (GETTS) \+251 11 553 4678/4379; m +251 911 233 289; f +251 11 553 4395; e getts@ethionet.et or yaredbz@yahoo.com; www.getts.com.et. This dynamic, responsive & competitively priced new company benefits greatly from the hands-on management style of the vastly experienced former guide Yared Belete – another good first contact for bespoke travels almost anywhere in Ethiopia.

Green Land Tours \+251 11 629 9252–44; m +251 911 203 614/613 016; f +251 11 629 9259; e greenplc@yahoo.com or dario@greenlandethiopia.com; www.greenlandethiopia.com. Italian-owned-&-managed Green Land Tours specialises in 4x4 expeditions to the southwest, where it has lodges in Turmi, Arba Minch & Langano.

Hess Travel \+251 11 661 4122/618 1868; f +251 11 661 3106; e hesstravel@ethionet.et; www.hesstravelethiopia.com. This is a highly regarded & experienced company with efficient German–Ethiopian management. It is recommended in particular to German- & French-speakers, & special-interest groups.

Image Ethiopia Tour & Travel Plc ↘+251 911 69 9473; e info@imageethiopia.com; www.imageethiopia.com. Offers a selection of itineraries & tailor-made programmes.

Imagine Ethiopia Tours & Travel ↘+251 911 10 9336; e info@imagineethiopiatours.com; www.imagineethiopiatours.com. An Ethiopian-owned tour company providing tailor-made trips, package tours & adventure holidays.

Inspiration Tour Operator ↘+251 911 314 034; e vacation@ethionet.et; www.ethiopianinspiration.com. Specialises in cultural & historical tours

Jacaranda Tours ↘+251 11 662 8625; f +251 11 662 7954; e jacarandatours@ethionet.et or info@jacarandatours.net; www.jacarandatours.net. Offers packages to breathtaking scenery & ancient civilisations.

Jenman African Safaris South Africa, ↘+27 21 683 7826; UK, ↘0871 284 5010; USA & Canada, ↘+1 866 487 4323; e info@jenmansafaris.com; www.jenmansafaris.com. Leaders in tailor-made & scheduled safaris & tours in Ethiopia.

Kibran Tours ↘+251 11 662 6214–5; f +251 11 662 6216; e info@kibrantours.com or kibran@ethionet.et; www.kibrantours.com. This top-end operator offers a wide range of well-planned itineraries throughout the country. Professional guides speak fluent English, Italian, German, French & Spanish per your requirement; side trips or extensions to neighbouring countries are available.

Noah Safari ↘+251 11 550 3948; m 0911 331 138; e info@travel.com.et; www.travel.com.et

NTO ↘+251 11 515 9274/3827; f +251 11 551 7688; e info@nto.com.et; www.nto.com.et. This former government tourism body once held the

monopoly of all tour & travel services in Ethiopia. Now privatised, the travel agency is surging ahead with a new dynamic young team at the helm.

Simien Adventure ↘+251 918 536 753; m +251 924 269923; e simienmountain@gmail.com; www.simien.com.et. Adventure trekking specialist offering unique experiences.

Solomon Berhe Tours ↘+251 11 661 4921; m +251 911 181 051; from UK 07710 285283; e sol2rs@yahoo.com; www.solomonberhetours.com. Specialises in birding trips, & also has carefully planned trips to the Danakil Depression, South Omo & elsewhere.

Timeless Ethiopia ↘+251 11 554 6707; e tours@timelessethiopia.com; www.timelessethiopia.com. An Addis Ababa-based company offering package & tailor-made tours.

Travel Ethiopia ↘+251 11 550 8870; f +251 11 551 0200; USA ↘+1 404 547 2843; e info@travelethiopia.com; www.travelethiopia.com. This reputable company, affiliated with Village Ethiopia, offers the usual packages, as well as specialist excursions to the remote tribes & Omo National Park on the west of the Omo River.

VAST Ethiopia Tours ↘+251 11 662 4997; m +251 912 071 695; e info@vastethiopiatours.com; www.vastethiopiatours.com. Offers a range of tour packages from birdwatching & mountain climbing to historical & cultural tours.

Village Ethiopia ↘+251 11 850 4592/550 8869/515 7486; f +251 11 551 1276; e village.ethiopia@ethionet.et; www.village-ethiopia.net. Small but well established wholly Ethiopian-owned company offering a range of tours to the Historic Route, Simien Mountains & Omo Valley as well as tours with an emphasis on birds, flowers & plants, butterflies or geology.

Yumo Tours ↘+251 11 551 8878/3451; e info@yumo.net; www.yumo.net. Specialists in customised tours in Ethiopia.

UK

Aardvark Safaris RBL Hse, Ordnance Rd, Tidworth, Hants SP9 7QD; ↘01980 849160; f 01980 849161; e info@aardvarksafaris.com; www.aardvarksafaris.com. Arranges cultural trips led by anthropologists.

Ethiopia Travel 7 Beechwood Av, Gosforth, Newcastle upon Tyne NE3 5DH; ↘0191 285 5383; e info@ethiopiatravel.co.uk; www.ethiotravel.co.uk.

Footloose Adventure Travel 3 Springs Pavement, Ilkley, West Yorks LS29 8HD; ↘01943 604030; f 01943 604070; e info@footloose.co.uk; www.footlooseadventure.co.uk. Trekking & tailor-made tours.

Fulani Travel ↘01212 102500; f 01212 102501; e info@fulanitravel.co.uk; www.fulanitravel.co.uk

Gane & Marshall International ↘01822 600600; e holidays@ganeandmarshall.co.uk;

www.ganeandmarshall.co.uk. Tailor-made itineraries; historical & cultural tours.

Journeys by Design 36 Park Crescent, Brighton BN2 3HB; ☏ 01273 623790; f 01273 621766; e info@journeysbydesign.com; www.journeysbydesign.com. Tour operator specialising in east & southern Africa.

Rainbow Tours 305 Upper St, London N1 2TU; ☏ 020 7666 1250; e info@rainbowtours.co.uk; www.rainbowtours.co.uk. Tailor-made itineraries for individuals or small groups; yearly trip to the Timket festivals in January.

Silk Steps Deep Meadow, Edington, Bridgwater, Somerset TA7 9JH; ☏ 01278 722460; f 01278 723617; e info@silksteps.co.uk; www.silksteps.co.uk. Quality tailor-made & group travel arrangements.

Steppes Travel 51 Castle St, Cirencester, Gloucs GL7 1QD; ☏ 01285 880980; e enquiry@steppestravel.co.uk; www.steppestravel.co.uk. Specialists in tailor-made & small group departures.

Tim Best Travel 1b The Village, 101 Amies St, London SW11 2JW; ☏ 020 7591 0300; f 020 7978 7222; e info@timbesttravel.com; www.timbesttravel.com. Tailor-made itineraries to the north & south of the country.

Wild Frontiers ☏ 020 7736 3968; e info@wildfrontiers.co.uk; www.wildfrontiers.co.uk. Independent travel company specialising in tailor-made holidays & small group adventure tours.

Wildlife Worldwide Long Barn South, Sutton Manor Farm, Bishops Sutton, Alresford, Hants SO24 0AA; ☏ 0845 130 6982; f 0845 130 6984; e sales@wildlifeworldwide.com; www.wildlifeworldwide.com. Specialises in tailor-made wildlife holidays.

SOUTH AFRICA South African tour operators with specialist experience in Ethiopia.

Africa Travel Co ☏ +27 21 385 1530/1573; e cpt@africatravelco.com; www.africatravelco.com. Branches in South Africa & Zimbabwe. Offers 2 group tours, including a trekking option, as well as tailor-made variations.

Unusual Destinations ☏ +27 11 706 1991; f +27 11 463 1469; e info@unusualdestinations.com; www.unusualdestinations.com

TOURIST INFORMATION

Very little information about Ethiopia is available outside the country. Ethiopian Airlines offices and Ethiopian embassies will be able to give you information about internal flight schedules and current visa and entry requirements. It is also worth consulting the websites run by the UK and US governments, respectively www.fco.gov.uk and http://travel.state.gov/travel/cis_pa_tw/cis/cis_1113.html, and other websites listed in *Appendix 5, Further information*, page 620.

IN ETHIOPIA The main tourist office is on Meskel Square in Addis Ababa. It sometimes stocks a few informative free booklets about Bale, Simien and Lalibela, but it tends to be weak when it comes to current practical advice. There is also a regional tourist office in every regional capital, as well as at some major tourist attractions. The best of these is the Tigrai tourist office in Mekele, which stocks some great booklets about the rock-hewn churches and other regional attractions, and can also give very detailed advice about more obscure churches. Otherwise, regional and local offices vary greatly in their usefulness, ranging from the well-informed office at Gondar, through the helpful if slightly disorganised offices in Dilla and Bahir Dar, down to the apparently pointless exercises in job creation to be found in Harar and Gambella.

In towns where there is no official tourist office, the Ministry of Sport and Culture is often worth a visit, though your luck will depend on the enthusiasm of the individual to whom you speak – in places that don't receive much tourism, this enthusiasm can be considerable.

RED TAPE

PAPERWORK A valid **passport** is required to enter Ethiopia, and entry may be refused is it is set to expire within six months of your intended departure date.

All visitors to Ethiopia require a **visa**, though citizens of the USA, Canada, Mexico, Brazil, New Zealand, Australia, South Africa, China, Japan, Korea, Israel, Russia, the UK and all other European Union nations can buy a one-month visa upon arrival at Bole International Airport (Addis Ababa) for US$20–30. Other passport holders will need to arrange a visa in advance – if you live in a country where there is no Ethiopian embassy, and travel with Ethiopian Airways, you can apply for a visa through the airline office.

Travellers coming overland to Ethiopia should be aware that a single-entry visa is usually only valid for entry 30–90 days after issue (the exact time frame seems to depend on where it is issued) and that it is increasingly difficult to obtain Ethiopian visas in neighbouring states such as Kenya or Sudan unless you are resident in that country. For this reason, it might be safest to buy a multiple-entry visa (valid for one to two years, once again depending on where it is issued) before you leave home.

Should you need to spend longer in the country than is stamped into your passport, extensions can be granted at the Immigration office on Churchill Avenue in Addis Ababa. These cost the birr equivalent of US$20, regardless of the length of the extension, and usually take 24 hours to process.

A **yellow fever** certificate is not required for entry into Ethiopia unless you are coming from a yellow fever endemic zone. However, some countries may insist you have a certificate upon returning from Ethiopia, so it's safest to ensure yours is still current and to bring it with you.

Should there be any possibility you'll want to drive or hire a vehicle while you're in the country, do organise an **international driving licence** (any AA office in a country in which you're licensed to drive will do this for a nominal fee).

For **security** reasons, it's advisable to detail all your important information on one sheet of paper, photocopy it and distribute a few copies in your luggage, as well as emailing it to a webmail address you can easily access on the road. The sort of things you want to include on this are travel insurance policy details and 24-hour emergency contact number, passport number, details of relatives or friends to be contacted in an emergency, bank and credit card details, camera and lens serial numbers, etc.

Should your passport be lost or stolen, it will generally be easier to get a replacement if you have a photocopy of the important pages.

IMMIGRATION AND CUSTOMS Arriving by air, you should whizz through the formalities without complication, provided that you have a return or onward ticket, and a valid passport (as well as a visa if you belong to a nationality that is required to obtain one in advance).

Arriving overland, the most common overland entry point is Moyale on the Kenyan border. This has a reputation as a very relaxed crossing – though the border does close from time to time and the situation seems to be fluid. The major complication arriving at this border from Kenya is that the Ethiopian Embassy in Nairobi sometimes only issues visas on production of an air ticket to Addis Ababa. If you're heading this way, it's advisable to speak to travellers coming the other way for current advice. Details of the crossing are included in the text box *Moyale to Nairobi* on page 512.

At the time of writing, travelling between Ethiopia and Eritrea is impossible, and it may be some time before the borders reopen. In the past, however, the crossing was straightforward, provided you had the appropriate visa, which could be obtained at the Eritrean Embassy in Addis Ababa. If you were returning to Ethiopia from Eritrea, you needed a multiple-entry visa for Ethiopia.

Overland travel between Ethiopia and Somalia is also difficult at the time of writing, the exception being the self-declared and peaceful independent state of Somaliland, whose capital Hargeisa is only about three hours by road from Jijiga in eastern Ethiopia. For further details, see the Bradt guide *Somaliland*, the first edition of which was published in 2012.

At the time of writing it was possible to cross the border from Ethiopia to Sudan via the Metema/Yohannes crossing near Gondar. A regular minibus services the route from Gondar to the border departing at 06.00 and takes about one hour. The crossing is straightforward, if rather time-consuming, provided you have the appropriate visa which is available through the Sudanese Embassy in Addis Ababa. The situation with Sudan however changes all the time, so it is advisable to check the situation before you attempt to make the crossing.

It is also possible to travel overland between Djibouti and Ethiopia, though few people do so. In the past the best way to cross between the countries was by using the rail service connecting Addis Ababa and Djibouti via Dire Dawa, but this service ceased operations in 2008. It is also possible to travel there along the surfaced road through the northern Rift Valley covered in *Chapter 17*.

EMBASSIES AND HONORARY CONSULATES

For additional consulate and embassy information, check the Ministry of Foreign Affairs of Ethiopia website (*http://www.mfa.gov.et*).

Ⓔ **Australia** Honorary Consulate, 38 Johnston St, Fitsroy, Melbourne, Victoria 3065; ☎+61 39417 3419; e ethiopia@consul.com.au; www.consul.com.au

Ⓔ **Austria** Ethiopian Embassy, Wagramer Str 14/1/2, A-1220 Vienna; ☎+431 710 2168; e office@ethiopianembassy.at; www.ethiopianembassy.at

Ⓔ **Belgium** Ethiopian Embassy, Av de Tervueren 231, 1150 Brussels; ☎+322 771 3294; e etebru@brutele.be; www.ethiopianembassy.be

Ⓔ **Canada** Ethiopian Consulate, 5080-3080 Young St, Toronto M4N 3N1; ☎+1 416 482 6637; e info@ethioconsulatecanada.org; www.ethioconsulatecanada.org

Ⓔ **China** Ethiopian Embassy, No 3, Xiu Shui Nan Jie, Jian Guo Men Wai, Beijing; ☎+8610 653 25258; e ethchina@public3.bta.net.cn; www.ethiopiaemb.org.cn

Ⓔ **Côte d'Ivoire** Ethiopian Embassy, Immeuble Nour-Al-Hayat, 8th Floor Plateau, Abidjan; ☎+225 20 21 3365; e ambethio@gmail.com; www. ethiopianembassyabidjan.org

Ⓔ **Egypt** Ethiopian Embassy, Mesaha Sq, Villa 11, Dokki, Cairo; ☎+202 335 3696; e ethio@ethioembassy.org.eg; www.ethioembassy.org.eg

Ⓔ **France** Ethiopian Embassy, 35 Av Charles Floquet, 75007 Paris; ☎+33 1 47 83 83 95; e embeth@free.fr or embeth.free.fr

Ⓔ **Germany** Ethiopian Embassy, Boothstrasse 20a, 12207, Berlin; ☎+49 30 77 2060; e emb.ethiopia@t-online.de; www.aethiopien-botschaft.de

Ⓔ **Ghana** Ethiopian Embassy, 2 Milne Cl, Airport Residential Area, Accra; ☎+233 21 775928; e ethioemb@4u.com.gh

Ⓔ **Greece** Ethiopian Embassy, 3 Georgiou Sourrri, 105 57, Sintagma; ☎+30 210 9403483; e ethemb@otenet.gr

Ⓔ **Ireland** Ethiopian Embassy, 26 Upper Fitzwilliam St, Dublin 2; ☎+353 1 6787062; e info@ethiopianembassy.ie; www.ethiopianembassy.ie

Ⓔ **Israel** Ethiopian Embassy, 48 Menaham Begin St, Tel Aviv 66184; ☎+972 3 6397831; f +972 9 639 7837; e info@ethioemb.org.il; www.ethioemb.org.il

Ⓔ **Italy** Ethiopian Embassy, Via Andrea Vesalio 16–18, 00161 Rome; ☎+39 06 44 161 6307; e embethrm@rdn.it; www.ethiopianembassy.it

Ⓔ **Japan** Ethiopian Embassy, 3-4-1, Takanawa, Minato-Ku, Takanawa Kaisei Bldg 2 FL; ☎+81 3

5420 6860; e info@ethiopia-emb.or.jp; www. ethiopia-emb.or.jp

E Kenya Ethiopian Embassy, State Hse Av, Nairobi; +254 2 2732050; e ethioemb@kenyaweb.com

E Russia Ethiopia Embassy, Orlovo-Davydovsky Per 6, 129041 Moscow; +7 095 6801616; e eth-emb@col.ru

E Senegal Ethiopian Embassy, 46 Bd Martin Luther King, Dakar; +221 824 3708; f +221 821 9895; e ethembas@sentoo.sn

E South Africa Ethiopian Embassy, 47 Charles St, Baileys Muckleneuk, Pretoria; +27 12 346 3067; e ethiopiata@iburst.co.za

E Sudan Ethiopian Embassy, Plot No 4, Block 384BC, Khartoum South; +249 11 349151; e eekrt@hotmail.com

E Sweden Ethiopian Embassy, Löjtnantsgatan 17, PO Box 10148, Stockholm 115 50; +46 8661 6311; e ethio.embassy@telia.com; www.ethemb.se

E Switzerland Ethiopian Embassy, 56 Rue de Moillebeau, 1211 Geneva 19; +41 22 919 70 10; e mission.ethiopia@ties.itu.int; www. ethiopianmission.ch

E Thailand Honorary Consulate, 954/32 Suite 406 Prannok Plaza, Bangkok 10700; +66 2583 3993; e vorasakdi@yahoo.com

E Uganda Ethiopian Embassy, off Kira Rd, Plot No 3L, Kampala; +256 41 348340; e ethiokam@ starcom.co.ug

E UK Ethiopian Embassy, 17 Princes Gate, London SW7 1PZ; +44 020 7838 3897; e info@ ethioembassy.org.uk; www.ethioembassy.org.uk

E USA Ethiopian Embassy, 3506 International Dr, NW, Washington, DC 20008; +1 202 364 1200; e ethiopia@ethiopianembassy.org; www. ethiopianembassy.org

E Zimbabwe Ethiopian Embassy, 14 Lanark Rd, Belgravia, Harare; +2634 70 15 14; e emb@ ecoweb.co.zw

GETTING THERE AND AWAY

BY AIR All international flights arrive and depart from Bole International Airport in Addis Ababa. Many airlines fly to Ethiopia. Ethiopian Airlines is Africa's oldest airline and has an excellent safety record, but may not be the cheapest option. Bookings can be made online at www.ethiopianairlines.com, or by emailing reservation@ ethiopianairlines.com. For a complete list of contact information for both international and domestic offices, see www.ethiopianairlines.com/en/info/contacts.

Other major airlines that fly to Addis Ababa are Alitalia, Emirates, SAA, KLM, Lufthansa and Kenya Airways. There are dozens upon dozens of travel agents in London offering cheap flights to Africa, and it's worth checking out the ads in magazines like *Time Out* and *TNT* and phoning around before you book anything.

An established London operator, well worth contacting, is **Africa Travel Centre** (*3rd Floor, New Premier Hse, 150 South Hampton Row, Bloomsbury, London WC1B 5AL;* 020 7387 1211; f 0845 450 5725; *www.africatravel.co.uk*).

Two reputable agents specialising in cheap round-the-world-type tickets rather than Africa specifically are **Trailfinders** (*38 Poultry Rd, London EC2R 8AJ;* 020 7628 7628; *www.trailfinders.com*) and **STA** (*52 Grosvenor Gdns, London SW1W 0AG;* 0871 702 9840; f 020 7881 1299; *www.statravel.co.uk*). There are STA branches in Bristol, Cambridge, Oxford and Manchester.

An **airport tax** of US$20 is levied when you fly out of Ethiopia. This is normally included in the price of your ticket; if not, it must be paid in hard currency; an extra commission is taken for travellers' cheques.

OVERLAND The main overland route south from Europe, often referred to as the Nile Route, goes through Egypt and Sudan, entering Ethiopia west of Gondar. This route was closed for many years due to political instability in Sudan, and it remains potentially volatile, but with Sudanese visa in hand, travellers have been getting through with relative ease since 2003. If you opt to head this way, do keep your ears to the ground, and be prepared to fly over troubled areas, for instance between

Cairo and Khartoum or Khartoum and Addis Ababa. It is no longer possible to cross between Ethiopia and Sudan via Eritrea, as the border between Eritrea and Ethiopia has been closed for some years and looks set to remain that way.

Travellers heading up to Ethiopia from more southerly parts of Africa have a more straightforward ride. In terms of safety, the route from South Africa to Kenya via Zimbabwe, Zambia and Tanzania has been good for over a decade. The most volatile part of this route is the Kenyan–Ethiopian border area, as northern Kenya is prone to spasmodic outbreaks of Somali-related banditry. Plenty of people get through from Kenya without a problem, but the situation is subject to frequent change. As always, your best source of information is travellers coming in the opposite direction.

WHAT TO TAKE

There are two simple rules to bear in mind when you decide what to take with you to Ethiopia. The first is to bring with you *everything* that you could possibly need and that might not be readily available when you need it. The second is to carry as little as possible. Somewhat contradictory rules, and finding the right balance depends on personal taste and experience as much as anything. Worth stressing is that most genuine necessities are surprisingly easy to get hold of in Ethiopia, and that most of the ingenious gadgets you can buy in camping shops are likely to amount to dead weight on the road. If it came to it, you could easily travel in Ethiopia with little more than a change of clothes, a few basic toiletries and a medical kit.

CARRYING LUGGAGE Assuming that you'll be using public transport, you'll want to carry your luggage on your back, either in a backpack or in a suitcase that converts into one, since you'll tend to spend a lot of time walking between bus stations and hotels. Which of these you choose depends mainly on your style of travel. If you intend doing a lot of hiking you definitely want a proper backpack. On the other hand, if you'll be doing things where it might be a good idea to shake off the negative image attached to backpackers, then there would be obvious advantages in being able to convert your backpack into a conventional suitcase.

Travellers carrying a lot of valuable items should look for a pack that can easily be padlocked. A locked bag can, of course, be slashed open, but in Ethiopia you are still most likely to encounter casual theft of the sort to which a lock would be a real deterrent.

CLOTHES Clothes may be light but they are also bulky, so it's advisable to take the minimum. You can easily and cheaply replace worn items in Ethiopia. A minimum guideline might be one or two pairs of trousers and/or skirts, one pair of shorts, three shirts or T-shirts, a couple of sweaters, a light waterproof windbreaker during the rainy season, enough socks and underwear to last five to seven days, one solid pair of shoes or boots for walking, and one pair of sandals, flip-flops or other light shoes.

Skirts and trousers are best made of a light natural fabric such as cotton. T-shirts are lighter and less bulky than proper shirts, though the top pocket of a shirt (particularly if it buttons up) is a good place to carry spending money in markets and bus stations, since it's easier to keep an eye on than trouser pockets. Despite its equatorial location, much of Ethiopia is decidedly chilly, especially at night, so a couple of sweaters or sweatshirts are essential. There is a massive used clothing industry in Ethiopia, and at most markets you'll find stalls selling jumpers of dubious aesthetic but impeccable functional value for next to nothing – you might consider buying such clothing on the spot and giving it away afterwards. Getting clothes made from local fabrics is also quick and relatively inexpensive.

Ethiopians are modest dressers and the country has a significant Muslim population – you should select your clothing with this in mind. Women should never expose their knees or shoulders in public, so shorts and sleeveless tops are out. It isn't entirely acceptable for women to wear trousers in Muslim areas, but neither will it cause serious offence. Men should always wear a shirt in public places. Trousers are generally more acceptable than shorts, though again this isn't rigid. Sensitivity about dress is more of a factor in the predominantly Muslim eastern regions than it is elsewhere in Ethiopia.

Socks and underwear must be made from natural fabrics, such as cotton. As for footwear, genuine hiking boots are worth considering only if you're a serious off-road hiker, since they are very heavy whether on your feet or in your pack. A good pair of walking shoes, preferably made of leather and with good ankle support, is a good compromise. It's also useful to carry sandals, flip-flops or other light shoes. Flip-flops are useful as protection from the floors of communal showers, and they are very light to carry. Just watch out for irregular pavements!

CAMPING EQUIPMENT With cheap rooms being so widely available, the case for taking camping equipment to Ethiopia is less than compelling, unless you plan to hike in remote areas. But if you do, try to look for the lightest available gear. It is now possible to buy a lightweight tent weighing less than 2kg, and you'll also need a sleeping bag and a roll-mat for insulation and padding.

OTHER USEFUL ITEMS Most backpackers, even those with no intention of camping, carry a sleep-sheet or a **sleeping bag** for emergencies, or to use as an alternative to the dirty bedding provided in some budget hotels. Some travellers also like to carry their own **padlock**: not a bad idea in Ethiopia, particularly if you intend to stay mostly in shoestring hotels or travel to small towns, where not all hotels will supply padlocks.

If you're interested in natural history, it's difficult to imagine anything that will give you such value-for-weight entertainment as a pair of light compact **binoculars**, which these days needn't be much heavier or bulkier than a pack of cards. For most purposes, 7x21 compact binoculars will be fine, though some might prefer 7x35 traditional binoculars for their larger field of vision. Serious birdwatchers will find a 10x magnification more useful.

Your **toilet bag** should at the very minimum include soap (secured in a plastic bag or soap holder unless you enjoy a soapy toothbrush), shampoo, toothbrush and toothpaste. This sort of stuff is easy to replace as you go along, so there's no need to bring family-sized packs. Men will probably want a **razor**. Women should carry enough **tampons** and/or **sanitary pads** to see them through, since these items may not always be immediately available. If you wear **contact lenses**, be aware that the various cleansing and storing fluids are not readily available in Ethiopia and, since many people find the intense sun and dust irritates their eyes, you might consider reverting to glasses. Nobody should forget to bring a **towel**, or to keep handy a roll of **loo paper**, which although widely available at shops and kiosks cannot always be relied upon to be present where it's most urgently needed.

A **torch** will be useful not only if you are camping or staying in towns where there is no electricity, but also for visiting old churches, which tend to be very gloomy inside. Also worth bringing are a **universal plug**, a **penknife**, a **travel washing line** and a compact **alarm clock** for those early morning starts. Increasingly important as more and more travellers carry electronic camera equipment is a **universal electric socket adaptor** for charging your batteries in hotel rooms. Also very useful are **a few metres of wraparound cloth**, which might serve as a towel, a bed sheet, something to cover up with after a trip to a common shower or a night-time loo excursion, a shoulder cover if local custom requires, a curtain in a bus, and better sun protection if you burn easily than any amount of suncream. Some travellers carry **games** – most commonly a **pack of cards**, less often chess or draughts or Travel Scrabble – to while away the hours between bus trips.

English-language **reading material** of any description is difficult to locate outside of Addis Ababa, and even there you'll find the range limited. Bring a good stock of reading matter with you.

You should carry a small **medical kit**, the contents of which are discussed in *Chapter 4*, page 111, as are **mosquito nets**. Two items of tropical toiletry that are surprisingly difficult to get hold of in Ethiopia are **mosquito repellent** for skin application, and **sun block**. In both cases, you are advised to bring all you need with you, though aerial repellents can be bought almost anywhere. A medically qualified reader writes: 'Thinking about *injera* (see *Ethiopian dishes*, page 98) and Ethiopian eating habits, I would advise all travellers to carry with them some sort of **anti-bacterial disinfectant hand-wash solution** which makes eating with your hands (as Ethiopians do) so much healthier.'

MONEY

The unit of currency is the birr, also referred to as the dux or, a little confusingly, the dollar. Notes are printed in denominations of birr 100, 50, 10, 5 and 1; and 50, 25, 10, 5 and 1 cent coins are minted. The birr has long been one of the strongest currencies in Africa, though in recent years it has devalued significantly. In June 2012 exchange rates were roughly US$1 = birr 18, €1 = birr 22 and £1 = birr 27.

FOREIGN EXCHANGE If you have cash, the quickest way to exchange money in Addis is at a foreign-exchange bureau. Rates are similar to banks, but there is much less paperwork. You can also exchange money at most branches of the Commercial Bank of Ethiopia (CBE) or Dashen Bank. In Addis Ababa, this is a straightforward procedure taking anything from ten to 20 minutes, though neither bank is as efficient as the foreign-exchange bureaux at the Hilton and Sheraton hotels. In other large cities, bank procedures are much faster than they used to be, comparable to Addis Ababa really, but in small towns it can take ages to change money at a bank. Banking hours in Addis Ababa are from 09.00 to 16.00 weekdays, with a lunch break between noon and 14.00. The CBE branch at Bole Airport is open every day of the week and there are now two ATMs in the terminal. There are also a few private banks that offer foreign-exchange services, but in our experience the rates are often worse than at the CBE.

It is worth noting that many smaller towns have no bank, or a bank not equipped to deal with foreign-exchange transactions, or one that can handle cash but not travellers' cheques. Common sense dictates that you try to plan ahead to avoid getting into a situation where you need to change money in a small town (even if facilities do exist, they will be slow). Try to limit any transactions to the following towns: Addis Ababa, Bahir Dar, Gondar, Axum, Adigrat, Mekele, Dessie, Adama, Hawassa, Moyale, Arba Minch, Jimma, Dire Dawa and Harar. Note that Lalibela has only one bank, and no reliable foreign-exchange facilities are available between

Hawassa and Moyale, or in Konso and South Omo, and that the CBE in Ziway can deal with cash only.

The only other places where money can sometimes be changed officially are at top-end hotels or former government hotels. This facility is open only to hotel residents and rates are rather poor compared with those of the CBE. Should you get stuck in Lalibela and the bank is closed, the Roha Hotel offers a fair rate and will deal with non-residents.

Since the devaluation of the birr in October 1992, the difference between the black market and official rates has been negligible – about 5% at best – but the black market can come in useful in Addis Ababa when you need to change money outside of banking hours. In this situation, avoid changing money on the street – rather speak to somebody at your hotel, or at a restaurant or curio shop, to set up a deal in a controlled environment. Travellers' cheques are not accepted on the black market, nor are any currencies other than US dollars.

PRICES QUOTED IN THIS GUIDE It is always difficult to decide whether to quote prices in local currency or in US dollars. The main argument for sticking with local currency is that it makes the book easier to work with in the country. The argument against it is that most African currencies are subject to sudden downward spirals in exchange rates, which tend to drag local prices with them. With prices in Ethiopia having doubled in birr terms since the last edition was published, much of it due to devaluation of the currency, we have opted to go with converting prices to USD in this edition, in the hope it will be more meaningful to use birr prices a couple of years down the line.

The prices quoted in this book were collected in mid 2011. Any changes to exchange rates and local prices after that are beyond my control, but you will find that prices in Ethiopia are reasonably consistent countrywide. Whatever happens, the rates quoted in this book will be a useful relative guideline once you have a feel for current prices.

ORGANISING YOUR FINANCES The Dashen and Wegagen banks now have ATMs throughout Addis and in several other cities around the country – the Dashen Bank alone has 30 ATMs in Addis (including one at Bole Airport and the Hilton Hotel) as well as regional centres such as Bahir Dar, Gondar, Mekele, Dire Dawa, Hawassa and Harar – making a credit or debit card an excellent option for obtaining money while in Ethiopia. (Visa and growingly MasterCard are accepted, though Visa is more reliable. A debit card is also preferable as most credit cards charge interest on cash advances. It is sometimes possible to get around this by paying extra money to your credit card company in advance so that you have a positive balance.)

Do note that withdrawals may be limited to birr 5,000 per transaction and the birr equivalent of US$400–500 per day. If an ATM is out of order, provided you are there during banking hours you can usually get a cash advance on your card inside the branch, but it is not nearly as convenient, and fees may be involved.

Credit cards have also become much more accepted as payment in recent years, but they are still of limited use in Ethiopia. The major cards will be accepted to settle room and restaurant bills at the Addis Ababa Hilton and Sheraton, and Visa, and growingly MasterCard, is accepted at most of the other top hotels in the capital and around the country, but a surcharge is often added.

Travellers' cheques remain a viable option, especially since they can be refunded if they are lost or stolen. Bring your receipts though, as most banks ask to see them; these of course should be carried separately from your cheques. Most major currencies are accepted in Ethiopian banks, but unless you have a strong reason for not doing so, it is probably a good idea to carry US dollar travellers' cheques. More obscure currencies may cause confusion at banks outside Addis Ababa or if you try to pay for government hotels or other services in hard currency.

It is advisable to carry a portion of your funds in hard currency banknotes, which are easier to exchange outside of the capital. If you are thinking of using the black market, it is essential to have US dollars cash; high denomination bills are preferable, but US$100 notes issued before the year 2002 may be refused. Banks can also be unwilling to accept older US dollar banknotes because of the number of forgeries in circulation. There seems to be less of an issue with smaller banknotes, so unless you can locate spanking new US$100 bills, then denominations of US$50 are probably the best overall compromise.

No matter how long you intend to spend in Ethiopia, bring whatever money you're likely to need with you, in order to avoid the cost and complications of having money sent to you. If you are in a pinch, Western Union and several other services offer money transfers. In Ethiopia, as in most other countries, you will have to accept your money in local currency and then change it back to hard currency on departure.

BUDGETING

Budgeting is a personal thing, dependent on how much time you are spending in the country, what you are doing while you are there and how much money you can afford to spend.

SHORT-STAY BUDGETS Short-stay tourists will find Ethiopia undemanding on their wallets. You can expect to pay an average of around US$40–60 per night for a room in a moderate hotel and, except perhaps in Addis Ababa, you'd struggle to top US$15 per day on food and drink. Most visitors with time restraints will want to fly between major places of interest, for which they can expect to pay around US$90–230 per leg if you purchase your ticket online (you can check current prices on expedia.com), but if you are prepared to buy your ticket at the last moment from within Ethiopia domestic fares are less than half the price. Add to that about US$20 per day on guide and entrance fees, and a daily budget of US$160 for one person or US$270 for two looks very generous. If you were prepared to stay in the sort of mid-range hotels that exist in most major towns, around US$120/200 for one/two people would still look generous.

Where Ethiopia does get expensive is when you take organised driving tours and safaris. The low volume of tourists means that arrangements tend to be personalised, and thus a safari to somewhere like South Omo will be far more expensive than an equivalent safari in Kenya or Tanzania.

There is nothing preventing short-stay visitors from operating on the sort of budget that you would normally associate with long-stay visitors, except that the distances between major attractions make flying virtually essential if you are to see much of the country in a short space of time.

LONG-STAY BUDGETS If you use facilities that are mainly geared to locals, Ethiopia is a very inexpensive country, even by African standards. You can always find a basic room in a local hotel for around US$5–10 and a meal for less than US$2. Buses are cheap, as are drinks. Rigidly budget-conscious travellers could probably keep costs down to US$15 per day per person, but US$25 would give you considerably more flexibility. At US$40 per day, you could, within reason, do what you like.

If you are on a restricted budget, it is often a useful device to separate your daily budget from one-off expenses. This is less the case in Ethiopia than most African countries, because few travellers will be doing expensive one-off activities such as safaris, gorilla tracking or climbing Kilimanjaro. Nevertheless, there are always going to be days that a variety of factors (historical site and guide fees, air tickets) conspire to make expensive. At current prices, a daily budget of around US$30 with a few hundred dollars spare for one-off expenses would be very comfortable for most travellers.

GETTING AROUND

BY AIR If your time in Ethiopia is limited, flying is far and away the most efficient way to get around. Even travellers who wouldn't normally do so might think about using a couple of flights in Ethiopia. For starters, the full spectacle of Ethiopia's ravine-ravaged landscape is best seen from the air (the leg between Gondar and Lalibela is particularly recommended). You could also save a lot of time by flying out to a far-flung destination – for instance Axum, Arba Minch or Gambella – and working your way back overland, rather than repeating a similar bus trip out and back.

Ethiopian Airlines runs a good network of domestic flights connecting Addis Ababa to most major tourist destinations. The best connections are in the north, where at least one flight daily goes in either direction between any combination of Addis Ababa, Bahir Dar, Gondar, Lalibela and Axum (flights to Mekele are slightly less numerous). There are also flights to other parts of the country, such as Arba Minch, Gambella, Jimma and Dire Dawa. The internal flights are generally efficient and they normally leave to schedule, but last-minute schedule changes are commonplace and you can probably expect on average one serious hold-up when you fly around the historical circuit. The soundest advice we can give in this regard is always to allow one non-travel day between flights, which eliminates the possibility of missing something important.

In the past it was the case that it was best to book flights before you travelled to Ethiopia, with domestic tickets booked in conjunction with international inbound flights with Ethiopian Airlines given substantial discounts. However, as of 2011 foreigners purchasing domestic tickets in Ethiopia were afforded the same discount as Ethiopian residents, so if you are prepared to leave things to the last minute you'll pay almost a third of the price of a ticket booked internationally or online. For example at the time of writing a ticket booked online to Bahir Dar cost US$158, while purchased through a local ticket agent in Addis Ababa cost US$40. Ticket prices throughout this guide have been quoted on purchasing them locally. International Ethiopian Airlines offices generally accept credit cards, as does the main office in Addis Ababa, but cards cannot be used at their offices elsewhere in the country.

Having booked domestic flights, Ethiopian Airlines is famously flexible about changes of date. It is never a problem to change a flight date with a day or two's notice, provided seats are available for the day on which you want to fly. The converse of this flexible policy is that every individual leg of your ticket *must* be confirmed at the point of departure the day before you fly.

The baggage limit on most domestic flights has been increased to 20kg following the modernisation of several airports and subsequent replacement of light 17-seat planes by small jets carrying upwards of 50 passengers. Flights to more remote areas, such as Jijiga and Gambella, may still impose a 10kg limit, depending on the plane being used. A nominal airport departure tax, payable in local currency, is charged on all domestic flights. Luggage and body searches are part of the Ethiopian Airlines experience; they are generally very thorough but done with a reasonable level of politeness. If you are carrying anything that could possibly be perceived to be an antiquity, it will be confiscated at Axum Airport.

BY BUS, TRUCK, MINIBUS Ethiopian road transport compares well with that in many other parts of Africa. Buses are rarely crowded, the driving is as sober as it gets in Africa and, because buses rarely indulge in the African custom of stopping every 100m to pick up another passenger, you can generally expect to cover 30km in an hour on dirt and 50km on surfaced roads. Also unusual for Africa are organised breakfast and/or lunch stops on longer runs. In fact, the only real problem with bus

ROAD MAP CODES

Road conditions in Ethiopia, as elsewhere in Africa, are extremely variable, which can make it difficult to predict driving times based purely on the distance involved. There are some (admittedly not many) stretches of Ethiopian asphalt so good that you could cover 100km in an hour without undue risk, while at the other extreme are rutted dirt tracks where it would be difficult to achieve an average driving speed of 20km/h, and nigh impossible after heavy rain. For this reason, all regional maps in this guide show not only the distance between two points, but also rate the road quality, using the following grading system:

A Good asphalt road, not too many curves or steep gradients; should be able to average 80–100km/h without driving recklessly.

B Asphalt, but the combination of pot-holes and/or steep gradients and/or sharp curves and/or other impediments will restrict you to a realistic average driving speed of 60–70km/h.

C Good dirt road, not too many curves or steep gradients; should be able to average 50–60km/h without driving recklessly.

D Adequate dirt road, but the combination of rutted stretches and/or steep gradients and/or sharp curves and/or other impediments will restrict you to a realistic average driving speed of around 30–50km/h.

E Poor dirt road, more or less passable all year through, but need high clearance, ideally 4x4; cannot expect to average more than 20–30km/h.

F Poor dirt road or track, 4x4 required, driving speed low but variable, dependent on weather; may be impassable during the rains.

Note that the accuracy of this grading system will of course be linked to the power and quality of your vehicle, and the skill of the driver. Furthermore, not all roads are consistent – even the best asphalt road might have the odd poor stretch, or curving ascent, and detours created by roadworks are often highly disruptive.

DRIVING IN ETHIOPIA

Extracted from an article by John Graham (see www.addistribune.com)

The countryside is full of quirky pedestrians. The children have devised a number of games to play with drivers. One of the more charming is 'Let's stand in the road defiantly and see if the car stops before we lose our nerve and run to the side'. This is only slightly more popular than 'Let me see if I can push my friend in front of a car'.

Shepherd boys have a pleasant way of passing their sometimes boring hours – making a line of sharp rocks across the road! Then there is the good old pastime of throwing rocks at cars, something that was not entirely unknown amongst the urchins where I grew up. One local official, trying to demonstrate to me the gratitude of the people for some good work we were doing, said that our organisation was so good that the children in his *woreda* didn't even throw stones at our cars! As we were driving out, sure enough, one did.

On the adult side, there is the curious criss-cross tradition. This stems from a rural belief that if a person crosses in front of a moving vehicle it will lengthen their life. Of course, if they fail to cross successfully, their life is considerably shortened. On almost every trip, we've had to brake abruptly at least a few times as some pedestrian suddenly hears us from behind and launches him or herself across the road metres in front of us. The loud skidding, honking and occasionally shouting which accompanies this event is usually greeted by the pedestrian with a big smile. I found this galling and irritating, until some kind and patient Ethiopian assured me that the smile was to show embarrassment, not amusement at the chaos they had caused.

The maze of obstacles that one has to negotiate to drive in rural Ethiopia used to leave me breathless in admiration of our drivers. Knowing me too well, my wife pointedly said on our first trip out of town that she felt that local drivers were essential for long trips and I shouldn't consider driving. At the time I sympathised. After a while the psychology of the people and animals at the side of the road, not to mention the manic drivers in the middle, became clearer. Now that I've driven myself all over rural Ethiopia, I recognise a sixth sense that tells me that this donkey is not going to launch itself in front of me, while that other one just might. There is nothing that can protect even the most experienced driver from the full-fledged unexpected dash onto the road by a pedestrian or animal – but the rest becomes relatively straightforward.

transport in Ethiopia is the size of the country. The northern historical circuit, for instance, requires more than 2,500km of road travel – and at an average progress rate of 40km/h this means that a daunting total of 60–70 hours, or the bulk of about seven waking days, must be spent on buses.

The best buses where they are available (which includes the main loop through the historical circuit, from Addis Ababa to Bahir Dar and Gondar, as well as from Addis Ababa to Adama and Dire Dawa in the east) are the recently introduced Selam (011 554 8800/1; e *selam.bus@ethionet.et; www.selambus.com*) and Sky Bus (011 156 8080/8585; *www.skybusethiopia.com*) services, both closer in style to a Greyhound-type coach than a typical African bus. On other routes, there are government buses and private buses. Where there is a choice, private buses are preferable for short runs (say up to 150km) and government buses are better for long runs. The reasoning behind this is that government buses are faster and better maintained, which is an advantage over a long distance, but private buses get going more quickly.

On some runs buses leave throughout the morning; on other runs buses leave at a specific time, which will normally be at 05.30 or 06.00. By leave, I mean you have to be at the bus station to buy a ticket; an actual departure before 07.00 is something to write home about. In some cases, you may be required to buy a ticket the day before departure, but you will still be told to be at the bus station at 05.30, and there's still very little chance of anything rolling much before 07.00. But it can happen! As far as possible, I've indicated local departure patterns throughout the regional section of this guide, but this sort of thing is subject to change. It is always advisable to check the current situation on the afternoon before you want to travel – and remember you'll generally, but not always, be quoted departure times in the Ethiopian clock (see box, *Ethiopian time*, page 37).

Light vehicles such as pick-up trucks and minibuses are less widely used in Ethiopia than in many other African countries. You can, however, rely on there being some form of regular light transport between large towns that are close together (for instance, Adwa and Axum, Goba and Robe or Dire Dawa and Harar). It is also possible to town-hop on light vehicles on some major routes (between Axum, Adigrat and Mekele; Addis Ababa and Adama; and Mojo and Hawassa). The other situation where light vehicles come into play is on routes where there are no buses, for instance between Goba and Negele Borena or Arba Minch and Jinka. Generally, these light vehicles are privately owned, are more crowded than buses, and fares are higher. That said, new government regulations which prohibit foreigners travelling in local ISUZU trucks, has made independent travel all but impossible.

Buses are cheap. Typically you are looking at around US$1 per 100km, though road conditions and travel time will also affect the fare. If you use light vehicles on routes where there are no buses, expect to pay considerably more than you would for a comparable distance on a bus route. As an example, Goba to Dola Mena costs around US$5 whereas a similar distance by bus might be around US$2. Another quirk is that on some routes you may be expected to pay full price for covering only part of the distance (for instance, if you ask a bus going from Shashemene to Ziway to drop you at Langano, you'll probably have to pay the full fare to Ziway). To avert potential paranoia, I should stress that in neither case is this because you are a foreigner. I cannot recall being overcharged on a bus in Ethiopia.

It is worth noting that Ethiopians are entirely irrational about opening bus windows, since they seem to associate wind with illness. Immediately after the bus departs, all the windows are closed and your fellow passengers will be very reluctant to open them again. Even if half the passengers are graphically suffering from motion sickness, merely cracking open your window will cause pandemonium in the rows behind you.

BY RAIL The only remaining rail service in Ethiopia, the French-built line between Addis and Djibouti, which stopped *en route* at Awash and Dire Dawa, had ceased operations at the time of writing. However, in mid 2010 the government announced plans to construct a new 4,780km railway complex that will link Addis Ababa to some 49 regional centres along eight main routes around the country, with the line to Djibouti given priority. We will post any news on our updates website: http://updates.bradtguides.com/ethiopia.

BICYCLES   *Edited from a letter by Arthur Gerfers*

Bicycle rental is very cheap in Ethiopia, and I personally prefer it to any other form of transport. I rented a bicycle in almost every place where one was available. I found it more pleasant to cover distances on a bicycle, not least because it enabled me to dodge the beggars and manoeuvre through crowds of yelling children with greater ease – though it is amazing how far some of those little chaps will run!

Always TEST DRIVE a bike before renting it. You can't get the feel of a bike if the seat is too high or too low. Often the seat is also too loose. Have the seat adjusted to suit you. Perseverance is the key here. The bike guy doesn't have anything else better to do anyway. Once you have taken the bike for a spin, and it catches your fancy, pay attention to a few other factors:

- Bent handlebars gripped such that the knuckles line up parallel to the legs are going to wear on your wrists more quickly than straight handlebars gripped such that the knuckles line up parallel to the handlebars. If you have a choice (and if you are in no hurry, you probably do) straight handlebars are recommended.
- Pedals are a must. Without pedals your feet will cramp up quick. If the pedals are broken, missing or do not adjust properly with the turning of the cranks, do not take the bicycle.
- Brakes are important. Make sure they work at least somewhat. Though most Ethiopian cyclists on the road get by without them, and some trips (like flat overland ones) don't require them, brakes are usually necessary in some form.
- Insist on a pump. The bike guy, or his brother or cousin, is bound to have one. And, should you have a flat tyre, you will be glad to have a pump too. Again, perseverance is the key here.

A final note on the day after: it is not unusual to have an especially sore bum on the day after a trying bike ride. The best way to overcome this mild irritation is to ride the bike again as often as possible. The pain will subside in another day or two. These few rules of thumb should ensure a more enjoyable biking holiday!

BY FERRY Two ferry services run on Lake Tana: a daily service between Bahir Dar and Zege, and a weekly overnight service between Bahir Dar and Gorgora. See *Chapter 7* for details.

BY BICYCLE Anybody thinking about cycling around Ethiopia should refer to the detailed online report (*www.owen.org/cycling/ethiopia*), written by Owen Barder and Grethe Petersen, who undertook a cycling holiday there in 2002. See also the box, *Bicycles*, above.

BY TAXI, *GARI* AND *BAJAJ* Taxis can be found in many larger towns. Except in Addis and towns with a high tourist turnover (for instance Gondar), they are very cheap but foreigners are frequently asked higher prices and you should expect to bargain. Taxis in Addis are expensive (though still cheap by international standards) and often drivers will refuse to drop their prices for foreigners. In towns with a cool climate, the horse-drawn cart or *gari* replaces taxis. These are even cheaper than taxis and very useful for reaching places a few kilometres out of town. Growing in number, however, outside of the capital, *bajajis* – small three-wheeled *tuk-tuks* imported from India – have replaced taxis in many of the country's flatter regional towns such as Bahir Dar, Gondar, Harar and Hawassa as the main means of local transportation. The standard fare for a short trip is birr 1, but you will undoubtedly be asked to pay more than five times this. You can also charter a *bajaj* for between US$0.60 and US$1.20, or even less if your negotiating skills are good.

BY CAR/CAR HIRE It is straightforward enough to hire a vehicle in Addis Ababa, but as a rule a driver will be supplied so in essence you are really organising a tailored tour or safari. Car hire in Ethiopia is expensive by any standards – the lowest rate you'll get will be about US$150 per day, and US$200 or higher is likely from a reputable tour company. Avis is represented in Ethiopia by Galaxy Express, but most other operators

ACCOMMODATION CATEGORIES

In order to guide readers of this sixth edition through the immense number of hotels in many Ethiopian towns, accommodation entries have been divided into six categories. The purpose of the categorisation is twofold: to break up long hotel listings that span a wide price range, and to help readers isolate the range of hotels in any given town that best suits their budget and taste. The application of categories is not rigid, and an element of subjectivity is inevitable, since it is based first and foremost on the feel of any given hotel rather than the absolute price (prices are quoted for all entries anyway) and does depend on what other accommodation is available in any given town. It should also be noted that assessments relating to the value for money represented by any given hotel are to be read in the context of the stated category, as well as the individual town.

A brief explanation of each category follows.

INTERNATIONAL This category includes the Addis Ababa Sheraton and Addis Ababa Hilton, international chains that provide secure compound living and enough amenities that you really have no need to leave. Prices are upwards of US$200.

LUXURY This category consists of hotels that are verging on international standards with all the bells and whistles as most listed in the above category such as pool, spas and good restaurants and bars as well as rooms endowed with modern extras such as flat-screen satellite televisions and free Wi-Fi, but with the hefty price tag. Prices are from US$86 to US$199.

UPMARKET This category lists hotels that are essentially aimed at tourists, and regularly used by package tours and such. In Addis Ababa, hotels in this category may be truly luxurious – judging by the rooms alone, many offer equal or better quality than the luxury hotels above, and at much more reasonable prices. Elsewhere in the country, hotels in this category typically have motel-standard rooms, and facilities such as hot water, satellite television, and restaurants serving Western food. While upmarket hotels in Ethiopia are generally very comfortable and quite efficiently run, one should not approach them with unreasonable expectations. Room rates are generally very reasonable for what you get and often quoted in US

in Addis Ababa can arrange car hire (see *Tour operators*, page 77). If you are thinking of driving yourself, be warned that Ethiopian roads are not what you are used to at home. Many Ethiopian roads are in poor condition, and the pedestrians and livestock share a quality of indifference I've encountered nowhere else in Africa when it comes to dawdling in the middle of the road while a hooting vehicle hurtles towards them at full tilt. See also the box, *Driving in Ethiopia*, above.

ACCOMMODATION

If you are not particularly fussy, finding a room in Ethiopia is rarely a problem, though genuine tourist-class hotels are limited to major tourist centres. Accommodation at all levels is inexpensive, even by most African standards. Few Ethiopian hotels distinguish between double and single occupancy. Almost without exception, rooms in private hotels will have a bed made to sleep two, and the price

dollars. This is the first category to look at if you simply want the best available accommodation irrespective of price. Prices are usually between US$56 and US$85.

MODERATE This category consists of superior local hotels, mainly but not exclusively privately owned. You can expect any hotel in this category to have clean and quite smart en-suite rooms with hot water and possibly television. Most will also have a decent restaurant and English-speaking staff. In many cases, moderate hotels are significantly cheaper than upmarket hotels. Outside of Addis most hotels in this range cost under US$30. This is the category to look at if your first priority is a reasonable level of comfort, but you also want to keep down accommodation costs. Prices usually range from US$20 to US$55.

BUDGET Hotels in this category are aimed largely at the local market and definitely don't approach international standards, but are still reasonably comfortable and in many cases have en-suite facilities. In other words, they are a cut above the shoestring dumps that proliferate in most towns. Budget hotels generally have clean rooms with cold and sometimes hot running water. In some cases, hotels without en-suite rooms are listed in this category, either because they are unusually clean and pleasant, or because accommodation in that town tends to be expensive. This is the category to look at if you are on a limited budget, but want to avoid total squalor! Prices in this category generally work out between US$10 and US$20, but there is a lot of regional variation.

SHOESTRING Shoestring accommodation consists of the cheapest rooms around, usually unpretentious local guesthouses that double as brothels and have common showers (or no shower at all). In many cases, these places are perfectly pleasant taken on their own terms, but just as often, they are flea-ridden dumps. Since no individual can properly assess every one of the dozens of shoestring hotels that are found in most Ethiopian towns, recommendations in this range should be seen as pointers rather than absolutes. This is the category for budget travellers who want to keep accommodation prices as low as possible, irrespective of what discomfort that might involve. Shoestring accommodation cannot generally be recommended to single female travellers. Prices in this range vary from US$3 to US$7.

FARANJI AND MILLENNIUM PRICES

In the past, it was only government hotels and government institutions that charged higher rates to foreigners than to Ethiopians. Though this practice antagonised many tourists, it could be seen as justified – Ethiopians generally earn a lot less than Westerners, and lower rates could be viewed as a discount allowing Ethiopians to see their own country. Over the past few years, the trend has been for most hotels to have discriminatory pricing. Again, when budget hotels cost US$2 or less, there was little reason for travellers to complain.

This all changed with the introduction of 'Millennium Fever', huge price hikes made in anticipation of the 2007 Ethiopian Millennium Celebration, and which remain in effect even though the celebration is now over. In some cases rates for foreigners were instantly doubled, often tripled, and sometime even quintupled! Thus it can no longer be argued that foreigners get fair value while locals get a discount – now even locals pay more, while tourists regularly and justifiably feel completely ripped off.

All of this would be less annoying were hotel owners more open to negotiation, but most would rather see a tourist walk away than compromise on the price. This arrogance seems to stem from two fundamentals. The first is that government hotels charge even more, the second that *faranjis* are all so rich (or stupid) that they will pay any rate asked of them. What a lot of hotel owners don't get is that their rooms aren't up to government hotel standards, and that travellers who favour private hotels over government hotels do so to save money. The silliest thing about wildly inflated faranji prices (up to five times the local rate) is that everybody loses out. On several occasions on our most recent trip, we ended up using an inferior hotel when we would have happily paid the non-faranji rate – or any reasonable price – to sleep at a better one. The hotel lost the customer, we lost out on a more comfortable room, yet both could have gained were the hotel owner not so inflexible.

Another frustration associated with faranji prices at hotels that see few tourists is that they are not market-driven in the way that rates for locals are, which means that prices are often thoroughly arbitrary. Likewise, in a town where one or two hotels opt not to charge an inflated faranji price, these anomalies can make all the other hotels in that town look like poor value.

It's easy to be philosophical about being asked a higher faranji price when the standard of the room is commensurate with that rate. More annoying are hotel owners that ask – and seem to expect – a price that both they and you know is plain silly. And watch out for the more devious approach wherein you take a room after being quoted a normal rate at reception, but are asked to pay a much higher rate by an aggressive hotel owner when you come to check out, on the basis his underling 'forgot' about the faranji price. To avoid being exposed to this sort of contrived misunderstanding, best pay for your room – at least for the first night – upon arrival.

Equally irksome is the practice of charging inflated faranji prices on food and drinks, which has become quite common in the south. A bait and switch method is often employed, in which the Ethiopian menu lists one set of prices but, when you go to pay, an English menu with higher prices is produced. The silver lining is that the food is still incredibly cheap, and your wallet does not take the same sort of beating it does with hotels. Nevertheless, many travellers prefer to seek out places that charge the same price for all.

of the rooms is the same whether it is occupied by one or two – or for that matter half a dozen – people. Even the most basic hotels in Ethiopia generally have electric sockets for charging mobile phones, digital cameras and similar devices in every room, though you might want to confirm they are working before taking a room in the budget and shoestring ranges.

TOURIST-CLASS HOTELS In the past, most tourist-class hotels were run by one of four government chains, all of which had at least one hotel in Addis Ababa. The Ghion Hotel Group ran all government hotels in the north, the Ras Hotel Group represented the southeast, the Wabe Shebelle Group ran hotels in the south, and the Ethiopia Hotel Group dominated in the west. Nowadays, however, many of the hotels in these chains have been privatised, and there are often newer, equally good if not better private hotels available, especially in major cities. In our listings, many of the former government hotels are no longer listed first, with many of the newer hotels representing best quality and value.

Outside of Addis, few hotels cost more than US$50 per room, and many – especially those in the south and west – are little more than US$20. Most will have rooms with private hot showers and bowl toilets. By international standards, few hotels would scrape much more than a one-star rating; they could generally be described as comfortable but tatty. That said the first thing you will notice when you arrive in Ethiopia is the boom in the construction of tourist-class hotels with newer, better-quality hotels opening all the time. The greatest problem these new hotels face however is upkeep, with many almost falling apart less than a year later. Note also that most (but not all) hotels will call a room with a double bed a single room, and a room with two singles a double.

In recent years the long-serving Bekele Mola Hotel Group, which has several hotels in southern Ethiopia, has dropped its standards significantly. This one-time popular private hotel group once had some 12 properties in the chain but due to lack of maintenance and financial difficulties several of the hotels have been forced to close, most recently the hotel in Langano. Of those that remain, most are now no better than shoestring hotels with their offering Moyale, in our view the worst in the chain. The marked exceptions however are the hotels at Adama (which remains the best), Arba Minch (which wins points mostly for its location) and Robe (which is still very reasonable). All of which have good rooms with private showers and bowl toilets for around US$6–15.

LOCAL HOTELS The vast majority of budget hotels in Ethiopia are straightforward local places with spartan furnishing, cell-like rooms, communal toilets and either communal showers or else no showers at all. Hotels like this are dubbed shoestring hotels in this book.

In larger towns, there are generally one or two budget hotels of superior standard. These are distinguished from the mass of shoestring places by having en-suite rooms (rooms with private showers and toilets, often referred to as self-contained in Ethiopia and elsewhere in east Africa) and also by being slightly more expensive. These hotels appear to be geared primarily to relatively well-heeled Ethiopians, so that the standard room prices reflect the local economy, though it is increasingly the case that tourists will be charged a special *faranji* price of around twice the local rate. Except for in a handful of major tourist centres, you can expect to pay around US$8–12 for a room in a superior budget hotel, which is usually a fair value for money. Travellers on a very tight budget should be aware that, although it will often be assumed that *faranji* prefer self-contained rooms, almost all superior budget hotels also have cheaper rooms using communal showers, and that these are generally similar in price but of a higher standard than rooms in true shoestring hotels.

The shoestring category embraces a good 85% of hotels in Ethiopia. In larger towns, there may be 30 or 40 such establishments. In the sort of small town where elsewhere in Africa you might expect at best one hotel, there may be half a dozen in Ethiopia. Hotels in this category can range from dirty, noisy, showerless brothels with flaking paint and sagging, flea-ridden beds, to bright and cheery family-run establishments with good communal showers and clean, comfortable rooms.

Rooms in this range generally cost US$3–7, dependent more on the town you are in than the quality of the hotel. In other words, in most towns there will be a standard price for hotels in this category, regardless of quality (in fact, I have often been asked more for a room in a dump than for a far nicer room a few doors down). It is difficult to imagine that many travellers, even those on the tightest budget, will worry too much about whether they're paying a birr or three or less, so in the regional part of the guide I have often not quoted individual prices for hotels in this category, but have instead listed the better places.

Bearing in mind that many large towns have dozens of shoestring hotels, and that prices are relatively uniform, it is worth choosing your hotel with care, and asking to see the shower and toilet before you take a room. Ethiopian hotel owners tend to devote little time to maintenance, so that the newest hotels are often the cleanest and brightest. As a rule, the exterior of a hotel is generally a fair reflection of the interior. Also, hotels with female owners, or a strong female presence, tend to be cleaner and friendlier than those run only by men. Note, too, that many cheap hotels in Ethiopia to some extent double as brothels, but – while it can be mildly disconcerting to wake in the night to the sound of quadraphonic orgasms and creaking beds in the surrounding rooms – such hotels aren't necessarily dirtier or less secure than others. However, they are best avoided by women travelling alone.

CAMPING The opportunities for organised camping in Ethiopia are limited to a few facility-free campsites in various national parks, the Wabe Shebelle Hotel at Wondo Genet and the Wabe Shebelle Hotel and the Welanesa and Langano lodges at Lake Langano and in Arba Minch. As such, the additional weight and hassle involved in carrying camping equipment is difficult to justify in Ethiopia (see *Camping equipment*, page 84).

EATING AND DRINKING

To anyone who has travelled elsewhere in Africa, Ethiopian food comes as a welcome revelation. Instead of the bland gristle and starch that is the standard restaurant fare in most African small towns, Ethiopian food is deliciously spicy and you can eat well virtually anywhere in the country. Contrary to many people's expectations, most of Ethiopia is fertile, food is easy to find and portions are generous and very cheap. You'll often find that one plate of food – which costs little more than a dollar – will be adequate to feed two.

ETHIOPIAN DISHES A wide variety of different dishes is available in Ethiopia. Most of them are unique to the country, so it is worth familiarising yourself with their names as soon as you arrive.

The staple source of carbohydrates in Ethiopia is *injera*, a large, pancake-shaped substance made from *tef*, a nutty-tasting grain that is unique to Ethiopia and comes in three varieties: white, brown and red. The *tef* dough is fermented for up to three days before it is cooked, the result of which is a foam-rubber texture and a slightly sour taste reminiscent of sherbet. *Injera* is normally served with a bowl of *wat* stew. The ritual is to take a piece of *injera* in your hand and use it to scoop the accompaniment into your mouth. If you dine with Ethiopians, it is normal for everyone to eat off the same plate.

Ethiopians will often tell you that *injera* is of little nutritional value. This is not the case at all. Gram for gram, *tef* supplies more fibre-rich bran and nutritious germ than any other grain, containing 15% protein, 3% fat and 82% complex carbohydrates. This is partly as a result of it being smaller than any other edible grain and having a proportionately larger husk, which is where most of the nutrients in any grain are stored. *Tef* contains almost 20 times more calcium than wheat or barley, it has two to three times the iron content of other grains, and it is the only grain to contain symbiotic yeast – which means that no yeast needs to be added during the preparation of *injera*.

There are two main types of *wat* sauce: *kai wat* is red in colour (*kai* literally means red), very hot and flavoured with *beriberi* (peppers), onions and garlic; *alicha wat* has a yellowish colour and is generally quite bland. There is a widely held belief among Ethiopians that they are the only people in the world who can tolerate spicy food, so unless you specify what you want you will generally be served with *alicha wat*. To my taste, *alicha wat* is pretty horrible, though in part this is because it is too bland to offset the sourness of the *injera*. If you're not overly fond of spicy food, order *wat misto*, which consists of half-portions of *kai* and *alicha wat*, sometimes served in separate bowls and sometimes mixed together. Conversely, if you want to spice things up, you can ask for *mitmita*, a spicy red powder, or *awaze*, a sauce made from *beriberi*.

Most *wat* is made from meat (*siga*). The most common meat in the highlands is lamb (*bege*), while in drier areas you will most often be served with goat (*figel*). Beef (*bure*) is also eaten, mostly in large towns. In towns near lakes, fish (*asa*) predominates. I have also come across *tripe wat* – which is the same as our tripe but pronounced *trippy*. The official national dish of Ethiopia is *doro wat*, made of chicken, but this is to be avoided if you are hungry, as it is traditional to serve only a lonely drumstick or wing in a bowl of sauce. Normally *kai wat* consists of meat boiled in the *kai* sauce, but you may also come across *tibs kai wat*, which means the meat was fried before the sauce was added. If the meat is minced prior to cooking, then the dish is known as *minje tabish*.

Vegetarian *wats* are served mainly on Wednesday and Friday, the Orthodox fasting days, and can be made from puréed beans (*shiro wat*), halved beans (*kik wat*) and lentils (*misr wat*). *Shiro tegamino* is an especially delicious thick paste, whereas standard *shiro wat* tends to have a liquid consistency. The normal dish on fasting days is *atkilt bayinetu*, which consists of dollops of various vegetarian *wats*, as well as piles of spinach (*gomon*), beetroot (*kai iser*) and vegetable stew (*atkilt alicha*) heaped discretely in a circle on the *injera*.

Fried meat (*siga tibs*) is also very popular in Ethiopia, as is boiled meat (*siga kekel*). *Shakila tibs* consists of fried meat served in a clay pot that contains a charcoal burner. Other dishes, found mainly in large towns, are crumbed meat or fish cutlet (*siga* or *asa kutilet*), roast meat (*siga arosto*), steak (*stek*) and a mildly spicy brown stew (*gulash*). Then there is *kitfo*, a very bland form of fried mince, and *kitfo special*, the same dish but uncooked, which should be avoided purely for health reasons as should *kurt* (pronounced court), which is raw sliced beef.

A popular breakfast dish, and a useful fallback in the evening if you don't fancy anything else that's on offer, is *inkolala tibs* – literally fried eggs, but more like scrambled eggs, cooked on request with slices of onion (*shinkuts*), green pepper (*karia*) and tomato (*tamatim*). Another common breakfast dish is *yinjera firfir*, which consists of pieces of *injera* soaked in *kai wat* sauce and eaten with – you guessed it – *injera*. Note that *firfir* literally means torn-up: *inkolala firfir* is exactly the same as *inkolala tibs*, but hacked at a bit before it is served. Also popular at breakfast is *ful*, a spicy bean dish made with lots of garlic, a refreshing change from eggs when you can find it.

Menus are normally printed in Amharigna script so you will have to ask what's available ('*Magi min ale?*'). As a rule, you won't understand a word of the rushed reply, so you'll probably have to suggest a few possibilities yourself. The way to phrase this is to start with the type of meat, or vegetable (prefaced with *ye*), then the type of dish. In other words, fried goat is *yefigel tibs*, fish cutlet is *yasa kutilet*, *kai wat* made with lentils is *yemisr kai wat*, and *alicha wat* made with beef is *yebure alicha wat*. If all else fails, ask for *sekondo misto*, which consists of small portions of everything on the menu.

The variety of food at local restaurants decreases during the fasting weeks of Ethiopian Lent, a period that generally occupies most of March and April, since Orthodox Christians will only eat vegetarian dishes during this period. Most non-vegetarians travelling in off-the-beaten-track areas get a bit frustrated by this, whereas vegetarians will find it a good time to travel. It doesn't affect travellers so much in Muslim areas, nor will it alter the variety of food on offer at tourist-oriented restaurants.

CHAT *Chat* is a mildly stimulating leaf that is traditionally popular with Muslims (who are forbidden from drinking alcohol) and is now chewed throughout Ethiopia. For readers who have visited Kenya, it is pretty similar to *miraa*, though I gather not exactly the same plant (and you see few Ethiopians with the manically glazed eyes I've come to associate with *miraa*-ed out Kenyans).

Chat ceremony is generally a social thing. The idea is for a few people to gather in a room, where you each grab a few branches, pick off the greenest leaves, pop them into your mouth one by one, mush it all up into a cud, chew for a few hours and then, with whatever strength is left in your jaw, spit out the remaining pulp. Ideally, you devote the afternoon to group mastication, then go for a few beers to neutralise the sleeplessness that the leaves induce. The leaves taste very bitter so a spoonful of sugar helps it all go down. *Chat* has its devotees among travellers, but most will find the effort involved in spending the afternoon chewing themselves into foul-tasting oblivion holds little appeal – especially when all sorts of cheap, pleasant-tasting, no-effort-required alcoholic substances are widely available in the country!

The centre of *chat* cultivation and chewing is the Muslim town of Harar – at the end of a bus ride in this area it looks as if the vehicle has been overrun by psycho-caterpillars – but you can get the stuff at markets all over the country. It's not expensive, but it's worth taking along an Ethiopian friend to ensure you locate the best-quality *chat* – prices do reflect quality and the youngest leaves are the best.

Sticking with leaves green and mind-altering, it should be clarified somewhere in this book that the link between Rastafarianism and Ethiopians is by and large a one-way thing. Smoking marijuana is illegal in Ethiopia and, generally speaking, it is less socially acceptable than in most Western countries. You should certainly not assume that an Ethiopian male with plaited hair is adorned for anything but religious reasons. Basically, if you must smoke dope in Ethiopia be as discreet as you would be at home, if not more so – not only to keep yourself out of jail, but also to maintain the good name of travellers.

WESTERN FOOD If you feel like a break from *injera* (and you will), many restaurants serve pasta (look out for variant spellings such as *spiggttii* or *makarronni*) skimpily topped with a spicy sauce. Even in the smallest villages you can usually find fresh, crusty bread (*dabo*) as an alternative accompaniment.

Many hotels in Addis, and government hotels throughout the country, serve standard Western food such as roast chicken, fish kebabs, roast meat and steaks. Generally this is a couple of birr more expensive than eating at local restaurants, but nowhere outside of Addis are you likely to pay much more than US$4 for a meal.

An attractive feature of Ethiopia is the numerous pastry shops in Addis and other medium-to-large towns. These generally serve a selection of freshly baked iced and plain cakes, wonderful biscuits and good bread, along with coffee, tea and puréed fruit juice. Pastry shops are great for sweet-toothed breakfasts and snacks, and you'll walk away with plenty of change from a dollar. Also on the snack front, look out for *ashet* (roasted maize cobs); the cry of the kids who sell it, which sounds remarkably like *shit*, should attract your attention. *Kolo* is a delicious snack of roasted grains or pulses, sometimes covered in spice, and sold by the handful for a few cents.

DRINKS Given that the Kaffa province of Ethiopia is thought to be where coffee originated, and the coffee bean accounts for more than half of Ethiopia's exports, it should be no surprise that Ethiopians are coffee mad. The local espresso-style coffee (*buna*), served with two spoons of sugar, is rich, sweet and thoroughly addictive. Coffee with milk is *buna watat*. In small towns, sweet tea (*shai*) is more widely available than coffee.

You'll often be invited to join a traditional coffee ceremony, in which the grains are roasted over charcoal, ground while the water is boiled, then used to make three successive pots of coffee. It's not advisable to accept if you're in a rush or want to get any sleep (it is rude to leave before the third round has been drunk), but you should certainly experience it at least once in your trip. Despite the pomp you might associate with the word 'ceremony', it's really just a social thing – instant coffee holds little appeal in a country where few people have jobs, or even television.

The usual soft drinks – Coca-Cola, Pepsi, Fanta – are widely available and very cheap. The generic name for soft drinks is *leslasa*. The Harar Brewery also produces a non-alcoholic malt beverage (apparently aimed at the Muslim population) called Harar Sofi, which tastes similar to cola and is said to be good for an upset stomach.

A little more surprisingly, carbonated mineral water is bottled locally and is widely available for around US$0.60 per 750ml bottle. It is best to ask for mineral water by brand name, which is Ambo in central, south and western Ethiopia, and Babile (pronounced 'bubbily' – not sure if this is coincidence!) in the east. Still water is also available. The major brand is called Highland, and you will often hear roadside children screaming this repeatedly in the hope that you will toss them an empty bottle (which you most certainly should not!). Another (and arguably better-tasting) top brand is Abyssinia.

Ethiopia's prime soft drink is fruit juice, which is really puréed fruit. What is available depends somewhat on season and location, but the most common juices are banana, avocado, papaya, orange and guava. I highly recommend the avocado, which sounds odd but is delicious with a squeeze of fresh lime and is sometimes layered with grenadine syrup. If in doubt, ask for *espris*, which consists of layers of all available juices. The result is thick, creamy, healthy and absolutely fantastic. A glass of juice generally costs around US$0.80.

The most popular local tipple is *tej*, a mead-like drink made from honey (*mar*) or sugar (*isukalama*). *Mar tej* is a considerable improvement on most African home brews, and very alcoholic, but personally I couldn't get into it on a daily basis. *Isukalama tej* is entirely avoidable. *Tej* is not served in normal bars; you will have to go to a *tej abet* to drink it. A 750ml bottle of *tej* costs around US$1. Locally brewed beer, made from millet or maize, is called *tella*. This is similar to the local brew of east and southern Africa, and no less foul in Ethiopia than it is elsewhere in the region.

Acceptable bottled lager is sold throughout Ethiopia. There are several brands, among them Castel, Bati, Bedele, St George, Harar and Dashen. A 350ml bottle of beer costs around US$0.80, with prices varying slightly, depending on where you buy it. Draught lager is available in Addis and quite a few other towns around the country, and it is very cheap. A beer journalist writes: 'Ethiopia now has a licensed Guinness Foreign Extra Stout, something beer geeks always seek, and it says "Guinness is Good for You" in Amharic on the neck label! Hakim Stout, from the Harare Brewery, isn't bad, although it's not really a stout.' Wine is brewed locally; the result is indifferent but affordable, especially if bought directly from a shop. Imported spirits are served in most bars at very low prices for generous tots.

PUBLIC HOLIDAYS AND FESTIVALS

In any country you should be aware of public holidays, as many shops will be closed. The most significant practical consequence of public holidays in Ethiopia is that banks close, something you should plan around when you change money, especially if you travel between March and May, when most of the holidays are concentrated. Public holidays that are also religious festivals generally involve colourful celebrations and processions, so it is worth trying to get to one of the main religious sites – Lalibela, Gondar or Axum – for the occasion. Check the moveable dates before you travel.

7 January	Ethiopian Christmas	**1 May**	International Labour Day
19 January	Ethiopian Epiphany	**5 May**	Patriots' Victory Day
2 March	Adwa Day	**28 May**	Downfall of the Derg
Moveable	Ramadan	**Moveable**	Moulid
Moveable	Ethiopian Good Friday	**11 September**	Ethiopian New Year
Moveable	Ethiopian Easter	**27 September**	Meskel

SHOPPING

Shops in Ethiopia are generally well stocked by African standards, though readers who are unfamiliar with African conditions should realise that this is a very relative statement. Basic goods are widely available, luxuries are not. Most medium-to-large towns have stationery shops, good pharmacies, music shops and general stores. Even in small towns you'll find kiosks that sell most things you're likely to want – batteries, pens, paper, soap, washing powder, dry biscuits, boiled sweets, bottled drinks, toilet rolls (which Ethiopians rather endearingly call *softi*), mosquito spray and incense (useful for rooms with drifting toilet smells).

Most towns and villages have markets. In larger towns these will be open every day but the main market day throughout the country is Saturday. In some towns, especially small towns that serve large rural areas, there is an additional market day. Market days are usually the best days to visit off-the-beaten-track areas, as there will be far more transport. Buying from markets rather than shops actively puts money into the hands of a local community.

EXPORTING SOUVENIRS AND ANTIQUES Many of Ethiopia's ancient treasures have been stolen or removed from the country in recent years, most infamously the 5–7kg gold Lalibela Cross that was stolen from the Church of Medhane Alem in Lalibela in March 1997 and returned two years later. But many smaller items have gone, too, and the Ethiopian authorities are understandably cracking down on what tourists can take out of the country. Indeed, individual tourists should think twice before they buy antiquities – aside from the fact that such behaviour is gradually depleting the country of its cultural resources, many genuine old items will have been stolen from their real owner for resale to tourists.

In this light, and with slight artistic licence, I'm quoting in full the advice of Tony Howard and Di Taylor on the subject:

Buying things to take out of the country can be a bit of a hassle. Anything that can be considered old or antique reportedly needs a permit whether it is silver, wood, cotton or whatever. Ivory is illegal (as, we were told, are three-legged wooden stools!). Old silver crosses and religious items are also a problem. Whatever you buy, first ask the shopkeeper if it's a permitted item (he may not know) and make sure you get a receipt.

Take the goods and receipts and then get hold of plenty of thick wrapping paper and good Sellotape (both available at any of the numerous stationery shops in Addis Ababa). Then go to the National Museum, where the office to the left of the main museum will approve your purchases or not, as the case may be. You must then wrap your purchases, and the museum staff will stamp the wrapping paper, and for less than US$0.50 per item, give you an export permit. This permit must be shown at the airport with the goods still wrapped and the paper intact, and you should be out with no further problem.

Or don't bother with the permit and just hope that you won't be stopped at the airport. If you are, you may lose the lot – it's up to you. Conversely, we went to all that trouble and nobody at the airport stopped us or asked to see what we had in our bags – such is life!

ARTS AND ENTERTAINMENT

Most Ethiopian towns can be relied upon to have a handful of lively bars, and it's easy enough to follow your nose if you are looking for a sociable drink. The atmosphere in Ethiopian bars is generally easy and inclusive, and locals who speak a bit of English will go out of their way to chat to you. Bars are also often the best place to hear Ethiopia's idiosyncratic traditional and contemporary music, though increasingly the hi-fi is subservient to the television when football is being broadcast live. (For more information about Ethiopian music, see page 41.)

If Ethiopian music is refreshingly odd, the dancing is plain bizarre, particularly the styles that originate in the north but which are now practised in most of the country. In some parts of Ethiopia people traditionally leap up and down like the Maasai of east Africa, or do the more standard hip wriggling of east Africa. But it is the women of Amhara and Tigrai that stick in the mind – fixed grins, hot-coal eyes and madly flapping breasts all held together by shuddering shoulder movements, creating a whirling demonic whole that manages to be robotic and erotic at the same time. Several government hotels in Addis have resident bands and dancers, and while these are inevitably a bit staged, there is no need to be just an observer. Spontaneous raves occur at bars throughout the country every night, and you'll always be welcome to join in – and to provide some amusement by attempting to emulate the moves!

MEDIA AND COMMUNICATIONS

NEWSPAPERS Except in Addis, where a couple of indifferent locally published English-language papers including the *Addis Tribune* and *Fortune* weeklies can be bought – as can magazines such as *Time* and *Newsweek* – you are unlikely to see a newspaper you can read in Ethiopia.

TELEVISION Ethiopia's domestic television service isn't much to get excited about. The nightly news service is in Amharigna, though you may catch the odd bit of international news in English. A recent development is the spread of satellite television in Ethiopia, especially the South African-based multi-channel service DSTV and the Arabsat service out of Saudi Arabia. This is something of a mixed

---

PHOTOGRAPHIC TIPS *Ariadne Van Zandbergen*

EQUIPMENT Although with some thought and an eye for composition you can take reasonable photographs with a 'point and shoot' camera, you need an SLR camera with one or more lenses if you are at all serious about photography. The most important component in a digital SLR is the sensor. There are two types of sensor: DX and FX. The FX is a full-size sensor identical to the old film size (36mm). The DX sensor is half size and produces less quality. Your choice of lenses will be determined by whether you have a DX or FX sensor in your camera as the DX sensor introduces a 0.5x multiplication to the focal length. So a 300mm lens becomes in effect a 450mm lens. FX ('full frame') sensors are the future, so I will further refer to focal lengths appropriate to the FX sensor.

Always buy the best lens you can afford. Fixed fast lenses are ideal, but very costly. Zoom lenses are easier to change composition without changing lenses the whole time. If you carry only one lens a 24–70mm or similar zoom should be ideal. For a second lens, a lightweight 80–200mm or 70–300mm or similar will be excellent for candid shots and varying your composition. Wildlife photography will be very frustrating if you don't have at least a 300mm lens. For a small loss of quality, teleconverters are a cheap and compact way to increase magnification: a 300mm lens with a 1.4x converter becomes 420mm, and with a 2x it becomes 600mm. NB: 1.4x and 2x teleconverters reduce the speed of your lens by 1.4 and 2 stops respectively.

The resolution of digital cameras is improving the whole time. For ordinary prints a 6-megapixel camera is fine. For better results and the possibility to enlarge images and for professional reproduction, higher resolution is available up to 21 megapixels.

It is important to have enough memory space when photographing on your holiday. The number of pictures you can fit on a card depends on the quality you choose. You should calculate how many pictures you can fit on a card and either take enough cards or take a storage drive onto which you can download the cards' content. You can obviously take a laptop which gives the advantage that you can see your pictures properly at the end of each day, edit them and delete rejects. If you don't want the extra bulk and weight you can buy a storage device, which can read memory cards. These drives come in different capacities.

Keep in mind that digital camera batteries, computers and other storage devices need charging. Make sure you have all the chargers, cables and converters with you. Most hotels/lodges have charging points, but it will be best to enquire

blessing – it's great when you want some news from home, or to watch live sport, but there are times when it seems impossible to find a bar or restaurant whose atmosphere isn't dominated by a television shouting at the clientele.

POST Ethiopia has a good internal and international post service, which celebrated its centenary in 1994. Mail between most parts of Europe and Addis Ababa takes around a week, but it can take longer from elsewhere in the world. Post offices can be found in most larger towns and cities, and rates are very cheap.

TELEPHONE The international telephone code for Ethiopia is +251. Ethiopia has a decent telephone service when compared with most parts of Africa. There are telecommunications centres in most towns, and even functional phone booths.

about this in advance. When camping you might have to rely on charging from the car battery.

DUST AND HEAT Dust and heat are often a problem. Keep your equipment in a sealed bag, and avoid exposing equipment to the sun when possible. Digital cameras are prone to collecting dust particles on the sensor, which results in spots on the image. The dirt mostly enters the camera when changing lenses, so you should be careful when doing this. To some extent photos can be 'cleaned' up afterwards in Photoshop, but this is time-consuming. You can have your camera sensor professionally cleaned, or you can do this yourself with special brushes and swabs made for this purpose, but note that touching the sensor might cause damage and should only be done with the greatest care.

LIGHT The most striking outdoor photographs are often taken during the hour or two of 'golden light' after dawn and before sunset. Shooting in low light may enforce the use of very low shutter speeds, in which case a tripod/beanbag will be required to avoid camera shake. The most advanced digital SLRs have very little loss of quality on higher ISO settings, which allows you to shoot at lower light conditions. It is still recommended not to increase the ISO unless necessary.

With careful handling, side lighting and back lighting can produce stunning effects, especially in soft light and at sunrise or sunset. Generally, however, it is best to shoot with the sun behind you. When photographing animals or people in the harsh midday sun, images taken in light but even shade may look nicer than those taken in direct sunlight or patchy shade which create too much contrast.

PROTOCOL In some countries, it is unacceptable to photograph local people without permission, and many people will refuse to pose or will ask for a donation. In such circumstances, don't try to sneak photographs as you might get yourself into trouble. Even the most willing subject will often pose stiffly when a camera is pointed at them; relax them by making a joke, and take a few shots in quick succession to improve the odds of capturing a natural pose.

Ariadne Van Zandbergen is a professional travel and wildlife photographer specialising in Africa. She runs 'The Africa Image Library'. For photo requests, visit the website www.africaimagelibrary.co.za or contact her direct at ariadne@hixnet.co.za.

Playing by the book, it is generally easiest to make international calls from the telecommunications centre on Churchill Avenue in Addis Ababa. Expect to wait anything between ten minutes and an hour for your call to be placed. International phone rates are very cheap.

Much less hassle are the officially forbidden VOIP internet kiosks which can be found in Addis and many larger towns; expect to pay around US$0.60 a minute to the US or Europe.

Cell/mobile phones have become extremely popular. In terms of geography, cell coverage is excellent, but due to high volume the network is often overloaded.

Obtaining an Ethiopian SIM card can also be difficult. Theoretically you should be able to buy one at a kiosk at Bole Airport. In reality, this kiosk only seems to be open at certain times, and is often out of stock. It's also reputably possible to get a SIM card at the ETC (Ethiopian Telecom) office next to Edna Mall for as little as US$4 with just a photocopy of your passport and two passport-size photographs. An excellent alternative, especially for short trips, is to rent a phone and SIM card from someone in Addis. Several hotels offer this service at a reasonable fee, or you can contact Red Zebra Executive Solutions (m +251 911 240 565; e info@redzebraes. com; www.redzebraes.com), which rents SIM cards from US$4/8 per day excluding/ including a phone. Airtime is bought through prepaid scratch cards, which are available in most towns in birr 50 and 100 denominations. Some international cell phones work in Ethiopia, but at much higher airtime rates.

INTERNET AND EMAIL The only server that currently operates in Ethiopia is the state-run Ethionet, which is effectively a monopoly protected by law, though there is some talk of private servers being permitted and introduced in the near future. This means that all locally hosted Ethiopian email addresses have the same suffix '@ ethionet.et' (though older references may still quote addresses that end @telecom. net.et, in which case just substitute it with @ethionet.et).

Reliable internet cafés are dotted all around Addis Ababa, and cost a very reasonable birr 0.30 to 0.40 per minute (around US$1.50-2 per hour). Elsewhere, internet usage and access lags far behind that of many neighbouring countries, though most large towns offer some sort of service, ranging from almost as good as Addis Ababa (Bahir Dar, Hawassa, Harar, Dire Dawa, Jimma, Gondar) to slow and costly (Lalibela, Axum). As things stand, short-stay travellers could waste a lot of time at a PC if they depend on having internet access or receiving email outside of Addis Ababa. That said, many of the better hotels in the larger centres including Bahir Dar, Gondar and Hawassa now offer free Wi-Fi as standard.

Almost every internet café in Ethiopia has its home page set to Yahoo!, and most Ethiopians seem to have a Yahoo! (as opposed to a hotmail or gmail) address. The downside of this is that getting onto the Yahoo! home page can be a slow process when half of Ethiopia's internet population is trying to do the same. If you have a Yahoo! ID or email address it will in fact work on any of the Yahoo! country sites and you will find it easier to check your mail via yahoo.co.uk, yahoo.ca, yahoo.de or yahoo.fr.

LOCAL INTERACTION

TIPPING AND GUIDE FEES The qualified guides who work in Ethiopia's main historical centres usually charge a fixed rate of birr 100–200 per party per day. They will sometimes be open to negotiation out of season. Elsewhere, for a knowledgeable professional guide, birr 20 for up to two hours and birr 10 for every hour thereafter is a fair-to-generous guideline. In both cases it is best to agree a price upfront. If you want to arrange informal guides in other areas, you should also discuss a fee in advance. It is difficult to generalise, but birr 10–15 for a youngster and twice that amount for an adult feels about right, depending on how long you are out, and whether you are in an expensive town or in a rural area where money goes further.

There are some tiresome guides (mostly non-professional) who will routinely go into a sulk after you have paid them in the hope they can manipulate a bit of extra cash out of you, often spoiling what might otherwise have been a good day out in the process. Never give in to this sort of manipulative behaviour! And if any guide happens to pull the old stunt of thrusting your payment back into your hands in feigned disgust at its paltriness, call his bluff – take the money, walk off, and you'll be amazed how quickly he decides that he actually would like the money after all.

Tipping waiters is not the established custom in Ethiopia, but it is acceptable and greatly appreciated by the recipient, who might well earn less than birr 200 per month in actual salary. At upmarket restaurants such as those in government hotels, the 10% tip that is customary in many Western countries is a fair-to-generous guideline (in fact, a service charge is levied at most such restaurants, but the odds of this ending up in the hands of the waiters and waitresses is negligible). In private restaurants and bars, it's entirely at your discretion: tipping is not expected, but leaving behind a coin or two in a coffee or pastry shop or local restaurant would be appreciated, while birr 1–2 would be a decent tip in a proper restaurant.

OVERCHARGING AND BARGAINING Hotel rates aside, overcharging tourists is relatively uncommon in Ethiopia, but it happens, especially in Addis Ababa and at certain major tourist centres. If you think you are being overcharged, rather than accusing the person of ripping you off, just query the price gently, or simply say it is too expensive for you. This gives the person the opportunity to save face and lower the price in a manner that seems generous.

Bear in mind, however, that bargaining is acceptable to Ethiopians in many situations, and that there *is* a difference between blatant overcharging and asking a flexible price. You will always need to bargain to get a decent price with taxi and *gari* drivers, and at curio stalls anywhere in the country. By contrast, overcharging is not a normal practice on buses and on other public transport, whereas it has become institutionalised in the form of non-negotiable '*faranji* prices' at many hotels and restaurants (see box, page 96).

GIFTS AND BEGGING There are beggars everywhere in Ethiopia, especially in Addis Ababa, and most of them make a beeline for foreigners. Ethiopians themselves often give loose change to genuine beggars, and there is no reason why tourists shouldn't follow suit. However, there are also plenty of chancers around – adults and children – who'll try to hit on any passing *faranji* for a handout, and for obvious reasons they are best ignored.

We are often surprised at how many tourists travel around countries like Ethiopia arbitrarily handing out gifts – be it sweets or biscuits, pens or money – to children. It is an understandable response to being in a poor country, and is often tacitly encouraged by tour operators and guides, but we feel strongly that it should be discouraged. For one thing, it reinforces a culture of begging and dependency that is already prevalent in Ethiopia, as epitomised by the common practice of begging for plastic water bottles (the usual refrain being 'Highland, Highland', the brand name of the most common bottled water), as well as more random treats such as biscuits and sweets (both of which can have a detrimental effect on teeth in a country where dental healthcare is minimal).

In several parts of Ethiopia, children now routinely skip school, preferring to dance and sing for tourists, or simply trail behind them, in the hope of earning some money or begging for treats. Indeed, in parts of the south, we've come across children lining across the road and refusing to move – doing the splits or dancing in the middle of the road as the car approaches – a scenario that seems bound to result in a fatal accident sooner or later. In addition, many young beggars are in fact controlled by adult relatives, who encourage them to abandon their education in order to supplement the family income.

Finally, and more selfishly, encouraging child beggars will only go to create increased hassles for the next group of tourists that passes by. In some Ethiopian towns, independent travellers might be asked for money or sweets or a pen 100 times per day. Equally, there are still places in Ethiopia where children are genuinely friendly and never ask for things. It requires only one naive tourist and a bag of sweets to change that.

See also *Women travellers* in *Chapter 4*, page 123.

RESPONSIBLE TOURISM

Bradt Guides is an advocate of Responsible Tourism, and readers unfamiliar with this concept are pointed to the excellent website of the British organisation Tourism Concern (*www.tourismconcern.org.uk*) for further details of what this entails, However, we also think it is important to note that the promotion of Responsible Tourism is not intended to imply that conventional travel is inherently irresponsible or damaging to developing countries. On the contrary, as the world's largest industry, tourism is an immensely powerful economic stimulant, with some 15% of jobs worldwide being tourism-related. All the more so in a poor country such as Ethiopia, where community tourist projects and more straightforward private developments such as hotels and restaurants all create employment and raise foreign revenue. Ultimately, almost any sustainable tourism venture in Africa falls into the category 'trade not aid' and will contribute to the economic development (and/or cultural and environmental preservation) of those countries where it is most needed.

ETHIOPIAN CHARITIES *Hilary Bradt*
Few visitors to Ethiopia can fail to be moved by the warmth and generosity of the people, despite their poverty, and the country has an impressive number of NGOs, often set up by people who originally came as tourists but stayed to help. The list below is by no means exhaustive; these are the organisations I came across during my two-week trip, and who provided me with a little extra information about their activities. All would welcome donations to help them further their work.

Ethiopia Education Aid (*www.ethiopiaeducationaid.org*) A small Christian charity, founded by Maurice and Susan Clarke in 2006, who fund students through school and college so they can gain a qualification or trade. Here are some of their success stories.

> Mulugeta Ababu is our first student to graduate. We gave him a new suit, tie, white shirt and cufflinks and he was thrilled. The graduation was a wonderful celebration of music, traditional dancing, receiving awards and much clapping – quite different from our own!

Mulugeta's story Mulugeta grew up in a rural area without education. He lost both parents (his mother died from rabid dog bite) and started school at 15 years. When we met Mulugeta in January 2006, he was 22 and working long hours in a shop to feed himself. He could not afford books or a school uniform and was struggling to stay at school. We visited his headmaster and teacher to find out about the education system and discuss his situation. On returning to the UK we started a charity, Ethiopia Education Aid, and sponsored Mulugeta's last year at school, followed by a nine-month course in English and computer studies to gain entry into Lion College to study Tourist Management for three years. Needless to say, we are enormously proud of him!

Birtukan Abate's story Birtukan left home when she was 16 to begin a job in Addis Ababa as paid help in an Ethiopian household. Three years later she was found ill-treated, downtrodden and earning a pit home. Initially we were asked to support her return home to Lalibela. Once her tance – insufficient to allow her to return confidence had returned we began to sponsor her at a further education college to train as a hotel receptionist. She is now learning English and Computer Studies and has a hotel placement one day per week. She is a transformed young woman for as little as £40 per month.

PLAN (*www.Plan-UK.org*) I learned about Plan from Dr Hugh Sharp, who has raised thousands of pounds for this NGO which is active in Ethiopia in health, education and community projects. They also do child sponsorships. Hugh and his wife came to Ethiopia as tourists and after seeing the poor conditions in the hospital in Lalibela, decided to get involved. Now they come to Lalibela every year, to 'keep an eye on things' and visit PLAN's office there.

The Donkey Sanctuary

(*www.thedonkeysanctuary.org.uk*) Visitors are often dismayed at the state of the working donkeys in Ethiopia (which has the second-largest number of donkeys in the world, after China). A Devon charity, The Donkey Sanctuary, has a highly effective project in Ethiopia, working with the owners to improve their understanding of donkey care, such as how to prevent harness sores by using the locally made padded pack-saddles, and reduce the currently high incidence of traffic accidents involving donkeys.

I talked to Asmamaw Kassaye, the head vet at the Donkey Sanctuary in Ethiopia. He told me its headquarters are in Debre Zeit but with mobile units in five different locations. With so much poverty around you would expect donkey welfare to be pretty low down in priorities, but of course to a rural person a donkey is the equivalent of a car; without one he loses his ability to earn money. Asmamaw showed me a photo of a donkey brought in strapped to a flat-bed cart, pulled by another donkey. The vets successfully cured it of its colic.

To learn more about their work while in Ethiopia or make a donation during your visit, phone the headquarters in Addis Ababa: ✆ +251 618 5708; m +251 91 333 3591 or +251 91 160 3911. Once home, donations can be made through the sanctuary website: www.thedonkeysanctuary.org.uk.

4

Health and Safety

with Dr Felicity Nicholson

Ethiopia boasts an impressive array of tropical diseases, but with some sensible precautions the chance of catching anything very serious is not great. Most travellers who spend a while in the country will become ill at some point in their trip, but this is most likely to be straightforward travellers' diarrhoea or a cold. There appears to be a greater risk of travellers contracting more serious sanitation-related diseases (such as typhoid and hepatitis A) in Ethiopia than in other parts of east Africa, but the risk is decreased by having the appropriate immunisations before you leave home. You should also avoid high-risk foods and drink safe water once you are in the country. This prevalence of sanitation-related diseases has to be balanced against the fact that there is less likelihood of contracting malaria in Ethiopia than in most other parts of tropical Africa. Before you travel to Ethiopia, ensure you receive the necessary immunisations and, if you plan on entering a malarial area, seek advice on which tablets are currently most effective and also consider how to prevent mosquitoes from biting you – subjects that are covered below.

PREPARATIONS

TRAVEL INSURANCE Don't think about visiting Ethiopia without comprehensive medical travel insurance: one that will fly you home in an emergency. The ISIS policy, available in Britain through STA Travel (✆ *0871 230 0040; www.statravel. co.uk*), is inexpensive and has a good reputation.

IMMUNISATIONS A yellow fever certificate is not required for entry into Ethiopia unless you are coming from a yellow fever endemic zone. The vaccine may be recommended if you are going into western areas of Ethiopia where there is risk of disease. The east of the country has very little disease so vaccine would not be advised for those areas. If the vaccine is contraindicated on health grounds then it may be necessary to obtain an exemption certificate to meet the entry requirements. To be fully effective yellow fever vaccine should be taken at least ten days prior to travel and lasts for ten years. It is also strongly advisable to be immunised against typhoid, polio, diphtheria and tetanus. Travellers should also be advised to have immunisation against hepatitis A, with hepatitis A vaccine (eg: Havrix Monodose, Avaxim). One dose of vaccine lasts for one year and can be boosted to give protection for up to 25 years. The course of two injections costs about £100, but may be available on the NHS. Acquiring hepatitis A could effectively end your travels and leave you ill for several months, and according to local doctors it is often caught by visitors to Ethiopia. If you intend travelling more than 24 hours away from medical facilities, consider rabies immunisation. Ideally three doses of vaccine

PERSONAL FIRST-AID KIT

A minimal kit contains:

- A good drying antiseptic, eg: iodine or potassium permanganate (don't take antiseptic cream)
- A few small dressings (Band-Aids)
- Suncream
- Insect repellent; anti-malaria tablets; impregnated bed-net or permethrin spray
- Aspirin or paracetamol
- Antifungal cream (eg: Canesten)
- Ciprofloxacin or norfloxacin, for severe diarrhoea
- Tinidazole for giardia or amoebic dysentery
- Antibiotic eye drops, for sore, 'gritty', stuck-together eyes (conjunctivitis)
- A pair of fine pointed tweezers (to remove hairy caterpillar hairs, thorns, splinters, coral, etc)
- Alcohol-based hand rub or bar of soap in plastic box
- Condoms or femidoms

should be taken and can be given over a minimum period of 21 days. However, if time is short even two or one dose of vaccine is better than nothing at all.

Hepatitis B vaccination should be considered for longer trips or for those working in situations where the likelihood of contact with blood is increased or when working closely with local children. Three injections are ideal, given over a minimum period of three weeks before travel. If more time is available then the doses can be spread over eight weeks or longer. Meningitis ACWY vaccine is ideally recommended for all travellers, especially if working and/or living with local people or for longer trips.

TRAVEL CLINICS AND HEALTH INFORMATION A full list of current travel clinic websites worldwide is available on www.istm.org. For other journey preparation information, consult www.nathnac.org/ds/map_world.aspx. Information about various medications may be found on www.netdoctor.co.uk/travel.

UK

✚ Berkeley Travel Clinic 32 Berkeley St, London W1J 8EL (near Green Park tube station); ☎020 7629 6233; ⊕ 10.00–18.00 Mon–Fri; 10.00–15.00 Sat

✚ Cambridge Travel Clinic 41 Hills Rd, Cambridge CB2 1NT; ☎01223 367362; f 01223 368021; e enquiries@travelcliniccambridge.co.uk; www.travelcliniccambridge.co.uk; ⊕ 10.00–16.00 Mon, Tue & Fri, 12.00-18.30 Wed & Thu, 10.00–15.30 Sat

✚ Edinburgh Travel Health Clinic 14 East Preston St, Newington, Edinburgh EH8 9QA; ☎0131 667 1030; www.edinburghtravelhealthclinic.co.uk; ⊕ 09.00–

19.00 Mon–Wed, 09.00–18.00 Thu & Fri. Travel vaccinations & advice on all aspects of malaria prevention. All current UK prescribed anti-malaria tablets in stock.

✚ Fleet Street Travel Clinic 29 Fleet St, London EC4Y 1AA; ☎020 7353 5678; www.fleetstreetclinic.com; ⊕ 08.45–20.00 Mon–Thu, 08.45-17.30 Fri. Injections, travel products & latest advice.

✚ Hospital for Tropical Diseases Travel Clinic Mortimer Market Centre, 2nd Floor, Capper St (off Tottenham Ct Rd), London WC1E 6AU; ☎020 7388 9600; www.thehtd.org. Offers consultations & advice, & is able to provide all necessary drugs & vaccines for certain travellers (see website).

Runs a healthline (📞 *020 7950 7799*) for country-specific information & health hazards. Also stocks nets, water purification equipment & personal protection measures.

✚ **InterHealth Travel Clinic** 111 Westminster Bridge Rd, London SE1 7HR; 📞 020 7902 9000; e info@ interhealth.org.uk; www.interhealth.org. uk; ⏲ 08.30-17.30 Mon–Fri. Competitively priced, one-stop travel health service by appointment only.

✚ **MASTA** (Medical Advisory Service for Travellers Abroad) London School of Hygiene and Tropical Medicine, Keppel St, London WC1 7HT; 📞 09068 337733; www.masta-travel-health.com. This is a premium-line number, charged at 60p per minute. For a fee, they will provide an individually tailored health brief, with up-to-date information on how to stay healthy, inoculations & what to take.

✚ **MASTA pre-travel clinics** 📞 01276 685040. Call for the nearest; there are currently 30 in Britain. They also sell malaria prophylaxis memory cards, treatment kits, bed-nets, net treatment kits, etc.

✚ **NHS travel website** www.fitfortravel.nhs. uk/home.aspx. Provides country-by-country advice on immunisation & malaria prevention, plus details of recent developments, & a list of relevant health organisations.

✚ **Nomad Travel Store** 3–4 Wellington Terrace, Turnpike Lane, London N8 0PX; 📞 020 8889 7014; f 020 8889 9528; e turnpike@nomadtravel.co.uk; www.nomadtravel.co.uk; walk in or appointments ⏲ 09.15–18.00 Mon–Wed & Sat, 11.45–19.30 Thu, 10.15–18.00 Fri. 6 stores in total countrywide. As well as dispensing health advice, Nomad stocks mosquito nets & other anti-bug devices, & an excellent range of adventure travel gear.

✚ **Trailfinders Immunisation Centre** 194 Kensington High St, London W8 7RG; 📞 020 7938 3999; www.trailfinders.com/travelessentials/ travelclinic.htm; ⏲ 09.00–17.00 Mon, Tue, Wed & Fri, 10.00–18.00 Thu, 10.00–17.15 Sat

✚ **Travelpharm** The Travelpharm website (*www. travelpharm.com*) offers up-to-date guidance on travel-related health & has a range of medications available through its online mini pharmacy.

Irish Republic

✚ **Tropical Medical Bureau** Grafton St Medical Centre, Grafton Bldgs, 54 Grafton St, Dublin 2; 📞 1 271 5272; e graftonstreet@tmb.ie. Has a useful website specific to tropical destinations: www.tmb.ie.

USA

✚ **Centers for Disease Control** 1600 Clifton Rd, Atlanta, GA 30333; 📞 (800) 232 4636; e cdcinfo@ cdc.gov; www.cdc.gov/travel; ⏲ 08.00–20.00 Mon–Fri. The central source of travel information in the USA. Each summer they publish the invaluable *Health Information for International Travel.*

✚ **IAMAT** (International Association for Medical Assistance to Travelers) 1623 Military Rd, #279 Niagara Falls, NY 14304-1745; 📞 716 754 4883; e info@iamat.org; www.iamat.org. A non-profit organisation with free membership that provides lists of English-speaking doctors abroad.

Canada

✚ **IAMAT** (International Association for Medical Assistance to Travellers) Suite 1, 1287 St Clair Av W, Toronto, Ontario M6E 1B8; 📞 416 652 0137; www. iamat.org

✚ **TMVC** Suite 314, 1030 W Georgia St, Vancouver, BC V6E 2Y3; 📞 604 681 5656; e vancouver@tmvc.com; www.tmvc.com. One-stop medical clinic for all your international travel medicine & vaccination needs.

Australia, New Zealand and Asia

✚ **TMVC** (Travel Doctors Group) 📞 1300 65 88 44; www.tmvc.com.au. 41 clinics in Australia, Indonesia, Japan, New Zealand, Singapore, Thailand & Vietnam, including: *Auckland* Canterbury Arcade, 170 Queen St, Auckland; 📞 9 373 3531; e auckland@traveldoctor. co.nz; *Brisbane* 75a Astor Terrace, Spring Hill, Brisbane, QLD 4000; 📞 7 3815 6900; f 7 3815 6901; e brisbane@ traveldoctor.com.au; *Melbourne* 393 Little Bourke St, 2nd & 3rd Floors, Melbourne, VIC 3000; 📞 3 9935 8100; f 3 9935 8199; e melbourne@traveldoctor.com. au; *Sydney* Dymocks Bldg, 7th Floor, 428 George St, Sydney, NSW 2000; 📞 2 9221 7133; f 2 9221 8401; e sydney@traveldoctor.com.au

✚ **IAMAT** 206 Papanui Rd, Christchurch 5, New Zealand; www.iamat.org

South Africa

✚ **SAA-Netcare Travel Clinics** e travelinfo@ netcare.co.za; www.travelclinic.co.za or www. malaria.co.za. 12 clinics throughout South Africa.

✚ **TMVC** NHC Health Centre, corner Beyers Naude & Waugh Northcliff; 📞 011 214 9030; f 011 214 9029; e info@traveldoctor.co.za; www.traveldoctor.co.za. Consult the website for details of clinics.

DIARRHOEA AND RELATED ILLNESSES Travelling in Ethiopia carries a fairly high risk of getting a dose of travellers' diarrhoea; perhaps half of all visitors will suffer and the newer you are to exotic travel the more likely you will be to suffer. By taking precautions against travellers' diarrhoea you will also avoid typhoid, paratyphoid, cholera, hepatitis, dysentery, worms, etc. Travellers' diarrhoea and the other faecal-oral diseases come from getting other people's faeces in your mouth. This most often happens from cooks not washing their hands after a trip to the toilet, but even if the restaurant cook does not understand basic hygiene you will be safe if your food has been properly cooked and arrives piping hot. The most important prevention strategy is to wash your hands before eating anything. You can pick up salmonella and shigella from toilet door handles and possibly bank notes. The maxim to remind you what you can safely eat is:

LONG-HAUL FLIGHTS, CLOTS AND DVT

Any prolonged immobility including travel by land or air can result in deep vein thrombosis (DVT) with the risk of embolus to the lungs. Certain factors can increase the risk and these include:

- Previous clot or close relative with a history
- Being over 40 but > risk over 80 years
- Recent major operation or varicose veins surgery
- Cancer
- Stroke
- Heart disease
- Obesity
- Pregnancy
- Hormone therapy
- Heavy smoking
- Severe varicose veins
- Being very tall (over 6ft/1.8m) or short (under 5ft/1.5m)

A deep vein thrombosis (DVT) causes painful swelling and redness of the calf or sometimes the thigh. It is only dangerous if a clot travels to the lungs (pulmonary embolus). Symptoms of a pulmonary embolus (PE) include chest pain, shortness of breath and sometimes coughing up small amounts of blood, and commonly start three to ten days after a long flight. Anyone who thinks that they might have a DVT needs to see a doctor immediately.

PREVENTION OF DVT
- Keep mobile before and during the flight; move around every couple of hours
- Drink plenty of fluids during the flight
- Avoid taking sleeping pills and excessive tea, coffee and alcohol
- Consider wearing flight socks or support stockings (see *www.legshealth.com*)

If you think you are at increased risk of a clot, ask your doctor if it is safe to travel.

TREATING TRAVELLERS' DIARRHOEA *Dr Jane Wilson-Howarth*

It is dehydration that makes you feel awful during a bout of diarrhoea and the most important part of treatment is drinking lots of clear fluids. Sachets of oral rehydration salts give the perfect biochemical mix to replace all that is pouring out of your bottom but other recipes taste nicer. Any dilute mixture of sugar and salt in water will do you good: try Coke or orange squash with a three-finger pinch of salt added to each glass (if you are salt-depleted you won't taste the salt). Otherwise make a solution of a four-finger scoop of sugar with a three-finger pinch of salt in a 500ml glass. Or add eight level teaspoons of sugar (18g) and one level teaspoon of salt (3g) to one litre (five cups) of safe water. A squeeze of lemon or orange juice improves the taste and adds potassium, which is also lost in diarrhoea. Drink two large glasses after every bowel action, and more if you are thirsty. These solutions are still absorbed well if you are vomiting, but you will need to take sips at a time. If you are not eating you need to drink three litres a day plus whatever is pouring into the toilet. If you feel like eating, take a bland, high carbohydrate diet. Heavy greasy foods will probably give you cramps.

If the diarrhoea is bad, or you are passing blood or slime, or you have a fever, you will probably need antibiotics in addition to fluid replacement. A dose of norfloxacin or ciprofloxacin repeated twice a day until better may be appropriate (if you are planning to take an antibiotic with you, note that both norfloxacin and ciprofloxacin are available only on prescription in the UK). If the diarrhoea is greasy and bulky and is accompanied by sulphurous (eggy) burps, one likely cause is giardia. This is best treated with tinidazole (four x 500mg in one dose, repeated seven days later if symptoms persist).

PEEL IT, BOIL IT, COOK IT OR FORGET IT.

This means that fruit you have washed and peeled yourself, and hot foods, should be safe but raw foods, cold cooked foods, salads, fruit salads which have been prepared by others, ice cream and ice are all risky, and foods kept lukewarm in hotel buffets are often dangerous. That said, plenty of travellers and expatriates enjoy fruit and vegetables, so do keep a sense of perspective: food served in a fairly decent hotel in a large town or a place regularly frequented by expatriates is likely to be safe. If you are struck, see box, *Treating travellers' diarrhoea*, above, for treatment.

MALARIA Malaria kills about a million Africans every year. Of the travellers who return to Britain with malaria, 92% have caught it in Africa. You are 100 times more likely to catch malaria in Africa than you are in Asia. In most African countries, visitors are urged to take malaria tablets as a matter of course. The situation in Ethiopia is less clear-cut, and is dependent on which parts of the country you intend to visit, and at what time of year you will be there. Malaria is present in most parts of tropical Africa below c2,000m, and the *Anopheles* mosquito which transmits the malaria parasite is most abundant near the marshes and still water in which it breeds. In other words, malaria is most prevalent in low-lying areas where there is water, and especially after rain.

Malaria is absent from most parts of the Ethiopian Plateau, for instance the Bale Highlands, the central highlands around Addis Ababa, and the western highlands around Jimma. It is not prevalent at most points along the northern historical circuit, the one notable exception being Bahir Dar and elsewhere on the shore of Lake Tana, which lies at 1,830m and is increasingly subject to outbreaks of the disease, particularly during the rainy season – though the risk of contracting it is slight by comparison with many popular safari destinations in east and southern Africa.

In the Rift Valley, malaria is generally seasonal, with spasmodic and localised outbreaks taking place during the rainy season. The severity of these outbreaks varies greatly from year to year and place to place, and usually they are well publicised by word of mouth because most residents of the Ethiopian Highlands have as little resistance to malaria as do Europeans. Nevertheless, it is safest to assume that an element of risk exists throughout the Rift Valley (which includes Dire Dawa, Awash National Park, Adama, the Rift Valley lakes, Arba Minch and Moyale) during the rains, even though the incidence of malaria is rarely comparable to that in many parts of east Africa. The same applies to other relatively dry low-lying areas, such as those east and south of the Bale Mountains. The two areas of Ethiopia that are most likely to be visited by tourists and where malaria is a definite year-round threat are the Omo Valley (Omo and Mago national parks) and the western lowlands around Gambella.

So should you take malaria pills or not? Definitely, if you are visiting a high-risk area like the Omo Valley or Gambella at any time of year, or if you are travelling in the Rift Valley during the wet season. On the other hand, if your travels will be restricted to highland areas, or you visit in the dry season and avoid high-risk areas, there is a case for not taking them. Having said that, it can be argued that even the slight risk present in some parts of the country is justification for taking all possible precautions. A visitor to Ethiopia who does not regularly visit the tropics would probably be wiser to err on the side of caution and to take malaria tablets. If you opt not to take tablets, you should be doubly aware of any symptoms that might be malarial, and take extra care to avoiding being bitten by mosquitoes (see page 119).

Mefloquine (Lariam) is one of the most effective prophylactic agents for Ethiopia but is not suitable for everyone, so should only be taken on a doctor's recommendation. If this drug is suggested, then start 2½ weeks before departure to check it suits you. Stop immediately if it seems to cause depression or anxiety, visual or hearing disturbances, severe headaches or changes in heart rhythm. Anyone who has been treated for depression or psychiatric problems, has diabetes controlled by oral therapy, who is epileptic (or who has suffered fits in the past), or has a close blood relative who is epileptic, should not take mefloquine. Malarone (paludrine and atovaquone) is now considered to be as effective as mefloquine. It has the advantage of having relatively few side effects and need only be started one to two days before entering a malarial area, whilst you are there and for seven days after. Although expensive, it is ideal for short stays, as you are more likely to complete the course. Paediatric Malarone is also available and is based on body weight (in kg). If your child is above 11kg but below 40kg then they will need this formulation. Malarone can be used safely for up to a year and probably longer although the licence has only been granted for 28 days in a malarial area. This is because it costs money to extend the licence and not for safety reasons.

Doxycycline (100mg daily) is a good alternative if mefloquine is unsuitable or Malarone is too expensive and need only be started one to two days before arrival in a malarial region. Like mefloquine and Malarone it can only be obtained from a doctor. There is a possibility of allergic skin reactions developing in sunlight in approximately 1–3% of people. If this happens the drug should be stopped.

Chloroquine (Nivaquine or Avloclor) and proguanil (Paludrine) are now considered to be the least effective. They should only be used if there is no suitable alternative.

All prophylactic agents should be taken after or with the evening meal, washed down with plenty of fluids and, with the exception of Malarone, continued for four weeks after leaving the last malarial area. Be aware, however, that resistance patterns and thus the effectiveness of particular drugs are prone to change. Your GP may not be aware of new developments, so you are advised to consult a travel clinic for current advice, or ↘ 020 7636 7921 for free information from the Malaria Reference Laboratory at the London School of Hygiene and Tropical Medicine.

Equally important as taking malaria pills is making every reasonable effort not to be bitten by mosquitoes. The fact is that drug resistance is widespread in Africa, and the most certain way to avoid malaria is to not be bitten by mosquitoes. This doesn't mean that avoiding bites is an alternative to taking pills – nobody will be able to prevent every potential bite – but that you should do both.

Even if you take your malaria tablets meticulously and are careful to avoid being bitten, you might still contract malaria. If you experience headaches, or even a general sense of disorientation or flu-like aches and pains, you may have malaria. However, the only consistent symptom is a high temperature (38°C or more). It is vital you seek medical advice immediately. Local doctors see malaria all the time; they will know it in all its guises and know the best treatment for local resistance patterns. Untreated malaria can rapidly be fatal, but even prophylactic-resistant strains normally respond well to treatment, provided that you do not leave it too late.

If you are unable to reach a doctor, you may have to treat yourself. For this reason, it may be advisable to carry a cure in your medical kit. Along with Co-arthemeter, Malarone is considered one of the safest and most effective treatments for malaria in Africa. Once again, this could change, so seek advice from a travel clinic before you leave for Ethiopia.

Malaria typically takes from six days to six months to develop but it can take as long as a year if you are taking prophylactic medication. This means that you may only display symptoms after you leave Ethiopia; you are advised to continue with prophylactics for at least four weeks after returning home (except for Malarone, which need only be continued for seven days). It is all too easy to forget your pills once you are in the everyday routine of life at home, but you should make every effort to remember. If you display symptoms which could possibly be malarial, even if this happens a year after you return home, get to a doctor and be sure to mention that you have been exposed to malaria.

Finally, if you have a fever and the malaria test is negative (though this does not exclude malaria), you may have typhoid, which should also receive immediate treatment.

AVOIDING BILHARZIA Schistosomiasis, more commonly known as bilharzia, is common throughout Africa. It is caused by parasitic worms which can penetrate the skin when wading, swimming, bathing, or washing in contaminated water.

- If you are bathing, swimming, paddling or wading in fresh water which you think may carry a bilharzia risk, try to get out of the water within ten minutes.
- Avoid bathing or paddling on shores within 200m of villages or places where people use the water a great deal, especially reedy shores or where there's lots of water weed.
- Dry off thoroughly with a towel; rub vigorously.
- If your bathing water comes from a risky source try to ensure that the water is taken from the lake in the early morning and stored snail-free, otherwise it should be filtered or Dettol or Cresol added.

- Bathing early in the morning is safer than bathing in the last half of the day.
- Cover yourself with DEET insect repellent before swimming: it may offer some protection.

HIV/AIDS The risks of sexually transmitted infection are extremely high in Ethiopia, whether you sleep with fellow travellers or locals. About 80% of HIV infections in British heterosexuals are acquired abroad. If you must indulge, use condoms or femidoms, which help reduce the risk of transmission. If you notice any genital ulcers or discharge, get treatment promptly since these increase the risk of acquiring HIV. If you do have unprotected sex, visit a clinic as soon as possible; this should be within 24 hours, or no later than 72 hours, for post-exposure prophylaxis.

MENINGITIS This is a particularly nasty disease as it can kill within hours of the first symptoms appearing. The telltale symptom is the combination of a blinding headache and usually a fever. Meningitis ACWY vaccine protects against the common and serious bacterial forms in Africa, but not against all of the many kinds of meningitis. Local papers normally report localised outbreaks. If you develop symptoms, get to a doctor immediately.

TICKBITE FEVER African ticks are not the rampant disease transmitters they are in the Americas, but they may spread tickbite fever and a few dangerous rarities in Ethiopia. Tickbite fever is a flu-like illness that can easily be treated with doxycycline, but as there can be some serious complications it is important to visit a doctor.

Ticks should ideally be removed as soon as possible, as leaving them on the body increases the chance of infection. They should be removed with special tick tweezers that can be bought in good travel shops. Failing that you can use your fingernails: grasp the tick as close to your body as possible and pull steadily and firmly away at right angles to your skin. The tick will then come away complete, as long as you do not jerk or twist. If possible douse the wound with alcohol (any spirit will do) or iodine. Irritants (eg: Olbas oil) or lit cigarettes are to be discouraged since they can cause the ticks to regurgitate and therefore increase the risk of disease. It is best to get a travelling companion to check you for ticks; if you are travelling with small children, remember to check their heads, and particularly behind the ears.

Spreading redness around the bite and/or fever and/or aching joints after a tickbite imply that you have an infection that requires antibiotic treatment, so seek advice.

RABIES AND ANIMAL BITES Rabies is carried by all mammals (anything with fur and teeth is an easy way to remember) and is passed on to humans through a bite, a scratch, or a lick of an open wound. It can even be transmitted through saliva in the eyes, nose and mouth. You must always assume any animal is rabid even if they look well, as there is a ten-day incubation period where they can appear healthy but are infectious. Seek medical help as soon as possible and in the interim scrub the wound with soap and bottled or boiled water, then pour on a strong iodine or alcohol solution. This helps stop the rabies virus entering the body and will guard against wound infections, including tetanus.

If you intend to have contact with animals and/or are likely to be more than 24 hours away from medical help, then vaccination is advised. Ideally, three pre-exposure doses should be taken over a minimum of 21 days. If you think you have been exposed to rabies then get treatment as soon as possible, but it is never too late to seek help, as the incubation period for rabies can be very long. Tell the doctors if you have had the three doses of pre-exposure vaccine, as this simplifies the treatment and means that you do not need to have the rabies immunoglobulin (RIG) treatment which is expensive and hard to come by. Remember, if you contract rabies the mortality rate is 100% and death from rabies is probably one of the worst ways to go.

TETANUS Tetanus is caught through deep, dirty wounds, so ensure that any wounds are thoroughly cleaned. Immunisation gives good protection for ten years, provided you do not have an overwhelming number of tetanus bacteria on board. Keep immunised and be sensible about first aid.

INSECTS

Even if you are taking malaria tablets, you should take steps to avoid being bitten by insects and by mosquitoes in particular. The most imperative reason for doing so is the increasing levels of resistance to preventative drugs. Whatever pills you take, there remains a significant risk of being infected by malaria in areas below 1,800m. Of much less concern, but still a risk, are several other mosquito-borne viral fevers that either are, or else might be, present in low- and medium-altitude parts of Ethiopia. Dengue, the only one of these diseases that is anything close to being common, is very nasty with symptoms that include severe muscle cramps, high fever and a measles-like rash; fatalities are exceptional but medical help should be sought. The other diseases in this category are too rare to be a cause for serious concern; nevertheless, they are difficult to treat, and some of them are potentially fatal. It is not only mosquitoes that might carry nasty diseases; leishmania, another difficult-to-treat disease, is spread by sandfly bites. Before you panic, it should be stressed that all these diseases, other than malaria, are most unlikely to be caught by travellers. I mention them mainly to illustrate that malaria pills on their own do not guarantee your safety against serious insect-borne diseases.

The *Anopheles* mosquito that spreads malaria emerges at dusk, as do sandflies and most other disease-carrying mosquitoes. The exception to this is the *Aedes* mosquito carrying dengue fever, which flies during the day, so use insect repellents (see below) during the daytime if you see any mosquitoes around. After dusk you will greatly reduce your chances of being bitten and contracting other insect-borne diseases if you wear long trousers and socks in the evening and cover exposed parts of your body with insect repellent, preferably a DEET-based preparation such as Repel (50–55% DEET). This strength DEET is also suitable for pregnant women and children. Sprays of this sort are not available in Ethiopia; bring one with you.

The *Anopheles* mosquito hunts mostly at ground level and it can bite through thin socks, so it is worth putting repellent on your ankles, even if they are covered. DEET-impregnated ankle-bands (marketed by MASTA at the London School of Hygiene and Tropical Medicine) are also quite effective, though they may get you some funny looks. When walking in scrub and forest areas, you should cover and spray yourself by day as well; the *Aedes* mosquito that spreads dengue is a day-biter. Solid shoes, socks and trousers will, in any case, protect you against snakes, sharp thorns, ticks and harmless but irritating biters like midges.

Like many insects, mosquitoes are drawn to direct light. If you are camping, never put a lamp near the opening of your tent, or you will have a swarm of mosquitoes and other insects waiting to join you when you retire. In hotel rooms, be aware that the longer you leave on your light, the greater the number of insects with which you are likely to share your accommodation.

Once you are in bed, the most effective form of protection against mosquitoes is an impregnated net. Basically though, once you're in Ethiopia, your only option is Mobil Insecticide Spray, which is for spraying rooms (not your body) and is available throughout the country. Far better, though, is to carry your own permethrin-impregnated net, which will protect you against everything (these are available at Trailfinders, MASTA and from good camping shops such as Blacks).

To balance the warnings, a reminder that in most parts of the Ethiopian Highlands you are unlikely to even encounter a mosquito, and that disease-carrying sandflies are only really likely to be found in rural villages. It should be stressed, too, that the overwhelming majority of insects don't bite people, and of those that do, most are entirely harmless – rather fortunate, as cheap hotels in Ethiopia tend to approach menagerie status on the insect front. Mattresses quite often contain bedbugs and fleas, which drive some people crazy, but they are both essentially harmless.

As much to guarantee a good night's sleep as anything, it's worth getting into the habit of spraying your room with insecticide before you retire. If bedbugs become a nuisance, a sleeping mat will insulate you from them. Again, an enclosed free-standing sleeping net, such as the ones put out by Long Road in the USA (↘ 510 450 4763), should keep all nocturnal insects out.

Flies are locally abundant in Ethiopia, particularly during and immediately after the rains, and Lalibela deserves some sort of award in this direction! Ultimately, there's not a lot you can do about flies – though I noticed they liked me most when I was sweaty, and least when I was freshly showered. You get used to them.

MEDICAL FACILITIES

Most doctors here speak good English and are very helpful. In larger towns there are hospitals where outpatients can be treated and there are basic laboratory facilities for blood and stool tests. Where there is no hospital or clinic, or you can't find a doctor, pharmacists generally speak good English and are often experienced diagnosticians (most Ethiopians consult pharmacists rather than doctors), and they will be able to tell you where laboratory facilities can be found. In Addis, the clinic opposite the Gandhi Hospital has an excellent laboratory.

Medication, consultations and tests are all very cheap when compared with Western countries – outside of Addis Ababa, a consultation, blood or stool test and medication are unlikely to set you back more than US$7 – so for goodness' sake don't let your budget put you off visiting a doctor.

OUTDOOR HEALTH

SUN AND HEAT The equatorial sun is vicious. Although it is impossible to avoid some exposure to the sun, it would be foolish to sunbathe needlessly. Tanning ages your skin and it can cause skin cancer. If you are coming to Ethiopia from a less harsh climate, let your body get used to the sunlight gradually or you will end up with sunburn. Take things too far, and sunstroke – a potentially fatal condition – may be the result. Wear sunscreen and build up your exposure gradually, starting with no more than 20 minutes a day. Avoid exposing yourself for more than two hours in any day, and stay out of the sun between noon and 15.00.

Always wear clothes made from natural fabrics such as 100% cotton. These help prevent fungal infections and other rashes. Athlete's foot is prevalent, so wear thongs in communal showers.

Even small cuts are inclined to go septic in the tropics. Clean any lesion with a dilute solution of potassium permanganate or iodine two to three times daily. Antiseptic creams are not suitable for the tropics; wounds must be kept dry and covered.

DANGEROUS ANIMALS There are very few parts of Ethiopia where you are likely to come into contact with potentially dangerous large mammals. Elephant, buffalo and black rhinoceros – the most dangerous of Africa's terrestrial herbivores – are practically restricted to the Omo Valley and remote border areas.

The large mammal that you need most concern yourself with is the hippopotamus, whose response to any disturbance whilst it is grazing is to head directly for the safety of water, and trample anything that gets in its way. Be cautious around any lake or large river where hippos might be present, especially towards dusk, in the early morning and in overcast weather.

Another animal to watch out for near water is the crocodile, though only a very large croc is likely to attack a person, and then only if you are actually in the water or standing right on the shore. Anywhere near a town or village, you can be fairly sure that potential man-eaters will have been disposed of by their potential prey, so the risk is greatest in water away from human habitation.

Most large predators are too thinly distributed to be a cause for concern in Ethiopia, except perhaps in the Omo region. Spotted hyenas are common, however, and frequently associated with human settlements. But even where large predators are reasonably common, sleeping in a sealed tent practically guarantees your safety – unless you do something daft like putting meat in your tent, or sleeping with your head sticking out of the flap.

SNAKEBITE Snakes rarely attack unless provoked, and bites in travellers are unusual. You are less likely to get bitten if you wear stout shoes and long trousers when in the bush. Most snakes are harmless and even venomous species will dispense venom in only about half of their bites. If bitten, then, you are unlikely to have received venom; keeping this fact in mind may help you to stay calm. Many so-called first-aid techniques do more harm than good: cutting into the wound is harmful; tourniquets are dangerous; suction and electrical inactivation devices do not work. The only treatment is antivenom. In case of a bite that you fear may have been from a venomous snake:

> **DUST** *From a letter by Arthur Gerfers*
>
> The one thing that made me sick during my seven weeks in Ethiopia was dust! The houses are made of it, many of the roads are made of it, the churches are full of it, and the air is heavily charged with millions of particles. At first, I paid no attention to the layers of red dust building up on my trousers during endless days of bus travel. But on the three-day journey from Lalibela to Gondar the dust began to weigh heavily in my lungs. It became difficult to breathe, as I began to register the state of my dust-clogged lungs after a good week of dusty travel. In Gondar, I spent four solid days convalescing in a hotel with gardens. Even afterwards, while strolling through town, the smell of dust made me sick to my stomach. It took a couple of weeks before I felt normal again. After that, I was very careful to tie a bandana around my nose and mouth during long dusty journeys. And though I may have looked like some Wild West train robber to the average European, my example was followed by a surprising number of locals; plus, most important of all, I never got sick again. Dust, especially on long, cramped bus rides, deserves attention, just as much as diarrhoea or dangerous animals any day!

- Try to keep calm – it is likely that no venom has been dispensed.
- Prevent movement of the bitten limb by applying a splint.
- Keep the bitten limb below heart height to slow the spread of any venom.
- If you have a crêpe bandage, wrap it around the whole limb (eg: all the way from the toes to the thigh), as tight as you would for a sprained ankle or a muscle pull.
- Evacuate to a hospital that has antivenom.

And remember:

- *Never* give aspirin; you may take paracetamol, which is safe.
- *Never* cut or suck the wound.
- *Do not* apply ice packs.
- *Do not* apply potassium permanganate.

If the offending snake can be captured without risk of someone else being bitten, take this to show the doctor – but beware, since even a decapitated head is able to bite.

SAFETY

Ethiopia is generally a very safe country. Casual theft and pickpocketing are fairly commonplace in parts of the country, most notably Addis Ababa, but this sort of thing is almost never accompanied by violence. In Addis Ababa, pickpockets might operate anywhere, but favoured areas are the Mercato, and in the vicinity of government hotels in the city centre. Violent crime isn't a cause for serious concern, but as in any large city one should not wander around at night with a large amount of money or important documents.

In other parts of Ethiopia, the risk of encountering pickpockets is mainly confined to bus stations and markets, and even then only in larger towns. At bus stations, this is most likely to be a loner operating in the surge of people getting onto a bus. In the streets, a favoured trick is for one person to distract you by bumping into you or grabbing your arm, while a second person slips his fingers into your pocket from the other side. It's advisable to leave valuables and any money you don't need in a hotel room, to carry the money you do need in a relatively inaccessible place, and to always turn quickly in the other direction if somebody does bump into you or grab you. A useful ruse is to stuff something bulky but valueless (a bit of scrunched-up tissue or an empty cigarette pack) as a decoy in a more accessible pocket. If you need to go out with important documents or foreign currency, carry it in a concealed money-belt, and carry some cash separately so that you need not reveal your money-belt in public.

Thieves often pick up on uncertainty and home in on what they perceive to be an easy victim. In Addis Ababa, where there are plenty of experienced thieves and con artists, always walk quickly and decisively. When you arrive in a new town by bus, stroll out of the bus station quickly and confidently as if you know exactly where you're going (even if you don't). Avoid letting the kids who often hang around bus stations latch on to you. Once through the crowds, you can sit down somewhere and check your map, or ask for directions.

One area of risk that is difficult to quantify is that of armed bandits – *shifta* – holding up a bus. This was quite commonplace a few years ago, but is no longer a serious cause for concern, except perhaps in eastern areas near the Somali border.

It is easy enough to let warnings about theft induce an element of paranoia into your thinking. There is no cause for this sort of overreaction. If you are moderately careful and sensible, the chance of hitting anything more serious than pickpocketing is very small. Far more remarkable than the odd bit of theft, especially when you consider how much poverty there is in the country, is the overwhelming honesty that is the norm in Ethiopia.

HASSLES The level of hassle experienced by visitors to Ethiopia is strongly dependent on how they travel. People on organised tours generally experience the country as almost entirely hassle-free, and those who fly or are driven around the country, and who make extensive use of upmarket hotels and professional guides, are also likely to have a smooth trip. By contrast, solitary independent travellers who bus between towns, who seldom explore sites with local guides, and who stay mainly in local hotels, often report the hassle factor to be the highest of any African country.

The most persistent irritant comprises groups of children who follow travellers around yelling '*faranji, faranji*', 'you, you, you', or a variant thereof. This may sound harmless enough, and it is, but the children's persistence can easily exhaust one's reserves of good humour! The best response to this sort of thing is to poke gentle fun at the kids. If a kid shouts 'you', yell 'you' back, or if they shout '*faranji*', respond with '*habbishat*' (Ethiopian). Humour may not always defuse the mob, but it is generally a more successful ploy than showing anger or irritation! (A *very* occasional but more inherently worrying problem is children throwing stones at travellers. Why they do this is anybody's guess, but the best way to deal with it is usually to appeal to an Ethiopian adult to get the children to stop.)

That aside, independent travellers may sometimes find it rather trying to operate in an environment where they have no privacy, and where every move seems to attract comment or attention. This manifests itself in many small ways: beggars will cross the street to catch your attention, arbitrary bores will monopolise your company, aspirant guides will latch on to you for no good reason and later expect to be paid for their imagined service, and even the most straightforward situations such as catching a bus or ordering a meal often entails fuss and complications.

There is no absolute way of dealing with this sort of thing. Generally, however, if you need help or directions on arriving in a town, it is far better to approach somebody yourself than allow yourself to become obliged to a bore, or an aspirant guide, or anybody else who comes across like they have an agenda. Also, when you are travelling rough for a long period, it genuinely helps to take the odd break – an afternoon with a book in the garden of a smart hotel can, for instance, be tremendously therapeutic.

WOMEN TRAVELLERS

Most feedback from female travellers suggests that Ethiopia is a relatively safe country for single women travellers. The risk of rape or seriously threatening harassment is probably lower than in many Westernised countries. From this female updater's perspective, Ethiopia has been the easiest, most non-threatening African country I have travelled in for work, and not once over the three months I conducted my research for this guide was I threatened or harassed in any way. If anything, I was probably shown more respect. As a fellow female traveller Hisako Tajima also claimed: 'As a solo female traveller, I found Ethiopia to be a very easy and friendly country, refreshingly free of amorous male advances that make countries like Egypt and Turkey such a chore.'

The most regular complaint from any female travellers is teenage boys yelling out 'Fuck you' from across the street, something to which male travellers are also subjected. Yelling out obscenities at tourists is not an everyday occurrence (unless you decide to live in Shashemene), and it is unlikely to happen when you are in the company of a respected guide or another local person. Although unpleasant, it is ultimately a less innocuous variation on the sort of verbal crap that all single travellers have to put up with from time to time in Ethiopia.

One place that several female travellers have found threatening is the Mercato market in Addis Ababa. Fran Gohd, who found the country safe and friendly in general, writes: 'We went to the market. We were the only women and were given hostile looks and hissed at repeatedly. I was told 'Fuck you' several times after I didn't give in to the men asking me for money. I was asked by a 12-year-old boy if I wanted to have sex. This got worse as we approached the part of the market where they sold *chat*. I felt like I could've been dragged off the street and disappeared without trace.'

Women travellers are naturally urged to avoid staying at hotels at the brothel-cum-barroom end of the price scale. Outside of Addis Ababa, no respectable Ethiopian woman would dream of going to a local bar, since Ethiopian men assume that any woman they see in a bar is a prostitute. While they might recognise that this isn't the case with a female traveller, hanging about in the lowest shoestring hotels does place you in an environment where motives might be misinterpreted.

On the subject of dress, Ethiopia has a substantial Muslim population, and in rural areas particularly both Muslims and Christians tend to dress modestly. In general it is good sense to look to what the local women are wearing and follow their lead. Anna Rank has this to say: 'If I wear sleeveless clothes then I tend to get a constant stream of comments and stares, although this does not particularly bother me in Addis. I would not dress in this manner in smaller towns where *faranjis* are few and far between.' Fran Gohd again: 'We came prepared with skirts and headscarves, but there was no need to wear them. We wore pants/trousers and that was acceptable. I saw some women travellers wearing shorts, but I'm not sure that I'd feel comfortable with that unless they extended below the knee and even then I'd think twice.'

A couple of readers have highlighted the problems specifically facing black female travellers in Ethiopia, where women retain a somewhat subservient role by Western standards. European women are not expected to fit the mould, but nobody seems quite certain on which side of the chasm to place black Western women. Black women who travel alone in Ethiopia are in for a strange time, and they will often experience African sexual attitudes at first hand. The obvious area of solution is to dress and carry yourself in a manner that precludes confusion: don't come with a rucksack full of flowing African dresses and bright blouses, but rather wear jeans or preppy clothes, things that would rarely be seen on an Ethiopian woman.

On a practical level female travellers should note that finding sanitary products, in particular tampons, is nigh impossible outside of the capital so stock up before you depart Addis.

One final point is that you should be aware that when Ethiopians ask you to play with them, they are not suggesting a quick grope but that you make conversation – the Amharic *techawot* means both to talk and to play.

DISABLED TRAVELLERS

Bradt Travel Guides holds extensive notes by Gordon Rattray offering advice for wheelchair travellers in Ethiopia. If you would like a copy, please contact Bradt (e *info@bradtguides.com*). In addition, the Ethiopian Centre for Disability and Development (*www.ecdd-ethiopia.org*) have produced a detailed guide entitled *Accessible Addis Ababa*. It is available in pdf format from the centre by contacting them via email (e *info@ecdd-ethiopia.org*). The centre also has plans to produce a countrywide guide in the future.

Part Two

ADDIS ABABA

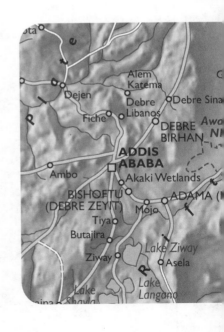

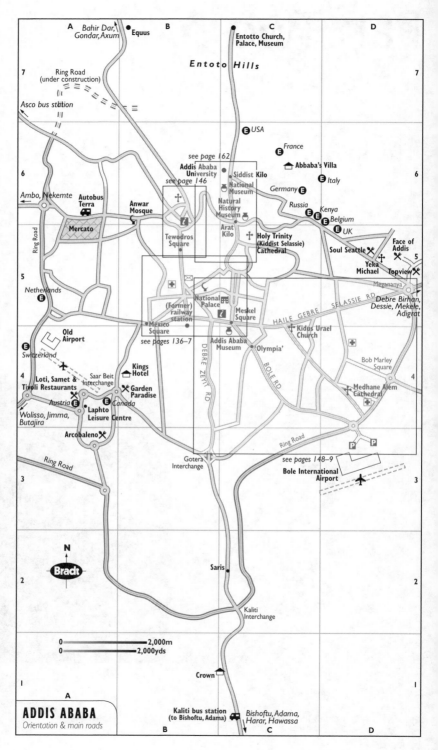

ADDIS ABABA
Orientation & main roads

5

Addis Ababa

The world's third-highest capital city, Addis Ababa (which somewhat improbably means 'New Flower', and is often shortened to plain 'Addis') lies in the central highlands of Ethiopia at an altitude of 2,400m. Climatically, this large city is a highly encouraging introduction to Ethiopia: characterised throughout the year, both day and night, by comfortable temperate weather, interrupted by the occasional torrential downpour, Addis Ababa will swiftly dispel any lingering preconceptions about Ethiopia being a searing desert. In most other respects, however, Addis Ababa and its three million residents can be rather overwhelming on first exposure, with beggars, cripples, taxi drivers and hawkers clamouring for your attention, and con artists and pickpockets doing their utmost to divert it. Visitors on organised tours will be reasonably sheltered from Addis's more bombastic elements, but independent travellers who haven't visited a large Third World city before – and, indeed, many who have – are likely to end their first day in Addis Ababa feeling somewhat besieged. A not unreasonable response to Addis Ababa would be to move on as swiftly as possible. Certainly, those who touchdown at Bole Airport in the morning or early afternoon could easily bus straight on to somewhere like Bishoftu (Debre Zeyit) or Adama (Nazret), and save prolonged confrontation with the capital for a later date.

Like most African cities, Addis does tend to grow on you. When I researched the first edition of this guide, I found it difficult to reconcile the notes I made after my first day in Addis with the city I eventually came to know and, if not exactly love, then certainly like and enjoy. It's difficult to pinpoint any single reason for this. One factor, particularly for those who travel rough, is that the capital's relatively Westernised facilities look a lot more inviting after a week or two bussing through the sticks than they do coming directly from Europe or wherever. Another is that Addis Ababa's less savoury elements – the pickpockets, con artists and bogus students – are far more easily handled and deflected once one has become attuned to Ethiopia more generally. Eventually, sadly, the visitor will even become somewhat if not entirely numbed to Addis's shocking parade of polio cripples, amputee war veterans, ragged street children, naked beggars and ranting loonies. More than anything, though, Addis Ababa grows on the visitor because it is all bark and very little bite. For all the hustlers and opportunistic thieves, the show-off teenagers who gratuitously yell 'Fuck off' or 'Fuck you' at travellers and make lewd propositions to single females, the actual threat to one's personal safety is negligible. I'd feel safer spending a month in downtown Addis Ababa than I would an hour in parts of Nairobi or Johannesburg – or parts of many Western capitals. And beneath the grotesquery and poverty there lies the infectious spirit that is characteristic of Ethiopia. Addis Ababa is a busy, bustling, exciting city; the hassle that one might occasionally receive comes from only a tiny fraction of its predominantly friendly population – don't let first impressions put you off.

Short-stay visitors to Ethiopia often see little more of the capital than a few blurred street scenes as they are whisked from airport to hotel and back before flying to the more noteworthy historical sights of the north. But travellers with more time on their hands will find it worth making the effort to like Addis Ababa. This is a city with a real buzz, one possessed of a sense of self-definition and place lacking entirely from the many African capitals whose governments have attempted – and largely failed – to create misplaced pockets of Western urbanity in otherwise under-developed nations. Perhaps the highest praise one can direct at this chaotic, contradictory and compelling city is this: Addis Ababa *does* feel exactly as the Ethiopian capital *should* feel – singularly and unmistakably Ethiopian.

Moreover, Addis Ababa is also one of the few African cities whose environs offer a wide variety of exceptional sightseeing. Although it is a relatively modern city, founded by Emperor Menelik II in 1887, the surrounding Entoto Hills have long been a major centre of Showan politics. Unconfirmed legend has it that the rulers of Axum fled to Entoto during the purgative reign of Queen Yodit, while the presence of two disused rock-hewn churches within 10km of the modern city centre highlights the strong medieval links between Entoto and the Zagwe capital of Lalibela. In addition to the above, there are several interesting museums in Addis, most notably the Ethnographic and National museums, respectively ranking with the best of their type in Africa. Further afield, but still within day-tripping distance of the capital, there is wonderful birdwatching and rambling in the Akaki Wetlands, lush highland forest rattling with birds and monkeys in the Menegasha, a field of seven crater lakes at Bishoftu, the atmospheric and historic monastery of Debre Libanos, and an extant rock-hewn church, fascinating prehistoric site, and field of medieval engraved stelae clustered along the Butajira road. Addis Ababa offers more than enough in the way of sightseeing and outings to keep a curious traveller going for a week, something you could not say of too many African capitals.

GETTING THERE AND AWAY

BY AIR Most visitors will first arrive in Addis by air. **Bole International Airport** [149 G1] is only 5km from the city centre and **taxis** can be hired at a kiosk in the airport building for around US$8–12 depending on which part of the city you are heading for, slightly more expensive if you arrive on the late-night flight. Private taxis can be hired outside the airport, and will be cheaper provided you negotiate, but this saving should be balanced against the added exposure of your luggage to theft. The risk is minimal, but perhaps not worth it at this early point in your holiday! If your flight arrives very late at night, it is advisable to book a hotel room in advance or failing that to stay at the airport until sunrise.

Minibuses, departing from the far end of the car park or the nearby Bole Bridge Minibus Station under the Ring Road flyover, run between the airport and city centre and charge a notional fare. These will generally follow Bole Road to Meskel Square, and then veer up Ras Desta Damtew Road past the Ambassador Theatre to the post office, from where they will follow Churchill Avenue to De Gaulle Square on the Piazza. While minibuses are convenient and cheap, you're unlikely to be very alert after a long flight, for which reason you should consider using a minibus only if you are heading to a hotel along the route described above. You really don't want to be plonked down in the city centre and have to take another minibus or walk to your hotel, and quite possibly get lost, or worse still have something stolen all just to save a few dollars. For more information on minibus safety, see the boxed text *Catching minibuses* on page 134.

Ethiopian Airlines' **domestic flights** depart from Terminal 1 at Bole International Airport.

Airline offices The head office of **Ethiopian Airlines** [149 G2] (↘*011 661 6666 for reservations, confirmations & arrival information; e addcto@ethiopianairlines.com; www.ethiopianairlines.com*) is on Bole Road close to the airport. For most purposes, you can visit one of the several Ethiopian Airlines' branch offices in the city centre and Piazza. The main office is on Churchill Avenue [146 D4] (*opposite the National Theatre;* ↘ *011 551 7000*), while the office at the Hilton Hotel [137 H5] (↘ *011 515 7226*) is very handy.

Other airlines that are represented in Addis are:

✈ **BMI** [148 D5] (British Midland International) Room 102, Axum Bldg, Ghana St; ↘011 551 5666; e addbmi@dlh.de; www.flybmi.com

✈ **Egyptair** [136 C6] 2nd Floor, Shashe Bldg, Churchill Av; ↘011 156 4494; www.egyptair.com

✈ **Emirates** [137 H1] 2nd Floor, Dembel City Centre Mall, Bole Rd; ↘011 518 1818; www.emirates.com

✈ **Gulf Air** [137 G2] Jomo Kenyatta St; ↘011 550 9034; e woldegebriel@gulfair.com; www.gulfair.com

✈ **Kenya Airways** [137 H8] Hilton Hotel, Menelik II Av; ↘011 551 3018/552 5547–8; e kenyaair@ethionet.et; www.kenya-airways.com

✈ **KLM** [137 H5] Hilton Hotel, Menelik II Av; ↘011 552 5541/5495; e yemeserch.habte@KLM.com; www.klm.com

✈ **Lufthansa** [148 D5] Axum Bldg, Ghana St; ↘011 551 5666; e addgtsal@dlh.de; www.lufthansa.com

✈ **South African Airways** Bole Rd (opposite Sunshine Bldg); ↘011 553 7880–1; www.flysaa.com

✈ **Turkish Airlines** Zimbabwe St; ↘011 662 7781–3; e turkishairlines@ethionet.et; www.turkishairlines.com

✈ **Yemenia** [136 D5] Ras Desta Damtew St; ↘011 551 5076; e addisababa@yemenia.com; www.yemenia.com

For charter flights within Ethiopia, try a private company called **Abyssinian Flight Services** (↘ *011 662 0622–4; e bookings@abyssinianflights.com; www.abyssinianflights.com*).

BY BUS The best bus services departing from Addis Ababa are Selam Bus and Sky Bus, both closer in style to a Greyhound-type coach service than a typical African bus. **Selam Bus** (↘ *011 554 8800–1; e selam.bus@ethionet.et; www.selambus.com*) has a booking office in front of the central railway station [136 D2], whilst the booking office for **Sky Bus** (↘*011 156 8080/8585; www.skybusethiopia.com*) is in the popular Itegue Taitu Hotel [146 D3].

Both companies offer a direct daily service in either direction from Addis Ababa north to Bahir Dar (US$18; around 9 hours), Gondar (US$22; 10–12 hours) and Dessie (US$12; 7 hours); east to Dire Dawa (US$20, 9 hours), Harar (US$20; 9 hours) and Jijiga (US$22; 12 hours); and west to Jimma (US$12; 5½ hours). Selam runs an additional daily service to Mekele (US$19.50, 1¼ days), staying overnight in Ataye, and a Tuesdays only service to Shire (US$27, 2 days), which involves an overnight stay in Gondar. All buses leave from Meskel Square at 05.30. Services to Hawassa may be added soon.

Other, cheaper bus services also cover these routes, but they are less reliable. Traditionally most of these buses left from **Autobus Terra** in Mercato. There is a plan to close this station and replace it with suburban bus stations on each of the major roads out of Addis. Two of these bus stations are now operational: **Kaliti** [126 C1], 15km south of the city centre on the Debre Zeyit road, which offers short-distance bus and minibus services to Bishoftu, Adama, Mojo, Ziway and Hawassa (a minibus from Meskel Square to Kaliti costs around US$0.40); and, **Asco Bus Station** [off map 126 A7], on the Ambo road, which runs minibuses and buses to Ambo and Nekemte. All other long-distance services still depart from **Autobus Terra** in Mercato including Arba Minch, Moyale, Goba, Robe, Yabello and Jinka.

BY RAIL As of 2008 Ethiopia's last serving rail line, to Djibouti, ceased operation. In 2010 the government announced plans to build a new 4,780km network, which will link Addis Ababa to some 49 regional centres. For updates see http://updates.bradtguides.com/ethiopia.

ORIENTATION

Addis Ababa is a large city, and many of its main roads and other landmarks have long gone by two or even three names, with the name shown on most maps differing from the one in common use. This confusing situation is further exacerbated by the decision to name 52 of the city's main roads after each of the non-Ethiopian member states of the African Union. All in all, then, Addis Ababa can be a bit confusing – so read through this with map in hand before you start exploring (see *Maps*, page 131). In its hotel and restaurant listings, this book now tries to use the official names that will be on any map of Addis you may buy, but elsewhere the everyday name may be used, for example Arat Kilo or Siddist Kilo.

The **city centre** is more or less rectangular, defined by **Mexico Square** [136 A2] in the southwest, **Meskel Square** [137 F2] (also called Abbiot, meaning Revolution Square) in the southeast, the **Hilton Hotel** [137 H5] in the northeast and **Tewodros Square** [146 B1] in the northwest. The main thoroughfare through the city centre is **Churchill Avenue** (the southern end of which is now officially called Gambia Road). This wide road runs downhill from north to south, starting just below the City Hall [146 B5] in the area known as the Piazza, and passing the immigration office, the central post office, the National Theatre and the Ras Hotel, to terminate at the square in front of the **railway station** [136 D2] (also known as the Lagar). The main thoroughfare from west to east is **Ras Mekonnen Avenue**, which runs from Mexico Square to the railway station, where it intersects with Gambia Road. It then continues east past the stadium and Meskel Square to become **Haile Gebrselassie Road**, which leads east out of the city centre via Adwa Square (more commonly known as **Megenagna**) towards Debre Birhan, Dessie and Mekele.

Two important roads run south from Ras Mekonnen Avenue. The first lies immediately west of Meskel Square and leads out of town to most destinations in the south and west. Somewhat confusingly, it is marked on maps as Ras Baru Avenue but is more commonly referred to as the **Debre Zeyit road**, the name that I will use in this chapter, even though the town formerly known as Debre Zeyit has reverted to its original name of Bishoftu. Immediately east of Meskel Square, the road marked on most maps as Africa Avenue but more commonly referred to as **Bole Road** terminates at Bole International Airport, 5km out of town.

The area known as the **Piazza** lies immediately north of the city centre, from where it can be reached by heading uphill along Churchill Avenue with the City Hall clear in your sights. The Piazza is a loosely defined area, centred on **De Gaulle Square** [146 C4], bounded by Haile Selassie Street and the Taitu Hotel to the east, by Kidus Giyorgis Church to the north, and the City Hall to the west. The Piazza is also a busy shopping area, with a great many budget hotels concentrated in the side streets south of De Gaulle Square.

Haile Selassie Street arcs east of the Piazza to **Megabit Square** [162 C3], a major four-way junction most commonly referred to as **Arat Kilo**. The road that runs north from Arat Kilo heads into the Entoto Hills via the National Museum, the university campus at Yekatit 12 Square (**Siddist Kilo**) [162 C6] and the US Embassy. The road running east from Arat Kilo passes the Russian and British embassies before reaching Adwa Square. The road running south from Arat Kilo passes the Gibbe or Old Palace, the Hilton Hotel, the National or Presidential Palace and Africa Hall before it intersects with Ras Mekonnen Avenue at Meskel Square.

About 1km west of the Piazza, Addis Ketema or **Mercato** [162 A5] is a tight grid of streets centred on what is reputedly the largest **market** in Africa. On Habte Giyorgis Street, the main road that runs along the north of Mercato, is the main bus station, known as the Autobus Terra [126 A6].

A ring road around Addis Ababa, likely to total more than 50km once complete, has been under construction for several years now, and most of it is fully operational, with the only missing link being across the top of what is currently a very rough U shape. At Adwa Square, in the northeast corner of the U, five major roads converge in a two-level interchange. From there the road heads south, passing Bob Marley Square (Imperial roundabout) and then running on a 400m elevated stretch above Bole Road (which connects the city centre to the airport). The road then runs south to the Kaliti Interchange, where it swings under the Debre Zeyit road, which is the main thoroughfare south out of Addis Ababa. From here it heads northwards, passing huge areas of new condominium developments, the Makenissa and Jimma Road roundabouts, the Torhailoc flyover, and the Kolfe roundabout (just west of Mercato) from which the new Ambo road leads off to the west before finally ending northwest of the city centre at Gulele/Wingate where it meets the 'old' Ambo road on its way to Asco Bus Station.

MAPS The best map of Addis, produced by GTZ, is out of print. If it appears again it will cost at least US$15 in the streets. An acceptable city map, sufficient for most tourist purposes, can be bought for US$6 at the souvenir shop in the Ghion Hotel. If you're in need of maps of remote places for trekking, go to the **Ethiopian Mapping Authority** [137 G6] opposite the Hilton Hotel. Take ID and be willing to wait in the queue. They also sell a reasonably up-to-date 1:25,000 map of the whole city, including the full ring road, for US$3.50. If it is vital that you have certain maps, then you should contact the EMA (*PO Box 597, Addis Ababa;* 011 551 8445) well in advance.

GETTING AROUND

An efficient network of **minibuses** services Addis Ababa's roads. Public transport starts running at around 05.00, and peters out at around 20.00–21.00. Once rarely crowded, the minibuses now tend to fill up during the morning and evening commute. There can be a lot of pushing and shoving for the last minibus of the day, in which case it may be easier to take a taxi. Minibuses are very cheap and overcharging uncommon (expect to pay between US$0.10 and US$0.30), but the crowds can make it easy for pickpockets, so take care (see boxed text on *Catching minibuses*, page 134). Overcharging foreigners is not the custom – it has happened to me twice in hundreds of minibus rides.

The **main minibus stops** are dotted around De Gaulle Square on the Piazza; at Arat Kilo; opposite the Autobus Terra near the Mercato; in front of the railway station; in front of and opposite the stadium on Ras Mekonnen Avenue; and

Addis Ababa, officially founded in 1887, is not the only African city to have sprung up from nothing little more than a century ago, to grow into a modern metropolis of several million people. However, it owes its modern status as one of the five largest cities in sub-Saharan Africa to the unlikely combination of a grandfather's prophecy, an empress's whim and the timely intervention of an Australian tree!

In the early 1880s, the King of Showa, the future Emperor Menelik II, abandoned his capital at Ankober in favour of the Entoto Hills. What inspired this is unclear, but the Entoto area had great historical significance to the Showan aristocracy before being occupied by the Oromo after the religious wars of the 16th century. It was Menelik's expansionist grandfather, King Sahle Selassie, who reclaimed the area for Showa, prophesying that his grandson would build a large house in the valley below Entoto, from which would grow a great city.

At the end of the cold rainy season of 1886, Menelik II and his royal entourage moved down from the chilly hilltops of Entoto, to set up camp around the hot springs known as Filwoha. The emperor's wife Taitu fell in love with natural hot baths and the abundance of mimosa trees, and suggested that her husband build her a house there. Menelik concurred, recognising this to be the site described in his grandfather's prophecy. The royal party soon retreated to the hilltop capital, but a house was built at Filwoha, and the emperor and his entourage returned to the site the empress would christen Addis Ababa – New Flower – after the rains of 1887.

Although posterity has settled on 1887 as the year in which Addis Ababa became the capital if not of Ethiopia then of its future emperor, the shift to Filwoha was more gradual. Most of Menelik's correspondence prior to 1891 was despatched from Entoto, and it was 1889, months before his formal coronation as emperor, when he set about building a proper palace in the valley. Outsiders seem to have regarded the move from Entoto as folly. A French visitor in 1887 described the suggestion this site might one day house a great city as 'fantasy'. A decade later, European visitors felt the growing lack of firewood – now transported 20km from Menegasha – would force the new flower to die before reaching full bloom. Indeed, Menelik made tentative plans to relocate his capital some 50km west to a forested site he christened Addis Alem – New World – and have a palace constructed there. Bizarrely, it was a stand of eucalyptus trees planted by a foreign resident in 1894 that would save Addis Ababa. Spurred by his Swiss adviser Alfred Ilg, Menelik II noticed how rapidly these trees grew, and instead of shifting the capital he decided to import vast quantities of eucalyptus seedlings. The residents of the nascent city were initially unimpressed, above all by the smell of the exotic trees, but their phenomenal growth rate soon swept such delicacies aside.

The Addis Ababa of Menelik's time bore scant resemblance to the city it has become. The palace was impressive and well organised: a $3km^2$ compound that enclosed 50 buildings, employed and housed some 8,000 people, and – courtesy of Ilg's engineering prowess – had piped water by 1894 and electricity by 1905. As early as 1894, Menelik II and Ilg were discussing plans to construct a railway to the French port of Djibouti. By 1897, the Saturday market – situated on the site of an older Oromo market not far from the modern Piazza below the recently completed Church of St George – attracted up to 50,000 people from the surrounding countryside.

For all that, Menelik's capital was essentially a compacted rural sprawl. Few modern buildings existed outside of the royal compound, and the population, according to one French visitor, stood at a mere 100,000 settled over an area of about 55km^2! The account of Herbert Vivian, who arrived in the Ethiopian capital in 1900, is typical:

> I happened to turn around and ask one of my men, 'When on earth are we ever going to reach Addis Ababa?'
> 'But sah'b, here it is.'
> 'Where?'
> 'Here, we have already arrived.'
> I looked around incredulously, and saw nothing but a few summer huts and an occasional white tent, all very far from each other, scattered over a rough hilly basin at the foot of steep hills. I would scarcely believe that I was approaching a village. That this could be the capital of a great empire, the residence of the King of Kings, seemed monstrous and out of the question. 'Then, pray, where is Menelik's palace?' I asked with a sneer. The men pointed to the horizon, and I could just make out what seemed to be a fairly large homestead with a number of trees and huts crouching on the top of a hill.
> The capital is a camp rather than a town … To appreciate Addis Ababa it is necessary to realise that this strange capital covers some 50 square miles, and contains a very large population, which has never been counted. Streets there are none, and to go from one point of the town to the other you must simply bestride your mule and prepare to ride across country. Three quarters of an hour at least are necessary for a pilgrimage from the British Agency to the Palace, and as much again to the market. On either of these journeys you must cross three or four ravines with stony, precipitous banks and a torrent-bed full of slippery boulders.

Fifteen years later Menelik II was dead, but his capital had become, in the words of one contemporary visitor, a 'mushroom city'. Another 15 years on, Haile Selassie was enthroned as emperor, and Addis Ababa entered the modern era as the most populous settlement in Africa between Cairo and Johannesburg – some maintain it still is.

And yet the city's rustic roots are evident to any visitor. In 1969, a Ministry of Information handbook to Ethiopia described the capital as a surprising mixture of:

> the Near East, the Mediterranean and the Wild West. Donkeys jostle with diplomatic Cadillacs; camels loaded with charcoal plod up the hills behind 14-ton Italian diesel lorries; dignified country gentlemen in jodhpurs, topi and fly whisk have to stand on traffic crossings waiting for buses loaded with schoolchildren to pass. Young Ethiopian executives dash from meeting to meeting in cars against a backdrop of modern office blocks and corrugated iron roof huts. Shop girls wear national costume and out of small cafés comes the smell of frankincense and the twang of the masenko, one of Ethiopia's most ancient instruments.

True, Cadillacs and jodhpurs may have gone the way of Rubik's cube and bell-bottoms, and Addis Ababa's post-war office blocks aren't quite the gleaming icons of modernist architecture they might have been a few years after they were built. But, otherwise, it sounds an awful lot like Addis Ababa today.

on Churchill Avenue opposite the post office. If you spend only a day or two in Addis Ababa, familiarising yourself with this network may not be worth the effort, given that taxis are relatively cheap, but it's easy enough to figure out if you have the time.

One of the most useful **minibus routes** to travellers, described using landmarks favoured by conductors, runs between Bole Airport and the Piazza via Olympia, Meskel Square, the Ambassador Theatre and the post office. Other significant routes emanating from the Piazza run to the Mercato and the Autobus Terra, to Mexico Square via the post office and Ras Hotel, and to Arat Kilo (where you can

CATCHING MINIBUSES *Frank Rispin*

Minibuses follow fixed routes along most major roads. They all have a conductor who opens the side door, collects fares and shouts out the name of the destinations. They will stop anywhere to pick you up. If the conductor asks '*Yet?*' he wants to know where you are going; reply 'Piazza', etc. If you want to get off before a major destination, say '*Woraj*' when you are there. If the conductor asks '*Chaf woraj alla?*', it means 'Does anyone want next stop?' Most locals riding minibuses will have some English, so as soon as you are on, ask your neighbour if it is definitely going to your destination.

After getting on, you know when it is time to pay, as the conductor will politely point his hand in your direction – or if you are in the front seat, tap on your shoulder. In early 2012 fares were birr 1.35/2.70/3.80/4.40, depending on the distance travelled, but they tend to increase regularly with fuel prices. Trips to distant suburbs, eg: Kaliti, may cost birr 5–6. Have plenty of birr 1 notes.

Minibuses heading into the city centre will almost always be going to one or more of the four major hubs which stand at the corners of the central Addis area – Arat Kilo in the northeast, the Piazza in the northwest, Mexico Square in the southwest and Stadium/Lagar for the southeast. (In-bound line minibuses may pass through Meskel Square but are not allowed to stop there.) Most hotels are on or near a main road with minibuses running into one of these city centre points. Each of these four hubs has several departure points for outgoing minibuses and you may need to ask for help, or look at the maps here to find the right one. If you are aiming for the National or Ethnographic museums, you must get to Arat Kilo, then change to a northbound Siddist Kilo minibus, or walk! If your hotel is on or near Bole Road you need a 'Bole' minibus on the way back; if on Haile Gebrselassie you need a 'Megenagna' taxi from Stadium/Lagar or from Arat Kilo a 'Kasainches, Megenagna' minibus.

A handful of the city's 10,000 minibus operators are crooks who may try to distract you in order to pick your pocket. To avoid this happening, follow these rules:

1 If a minibus stops to ask where you're heading, ignore it.
2 If you are on your own, only get on a minibus where other people are getting on.
3 Once on a minibus, if you are asked to move from the front to the back row, or from an aisle to a window seat, refuse or get off.
4 If you are asked to open a window, be aware it might be a ruse allowing someone to pick your pocket or bag while you are wrestling with the stuck window.

change minibus for Siddist Kilo or for Urael Junction on Haile Gebrselassie Road) via Adwa Avenue.

There are also minibuses between Bole Road and Mercato via Olympia, Meskel Square and Mexico Square; Ras Mekonnen Avenue opposite the stadium and Arat Kilo via Meskel Square and the Hilton Hotel; Ras Mekonnen Avenue and Saris (on the Debre Zeyit road); Ras Mekonnen Road and Adwa Square (Megananya) via Haile Gebrselassie Road; and Arat Kilo and Siddist Kilo. People hop on and off minibuses the whole time; you'll rarely wait more than five minutes for a ride along any of these routes.

A recent change has been the introduction of mid-sized cream-and-green minibuses commonly known as *higers*. These have about 25 seats and behave much the same as minibus line taxis, except they do not stop everywhere and anywhere! Most have two touts collecting the fares and shouting out their destination. Fares will be a little less than minibus taxis and more likely to be in round figures of, eg: exactly birr 1, 2 or 3.

Bright yellow-and-red Anbessa (Lion) **buses** also trundle around Addis. They are even cheaper than minibuses, but slower, less frequent and often overcrowded. Buses also have a bad reputation for pickpockets and snatch thieves. You are strongly advised against using them.

Private **taxis**, usually blue Ladas, can be found at ranks in front of all the main government hotels, as well as at the airport, on Ras Mekonnen Avenue in front of the stadium and at De Gaulle Square on the Piazza. Taxis are very inexpensive by international standards, even at the inflated rates generally asked of foreigners, and are even cheaper if you are prepared to bargain.

TOURIST INFORMATION

The **Ethiopian Tourist Commission (ETC)** [137 F3] headquarters on Meskel Square (\ *011 551 7470*) sporadically stocks free booklets on Lalibela, Simien and Bale national parks, as well as pamphlets on other parts of the country. The staff at the **National Museum** [162 C5] (\ *011 551 2310 or 618 4290 (airport)*) are a good source of practical information relating to obscure historical and archaeological sites.

Several **tour operators and booking agencies** are based in Addis Ababa. For details see *Chapter 3*, page 77.

WHERE TO STAY

One thing you don't need to worry about is finding a hotel room in Addis Ababa. In recent years there has been a building boom, particularly at the highest level. Thus, while the world-class Addis Ababa Sheraton still tops the list in terms of sheer magnitude and price, there are now some serious contenders providing high-quality accommodations.

Perhaps 100 hotels fall between the moderate and luxury brackets, offering accommodation adequate to most tourists at prices ranging from US$30 to US$200. Lower on the comfort rung is a good choice of decent budget hotels falling in the US$12–30 range, while shoestring hotels under US$12 that still meet backpacker standards are becoming increasingly rare. The following listings are as exhaustive as time, space and common sense allow (most readers will, after all, stay in only one or at most two hotels in the capital), but there are doubtless further gems awaiting discovery.

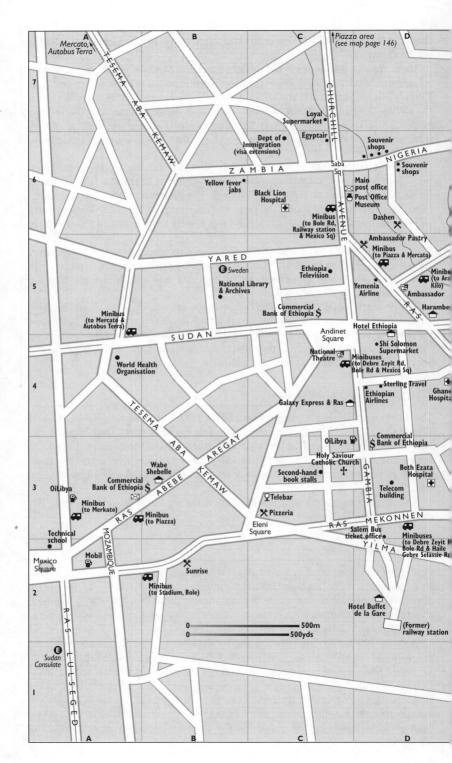

F *Siddist, Arat Kilo*

G

GIBBE/
OLD PALACE

H

7

Minibus
(to Arat Kilo)

Kidus Gebriel †

WENDMENEN

Kechene

NIGER ST

ZEWDITU

Sheraton

6

Ethiopia
Mapping
Authority

Shemuna Pub

TAITU

St George's
Art Gallery

Mosque

MENELIK II

MENELIK II

N

Bradt

Hilton

5

Filwoha

YOHANNIS

Fin Fin

Kasainches

Serbia

TITO STREET

Radisson Blu

otal

Cottage

National
Palace

0   500m
0   500yds

4

† 7th Day Adventist church

DESTA

December 19

Poly Clinic

Yeshi Coffee

Bank of
byssinia

Gishen 24hr
pharmacy

Africa Hall

Ireland

OiLibya

National Tourist
Organisation

Ghion

Stadium

DAMTEW

Bantyiketu

Finfine
Bridge

3

China Bar

Minibus
(to Piazza
& Mercato)

National

OiLibya

Minibus
(to Mexico Sq
& Mercato)

Lalibela

Ethiopia Tourist
Commission

Total

Square
Garden

Bekele Mola
booking office

Kidus Istifanos

Megananya,
Kasainches,
Debre Birhan

Meskel
Square

Red Terror
Martyr's Memorial
Museum

Gulf Air

Minibus
(to Piazza, Mercato
& Post office)

JOMO KENYATTA STREET

Carnivore Addis

2

BRU)

DEMISE

Japan

Joseph

Linda's at
Juventus

Addis Ababa
Museum

Greek Club

Minibus
(to Piazza, Mercato
& Mexico Sq)

Lion's Den

Oromia
State Council

DEBRE ZEYIT (RAS

Exhibition
Centre

BOLE

Zebra
Grill

1

Memos ☆

Dawit Music Shop

*Bishoftu, Adama,
Harar, Dire Dawa,
Assaita, Shashamene,
Arba Minch, Goba*

Dembel Centre Mall
(NIB Bank)

E

F

G

H

Bole Airport

INTERNATIONAL HOTELS (US$200+)

⌂ **Addis Ababa Sheraton** [137 F6] (293 rooms) Taitu St; ☎011 517 1717; e reservationsaddisababa@luxurycollection. com. The top hotel in Addis Ababa is the plush & architecturally inspired Sheraton, which has been justifiably praised as one of the finest city hotels anywhere in Africa. The feeling upon entering the lavish reception area is rather like stepping out of downtown Addis Ababa into a European hotel. It has several excellent restaurants, ranging from the poolside Breezes Restaurant (fantastic light show at the fountain in the evening) to the wonderful but pricey east Indian Shaheen Restaurant. There is a nice piano bar near the entrance, a high-priced nightclub, some shops & a bank. Rooms & service are immaculate. *US$650/732 club/ executive sgl occupancy, US$713/794 dbl occupancy; US$1,375/1,550/9,325 classic suite/junior suite/ executive suite.*

⌂ **Addis Ababa Hilton** [137 H5/148 B7] (400 rooms) Close to Africa Hall; ☎011 517 0000; e hilton.addis@ethionet.et. At present, the other main international hotel is the Hilton, which lies in 15 acres of landscaped grounds. Built in 1968, it is beginning to show its age, & it gets mixed reviews from readers. Still, it has all the amenities you would expect, including full business services, closed-circuit TV, a thermal swimming pool, tennis courts, jacuzzi, sauna, gym & several highly rated restaurants. *US$314/435 standard/executive, US$430/580/830 duplex/corner suite/President's Suite.*

⌂ **Radisson Blu** [137 H4] (220 rooms) Tito St; ☎011 515 7600; e info.addisababa@radissonblu. com; www.radissonblu.com. This likely rival to the Sheraton and Hilton is due to open in 2012; see the website for details.

LUXURY (approx US$86–200)

⌂ **Addis Regency** [off map 146 C7] (29 rooms) Off Benin St; ☎011 155 0000; m 091 314 1583; e info@addisregency.com; www.addisregency. com. Only 600m northeast of Menelik Sq, this relatively new hotel has rapidly established itself

---

THEFT AND SAFETY

A bit of a bad-news-and-good-news scenario, this! The bad news is that Addis Ababa is one of the worst cities in sub-Saharan Africa when it comes to casual theft and con tricks. The good news is that violent crime of the sort you get in Nairobi or Johannesburg is very unusual. People who have travelled in north Africa reckon that Addis Ababa is relatively sedate by comparison with large cities in Morocco and Egypt. Pickpockets are the major threat to travellers, and few people will spend long in Addis without having an attempt made on them.

Pickpockets and con artists like to prey on Ethiopian Airlines transit passengers and other newcomers, so they tend to congregate where there are plenty of tourists and in other crowded places. Traditional hotspots for con artists and pickpockets include the immediate vicinity of established hotels such as the Ghion and Ras, but these days you might encounter them anywhere in the city centre or along Bole Road. There are also plenty of less discriminating pickpockets around the railway station, any crowded minibus stand, the Mercato area and on the buses that operate within the city.

The modus operandi of Addis's pickpockets is a twin-pronged attack wherein the first person bumps into you, grabs your legs, clings on to your arm or distracts you in some other way while a second person fishes in your pocket. So, if somebody distracts you on one side, you should not respond directly but instead immediately check out what is happening on your other side. It's not a bad idea – as I said earlier – to stuff your trouser pocket with something useless such as a wad of tissue or an empty cigarette box, which serves nicely as a decoy. And note that the kids who sell cigarettes and chewing gum are not above playing the distracting role, so buy such odds and ends from shops. Bag slashing is also a bit of a problem, so if you're carrying anything important (passport or travellers'

as the number-one choice at this price level due to excellent value-for-money rooms & outstanding customer service. Breakfast, airport shuttle & Wi-Fi in rooms are included. *US$75 standard, US$85/95 deluxe with minibar/super deluxe.*

🏠 **Bole Ambassador Hotel** [149 F2] (52 rooms) Off Bole Rd; ☎011 618 7098/8281; e reservations@boleambassadorhotel.com; www. boleambassadorhotel.com. This is an all-suite set-up, & all rooms have DTSV, Wi-Fi & kitchen with stove. There is a restaurant/bar, & prices include airport shuttle, gym, & breakfast. *US$109/135 sgl/ twin, US$140 king.*

🏠 **Ceasar's Court** [149 F2] (16 rooms) Off Bole Rd; ☎011 618 9600; m 091 125 0637; e ceasars@ethionet.et. This boutique hotel near the airport offers luxury suites. Perfect for the business traveller, each room has its own internet-connected computer with 21-inch flat-panel monitor, printer & fax machine. It has an elegant Italian restaurant with a great menu. Discount for longer stays. *US$87/115 sgl/suite.*

🏠 **Desalegen Hotel** [148 D4] (60 rooms) Miky Leyland St; ☎011 662 4524; e desalegn2@ gmail.com. This has quality bathrooms, & its other facilities include a gym, sauna, steam rooms & a superb jacuzzi, but these are at extra cost. Wi-Fi, airport shuttle & breakfast are included. *US$87/90 standard/twin sgl occupancy, US$89/103 dbl occupancy; US$152 family suite.*

🏠 **Dreamliner Hotel** [148 B3] (96 rooms) Meskel Flower Rd; ☎011 467 4000; e dreamlinerhotel@ethionet.et; www. dreamlinerhotel.com. The 8th-floor gym & bar have superb views. Ask for a rear room as the front faces the road with nearby bars & restaurants. Airport shuttle & breakfast included. *US$101/152 sgl/dbl, US$284 suite.*

🏠 **Harmony Hotel** [149 E3] (63 rooms) Off Cameroon St, Bole Medhane Alem; ☎011 618 3100; e info@harmonyhotelethiopia.com; www. harmonyhotelethiopia.com. One of the best of the city's new batch of upmarket hotels, with an excellent restaurant. All rooms have a minibar,

cheques) keep it in your money-belt. Carrying a daypack in Addis definitely marks you out as a tourist.

The chancers who hang out near places like the ETC, Churchill Avenue and in front of the Ghion and Taitu hotels are relatively harmless; their basic agenda is to get you talking, sucker you into feeling sorry for them, then ask you for something. Typical approaches include a standard 'How do you like Ethiopia?' questioning, or claiming to be the waiter or gardener at your hotel, or asking 'Do you remember me?' Once hooked, you may be in for a straightforward request for money, or something more insidious. A common trick is to ask you for a drink at a private bar, then to present you with a huge bill (see box, *Friendly students*, page 153). Another ploy is to tell you about some one-off happening that you can only see today. Con artists in Addis excel when it comes to manipulating foreigners' emotions, and the longer you indulge them the more difficult they become to shake off. If you live in any large city, you know that when a stranger approaches you in the street they are almost always lost, irritatingly drunk, or a beggar with a sob story. Addis is no different – except that no resident of the city is going to stop to ask a tourist directions.

Even if the sort of minor hassles mentioned above are part and parcel of visiting Addis, it is a safe city in terms of violent crime, though it would be silly to carry large amounts of money at any time, or to disregard warnings from other sources about any particular trouble spots.

As for beggars, Tony Howard and Di Taylor offer the following sensible advice: 'Hope Enterprises opposite Haile Selassie Handicrafts on Churchill Avenue just below Tewodros Square sells meal tickets for the destitute: eight for a few birr. You may prefer to give these to beggars rather than money – they certainly seem happy to get them!'

satellite TV & safe. Prices include use of internet, gym, sauna & steam rooms as well as airport shuttle & buffet breakfast. *US$140/143 standard/queen sgl occupancy, US$170/173 dbl occupancy; US$187/260 king/suite sgl occupancy, US$217/290 dbl occupancy.*

🏠 **Jupiter International Bole** [149 F2] (42 rooms) Off Bole Rd; ☎ 011 661 6969; e info@jupiterinternationalhotel.com; www. jupiterinternatonalhotel.com. Less grandiose than the Jupiter Kazanchis, but still excellent. Airport shuttle, breakfast & Wi-Fi are included. *US$115/135 standard/deluxe sgl occupancy, US$135/155 dbl occupancy; US$150 twin; US$155 suite sgl occupancy, US$175 dbl occupancy.*

🏠 **Jupiter International Hotel Kazanchis** [148 C7] (102 rooms) Tito St; ☎ 011 552 7333; e jupiter@ethionet.et; www. jupiterinternationalhotel.com. Located in the central & recently redeveloped Kazanchis area, this new towering glass high-rise lacks the giant compound feel of the Hilton or Sheraton, yet offers superior rooms at a fraction of the price. Amenities include an elegant restaurant, lobby bar & lounge, business & fitness centres, Wi-Fi, & free airport shuttle. *US$100/135 standard/king sgl occupancy, US$115/155 dbl occupancy; US$150 twin; US$175–220 suites.*

🏠 **KZ Hotel** [149 E3] (32 rooms) Bole Rd; ☎ 011 662 1677/81; e kzhotel08@yahoo.com; www. kzfamilyhotel.com. Only 5mins from the airport, & opposite a 24/7 supermarket, this newish hotel has very helpful staff & a reputation for efficiency. All rooms have bath, fridge & safe. The bar, restaurant & reception are upstairs; & there is 24hr room service. Prices include breakfast, airport shuttle & Wi-Fi, & are seasonably negotiable. *US$80/80–95 standard/ dbl, US$90–100 suites.*

🏠 **Panorama Hotel** [149 H7] (65 rooms) Equatorial Guinea St (the eastern end of Haile Gebrselassie St); ☎ 011 661 6070; m 091 183 6692; e panoramahotel@ethionet.et; www. panoramaaddis.com. This fairly new hotel doesn't feel as quite as polished as some of the hotels above, but still offers expected upscale features such as in-room safe & minibar, Wi-Fi, business centre, free airport shuttle & breakfast. Some rooms face a courtyard, so make sure you get an outside view. *US$76/95 standard/twin, US$102 suite.*

🏠 **Yoly Addis Hotel** [149 E5] (19 rooms) Miky Leyland St; ☎ 011 663 2828; e contact@ yolyhotel.com; www.yolyhotel.com. With easy

access to local restaurants, this high-rise hotel has its own ATM, the largest nightclub in Addis now called H2O in the basement, the excellent **London Café** & **Don Vito Pizza** on the ground & 1st floor respectively, & the **Ker Fitness Centre**, one of the best workout facilities in the country, on the 2nd floor. Rooms are very luxurious, all have a bath & safe. Prices include airport shuttle, breakfast, Wi-Fi & gym. *US$80/96 standard/dbl; US$105/148 suite/ family suite.*

UPMARKET (US$56–85)

🏠 **Abbaba's Villa** [126 C6] (8 rooms) French Embassy area; m 0911 430 641; e eyogedlu@ yahoo.com; www.abbabasvilla.com. An amazing atmospheric 1930s Addis villa, set in a large wooded compound northeast of Siddist Kilo, is perfect for a taste of the old imperial Addis. There is wheelchair access throughout & a lovely tree-shaded rear patio. Owner Jerusalem will provide evening dinner on request. Prices which include breakfast & airport shuttle are seasonally negotiable. *US$50/75 sgl/dbl.*

🏠 **Axum Hotel** [149 E7] (63 rooms) Haile Gebrselassie St; ☎ 011 661 3916; e axum.d@ ethionet.et; www.axumhotels.com. Situated 3km east of Meskel Sq, close to several new malls with restaurants, this combines comfortable modern rooms with traditionally decorated common areas. Prices include airport shuttle, breakfast & Wi-Fi. *US$60/83 sgl/semi suite in older section, US$76/102–114 new wing sgl/suites.*

🏠 **Ghion Hotel** [137 F3/148 A6] (190 rooms) Ras Desta Damtew Av; ☎ 011 551 3222; e ghion@ethionet.et; www.ghionhotel.com.et. The established & very central Ghion Hotel has large, attractive, ambling gardens which serve as a huge oasis from the dust, noise, traffic & beggars outside. Offers some of the best birdwatching in the city & the chance to see colourful wedding parties. There is also a huge swimming pool in the complex, along with 4 restaurants, a nightclub & a casino. Other facilities include Wi-Fi, forex & ATM. The rather run-down rooms are indifferent value, & the service can be moderate. *US$79/93 sgl/dbl, US$117 suite.*

🏠 **Global Hotel** [148 A4] (52 rooms) Debre Zeyit Rd; ☎ 011 466 4766/3906; e globalhotel@ ethionet.et; www.globalhotel.com.et. This older hotel has very friendly staff & large comfortable en-suite rooms with TV, fridge & balcony. The ground floor has a restaurant & piano bar, whilst upstairs are a sauna & steam room. Breakfast, airport shuttle & Wi-Fi are included. *US$70/82 standard/studio, US$110 suite.*

🏠 **Hotel de Leopol International** [148 C6] (74 rooms) Off Haile Gebrselassie St; 011 550 7777; e hoteldeleopol@ethionet.et; www. hoteldeleopolint.com. All rooms are tastefully decorated & have in-room safe & fridge. Rates include breakfast & broadband internet. In addition to the classy **Robin Restaurant** & Duke Bar, the excellent **Khyber Indian Restaurant** is located on the 11th floor. *US$56/86 studio sgl/ standard sgl, US$96–120/150 dbl/suite.*

🏠 **Kings Hotel** [126 B4] (34 rooms) Roosevelt St; 011 371 1300; m 0911 699 499; e kingshotel@ethionet.et; www. kingshotelethiopia.com. The only hotel in these listings in the southwest suburbs is 1km south of Mexico Sq very close to Adams Pavilion Mall. Prices include breakfast & Wi-Fi. There is live music in the piano bar 18.30–21.00 daily. All rooms have deluxe king-size beds & flat-screen TVs. *US$50/62 dbl/suite.*

🏠 **Lions Den Hotel** [137 H1] (16 rooms) Olympia; 011 554 7734–5; e info@ thelionsdenhotel.com; www.thelionsdenhotel. com. All rooms at this popular spot are identical suites with a lounge & large kitchen. It has a central location in a side street near Olympiacos, the Greek club. Prices include Wi-Fi, airport shuttle & breakfast. *US$65/75 sgl/dbl occupancy.*

🏠 **Nigist Tower Apartments** [148 C6] (32 rooms) Guinea Conakry St; 011 550 9770; e info@nigisttowers.com; www.nigisttowers.com. The only furnished apartments in these listings are located in the rapidly developing area of new hotels & international organisations just behind UNECA in Kazanchis & close to the city centre. The Nigist does not have a restaurant but room service is provided from one in the same building. There are 3 apartment sizes: studio flat, 1-bedroom suite & 2-bedroom suite. Discounts available for UN & corporate customers. *US$70/90/120 studio/1 bed/2 bed.*

🏠 **Queen of Sheba Hotel** [148 D6] (40 rooms) Haile Gebrselassie Rd; 011 618 4000; e QueenShebaHotel@ethionet.et. This lacks slightly for atmosphere, but has a rare aura of efficiency & combines elements of traditional décor with upscale facilities. Breakfast & airport shuttle

are included, & some rooms have kitchenettes. *US$65/79 sgl/standard, US$89/99/120 suite/twin/ family suite.*

🏠 **Soramba Hotel** [146 B7] (60 rooms) Dej Beley Zeleke St; 011 156 5633; e sorambahotel@ ethionet.et; www.sorambahoteladdis.com. This new hotel is already popular with tour companies. It is only a 5min walk north of Menelik Sq & St George's Cathedral at the northern end of the Piazza. There is a pleasant piano bar on the 1st floor next to the restaurant. All rooms have web access & breakfast is included. *US$62/70 dbl/twin.*

🏠 **Weygoss Guest House** [148 C4] (31 rooms) Bole Rd; 011 551 2205; m 091 151 7487; e reservation@weygossguesthouse.com; www.weygossguesthouse.com. This popular place is behind the Mega Building, but due to construction in 2012, road access is from the rear only. Prices include airport shuttle, internet & breakfast but there is no restaurant so meals come from the excellent Makush next door. *US$45/65 standard/twin, US$65/110 junior/master suite.*

MODERATE (approx US$31–55)

🏠 **Addis Guest House** [149 F5] (20 rooms) Djibouti St; 011 618 9491; m 0911 511 569; e addis_guest_house@yahoo.com. Top ranked of the city's newer guesthouses, this place is renowned for Californian standards of customer service. All rooms have a mini kitchen with kettles & other cooking equipment available on request. The excellent ground-floor restaurant/bar provides 24hr room service. Edna Mall, supermarkets & restaurants are within walking distance. Breakfast, Wi-Fi, airport shuttle & laundry are all included. Prices vary with season & length of stay. *US$40–55 standard, US$55–70 twin, dbl, apt.*

🏠 **Altitude Guest House** [148 D2] (5 rooms) Off Bole Rd; m 0912 933 755; e info@altitudeguesthouse.com; www. altitudeguesthouse.com. A 300m walk off Bole Rd into the Ruanda area brings you to 'compound 3' where you will find this small friendly place with resident Ethiopian–Irish owners. Prices include breakfast but airport shuttle may be chargeable. Some smaller rooms not en suite. *US$22/36 backpackers/sgl, US$50–55 dbl, US$140 whole top floor (sleeps 7).*

🏠 **Biruk B and B** [149 E4] (7 rooms) Off Bole Rd; 0911 486 340; e bbbreakfast@gmail.com; www.birukbandb.com. In the very quiet, upmarket area between Bole Rd & Medhane Alem, this family-run guesthouse has mainly ground-floor rooms with a shaded front patio. Airport pick-up at US$6. *US$30/40 sgl/twin, US$50/60 dbl/family.*

🏠 **Damu Hotel** [148 C4] (20 rooms) Bole Rd; 📞011 550 9828/29/35; e damuhotel@ethionet.et; www.damuhotel.com. This is well designed so all rooms have good views & none faces onto the busy Bole Rd. It has a national food restaurant on the 8th floor whilst the main restaurant is on the 1st. Wi-Fi, airport shuttle & buffet breakfast included. *US$$45/65/85 sgl/twin/suite.*

🏠 **Mimosa Hotel** [149 E5] (16 rooms) Bole; 📞011 661 6690/92; m 0911 201 252; e mimosahotel@ethionet.et; www.mimosahotel. com. Found in a quiet part of Bole between Yonas Kitfo Beit Rd & Miky Leyland St, Mimosa is only a 5min walk to the Yoly-Atlas-area restaurants. It has its own ground-floor restaurant & bar area with a large-screen TV. The spacious rooms all have a large TV & mini fridge. Its resident owner-managers give more of a guesthouse atmosphere, but the attractive, well-equipped rooms are of excellent hotel quality so it is really good value for money. All prices include airport shuttle, breakfast & laundry. *US$30/50/60/70 sgl/dbl/twin/deluxe.*

🏠 **Plaza Hotel** [148 D6] (39 rooms) Haile Gebrselassie St; 📞011 661 2200; e plazahotel@ ethionet.net; www.plazaaddis.com. The Plaza was the first private hotel of any quality to be established in Ethiopia in the post-Derg era. It remains a useful first base for budget-conscious travellers seeking friendly, comfortable & reasonably central accommodation at a fair price. Facilities include 24hr bar & restaurant room service. *US$45/55 sgl/dbl.*

🏠 **Toronto Guest House** [148 D5] (12 rooms) Miky Leyland St; 📞011 662 2742; m 0911 208 568; e shewalia@hotmail.com. Found halfway up between Atlas & Lex Plaza, & behind Protection Hse, this friendly place has baths in all rooms except the 'compact'. With a pleasant ground-floor café, & a rooftop patio, there is internet, laundry, 24hr room service & dinner provided on request. Breakfast is included. *US$30/35 compact sgl/ standard dbl, US$50 suite.*

BUDGET (approx US$12–30)

🏠 **Ankober Guest House** [146 C3] (15 rooms) Muniyem, Piazza; 📞011 111 2350; e ankober.g.house@gmail.com. New on the Piazza scene, at the junction below the Baro, this has nice rooms either side of the ground-floor corridor. There is no catering but it is close to Wutma & Taitu hotels & many restaurants, & has a well equipped laundry room. *US$22/30 small dbl/twin, US$40 family room.*

🏠 **Buffet de la Gare** [136 D2] (7 rooms) 📞011 553 6286–7; m 091 238 7360. This pleasantly time-worn small hotel is tucked away in rather neglected green grounds in front of the central railway station. *US$12/15 sgl/dbl.*

🏠 **Central Showa Hotel** [149 G7] (53 rooms) Haile Gebrselassie Rd; 📞011 661 1454/663 2554; e centralh@ethionet.et. One of several decent hotels strung along this road, this popular but middle-aged high-rise is only 7mins' walk from an area of new malls & restaurants. Its en-suite rooms have fridge & TV. *US$21/25 dbl/twin with a fridge, phone, DSTV & hot shower; US$27/33 sgl/dbl.*

🏠 **Concorde Hotel** [148 A2] (23 rooms) Debre Zeyit Rd; 📞011 465 4959; e hotelconcorde@ ethionet.et. Situated about 2km south of Meskel Sq, the Concorde is best known perhaps for the **Dome Nightclub** in its basement, but it also now offers refurbished, value-for-money accommodation. There are new corridor carpets & rooms have been pleasantly updated with wooden floors, large-screen TVs, & fridges. An airport shuttle is available. Breakfast is included & the ground floor has the excellent **China Paradise Restaurant** & a piano bar with live music from 18.00 daily. *US$32/38 standard dbl/suite dbl; US$125 family villa at rear.*

🏠 **Debre Damo Hotel** [149 E7] (28 rooms) Haile Gebrselassie Rd; 📞011 661 2630/662 2921; e debredamo@ethionet.et. Its restaurant serves Indian, Ethiopian & Western dishes & it is right in the heart of a group of new malls & restaurants. A new high-rise addition is still currently under construction. *US$10 small non en-suite dbl, US$18/24 dbl/suite.*

🏠 **Dream Palace Guest House** [149 E7] (9 rooms) Off Haile Gebrselassie Rd; 📞011 663 5972; m 091 113 3232; e dreampalaceguesthouse@yahoo.com. Located in a side street just behind the Axum Hotel, this place has no restaurant but is good value & very close to the bunch of new malls, restaurants & supermarkets at the top of Haya Hulet. Free tea & coffee always available in the lounge. *US$12/27 small dbl/big dbl, US$45 family.*

🏠 **Family B&B** [148 C2] (11 rooms) Ethio Chinese Av; ☎ 011 850 5276/552 8413; e familybedandbreakfast@gmail.com. This guesthouse is in Bole opposite the Ibex Hotel, & immediately adjacent to their restaurant. Rooms are bright & colourful with some non en-suite rooms at budget prices. There is a guest lounge with internet, a kitchen & laundry facilities. Rooms can be booked on www.hostelworld.com or www.hostelbookers.com. Prices vary with length of stay & season. *US$22–28 smaller non en suite, US$45–55 en-suite dbl, twin.*

🏠 **Holiday Hotel** [149 E7] (25 rooms) Haile Gebrselassie Rd; ☎ 011 661 2081; e holidayhotel@ethionet.et. Currently under expansion. This stalwart favourite is 2km from Meskel Sq, very near to new malls with restaurants, & has clean compact en-suite rooms. A ground-floor restaurant with helpful friendly staff serves good local food. *US$15/18 sgl/twin, US$19/25 dbl/family.*

🏠 **Itegue Taitu Hotel** [146 D3] (73 rooms) Off Dej Jote St, Piazza; ☎ 011 156 0787; e reservations@taituhotel.com; www.taituhotel.com. The hub of backpacker activity in Addis Ababa this is also the city's oldest hotel, & was constructed for Empress Taitu (wife of Menelik II) in 1907 to a design by the locally celebrated Armenian architect Minas Kherbekian. The Taitu retains much of its original character, with an exterior instantly recognisable from a photograph taken in 1909 & a spacious interior of high ceilings, creaky wooden floors & period furnishing. The restaurant, which serves Ethiopian cuisine in traditional décor, is recommended. Within the grounds are an ATM, a bank, a jazz café, several tour companies & the Sky Bus ticket office. Rooms are individually priced according to age, size, facilities & location. The rooms in the main building, though run-down, are steeped in period character & seem excellent value. The cheaper rooms in various annexes are also good value, though lacking in character. *US$9–11 with common showers, US$20–25 standard dbl, US$40–50 superior.*

🏠 **Ras Hotel** [136 C4] (60 rooms) Gambia St; ☎ 011 551 7060; e rashotel@ethionet.et; www.rashotels.com. With a superb central location, & street-side patio bar for watching the world go by, this now has completely renovated rooms with wooden floors & excellent bathrooms. You can even rent the Mandela Suite, where the great

man stayed in the '60s, complete with jacuzzi. New gym, sauna & steam room are about to open. It has 2 restaurants, an ATM & even a post box! Prices include buffet breakfast & airport shuttle on request, but will increase soon. *US$23–26 standard, US$100 Mandela Suite.*

🏠 **Rita Guest House** [148 C5] (11 rooms) Olympia; ☎ 011 553 0979; e pen@ethionet.et; www.ritaguesthouse.com. Rooms are all on the ground floor round a pleasant courtyard. There is no restaurant but the free breakfast is served in your room, & internet is available in reception. All rooms are en suite & prices seasonable. *US$20/23/35 small sgl/larger sgl/dbl or twin.*

🏠 **Yonnas Hotel** [148 F7] (28 rooms) Haile Gebrselassie Rd; ☎ 011 663 3988; e yonnashot@ethionet.et. 3km from Meskel Sq & located near the Central Shoa, this has a pleasant ground-floor restaurant & bar. Rooms are all en suite & very acceptable at these prices. *US$14/18 sgl/dbl, US$20 suite.*

🏠 **Z Guest House** [162 A6] (4 rooms) Welete Yohannes St; ☎ 011 155 9860; m 0911 123 903; e stay@zguesthouse.com; www.zguesthouse.com. Within walking distance of the major museums this has a lovely garden. Prices include breakfast & airport shuttle, & internet is available. Standard rooms have a double bed, TV & minibar, whilst suites sleep up to 4 & have a large lounge & kitchenette. *US$29.95/59.95 standard/suite.*

SHOESTRING (under US$12)

🏠 **Almaz Pension** [148 C5] (21 rooms) Off Democratic Republic of Congo Rd; m 0911 195 473; e almaztadessepension@yahoo.com; www.almaztadesse-guesthouse.com. This centrally located budget option has a friendly reception office with good English. All rooms have a queen-size bed & 15 are en suite. Take the side road by the Wanza Hotel. Almaz is behind a yellow gate. *US$11/15 non en suite/standard.*

🏠 **Baro Hotel** [146 C3] (26 rooms) Muniyem St; ☎ 011 157 4157/155 9846 e baro@ethionet.et. This is a safe, friendly & affordable place to adjust to Addis Ababa & well equipped to deal with such practicalities as changing money, phone calls, internet access, safe luggage storage & 4x4 rental. Some rooms are much larger & better than others, so ask to see one first. *US$8–11/10–15 sgl/dbl.*

🏠 **Mr Martin's Cozy Place** [148 D5] (10 rooms) ☎ 011 663 2611; e coze376@yahoo.com;

www.cozyplaceaddis.com. Set back from the road across Miky Leyland St from the Atlas Hotel, this is the only place in the area in this price range. It is near several good restaurants. All rooms share 3 clean common bathrooms. US$11/12 sgl/dbl, US$14–18 family.

⌂ **National Hotel** [146 C3] (20 rooms) Not to be confused with the hotel of the same name below Africa Hall, this is the pick of the cluster of cheaper hotels that lie along the short road in Piazza between the Taitu Hotel & De Gaulle Sq. If you really want a cheapo, this is it. Rooms are small dark singles, using good common showers & the staff are very helpful. There is no email or working phone, so just turn up. US$6.

⌂ **Wanza Hotel** [148 C5] (16 rooms) Democratic Republic of Congo St; ☏ 011 515 6177. The clean tiled rooms are all en suite with hot water & have a proper double bed. The restaurant serves good local dishes at fair prices. US$8.

⌂ **Wutma Hotel** [146 C3] (15 rooms) Muniyem St; ☏ 011 156 2878; m 093 001 3114; e wutmahotel@yahoo.com. Located across the street from the Baro, this has a pleasant ground-floor restaurant & internet is available. All rooms are en suite with a large bed. Breakfast not included. US$9.

✗ WHERE TO EAT AND DRINK

If finding a room in Addis is straightforward, then locating a decent meal is even easier. Top-quality restaurants specialising in most recognised international cuisines are to be found dotted around the city, with main courses typically costing US$3–7 plus VAT and usually service charge. Most hotels have reasonable restaurants serving inexpensive Western dishes such as roast meat and steak, and there are also many budget restaurants specialising in Italian-influenced dishes or else local cuisine. For snacks, there are hundreds of cake, coffee and pastry shops, many of which serve savoury mini pizzas and spicy hamburgers in addition to the usual cakes and biscuits. Amongst the best known are the upmarket 'Starbucks imitating' Kaldis chain, the Parisienne chain (no service charge) and the Yeshi Coffee group with staff in traditional dress. Some of these are marked on the maps but in Addis you are never very far from one.

Given that few restaurants in Addis Ababa are seriously expensive, and that it is often convenient to eat near your hotel or in a part of town you're visiting for another reason, I've grouped restaurants by area rather than price or the type of cuisine. The collection of restaurants in the Sheraton and Hilton hotels is world class, but a lot pricier than other restaurants.

KAZANCHIS CITY CENTRE/PIAZZA

✗ **Addis Ababa Restaurant** [off 146 C7] Off Benin St; ☏ 011 656 6157; ☉ 12.00–22.00 daily. Situated in a large circular *tukul* building with very traditional décor, this old favourite offers possibly the best ambience in Addis for national food. Customers sit on *jimma* stools at *mesobs* (basketware tables) to enjoy the best of Ethiopian cuisine & good *tej* at very reasonable prices. US$3–5; *tej* US$4 a bottle.

✗ **Alliance Francaise-La Petite France** [off 146 A3] Umma Semetar St; ☏ 011 554 9044; m 0911 805 656; ☉ 09.00–22.00 Mon–Sat. This excellent French-style restaurant, complete with menu de jour is a great place to stop if you are visiting Mercato. It is southwest of Piazza behind the Ries car dealership. Now under new independent management, with a new name, it has a nice shaded decking area outside for lunchtime. US$3–5.

✗ **Buffet de la Gare** [136 D2] Railway Station Sq (Lagar); ☏ 011 553 6286; ☉ 12.00–15.00 & 18.00–24.00 daily. This place is very popular at lunchtimes for its quality Italian cuisine, but its pleasant gardens have been neglected. US$3–6.

✗ **Castelli's** [146 C3] Gandhi Rd; ☏ 011 157 1757/156 3580; ☉ 12.00–14.30 & 19.00–22.00 Mon–Sat. Established around 1942 & still run by the same Italian family, Castelli's is without a doubt Addis's most famous restaurant; so for an evening, booking is advisable. Dining is in various different-sized rooms where you can sometimes spot celebrities if the likes of Bob Geldof or Brad Pitt are in town. Seafood is flown in from Djibouti, at a price, & the renowned antipasti are by self-service in the foyer. It is found just to the south of the Piazza one-way system. *US$5–12*.

X **China Bar** [137 F3] Ras Desta Damtew Rd; \011 551 3772; ⊕ 11.30–15.00 & 18.00–22.30 Mon–Sat, 11.30–22.20 Sun. Conveniently located just 30m from the Ghion Hotel main gate; service is good & portions are generous, but the chicken, beef & vegetable dishes may be better than the pork. *US$4–5*.

X **The Cottage Restaurant and Pub** [137 E4] Ras Desta Damtew Rd; \011 551 6359/554 1532–3; ⊕ 12.00–14.30 & 17.30–23.00 daily. The emphasis is on European dishes as well as normal Addis favourites; try the delicious special fish. There is a large car park. *US$4–6*.

X **Dashen** [136 D6] Off Nigeria St; \011 552 9746; ⊕ 10.00–22.00 Mon & Tue, 10.00–24.00 Wed, 10.00–late Thu–Sun; live music & dance Wed–Sat. One of the best places for lunchtime local cuisine, it is found in a small street behind the main post office. Wrap up for evenings. *US$2–5*.

X **Fin Fin** [137 E5] Yohanis St; \011 551 4711; ⊕ 07.00–midnight daily. This old atmospheric hotel is a great place for local food. Eat upstairs in the evening or in the rear gardens at lunchtime. If you are driving beware of the powerful *tej*. *US$3–5*.

X **Itegue Taitu Hotel** [146 D3] Off Dej Jote St, Piazza; \011 156 0787; ⊕ 07.00–22.00 daily. Vegan buffet lunch. (See also hotels section.) *US$3–5*.

X **Limetree Kasa** [136 C6] Guinea Conakry St; ⊕ 06.00–22.00 daily. This 2nd Limetree is in the same building as Liquid Lounge, just south of the Intercontinental Hotel. Cuisine details, see Bole – Limetree. *US$2–6*.

X **Linda's at Juventus Italian Club** [137 G2] Off Meskel Sq; m 0911 219 729; ⊕ 12.00–14.30 & 19.00–21.30 Tue–Sat. Juventus is behind the huge billboards at Meskel Sq, so for pedestrian access, go up the central steps through the terracing, & it is immediately on your left. Linda's is a first-class restaurant within the buzzing centre of the Italian community. It is advisable to book on Fri nights. *US$4–9*.

X **Liquid Lounge** [148 C6] Guinea Conakry St; m 0913 080 104; ⊕ 09.00–23.00 daily. This has a Japanese flavour & specialises in *teppanyaki* grills & pizzas. Drinks are a bit pricey for Addis but main meals reasonable. *US$3–8*.

X **Serenade** [162 B4] Off Haile Selassie St; m 0911 200 072; ⊕ 12.00–15.00 & 18.00–22.00 Tue–Sat, 15.00–18.00 Thu–Sat high tea, 10.30–12.30 Sun brunch. This features Mediterranean cuisine & in 2012 had recently reopened with art displays as an added attraction. For easiest pedestrian access go up steps east of Ras Makonnen Bridge; vehicles best via Sahle Selassie St. *US$6–15*.

X **Square Garden** [137 G3] Meskel Sq, north side; ⊕ 09.00–21.00 daily. Handy for lunch or pizzas if you can ignore the 7 lanes of eastbound traffic a few metres away. *US$2–4*.

BOLE/MEDHANE ALEM/WOLLO SEFER

X **Aladdin** [149 E3] Zimbabwe St; \011 861 7731/661 4109; ⊕ 12.00–15.00 & 19.00–22.30 Mon–Sat; e t_kevorkian@hotmail.com. This is the top place in town for Armenian specialities, & is best known for its mezes. *Mezes US$3, kebabs US$7*.

X **Al Yemen Al Saed** [148 C3] Ethio China St; m 0913 505 058; ⊕ 07.00–midnight daily. This friendly, Yemeni-style eatery does fabulous chicken *mendi* with rice. It is also a great place for a breakfast of scrambled eggs & freshly cooked *khoubz* bread. *US$4–7*.

X **Antica** [148 D3] Just off EU Rd; \011 634 841/661 5815; ⊕ 12.00–23.00 daily; www.anticaddis.com. Some of the best pizzas in Addis, in 15 varieties, are to be found here. Downstairs is the Vuvuzela Nightclub should you wish to make a long evening of it! *US$3–6*.

X **Ceasar's Court** [149 F2] Bole Rd; \011 618 9600; m 0911 250 637; ⊕ 07.00–23.00 daily. This small but elegant Italian restaurant is on the ground floor of the hotel of the same name. Turn off Bole Rd with DH Geda Tower on your right, & then take the first left. *US$3–6*.

X **Diplomat** [149 E2] Bole Rd; \011 618 4363; m 0920 959 697; ⊕ 11.30–15.00 & 17.30–23.30 daily. This upmarket establishment brings in chefs from around the world for month-long menus from different nations, so it is worth phoning to find out what month it is! *US$5–10*.

X **Family Restaurant** [148 C2] Ethio China Rd; \011 371 3238; e familyrestaurant@gmail.com; ⊕ 07.00–22.00 daily. Opposite Ibex Hotel, this has one of the most interesting menus in Addis, with great ice creams. *US$2–6*.

X **Four Seasons** [149 E5] Johanes Kitfo Beit Rd; \011 618 0285; ⊕ 12.00–15.00 & 18.00–22.30

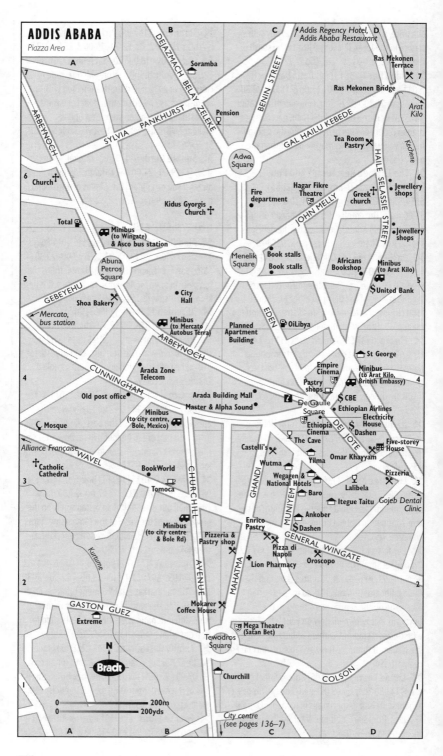

ADDIS ABABA
Piazza Area

A   B   C   D

Addis Regency Hotel,
Addis Ababa Restaurant

Soramba

Ras Mekonen
Terrace

7

DEJAZMACH BELAY ZELEKE

BENIN STREET

Ras Mekonen Bridge

Arat
Kilo

Pension

SYLVIA PANKHURST

GAL HAILU KEBEDE

Kechene

Tea Room
Pastry

Adwa
Square

Church †

6

Fire
department

Hagar Fikre
Theatre

Greek
church †

Jewellery
shops

HAILE SELASSIE STREET

JOHN MELLY

Kidus Gyorgis
Church †

Jewellery
shops

ARBEYNOCH

Total

Minibus
(to Wingate)
& Asco bus station

Menelik
Square

Book stalls

Book stalls

Africans
Bookshop

Minibus
(to Arat Kilo)

5

Abuna
Petros Square

United Bank

GEBEYEHU

Shoa Bakery

City
Hall

St George

Mercato,
bus station

Minibus
(to Mercato
Autobus Terra)

ARBEYNOCH

Planned
Apartment
Building

EDEN

OiLibya

Empire
Cinema

Minibus
(to Arat Kilo,
British Embassy)

4

CUNNINGHAM

Arada Zone
Telecom

Pastry
shops

CBE

Old post office

Arada Building Mall

Master & Alpha Sound

De Gaulle
Square

Ethiopian Airlines

Electricity
House

Mosque

Minibus
(to city centre,
Bole, Mexico)

Ethiopia
Cinema

Dashen

Five-storey
House

DEJOTE

Castelli's

The Cave

Omar Khayyam

Alliance Française

WAVEL

Wutma

Yilma

Pizzeria

3

Catholic
Cathedral

BookWorld

Wegagen &
National Hotels

GHANDI

Lalibela

MUNIYEM

Tomoca

Baro

Itegue Taitu

Gojeb Dental
Clinic

CHURCHILL

Ankober

Kurtume

Minibus
(to city centre
& Bole Rd)

Enrico
Pastry

Dashen

GENERAL WINGATE

Pizzeria &
Pastry shop

Pizza di
Napoli

Oroscopo

MAHATMA

2

Lion Pharmacy

GASTON GUEZ

AVENUE

Mokarer
Coffee House

Extreme

Mega Theatre
(Satan Bet)

N

Bradt

Tewodros
Square

Churchill

COLSON

1

0   200m
0   200yds

City centre
(see pages 136–7)

A   B   C   D

146

Mon–Sat, 18.00–22.30 Sun. This probably has the most authentic & upmarket Japanese menu in Addis. *Soups US$4–6, teppanyaki & terryaki US$7–13, sushi rolls US$8–11.*

✗ **Gati Thai** [149 E3] Bole Rd; ☎011 662 0853; m 0910 154 458; e saiyood_2520@hotmail.com; ⏱ 11.30–22.00 daily. Gati is in a villa on a side street behind KZ Hotel. It is very Thai & very good, serving specialist Thai soups, plus a normal Thai menu with red & green curries. *US$4–6.*

✗ **Greenview** [148 D4] EU Rd; ☎011 665 6347; e gvrestaurant@yahoo.com; ⏱ 12.00–22.00 daily. This pleasant first-floor restaurant is a reliable place for good pizzas. *US$3–6.*

✗ **Habesha Cultural Restaurant** [148 C4] Bole Rd; ☎011 551 8358; m 0912 339 984; e habesharesturant@yahoo.com; www. habesharestaurant.com; ⏱ 11.30–15.00 & 18.00–24.00 daily. Smaller & more intimate than the other cultural restaurants, it is also cheaper. Look for blue double gates across Bole Rd from a giant Coke bottle. *US$3–5.*

✗ **Habesha 2000 Cultural Restaurant** EU Rd; ☎011 618 2253/58; m 0911 635 296; e negasy_s@yahoo.com; ⏱ 09.00–24.00 daily. This has excellent music & dance. Go à la carte if you know your dishes, as the buffet is fine but costs more. *US$3–6, buffet US$8.*

✗ **Hebir Cultural Restaurant** [149 E3] Bole Rd; ☎011 662 0922; ⏱ 12.00–15.00 & 19.00–23.00 daily, but no dance show on Sun evenings. This very spacious cultural restaurant allows the dance group plenty of room to perform. *US$4–6.*

✗ **Han Kuk Korean Restaurant** [149 E5] Miky Leyland St; m 0910 568 860; ⏱ 08.00–22.00 daily. The city's newest Korean is at the Atlas junction. Its menu is also in Chinese & Japanese & is broad in tastes & prices. *US$4–16.*

✗ **La Mandoline** [149 F3] Off Cameroon St; ☎011 662 9482; m 0921 328 507; e LaMandoline@hotmail.fr; ⏱ 12.00–15.00 & 19.00–23.00 Tue–Sun. At this new French eatery most of the tables are outside on the wide pavement with quality shade for lunchtimes. *US$5–7.*

✗ **Limetree** [149 E2] Bole Rd; ⏱ 08.00–22.00 daily. This very popular place is perhaps more of a daytime snack location than an evening restaurant. *B/fasts US$2–3, snacks US$2–4, burgers US$3–4, desserts US$1–2.*

✗ **Makush** [148 C4] Bole Rd; ☎011 552 6848; ⏱ 11.30–23.30 daily. Upstairs in the Mega Building,

it is reached by walking through its own art gallery & offers good-quality Italian cuisine. *US$3–6.*

✗ **Pamukkale** EU Rd; m 0910 174 728; e sibiryalimemo@hotmail.com; ⏱ 12.00–22.00 daily. Offers various Turkish dishes & pizzas & unusually for Addis, menu prices are inclusive of VAT, & there is no service charge. *US$4–6.*

✗ **Yod Abyssinia Cultural Restaurant** [149 G3] Off Cameroon St; ☎011 661 2985; ⏱ 09.00–24.00 daily; e yod@ethionet.et; www.yodabyssinia.com. Currently this is the most popular of the city's traditional Ethiopian restaurants. Its daily music & ethnic dancing show starting around 19.45 is equally popular with locals & tour companies. The restaurant area is very large but it is still best to book for evenings if you want a good view. It has a handy location if you have a late flight on your last night in Addis! *Buffet US$8, à la carte US$4–7.*

✗ **Zebra Grill** [137 H1] Bole Rd; ☎011 554 5616; ⏱ 07.00–23.00 daily. There are superb views of the city centre from here as it is on the 9th floor of the Bedesta Building. It serves a normal Addis menu plus some Caribbean specialities. *US$3–6.*

HAILE GEBRSELASSIE STREET/HAYA HULET

✗ **Pizza Hut** [149 E7] Haile Gebrselassie St; m 0911 430 926/425 545; ⏱ 08.00–21.30 daily. It has a spacious 3rd-floor location in Lex Plaza Mall. *Soups US$1, pizzas in 3 sizes US$3–4.*

✗ **Sichuan** [148 D6] Haile Gebrselassie St; m 0911 603 926; ⏱ 12.00–15.00 & 18.30–22.00 daily. This excellent Chinese has great views of eastern Addis from the top floor of the Waf Building, just west of Lex Plaza Mall. *US$4–7.*

✗ **Zebra Grill** [149 F6] Djibouti St; ☎011 662 3630; ⏱ 07.00–23.00 daily. Found on the northern section of Haya Hulet a bit north of St Gabriel's Hospital, this was the original Zebra Grill (see Bole section for cuisine). *US$3–6.*

NORTHEAST

✗ **Armenian Club (aka Ararat)** [162 B5] Welete Yohannis St; ☎011 111 3572; ⏱ 12.00–14.00 & 18.00–22.00 daily. Most people buy a selection of mezes to share but lentil soup & good kebabs are also on the menu. It is best accessed in a car from Amist Kilo lights; go west, then fork right. *US$3–5.*

✗ **Face of Addis (aka Portuguese Restaurant)** [126 D5] Above Upper Megenagna

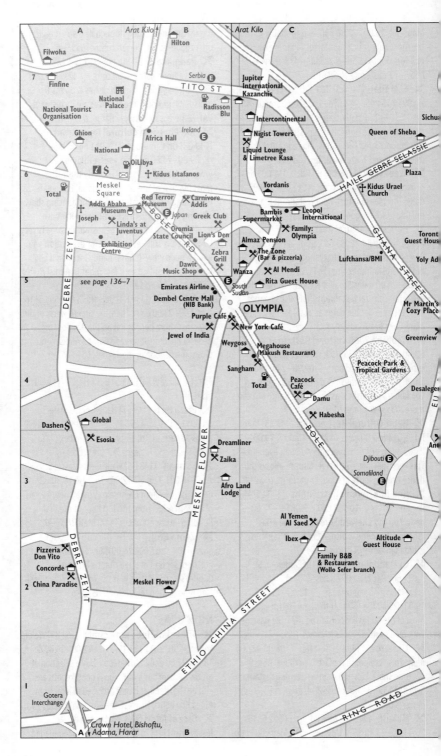

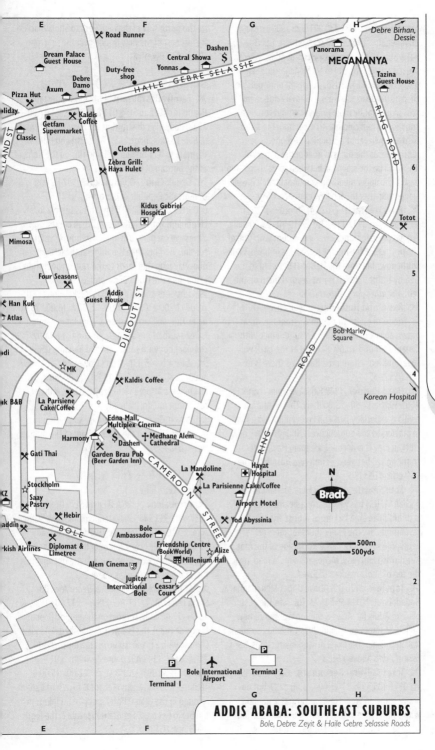

ADDIS ABABA: SOUTHEAST SUBURBS
Bole, Debre Zeyit & Haile Gebre Selassie Roads

Road Runner
Dream Palace Guest House
Dashen
Central Showa
Yonnas
Duty-free shop
Debre Damo
Axum
Pizza Hut
oliday
Classic
Getfam Supermarket
Kaldis Coffee
Clothes shops
Zebra Grill: Haya Hulet
Kidus Gebriel Hospital
Mimosa
Four Seasons
Han Kuk
Atlas
odi
Addis Guest House
MK
k B&B
La Parisiene Cake/Coffee
Kaldis Coffee
Edna Mall, Multiplex Cinema
Harmony
Dashen
Medhane Alem Cathedral
Gati Thai
Garden Brau Pub (Beer Garden Inn)
La Mandoline
Hayat Hospital
KZ
Stockholm
Saay Pastry
La Parisienne Cake/Coffee
Hebir
Airport Motel
addin
Yod Abyssinia
Bole
kish Airlines
Diplomat & Limetree
Bole Ambassador
Friendship Centre (BookWorld)
Alize
Millenium Hall
Alem Cinema
Jupiter International Bole
Ceasar's Court
Terminal I
Bole International Airport
Terminal 2

HAILE GEBRE SELASSIE
Panorama
MEGANANYA
Debre Birhan, Dessie
Tazina Guest House
RING ROAD
Totot
Bob Marley Square
Korean Hospital
DJIBOUTI ST
CAMEROON STREET
RING ROAD
BOLE
N
Bradt

0 ——— 500m
0 ——— 500yds

roundabout; m 0911 230 001/525 790; e bella@ethionet.et; ⏰ 16.00–23.00 Mon–Fri, 12.00–22.00 Sat & Sun. This has the best views in Addis; you can see right across the city to Mt Menegasha, 25km away. Go around 17.30 for a daylight drink outside, then go inside to eat. It has a normal Addis menu plus some slightly more pricey Portuguese items such as peri peri chicken. Access is from the same road as Topview but it is higher. Best photos at lunchtime, as the sun is in front of the camera at 17.30. Go up the steep hill between some shops 30m east of the upper Megenagna roundabout. It is well signposted after the Topview entrance. *US$4–12.*

✕ **Pizzeria Italia** [162 C4] Entoto Av; 011 123 2935; m 0912 139 810; ⏰ 10.30–23.00 daily. A good place for lunch after a museum visit. One of the best value-for-money pizza *beits* in town. Walk south downhill from the National Museum to the nearby traffic lights; it is just beyond them on the left. *Medium & large pizzas US$3–4.*

✕ **Ras Amba Hotel Bar** Queen Elizabeth St. The semi open-air bar on the roof has great views, so is a good place for a sundowner with canapés around 18.00. Parking at the back will save your legs climbing 2 floors, as there is no lift! *US$2–5.*

✕ **Road Runner** [149 F7] Haya Hulet; m 0911 750 909; ⏰ 11.00–23.00 daily. This restaurant in a villa is especially lively on Fri evenings with fires in braziers in the outdoor areas. It does a very nice chicken Kiev & is north of the main Haya Hulet traffic lights, between Demberwa Hospital & the VSO office. *US$3–5.*

✕ **Soul Seattle** [126 D5] Fikre Mariam Aba Techan St. This has very reasonable prices for food & drinks in an area lacking in tourist-friendly restaurants. Try the Philly cheeseburgers or vegetable soup. It is on the north side of the Arat Kilo, British Embassy, Megenagna main road, near the top of Shola Market. *US$2–4.*

✕ **Topview** [126 D5] Above Upper Megenagna Roundabout; 011 651 1573. This was the best place in Addis for views & photographs until new buildings somewhat spoilt this. It still has excellent Italian cuisine. (For exact driving instructions, see *Face of Addis* above.) *US$3–7.*

✕ **Totot Cultural Restaurant** Gerji [149 H5] m 0911 105 399; ⏰ 11.00–23.00 daily, but no dance show on Wed. This is a cultural restaurant with a difference in that the menu & the dancing reflect predominantly the Gurage ethnic group. It is

on the north side of the new Gerji to Shola Market Rd just east of the new bridge over the ring road. *US$3–7.*

OLYMPIA/MESKEL FLOWER ROAD

✕ **Family Restaurant** [148 C5] Democratic Republic of Congo St; 011 850 0279; ⏰ 07.00–22.00 daily. (For description see *Family Restaurant* in *Bole* section, page 145.) When driving from Olympia to Bambis you will find this on the right, at the bottom of the hill. *US$2–6.*

✕ **Greek Club – Olympiakos** [137 H2] Off Democratic Republic of Congo Rd; 011 553 0485; ⏰ 09.00–23.00 daily. This is set in a lovely compound with tennis & basketball courts, plus a massive car park. Driving north from Olympia towards Bambis, take the third on the left onto a one-way loop that leads to the club on your right just before the Lion's Den Hotel. *US$3–6.*

✕ **Jewel of India** [148 B5] Meskel Flower Rd; m 0911 200 230; ⏰ 11.00–15.00 & 18.00–23.00 daily. This well-established & popular restaurant is just south of the Olympia junction. It is fairly compact but with some off-road parking. *US$4–7.*

✕ **Zaika** [148 B3] Meskel Flower Rd; 011 467 4000; ⏰ 11.00–16.00 & 17.00–23.00 Mon–Sat. The newest & some would say the best Indian restaurant in Addis; already has a very good reputation. Some dishes are very spicy & service is excellent. It is on the ground floor of Dreamliner Hotel. *US$4–9.*

SOUTH/DEBRE ZEIT ROAD/ SOUTHWEST

✕ **Arcobaleno** [126 A3] Egypt St; 011 371 3257; m 0911 248 121; e lemlemkahessay@yahoo.com; ⏰ 10.00–24.00 daily. This would certainly rank very highly in any survey of Italian cuisine in Addis. From Mexico Sq go south & straight on under the Saar Beit interchange. *US$4–6.*

✕ **China Paradise** [148 A2] Debre Zeyit Rd/Sierra Leone St; 011 465 4959; ⏰ 12.00–15.00 & 18.00–22.00 daily. Located on the ground floor of Concorde Hotel, this is a well-established & popular Chinese with a piano bar across the foyer. *US$4–7.*

✕ **Esosia** [148 A3] Debre Zeyit Rd; 011 466 1821; m 0911 202 821; ⏰ 12.00–15.00 & 18.00–23.00 daily. This elegant & excellent Italian is found in the Global Hotel group of buildings in the Beklo Bet area. Service is first rate & the food really hot. *US$3–6.*

✖ Garden Paradise [126 B4] Saar Beit Sq, Adams Pavilion Mall; ☎ 011 372 0065; m 0911 825 882; www.gardenparadise.com; ⏰ 07.00–21.00 daily. This 3rd-floor restaurant has an American chef & a very wide menu including normal Addis favourites plus South American fried chicken, & west African pepper soup! *US$3–8.*

✖ Loti [126 A4] South Africa St; ☎ 011 372 9254; m 0911 216 140; ⏰ 10.00–23.00 daily, with Sun brunch. This very French-flavoured restaurant is now just south of Karl Sq (Saar Beit Tele roundabout). *US$4–10.*

✖ Samet [126 A4] South Africa St; ☎ 011 371 0317; m 0911 874 507; www.sametrestaurant.

com; ⏰ 11.00–15.00 & 17.30–22.00 daily. Found on the right-hand side, some 200m south of Loti, this is best known for its large tasty pizzas. *US$2–6.*

✖ Tivoli Pizza and Coffee Bar [126 A4] South Africa St; ☎ 011 320 3918; ⏰ 07.00–24.00 daily. This newish place could be described as a cross between a cake/coffee shop & a full restaurant. Just south of Samet, it has a US$1 kids' menu. *US$3–5.*

✖ Yod Abyssinia 2 Seychelles St; ☎ 011 372 0607/371 4171; ⏰ 09.00–24.00 daily. (See Yod under *Bole* for description, page 145.) This smaller branch of Yod is found just east of Karl Sq (Saar Beit Tele roundabout). *Buffet US$8, à la carte US$4–7.*

ENTERTAINMENT AND NIGHTLIFE

Addis is remarkably lively at night, with the emphasis on drinking draught beer till it dries up at around 22.00, then switching to the bottled stuff. A good way to start a night out is with a meal at one of several cultural restaurants that do traditional Ethiopian food accompanied by live music and dancing. If you and your stomach are very new to Addis, they will provide a less spicy alternative such as fish, rice and salad. In most cases, and contrary perhaps to expectations, such restaurants cater not to a primarily Western audience, but to locals out on the town for the night. In terms of quality of performance, costumes and variety, the pick at present is probably Yod Abyssinia at Bole Brass, though the Crown Hotel on Debre Zeyit Road is also recommended. With musical styles that range from Afar wailing to meaty contemporary Amharigna pop, and dancing that ranges from the Walaita hip-shake to the Amhara/Oromo shoulder-shudder, through the more gentle Tigrai small steps, and often climaxing in the fantastically energetic Gurage horseriding, this is a great opportunity to get to grips with the extraordinarily diverse thing that is Ethiopian music and dance. Other possibilities include the Habesha, Habesha 2000, Hebir and Totot restaurants – all covered in the *Where to eat and drink* section, pages 144–51.

YOHANNIS KITFO   *From a letter by Des Blonyal*

I became very partial to the Ethiopian *kitfo* dish (spiced raw minced beef) while I lived in Addis Ababa. Typically, it's served raw (*terea*) or partially cooked (*lublub*). I prefer it to be fully cooked (*yebesela*). The best kitfo house by far is Yohannis kitfo, located somewhere off Haile Gebrselassie Road (you'll have to take a taxi as it's difficult for the average tourist to find). The special kitfo dish comes with *gomen* (a type of cabbage, almost like spinach), *eib* (cottage cheese) and roasted *kocho* (bread-like rubbery stuff made from the stem of the *enset* or false banana tree). I recommend the special kitfo. There are also other good kitfo houses in town but this is the best and probably most expensive at birr 20 for the special kitfo. The butter used is of the special pure Gurage variety, not mixed with oil. If you don't ask for *yebesela kitfo*, you will more than likely get *terea* or *lublub kitfo*. Beware though, it can be very spicy – it's wise to order a couple of cold beers with it!

If you feel like moving on, the best downmarket option – especially if you are staying in the area anyway – is the row of bars below the Piazza around the Taitu and National hotels. There's a strong Tigraian element here, plenty of dancing – you'll be urged to join in and you'll make a lot of friends if you do – and a surprising amount of English is spoken. The activity seems to shuffle from pub to pub as the night progresses, and more than once I have found myself emerging from the last drinking hole at sunrise. I never sensed any threat of theft along this road, but as always it would be sensible to carry only the money you need.

NIGHTCLUBS The nightclub scene in Addis is lively and constantly changing, so check the latest with locals at your hotel. Entrance may be free, and if not prices are low, usually around US$2–4. The nearest nightspot to Bole Airport is the popular **Alize** [149 G2], in the basement of a building on the slip road by the airport flyover, and described by a recent visitor as an interesting mix of disco, Motown and Ethiopian sounds. Off Bole Road behind Saay Pastry is **Stockholm** [149 E3] on two floors with live bands. **Memos** [137 G1] near Meskel Square is popular with *faranjis*, and further into the city centre is **Illusion**, under the Ambassador Theatre [136 D5].

Right now the hub of clubs is in the Edna Mall area [149 F3]. Here you will find the well-established **Farenheit**, usually with live bands, as well as the recently moved **Platinum**, which some would say is the closest to a European club, with its world-class décor, but does not normally have live bands and gets very full on Saturdays. Inside the mall building itself is **Wube Bereha**, whilst round the corner opposite Harmony Hotel is **Flirt**. Still in this area, but behind BoleTele is **MK** [149 E4], a sports bar with a band on Sundays and great breakfasts.

At Arat Kilo, next door to the post office, you will find **Jolly Bar** [162 C3], which sometimes hosts live bands. Inside the Piazza's Itegue Taitu Hotel, the recommended **Jazz Cafe** [146 D3] has some of the best local singing stars as well as occasional international visiting performers. On the Debre Zeyit road the long-established **Dome** still runs in the basement of the Concorde Hotel [148 A2]. If you want to pay considerably more and not catch the local flavour – retreat into **Gaslights** at the Sheraton [137 F6].

CINEMA AND THEATRE For first-run international films, the new multiplex in the Edna Mall [149 F3] (*opposite Bole Medhanealem Church;* \ *011 661 6207/6278*) is the place to go, charging US$3 per ticket. The **Ambassador Theatre** [136 D5] (\ *011 553 7637*) near the Harambee Hotel often shows good films, but it isn't always easy to establish what will be showing in advance. Other possibilities are the **Alem Cinema** [149 F2] (\ *011 213 0022*) at the airport end of Bole Road and the **Empire Cinema** [146 D4] (\ *011 157 9467*) and **Ethiopia Cinema** [146 C4] (\ *011 111 6690*) on the Piazza. Two new cinemas are due to open in 2012 in the Bisrat Gabriel area of southwest Addis.

Unlike the cinemas in Addis Ababa, the theatres generally stage productions in Amharigna, which can make them rather heavy-going for foreigners who don't speak the language. The **Mega Theatre** [146 C2] (\ *011 111 8084/155 3577*) on Tewodros Square is the oldest in town, built circa 1920, while other possibilities include the **National Theatre** [136 C4] (\ *011 515 8225/4147*) further south along Churchill Avenue and the **Hagar Fikre Theatre** [146 C6] (\ *011 111 9820/112 4158*) near the Piazza.

Also worth checking out is the **Alliance Ethio-Française** (\ *011 156 9893;* e *aef@ allianceaddis.org; www.allianceaddis.org*) on Wavel Road south of the Piazza, which regularly hosts plays, art exhibitions, local musical evenings and other cultural activities, as does the **Goethe Institut** (✆ *011 124 2345–6;* e *info@addis.goethe.de; www.goethe.de*) located in the Faculty of Business and Economics compound in Siddist Kilo.

SHOPPING

Shops in Addis are well stocked and they compare favourably with those of most African cities. There are loads of different shops along the lower half of Churchill Avenue, and along Adwa Avenue in the Piazza area. Bole Road is packed with high-rise malls offering a wide range of goods and services.

CURIOS For curio shopping, try the well-stocked stalls and shops that lie near Tewodros Square on Churchill Avenue and on Nigeria Street, just off Churchill Avenue facing the side of the central post office. There are also curio kiosks in most of the smarter tourist-class hotels. Prices at the stalls on and around Churchill Avenue are highly negotiable, but are generally fixed at hotels and the more upmarket shops in the city centre. Most shops and offices close for an hour or two at some point between 12.00 and 14.00 – there is little point in trying to get anything done during these hours. For a good selection of locally manufactured **CDs** (which cost birr 25–30) try the many music shops on the Piazza, Haile

FRIENDLY STUDENTS

The scam most frequently tried on newcomers to Addis involves being accosted by a friendly 'student' who invites you a traditional ceremony – coffee or *tej* – at the end of which you are presented with a bill totalling as much as US$100 or more. I've had more than a dozen letters from readers who fell victim to this trick, so it seems worth repeating one encounter in full.

After checking into the Wutma Hotel, we went for a walk around the city. We were approached by a pleasant young student, who offered to show us around. Having said he worked at the Wutma, we thought this may not be a bad idea, and so the next day we took him as an escort to the Mercato Market, where one needs to be on guard against pickpockets. At the end of this trip, he invited us to a coffee-making ceremony that evening. *Beware* all travellers: do not go to one of these in Addis Ababa! I should have known better, having done a considerable amount of travelling, but against my better judgement we went to a house where we met 'local' girls in national dress, performing Ethiopian dances and serving Ethiopian food. Unfortunately they were also drinking imported brandy! After a couple of hours we decided to leave and were presented with a bill of US$100! Not a good start! We met other travellers who had also been conned similarly in Addis, so it is becoming quite a scam in the city.

The moral is quite simple. Don't trust any supposed student you meet in Addis Ababa. Assume that anybody who says they work at your hotel, or who remembers meeting you yesterday, is a liar. Don't be lured to a coffee or any other ceremony. And remember always that plausibility is the con artist's most valuable asset!

Gebrselassie Street or on Bole Road. Many CDs and DVDs are sold by boys in the street, on the Piazza.

BOOKS The best shop for new books is **BookWorld** (⊠ *011 155 9010/3*), which has two main branches, one on Wavel Street below the Piazza [146 B3] and the other in Friendship Centre on Bole Road [149 F2]. In addition to a good range of books about various aspects of Ethiopia, BookWorld stocks a fair selection of paperbacks and imported magazines. For non-fiction titles about Ethiopia, other possibilities are the bookshop under the German Cultural Institute between Arat Kilo and the National Museum, the bookshop off Bole Road around the corner from KZ Hotel and the **Africans Bookshop** [146 D5] on Haile Selassie St.

Several clusters of **permanent secondhand bookstalls** with a fair selection of secondhand novels and books about Ethiopia are dotted around Addis. One of the best lies [136 C3] in the back roads behind the Ras Hotel. Another one lies on John Melly Road where it joins Menelik Square above the Piazza. Prices are negotiable at all these stalls.

SUPERMARKETS As in so many other ways, Ethiopia is different when it comes to malls. The average Addis mall is a tower block where the bottom three or four floors are shops and cafés, while the upper floors are offices. The two nearest malls to the airport, **DH Geda Tower** and **Friendship**, are found on Bole Road [149 F2] opposite the Millenium Hall. Friendship Mall is one of the best in town with a branch of BookWorld, a large supermarket in the basement and an excellent shop for local textiles and dresses. Along Bole Road you will also find several supermarkets including a small one open 24/7 opposite KZ Hotel [149 E3]. At Olympia towards the city end sits the yellow-faced **Dembel Mall** [148 B5] (⊕ *Mon–Sat*) which was the first to be built in the city, and has mainly upmarket shops selling imported goods but upstairs in the rotunda, is a high-quality art and souvenir retailer. It also has ATMs and a Nib Bank.

If you need a supermarket in the city centre, try **Shi Solomon** [136 D4] (⊕ *07.30–19.30 Mon–Sat*) opposite the National Theatre, or **Loyal Supermarket** [136 C7] (⊕ *08.00–19.30 daily*) across from the central post office. In Arat Kilo, just north of the roundabout, is **Bellonias** (⊕ *07.30–19.30 Mon–Sat*). If your hotel is on or near Haile Gebrselassie Road your trip into the centre will take you past **Bambis** [148 C6] (⊕ *08.00–19.00 Mon–Sat*) – the city's original Western-style supermarket – on the north side of the road close to Hotel De Leopold. Further east near the Axum and Plaza hotels is **Getfam Supermarket** [149 E7] (⊕ *07.30–19.30 Mon–Sat*). The area near here is possibly the best in town for buying Western clothes. The northern end of Haya Hulet between St Gabriel's Hospital and Debre Damo Hotel is also lined with small clothing retailers.

OTHER PRACTICALITIES

FOREIGN EXCHANGE The best banks for changing money are the **Commercial Bank of Ethiopia** (CBE) [146 D4] or, more efficiently, the **Dashen Bank** [146 D4]; both have several branches around the city including in the Piazza area. Generally though, the quickest way to change money is at a foreign-exchange bureau – the ones at the Hilton, Sheraton and Ghion hotels are recommended. Visa and MasterCard are widely accepted at upmarket hotels in Addis, if the machine is working. You can also draw local currency with either Visa or, less reliably, MasterCard at about 30 Dashen ATMs citywide including those at the Hilton and at Bole Airport.

EMBASSIES Travellers heading south by road from Ethiopia to Kenya may want to note that Kenyan visas are available at Moyale. Sudanese visas normally take 48 hours from their consulate [136 A1] south of Mexico Square.

Ε Austria [126 A4] South Africa St, PO Box 1219; 011 371 2144/2445; e addis-abeba-ob@bmaa.gv.at; www.aussenministerium.at/addisabeba; 09.00–12.00 Mon–Fri

Ε Belgium [126 D6] Comoros St, Kabana, PO Box 1239; 011 662 1291/3420; e addisababa@diplobel.org; www.diplomatie.be/addisababa; 08.00–13.00 & 13.30–16.00 Mon–Thu, 08.30–14.00 Fri

Ε Canada [126 A4] Seychelles St, Saar Beit, PO Box 1130; 011 371 3022; e addis@international.gc.ca; www.ethiopia.gc.ca; 08.00–12.15 & 13.00–17.00 Mon–Thu

Ε Djibouti [148 D3] Off Bole Rd, PO Box 1022; 011 155 3077; e ibrahimkamil@hotmail.com

Ε Egypt PO Box 1611; 011 155 3077/0021; f 011 155 2722

Ε France [126 C6] Quartier Kabana, PO Box 1464; 011 140 0000; e presse@france-ethiopie.org; www.ambafrance-et.org

Ε Germany [126 C6] Kabana, PO Box 660; 011 123 5162; e german.emb.addis@ethionet.et; www.addis-abeba.diplo.de; 07.45–13.00 & 13.30–17.00 Mon–Thu, 07.45–13.45 Fri

Ε Ireland [137 H3] Kazanchis, behind Intercontinental Hotel, PO Box 9585; 011 518 0500, consulate 011 518 0513, emergency 011 518 0500; e addisababaembassy@dfa.ie; www.embassyofireland.org.et

Ε Israel East of Megenagna on Kotebe Rd, PO Box 1266; 011 646 0999; e embassy@addisababa.mfa.gov.il; http://addisababa.mfa.gov.il; 09.00–13.00 Mon–Thu, 09.00–12.30 Fri

Ε Italy [126 D6] Villa Italia, Kabana, PO Box 1105; 011 123 5717/5685; e ambasciata.addisabeba@esteri.it; www.ambaddisabeba.esteri.it; 08.00–14.00 Mon, Wed & Fri, 08.00–14.00 & 15.30–18.30 Tue & Thu

Ε Japan [137 H2] Kirkose Kifle, Ketema, PO Box 5650; 011 551 1088; www.et.emb-japan.go.jp

Ε Kenya [126 C6] Comoros St, Kabana, PO Box 3301; 011 661 0033; e kengad@ethionet.et

Ε Netherlands [126 A5] Ring Rd, Torhailoch, PO Box 1241; 011 371 1100; e add@minbuza.nl; www.ethiopia.nlembassy.org; 08.00–13.00 & 14.00–17.00 Mon–Fri

Ε Russia [126 C6] Comoros St, PO Box 1500; 011 661 2060/1828, consular 011 661 2054; e russemb@ethionet.et

Ε Serbia [137 H5] Tito St, PO Box 1341; 011 551 7804; e yugoslav.embassy@ethionet.et

Ε Somaliland See box, *The Somaliland Embassy in Addis Ababa*, page 156.

Ε South Sudan [148 B5] Schuadapo Bldg, nr Dembel Mall, Bole Rd, PO Box 3140/1250; 011 552 2636; e addis_addis@ethionet.et

Ε Sudan [136 A1] Ras Lulseged St, PO Box 1110; 011 551 6477; e sudan.embassy@ethionet.et; www.gossethiopia.org (goss = Government of South Sudan)

Ε Sweden [136 B5] Yared St, PO Box 1142; 011 518 0000; e ambassaden.addis.abeba@sida.se; www.swedenabroad.com/addisabeba; 09.30 –12.00 Mon, Tue, Thu & Fri

Ε Switzerland [126 A4] Ring Rd, PO Box 1106; 011 371 1107/0577/0483; e vertretung@add.rep.admin.ch; www.eda.admin.ch/addisababa

Ε UK [126 D5] Comoros St, PO Box 858; 011 661 2354; e britishembassy.addisababa@fco.gov.uk; www.ukinethiopia.fco.gov.uk

Ε USA [126 C6] Algeria St (Entoto St), PO Box 1014; 011 517 4000; e usemaddis@state.gov; http://addisababa.usembassy.gov/; 08.30–12.00 & 13.30–15.30 Mon–Fri

For additional embassy information, check http://embassy-finder.com/.

MEDICAL AND EMERGENCIES The local name for a GP/doctors' surgery is a 'higher clinic'. Most doctors speak passable English and many have in-house laboratories able to perform most straightforward blood, stool or urine tests. In an emergency, contact the **Panorama Clinic** (*011 465 1666 or 24hr call-out* m *0911 22 3700*). For any tests that an ordinary GP is unable to do, visit the excellent **Ras Desta Damtew Laboratory** (*011 155 3399*), which lies on the road of the same name opposite the **Gandhi Hospital**. Other recommended clinics and hospitals include the **Africa Higher Clinic** (⊙ *011 276 6817–8*), **Bethezata Higher Clinic** (⊙ *011 551 4470;* m *0911 201 279*), **St Gebriel Hospital** (⊙ *011 661 4400/7622*) and the **Korean Hospital** (⊙ *011 629 2963*), east of Bob Marley Square [off map 149]. To contact the Red Cross, dial 92 or 907. For other emergencies dial 91. One of the best dentists in town is the **Gojeb Dental Clinic** [162 A2] (⊙ *011 156 6521*) on the Piazza.

Pharmacists in Addis are generally well stocked and helpful. I can recommend the **Lion** [146 C2] on the lower part of Mahatma Gandhi Road and **Gishen** [137 E4] opposite Stadium OiLibya, which is open 24 hours.

MEDIA AND COMMUNICATIONS

Internet and email Internet cafés are dotted all around Addis Ababa. The standard charge is 0.30–0.40 Ethiopian cents per minute, which works out at around US$1–1.50 per hour, though it is worth noting that many upmarket hotels charge double or triple that rate. Particularly popular with travellers are the inexpensive internet cafés attached to the Baro and Wutma hotels, but there are numerous other cafés concentrated along Bole Road (try MKTV Business Centre opposite the Angola Chancery), the Piazza, the city centre and the Arat and Siddist Kilo areas.

Newspapers There are two English-language weekly business papers that come out on Sundays – *Fortune* and *Capital* – and these are sold mainly in the streets and supermarkets. Young children will also try to sell you *Newsweek* and *The Economist*, especially outside Shi Solomon Supermarket on Churchill Avenue. It is now very difficult to find newspapers from outside the country.

Post The central post office is on Churchill Avenue, while the original city centre post office is on the Piazza one-way loop. There are several branch post offices dotted around the city, and the queues are rarely daunting. Sending freight out of Addis Ababa is very cheap, but best arranged with your airline.

SWIMMING POOLS Addis Ababa is not often so torrid that making a beeline for the nearest swimming pool is likely to be a high priority. But, should the urge strike, the swimming pool at the Ghion Hotel (with 10m diving platform) is a reliable bet, and only costs US$2.50 The swimming pools at the Hilton (US$8–13) and Sheraton (US$9–15) hotels are fabulous, and very popular with wealthy Ethiopians and expatriates. Other options include the rooftop pool at the Intercontinental (US$6–

THE SOMALILAND EMBASSY IN ADDIS ABABA

The world's only Somaliland embassy [148 D3] (⊙ *011 453 4998/101 0998;* ⊙ *08.30–14.00 Mon–Fri*) is situated in Addis Ababa, right next to the Namibian Embassy, about 200m from Bole Road. To get there, walk or catch a shared minibus to the well-known Saay Cake pastry shop, on the left side of the road coming from the city centre. The junction to the embassy, clearly signposted, is also on the left, between the pastry shop and the boldly painted red-and-yellow Wassamar Hotel. A visa can usually be issued on the spot, though this may be dependent on the presence of the ambassador, so it is probably safest to plan on an overnight wait, longer if you arrive in Addis over a weekend or on a public holiday. Two passport photographs are required and the visa costs US$40.

9), the outdoor pool at the Laphto Leisure Centre [126 A4 A3] (US$7), which also has a tenpin bowling alley in its basement (US$2 per game), and the indoor pool at the Bole Rock Sports Centre [149 F3] (US$4).

GREAT ETHIOPIAN RUN Reputedly the largest road race on the continent, this now takes place in Addis, usually on the last Sunday in November. This 10km event with 38,000 participants in 2011 was started in 2001 by the Olympic gold medallist runner Haile Gebreselassie and others. It is now so popular local tickets are usually sold out by the end of September. For details on how to enter see www.ethiopianrun.org.

VISA EXTENSIONS These can be obtained at the **Department of Immigration** on Churchill Avenue. This is normally a straightforward procedure, but note that a passport-sized photograph is required (there's a photo kiosk outside) and a fee of approximately US$20 must be paid (in local currency). Visa extensions normally take 24 hours, but they can be done on the same day by special request, provided you make the application in the morning.

WHAT TO SEE AND DO

An excellent companion to any pedestrian exploration of the capital is Milena Batistoni and Gian Paolo Chiari's revelatory book *Old Tracks in the New Flower: A Historical Guide to Addis Ababa*, which describes more than 130 of its more interesting buildings along a series of different day walks. Rich in historical detail with regard to the city's formative years, this book was published by Arada Books in 2004 and can be bought at any bookshop in Addis Ababa for birr 100.

CITY CENTRE WALKING TOUR Addis Ababa's relatively modern city centre started to take shape following the arrival of the railway at the south end of what is now Churchill Avenue in 1917, and its present-day street plan was finalised during the Italian occupation. The city centre is arguably of interest more for its cafés, restaurants and shops than for riveting sightseeing. All the same, one could easily spend a day exploring the various small museums and other landmarks that dot central Addis Ababa. A suggested walking itinerary, taking in most such landmarks, might start at Tewodros Square, continuing south along Churchill Avenue past the central post office to the junction with Ras Mekonnen Avenue, and following this eastward past the stadium to Meskel Square and the nearby Addis Ababa Museum. From Meskel Square, you could continue northwards up the shady Menelik II Avenue, then head along Taitu Street, passing the Sheraton and possibly the Filwoha Hot Springs *en route* back to your starting point at Churchill Avenue.

For the sake of coherency, the major sites in the city centre are described following the above route, but one could pick up this loop at another point, or visit any one place of interest by taxi or minibus. Travellers exploring the city centre on foot are urged to carry no more money than they will need for the day, and to leave other valuables and important documents behind in their hotel – pickpockets are rife in several areas. Note, too, that we've had recent reports of travellers being stopped by the police for taking photographs of the 'very secret area' looking uphill along Churchill Avenue towards the town hall – one person reports having had their film destroyed by the police.

One of the most interesting buildings in this part of town is the **Mega Theatre** [146 C2], a rectangular double-storey stone construction that dates to the 1920s and was originally named the Club de l'Union. A combined cinema, bar, dance hall and casino, the French-owned club acquired a rather seedy reputation that earned it the soubriquet of **Satan Bet** – Devil's House – from suspicious Ethiopians, a name that is still in casual use today.

Heading downhill, on the left of Churchill Avenue is the **Postal Museum** [136 D6] next to the central post office, which will be of great interest to philatelists, as it displays examples of every stamp ever issued in Ethiopia since the postal service was founded over a century ago. On the opposite side of Churchill from the post office complex is the **Tiglachin Memorial**, a tall column topped by a red star commemorating those who died in the Ethio-Somalia War of 1978. The nearby **National Library** [136 B5], reached along Yared Road, houses the country's largest collection of ancient church manuscripts – 355 at the last count. Most of these have been recovered from old churches and monasteries; the oldest manuscript is a 15th-century document retrieved from the monastery of Hayk Istafanos. The National Library also claims to possess a copy of every book ever written about Ethiopia.

Back on Churchill and south of the traffic lights, is the **National Theatre** [136 C4], of little architectural merit, but it does stage Amharigna plays in the evenings, and marks the beginning of a row of cafés. South of the junction with Ras Mekonnen Avenue, in a small garden, stands the **Lion of Judah** statue, and beyond that the bombastic, but run-down, neocolonial-style **railway station** [136 D2], which was built by the Parisian architect Paul Barria over 1928–29 and inaugurated by the Empress Zawditu months before her premature death.

Heading eastward along Ras Mekonnen Avenue, you pass to your left the large **Addis Ababa Stadium** [137 E3], built in the mid 1960s, and the site of most international football matches – including Ethiopia's fondly remembered home victory in the third Africa Nations Cup. A few hundred metres further, you arrive at **Meskel Square** [137 F2], an important landmark, and notable among other things for one of the scariest pedestrian road crossings you're ever likely to navigate. The **tourist office** is situated on the northern side of Meskel Square, below the podium used by Mengistu to address the masses in the days when it was known as Revolution Square, as is the excellent Square Garden Restaurant.

The worthwhile **Red Terror Martyrs' Memorial Museum** [137 G2] (☏ 011 850 6730; www.rtmmm.org; ⊕ 08.30–16.30 daily; entrance free) officially opened on the corner of Meskel Square and Bole Road in March 2010. It is dedicated to the victims of the red terror campaign under President Mengistu and the Derg regime, and displays include some riveting black-and-white photos dating to the 1975 coup as well as some more chilling relics – skulls and clothes removed from mass graves, torture instruments – of this genocidal era in modern Ethiopian history. Off Bole Road, housed in a former royal residence five minutes' walk south of Meskel Square, the **Addis Ababa Museum** [137 G2] (☏ 011 551 3180; ⊕ 08.30–12.30 & 13.30–17.30 Mon–Fri, 08.30–12.30 Sat & Sun; entrance US$0.60) is worth a couple of hours' investigation. Besides a collection of old ceremonial and official clothes, the museum displays a marvellous collection of photographs from the early days of Addis Ababa, providing an interesting contrast to the more modern images that are also on display. Rising uphill to the northeast of Meskel Square, the shady Menelik II Avenue, bisected by a green traffic island, is lined by a number of historic buildings. On the east of the avenue, the modern **Church of Kidus Istafanos** [137 G3] stands in an attractive green garden overlooking Meskel Square. Built during the Haile Selassie era, this church is notable for the mosaic above the main entrance, depicting the martyrdom of its namesake St Stephen. On festival days and Sundays, white-robed worshippers congregate in the large grounds, a scene characteristic of rural Ethiopia, but transplanted to the big city.

Uphill from the church, the imposing **Africa Hall** was also constructed by Haile Selassie, to serve as the headquarters of the Organisation of African Unity. The Italian architecture of Africa Hall seems somewhat divorced from its Ethiopian setting, but the immense stained-glass mural, created by the lauded local artist Afewerk Tekle, more than justifies a look inside. Further uphill, to the left, a pair of steel gates guard the verdant grounds of the **National Palace** [137 G4], built in 1955 to mark the occasion of Haile Selassie's 25-year jubilee. The palace, now the official home of the president, is closed to the public, and pulling out a camera in the vicinity of the gates is emphatically forbidden.

At the junction immediately north of the palace, you have three onward options. The first is to follow the dual Yohannis Street back towards the city centre, passing *en route* the attractively time-warped **Fin Fin Hotel** [137 E5] and nearby **Filwoha Hot Springs** [137 E5] (in the hotel of the same name), the presence of which first encouraged Menelik to move his capital down from the Entoto Hills. The second option is to continue north up Menelik II Avenue, passing the **Hilton Hotel** [137 H5] to your right and the **Ethiopia Mapping Authority** [137 G6] amid a row of other government buildings to your left. After 200m or so, turn left into at the T-junction onto the wide curving Niger Street. Then after another 100m or so turn left into Taitu Road, passing the **Sheraton Hotel** [137 F6] *en route* back to the city centre. The third option, assuming that you want to move on to the museums near the university, or to the Piazza area, is to pick up one of the regular minibuses to Arat Kilo or Siddist Kilo at the T-junction. On your right on Niger Street is the well-guarded Gibbe or Old Palace, the former palace of Menelik, today still the seat of government.

THE CHURCHES OF KIDDIST MARYAM, KIDANE MIHRET AND KIDDIST SELASSIE

This trio of historical churches is situated to the north of Menelik II Avenue, tucked away in a substantial forested area behind the Gibbe. To reach these walk north, then take the wide first right passing between the Parliament building on your left and the prime minister's office block on the right, and take the next right which leads to the gate. Enter at the guarded gate, past the uninteresting modern church of St Gabriel. Once inside the complex, head towards the tacky statue of St Mary and the disciples that was donated by the Italians during the occupation, and the tall bell tower which is shaped like an Axumite obelisk – looking out for squawking flocks of the endemic black-winged lovebird on the way.

Near this statue stands the oldest of the churches, **Kiddist Maryam** [162 C4], built by Empress Zawditu in 1911. This attractive square stone church has four Axumite-style colonnaded arches on each of its exterior walls and carved lions guarding the entrance, and it is topped by a large central dome and one smaller dome on each corner. Below the church, reached via a low staircase, the eerie subterranean **Menelik II Mausoleum** [162 D1] encloses the carved marble tombs of Emperor Menelik II, his wife Empress Taitu and their daughter Empress Zawditu. Also buried here is Abuna Matthias, the patriarch of the Ethiopian Orthodox Church who presided over the coronation of Menelik II, and a daughter of Haile Selassie who died at the age of 22. The remains of Haile Selassie were held in this church prior to his formal burial in November 2000, 25 years after his death. Church treasures include an illuminated Bible that belonged to Emperor Yohannis IV. In the main part of the church, a series of murals depicts several important events in Ethiopian history. To the left of Kiddist Maryam, **Kidane Mihret** is a circular church noted for its interior paintings and nearby sacred springs, which produce holy water used for baptism ceremonies.

From Kiddist Maryam, a short walk north leads to the **Holy Trinity (Kiddist Selassie) Cathedral** [162 D2] (⊕ *08.30–12.30 & 13.30–17.30 Sun–Fri; entrance US$1.80, video US$1.80*), the cornerstone of which was laid by Haile Selassie in 1933. This very large church has a rather Arabic façade, while the interior is lavishly decorated by ecclesiastical paintings in both the modern and medieval Ethiopian styles. Within the grounds lie stone monuments dedicated to the first victims of the Derg regime, to the soldiers who died while resisting the Italian occupation, and to the British officers who died during the Allied campaign that ended the occupation. Several members of the Ethiopian aristocracy are buried here, as is the famous suffragette and Ethiopian sympathiser Sylvia Pankhurst. There is also now a small museum.

The Holy Trinity Cathedral's biggest and most recent claim to fame is as **the final resting place of Emperor Haile Selassie**, who was reburied within the church grounds on 5 November 2000, 25 years after his death. Originally buried next to a toilet by his killers, the emperor's exhumed remains were later housed for several years in a small coffin within the Menelik II Mausoleum. The colourful reburial procession, which ran uphill from Meskel Square, was attended by a substantial international Rastafarian contingent, headed by Rita Marley (the widow of Bob Marley), who said: 'Rasta people will be all loving his Imperial Majesty, Emperor Haile Selassie I. There is no end of his reign.' Now open to the public, Haile Selassie's granite tomb stands next to an identical tomb holding the remains of his wife.

ARAT KILO AND SIDDIST KILO
These two major traffic roundabouts are respectively situated – as their Amharigna names suggest – about 4km and 6km from the city centre, and are easily reached by minibus from the city centre or the Piazza area. Two of Ethiopia's best museums lie in this area, which also forms a major centre of student activity, with various departments of the University of Addis Ababa lining the road between the two roundabouts.

Coming from the city centre or Piazza, you'll first hit **Arat Kilo**, a large roundabout, which serves as a key minibus hub, and has many shops and cafés. The monument in the middle of the roundabout commemorates the day in 1941 on which Haile Selassie returned from exile to his liberated nation, so if you are in Addis on Patriots' Day (5 May) the main celebration is held here in the morning. To the east of the roundabout, the **Museum of Natural History** [162 D3] (⊕ *09.00–11.45 & 13.30–16.30 Tue–Sun; entrance US$1.20*) contains a collection of stuffed animals that struck me as pretty uninspired by comparison with similar museums in other African capitals, which doesn't mean it won't be of passing interest to some first-time visitors to Africa.

A ten-minute walk uphill from Arat Kilo towards Siddist Kilo leads to the **National Museum of Ethiopia** [162 C5] (⊕ *08.30–17.30 daily; entrance US$0.60*), housed in green grounds on the left-hand side of the road. This is one of the best museums of its type I've seen in Africa, not only for the quality and diversity of the exhibits, but also for the knowledgeable guides who work there. Archaeological exhibits include a realistic replica of the 3.5-million-year-old skull of Lucy (or Dinquinesh – 'thou art wonderful' – to Ethiopians), a hominid woman of the species *Australopithecus afarensis*. The discovery of this skull in 1974 forced a complete rethink of human genealogy, proving that our ancestors were walking 2.5 million years earlier than had previously been supposed. The national museum also contains some wonderful artefacts dating to the south Arabian period of the so-called pre-Axumite civilisation of Tigrai. These include a number of large stone statues of seated female figures, thought to have been fertility symbols of a pre-

Judaic religion. It is interesting that the figures have plaited hair identical to the style worn by modern Ethiopians (it has been suggested that the mythological Medusa of ancient Greece was simply a dreadlocked Ethiopian woman). One almost perfectly preserved statue, thought to be about 2,600 years old and unearthed at a site near Yeha, is seated in a 2m-high stone cask adorned with engravings of ibex. Many of the other statues are headless – probably decapitated by early Christians, who converted many pagan temples to churches. Other items include a sphinx from Yeha, once again emphasising Axumite links with the classical world, a huge range of artefacts from Axum itself, and a cast of one of the Gragn stones from Tiya.

Before heading on north to Siddist Kilo, you might want to have a drink in Lucy's within the National Museum grounds or a good place for lunch after or between visiting the museums is Pizzeria Italia at Amist Kilo lights (see *Where to eat and drink, Northeast*, page 161).

Siddist Kilo itself is dominated by the **Yekatit 12 Monument** [162 C6], a towering column topped by a statue of a lion and dedicated to the Ethiopians who died in a massacre initiated by the attempted assassination of the Italian Viceroy Graziani on 19 February 1937. Also situated at Siddist Kilo is the **Lion Zoo** [162 C6] (*entrance US$1.25*), the one place in Ethiopia where you can be certain of seeing the Abyssinian lion, a highland race that is reportedly smaller than other lions and definitely has a much darker mane. But don't get over-excited – when all's said and done, they are simply lions in cages, descendants of the pride that accompanied Haile Selassie.

Continuing straight uphill north past Siddist Kilo for perhaps 500m, a left turn through a tall gateway leads into the main campus of the University of Addis Ababa. Walk straight ahead for three minutes to find the excellent **Museum and Library of the Institute of Ethiopian Studies** (often known as the Ethnological

ART GALLERIES

The popular **Asni Gallery** [just off 162 D3] (\ *011 111 7360; e asnigallery@ hotmail.com;* ⊕ *09.00–19.00 Mon–Sat; appointments for other times*) has recently moved to its new home near the Ras Amba Hotel. Entrenched as an essential fixture on the itinerary of any tourist with a passing interest in contemporary Ethiopian art, the gallery displays a wide variety of contemporary Ethiopian art, which generally combines elements of traditional painting with contemporary international influences. It also has a small café.

In the area of Asni's previous home, near the French Embassy, is the new **Netsa Art Village** (m *0911 941 678; e netsaartvillage@gmail.com; www. netsaartvillage.com*), a collective of Ethiopian artists working in Ferensay Park. There is a café serving a mix of local and foreign food and the artists have built their own space out of recycled metal where they hold exhibitions and art talks, festivals and numerous other events. In the southwest of the city, in a well-signposted villa near the Chinese Embassy, the **Lela Gallery** (m *0911 300 756; e lelagallery@gmail.com*) showcases contemporary art and regularly has various exhibitions.

Another place worth a look is **St George's Gallery** [137 E6] (\ *011 551 0983; e addis@stgeorgeofethiopia.com; www.stgeorgeofethiopia.com;* ⊕ *09.00–13.00 & 14.30–18.30 Mon–Sat*) on Taitu Street just below the Sheraton. The gallery, which features paintings, furniture, jewellery and other examples of local craft and interior design, was one of the first galleries to open in Addis Ababa.

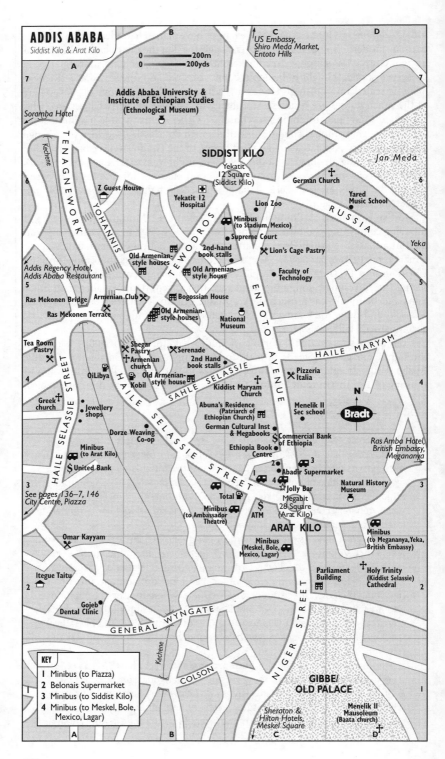

ADDIS ABABA
Siddist Kilo & Arat Kilo

0 _____ 200m
0 _____ 200yds

US Embassy,
Shiro Meda Market,
Entoto Hills

Soramba Hotel

Kechene

TENAGNEWORK

YOHANNIS

Addis Ababa University &
Institute of Ethiopian Studies
(Ethnological Museum)

SIDDIST KILO

Jan Meda

Yekatit
12 Square
(Siddist Kilo)

German Church

Yared
Music School

RUSSIA

Yeka

Z Guest House

Yekatit 12
Hospital

Lion Zoo

Minibus
(to Stadium, Mexico)

Supreme Court

Lion's Cage Pastry

TEWODROS

Addis Regency Hotel,
Addis Ababa Restaurant

Old Armenian-
style houses

2nd-hand
book stalls

Old Armenian-
style house

Faculty of
Technology

Ras Mekonen Bridge

Armenian Club

Bogossian House

ENTOTO AVENUE

Ras Mekonen Terrace

Old Armenian-
style houses

National
Museum

HAILE MARYAM

Tea Room
Pastry

Shegar
Pastry

Serenade

2nd Hand
book stalls

Pizzeria
Italia

HAILE SELASSIE STREET

Greek
church

OiLibya

Armenian
church

Old Armenian-
style house

SAHLE SELASSIE

Kiddist Maryam
Church

Menelik II
Sec school

N

Bradt

Kobil

Jewellery
shops

Abuna's Residence
(Patriarch of
Ethiopian Church)

Ras Amba Hotel,
British Embassy,
Megananya

Dorze Weaving
Co-op

German Cultural Inst
& Megabooks

Commercial Bank
of Ethiopia

Minibus
(to Arat Kilo)

United Bank

Ethiopia Book
Centre

2

Abadir Supermarket

HAILE SELASSIE STREET

See pages 136–7, 146
City Centre, Piazza

4

Jolly Bar

Natural History
Museum

Total

Megabit
28 Square
(Arat Kilo)

Minibus
(to Ambassador
Theatre)

ATM

ARAT KILO

Minibus
(to Meananya, Yeka,
British Embassy)

Omar Kayyam

Minibus
(Meskel, Bole,
Mexico, Lagar)

Itegue Taitu

Parliament
Building

Holy Trinity
(Kiddist Selassie)
Cathedral

NIGER STREET

Gojeb
Dental Clinic

GENERAL WYNGATE

Kechene

GIBBE/
OLD PALACE

COLSON

Sheraton &
Hilton Hotels,
Meskel Square

Menelik II
Mausoleum
(Baata church)

KEY
1 Minibus (to Piazza)
2 Belonais Supermarket
3 Minibus (to Siddist Kilo)
4 Minibus (to Meskel, Bole,
   Mexico, Lagar)

Museum) [162 B7] (⏲ *08.00–17.00 daily; entrance US$3*). Very different from the National Museum, but no less absorbing, this is an exemplary ethnographic museum, housed on the upper floors of a former palace of Haile Selassie, within the green university grounds. The first floor of the building is dedicated to a varied array of artefacts and daily objects relating to most ethnic groups in Ethiopia, not only the monotheistic highlanders, but also the fascinating animist cultural groups of South Omo and the Afar people of the eastern deserts. On the second floor is a new exhibition on Ethiopian musical instruments and visual art through the ages, an impressive selection of Ethiopian crosses and a unique collection of icons dating back to the Middle Ages. Outside the museum building, look out for the displaced 'head' of the largest of the Tiya stelae in the gardens. On the ground floor of the building, the IES Library hoards one of the world's most comprehensive collections of books and photocopied articles about Ethiopia. Despite the archaic and occasionally frustrating card indexing system, this is an invaluable resource for anybody undertaking research on any aspect of Ethiopian culture and history. An attached gift shop sells a remarkable range of carefully selected tourist and gift items at reasonable prices, and is a way of supporting the museum.

The back roads running west from Arat Kilo and Siddist Kilo host one of the oldest residential quarters in Addis Ababa. This area is strongly associated with the Armenian Orthodox community that took refuge in the nascent city at the invitation of Menelik II in response to its persecution by Turkish Muslims. These Armenian settlers – whose descendants retain a strong presence in the area today – proved to be an important influence on the development of Addis Ababa's music scene, as well as on its pre-Italian occupation architecture. A great many characterful old **Armenian buildings** [162 B5] are dotted around this quiet suburb, many close to the junction of Tewodros and Welete Yohannis streets. Possibly the oldest extant house in Addis Ababa, dating to around 1886, the thatched one-storey residence built by **Krikorios Bogossion** [162 B5] on Welete Yohannis Street is still owned by the Bogossion family, and interested visitors may be invited to take a look around the period-furnished interior.

THE PIAZZA Prior to the 1938 Italian construction of a 'Grand Mercato Indegeno' (the present-day Mercato) and simultaneous expansion of the modern city centre, the Piazza – or more correctly Arada – was the economic pulse of Addis Ababa and site of the city's most important bank, market, hotel and shops. Arada Market, described by one European visitor as 'picturesque chaos', was held around a sprawling sycamore fig on what is today De Gaulle Square, peaking in activity on Saturdays, which is also when public executions were held right through until the early years of Haile Selassie's rule.

Today, the Piazza, though dominated by post-Italian occupation constructions, is also studded with Armenian-influenced relics of the Menelik era. Most of the older buildings are in poor repair, though the area as a whole seems to have undergone a striking facelift of late. One of the few buildings that does remain in pristine condition is the **Itegue Taitu Hotel** [146 D3], which is the oldest hostelry in the city, practically unchanged in appearance since 1907, and definitely worth a look in for the spacious architecture, period furnishings and excellent national restaurant.

Other interesting buildings in the area include the stone **Bank of Abyssinia**, which dates to 1905 and lies on the south side of General Wingate Street behind the Taitu. Next door, the **Foalklands Bar** (which one last-minute report suggests has been demolished) has gone somewhat downhill since it was consecrated as a Greek Orthodox church to accommodate the Greek manager of the Taitu c1915.

Around the corner, next to the Omar Khayyam Restaurant, a fabulously sprawling five-storey house designed by Minas Kherbekian (the Armenian architect who also designed the Taitu) stood as the tallest in the city prior to the Italian occupation.

Another important landmark, hidden by trees on the northwest side of Menelik Square, at the northern edge of the Piazza area is **St George's Church** [146 B6], founded by Menelik in 1896 to commemorate the victory over Italy in the Battle of Adwa, though the church itself dates to 1905–11. Subsequent emperors of Ethiopia were crowned in this, the oldest of Addis Ababa's churches. The walls of the church are graced by some fine paintings and tile murals by Afewerk Tekle, commissioned during post-World War II restoration work initiated by Haile Selassie. The interesting **museum** is concerned mainly with his 1930 coronation (⏱ *08.30–12.30 & 14.00–17.00 daily; combined entrance to cathedral & museum, with guide US$3, video extra US$6*). It stands in the church grounds, as does the engraved tomb of the popular singer Mary Armide.

MERCATO [126 A5] This is the biggest shopping area in Addis – and I'm told the largest market on the African continent. Mercato is wistfully described elsewhere as having 'pungent aromas of incense and spices ... [that] ... make a stunning impact on the senses'. On the pungency front, I must admit that I was more impacted upon by rotting vegetables and human excreta. Perhaps it was just a hot day.

Whiffy or not, Mercato is the real commercial hub of Addis, a vast grid of roads lined with stalls, kiosks, small shops and new malls, where you can buy just about anything you might want: the latest local cassettes; traditional crosses, clothes and other curios; vegetables, spices and pulses; custom-made silver and gold jewellery – there is even an entire street devoted to selling *chat*! Needless to say, prices are generally negotiable, and pickpocketing and bag-snatching can happen. As with everywhere in Addis be careful and do not present pickpockets with easy opportunities.

WASHA MIKAEL CHURCH Given that there is so much interest in the rock-hewn churches of Lalibela and Tigrai, you might expect that a rock-hewn church lying within easy walking distance of the capital would be a major tourist attraction. In fact, there are two such churches, of which the easier to walk to is **Washa Mikael**, and both go unvisited by the vast majority of visitors to Addis Ababa. I considered Washa Mikael to be a fine church and well worth the walk when I visited it a few years ago, a reaction that might well have been influenced by the fact I had no idea what to expect from it. Reader consensus appears to be that it's a disappointment. Either way, subsequent to my visit, several tourists have been mugged along the road up, some of them by 'guides' they picked up at the base to avoid such a fate. For this reason, unless you have a 4x4 to drive up in, it would be advisable either to take a guide from town, or to carry nothing worth stealing with you.

According to the priests at nearby **Tekle Haymanot Church**, Washa Mikael was excavated by Abreha and Atsbeha in the 4th century. The 12th or 13th century seems more likely, especially as it is far closer in execution to the 12th-century churches at Lalibela than to older churches in Tigrai. Washa Mikael is a semi-monolith – freed from the surrounding rock on three sides. It is excavated entirely from below the ground, and its enclosure is reached via a short tunnel through the rock. Locals may tell you that the church was used as a hideout during the Italian occupation, when it lost its roof to an Italian bomb and fell into disuse, to be replaced by Tekle Haymanot Church. Academic opinion is that the roof collapsed more than a century ago, while another story has it that it was de-sanctified in 1897 by Emperor Menelik II, who sent the *tabot* to Yeka Mikael Church down the road.

Paradoxically, this roofless condition of the church allows you to get a far better idea of the layout than is normally possible. The pillars and walls are still standing, and you can scramble over the rocks into what used to be the Holy of Holies where the *tabot* was stored. There are several windows and candle niches along the walls, and there is a holy pool fed by underground springs. Overgrown it may be, but Washa Mikael is in my opinion a very impressive excavation – though take heed that one reader has accused me of being over-imaginative in this description.

To get to the church, take a Kebena, Shola, Megenagna minibus eastwards from Arat Kilo. Get off at Shola Market about 1km past the British Embassy, and cross the eight-lane main road. Take the non-tarmac side road that goes gently uphill with Yeka Park on your right – follow it straight through the famous Beg Terra sheep market. When you hit a T-junction with another unsurfaced road, turn right. You should follow this road for about ten minutes, across a bridge, then climb steeply before you reach a left fork immediately before another bridge. From here, there are two options: on the way out I would advise you to take the longer but more straightforward route, which means ignoring the left fork and continuing straight along a road that climbs a eucalyptus-clad hill. After about 500m, the road descends towards a tin-roofed village. At the base of the hill, just before you enter the village, the road crosses a small watercourse where there is a distinctive small hill to your right. Immediately after the watercourse, take the road to your left, and follow it for about 300m till you reach a T-junction, where you need to turn left. From here it's a straightforward 1–2km slog along a road that curls steeply uphill through eucalyptus forest. At the top of the hill, you come out in a meadow. The road turns sharply left, and after about 200m there is a small rocky peak to your left. The church is here, in a fenced enclosure near the road but not visible from it. If in doubt, you'll see plenty of locals along the walk out – just keep asking for directions (better to ask for Tekle Haymanot than Washa Mikael). People have recently been asked an entrance fee of US$3–4.

Once you're at the church, it will be evident that you can reduce the return distance by as much as 50% by cutting downhill through the forest behind Tekle Haymanot back to the road, and then, about 500m further, at the sharp left turn that marks the end of the steepest part of the descent, by crossing through the light forest back to the fork near the bridge. You could, of course, try to go out to the church by using these short cuts, but you risk getting lost – the short cuts are only obvious once you have your bearings.

ENTOTO MARYAM The Entoto Hills were the site of Menelik's capital before Addis Ababa was founded in 1887. The only obvious relic of this era, the still-functional **Entoto Maryam Church**, is an octagonal building with a traditionally painted interior, where Menelik was crowned in 1882. The interior can only be seen during and immediately after the church services, which are held every morning ending at around 09.00. In the church compound, the **Entoto Saint Mary, Emperor Menelik and Empress Taitu Memorial Museum** (⊕ *Tue–Sun*), which opened in 1987, houses an interesting collection of religious items and ceremonial clothing dating from Menelik's time.

Entoto Maryam can be reached by private taxi, or else by catching a bus from Arat Kilo northwards past Siddist Kilo to the terminus at the footslopes of the Entoto Hills. At about 100m and signposted from this terminus, the local women (under the auspices of the **Women Fuel Wood Carriers Project**, supported by the International Labour Organization (ILO)) have established a souvenir and gift shop selling hand-woven cotton shawls, traditional *gabbis* and *netelas*, and sisal hats, baskets and much more. From here, you can follow the main road uphill on foot for about 2–3km, a tough slog that will take at least an hour. The alternatives are to wait at the terminus for one of the occasional minibuses that go all the way up to the church (as, I'm told, do number 17 buses), or to catch a private taxi. About 2km past Entoto Maryam, there is a disused 13th-century rock-hewn church called **Kidus Raguel** which, like Washa Mikael, was partially destroyed during the Italian occupation. Marie Hogervost writes: 'One of my friends went to an **exorcism** at Entoto Maryam. These take place on Sundays at 05.00, and last for about an hour. People that are suspected of being possessed by the devil are cured with holy water, and many other diseases like AIDS are cured. You are supposed to become religious as soon as you have seen this, according to many Ethiopian friends, but even if you don't it is an interesting spectacle.'

SHORT TRIPS FURTHER AFIELD Unusually for an African capital, Addis Ababa lies at the centre of an area rich in places of interest, most of which can be visited either as a day trip from the capital or else as a preliminary to travels further afield. Many such places of interest are overlooked by tourists in their rush to get to Ethiopia's more renowned attractions. They are also, for the most part, highly accessible, and offer what amounts to some excellent off-the-beaten-track travel with a minimum of effort. These places are described along routes covered elsewhere in this book, but it is worth giving a quick overview here.

The main string of attractions lies on the road to Adama, a large town about 100km southeast of the capital and a useful springboard to most parts of east and southern Ethiopia. Attractions along the Adama road include the Akaki River Wetlands, the crater-lake field at Bishoftu, and mounts Yerer and Zikwala. From Adama, you can also visit the popular hot-springs resort at Sodore.

A second cluster of attractions, mostly with a historical bent, lies around Melka Awash and Tiya on the Butajira road. From Melka Awash you could, at a push, visit in a day an ancient rock-hewn church, a field of mysterious engraved tomb-markers, which date to the 14th century or thereabouts, and the prehistoric Stone Age site at Melka Kunture.

North of Addis, the Durba Waterfall is one of the highest in the country, and the surrounding area offers wonderful views across the Muger Valley Gorge, as well as a good chance of close-up views of the endemic gelada baboon. The monastery of Debre Libanos is also a feasible site for a day trip.

To the west, Ambo is a hot-springs resort mostly of interest to Addis weekenders. On the way there you pass Gefersa Reservoir and Menelik's turn-of-the-century proposed capital at Addis Alem. Ambo is also a base from which you can visit forested Lake Wenchi.

Another excellent day or overnight goal to the west of the city is the Menegasha Forest. The monthly day or weekend excursions run by the Ethiopian Wildlife Society go to most of the places mentioned above and they sometimes run longer trips to the northern circuit and even Moyale tourists are welcome to join these excursions by contacting their office on ℡ 011 663 6792. The Ethiopian Horticultural Society organises visits to gardens in Addis and as far away as Arba Minch; contact Liz Asfaw on m 092 033 6420.

ADDIS REGENCY
HOTEL

Tel. +251 111 550000
Mob. +251 913 141583, Fax. +251 111 550017
www.addisregency.com

Addis Regency Hotel is located in the heart of Piazza in Addis Ababa, Ethiopia. We offer single, double, twin and family suites. Our rates include buffet breakfast, transfers to/from the airport and free wi-fi internet access throughout the hotel. We also have a 24 hour Bar and Restaurant, onsite laundry services and a hall for special events and conferences.
Visit us at **www.addisregency.com** to make your booking!

Your Comfort is our Business!

Part Three

NORTHERN ETHIOPIA

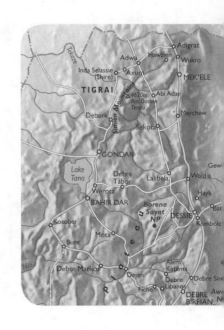

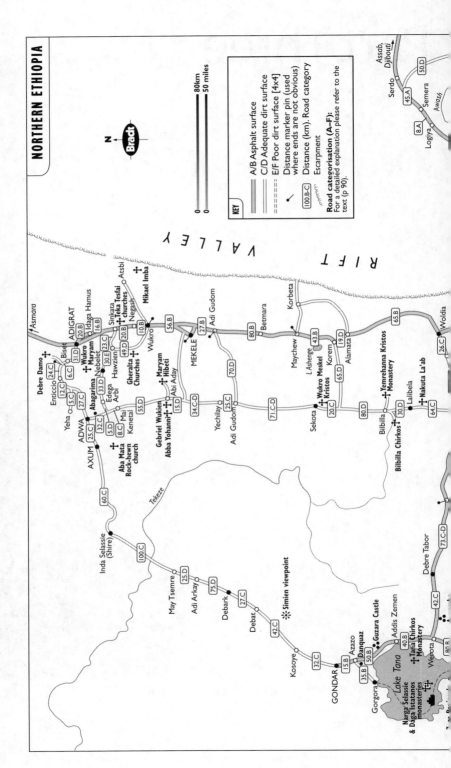

NORTHERN ETHIOPIA

KEY

▬▬	A/B Asphalt surface
▬▬	C/D Adequate dirt surface
┄┄	E/F Poor dirt surface [4x4]
╱	Distance marker pin (used where ends are not obvious)
100-B-C	Distance (km). Road category
⌐⌐⌐	Escarpment

Road categorisation (A–F):
For a detailed explanation please refer to the text (p 90).

0 80km
0 50 miles

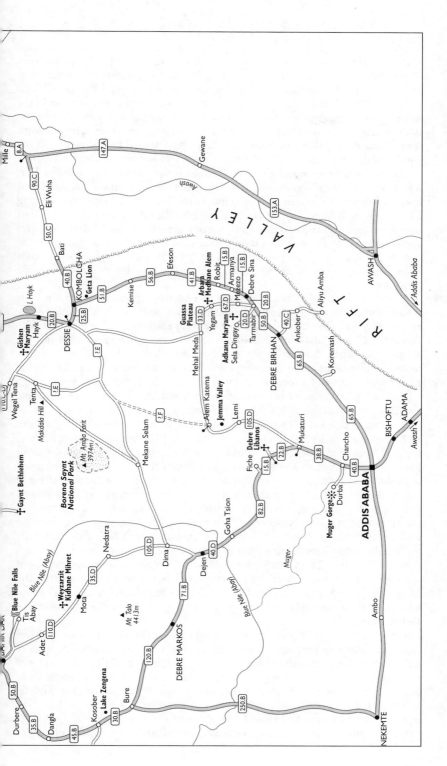

The well-defined 'historical circuit' through northern Ethiopia forms the core of the country's tourist industry. It is probably no exaggeration to say that 90% of travellers to Ethiopia base the bulk of their itinerary around this circuit, and rightly so. There is nothing in sub-Saharan Africa – in a sense, nothing else in the world – that prepares the visitor for the wealth of historical and cultural treasures, both ancient and living, contained in northern Ethiopia. The circuit pivots around **four cities**, all very different from the others, and followed in this section in the **clockwise direction** favoured by most tour operators and independent travellers.

The standard **first stop** in northern Ethiopia is the modern city of **Bahir Dar**, a bustling commercial centre set on the southern shore of Lake Tana, the largest body of water in Ethiopia and official source of the Blue Nile. In addition to hosting a fascinating traditional daily market and rich birdlife, Bahir Dar forms the obvious base for several day trips: to the multitude of atmospheric medieval **monasteries** dotted around the forested islands and peninsulas of Lake Tana, as well as to the sensational **Blue Nile Falls** (sensational, that is, on the increasingly rare occasions when the Nile's water hasn't been diverted to fuel a neighbouring hydro-electric generator).

To the north of Lake Tana, a popular **second stop** on the northern circuit is **Gondar**, which served as Ethiopia's capital for almost 300 years from 1635 onwards, and is today noted for its impressive **16th-century castles** as well as the beautifully decorated **Church of Debre Birhan Selassie**. To the north of Gondar, lies the staggeringly scenic **Simien Mountains National Park**, home to the country's main concentrations of the endemic gelada baboon and Walia ibex. Following the recent construction of a rough road into the Simien Mountains, this lovely range – traditionally the preserve of hardened trekkers and hikers – also forms a feasible goal for a day or overnight 4x4 trip out of Gondar.

A common **third stop** on the historical circuit is the ancient capital of **Axum**, which lies close to the Eritrean border at the heart of the former Axumite Empire, the dominant economic and political force in the region for about a millennium prior to its collapse circa AD700. Axum is best known today for the **giant engraved obelisks** (stelae) that tower over the northeast of the town. But the entire city stands above a fascinating miscellany of ancient relics – dingy catacombs, ruined palaces, rock engravings and inscribed tablets – that pay collective testament to the enterprise and complexity of what is perhaps the most enigmatic of all the ancient civilisations of the Old World. This enigma is amplified when one visits the nearby **Yeha Temple**, estimated to have been constructed 2,500 years ago. Axum's **Church of Tsion Maryam** – claimed by Ethiopians to house the Ark of the Covenant – has for more than 1,600 years lain at the spiritual heart of the Ethiopian Orthodox Church; the Axumite architectural legacy lives on in several ancient churches, notably the male-only clifftop gem that is the **Monastery of Debre Damo**.

For most visitors to Ethiopia, the **highlight** of the northern circuit is the medieval capital of **Lalibela**, where high in the chilly mountains of Wolo stands a complex of a **dozen rock-hewn churches** often and justifiably ranked as the eighth wonder of the ancient world. Reachable only on foot or by mule until a couple of decades back, but now serviced by daily buses and flights, these churches stand as an inspirational active shrine to a Christian civilisation that pre-dates its northern European equivalent by centuries. And around Lalibela lie several more ecclesiastic gems: the beautiful Axumite cave church of **Yemrehanna Kristos**, the isolated monasteries and churches around **Bilbilla**, the remote montane retreat of **Asheton Maryam** … all set amid some of the most fantastic mountain scenery on the African continent.

The majority of travellers take one of three approaches to exploring the 'big four' cities of the northern circuit. The first, and less strenuous, approach is to **fly** between the aforementioned stops, exploring the towns, and sometimes arranging day excursions to nearby places of interest. One could, in theory, see the best of the northern circuit over five days, since flights generally take only an hour or so, leaving one with plenty of time to explore in between. In practice, however, the combination of sudden schedule changes, occasional delays and the need to reconfirm all domestic flights at the point of departure, makes it advisable to dedicate about eight days to a flying excursion around the northern circuit. This will allow for a full day between flights to explore each of the major towns at leisure.

A more demanding option is to **drive** around the historical circuit in a rented 4x4 with a driver and/or guide, or – tougher still – to do the whole circuit using **buses** and other public transport. The disadvantage of road travel is that it is time-consuming and sometimes exhausting – recent improvements notwithstanding, a realistic minimum of 12–14 days is required to cover this circuit by road, and three weeks or longer would be better, especially if you are using public transport. The main advantages of driving over flying are firstly that you get to see far more of the beautiful mountain scenery, and secondly that you have the opportunity of escaping the relatively well-trodden tourist trail to visit areas where tourists remain an infrequent sight. As a thorough read through this section will make abundantly clear, there is infinitely more to northern Ethiopia than its four established historical cities. The list of off-the-beaten-track possibilities is practically endless; to name one example, the vastly underrated rock-hewn churches of Tigrai alone could keep an interested traveller busy for weeks.

6

Addis Ababa to Lake Tana by Road

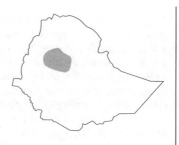

This chapter follows the two road routes between Addis Ababa and Bahir Dar, the latter being the principal town on Lake Tana and a popular first stop along the historical circuit. The main 560km road between these cities – via Dejen and Debre Markos – is now sealed in its entirety including the steep 30km stretch that passes through the Blue Nile Gorge between Goha Tsion and Dejen. The road can easily be driven in a private vehicle in one day, or covered by any of several direct bus services, but for those who prefer to dawdle, the route is also endowed with a number of little-visited potential diversions.

The most significant geographical landmark between Addis Ababa and Bahir Dar is the **Blue Nile Gorge**, which can, at a push, be visited as a round day trip from the capital in a private vehicle. Between Addis Ababa and the Blue Nile Gorge, the main sites of interest are the spectacular and underrated **Muger River Gorge** (a potential day trip from Addis even on public transport) and the famous medieval monastery of **Debre Libanos**.

Roughly 230km north of Addis Ababa, shortly after passing through Dejen on the northern rim of the Blue Nile Gorge, there is a major fork in the road. Both routes north from here lead to Bahir Dar. The eastern route, via Mota, is the less interesting of the two, and the road is unsealed, but is shorter at around 240km. The western route, about 90km longer, passes through Debre Markos, the largest town covered in this chapter and former capital of the defunct Gojjam region, and offers some interesting yet accessible off-the-beaten-track possibilities in the vicinity of Kosober, including montane forests, crater lakes, waterfalls and the 'true' source of the Nile as identified by James Bruce.

FROM ADDIS ABABA TO DEJEN

CHANCHO AND THE MUGER GORGE On leaving Addis Ababa, the Bahir Dar road climbs the eucalyptus-clad Entoto Hills into high moorland. The first stop, **Chancho**, lies 40km from the capital in an area of rolling grassland and babbling streams. Chancho is of little interest in itself, but it's a reasonably large town in attractive surrounds and, more significantly, the springboard for visits to the immense Muger River Gorge – a good day trip from the capital, or possible first stop along the historic route. Public transport between the Autobus Terra in Addis and Chancho runs all day through, taking about one hour in either direction. If you're looking to overnight in Chancho before heading further north, there is no shortage of shoestring accommodation including the **Hotel Awash** (*11 rooms*) in the centre of town which offers basic rooms with common shower for US$2.50. A more promising option is a new hotel less than 1km from the centre on the Addis Ababa side of town, which was under construction and should be completed by the time this book is published.

Access to **Muger Gorge** is from the village of Durba, where there is a waterfall, which, although it carries a low volume of water, makes a dramatic plunge of around 100m into a side gorge. Just past the village, the Durba Cement Factory stands on a rock promontory with wonderful views in three directions. The Durba area is at its best in September and October, when the water is high and the countryside is a patchwork of colourful flowers, mostly the yellow meskel flower but also several other varieties coloured blue, pink, white and purple. An incentive for visiting the region at any time of year is the presence of gelada baboons, which are often seen just outside the village. There is also good birdwatching: a pair of lammergeyers breed on the cliffs near the waterfall, while other birds worth looking out for include black eagle, gymnogene, Hemprich's hornbill and the endemic white-billed starling. **Durba** is a peaceful, leafy village, with at least one shoestring hotel. It only takes a glance at the surrounding area to see it has enormous potential for walking and hiking – a footpath leads from the cement factory to the base of the gorge, or you could follow the rim north of Durba for several kilometres. If you are looking for some off-the-beaten-track hiking in the Addis area, the Muger Gorge feels like an excellent option. Take some food along, as there's not much available in Durba.

Durba lies about 20km west of the Bahir Dar road, and can be reached via a turn-off at the southern end of Chancho. The light vehicles that serve as erratic public transport between Durba and Chancho can usually be located at the junction, and are most prolific on Saturday (market day). On other days, the earliest possible start is recommended, or you could get stuck in Durba. In fact, with an early enough start, you could think about walking back: it's a 20km hike but the slopes are gentle, the scenery is good, and you cross several babbling streams. If you are on foot, or are driving yourself, do stop at the Sibale River about 2km out of Chancho, as it has a reputation for attracting unusual migrant birds alongside endemics such as black-headed siskin, wattled ibis and Abyssinian longclaw.

JEMMA VALLEY

Lying to the east of the Debre Libanos road, the pretty Jemma Valley is named for the river that formed it, a tributary of the Blue Nile. The area is of great interest to birders as the most accessible place to tick Harwood's francolin, an Ethiopian endemic restricted to a handful of sites in the Blue Nile watershed region. Lying at an altitude of between 1,300m and 2,000m, the valley is dominated by acacia woodland, and also supports other interesting birds including the endemic Rüppell's cliff-chat, white-billed starling and white-throated seedeater, as well as vinaceous dove, foxy cisticola, speckle-fronted weaver, black-faced firefinch and stone partridge.

The valley is reached by turning right from the main road to Lake Tana at Mukaturi, which lies roughly 40km north of Chancho and 20km south of the junction for Debre Libanos, and can be reached from Addis Ababa by direct buses. From the junction at Mukaturi, a 105km road descends via Lemi to the small town of Alem Katema, which lies at the base of the valley next to a stretch of the Jemma River where the range-restricted francolin is very common. Two buses daily run along this road, leaving Mukaturi at about 05.30 and 08.00 and arriving at Alem Katema about four hours later. Basic accommodation is available in Mukaturi, Lemi and Alem Katema. From Alem Katema a very rough gravel road leads northwards to Tenta and Lalibela.

DEBRE LIBANOS AND RAS DARGE'S BRIDGE

Past Chancho, the Bahir Dar road continues through high moorland swathed in unusual heather-like vegetation and, particularly after Debre Tegist, offering some impressive views across rugged montane scenery. After some 57km, you'll pass a viewpoint to the right and a parking lot to the left, the latter adorned by a plaque erected in 2005 to commemorate Ethio-Japanese co-operation in the construction of this (excellent) 200km asphalt road between Addis Ababa and Goha Tsion. Another 3km further, precisely 100km out of Addis Ababa, a rough side road leads eastward to the renowned medieval monastery of **Debre Libanos**, which stands at the base of a magnificent 700m-high canyon known (for reasons that are unclear) as Wusha Gadel (Dog Valley).

A reliable tradition states that Debre Libanos was founded in 1284 by Abuna Tekle Haymanot, the priest who was instrumental to the contemporaneous spread of Christianity through Showa. Tekle Haymanot spent roughly a decade studying the Scriptures at each of two of northern Ethiopia's most important monasteries, Hayk Istafanos and Debre Damo, and his influence is widely associated with the reinstatement of the so-called Solomonic dynasty after centuries of Zagwe rule. One of the many bizarre legends associated with this important figure, who is usually depicted as having one leg and six wings, is that he spent seven years standing on one leg praying, and subsisted on one seed a year (fed to him by a bird), before eventually his spare leg withered away and fell off!

Originally known as Debre Asbo, Debre Libanos was given its present name by Emperor Zara Yaqob in 1445. At around the same time, Debre Libanos usurped Hayk Istafanos as the political centre of the Ethiopian Church, a position it consolidated under the powerful leadership of Abbot Marha Kristos from 1463 to 1497. It was here, in 1520, that Emperor Lebna Dengal formally received the first Portuguese mission to Ethiopia; here, too, that the priest Francisco Alvarez, a member of that mission, made contact with Pero de Covilhão, the 'spy' who had been sent overland by King John of Portugal to explore the Land of Prester John three decades earlier. Debre Libanos retained its political significance until as recently as the Italian occupation, when – as a perceived hotbed of patriotic anti-Italian sentiment – both the monastery and its inhabitants were destroyed by the fascist troops (see box, *Graziani's revenge*, page 178). It remains an important pilgrimage site for Orthodox Christians.

The modern church, built in the 1950s by Haile Selassie to replace the one destroyed by the fascists, is tucked away in a small wooded gorge that feels intimate and secluded next to the surrounding canyon. The rather bombastic exterior is typical of latter-day Ethiopian churches, but the attractive marble interior, decorated with stained-glass windows of various saints, compensates. Entrance costs a rather steep US$6, including a US$3 charge levied for use of a video or camera. A signpost stipulates that entry to the church is forbidden to menstruating women and to anybody who has had sexual intercourse within the previous 48 hours.

The church aside, there is a definite aura about Debre Libanos, especially if you follow the footpaths along the stream – boosted by several waterfalls tumbling over the gorge's edge – that runs past the new church to its derelict predecessor. There is a small woody village about 1km towards the main road from the church. It's all very beautiful and serene; in the right frame of mind one could spend several days wandering around the valley. On the opposite side of the stream to the main church, the cave where Tekle Haymanot prayed until his death (aged 98, according to tradition) is now maintained as a shrine. The caretaker priest here will gladly bless visitors with holy water from the cave, provided that they haven't eaten anything yet that day. Some of the monks and nuns live in nearby caves.

Little more than 100m north of the turn-off to Debre Libanos, a 500m footpath leads east from the Bahir Dar road to a lichen- and moss-stained stone bridge that spans the Gur River before it plunges for several hundred metres over a cliff

During the Italian occupation, Debre Libanos was the target of one of the most heinous atrocities committed by the fascists, who believed some of its monks to have been involved in a failed attempt on Viceroy Graziani's life. On 20 May 1937, the fascist troops descended on a Tekle Haymanot Day celebration close to Fiche, seized 297 monks, and shot them. A few days later, more than 100 young deacons attached to the monastery were slaughtered, and Graziani telegraphed Mussolini in Rome to say that: 'Of the monastery nothing remains.'

In 1998, an article by Ian Campbell and Degife Gabre-Tsadik revealed that a third related massacre took place about a week later. At least 400 lay people who had attended the celebration for the saint were detained by the Italians, separated from the monks, tied together, and transported by truck to the village of Engecha on the old Ankober road. According to two eyewitnesses interviewed by Campbell, the prisoners were lined up along the edge of two 10m-long trenches, and then mowed down with machine-gun fire. The lay victims of this massacre were buried, without ceremony, where they fell. The bones of the martyred monks and deacons can still be seen at the monastery.

Debre Libanos had served as the head of the Ethiopian Church for four centuries prior to this massacre, but as John Graham points out: 'Graziani not only killed the priests, he also killed Debre Libanos as the centre of the Church. It never recovered from the loss of the priests and teachers. Although it was resurrected, and a new and wonderful church was built there in the 1950s, it could never become the centre of learning it had previously been.'

edge to eventually flow into the Jemma, a tributary of the Nile. Presumably as a result of confusion with the two 17th-century bridges that span the Nile below the Blue Nile Falls, this is now widely referred to as the '**Portuguese Bridge**'. Despite a convincingly time-worn appearance, however, it was actually built at the cusp of the 19th and 20th centuries by Ras Darge, a relation of Menelik II, using the traditional sealant of limestone and crushed ostrich shell instead of cement. Not only is Ras Darge's Bridge of some historical interest, but the view from the lip of the gorge is fantastic. Cross the bridge and follow the cliff edge to your right for a view back to the waterfall and the Washa Gelada – Gelada Cave – where a troop of these striking primates sleeps most nights. Keep an eye open, too, for highland birds such as lammergeyer, auger buzzard, Abyssinian ground hornbill and the endemic banded barbet, Abyssinian woodpecker, Rüppell's black chat and white-winged cliff-chat.

Getting there and away The junction to Debre Libanos lies on the main road between Addis Ababa and Bahir Dar some 60km north of Chancho and 15km south of Fiche, the closest town. The church lies 4km along the junction along a partially surfaced road from where several troops of relatively habituated gelada monkeys are regularly observed. With your own vehicle, the monastery is a perfectly feasible day trip from either of these towns, or from Addis Ababa – the drive from the capital would take about 90 minutes to two hours each way – and it could also be visited *en route* between Addis and points further north. When you are ready to leave Debre Libanos bear in mind it may only be a 4km walk back to the junction but it's a *very* steep walk. Still, if you're staying at one of the nearby hotels you'll have the whole afternoon to do it, and there are great views over the sandstone canyon and terraced cultivation of the slopes.

Debre Libanos can be visited from Addis Ababa as a day trip using public transport with two buses daily departing Addis Ababa (US$2; 2½ hours). Henk Klaassen provides details: 'I made the trip to Debre Libanos in one day. The morning bus from Addis Ababa drops you off direct in front of the church by 10.00. I walked the area until 13.00, and was fortunate to get a hitch all the way back to Chancho. I caught a pick-up from there, and was back in Addis by 16.00.'

The short footpath to Ras Darge's bridge is clearly signposted 'Portuguese Bridge' about 100m past the junction. A few curio-seller-cum-aspirant-guides hang around the signpost but the bridge is easy to find without assistance (the footpath is clear enough) and most locals speak insufficient English to make any contribution beyond stating the blatantly obvious. If you take a guide – or let one tag along – they'll expect a tip of US$1.50.

Where to stay and eat In addition to the hotels listed below several decent options, including the **Anbesa International Hotel** (*40 rooms;* \ *011 135 2197;* e *abidointernational@yahoo.com*) and **Alem Hotel** (*34 rooms;* \ *011 135 0003*), are available at the small town of Fiche, only 15km further north.

🏠 **Ethio-German Park Hotel** (14 rooms) \011 656 3213. Perched on the clifftop a short walk from the Portuguese Bridge, this hotel offers fantastic views of the gorge below. The view comes with a price, though – food & drinks are double the price of comparable establishments & non-guests have to pay US$1.50 to park in the car park (even if eating in the restaurant) & a further US$1.50 to walk down to the Portuguese Bridge. *US$12/15 en-suite dbl without/with view.*

🏠 **Hotel Haile Maryam** (10 rooms) Situated alongside the main Bahir Dar road immediately south of the junction to Debre Libanos, this

GRAND PLANS FOR NEW DAMS

In mid 2011, the Ethiopian government began construction on a controversial multi-billion-dollar dam on the Blue Nile in the Benishangul-Gumuz region some 40km east of Sudan. The government hopes that their grand dam – originally known as the Millennium Dam and subsequently renamed Grand Ethiopian Renaissance Dam – will supply more than 5,000 megawatts of electricity for Ethiopia and its neighbours. When completed the dam will be the largest hydro-electric power plant in Africa and the tenth largest in the world. With a capacity of 63 billion cubic metres of water, the artificial lake created will also be twice the size of Lake Tana. While the government has been quick to move forward with construction of the US$4.7 billion project – which includes the building of an additional four smaller dams on the Blue Nile – neighbouring countries including Egypt and Sudan have expressed deep concern that the mega-dam project could seriously impact upon their water resources. Conservationists too are worried about the environmental impacts of the dam. It however doesn't bode well that the Ethiopian government has a reputation for forcing large numbers of tribal people off ancestral land to make way for private agricultural irrigation schemes, most notably the Gibe III Dam in South Omo, which is feared will affect as many as half a million people living in Ethiopia and Kenya, not to mention threaten the region's wildlife.

basic but not unpleasant hotel was closed for renovations when visited in late 2011.

✕ **Top View Resort** ⊕ 08.00–14.00 daily. This new restaurant located immediately on the right as you turn off the main road towards Debre

Libanos is an ideal spot for a quick snack with a small menu of local dishes & cold drinks & beer served alongside sweeping views overlooking the valley below. *US$1–2*.

BLUE NILE GORGE This truly magnificent gorge, which spans altitudes of around 2,500m to 1,200m, is comparable in scale to America's Grand Canyon, and – quite how one measures these things I don't know – is often cited to be the largest canyon in Africa, a title also frequently bestowed on Namibia's Fish River Canyon. The gorge follows the course of the Blue Nile as it arcs south of Lake Tana before it gushes out of Ethiopia into Sudan. Travelling between Fiche and Debre Markos, you will cross the gorge on one of the most chilling roads I have ever seen. Originally built by the Italians, and supported by viaducts in several places, it is an awesome feat of engineering; there are places where you can barely see the road's edge from a bus window, only a sheer plunge of perhaps 100m.

The 40km tarred road between Goha Tsion and Dejen typically takes up to an hour to cover – which gives you plenty of time to admire the expansive views over terraced slopes and euphorbia-studded cliffs to the opposite wall. As you descend, there is a corresponding rise in temperature and humidity. At the bottom a second new Ethiopian–Japanese bridge crosses the river taking the traffic, so it is now possible to park and walk over the old Italian bridge and take photographs.

The first stop after crossing the gorge is **Dejen**, which lies at an altitude of around 2,400m, yet is still close enough to the gorge to make a viable base for further exploration on foot. There is plenty of **shoestring accommodation**: the double-storey pale pink and blue **Alem Hotel** (*27 rooms;* \ *058 776 0010*) behind the town's only filling station looks comfortably the most attractive option with clean common shower rooms US$5 and en-suite doubles for US$12. A few kilometres north of Dejen, the main road splits into the direct route to Bahir Dar and a longer route to the same destination via the regional capital of Debre Markos. Whichever way you go, the pretty rolling countryside seems rather pedestrian after the gorge, though the highland cool comes as a major relief. From Dejen it is also possible to drive to Lalibela on graded gravel through Dima and Mekane Selam, via the newly designated Borena Sayint National Park (see *Chapter 12*, page 320).

DEJEN TO BAHIR DAR VIA MOTA

This is the shorter of the two routes between Addis Ababa and Bahir Dar, but also the less popular one, since the road is unsurfaced and generally in mediocre condition. Some buses between the cities do, however, head this way, presumably because it saves on fuel, overnighting either at Mota, a small town situated some 110km south of Bahir Dar, or else at whichever other village takes the driver's fancy. The most notable tourist attractions along this road are in the vicinity of Mota, at the southern end of an area that was an important royal fiefdom during the early Gonderine period.

Several significant but seldom-visited churches lie along the road between Dejen and Mota, or within striking distance of it. The disused church of **Weyname Kidane Mihret**, situated no more than 5km north of Bichena, was renowned for the superb 200-year-old cloth paintings that decorated its every wall, as described in an *Ethiopian Observer* article by Walter Krafft, who in 1971 had been the church's first European visitor. Sadly, just three years later, thieves tore every last painting from the church walls, and the cloth was cut into fragments that later turned up as curios in Addis Ababa.

Also of interest is the medieval monastery of **Dima Giyorgis**, which stands on the rim of the Blue Nile Gorge some 14km along a track that branches to the east 15km north of Bichena. The hilltop Monastery of Debre Work Maryam, which lies some 30km north of Bichena, and was reputedly founded in Axumite times, holds several important treasures including an icon said to have belonged to St Luke. Another 20km northwest of this, **Dingayama Maryam** (literally 'Mary on the Rocks') is an elaborately decorated hilltop church built in the time of Emperor Susneyos, a painting of whom graces the walls. Set on the rim of the Blue Nile Gorge about 25km east of the main road near Wofit, the remote but palatial stone church of Mertule Maryam, site of Emperor Susneyos's coronation, is probably the oldest European-influenced building in Ethiopia – it was constructed in the dying years of the 16th century by Empress Eleni, the long-lived and highly influential wife of Zara Yaqob, with assistance from the Portuguese spy Pero de Covilhão. All these churches are described in some detail in Paul Henze's *Ethiopian Journeys* (see *Appendix 5, Further information*, page 613).

Mota itself is the closest town to **Sebara Dildi**, the 17th-century footbridge over the Nile built during the rule of Emperor Fasilidas, and the subject of an aborted search by Thomas Pakenham, described in his book *The Mountains of Rasselas*. All things considered, four hours in either direction by mule or foot does seem a long, long way to go to see a broken bridge, but for those in pursuit of the truly esoteric it might be an irresistible option!

More alluring is the little-visited church of **Weyzazirt Kidhane Mihret**, which lies about 5km east of the Bahir Dar road some 15km past Mota. Constructed for Princess Seble-Wengiel, daughter of Emperor Fasilidas, this church is adorned with some superb 17th-century paintings – including a series depicting the 12 Apostles on the colonnades – and also houses the mummified remains of its founder and her husband.

Gonji Tewodros is another interesting Gonderine church, built on the rim of the Blue Nile Gorge by one of the sons of Emperor Fasilidas, and reached by continuing along the main Bahir Dar road for 8km past the turn-off to Weyzazirt, then following a side road to the east for 9km.

Near Debre Mai, some 30km before you reach Bahir Dar, stand the ruins of the 17th-century **Gimbe Maryam** and **Yebada** palaces, constructed respectively by emperors Susneyos and Fasilidas. The former palace lies about 5km west of the town and the latter 3km from town; both are accessible on foot or by mule only.

DEJEN TO BAHIR DAR VIA DEBRE MARKOS

DEBRE MARKOS Assuming that urban facilities feature highly in your priorities, the former capital of the defunct province of Gojjam, set at an altitude of 2,410m in the moist highlands north of the Blue Nile Gorge, is the obvious place to break up the long bus trip from the capital to Bahir Dar. With a breezy highland ambience – the town was formerly known as Mankorar (cold place) – and a neatly laid-out town centre supporting a population of around 65,000, Debre Markos is an attractive enough stopover, albeit one with few compelling sights.

Historically, Debre Markos's main claim to fame is as the site of the surrender of some 14,000 Italian troops to a mere 300 members of the combined Ethiopian–Allied army in April 1941, a key event in the collapse of the Italian occupation. The closest thing to a must-see in Debre Markos is the impressively decorated church

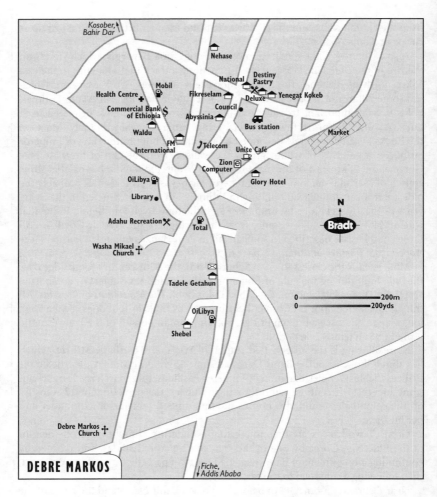

DEBRE MARKOS

for which the town is named, which was constructed in the last years of the 19th century by a local prince. Set in an attractive wooded compound, the church and its outbuildings lie about ten minutes' walk along the dirt road that slopes uphill in a southerly direction between the Total garage and the Adahu Recreation Centre on the central traffic roundabout.

Getting there and away Debre Markos lies 300km northwest of Addis Ababa along a road that is now surfaced in its entirety. The drive should take around four to five hours in a private vehicle, though you ought to allow another hour or two for stops. Direct buses to Debre Markos leave Addis Ababa at 05.30 daily. There is no direct transport if you are coming to Debre Markos from somewhere like Fiche or **Dejen**, so you will be reliant on finding an empty seat on a bus coming from Addis. If this proves to be difficult, hitching is a reasonably feasible option along this route.

Heading on to Bahir Dar, you will need to be at the bus station at 05.30 to stand much chance of getting a ticket on the council bus, though the complicated and chaotic booking procedure means you'll be lucky if you depart much before 08.00. If you fail to get a ticket straight through to Bahir Dar, a bus or two leaves Debre Markos for Dangla via Kosober at 09.00, and there is plenty of transport from Dangla to Bahir Dar. Overall, this is a better option than the council bus, and there is plenty of budget accommodation in Dangla in the unlikely event you were to get stuck there overnight – the Hahu Hotel on the Addis Ababa side of town looks the best bet.

Where to stay

FM International Hotel (30 rooms) ☎058 771 3227. On the main roundabout opposite the Bank of Abyssinia, this flash new cylindrical hotel is hands down the best place to stay in Debre Markos. The rooms each with flat-screen TV, hot-shower en suite & private balcony radiate out from a central marble staircase which winds its way up the middle of the hotel. There's a bright café serving fresh pastries & coffee as well as an internet café on the ground floor & a smart restaurant (dishes US$2.50–4.50) on the 1st floor. *US$12/14/28 sgl/dbl/twin.*

Shebel Hotel (31 rooms) ☎058 771 1410; e shebeit@ethionet.et. Tucked away behind the OiLibya garage on the Addis Ababa road around 200m from the main traffic roundabout, this faded multi-storey hotel was once the smartest hotel in Debre Markos. Hard to believe given the fraying state of the rooms – all with carpet, TV & hot-shower en suite. On the plus side, the popular ground-floor bar & restaurant serves a selection of local & Western dishes in the US$2–3 range. *US$8/10 sgl/dbl.*

Tadele Getahun Hotel (16 rooms) ☎058 771 2725. A little further down the road from the Shebel & a step down in quality, this place offers en-suite rooms with hot shower & satellite TV. A rather dreary bar & restaurant is attached. *US$7.50/9 dbl/twin.*

Fikreselam Hotel (22 rooms) ☎058 771 1922. This place near the bus station is good value. All rooms come with ¾ bed, private hot shower & satellite TV. *US$7.50.*

Delux Hotel (22 rooms) ☎058 771 4198. This retro-'80s throwback opposite the bus station offers small but clean rooms all with hot-water shower. Rooms facing the street have large full-length windows overlooking the bus station, so you might want to choose one facing the back. *US$4.50/6.50 sgl/dbl.*

Where to eat

Beyond the hotel restaurants – the best being the **FM International** and **Shebel** – there are a few excellent patisseries dotted around the centre including **Unite Café** near the old Tourist Hotel which is a good spot for a drink or light meal, with sandwiches and burgers costing around US$1.50–2.50, and the bright-and-breezy **Destiny Pastry** directly opposite the bus station with a sweet range of cakes and buns for less than US$1.

KOSOBER AND AWI ZONE The autonomous administrative zone of Awi, home to the Agaw people since Axumite times, lies to the northwest of Debre Markos, where it is bisected by the main asphalt road to Bahir Dar. The Agaw, whose neatly fenced compounds and circular homesteads – tall thatched roofs bound tightly by entwined bamboo sticks – form such a prominent feature of the countryside, are also known for their ecologically sustainable and highly productive traditional agricultural practices. Indeed, thanks to the communal monitoring of resources such as water and forests in Awi over several centuries, few if any other comparably cultivated parts of Ethiopia retain such a significant cover of indigenous woodland.

Blessed with a bountiful rainfall (more than 2,000mm per annum at higher altitudes) and fertile red soil, the landscape of Awi, though geologically subdued today, is – like that of Bishoftu closer to Addis Ababa – overtly volcanic in origin. Indeed, the area has experienced extensive eruptive activity within the last million years, as evidenced by the black basaltic rocks strewn like porous cannonballs across its green fields, the gigantic plugs that jut skywards from the surrounding hills, and a sprinkling of extinct craters, several of which support perennial or seasonal lakes.

Despite its wealth of low-key natural attractions and highly accessible location along the main road between Addis Ababa and Bahir Dar, Awi is generally bypassed by tourists in their haste to reach Lake Tana and the other big guns of the northern circuit. And fair enough, if your time is limited and your tolerance of basic conditions low, then Awi probably doesn't warrant your attention. Equally, the area is rich in potential for birdwatchers, ramblers and other nature lovers, and it will provide a refreshing rustic break from 'touristy' Ethiopia to those for whom travel is about the journey as much as the destination.

The obvious base from which to explore Awi is the small junction town of Kosober, which straddles the asphalt Bahir Dar road some 5km south of a magnificent volcanic plug called Mount Zivixi. Often referred to (and signposted as) Injibara, the name of the surrounding district, Kosober boasts good public transport connections in most directions, and is well endowed with small hotels and eateries, albeit none that comes close to conforming to tourist-class standards. Other significant settlements include Kesa, Tilili and Bure, which respectively lie 8km, 15km and 30km southeast of Kosober along the main road towards Debre Markos. All three towns boast a few basic hotels, while Bure is of minor logistical note as the northern terminus of a 250km unsurfaced road to Nekemte.

Getting there and around Kosober lies exactly 150km northeast of Debre Markos along the road to Bahir Dar. Coming from the south, buses from Debre Markos to Dangla leave at around 09.00 and stop in Kosober. Buses from Debre Markos to Bahir Dar also stop at Kosober, and will also drop travellers at the other towns mentioned above, but it would be customary to pay the full fare even if you hop off halfway. There is also quite a bit of local public transport connecting Kosober to other small towns in the area, as well as to Dangla 35km further north, from where there is plenty of transport on to Bahir Dar.

Where to stay and eat

Megenagna Pension (36 rooms) ☎058 227 0430. Located next to the OiLibya filling station, this friendly lodge has decent en-suite rooms with a private cold shower as well as smaller less-attractive common shower rooms, both with full-size beds. *US$2/6 without/with shower.*

Yordanis Hotel (15 rooms) ☎058 227 0431. This quiet, clean & pleasant little guesthouse, clearly signposted on the right side of the road towards Bahir Dar about 500m past the central junction in Kosober, has large rooms with ¾ bed using powerful common showers. A limited choice of food & drinks is available. *US$3.*

Family Café Fresh bread, doughnuts, coffee & other snacks served next to the Total garage on the Debre Markos road.

What to see

Fang Waterfall Situated on the Fetam River some 3km south of Tilili, this attractive waterfall is most notable perhaps for the striking rock formations it has exposed – a grid of shiny black hexagonal basalt columns whose crystalline shape is associated with lava that has cooled unusually quickly. The waterfall stands about 15m high, and can be very impressive after heavy rain, while in less torrential circumstances the pool at its base looks safe for a chilly dip. To get there, follow the road towards Kosober out of Tilili for about 500m after crossing the Fetam River, then turn left into a motorable track at the faded orange signpost that reads 'Stay at Interesting Fang Waterfall'. About 2km along this track, a marshy area to the right looks promising for endemics such as Rouget's rail and blue-winged goose, then after another 1km, you should hear the waterfall – and see the outline of the tree-lined gorge into which it tumbles – some 300m to your left. A couple of **basic lodges** can be found in Tilili.

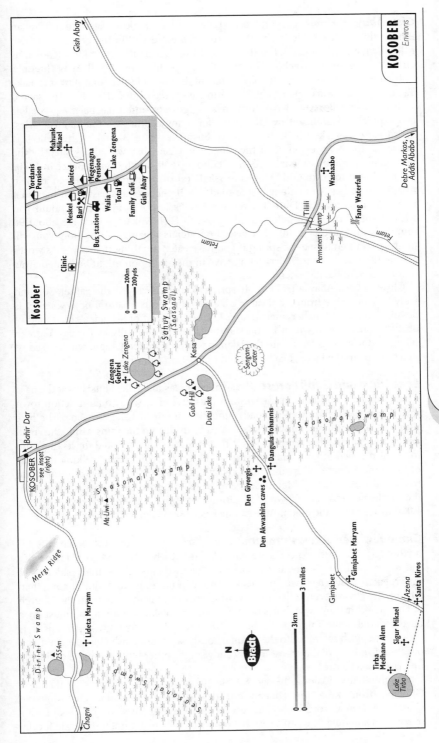

KOSOBER
Environs

Kosober

Yordanis Pension
Mahunk Mikael
United
Negenagna Pension
Lake Zengena
Meskel
Bari
Bus station
Walia
Total
Family Café
Gish Abay
Clinic

0   200m
0   200yds

Gish Abay The most geographically poignant landmark in Agaw country is an inherently unremarkable freshwater spring protected within the grounds of Gish Mikael Monastery some 30km due east of Kosober as the crow flies. Known as Gish Abay or Abay Minch, this is the starting point of the Gilgil Abay (literally, Calf Nile), which, as the most voluminous of the 60-odd rivers that flow into Lake Tana, is generally accepted to be the ultimate source of the Blue Nile. The sacred spring is also believed to have strong healing powers, and it has been regarded as geographically significant by Ethiopians for many centuries – the Spanish priest Pedro Páez was taken there by Emperor Susneyos in 1613, making him the first European to visit the source of the Blue Nile. Gish Abay was also visited by the Portuguese Jesuit missionary Jerónimo Lobo in 1629, and by James Bruce in 1770.

The closest town to Gish Mikael is Sekala (also sometimes referred to as Gish Abay), which lies 35km along a side road that branches northeast from the main Debre Markos road at Tilili. There are a few basic hotels in Sekala, should you wish to spend the night before heading out to Gish Mikael, which lies about 90 minutes' walk further south. Because the water is regarded to be holy you will not be permitted to see the spring if you have eaten anything that day – it's worth getting there early, as travellers who arrive in the afternoon might be turned away on suspicion of having eaten.

Close to Gish Abay, a trio of holy springs known locally as the Father, Son and Holy Spirit emerge from a hole above a cave into a warm natural pool where it is possible to swim. Further afield, some 15km northwest of Sekala, a small field of obelisks, only one of which is still standing, is known locally as Dingay Yegragn (Gragn's Rocks) in reference to the Islamic warlord Ahmed Gragn, who caused so much havoc in the Lake Tana hinterland in the 16th century.

Lake Dutsi and Gubil Forest The small and seasonal Lake Dutsi lies at the base of the domed Gubil Hill on the western outskirts of Kesa, a small junction town that flanks the Debre Markos road some 2km south of Lake Zengena. The lake supports large numbers of water-associated birds during the rains, while the small and readily accessible evergreen forest that swathes Gubil is noted for its highland forest birds. Two other points of natural interest lie within easy walking distance of Kesa: the Sahuy Floodplain and associated seasonal lake northeast of the main road, and the imposing Mount Sengem, whose wooded slopes, which rise from the southern outskirts of town to an altitude of above 2,500m, hide an impressive 1,000m-deep volcanic crater. At least one basic **hotel** is to be found in Kesa.

Gimjabet, Den Akwashita and Lake Tirba Given the Ethiopian gift for mythologising, you'd expect a decent tall story to be attached to a town with the name Gimjabet – literally 'Treasury'. But evidently not – the residents we interrogated about the town's name came up with nothing more illuminating than a blank 'It's always been called that'. Most likely the name derives from the Church of Gimjabet Maryam, which lies on the southern outskirts of town and must once have secured some important Church treasures. But who knows: perhaps it is simply a waggish reference to the incongruously large and plush Commercial Bank of Ethiopia edifice that rises assertively above every other building in the decidedly low-rise town centre?

Roughly halfway along the serviceable 10km dirt road that runs southeast to Gimjabet from Kesa, immediately outside the stone compound enclosing the Church of Den Giyorgis, the Den Akwashita Caves consist of a series of four overgrown sinkhole-like entrances that open into a large natural tunnel said locally to run for several kilometres underground. In times of war, the cave system has often served as a refuge (perhaps treasure was stored there too?), and the subterranean river that passes within 50m of the last entrance is regarded as holy by the local clergy, though you need a torch to see it.

The other attraction in the Gimjabet area is the pretty Tirba Crater Lake, 153m deep and nestled in a 1km² caldera some 4km west of town as the crow flies. To get there, you must first follow the road to Azena southwest for 3km until you see the Church of Sahta Kiros to the left. From here, it's a roughly 30-minute walk northwest to the lakeshore Tirba Medhane Alem, following a footpath that starts opposite Sahta Kiros and passes the Church of Sigur Mikael on the way.

Lake Zengena (*Entrance US$1.50 pp, US$1 for video cameras*) Foremost among Awi's beauty spots, situated just 6km south of Kosober practically alongside the Debre Markos road, is the spectacular freshwater Zengena Crater Lake. The forested rim of this near-perfect crater is set at an altitude of 2,500m, and the lakeshore lies perhaps 30m below this, but the lake itself is 166m in depth, making it the second deepest in the country. The northern slopes of the crater support an artificial cypress plantation as well as the recently constructed Church of Zengena Gebriel, but the southern slopes retain a cover of lush indigenous acacia woodland. Grivet monkeys are much in evidence, and there is plenty of birdlife too.

To get to Zengena from Kosober, follow the Debre Markos road south for 6km until you see a cypress-covered slope to your left, then follow the rough dirt track that leads through the plantation for about 200m to a shady parking area. Coming from the south, the track lies to the right about 2km after you pass through Kesa. Either way, the lake itself is invisible from the main road – and, for that matter, from the parking area, from where a steep 50m footpath leads downhill to the shore. Local authorities hope eventually to build a tourist lodge on the crater rim – until such time as that happens you can camp here for US$2 per tent, but there are no facilities and you must bring all your own supplies. You can also hire a horse for US$3 per person for a one-hour ride around the lake. It also makes for an idyllic picnic spot *en route* to Bahir Dar.

Dirini Swamp Situated within a collapsed caldera opposite the Church of Lideta Maryam, exactly 9.5km from Kosober along the unsealed road to Chagni, the perennial Dirini Swamp is of interest primarily for a varied selection of water-associated birds, including Rouget's rail, black-crowned crane, blue-winged goose and other waterfowl, as well as various herons, ibises and waders. Although the swamp lies no more than 500m north of the Chagni road, its existence is obscured by the crater walls during the dry season, so you could easily drive right past! During the wet season, the swamp often spills out from the crater to fill a second (non-volcanic) depression south of the road, in which case it can't be missed. An impressive volcanic plug juts skyward from a thicket of indigenous woodland on the north shore of the swamp – it looks climbable, but not easily, yet the views from the top should be excellent! Chagni, incidentally, is the largest town in Awi, supporting a population of around 25,000, and there is plenty of public transport there from Kosober – the only potential attraction I'm aware of in its immediate vicinity, however, is the seldom-visited Dondar Waterfall.

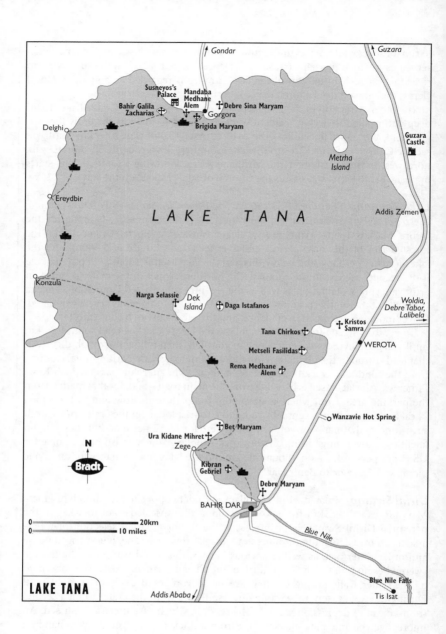

LAKE TANA

7

Bahir Dar and Lake Tana

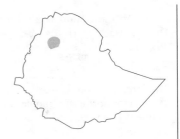

Set at an altitude of 1,830m, **Lake Tana** is the largest lake in Ethiopia, with a surface area of 3,673km², and it is also the source of the Blue Nile, a connection that explains many of Ethiopia's links with the ancient world. Tana was known to the ancient Greeks as Pseboe, and to the ancient Egyptians as Coloe; it was described by a 5th-century Greek dramatist as the 'copper-tinted lake ... that is the jewel of Ethiopia'. Even today, the papyrus *tankwa* that sail the lake bear a striking resemblance to the boats of ancient Egypt.

Aside from the southern spur from which the Nile flows, and on which Bahir Dar is situated, Tana has a broadly circular shape measuring some 65km in diameter. It was formed at least 20 million years ago, by an ancient lava extrusion that effectively functions as a natural dam. Averaging some 14m in depth, and dotted with more than three-dozen islands, many of which are inhabited, Tana harbours at least 26 different fish species, of which 17 are endemic to the lake. Tana is also renowned for its varied birdlife – flotillas of white pelican being a particularly common sight – while the shallows support small pods of hippos. As of early 2012 plans were under way to implement a Biosphere Reserve around Lake Tana which could have a significant impact on the future of tourism in the area.

The Tana area is the traditional home of the Amhara, a Christian people whose language was for many years the national language of Ethiopia. Tana was also the homeland of the Falasha who, although they are ethnically identical to the Amhara and speak the same language, practise a form of Judaism that appears to have been severed from the Jewish mainstream before 650BC. There are now very few Falasha people left in the Tana region; after centuries of persecution, most of them were airlifted to Israel in 1991.

Between the collapse of the Zagwe dynasty in the late 13th century and the establishment of Gondar as a permanent capital in the early 17th century, Tana was the political and spiritual focus of the Christian empire. Several temporary capitals were established on or near the lake's shore, and it is here where the Portuguese force led by Christopher Da Gama spent most of its time in Ethiopia. Many of the island monasteries which dot Lake Tana date to this time, though some are older – the monastery at Tana Kirkos, for one, appears to have served as a spiritual retreat long before Christianity was established in the region.

The largest city and most important tourist centre in the Tana region is **Bahir Dar**, which lies on the southern lakeshore close to the Nile outlet, and is connected by regular flights to Addis Ababa and the other major tourist centres of northern Ethiopia. In addition to being an attractive city in its own right, Bahir Dar serves as the obvious base from which to explore the region's other main attractions: the **Blue Nile Falls** and myriad **monasteries** dotted around the lake. Bahir Dar aside, the only significant lakeshore settlement is Gorgora, which lies on the northern shore 60km from the city of Gondar, and is connected to Bahir Dar by a weekly ferry service.

BAHIR DAR

This large town on the southern shore of Lake Tana has a sticky tropical ambience unusual for northern Ethiopia and more similar to somewhere like Hawassa in the southern Rift Valley. Palm-lined avenues and pretty lakeside vistas make Bahir Dar a decidedly attractive town, and it is also the base for visits to the Blue Nile Falls and Lake Tana's many monasteries. With tourist amenities that are among the best in the country, Bahir Dar is an excellent place to settle into for a few days.

As recently as the early 1950s, Bahir Dar was little more than a sleepy lakeshore village, overshadowed politically and economically by Gondar to the north and Debre Markos to the south. The initial stimulus for its subsequent rapid growth was the decision to build a hydro-electric plant at nearby Tis Abay. Subsequent to this, Bahir Dar has become one of Ethiopia's most important industrial centres and the country's seventh-largest town, with a population approaching the 185,000 mark – and western outskirts that have visibly expanded since 1994, when the first edition of this guide was researched. In 1995, Bahir Dar leapfrogged ahead of Gondar, Dessie and Debre Markos – the respective former administrative capitals of the defunct provinces of Gondar, Wolo and Gojjam – when a capital was selected for the redrawn Federal Region of Amhara.

Although the town itself is modern, the waterfront **Church of Bahir Dar Giyorgis**, situated near the main traffic roundabout, was founded at least 400 years ago. The original church was knocked down to make way for a larger and more modern but not unattractive edifice in the Haile Selassie era, but the compound also houses a disused two-storey stone tower, architecturally reminiscent of the Gonderine palaces, and whose construction is attributed to the Jesuit priest Pedro Páez during the reign of Susneyos.

As with so many large Ethiopian towns, the juxtaposition between urban modernity and rustic traditionalism is a striking feature of Bahir Dar, no more so than in the bustling daily **central market**, which ranks as one of the finest in the country and well worth a couple of hours. The goatskin *injera*-holder called an *agelgil*, traditionally used by herdsmen as a 'picnic basket', makes for an unusual and inexpensive souvenir, as does the locally produced white *shama* cloth.

Many travellers love Bahir Dar without reservation, but others reckon that their time there was marred by the histrionics of various guides, fixers and compulsive yellers. The 'hassle factor' has died down considerably in recent years, but it remains the case that initial impressions tend to be influenced by whether you arrive by air or by bus. The reception committee at the bus station is notorious for latching onto travellers and trying to set up their accommodation in the hope of a commission from the hotel, which the traveller will cover by paying more than they would have otherwise – and be warned that such touts often claim any hotel that doesn't give commissions is full. Staying at a slightly more expensive hotel, or away from the town centre, will definitely help protect you from unwanted attention. So, too, will exploring the town in the company of a local guide.

GETTING THERE AND AWAY
By air   Daily flights by **Ethiopian Airlines** [194 D5] (\ *office 058 220 0020;* \ *airport 058 226 0036;* e *bjrtsm@ethiopianairlines.com*) connect Bahir Dar and Addis Ababa in either direction (US$50). There is also at least one flight daily in either direction

between Bahir Dar and Lalibela (US$40) with connecting flights to Axum (US$85). Onward tickets *must* be reconfirmed a day ahead of schedule at Ethiopian Airlines' city office, which keeps normal business hours seven days a week.

The airport lies about 3km west of the town centre, and unless you are booked into a hotel with a shuttle service, or being met by a tour operator, you'll have to get a taxi into town, which shouldn't cost more than US$5. It's worth noting here that many hotels, including the Ghion, Ethio-Star and Summerland, now offer free airport transfers.

By road Bahir Dar lies 560km from Addis Ababa along the surfaced road through Debre Markos and Kosober. A significantly shorter route through Mota also connects Addis Ababa and Bahir Dar, and offers more in the way of sightseeing for aficionados of arcane churches, but this road is unsurfaced north of Goha Tsion, so it takes longer to drive than the Debre Markos route. In a private vehicle, the drive from Addis Ababa to Bahir Dar via Debre Markos (see *Chapter 6*, page 181) can be undertaken in one long day, even allowing for the popular diversion to Debre Libanos, but two days would allow for a more relaxed drive as well as further sightseeing.

Both Selam and Sky Bus run direct daily buses between Addis Ababa and Bahir Dar, which leave in either direction at around 05.30 (US$18; around 9 hours). If the prospect of spending a whole day on a bus doesn't grab you it is possible to split the trip into two separate day-long bus rides, stopping at Debre Markos, Kosober or Mota. Potential stops on the road between Addis Ababa and Bahir Dar are discussed more fully in *Chapter 6*.

Bahir Dar and Gondar lie 180km apart via a road that is now surfaced in its entirety. The drive takes about three hours in a private vehicle, not allowing for possible diversions to Awramba or Guzara Castle. Buses leave in either direction at 06.00, 08.00 and 16.00 (US$4; 4 hours). A regular minibus service also departs throughout the day from the bus station (US$4.50). To get to Lalibela on public transport, you need to catch the 06.00 bus to Dessie, disembark at Gashena, and hope for a lift from there.

By boat A daily ferry service runs between Bahir Dar and the Zege Peninsula costing US$3.20 one-way. If you are looking for a longer trip, the inexpensive weekly ferry across Lake Tana to Gorgora, a short bus ride away from Gondar, is described in *The Lake Tana Ferry* box, page 198. Possibilities for exploring the Lake Tana monasteries as a day trip are discussed elsewhere in this chapter, but it is worth mentioning here that one could extend such a trip to terminate at Gorgora – not a cheap option at US$236 and up, but reasonably affordable if it is divided amongst a group.

GETTING AROUND Minibuses run from the main roundabout along the Gondar road past Abay Minch Lodge. Plenty of cheap *bajajis* clog Bahir Dar's streets and can easily be chartered for around US$1–1.50. Bicycles can be hired at the Ghion Hotel or along the road between the main roundabout and the market; expect to pay around US$1.80 per hour. Details of organising boat trips to the various Lake Tana monasteries, and of reaching the Blue Nile Falls, are included under the sections on these excursions.

Boat hire Bahir Dar has several reliable operators that can arrange trips to the monasteries. Rates vary from season to season and are to some extent negotiable; the prices listed overleaf should only be used as a guideline. Beyond price, another

A worthwhile short excursion if you have a few hours to spare in Bahir Dar is to the **Blue Nile**, which exits Lake Tana on the eastern outskirts of town. To reach the outlet, you can walk, cycle or catch a charter taxi or local *bajaj* to about 1km past Abay Minch Lodge, where a large bridge crosses the river. The wide river here provides ideal conditions for hippos and crocodiles, both of which are occasionally seen from the bridge, and the **Monastery of Debre Maryam** can be reached easily and affordably (see page 203).

A popular onward option from here involves taking the first right turn after the bridge and following it for about 2.5km to the top of **Bezawit Hill**, which is dominated by an ostentatious split-level **palace** built for Haile Selassie in 1967 and used by him on only two occasions during the remaining seven years of his rule. Entrance to the disused palace is forbidden, as is photography of the exterior, but the hill does provide an excellent vantage point over the town and Lake Tana, especially at dusk, and there's a chance of seeing **hippos** in the river below.

factor to consider is the horsepower rating on the boat's engine. A boat with a smaller engine might seem like a better deal, but it could be much slower. Even with a sunshade it can get very hot out on the water. Especially for longer trips, a faster boat is worth the extra expense. Before heading out, make sure that your boat has enough life vests for all passengers on board. Sunscreen and hats are essential, as are food and plenty of drinking water for full-day trips. Finally, note that boat prices *do not* include church entrance fees.

Lake Tana Pontoon Operations [195 F5] (℅ *058 226 4509;* m *0911 43 14 15;* e *tanaboats555@yahoo.com*) have four pontoon boats, some with 60hp engines, and a larger boat with a 150hp engine. These boats hold up to 25 people, making them ideal for larger groups. For a group of one to five the pricing is US$89/265 half/full day with prices going up incrementally as you add more passengers. (A full-day trip for 20–25 passengers costs US$324 at the time of research.) Tourist boats operated by **Lake Tana Transport Enterprise** [194 C6] (℅ *058 220 0730/0027*) are similarly priced. Cheaper rates are available through private operators at several of the hotels in town including the **Ghion Hotel** [194 B6] but again make sure that your boat has enough life vests for all passengers on board. All three operators offer trips to Gorgora on the northern lakeshore, with prices starting at US$412 for a two-day crossing.

Guides Travellers on pre-booked packages will generally be allocated local guides working for the company they have booked with. For independent travellers, there is little inherent need to take on a guide in town or to visit the Blue Nile Falls (though it can be argued that a good local guide will deflect a lot of hassle). A guide isn't far short of necessary if you want to set up a trip to the lake monasteries. Although no shortage of 'guides' wander the streets of Bahir Dar offering their services to independent travellers, it's worth asking around for an official guide at the Ghion Hotel or **Galaxy Express Services** (m *0911 023 242/0918 023 242*) office at Blue Nile Resort Tana Hotel.

TOURIST INFORMATION The **Amhara Regional Tourist Office** [194 B5] (℅ *058 220 1686/2650*; e *amhtour@ethionet.et*) is conveniently located along a back road behind the Commercial Bank of Ethiopia. It stocks a couple of useful brochures covering local tourist attractions, though for practical local travel advice you would be better off picking the brains of one of the private tour operators at one of the bigger hotels.

WHERE TO STAY

Luxury

Kuriftu Resort & Spa [194 B6] (28 rooms) \058 226 4868; e contactbl@kurifturesortspa.com; www.kurifturesortspa.com. This high-end resort next to the Ghion Hotel is owned by the same American-backed group that created the Boston Day Spa in Addis & the Kuriftu Resort & Spa in Bishoftu. The beautifully decorated private waterfront stone bungalows are similar quality & style as their counterparts – all with DSTV, rain showers, minibar with wine & private patio with a fireplace. Other facilities include a spa, restaurant & bar, a stunning guests-only swimming pool & outdoor terrace overlooking the lake & airport shuttle. Future plans include a new gym & cinema. Rates include a complimentary massage, manicure & pedicure. *US$188/198/229 dbl/twin/suite FB, US$119/126/150 dbl/twin/suite HB.*

Upmarket

Abay Minch Lodge [off map 195 H7] (44 rooms) \058 218 1039 (Bahir Dar)/011 515 4310 (Addis); f 058 218 2223; e sandmp@ethionet.et or sime@ethionet.et; www.abayminchlodge.com. Previously a recreation centre, this pleasant new lodge is located on a secluded section of the lake north of the Blue Nile Resort Tana Hotel, just out of town. Accommodation is in one of 22 stone bungalows each housing 2 separate units with small balcony & the flashiest en-suite showers we've seen outside side of Addis Ababa featuring a radio & rain shower. Facilities include airport shuttle, business centre, & restaurant & bar serving both Continental & Ethiopian cuisine, Visa & MasterCard are accepted & rates include breakfast. *US$76/89/89 sgl/dbl/twin.*

Homland Hotel [off map 194 A6] (28 rooms) \058 220 4545; m 0918 341 110; e rahel.belay@gmail.com. This new hotel conveniently located opposite Trade & Transport Bureau on the road to the airport caters well to business travellers. The suitably modern & orderly rooms all have tiled floors, flat-screen TVs, fridge, en suite & private balcony. The terrace restaurant & bar on the first floor serves the usual Ethiopian/Continental

fare in the US$2–5 range. Rates include free breakfast, Wi-Fi & airport shuttle. *US$47/65/76 sgl/dbl/twin.*

Moderate

Blue Nile Resort-Tana Hotel [195 F7] (62 rooms) \058 220 0554/0626. Previously part of the government-owned Ghion chain, the now privately run hotel is situated a couple of kilometres out of town along the Gondar road. The first choice of most tour operators, the Tana boasts one overwhelming selling point: the large, thickly wooded lakeshore grounds, which offer genuine respite from the nearby city & host a rich variety of birds ranging from giant kingfisher & various herons to colourful woodland dwellers such as double-toothed & banded barbet, Bruce's green pigeon & white-cheeked turaco. The en-suite rooms, while dated, all have lake views. The food is nothing to write home about though if you're staying a couple of nights you might want to spice things up by asking the kitchen to prepare a traditional buffet. Future plans include Wi-Fi & airport shuttle. *US$38/51/75 sgl/dbl/suite.*

Papyrus Hotel [194 D1] (100 rooms) \058 220 5100; f 058 220 5047; e papy@ethionet.et or info@papyrushotelethiopia.com; www.papyrushotelethiopia.com. Situated at the tail end of the city centre, with a less-than-captivating view of an OiLibya garage, this blandly functional & relatively modern multi-storey building lies some distance from the lake, but arguably compensates by being centred on a large, fairly clean – & in this sweaty climate rather welcome – swimming pool (available to non-guests for US$2). It also has 3 restaurants including a decent traditional restaurant with music on Sat & Thu evenings. Visa & MasterCard accepted. *US$41/47 sgl/dbl, US$50–59 suite inc breakfast.*

Summerland Hotel [195 E5] (40 rooms) \058 220 6566; e gogobahirdar@yahoo.com. The 5-storey Summerland Hotel opened in early 2005 & has a great water-view location – or rather, would have were the view not compromised by

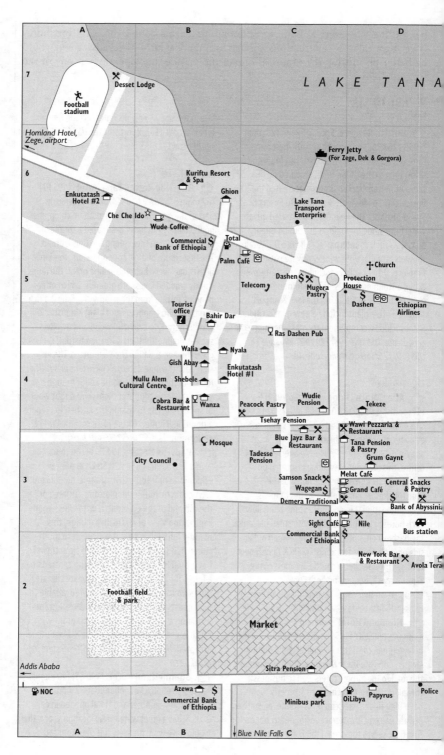

LAKE TANA

Football stadium

Desset Lodge

Homland Hotel, Zege, airport

Ferry Jetty (For Zege, Dek & Gorgora)

Kuriftu Resort & Spa

Ghion

Lake Tana Transport Enterprise

Enkutatash Hotel #2

Che Che Ido

Wude Coffee

Commercial Bank of Ethiopia

Total

Palm Café

Church

Protection House

Dashen

Mugera Pastry

Telecom

Dashen

Ethiopian Airlines

Tourist office

Bahir Dar

Ras Dashen Pub

Walia

Nyala

Gish Abay

Shebele

Enkutatash Hotel #1

Mullu Alem Cultural Centre

Cobra Bar & Restaurant

Wanza

Peacock Pastry

Wudie Pension

Tekeze

Tsehay Pension

Wawi Pezzaria & Restaurant

Mosque

Blue Jayz Bar & Restaurant

Tana Pension & Pastry

City Council

Tadesse Pension

Grum Gaynt

Melat Café

Samson Snack

Central Snacks & Pastry

Wagegan

Grand Café

Demera Traditional

Bank of Abyssinia

Pension

Sight Café

Nile

Commercial Bank of Ethiopia

Bus station

New York Bar & Restaurant

Avola Tera

Football field & park

Addis Ababa

Market

Sitra Pension

NOC

Azewa

Commercial Bank of Ethiopia

Minibus park

OiLibya

Papyrus

Police

Blue Nile Falls

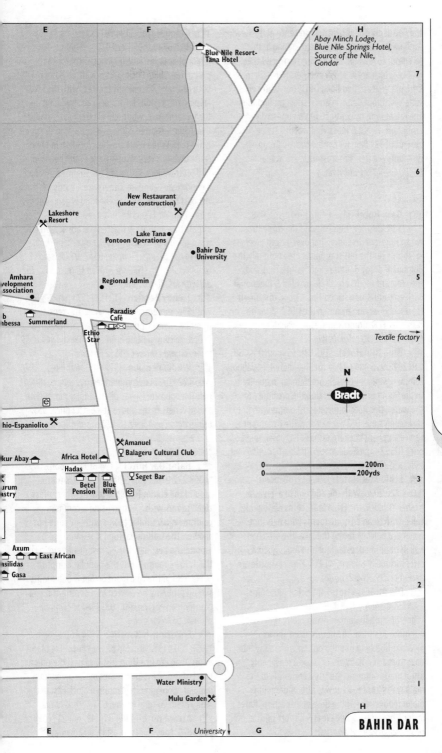

Blue Nile Resort-
Tana Hotel

Abay Minch Lodge,
Blue Nile Springs Hotel,
Source of the Nile,
Gondar

New Restaurant
(under construction)

Lakeshore
Resort

Lake Tana
Pontoon Operations

Bahir Dar
University

Amhara
Development
Association

Regional Admin

Summerland

Paradise
Café

Ethio
Star

Textile factory

N

Bradt

 E

hio-Espaniolito

Amanuel
Balageru Cultural Club

ukur Abay

Africa Hotel

Hadas

Seget Bar

rum
astry

Betel
Pension

Blue
Nile

e

0   200m
0   200yds

Axum

East African

asilidas

Gasa

Water Ministry

Mulu Garden

University

BAHIR DAR

the decidedly eye-distracting presence of the new Amhara Development Building looming in the foreground. It would be churlish to criticise the rooms, which are as plush as it gets in northern Ethiopia – clean tiled floor, DSTV, hot-water en suite – without being in any respect memorable. The restaurant, by contrast, has an unusually ambitious menu, & looks well worth a try at around US$3–5.50 for a main course. Group discounts & a free airport shuttle are available. *US$30/39/43 sgl/dbl/twin.*

Budget

🏠 **Gasa Hotel** [195 E2] (31 rooms) ☎058 226 3568. This new hotel around the corner from Axum Hotel seems somewhat over-priced given its location near the bus station, an area normally the domain of dingy dollar-a-night joints. That said, the pleasant rooms are all clean, tiled & functional with en suite & flat-screen TVs. A good restaurant is attached serving dishes in the US$2–5 range & free Wi-Fi & airport shuttle are available. *US$24/27/32.50 sgl/dbl/twin.*

🏠 **Blue Nile Hotel** [195 F3] (55 rooms) ☎058 220 2028/226 4093–4; e thebluenilehotel@yahoo. com; www.bluenilehotel.com. Similar in quality to the Summerland but lacking the proximity to the water, this hotel offers decent rooms with hot-shower en suite, DSTV & balcony. The restaurant serves excellent Western dishes at a reasonable price (US$2–4). *US$22.50/26.50/29.50 sgl/dbl/ twin, US$33 suite.*

🏠 **Ethio Star Hotel** [195 F5] (62 rooms) ☎058 220 2026. With the addition of a new fresher 'B' block, the Ethio Star seems reasonable value with clean en-suite rooms with nets, hot water & a balcony facing the lake. The attached Kokeb traditional restaurant also looks good & rates include breakfast; Wi-Fi & airport shuttle are available. *US$21/27 sgl/dbl.*

🏠 **Dib Anbessa Hotel** [195 E5] (60 rooms) ☎058 220 1436; f 058 220 1818; e bearlionhotelbahirdar@yahoo.com. Older & not quite so slick as the hotels listed above, this pleasant hotel – a popular option with many tour operators & regular visitors – has a reasonably attractive location on the city-centre side of the main waterfront road. It was also undergoing major renovations at the time of inspection. Rates include breakfast & free Wi-Fi & airport shuttle. *US$18/22.50/24 sgl/dbl/twin.*

🏠 **Ghion Hotel** [194 B6] (33 rooms) ☎058 220 0111/0740; f 058 220 0303; e ghionbd@ ethionet.et or bisratwel@yahoo.com. Formerly part of the Ghion chain, this privatised hotel is both centrally & scenically located, with the lake lapping its gracious lawns, pelicans huddling on the waterfront, & white-cheeked turaco, paradise flycatcher & spotted eagle owl resident in the giant ficus trees. While it has the best location in town & the owner is very sympathetic to the needs of budget travellers, the rooms are shabby & need of a good clean & update. Otherwise it easily ranks as the best deal in Bahir Dar. The food is good, there's a free 24hr Wi-Fi service, hotel residents get a free airport transfer, Visa & MasterCard are accepted & it's as good a place as any to set up reliable boat trips to the islands. *Camping US$2, US$6 using common shower, US$9 sgl with en suite, US$12/15 dbl with lake/back view.*

🏠 **Tsehay Pension** [194 C4] (57 rooms) ☎058 222 1550; e meritam@ethionet.et. This central hotel is somewhat over-priced with clean rooms with a ¾ bed, balcony, netting & en-suite hot shower. *US$9 using common shower, US$12 en suite.*

🏠 **Wudie Pension** [194 C4] (36 rooms) ☎058 220 0335. Recommended by readers, this pension opposite Tsehay offers similar rooms with ¾ bed & nets to the above at a better price. *US$7 using common shower, US$12 en suite.*

Shoestring

🏠 **Bahir Dar Hotel** [194 B5] (23 rooms) ☎058 222 0788. This pleasant hotel, situated around the corner from the tourist office offers clean rooms with a ¾ bed using a common cold shower & similar rooms with en-suite hot shower. The traditional food is regarded to be among the best in town – most dishes are in the US$1.50–3 range – but the popular campfire party held in the courtyard on Sat & Sun nights should probably be viewed as a deterrent if you're planning an early night. *US$5 using common shower, US$6 en suite.*

🏠 **Enkutatash Hotel #2** [194 A6] (9 rooms) ☎058 220 4435. Situated on the south side of the Addis Ababa road a short distance past the Ghion Hotel, this place is an offshoot of the perennially popular eponymous restaurant a block east of the Mullu Alem Cultural Centre. *US$6/9 dbl/twin.*

🏠 **Azewa Hotel** [194 B1] (41 rooms) ☎058 220 3820. Lousy location aside, an adequate room with a queen bed & en-suite cold shower. The downstairs terrace restaurant is popular & known for its fish dishes. *US$4.50/6 sgl/twin using common shower, US$5.50 dbl en suite.*

🏠 **Tana Pension** [194 D3] (12 rooms) 📞 058 220 1302. The best cheapie in town, simply because it declines to charge a discriminatory

faranji price, this friendly pension is situated on the main north–south road through town, close to the bus station, & right above a good pastry shop & restaurant. This hotel has adhered to a one-price-for-all policy for years, & it deserves our support so long as this remains the case! *US$4 using common shower, US$5 en suite.*

✖ **WHERE TO EAT AND DRINK** The upmarket and moderate hotels listed previously all have decent restaurants serving local and foreign dishes. The restaurants at the **Dib Anbessa** [194 E5] and **Papyrus** [194 D1] hotels have good reputations, the new **Summerland** [195 E5] and **Blue Nile** [195 F3] hotels have a more interesting menu, and the out-of-town **Blue Nile Resort – Tana Hotel** [195 F7] is slightly pricier but comes with a far more attractive setting. The food at the relatively inexpensive **Ghion Hotel** [194 B6] is also pretty good, with a menu as varied as any, and you can eat on the shady veranda or in the atmospheric grounds, while the **Azewa Hotel** [194 B1] is renowned for serving some of the best and most inexpensive fish goulash around.

For good Ethiopian food, reliable bets include the stalwart **Tana Pension** [194 D3], the Kokeb traditional restaurant at **Ethio Star Hotel** [195 F5] and **Bahir Dar Pension** [194 B5] – the last is a nice place to hang out on Saturday and Sunday nights.

Bahir Dar also has its fair share of decent pastry shops, of which the excellent **Cloud Nine Pastry** [194 C4] below the Tsehay Pension stands out for its tasty confectionaries and good selection of juices. Also worth a try are the **Tana Pastry** [194 D3] on the main road, **Mugera Pastry** [194 C5] near the Dashen Bank, **Paradise Café** [194 F5] next to the Ethio Star Hotel, and **Central Pastry** [194 D3] opposite the bus station.

✖ **Blue Jayz Bar & Restaurant** [194 C4] m 0918 760 087; ⏰ 06.30–22.00 daily. Just down from the Tsehay Pension, this friendly place has a faithful crowd & offers sandwiches & salads in addition to the typical fare. *US$1.50–3.*

✖ **Desset Lodge** [194 A7] m 0918 340 199; ⏰ 06.00–22.00 daily. Located near the football stadium, this new restaurant with its beautiful lakeside spot, shady fig trees & prettily landscaped gardens is an attractive place to while away an afternoon with both inside & outside dining, a lengthy menu of Ethiopian & Continental dishes as well as coffees, beers & light snacks all on offer. In the near future it will also host accommodation with 8 rooms currently under construction. *US$2–4.50.*

✖ **Enkutatash Restaurant** [194 B4] ⏰ 11.00-22.00 daily. Tucked away in the back roads just east of the Mullu Alem Cultural Centre, this popular local eatery (house speciality fish cutlet) has for some years been entrenched as one of Bahir Dar's top tourist spots – unfortunately it appears to have responded to the ubiquitous guidebook recommendations by charging discriminatory *faranji* prices. *US$2–4.*

✖ **Ethio-Espaniolito** [195 E4] 📞 058 220 5156; ⏰ 07.00–22.00 daily. Located behind the Dib Anbessa Hotel, this is another good local restaurant serving a variety of local & Western dishes. *US$2–4.*

✖ **Lakeshore Resort** [195 E6] m 0918 340 666; ⏰ 06.00–midnight daily. Perched on a hillside overlooking the lake, this new place is already drawing the crowds with its combination of good location & good food. Live music on Thu, Sat & Sun. *US$1.50–4.*

✖ **Mulu Garden** [195 G1] m 0918 787 790; ⏰ 07.00–21.00 daily. On the road to the university, this new place is unsurprisingly popular with local students. Serves a variety of light snacks & drinks. *US$1.50–3.*

✖ **Wawi Pezzaria & Restaurant** [194 C4] m 0918 763 219; ⏰ 07.00–22.00 daily. Inability to spell aside, this popular restaurant does a decent job at imitating Italian fare. It also offers a small selection of Ethiopian dishes as well as sandwiches & breakfast. *Pastas US$1.50–2.50, pizzas US$2–4.*

✖ **Wude Coffee** [194 B6] m 0918 765 662; ⏰ 06.30–22.00 daily. Similar in style to Teshi

Buna in Addis, this smart new café-cum-restaurant opposite Kuriftu Resort & Spa serves excellent coffee (US$0.25–0.40) as well as a small selection of Western dishes & what one reader claims is the best *shiro tegabino* in the country. *US$1.50–2.*

ENTERTAINMENT AND NIGHTLIFE The recently opened **Che Che Ido** [194 B6] near Wude Coffee is the in place for live music with nightly performances starting at 20.00; the atmosphere is very informal, the clientele predominantly local, and you can come and go as you please. The **Balageru Cultural Club** [195 F3] (\ *058 220 2448*) next to the Amanuel Restaurant also stands out for its lively traditional music and dancing from all over Ethiopia. It is customary to tip the dancers at the end of the show.

Situated close to the tourist office, the more ostentatious municipal **Mullu Alem Cultural Centre** [194 B4], despite the fancy name, serves as little other than a cinema, showing foreign films on Saturday and Sunday only.

OTHER PRACTICALITIES
Foreign exchange The **Dashen Bank** [194 D5] opposite St George's Church has a fairly reliable ATM accepting Visa and MasterCard, while the ATM at the **Wagegan Bank** [194 C3] accepts Visa. US dollar and other major denomination travellers'

THE LAKE TANA FERRY

The MV *Tananich* crosses the lake between Bahir Dar and Gorgora once a week. There are several reasons why you might want to use this ferry. There's the aura of romance attached to sailing across any large lake, particularly when that lake happens to be the source of the Nile River and very beautiful to boot. For travellers who are bussing through northern Ethiopia, the fact that the ferry is the sole opportunity to take a break from road transport should be enough. The trip as a whole offers a mellow, cheap respite from the more frenzied aspects of travelling, as well as a wonderfully low-key glimpse of a part of Ethiopia that lies well clear of any established tourist itinerary. If you can fit it in, then do it.

The MV *Tananich* leaves Bahir Dar at 07.00 every Sunday and arrives in Gorgora around 16.00 on Monday. It starts the return trip at 07.00 on Thursday (but ticket sales start at 06.00) and arrives in Bahir Dar on Friday afternoon. In both directions, there is an overnight stop at Konzula. A first-class seat in the salon costs US$15 for foreigners, which is a lot more than locals pay to be on the deck, but still a good deal for two days' travel on Ethiopia's largest lake. Apart from seats and tables, the salon's only facilities are lights and running water. There is also a toilet for exclusive use of staff and salon passengers. It would be sensible to bring some food and drinking water with you, though the ferry does stop for an hour or so at Zege and several small villages where you can disembark for *wat*, sodas and tea.

I did the trip from south to north and will describe it that way. After leaving Bahir Dar at 07.00 on Sunday, the ferry arrives at Zege at 08.00 and departs from there an hour later. The next stop is at the village of Gurer on Dek Island, which the boat reaches at around 11.00. Gurer is little more than a collection of mud huts, but hippos are often seen in the area, and a short walk inland revealed dense thicket, forest and swamp. There are several other islands in this group, including the one housing Daga Istafanos Monastery. There is no hotel in Gurer, but with a tent, some food and – ideally – a map, it could be an interesting place to explore, secure in the knowledge that the boat will return in four days' time.

cheques and cash can also be exchanged into local currency at the Dashen Bank or (rather less efficiently) at **Commercial Bank of Ethiopia** [194 B5 & B1] branches opposite the Ghion Hotel and a block up from the Papyrus Hotel. At other times, your only option is to try to exchange US dollars cash with one of the smarter hotels – a service generally offered to hotel residents only.

Internet and email Numerous internet cafés are now dotted all around Bahir Dar and charge less than US$0.05 per minute. The internet café in Protection House on the main waterfront road is recommended, as is the one in the Ghion Hotel.

THE BLUE NILE FALLS

About 30km after it exits Lake Tana, the Blue Nile plunges over a 45m-high rock face to form one of Africa's most spectacular waterfalls, known locally as Tis Abay (Smoke of the Nile) or Tis Isat (Water that Smokes). Tis Abay consists of four separate streams and is most impressive for the sheer volume of water that pours over it, particularly during the rainy season. The Nile is 400m wide above the waterfall; in the gorge below, it follows a much narrower course estimated to be 37m deep!

When the boat arrives in Konzula at around 16.00, your first priority should be a mad dash to find a room at the only hotel. The village gets visitors only twice a week, and it's not braced for the influx. There's no need to panic, just get to the village quickly – plenty of rooms were available when I arrived, but they had run out ten minutes later. It's a fairly steep ten-minute walk from the pier to the village, so it might speed things up to lock your luggage in the salon and collect it later (for that matter, I would have few qualms about locking it there overnight and just taking up a daypack). Once there, the hotel is predictably basic, predictably over-priced – at least for *faranjis*, who pay US$3 a room that wouldn't fetch half that price were there any choice in the matter – and lacking any running water. The attached restaurant serves fried eggs and tasty *asa wat*.

There's not anything compelling to do or see in Konzula, aside from the small church with its attractively wooded grounds, and if you arrive at dusk you're unlikely to be in much of a mood to explore. Even if you are, the mass of children that will follow your every step might be a little daunting. I've never seen anything like the kids here: I must have had a pack of 100 trailing behind me. To be fair, there wasn't any request for money or anything like that. Konzula seems a friendly place, but it doesn't see too many *faranji* visitors.

The ferry departs from Konzula at 07.00 on Monday and arrives at Eseydbir around two hours later. This is a pretty if unremarkable town, where you should be able to locate a soda and something to eat. The next stop, at around 12.00, is at Delghi, a larger town on a rather bland stretch of shore. Delghi has a restaurant, and even a hotel. From Delghi, the ferry takes about three hours to reach Gorgora (see page 211).

Note that this is Ethiopia, not Switzerland, and while the ferry schedule is reasonably reliable, exact timings may vary according to the amount of cargo to be loaded, mechanical problems or the captain's whim.

The 18th-century Scottish traveller James Bruce is often, but incorrectly, credited as the first European to see Tis Abay. In fact, Bruce was two centuries too late to claim that distinction, as the first description of the waterfall is included in the memoirs of the Portuguese priest João Bermudes, which were published in 1565. Nevertheless, Bruce is responsible for the most famous description of the Blue Nile Falls: 'a magnificent sight, that ages, added to the greatest length of human life, would not efface or eradicate from my memory; it struck me with a kind of stupor, and a total oblivion of where I was, and of every other sublunary concern.' After reading this, I was a little disappointed by the actuality when I first saw Tis Abay in 1994 – it isn't in the same league as Victoria Falls, to which it is often compared – but, with less fanciful expectations, Ethiopia's premier waterfall in full flow has to be classed as a sight not to be missed.

Whatever mild disappointment I experienced back then cannot be compared to that of more recent visitors to Tis Abay. In the words of Steve Rooke, a tour leader who visits Ethiopia annually: 'The Blue Nile Falls are no more! Gone are the thundering waters and clouds of spray with their attendant rainbows. All that is left is a small narrow trickle across a vast expanse of bare rock – frankly, the waterfall at Awash is more impressive!' The reason for the falls' demise is the completion of a hydro-electric plant that diverts something like 95% of the water when it is operating. On our most recent visit in 2011 the falls were again flowing, but this possibly had more to do with luck in timing our arrival at the end of the rainy season. Various rumours however were doing the rounds about the long-term status of the waterfall – among them that the hydro-electric plant is currently only working at 75% capacity and that it will cease operating once the new Grand Ethiopian Renaissance Dam (see boxed text, *Grand plans for new dams* in *Chapter 6*, page 179) to be built further upstream on the Blue Nile in the Benishangul-Gumuz region is completed, allowing Lake Tana to continue to feed the falls. Either way, as Steve Rooke points out: 'Reducing the Blue Nile Falls to a Disneyland-type attraction that is turned on and off at will detracts from the whole experience; more important perhaps is that the lack of water is devastating a spray-soaked ecosystem that has taken thousands of years to evolve.'

As things stand, the unfortunate reality is that so long as the plant keeps running, the Cliff Formerly Known as the Blue Nile Falls is not worth making a special effort to see unless you time your visit directly after the rainy season – with devastating consequences for Bahir Dar's nascent tourist industry. Full details of visiting the falls are retained below, in the hope that the water will come back online during the lifespan of this edition, but this is far from certain.

To the west of Tis Abay, in the Yagume Escarpment some 7km off the road, stands Dengai Debelo, an impressive rock-hewn church said to have been carved by King Lalibela before his coronation.

GETTING THERE AND AWAY The most straightforward way of visiting the waterfall is to organise a half-day excursion from Bahir Dar with a reputable tour operator. It's also very easy to visit the waterfall independently. There are four buses daily between Bahir Dar and the village of Tis Abay (US$0.80). These leave the main bus station at roughly 06.00, 09.00, 12.00 and 13.00. The trip takes an hour and, upon arriving in Tis Abay, the buses fill up immediately and return to Bahir Dar. The last bus out of Tis Abay will leave at around 15.00. Aside from the obvious advantage of allowing you more time to get back, catching the 06.00 bus out of Bahir Dar also means you will be walking out to the waterfall before the heat of the day sets in. Alternatively, many of the hotels in Bahir Dar, including the Ghion Hotel, offer tours to the falls starting at around US$9 per person.

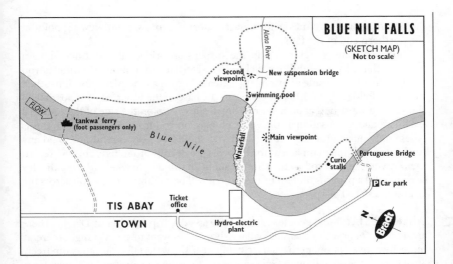

Once at the village, you need to visit the ticket office, where you pay a very reasonable entrance fee of US$1.80 – on a good day, this includes a useful map with some informative text. There is no additional charge for still photography, but a video camera attracts a US$3 filming fee. Independent groups are not obliged to pay extra to hire a guide, but the alternative is pretty gruesome – a train of children and souvenir sellers demanding money, yelling, and generally doing their utmost to ensure they spoil the experience. Should you arrive with a tour operator, hiring an additional guide now appears to be mandatory at a cost of US$3 for groups of one to five people and US$5 for groups of six and over.

It's a 30-minute walk from the village to the main viewpoint over the waterfall. From the ticket office, follow the road towards the hydro-electric plant and, about 50m before the plant's metal gate, cross the 'bridge' (basically just a couple of wooden planks) over the water channel running parallel and to the right of the road. From here, a path leads out of the village across porous-looking rocks. Once you exit the village, there's a eucalyptus plantation to your right, and you cross two more unspectacular bridges. Immediately after the second bridge, perhaps 1km out of the village, take the indistinct left fork that leads down a slight slope. You will know you're on the right path if the fence of the hydro-electric plant lies to your left and a church is briefly visible through the trees to your right.

This slope leads down to the Nile. You will cross the river on a large stone bridge called Agam Dildi, built by the Portuguese c1620 during the reign of Emperor Susneyos. There's some dense riverine woodland here, and enough birds to delay enthusiasts for a good hour – African thrush, white-headed babbler, blue-breasted bee-eater, northern crowned crane and the endemic wattled ibis, white-cheeked turaco, white-billed starling, black-winged lovebird and yellow-fronted parrot. Once across the bridge, the path curves uphill to the right then immediately veers back to the left past a few huts, from where you can more or less follow the contour to the viewpoint opposite the falls – if your ears aren't an adequate guide, then the hydro-electric plant, visible to your left on the opposite bank of the river, surely will be. The series of viewpoints here is directly opposite the waterfall and offers dramatic views. From the main viewpoint you can often see a rainbow in the spray. Don't be tempted to return from here though, because a little further along the path a newly constructed suspension bridge built by the

Swiss across the gorge makes for a quick short cut to a second viewing point at the northern end of the falls.

Those with the energy can skip the suspension bridge and continue along a footpath that runs downhill parallel to the waterfall. After about 15 minutes you need to turn left to wade across a large stream known as the Alata, and must then turn back following the stream's course to the base of the waterfall. It is possible to shower in a waist-height pool below a small slipstream on the side of the waterfall – a breathtaking sensation as the water plunges on you from 40m above – but this is safe only during the dry season, and you should be very careful not to go any further towards the main fall, as the currents are deadly. From here, you can return the way you came, or follow the Nile for about 20 minutes to where (during the dry season only) a papyrus *tankwa* or motorboat will be waiting to carry you across the river for US$0.60 per person.

WHERE TO STAY Most people visit Tis Abay as a day trip from Bahir Dar, but there are a couple of basic hotels in the village should you want to spend a night there. A more attractive option, perhaps, is to camp near the waterfall. You can camp freely anywhere in the area, though you are advised to bring all your food with you from Bahir Dar, and might want to organise a guard from the police station, which costs around US$6.

THE LAKE TANA MONASTERIES

The islands and peninsulas of Lake Tana collectively house more than 20 monastic churches, many of which were founded during the 14th-century rule of Amda Tsion, though some are possibly older, and at least two (Narga Selassie and Metseli Fasilidas) date to the Gonderine period. A popular local legend has it that seven of the most important 14th-century monasteries were founded by a loosely allied group of monks known as the Seven Stars. These are Daga Istafanos (founded by Hirute Amlak), Kibran Gebriel (Abuna Yohannis), Ura Kidane Mihret (Abuna Betre Maryam), Bahir Galila Zacharias (Abuna Zacharias), Mandaba Medhane Alem (Ras Asai), Gugubie (Afkrene Egzi) and Debre Maryam (Tadewos Tselalesh).

Many of the Lake Tana monasteries remained practically unknown to outsiders prior to Major Robert Cheesman's pioneering 1930s expedition during which he became the first European to visit all the islands on Lake Tana, as documented in his definitive (but out of print and maddeningly difficult to locate) book *Lake Tana and the Blue Nile: An Abyssinian Quest*. Architecturally, none stands comparison to the rock-hewn and Axumite churches of Tigrai and Lasta, but several are beautifully decorated, none more so than the relatively accessible Ura Kidane Mihret on the Zege Peninsula, covered from top to bottom with paintings that collectively serve as a visual encyclopaedia of Ethiopian ecclesiastical concerns. Also highly impressive in this regard is the more remote, and modern, Gonderine-era church of Narga Selassie.

Many of Lake Tana's monasteries have fascinating treasure houses. For bibliophiles, Kibran Gebriel, the closest true island monastery to Bahir Dar, is of particular interest for its library of almost 200 old books. At Daga Istafanos, visitors can be taken to see the mummified remains of five former emperors of Ethiopia, notably Fasilidas (the founder of Gondar), while on Tana Kirkos there stand three Judaic sacrificial pillars, claimed by the author Graham Hancock to support a legend that this island was for 800 years used to store the Ark of the Covenant.

Steeped in mystery and legend, the old churches of Lake Tana form peaceful retreats for their monastic residents and visiting tourists alike. As in so many parts of Ethiopia, the strong conservationist element in Orthodox Christianity has ensured that the monasteries practically double as nature sanctuaries. The Zege Peninsula, which supports by far the largest remaining tract of natural forest on Lake Tana, still harbours monkeys and various forest birds, while most of the monastic islands, considering their dense population, remain remarkably undisturbed in environmental terms. Combined with the romance attached to being afloat in a beautiful tropical lake that is not only the largest in Ethiopia, but also the source of the world's longest river, a day trip to at least one of these monasteries will be a highlight of any stay in Bahir Dar.

GETTING THERE Monastery-hopping on Lake Tana can be easily arranged. In addition to the tourist boats operated by Lake Tana Transport Enterprise [194 C6] (⚲ 058 220 0730/27) costing US$64–249 for one to five people for a half/full-day tour, several private operators offer much more realistic deals starting from US$35 per group of one to five people for a half-day trip to the southern monasteries, and US$118 for a full-day trip to the central monasteries. The only monasteries that can be visited more cheaply by independent travellers are Debre Maryam, a short walk and ten-minute ride by *tankwa* from Bahir Dar, and those on the Zege Peninsula, which is accessible by public ferry, and can also be reached by road public transport.

In addition to the boat charter fee, all the monasteries charge an entrance fee. The standard entry fee is now US$6 per person across the board for all monasteries with the exception of budget-friendly Debre Maryam, which charges US$3. Still cameras are free but a video camera costs US$6.

It should be noted that women are not and have never been permitted to enter most of the monasteries – a nugget of information that local tour operators have been known to divulge only once a trip is paid up and in progress, thus meaning women travellers may pay to see a monastery they are not permitted to see! Many female travellers find this ruling offensive, but it does date back several centuries and, as a well-meaning brochure produced by the monks of Daga Istafanos notes, 'it is not meant to belittle women.' To elaborate:

> The reason why women and all domestic animals are not allowed is the thinking that creatures of the opposite sex could be bad examples for the monks, especially those young at age. These young virgin hermits should subdue their body to the service of their God, and the devil should not attack them with the spear of adultery, like the Apostle Saint Paul said: 'Younger widows may not be placed on the roll.'

The exceptions to the men-only rule are the less isolated monasteries that lie on peninsulas or islands where the monks routinely interact with secular communities, ie: Debre Maryam, Narga Selassie and the monasteries on the Zege Peninsula.

Southern monasteries The most accessible monasteries from Bahir Dar are those on the southern part of the lake. All of the monasteries mentioned below could be visited over the course of a long half-day by boat, though generally speaking Debre Maryam is visited only by independent travellers with limited time or money, while package tours tend to aim for Ura Kidane Mihret on the Zege Peninsula. If you are setting up your own boat trip to the southern monasteries, a good combination is Kibran Gebriel, Ura Kidane Mihret and possibly Azwa Maryam.

Debre Maryam Founded by Abuna Tadewos Tselalesh near the Nile Outlet during the 14th-century reign of Amda Tsion, Debre Maryam is the only monastery that can easily be visited independently without significant effort or expense. The temple is reputedly very ancient; the rest of the church – rather plain in appearance – is little more than a century old, having been rebuilt during the rule of Emperor Tewodros. In terms of treasures, the church is also relatively impoverished, though there are at least three ancient Ge'ez goatskin manuscripts stored inside. It is said that the monastery grounds are inhabited by many invisible saints. The priest here is very friendly, used to budget travellers, and evidently enjoys modelling for photographs. While by no means the finest of the monasteries, Debre Maryam is agreed by all to be a good day's outing!

The cheapest way to visit Debre Maryam is to follow the Gondar road out of town for about 20 minutes, turning left onto a clear track just before the bridge across the Nile. From here, it's a five–ten-minute walk to a stretch of shore where you'll find a few boatmen and their papyrus *tankwa* boats ready and willing to take you across the water to the monastery – a five–ten-minute boat ride which should cost no more than US$2 for the return trip. It's advisable to head out early in the day, before the wind starts up, or the water might be too choppy for a *tankwa* to cross.

Debre Maryam can also be visited relatively cheaply from town by motorboat, in conjunction with a spot close to the outlet of the Nile where hippopotami are resident. The round trip takes two to three hours and should cost around US$18–20.

Kibran Gebriel The closest monastery to Bahir Dar, and visible from the town, Kibran Gebriel lies on a tiny, forested crescent – presumably part of the rim of an extinct volcano – which, somewhat incredibly, provides sanctuary to as many as 40 monks. It was founded in the 13th century by a hermit called Abuna Yohannis, who named it after the married couple – Gebriel and Kibran – who rowed him out to the island and later returned there to check on his health. The church, on the highest point of the island, was rebuilt in the 17th century by King Dawit II to a similar design to the better-known Ura Kidane Mihret on Zege. Kibran Gebriel boasts no paintings of note, but it houses the largest library of ancient books of any church in the region – almost 200 volumes in total including a beautifully illustrated 15th-century Life of Christ.

The island can easily be visited in conjunction with the monasteries on the Zege Peninsula, and is no more than 30 minutes by boat from Bahir Dar. Women are forbidden from setting foot on the island, though a legend that Empress Mentewab once visited it, but declined to enter the church because she was menstruating, would suggest that this has not always been the case. The smaller forested island of Entons immediately south of Kibran used to be a nunnery but was abandoned some years ago – however, a recent report from a traveller who was offered to be shown the 'women's monastery' adjacent to Kibran Gebriel suggests that the disused church might still be worth a look.

Ura Kidane Mihret and the Zege Peninsula The forested Zege Peninsula is studded with medieval churches, of which Ura Kidane Mihret ranks not only as the most impressive of the southern monasteries, but also possibly the most beautiful church anywhere in the Tana region. This, combined with its relative proximity to Bahir Dar, has made it the most frequently visited church on the lake. Set within bleak stone walls, the monastery was founded in the 14th century by a saint called Betre Maryam, who hailed from the Muger River in Showa and started training as a priest after being visited by two angels at the age of seven (Betre Maryam literally means 'Rod of Mary', and is a reference to the saint's steeliness when it came to beating off the devil and other demons).

The circular church was built in the 16th century. The walls are covered in an incredible jumble of murals, painted between 100 and 250 years ago (the most recent were executed by an artist called Engida during the dying years of the reign of Menelik II), and many of which have been restored in the last few decades. These paintings are positively Chaucerian in their physicality, ribaldry and gore, and it is no hyperbole to say that they offer a genuinely revealing glimpse into medieval Ethiopia – so do give yourself time to look at them closely. There are also some intriguing line drawings on one of the doors, and the museum has a few old crowns of Ethiopian kings, leather-bound Bibles and other ancient treasures.

Reachable from Ura Kidane Mihret by boat, or by following a 2km footpath through thick forest, stand the disused churches of **Mehal Giyorgis** and **Bet Maryam**. Mehal Giyorgis is little more than a shell but there are some 18th-century murals on the standing walls. There are several antiquities locked away in Bet Maryam. Another interesting church on the peninsula is **Azuwa Maryam**, which lies closer to Ura Kidane Mihret, and also boasts several animated 18th-century paintings.

A charter boat is still the quickest way to visit Ura Kidane Mihret. This takes about an hour, terminating at a jetty five–ten-minutes' easy walk from the monastery itself. Here you are likely to be greeted by guides wanting to direct you to the monastery. A guide is not really necessary to reach the church, but they can provide interesting information about the paintings within. Finally opened to foreigners, the daily Zege ferry stops at this same jetty and is a more economical option at US$5 round trip, the main drawback being that you are subject to the ferry schedule. It is also quite easy to visit the peninsula by a recently renovated road from Bahir Dar, whether by private vehicle or public transport. For more details see box, *The Zege Peninsula*, page 206.

Central monasteries Although less easily accessible from Bahir Dar than the Zege Peninsula, the string of monasteries that runs from east to west across the centre of Lake Tana is arguably more intriguing. These monasteries fall into two main clusters: one close to the eastern lakeshore, of which Tana Kirkos with its mysterious sacrificial stones is without doubt the most important; and the other dead central, of which the beautifully decorated Narga Selassie on Dek Island, and Daga Istafanos – housing the mummified remains of five former emperors – are the highlights.

With a very early start from Bahir Dar, it is possible to visit the three monasteries mentioned above (but no others) in one long day. A more popular option, however, is to head for one or other cluster, which allows for a slightly later start. Women travellers should be reminded that, with the exception of Narga Selassie, all the central monasteries permit male visitors only.

Tana Kirkos This small island monastery, separated from the eastern shore by a narrow marshy corridor, is dominated by a striking spine of rock perhaps 30m high, and fringed by riparian forest supporting several pairs of fish eagle. It has acquired something approaching cult status since the publication of Graham Hancock's book *The Sign and the Seal*, which attempts to substantiate an ancient tradition that the Ark of the Covenant was stowed on the island for some 800 years before it was transferred to Axum in the 4th century AD by King Ezana.

One tradition has it that the Christian monastery was founded on the site of an older temple during the 6th-century reign of Gebre Meskel by St Yared and Abuna Aregawi. Another tradition holds that the monastery was founded two centuries earlier by Frumentius, the first Bishop of Axum, who was buried there. Other sources suggest that the island converted to Christianity a mere 540 years ago.

Whenever the monastery was founded, the architecturally undistinguished church, which was built about 100 years ago with funding from Ras Gugsa of Debre Tabor, looks more time-worn than it does ancient, and none of the paintings that adorn it looks significantly more than a decade old.

Far more interesting than the monastery itself is a trio of hollowed-out sacrificial pillars that stand alongside it, testifying to the island's importance as a Judaic religious shrine in pre-Christian times. The local priests say that the pillars date from King Solomon's time and were used to make dyes. Given the Ethiopian predilection for mythologising – one local tradition has it that the Virgin Mary rested here on her (presumably somewhat circuitous) return from Egypt to Israel, and a 'footprint' on one of the island's rocks is claimed to be that of none other than her immaculately conceived firstborn son – it is stretching a point to conclude, as Hancock does, that these pillars provide circumstantial support for the Ark once having resided on the island.

Tana Kirkos lies some three hours from Bahir Dar by boat; the walk from the jetty to the monastery takes no more than five minutes. On the way to the island (or coming back) it is possible to look at two further monasteries, both on small,

THE ZEGE PENINSULA   *Updated with the help of Christian Sefrin*

The forested peninsula of Zege, together with the eponymous village, is one of the most accessible points on the Lake Tana shore using public transport with the public ferry the easiest way to access the peninsula. Ferries stop both at Zege village and at a jetty that is only a ten-minute walk from the Ura Kidane Mihret Monastery. The cost for tourists is US$3.20 each way. Should you prefer to stick to a land route, there is a reasonably good 22km track to Zege covered by reliable public transport from Bahir Dar.

The main attraction of Zege is of course the monasteries that dot the peninsula (see *Ura Kidane Mihret and the Zege Peninsula*, page 204), which would collectively take the best part of a day to check out on foot from Zege village. The most interesting and popular of these monasteries, Ura Kidane Mihret, lies only 3km from the village, and could therefore be visited as a round trip in two to three hours. To get there, follow the steep footpath out from the central market to the top of the peninsula, from where you take a left fork to enter the forest and head west towards the churches. You can't really go wrong from here: there are a couple of small side paths, but the main track is wide and clear – indeed, with a private vehicle you can drive to within 200m of the church – and there are plenty of people to direct you along the way. You'll find plenty of youngsters hanging around the compound offering their services as guides. You can safely ignore them, as the monks will show you everything anyway (but most of them do not speak English).

The forest itself is worth taking slowly. It's one of the few large indigenous forests in this part of Ethiopia, and it makes an appealing change from the characteristic open grassland of the region. Wild coffee dominates the undergrowth, vervet monkeys shake the canopy, parrots screech and hornbills explode into cacophony, and colourful butterflies flutter at your feet. With glimpses of the lake to your right, this is a lovely walk, even if you elect not to visit the monasteries. There is a beautiful viewpoint over Lake Tana on the hill near Yiganda Tekle Haymanot church (no entrance for *faranjis*!) – ask for someone to show you the way there.

On first impressions, Zege village isn't much of a place: a couple of roads lined with mud houses radiating from a large central marketplace. The surrounding

forested islands about 30 minutes from Tana Kirkos. These are Rema Medhane Alem, a recently rebuilt church in which are stored a few interesting old paintings, and Mitseli Fasilidas, founded during the rule of the emperor after whom it is named, and architecturally undistinguished – though the surrounding forest is rich in birdlife.

With a private vehicle, and ideally a local guide, Tana Kirkos can also be visited by taking the main road to Gondar from Bahir Dar for about 70km, then following rough tracks for about 5km east to the mainland church of Kristos Samra, itself an important pilgrimage site in honour of the nun after whom it is named. From the mainland, a papyrus *tankwa* can easily be arranged to Tana Kirkos, a ten-minute trip that shouldn't cost more than US$3 return.

Daga Istafanos The largest monastery on the lake, and home to as many as 200 monks, Daga Istafanos lies on a small wedge-shaped island immediately east of the much larger Dek Island. A reliable (and for once apparently uncontested) tradition states that the monastery was founded in the late 13th century by Hiruta Amlak, a nephew of Emperor Yekuno Amlak who served his apprenticeship under Iyasu Moa at Hayk Istafanos at the same time as the future Archbishop Tekle Haymanot. A

forest gives it some ambience, especially at night when it's all bobbing candles and chirping cicadas – there's no electricity or cars. If idling is on the agenda, no better place to do so than on the attractive pier, with the lake stretching in front of you and the forested peninsula to your left. More acquisitively, you can buy goatskin *injera* baskets on Zege for about half of what you would pay in town.

Minibuses to Zege cost US$0.80 one-way, and leave Bahir Dar a few times daily from the main bus station in town. If you take the ferry, it normally leaves Bahir Dar at 07.00 daily and passengers need to be at the compound 30 minutes earlier. Get off at Yiganda jetty and from here it returns to Bahir Dar at around 10.00. There may be additional ferries leaving later in the day, making it worthwhile to ask about the current schedule. Whether by land or by water, the trip to Zege takes about one hour. If you want to overnight in Zege, the pick of the lodges is the new **Wendemamachuch Hotel** (*94 rooms;* m *0918 012 486*), which charges US$2–3 for a basic room using a common shower and serves acceptable food and drink, followed by the Hebiste Erko Hotel, an even more basic, family-run lodge charging US$2 for a cramped room (bucket showers only). The other hotels in town are no better and charge silly *faranji* prices.

The road between Bahir Dar and Zege is now passable all year through, so it is possible to drive there in a private vehicle from Bahir Dar, as well as to cycle there, which takes two to three hours in either direction. Bicycles can easily be hired in Bahir Dar for around US$1.80 per hour, but try to get reasonably sturdy ones, and insist on a pump and tyre-repair kit. To get to Zege, take the surfaced main road west out of town, past the Ghion Hotel, and climb the slightly hilly road towards the airport for 4.5km until you see a water tower to your right and a small hill to your left. Turn right here, then after another 4.5km you'll reach a Y-junction where you must turn right again, in the direction of the lake. About 2km further, turn right at a T-junction, then after another 2.5km cross the recently constructed bridge across the Efransi River. After the river crossing, you need to keep going for another 8–9km – the small tracks through the area sometimes cross each other, but if you stick to what appears to be the main track, then you can't really go wrong.

somewhat less probable tradition has it that Hiruta Amlak was guided to the shores of Lake Tana by Istafanos from Hayk, and was then ferried from mainland to island on a pair of divine stones that can still be seen in the grounds of the monastery he founded. The church on the island's conical peak is relatively uninteresting and not especially old – it was rebuilt after the original burnt to the ground in the 19th century – although there is a rather unusual monochrome painting of an angel on one of the inner doors. Tradition has it that Daga Istafanos is where the Ark of the Covenant was hidden during Ahmed Gragn's 16th-century occupation of Axum.

The main point of interest at Daga Istafanos today is the mausoleum, which contains the mummified remains of at least five Ethiopian emperors: Yakuno Amlak (1268–93), Dawit I (1428–30), Zara Yaqob (1434–68), Susneyos (1607–32) and Fasilidas (1632–76). The glass coffins in which the mummies now lie are recent acquisitions, donated by Haile Selassie after he visited the monastery in 1951. The mummy of Fasilidas is the best preserved of the five, and his facial features are still eerily discernible. A tiny skeleton next to this is said to be the remains of Fasilidas's favourite son, who was crowned as his father's successor but collapsed and died under the weight of the crown.

It is something of a mystery as to when, why and how the mummies ended up on this remote island: some say during the Mahdist invasion of Gondar in the late 19th century, others during the Italian occupation, but there also seems to be good reason to believe that the dead kings were brought here for mummification shortly after they died. Certainly, Daga Istafanos was a popular retreat for several of the abovementioned kings, and its tranquillity was reputedly also favoured by Tewodros II, who took communion there on several occasions. Several other treasures associated with these kings are stored in the mausoleum: old crowns, a goatskin book with some line drawings dating from the 14th century, and two immaculately preserved 15th-century paintings of the Madonna with uncharacteristically detailed and non-stylised facial features.

Daga Istafanos lies about three hours by boat from Bahir Dar, 90 minutes from Tana Kirkos and an hour from Narga Selassie. The walk from the jetty to the church is quite steep, and takes about 15 minutes, with a chance of encountering the odd monkey along the way. It can be visited in conjunction with the nearby monastery of Metseli Fasilidas, which was founded by Emperor Fasilidas of Gondar and reputedly contains an interesting collection of old books and manuscripts.

Narga Selassie Situated on the western shore of Dek, the largest island on Lake Tana, Narga Selassie is, with the possible exception of the much older Ura Kidane Mihret, the most ornately decorated of all the lake monasteries. Built in the 18th century for Princess Mentewab (regent for Emperor Iyasu II), the stone walls surrounding the compound, with their domed turrets, are typically Gonderine, and not dissimilar in appearance to the walls surrounding the church next to Mentewab's palace at Kuskuam outside Gondar. The compound, its 'old grey towers, forgotten on this lonely island' looked somewhat neglected when Cheesman visited it in the 1930s, but the church was restored with funding by Haile Selassie in 1951 and the roof was renovated again in 2001.

The main church is circular in shape and surrounded by stone pillars (one of which is decorated by an etching of the pipe-puffing explorer James Bruce, a close associate of Mentewab). As with Ura Kidane Mihret, the inner walls are covered from top to bottom with a riotous and absorbing collection of paintings, most thought to date from the 18th century. In addition to the usual pictures of saints and their exploits, there is a painting of the church's founder lying prostrate before

Mary and the Baby Jesus, probably the only contemporaneous portrait of Mentewab to survive. Another interesting one shows a church on a fish, the latter about to be speared by an angel – evidently relating to a legend about a town on Lake Tana that was being harassed by a big fish until the angel intervened.

Narga Selassie lies some three hours from Bahir Dar by boat, and an hour from Daga Istafanos. The monastery is practically next to the jetty. There are two other monasteries on Dek Island – Arsema Semaetat and Mota Maryam – but neither is regularly visited by tourists.

Northern monasteries Four ancient but seldom-visited monasteries dot the islands off the northern shore of Lake Tana, all of them somewhat remote from Bahir Dar – a boat charter from there would cost US$442 minimum – but situated within easy striking distance of the northern ferry terminal of Gorgora. The best way to explore these monasteries is to charter a boat from Gorgora, which can be organised through the Lake Tana Transport Enterprise (❨ 058 220 0730/0027) for US$64 for up to five people, depending on which churches you opt to visit, or for about half that price through one of a handful of private boat owners. The monasteries, which can be visited in conjunction with the port of Old Gorgora, generally ask for an entrance fee of US$3 apiece, but do note that women are not allowed on any of the islands. A good contact for making arrangements in the Gorgora area is the locally based guide Tesfaye Mekonnen (❨ 058 111 5679).

Probably the most venerated of the northern monasteries is **Mandaba Medhane Alem**, which lies about 30 minutes from Gorgora by motorboat. The monastery was founded in the 14th century by Ras Asai, the ascetic son of Emperor Amda Tsion, and its monks, among the most devout and virtuous in Ethiopia, are considered to be angels made flesh. The church is of greatest interest for its superb collection of old manuscripts, paintings and other antiquated treasures. The church itself underwent major reconstruction in the 1950s, but parts of the interior, including the painted door frame, are very old.

Much the same goes for **Brigida Maryam**: built by Amda Tsion in the 14th century but reconstructed three times since owing to fire damage, the church is of limited architectural interest, but it does host some genuine treasures, most notably perhaps a superb 16th-century painting of Mary. Nearby **Angara Tekle Haymanot** has few treasures and the present-day church dates to the Haile Selassie era.

Somewhat further afield, about an hour by boat from Gorgora, **Bahir Galila Zacharias** has the oldest church of the northern island monasteries, possibly dating to the 14th century, though it is currently under scaffolding. Bahir Galila is Amharic for 'Sea of Galilee', and it was founded in the 14th century by a monk called Zacharias, who could reputedly walk on water. The monastery is remembered for the massacre of most of its monks by Ahmed Gragn in the 16th century.

BAHIR DAR TO GONDAR BY ROAD

With the surfacing of the 185km road that runs east of Lake Tana between Bahir Dar and Gondar, even tourists who fly between all other points of interest in northern Ethiopia might regard driving between these two cities to be an attractive prospect. The drive is not particularly time-consuming – you're looking at about four hours on public transport, no more than three (excluding breaks) in a decent private vehicle. Furthermore, tackling this one domestic journey by road offers short-stay visitors to Ethiopia an experience of the countryside away from the towns and historical sites.

If time is a factor, you could easily leave Bahir Dar after breakfast and be in Gondar for lunch, or vice versa. But if you're not in a rush, there are a few worthwhile minor diversions *en route*. First among these, set in a thickly wooded grove to the east of the main road some 50km from Bahir Dar, is the **Wanzaye Hot Springs** (*entrance US$1.50*), which bubble from beneath the earth at temperatures in excess of 42°C to feed a series of pools that empty into the Gumara River. Regarded as holy by Ethiopians, and popular for its therapeutic qualities, Wanzaye is also of interest for the colourful birds and monkeys that inhabit the surrounding riparian vegetation. It's possible to stay at the former government hotel, which offers eight basic rooms with common shower for US$2.50, while camping costs US$2 per tent.

Altogether different in nature is the weaving co-operative at **Awra Amba Community** (✆ *058 231 0108; www.awraamba.com*), which can be reached by turning right onto the Woldia road about 60km from Bahir Dar (and less than 1km north of Werota). Follow the Woldia road for 8km until you reach a (poorly) signposted junction to the right, and then follow this rough road for another 2km to the village. Awra Amba was founded in 1985 by a group of 20 people to demonstrate to its members and to other Ethiopians that the best escape route from poverty and hunger is not religion or prayer but education and plain hard work. Remarkable simply for being the only overtly atheistic society I've come across anywhere in Africa (pride of place is given not to a mosque or a church but to a surprisingly well-stocked school library), this isolated community, which now consists of about 129 families totalling 462 individuals, also prides itself on an egalitarian non-sexist, non-racist policy (the weaving work is shared between men and women), on the formal health care and support it provides to the elderly, and on a pre-school aimed primarily at children under the age of seven, but also attended by older people seeking to attain a basic level of literacy.

Better known to Ethiopians than to tourists thanks to a television appearance in which the village chairman unveiled his unorthodox religious views to a somewhat startled nation, Awra Amba welcomes foreign visitors, though it's rather quiet on Wednesdays and Saturdays when most inhabitants are at the market. Ask to be shown the school, the library, the dormitories for aged members of the community, the innovative *injera* cookers in the adobe houses (whose curvaceous design rather reminds me of Mali's Dogon country), and the communal weaving area with its 20 handmade looms.

A small, one-price-for-all entrance fee of US$0.50 is charged at Awra Amba. Begging is actively frowned upon; if you want to contribute more, the most appropriate way would be to buy some of the handspun cotton and wool items in the warehouse – a range of shamas, scarves, shirts and blankets costs half what you'd pay in most other parts of the country. Book donations to the communal library are also greatly appreciated. It is worth noting that this must be the only place we've been in Ethiopia where not one child yelled at us or approached us asking for money or a pen or sweets – an utterly refreshing experience, so please, please, please can those who follow in our footsteps help keep it that way by resisting the temptation to hand out trinkets indiscriminately.

Should you wish to stay overnight, simple dorm-style rooms with clean shared showers are available for US$2 per person and camping costs US$1 per tent.

Back on the surfaced road, **Addis Zemen**, about 40km north of Werota, is the most substantial town between Bahir Dar and Gondar – which isn't saying a great deal, but does make it the best place to stop for a meal, a cold drink, or a bed for the night. North of Addis Zemen, the road ascends into hillier territory, passing a striking isolated rock formation known as the Devil's Nose after about 4km.

Some 25km further, past the small village of Emfraz, a short but rough track to the right leads uphill to **Guzara Castle** (📞 *058 112 2586*; **e** *ngzct@yahoo.com; entrance US$3; guide US$2*), which is generally regarded to have been built for Emperor Sarsa Dengal in 1571–72. Easily visible from the main road, and offering grand views across to Lake Tana, this imposing building, evidently built with a strong Portuguese input, comes across as a clear stylistic precursor of the more famous castles built half a century later by Sarsa Dengal's grandson Fasilidas and his successors at Gondar. Indeed, Guzara's architectural resemblance to the Gonderine castle has led to recent expert speculation that it was built by Susneyos or Fasilidas rather than Sarsa Dengal. Despite years of neglect, the castle is still in fair shape, and is in the process of being restored to its full former glory with US funding.

About 30km further north, easily visible from the main road about 5km past the village of Maksegno Gebeya (which translates somewhat prosaically but thoroughly accurately as 'Tuesday Market'), **Bet Bahari Mikael** is an impressive fortress-like stone church built during the early 16th century (more than 100 years before the Gonderine castles) by Emperor Lebna Dengal with some architectural input from his Portuguese adviser Pero de Covilhão. The church boasts two domes – one as originally constructed by Lebna Dengal, one added in the 1960s by Haile Selassie – and parts are in urgent need of maintenance after having been bombarded during fighting between government and rebel forces in 1990.

Crowned as a child, Lebna Dengal's was an eventful rule – it started under the regency of the former Empress Eleni in 1508, was punctuated by the reception of the first Portuguese envoy to Ethiopia in 1520, and ended in 1540 at the Tigraian monastery of Debre Damo, where the emperor died of illness and exhaustion following 12 years of bitter war with the Islamic army of Ahmed Gragn. Three years after Lebna Dengal's death, on 11 February 1543, Gragn himself was killed in the Battle of Weyna Daga, to be buried, somewhat fittingly, a mere 20km from Bet Bahari Mikael at a place called **Sentara**.

Some say that the fatal blow to Gragn was struck by a Portuguese musket ball fired by the army of Lebna Dengal's son Galawdewos, others that he was stung to death by one of those bee swarms that turn up habitually during critical junctures in Ethiopian history. Either way, the Tomb of Ahmed Gragn still stands at Sentara today, and can be reached along a 20km side road east from the Bahir Dar–Gondar road between Maksegno Gebeya and Bet Bahari Mikael. Many Ethiopian Muslims make the pilgrimage to the tomb on the anniversary of Gragn's death, although this being a predominantly Christian area, shrines erected at the site have a habit of vanishing before the next anniversary comes around! Some 4km before reaching the tomb, the road passes an extant tree stump where Gragn is said to have rested whilst mortally wounded.

GORGORA

The little-visited town of Gorgora, situated on the northern shore of Lake Tana, is today dominated by the large, leafy Lake Tana Transport Authority compound, an attractive spot that will prove highly rewarding to birdwatchers. Founded in medieval times, when it served as one of the many temporary capitals of the period, Gorgora has strong historical associations with Gondar 60km to its north. Even today it doesn't really seem to belong in the standard Lake Tana tourist circuit, but feels more like a lakeshore satellite to Fasilidas's former capital (to which it is linked by regular road transport). Gorgora was an important port during the Italian occupation, the most obvious relic of which is the so-called Mussolini Pillar – so far as I can ascertain, a lighthouse-like construction that helped guide ships towards the harbour – that stands on a hill above the town and is clearly visible on the road in from Gondar.

A highlight of any visit to Gorgora will be a visit to the **Monastery of Debre Sina Maryam** (*entrance US$3*), which lies along a motorable track five minutes' walk from the town centre, and permits women visitors. As is so often the case, the history of this church varies with the telling, but most likely it was founded c1334 by a monk called Hesterus who hailed from the town of Debre Sina further southeast. The present building, a fine example of a thatched circular church, probably dates to the 16th century, though the carved Axumite windows and frames might well have been lifted from an earlier building.

The murals on Debre Sina Maryam rank with the most complex and vivid to be seen in the Tana region. Local tradition claims them to be medieval in origin, but the greater probability is that they were executed in the early Gonderine period under the patronage of the noblewoman Melako Tawit, who is depicted on one mural. According to the priests, the woman in question was the elder sister of Emperor Fasilidas, but more likely perhaps she was the wife of Iyasu I – evidently both women had the same name. Either way, the most recent murals were painted at least 300 years ago, making them significantly older than their counterparts at Ura Kidane Mihret or Narga Selassie. What's more, the lowest row of paintings does look significantly older than the one that includes the portrait of Melako Tawit, and it's also very different stylistically – compare the facial detail of the lower and higher portraits of Mary on the wall as you enter – so it could be that some paintings are older than others.

Two of the church's most striking wall panels depict the devil rolling about in laughter as Adam and Eve sample the forbidden fruit, and a decidedly smug-looking King Herod and cronies making bloodthirsty work of the newly born children of Israel. The church's greatest treasure is a glass-covered portrait known as the 'Egyptian Saint Mary': an utterly implausible legend has it that this painting was made when Mary was exiled to Egypt, and the local priests claim that it lights up spontaneously from time to time, and has the capacity to revive dead children.

Also of interest is the **Gorgora Cathedral** built by the Jesuit priest Pedro Páez after he was granted land there by his friend Emperor Susneyos. The church was abandoned after Fasilidas booted all Portuguese and other Catholic settlers out of his empire. The cathedral is now an overgrown ruin, but what does remain – tall walls, pillars and archways engraved with flowers and crosses – is sufficient to hint at its former grandeur. And there is talk of restoring the church with UNESCO help. To reach the cathedral, you can either walk east along the lakeshore for several hours, or head out of Gorgora for 8km along the Gondar road, then turn left at a small village and follow a track back towards the lake for about 15km – the track isn't very clear so keep asking for directions.

On a peninsula roughly 10km west of Gorgora stands '**Old Gorgora**' and the ruined palace constructed by Emperor Susneyos between 1625 and 1630 with Portuguese assistance. The building isn't in the greatest shape, but it is of some interest architecturally as an immediate precursor to the more renowned palaces of Gondar. Old Gorgora can only be visited by boat – these can be chartered through the Lake Tana Transport Authority for US$64, or more cheaply through a private operator – and the excursion can be combined with stops *en route* at some of the northern monasteries described on pages 202–9.

GETTING THERE AND AWAY Gorgora is the northern terminus of the weekly ferry to and from Bahir Dar (see box, *The Lake Tana Ferry*, page 198). It is also possible to charter a private boat from Bahir Dar for around US$442 for up to six people. The port lies 60km south of Gondar along a reasonable dirt road and the drive takes slightly longer than one hour. Two buses ply the Gondar road every day, the first leaving at 06.00 and the second at around 12.00, and there are also regular minibuses – the trip takes one–two hours and tickets cost US$2. Coming from Gondar, minibuses to Gorgora leave from the bus station near the Axum Hotel.

WHERE TO STAY AND EAT

Gorgora Port Hotel (19 rooms) \058 497 0003. The most attractive aspect of this government-owned hotel is its position on the lakeshore. The rooms are run-down, musty & overpriced – and that's being generous! The restaurant meals while affordable are nothing to write home about. Our advice: pitch a tent or pray the new resort below opens before this book goes to print. *US$4.50 tent, US$4/8 sgl/dbl with common shower, US$12 dbl en suite, US$27 suite.*

Gorgora Rock Resort (25 rooms) www.gororanovarockresort.com. This new luxury resort set to open in early 2013 is a much more tempting option. An initiative of the GreenDreamCompany (*www.greendreamcompany.com*) from the Netherlands, the resort is being built in a socially & environmentally responsible way using natural materials & traditional techniques. When complete it will house 25 guestrooms with private en suite, a wellness centre, a restaurant, conference room & pool. *US$120 dbl, US$160 suite.*

8

Gondar and the Simien Mountains

The city of Gondar was, until 1994, the capital and principal town of an eponymous province that was subsequently absorbed into the Federal Region of Amhara. Founded by Emperor Fasilidas in 1635, the city served as the imperial capital for 250 years prior to the rise of Emperor Tewodros and the associated power shift southward to Showa. Gondar is one of the main tourist attractions on the northern historical circuit, best known for its 17th-century castles and palaces, but studded with several other points of interest, most notably the fantastically decorated **Church of Debre Birhan Selassie** ten minutes' walk from the town centre. Gondar is also the obvious base from which to stage day trips or longer treks into the scenic **Simien Mountains National Park**, Ethiopia's most popular hiking destination.

The city of Gondar is the main travel gateway to the region, serviced by daily Ethiopian Airlines flights, a few buses daily from Bahir Dar, and less regular buses northwards towards Axum. The region can also be approached through Gorgora, the northern terminus of the Lake Tana Ferry, and linked to Gondar by regular public transport (see *Chapter 7*, page 211).

GONDAR

Gondar is probably the most immediately impressive of Ethiopia's major ex-capitals, but its antiquities are for the most part less enduringly memorable than those at the more ancient towns of Axum or Lalibela. The city was founded in 1635 by Emperor Fasilidas (often abbreviated to Fasil) in the aftermath of a tumultuous century during which the Abyssinian Empire had virtually collapsed under the onslaught of the Muslim leader Ahmed Gragn, and was then torn apart by internal religious conflict after Emperor Susneyos converted to Catholicism in 1622. Influenced by the Portuguese Jesuits, who had settled around his temporary court on the shores of Lake Tana, Susneyos imposed Catholicism on his subjects by declaring it the state religion and attempting to close down the Orthodox Church. The result of this unpopular policy was a period of violent instability during which an estimated 32,000 peasants were killed by the royal army. In 1632, Susneyos partially redeemed himself when he abdicated in favour of his son Fasilidas, who immediately reinstated the traditional state religion and expelled the Portuguese from the empire.

After a period of several centuries during which Ethiopia was ruled from a succession of temporary capitals, the last of which, Danquaz, lay some 20km from Gondar, Fasilidas recognised that a permanent capital might help provide greater internal stability. He settled on the small village of Gondar, with its strategic hilltop location at an altitude of 2,120m in the southern foothills of the Simien Mountains. One oft-repeated story has it that Fasilidas selected Gondar because it fulfilled an ancient tradition by having the initial letter of G (some historians maintain that this 'tradition' was manufactured by the royal myth-machine subsequent to the adoption of Gondar as capital). By the time of Fasilidas's death in 1667, Gondar had become the largest and most important city in the empire, with a population in excess of 60,000. It retained its position as the capital of Ethiopia for 250 years, though this status was increasingly nominal from the late 18th century onwards as the central monarchy gradually lost importance to powerful regional rulers.

Having enjoyed something of a revival during and subsequent to the Italian occupation, Gondar is today the fourth-largest city in Ethiopia, with a population thought to exceed 214,000. It is also a very pleasant city, with a friendly, laid-back, almost countrified mood by comparison with Addis Ababa or even Bahir Dar. The walled Royal Enclosure that dominates the city centre contains several well-preserved castles and other buildings, and definitely warrants a half-day's exploration. Also of interest in Gondar are Fasilidas's Bathing Pool, the elaborately decorated Debre Birhan Selassie Church, and out-of-town palaces built by Princess Mentewab and Emperor Susneyos. Juxtaposed against this distinctive Gonderine architecture, much of the modern town centre dates from the Italian occupation of 1936–41, and hints of Art Deco and other pre-war European styles can be detected in many of the run-down buildings that line the central Piazza.

GETTING THERE AND AWAY

By air Ethiopian Airlines flies daily between Gondar and Addis Ababa (US$65), Axum (US$43) and Lalibela (US$48). The airport is about 20km out of town, just off the main Bahir Dar road, so you'll have to catch a taxi or try to make an arrangement with one of the tour buses that meet most flights. Fares are negotiable as always, but should not exceed US$8 for a taxi charter. Air tickets out of Gondar can and should be reconfirmed at the **Ethiopian Airlines office** [218 D1] (\ *058 111 7688*; e *gdqtsm@ethiopianairlines.com*) on the Piazza below the Royal Enclosure.

By boat For details of the ferry connecting Bahir Dar to Gorgora, 60km south of Gondar, see *Chapter 7*, page 198. There is regular road transport between Gorgora and Gondar.

By road Coming from the south, Selam and Sky Bus run direct buses from Addis Ababa to Gondar, departing around 05.30 (US$22; 10–12 hours). Direct buses to Gondar are not used by many tourists, since it would mean passing straight through Bahir Dar. More normal therefore is to catch one bus to Bahir Dar, spend a night or two there, and then bus on to Gondar. At least three buses daily run between Bahir Dar and Gondar (US$4; 4 hours), while minibuses, also departing from the bus station, run regularly throughout the day (US$4.50; 3–4 hours). The 185km trip takes about three hours without breaks in a private vehicle – see also *Bahir Dar to Gondar by road* in *Chapter 7*, page 209.

Heading north from Gondar, a couple of buses leave at around 05.30 daily for Debark (US$2.50; 4 hours), which is the base for hiking in the Simien Mountains. If you are heading directly to Axum, then your best bet is to catch the 06.30 bus to Shire (Inda Selassie; US$7.50). (See *Gondar to Axum by road,* page 231.) There is plenty of accommodation in Shire, and regular transport on to Axum.

Details of travelling directly from Gondar to Lalibela by road are included in *Chapter 12*, page 309.

Buses out of Gondar generally need to be booked the afternoon before departure.

GETTING AROUND Cheap minibuses cover most main roads between central and suburban Gondar. *Bajajis* are readily available – you should pay about US$1–1.50 within the city centre. For suburban destinations such as Fasil's Bath or Debre Birhan Selassie Church you can charter a taxi for around US$3 but will invariably be asked a lot more. Alternatively, reputable local guide **Sisay Assefa** (m *0918 712 125;* e *asefa_sisay@yahoo.com*) can arrange a city tour to three of the major sites for US$38.50 including transportation.

Guides Gondar has the usual crew of freelance guides who hang around the Piazza. In the past, one of these guides was almost a necessity to keep street kids and other wannabe guides at bay. Thankfully, the hassle factor has greatly decreased. On this visit we were able to walk around everywhere in relative peace. Official guides can be easily found at the **Gondar Guides Association** (m *0918 773 916/0019;* e *gondarlocalgu@yahoo.com*), which has its permanent headquarters within the Royal Enclosure. It is not essential to take a guide to the better-known historical sites around town, though it may simplify things linguistically. Most guides can organise day trips to the Simien Mountains, but do check prices against those offered by the tourist office and private tour operators before agreeing to anything.

TOURIST INFORMATION A knowledgeable and helpful former guide runs the **tourist office** [218 D2] (⏰ *08.30–12.30 & 13.30–17.30 weekdays*) above the Piazza. The office stocks a fair selection of brochures about Gondar and places further afield. The prices quoted for motorised day trips out of Gondar are far lower than those offered by most private guides and tour companies.

TOUR OPERATORS If you want to organise your Simien hike through a proper tour operator, recommended local specialists include the **Galaxy Express** branch office (☎ *058 111 1546;* m *0918 770 347;* e *gahaws2000@yahoo.com*) based in the new Taye Hotel, **Explore Simien Tours** (☎ *058 111 9066;* m *0918 770 280;* e *fasilm_675@ yahoo.com*) in the Quara Hotel, and the **NTO** [218 B2] (m *0918 775 948; www. nto.com.et*) located near the Kebele administration offices. Typical all-inclusive rates for a five-day hike out of Gondar with any of these companies will be around US$300/600 each for four/two people.

WHERE TO STAY In recent years, the number of hotels in Gondar has increased dramatically. There are now several decent hotels in the moderate range, filling a much-lamented gap. However, there is a tendency for more basic hotels to charge absurdly inflated *faranji* prices by comparison with, say, Axum or Bahir Dar. As a result, few hotels listed below would rank as good value for money anywhere else in Ethiopia except perhaps Lalibela. Some of the cheaper places will offer off-season discounts if you look convincingly disgruntled. Most hotels charge an even more inflated rate over the week building up to Timkat (20 January).

Upmarket
🏠 **Goha Hotel** [off map 218 A2] (66 rooms) ☎ 058 111 0358; f 058 111 1920; e gohahotel@ yahoo.com; www.gohahotel.com.et. Rated by many as the best hotel in the former government Ghion chain, the Goha is perched attractively on a hill about 1.5km from the town centre. The great view over town & the above-average service make this one of the better hotels in northern Ethiopia. For those who are staying in the town centre, & who don't mind the stiff 30min walk or are prepared to pay for a taxi, the Goha is a nice place to head to watch the sunset & enjoy a smart dinner – the 3-course set menu costs around US$8. *US$59/73/98 sgl/dbl/suite inc b/fast.*

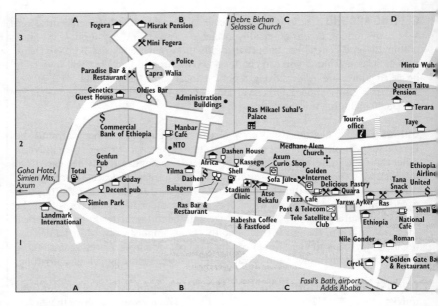

Landmark International Hotel [218 A1] (80 rooms) ☎058 112 2929; f 058 112 2931. This hotel was in the midst of a huge upgrade on our most recent visit in late 2011 – plans are ambitious & include a cable car to a panoramic revolving hilltop restaurant, a cinema, conference hall, gym, spa, pool & shopping complex. Hopes are high that it will reopen during the life of this edition of the guide.

Taye Hotel [218 D2] ☎058 111 2180/2252; f 058 111 2175; e tayehotel@gmail.com; www. tayehotel.com. This newly opened hotel in the centre aims to be of international standard & is pretty close to the mark. The nicely decorated rooms all have hot-water en suite, DSTV & balconies with views of the castle, but the beds feature 'medical mattresses' which might be too firm for some (this updater included). There's a restaurant & bar attached. Other amenities include free Wi-Fi, 24hr room service & airport shuttle, with gym, spa, sauna & outdoor pool set to open before this book is published. *US$60/70 sgl/dbl, US$75/85 junior suite/suite inc b/fast.*

Moderate

Florida International Hotel [off map 219 E1] (64 rooms) m 0918 775 648; e mullern@ yahoo.com; www.hotelfloridagonder.com. This new multi-storey hotel near the university was completing the final pre-opening touches on our most recent visit to Gondar. Fresh-out-of-the-wrapper accommodation consists of compact economy rooms with DSTV & hot-water en suite & spacious suites with an added jacuzzi & steam bath. There's also a swimming pool, ballroom & health centre as well as a restaurant, bar & café & free Wi-Fi & airport shuttle. *US$50 economy rooms, US$75–80 suites.*

Quara Hotel [218 C1] (48 rooms) ☎058 111 0040/3808; e quarahotelgonder@yahoo. com; www.quarahotelgonder.com. Now privatised this former government hotel boasting a great location on the Piazza has undergone a major transformation since the last edition. 32 new rooms have been added & old rooms have been upgraded – all now have private en suites & DSTV. Facilities include an internet café, travel agent, rooftop terrace, hair salon, sauna & free airport shuttle. They also accept Visa, & the restaurant has a varied menu including vegetarian dishes, pizzas, ice cream & sandwiches as well as the standard Ethiopian/Continental fare. *US$ 40/43/43 sgl/dbl/ twin inc b/fast.*

Hotel Lammergeyer [off map 219 E1] (20 rooms) ☎058 112 2993; e belayadu@yahoo. com. In spite of an out-of-town location & limited secure parking, this hotel is one of the better picks in Gondar. En-suite rooms with a tub & DSTV are clean & reasonably priced. The restaurant has good food, which can also be served on a patio or in the

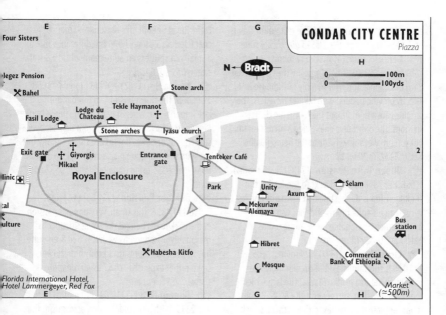

GONDAR CITY CENTRE
Piazza

Four Sisters

legez Pension

✕ Bahel

Fasil Lodge

Lodge du Chateau

Tekle Haymanot ✝

Stone arch

Stone arches

Iyasu church ✝

Exit gate   ✝ Giyorgis Mikael

Entrance gate

Tenteker Café

Royal Enclosure

linic ✚

Park

Unity

Axum

Selam

Mekuriaw Alemaya

cal

ulture

Bus station

✕ Habesha Kitfo

Hibret

Mosque

Commercial Bank of Ethiopia $

Florida International Hotel,
Hotel Lammergeyer, Red Fox

Market (≈500m)

N ◄ **Bradt** ►

0 ──── 100m
0 ──── 100yds

---

relaxing garden out the back. *US$35/45/45 sgl/
dbl/twin exc b/fast.*

🏠 **Lodge du Chateau** [219 F2] (13 rooms)
m 0911 021 025/0918 152 001; e lodge@
lodgeduchateau.com; www.lodgeduchateau.
com. This small new lodge located near the
Royal Enclosure is already receiving rave reviews.
The beautifully decorated rooms using locally
made furniture each have private en suite &
are all built around a lovely central garden.
The breezy upstairs breakfast restaurant has
wonderful views; other dishes may be available
on request. Budget beds are also available in
a 5-bed basement dorm – accessed by a very
rickety staircase. Wi-Fi is free. *US$12 dorm,
US$36/40/40/70 sgl/dbl/twin/trpl.*

🏠 **Fasil Lodge** [219 E2] (13 rooms) ☎ 058
111 0637; m 0911 017 991; e beffrem@yahoo.
com. Another good new lodge located near the
exit to the Royal Enclosure, this lodge offers good-
quality clean rooms with tiled floors & hot shower
en suite. A thatched-roof restaurant & bar are
attached. *US$25/35/40 sgl/dbl/twin inc b/fast.*

🏠 **Atse Bekafu Hotel** [218 C2] (24 rooms)
☎ 058 111 7711; e atsebekafahotel@yahoo.
com. With a prime in-town location, this smart
multi-storey hotel has quickly become a favourite
with tour operators. A rooftop deck & a menu that
includes pizzas & salads are other strong selling
points. All rooms are en suite with DSTV. Suites

have 2 beds, carpet & a fridge. *US$25/30/30/35
sgl/dbl/twin/suite.*

🏠 **Capra Walia Inn** [218 B3] (16 rooms)
☎ 058 112 0314–15; e caprawaliainn@yahoo.
com. Another good central choice, this inn offers
pleasant en-suite singles & doubles with TV.
Twin rooms are much posher & have 2 ¾ beds &
a bathtub. Visa is accepted, they have internet
access, & the attached restaurant serves good juice.
US$20/25/30 sgl/dbl/twin.

🏠 **Fogera Hotel** [218 A3] (12 rooms) ☎ 058
111 0405. This former government establishment
lies in a compact green garden about 5mins' walk
from the town centre. Originally built as a villa by
one of Mussolini's fascists, the Fogera though still
possessing a time-warped aura common to many
former (& extant) government hotels, has recently
been renovated. The 6 bungalows each have 2
separate rooms with clean, tiled floors & hot water
en suite. The restaurant serves decent hotel fare
at US$1.50–3 for a main course. *US$25/30/30 sgl/
dbl/twin.*

Budget

🏠 **Red Fox Hotel** [off map 219 E1] (14
rooms) ☎ 058 114 0581–2. Located about 5km
from the town centre this quiet hotel features
spacious rooms with queen bed, balcony, DSTV
& wonderfully large & surprisingly modern hot
shower en suite. Several suites have 2 queens &

accommodate up to 4 people. The restaurant & bar both have big-screen TVs. *US$15 dbl, US$24 suite.*

🏠 **Genetics Guest House** (12 rooms) [218 A2] **m** 0918 049 191. Opposite the Commercial Bank of Ethiopia, this new friendly guesthouse is already proving popular with budget travellers. The en suites are a tight fit, but the rooms are clean & spacious. The only downside is there's no restaurant, but you can wet your whistle at the nearby Oldies Bar. *US$15/20/20 sgl/dbl/twin.*

🏠 **Queen Taitu Pension** [218 D2] (19 rooms) 📞 058 112 2898. Located next to the Terara, this small pension is the best deal in town offering very clean en-suite rooms with hot water & TV for extremely reasonable rates. Some rooms have balconies. *US$9/12 sgl/dbl.*

🏠 **Circle Hotel** [218 D1] (24 rooms) 📞 058 111 1991. This unmistakable circular high-rise building is set just off the Piazza. The large, tiled rooms all have hot-shower en suite & DSTV. Some rooms are rather more frayed than others, so ask to check your room before you register. The 1st-floor restaurant receives mixed reports, & there's a breezy rooftop restaurant/bar as well. *US$9/10 sgl/dbl.*

🏠 **Embassy Hotel** (18 rooms) 📞 058 114 0868. Its out-of-town location south of the main centre is less than convenient, but the price is right – at least for the single rooms, which come with full bed, DSTV & hot shower, while the doubles are cramped & overpriced. As with most hotels around Gondar, 27 new rooms are under construction. The restaurant/bar is popular with locals & has plenty of 'loveseat' couches as well as a pleasant covered veranda out back. Apparently constructed without the benefit of a measuring tape, the stairs are very uneven in height & require due care! *US$9/15 sgl/dbl.*

Shoestring

🏠 **Merkuriaw Alemaya Hotel** [219 G1] (35 rooms) 📞 058 111 6677. Boasting a convenient (if potentially noisy) location between the bus station

& the Royal Ghebbi, this reasonably smart & characterless 5-storey hotel is indifferent value for a small but spotless en-suite room with TV & hot water. *US$6/7.50 sgl/dbl.*

🏠 **Terara Hotel** [218 D2] (31 rooms) 📞 058 111 0153. The finest hostelry in Gondar during the late Imperial era, when it went by the name Itegue Menen, this has suffered badly from neglect over subsequent decades. Rooms are small & dingy but the garden bar is quite nice. Camping is permitted. *US$4 tent, US$5 using common shower, US$7 en suite.*

🏠 **Belegez Pension** [219 E3] (14 rooms) 📞 058 111 4356. This small, very popular pension in the back roads behind the Royal Ghebbi has reasonably priced rooms with a ¾ bed & en-suite hot shower. The rooms using common showers seem rather expensive. *US$7 using common shower, US$10 en suite.*

🏠 **Roman Hotel** [218 D1] (10 rooms) 📞 058 112 2315. With a central location across from the Circle Hotel, the Roman offers adequately clean rooms with hot water, but is better known for its café & restaurant. *US$6/8.50 sgl/twin using common shower, US$7.50 with ¾ bed & en suite.*

🏠 **Misrak Pension** [218 B3] (11 rooms) 📞 058 111 0069. Set in a quiet green compound next to the Fogera Hotel, this once popular pension is a textbook example of a place that's responded to ubiquitous guidebook recommendations by screwing over the books' readerships. It remains adequately clean & friendly, but the small en-suite rooms with ¾ bed & cold shower are poor value at the inflated (albeit seasonally negotiable) *faranji* price. *US$7.50.*

🏠 **Ethiopia Hotel** [218 D1] (21 rooms) 📞 058 111 2004. This is the established shoestring favourite by virtue of its central location on the Piazza, & the paucity of notable alternatives. It no longer charges the same rate to all comers, but still seems quite reasonable for a no-frills room & access to sporadically functioning common showers. *US$5/6 sgl/dbl.*

✖ **WHERE TO EAT AND DRINK** Gondar boasts a pretty decent selection of eateries. Of the hotels, the **Goha Hotel** [off map 218 A2] tops the list with its three-course set dinners and lunches at US$7–8 per head, but it's not madly convenient unless you are sleeping there. The restaurants at the **Fogera Hotel** [218 A3] and **Quara Hotel** [218 C1] are also recommended. As for the **Terara Hotel** [218 D2], the garden bar is as good a place as any to knock back a pre- or post-dinner tipple, but you'd have to pay me to try the food! If you adhere to the maxim of following the locals, the **Circle**

Extracted from a letter by Raoul Boulakia

Gondar is a great town to go to a bar and enjoy traditional praise singing. Young couples (a man playing *masinko* and a woman singing) perform. You give them money as they sing, to encourage them, and they sing traditional and spontaneous praise in Amharic. The singing is really soulful and pleasant. Even if you are the only guests it turns into a party. I'd rate that as a trip highlight, and a 'must' activity to enjoy local culture. Guests can suggest lines to the singer as she goes on and she will incorporate them into her song. My favourite line was 'Your mother should be summoned to court and convicted for having such a handsome son'. Of course you'll need to make friends who can translate. People were super-friendly at these bars.

Hotel [218 D1] used to be the place to head for, and the rooftop bar still affords a pleasant view over the Piazza and the roofs of the Royal Enclosure. The food at the **Roman Hotel** [218 D1] next door is also good, and they advertise ice cream.

✕ **Four Sisters Restaurant** [219 E3] ☏058 112 2031; www.thefoursistersrestaurant.com. et; ⏱ 06.00–late daily. Located 200m from the exit to the Royal Enclosure, this new traditional Ethiopian restaurant, aptly owned & run by 4 very amiable sisters, had barely opened before we started receiving glowing recommendations from readers. The story behind its opening is that one of the sisters apparently gave such good service to a customer she was waiting on at the Goha that he helped her & her sisters start the restaurant. The food, while on the expensive side, is delicious & indeed made from the sisters' hearts with most dishes averaging around *US$4*.

✕ **Habesha Coffee & Fastfood** [218 C2] ▯ 0922 709 454; ⏱ 06.00–22.00 daily. Previously the site of the popular Tuscany Italian restaurant, this fresh new café is a popular spot for coffees, pastries & light meals including sandwiches, hamburgers & pizzas. *US$2.50–4.50*.

✕ **Habesha Kitfo** [219 F1] ▯ 0911 563 511; ⏱ 06.00–22.00 daily. Opposite the old entrance to the Royal Enclosure and noted for its attractive traditional décor & good *kitfo*. Their *shiro tegabino* is some of the best you will find anywhere, while

the several tame ducks that wander about make for a fun atmosphere. *US$2–5*.

✕ **Golden Gate Bar & Restaurant** [218 D1] ⏱ 07.00–22.00 daily. This long-time popular expat hangout features Chinese food which is a welcome break from the usual culinary monotony.

✕ **Mini Fogera Restaurant** [218 B3] On the same square as the Fogera Hotel, this small place may not be as attractively decorated as Habesha but is just as good when it comes to Ethiopian cuisine.

✕ **Tele Satellite Clb** [218 C1] Below the post office, this is a popular breakfast spot (the speciality is *nashif*, egg fried in a spicy red chilli sauce, topped with a cup of cultured milk), & the owner is a useful source of local information.

▭ **Delicious Pastry** [218 C1] ⏱ 06.30–21.00 daily. Next to Pizza Café, this patisserie is the pick when it comes to sugar-laden cakes.

▭ **Pizza Café** [218 C1] ⏱ 07.00–22.00 daily. This new café next door to Golden Internet serves a small menu of pizzas as well as coffee, sandwiches & burgers in the US$2.50–4.50 range.

▭ **Sofa Juice** [218 C2] ☏058 111 4026; ⏱ 06.00–21.30 daily. This friendly place serves the widest variety of always-fresh fruit juices, as well as tasty mini pizzas.

ENTERTAINMENT AND NIGHTLIFE Gondar is well known for its nightlife, with the greatest density of seedy and seedier bars clustered in the backstreets behind the NTO office. It almost goes without saying, but **Dashen House** [218 B2] is the best place (apart from the factory) to sample the locally made ale, served on tap or by the bottle. Meanwhile traditional music and dancing can be enjoyed on most nights from 20.30 at the **Balageru Bar** [218 B2] (☏ *058 111 5133*) next to the Dashen Bank, at the **Atse Bekafu Cultural Club** [218 C2] (✎ *058 111 7711*) next to the hotel of the same name some 50m closer to the town centre and on Thursday and Saturday evenings at **Four Sisters Restaurant** [219 E3].

OTHER PRACTICALITIES
Foreign exchange Both branches of the **Commercial Bank of Ethiopia** [218 A2/219 H1] offer a foreign-exchange service, as does the generally more efficient **Dashen Bank** [218 B2] which also·has an ATM. Cash and travellers' cheques in most major currencies are accepted. The service is quicker than in most other parts of Ethiopia.

Internet and email Most of Gondar's better hotels offer free Wi-Fi or have internet cafés. Beyond that your best bet is **Golden Internet** [218 C2] (next to Sofa Juice), which charges less than US$0.05 per minute.

Meal tickets In Gondar (just like in Addis Ababa) it is possible to buy meal tickets for beggars. They are available from Habesha Kitfo opposite the entrance to the Royal Enclosure. A bundle of ten meal tickets costs US$1. For each ticket somebody can get two small loaves of bread at any participating bakery.

A ROYAL BANQUET AT GONDAR

When James Bruce published the five-volume account of his Ethiopian journey under the title *Travels to Discover the Source of the Nile* in 1790, its contents seemed so outrageous to polite European society that they were widely dismissed as fabrication. Of all the passages in the book, none proved to be as controversial as an account of a banquet held at the Royal Ghebbi in Gondar, from which the following edited extracts are drawn.

A long table is set in the middle of a large room, and benches beside it for the guests. A cow or bull, one or more, is brought close to the door and carved up alive. The prodigious noise the animal makes is the signal for the company to sit down to table.

There are then laid out before every guest – instead of plates – pancakes, and something thicker and tougher. It is unleavened bread of a sourish taste, far from being disagreeable, and very easily digested, made of a grain called tef. Three or four of these cakes are put uppermost, for the food of the person opposite to whose seat they are placed. Beneath these are four of five of ordinary bread, which serve the master to wipe his fingers on, and afterwards the servant for bread to his dinner.

Three or four servants then come, each with a square piece of beef in their bare hands, laying it upon the cakes of tef, without cloth or anything else beneath them. By this time all the guests have knives in their hands. The company are so ranged that one man sits between two women. The man with his knife cuts a thin piece, which would be thought a good beefsteak in England, while you see the motion of the fibres yet perfectly distinct, and alive in the flesh. No man in Abyssinia, of any fashion whatever, feeds himself or touches his own meat. The women take the steak and cut it lengthwise like strings, about the thickness of your little finger, then crossways into square pieces, something smaller than dice. This they lay upon a piece of tef-bread, strongly powdered with black pepper and salt; they then wrap it up in the tef-bread like a cartridge.

WHAT TO SEE Gondar's most important tourist attraction is the Fasil Ghebbi or **Royal Enclosure** (☏ *058 111 1536;* ⊕ *08.00–17.00 daily; entrance US$6; US$5 video camera*), a walled compound of 17th-century castles and buildings lying in the city centre at the southern end of the Piazza. Similar in vintage and architectural style is Fasilidas's Pool (see page 226), a couple of kilometres from the city centre. The entrance ticket to the Royal Enclosure is valid for the day of purchase only. If you have a couple of days in town, it's worth planning your sightseeing around the fact that this ticket also covers entrance to Fasilidas's Pool, but not to other historical sites.

Of several old churches dotted around Gondar, the most beautiful is the lavishly decorated Debre Birhan Selassie, 1km from the city centre, and regarded by some experts to contain the finest art of its period anywhere in Ethiopia. Also well worth a visit is Kuskuam Maryam, set on a hill 5km from the city centre: the church itself is modern and undistinguished, but the adjoining residence of the Empress Mentewab is both architecturally interesting and atmospheric, as well as offering a great view over the city centre. Of minor interest are the central church of Medhane Alem and suburban church of Kidus Yohannis. Probably of greater interest to scholars than to tourists is the former capital of Danquaz, established by Emperor Susneyos but abandoned by his son Fasilidas in favour of Gondar.

In the meantime the man, having put up his knife, with each hand resting upon his neighbour's knee, his body stooping, his head low and forward, and mouth open very like an idiot, turns to the one whose cartridge is first ready, who stuffs the whole of it into his mouth, which is so full that he is in constant danger of being choked. This is a mark of grandeur. The greater the man would seem to be, the larger the piece he takes into his mouth; the more noise he makes in chewing it, the more polite he is thought to be. They indeed have a proverb that says: 'Beggars and thieves only eat small pieces, or without making a noise.'

Having dispatched this morsel, which he does very expeditiously, his next female neighbour holds forth another cartridge, which goes the same way, and so forth, until he is satisfied. He never drinks before he has finished eating, and before he begins drinking, in gratitude to the two fair ones that feed him, he rolls up two small cartridges of the same shape and form, and each of his neighbours opens her mouth at the same time, while with each hand he puts the portions into their mouths. He then falls to drinking out of a handsome horn; the ladies eat until they are satisfied, and they all drink together. A great deal of joy and mirth goes around, very seldom with any mixture of acrimony or ill humour.

Those within are very much elevated: love lights all its fires, and everything is permitted with absolute freedom. There is no coyness, no delays, no need of appointments or retirement to gratify their wishes. There are no rooms but one, in which they sacrifice both to Bacchus and to Venus. The two men nearest the vacuum a pair have made on the bench by leaving their seats, hold their upper garments like a screen before the two that have left the bench; and, if we may judge by sound, they seem to think it as great a shame to make love in silence as to eat.

Replaced in their seats again, the company drink the happy couple's health, and their example is followed at different ends of the table, as each couple is disposed. All this passes without remark or scandal, not a licentious word is uttered, nor the most distant joke made upon the transaction.

Although the ideal way to explore the Simien Mountains is over several days' hiking or trekking, the tar road to Debark on the outskirts of the national park makes a full-day trip from Gondar a realistic and increasingly popular excursion. A more affordable alternative is the half-day trip to Kosoye viewpoint 32km from town along the Simien road. In order that fly-in visitors to Gondar don't overlook these options, they are briefly covered below as excursions from the city, rather than under the full section on the Simien Mountains later in the chapter.

Fasil Ghebbi (Royal Enclosure) and the city centre

The Fasil Ghebbi lies at the heart of modern Gondar and gives the city much of its character. Surrounded by high stone walls, the enclosure covers an area of 70,000m² and contains six castles, a complex of connecting tunnels and raised walkways, and several smaller buildings. It's a fascinating place to explore, and one could easily spend several hours here. At the gate an entrance fee of US$6 is levied. Tickets are only valid for the day of purchase and include still photography. A video camera attracts an additional fee of US$5. For a first-time visitor, hiring an official guide is recommended. They are generally quite knowledgeable and will point out features that might otherwise be missed. Guide fees start at around US$9 for a group of one to five persons; it is best that you first walk around under their tuition, then return on your own later to soak up some of the atmosphere.

The most impressive castle within the enclosure is the original built by Fasilidas, c1640, partially restored in the mid 20th century, and more fully restored, using the original construction methods, with UNESCO funding between 1999 and 2002. **Fasilidas's Castle** is made of stone and shows a unique combination of Portuguese, Axumite and even Indian influences. The ground floor consists of reception and dining areas. The walls are decorated with a symbol similar to the Star of David, which became the emblem of the Ethiopian royal family after the Solomonic dynasty reclaimed the throne in the 13th century. The first-floor roof of the castle was used for prayer and religious ceremonies, and it is also where Fasilidas addressed the townsfolk. Fasilidas's prayer room, also on the first floor, has four windows, every one of which faces a church. Stairs lead from the roof to the small second-floor room that Fasilidas used as his sleeping quarters. Above this is an open balcony, which was probably the watchtower. This third-floor platform, 32m above the ground, offers views in all directions; on a clear day, you can even see Lake Tana on the horizon, emphasising the strategic advantage of choosing Gondar as a capital.

The other major relic of Fasilidas's reign is the **Royal Archive Building**. This was partially destroyed during World War II when Britain bombed the Italian headquarters, which lay within the compound. There are also several crumbling buildings behind the castle and a bathing pool, all of which are thought to have been built by Fasilidas. Near to Fasilidas's Castle, the tiny castle built by Fasilidas's successor Emperor Yohannis I (1667–82) is the least interesting building in the compound.

Yohannis I was succeeded by Emperor Iyasu (1682–1706), who is regarded as the greatest ruler of the Gondar period. Iyasu was a popular and peace-loving emperor, who nevertheless spent much of his rule at war with the Oromo of southern Ethiopia. **Iyasu's Castle** is one of the largest in the compound, and the most ornately constructed. In its prime it was extremely beautiful, decorated with ivory, gold leaf, precious stones and paintings. Unfortunately it was partially damaged by an earthquake in 1704, and the ground-floor ceiling collapsed under the British bombardment in World War II. It is now little more than a shell. In rather better condition is the three-room sauna that was constructed by Iyasu alongside his castle. The guide will demonstrate how the various chambers were used to create steam. Iyasu is also credited with the construction of the raised walkways that connect Gondar's three oldest castles.

In 1699 Iyasu was visited by a French doctor called Poncet, who described the emperor as a 'lively and sagacious genius' and also left an account of a ceremony that gives some flavour of 17th-century Gondar. According to Poncet, an assembly of 12,000 soldiers in battledress attended the ceremony, and the emperor arrived with 'two princes of the blood in splendid dresses ... holding a magnificent canopy under which the emperor walked, preceded by his trumpets, kettledrums, fifes, harps and other instruments'. Poncet's visit led indirectly to greater contact between Iyasu and European Catholics, a cause of great concern to the Orthodox clergy coming less than a century after the religious strife under Emperor Susneyos. In 1706, the emperor was ousted by his son Tekle Haymanot with the support of the clergy, setting the scene for another phase of Catholic–Orthodox tension.

Four kings were crowned and then assassinated in the 15 years after Iyasu was ousted. Only one of them, Dawit III (1716–21), another of Iyasu's sons, left his mark on the Royal Enclosure in the form of a **lion cage**. The black-maned Abyssinian lion was an important royal symbol right through to Haile Selassie's rule in the 20th century, and I'm told that this cage held live lions until the last one died in 1992. Dawit III also built a large **concert hall**, which is still standing today.

Emperor Dawit III was poisoned in 1721, to be succeeded by his brother Bakafa, who ruled Ethiopia for nine years, and left his mark on the Royal Enclosure by building **Bakafa's Castle**, some **stables**, and an immense **banquet hall**. This hall was the victim of a British or Italian raid, depending on whom you believe (and has since been rendered unrecognisable by a feeble attempt at restoration using concrete!). Bakafa was a powerful but heavy-handed ruler, and his attempts to restore the strength of the monarchy, which had been badly affected by 15 years of intrigue and ineffective rule, alienated his most powerful subjects.

Bakafa's son, Iyasu II (1730–55), ascended the throne under the regency of his mother Mentewab, who proved to be the last of Gondar's castle builders. **Mentewab's Castle** is a fine building, decorated with Gondar crosses, and in such good condition that it is now used as a gift shop. Mentewab's Catholic leanings only furthered the religious divisions in the empire, and her artistically inclined son proved an ineffective ruler. After 1755, the monarchy decreased in importance as it became a puppet of powerful regional princes, and no further building took place in the Royal Enclosure.

Three churches lie within separate compounds within the main walls of the Royal Enclosure. The oldest, **Gemjabet Maryam**, was founded by Fasilidas, who was buried there in 1767. The modern church building is of limited interest, though it is the site of the grave of Walter Plowden, a close associate of Emperor Tewodros, and its treasury holds some excellent 19th-century paintings. The churches of **Elfin Giyorgis** and **Asasame Kidus Mikael** are also modern, built over destroyed churches respectively attributed to emperors Dawit II and Fasilidas.

Also in the city centre, but outside of the Royal Enclosure, there are a few other historical sites worth looking at. One such building is **Ras Ghimb**, the palace built by Ras Mikael Suhul in the late 18th century, and subsequently used as a holiday residence by Emperor Haile Selassie and as an interrogation hall under the Mengistu regime. Judging by outward appearances, this impressive building is still in reasonable shape, and it now houses the offices of a UN Project for Forest Plantation and Integrated Development. It has been closed to visitors for as long as anybody can remember.

Close to Ras Ghimb, but obscured behind a swathe of tall juniper trees, the **Church of Medhane Alem** is the seat of the Bishop of Gondar, and one of the few churches in the city to have survived the Mahdist invasion more or less untouched.

THE EMPEROR'S HORSE

Outside the enclosure of Fasilidas's Pool stands a small domed pavilion that is supported by six pillars and not unlike a disused bandstand in appearance. Local tradition has it that this was the mausoleum built by Emperor Iyasu I for a horse called Suviel. According to legend, the injured Suviel was captured by Muslim foes after its owner Emperor Yohannis I was killed in battle in the Sudan. The horse was healed by a disguised 'stranger' – in fact, Yohannis's son, the future Emperor Iyasu I, who tricked the Muslims into letting him ride Suviel, then fled away on horseback. When the Muslims gave chase, Suviel leapt across a gorge too wide for a lesser horse to cross, and both he and the future emperor returned safely to Gondar. This story seems wildly far-fetched, given that no evidence exists to suggest Yohannis died in the Sudan. It is more likely the little pavilion is where the early emperors of Gondar stood during ceremonies held at the pool.

Founded by Fasilidas, and originally part of the imperial palace, the restored church is faithful to the original design, but the extensive paintings on the outer wall of the sanctuary probably date to the late 19th century but may well replicate much older paintings that preceded them.

Fasilidas's Pool and surrounds About 2km out of the town centre, along the Bahir Dar road, lies the 2,800m² sunken bathing pool generally attributed to Emperor Fasilidas. Enclosed by a tall stone wall with six turrets, the pool is overlooked by a two-storey building widely said to have been Fasilidas's second residence. Some sources attribute the pool to the later reign of Emperor Iyasu I, while others suggest it may in fact be the earliest of Fasilidas's constructions, pre-dating his famous castle. You can walk out to the pool from the town centre, or else take a local minibus. Entrance to the pool is included in the price for visiting the Royal Enclosure, so take your ticket with you (tickets cannot be bought at the pool itself).

Often referred to as a swimming pool, the sunken construction – which is dry most of the year through – has probably always been used ceremonially rather than for royal leisure pursuits. The pool is the central stage on which the Timkat or Epiphany Festival is celebrated in Gondar. This takes place on the 11th day of Tir (variably between 18 and 20 January) and – should you be around at the time – is a sight not to be missed. Led by colourfully attired priests carrying *tabots* and crosses, thousands of white-robed worshippers converge around the pool in the afternoon, where they are blessed and sprinkled with its holy water.

Another low-key stone building close to the pool is popularly known as the **House of Chickens**. Local legend somewhat improbably claims that this served as a royal chicken run under Fasilidas; a pre-Mengistu ETC brochure suggests, more plausibly, that it might have housed a 'sweating house isolated for the cure of contagious diseases'.

A short walk away from Fasil's Pool, the **Church of Kidus Yohannis** was founded under Iyasu II and destroyed by the Dervish in 1888. The outer walls are still standing, however, and a well-preserved vestry in one of the turrets now serves as the sanctuary of what is otherwise in effect an open-air church!

Kuskuam Set at an altitude of 2,234m on Debre Tsehai (Mountain of Sun), which overlooks the city of Gondar, the palatial stone complex known as Kuskuam – after a

Coptic convent in Egypt – was constructed as the residence of the Empress Mentewab after the death of her husband Emperor Bakafa in 1730. Mentewab served for many years as regent for her young son Iyasu II, so that her out-of-town residence took over from the old Royal Enclosure as the centre of imperial affairs in the mid 18th century. It is here, at Kuskuam, that the Scots explorer James Bruce spent several sociable months waiting for permission to visit the source of the Nile at Gish Abay, in the process becoming a close friend and confidant of Mentewab. (It has also been claimed that Bruce had an affair with one of the empress's married daughters, who bore him a child at Kuskuam, though it died before it could be christened.)

Although in a state of partial ruin, Kuskuam makes for a fascinating excursion from central Gondar. The overall shape of the main palace is clearly discernible, with most of the first-floor walls still intact, as is one staircase and part of the first floor. An ornate Gonderine cross is carved over the door to Mentewab's bedroom. Little remains of the queen's personal chapel, which was once adorned with paintings as impressive as those at Debre Birhan Selassie, representing every saint venerated by the Ethiopian Church. A round building ingeniously designed to get around the prohibition on menstruating women entering a church, the chapel has 12 alcoves, which the queen would visit in turn every hour to pray when 'unclean', while a priest stood outside praying and swinging incense. Better preserved is the impressive banquet hall, which must be at least 10m high. Engravings of animals and crosses decorate the outer wall of the banquet hall; there is also an etching of Abuna Yohannis, Patriarch of the Ethiopian Church during Mentewab's regency. The almost cartoon-like style of some of these etchings is similar to those (including one of James Bruce) at the Lake Tana monastery of Narga Selassie, also built by Mentewab.

The church of Kuskuam Maryam, set alongside the royal residence, suffered the same fate as most Gonderine churches during the Mahdist War. Rebuilt during the Italian occupation, it is elaborately decorated, though none of the paintings dates to before 1970. The bones of Mentewab and Iyasu II were retrieved from the ground during the church's reconstruction, and are now housed in a glass coffin within the anterooms. There is a big celebration at the church every 15 November.

Entrance to Kuskuam costs US$3. The complex lies about 5km from the city centre. To get there, drive or catch a shared minibus from the Piazza to the Medical College, from where a road signposted to the right leads uphill for about 1.5km to the church and ruined palace. If you don't fancy walking the last, rather steep stretch, a taxi from the Piazza should cost around US$3 one-way. There are great views over the city centre on the way up, and the juniper and olive trees around the ruined palace host a variety of colourful birds.

Debre Birhan Selassie

There are said to be 44 churches in Gondar, at least seven of which date from Fasilidas's rule, but most of the original buildings were destroyed in 1888 when Gondar was attacked by the Dervish or Mahdist of Sudan. The only Gonderine church that escaped entirely untouched was Debre Birhan Selassie ('Mountain of the Enlightened Trinity'), saved from the Dervish by the intervention of a swarm of bees ... or so they say in Gondar.

Founded by Iyasu I in the 1690s, Debre Birhan Selassie was the most important church in 18th-century Gondar, when it was the site of several royal burials. The dating of the modern building is open to question: the original church was almost certainly circular in shape, and remained so after it was restored following a fire in 1707. It is likely that the modern rectangular building was constructed in the late 18th century, following the destruction of the original building by lightning. Whenever it was built, this beautiful church, along with the much more imposing

THE BEAUTIFUL EMPRESS

Paul Henze has described the Empress Mentewab as 'a subject awaiting a biographer'. And certainly the fondly remembered builder of Kuskuam and Narga Selassie must rank among the most charismatic figures of the Gonderine era – as well, folklore has it, as a queen of great generosity, wit, comeliness and political savvy.

Two contradictory stories relate to Mentewab's union with Bakafa. One legend has it that Mentewab was raised in humble circumstances in a district called Quara to the west of Lake Tana. In the early 1720s, Bakafa happened to be travelling through this district when he fell seriously ill. The ailing emperor was taken in by a local farmer, and was nursed back to health by the farmer's beautiful daughter Birhan Mogasa ('Splendour of Light'). And Bakafa was so enamoured with his saviour that he married her as soon as he was fit enough to return to Gondar.

. The other version, as told by Mentewab's official chronicler, is that she was the daughter of a princess called Yolyana, who dressed her up in the finest cloths and golden jewellery and arranged for her to be introduced to the king. 'When Bakafa saw her he was very happy because she was so completely beautiful, and he said to her "You have no fault at all!"' recalls the chronicler: 'Then he made her sit beside him and had delicious foods brought, and they ate and drank together. That day he knew her as Adam knew Eve, and she conceived immediately.'

Whichever story is true, there is no doubting Bakafa's appreciation of the wife who would outlive both him and their eldest son, the Emperor Iyasu – it was he who bestowed upon her the exclamatory throne name Mentewab, which translates as 'How Beautiful Thou Art!'.

---

one built by Fasilidas in Axum, which it resembles, offers some idea of what other treasures might be in Gondar today had it not been for the Mahdist War.

While Debre Birhan Selassie is not without architectural merit, it is of greatest interest for the prolific paintings inside. The much-photographed ceiling, decorated with paintings of 80 cherubic faces, is probably the most famous single example of ecclesiastical art in Ethiopia. The walls are also painted with dozens of separate scenes: the southern wall concentrates on the Life of Christ, while the northern wall depicts various saints. One of the most striking individual paintings is an unusually fearsome depiction of the devil surrounded by flames, to be found on the wall to the left of the main door, while next to this door is a striking image of a captive Muhammad being led by the devil. The paintings are traditionally held to be the work of the 17th-century artist Haile Meskel, but it is more likely that several artists were involved and that the majority were painted during the rule of Egwala Tsion (1801–17), who is depicted prostrating himself before the Cross on one of the murals.

The church lies about 1km out of town, a ten-minute walk from the stairs below the administrative offices. After climbing the stairs, simply continue straight ahead along a rolling country road with views back to the Royal Enclosure. You can't miss the church – it's enclosed by a high stone wall and surrounded by juniper trees. An entrance fee of US$3 is charged and an additional US$5 for a video camera. The caretaker of several years' standing is very helpful and not at all pushy; a small tip will be appreciated but is not expected. Flash photography is forbidden; to photograph the famous roof without tripods you'll have to use a table as support.

A good time to visit the church is around 30 minutes before sunset, when the sun's rays penetrate the interior to enhance the spiritual atmosphere. Don't be late – once the sun has gone down the paintings are difficult to see, especially when there is no power to light up the few fluorescent bulbs.

Danquaz Situated some 20km south of modern Gondar, Danquaz was the last of several semi-permanent capitals established by Emperor Susneyos in the early 17th century, and it was also used by Emperor Fasilidas for the first three years of his reign, after which he relocated his capital to Gondar. Contemporary accounts and archaeological research indicate that Danquaz was an impressive and well-built complex – in many senses the precursor to the foundation of a permanent capital at Gondar.

Sadly, little of the former capital remains today. Susneyos founded the Church of Azusa Tekle Haymanot, perched atop a small hill, but as with so many Gonderine churches the original building was destroyed during the Mahdist War. Rebuilt in the 1950s, it is of limited historical interest, though the original stone walls enclosing the compound do survive intact. There are a couple of engraved crosses with 16 arms each on the outer wall to the right of the main gate, while a small house built into the wall and reputedly once lived in by Susneyos stands on the other side of the gate.

A five-minute walk downhill from the church is the pool (ask for Atse Mawegna – the King's Pool) built by Susneyos and believed to be the model on which Fasil's Pool in Gondar was based. Now dry and somewhat overgrown, the sunken walls of the pool are still clearly discernible. Recent excavations suggest that the pool was filled via a subterranean channel leading from the nearby river.

Historically important as this site may be, there isn't much left to capture the imagination of the casual visitor. It is, however, accessible enough, and would make an easy side trip in a vehicle on the way to or from the airport. Azazo lies on the

SYMBOLIC ARCHITECTURE OF DEBRE BIRHAN SELASSIE

Extracted from a letter by John Moore

Debre Birhan Selassie is certainly one of the, if not the, most beautiful of the Ethiopian churches. Perhaps the reason it's so special and that such care and effort was put into it is that the emperor intended to move the Ark of the Covenant there from Axum. As a result, it is not round like all the other churches in the Gondar region but rectangular and you can still see clearly the foundations of the round church previously on the site. It was built roughly to the same directions as Solomon's Temple in Jerusalem, where the Ark came from. The perimeter wall has 12 equidistant round towers representing the 12 Apostles, one of which is larger than the rest and was intended to house relics associated with the Ark. The gateway is the '13th tower' and represents Christ. The gateway's superstructure is built to look like a royal lion couchant, which it does more or less, and the tail of the lion, which looks like a comma, is carved on the keystone of the arch in the wall to the west of the church, signifying the omnipresence of Christ. Near the top of the south end of the roof are seven niches supporting a seven-pronged medallion, with an ostrich egg on each prong. Seven signifies the seven days of creation and eggs represent the power of the creative spirit.

junction of the airport and Bahir Dar roads. To get to the church, follow the Bahir Dar road from the junction for about 1km, then take a right turn along a clear side road, which after another 1km or so leads uphill to the church. There is regular public transport between Gondar and Azazo.

Ploughshare Women's Training Centre (e *tesfalemabera@yahoo.com*; ⏱ *08.30–18.00 Mon–Sat*) Located only 3km out of Gondar on the right side of the Axum road, this is a good place to pick up traditional black pottery such as coffee ceremony pots and incense burners. Weaving is another activity; tapestries and other small handicrafts are available in the gift shop. The curator here speaks excellent English and is truly excited to show people around.

Wolleka (Falasha village) Situated roughly 5km from Gondar along the Axum road, this formerly famous Falasha village is the only accessible place where you can check out something of the tradition of Ethiopian Judaism. Even so, it has to be classed as something of a let-down. Wolleka was vacated by its original occupants between 1985 and 1992, when most of Ethiopia's 'Black Jews' were airlifted to Jerusalem by the Israeli government to liberate them from the repressive Mengistu regime. All that remains today is the old synagogue, the design of which mimics a typical circular Ethiopian church, but with a Star of David rather than a cross on its roof.

Kosoye It is said that this viewpoint, 32km from Gondar, so appealed to Queen Elizabeth II that she instructed her driver to stop there for tea while travelling between Gondar and Axum in 1965. Legend or not, it is a great spot, with a sweeping view across the lowlands to the Simien Mountains, and a recommended half-day excursion for those who don't have time to get to the Simiens proper. The one-hour walk along the cliff offers a good chance of seeing gelada and guereza monkeys, as well as birds of prey such as lammergeyer. Transport can be arranged through one of the private tour operators in Gondar for around US$36 per group. You can also get there easily by taking the bus going to Debark. At the time of writing two new lodges were under construction along this stretch of road: **Kosoye Lodge** (*14 rooms;* m *0918 770 347;* e *gashaws2000@yahoo.com*) overlooking the valley right near the viewpoint, and **Befikir Kosoye Ecolodge** (*14 rooms;* m *0911 250 828;* e *befikirdd66@yahoo.com*) 4km further along the road from the lookout towards Debark.

DEBARK

This sprawling town of nearly 30,000 straddles the main Gondar–Axum road 100km north of Gondar and 250km southwest of Axum at a chilly altitude of around 2,800m on the western base of the awesome Simien Mountains National Park. Debark is the traditional trailhead for Simien hikes and treks, and – although many hikers now drive deeper into the park to start their hike – all prospective visitors must stop in at the park headquarters on the Gondar side of Debark to buy the necessary permits. Despite its proximity to Ethiopia's most popular trekking destination, the town itself is rather nondescript and lacking in scenic qualities. Facilities include a couple of decent budget hotels, what must surely be the world's most persistent shoeshine boys, and a decent market and bakery where 'helpful' youngsters try to insinuate themselves into any and every transaction with a *faranji* in the hope of bolstering the price to gain a commission. Surprisingly, Debark has acceptably fast internet access, albeit at a high cost of birr 1 per minute.

GETTING THERE AND AWAY If you are making your way to Debark independently, two buses daily head there from Gondar, leaving at around 06.00 and 10.30 (US$2.50; 4 hours). Alternatively, organise your whole trek with a tour operator, including private transport to and from Debark – or, for that matter, directly to and from one of the national park campsites.

In a private vehicle, the drive between Debark and Axum takes about six hours, longer if you stop along the way. Coming from Axum on public transport, catch a minibus to Shire (Inda Selassie), which costs around US$2.50 and takes about 90 minutes, and spend the night there before catching the early morning bus to Gondar, which will drop you in Debark. Heading northwards from Debark to Axum, the first bus from Gondar to Shire arrives in Debark at around 09.00 and it is often full. To be certain of a seat, you could ask somebody to go to Gondar the day before and buy your ticket. The bus usually arrives in Shire in the mid afternoon, leaving you time to catch a minibus on to Axum the same day.

TOURIST INFORMATION A visit to the **national park office** (↺ *058 117 0407/0016;* e *walia.smnp@ethionet.et;* ⊕ *08.30–12.30 & 13.30–17.30 Mon–Thu, 08.30–11.30 & 13.30–17.30 Fri, 08.30–12.00 & 14.00–17.00 Sat & Sun*), which lies on the Gondar road a few minutes' walk from Simien Park Hotel, is essential for anyone wanting to plan a visit to the Siemiens. It is here where you pay your fees and organise scouts and guides. In spite of what the surly staff may say, it is *not* essential to hire a guide.

WHERE TO STAY AND EAT

🏠 **Hotel Imet Gogo** (32 rooms) ↺058 117 0634. This hotel provides much-needed mid-range en-suite rooms with hot water & TV. The smart bar features flat-screen DSTV & it serves food as well. *US$17/20/22.50 sgl/dbl/twin.*

🏠 **Hotel Giant Lobelia** (39 rooms) ↺058 117 0560; m 0918 763 002; e globeliahotel@yahoo. com. This brand-new hotel with clean en-suite rooms located near the filling station would be a good deal apart from the fact that there is no hot water. Only a couple of the rooms actually have working boilers; these are the ones you'll be shown when you ask. But then you'll be checked into a room without one as we & several other guests unhappily discovered. *US$13.50/18/23 sgl/dbl/twin.*

🏠 **Unique Landscape** (44 rooms) ↺058 117 0152; m 0918 236 075; e shmels.ayalewu12@ gmail.com. Located opposite the NOC filling station, this new hotel is the hotel of choice for many tour operators. The tiled en-suite rooms are neat & clean & – more importantly – have working hot-water systems. Common showers are also available, but ridiculously over-priced. There's a popular café-cum-

bar on the ground floor & an OK restaurant on the 1st floor serving the standard Ethiopian/Continental fare for US$2–4. *US$11.50 using common shower, US$13/15/18/27 sgl/dbl/twin/trpl.*

🏠 **Simien Park Hotel** (24 rooms) ↺058 117 0055/0406; m 0911 457 516; e zlife96@ yahoo.com; www.simenparkhotel.com. It's easy to see why this long-serving lodge on the main road through Debark is the top choice for budget travellers. The 12 new en-suite rooms, all with hot water & TV, are the cleanest, nicest & most reasonably priced rooms in town. Meanwhile the older shared shower rooms also have hot water & while worn we've been told they're due for a facelift. Camping is also permitted in the back garden, & the hotel can rent out most of the camping gear required for a Simien hike. It has a decent restaurant serving excellent roast lamb (except during fasting periods) as well as other Ethiopian & Western dishes & a new café & bar were under construction when we visited. *US$5/6/9 using common shower, US$12/15/18/24 sgl/dbl/twin/trpl.*

GONDAR TO AXUM BY ROAD

The drive between Gondar and Axum takes around eight hours in a good private vehicle, not allowing for breaks. There is no direct bus service between the cities, but there are direct buses between Gondar and Shire (Inda Selassie), leaving at 06.30 in either direction, taking around ten hours, and stopping at Debark (the base for climbing the Simien Mountains). Minibuses between Shire and Axum leave throughout the day and take about 90 minutes. So it is easy enough to bus between Gondar and Axum in a day, but for those who would prefer to dawdle along this scenic route rather than spend a full day cooped up in a bus, I'm retaining an edited and updated version of the section on travelling between Gondar and Axum that appeared in the first edition.

Buses between Gondar and Adi Arkay leave at around 06.00 to 06.30 in either direction and take about eight hours, stopping at Debark *en route* to drop off and pick up passengers. The road between Gondar and Debark climbs through a typically pretty highland landscape of rolling hills, brightened in September by profuse wild flowers. Immediately after Debark, you plunge into the Simien foothills along a road that I would rate as the most dramatic I've seen in Africa, and perhaps the most scary as well. The Italian-built road clings giddily to the slopes, and the drama is increased by the presence of the jaggedly evocative spines of the Simiens towering to your left. The altitude drop between Debark and Adi Arkay is close on 2,000m, and the 70km drive takes up to three hours of endless switchbacks! At the time of writing the road was slowly being upgraded by the Chinese and will hopefully be tarred by the time this book goes to press.

Adi Arkay is a pleasant enough town, stunningly situated, reasonably free of *faranji* hysteria, blessed with a striking little stone church, and with a higher fly count than most. A possible off-the-beaten-track excursion from here is to Waldiba Monastery towards the remote Tekaze Valley. One of the oldest monastic schools in Ethiopia, Waldiba was established at a site that, legend has it, was visited by Joseph, Mary and Jesus during their time in Egypt. While at Waldiba, they received a divine message to return to Jerusalem, which they did by taking a subterranean passage via Eritrea or Yemen. The monastery cannot be reached in a vehicle, and makes for a long day trip on muleback. Several other interesting monasteries lie in the area, and can be visited over a few days from the village of Sekwar Maryam, which has accommodation and lies close to Waldiba.

You have a few rather basic **hotels** to choose from in Adi Arkay. The most obvious pick is the **Ras Dashen Hotel** (*10 rooms;* m *0918 731 952*), but it is madly over-priced at US$4.50 for a very basic room using a common cold shower. Further up the road the unsigned **Tekaze Hotel** has newer, though decidedly scruffy, share-shower rooms for US$5 and also serves reasonably good local food. Remarkably, one letter mentions seeing a lammergeyer perched on a tree right outside the Ras Dashen Hotel.

Bus tickets between Adi Arkay and May Tsemre can be hard to come by, so it might be worth asking around at the overnight truck stop when you arrive for a lift the next day. If this doesn't work, beg the driver of the Axum bus to take you as far as May Tsemre the next morning. This is only 25km further down the road, and he may give you standing room on the basis that there are no police checks on the way. From May Tsemre, you should quickly enough find transport to Shire, but if not there are a few very basic hotels lining the main road.

SHIRE Marked on most maps as Inda Selassie, Shire is a sizeable and reasonably attractive town in the midst of an unforeseen building boom. At the forefront is the **Gebar Centre**, a large, gleaming white complex that would look much more at home in Addis. In addition to two banks, the centre is home to a hotel (see opposite). Selam runs a weekly bus service from Addis Ababa to Shire departing on Tuesdays at 05.30, which involves an overnight stay in Gondar (US$27; around 18 hours). More locally, there are regular daily services heading eastward to Axum (US$2.50). The best place to stay is **Gebar Shire Hotel** (*52 rooms;* ✆ *034 444 3127/4264;* e *gebshire@ethionet. et; www.gebarshirehotel.com*), which offers a level of luxury that greatly surpasses anything around. All of the well-sized rooms are tastefully decorated, have DSTV and refrigerators, and are excellent value at US$18.50/21.50/25.50/27.50 for a single/ double/twin/suite, while a clean common shower costs US$8.50–12 depending on the size of the room. Of even greater note is the elegant restaurant, which has a vast menu containing pages of interesting entrées including chicken, fish, veal, steak, lamb, pasta and rice dishes, as well as a full page of soups and salads. If your budget doesn't stretch that far, **Africa Hotel** (*41 rooms;* ✆ *034 444 0101*) located on the Axum side of town before the Gebar Centre, offers well-priced en-suite rooms with full bed, hot water and television for US$9.50. The restaurant is good, there's internet access, and they have a covered outdoor pool table.

SIMIEN MOUNTAINS NATIONAL PARK

Expanded from text originally written by David Else and Ariadne Van Zandbergen (*Entrance US$5.50 pp per day, US$1.50/2.50 for up to/greater than 12-seat vehicle; US$5 mandatory scout*) Situated about 100km north of Gondar to the east side of the Axum road, the Simien Mountains are one of Africa's largest ranges, studded with at least a dozen peaks topping the 4,000m mark. These include Ras Dejen (also spelt Ras Dashen), the highest point in Ethiopia and possibly the fourth-highest peak in Africa (see box, *On Top of the World,* page 241). The western side of the range, excluding Ras Dejen, was designated as the Simien Mountains National Park in 1969, and the entire range was listed as a UNESCO World Heritage Site in 1979.

A single dirt road runs through the park, branching eastward from Debark, and then passing through Sankaber and Chennek camps *en route* to the Bwahit Pass, where it branches southward to terminate some 10km outside of the park boundary at the small town of Mekane Birhan. This road is open to tourist vehicles, and it provides the opportunity to see most of the park's key habitats in a short space of time (even as a day trip from Gondar), as well as offering almost certain sightings of gelada. For further details, see the box, *The Simiens by Road,* page 239. At the time of writing a new road was being planned running from Sawre (the park gate) to Janamora, which will bypass the main escarpment and ease traffic on the escarpment road.

A less efficient but more satisfactory way to explore the Simiens is on foot or by mule, following an extensive network of tracks used by local people to travel between the villages on the lower slopes or to reach the high pastures for grazing animals. These tracks are ideal walking routes and, combined with the range's impressive scenery, make the Simiens an excellent area for trekking. Most trekking routes take you through small villages and terraced fields in the lower valleys, before reaching a series of dramatic cliffs and escarpments. Beyond the escarpments you reach the beautiful alpine meadows and the rugged wilderness of the high peak areas.

GEOGRAPHY The Simien range consists of several major plateaux divided by large river valleys. The western plateau is bounded on the north and east by a massive escarpment, many kilometres long and over 1,000m high in places, and cut along its length by steep gorges. The views from the top of the escarpment look north over the vast plains towards Eritrea. At their foot are the remains of ancient hills, now eroded into hundreds of pinnacles and buttresses that were described so eloquently in *From Red Sea to Blue Nile – A Thousand Miles of Ethiopia* by Rosita Forbes, the formidable traveller who first reached this region in the 1920s:

The most marvellous of all Abyssinian landscapes opened before us, as we looked across a gorge of clouded amethyst ... A thousand years ago, when the old gods reigned in Ethiopia, they must have played chess with these stupendous crags, for we saw bishops' mitres cut in lapis lazuli, castles with the ruby of approaching sunset on their turrets, an emerald knight where the forest crept up on the rock, and far away a king, crowned with sapphire, and guarded by a row of pawns. When the gods exchanged their games for shield and bucklers to fight the new men clamouring at their gates, they turned the pieces of their chessboard into mountains. In Simien they stand enchanted, till once again the world is pagan and the titans and the earth gods lean down from the monstrous cloud banks to wager a star or two on their sport.

Much of this escarpment area is contained within the Simien Mountains National Park, which covers the western side of the range, running east as far as the 4,430m Mount Bwahit, and includes some of the most dramatic sections of trekking along the edge of the escarpment. Ras Dejen, the highest point in the range, lies about 10km east of the national park, and is separated from it by the massive gorge carved by the Masheha River.

WILDLIFE Three of Ethiopia's endemic large mammals are resident in the Simiens. The gelada monkey is the most common of these, with an estimated population of at least 7,000 often to be seen congregating in grazing herds of up to 400 individuals, especially in the vicinity of Sankaber. By contrast, the Ethiopian wolf is now very rare in the mountains, with an estimated population of around 40 individuals concentrated mostly in the Afro-alpine moorland on the upper slopes of Bwahit, Ras Dejen and Kidus Yared.

The Walia ibex, whose range is now restricted entirely to the Simiens, was poached close to extinction in the late 1960s, when just 150 animals survived. The estimated number of ibex had increased to 400 by 1989, but it declined to 250 in the aftermath of the collapse of the Derg. The population is once again on the rise, however, with recent counts estimating 600 individuals. Hikers quite often see ibex from the trail running along the ridge between Gich and Chennek via Imet Gogo.

Of the non-endemic mammals, klipspringer and bushbuck are present, but seldom seen. Nor are you likely to see spotted hyena, even though their droppings are often scattered around the camps. You're more likely to see common jackal, which also haunts the camps. Unfortunately, predators such as jackal, hyena and serval are being discreetly eliminated by the people living in the Simiens because of the threat they pose to domesticated animals.

The number of birds recorded in the Simiens is not high – about 180 species to date, if one includes the lower slopes – and endemics are not as well represented as they are at Bale. The mountains are noted for cliff-nesting birds of prey, in particular the large and powerful lammergeyer, which can often be seen soaring above the escarpments on the north side of the national park, and is also a regular sight at Sankaber and Gich camps.

GETTING THERE Debark is the obvious place to organise a hike, and the people here set up treks all the time, so things normally fall into place very smoothly. The chances are you'll quickly be approached by one of the official guides when you arrive in town, but if not, just head to the national park office, which lies along the Gondar road less than ten minutes' walk from the Simien Park Hotel. Although Debark is well organised, nothing happens that quickly, so if you are making independent arrangements, you should ideally leave yourself enough time to complete formalities on the afternoon you arrive, spend the night there, and then set off into the mountains the following morning.

The entrance gate to the park lies near Buyit Ras, some 15km from Debark along the road to Sankaber, but all park fees must be paid at the national park office in Debark. Receipts are checked at the entrance gate.

Many travellers now make their initial trekking arrangements in Gondar. The basic set-up is that somebody in Gondar will approach you offering to organise a hike. He will check what, if any, extra equipment you need and advise you about routes, stocking up on food, and all other aspects of a hike. He will then ring your requirements through to Debark, and arrange for somebody to meet your bus. By all accounts, this is a very smooth procedure, and because you pay nothing until you get to Debark, no risk is attached. Depending on group size, a five-day hike organised in Debark or Gondar will typically work out at around US$240–300, exclusive of transport between Gondar and Debark, but inclusive of park fees, scout, guide, mules, and mule drivers. You can cut the cost by omitting some of the above. A cook, stove, tent and sleeping bag can be arranged if required.

Several tour operators in Gondar (see *Tour operators*, page 77) offer more expensive packages inclusive of a cook, good food and private transport between Gondar and Debark in one or both directions. If you opt for such a package, you might as well arrange to be driven as far as Sankaber on the first day of your trip, and to be picked up at Sankaber or Chennek on the last day – this will cut the duration of the trip by two or three days. A five-day trip of this sort, taking in Sankaber, Gich, Imet Gogo, Chennek and Bwahit Pass, is likely to cost upwards of US$300 per head.

Even if you don't have a private vehicle, it is increasingly easy to pick up transport along the road from Debark to Sankaber and Chennek, and while nothing is certain, you can plan on this basis with a reasonably secure mind. At least one bus daily runs between Debark and Mekane Birhan via the two camps, and there is also occasional truck transport. Heading out to the mountains, you can ask around at the market in Debark or wait for a lift at the clearly signposted junction to the national park. Heading back to Debark, you can assume that any vehicle heading west along the road through the Simiens is bound for Debark. Another possibility is a lift with other tourists, which you can ask about at the either the Simien Park or Red Fox hotel.

Whether you arrange things in Gondar or Debark, it is all pretty straightforward and readers' feedback has been consistently positive about the guides, but going by our most recent experience, the same can't be said for the brusque staff at the national park office.

GETTING AROUND
Guides and scouts The park rules stipulate that an armed scout must accompany all visitors. This costs US$5 per day. In theory, the scout should be self-sufficient in food. In practice, he'll probably run out of food after a few days, if he brings any food at all, so consider buying extra rice and salt. If you go all the way to Ras Dejen, the park officials will suggest you take two scouts for extra safety, so that one can guard your camp while the other comes with you to the summit. This is recommended but not obligatory.

Indeed, in spite of what the staff at the national park office say, a guide, while recommended, is not obligatory. The Simien guides are not park employees, but they are officially organised into a co-operative, and take tourists into the park on a rotational basis. The official guides are all trained by the tourist office in Gondar, speak good English and charge a standard US$12 per day. It is not compulsory to trek with a local guide, and the scouts know all the paths. Most readers have showered their Simien guides with praise, but a few have complained that the guides do little but state the blindingly obvious – one dissenter asks, 'Why would you want to pay somebody to babble in your ear incessantly?'

Mules Unlike on most other mountains in east Africa, porters are not available for the Simiens, so it is conventional to take mules as pack animals. Carrying all your own gear and food is not recommended (unless you're used to backpacking), as distances are long and routes undulating. The scout and guide will expect you to hire at least one mule to carry their food and blankets. With the mule you have to hire a driver (horseman), who loads them up, makes sure they're fed and watered, and chases after them when they run away. Each mule will cost US$4 per day, while each driver costs US$5.

You can also hire a mule to ride. If your time is limited and you want to do a long trek this is recommended. Even if you ride for only a few short stretches during the day, it makes the trek much more enjoyable and increases the distance you can cover. It's also good fun. Before hiring a mule check that it's in good condition. Make the driver lead it up and down; if there's a hint of a limp, don't hire it. Local saddles are basic and often used without a blanket underneath. Lift up the saddle and check the mule's back; if there are cuts or sores, don't hire it. And insist that any mule you hire for riding or carrying gear has a blanket under the saddle for padding.

WHERE TO STAY

Simien Lodge (20 rooms) ☎ 058 231 0741, ☎ 011 552 4758 (Addis Ababa), European bookings ☎ +33 6 10 29 96 35; e lodge@simiens.com; www.simiens.com. Located within the park at Buit Ras, 22km from Debark, this eco-friendly lodge fills an important niche by providing comfortable accommodation to those wishing to explore the mountains from a relatively upmarket base. At an elevation of 3,260m, the lodge bills itself as 'the highest hotel in Africa', but that also means afternoon clouds often impair advertised solar-powered features such as hot water & underfloor heating. The private *tukul*-style rooms – each with warm duvets, extra blankets & hot-water en suites complete with hairdryers – are very comfortable, but feel somewhat over-priced. The modern kitchen serves good-quality meals from a daily set menu & the setting is fantastic. The surrounding area is populated by habituated geladas, & the lodge can organise foot & horse treks. High-quality

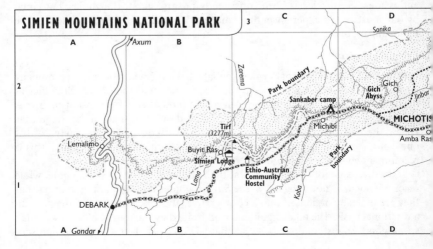

SIMIEN MOUNTAINS NATIONAL PARK

mountain bikes can also be rented. Beds in a dormitory *tukul* with access to a hot shower are meant for drivers & guides, but are available to tourists in low season. *US$160/170 sgl/dbl, US$250 family suite (sleeps 4).*

Huts and camping The hutted national park camps at Sankaber, Gich and Chennek were destroyed during the fighting in the 1980s. The huts have been since rebuilt and are open to tourists – with the exception of Chennek which is now for the exclusive use of park employees – offering very basic dormitory-style accommodation costing US$5 per person per night. The misleadingly named Ethio-Austria Community Lodge, located just past the Simien Lodge, also offers very basic accommodation at US$5 per night and will let you pitch a tent for US$1.50 per night. Take note there are no showers or toilet facilities at this so-called lodge.

Elsewhere, this leaves you two options: either you must be completely self-contained with tent and camping equipment, including sleeping bag, stove and cooking gear; or else you can lodge with local people in the villages. Most local people are happy to make space in their hut for a visitor, as it provides a bit of extra income (you should pay US$1.50 or less per night). Be warned that conditions are basic: you'll sleep on the floor or maybe on a bed (a wooden platform with goats or cows underneath to provide warmth), and you're in for a rough time if you're sensitive to flea bites. Your guide will find you a hut to stay in, if you take this option.

If you camp, it's usual to pitch near a village, so that your guide and scout have somewhere to sleep. When the park is busy, the guides tend to plonk their clients village-style in the closest possible proximity to each other – do feel free to point out that the campsites are large and it's not necessary to trip over your neighbour's guy ropes every time you leave your tent. There is a shower at each of the camps, but no running water. The toilets are filthy.

EQUIPMENT AND SUPPLIES Debark has a few shops and stalls where you can buy basic items such as rice, lentils, bread, biscuits, rope, candles, soap and plastic water containers. Rather than buying food in Debark, however, small groups who plan on staying in or near villages seem to have little difficulty arranging basic meals and things like eggs and *injera* as they go along, though I'd be hesitant about relying on this completely. Better to stock up in Gondar, where several shops stock pasta, salt, sugar, tea, coffee and biscuits, plus tins of fish, meat and chicken. If your tastes are

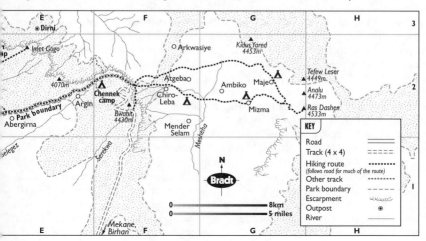

more elaborate, you can buy imported goods like chocolate, porridge oats, cheese, jam and custard creams in Addis Ababa.

If you don't have all the equipment you need, you can rent most obvious items of trekking gear at park headquarters or at the Simien Park Hotel in Debark. This includes tents, sleeping bags, roll mattresses, simple kerosene stoves and aluminium cooking pots. Expect to pay around US$12 per day for the full kit. Deforestation is a real problem in Ethiopia generally and in the Simien Mountains specifically. Travellers are therefore urged to rent a stove rather than depend on fires for cooking, and are certainly discouraged from making large wasteful bonfires to keep themselves warm at night. *Note that it is forbidden to light fires outside the designated campsites.*

A good sleeping bag and warm clothing are essential in the chilly peaks of the Simiens. A thick windbreaker or other heavy waterproof jacket will be ideal, but many travellers won't be willing to carry something like this all the way around Ethiopia for just a few days' use. Secondhand clothes are available very cheaply in markets throughout Ethiopia: one option would be to buy a couple of thick jumpers before you set off, and to leave them with a local when you are through with them. Waterproof gear is necessary between May and October.

We've received several reports of people becoming ill through drinking untreated water in the mountains, and I'm told that the cooks may not be aware of the importance of boiling rather than just warming drinking water. You should thus personally ensure this is done properly. Given that water takes some time to boil at this altitude, it might be worth carrying some purifying tablets – inferior though they are to boiling water – as a fallback.

TREKKING ROUTES There are several route options, depending on the time you have, the distance you want to cover, and whether or not you drive part way into the park. Your route is also determined by the places where you can sleep the night and find water. Most visitors stay at or near the national park camps. With the exception of Sankaber, there are no longer huts for tourist use, but the water supply at the camps is reliable and the positions good (spaced a day's walk apart). The park camps are at Sankaber, Gich and Chennek. Distances between camps can be long and most days require between four and eight hours of walking. You need to be reasonably fit. However, as the trekking route described here follows paths and tracks for most of the distance, conditions underfoot are not too hard. It may be worth planning your hike in conjunction with the excellent 1:100,000 *Simien Mountains* map published by the University of Bern in 2003 – all names used in the trail descriptions below conform to this map. Now out of print and no longer so easy to find, at the time of writing it was available through the Addis Ababa-based agent (m *0911 222 707*) for the map's author at the steep price of US$35.50. Copies may be available in Debark.

You should not underestimate the effects of altitude when planning your route, especially if you have flown in direct from Europe and have had little time to acclimatise. This is particularly important if you are going all the way to the summit of Ras Dejen. Although severe altitude-related illnesses (of the type suffered by trekkers on Mount Kenya and Kilimanjaro) are unlikely, you may experience headaches, shortness of breath, loss of appetite and general lethargy at higher altitudes. The best way to avoid these symptoms is to acclimatise properly by making a steady ascent. Do not try and rush to conquer Ras Dejen in four days: spend an extra night at one of the high camps (such as Chennek or Gich) and take a rest day. This will make your trek much more rewarding and enjoyable.

THE SIMIENS BY ROAD

Although trekking remains the best way to see the Simiens properly, a good 4x4 road runs via Sankaber, Chennek and the Bwahit Pass, allowing more sedentary travellers, or those with limited time, to get a good feel for the scenery and wildlife in the space of a few hours. Indeed, with an early start, it is possible to cover this road as far as Bwahit as a day trip out of Gondar, though this is hardly the most satisfactory approach, and the rushed timeframe might arguably encourage the driver to speed in what is a fragile environment. A full-day trip in a 4x4 will cost US$70–100 per group excluding park fees, and can be arranged through any tour operator in Gondar at short notice. If you have more time, however, it would be preferable to overnight in Debark, at the new upmarket Simien Lodge, or at one of the camps within the park, and to return to Gondar the next day. With a one- or two-night stop in Debark, the park could also be explored by vehicle *en route* between Gondar and Axum.

Some people are happy to visit the park for just two days, doing a short walk and staying one night at Sankaber. Other people spend ten days or more in the mountains, doing a long trek all the way to Ras Dejen, and diverting to several of the smaller peaks. In between these two extremes are several other options. Here are some suggestions:

- **Four days** (three nights) Sleeping at Sankaber, Gich and then at Sankaber again.
- **Five days** (four nights) Sleeping at Sankaber, Chennek (for two nights, going to the summit of Bwahit or the viewpoint on the way to Ras Dejen, on the day in between), then at Sankaber again.
- **Seven days** (six nights) Sleeping at Sankaber, Chennek, Ambiko (for two nights, going up Ras Dejen in between), then back to Chennek and Sankaber again.

Route stages In this section the various trekking routes have been broken into stages. Each is one day long. You can combine all of them to create a major trek, or combine just a few of them for a shorter trek. Times given are walking times only; you should allow extra time for lunch stops, photographs, rests or simply looking at the view. Times will also be shorter if you ride your mule a lot.

Stage one: Debark to Sankaber (5–7 hours) Leave Debark (2,800m) on the dirt road that leads through the market and then heads in an easterly direction through the outskirts of the town. The dirt road passes through fields, then crosses the Lama River and climbs steeply onto the western plateau. You reach the plateau's northern escarpment near Chinkwanit and follow this to reach the village of Michibi and Sankaber Camp (3,250m). You may cross or follow the road during this stage, but don't let your guide follow it all the way as you'll miss the views between Chinkwanit and Michibi. Worth noting, if you don't want to do this hike in one day, is that there is a camp called the Ethio–Austria Community Hostel (3,230m; see page 237) about halfway between Debark and Sankaber, close to the site of the Simien Lodge.

Stage two: Sankaber to Gich (5–7 hours) Follow the track eastward along a narrow ridge, with the escarpment to the north and the Koba river valley to the south. Drop into the Koba, and then climb steeply up through an area called

Michotis. To your left is the Gich Abyss, as well as a large waterfall where the Jinbar River plunges into it. About three to four hours from Sankaber, the paths divide. Keep left and drop into the valley, across the Jinbar River, then steeply up through Gich village to reach Gich Camp (3,600m). From Gich Camp it's one to two hours to the summit of Imet Gogo (3,925m), a large peak to the east of the camp, with spectacular views north and east across the foothills and plains.

Stage three: Gich to Chennek (5–7 hours) Assuming that you use the track running south along the western escarpment via Imet Gogo rather than the main road marked on most maps, this is possibly the most spectacular stage anywhere in the Simiens, offering superb views to the valleys below. Other major peaks you pass on the way are Shayno Sefer (3,962m) and Inatye (4,070m). It's also a good area to look for gelada, lammergeyer and the rare Walia ibex. Alternatively, you can miss Gich and go direct from Sankaber to Chennek (3,620m), as described in stage four.

Stage four: Sankaber to Chennek (6–8 hours) Follow the directions in stage two to pass through Michotis. Where the routes divide (left goes to Gich), keep right and up, and follow the track along the crest of a broad ridge. This area is called

Abergirna. About four to six hours from Sankaber the track starts to descend into the huge Belegez river valley. The track zigzags steeply down, crossing several streams, then climbs up again slightly, passing on the left a U-shaped gap in the escarpment wall (through which you get splendid views), to reach Chennek Camp. Chennek is one of the most spectacular spots on this trekking route through the Simiens, and the surrounding slopes are thick with giant lobelias and other Afro-alpine scrub. The views are stunning in all directions, out from the escarpment edge, across the foothills, up to the surrounding peaks of Imet Gogo and Bwahit (4,430m), and westward down the Belegez Valley. It's also a good place to observe wildlife; the surrounding cliffs are a favoured haunt of lammergeyers and gelada monkeys.

If you stay two nights at Chennek and then return towards Debark, a good destination for the day in between is the viewpoint overlooking the Mesheha River described in *Stage five*.

Stage five: Chennek to Ambiko (6–8 hours) Heading east from Chennek, you leave the national park. The track climbs up a valley to the left (north) of Bwahit Peak, which overlooks the camp. About 1½ hours from Chennek, after crossing the Bwahit Pass (4,200m), you reach a viewpoint. To the east, across the vast valley of the Mesheha River and its tributaries, you get your first sighting of Ras Dejen (4,533m) – the highest point in a wall of cliffs and peaks on the skyline on the far side of the valley. From the viewpoint the path drops steeply down, passing through the village of Chiro-Leba (3,300m; the tin-roofed school is a good landmark), and continues down through tributary valleys to reach the Mesheha River (2,800m; five to seven hours from Chennek). The path goes steeply up again to reach the village of Ambiko (3,200m) after another hour.

Stage six: Ambiko to Ras Dejen summit and return (7–9 hours) It's usual to stay two nights at Ambiko, going up to the summit of Ras Dejen on the day in between. A dawn start is advised. From Ambiko, continue up the valley to reach the small village of Mizma (3,500m), where the path swings left and climbs steeply to reach a ridge crest overlooking a larger valley. Keeping this larger valley

ON TOP OF THE WORLD

During the course of updating the fourth edition, I noticed that the new 1:100,000 map of the Simiens gives the height of Ras Dejen as 4,533m rather than the 4,620m quoted in previous editions of this guide. Initially I assumed this to be a blip on my part, but this is not the case: almost every official source I can locate, including various EMA maps, the National Atlas of Ethiopia, government handbooks dating back to the 1960s, and the official website of the Federal Region of Amhara, also gives the altitude of Ras Dejen as 4,620m! A quick google search also came down slightly in favour of the higher figure, with a few deviants settling on 4,543m. However, while the truth is difficult to ascertain, my best guess – based on the credibility of the various sources – is that 4,533m is the correct altitude, in which case it is not, as is often claimed, the fourth-highest mountain in Africa, but the fifth, falling one place behind Tanzania's Mount Meru. Furthermore, occasional queries about whether tourists are actually taken to the highest peak can be explained by a trick of perspective, as the peaks of Analu and Tefew Leser, just 1km and 2km further north respectively, both rise to within 60m of Ras Dejen itself.

down to your left, follow the path eastward, and head towards Ras Dejen's rocky west face, visible at the head of the valley. About three to four hours from Ambiko you pass through a gap in an old stone wall, then swing left up a broad ridge to enter a wide semicircular corrie, surrounded by three major buttresses with steep sides of exposed rock. From this point it's impossible to see which buttress is the highest. The summit of Ras Dejen is on the top of the buttress on the left. To reach it, scramble up a gully through the cliffs to reach the cairn (pile of rocks) marking the summit (about four to five hours from Ambiko). Return to Ambiko by the same route (allow three to four hours).

Stages seven to nine From Ambiko it's usual to return to Debark by the same route: stage seven – Ambiko to Chennek (six to eight hours); stage eight – Chennek to Sankaber (five to six hours); stage nine – Sankaber to Debark (six to seven hours) – though nine days out of ten you should have no problem hitching a lift with a truck from Chennek to Debark if you want to cut out the last two days.

After the trek to Debark, you can return either to the park office or to the Simien Hotel to unload your mules and pay off the guide. It is polite to buy your 'crew' some tea and bread, while sorting out these final matters. If service has been good, a small tip to the guide, horseman and scout is appropriate and always appreciated. As a rule of thumb, a tip should be an extra one to two days' wages per every five to seven days of work.

9

Axum and the Adigrat Road

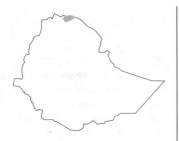

The present chapter covers the far north of the Federal Region of Tigrai, starting with the ancient city of **Axum** in the west, then following the main road east through Adwa as far as the junction town of **Adigrat**. Together with neighbouring Eritrea, it is an area that might be regarded as the fulcrum of Ethiopian culture. Axum (also spelt Aksum) was in existence at least three centuries before the birth of Christ, when it emerged as the imperial capital of the mighty Axumite Empire. The ancient city is also the site of Ethiopia's oldest Christian sanctuary, the Cathedral of Tsion Maryam, founded in the 4th century and still regarded as the spiritual home of Ethiopian Orthodox Christianity.

Tigrai has a distinctly different character from the rest of Ethiopia. Historically and culturally, it shares strong links, both ancient and modern, with neighbouring Eritrea, which together with Tigrai formed the core of the ancient Axumite Empire. The mountainous sandstone rockscapes of Tigrai have an angular, wild quality quite distinct from the more curvaceous green hills seen elsewhere in the Ethiopian Highlands. A memorable feature of this harsh and dry landscape is the prolific stone terracing which is used to cultivate the slopes, though it is rather ineffective in years of drought, which generally occur once every decade. Tigraian houses, too, are built of stone, and they give the towns and villages a sense of orderly permanence that is rare in Africa.

The Tigraian people were persecuted under the Mengistu government, which, by frustrating all attempts at food distribution, must take a large share of the blame for the notorious famine of 1985. It is largely through Tigraian resistance that Mengistu was toppled in 1991, and that Eritrea was granted the independence for which it had fought for over two decades. Historical and cultural links notwithstanding, relationships between the two regions have yet to recover from the bloody border war of 1998–2000, which pitched the predominantly Tigraian leadership of Ethiopia against its former comrades in Eritrea.

AXUM

My initial response upon arriving at Axum in the course of researching the first edition of this guidebook was how small and inauspicious the town appeared to be given its estimable pedigree. And so has it been since the mid 16th century, when Ahmed Gragn led a destructive attack on the former capital of the Axumite Empire and razed its premier church. Francisco Alvarez, who visited Axum perhaps a decade before Gragn's arrival, described it as 'a large town of very good houses, such that there are none like them in the whole of Ethiopia, and very good wells of water, and worked masonry, and also in most of the houses ancient figures of lions, dogs and birds, all well made in stone'. A century later, according to Manuel de Almeida, Axum had been reduced to 'a place of about a hundred inhabitants [where] everywhere there are ruins to be seen'.

Of course, Axum has grown vastly since Almeida's day. Panoramic photographs taken by the Deutsche-Aksum Expedition suggest it harboured a population of a few thousand in 1909, though – somewhat disorientating at first glance – it appears that the town was then concentrated to the northwest of Maryam Tsion, while what is now the city centre, to the east of the watercourse called Mai Hejja, consisted of unsettled plains. This eastward expansion has continued over the past two decades – much of the development east of the Commercial Bank of Ethiopia post-dates my 1994 visit, since when the modern town of 50,000 inhabitants has also gained a more urbanised presence as a result of the main road being surfaced and adorned with a neat row of young palms. All the same, on first contact with Axum, one can empathise with Bob Geldof, who on landing in Timbuktu (arguably west Africa's answer to Axum) reputedly took a quick look around and muttered 'Is that it?'

Fortunately, in Axum's case, a strip of fresh asphalt lined by standard-issue Ethiopian shops and houses is decidedly not 'it'. True, Axum may lack the immediate impact of Lalibela or Gondar, but this most ancient of Ethiopian capitals, the holiest city of the Ethiopian Orthodox Church, does boast a wealth of quite startling antiquities: the extensive stelae field on the outskirts of town, subterranean catacombs high enough to walk in, mysterious ruined palaces, multi-lingual tablets dating from the time of Christ – and much more besides. It also boasts two superb Saturday markets: one in the town centre above the stadium, and the other (livestock only) at the old airstrip on the southern outskirts. A guided tour of Axum takes several hours; at least two days are required if you want to visit most places of interest in its immediate vicinity, and the questions that arise during the course of exploring the capital of the little-understood Axumite Kingdom will linger on for months.

The history of Axum is integral to that of the Axumite Kingdom and Ethiopia from around the time of Christ to the 10th century AD. Rather than reproduce an abbreviated history here, readers who want to get the most from Axum's historical sites are pointed to the first half of the general *History* section in *Chapter 1*, which focuses on Axum and Ethiopian traditions relating to the city.

GETTING THERE AND AWAY

By air Regular services connecting Axum to Gondar (US$43), Lalibela (US$44) and Addis Ababa (US$69) are offered by **Ethiopian Airlines** [247 E3] (✆ *034 775 2300;* e *axutsm@ethiopianairlines.com*). The airstrip used to verge on the town centre, but – in keeping with the expansionist spirit that has overtaken Axum – a new, modern airport is located 5km out of town along the Adwa road. A taxi to the town centre shouldn't cost more than US$5. All onward flights must be reconfirmed at the Ethiopian Airlines office opposite King Ezana Park a day ahead of the date of departure.

By road Coming from or heading to Gondar or the Simien Mountains, there are no direct buses. You will need to switch buses at Shire (Inda Selassie), where you may need to spend the night, particularly if you are travelling towards Gondar, as buses there from Shire leave at 06.30. See also the section *Gondar to Axum by road* in *Chapter 8*, page 231.

Heading east from Axum, at least one local bus leaves daily for Mekele (US$5.50) at 06.00 and stops at Adigrat (US$4.50) *en route*. There is also a daily bus from Shire to Adigrat, which passes through Axum (US$2.50) at around 09.00. From Adigrat, it is easy to find transport through to Mekele. If you are coming to Axum *from* Adigrat, you have the choice of catching the early morning bus to Shire, or else waiting till mid morning for buses to come through from Mekele. You can also travel between Axum and Adigrat in hops, as there is a fair amount of local public transport between the various small towns *en route*. Minibuses between Axum and nearby Adwa leave on a fill-up-and-go basis throughout the day.

Note that buses heading west from Axum towards Shire depart from the old central bus station, essentially a patch of open ground on the traffic roundabout immediately north of the King Ezana Hotel. All buses to easterly destinations such as Adwa, Adigrat and Mekele depart from the smart new bus station, which has a rather inconvenient location about 1.5km out of town along the Adwa road. Regular minibuses run between the old and new bus stations for the princely fare of US$0.50.

Before the border war between Ethiopia and Eritrea, daily buses ran directly between Axum and Asmara, leaving in the early morning, while one bus between Shire and Asmara passed through Axum at around 09.00. These services will presumably resume if and when the border between the two countries reopens.

Most visitors who travel by road arrive at Axum from Gondar and depart in the direction of Adigrat (or vice versa). Two other little-known but potentially interesting onward options exist, however, both of which initially involve heading south at Adwa along the road towards Adi Arkay. The first option is to continue southward from Adi Arkay to Sekota and Lalibela – with an early start and a private vehicle, the full trip from Axum to Lalibela can be covered in one long dusty day (the drive would take about eight hours not allowing for breaks, or breakdowns!), but there is enough to see on the way to justify an overnight stop at Abi Aday (for more information see *Chapter 12*, page 309). Alternatively, if you are heading on to the rock-hewn churches of Gheralta, the little-used route to Hawzien via Adwa and Nebelet, the closest town to the remote rock-hewn church of Maryam Wukro, can be covered in four to five hours from Axum without breaks or diversions (see box, *Hawzien to Axum via Maryam Wukro* in *Chapter 10*, page 283).

GETTING AROUND Plenty of *bajajis* ply the streets of Axum costing around US$1 for a short charter trip within the city centre. For day excursions from Axum, the Abinet Hotel has a modern minibus it rents out. Rates are to some extent negotiable, but expect to pay around US$60 per group of up to four people to visit Yeha, or US$115 to visit Debre Damo and Yeha. Minibuses can also be arranged through local tourist guides.

TOURIST INFORMATION The **Aksum Tourist Information Office** [246 D3] (⎯034 775 3924; e *aksumtour@ethionet.et; www.aksumtourism.com;* ⊕ *07.00–18.00 daily*) is located along the road towards the stelae field, just east of the Total petrol station at the main roundabout. It is a good source of local information and is where you pay the US$3 entrance fee that covers the various secular historical sites dotted around town. As well as arranging official guides (US$15 per day), the newly formed **Axum Guides Association** [246 B6] next to the entrance to the main stelae field is also a good source of information.

TOUR OPERATORS Conveniently located on the main road on the way to the stelae field, **Covenant Tours** [246 C5] (⎯ *034 775 4226;* m *0913 709 926; www. covenantethiopia.com*) can organise excursions to the rock-hewn churches of Tigrai as well as car rental and guided city tours of Axum. **Abune Yemata Tours** [247 G3] (⎯*034 775 3700;* m *0911 532 526; www.abuneyematatours.com*) based at the Africa Hotel offers a similar range of services.

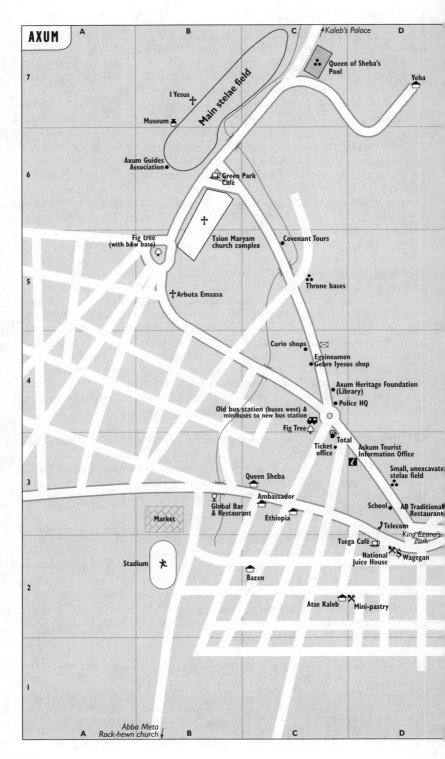

AXUM

A B C D

Kaleb's Palace

Queen of Sheba's Pool

Yeha

7

I Yesus

Main stelae field

Museum

Axum Guides
Association

Green Park Café

6

Tsion Maryam
church complex

Covenant Tours

Fig tree
(with b&w base)

†Arbuta Emsasa

Throne bases

5

Curio shops

Egzineamen
Gebre Iyesus shop

Axum Heritage Foundation
(Library)
Police HQ

4

Old bus station (buses west) &
minibuses to new bus station

Fig Tree

Total

Ticket
office

Askum Tourist
Information Office

Small, unexcavate
stelae field

Queen Sheba

Ambassador

School

AB Traditional
Restaurant

3

Global Bar
& Restaurant

Ethiopia

Telecom

Market

Tsega Café

*King Ezana's
Park*

National
Juice House

Wagegan

Stadium

Bazen

2

Atse Kaleb

Mini-pastry

1

A B C D

*Abba Meta
Rock-hewn church*

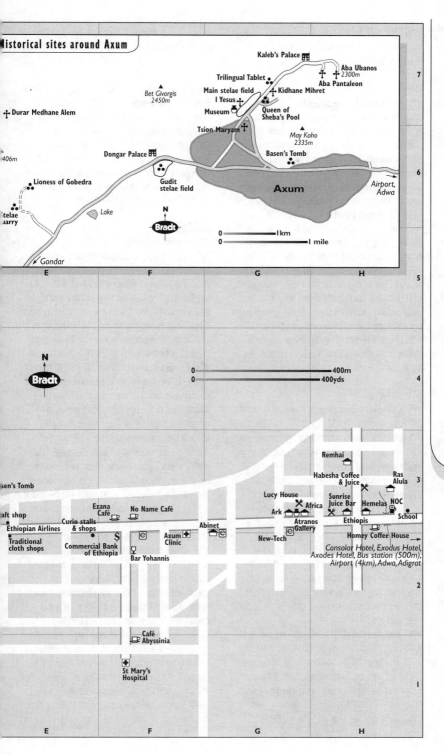

Historical sites around Axum

Kaleb's Palace

Aba Ubanos
2300m

Trilingual Tablet

Main stelae field · Kidhane Mihret · Aba Pantaleon

I Yesus

Bet Givorgis
2450m

Durar Medhane Alem

Museum

Queen of
Sheba's Pool

Tsion Maryam

May Koho
2335m

Dongar Palace

Basen's Tomb

406m

Lioness of Gobedra

Gudit
stelae field

Axum

Airport,
Adwa

telae
Jarry

Lake

N

Bradt

0 ———— 1 km
0 ———— 1 mile

Gondar

E   F   G   H   5

Axum and the Adigrat Road   AXUM   9

N

Bradt

0 ———— 400m
0 ———— 400yds

4

Remhai

Habesha Coffee
& Juice

Ras
Alula

3

sen's Tomb

Lucy House

Sunrise
Juice Bar

Hemelas   NOC

aft shop

Ezana
Café

No Name Café

Ark   Africa

Ethiopis

School

Ethiopian Airlines

Curio stalls
& shops

Abinet

Atranos
Gallery

Homey Coffee House

Traditional
cloth shops

Commercial Bank
of Ethiopia

Axum
Clinic

New-Tech

Consolar Hotel, Exodus Hotel,
Axodes Hotel, Bus station (500m),
Airport (4km), Adwa, Adigrat

Bar Yohannis

2

Café
Abyssinia

St Mary's
Hospital

1

E   F   G   H

247

WHERE TO STAY Axum boasts a good variety of accommodation by Ethiopian standards, and seems particularly well equipped with attractive and sensibly priced budget hotels.

Upmarket

Yeha Hotel [246 D7] (63 rooms) \034 775 0605; e yehaxum@yahoo.com. Previously part of the government Ghion chain, this rather time-warped but well-managed hotel is most notable for its wonderful situation on a wooded hilltop that overlooks the town centre. Now under private ownership, it is slated for major renovations with new facilities including a pool, gym, hair salon, & business centre all on the wish list for 2012. In the meantime, the functional en-suite rooms seem a little over-priced. A good tar road leads to the hotel, or you can walk there from the stelae field in 10 (steep) mins, passing the Queen of Sheba's Pool *en route*. The restaurant serves a reasonable variety of Ethiopian & Continental dishes with a 3-course meal costing around US$6, while the outside patio is a classic spot for sundowners with the stelae field below & plenty of birds rattling around in the fig trees above. *US$57/76/101 sgl/dbl/suite, exc b/fast.*

Moderate

Consolar International Hotel [off map 247 H3] (33 rooms) \034 875 0210/775 5306; f 034 775 4960; e info@consolarhotelaxum.com; www.consolarhotelaxum.com. This smart & stylish new multi-storey hotel located opposite the Pantaleon Monastery on the road to the airport easily ranks as the best hotel in town in terms of facilities & services, but comes a poor second to the Yeha in terms of location & atmosphere. Aimed squarely at the business market – ironic considering its oddly misspelt name – the hotel's rooms all feature electronic safes, broadband internet, minibar, DSTV & hot-water en suite. Other facilities include a free airport shuttle, bar & excellent restaurant. *US$55/60 standard dbl without/with view, US$75 twin, US$80 suite, exc b/fast.*

Remhai Hotel [247 H3] (65 rooms) \034 775 2168/1501/3210; f 034 775 2894. This sprawling hotel on the eastern fringe of the town centre seems a tad forlorn these days. Tellingly only 42 of the hotel's rooms were open for use on our most recent visit & staff – & guests – were thin on the ground. That said, the available rooms – all with DSTV, fridge & phone – are good

value & arguably better than the ones at the Yeha. Facilities include an internet café, a good curio shop, & a free airport shuttle. A good Western restaurant in the main building serves meals in the US$2.50–5 range, while a traditional *tukul* next to the swimming pool (US$2.50 for non-guests) serves local food accompanied by traditional music & dancing from 18.30 onwards on Thu & Sat. *US$21.50/36.50/58.50 sgl/dbl/suite.*

Budget

Abinet Hotel [247 G2] (30 rooms) \034 775 3857; e abinethotel2@yahoo.com. This friendly hotel on the eastern side of town, offers clean & spacious rooms with tiled floor & en-suite hot showers. The first-floor restaurant is one of the best & busiest in town, with a menu including pizzas & burgers & dishes costing US$2–4. There's a free airport shuttle & internet is available for less than US$0.05 per minute. *US$18/25/30 sgl/dbl/twin.*

Exodus Hotel [off map 247 H3] (22 rooms) \034 775 2498; e info@exodushotel.com; www.exodushotel.com. This pleasant hotel is situated directly next to the bus station on the road to the airport. The clean en-suite twins all with TV, fridge & balcony are good value, while some of the double rooms are much better appointed than others, so it is a good idea to ask to see the room before committing. Slightly less expensive rooms are available at the back of the hotel, but the *tej* bar right outside could be noisy. There is also a decent restaurant with entrées in the US$2.50–4.50 range. *US$7.50 back rooms, US$12.50 dbl/twin.*

Africa Hotel [247 G3] (40 rooms) \034 775 3700–1; f 034 775 3701; e africaho@ethionet.com; www.africahotelaxum.com. Consistently popular with travellers since it opened in the mid 1990s thanks to a high standard of cleanliness, reasonable prices & a helpful hands-on owner-manager, the Africa Hotel ranks among our favourite budget lodgings anywhere in Ethiopia. Recently updated it boasts excellent facilities in the form of a free airport shuttle (just phone when you land), DSTV (in all rooms), tour agency, free Wi-Fi, & a good restaurant & juice bar, & the staff can hook you up with reliable local guides for a city tour. *US$11/12/14 sgl/dbl/twin.*

🏠 **Aste Kaleb Hotel** [246 C2] (20 rooms) 🕽034 775 2222; e astekalebhotel@yahoo.com. Another long-serving favourite (indeed, it's been owned & managed by the same family for more than 30 years), this friendly hotel is set around a large green courtyard in the back roads east of the market. The well-maintained rooms all have a hot-water en suite & TV with an additional 8 new rooms slated for construction. Food & drinks are available, but it serves primarily as a pension. *US$9/11 dbl/twin.*

Shoestring Aside from the exceptions listed below, there is a cluster of perhaps a dozen basic lodgings running south from the old bus station – & if cheap & grotty is what you want, then cheap & grotty they most certainly are.

🏠 **Ark Hotel** [247 G3] (20 rooms) 🕽034 775 2676; e daniark.2003@yahoo.com. This hotel on the eastern side of the town centre has reasonably clean rooms all with hot-shower en suite & TV. There is a decent restaurant, an internet café on the ground floor, & the management is very

friendly. Room rates are usually negotiable out of season. 10 new rooms were under construction at the time of writing. *US$6/7.50/9 sgl/dbl/twin.*

🏠 **Ethiopis Hotel** [247 H3] (20 rooms) 🕽034 775 2365; m 0911 698 444. This multi-storey hotel offers clean en-suite rooms with hot water & balcony. A bar/restaurant is attached. *US$6/9/11 sgl/dbl/twin.*

🏠 **Hemelas Hotel** [247 H3] (33 rooms) 🕽034 775 3106. This double-storey hotel, situated 2 blocks up from the Africa, is a definite notch down from any of the places listed previously. In spite of a recent change of management, not much has changed since the last edition, with both en-suite & common-shower rooms musty, run-down & over-priced. *US$5 with common shower, US$7.50/9 sgl/dbl with hot-water en suite.*

🏠 **Ras Alula Hotel** [247 H3] (20 rooms) 🕽034 775 3622. Located on the east end of town behind the NOC gas station, this place offers acceptable en-suite rooms with ¾ bed & hot shower. The attached restaurant/bar is popular with locals, & though his English is limited, the gregarious owner may join you for a drink. *US$9 dbl.*

✕ **WHERE TO EAT** Several of the hotels listed above have decent restaurants. Top of the range is the **Yeha Hotel** [246 D7], especially considering its superb view from the patio, closely followed by the **Remhai Hotel** [247 H3] and **Consolar Hotel** [off map 247 H3]. The restaurant at the **Africa Hotel** [247 G3] is pretty good, too, combining Western dishes with local fare in the US$1.50–4 range, and it also serves excellent fruit juice. The **Ark** [247 G3] and **Abinet** [247 G2] hotels are comparable in standard, though the former doesn't prepare meat dishes during fasting times.

✕ **AB Traditional Bar & Restaurant** [246 D3] m 0912 955 022; ⊕ 07.00–late daily. Located near the Ethiopian Airlines office, this new place features traditional décor & serves good Ethiopian fare along with a smattering of *faranji* dishes. There's music & dancing on Sat nights. *US$2–4.*

🍺 **Homey Coffee House** [247 H3] 🕽034 775 2263; ⊕ 07.00–21.30 daily. This cheery café opposite Hemela Hotel is another good spot for breakfast, coffee & juice. It also offers a small menu of sandwiches. *US$2–4.*

🍺 **Central Café** [246 D2] m 0911 030 468; ⊕ 06.00–22.30 daily. On the 1st floor above the Wagegan Bank, this breezy new café serves

excellent coffee & pastries along with a great view of King Ezana's Park. The café also has DSTV as well as both pool & table tennis tables. Football matches on big screen. *US$1.50–4.*

🍺 **Ezana Café** [247 F3] ⊕ 07.00–22.00 daily. Next door to the No Name Café, this friendly new café serves cheap & filling breakfasts including delicious, spicy *fitfit* with yoghurt (proof dairy products do exist in the north!) as well as the ubiquitous juice & coffee. *US$1.50–3.*

🍺 **National Yared Juice House** [246 D2] 🕽034 775 3355; ⊕ 06.00–22.30 daily. On the opposite side of the road, serves inexpensive & wholesome juices. *US$1.50.*

SHOPPING Axum is particularly well endowed with shops selling Ethiopian handicrafts, ranging from religious icons and other old artefacts to modern carvings and cotton *shama* cloth. Situated between the Ark and the Africa hotels, the modern **Atranos Gallery** [247 G3] (✆ *034 775 3190*; ⏰ *09.00–20.30 daily*) comes highly recommended, but there are several other good shops, including **Egzineamen Gebre Iyesus** [246 C4] (✆*034 775 2240*; ⏰ *07.00–20.00 daily*) running along the road towards Maryam Tsion.

OTHER PRACTICALITIES
Further reading An excellent companion for anybody with a serious interest in Axum's archaeological sites is Gian Paulo Chiari's *Guide to Aksum and Yeha*, published in 2009 by Arada Books (*www.aradabooks.com*) and widely available in bookshops in Addis Ababa as well as through the Anglo-Ethiopian Society in London (*www.anglo-ethiopian.org*). More than 250 pages in length, and lavishly illustrated with more than 300 photographs, it is particularly strong on detail for the main stelae field, the Church of Maryam Tsion, and Axum Museum, reflecting the most recent archaeological research available, but it also covers all outlying sites in considerable depth.

Internet and email Internet facilities exist at the main tourist hotels including the Remhai, the Ark and the Africa. There are a handful of independent internet cafés dotted around the centre including **New-Tech Internet Café** [247 G3] (✆*034 775 2001*; ⏰ *08.00–22.00 daily*) opposite the Ark Hotel, all charging less than US$0.05 per minute.

Library Situated in a former palace between the main traffic roundabout and the Cathedral of Maryam Tsion, the **Axum Heritage Foundation** [246 C4] (✆ *034 775 2871/2554*; e *axumite_heritage@yahoo.com*; ⏰ *08.30–22.00 Mon–Sat*) houses an excellent library including a collection of several hundred titles about Ethiopia, many of which are rare or out of print. Casual visitors are welcome to browse through the collection.

Swimming Axum is tangibly warmer than most other places of interest in Ethiopia, for which reason an afternoon at the swimming pool at the Remhai Hotel might be tempting – it costs US$2.50 to swim for non-hotel guests.

WHAT TO SEE To see Axum's main cluster of antiquities, walk out past the old bus station towards the stelae field on the northwestern outskirts of town. *En route*, you need to stop at the Aksum Tourist Information Office (see page 245) to purchase a ticket that allows access to all the secular historical sites within walking distance of the town (excluding Tsion Maryam). These tickets cost US$3, with a 50% reduction in price on presentation of a student card, and a rather less significant discount for groups of five or more people. Knowledgeable guides are provided by both the tourist office and the Axum Guides Association on request and ask around US$15 per day per group. The unofficial guides are best avoided. Don't forget to bring along your torch. Note that there is a separate charge to visit the church compound.

The notes here will be better understood if read in conjunction with the *History* section in *Chapter 1*, page 3.

The stelae field A tour normally starts at the main stelae field opposite the Church of Tsion Maryam, which consists of some 75 or more stelae of various shapes and sizes, concentrated within an area of less than 1,000m². Do note that while most of the larger stelae are linked by local tradition to specific kings, and these traditions are referred to in the text that follows, these associations have little scholarly basis.

The modern view of the stelae field is dominated by the stele accredited to King Ezana, the third-largest ever erected at Axum. This engraved block of solid granite, which stands some 23m high, was transported from a quarry 4km distant, most probably by elephants. No satisfactory explanation has been postulated for how such a massive block of stone was erected – one Axumite tradition has it that it was the work of the mysterious powers of the Ark of the Covenant. The stele is carved with a door and nine windows, which are thought to symbolise the door and nine chambers of Ezana's Tomb, and the nine palaces built by the king. Ezana's stele is slightly tilted, and at one point there were fears it might eventually topple over, but recent measurements compared with those taken 100 years ago suggest it was erected at this angle. Unfortunately, the nearby Tomb of the Arches is no longer open to the public due to worries about instability, but you can still look down to see the first archway.

The largest of Axum's stelae, credited by tradition to the 3rd-century **King Remhai**, now lies shattered on the ground. Its collapse is linked by tradition to Queen Yodit, who destroyed many of Axum's finest buildings, but scholarly opinion is that it toppled over either while it was being erected or soon afterwards, probably because the base of the stele was too small to support it. Remhai's stele still lies where it fell. It weighs 500 tons and would be over 33m high were it standing. It is decorated with a door and 12 windows.

Not far from this stele, **Remhai's Tomb** consists of 12 underground vaults that are high enough to walk through. The most striking thing about this tomb is the precision of its masonry, which consists of large blocks of granite held together by metal pins. In the back vault, Remhai's sealed stone coffin lies where it was abandoned after Neville Chittick's excavations were aborted following the 1974 revolution. Another nearby excavation that should not be missed is the Tomb of the Mausoleum. Opened to the public for the 2007 millennium celebration, this tomb has two entrances connected by a corridor. The entrance doors are rock-hewn and feature a common design with doors found at the churches of Tigrai. The west entrance door was damaged (along with many lintel beams) at the time the big stele collapsed, but the east door remains intact. Three 'shaft tombs' serve as skylights that illuminate the stack-stone constructed passage, and five burial chambers line each side.

During the Italian occupation, the second-largest Axumite stele, which stands 26m high and whose builder is unknown, was cut into three blocks for ease of transportation and reassembled on the Piazza in Rome. Several years of negotiation between the Ethiopian and Italian governments have culminated with the recent return of the looted stele to its rightful home. The first block arrived in Axum to scenes of public jubilation on 19 April 2005, and the other two blocks followed shortly afterwards. Now it's in the process of being re-erected, the site is currently surrounded by an elaborate jungle of scaffolding. The construction effort also affects King Ezana's stele, which is being stabilised with a sling attached to a metal pole to prevent it from shifting or tipping over. To the great appreciation of photographers, this work should be completed by the time of publication.

Ezana was the first Christian ruler of Axum, and the last one to build a stele. The stelae of Axum are not, however, thought to have any religious significance, but to have demonstrated the power and importance of the ruler who built them. It is not surprising, then, that Ezana, the conqueror of Yemen and parts of modern-day Sudan, is credited with building such an impressive monument. There are many smaller stelae scattered around the site, and a few other places in town where a few

The earliest excavations at Axum were conducted during the first three months of 1906 by the Deutsche-Aksum Expedition (DAE), led by Dr Enno Litmann and funded by the German Kaiser. The massively detailed report of this expedition, which includes extensive notes on the two main stelae fields, Kaleb's Palace and several churches, was published in German in 1913. It had long been out of print when an English translation, edited and annotated by leading archaeologist and Axum expert Dr David Phillipson, and lavishly illustrated with line drawings and photographs taken in 1906, was published as *The Monuments of Aksum* by the Addis Ababa University Press in 1997. While aspects of the DAE report are inevitably dated, it remains a marvellously detailed and informative introduction to the main historical sites dotted around the modern town; it costs around US$9.50 and is more easily obtained in Addis Ababa than in Axum.

Between 1906 and 1992, only two significant series of excavations took place at Axum, both of which were terminated after the assassination of Haile Selassie in 1974. The French excavations at Dongar Palace and several other sites, initiated in 1952 and supervised by Francis Anfrey, resulted in several sketchy preliminary accounts but have as yet yielded no detailed report. Stuart Munro-Hay published a full account of the excavations at the main stelae field undertaken by Neville Chittick for the British Institute in East Africa in the early 1970s after Chittick's death. In 1991, Munro-Hay published the most detailed and readable existing account of Axumite society, a book entitled *Aksum: An African Civilisation of Late Antiquity*. In this book, Munro-Hay writes:

> Of all the important ancient civilisations of the past, that of the ancient Ethiopian kingdom of Aksum still remains perhaps the least known … Its history and civilisation has been largely ignored, or at most accorded only brief mention, in the majority of recent books purporting to deal at large with ancient African civilisations, or with the world of late antiquity … When this book was in preparation, I wrote to the archaeology editor of one of Britain's most prominent history and archaeology publishers about its prospects. He replied that, although he had a degree in archaeology, he had never heard of Aksum.

The subsequent decade has seen a number of important new excavations undertaken in and around Axum, the results of which generally remain unpublished. Only a tiny fraction of known sites around Axum have been excavated, and new sites are being discovered at a faster pace than the established ones are being investigated. It is thus safe to say that almost anything written about Axum today is based on relatively sketchy archaeological foundations. One can only guess at what further excavation of this mysterious city might yet reveal.

smaller and in most cases collapsed stelae can be seen, for instance on the opposite side of the road to the school next to King Ezana's Park.

Axum Museum [246 B7] Exploring the stelae field conveys something of the majesty of ancient Axum, but it is the tour through the marvellous site museum that illustrates just how cosmopolitan and technologically advanced the city was. With a new location directly behind the stelae field, this is an exemplary museum and it deserves thorough investigation. Surprisingly, even though it was built recently, the future of this museum is already uncertain. Important tombs have been located beneath it, and it may move again.

The first display is a selection of ancient rock tablets, which are inscribed in a variety of languages including a form of Sabaean that preceded the Ge'ez of Christian Axum. This early Sabaean writing consisted of consonants only, but it is similar enough to the modern Amharigna script that the letters (though obviously not the meaning of the words) are intelligible to Ethiopians today.

The museum also contains an array of Axumite household artefacts, ranging from a water filter to a set of drinking glasses that were imported from Egypt. There is a collection of Axumite crosses and coins, the latter minted up until the 6th century AD. A more recent artefact is a 700-year-old leather Bible, written in Ge'ez and decorated with illuminations.

Some new explanatory posters have been added recently, funded by an American–Italian archaeological research project. They give an overview of the history of Axum, its major archaeological sites and the various artefacts found. This will help you to get a broader and better picture of what is of archaeological relevance in Axum and the surrounding area, in a context that contrasts with the more outlandish myths and legends that are recounted by guides in Axum as if they were accepted fact.

Next to the museum you can visit a typical Axumite house. Although this is a new building and not historical, it is built true to form – be sure to check out the basement where the large beam construction can be observed in detail. The Axumite Women's Association has also opened a small traditional coffee house here serving coffee and cool drinks. In the hills behind the museum, Boston University researchers are in the process of discovering many significant pre-Axumite sites. It seems with each visit something new is being uncovered, making Axum the most dynamic of the historic route's cities.

Mai Shum

Mai Shum Often referred to as the **Queen of Sheba's Swimming Pool** [246 C7], Mai Shum is a small reservoir situated alongside the northern end of the stelae field at the junction of the tracks that lead to the Yeha Hotel and to the Tomb of Kaleb. Traditions regarding the excavation of the pool are, even by Ethiopian standards, somewhat divergent. At one end of the timescale is the popular legend that Mai Shum was created some 3,000 years ago as a bathing place for the Queen of Sheba. At the other is the more credible story that it was dug by Abuna Samuel, Bishop of Axum during the early 15th-century reign of Emperor Yishak. The notion that the Queen of Sheba ever unrobed and took a dip in Mai Shum has to be classified as fanciful, but there is reason to think that the pool was excavated in Axumite times, as were the stone steps leading down to it, and that Abuna Samuel's contribution consisted of clearing and possibly enlarging the existing basin. Suggestively, the name Axum is thought to derive from the phrase 'Ak Shum', which consists of a Cushitic word meaning water and a Semitic word for chief, while 'Mai' is the Tigrigna equivalent to 'Ak' – so that both Mai Shum and Axum translate as 'Water of the Chief', leaving open the possibility that the town is named after the pool alongside which it was founded.

Cathedral of Tsion Maryam

Cathedral of Tsion Maryam [246 B6] From the museum, you'll probably move on to the compound of the Cathedral of Tsion Maryam (St Mary of Zion), where a church of that name was constructed above an old pagan shrine by King Ezana in the 4th century. Ethiopia's first church, the original Maryam Tsion church, which consisted of 12 temples, has been destroyed, most probably by the 16th-century Muslim leader Ahmed Gragn, though one version of events is that it was a victim of the rampages of Queen Yodit, and that Gragn destroyed a later replacement church.

Francisco Alvarez, who visited Axum in 1520, penned what is, so far as I'm aware, the most detailed surviving description of the church destroyed by Gragn. It was, the Portuguese priest wrote,

> a very noble church, the first there was in Ethiopia ... named Saint Mary of Zion ... because the apostles sent [its altar stone] from Mount Zion. This church is very large. It has five aisles of good width and of great length, vaulted above, and all the vaults closed; the ceilings and sides are painted. Below, the body of the church is well worked with handsome cut stones; it has seven chapels, all with their backs to the east, and their altars well ornamented.
>
> This church has a large enclosure, and it is also surrounded by another larger enclosure, like the enclosing wall of a large town or city. Within the enclosure are handsome groups of one-storey buildings, and all spout out water by strong figures of lions and dogs of stone. Inside this large enclosure there are two mansions ... which belong to two rectors of the church; and the other houses are of canons and monks. In the large enclosure, at the gate nearest the church, there is a large ruin, built in a square, which in other time was a house, and it has at each corner a big stone pillar, squared and worked. This house is called Ambacabete, which means house of lions. They say that in this house were the captive lions, and there are still some always travelling, and there go before the Prester John four captive lions.

The oldest-functioning church in the compound today resembles the castles of Gondar – not surprising, as Gondar's founder, Emperor Fasilidas, built it. There are some good paintings and musical instruments inside the church, but entrance is forbidden to women. The foundations of one of the original 12 temples have been left undisturbed as a mark of respect, and there is some talk of archaeological excavation taking place below it in the near future. As for the rather overblown piece of 20th-century architecture that now forms the largest church in the compound, this was built in the 1960s under Haile Selassie – sadly, its ugly spire competes with the ancient stelae for horizon space. Haile Selassie's wife had the museum built next to the old church, which is worth visiting for its collection of ancient crowns, crosses and other church relics. Behind the old church stands the so-called Throne of David, which is where the Axumite emperors were crowned, as well as the Thrones of the Judges, a row of a dozen old throne bases that suffered some damage at the hands of Gragn's army.

Axum's most famous religious artefact, the Tabot or supposed Ark of the Covenant, is currently kept in a sanctified outbuilding within the compound, but plans are afoot to move the Ark of the Covenant to the museum. Still, there's not much chance of being allowed to see it – indeed, only two Westerners claim to have had the privilege! Yohannis Tomacean, who viewed it in 1764, described it as 'a piece of stone with a few incomplete letters on it'. A century later, R P Dimotheos, was shown 'a tablet of pinkish marble of the type one normally finds in Egypt ... quadrangular, 24cm long by 22cm wide [on which] the Ten Commandments, five on one side, five on the other [were] written obliquely in Turkish fashion'. Dimotheos thought the 'nearly intact' tablet to be perhaps 600 years old, and quite clearly he was shown a different artefact from the one seen by Tomacean – almost certainly, both men were allowed to view *a tabot*, but not *the* Tabot.

Entrance to the church compound costs US$12, a somewhat steep fee by comparison with that charged for the other historical sites, especially for female visitors (women have been banned from entering the most interesting church in the compound since its predecessor was attacked by Queen Yodit in the 10th century). There is no charge for visiting the nearby Church of Arbuta Insesa (Four Animals), a circular church constructed in the 17th century by Iyasu I and rebuilt in its present rectangular style in 1962, when several ancient tombs were found underneath it. Refreshingly low-key by comparison with the contemporaneous eyesore built by Haile Selassie next door, Arbuta Insesa is worth visiting for the interesting modern paintings that adorn its walls.

King Ezana's Park and King Basen's Tomb [246 D2/247 E3] There are two

major historical sites within the modern town centre. In King Ezana's Park, a tablet inscribed in Sabaean, Ge'ez and Greek stands where it was originally placed in the 4th century AD. Other relics in the park include standing pillars from what was presumably Ezana's palace, a stele, what looks like a tomb, and an innocuous-looking slab of stone that could be mistaken for a park bench but was in fact used for cleaning corpses. This site, like several others that have been fenced off around the town, has never been excavated.

Not far from the park, marked by the customary stele, is King Basen's Tomb. According to the chronology of Axumite kings, Basen would have been ruling over Axum at the time of Christ's birth. His tomb lies underground and is entered via a man-high tunnel, but it differs from the tombs in the main stelae field in that it is hewn out of rock as opposed to being built from stone blocks. The graves chiselled into the side of the entry tunnel are probably where Basen's family were laid to rest. At the end of the tunnel are two much larger vaults in which the king and his wife are thought to have been entombed. Discrete from the king's tomb is a series of graves carved into the rock, reminiscent of the similar but much more recent graves carved into the surrounding walls of the churches at Lalibela.

EXCURSIONS FURTHER AFIELD Several important sites lie within a 5km radius

of the city centre, and most can be visited on foot if you so choose, or in a rented vehicle or taxi.

The tombs of Kaleb and Gebre Meskel On a hilltop some 2km north of the

town centre stand the 'two houses under the ground, into which men do not enter without a lamp' as mentioned in the writings of Francisco Alvarez. Local tradition has it that these tombs, whose entrances lie just 23m apart, were excavated below the palaces of the powerful 6th-century Emperor Kaleb and his son and successor Gebre Meskel, and the two emperors were entombed within them. While these assertions are difficult to verify, there is no strong reason to doubt them either (except perhaps that contradictory legends claim Kaleb was buried at Pantaleon Monastery and Gebre Meskel at Debre Damo) and the set of raised stone crosses on one tomb, together with the absence of any stelae, implies it dates to the Christian era.

Dr Littman excavated the site in 1898, at which time the whole construction was buried. Little remains of the palace itself, but the burial vaults underneath it are in excellent condition, though grave robbers have cleared out their contents – all that remain are the stone sarcophagi referred to by Alvarez as 'the treasure chests of the Queen of Sheba'! The subterranean architecture is similar to that of Remhai's Tomb, which was constructed below the stelae field some 300 years earlier. The most obvious difference lies in the masonry: whereas Remhai's Tomb was constructed by riveting together cubed stone blocks, this one is made of freely interlocking blocks of irregular shape. Legend has it that a secret tunnel goes all the way from the tombs to Eritrea and/or Yemen.

To get to the twin tombs, start from the square in front of the stelae field and (assuming that you are facing the stelae) follow the asphalt road to your right. After no more than five minutes, after passing the rightward fork to the Yeha Hotel, you will pass the pool known as Mai Shum on your right. From here, it's a fairly straightforward 20-minute hike to the ruined palace, following a motorable track that offers some fine views over the stelae field, dwarfed though it is by the singularly ugly spire of the 20th-century Tsion Maryam Church.

About halfway up the hill is a reminder of just what may lie undiscovered beneath the soil around Axum. In the 1980s, a farmer discovered a **trilingual tablet** that had been inscribed under King Ezana. The tablet praises God for his help in the conquest of Yemen. It also warns that anybody who dares move the tablet will meet an untimely death. The tablet lies exactly where it was found, but is easy to miss because it is protected in a makeshift hut. As with Kaleb's Tomb, the entrance fee for the museum and stelae field covers the tablet too.

Debre Liqanos Monastery From Kaleb's Palace, a clear path to your right leads after 20–30 minutes to a hilltop monastery founded by Abba Liqanos, a Constantinople-born member of the 'Nine Saints' who evangelised in the vicinity of present-day Adwa in the 6th century. The original Axumite church, thought to have been converted by Abba Liqanos and his followers from an older non-Christian temple, was replaced several centuries ago, but fragments such as the pillar next to the baptismal font can still be seen. Women may enter the monastery compound and look at the various holy crosses and books, but the church interior is accessible to men only. Many people feel this walk is worthwhile just for the scenery and the opportunity to escape the yelling kids and wannabe guides. Instead of returning to Axum the way you came, a steep short cut leads down the hill to bring you out on the road between Basen's Tomb and Maryam Tsion. Entrance costs US$3.

Pantaleon Monastery This attractive monastery, situated 5km out of town on a euphorbia-clad 40m-high pinnacle known as Debre Katin, boasts one of the oldest and most historically important churches in the country. Pantaleon was founded in the early 6th century by Abba Pantaleon, a son of a Byzantine nobleman who entered the monastic life as a child and later became one of the 'Nine Saints' who fled to Ethiopia when the Monophysitic doctrine was proclaimed to be heretical. Local tradition has it that Pantaleon spent the last 45 years of his life praying and healing the sick from the confines of a tall, narrow monastic cell in which he was forced to spend 24 hours a day in a standing position. Pantaleon was an adviser to King Kaleb, who joined the monastery after he abdicated in favour of his son Gebre Meskel in roughly AD550. Another plausible local tradition claims that Abba Yared, the contemporary of Gebre Meskel who invented the notation of Ethiopian ecclesiastical music and compiled the *Mazgaba Degwa* (Treasury of Hymns), spent much of his life at Pantaleon.

As with its counterpart at Debre Libanos, the hilltop church at Pantaleon is thought to have been built on the site of an older non-Christian temple and is open to men only. According to the priests, the church's sanctuary – which is off-limits to the laity – stands atop a stone staircase leading to a subterranean rock-hewn pit that formed part of the original temple. Visitors can be taken to the stone pit where Abba Pantaleon endured his hermitage, and to the nearby rock where King

Kaleb sat when he sought the priest's blessing or counsel. Both men are said to have been buried in the stone cemetery in the church compound. Women may enter the brightly painted modern church that stands below the original.

Pantaleon can be reached on foot from the Monastery of Debre Liqanos, a roughly 45-minute walk through lovely countryside. A quicker way back to town is to descend the southern slope of the hill via a footpath that leads to a motorable track that emerges on the Adwa road roughly 100m past the Africa Hotel. You can, of course, visit the monastery as a stand-alone excursion by using this second track, either on foot or by vehicle – the monastery is clearly visible and signposted from the Adwa road. Entrance costs US$3.

Dongar and the Gudit Stelae Field
Another important site that lies outside of the modern town is Dongar, popularly known as the Queen of Sheba's Palace, which was discovered as recently as 1950. As with so many sites in Axum, many questions surround the construction of this palace, but it is unlikely to have anything to do with the Queen of Sheba. The French archaeologist Francis Antrey, who excavated the site in 1952 but never published the bulk of his findings, concluded that the palace was most probably built in the 7th century AD. I'm told that more recent excavations and carbon-dating tests, the results of which are not yet published, indicate that the palace may in fact date to the pre-Christian era.

Whenever it was built, the intact floor plan and entrance stairs are sufficient to confirm that it was probably the most impressive palace ever built in Axum, consisting of more than 50 rooms, and boasting an elaborate drainage system. It is also where many of the more unusual relics now housed in Axum's museum were found. The palace stands 20–30 minutes' walk from the town centre on the northern edge of the Gondar road. You will need your ticket from the tourist office to enter the site.

On the opposite side of the road to the palace is a field of hundreds of relatively small and unadorned stelae, which aside from one 22.5m stele and another 7.5m stele are generally not much more than 2m high. This is referred to locally as the Gudit Stelae Field, Gudit being an alternative rendition of Yodit, the Falasha queen traditionally said to have razed much of ancient Axum. The traditional link between Gudit and these stelae has yet to be explained to me, but one popular tradition does maintain that the largest stele within the field marks the grave of Makeda, the Queen of Sheba. Based on limited archaeological exploration in 1974 and 1994–96, these stelae have been confirmed to mark graves of some sort. One tomb contained several artefacts that appear to date from the 3rd century AD, suggesting that this field was broadly contemporaneous with the main stelae field in town. A likely explanation is that it was a burial ground for dignitaries considered less important than those buried at the main stelae field.

Ad Hankara and the Gobedra Lioness
Also along the Gondar road, reached via a 1km side road running to the north opposite the electrical substation at Ad Hankara, some 2–3km or so past Dongar, is the hillside quarry from whence came the stelae that stand outside Axum. Amongst the broken rock that litters the hill can clearly be seen rocks from where some of the larger stelae were cut, and there is also one partially carved stele that lies *in situ*.

A short walk further uphill, etched into a flat rock face with a southwest orientation, there is a 3.27m-long outline figure of a crouching lion known as the Gobedra Lioness. The story behind this isolated and singular carving has long been a source of speculation. Tradition asserts that the Archangel Mikael was attacked by a lion here, and that he repelled the lion with such force it left an outline in the rock. The presence of a carved cross alongside the carving was for some time thought to indicate a post-Christian date, but it is more likely that the lioness was carved in pre-Christian times and the cross was carved next to it later. In *The Sign and the Seal*, Graham Hancock suggests it was the work of the Knights Templar who he believed visited the area in medieval times, but it was more probably carved during the reign of Gebre Meskel. Whether the carving has any deep significance or was merely decorative is anybody's guess.

There is a small lake on the way between Dongar and Ad Hankara where pelicans and a variety of storks and wintering ducks and waders are seasonally abundant.

Dereka Abba Meta

Axum, with its elevated ecclesiastical status, ancient tomb-carving tradition and local abundance of suitable sandstone outcrops, might reasonably be expected to lie at the epicentre of a cluster of rock-hewn churches similar to those that surround Wukro or Lalibela. Oddly, however, the opposite is the case. Aside from the subterranean chamber rumoured to lie beneath the sanctuary of Pantaleon Monastery, the only rock-hewn church I'm aware of within day-tripping distance of Axum is the little-known Abba Meta, carved into the eastern wall of a wooded gorge near Dereka, some 9km south of the town centre.

Abba Meta is named after its Roman-born excavator, a rather shadowy 6th-century figure who (like the church itself) is also sometimes referred to as Abba Libanos (not to be confused with Abba Liqanos) and whose name replaces that of Abba Aregawi in some lists of the 'Nine Saints'. Tradition has it that Abba Meta was exiled to Dereka after he accused the Patriarch of the Ethiopian Church of corrupt practices, and spent several years there secluded in a monastic cell – quite possibly one of the artificial caves carved into the cliff above the church that today bears his name. Eventually, the patriarch received a divine message instructing him to accept Abba Meta's criticisms, and the pardoned priest left Dereka for Gunda Gundo, where he founded a monastery with the support of Emperor Gebre Meskel.

As with many other Tigraian rock churches, Dereka Abba Meta is not as straightforward to visit as it could be. I failed to gain entry on two separate attempts, mainly because no key was available – I'm told that the caretaker priest lives some distance away, is normally absent on Saturdays (market day in Axum), and is a reliable presence only before 09.00 on Sundays and special mass days. Even when he is available to unlock the church, entry is forbidden to women. I have no reliable information about the church interior, but one deacon told me that it consists of a single chamber large enough to seat 100 people, and contains two engraved rock columns but no paintings. According to the same deacon, the artificial caves in the nearby cliff represent failed early attempts to excavate a church into unyielding rock, but to me they look more like disused monastic cells. Even if you fail to enter the church, the surrounding euphorbia-studded rockscapes are quite magnificent, and the lush forest in the gorge – fed by a holy spring – supports plenty of monkeys and birds.

Dereka Abba Meta can be approached to within a few hundred metres by 4x4. From central Axum, follow the Gondar road as far as the Tsehai Berki Hotel, then turn left immediately afterwards, following a dirt road that runs slightly downhill past the stadium and market (both to your right) before it curves through a shallow watercourse to cross the old airstrip after about 700m. About 800m after crossing the airstrip, the road forks, and you need to take the rather rough-looking track to your right. Follow this track for another 5.5km (passing an electric pylon some 2km past the junction), then turn right again at another fork. About 500m further, watch out for the marshy patch in the road – you could easily get bogged down in it, so consider walking. Then, after another 1km, there is a spot where you can park your car before walking the last stretch to the top of the gorge, from where a short but steep path runs through the base of the gorge to the prominent blue-and-white church door.

FROM AXUM TO ADIGRAT

If you want, the 122km trip between Axum and Adigrat, Tigrai's second-largest town, can be done as a straightforward three–four-hour drive or bus ride. There are, however, several places of interest along the way, most notably the ruins at Yeha, the ancient clifftop monastery of Debre Damo and the town of Adwa. Light vehicles run throughout the day between Axum and Adwa, Adwa and Enticcio, Enticcio and Biset, and Biset and Adigrat, so hopping between places of interest is reasonably easy, provided that you're not in a rush!

The road between Axum and Adigrat passes through rugged sandstone terrain. This is most spectacular between Biset and Adigrat, where it climbs to above 3,000m, offering terrific views over terraced slopes and the cliffs of the Hista river gorge, and then snakes down a mountain pass to Adigrat 600m below.

ADWA Slightly larger than Axum, and a more important centre of industrial and population growth, the neat little town of Adwa has an attractive setting amid the stark granite hills so typical of Tigrai. Adwa is of limited interest to tourists, but of tremendous significance to Ethiopians: it was in the surrounding hills that Emperor Menelik II defeated the Italian army on 1 March 1896, thereby ensuring that his empire would be the only African state to enter the 20th century as a fully independent entity.

The most likely reason why an independent traveller might want to overnight in Adwa is to get a head start visiting the Yeha ruins the next morning or to pick up early morning transport southward to Abi Aday. If you do need to spend a night, it is a pleasant enough place, and remarkably unaffected by tourism considering its proximity to Axum. The main point of interest in the town centre is the Church of Adwa Inda Selassie, which was built by Emperor Yohannis IV and is decorated with some superb late 19th-century murals.

Getting there and away Adwa lies 22km east of Axum along a good road that is now asphalted the whole way. The drive takes about 20 minutes in a private vehicle, and about 30 minutes in one of the regular minibuses that nip backwards and forwards between the two towns throughout the day. There is plenty of transport from Adwa east through to Adigrat, Mekele and points along the main road in between. One bus daily connects Adwa to Mekele via Abi Aday, leaving Adwa at around 06.00 and passing through Abi Aday about five hours later (see also *From Axum/Mekele via Abi Aday and Sekota* and *Axum to Hawzien via Maryam Wukro* on pages 314 and 283 respectively).

⌂ **Where to stay and eat** At the time of writing a new multi-storey hotel was under construction next door to the Shewit Bar & Café. Until complete the following are Adwa's best offerings.

⌂ **Semayata Hotel** (26 rooms) ☎034 771 2153. With a pastry shop, restaurant & bar on the ground floor, & an internet café charging around US$0.05 per minute next door, this hotel offers clean bright en-suite rooms with hot water – some rooms have TV & tub. *US$4 small sgl, US$5.50/7.50/11 sgl/dbl/twin.*

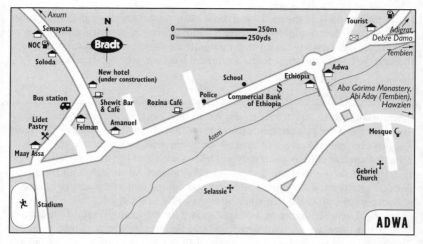

Soloda Hotel (35 rooms) ☎ 034 771 1063/1783/1794; e solodahot@ethionet.net. Located near the NOC filling station, this hotel is similar in quality & amenities to the Semayata. All rooms have hot-water en suite & a good restaurant & bar attached. *US$5–6 sgl, US$9 dbl or twin.*

Maay Assa Hotel (20 rooms) ☎ 034 771 3161/4390. This hotel near the stadium offers smart rooms with hot-water en suite & DSTV (rooms with bathtubs are more expensive), as well as smaller singles with cold-water showers. The

food at the attached restaurant is not the greatest – you may have better luck at their pastry shop. *US$4.50 sgl, US$6–12 dbl, US$15–18 twin.*

Tourist Hotel (27 rooms) ☎ 034 771 1054. This time-worn hotel is about the best place for cheap central lodging. Bear in mind: you do get what you pay for. *US$1.50–2 with ¾ bed & common cold-water shower.*

Shewit Bar & Café Situated not far from the bus station on the road to Axum, this small café serves decent pastries, juice & coffee.

MADERA ABBA GARIMA The monastery of Abba Garima at Madera, 5km east of Adwa as the crow flies, was founded during the 6th century by the eponymous member of the 'Nine Saints'. According to legend, Abba Garima was of royal Byzantine birth, and he served as the reluctant king of his homeland for seven years before Abba Pantaleon summoned him to evangelise in Axum. There he arrived three hours later, on the back of the Archangel Gabriel. The Monastery of Abba Garima was reputedly built by the Emperor Gebre Meskel, and its namesake lived there for about 20 years, performing miracles and healing the sick, until one day he ascended to the sky and was never seen again. A holy spring on the hill above the monastery is said to have started life when Abba Garima spat on the spot from where it emerges.

More recently, it was from Abba Garima that Menelik II observed the Italian troops as they approached Adwa prior to Ethiopia's decisive victory over the aspirant colonists in 1896. A year later, Ras Alula, the Governor of Hamasien and accomplished military tactician who famously defeated a contingent of 500 Italian troops at Dogali in present-day Eritrea in January 1887, died at Abba Garima of wounds sustained at the Battle of Adwa. Ras Alula's modest tomb still stands outside the rear entrance of the church, and several of his possessions are now held in the treasury.

The church at Abba Garima is said to be 1,500 years old. It looks far newer than that, but the twin stelae and bowl-like rocks that stand in front of its main door might well date to Axumite times. Abba Garima is today best known for its treasury, which contains a fantastic collection of ancient crowns, crosses and other artefacts donated by various emperors and nobles over the centuries, including a silver cross with gold inlays that once belonged to Gebre Meskel, and the crown of Zara Yaqob. The extensive library includes an illuminated Gospel supposedly written and illustrated in one day by Abba Garima himself (it's probably not *quite* that ancient, but some experts reckon it dates to the 8th century, which would make it the oldest-known manuscript in Ethiopia), as well as an equally antiquated history of the monastery's early days written by a priest called Hawi. Stored somewhat perversely in the midst of these treasures is a modern wall clock of the sort you'd find in any suburban Western kitchen – when I asked what it was doing there, I received the deadpan answer that it was yet another precious item the church had received as a gift!

Abba Garima lies about 10km from Adwa by road. To get there, follow the Adi Abay road southeast from Adwa for 7km, and then take the rough 3km track signposted to your left. Women are not permitted to enter the church or the treasury, but the priests will sometimes take the most important treasures outside to show female visitors. Equally, sometimes they won't. Male visitors are sometimes welcome to look around the church and treasury, but on other occasions they may be refused entry to one or the other – or to both – unless they can produce a letter of authority. It could well be that your willingness to pay more than the official church entry fee of US$6 plus an additional US$3 for a local guide is the determining factor – you may be asked for more to see the Gospel of Abba Garima, which is stored in a glass container to protect it from further wear and tear! But the set-up does come across as rather whimsical, so, as one reader notes: 'Be warned – you could be in for a lot of fuss for a very meagre result!'

YEHA Of main interest to those interested in pre-Axumite Sabaean culture, Yeha cannot compare to nearby sites such as Debre Damo or the rock-hewn churches near Hawzien. Not so much a village today as a small cluster of rustic stone houses, Yeha was once the most important city in Tigrai. Situated about 50km northeast of Axum, the ruined city was founded at least 2,800 years ago, and it served as the capital of a pre-Axumite empire called Damot for centuries prior to being usurped by Axum c100BC. The relationship between the two ancient Tigraian capitals is little understood. Rock-hewn tombs similar to those of King Basen in Axum demonstrate that Yeha had its own dignitaries and rulers. But it is a matter for conjecture whether Yeha and Axum were always independent political entities, or whether one town ruled over the other. What is clear is that by the time the Axumite Empire entered its most influential period, Yeha was a town of little political significance.

Yeha's single most remarkable antiquity is a well-preserved stone temple that stands 12m high, consists of up to 52 layers of masonry, and was built at least 2,500 years ago. Nobody knows what religion was originally practised in the temple, but appearances suggest links with the pagan faith of the Sabaean civilisation of south Arabia and inscriptions refer to a deity called Ilmukah. Abundant engravings of ibex suggest this animal was of some religious significance. Yeha also had a fertility cult of sorts and was once decorated by large statues of plump, dreadlocked women, but these statues are now mostly housed in the National Museum in Addis Ababa. A persistent local tradition, related to Alvarez in 1520 and to Henry Salt almost three centuries later, is that the Ark of the Covenant was kept here for a period prior to being taken to Axum.

One of the reasons why the temple at Yeha is in such good condition is that it became the centre of a monastic Christian community in the early 6th century. This church was founded by Abba Afse, one of the 'Nine Saints', who was guided there by an angel after having spent 12 years living at the monastery of Abba Garima. It seems entirely credible that the high stone monastery surrounding the ancient temple dates to this era; certainly it boasts one of the most remarkable treasure houses of any Ethiopian church, containing many ancient illuminated manuscripts and crowns. In addition to the temple and church treasures, Yeha is attractive for its scenic surrounds and characteristically Tigraian sandstone homesteads.

The turn-off to Yeha is clearly signposted on the left side of the Adigrat road some 27km past Adwa. Yeha lies 5km north of the main road. Light vehicles travelling between Adwa and Enticcio will be able to drop you at the turn-off, and to pick you up later in the day. There is no public transport to Yeha itself, but there's enough tourist traffic that you'd be unlucky not to get a lift in at least one direction – if the worst comes to the worst, it takes about 90 minutes to reach the site on foot. An early start is recommended to ensure you don't get stuck along the roadside, and be warned that it can get very hot, so you ought to carry some water if you are thinking of walking. There is no restriction on women visiting the church, and an entrance fee of US$6 covers both this and the old temple. A small 'resort' next to the church car park serves basic meals and cold drinks – and if you are really desperate for somewhere to crash, it also offers very basic accommodation for around US$1.50.

ENTICCIO This small town on the Inguya River lies on the Adigrat road about 12km east of the Yeha turn-off. If you end up spending the night, your best bet is the Debre Damo Hotel, a friendly double-storey lodge whose owner speaks good English and charges US$2 for a basic but clean room with a three-quarter bed and common showers. Food and drinks are also available at the hotel. Transport out of Enticcio is easy to find in either direction.

DEBRE DAMO MONASTERY One of the highlights of the north, the monastery of Debre Damo is notable for its 6th-century Axumite stone church, as well as for its impregnable clifftop position. The isolated monastery lies on a 3,000m-high *amba* (flat-topped hill) covering an area of 0.5km² and surrounded by sheer cliffs. It is something of a mystery how the founder of the monastery, Abba Aregawi, reached the top, and also how the monks carried up the stones with which the church was built. One tradition has it that a flying serpent carried the founding monk to the top. It is also said that Abba Aregawi's disciple, Tekle Haymanot, sprouted wings to escape when the devil cut the rope on which he was climbing up – after which he was able to make regular flying trips to Jerusalem! Today, the only way to reach Debre Damo – unless you happen to have a helicopter or flying serpent to hand – is by ascending a 15m-high cliff with the aid of a leather rope.

The double-storey main church, named after Abba Aregawi, is widely regarded to be the oldest extant non-rock-hewn church in Ethiopia. Legend has it that it was built by Aregawi himself, but much of it probably dates to the 10th and 11th centuries, and it was refurbished in the 1950s under the direction of David Buxton, a leading expert on Axumite architecture. The architecture shows strong Axumite influences, built up with layers of thick wood and whitewashed stone, and the wooden ceiling is decorated with animal engravings. Note that only the portal and narthex are open to the public.

Other ancient buildings include a secondary church, built on the spot where Abuna Aregawi is said to have vanished into thin air at the end of his mortal existence. Near this church are a number of rock-hewn tombs. On the main cliff there are several cramped hermit caves, the inhabitants of which subsist on bread and water lowered from the monastery by rope. In 1540, Emperor Lebna Dengal, in exile after his defeat by Ahmed Gragn, died at Debre Damo. It is also said that the 6th-century Axumite ruler Gebre Meskel is buried at the monastery. Debre Damo, like Gishen Maryam after it, served for some centuries as a place of imprisonment for princes with a claim to the imperial throne. When Queen Yodit overthrew Axum, she reputedly massacred all the princes at Debre Damo – up to 400 of them according to some accounts.

Debre Damo lies 11km north of the Adigrat road, along a poorly signposted turn-off some 24km east of Enticcio, 6km west of Biset and 37km from Adigrat. In a private vehicle, the monastery can easily be visited as a day trip out of Axum, Adwa or Adigrat, or *en route* between Axum and Adigrat. If you are renting a vehicle for the express purpose of visiting Debre Damo, Adigrat is likely to be the cheapest option – expect to pay around US$32 for a 4x4 or minibus as compared with around US$95 from Axum or Adwa.

There is no formal public transport along the road to Debre Damo, so most backpackers catch a bus between Adigrat and Adwa, ask to be dropped at the turn-off, and improvise from there. You could also visit the monastery out of Biset, where there are a few hotels, all fairly basic. The first hotel to the left as you enter town from the direction of Adwa has been recommended as clean and friendly, and the attached restaurant serves good *tibs*. Once at the junction, hitching or otherwise finding a lift certainly isn't out of the question; indeed many travellers get lucky in both directions, but nor can it be guaranteed. So be prepared for a long, hot 11km walk in either direction, take plenty of water, sunblock and a hat, and also maybe some food. If you need to, you can sleep at the monastery, but no food is available, the drinking water is dubious and the insects are prolific.

Before ascending to Debre Damo, you will need to pay a fee to the priest who pulls the strings – US$9 is the official non-negotiable rate, but a tip will also be expected. Women are forbidden from visiting Debre Damo, and prospective male visitors should expect to be interrogated about their faith before being allowed to visit.

ADIGRAT

Adigrat is the second-largest town in Tigrai, with a population of around 70,000, and it stands at the pivotal junction of the roads to Axum, Mekele and Asmara, the capital of Eritrea. It's a bustling, friendly, rather cosmopolitan town, where plenty of English is spoken, and it has strong historical and cultural links to Eritrea. Since the recent war with Eritrea, in which Adigrat played a frontline role, loss of cross-border trade has diminished the importance of this town. Nevertheless, the town has expanded, and as of 2008 there is a strong UN presence, and an ongoing archaeological project as well. Economically buoyant though it might be, Adigrat offers little in the way of sightseeing, but its distinctively Tigraian character and wonderful mountain setting make it an easy place to settle into for a night or two.

The busy **market** is definitely worth visiting. It's a good place to buy Tigraian coffee pots and local cloths as well as the nationally renowned honey that comes from Alitena. Just behind the market lies **Adigrat Chirkos Church**, covered in fine 19th-century paintings depicting angels and with a balcony offering a great view over the town. There is also a large **Catholic church** that bears a strong resemblance to a church in Florence. Equally unusual is the **Medhane Alem Church**, a rectangular sandstone building that more closely resembles a fort than any other church I've seen in Ethiopia. The park between the main roundabout and the Catholic church has been developed as a recreational centre with a swimming pool, albeit one predictably bereft of water when we last dropped in!

Adigrat would serve as a good base for exploring some of the rock-hewn churches described in the next chapter. It is closer to most of these churches than is Mekele, and even without a private vehicle it could be used as a base from which to visit churches along the main Mekele road as far south as Wukro. Aside from the rock churches covered in the next chapter, there are a couple more that lie very near to Adigrat. The closest, **Mayaba Samuel**, was badly burnt at some unspecified time in the past and has since fallen into disuse. It is basically an extended cavern, about 2.5m high but with a very low entrance. A few paintings survived the fire, including an orange painting of Christ. The church is in a rock face in the hills west of the Mekele road, and takes less than an hour to walk to from the town centre. You will probably need a guide to find it.

In the village of Kirsaba, about 7km along the Asmara road, **Mikael Kirsaba** is rather unusual in that it consists of a modern church with an older four-chambered rock-hewn church built underneath it. The story goes that the original church

TESFA TREKKING IN TIGRAI
Information provided by Mark Chapman

Tesfa has started doing community tours and treks in Tigrai, in the Agame Mountains around Adigrat. These red sandstone mountains are home to a number of less known rock churches. As with the trekking in Wolo, the communities own and operate simple guesthouses and receive a substantial proportion of the income for their services. Guests are guided through the mountains by specially trained guides from Adigrat, with their luggage carried on donkeys. Each guesthouse has a simple eco-toilet and wash facilities with accommodation for six guests in three rooms. The community cook simple but tasty food along with coffee and tea, while bottled drinks – water, beer and soft drinks – are available for purchase.

The trekking takes you up onto the sandstone ridges and through the farmed valleys. The most southerly community-run guesthouse, Shimbrety, is some 20km north of Hawzien and can be reached from Gheralta Lodge (using transport to drop you halfway). This is on the western ridge of the Agame Mountains. A little further along the ridge there is an interesting rock tunnel that has been carved through the ridge to give villages on the western side access to the lovely rock church of Maryam Buzuhan.

The nearest community guesthouse to Shimbrety is Gohgot, a few hours' walk to the east tucked under the cliff but above the villages. The nearby rock church of Gohgot Eyesus, positioned above indigenous woodland at the head of the valley, is roughly 90 minutes' walk away. Gohgot can be accessed either from Shimbrety, or nearby if taking a transfer by vehicle from the Hawzien area. It's a four–five-hour walk to Gohgot from the main road starting from the village of Idega Hamus just south of Adigrat.

Gohgot also connects to the highest guesthouse in the area: Enaf Enaf. At 3,000m it has stunning views across the Agame massif and its valleys. The walk from Gohgot takes around six–seven hours and goes past some lovely churches – notably Debre Giyorgis, which is a built-up church in the ancient tradition of Debre Damo and Yemrehanna Christos. It is perched on a ledge three-quarters of the way up the escarpment and is a challenging climb up via sturdy ladders. The walk has some steep sections on it so you need to be fit. From Enaf it's a four-hour walk down to the Agoro Lodge on the edge of Adigrat, built to support local community groups, but with a high standard of service and comfort.

The Erar community guesthouse can be reached from Shimbrety (about 4 hours) Gohgot (about 5 hours) Enaf (about 7 hours), and from a drop point on an access road leading from the Axum–Adigrat main road. Constructed on an isolated

(excavated in the 5th century by the horns of an agitated bull, if the local priests are to be believed) was doused with petrol by the Italians on their way to Adwa in 1896, but that the petrol miraculously turned to water before the church could be set aflame. The waterlogged church was not drained because the water was regarded as holy, so a new church was built above it by Menelik II. Any vehicle heading towards Asmara will be able to drop you at Kirsaba, but be aware that women are forbidden from entering the church and the priest with the key is often difficult to locate. Even if you surmount this obstacle, there is really very little to see other than a gloomy, waterlogged pit and some attractive 20th-century paintings.

GETTING THERE AND AWAY There are good bus connections between Adigrat, Axum and Mekele. In addition to buses that start their trip in Adigrat, buses

section of the escarpment with wonderful views westward to the mountains of Adwa and the Nebulet pillars, there are gelada monkeys around, and birds of prey soaring on the thermals. Just to the north in the village of Kiat is the famous rock church of Maryam Kiat, which has many natural springs and lots of fields with all manner of crops.

Further north along on a spur running off the ridge is a new community guesthouse perched above the village of Mugulat. Mugulat can be reached from Erar – about four hours' walking depending on the route selected as well as via Maryam Kiat. It's also possible to reach Mugulat from the other sites, but with a longer walk.

Mugulat is 40 minutes' walk from the access road that turns off the Adigrat–Axum road, some 20km west of Adigrat. From Mugulat a new trail has been developed. It crosses the Adigrat–Axum road and runs to Chehat community guesthouse with views over Young Gorge and the surrounding mountains. The walk is a ridge-top walk – without too many ups and downs – but is quite long.

From Chehat the trail winds north and east to join the road north from Adigrat. Just off this road is Amba Fekada Mountain where the local Menebayti community have built a guesthouse. It's a magnificent place for views and walking in the area. From here you can see the Debre Damo Amba to the west and the gorges to the east that drop into the Rift Valley.

Around the northern edge of the mountain there is a rock painting depicting oxen ploughing a field – but these are hump-less long-horned oxen which some experts conclude date from the early Axumite period (100BC–AD300). The painting also depicts three 'felines' (leopards?) and some humans – some with bows and spears.

Down in the valley is Enda Tekle Haymanot church, in the compound of which are ruins from the Axumite period – pillars and large stone slabs. Oral history claims these to be the ruins of the Queen of Sheba's palace, and also the palace where the Ark of the Covenant rested on its way to Axum. In fact the local district is called Gulo Makeda, meaning enclosure of Makeda (the traditional name for the Queen of Sheba).

The price per person per full day is US$55 including food, accommodation, guide and pack animal but excluding bottled drinks, transport and church entry. Advance booking is required. For more information contact Tesfa Tours (\011 810 0920; m 0923 490 495; www.tesfatours.com).

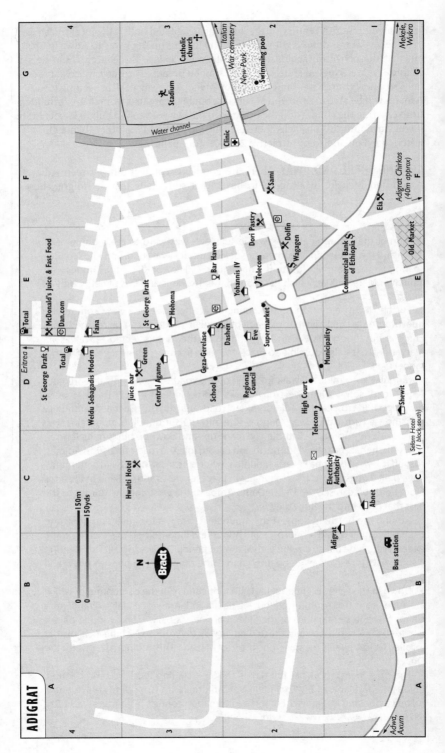

ADIGRAT

between Mekele and Axum or Asmara pass through Adigrat *en route*, generally in the mid morning, so there is less pressure than normal to get an early start.

A variety of light vehicles runs throughout the day between Adigrat and more local destinations such as Frewenyi (Sinkata), Wukro and Biset.

WHERE TO STAY

Budget

Geza-Gerelase Hotel [266 D3] (29 rooms) 034 445 2500. This place has clean, compact, carpeted rooms with private hot bath & DSTV. The restaurant has good salads & is a popular hangout for UN workers stationed in town. In the back there is a second *tukul* restaurant that serves traditional food including *kurt*, raw meat sliced very thin (try at your own risk!). Like many hotels throughout the region, the Geza was undergoing major expansions on our most recent visit with 31 more rooms under construction. *US$18.50/26/37 sgl/dbl/twin.*

Eve Hotel [266 D2] (26 rooms) 034 445 1120/845 0034; e evehoteladigrat@yahoo.com. This pleasant-looking hotel offers neat & clean en-suite rooms with hot water & TV. A restaurant & bar is attached & internet is available. *US$12/15/15 sgl/dbl/twin, US$18 suite.*

Weldu Sebagadis Modern Hotel [266 D4] (24 rooms) 034 445 2275; e helenzz2002@yahoo. com. This long-serving & friendly travellers' favourite offers large, clean rooms with ¾ bed & en-suite hot shower, as well as smaller common shower rooms. Some rooms have TV. The restaurant serves *faranji* & local dishes & is a good place to try *tholoh*, a dish specific to this part of Ethiopia, which is eaten like Swiss fondue – small balls of cooked barley are taken on the tip of a forked stick & dunked into a spicy sauce thick with butter & yoghurt. *US$4 using common shower, US$7.50/9.50 sgl/dbl en suite.*

Hohoma Hotel [266 E3] (7 rooms) 034 445 2469/2605. This hotel is one of the better budget options in Adigrat, but it is often full. The motel-style rooms are neat & compact with proper double beds, TV & en-suite hot shower. The ground-floor restaurant has a good selection of local & Western dishes in the US$2–4 range, & is one of the few places in town to serve meat during fasting periods. *US$7.50 standard dbl, US$9 suite.*

Shoestring

Shewit Hotel [266 D1] (7 rooms) 034 445 3028. This rather scruffy hotel has the solitary advantage of lying close to the bus station. *US$4–4.50 room with ¾ bed & common shower.*

Central Agame Hotel [266 D3] (27 rooms) 034 445 2466. This decent hotel offers clean & quite spacious rooms with ¾ bed, TV & en-suite hot shower, as well as smaller rooms with common shower & no TV. The restaurant here is good. *US$3/6 with common shower/en suite.*

Selam Hotel [off map 266 C1] (17 rooms) 034 445 0385. Conveniently located a block or 2 from the bus station, this 3-storey hotel is clean, friendly & decent value. *US$2–3 room with ¾ bed & common showers.*

Yohannis IV Hotel [266 E2] (25 rooms) 034 445 0170. This friendly place opposite the Ethiopia Hotel is a pleasant & safe option. *US$3 with common shower, US$6 en suite.*

WHERE TO EAT The smarter hotels listed above all serve good food, in particular the **Geza-Gerelase Hotel** [266 D3] which is noted for its traditional Ethiopian fare. The **Sami Restaurant** [266 F2] is the best stand-alone eatery, serving a variety of local meat, fish and vegetarian dishes. For between meals, the **Dori Pastry and Bakery** [266 F2] was for some years the only pastry shop in Adigrat, but it has recently been joined by the **Yohannis IV Café** [266 E2] on the ground floor of the eponymous hotel – both places serve cakes, bread, juice and coffee.

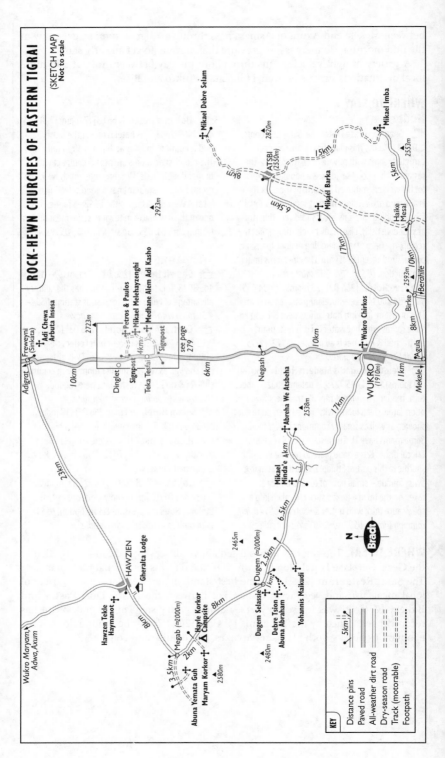

ROCK-HEWN CHURCHES OF EASTERN TIGRAI

(SKETCH MAP)
Not to scale

KEY

Distance pins — 5km
Paved road
All-weather dirt road
Dry-season road
Track (motorable)
Footpath

N Bradt

see page 279

10

Rock-hewn Churches of Northeast Tigrai

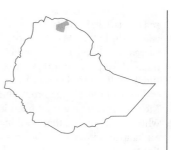

The epithet of 'best-kept secret' has been applied to so many modern mediocrities that it seems ludicrously inadequate when confronted by religious sanctuaries as magnificently obscure as the churches carved into the sandstone cliffs of Tigrai. Practically unknown to other Ethiopians – let alone the outside world – before 1966, the **rock-hewn churches** of Tigrai have been described by the British academic Ivy Pearce as 'the greatest of the historical-cultural heritages of the Ethiopian people'. Most of these architectural gems remain in active use today, several house paintings and other sacred medieval artefacts, and every one of them is imbued with an aura of spirituality that seeps from the very rock into which they are carved.

The rock-hewn churches of Tigrai do not function primarily as tourist attractions. A select crop of about 20 churches is described in brochures compiled by the Tigrai Tourist Commission (TTC). The most popular and accessible of these churches might be visited by outsiders once or twice a week, the rest perhaps every two or three months. As for the rest – well, it would not surprise me to learn that half of the rock-hewn churches in Tigrai have gone unseen by foreigners since the 1974 revolution. Visits by foreigners are generally tolerated, sometimes welcomed, and occasionally met with visible distrust. Fortunately, because the Tigraian churches are more scattered and less accessible than their counterparts at Lalibela, it's difficult to envisage their spiritual integrity ever being threatened by coaches full of prying tourists.

Sensitivity towards an older way of life is a prerequisite for exploring the Tigraian churches. So, too, is patience and humour. Many of the priests will not allow foreigners into their churches during mass, nor, as is customary in Ethiopia, will they open up the church if a mass has already been held on that day. At more inaccessible churches, the priests are understandably loath to undertake the long trek up from the plains unless a large pre-agreed tip is added to the official entrance fee. Then there is the small matter of locating the priest who keeps the key. Though, in recent years this has become increasingly easier.

With sufficient time, and a philosophical frame of mind, exploring these churches is likely to be a highlight of any trip through Ethiopia. True, none of the individual churches compares in architecture or impact to the complex at Lalibela. But, balanced against this, these remote churches do retain an aura of isolation and mystery that many people – I am not one of them – feel Lalibela has sacrificed as it has grown in accessibility and popularity. Furthermore, it is in Tigrai, more than anywhere else, that one is confronted by the radical nature of Ethiopian Christianity. During mass, or at festivals, these remarkable rock edifices witness scenes straight out of the Bible: white-robed worshippers chanting and swaying in prayer, prostrating themselves before the altar, or standing outside the church sharing thick, rough *injera* and beakers of alcoholic *t'ella*. This, one senses, is Christianity much as it would have been practised before the Vatican was built, before Martin Luther or Henry VIII, before Billy Graham – an almost surreal reminder that the religion we associate with American televangelism and quaint European country churches is at root every bit as Middle Eastern as Islam or Judaism. It is utterly fantastic!

Many of the Tigraian rock churches lie along the main road between Adigrat and Mekele, or can be visited from it. Four main clusters are covered in this chapter, of which the churches that lie along the main road between Freweyni (formerly called Sinkata) and Wukro are the most accessible to those without private transport or with limited time. The pick of these churches is undoubtedly **Adi Kasho Medhane Alem**, part of the highly accessible Teka Tesfai cluster 10km south of Freweyni/Sinkata. A second rather loose cluster consists of **Wukro Chirkos** – the most accessible of all the Tigraian churches, as it lies 500m from the main road in the town of Wukro – and the magnificent **Abreha we Atsbeha Church** along the Hawzien road. The most extensive cluster is found in the Gheralta region, which lies to the south of Hawzien and includes some of the most stunningly situated churches anywhere in Ethiopia. Gheralta can easily be explored out of Hawzien with a vehicle or from Gheralta Lodge, arguably one of the finest boutique resorts in the country. It could also be explored over a few days of hiking, bearing in mind that the region's finest churches are reached by long, steep walks that require a fair level of fitness. A fourth and more dispersed cluster lies in the Atsbi area, to the east of Wukro. With one exception, the **Atsbi churches** can be explored only with a vehicle. Finally, there are the churches in the Tembien, as covered in the section *From Axum/Mekele via Abi Aday and Sekota* in the chapter *Through Routes to Lalibela*, page 309.

Note that churches may be referred to either by their church name or else by the name of the place where they are situated. Medhane Alem Church at Adi Kasho, for instance, is sometimes referred to as Medhane Alem and sometimes as Adi Kasho. To ease confusion – and it can become very confusing – I've always strung the two names together.

BACKGROUND

It is anybody's guess as to why the rock-hewn churches of Tigrai were so often carved into relatively inaccessible cliff faces – was it for security, or for spiritual isolation, or simply because cliff faces are inherently good places to carve churches, and cliff faces are inherently inaccessible? Certainly, if keeping away outsiders *was* the objective, then the excavators of these churches did an admirable job, judging by the obscurity in which many of these churches languished throughout the first century of regular European presence in Ethiopia. Several 19th-century visitors to Tigrai – for instance Henry Salt, Nathaniel Pierce and Frances Harrison Smith – must have passed within a kilometre of some of these churches without ever suspecting that they existed.

In 1868, the British expedition led by Napier passed through the small Tigraian village of Wukro where they were shown an astonishing church carved into a rocky outcrop. For six full decades after this, it was assumed by the outside world that this church was the only one of its type in Tigrai. In 1928, Dr Enza Parona visited the monastery of Abba Yohanni in the Tembien, and four further churches were 'discovered' and described by Antonio Mordini during the Italian occupation, among them Maryam and Giyorgis Wukro to the southeast of Adwa. The list was added to in 1948, when Beatrice Playne visited several rock-hewn churches in Tigrai, including the formerly undescribed Mikael Imba near Atsbi and Tekle Haymanot in Hawzien.

Nevertheless when Sauter published an exhaustive list of all known Ethiopian rock-hewn churches in 1963, fewer than ten were listed for Tigrai.

All of which provides context to the veritable buzz that followed the 1966 Conference of Ethiopian Studies, during which Dr Abba Tewelde Medhin Josief, a Catholic priest from Adigrat, announced the existence of at least 123 rock-hewn churches in Tigrai, more than three-quarters of which were still in active use. Dr Josief died soon afterwards, but his findings were pursued by the Swiss photographer Georg Gerster, who travelled to eight churches (including Petros and Paulos Melehayzenghi, which was apparently overlooked by Josief) to produce a fantastic photographic essay entitled 'Rocks of Faith' for the British *Sunday Times*. Over the next three years, the British academics David Buxton, Ivy Pearce and Ruth Plant collectively visited 75 Tigraian rock-hewn churches and published several papers based on their formative research. The most useful of these first appeared in a 1971 issue of the *Ethiopian Observer* (vol XIII, no 3), which was devoted exclusively to the Tigraian churches and described more than 70 individual churches in full. By 1973, when Ivy Pearce published a supplementary list describing another 17 churches in the *Ethiopian Observer* (vol XVI, no 1), the full list of confirmed rock-hewn churches in Tigrai had been extended to 153, of which all but 26 were still in active use, and several other churches were known of by word of mouth only. The 1974 revolution put paid to any further research in the region, and nothing of consequence has been published about the Tigraian churches since that time. Nor, so far as I'm aware, has any further research been undertaken into the comparative or absolute dating of these fascinating edifices. These pre-revolution publications mentioned above, now long out of print, have all been used extensively in compiling this chapter.

The churches of Tigrai were generally excavated using a very different method from that favoured at Lalibela. The most impressive churches in and around Lalibela were generally created in two phases: first of all a moat-like subterranean trench would be excavated deep into a horizontal rock, then the church itself would be chiselled into the monolithic block of rock created at the centre of the trench. More characteristic of the Tigrai region, however, are churches carved into a vertical cliff face or from an outcrop, the former sometimes expanding onto a ledge where a false entrance has been added. So far as I'm aware, not one monolithic church is to be found in Tigrai, and the only major church that qualifies as a three-quarter monolith (where three full walls have been carved free of the original rock) is Mikael Imba.

The antiquity of most of the Tigraian rock-hewn churches remains largely a matter of conjecture. Every church has its own oral tradition regarding its excavation; in many cases, the church is dated to the rule of Abreha and Atsbeha, the twin emperors of Axum who converted to Christianity in the middle of the 4th century. Often, these anecdotal claims are riddled with apparent inconsistencies. In some instances, I was told that a church had been hewn by a specific emperor, but at a date centuries before or after that emperor ruled. At several churches, the traditions related to me personally were very different from those mentioned in the Tigrai Tourist Commission publication about the same church. There seems also to be a competitive element in the traditional accounts. At several of the churches ascribed to Abreha and Atsbeha, the priest told us that the church we were visiting was the first carved by the twin emperors, and mentioned by name other churches that make similar but – according to him – erroneous claims. To anybody who has travelled extensively in Ethiopia, and read widely about the country, such inconsistencies will not be unfamiliar terrain. Nevertheless, it makes it difficult to treat the local traditions very seriously.

It can be said with confidence that the overwhelming majority of the Tigraian churches were excavated prior to the 16th century. Subsequent to his own exploration of the area, David Buxton recognised that many churches in Wukro, Tembien and Gheralta had been accurately located in the writings of the Jesuit priest, Manuel Barradas, who lived in Ethiopia in 1624–40. And, as Ruth Plant points out, it can reasonably be assumed that Christian Ethiopia in the 16th century was too preoccupied with the immediate survival of the empire against the onslaught of Ahmed Gragn to have expended much energy in excavating houses of worship. Beyond this, however, the dating of the churches is open to speculation.

David Buxton, a leading authority on Axumite architecture, has thus far produced the only coherent attempt to place the churches within a formal chronological framework. In a 70-page essay, published in the Italian periodical *Archologia* in 1971, Buxton divides the churches into five broad chronological styles. The earliest style, which he calls Archaic Ethiopian Basilica and which he ascribes to the 10th and 11th centuries, consists of relatively crude attempts to reproduce the classic built-up Axumite church style in rock. In Buxton's view, the only church that can be placed unambiguously in this prototypical category, based on such archaic features as its colonnaded portico, is Adi Kasho Medhane Alem. He does describe several other superficially similar churches, notably Maryam Hibeti in the Tembien, but reckons that all of them display anachronistic features suggesting they are later imitations.

The next chronological architectural style as identified by Buxton is the Inscribed Cross Church, which peaked in popularity in the 11th and 12th centuries. The layout of all churches in this category consists of a cruciform plan within a larger square, a distinctively Tigraian style that seems to have no obvious precursor in built-up churches. Several of the best-known churches in Tigrai fall clearly into this category, for instance Wukro Chirkos, Mikael Imba and Abreha we Atsbeha (the last described by Buxton as 'the most perfect example of the cross-in-square layout'). Buxton believes that these churches clearly pre-date the excavations at Lalibela, and raises the intriguing possibility that the Bet Giyorgis in Lalibela, with its uniquely cruciform exterior, is the product of a conscious attempt to externalise the form of an Inscribed Cross Church.

Buxton goes on to describe three further styles, of which the Classic Ethiopian Basilica, a direct architectural progression from the Archaic Ethiopian Basilica, is probably roughly contemporaneous with the churches at Lalibela. The churches in what he refers to as the earlier series of the Tigraian Basilica style, which includes many of those in the Gheralta region, probably date to the 13th and 14th centuries, and thus post-date Lalibela. The later series of Tigraian Basilica includes several churches in the Tembien, the one area where oral tradition and academic opinion are in broad agreement, dating most of the excavations to the 14th- and 15th-century reigns of emperors Dawit and Zara Yaqob.

An interesting pattern that seems to emerge from Buxton's relative chronology is a broad westward movement in the excavation of Tigraian churches, with those lying to the east of what is now the main Adigrat–Mekele road generally pre-dating the Gheralta churches, which in turn pre-date those in the Tembien. If that is the case, might not the absolute dating of these churches be linked to the as yet poorly understood shifts of imperial power bases between the collapse of Axum and the rise of Lalibela four centuries later? For that matter, could it not be that some apparent chronological differences are also a reflection of regional variations in style? In this context, it's worth noting that the travelling time between, say, Abi Aday and Atsbi was far greater in previous centuries than it is today, and that many of the churches in question were practically invisible from the outside prior to the recent addition of built-up exteriors. Buxton himself notes that 'both the monolithic church and the elaborated exterior were specialities of Lalibela, and neither the one nor the other was ever adopted as an ideal by the Tigraian rock-hewers'. Much the same might be said for the cross-in-square style, which seems to have its epicentre in Wukro, and the various basilica styles that are predominant farther west.

Another potential stumbling block in dating the churches is that many might have been extended or redecorated one or more times in their history, thereby resulting in apparently anachronistic architectural features. It is clearly the case that many church paintings, though very old, are far more modern than the edifices that house them, while the southern third of Mikael Melehayzenghi is accepted to be a relatively recent addition to a much older church. It is possible, too, that some churches might have started life as partially hewn cave temples in pre-Christian times – a tradition of this sort is attributed locally to the church of Tekle Haymanot in Hawzien. A further circumstantial argument for supposing that some of the rock-hewn churches of Tigrai might have roots in the earliest Christian or even pre-Christian times is the presence of similar, albeit more primitive, rock-hewn tombs in Axum. It seems reasonable to start from the basis that some sort of architectural continuum links Ethiopia's various rock-hewn edifices.

The dates of excavation suggested by Buxton, like those ascribed to the churches by oral tradition, are often quoted as immutable fact. It should be noted, therefore, that Buxton himself takes great pains to emphasise that his chronological scheme is no better than provisional, and he frequently phrases his opinions in the guise of educated guesses. How the churches were excavated is not in question. The broad reason why they were carved will be clear to anybody who visits one of these active shrines of Christian worship today. But as for when, who knows? The temptation to look for reasons why some Tigraian churches might be as old as the traditions claim is irresistible. Yet it is interesting to note that while no suggestion has ever been made that any Ethiopian rock-hewn church dates to the post-Gragn era, at least two such churches (the 'new' Petros and Paulos in Tigrai and a church near Debre Tabor in Amhara) were excavated over the last 20 years. The work of latter-day glory hunters, or evidence that the rock-hewing tradition is not as frozen in the past as people tend to think: who knows? As Ruth Plant wrote in the introduction to the most exhaustive inventory of Tigraian rock-hewn churches yet published, 'it is vital to keep an open mind as to dates.'

BUREAUCRACY

One of the things that make the rock-hewn churches of Tigrai so absorbing is that they are not primarily tourist attractions, but active sites of worship. The more accessible and publicised churches might go for weeks without being visited by a tourist; there are probably many churches that haven't been seen by as many as a dozen foreigners ever. But, if the remote and often parochial character of the churches enhances the sense of privilege experienced by the occasional visitor, it can also lie at the root of several areas of bureaucratic frustration. Absent priests and silly attempts at over-charging are all part and parcel of the Tigraian church experience. All this will be simplified if you are travelling with a vehicle and a local Tigrigna-speaking guide, though even they may not always be able to locate a priest who's gone walkabout. If you are travelling independently it's probably fair to say that there are no hard and fast rules when it comes to dealing with the issues addressed on page 274 – a degree of flexibility and forbearance is a prerequisite!

FINDING THE PRIEST At any given church, there is generally only one priest who carries a key for the front door. If that priest isn't around, nobody can get into the church, and that's that. In our experience, the worst time to visit any church is on the local market day (Saturday in Atsbi and the Tembien; Wednesday in Gheralta), when the priest will reliably be off on a shopping spree. It is also the case that while some priests live close to their church, others live some way away, and will almost always never be around except during services. Another factor is that some priests will visit a church dedicated to a particular saint on the day dedicated to that saint, the implication of which is that visiting a church dedicated to St Maryam on St Maryam's Day is a good idea, but any church dedicated to another saint might just be one priest short of an open door.

This isn't complicated enough? Well most priests will not allow tourists into their church during any special mass (which generally runs from about 10.00 to 15.00), and it is customary to lock up the church for the rest of the day after a special mass has been held. In other words, if you want to visit a church on a mass day, then you need to be there before 10.00 to be reasonably certain of gaining entrance.

The net result of all this, based on our visits to the area, is that you've about a 50% chance of getting into any given church on any given day. With a vehicle, you can at least establish when the priest is likely to be around and return later. Without one, your best bet is to try to establish in advance whether there is any reason why the priest is likely not to be at the church that you intend to visit. This, I'm afraid, is far from foolproof.

PERMITS AND FEES In the past to visit the churches you required an official permit issued by the Tigrai Tourist Commission (TTC) (*www.tigraitourism.com*). This is no longer the case. However, if you want to visit any of the churches you must be in the company of an official badge-wearing guide (see below for details). The official TTC fee for entering any church is US$6 per person for all churches. This is truly a shame; while US$6 is a reasonable fee for the more spectacular churches, it will likely discourage tourists from visiting the less spectacular ones.

In addition to the entrance fee, for which you should in theory be given a receipt, the priest who holds the key and shows you around will normally expect a tip of around US$1.50–2, and he may ask for this before you go into the church. At churches where the priest has to walk with you for 30 minutes or longer before actually reaching the church, the tip is thoroughly deserved.

It's worth noting here that in addition to tipping the priest himself, you will be expected to slip a note to the person who locates the priest, and in the direction of anybody you photograph in or around the churches. Local kids who offer to carry your daypack or any other luggage will also expect a tip. So, too, come to think of it, may anybody else who accompanies you to the church, whether or not they actually contributed to the expedition.

GUIDES

The churches at Wukro, Freweyni/Sinkata, Hawzien and Teka Tesfai can easily be visited using public or private transport, with no strenuous legwork involved. The other churches in the region require greater effort and/or expense to visit. To visit any of the churches you must now be accompanied by an official guide or you will be refused entry. There are of course several reasons why a knowledgeable guide will come in handy. Firstly, there are no reliable maps of the region. Secondly, it can be very time-consuming finding the priest who keeps the key unless you speak Amharigna (or better Tigrigna). Finally, you are unlikely to be pressured into paying an exorbitant unofficial entrance fee. For the Gheralta, Atsbi or Abi Aday churches, you need to arrange a guide through the newly formed **Gheralta Guides Association** (m *0914 263 799;* ⊕ *08.00–17.30 daily*) in the small village of Megab, around 8km from Hawzien. Fixed fees are US$15/21 for a group of one to five people/six to ten people per day. Knowledgeable guides can also be hired through the TTC office in Mekele or Wukro.

Most churches can be approached in a 4x4 vehicle (though as they tend to be on cliffs, you will always have to walk the final stretch). You can hire a vehicle in advance out of Addis Ababa, or else fly or bus to Mekele and arrange to have a vehicle meet you there. Alternatively, the TTC office in Wukro can arrange minibus or 4x4 hire to visit Gheralta or Atsbi for around US$60 per day.

In order to see the interior of any of these churches properly, you need a torch or a candle. Don't forget to bring a torch, some food and water, and a stash of change for tips and church entrance fees! Readers are urged to resist the temptation to use flash photography on old paintings, as repeated exposure to a flash can damage them – in any event, the combination of ambient light and a tripod will generally produce far richer colours and more atmospheric results.

FURTHER INFORMATION

For further information, particularly regarding less frequently visited churches, the TTC offices in Mekele and Wukro are usually knowledgeable, enthusiastic and helpful. For contact details, see the *Wukro* and *Mekele* listings on pages 287 (this chapter) and 296 (*Chapter 11*) respectively. The TTC also stocks a detailed series of pamphlets about the churches, one dedicated to each of the main clusters. Note, however, that the 1:50,000 maps of the region compiled by the Ethiopian Map Authority are notoriously unreliable. The map in this book, though not definitive, is the most reliable in print.

THE ADIGRAT–WUKRO ROAD

The most accessible rock-hewn churches in Tigrai are the seven that lie within easy walking distance of the main road between Adigrat and Mekele. With a private vehicle, it would be possible to check out most of these churches over the course of a long day driving between Adigrat and Mekele. Even on public transport you could probably see most of them over two days, spending a night *en route* at Freweyni/Sinkata, Negash or Wukro, the main towns along this road.

Four of the churches along this road are clustered within about 2km of each other east of Teka Tesfai: the 'new' and 'old' Petros and Paulos Melehayzenghi, Mikael Melehayzenghi and Medhane Alem Adi Kasho. The last of these churches is regarded to be the oldest and one of the finest churches in Tigrai by some authorities, and the whole cluster makes for such a rewarding half-day walking excursion that it is worth looking at even if you visit no other church in the region. Two further churches, Gebriel Tsilalmao and Adi Chewa, lie to the north of Teka Tesfai, about 20 minutes' walk from the main road. Both are isolated from other rock-hewn churches, and are less attractive to travellers with limited time than the Teka Tesfai cluster. The last of the seven churches is Wukro Chirkos, which lies on the outskirts of the town of Wukro, and is covered under *Wukro* on page 287.

IDAGA HAMUS This is an unremarkable small town straddling the main Mekele road roughly 20km south of Adigrat. About 1km south of town, 100m east of the main road and visible from it, is what appears to be an abandoned and partially collapsed rock-hewn church. It's not the most riveting example of the architectural style, it has to be said, but on the other hand there is no charge for taking a quick poke around. The **Behre Negash Hotel** (*15 rooms;* ✆ *034 773 0210*) on the main junction in Idaga Hamus looks a more appealing prospect than any other hotel between Adigrat and Wukro with common shower rooms, costing US$3. If you stay, ask to use the separate *faranji* bathroom, which has a Western toilet and is marginally cleaner. Cold drinks and basic dishes such as eggs and pasta are available. Note, too, that the 6th-century monastery of Gunda Gundo Maryam, signposted blithely to the left as you enter town from the Adigrat side, is actually the best part of half a day's travelling distance away in either direction, first by road, then by muleback or on foot!

GEBRIEL TSILALMAO The most northerly extant church close to the main Adigrat–Mekele road is Gebriel Tsilalmao, which lies about 3km north of the small village of Mai Megelta. It is a reasonably large church of unknown antiquity, supported by unusually thick cruciform columns with double-bracket capitals covered in recent-looking paintings – when I asked the priest whether the artwork was new or restored, the priest said simply that it had always been there! Other notable features include the neatly cut arches, the engraved roofs of the six bays, two windows cut in Axumite style, an entrance with a built-up porch, and a large room in the back bisected by a column. A pair of evidently disused hermit cells is carved into the outer wall.

To reach Gebriel Tsilalmao, look out for the clearly signposted turn-off to the east roughly 8km south of Idaga Hamus or 8km north of Freweyni/Sinkata. Follow this track eastward for 2km, crossing a seasonal area of marsh, into a narrow gorge ringed by steep wooded hills. The church lies immediately to your right, less than five minutes' walk up a staircase. The priest lives about 30 minutes' walk away, and if he isn't around when you arrive, you might have to wait for somebody to fetch him. You can distract yourself by exploring the riparian woodland around the church and permanent marsh patch on the opposite side of the gorge; the trees harbour grivet monkeys, squirrels and numerous birds (look out for the gorgeous white-cheeked turaco), while Rouget's rail appears to be resident in the marsh.

FREWEYNI/SINKATA AND ADI CHEWA ARBUTA INSESA Situated 36km south of Adigrat at the junction of the Mekele road and the side road to Hawzien (see *Hawzien and the Gheralta*, page 280), Freweyni/Sinkata is a quietly attractive village of stone houses, looked over by sandstone cliffs to the east, and offering stunning views over the Gheralta Plains. There's plenty of transport through Freweyni/Sinkata along the main road, but transport to Hawzien is erratic and might leave at any time – or not at all! There are a few basic hotels in Freweyni/Sinkata charging a standard birr 6 for a room. The **Walwalo Hotel** (*7 rooms*), one block from the main road, looks about the best option with passably clean rooms using a common shower for US$2.50. A small restaurant is attached serving dishes in the US$2–5 range.

Immediately east of Freweyni/Sinkata, the rock-hewn church of **Arbuta Insesa** (The Four Animals) at **Adi Chewa** can easily be reached on foot or by vehicle from the village. This is a large church with several unusual features, most notably a domed ceiling almost 5m in height (the deepest of its kind in any Tigraian church) and strange red-and-yellow stencil-like figures on the thick columns. There are also more typical paintings in the church. To get to the Arbuta Insesa by road, follow the Mekele road south of town for about 500m, then turn left onto a side road directly opposite the signpost for 'World Vision Ethiopia'. After 800m, you'll hit a T-junction where you need to turn right, from where it's another 1km to the base of the cliff. The church lies about 20m up the cliff face, and it can be reached in less than five minutes along a moderately steep footpath. If you are walking from Freweyni/Sinkata, you could cut through the village and walk directly across the fields to the church in 20 minutes – the whitewashed exterior and bright green door will be clearly visible as soon as you've crossed the first rise at the edge of the village.

THE TEKA TESFAI CLUSTER

Also known as Tsaeda Imba, this is the most accessible cluster of churches in Tigrai, sited only 2km east of the main Adigrat–Mekele road. There is no accommodation in the immediate vicinity, though rooms are available in nearby Freweyni/Sinkata and Negash. The cluster is easily visited as a day trip from either Adigrat or Wukro on public transport, and could be covered as a day trip from Mekele in a private vehicle. It consists of three old churches and one new one, each very different and all within 2km of each other.

The finest of the Teka Tesfai churches is **Medhane Alem Adi Kasho**, described by Ruth Plant as 'one of the truly great churches of the Tigrai'. It is, I think, most impressive for its size and complex architecture. The imposing exterior is cut free from the rock behind, with four columns in front and two large doors, and it is covered in recent but very attractive paintings. The interior has a cathedral-like atmosphere, and the magnificent roof is dense with patterned etchings. Although experts regard Medhane Alem to be less perfectly executed than the churches of Wukro Chirkos and Abreha and Atsbeha, I felt that, along with Mikael Imba, it is the most atmospheric of the Tigraian churches east of Gheralta. For photographers, the airy front cloister offers excellent possibilities for moody interior shots, while the west-facing exterior is ideal for late afternoon light. Note that the priest here usually asks an entrance fee of US$6, and is not open to amiable negotiation.

Medhane Alem is quite possibly the oldest rock-hewn church in Tigrai, or anywhere in Ethiopia. Writing in the late 1960s, David Buxton noted that Medhane Alem is 'the only church I know that can be placed with confidence in the earliest category of rock-churches'. Buxton regarded it to combine 'all the features to be expected in a very early Ethiopian church and not a single one that could point to a later date'. Unsurprisingly, one local tradition links the excavation of the church to the time of Abreha and Atsbeha. Rather less expected is a tradition claiming it to be the work of Jesus Christ himself – echoing (or pre-empting) a tradition at Lalibela's Beta Giyorgis, it is said that the holes in the rock path leading to the church were made by Christ's horse. On somewhat firmer academic ground, Buxton regarded Medhane Alem to most likely date to the late 10th or early 11th century, and thought that it formed the Zagwe dynasty's 'earliest-known attempt to copy a Debra-Damo-type church in solid rock'.

Very different in style, **Petros and Paulos Melehayzenghi** lies halfway up a cliff, and it is visible from the main road. Petros and Paulos isn't truly rock-hewn, as only the sanctuary lies within the rock – the rest of the church has been built out onto a ledge. It does, however, boast some fascinatingly primitive paintings of angels and saints, which can be seen clearly because the church has fallen into disuse and the damaged roof lets in a fair amount of light. Reaching the church involves a vertiginous ascent up footholds; this rather tested my not-too-good head for heights, but it is not really dangerous if taken slowly and carefully. The view from the ledge, deep into the heart of Gheralta, is superb. Entrance to the church used to be free, and should really still be since it is disused, but an official entrance fee of US$6 is now required. It is to be hoped that some of this money will be used to help preserve the paintings, which have faded dramatically as a result of exposure over the past decade.

The original church of Petros and Paulos Melehayzenghi was evidently still in use in the late 1960s, when Ivy Pearce met the priests and was shown 'a large number of very interesting books and manuscripts', as it was a few years later when Paul Henze visited. At some point in the interim, the *tabot* has been moved to the **new Church of Petros and Paulos**, which is carved into the base of the ledge. This church, carved between 1982 and 1996, is the work of Halefom Retta, who claimed to have received instruction from the Archangel Gabriel (when I asked him what motivated him to build the new church, he said that the old one was too difficult for women to reach!). Sadly, the engaging Ato Halefom passed away in early 2005 – and frankly, without his enthusiastic presence, the additional fee of US$3 seems steep for a church of no historical interest and little aesthetic merit.

The last of the Teka Tesfai churches is **Mikael Melehayzenghi**, which lies within a domed rock outcrop between Medhane Alem and Petros and Paulos. Very different in execution from any other rock-hewn church I've seen in Ethiopia, Mikael Melehayzenghi is entered via a low doorway, which gives way to a surprisingly large interior with a finely carved dome almost 3m in height. This church is said locally to date to the 8th century, though the southern third was added in the 19th century. A notable decoration is a vivid painting of unknown antiquity that depicts Christ saving Adam and Eve from (or possibly abandoning them to) a pair of ferocious dragon-like creatures at the Last Judgement. The official entrance fee is US$6 per person.

Getting there and away The Teka Tesfai cluster is located to the east of the main Adigrat–Wukro road, roughly 10km south of Freweyni/Sinkata and a similar distance north of Negash.

From the main road, there are two different turn-offs, which lead to the cluster. If your goal is Petros and Paulos or Mikael Melehayzenghi, you should take the signposted turn-off located 200m south of the village of Dinglet. If your goal is Medhane Alem Adi Kasho, there is another signposted turn-off 4km further south (6km north of Negash). On foot, all three churches can be reached from either turn-off; if you plan to visit all three, it may be easiest to do a loop as described below.

If you are using public transport, ask to be dropped off at Dinglet. To visit the churches you will need to take a local guide, most helpful in locating the priests who keep the church keys, and to avoid getting more involved than necessary with the rather avaricious family that lives at the base of Petros and Paulos.

From the Petros and Paulos signpost, you can follow any of several footpaths across the fields towards the cliffs to the east of the road. You'll soon see Petros and Paulos Melehayzenghi halfway up the cliff, and can walk there from the road in 20–30 minutes. From Petros and Paulos, it's a 20-minute walk southward across relatively flat fields to the prominent euphorbia-studded rock outcrop that houses Mikael Melehayzenghi. Medhane Alem can be reached from Mikael by continuing southwards towards a low rocky hill until you come to a rough semi-motorable track, where you want to cut to your left, over the low hill, to a second, larger hill covered in olive and juniper trees. The track takes you to the base of the second hill. From there, it's a steepish hike along a clear footpath to the top of the hill. The church lies just below the rise, in a grove of olive trees.

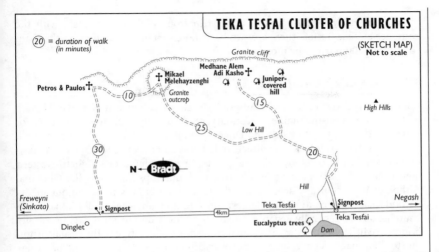

TEKA TESFAI CLUSTER OF CHURCHES

(20) = duration of walk
(in minutes)

(SKETCH MAP)
Not to scale

Granite cliff

Medhane Alem
Adi Kasho †

Mikael
Melehayzenghi †

Juniper-
covered
hill

Petros & Paulos †

Granite
outcrop

(10)

(15)

High Hills

(25)

Low Hill

(30)

N — **Bradt**

(20)

Hill

Freweyni
(Sinkata)

Signpost

4km

Teka Tesfai

Signpost

Negash

Teka Tesfai

Dinglet

Eucalyptus trees

Dam

Once you've seen Medhane Alem you can return the way you came, but you might prefer to take a short cut (about 40 minutes as opposed to one hour). This involves following the motorable track back to the low hill, where you should take the left fork, and basically follow it straight ahead for ten to 15 minutes until you come to a marshy area and stream. Follow the footpath that runs roughly parallel to the stream until, after about ten minutes, you cross a rocky ridge. The main road is clearly visible from here, as is the dam on the opposite side of it. You shouldn't have a problem picking up a lift from here to Wukro or Freweyni/Sinkata.

With private transport, you can drive right to the base of Petros and Paulos, and to within about 300m of Mikael Melehayzenghi. The motorable track from Mikael Melehayzenghi to Adi Kasho has deteriorated in recent years, so that even with a private vehicle, you'll need to walk there. This takes about 30 minutes, and is reasonably flat except for a final scramble up a 45° rock face. If Medhane Alem Adi Kasho is your only goal, then you can approach from the southern turn-off where a 6km drive will put you within a ten-minute walk of the church.

NEGASH Something of an anomaly in the heart of Ethiopia's main concentration of rock-hewn churches is the small hilltop village of Negash, which straddles the main Adigrat–Mekele road about 10km south of Teka Tesfai and 10km north of Wukro. Negash was the site of the first Muslim settlement in Ethiopia, granted to more than 100 early Islamic refugees (including Muhammad's daughter Rukiya and his future wives Uma Habiba and Uma Salama) by the Axumite Emperor Asihima in AD615. The name of the town is an Arabic corruption of the Ethiopian *negus* (emperor or king), and may simply have been chosen as a token of thanks by the Muslim refugees. There is, however, an obscure, probably untrue, but nevertheless persistent Muslim tradition that Negus Asihima converted to Islam under the influence of Muhammad, and there is some reason to think he was buried at Negash after his death in AD630.

Ancient Negash may be, and sacred too – some Ethiopian Muslims regard it as the most holy Islamic town after Mecca – but the town has little to show for it today. The large modern mosque, reputedly built on the site of the 7th-century original, is the target of an annual pilgrimage and festival, but it's nothing to look at – a US$1.50 fee is charged if you want to go inside. More interesting, assuming that you can find it, is the elusive 7th-century Muslim graveyard that was recently discovered in the town.

You can easily visit Negash as a day trip from Wukro, in tandem with the churches at Teka Tesfai. There are two basic hotels facing each other on the main road about 100m from the mosque.

HAWZIEN AND THE GHERALTA

Looping to the west of the main Adigrat–Mekele road, between Freweyni/Sinkata and Wukro, a well-maintained secondary road runs through the small town of Hawzien, the villages of Megab and Dugem, and the church of Abreha we Atsbeha. More than twice as long as the direct route between Freweyni/Sinkata and Wukro (72km as opposed to 30km), this road passes through a fantastic spaghetti-western landscape of flat dry plains and towering rock outcrops known as the Gheralta. Although it is scenically spectacular, the Gheralta region is most famous for its 35-odd rock-hewn churches, the largest concentration anywhere in Ethiopia. These churches aren't generally regarded to be the oldest or the most architecturally impressive in Tigrai, but they are probably the most captivating to the casual visitor, due to their magnificent setting, atmospheric interiors, and wealth of old paintings and church treasures.

Exploring the Gheralta region is not quite as straightforward as visiting the churches along the main Adigrat–Mekele road. For a start, the region's finest churches are situated in high isolation on the outcrops of the Gheralta ridge. This means that a relatively strenuous ascent is involved in getting to see any given church, and that only the fittest of travellers will be in a position to consider visiting more than two such churches in the course of one day. That said, with a private vehicle, a Tigrigna-speaking guide and a reasonable level of fitness, the Gheralta churches are as accessible as anywhere else in Ethiopia.

Independent travel in Gheralta is to some extent restricted by the limited amount of public transport. This problem, by no means insurmountable, is addressed in further detail below, but it's worth noting upfront that Gheralta will almost certainly prove frustrating to independent travellers who aren't prepared to approach transportation with a degree of flexibility. On the other hand, Gheralta is practically custom-made for any traveller who is attracted to the prospect of heading off the beaten track into an area as rich scenically as it is culturally.

GETTING AROUND Hawzien is most easily reached along a well-maintained 23km-long side road that branches west from the main Adigrat–Mekele road at Freweyni/Sinkata. The roughly 50km-long road between Hawzien and Wukro through Gheralta is also in a good state of repair, and since all the major Gheralta churches lie within 20km of Hawzien by road, they can easily be explored in a private vehicle using Hawzien as a base. Another possible base for exploring Gheralta with a private vehicle is Wukro, which lies about 30km from Dugem and 40km from Megab, the two villages closest to the best churches. Any one church in the Gheralta could be driven to as a day trip from Adigrat or Mekele, or even *en route* between these towns. Given that the walk to most of the more important churches takes 30–60 minutes in either direction it would be unrealistic to attempt to see more than one or maybe two churches in this way.

For travellers dependent on public transport, a few light vehicles and trucks run along the Freweyni/Sinkata–Hawzien road daily. Traffic is heaviest on a Wednesday, the main market day both in Hawzien and in the villages of Gheralta, but this is also when the priests are most likely to be on walkabout. A daily bus service connecting Hawzien to Mekele via Megab, Dugem and Wukro departs at around 06.00 in either direction and will drop you off anywhere *en route*, though you may have to pay full fare. With a few days available, it would be more than possible to walk from Hawzien to Megab and Dugem, the closest villages to the more interesting churches. Megab lies only 8km from Hawzien by road, and Dugem another 10km towards Wukro; basic rooms are available in both villages, and camping is permitted. If walking doesn't appeal, you could explore the possibility of hiring a bicycle, mule or horse-drawn *gari* out of Hawzien. If you are thinking of hiring a 4x4 vehicle to visit one or two of the Gheralta churches as a day trip, expect to pay around US$65 for a full day. A vehicle is more easily hired in Wukro than in Hawzien, with the advantage that you could stop at Abreha we Atsbeha church *en route* (see page 290).

A little-used alternative route to Hawzien and the Gheralta leads from Adwa via Nebelet, the closest town to the remote rock-hewn church of Maryam Wukro. Although the road is rough in parts and requires a 4x4, especially the stretch between Hawzien and Nebelet, you could probably drive between Axum and Hawzien in about five to six hours using this route, adding another two hours for the excursion to Maryam Wukro.

HAWZIEN The small town of Hawzien lies 23km from the Adigrat–Mekele road, and is reached by a side road that branches westward at Freweyni/Sinkata. Hawzien is of greatest interest as the gateway to the Gheralta region, but it is also of some historical interest in its own right. The town, which appears on the oldest-known maps of Tigrai, was reputedly founded by the Sadqan – 'the Righteous Ones' – a group of zealous Christian exiles said to have been as numerous 'as the army of a king' and to have subsisted on grass only. The Sadqan fled the worldly Roman Church in the late 5th century to preach their ascetic 'heresies' to Ethiopians. Legend has it that the Sadqan were persecuted by local animist tribes and, despite the protective efforts of King Kaleb of Axum, they were eventually massacred. Heaps of bones believed to date from this genocide are preserved at several sites associated with the Sadqan.

In 1988, Hawzien was the target of one of the most vicious public excesses of the Mengistu regime, when its marketplace was bombed from the air. An estimated 2,500 people died in this tragic and apparently unprovoked civilian massacre. The walls of several buildings destroyed in the bombing still stand on the outskirts of town, along the footpath to Tekle Haymanot church. In the marketplace, four ancient stelae – judging by appearance, of similar vintage to the so-called Gudit stelae outside Axum – were knocked over by the bombing. The stelae are still intact, however, and a couple of them have been re-erected.

Also of interest in Hawzien is the **Church of Hawzien Tekle Haymanot**, which lies about five minutes' walk from the town centre in a wooded grove next to a river. The modern built-up church encloses a small rock-hewn church, thought to be one of the oldest in Tigrai based on the finely carved capital and columns, which according to Ruth Plant, bears a strong resemblance to the original throne in Axum. If local traditions are to be believed, this church might well have started life as a partially hewn temple in pre-Christian times. Unfortunately, the rock-hewn section now forms the sanctuary, and is thus off-limits to lay visitors. I was allowed to peek into the sanctuary through the door, and the priest was kind enough to light it up for my benefit, but on the whole the experience seemed a relatively underwhelming return for the birr 50 investment.

Details of reaching Hawzien are given under the heading *Getting around*, opposite.

Where to stay and eat At the time of writing a new multi-storey hotel located next door to the police office was near completion. When open the garishly orange-coloured hotel with its shiny blue windows will undoubtedly provide the best accommodation in Hawzien.

⌂ **Adulis Hotel** (26 rooms) ✆ 034 667 0385; m 0914 701 093. This recently extended hotel next to the Commercial Bank of Ethiopia currently offers the best place to stay in town. The new rooms on the 1st floor are all spacious with tiled floors, private en-suite & hot-water shower (rooms with bathtubs are more expensive), while the older ground-floor rooms are somewhat scruffier & have a common shower. No restaurant or bar is attached. *US$6/9 sgl/ dbl with common shower, US$9/12 sgl/dbl en suite.*

⌂ **Tourist Hotel** (10 rooms) ✆ 034 667 0238. Located next to the Adulis, this place has compact en-suite rooms with tiled floors, ¾ beds & hot water, though is not exactly a bargain in comparison with its neighbour. The thatched roof bar in the large green courtyard serves beers & other cold drinks & a restaurant is planned. *US$11/14 sgl/dbl.*

MEGAB AND NEARBY CHURCHES The small village of Megab lies at the base of the northern tip of the Gheralta Mountains, precisely 8km from Hawzien along a gently undulating dirt road. The drive from Hawzien takes 15–20 minutes, and you could walk it in less than two hours, with the only significant slopes occurring over the 1–2km after you leave Hawzien. In addition to having a superlative setting below a row of dramatic rock outcrops, Megab lies within easy walking distance of a clutch of wonderful rock-hewn churches, described below. It is also here at the **Gheralta Guides Association** (m *0914 263 799;* ⊕ *08.00–17.30 daily*) thate you need to arrange an official guide to visit the churches. The office is located on the left-hand side of the road coming from Hawzien just before the junction for Abuna Yemata Guh. The Werkanash family run a small informal and unsignposted **guesthouse**, opposite the guides association; it has four basic single rooms at US$4 apiece, bucket showers are available, and the attached restaurant can prepare local dishes and pasta. It's also possible to pitch a tent in a new campsite located around 2.5km from Megab in the shadow of Debre Maryam Korkor (see the section *Debre Maryam Korkor* on page 284 for details).

Abuna Yemata Guh The most compelling church in the Megab area – indeed, probably the most spectacularly situated rock-hewn church anywhere in Ethiopia – is Abuna Yemata Guh. This small but very beautiful church has been carved into the top of one of the tall perpendicular rock pillars that dominate Megab's southwestern horizon. The interior of the church, reached via a small crack in the rock, is notable for its extensive and perfectly preserved wall and roof murals, thought to date from the 15th century and regarded by Ruth Plant as 'the most sophisticated paintings found so far in Tigrai'. Nine of the Apostles are depicted in a circle in one of the roof domes, while the nine Syrian monks are depicted in the other. The wall paintings include one of the remaining three Apostles, as well as a large frieze of the church's namesake, Abuna Yemata, on horseback. There are stunning views from the narrow ledge that leads to the church, looking over a sheer drop of roughly 200m. To get to Abuna Yemata Guh from Megab, you must first follow the signposted track that forks southwest from the Dugem road next to the Fitsum Bar. The footpath to the church lies about 3.5km along this track: a flat 45 minutes for pedestrians, or ten minutes in a vehicle. Having located the priest, the hike up to the church takes 40–60 minutes, climbing roughly 500m in altitude.

The last part of the ascent to Abuna Yemata Guh involves clambering up a sheer cliff face using handgrips and footholds. It is probably not dangerous provided that you are reasonably fit and agile, and have a good head for heights.

The little-used 110km back route that connects Hawzien to Adwa via the hamlets of Nebelet and Edaga Arbi is of potential interest to travellers for two reasons: first, is as a rough but relatively direct route to the Gheralta churches from Axum, it can be covered in about half the time it takes to traverse the more normal (and less bumpy) road via Adigrat; second, to visit what must rank as one of the most remote of the major Tigraian churches, Maryam Wukro, situated to the north of Nebelet, some 37km from Hawzien (about two hours' drive in either direction if you are thinking of doing it as a round trip).

Starting from Hawzien, the hilly 30km road to Nebelet is in poor shape, with some stretches that are rough and rocky, and others that are deep with sand, so you're unlikely to get through in less than 90 minutes, longer after rain, though this will change once proposed roadworks are completed. Nebelet itself is a typical small Tigraian village of neat sandstone houses, set in spectacular isolation below a tall rock outcrop reminiscent of Gheralta. There's no accommodation in town, nor does there seem to be any public transport in either direction, but a few small shops sell basic local food and water-cooled drinks. The 7km track from Nebelet to Maryam Wukro is unambiguously 4x4 territory and not always easy to follow. It takes around 30 minutes to traverse, ideally having picked up somebody in Nebelet to act as a guide. On the plus side, you can drive to within 10m of the church compound, the priest with the key lives very nearby.

It is odd to think that this remote church, with its unflattering exterior, was one of the first Tigraian rock-hewn edifices to be visited by a foreigner (Professor Mordini in 1939). Maryam Wukro was subsequently described by Ruth Plant as 'a great example of Tigraian architecture' and by David Buxton as 'the most elaborate and even fantastic cliff church I know'. As with Mikael Debre Selam near Atsbi, Maryam Wukro combines elements of rock-hewn and built-up Axumite architecture, though the rock-hewn part of the church is much larger and airier, with a 10m-high interior in parts, and comprising three aisles and bays. Notable features include an unsupported double arch, several thick pillars, ancient rock etchings and more modern paintings. The church is said to have been excavated by angels during the reign of Abreha and Atsbeha, who were regular visitors, and there is also a niche in the back where Maryam herself sometimes comes to pray and weep. Reached via a wooden ladder, a more crudely hewn chapel, Wukro Giyorgis, is carved into the cliff face above Maryam and has a few floor-level openings looking into the larger church. David Buxton indicated that this church might have been modelled on the Axumite church at Debre Damo, and had some influence on the architecture of the cliff churches in Lalibela.

If you are continuing on towards Axum, it's 33km by road from Nebelet to Edaga Arbi, a small town set below the ancient hilltop monastery of Abuna Tsama. A little-known site of interest in this area, only 15km from town but so far as I can ascertain inaccessible by road, is a field of some 140 Axumite stelae at Henzat. There's plenty of public transport from Edaga Arbi through to Adwa, then on to Axum, following a good 12km dirt road that intersects with the Abi Aday road some 32km south of Adwa and 8km north of Mai Kenetal. In a private vehicle, expect the drive from Edaga Arbi to Axum to take about 90 minutes.

GHERALTA LODGE

(*16 rooms;* ☎ *034 667 0344, in Addis* ☎ *011 554 5489;* f *011 554 0023;* e *info@ gheraltalodgetigrai.com; www.gheraltalodgetigrai.com*) This lovely family-style resort, 1.5km from the centre of Hawzien along the Megab road, does everything right. For starters, the location is fantastic. The lodge features panoramic views of the stunning rock formation after which it is named. The grounds and gardens are immaculate, while the buildings feature traditional stacked-rock construction, which blends effortlessly with the environment. Rooms are simply but tastefully decorated, and the freshly prepared meals are delicious. Yet what truly makes the lodge stand apart is the world-class hospitality of owners Enrica and Silvio Rizzotti. Guests are made to feel at home, beginning with complimentary cocktails and conversation upon the night of your arrival. This is followed by a five-course meal prepared from local ingredients, with an Italian touch thrown in. Set lunch/dinner menus cost US$6/7.50 and picnic lunches are available for US$6 per person. Activities include hikes around the property as well as visits to the surrounding churches. English- and Italian-speaking guides are available. Car hire can also be arranged for day trips for US$65–95 per day. Three types of rooms are available: smaller square bungalows for one person; larger, round bungalows with two full beds for one or two persons; and a 'Farmer's House' with three single beds. Rates include breakfast and are very reasonable. Discounts are available for organisations. Airport pick-up is available from both Axum and Mekele. For more details visit their website. *Sgl rooms US$21/29.50/32.50 low/ medium/high season; bungalows US$29.50/47.50/53 low/medium/high season sgl occupancy, US$41.50/59/65 low/medium/high season dbl occupancy; trpl rooms US$53/71/77 low/medium/high season.*

But it should emphatically not be attempted by anybody who has doubts about their agility, or who has even the mildest tendency towards vertigo – were you to panic or freeze on this face, you would be in serious trouble indeed. And if you do decide to abstain, you will be in good company. Ivy Pearce, the first *faranji* to visit several of the Tigraian rock-hewn churches, wrote of the ascent to Guh that: 'I came face to face with a cliff face with only footholds and handgrips at irregular intervals. The climb I could not manage as my arms were not long enough [and] the handgrips too wide to grasp firmly. I didn't want to take risks, so gave it up and sat on a small ledge below.'

Abuna Gebre Mikael Situated on the Koraro Escarpment about 15km southwest of Guh, the little-visited church of Abuna Gebre Mikael, reputedly carved by its namesake in the 4th century, is regarded to be one of the finest in the Gheralta. Set in the base of a 20m-high cliff, the church has an unusually ornate carved exterior, and a large cruciform interior supported by eight columns. Both the columns and the neatly hewn ceiling cupolas are decorated with brightly coloured paintings lit by four windows and an imposing wooden doorway. The steep walk to the church takes about 45 minutes and involves some clambering and jumping between rocks, though nothing as dodgy as the ascent of Abuna Yemata Guh.

Debre Maryam Korkor This monastic church is set on a small plateau atop a sheer-sided 2,480m-high mountain a short distance southeast of Guh. The built-up façade, recently painted bright green, is rather off-putting, but the interior is very atmospheric and large, almost 10m wide, 17m deep and 6m high. Architectural features include 12 cruciform pillars with bracket capitals, and seven arches stylistically reminiscent of those at Abreha we Atsbeha. Predictably, local tradition links the excavation of Debre Maryam Korkor with the twin emperors (Buxton placed it in the early series of Tigraian Basilica churches, carved after those at Lalibela). The fine artwork on the walls and columns is said locally to date from the 13th century. Ivy Pearce and Ruth Plant both felt that it was probably painted in the 17th century, citing a painting of the Virgin Mary with a circle around her abdomen (indicating the development of the foetal Jesus Christ) as typical of that era.

On the way up to Debre Maryam Korkor, the footpath passes a disused and partially collapsed rock-hewn church that is said to have served as a nunnery before the monastery attached to the church was founded, probably during the reign of Zara Yaqob. Two or three minutes' walk from Debre Maryam Korkor, another rock-hewn church called Abba Daniel Korkor is set above a sheer precipice with stunning views over the surrounding plains. This church, which consists of only two small rooms, has also fallen into disuse. Lay visitors can therefore enter the former sanctuary, the walls of which are covered in old paintings. The entrance fee of US$6 covers both the extant church and the two disused ones.

The track to Debre Maryam Korkor is clearly signposted 2km from Megab on the southwest side of the Dugem road. The first 1km of this track, bordered by a hedge of euphorbia shrubs, is motorable. The priest with the key lives in the village at the end of the motorable track. Having located him, the hike to the church takes the best part of an hour. After crossing the fields to the base of the mountain, the footpath rises steeply through a natural rock passage (watch out for loose rocks underfoot), coming out at the abandoned nunnery. From here, you can use the shorter 'men's route', which involves scrambling up footholds and handgrips on a 60° rock face, or the slightly longer but less vertiginous 'women's route'.

It's now possible to stay nearby Debre Maryam at the **Hayle Korkor Campsite** (m *0910 455 135*) where you can pitch a tent on the grass for US$2. Facilities currently consist of a not-so-private bucket shower, but three new rooms and new amenities are planned. There is no restaurant as such, but simple meals can be arranged for US$2–3; coffee, cold drinks and fresh honey are also available. The campsite is located 300m along the dirt track to Debre Maryam Korkor.

DUGEM AND NEARBY CHURCHES

The village of Dugem straddles the road between Hawzien and Wukro, precisely 10km from Megab (two hours on foot along a very flat stretch of road), and a more undulating 14km from the church of Abreha we Atsbeha. Like Megab, Dugem has a scenic location at the base of the Gheralta Mountains. In addition to being the springboard for hikes to a number of interesting churches, Dugem boasts a small rock-hewn church of its own called Dugem Selassie, unusual in that it is situated on the plain rather than high in the mountains. Dugem Selassie is carved into a granite outcrop within the compound of the eponymous modern church, and there is a bath of holy water at its entrance. The small size of this church, together with features that Ruth Plant found reminiscent of King Kaleb's tomb in Axum, has led some experts to think it was originally carved as a tomb. It is possible to camp within the compound of Dugem Selassie. Otherwise, no formal accommodation exists in Dugem, though the friendly folk at the Andinet Snack Bar can roll out a mattress or two for a few birr if required.

Abuna Abraham Debre Tsion Few who visit Debre Tsion will disagree with Ruth Plant's estimation that it is 'one of the great churches of the Tigrai, both from the architectural and devotional aspect'. Debre Tsion is a monastic cliff church, carved into a rusty sandstone face high above the village of Dugem; it has an impressive and unusually ornate exterior, currently despoiled by the corrugated-iron shelters, designed to limit seepage, that cover the doors. Debre Tsion must have the largest ground plan of any rock-hewn church in the region. The main body of the church is itself fairly large, and consists of four bays with decorated domed roofs, supported by pillars and walls covered in murals of various Old Testament figures. Arcing behind the main church is a tall, deep rock-hewn passage, which leads to a decorated cell said to have been the personal prayer room of Abuna Abraham. Amongst the church's treasures is a beautiful 15th-century ceremonial fan, 1m in diameter, and comprising 34 individual panels, each painted with a figure of a saint. Although the priests will open it up for a small additional payment, the fan is starting to fray and tear in places, and it seems unlikely to survive much longer if it is regularly opened and closed.

Debre Tsion is named for Abuna Abraham, the monk who is said to have founded and excavated the church in the time of Abreha and Atsbeha. Experts believe the church to date from the 14th century or thereabouts. On the way up, the priest can show you a much smaller church that was hewn into an existing cave. Now disused, this is said to have been Abuna Abraham's first attempt at carving a church in the area. As with many other Ethiopian saints, Abraham was partial to demonstrating his faith through self-abuse: close to the old church lies a natural bed of jagged rocks on which the saint would writhe around while he prayed. Abuna Abraham is reputedly buried beneath the floor of Debre Tsion. There is a festival here on 21 Hidar (normally 30 November).

A motorable track to Debre Tsion is signposted to the southwest of the Wukro road 3.5km southeast of Dugem. You can drive the first 1km or so. From there you need to walk for about 20 minutes across flat fields to the back of the mountain. A steep but otherwise quite easy 30–40-minute hike brings you to the summit and the church – pausing, as is the convention, at the spot where Abuna Abraham is said to have stopped to pray whenever he climbed up. As with other churches that involve a long hike, it's important to locate the priest at the base. The standard US$6 entrance fee is charged.

Yohannis Maikudi Situated 2km southeast of Debre Tsion as the crow flies, Yohannis Maikudi has been described by David Buxton as 'the most interesting [church dedicated to Yohannis] I have seen, and memorable, too, for its means of access, which is a narrow cleft between bulging walls of bare, glaring sandstone'. Ivy Pearce felt that Yohannis Maikudi had a more 'reverent and holy atmosphere' than any other church she visited in the Tigrai. The 130m² rectangular church is notable architecturally for its Axumite doors, one of which is reserved for male worshippers, the other for females. The walls and roof are densely covered in primitive but evocative paintings of Old and New Testament scenes. These exceptionally well-preserved murals are thought to be at least 300 years old, and are very different in style from any other church paintings found in Gheralta. Dale Otto, a member of Ivy Pearce's expedition to Tigrai, thought that they displayed both Byzantine and Nubian influences.

Yohannis Maikudi can be visited on its own or in conjunction with nearby Debre Tsion. The walk, whether from Debre Tsion or from the end of the motorable track used to reach Debre Tsion, takes about one hour.

WUKRO AND SURROUNDS

The only sizeable town between Adigrat and Mekele, Wukro supports a permanent population of around 30,200, as well as a more transient military quota associated with its strategic importance in the wake of the border war with Eritrea – there's a large military base on the outskirts of town and soldiers are to be seen everywhere. With its relaxed if rather nondescript character, Wukro forms a convenient base from which to explore a number of rock-hewn churches. There is a major rock-hewn church on the outskirts of town, and the town is situated a mere 20km by road from the fine Teka Tesfai churches described previously. It also stands at the pivotal junction of the main Adigrat–Mekele road, the branch road east to the Atsbi churches and the Danakil Desert, and the branch road west to Hawzien via Abreha we Atsbeha and the Gheralta churches.

The well-run branch of the **Tigrai Tourist Commission** [289 C2] (⟨ 034 443 0340; e *tigrai.tourism@ethionet.et*; *www.tigraitourism.com*; ⊕ *08.00–17.00*), is clearly signposted on the Mekele side of town, on the opposite side of the main road to the bus station. The office stocks a good range of brochures and the guides who staff it are very knowledgeable about local attractions and helpful when it comes to arranging car hire and other activities. Sadly, Wukro's enormous potential as a tourist focus is not otherwise reflected by its amenities – particularly disappointing is a selection of hotels that are uniformly dire even by small-town Ethiopian standards, and in most cases exist purely to service a by-the-hour market amplified by the recent heightened military presence. Market day is Thursday.

GETTING THERE AND AWAY Wukro is an important junction town, connected by regular transport to Adigrat, Mekele and intermediate points. With an early start, you could easily stop off in Wukro just to see the church and still get between Adigrat and Mekele in a day. Heading east, a few 4x4 vehicles daily ply up and down the road between Wukro and Atsbi. Public transport between Wukro and Hawzien (via Abreha we Atsbeha, Megab and Dugem) is rather less frequent, but at least one bus daily passes through at around 09.00 *en route* from Mekele to Hawzien. There may be additional buses on Wednesday (market day in Gheralta).

WHERE TO STAY
Budget

Top View Guesthouse [289 D5] (9 rooms) ⟨034 443 1167; e topview_gh@peoplepc. com. Located on a hillside above the stadium, this impressive-looking establishment is hands-down the nicest place to stay in Wukro. 5 of the rooms are in a converted house surrounded by a pleasant courtyard. Rooms on the 1st floor are marginally more expensive than those on the ground floor. Though not en suite, each floor has a private bathroom with tub. For a few dollars more, an en-suite master bedroom is available – the tacky mauve & gold bathroom set alone is worth the extra expense! Out the back there is an additional block of 4 clean rooms with common cold shower. No food or drink is available, but there is a nice dining room if you bring your own

eats. Unfortunately the guesthouse was closed on our most recent visit, though a room should cost *US$12–13.50*.

Lwam Hotel [289 C1] (59 rooms) ⟨034 443 0042. Located directly opposite the NOC filling station, this new multi-storey hotel is an easy second choice, & may be preferable for travellers without a vehicle. Rooms are clean & neat, hot water is available & there's a good restaurant, internet café & pool house attached. *US$4 using common shower, US$10.50/11.50 sgl/dbl en suite.*

Lwam Pension [289 C2] (13 rooms) ⟨034 443 0126. Under the same ownership as the above this small pension located directly behind the Tigrai Tourist Commission office offers slightly older rooms of similar price & standard. *US$4 using common shower, US$10.50/11.50 sgl/dbl en suite.*

Shoestring

🏠 **Kalu Hotel** [289 C2] (15 rooms) **m** 0914 769 618. A notable step down from the budget places, but still a standout cheapie, this place offers reasonably clean en-suite rooms with hot-water shower as well as smaller rooms with common cold showers. The restaurant & café are both good. *US$3 using common shower, US$5/6 sgl/dbl en suite.*

🏠 **MS Pension** [289 C5] (14 rooms) ✆034 443 0284. This place, with its pleasant garden, doesn't serve food, but the common showers are hot. *US$3–4 using common shower.*

🏠 **Tekle Millennium Pension** [289 C3] (10 rooms) At the bottom end of the scale, this establishment offers cheap-&-no-so-cheerful smelly rooms with ¾ bed & common cold shower. *US$2.*

✖ **WHERE TO EAT** The restaurant at the new **Lwam Hotel** [289 C1] is the smartest place to eat with a clientele dominated by local businessmen and a reasonably varied menu including Ethiopian and European fare for around US$2–4, while the bar and restaurant at the **Kalu Hotel** [289 C2] serves tasty *tibs*, *kai wat* and other dishes in the US$2–3 range – meat is also available even during fasting periods.

The **Frye Selam Pastry Shop** [289 C5], situated on the main street at the Adigrat end of town, serves a welcome selection of pastries, cakes, coffee and fruit juices, as well as tasty fried eggs and mini pizzas. They also serve excellent *ful*, a breakfast dish made from beans. Just a few doors up, the popular **Zebib Pastry Shop** [289 C5] offers a similar range of treats.

Other places worth trying are the **Hill Top Snack Café** [289 C4] on the main circle opposite the war memorial and the new **Rubane Café** [289 C4], two blocks further south of the circle.

CHURCHES AROUND WUKRO In addition to Wukro Chirkos, which lies on the outskirts of town and is described below, Wukro makes a good base for day trips to any of the churches situated back along the Adigrat road, whether on public transport or in a private vehicle. Also described below is the important church of Abreha we Atsbeha, which lies about 17km from Wukro along the road to Gheralta and Hawzien, as well as Mikael Minda'e, 4km further along the same road. All the churches listed under the heading *Churches around Atsbi* (see page 291) form realistic goals for a day trip out of Wukro: Mikael Barka on public transport, the rest with a private vehicle only. With a private vehicle, the churches of Gheralta can also be explored from Wukro, though Hawzien and the Gheralta Lodge are closer bases.

Some 3km south of Wukro there is a new site known as **Queen Yodit's Royal Grave**. Still under excavation, no entrance fee has been set. A visit may be possible, but a permit would be required from the TTC as the site is not yet officially open to the public. This situation may change during the lifetime of this edition – it is a good idea to check at the tourist office in either Wukro or Mekele for updated information.

Wukro Chirkos [289 B7] Jutting out from a low cliff in mock-monolithic style, Wukro Chirkos lies about 500m out of town on a low hill east of the main road. The church is believed by locals to date from the 4th-century rule of Abreha and Atsbeha, but is thought by David Buxton to have been excavated at a later date than Adi Kasho Medhane Alem and perhaps a century before the churches of Lalibela. The lovely line drawings on the ceiling must date to the 15th century or earlier, since they were partially destroyed when the Muslim leader Ahmed Gragn burnt the church. The external roof and raised porch were added in 1958 due to seepage. The inside consists of a large domed reception area and three 'rooms'. My reactions to Chirkos when I first saw it back in 1994 must be tempered against the fact it was the first rock-hewn church I visited, but I was awe-struck by its size, and by

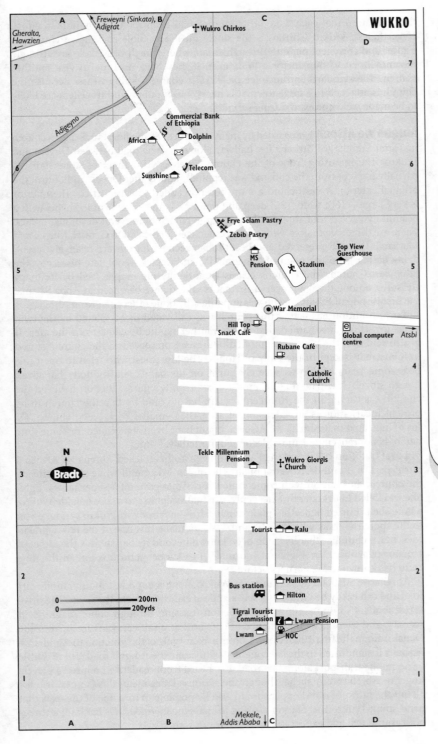

10

WUKRO

+ Wukro Chirkos

Freweyni (Sinkata),
Adigrat

Gheralta,
Hawzien

Adigeyno

Commercial Bank
of Ethiopia

Africa $
Dolphin

Telecom

Sunshine

★ Frye Selam Pastry
★ Zebib Pastry

MS
Pension

Stadium

Top View
Guesthouse

War Memorial

Hill Top
Snack Café

Global computer
centre

Atsbi

Rubane Café

+ Catholic
church

Tekle Millennium
Pension

+ Wukro Giorgis
Church

Tourist   Kalu

Mullibirhan

Bus station

Hilton

Tigrai Tourist
Commission

Lwam Pension

Lwam

NOC

N

Bradt

0 ———— 200m
0 ———— 200yds

Mekele,
Addis Ababa ↓

the realisation that each flake of its interior had been removed by human effort. Nevertheless, Wukro Chirkos is the single most accessible rock-hewn church in Tigrai, and travellers bussing through to anywhere north of Mekele are strongly recommended to pop in for a look, even if they have no time to visit another church. The standard entrance fee of US$6 is charged without fuss. Because the church is attached to a large town, it is nearly always open and travellers are likely to be made welcome even during services.

Abreha we Atsbeha Regarded by many experts to be the finest rock-hewn church in Tigrai, Abreha we Atsbeha lies halfway along the new road between Dugem and Wukro. The imposing front of the church, reached via a flight of stone stairs, is partially free-cut from the cliff and was reputedly added after Queen Yodit burnt the original exterior. It lies behind a more recently added Italian portico. The interior is very large – 16m wide, 13m deep and 6m high – and cruciform in shape, with a beautifully carved roof supported by 13 large pillars and several decorated arches. There are three sanctuaries, with *tabots* respectively dedicated to Gebriel, Mikael and Maryam. The well-preserved and beautifully executed murals are relatively recent, many dating from the reign of Yohannis IV, and depict a complete history of the Ethiopian Church. The church's claims to antiquity are emphasised by its many treasures, among them a prayer cross that is said to have belonged to Abba Salama, the first Bishop of Ethiopia, who was appointed by none other than King Abreha.

Local tradition has it that this church was excavated in AD335–40 by the twin kings for whom it is named, and whose mother reputedly came from the area. It is also said that the kings' mummified bodies are preserved in the church, stored in a box that is kept in the Holy of Holies. The last priest who tried to open this box, some years back, was severely burnt on his hands, and nobody has given it a go since! How true these claims are is anybody's guess. Buxton believed the church was carved in the 10th century AD, but it could be that the church in its present incarnation is an extension of an earlier, smaller rock-hewn church. Dr Josief indicated that Abreha we Atsbeha might have been abandoned for some time before being reoccupied and redecorated in medieval times.

Local tradition has it that the Falasha Queen Yodit attacked Abreha we Atsbeha, burnt part of it and destroyed a pillar. The queen became ill while she was inside the church, and ran off with some sacred rocks that gave off a supernatural light. She was killed hours later by a heavenly gale that swept her to a spot outside Wukro, where she is buried beneath a plain stone cairn – anybody in Wukro can take you to the spot. The links with Abreha and Atsbeha make this one of the few Tigraian rock-hewn churches that has long been known beyond its parish. It is the target of a major pilgrimage on 4 Tekemt (normally 14 October) and it is one of the nine churches known to Westerners before 1966.

Abreha we Atsbeha lies 17km from Wukro along a good but mountainous dirt road and can easily be visited as a self-standing excursion from the town. The drive takes about 45 minutes in either direction, passing through some magnificent scenery, and there is a good chance of encountering salt caravans fresh from the Danakil along the first 10km or so. Coming from Wukro, the junction to Abreha we Atsbeha is signposted to the left roughly 500m along the Adigrat road. There is little or no public transport along this road. I've heard from readers who hired a bicycle to get to Abreha we Atsbeha, though the serious slopes mean this is not a trip for all but the fittest of travellers. It should also be possible to hire one of the 4x4s that hang about Wukro Bus Station waiting for passengers to Atsbi – bank on a three-hour round trip and expect to pay US$15 or upwards.

Abreha we Atsbeha can also be visited as an extension of the Gheralta circuit, since it is situated only 14km from the village of Dugem. The Wukro–Dugem road runs almost past Abreha we Atsbeha, along a 500m side road leading through a small village which is apparently named for the church. Vehicles can be parked in an open area, from where a three-minute walk up a short but steep staircase leads to the church itself. There is no accommodation in the area.

Mikael Minda'e This relatively unknown church, perched on a low cliff about 200m north of the Wukro–Dugem road roughly 4km past Abreha we Atsbeha, is easily picked out owing to the whitewashed built-up exterior added in the year 2000. Architecturally, Mikael Minda'e isn't a particularly interesting representative of the genre – the interior is rather small, with large pillars but no noteworthy paintings or etchings – but it's an atmospheric church. We enjoyed our first visit as much as anything for the priests, who at the time were so unused to tourists that we actually had to explain to them about the entrance fee. The priests were in an amiable post-mass state of inebriation, and bounced around the church telling us tall stories in slurred Tigrigna, leaping in front of the camera at inappropriate moments, and offering us glasses of *tella*.

One of the priests – admittedly not the most sober among them – told us an interesting tradition relating to Mikael Minda'e. If I understood him correctly, the church was partially excavated by Abreha and Atsbeha before they went off to fight a war in which Abreha was killed. Atsbeha returned to the unfinished church carrying Abreha's body, with the intention of burying his brother there when it was completed. While Atsbeha was busy chiselling, however, a bird picked up Abreha's body and took it to a nearby cliff face. Atsbeha took this as a sign to start excavating a new church in which to bury his brother, at the place selected by the bird – now the church of Abreha we Atsbeha, 4km from Mikael Minda'e. Nowadays a US$3 entrance fee is charged.

ATSBI AND SURROUNDS

The town of Atsbi consists of a characteristically attractive Tigraian assemblage of traditional stone houses situated at an altitude of around 2,500m on a plateau some 25km east of Wukro. In addition to lying along the ancient salt caravan route and modern road between Wukro and the Danakil Desert, Atsbi lies at the epicentre of a loose cluster of important rock-hewn and Axumite churches. Marked on some maps as Inda Selassie, Atsbi is connected to Wukro by a good unsurfaced road (and reasonably regular public transport) offering some magnificent views as it ascends the plateau. Should you elect to spend the night in Atsbi, there are at least two indifferent dollar-a-night hotels to choose from. Realistically, however, motorised travellers who intend visiting some of the churches around Atsbi can easily do so using Wukro as a base, while travellers without a vehicle will need to be prepared for some serious hiking or trekking to see the more interesting churches in the area. The town is at its most colourful on market day, which is Saturday, and this is also when transport from Wukro is most regular. Unfortunately, however, Saturday is a bad day to visit churches in the Atsbi area, as the priests will in all probability be at the market. We were not asked for a permit at any of the Atsbi churches.

CHURCHES AROUND ATSBI
Mikael Barka The most accessible of the churches in this area is Mikael Barka, visible from the main road between Atsbi and Wukro. An uninspiring built-up portico, built in the 1960s and painted luminous green, gives little indication of

what lies inside. Mikael Barka is a cavernously gloomy but very atmospheric rock-hewn church, excavated in a cruciform shape, and decorated with numerous murals on the domed roof, and a large etched cross on one of the 12 columns. The priest told me that the church was founded during the 9th-century reign of Emperor Dil Ne'ad; other oral traditions associate Mikael Barka with Abuna Abraham, who was active in the 6th century, while David Buxton felt it probably post-dated the Lalibela churches. So no ambiguity about that, then! The scorching over the roof is linked by tradition with an attack by Queen Yodit in the 10th century.

Mikael Barka is signposted at the base of a small isolated hill precisely 18.5km from Wukro and 6km from Atsbi. The footpath that leads to the church is fairly steep, but not arduous, and the walk up takes no more than 15 minutes. This is one church that independent travellers can reach quite easily, using public transport between Wukro and Atsbi, though an early start is advised to be certain of finding transport back. It would also be possible to overnight in Atsbi and walk to and from the church. The family that lives in a stone house opposite the signpost to the church should know whether the priest is around. The standard US$6 entrance fee is charged.

Mikael Imba This superb three-quarter monolith, first reported to the outside world by Beatrice Payne in 1948, boasts what is probably the most impressive exterior of any rock-hewn church in Tigrai. Outwardly, the west-facing façade of Mikael Imba looks more like a transplant from Lalibela than it resembles any other Tigraian church (photographers should visit the church in the afternoon when the façade catches the sun). The monks here predictably claim that Mikael Imba dates from the rule of Abreha and Atsbeha, while David Buxton regarded it to be an 11th- or 12th-century excavation. Either way, Mikael Imba must have been the closest thing to a true monolith in existence at the time it was excavated, and it seems likely to have served as a model for the style of rock-hewn church now associated with Lalibela and surrounds. The vast interior is magnificent, and unusually well lit owing to the large frontal windows. A total of 25 pillars support the 6m-high ceiling, and although modestly decorated by comparison with the Gheralta churches, the precision of the workmanship is such that it looks as if it was excavated yesterday. Notable features include a large Greek cross hewn into the ceiling, the decorated wooden doors, and a treasure house containing an ancient metal cross and several old manuscripts. There is a pool containing holy water outside the church.

Mikael Imba is situated at an altitude of 2,329m on an *amba* (flat-topped hill) some 15km south of Atsbi along a rough and occasionally unclear dirt track (a local guide might be useful). The last 1km of the track is very rough, so even with a 4x4 it would be advisable to walk this stretch, which passes through a memorable landscape of glowing sandstone cliffs, patches of juniper and euphorbia trees, and layered mountains receding to the horizon. From the base of the hill, the steep ascent takes about ten minutes, and involves using safe footholds on one short stretch, as well as climbing up an old but solid wooden ladder to the summit.

If you do not plan to visit the other Atsbi churches, a more direct route to Mikael Imba is possible. Instead of turning off in Wukro, take the main Mekele road 11km south to the small town of Agula. Here a dirt road leads off to the right. After 8km this road branches at the small village of Birke, with one branch heading towards the Danakil border town of Berahile (see page 303), and the other continuing on towards Mikael Imba. Taking the Mikael Imba branch, you will come to a second village called Haike Mesal, a distance of 10km from Birke. From Haike Mesal it is another 15km to the church. If you have not already done so, it is recommended that you pick up a guide here; the route is not at all clear, and there may be a short cut once a new bridge has been completed.

When we visited Mikael Imba the 'treasurer' charged us the then standard birr 20 fee, and did not ask to see a permit, but he was neither co-operative nor friendly, and admitted that he didn't like tourists visiting the monastery. Whether this attitude extends to the normal priest, I cannot say, but it marred what was otherwise a highlight of our time in the region.

Mikael Debre Selam Photographed in 1966 by Georg Gerster, the first *faranji* to visit it, Mikael Debre Selam is unusual if not unique in combining a fine rock-hewn church with the Axumite sandwich architectural style associated with the monastery of Yemrehanna Kristos near Lalibela. Described by Ivy Pearce as an 'extraordinary ... church within a church', Debre Selam outwardly consists of a built-up cave church, protected within a relatively modern whitewashed portico. The church was built using alternating layers of whitewashed stone and wood, the latter decorated with geometric patterns, while one of the wooden window shutters is decorated with a very old cloth painting of the Virgin Mary and Child. The rock-hewn part of the church, which includes the sanctuary, is small and rather gloomy due to a lack of exterior windows, but the precise execution of the carved arches and pillars echoes the skilled workmanship of Mikael Imba. A sealed cave in the cliff above the church is said locally to be the tomb of the 6th-century Emperor Gebre Meskel, during whose reign the church was reputedly constructed. While certain archaic features superficially support this local tradition, academic opinion is that Debre Selam post-dates the Lalibela churches.

Mikael Debre Selam is situated at an altitude of 2,670m, high on a cliff face about 7km north of Atsbi town as the crow flies. To get there, follow the main road north out of town, which soon deteriorates to become an occasionally unclear track suitable for 4x4 only. After about 5km, a signpost to the left points along the track to the church. This track is motorable until you reach the Hidar River, after another 3km. The white portico of the church is clearly visible for some distance before you reach the river. Although there is a potentially fordable track across the Hidar, it should probably only be attempted when the water is very low. A safer bet is to leave your car here and wade through the chilly river on foot. Having crossed the river, the walk to the church takes about 30 minutes along a steepish footpath offering great views over the valley below.

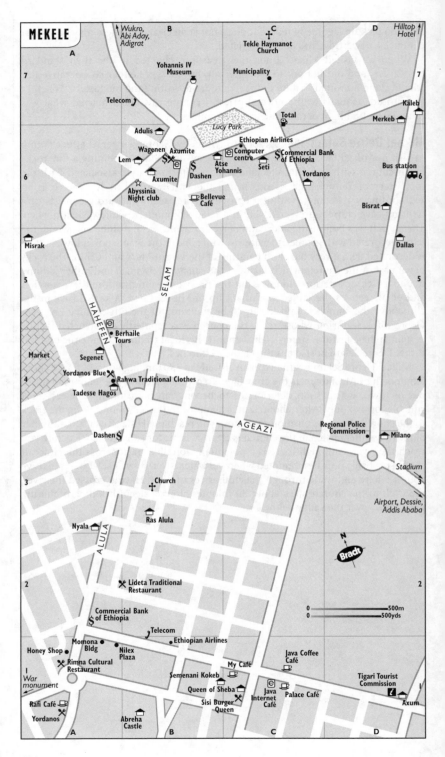

MEKELE

Wukro,
Abi Aday,
Adigrat

Hilltop
Hotel

Tekle Haymanot
Church

Yohannis IV
Museum

Municipality

Telecom

Kaleb

Total

Merkeb

Adulis

Lucy Park

Wagenen   Axumite

Ethiopian Airlines

Computer
centre

Bus station

Lem

Atse
Yohannis

Commercial Bank
of Ethiopia

Axumite   Dashen   Seti

Yordanos

Abyssinia
Night club

Bellevue
Café

Bisrat

Misrak

Dallas

SELAM

HAHEFEN

Berhaile
Tours

Market

Segenet

Yordanos Blue   Rahwa Traditional Clothes

Tadesse Hagos

AGEAZI

Regional Police
Commission

Milano

Dashen

Stadium

Church

Airport, Dessie,
Addis Ababa

Ras Alula

N

Nyala

Bradt

ALULA

Lideta Traditional
Restaurant

0   500m
0   500yds

Commercial Bank
of Ethiopia

Honey Shop

Momona
Bldg

Telecom

Ethiopian Airlines

Java Coffee
Café

Nilex
Plaza

My Café

Rimna Cultural
Restaurant

Semenani Kokeb

Tigari Tourist
Commission

War
monument

Java
Internet
Café

Palace Café

Queen of Sheba

Rafi Café

Sisi Burger
Queen

Axum

Yordanos

Abreha
Castle

294

11

Mekele and the Danakil

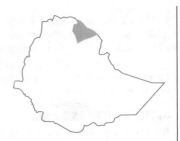

This chapter covers the Tigraian capital city of Mekele, together with the remote Danakil Depression to its east, and various minor points of interest along the 230km road that connects Mekele to Woldia on the junction of the main road between Addis Ababa and Asmara and the China Road to Lalibela. Mekele is of limited interest to tourists, although as the most modern city in northeast Ethiopia it is a great place for backpackers to take a break between long bus rides. Mekele is the only city with genuine tourist-class accommodation and amenities to lie within striking distance of the rock-hewn churches described in the previous chapter.

MEKELE

In 1944, David Buxton dismissed the Tigraian capital as 'a dreary place set in a featureless landscape'. Three decades later, Paul Henze wrote that it was 'a scattered town which, in spite of its solid stone houses, has a chronically unfinished look' and 'small, even in comparison to most Ethiopian provincial capitals' but also 'lively and developing rapidly'. Today, it is those last four prophetic words that most aptly describe Mekele as it sprawls energetically across a hill-ringed basin at an altitude of roughly 2,200m in the rocky Tigraian Highlands.

Mekele today is a large, burgeoning city whose contradictions seem to encapsulate those of Ethiopia in the early 21st century – flash, modern high-rise buildings tower above rows of rustic stone homesteads, while neatly suited, cellphone-clasping businessmen hurry past rural Tigraians as they amble towards the market in their traditional attire. Yet, paradoxically perhaps, Mekele is also possessed of a satisfying sense of cohesion unusual for urban Ethiopia – clean, orderly, vibrant, overwhelmingly Tigraian, largely unaffected by tourism, and refreshingly free of chanting children and self-appointed guides. True, the city boasts few compelling tourist attractions, but a great selection of affordable accommodation, decent restaurants and tempting pastry shops makes it an attractive place to rest up between bus trips or from which to explore the rock-hewn churches around Wukro in a hired vehicle.

Mekele is of little historical importance by comparison with many smaller Tigraian towns. Unlike Adwa, or even Wukro and Hawzien, it doesn't appear on early maps of the area, nor is it referred to in any document written before the 1830s. The modern city owes its pre-eminence to Emperor Yohannis IV (reigned 1871–89), who believed he had been conceived in the area, and treated it as his de facto capital. During the early years of his reign, when he was based at Tewodros's former capital of Debre Birhan, Yohannis IV founded a number of churches in Mekele. He relocated to Mekele in 1881, and the palace he constructed there over 1882–84, now a museum, served as the main imperial residence during the latter part of his reign.

Mekele has served as the capital of Tigrai ever since, but even as recently as 1970 it was a rustic small town with a population of fewer than 20,000. Mekele didn't feature among Ethiopia's ten largest towns in the 1984 census, but – in large part because of its favoured status with the (largely Tigraian) post-Derg national government – it is now the sixth-largest city in Ethiopia, with a population estimated at 169,200.

GETTING THERE AND AWAY

By air Daily flights with Ethiopian Airlines connect Mekele to Addis Ababa (US$63). There are also flights most days to Shire. The recently upgraded airport lies about 5km from the city centre. Taxis to the airport are available from the city centre. All outward flights should be confirmed a day in advance at the **Ethiopian Airlines** office [294 B1] (**✆** *034 442 0437;* e *mqxtsm@ethiopianairlines.com*) on the main roundabout opposite the museum.

By road Mekele lies 780km from Addis Ababa along an asphalt road through Debre Birhan, Dessie and Woldia. It is feasible, with a very early start, to drive between the two cities in one day, but it would certainly be preferable to break up the trip with an overnight stop at Dessie or elsewhere. Several road routes exist between Mekele and Lalibela: the most direct option, via Abi Aday and Sekota, could be covered in a day at a push (better, however, to take a night's break at Abi Aday and check out some of the Tembien churches), but most tourist vehicles prefer the longer though smoother route via Woldia.

The road northward from Mekele to Adigrat takes about 90 minutes to two hours to cover in a private vehicle without breaks, but most tourists opt to stop at Wukro Chirkos and/or some of the other rock-hewn churches in the vicinity. It is possible to drive between Mekele and Axum in one long day, either via Adigrat or Hawzien, routes covered in the previous two chapters, but in both cases it would be a long slog without any opportunities for sightseeing.

Mekele's main bus station [294 D6] is located at the east end of Ageazi Street, across from the Bisrat Hotel. Early morning buses run daily in both directions between Mekele and Hawzien, Adwa, and Axum to the north, and Woldia and Dessie to the south. There is transport between Mekele and Wukro or Adigrat throughout the day, as well as a few vehicles daily between Mekele and Adi Aday on the Axum–Lalibela road. **Selam Bus** (**✆** *034 441 8853*) runs daily services from Mekele north to Shire (US$7.50; 5 hours) stopping via Axum (US$6; 3–4 hours), and south to Addis Ababa (US$19.50; 1¼ days) overnighting in Ataye. Both services depart at 05.30 from outside the Seti Hotel.

TOURIST INFORMATION An excellent Mekele map and city guide is available for purchase at the Axum Hotel. The very organised and helpful **Tigrai Tourist Commission** (TTC) [294 D1] (**✆** *034 441 9916;* e *tigrai.tourism@ethionet.et; www. tigraitourism.com;* ⊕ *08.30–12.30 & 13.30–17.30 daily*), recently relocated to a new office next to the Axum Hotel, and stocks a series of useful illustrated brochures covering the major rock-hewn churches in the province. It can also supply advice about visiting less-known historical sites in Tigrai, and will provide travellers with a local guide for around US$15–18 per day as required. (Guides to the Danakil cost US$36 per day.)

TOUR OPERATORS A couple of companies organise 4x4 excursions to the rock-hewn churches around Wukro as well as to the Danakil: **GK Ahadu Tours** (**✆** *034*

440 6466–7; **e** gkahadu@ethionet.et) and **Danakil Tour and Travel Agency** (☎ 034 440 7414; **m** 0914 702 648).

⊿ WHERE TO STAY
Upmarket
⌂ **Axum Hotel** [294 D1] (180 rooms) ☎034 440 5155–7; **f** 034 440 6115; **e** axum.d@ethionet. et. This monstrous high-rise hotel is the best overall bet in Mekele, with a reasonably central location, an excellent traditionally decorated restaurant, & a gym with sauna & steam room. While the large carpeted rooms in the main building have a stale 1970s feel about them, the 120 plush new rooms in a recently opened annex are as close as you'll get in Ethiopia to being on par with international standards each with phone, flat-screen DSTV, hot shower en-suite – some even wheelchair accessible. Future additions include a rooftop terrace bar, an indoor pool, beauty salon & nightclub. Suites have separate sitting room & bathtub. All rates include free Wi-Fi, airport shuttle & breakfast. Visa accepted. *Old rooms US$50/55/65/90 dbl/twin/semi suite/suite inc b/ fast; new rooms US$132/125/150/180 twin/deluxe suite/superior suite/executive suite.*

Moderate
⌂ **Yordanos Hotel** [294 C6] (19 rooms) ☎034 441 3370/3722; **e** yordares@yahoo.com; www.yordanoshotels.com. This smart hotel, a block south of the Lucy Park, is the popular choice for many business travellers. The en-suite rooms – each with phone, DSTV & fridge – are clean & bright. Larger suites come complete with jacuzzi. Owned by the same people that own the 2 popular Yordanos restaurants in town, the restaurant also rates very highly. Room prices include breakfast, & internet is available. *US$44/55/72 standard sgl/dbl/twin, US$99/121/161 standard/deluxe/ executive suite.*

Budget
⌂ **Abreha Castle Hotel** [294 B1] (24 rooms) ☎034 440 6555–7; **f** 034 440 2258. Set in a 19th-century stone castle built by a nobleman called Abreha Aria, this prominent local landmark was restored & converted to a hotel in the 1960s by a grandson of Yohannis IV. It's an attractive hotel, with plenty of character & a winning setting in green gardens overlooking the town centre, all of which compensates for the superior facilities

& more modern feel of its competitors. *US$18/23 sgl/dbl using common shower, US$27/31 sgl/dbl en suite & TV, US$33/45 sgl/dbl.*

⌂ **Hilltop Hotel** [off map 294 D7] (27 rooms) ☎034 440 5683–6; **f** 034 440 5687. The Hilltop is – as its name suggests – perched on a suburban rise about 1km from the town centre, & it offers what would be an attractive view were it not for the factories that loom in the foreground. The large semi-detached rooms are comfortable & clean, albeit a touch frayed at the seams, & they all have a proper double bed, a fridge, DSTV & an en-suite hot bath. The terrace bar is a good spot for a drink, & the restaurant serves decent meals. *US$12/16 dbl/twin, US$18.50/25.50 semi suite/suite.*

⌂ **Milano Hotel** [294 D3] (104 rooms) ☎034 441 8724/30; **e** hotelmillano@yahoo. com. Located opposite the Regional Police Commission on the site of the former Hawzien Hotel, this place may not be as impressive as the Axum Hotel, but it offers perfectly acceptable en-suite rooms with TV at less than half the price! A restaurant, bar & nightclub are attached. *US$12/13.50 dbl with ¾/queen bed, US$15 twin, US$27/35 semi suite/suite.*

⌂ **Atse Yohannis Hotel** [294 B6] (64 rooms) ☎034 440 6760/22; **f** 034 440 6761. Situated in a high-rise building above the Nyala Insurance Co, this pleasant hotel is a perennial budget favourite – and justifiably so. The well-kept carpeted rooms each with DSTV, en-suite hot shower & private balcony are great value. What's more room rates include a full breakfast & free Wi-Fi – a rare find in this price bracket. The restaurant offers good Western fare, & the lively patio bar on the 1st floor is a great place to socialise over beers & French fries. *US$12/14/17/22.50 sgl/dbl/ semi suite/suite.*

Shoestring
⌂ **Ras Alula Hotel** [294 B3] (21 rooms) ☎034 440 6675. The quiet hotel tucked away in the cobbled back streets east of Alula Rd is another excellent budget choice with large, well-priced rooms all with clean, tiled floors & hot water en suites. *US$7.50 dbl.*

⌂ Axumite Hotel [294 B6] (13 rooms) ✎ 034 440 3671; f 034 440 3670. A step down in standard from those listed previously, this centrally located place offers reasonably clean doubles with en-suite hot shower & TV. A restaurant is attached, & the glass-enclosed bar provides good views. *US$4.50/5.50 sgl/dbl.*

⌂ Seti Hotel [294 C6] (55 rooms) ✎ 034 440 0608. This long-standing hotel has a useful location on the main square opposite the museum, but the cavernous rooms are seriously run-down & the plumbing unreliable. Meanwhile, the dimly lit ground-floor restaurant looks no less seedy once your eyes adjust to the dark. *US$4/6 sgl/dbl using common shower, US$6/8 sgl/dbl en suite.*

⌂ Merkeb Hotel [294 D7] (46 rooms) ✎ 034 441 0360. This hotel situated on the opposite side of the road to the bus station is fair value with compact but clean tiled rooms with en-suite hot shower & a ¾ bed. The snack bar here is popular with locals. *US$7.50/9 sgl/dbl.*

⌂ Dallas Hotel [294 D5] (34 rooms) ✎ 034 441 4100. Another hotel located alongside the bus station, this place offers clean en-suite room with ¾ bed, hot water & toilet, as well as smaller rooms with common shower. *US$4/6 with common shower/private en suite.*

⌂ Tadesse Hagos Hotel [294 A4] (32 rooms) ✎ 034 440 2690. The best of several cheapies clustered along Alula Rd around what used to be the bus station, between the Abreha Castle Hotel & the Commercial Bank of Ethiopia, this place offers adequately clean rooms with hot-water en suites. *US$4.50/6 sgl/dbl.*

⌂ Queen of Sheba Hotel [294 C1] (30 rooms) ✎ 034 441 1718. This rather pompous-sounding hotel close to the Mekele Health Centre offers unpretentious clean rooms in a good central location. *US$6/7.50 with common shower/private en suite.*

✕ WHERE TO EAT All of the hotels listed in the moderate and budget categories have restaurants serving local and Western dishes at reasonable prices. Of the more central places, the **Atse Yohannis** [294 B6] and **Axumite** [294 B6] hotels are both worth trying, and are excellent value at around US$3 for a substantial main course. A notch up from these is the smart restaurant at the **Axum Hotel** [294 D1], which serves the same excellent Western food as its sister hotel in Addis. The **Abreha Castle Hotel** [294 B1] has the most attractive location and view if you feel like eating outdoors.

✕ Bellevue Café & Restaurant [294 B6] ⊕ 07.00–21.00 daily. This friendly restaurant has been recommended for its well-priced local food. A small menu of continental dishes is also available. *Mostly <US$2.50.*

✕ Lideta Traditional Restaurant [294 A2] m 0914 373 011; ⊕ 09.00–late daily. Tucked away just off Alula Rd, this appropriately decorated restaurant is the perfect place to sample traditional Ethiopian food. Prices though, are on the high side. Music & dancing on Thu, Sat & Sun nights. *US$4.50–8.*

✕ Rimna Cultural Restaurant [294 A1] m 0914 731 835; ⊕ 0.700–late daily. The setting may not be as attractive as the Lideta, but the Rimna still delivers, serving the usual selection of Ethiopian staples often accompanied by live music & dancing. *US$1.50–3.*

✕ Sisi Burger Queen [294 C1] m 0914 379 807; ⊕ 08.00–21.00 daily. Next to the Queen of Sheba Hotel, this bright new American-style burger joint offers a good range of burgers, sandwiches & light snacks. Take-away is also available. *<US$2.50.*

✕ Yordanos Restaurant & Pizzeria [294 A1] ✎ 034 440 5199; ⊕ 11.00–23.00 daily. This popular restaurant at the southern end of Alula Rd has a great atmosphere, with several small *tukuls* in the courtyard & a smart indoor area. It serves a variety of Ethiopian & Italian dishes, including pizzas & grills. Ice cream & fruit salad are also available. There's a second branch of the restaurant – **Yordanos Blue** [294 A4] – near Tadesse Hagos Hotel, but it doesn't serve pizzas. *US$3–4.*

⎍ Palace Café [294 C1] ⊕ 06.00–21.00 daily. Of the dozen or so pastry shops dotted around the city centre the Palace remains a strong favourite serving sweet treats. *US$1.*

SHOPPING Supermarkets in Mekele are unusually well stocked with sweets, biscuits, tinned foods and the like, making it a good place to stock up if you plan to hike around Gheralta or head into the Danakil. The no name **honey shop** [294 A1] next to Rimna Cultural Restaurant is a good place to purchase some of the region's famous white honey. Mekele is also a great place to buy traditional dresses with an unusually high number of dressmakers lining the streets around the Alula/Selam circle. We recommend **Rahwa Traditional Clothes** [294 A4] (⟍ *034 440 1908*) near Yordanos Blue Restaurant. Prices aren't cheap though, with the beautiful handmade garments costing upwards of US$60.

OTHER PRACTICALITIES

Foreign exchange Cash and travellers' cheques in US dollars and other major currencies can be converted to local currency at any major bank. The branch of the **Commercial Bank of Ethiopia** [294 A2/C6] on the junction of Alula and Ageazi roads is unusually efficient, but the **Dashen Bank** [294 A3/B6] on the main square is better – it also has an ATM accepting Visa and MasterCard.

Internet and email Browsing facilities are available for around US$1 per half-hour at several internet cafés. The **Java Internet Café** [294 C1] and the **Mekele Computer Centre** [294 C6] next to the Atse Yohannis Hotel are both good.

WHAT TO SEE

City centre The premier attraction is the **Yohannis IV Museum** [294 B7] (⊕ *08.00–12.30 & 13.30–17.00 daily except Mon & Fri; entrance US$1.50*), sited in the palace built for the emperor by a European architect, and described by the British envoy Francis Harrison Smith, who visited Mekele in 1886 as being 'like an old-fashioned English church'. Still architecturally impressive, the rather esoteric displays of royal paraphernalia justify the nominal entrance fee, and there is a great view from the palace roof, one that Yohannis, who had a phobia about climbing stairs, may never have enjoyed personally. Photography is forbidden inside and outside, although with permission I was allowed to take some photos of the surrounding scenery. Other relics of the Yohannis era in Mekele are the churches of Tekle Haymanot, Medhane Alem and Kidane Mihret, all of which were built by the emperor in the 1870s.

Mekele's legendary **market** [294 A4], situated a couple of blocks west of the city centre, is the urban terminus of the traditional salt caravan route from the Danakil Desert. Slabs of salt are mined in the Arho region of this inhospitable area, and carried on camelback by caravans through Atsbi to Mekele. The journey between Arho and Mekele takes longer than a week, during which time the Arhotai (the name given to the Afar and Raya people who make the journey) subsist on a type of dry bread called *bircutta*. With luck, you can see these caravans arriving – the main market day is Monday, but the salt traders might arrive on other days.

The **Tigraian People's Liberation Front Monument** [off map 294 A1] (⊕ *08.00–12.00 & 13.30–17.30 daily; entrance US$1*), visible throughout much of Mekele, is a short 15-minute walk from the Abreha Castle Hotel. The centrepiece for a sprawling memorial encompassing a museum and conference complex, it's well worth making the effort to see.

Chelekot The small village of Chelekot (aka Celicut), set on a green hill 17km south of Mekele, was a far more important settlement than the modern capital in the early 19th century. Chelekot housed the court of the Tigraian Ras Wolde Selassie, who, prior to his death in 1816, was probably the most powerful regional ruler in

Ethiopia at a time when the imperial court at Gondar had little influence beyond its immediate vicinity. A staunch supporter of Solomonic rule, Wolde Selassie was notable among other things for having been served as aide by Nathaniel Pearce, a young Englishman who found his way to the Tigraian court in 1810, married an Ethiopian woman, and stayed on there for three years after the ras's death.

Henry Salt, the first European to write about the Ethiopian interior since James Bruce's day, visited the court of Wolde Selassie in 1805 and 1810. Built between Salt's visits, the main point of interest in the village today is the church of Chelekot Selassie. This architecturally impressive example of the circular *tukul* style of churches is covered in beautiful 19th-century paintings, and it houses several treasures dating to the rule of Wolde Selassie.

There's no public transport to Chelekot, but it's a recommended excursion if you have your own vehicle or can afford a taxi.

Chele Anka Waterfall

This tall, narrow waterfall on the Chele Anka (aka Chelanqua) River tumbles for around 60m into a gorge 8km southwest of Mekele, and is particularly dramatic during the rainy season. The waterfall is located about 1.5km from Debir, itself a rather interesting and picturesque village of traditional Tigraian stone houses. To get there, follow the main road west of Mekele, past the war memorial and new University for Business and Economy, and as you reach the outskirts of town follow the tracks south asking for Debir. Once at the village, anybody will lead you to a viewpoint over the gorge and waterfall next to the attractive old church of Debir Maryam. A steep footpath leads from the lip of the gorge to the base of the waterfall, where there is a pool said by locals to be safe for swimming. There is no public transport to Debir, nor would the track be passable in an ordinary saloon car, so the best way to get there is in a private 4x4 or by horse-drawn *gari*.

Eyesus Hintsa rock-hewn church

Located 60km south of Mekele, this rediscovered church devoted to Jesus has recently been refurbished with the assistance of the UK-based Eyesus Hintsa Trust (*www.eyesushintsatrust.co.uk*). Carved out of sandstone, most likely during the 14th century, Eyesus Hintsa is impressive both for its size and unique design features. The façade features five large round windows which are reminiscent of the portholes of a modern ship. Inside, the church is elaborately carved in the style of Axumite architecture, with six massive stone pillars topped by arches and a large domed ceiling. Much of the interior was originally covered in frescoes, but tradition holds that these were destroyed by the Muslim invader Ahmed Gragn in the 16th century. Recent improvements include solar-powered lighting to illuminate the interior of the church, and a protective roof to prevent further water damage due to seepage. A nearby museum houses church antiquities, and a second rock-hewn church, the Church of St Michael, is built into a limestone cave a short distance away. The entire site is situated in a scenic river valley that is teeming with birds and wildlife.

Eyesus Hintsa makes for an excellent day trip out of Mekele. Camping is permitted should you want to stay longer, and a few simple huts are available if you do not have a tent. The local people here are friendly and more laid-back than at many of the other sites, making for a relaxing and rewarding experience.

To get to the site, first head south from Mekele to the small village of Gijet. In a private vehicle this should take about two hours using reasonably good dirt roads. From here it is another 4km to the site, but the road is poor, and a 4x4 is required. If you don't mind the walk, it may be quicker to take a short cut across the fields – village children can show you the way, but you may want to find an official guide.

To save yourself disappointment, it is also important to locate the priest with the key before heading onward from Gijet. Better yet, contact the Tigrai Tourist Commission a day in advance and they will call ahead so that the priest can be made available. If you do not call ahead, your best chance of finding the priest and gaining entrance is right after the morning service, usually 06.00–08.00, or after the evening service at 17.00. The standard US$6 entrance fee is charged, and the priest will certainly want a tip. Additional information can be found in the small book *Eyesus Hintsa: An Ethiopian Journey through Landscape and Time* by Louise Schofield, which is available at the TTC office in Mekele and at the on-site museum. A useful brochure with a good map can also be picked up at the TTC office in Mekele.

THE DANAKIL DEPRESSION *with Ariadne Van Zandbergen*

The Danakil (or Dallol) Depression, which straddles the Eritrean border to the east of the Tigraian Highlands, is renowned as the hottest place on earth, with an average temperature of 34–35°C. Much of this vast and practically unpopulated region lies below sea level, dipping to a frazzled nadir of -116m at Dallol, near Lake Asale, the lowest spot of terra firma on the African continent. One of the driest and most

DANAKIL TRAVEL WARNING

In January 2012, a group of foreign tourists was attacked by gunmen approximately 30km from the Ethiopian–Eritrean border, near the site of the Erta Ale Volcano. The attack resulted in the death of five tourists, with two others injured and four people including two tourists and a local driver and police escort kidnapped. This region is a high-risk area and has been the subject of Foreign Office warnings for a number of years. In 2007, a group including British Embassy staff from Addis Ababa was taken hostage in the region and released a week later, and in 2004 a French tourist disappeared without a trace. Before arranging any visit to the Danakil or Afar region, we urge you to contact your embassy for up-to-date information or make enquires with the tourist office in Addis Ababa.

tectonically active areas on the planet, the Danakil is an area of singular geological fascination: a strange lunar landscape studded with active volcanoes, malodorous sulphur-caked hot springs, solidified black lava flows and vast salt-encrusted basins.

The Danakil is effectively a southerly terrestrial extension of the rifting process that formed the Red Sea, set at the juncture of the African, Arabian and Somali tectonic plates, and its low-lying surface was once fully submerged by saline water. Relics of those distant days include lakes Asale and Afrera, both of which lie at the centre of an ancient salt-extraction industry (seismic studies indicate that the thickness of the salt at Lake Asale is around 2km) linking the somewhat restricted economy of the Danakil to the more naturally bountiful Tigraian Highlands around Mekele.

It is some measure of the Danakil's geological activity that more than 30 active or dormant volcanoes – roughly one-quarter of the African total as listed by the Smithsonian Institute Global Volcanism Program – are shared between its Ethiopian and Eritrean components. Following a series of fault lines running in a north-to-northwesterly direction, these volcanoes are all geological infants, having formed over the past million years, and a great many took their present shape within the last 10,000 years.

The most substantial range is the so-called Danakil Alps, also known as the Danakil Block or Danakil Horst, whose highest peak, the 2,219m Mount Nabro, lies within Eritrea some 8km northeast of Mallahle (1,875m) on the Ethiopian border. In June 2011, Mount Nabro erupted violently killing 31 people and causing major disruptions to air traffic. Other notable volcanoes include the spectacular peaks of Borale (812m) and Afrera (1,295m), both of which rise in magnificent isolation from the sunken (-103m) shoreline of Lake Afrera, and the more westerly Alayita, a vast massif that rises to 1,501m and last erupted in 1901 and 1915.

The most regularly visited volcanic range in the Danakil is Erta Ale (sometimes spelt Ertale or Irta'ale), which consists of seven active peaks extending over an area of 2,350km² between Kebit Ale (287m, on the west shore of Lake Asale) to Haile Gubbi (521m, about 20km north of Lake Afrera). Of the three peaks that top the 600m mark, most remarkable is Erta Ale itself, which is noted as being one of the most active volcanoes in Africa, having hosted a permanent lava lake for longer than 120 years, and which has been in a state of continuous eruption since at least 1967, when scientific observation commenced.

The Danakil's climatic inhospitality is mirrored by the reputation of its nomadic Afar inhabitants (see box *The Afar* in *Chapter 17*, page 398), who as recently as the Italian occupation had the somewhat discouraging custom of welcoming strangers by lopping off their testicles. While scrotal intactness is no longer a cause for concern, the Danakil remains a challenging travel destination: daytime temperatures frequently soar above 50°C, there's no shade worth talking about as alleviation, the heat is often exacerbated by the fierce gale known as the Gara (Fire Wind), and creature comforts are limited to what you bring in yourself. The best time to visit is the relatively cool season between November and March.

Following the airing of the 2009 BBC documentary *The Hottest Place on Earth*, the Danakil has become – pardon the pun – Ethiopia's hottest tourist attraction, though interest is likely to wane slightly following the killing of five tourists in the region in 2012 (see box, page 301). Along with its growing popularity, prices to visit the region have increased exponentially in recent years, making it now near impossible to visit independently. At a bare minimum you'll require a private vehicle and a knowledgeable guide as well as a back-up vehicle and driver – if only to carry the required local guides and scouts you'll need to pick up along the way! In short, you're looking at around US$2,200 for a five-day trip. Visitors should also be self-sufficient in food and water (bank on a minimum of five litres of drinking water each per day, and carry enough excess in jerrycans to last a few days extra) and will need to take camping and cooking gear, since no accommodation or firewood are available. The desert nights can be refreshingly chilly, so bring a light jumper or a sweatshirt.

There are **two main access points** to the Danakil. The first, situated about 120km from Mekele along the salt caravan route to Lake Asale, is the small town of Berahile, which offers good access to Dallol, Lake Asale and Erta Ale. The second leads to the small junction town of Serdo on the Assab road, which lies around three hours' drive from Lake Afrera and two days' drive from Erta Ale. The more southerly route out of Serdo is longer and less trafficked, whereas the route through Berahile attracts a stream of salt caravans (an estimated one million camels pass through annually), a reassuring thought in the event of an irreparable vehicle breakdown. It would be perfectly possible to do the trip as a loop, starting in Mekele then continuing to Berahile, Hamed Ela, Dallol, Lake Asale, Erta Ale, Lake Afrera and finally Serdo – or vice versa. However you go about it, you would ideally be looking at a minimum of three nights' camping in the desert.

Coming from the south, permission to travel to the Danakil must be obtained from the tourist office at Semera, which lies 48km before Serdo coming from Addis. Coming from Mekele, you can obtain advance permission from the **Afar Tourism Commission** (\ *033 666 0181;* f *033 666 0488*) or else visit the helpful Tigrai Tourist Commission office in Mekele for directions to the relevant authority. Either way, you will also need to check into the regional tourist office 1km before Berahile on the Mekele road, which is also where you'll need to pick up a local Afar guide (US$12 per day) and scout (US$12 per day) and pay the necessary permissions (US$6 per day). In theory the guide and scout should bring all their own food and water, but in practice they'll probably plan on scavenging both resources from friends along the way – or, failing that, from their clients.

For further information about the geology of Danakil, as well as some tantalising pictures of its volcanoes and other landscapes, check out the website www.dankalia. com, or watch the BBC's *Hottest Place on Earth* documentary on YouTube (*http:// www.youtube.com/watch?v=ebM7G4hyFFw*).

BERAHILE Situated at an altitude of around 1,000m, this unexpectedly large and attractive town, set in a valley below stark twin peaks, is neither truly of the highlands nor truly of the desert. Nevertheless, with its combination of typically Tigraian stone houses and more austere Afar huts, it is an agreeable point of transition between the two natural realms. The town also serves as an important stop on the salt caravan trail between Danakil and Mekele: if you spend the night here, it's worth checking out the encampment on the outskirts of town where the traders unload their camels for the night and feed them fresh fodder transported from the highlands.

If you arrive at Berahile in a private vehicle, you're unlikely to stick around much longer than it takes to organise your guide and permits at the tourist office 1km from town, perhaps grab a bite to eat, and knock back the last cold (water-cooled, that is) drink you'll see for a while. Beers are sold at a bar on the hill – something of a military hangout, as the genuine locals are mostly Islamic and don't drink. Arriving by bus – at least one covers the road from Mekele every three days, but you'll need to check when it next departs at the bus station in Mekele – your only viable next move would be to try to hook up with a camel caravan heading towards the salt lakes.

With the road now upgraded the drive from Mekele to Berahile shouldn't take more than two hours. To get there, head north out of Mekele for 15km, joining the main Adigrat road at Mai Mekdan, then continue northward for another 15km to Agula, where you need to turn right onto a dirt road signposted for the rock-hewn churches around Atsbi. A few kilometres later, turn right again, at a village that may (or may not) be called Birki Birki, from where it's a straightforward run of about 80km to Berahile, passing some attractive aloe-strewn slopes (and usually a caravan or three) along the way. There is no formal accommodation in Berahile, but you should be able to make a plan to camp or to sleep in a local family compound.

HAMED ELA, DALLOL AND LAKE ASALE
The small village of Hamed Ela, which lies 48km east of Berahile along a rough caravan track, is the usual springboard for visits to Dallol and Lake Asale, whether you are a tourist or a caravan trader. It is a hot, dirty place with no toilet facilities, bordered by a pair of deep wells where you can watch the industrious local Afar draw up a meagre catch of muddy water in a goatskin container. There is no formal accommodation, but you can hire a local house complete with makeshift shower for US$12–15 a night. Lukewarm soft drinks and basic food are normally available if you don't have your own.

The 48km track from Berahile to Hamed Ela, while rough, has improved in recent years, and the drive shouldn't take more than two hours in a good 4x4. The same track is used by the camel caravans, which usually overnight at an encampment known as Asa Bolo – basically a few makeshift Afar huts set near a permanent pool. The track follows a seasonal river gorge for much of its length, and passes some impressive rock formations along the way. About 3km before Hamed Ela, there stands a small rock formation that locals claim marks the sea-level point, but my map reading would suggest that you are already well below sea level at this point.

It's worth spending two nights at Hamed Ela to give yourself time to visit the lowest point of the Danakil, which lies about 20km further north of Hamed Ela along a rough but flat track to the once abandoned American phosphate-mining encampment which has recently started up again under a joint Indian–Canadian venture and marked on many maps as a village called Dallol. The main attraction of this area – indeed, a highlight of any Danakil adventure – is a surreal multi-hued field of sulphurous hot springs studded with steaming conical vents, strange ripple-like rock formations, and sprinkled with a rather adhesive, coarse orange deposit that looks something like dyed icing sugar. Try to get here in the early morning, when the light is fantastic and the temperature not too unbearable.

You can return via Lake Asale, the shore of which lies about 13km from Dallol and 8km from Hamed Ela, and is sometimes referred to as Regut by the salt traders. The salt-mining activity moves seasonally, but your guide should be able to locate it – though it cannot always be approached too closely in a vehicle, as it might sink! The site consists of literally hundreds of Afar cameleers chipping at the salty crust to extract neat 30x40cm rectangular tablets. One bar costs birr 1.25 at source, but in Mekele it will fetch birr 12 and more again in more distant parts of the highlands. Each bar weighs about 6.5kg; one camel carries up to 200kg, or about 30 bars. The saltpans are supposed to be haunted at night by a devil or evil spirit called Abo Lalu.

Before heading on anywhere from Hamed Ela, you will need to pick up one or maybe two armed scouts or police. Given half the chance, however, the local Afar will attempt to swell your party further with additional guides, police and 'secret guards'. If you are travelling with a decent company, it shouldn't get out of hand and if it does it shouldn't become your problem. On the other hand, if you are personally paying the guide fees, etc, then expect every effort to be made to fill every available seat (and quite possibly the roof too). Space permitting, you could be looking at half-a-dozen Kalashnikov-toting freeloaders expecting to be paid US$12 apiece per day to weigh down your vehicle, drink your water, chatter incessantly, stop the vehicle to greet their pals at every roadside settlement, and collaborate with the driver and guide in dreaming up obstacles to anything you might want to do that interferes with their party.

ERTA ALE Earmarked by the Afar regional government as the centrepiece of a forthcoming 'crater national park', Erta Ale ranks as one of the most alluring – and physically challenging – natural attractions anywhere in Ethiopia. Rising from below sea level to an altitude of 613m, Erta Ale is a shield volcano with a base diameter of 30km and a 1km² caldera at its summit. Nestled within the caldera are two pit craters: the larger, more northerly one, though currently inactive, held a lava lake in 1968 and 1973, while the smaller ellipsoid central pit contains the world's only permanent lava lake, which measures about 60m across and is 100m long.

Scientists think the lake must have a continuous link to a shallow magma chamber, which is itself fed on a regular basis by magma associated with the formation of the Rift. Significant changes in activity were noted at Erta Ale over 2004–05, including high levels of degassing, fissure eruptions on the northern flank, and a fresh breach on the southern crater that has caused the lava to overflow its terrace and rise up to within 20m of the crater rim. Several earthquakes have also been recorded in the vicinity of Erta Ale in recent years, suggesting that a major eruption may be imminent.

To reach Erta Ale from Hamed Ela, follow the rough and sometimes indistinguishable track that heads almost directly due south towards Lake Afrera, running roughly parallel to the Erta Ale range, whose peaks – Allu (429m), Dala Filla (613m), Borale Ale (668m), Erta Ale itself and Ale Bugu (1,031m) – stand 10–20km away on the eastern horizon. There are several small Afar settlements along the track, which passes through an ever-changing landscape of sand, rocks, scrubland and even the occasional palm-lined oasis. Depending on the strength of your 4x4, the skill of your driver, the competence of your guide, and the number of friends your guards need to visit, this drive might take anything from five hours to a full day. After about 60km, the track brings you to a small village that lies almost directly due west of the prominent peak of Ale Bugu, and goes by several different names, among them Gadala, Jelibahi and Durubu.

From here you need to veer east for 20km, across solidified lava flows and passing the northern base of Ale Bugu, to the village of El Dom at the base of Erta Ale. The volcano can be ascended by foot or on camelback from El Dom over three to four hours. No actual climbing is involved, and the slopes are generally quite gentle, but it's a tough hike all the same, due to the hard underfoot conditions, blistering heat and lack of shade. For this reason, it's a good idea to ascend in the late afternoon, leaving El Dom at around 17.00 and then spend the night on the top of Erta Ale, returning around 06.00 the next morning. The Afar people have constructed basic 'houses' – horse-shape structures made of stones piled on top of each other, just over a metre high with no roof – on the top of the caldera, which they hire for a steep US$12 per night. You'll have to bring everything else with you though including bedding, food and water. Camels can also be hired at the bottom for around US$30 for a round trip to carry all supplies.

LAKE AFRERA Lake Afrera, which extends over almost 100km² some 30km southeast of Erta Ale as the crow flies, is a highly saline body of water fed by the abundant thermal springs that rise on its northeastern and southeastern shores. It is also known as Lake Giulietti, in honour of the Italian explorer Giuseppe Maria Giulietti, whose pioneering 1881 expedition to the Danakil was curtailed when his entire party was slaughtered by Afar tribesmen in present-day Eritrea. Afrera lies at an altitude of 103m below sea level, and the solitary island in the southern half of the lake (which goes by the rather apt name of Deset) is noted as being the lowest-lying in the world.

Lake Afrera is a stunning apparition, with its emerald-green waters overshadowed by the looming black basalt of mounts Borale and Afrera, the dormant volcanoes that respectively rise to 812m and 1,295m above its eastern and southern shores. As with Lake Asale, Afrera is an important source of coarse salt, which is extracted for transportation to the highlands from the extensive crusts that divide its southernmost shore from Mount Afrera.

The western shore of Afrera can be reached from El Dom (at the base of Erta Ale) along a rough road that involves retracing your tracks in a westerly direction for some 20km, passing Ale Bugu to your left, and then heading southeast for 60km. This track is rough and difficult to follow in parts, and it can take anything from five to ten hours to cover, so the earliest possible start is recommended. With a new asphalt road recently laid, Lake Afrera is now around three hours' drive (about 180km) northwards from Serdo, a small junction town on the Assab road some 40km northeast of the regional capital Semera.

MEKELE TO WOLDIA BY ROAD

Most travellers will probably want to travel directly between Mekele and Woldia, a straightforward 230km run on a recently asphalted road that takes about four hours in a private vehicle and up to six hours by bus. Buses to Woldia leave Mekele at around 06.00. If you can't find a bus specifically going to Woldia, take one that is heading on to Dessie or Addis Ababa. Buses coming from Adigrat may pass through Mekele later in the day – your chances of getting a seat are good, but cannot be relied upon fully. Travelling in the opposite direction, you should be able to find a seat on a bus running from Dessie to Mekele; these generally pass through Woldia in the mid morning.

It is equally possible to do the Mekele–Woldia run in hops and dribbles over two or more days. The most convincing reasons to break up this trip would be to stop at Lake Ashenge, or – somewhat more esoterically – to visit the town of Maichew, the site of the decisive battle that led to the Italian occupation of Ethiopia in 1936. Travelling in stages also allows for a later start, breaks a very scenic route into comfortable travel bites, and adds an element of chance to your itinerary – never a bad thing if you have the time. Many of the small towns and other sites described below might be of interest to motorised travellers.

ADI GUDEM AND BETMARA Adi Gudem is the first town south of Mekele, situated some 35km from the regional capital. A small bus runs back and forth along the connecting road throughout the day (there is generally a departure at around 09.00), taking just over an hour in either direction. Adi Gudem is a typically Tigraian small town of sandstone houses and puzzled stares. A couple of small hotels can be relied upon for a friendly reception and a cup of hot tea, if not much else. Early morning buses aside, there's something of a public transport vacuum between Adi Gudem and Maichew, 80km further down the road, but there are plenty of trucks and it's easy to organise a lift.

The small, breezy town of **Betmara**, about halfway between Adi Gudem and Maichew, is where the buses generally stop for a tea break. If you've been in Tigrai for some time, the road south of Betmara climbs into the greenest hills you'll have seen in a while. Betmara marks the beginning of a stretch of road as awesome as any in Ethiopia, a 100km succession of dizzying hairpin climbs and descents through Maichew and Korem, culminating in a breathtaking drop of perhaps 1,000m to Alamata – thrilling stuff in dry weather, terrifyingly slippery when the road is wet. Technically, you will still be in Tigrai until you head south of Alamata, but scenically you leave it behind at Betmara.

MAICHEW Maichew – pronounced *macho* – is atypical of Tigraian towns in that there are few sandstone buildings, and it lacks an identifiable shape or centre. Before I arrived, Maichew was described to me as a one-street town – a little unfair, as the street stretches for a good 2km – but nevertheless it has an untidy, dusty feel that reminded me of similarly amorphous towns in southern Ethiopia, such as Robe and Dodola.

On 31 March 1936, the hills around Maichew were the scene of the final, decisive battle in Mussolini's bid to conquer Ethiopia, a 13-hour confrontation whose outcome was virtually predetermined by Italy's overwhelming dominance of the air. The Battle of Maichew is remembered as the start of the occupation of 1936–41, the one period in its 3,000-year history when outsiders ruled Ethiopia.

The Maichew area is wonderfully green and hilly, and it strikes me as having enormous potential for off-the-beaten-track hiking and rambling. If you feel like exploring, there is no shortage of affordable **accommodation**. The new multi-storey green-and-cream-painted **Tadele Hotel** (*20 rooms;* ☎ *034 777 0899*) just off the first roundabout coming from Mekele is the pick with clean spacious rooms with tiled floors and hot water en suite for US$11/13.50/15 for a single/double/twin. It also has a decent restaurant. The **Lemlem Hotel** (*28 rooms;* ☎ *034 777 0873*) next door is marginally cheaper though the rooms aren't as nice.

TO ALAMATA VIA LAKE ASHENGE Two roads connect Maichew to Alamata. The new road via Mehoni is no shorter than the old road via Korem, but it is flatter, better maintained and therefore faster and safer – you'll whizz through in an hour in a private vehicle, and public transport doesn't take much longer. Unfortunately, the new road is also far less scenic than the 62km old road to Alamata. If you opt for the old road, light vehicles trot back and forth throughout the day, stopping at Korem – Maichew revisited, but scruffier, and with plenty of gaudy hotels along the main street – about two-thirds of the way to Alamata. A very new and spanking-clean **hotel** on the roundabout when coming from the Adigrat road immediately on entering the village charges US$4 for a room.

A more alluring attraction than Korem, Lake Ashenge achieved some historical notoriety as the site of the Battle of Afla, which resulted in the capture and eventual grisly execution of the Portuguese commander Christofe da Gama by Ahmed Gragn in 1542. Situated at an altitude of 2,400m about halfway between Maichew and Korem, and clearly visible from the roadside, Ashenge is a beautiful mountain-ringed stretch of slightly saline water that covers an area of 14,000ha in an old volcanic crater, and is fed by several small streams but has no known outlet. The lake forms an excellent target for birders, particularly during the European winter when more than 20,000 waterbirds congregate around it, including ferruginous and maccoa duck, northern shoveler, southern pochard and great-crested grebe. At all times of year, endemics such as wattled ibis, Rouget's rail and black-headed siskin

11

are likely to be seen alongside other resident grassland species. Several footpaths lead from the road to the lakeshore.

Practically bordering Lake Ashenge, the **Hashengu Forest Reserve** (aka Hugumburda State Forest) is the highest portion of an extensive area of indigenous coniferous forest spanning the Alamata Escarpment from an altitude of 1,600m to 2,600m. It is one of the few substantial forests left in Tigrai, notable among other things for harbouring the rare endemic plant *Delosperma abyssinica* and more than a dozen forest birds not normally associated with Tigrai, for instance the Abyssinian catbird. An all-weather road runs through part of the forest – ask for the turn-off about 2km north of the lake – and camping is permitted at the guard's encampment.

ALAMATA The descent from Korem to Alamata is simply spectacular, and the sharp drop in altitude brings you to a hot plain that couldn't be more different from the green highlands you've just passed through. Alamata is calmer than either Maichew or Korem, and it feels smaller – or at least more compact – with a dusty frontier atmosphere, enhanced by the towering presence of the wildly majestic escarpment to the north.

Not least among Alamata's assets is the **Meaza Hotel** (*48 rooms;* ℡ *034 774 1230–2*). This large multi-storey pink building with white balustraded balconies would be hard to miss, and it also apparently holds the distinction (don't get too excited) of being voted the third-best hotel in Tigrai – a claim that seems over-zealous given the faded state of the rooms. An en-suite double or twin room with hot water, nets and television costs US$11. The restaurant is excellent, and the shady courtyard is a nice place for an afternoon tea. Internet is available. The older **Tewodros Belai Hotel** (*50 rooms;* ℡ *034 774 0321*) is a cheaper option at US$6 for a room with a common shower, or US$7.50 for an en-suite room with hot water. There's a pleasant outdoor bar, and the restaurant serves good *shiro tagamino*, which is a delicious spicy dish made from crushed beans cooked with oil. Directly facing the Tewodros Belai, the **Raya Hotel** (*30 rooms;* ℡ *034 774 0242*) is a step down again from the above hotels in terms of both quality and price, charging US$3 for a room with a common shower, and US$4.50 for a self-contained double with cold/hot shower.

right Outside Harar Gate, the
main entrance to Harar's
walled city (KW) page 420

below Holy Trinity Cathedral in
Addis Ababa is the final
resting place of Haile
Selassie (AVZ) page 160

bottom En route to the market in
Bati (EL) page 356

above left Yeha is home to a large, well-preserved stone temple estimated to be at least 2,500 years old (AVZ) page 261

above & left Once the capital of Ethiopia, Gondar is renowned for the castles that stud the central royal compound, and the church of Debre Birhan Selassie, which boasts some of the finest murals anywhere in the country (AVZ) page 215

left The fortress-like appearance of Bet Gebriel-Rafael in Lalibela has led some experts to believe that it was originally built as the residence of King Lalibela (AVZ) page 334

above   The Tutu Fela stelae field is the site of about 300 stelae marking ancient graves (AVZ) page 505

right   The 100-odd rock-hewn churches of Tigrai reach their architectural apex along the majestic sandstone cliffs of the Gheralta Escarpment (AVZ) page 280

above Officially the hottest place on Earth, the Danakil Depression features stunning landscapes, including live lava lakes, sulphurous multi-hued geysers and remote salt pans (AVZ) page 301

left The very steep and windy road from Gonder to Axum, Northern Circuit (KW) page 231

below The area around Dodola offers some of the best trekking in the country, with lush *tef* farming land, forest and moorland (AVZ) page 476

above The Sanetti Plateau supports heath-like vegetation which is typical of the Afro-Alpine habitat on Africa's highest mountains (AVZ) page 489

right Sightings of Swayne's hartebeest (*Alcelaphus buselaphus swaynei*) are practically guaranteed in Senkele Game Sanctuary (AVZ) page 466

below The crater lake of Chitu Hora, in Abiata-Shala National Park, harbours a semi-resident flock of up to 10,000 flamingoes (AVZ) page 458

top left | The Ethiopian wolf (*Canis simensis*) is the rarest of the world's canid species (AVZ) page 54

top right Black-and-white colobus monkey (*Colobus guereza*) (AVZ) page 55

above left Mountain nyala (*Tragelaphus buxtoni*) (AVZ) page 61

above right Beisa oryx (*Oryx beisa*) (AVZ) page 60

below Burchell's zebra (*Equus burchellii*) (AVZ) page 62

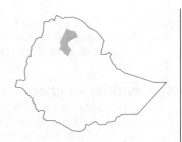

12

Through Routes to Lalibela

When Thomas Pakenham visited Lalibela in 1955, it was legendarily inaccessible. There was no proper road to the village, which typically received about five parties of foreign visitors annually, a muleback excursion that took four days from Dessie. Even as recently as the mid 1990s, air access to Lalibela was strictly restricted to the dry season, and the only road there was frequently impassable after heavy rain.

All that has changed in recent years. True, Lalibela is still not connected to any other town by a completed asphalt road, but the opening of a surfaced airstrip in 1997 has allowed flights there to run all year, while the construction of all-weather gravel roads south to Gashena and north to Sekota allows a road approach from any of several directions, depending on how they slot in with your other travel plans. However, you work it, the direct drive from Addis Ababa to Lalibela requires two days. But it is now only a one-day drive from Bahir Dar, Gondar or Dessie, whether you use public or private transport. In a private vehicle, it is just about possible to reach Lalibela in one day from Mekele or Axum, but two days would make for a more relaxed trip – and it would be the minimum travel period on public transport.

These routes are discussed in greater detail in the main body of this chapter, but a brief overview may be useful.

The most popular access route to Lalibela, and the easiest option coming from Addis Ababa, or anywhere else along the main eastern road connecting it to Mekele, is the graded 175km road from Woldia via Dilb. Coming from Bahir Dar or Gondar, the best route is the roughly 250km road from Werota via Debre Tabor. Both these routes utilise the so-called 'China Road', which was constructed by the Chinese in the 1970s to connect the Lake Tana region to Woldia via Werota, Debre Tabor and Nefas Mewcha. In both cases, the junction town is Gashena (often mistakenly marked as Bete Hor on maps), from where a 64km road runs north to Lalibela.

A less used option, coming from Axum or Mekele, is the 380km road from Adwa via Adi Abay and Sekota, a scenic delight that offers easy access to several little-visited rock-hewn churches. Finally, the most obscure option at present, but one that might well take off once it is fully upgraded (most likely during the lifespan of this edition) is a new road running north from Dejen, via Mekane Selam and the recently proclaimed Borena Sayint National Park, to connect with the China Road at Gashena. A variation on this same route runs west from Dessie to Mekane Selam.

WOLDIA AND THE MAIN EASTERN APPROACH

A medium-sized and largely unremarkable hillside town, **Woldia** sees a solid trickle of traveller through-traffic simply because it is the most popular springboard for road trips to Lalibela. It lies amongst pretty rolling hills, but otherwise it might most favourably be described as humdrum and amorphous, and more accurately perhaps as a tedious and scruffy urban sprawl. It is most lively on the market days of Tuesday and Saturday. Within Ethiopia, Woldia is perhaps best known these days as the birthplace of the tycoon Al Amoudi, the owner and constructor of the Addis Ababa Sheraton.

GETTING THERE AND AWAY Woldia straddles the asphalt Adigrat road some 520km from Addis Ababa, 120km north of Dessie and 230km south of Mekele. When you arrive in Woldia, you might want to use a *gari* to get you and your luggage up the 1.5km climb between bus station and town centre.

To/from Dessie or Mekele
Buses between Woldia and Dessie or Mekele leave at around 06.00 in all directions. If you don't feel like the early start, plenty of buses and trucks run along the main Addis Ababa–Mekele road, and they all stop at Woldia, so you shouldn't have any difficulty finding transport before noon. Heading south from Woldia, there is plenty of transport to Dessie, which lies 120km and about two hours away along what is now a good tar road. From Dessie, there are direct daily buses that run through to Addis Ababa in a day taking around ten hours.

To/from Lalibela
This route entails following the so-called China Road towards Debre Tabor west out of Woldia, first passing through the small town of Dilb (set in a river valley 25km from Woldia), and then tackling a spectacular 1,500m ascent to the breezy footslopes of Mount Abuna Yosef. Roughly 110km out of Woldia, turn right at the junction town of Gashena, which lies at an altitude of around 3,000m some 64km from Lalibela. About 20km before you reach Lalibela, turn right onto the asphalt road connecting the town to the airport.

This road can usually be covered in four hours in a private 4x4, depending on how recently it was graded and how much rain has fallen since, but it takes a couple of hours longer on public transport. A direct daily bus service travels the route between Woldia and Lalibela (US$3.50; 5–7 hours), leaving at around 06.00 in either direction. A second service, also departing around 06.00, continues on to Addis Ababa (US$12.50; 2 days) after stopping overnight in Dessie (US$6; 9–10 hours). The odd Land Rover also runs in either direction between Woldia and Lalibela (US$3.50; 5–7 hours).

WHERE TO STAY IN WOLDIA

Budget

🏠 **Lal Hotel** (54 rooms) ☎033 331 0367/0314 or 011 662 3731; e lato@ethionet.et; www.lalhotelsandtours.com. The presence of the multi-storey Lal Hotel – country cousin to its smarter Lalibela namesake – in a town not otherwise distinguished by comely accommodation comes as a welcome surprise. It's supposedly the best lodging in town, but the rooms seem rather bare for the asking price & the hotel as a whole is poorly maintained, perhaps because improvements in the roads south to Dessie & west to Lalibela have turned it into something of a white elephant. The restaurant is good, & the bar a popular meeting place. *US$13/18.50 sgl/dbl with hot shower en suite.*

🏠 **Arsema Hotel** (27 rooms) ☎033 331 3395. This place has a smart exterior with mirrored glass windows, but the rooms fail to live up to expectations. Rooms are indifferent & seem over-priced. *US$6 using common shower, US$9/12 with hot shower en suite.*

Shoestring

🏠 **Yordanos Hotel** (41 rooms) ☎033 331 1357/0034; e damayile@yahoo.com or yorda@yahoo.com. Centrally located behind the Total petrol station & catering to a mainly Ethiopian crowd, this hotel does not go out of its way to impress; rather it just does things right. The staff are very friendly & often dressed in a uniform T-shirt which reads 'Eat, Drink, Relax', a perfect statement of what this comfortable place is all about. The restaurant serves excellent *shakila tibs* – ask to have the meat cut into smaller pieces & it will be easier to eat. A one-price-for-all policy makes rooms here a bargain. Internet is available in the same building. *US$4/6 sgl/dbl with hot shower en suite.*

🏠 **Selam Hotel** (27 rooms) 📞033 331 1968; 📠 033 331 0120. Situated more or less opposite the Lal, this 3-storey hotel offers reasonably clean rooms with en suite & TV. *US$5/6 sgl/dbl.*

🏠 **Mechare Hotel** (24 rooms) 📞033 331 0233. The rooms at this centrally located hotel have seen better days. The attached restaurant serves a basic menu. *US$4/6 sgl/dbl using common hot shower, US$5/6/7.50 sgl/dbl/twin with hot shower en suite.*

🏠 **Wolde Yohannis Alula Hotel** (18 rooms) 📞033 331 1080. Probably the best of the real cheapies in town is this orange double-storey hotel on the Mekele road. *US$3 clean room with proper dbl bed & en-suite cold shower.*

🏠 **Genet Hotel** (29 rooms) 📞033 331 0327. Situated next door to the Wolde Yohannis Alula Hotel, this place has similar en-suite rooms, as well as decent rooms using a common shower. *US$2.50/3 with common/private shower.*

✖ **WHERE TO EAT** The restaurant at the **Lal Hotel** is the best in town, and serves a variety of Western and local dishes in the US$2–5 range. The **Extreme Café** next to the Selam Hotel serves juice, coffee, a few cakes and fresh bread. The nearby **Sami Supermarket** is quite well stocked. For local food, try the restaurants at the **Yordanos** and **Mechare** hotels.

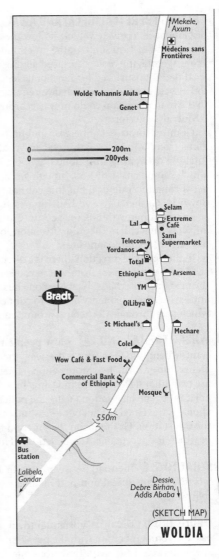

WOLDIA

THE CHINA ROAD FROM BAHIR DAR OR GONDAR

Based largely on a series of articles written by John Graham for the Addis Tribune, with additional input from the staff of Four Seasons Travel Agency

Travellers who head directly between Lalibela and Bahir Dar or Gondar will follow the 'China Road', which runs east from Werota, via Debre Tabor, Nefas Mewcha and Gashena (junction town for Lalibela) to Woldia. Originally built by the Chinese in the late 1970s, it was for years the best gravel road in Ethiopia (despite traversing some very scenic but seriously mountainous terrain) and a recent upgrade, also by the Chinese, means it is now asphalted all the way from Bahir Dar to Gashena. In addition to being a popular access route to Lalibela, the China Road between Werota and Gashena provides access to several infrequently visited churches and points of interest.

GETTING THERE (LALIBELA) AND AWAY Coming from the direction of Bahir Dar or Gondar in a private vehicle, follow the asphalt road between these two towns to Werota, about 1km south of the junction for the eastbound China Road to Woldia. From Werota, the road is surfaced all the way to Gashena, 64km from Lalibela on a road that is unsurfaced for most of its length. The drive from Bahir Dar or Gondar to Lalibela used to take a full day, requiring a very early start, but recent upgrades to the road mean you could now get through in five hours or so, depending on how frequently you stop.

Coming towards Lalibela on public transport, this route will entail catching a bus from Gondar or Bahir Dar to Woldia, disembarking at Gashena, and then hitching or waiting for public transport north along the 64km road to Lalibela, which should cost US$1.50, though *faranjis* are often overcharged. Most travellers get through in one day, but this cannot be guaranteed, so you may need to bed down in Gashena. We've had reports from travellers of a major overcharging scam operating with bus services in Gashena and also reports of buses stopping at Nefas Mewcha in the mid afternoon for no apparent reason and staying there overnight (see box, opposite).

In the opposite direction, there is a direct daily service from Lalibela to Bahir Dar (US$7.50; 9–10 hours) from where you can catch a bus to Gondar (US$4; 4 hours) the next day. Alternatively, at least one bus to Gashena leaves Lalibela at 06.00 daily, and arrives there in plenty of time to connect with the buses from Dessie to Gondar, which pass through Gashena at around midday.

WHERE TO STAY AND EAT Most people travel through in a day, but should you want accommodation along the way, there are a few options. The best place in **Debre Tabor** is the two-storey Guna Hotel, which has good en-suite rooms. There are two other decent hotels in Debre Tabor, one in front of the Guna and the other adjacent to the bus station facing the police station. In **Nefas Mewcha**, the place of choice is the Hotel Mullu, but if it is full there are a number of other hotels around the bus station. **Gashena**, on the junction to Lalibela, also has several basic lodges, of which the acceptable Adani Demisay Hotel charges US$3 for basic rooms.

WHAT TO SEE The road between Werota and Gashena provides access to several worthwhile historical and natural sites. Running from west to east, these are as follows.

Debre Tabor The first substantial town along this road, Debre Tabor lies 42km east of Werota junction, with the possibility of making a short diversion *en route* to Awramba (see page 210). Emperor Seife Ara'ad founded Debre Tabor in the 13th century, but the town rose to prominence only in the early 17th century, when it was used as a base to contain the Oromo incursions. Debre Tabor effectively served as capital of Ethiopia for much of the turbulent 19th century: it emerged as the successor to Gondar in 1803 during the reign of a local nobleman called Ras Gugsa Mursa, briefly the most powerful political figure in Ethiopia, and it retained this status until 1889, when Menelik II was crowned emperor. The only relics of Debre Tabor's heyday are two old churches. The first, **Tabor Iyasus**, lies on a forested hill 3km from the town centre. Although almost as old as the town itself, the present building – a magnificent circular construction enclosed by a large stone wall – was built by Ras Gugsa in the early 1800s. The interior has intricately carved pillars and fine 19th-century paintings. It also houses several treasures, including Ras Gugsa's ceremonial robe, and a throne-bed that belonged to Empress Taitu. The second, less remarkable church is **Tabor Maryam**, constructed with the support of Tewodros II in the 1860s.

Gafat The hamlet of Gafat, to the north of Debre Tabor, is associated with the most critical and bizarre episode in Tewodros's reign – the hostage-taking of missionaries who were then forced to manufacture a cannon. Local people will point you towards the foundations and walls of the buildings used as foundries, and to the hill where the soldiers who guarded the missionaries were camped. The cannon built by the missionaries – which didn't work, despite their best efforts – now stands on Makdala Hill over 100km away.

To get to Gafat, you must drive for 2km along the main road east of Debre Tabor, then follow a rough dirt turn-off heading north, then – when the road peters out – walk for another 1km or so.

Mount Guna This 4,231m mountain east of Debre Tabor supports 40km² of Afro-alpine moorland above the 3,800m contour, home to an isolated and highly vulnerable population of around 20 Ethiopian wolves, one of only four viable populations of the race that occurs northwest of the Rift Valley. Although we've not heard of any traveller visiting this mountain, it lies a short distance south of the main road, and local shepherds might act as guides.

Wukro Medhane Aleis This spectacular rock-hewn church was reputedly excavated by King Lalibela and is sometimes referred to as Wukro Lalibela. Unusually, this church – which consists of several different parts – contains four *tabots*, as well as a treasury of old crosses, manuscripts and other relics. The workmanship is excellent, with several fine carvings on the ceiling and walls.

Follow the Nefas Mewcha road for 20km out of Debre Tabor to a signposted turn-off at Kimer Dingay. Proceed for 300m, then turn left across a large ditch onto a sparkling white road that is reduced to rough rock after a few hundred metres. Although the road is scheduled for improvement, it is impassable after 4km, so you must walk the remaining 4km.

GASHENA TICKET SCAM

A reader forwarded us details of the following experience catching a bus from Gondar to Lalibela in late 2011:

We were fortunate and easily bought tickets for the Woldia bus (number 1181) and got to Gashena in six hours to catch the Lalibela bus. Others we met were not so lucky and were sold tickets to Gashena but their buses terminated earlier leaving them to buy tickets on connecting buses. However at Gashena there is a scam run where local people 'tell' the ticket seller to charge vastly inflated prices to Westerners; they then collect the additional cost from the ticket seller. We argued and the ticket seller accepted our offer. We then discovered the scam while talking to fellow passengers (who would say nothing while in Gashena). In Lalibela I complained to the police who forced the ticket collector to return the additional 'charge'. The fare is birr 20 per person. Initially the ticket seller wanted 100 per person; my wife would only pay 100. The ticket seller then gave birr 60 to the gang. The police were not happy with returning our money but they were supported by fellow passengers.

Gaynt Bethlehem The most singular and perhaps the finest church that can be reached from the China Road west of Gashena is Gaynt Bethlehem, a seminary specialising in advanced studies on St Yared, who wrote most of the praise songs used by the Orthodox Church. Enclosed with an unflattering circular thatched *tukul*, Bethlehem is built-up in the ancient Axumite style with a rectangular 200m² floor plan. Notable features include three old juniper doorways, fantastic carvings in the wooden beams holding up the roof, two basilica domes with ornate designs, plenty of old Ge'ez Bibles, and several wonderful old paintings on deteriorating cloth depicting scenes from the life of Jesus. Outside the church lies a 7m-long fallen Axumite pillar. Not unpredictably, oral tradition dates Bethlehem to the rule of Abreha we Atsbeha, but Thomas Pakenham, the first outsider to see this church, felt that the combination of Axum and Constantinople styles indicated a construction date between the 9th and 11th centuries, while other sources date its construction to the late 14th century. Pakenham's wonderful book *The Mountains of Rasselas* (see *Appendix 1, Further information*, page 615) contains a full chapter about the church, as well as some great photographs.

Getting to Bethlehem today is less of a mission than it was in the 1950s, but is still a considerable side trip. It is reached along a rough road that heads southward from the China Road at the western edge of Nefas Mewcha. Follow this for 50km, passing through the small market town of Arb Gebeya after 23km.

Zur Amba Abba Aragawi Sihar Aryam Built into an *amba* visible from the China Road some 20km before Nefas Mewcha, this church is of minor architectural interest, but it has a fascinating history, and houses several old treasures. Tradition has it that the original church at Zur Amba was built in memory of Abba Aregawi in the 6th-century reign of Gebre Meskel, abandoned in the time of Ahmed Gragn, and resurrected by Libawi Christos about 200 years later. From Salli, a rough 3.5km track leads to the base of the *amba*, followed by a steep 30-minute hike.

Checheho Gebriel and Bal-Egziabher Situated close to Checheho 25km east of Nefas Mewcha, these two new churches are being excavated by Abba Defar, who started work on them after receiving a holy vision. The larger church measures about 10m deep by 5m wide, and has several large central pillars. The rock is unusually soft and chalky, giving the interior an attractive white appearance.

FROM AXUM/MEKELE VIA ABI ADAY AND SEKOTA

Oddly under-utilised by tourists, the 380km gravel road that runs through the remote heartland of northern Ethiopia to connect Adwa and Lalibela via Abi Aday and Sekota is one of the most wildly attractive routes in the country, passing through a remote and rather arid area studded with significant rock-hewn churches. Though the final 130km stretch between Sekota and Lalibela is problematic on public transport, this road forms a perfectly viable route between Axum and Lalibela in a private vehicle, and it can also be used to drive between Mekele and Lalibela, cutting west from the main Adigrat road either at Mekele (for Abi Aday) or at Korem (for Sekota).

With a private vehicle, a very early start and a strict no-sightseeing policy, it should be possible to get from Axum or Mekele through to Lalibela in one long day. Allow 2½ hours to cover the 115km from Axum to Abi Aday (via Adwa and Mai Kenetal) or 95km from Mekele to Abi Aday (via Hagare Selam), another 3½ to 4½ hours to cover the 155km between Abi Aday and Sekota, and then about three hours for the 130km from Sekota to Lalibela itself. Alternatively, you could overnight at Abi Aday or Sekota to break things up – the former has better facilities, the latter is the more inherently interesting town, and both lie close to some worthwhile churches.

ABI ADAY AND THE TEMBIEN Abi Aday literally means 'Big Town', and although not quite the metropolis this might suggest, it is the largest town along the road between Adwa and Lalibela, a reasonably substantial and rapidly expanding settlement set in a dusty valley below an impressive cliff. The town is divided into two parts by a small bridge across the Tsechi River. The lower part of town is where the better hotels are, and where buses stop. The upper part of town is where you'll find the marketplace, Elsa's Hotel, and the seedier bars in which you're most likely to see Awri dancing as the *tej* hits the mark.

Abi Aday is the principal town of the Tembien region, which was until recently regarded as one of the remote parts of Tigrai, and it probably still should be, the recent construction of an all-weather dirt road connecting it to Mekele and Adwa notwithstanding. Historically, the region is remembered as the birthplace of emperors Yohannis IV and Ras Alula, while other Tigraians know it for its delicious honey and hyperactive Awri dancing. In addition, the Tembien probably houses the highest concentration of rock-hewn churches outside of Lalibela and Gheralta, most of which can be visited as a day trip out of Abi Aday.

Getting there and away Access to Abi Aday is relatively straightforward. Good roads lead to Mekele, Adwa, Sekota and Lalibela, and there are regular public transport connections with the first three towns. The main road between Adwa and Abi Aday via Mai Kinetel is 95km long and takes no more than two hours in a private vehicle (add 20–30 minutes coming to or from Axum). The unsurfaced road from Mekele, also 95km, passes through the bustling highland market centre of Hagare Selam, before descending along a spectacular mountain pass to the junction with the roads north towards Adwa and south towards Sekota and Lalibela (if you are driving yourself, you need to head right – towards Adwa – at this junction).

Regular minibuses to Abi Aday leave Adwa from a junction about 200m west of the main square and take around four hours. At least two buses run between Mekele and Abi Aday daily. However, most of the surrounding rock-hewn churches are accessible only to travellers with private transport.

Where to stay

Mylomin Lodge Botanical Garden (6 rooms) 034 446 0754; m 0911 110 132; e yeshiwoldehiwot@gmail.com. This newly opened lodge located around 1km from the bus station near the hospital provides welcome accommodation in nicely furnished traditional *tukuls* all with hot shower en suites. Massage & sauna bath are also available on request, while the attached Aba Geda Restaurant serves a wide variety of food & drinks. Group discounts are also available. *US$28/34 sgl/dbl.*

Ras Alula Hotel (20 rooms) 034 446 0621. Situated on the outskirts of town opposite the hospital about 1km along the Adwa road, this

unexpectedly comfortable 3-storey hotel is the next best option offering decent rooms with ensuite hot shower & a ¾ bed. There is a ground-floor bar, but no food is available at the time of writing. *US$5 en suite.*

Debre Selam Pension This friendly family-run place in the town centre, just 200m from the bus station, has elevated itself from a standard 1-floor lodge centred on an open courtyard by the addition of a smarter 2-storey annex. Rooms with a ¾ bed are simple but clean. *US$2.50 using common cold shower, US$4 with cold shower en suite.*

✕ Where to eat The best place for a full meal is **Mylomin Lodge**. Unexpectedly, there is a rather good juice shop on the main junction more or less opposite the Debre Selam; the English-speaking owner is articulate and helpful, and video shows are sometimes held here at night.

Churches around Abi Aday
Numerous rock-hewn and other historic churches are dotted around the Tembien and visitable as a day trip from Abi Aday. Note, however, that you *must* be accompanied by an official TTC guide to gain entrance to any of these churches, which basically rules out any option that doesn't see you arriving here *after* having passed through Wukro or Mekele.

Abba Yohanni This remote but fantastically situated monastery, visited by Dr Enzo Parona in 1928, lies midway up a tall west-facing sandstone cliff on a mountain called Debre Ansa. The façade, partially built after the original rock collapsed during excavation, is visible for miles before you arrive at the cliff base. It is one of the more photogenic exteriors, set high on a golden cliff, but does require afternoon light. The main church is reached via an atmospheric labyrinth of tunnels and nooks, incorporating the de-sanctified rock-hewn church of Kidane Mihret, and opening onto a series of ledges offering great views to the plains below. The rock-hewn church itself is very large, consisting of four domed bays standing up to 9m high and 14 carved columns, and is named after its founder Abba Yohanni, who is believed to have excavated it in the 14th century. Because the church is monastic, women are forbidden from entering the main building. Based on our experience, however, women are permitted to wander through the tunnel complex that leads up to the church.

To reach Abba Yohanni from Abi Aday, follow the Adwa road for 8km, then turn left onto a side road signposted for the church. After roughly 7km, you should park at the village of Menji at the base of the cliff. It's an easy ten to 15-minute walk from the road to the monastery. There is no public transport to Menji.

Gebriel Wukien The most accessible of the Tembien churches, Gebriel Wukien lies within easy walking distance of the main road between Abi Aday and Adwa. It appears to me to be a subterranean monolith, sunk within an excavated trench in a manner similar to several churches at Lalibela, although it is difficult to be sure of this because of the 20th-century stone roofing and mortar walls that cover and enclose the trench. Ruth Plant regarded Gebriel Wukien to be 'undoubtedly the most remarkable church' of the 15 she visited in the Tembien, and thought the quality of the carving of the four bays and several arches to be comparable to Adi Kasho Medhane Alem. Carved into a cliff behind the church are several monastic cells, as well as a kitchen and eating room where we were invited to drink *tella* with the friendly monks.

David Buxton placed Gebriel Wukien in the later series of Tigraian Basilica churches, which ties in with the oft-quoted tradition that this church was excavated during the 15th-century reign of Emperor Zara Yaqob. Undermining this rare instance of apparent academic and traditional concord, the priest who showed us around Gebriel Wukien told us that the cloth in front of the altar was a gift from Zara Yaqob, but the church itself was excavated during the 6th-century reign of Emperor Gebre Meskel. Accurate or not, this would appear to be a firmly established tradition, since we were shown the tomb of the church's purported founder, Abba Daniel, as well as a magnificent gold-plated diamond cross which reputedly belonged to him. The cloth paintings on the main door are also, and somewhat improbably, said to date to the time of Gebre Meskel.

To reach Gebriel Wukien from Abi Aday, follow the main Adwa road north for 16km, then turn left along a side road signposted for the church. After about 1km, you will reach a stand of fig trees and a water pump, where you can park your car in the shade. From the water pump, a footpath leads to the church, which despite its proximity to the road is very well hidden in a thicket of euphorbia and other scrubs. The walk takes no more than ten minutes, and the gradient is among the gentlest of any approach to a rock-hewn church in Tigrai. Entrance costs US$6 per person.

Maryam Hibeti This little-visited and rather lovely church, a close structural relative of Medhane Alem in Adi Kasho, is regarded by David Buxton to be a 15th-century replica of that prototypal church, a date which ties in with the local tradition ascribing it to the reign of Emperor Zara Yaqob. Maryam Hibeti translates as 'the Hidden Maryam', an apt name for an excavation that lies in a wooded enclave on the side of a gorge, invisible until you are within metres of the imposing façade. The interior, though large, is gloomy and unadorned, dominated by six arched columns, and a natural pool of therapeutic holy water immediately inside the main door. The well-lit and partially sunken cloister, by contrast, is atmospherically earthy because of the lack of adornment, and very photogenic.

To get to Maryam Hibeti from Abi Aday, follow the Adwa road north for roughly 18km, then take a right turn, which after 2km leads to Werkamba. This is a small, characteristically Tigraian town of stone houses, centred around a large marketplace and boasting a few shops and local restaurants but, so far as we could establish, no accommodation of any description. Continue along the main road through Werkamba for 4km until you reach another small village dominated by a war memorial. Turn left at the fork immediately past this village, following an occasionally unclear 4x4 track along a fertile plain for about 10km to the sizeable village of Adeha, where you can park your car. You'll need to find a guide here to help you locate the priest, who lives some distance from the village. Using a rather circuitous route past the priest's house, it took us a good 90 minutes to reach the church, and about an hour to walk back to Adeha. The footpath, much of which runs through the flat base of the gorge, is rough in places, but it doesn't involve any serious clambering except arguably along the short final ascent to the actual church. The area is, however, relatively low-lying and hot, and we regretted not taking any water with us.

It is worth noting, that although the church's name is more normally written as Maryam Hibito, locals definitely know it as Maryam Hibeti.

Emanuel Maibaha Situated on the slopes of Mount Zala, Emanuel Maibaha lies close to the old road between Hagere Selam and Abi Aday, for which reason it was one of the more accessible churches in the Tembien prior to the construction of the new road. The church is reputedly where Maibaha's most famous son, the Emperor Yohannis IV, was baptised as a child. Hidden within a prominent whitewashed built exterior, the rock-hewn church measures 9m wide and 10m deep, is supported by four large pillars, and is notable for the Croix Pautée on the domed ceiling. We were told that Emanuel Maibaha can be reached by following the same directions to Maryam Hibeti, but turning left instead of right at the fork after the village with the prominent war memorial 4km past Werkamba. So far as we could see, however, this road petered out after about 2km. Another, more reliable, possibility would be to follow the old Abi Aday road out of Hagere Selam for 13km; Emanuel Maibaha lies on the side of this road and its bold white exterior would be difficult to miss.

This 155km stretch of road, drivable in around four hours without stops, passes through some very remote scenery. Heading southward from Abi Aday towards Sekota, you need to turn right after 15km, at the junction with the road to Mekele via Hagare Selam. Another 19km and an altitudinal plunge to around 1,500m brings you to **Yechilay**, set in an otherwise unexpectedly austere landscape of spindly acacia scrubland populated by the odd herdsman and his coterie of skinny goats and long-horned cattle. The double-storey Tekaze Hotel on the Abi Aday side of Yechilay is probably the smartest lodging between here and Lalibela; if nothing else, this probably says all you need to know about accommodation standards in Sekota!

Between here and Tinarwa, 25km further south, the road bisects an isolated enclave of relatively low-lying Sahelian savanna, whose parched appearance – thick red sand, foreboding black rock, dry riverbeds, scraggly trees – comes as a real contrast even to the relatively dry highlands of northern Tigrai. It comes as no surprise to learn that this searing semi-desert, so visually reminiscent of the arid badlands of the Ethiopian–Kenyan border region, lay at the epicentre of the dreadful famine of 1985 – indeed, the television footage that first drew global attention to this tragedy was of victims who had evacuated the area between here and Sekota to hike to the main road at Korem.

After passing through the village of **Abegele** about 8km further on, the road crosses a series of watercourses that form part of the Tekaze drainage basin, the most impressive of which is the Tserari River, set at around 1,200m close to the isolated and venerable monastery of **Bar Kidane Mihret**. A striking feature of this area is the immense baobabs that line the rocky slopes. With bare contorted branches reaching skyward from squat, bulbous trunks, these ancient and obese trees – some must surely be thousands of years old – come across as if they have sucked the last drop of life from what was already a cruelly parched landscape. It comes as a relief when, after another 50km or so, the road ascends back into the highlands of Wag to the small town of Sekota.

SEKOTA

The remote highland town of Sekota is reminiscent of Lalibela as it used to look 20 years ago, before tourism took off and many of its characteristic traditional two-storey stone dwellings made way for more modern constructions. Sekota is the principal town of Wag, an ancient Agaw principality that converted to Christianity as early as the 6th century, possibly under the influence of the Syrian saint Abba Yemata. Wag is thought by many historians to have been an important centre of political power during the little-documented era that followed the collapse of the Axumite Empire and preceded the rise of the Zagwe Dynasty at Lalibela. Indeed, it is probable that Wag will eventually turn out to be the site of the mysterious Kubar, referred to by the 10th-century Arab writer Al-Masudi as 'capital of Abyssinia ... a great city [with] extensive territories stretching as far as the Abyssinian Sea [including] the coastal plain beyond Yemen'. The town's most noteworthy landmark, situated on the main traffic roundabout, is the **Church of Webila Maryam**, which is at least 200 years old and reputedly contains several interesting 19th-century paintings, though there was nobody around to open it up when I tried to check. More recently, Wag lay at the heart of the area affected by the terrible famine of 1985.

GETTING THERE AND AWAY The road route from Abi Aday is described opposite. Buses cover this route, but they are very slow. There is also an 85km road connecting Sekota to Korem (on the main road between Mekele and Woldia). The junction for the Korem road lies about 20km south of Sekota, where you need to fork left for Korem and right if you are heading for Lalibela. It is then a straight 110km drive to Lalibela, with the possibility of diverting to the churches around Bilbilla *en route*. There is no public transport between Sekota and Lalibela.

WHERE TO STAY AND EAT There isn't a great deal of choice on the accommodation front. The best bet is the Tadesse Hotel on the main roundabout, which charges an inflated *faranji* price of US$4 for a seriously basic room using common showers, and it serves adequate meals, decent coffee and the usual chilled drinks.

EXCURSIONS The near-monolithic rock-hewn church of **Wukro Meskel Kristos** lies about 6km south of Sekota, just ten minutes' walk east of the road to Korem/Lalibela. Tradition holds that Wukro Meskel Kristos pre-dates the Lalibela churches (some say it was excavated during the medieval reign of Yemrehanna Kristos, others that it dates to the 6th-century rule of Kaleb), and was the inspiration for many of them, which – if it is true – could mean it is the oldest near-monolith in Ethiopia. The rock-hewn church expert David Buxton, who visited Wukro Meskel Kristos in the 1960s, was of the opinion that the church is more recent, probably excavated in the 14th century. Either way, it's an atmospheric little church, and the ornate façade and decorated interior make it well worth the small effort required to reach it from the main road. Entrance costs US$6, women are forbidden and the church has been covered in scaffolding since 1998.

Six ancient coffins are stowed in the main church, while another stash of perhaps 50 coffins containing ancient mummies lies in an adjacent cave mausoleum. As usual, how they got there is a matter for conjecture. According to the priest I spoke to, the six coffins in the church house the bodies of former governors of Wag, while the mummies in the cave were Kaleb-era administrators who were carried to the church by angels after their death. When David Buxton visited the church in the 1950s, he was told that the mummies were former Wagsuns – Kings of Wag – who were customarily exhumed from their original graves about 20 years after their death and reburied in smaller caskets. Another legend has it that these are the bodies of priests who committed an unspecified sin and were struck down violently by God – certainly the few mummies that have spilled out of their coffins don't look like they died a peaceful death!

EXPLORING THE SOUTH WOLO HEARTLAND

Based on an article written by Mark Chapman
Travellers wanting to divert from the beaten tourist path can now travel between Lalibela and Addis Ababa or Dessie via Mekane Selam and the new Borena Sayint National Park. The details below are based largely on a 2011 trip undertaken by Mark Chapman, from north to south, but there is presumably no obstacle to travelling it in the other direction. It seems almost certain this road will be upgraded to all-weather gravel in its entirety during the lifespan of this edition, with potentially significant consequences for travellers, including the possibility of a direct bus service between Lalibela and Addis Ababa. Check our update website for news.

From Lalibela, you follow the main road heading south, which is asphalted until just near the airport where it turns off to the left and crosses the wide river bed

Based primarily on an article written by Mark Chapman, with additional information from an article by John Graham

Mekane Selam is the capital of Debre Sina *woreda*, an area of great historical and cultural significance to the Amhara people. The area around Mekane Selam is dotted with five-sided pillars not unlike the Axumite stelae in appearance and easily mistaken for manmade artefacts. In fact, the source of these pillars, possibly unknown to outsiders until John Graham was taken to see it a few years ago, is a magnificent natural rock formation in a river valley close to Mekane Selam. Reminiscent of the famous Giant's Causeway in Ireland, the rocks are basaltic columnar pillars, formed by lava that has effectively been crystallised into tightly packed pentagons. Some of the pillars must be close to 10m high. The formation stretches for about 30m on either side of the river. Several local buildings have been constructed using pillars removed from this formation, including the Mekane Selam branch of the Commercial Bank of Ethiopia.

Though somewhat remote, it is connected to Dessie by 180km of very bad road (through Kabi and Aksta), and can also be reached from the west following a road across a new bridge over the Blue Nile east of Dejen. Accommodation offerings here are few and far between, with the best being a **no-name hotel** in the Geteneh Building (the only concrete multi-storey place in town) in which in the top two floors reside basic bedrooms for between US$2 and US$2.50. Unfortunately the architect has forgotten to add bathrooms and the only communal bathroom on the lower of the two floors is not for the faint-hearted.

Mekane Selam is also the base for visits to the new **Borena Sayint National Park** (*entrance US$5.50 pp; US$1.50/3 per car/minibus*), which was officially designated in 2009. The park covers about 45km² of dense Afro-montane forest, which harbours around 23 large mammals including klipspringer, caracal, black-and-white colobus, jackal and bushbuck. At least 57 bird species have been recorded, including the endemic Abyssinian catbird, Abyssinian woodpecker, black-headed siskin and Harwood's francolin. At higher altitudes are open moorlands and forests of giant heather *Erica arboreal*, where the endemic Ethiopian wolf and gelada might be present.

The park headquarters is on the western side of town on a small road running north off the main gravel road. The 18km road to the park where the Frankfurt Zoological Society (FZS) has built an information centre is very rough and takes at least two hours driving mostly in low ratio to deal with the big bumps and loose surface. Along the way you'll pass many farmers heading to the Saturday market with their very healthy livestock. At the top you'll see the boundary of the park – there are markers here and there but the vegetation is full and ungrazed.

Five trekking routes have been created within the park, ranging from 8km to 16km in length. There are also some hikers' huts, built at an altitude of 3,300m, but these are currently unused and unfurnished, though have a good pit latrine toilet. Camping is definitely possible, however, and proper accommodation may soon be available. For more information contact the FZS (*www.fzs.org*).

of the Tenish Ababa (Little Flower). Soon after you will cross the young Tekezé River as it enters into a narrow gorge and goes on to become one of Ethiopia's mighty rivers. The well-graded dirt road winds through various lowland villages before climbing up onto the plateau – a ridge that is the watershed between the Tekezé River system and the Blue Nile. Continuing on you'll reach the unattractive crossroads settlement of **Gashena** on the China Road about 65km from Lalibela at a cool altitude of 3,000m.

At Gashena, head straight across at the junction with the China Road and follow the rutted 10km gravel road to Kon, the capital of the area. About another 10km on you'll have reached the southern edge of the plateau and began a remarkable 13km descent to the Jitta River. The bottom is at about 1,830m altitude. The 17km ascent up the other side to the plateau is equally steep and dramatic. The road flicks east before arriving at **Wegel Tena**, the main town in the area around 140km from Lalibela. There is no fuel station here, but food and snacks are available.

From here the road drops down to the second major river crossing – the Tukur Abay (Black Nile). It takes about an hour's drive, including photo stops, to cover the 27km. The bridge at the bottom is at an altitude of 1,690m from where you'll wind your way back above 2,900m to the roadside church of **Tash Tenta Mikael** and – only 5km further on – the small centre of **Tenta**, which is 196km from Lalibela and is best known as the junction town for Makdala Hill (see *Makdala Hill*, page 353).

From Tenta, you'll drive through a succession of South Wolo towns: Ajbar (in Tenta *woreda*) Amba Mariam (in Medela *woreda*) and a big junction town called Gimba, some 53km from Tenta where you'll join a bigger gravel road sweeping in from the east and follow it heading west. Along the way you'll notice the houses change to a conical design with walls only a foot or so high topped by a large conical dome. The altitude here is over 3,200m – so the house design is perhaps a way to protect against the intense cold of the mountain.

The next big town you'll pass through is Akasta, before arriving at **Mekane Selam** (see box, *Mekane Selam and Borena Sayint National Park*, opposite), which is 270km from Lalibela, a ten-hour drive including stops. From Mekane Selam, you need to head west for about 50km to the new bridge over the Blue Nile, along a road that descends from 2,680m to 1,167m at the bridge. The bridge is not yet open to commercial traffic and the road is still being completed, but is passable and should be finished sometime in 2012. It takes around two hours to drive to the bridge, and another hour to the top of the plateau on the Gojam side – a further 26km away.

The landscape on the Gojam side changes to fields full of crops peppered with acacia trees. From here the new road speeds through the countryside to **Mertule Mariam**, 143km from Mekane Selam, where there is a fuel station. Another 28km takes you to the junction with the old gravel road that leads from Dejen to Bahir Dar, and again another 99km to the asphalt road 8km outside **Dejen**. From here it is around another 287km on the main highway south to Addis Ababa. Depending on what time you arrive you may need to overnight in Dejen (see *Chapter 6*, page 180, for hotel recommendations).

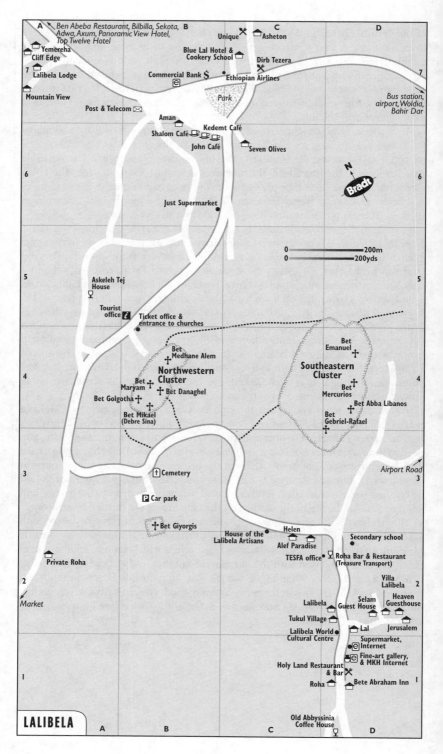

LALIBELA

Ben Abeba Restaurant, Bilbilla, Sekota,
Adwa, Axum, Panoramic View Hotel,
Top Twelve Hotel

A   B   C   D

Yemereha
Cliff Edge

Unique   Asheton

Blue Lal Hotel &
Cookery School

Labela Lodge

Dirb Tezera

Commercial Bank $

Ethiopian Airlines

7

Mountain View

Bus station,
airport, Woldia,
Bahir Dar

Park

Post & Telecom ✉

Aman

Kedemt Café

Shalom Café

John Café

Seven Olives

6   N   6

Bract

Just Supermarket

0   200m
0   200yds

5

Askeleh Tej
House

Tourist
office ℹ

Ticket office &
entrance to churches

Bet
Medhane Alem

Bet
Emanuel

Northwestern
Cluster

Southeastern
Cluster

4

Bet
Maryam

Bet Danaghel

Bet
Mercurios

Bet Golgotha

Bet Abba Libanos

Bet Mikael
(Debre Sina)

Bet
Gebriel-Rafael

Airport Road

3

Cemetery

P Car park

Bet Giyorgis

Helen

House of the
Lalibela Artisans

Secondary school

Alef Paradise

TESFA office

Roha Bar & Restaurant
(Treasure Transport)

Private Roha

Villa
Lalibela

2

Market

Lalibela
Guest House

Selam

Heaven
Guesthouse

Tukul Village

Lalibela World
Cultural Centre

Lal

Jerusalem

Supermarket,
Internet

Fine-art gallery,
& MKH Internet

Holy Land Restaurant
& Bar

1

Roha

Bete Abraham Inn

Old Abbyssinia
Coffee House

A   B   C   D

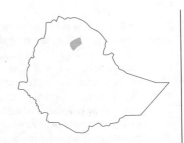

13

Lalibela and Surrounds

The strange, isolated town of Lalibela, set high in the mountains of Lasta, is famed for its rock-hewn churches, and is arguably the one place in Ethiopia that no tourist should miss. Known as Roha until recent times, Lalibela was the capital of the Zagwe dynasty, which ruled over Ethiopia from the 10th century to the mid 13th century, and its modern name derives from that of the most famous of the Zagwe rulers, the 12th-century King Lalibela.

According to local legend, Lalibela was born the brother of the incumbent king. As a young child he was covered by a swarm of bees, which his mother took as a sign that he would one day be king himself. (One reported translation of Lalibela is 'the bees recognise his sovereignty', which isn't at all bad for four syllables; another more mundane and succinct translation is 'miracle'.) The king was none too pleased at this prophecy, and eventually tried to poison his younger brother, but instead of killing him he cast him into a deep sleep that endured for three days. While sleeping, Lalibela was transported to heaven by an angel and shown a city of rock-hewn churches, which he was ordered to replicate. Rather neatly, his elder brother had a simultaneous vision in which Christ instructed him to abdicate in favour of Lalibela. Another version of the legend is that Lalibela went into exile in Jerusalem, and was inspired by a vision to create a 'new' Jerusalem of rock at Roha.

As soon as he was crowned, Lalibela set about gathering the world's greatest craftsmen and artisans in order to carve the churches. Legend has it that at least one of the churches was built in a day with the help of angels – or, as Graham Hancock suggests in *The Sign and the Seal* (and not a great deal more plausibly), with the assistance of Freemasons! In fact, the excavation of the churches *is* something of a mystery – some sources estimate that in the order of 40,000 people would have been required to carve them – so it's not surprising that their origin has been clouded in legend. If anywhere I have visited would make me start contemplating supernatural intervention – or, for that matter, the timely arrival of a bunch of bearded Grail-seekers – it would have to be Lalibela.

LALIBELA

Even before you visit the churches, Lalibela is a strikingly singular town. The setting alone is glorious. Perched at an altitude of 2,630m, among wild craggy mountains and vast rocky escarpments, there is a stark cathedral-like grandeur to Lalibela that recalls the Drakensberg Mountains of South Africa and Lesotho. The houses of Lalibela are of a design unlike anywhere else in Ethiopia, two-storey circular stone constructs that huddle in an amorphous mass over the steep slopes on which the town is built.

But people visit Lalibela for the churches. And, no matter if you have visited other rock-hewn churches in Ethiopia, nothing will prepare you for these. The Lalibela churches are *big* – several are in excess of 10m high – and, because they are carved below ground level, they are ringed by trenches and courtyards, the sides of which are cut into with stone graves and hermit cells, and connected to each other by a tangled maze of tunnels and passages. In size and scope, the church complex feels like a subterranean village. Yet each individual church is unique in shape and size, precisely carved and minutely decorated. Lalibela is, in a word, awesome. When the Portuguese priest Francisco Alvarez was taken to Lalibela in 1521, he doubted that his compatriots would believe what he had seen. In his narrative *Prester John of the Indies* he wrote: 'It wearied me to write more of these works, because it seemed to me that they will accuse me of untruth … there is much more than I have already written, and I have left it that they may not tax me with it being falsehood.'

Were it virtually anywhere but in Ethiopia, Lalibela would rightly be celebrated as one of the wonders of the world, as readily identified with Ethiopia as are the pyramids or the Sphinx with Egypt. As it is, Lalibela is barely known outside Ethiopia, and Ethiopia itself is associated first and foremost with desert and drought – not a little ironic, when you consider that the fertile Nile Basin, on which Egypt depends, receives 90% of its water from the Ethiopian Highlands.

Lalibela's obscurity is shameful but for those who visit the town it is part of the charm. These churches are not primarily tourist attractions, being prodded and poked away from their original context, nor are they the crumbling monuments of a dead civilisation. What they are, and what they have been for at least 800 years, is an active Christian shrine, the spiritual centre of a town's religious life. It is naive, and perhaps a bit patronising, to think in terms of unchanging cultures. Nevertheless, if you wander between the churches in the thin light of morning, when white-robed hermits emerge Bible-in-hand from their cells to bask on the rocks, and the chill highland air is warmed by Eucharistic drumbeats and gentle swaying chants, you can't help but feel that you are witnessing a scene that is fundamentally little different from the one that has been enacted here every morning for century upon century. The joy of Lalibela, the thing that makes this curiously medieval town so special, is that it is not just the rock-hewn churches that have survived into the modern era, but also something more organic. The churches breathe.

More prosaically, many of the churches have been damaged by seepage. For years the churches were individually covered with basic shelters of iron and

LALIBELA AT ETHIOPIAN CHRISTMAS

Extracted from a letter by Raoul Boulakia

We saw the Christmas service, which was interesting, and not what I expected when people told me the monks would dance, as they really mournfully sway and march in procession. What I found most impressive was the devotion of the rural people, hiking for days and even weeks to get there, and sleeping on the ground outside the churches. The multitude of pilgrims is really amazing. However, I expect there would be far fewer lodging and transportation hassles coming at other times. Either way is a trade-off. If you go at Christmas or Timkat, you get to see the magnitude of how important a religious site it is. If you go at other times, it should be calmer and easier to arrange. Rates also go up for Christmas and Timkat, sometimes during the course of a day as hotel owners realise everything is sold out. Whatever, it's still one of the manmade wonders of the world.

wood in order to protect them from the elements and to preserve them for future generations. With funding from the European Union, these piecemeal structures have recently been replaced by four large white translucent shelters, which cover each of the major churches in the two main clusters. Reviews of these new structures are mixed; the modern design is certainly eye-catching, but some feel it clashes with the ancient architecture that lies beneath. Fortunately these new shelters are designed to be temporary, and may be replaced if and when a more suitable design is approved.

GETTING THERE AND AWAY

By air Daily flights connect Lalibela to Addis Ababa (US$71, via Bahir Dar), Gondar (US$48), Bahir Dar (US$40) and Axum (US$44) throughout the year. The airport, with its surfaced airstrip, lies about 25km from the town centre along a tarred road passing below the monastery at Nakuta La'ab. All flights are met by most private operators, which generally charge US$4.50 per person for a one-way transfer to town. As with all domestic flights, it is necessary to confirm your ticket out of Lalibela a day in advance; the **Ethiopian Airlines office** [322 B7] (\ 033 336 0046; e llitam@ ethiopianairlines.com) is situated on the main square close to the Blue Lal Hotel.

By road Despite its isolation, Lalibela is now accessible by several different road routes, all of which are discussed in further detail in the previous chapter *Through Routes to Lalibela*. All buses to/from Lalibela now arrive and depart from the new bus station a few kilometres downhill from the centre. It's a steep hike, so your best bet is to hitch a ride on a *gari* or to call ahead and arrange a pick-up with your hotel.

GETTING AROUND Based at the Roha Bar and Restaurant, **Treasure Transport** [322 D2] offers car hire for trekkers, trips to the outlying monasteries, and group trips for budget travellers. Transportation to Gondar and Bahir Dar is also available. For reservations contact Habtamu Baye (\ 033 336 0038; m 0911 02 89 53; e b_h2007@yahoo.com).

Based in the Roha Hotel, **Pride Ethiopia Tours** [322 D1] (\ 033 336 0090/0952; m 0911 718 331) can also arrange vehicle rental and guided tours to churches outside Lalibela.

TOURIST INFORMATION The **tourist office** [322 D3] (\ 033 336 0119/0441; ⊕ 08.30–12.30 & 13.30–17.30 Mon–Fri) recently relocated to a more central position in a rather improbable-looking blue metal shed opposite the ticket office. The people who work there seem to be very helpful and they usually stock a few useful brochures and maps. The official **Lalibela Guides Association** (\ 033 336 0065; e syhlal@ethionet.et) has an office near the Roha Hotel, where registered guides can be arranged for US$18 per day for groups of up to three or US$25 per day for larger groups. The newly formed **Community Tourism Guiding Enterprise** (\ 033 336 1095; m 0913 783 557; e info@lalibelactge.com; www.lalibelactge.com), can also arrange guides.

An ancient but nevertheless exceptionally informative 32-page free booklet on Lalibela was reprinted by the ETC in 2000. Also worth looking out for is Tilahun Assefa's very useful booklet *Lalibela: World Wonder Heritage*, which used to be available for a small charge in Lalibela, but may be out of print.

WHERE TO STAY Hotels in Lalibela are uniformly over-priced by comparison with anywhere else in Ethiopia, probably because this is one place where tourists rather than locals constitute the bulk of the customers at all levels. You might be asked double the price quoted below when large numbers of tourists are in town, and four or five times that price during any important festival such as Timkat or Meskel. At such times camping may be permitted on the grounds of most hotels; the cost to pitch a tent then often exceeds the standard room rates. By contrast, most hotels will negotiate downwards when things are quiet. In recent years there has been a construction boom of mostly upmarket places, while unfortunately, budget accommodations remain thin on the ground.

Upmarket

Mountain View Hotel [322 A7] (30 rooms) \033 336 0804; m 0911 983 396; e info@mountainsviewhotel.com; www.mountainsviewhotel.com. Situated on a promontory just out of town, this architecturally designed luxury hotel offers stunning panoramic views of the expansive valley below. The rooms each with hot-water en suite & private balcony while comfortable & clean may lack the wow factor of the hotel's design, but are still better than or equal to the other offerings in this price range – they also have the added bonus of that amazing aforementioned view. Facilities include Wi-Fi, an expansive rooftop terrace bar (perfect for that sunset drink), & a first-class restaurant boasting internationally trained cooks. The reception is open 24hrs & a shuttle service to the airport is available. The helpful hotel staff can also organise tours, registered local guides & 4x4 & minibus hire. Future plans include a swimming pool as well as an additional 30 new rooms. *US$64/77/77 sgl/dbl/twin inc b/fast.*

Tukul Village Hotel [322 D2] (12 rooms) \033 336 0564/0565; m 0911 104 944; f 033 336 1180; e nora.wakim@tiscali.nl or messay_2005@ yahoo.co.uk; www.tukulvillage.com. This joint Dutch–Ethiopian venture, situated opposite the Lal Hotel, skilfully combines traditional stone-&-thatch *tukul*-style architecture with fully modern amenities. The large, spotless rooms are the best in town, featuring floor-to-ceiling windows & balconies offering superb views over Bet Giyorgis. Each room takes up an entire floor of the double-storey *tukuls,* putting them a class above other places with similar-looking exteriors. The palatial bathrooms with enclosed showers & 24hr hot water win the most spacious bathroom award in Ethiopia. At the time of writing 12 new *tukuls* each to feature locally hand-crafted furnishings were under construction. The restaurant features an inspired mix of European dishes as well as superb traditional food. A massage service is available,

& there is a book exchange with a fair number of titles in several languages. Rates include breakfast & free Wi-Fi. Visa & MasterCard are accepted. *US$57/77/77 sgl/dbl/twin, US$104 family room.*

Roha Hotel [322 D1] (64 rooms) \033 336 0009; m 0913 012 594; f 033 336 0156; e info@rohahotels.com; www.rohahotels.com. Situated about 2km from the town centre & the main cluster of churches, this one-time government hotel lacks the grand views of some of its sister hotels from the former Ghion chain such as the Goha Hotel in Gondar, but feels especially well managed, providing for an altogether pleasant experience. Like its former siblings, the Roha is slated for a full makeover, with an additional 86 new rooms to be added & current facilities (including the swimming pool which was empty on our most recent visit) updated & modernised. Even without the changes, it still remains one of the smartest places in town. Meals are good & cost US$3–5 per dish. Rates include breakfast, internet is available, & the gift shop well stocked – if you can't find what you are looking for there is a whole row of independent souvenir shops out front. *US$51/76/76 sgl/dbl/twin, US$101 suite.*

Bete Abraham Inn [322 D1] (53 rooms) \033 336 1065; m 0911 320 051; e beteabraham@yahoo.com; www.beteabrahaminn.com. This multi-storey hotel with its colourful exterior frescoes is located at the southern end of town opposite the Roha Hotel. Administered by the Church, the proceeds from the hotel purportedly go to supporting the region's 850 priests. The en-suite rooms each with over-sized furniture, tiled floors, DSTV, phone & private balcony are generally adequate, but seem somewhat overpriced when viewed in comparison to the other hotels in this price range. Tour guides can be arranged as can car hire & airport shuttles. A restaurant, bar & souvenir shop are attached & prices are negotiable during the low season. *US$50/60/60/85 sgl/dbl/twin/suite.*

🏠 **Jerusalem Hotel (aka Lasta Hotel)**
[322 D2] (26 rooms) 📞033 336 0047/0480;
📱 0911 435 432; e lastajerusalem@ethionet.
et; www.lalibelajerusalemhotel.com. This highly
regarded 3-storey hotel lies about 200m from the
Lal, along a cul-de-sac from where there are stirring
views over the rolling mountains of Lasta. The
huge tiled rooms come complete with king beds &
en-suite hot shower. Rates include breakfast & free
Wi-Fi & an airport shuttle is available for a small fee.
A 30% discount is available during the low season.
The restaurant is well known for its good traditional
& Western dishes priced in the US$2.50–6 range &
the English-speaking management is very helpful.
At the time of writing, the hotel was planning on
building a new 5-star annex close to the World
Cultural Centre. *US$45/60/70 sgl/dbl/twin inc
b/fast.*

Moderate

🏠 **Cliff Edge Hotel** [322 A7] (18 rooms)
📞033 336 0606; e info@cliffedgehotel-lalibela.
com; www.cliffedgehotel-lalibela.com. This
recently opened 3-storey hotel just down from
the Yemereha Hotel is already receiving good
feedback. As its name suggests it's perched right
on the edge of the mountain range overlooking
the valley below. The simply furnished rooms all
have hot-water shower en suites & are afforded
stunning views from private balconies. There's
a good restaurant serving both European &
Ethiopian dishes (a 3-course meal will set you
back around US$5.50), internet is available, pick-
ups from the airport can be arranged & Visa is
accepted. *US$45/55/55 sgl/dbl/twin inc b/fast.*

🏠 **Panoramic View Hotel** [off map 322
A7] (36 rooms) 📞033 836 0000; 📱 0911
022 398/042 247; e amdaya10@gmail.com
or info@panoramicviewhotel.com; www.
panoramicviewhotel.com. This multi-storey hotel
located on the hillside behind the Mountain
View Hotel is still under construction, but should
be completed before this book goes to print. It
will have 36 rooms each with private hot-water
en suite & balcony, a restaurant & rooftop bar &
airport transfers will be available. *US$40/50 sgl/
dbl inc b/fast.*

🏠 **Lalibela Lodge** [322 A7] (10 rooms)
📱 0911 534 900; e info@ethiopiasnewfaces.com;
www.ethiopiasnewfaces.com. This lodge next door
to Mountain View, owned & managed by a young

& enthusiastic ex-guide, was also in the final
stages of construction when we visited. All rooms
have phone, fridge, private hot-water shower en
suite & balconies facing the view. 3 of the rooms
have king-size double beds & the remainder have
twin beds. The owner's mother, an ex-cook from
Seven Olives Restaurant, will also be on hand
to whip up meals for guests. The lodge will also
double as a base for New Faces of Ethiopia Tours, so
it goes without saying this should be a very good
contact for arranging local tours, etc. *US$37/50 sgl/
dbl inc b/fast.*

🏠 **Top Twelve Hotel** [off map 322 A7]
(12 rooms) 📱 0911 930 217/0920 190 165;
e andebtlalibela@yahoo.com. Yet another new
hotel near completion in Lalibela's current building
boom on the hillside behind the Mountain View
Hotel, this place is again due to be open by the
time this guide sees light. It will offer spacious
rooms – 6 on the upper level & 6 on the lower level
– all with hot-shower en suite & balcony. 2 of the
rooms will also feature a small kitchenette for self-
caterers & free Wi-Fi will be available. *US$29/48/48
sgl/dbl/twin, US$59 suite inc b/fast.*

🏠 **Yemereha Hotel** [322 A7] (42 rooms)
📞033 336 0862/0864; e reservations@
yemerehahotel.com; www.yemerehahotel.com.
Part of the Green Land Hotels Group, this lodge
is situated on a newly cobbled road behind the
Mountain View Hotel. The traditionally furnished
rooms each have full-size beds & en-suite hot
bath. A breezy thatched-roof bar & restaurant
is attached, offering meals in the US$26 range,
& tours to outlying churches can be arranged.
US$30/40/40 sgl/dbl/twin.

🏠 **Lal Hotel** [322 D2] (105 rooms) 📞033
336 0008/0044/0183 or 011 662 6586; e lato@
ethionet.et or info@lalhoteltour.com; www.
lalhoteltour.com. Situated about 200m from the
Roha back towards the town centre, this hotel
offers 2 levels of accommodation: adequate
but uninspiring bungalow rooms with en-suite
hot shower, & newer *tukul* rooms which are
a bit fresher, but cannot be compared to the
much larger & better-appointed rooms at Tukul
Village. The Lal is a good place to arrange 4x4
transport to the outlying monasteries, & the
tukul-style restaurant is far better than that at
the Roha. Internet is available & a free airport
shuttle is offered for stays of 2 nights or more.
Like many of the hotels in Lalibela – and

throughout Ethiopia for that matter! – the Lal is in the process of expansion with 40 new rooms, a meeting hall, gallery, swimming pool & watchtower on the cards for the future. *Bungalow rooms US$31/36/36 sgl/dbl/twin, Tukul rooms US$36/42/42 sgl/dbl/twin.*

🏠 **Aman Hotel** [322 B6] (28 rooms) ✆033 366 0076; m 0911 756 450; e cheru_abebe@ yahoo.com. This multi-storey hotel boasts a central location in the upper part of town just metres from both the Commercial Bank of Ethiopia & the Ethiopian Airlines office. The smart rooms each have a breezy balcony & a compact en suite with hot-water shower. Other facilities should include a ground-floor internet café & supermarket, & 3rd-floor open-air bar & glassed-in restaurant offering 360° views. *US$35/40 sgl/dbl inc b/fast.*

🏠 **Villa Lalibela** [322 D2] (4 rooms) ✆033 336 0246; m 0911 343 113. This clean, modern new guesthouse offers huge garishly bright green rooms with good hot water en suites. There's a large downstairs lounge-cum-dining room & a good-sized kitchen perfect for self-caterers. *US$35 dbl inc b/fast.*

🏠 **Seven Olives Hotel** [322 C6] (18 rooms) ✆033 336 0020; e sevenoliveshotel@yahoo.com. Owned & managed by the Ethiopian Orthodox Church, this is the oldest hotel in Lalibela, set in mature well-wooded grounds that come as a pleasant surprise given the central location. The en-suite rooms with hot shower are also looking a little mature – well, not so much mature as past the sell-by date – making them feel very over-priced. Even so, the Old-World ambience & green flowering grounds should make the Seven Olives the first choice for romantically minded travellers who can see past the decaying state of the rooms to embrace the charm. And even if you don't stay overnight, it is worth dropping in for a tranquil meal, a chilled drink or a pot of strong coffee. (The food ranks as some of the best in town.) Internet is available. *US$24/34/42 sgl/dbl/trpl.*

🏠 **Alef Paradise Hotel** [322 C2] (22 rooms) ✆033 336 0023; e alparahotel@yahoo.com. Situated at the southern end of town near Helen Hotel, this friendly place offers good-quality rooms with hot-water en suite & spacious balconies with views of St George's Church at a very affordable price. There is a restaurant, internet café & terrace bar, as well as free airport pick-up. Additionally, tours & car hire can be arranged. *US$25/30/40 sgl/dbl/trpl.*

Budget

🏠 **Heaven Guesthouse** [322 D2] (9 rooms) ✆033 336 0075. Situated alongside the Lasta/Jerusalem Hotel, this modest guesthouse offers clean, compact rooms with a genuine double bed & en-suite hot shower. Tack on another US$3 if you want breakfast included – other meals are not served, but you can eat next door. *US$12/15 sgl/dbl.*

🏠 **Selam Guest House** [322 D2] (4 rooms) ✆033 336 0074; m 0913 840 116; e selamguesthouselalibela@gmail.com. Tucked away in a back street not far from the Lal Hotel, this unpretentious little guesthouse offers accommodation in unfussy rooms (3 are twins & 1 a standard dbl) all with private en suite. There's no restaurant, but cold drinks are available. *US$9/18/18 sgl/dbl/twin inc b/fast.*

🏠 **Blue Lal Hotel** [322 C7] (14 rooms) ✆033 336 0380; m 0911 974 812; e blulalhotel@yahoo. com. Aka Chez Sophie, the name of its French-speaking owner, this once-popular restaurant has relocated from the main square to a site 20m away along an alley leading behind Ethiopian Airlines, & morphed into an equally popular budget hotel. Accommodation is basic at best, yet while the common shower rooms are reasonable value, the en-suite rooms with their irregularly working hot-water showers seem somewhat optimistically priced in our view & only 3 rooms (rooms 2, 3 & 4) have a balcony. The hotel also runs a small cooking school (see under *Other practicalities* on page 330 for details). *US$7.50/9 sgl/dbl with common shower, US$12/15 sgl/dbl en suite.*

🏠 **Lalibela Hotel** [322 D2] (20 rooms) ✆033 336 0036/0027; m 0911 095 004; e lalibelahotels@gmail.com. Situated next to the Tukul Village on a plot overlooking Bet Giyorgis, this friendly hotel charges offers clean rooms with en-suite hot shower. The *tukul*-style restaurant has good food, & there is a well-stocked supermarket on site that carries supplies for trekking including cheese & camera batteries. The manager speaks excellent English & can help arrange tour guides or car hire. The gift shop here has fair pricing, & internet costs US$2 per half-hour. *Camping US$5 per tent, US$10/15/15/20 sgl/dbl/twin/trpl.*

🏠 **Asheton Hotel** [322 C7] (14 rooms) ✆033 336 0030. Lalibela's longest-serving budget hotel offers reasonably clean, though arguably bedraggled, rooms with hot water shower en-suite. The restaurant has been remodelled & has DSTV & decent food. *US$11/14 sgl/dbl*.

Shoestring

🏠 **Helen Hotel** [322 C2] (9 rooms) ✆ 033 336 0050; e helenhotel28@yahoo.com. The scruffy but reasonably priced little rooms here have a good view. 15 more rooms should be completed during the lifespan of this book. *US$6/7.50 sgl/dbl with hot-water en suite*.

🏠 **Private Roha Hotel** [322 A2] (10 rooms) ✆ 033 336 0094. This established favourite with budget travellers is commendable for the friendly management, the house speciality of spicy pasta, genuinely hot common showers & the legendary toilet with a view across to the churches. Like the Helen Hotel above, rates have remained the same such that the asking price for a very basic & not-as-clean-as-it-used-to-be room with common hot water shower represents decent value. *US$5/7.50 sgl/dbl*.

❌ **WHERE TO EAT** Most of the more tourist-oriented hotels serve a good mix of Ethiopian and Western dishes, with the **Mountain View Hotel** [322 A7] probably the standout in pure culinary terms, the **Lal Hotel** [322 D2] running it a close (and more affordable) second, and the **Seven Olives Hotel** [322 C6] scoring top marks for al fresco ambience. Also recommended is the restaurant at the **Blue Lal Hotel** [322 C7], which is owned and managed by an Ethiopian woman who lived in France for a decade, and who still transports many of her ingredients personally from Addis Ababa – spaghetti and fruit juice are the specialities.

❌ **Ben Abeba** [off map 322 A7] ✆ 033 336 0215; www.benabeba.com; ⏰ 11.00–23.00 daily. This rather magical new restaurant run by a Scottish expat & her Ethiopian partner, sits atop a conical-shaped hill at the northern end of town. The surreal-looking restaurant, somewhat reminiscent of witch's hat, has views to die for & at night lights up Lalibela. And the food, which includes both Ethiopian & European dishes (the shepherd's pie is not to be missed!), is superb. Scones with jam & cream are a speciality as are fresh juices & homemade chutney. Accommodation is also planned. *Snacks & burger US$2–4, US$6–7.50 3-course meal*.

❌ **Holy Land Restaurant & Bar** [322 D1] ⏰ 08.00–21.00 daily. This friendly new restaurant

has been recommended by readers. There's a varied menu & good terrace area with nice views, but service can be slow. *US$2–4*.

❌ **Roha Bar & Restaurant** [322 D2] ✆ 033 336 0329; ⏰ 06.00–22.00 daily. Located next to the Lalibela Hotel, this good local eatery serves decent meals. *US$2–4*.

❌ **Unique Restaurant** [322 C7] ✆ 033 336 0125; ⏰ 07.00–21.00. This unassuming little place, directly opposite the Asheton Hotel, doesn't entice from its outward appearance. But the 'Recommended by Faranji' sign on the front intrigued this updater enough to enter. Inside is a homely local restaurant serving tasty pizzas, Ethiopian specialities & roast meat. *US$1.50–3*.

NIGHTLIFE For nightlife, the **Old Abyssinia Coffee House** [322 D1] (m *0912 027 992*) is an excellent bar housed in an authentic mud-wall *tukul*, tastefully decorated with locally made furniture and wall hangings. It is well worth the ten-minute walk past the Roha Hotel; music usually starts from 19.00. Should you wish to try the local tipple for which Lalibela is justly famed, the **Askelech Tej House** [322 A5] is strongly endorsed by local guides, while the *tej* at the **Helen Hotel** [322 C2] has been described as 'heavenly'.

ENTERTAINMENT Thanks to funding from the European Union, an old building once shared by the local police and the cultural association has been revitalised and reopened as the impressive-looking **Lalibela World Cultural Centre** [322 D1] (m *0912 157 663*; ⏰ *08.30–18.00 daily*). Located at the southern end of town opposite the Lal Hotel, the new cultural centre houses a large conference hall which doubles as a cinema and concert hall, a library and computer room and a soon-to-be-opened ground-floor bar and restaurant. On the top floor of the main building is a museum hosting a permanent exhibition on the archaeology and history of Lalibela.

SHOPPING

Crafts The main clusters of craft stalls are on the main square and along the road between the Lal and Roha hotels. Also close to the Roha Hotel is the fine-art shop run by the self-taught local artist Tegegne Yirdaw, who sells watercolours and monochrome sketches for birr 150–200. Located next to Helen Hotel, the **House of the Lalibela Artisans** [322 C2] (\ *033 336 1203;* ⊕ *08.00–18.00 daily*) sells locally made cloth, pottery and baskets, with proceeds benefiting the community.

Supermarkets To stock up on dried food before trekking to one of the monasteries, **Just Supermarket** [322 B6] south of Seven Olives Hotel has a fair range of imported goods such as processed cheese, biscuits and chocolate. If you are staying closer to the Roha, then there are a few more conveniently located small **supermarkets** [322 D1] lining the road south of the Lal Hotel, or try the supermarket at the Lalibela Hotel.

OTHER PRACTICALITIES

Internet and email Email and internet services are now widely available at most hotels for free. There are also a number of small internet cafés dotted around town charging a fairly steep price of US$2 per half-hour. Service availability can be an issue, as can connection speed, but if you get lucky it is sometimes reasonably fast!

Foreign exchange The **Commercial Bank of Ethiopia** [322 B7] (⊕ *08.00–16.00 Mon–Fri, 08.00–13.00 Sat*), located next to the Ethiopian Airlines office, is the most reliable place to change foreign currency. If the bank is closed and you're stuck, speak to the receptionist at the Roha Hotel, who will generally change US dollar bills at a rate only marginally lower than the bank rate.

Cooking The Blu Lal Hotel (see page 328) has recently started a small **cookery school** [322 C7] in its kitchen where you can learn how to make your own Ethiopian staples including *injera* and *wat* for US$50/30 for one person/group of two–three. Don't expect a flash Jamie Oliver-style cooking school – this is a real local kitchen where cooking is done traditional-style on an open fire. Bookings can be made through the hotel.

WHAT TO SEE

The churches Lalibela's churches are divided into two clusters, separated by the Jordan River – one local legend has it that the river was given this name after King Lalibela returned from Jerusalem. The **northwest cluster** comprises seven churches: Bet Medhane Alem, Bet Maryam, Bet Meskel, Bet Danaghel, Bet Debre Sina, Bet Golgotha and the Selassie Chapel. The **southeast cluster** consists of five churches: Bet Emanuel, Bet Mercurios, Bet Abba Libanos, Bet Lehem and Bet Gebriel-Rafael. A 13th church, **Bet Giyorgis**, stands discrete from the two main clusters.

The various churches of Lalibela were constructed using one of two different methods. Bet Giyorgis and the churches in the northwest cluster are mostly excavated from below the ground, and are surrounded by courtyards and trenches, so that they mimic normal buildings. Several of these churches are monoliths or three-quarter monoliths – free from the surrounding rock on three or four sides – a style of excavation that is unique to Ethiopia. The churches of the southeast cluster are similar to many churches in Tigrai, in that most of them were excavated from a vertical rock face by exploiting existing caves or cracks in the rock.

Tour practicalities Tours of Lalibela start at the northwest cluster of churches, which lies a short walk downhill from the Seven Olives Hotel. Here you must buy a ticket at the **official ticket office** [322 B4] (✆ *033 336 0021*) for US$21 allowing access to all the churches in town (but not the monasteries outside town). Hang on to this ticket, because it's valid for four days.

Although it is reasonably easy to find your own way around the church complex, especially with a copy of Tilahun Assefa's *Lalibela: World Wonder Heritage* booklet, there is a strong case for organising a guide. Firstly, the guides – the official ones anyway – are generally very knowledgeable and informative. They also know all the priests, and so you'll be spared the hassle of having to raise the priest who keeps the key for each church. No less compelling is that the moment you appoint a guide the others will leave you in peace (and the guides at Lalibela – or rather the non-official guides – are increasingly becoming an irritant in this respect).

One of the official guides registered by the Lalibela Guides Association can be contacted through any of the hotels. The official guides are more knowledgeable than their unofficial counterparts, and are held in greater respect by the priests. Rates are negotiable, starting at around US$25 daily for a large group or US$18 daily for up to three people. Off-season, the official guides are often happy to take backpackers around at a better rate, while rates generally escalate during busy periods. If you are happy with the service provided, by all means tip, but you are under no obligation – the guides association forbids its members from asking for tips.

Unofficial guides ask less than official guides, but they are unlikely to be as knowledgeable, and it is often impossible to get into the churches with them. Many, too, are masters of the manipulative sulk – they will as a matter of course look insulted and start muttering about tips when you pay them the agreed fee, and so, also as a matter of course, will taint what was probably otherwise a fine day. Make it clear from the start that the rate you have agreed is final. If you are in town for a few days, make the guide aware of this, and that you will appoint him on a day-by-day basis.

Except when it comes to the subject of money, most guides (official or not) are genuinely helpful, and they'll sort out anything you want from a good local meal or a better hotel to helping you bargain for curios. Many people leave Lalibela very pleased with their guide, and quite a number have written to me commending a

TOURISM FOR EDUCATION AND DEVELOPMENT ASSOCIATION

In the past, Lalibela was known for its particularly persistent beggars and street children whose constant presence served as an unwelcome distraction to visiting tourists. During the past few years this situation has been significantly remedied by a programme aimed to get beggars and orphans off the streets and into homes. Tourists are now advised not to give any money or sweets directly to beggars or children. Instead, collection boxes have been stationed at most tourist hotels where visitors can make a donation to provide food and housing for people on the streets, as well as schooling and skills training. Funding also goes towards improving sanitation and building toilets, to curb the fly population and prevent the spreading of disease. For additional information contact the Tourism for Education and Development Association (m *0911 019 491;* e *tourismcommunity@yahoo.com*).

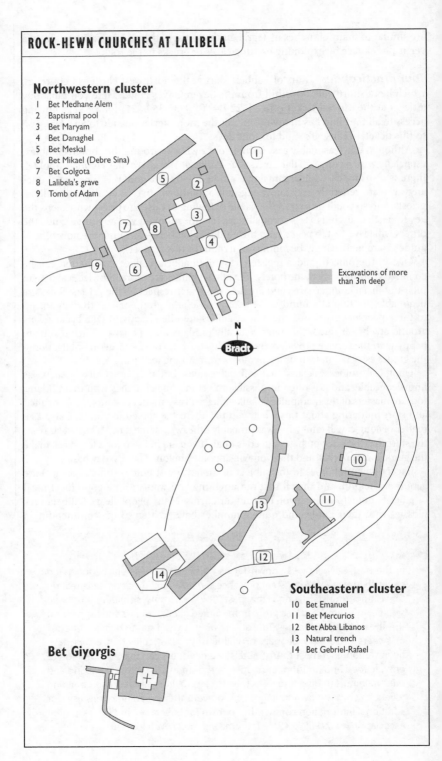

ROCK-HEWN CHURCHES AT LALIBELA

Northwestern cluster

1 Bet Medhane Alem
2 Baptismal pool
3 Bet Maryam
4 Bet Danaghel
5 Bet Meskal
6 Bet Mikael (Debre Sina)
7 Bet Golgota
8 Lalibela's grave
9 Tomb of Adam

Excavations of more
than 3m deep

N

Bradt

Southeastern cluster

10 Bet Emanuel
11 Bet Mercurios
12 Bet Abba Libanos
13 Natural trench
14 Bet Gebriel-Rafael

Bet Giyorgis

specific individual. I have, however, resisted the temptation to pass on names; that sort of licence can easily be abused, and there is always an element of personal chemistry in such matters.

Having appointed a guide, you may also be latched onto by a shoe-bearer when you enter the church complex (somewhat surprisingly, this practice appeared to have all but ceased on our most recent visit in late 2011). The shoe-bearer is a man or child who will take responsibility for your shoes while you are inside the churches, carry them between nearby churches, personally assist in putting them back on your feet at appropriate moments, and leer at you for good measure when the mood takes him. If you are approached by a shoe-bearer it is probably easiest to take the point of least resistance and hire one; once you've appointed him and agreed to give him a tip at the end of your tour, you can relax.

Assuming you've paid your entrance fee, you're free to walk where you like and photograph what you like anywhere in the complex (with the obvious exception of the Holy of Holies at the back of each church). It is, however, customary to slip a birr or two to any person you put centre frame – your guide will be able to advise you on this. Video photography is permitted only upon payment of around US$25 filming fee, US$50 if you have one of the larger professional recorders. Also, note that toilet facilities are available near the northwest cluster, but there are no toilets near the southeast cluster or Bet Giyorgis.

The northwest cluster The most easterly church in this cluster is **Bet Medhane Alem** [322 B4]. This is the largest monolithic rock-hewn church in the world, measuring 11.5m in height and covering an area of almost 800m². A plain building, supported by 36 pillars on the inside and another 36 around the outside, Bet Medhane Alem has a classical nobility reminiscent of an ancient Greek temple, a similarity that has led some experts to think it was modelled on the original St Mary Zion Church built by King Ezana at Axum. The interior of the church is also plain, and its vast size creates a cathedral-like austerity. Several graves have been carved into the rock floor; they are no longer permanently occupied, but when I visited, a helpful priest leapt into one and played possum for my benefit. Bet Medhane Alem has its own wide courtyard whose walls are pockmarked with niches that originally served as graves or hermits' caves.

A short tunnel leads to a second courtyard enclosing three more churches. The largest of these, **Bet Maryam** [322 B4], is thought to have been the first church built in Lalibela. Because of its association with the Virgin, it remains the most popular church in the complex among Ethiopians. Smaller and less imposing than Medhane Alem, but also a monolith, Bet Maryam has a more intimate and elaborately carved interior, with carvings of the original Lalibela Cross and of the Star of David, and dense paintings on parts of the roof. The church is 13m high and its upper floor has seven rooms used to store church treasures. Above the entrance is a relief of two riders fighting a dragon. Within the church, one veiled pillar is reputedly inscribed with the Ten Commandments in Greek and Ge'ez, as well as the story of how the churches of Lalibela were excavated, and the story of the beginning and end of the world. The local priests say that this pillar glowed brightly until the 16th century, and they claim it would be too dangerous to lift the veil and show it to researchers.

Carved into the northern wall of Bet Maryam's courtyard, the tiny chapel of **Bet Meskel** is barely 40m² in area. In the southern wall, and even smaller, the atmospheric chapel of **Bet Danaghel** (House of the Virgin Martyrs) was reputedly constructed in honour of 50 Christian maiden nuns murdered by the Roman ruler Julian the Apostate in the 4th century, a legend recorded in the Ethiopian *Book of*

Martyrs. Also in the courtyard is a pool that is believed to cure any infertile woman who is dipped into the water three times on Ethiopian Christmas – the water is certainly green and slimy enough to suggest a favourable effect on procreativity. The water level is about 2m below the courtyard, so the women have to be lowered down on a harnessed rope – a rather comic sight!

The third courtyard in the northwest cluster contains the twin churches of **Bet Debre Sina** [322 B4] (also called **Bet Mikael**) and **Bet Golgotha** [322 B4]. These churches share an entrance and together they form a semi-monolith. I found these churches the most atmospheric in Lalibela, with a dank dungeon-like atmosphere and a pervasive air of sanctity. The historical relationship between the twin churches is confused by the presence of several *tabots*, but the structure suggests they have always functioned separately. The interior of Bet Golgotha (the one church in Lalibela that women are prohibited from entering) is remarkable in that it has seven life-size reliefs of saints carved around its walls. There is also a legend that King Lalibela is buried beneath a slab on the floor of this church, and that the soil of this supposed grave has healing powers. The **Selassie Chapel**, which lies within Bet Golgotha, is considered the holiest place in Lalibela. Few visitors have ever been permitted to enter it. The western exit from the courtyard lies at the base of the **Tomb of Adam** [322 B4], a cruciform hermit's cell decorated by mutilated paintings of the kings of Lalibela. Some of the rock-hewn caves near this were recently converted into a church.

The southeast cluster Whereas the northwest cluster of churches possesses a sense of cohesion that suggests it was conceived as a whole, quite possibly by King Lalibela as the legends suggest, the southeast cluster comes across as more hotchpotch in design. Several of the individual churches in this cluster are thought to have been secular in origin and some pre-date the reign of Lalibela by five centuries.

Bet Gebriel-Rafael [322 D4] is a strange church, surrounded by a rock trench of perhaps 5m in depth. In effect, this trench is rather like a dry moat, and it must be crossed on a rickety wooden walkway. This fortress-like appearance, combined with the unusual alignment of the church, has long led experts to think that it was originally built as the residence of King Lalibela. More recent architectural studies by the British archaeologist David Phillipson indicate that both it and the nearby Bet Mercurios were excavated as the core of a fortified palatial complex during the politically unstable 7th and 8th centuries, when the Axumite Empire was in the process of disintegrating. From the outside, Bet Gebriel-Rafael is a very imposing and memorable sight. The northern façade, its height greatly exaggerated by the trench below, is distinguished by a row of arched niches, which, although they show strong Axumite influences, give the building a somewhat Islamic appearance. Inside, the church is surprisingly small and plain, decorated only by three carved Latin crosses. The priest spun me an intriguing story about a secret tunnel that leads to a second set of rooms underneath the church. These rooms, if they exist, are presumably on a level with the floor of the surrounding trench. The priest also said that nobody knows where this tunnel is any longer!

According to the legends, **Bet Abba Libanos** [322 D4] was built overnight by Lalibela's wife Meskel Kebre, assisted by a group of angels. The church has been built around a cave in a vertical face, and although the roof is still connected to the original rock, the sides and back are separated from the rock by narrow tunnels. The pink-tinged façade, which once again shows strong Axumite influences in its arched and cruciform windows, lies under an overhang in a way that is reminiscent of some churches in Tigrai. The interior of the church is most notable for a small light in the altar wall which, according to the priests, shines of its own accord 24 hours a day. A tunnel of about 50m in length leads from the right aisle of this church to the chapel of **Bet Lehem**, a small and simple shrine that could well have been a monastic cell used for private prayers by King Lalibela.

Bet Emanuel [322 D4] is a 12m-high monolith – the only church of this type in the southeast cluster – and it is considered by art historians to be the finest and most precisely worked church in Lalibela, possibly because it was the private church of the royal family. The exterior of the church imitates the classical Axumite wood-and-stone built-up church typified by Yemrehanna Kristos outside Lalibela. An ornamental frieze of blind windows dominates the church's interior.

Bet Mercurios [322 D4] is a cave church. It was originally used for secular purposes, and may well be around 1,400 years old. The presence of iron shackles in a trench suggests it may have served as a jail or courtroom. The interior is partially collapsed – the entrance was rebuilt from scratch in the late 1980s – but it does boast a beautiful if rather faded 15th-century wall frieze of what looks like the three wise men or a group of saints. There is also a recently restored painting displayed in the church, in which a most beatific-looking St Mercurios is depicted amidst a group of dog-headed men, his sword trailing through the guts of the evil King Oleonus.

Bet Giyorgis [322 B3] This isolated monolith – the only church in town not covered by a modern shelter – is the most majestic of all Lalibela's churches. It must measure close to 15m in height and, like the churches of the northwestern group, it is excavated below ground level in a sunken courtyard enclosed by precipitous walls. The most remarkable feature of this church is that it is carved in the shape of a symmetrical cruciform tower. The story is that Giyorgis – St George as he is known to us – was so offended that none of Lalibela's churches were dedicated to him that he personally visited the king to set things straight. Lalibela responded by promising he would build the finest of all his churches for Giyorgis. So enthusiastic was the saint to see the result of Lalibela's promise that he rode his horse right over the wall into the entrance tunnel. The holes in the stone tunnel walls are the hoof prints of St George's horse – or so they tell you in Lalibela.

CHURCHES OUTSIDE LALIBELA

The mountains around Lalibela are studded with medieval monasteries and churches, many of which are very different from their Lalibela counterparts, and are infrequently visited by tourists. With the exception of the monasteries at Nakuta La'ab and Asheton Maryam, both of which can be visited as affordable and relatively straightforward day trips from Lalibela, access to many of these churches is not easy unless you are prepared to spend several days trekking in the mountains, or have access to a 4x4 vehicle. For those who want to see a good selection of churches and monasteries in one go, the Bilbilla circuit to the north of Lalibela forms the obvious first choice, affording access to four different churches over a day by vehicle. The churches to the south and east are more scattered: Nakuta La'ab is traditionally very popular with backpackers, since it can be reached on foot without a guide, while the mule ride to Asheton Maryam also forms a straightforward day trip out of Lalibela. The other churches to the south and east of Lalibela are more difficult to access, and there is no vehicular circuit comparable to the one around Bilbilla.

The entrance fee to these outlying churches is *not* included in the price of the ticket for the churches within Lalibela. Yemrehanna Kristos charges a fixed entrance fee of US$9 per person and US$6 for video cameras. Fees for all the other churches around Lalibela including those near Bilbilla are now fixed at US$6 per person with an equivalent fee attracted for video cameras. Women are permitted to visit all of the churches and monasteries described below.

CHURCHES NEAR BILBILLA This relatively compact and very varied circuit of churches comprises Yemrehanna Kristos, Arbuta Insesa, Bilbilla Chirkos and Bilbilla Giyorgis. These churches all stand within 10km of the village of Bilbilla, itself some 30km from Lalibela off the road northwards to Sekota and Adwa. To explore all four churches along this circuit by vehicle takes about eight hours, including walking times of five to 20 minutes each way to the various churches. The vehicle hire will cost upwards of US$80 in Lalibela, and can be arranged through any of the more expensive hotels or through an official guide. Any one of these churches can be visited from Lalibela by mule as a ten–15-hour round day trip, for which you should expect to pay a guide fee of US$9 as well as a mule-hire fee of US$9. Yemrehanna Kristos qualifies as first choice for a day trip of this sort. To trek to all of the churches would require three to four days; official guides in Lalibela will be able to advise you about setting up a trip.

The turn-off to **Bilbilla Chirkos** branches left from the Sekota road 27km past the main square in Lalibela and about 2km before Bilbilla. The church, 6km from the main road, is covered in scaffolding which is clearly visible to the right before you reach the parking area, from where a gentle 500m footpath through a small forest patch and across a stream leads to the church. A tall semi-monolith encircled by deep trenches, Bilbilla Chirkos is architecturally reminiscent of Bet Gebriel-Rafael in Lalibela, with its intricately worked pink-tinged façade. Notable features of the interior include the 12 thick pillars, some very old paintings of Maryam and Giyorgis (with dragon) and various other saints, and the cross that is carved into the dome in front of the sanctuary. Several beehives lie within the church; the 'holy honey' they produce is said to have curative powers. Treasures include several goatskin books including an illustrated 800-year-old Ge'ez history of Kidus Chirkos. The age of Bilbilla Chirkos is unknown. One tradition holds that it is the oldest rock-hewn church in Lasta, excavated during the 6th-century rule of Emperor Kaleb. Other sources suggest it is roughly contemporaneous with the Lalibela churches. Unlike many other outlying churches, no monastery is attached to Bilbilla Chirkos. An interesting site that can be reached by driving another 15km past Bilbilla Chirkos then hiking for another two hours into the hills is **Kiddist Arbuta Washa**, the cave in which Lalibela was reputedly born.

Back on the main Axum road, the turn-off to Bilbilla village lies to the right about 2km past the Bilbilla Chirkos turn-off. The village is about 1km from the Axum road and visible from it. The road to Bilbilla crosses a stream that can only be forded by a vehicle with good clearance, ideally a 4x4. Signposted from the village, a 15–20-minute walk leads through the marketplace and uphill to **Bilbilla Giyorgis**, also covered in scaffolding. Carved into the rock face, Bilbilla Giyorgis has an imposing façade decorated with a frieze said to represent the 12 vaults of heaven, and it is surrounded by a tunnel in a manner reminiscent of Bet Mercurios in Lalibela. As with Bilbilla Giyorgis, there are several holy beehives in this church.

Continuing for 6km east along the side road through Bilbilla, you will come to **Arbuta Insesa**, reached on foot in five minutes following a gently sloping path uphill through a patch of euphorbia and other trees. This small, sunken semi-monolith is neither as beautiful nor as imposing as similar churches in Lalibela town. Previously, the absence of scaffolding made it easier to photograph than some, but this sadly has now been erected. A small spring within the church produces holy water. This appears to be a very old church, with pillars and doors mimicking the Axumite design of some built-up churches, and it is dedicated to the four beasts, symbols of the four evangelists who followed Kidus Yohannis (St John). A lengthy walk from here leads to the little-visited monastery of **Gedamit Maryam**, where there is an interesting built-up church.

The indisputable gem among the churches around Bilbilla, not least because it is so fundamentally different from anything in town, is the **Monastery of Yemrehanna Kristos**. Situated at an altitude of around 2,700m and protected by an unflattering modern outer wall, Yemrehanna Kristos is an old built-up church within a large cavern. It is a particularly fine example of late-Axumite architecture, built with alternating layers of wood and granite faced with white gypsum that give it the appearance of a gigantic layered chocolate cream cake. Among many interesting architectural features are the cruciform carved windows, an etched wood-panel roof, a coffer ceiling with inlaid hexagons and a large dome over the sanctuary. A reliable tradition has it that this church was built by its namesake, Yemrehanna Kristos, the third Zagwe ruler and a predecessor of King Lalibela, recorded as ascending to the throne in AD1087 and ruling for about 40 years. Yemrehanna Kristos is credited with restoring links between Ethiopia and the Coptic Church (an unverified legend states that he visited Egypt during his reign, and the priests at the monastery claim that all the wood used in the church's construction was imported from Egypt, while the gypsum was brought from Jerusalem). The church and its curative holy water formed an important site of pilgrimage in medieval times.

Behind the main building, adding an eerie quality to the already dingy cavern, lie the bones of some of the 10,740 Christian pilgrims who, it is claimed, travelled from as far afield as Egypt, Syria and Jerusalem to die at this monastery. In front of the church, a small opening reveals muddy soil, said to be part of a subterranean freshwater lake below the cave.

By road, Yemrehanna Kristos can be reached by continuing 9km eastwards from Arbuta Insesa (ie: 15km from Bilbilla village) to a parking area on the right side of the road. From here, a rather steep 15-minute walk – watch out for loose rocks underfoot – leads uphill to the monastery through a lovely patch of juniper forest. Reasonably fit travellers unable or unwilling to hire a vehicle might think seriously about visiting this monastery on muleback – a ten–12-hour round trip from Lalibela.

Between Lalibela and Bilbilla, a road leads westwards to **Sarsana Mikael**, a damaged and almost disused monolith reached by a tunnel, notable for the black stone on its door, which is said to kill immediately any sinner who touches it. The road to this church was impassable on last inspection, but may eventually be repaired. You can visit the church on foot or on the back of a donkey or mule.

NAKUTA LA'AB MONASTERY

The easiest of all the outlying churches to reach is the Monastery of Nakuta La'ab, named after its constructor, the nephew and successor of King Lalibela. One tradition has it that Nakuta La'ab ruled from this church, which he called Qoqhena, during an 18-month break in Lalibela's monarchy; another is that he took refuge here after he was deposed. Along with Lalibela, Nakuta La'ab is the only Zagwe ruler to be included under a recognisable name in all the available lists of Ethiopian kings. He ascended to the throne upon the death of Lalibela; some sources place his period of rule at 40–48 years, others indicate that he might have been forced from the throne within a few years of becoming king.

The monastery accredited to Nakuta La'ab consists of a relatively simple church built around a shallow cave in which several holy pools are fed by natural springs. The church has many treasures, some of which are claimed to have belonged to Nakuta La'ab himself. These include paintings, crosses and an illuminated leather

Bible. There are also some great paintings in the church. One advantage over the churches in town is that the treasures are brought out into the open where they can be examined in decent light.

Nakuta La'ab is roughly 6km from Lalibela, and is seen from a distance along the road between the airport and the town. It can be reached on foot by following the surfaced airport road out of Lalibela, a straightforward walk that will take an hour to 90 minutes. About halfway out, you'll pass a small gorge where birders might want

TESFA TREKKING: COMMUNITY TOURISM IN NORTH WOLO

Working with local communities, Tesfa Tours (☏ *011 810 0920;* m *0923 490 495; www.tesfatours.com*) has developed an extremely well-run trekking programme for tourists who wish to get off the beaten trail, trek in breathtaking scenery and see the real culture of the highlanders.

As of early 2012 there were a dozen communities running simple guesthouse facilities in the mountains around Lalibela. The communities own and manage the guesthouses and proceeds from their business go to promote economic and social development.

The original three community-run guesthouses are in western Meket (a district adjacent to Lalibela) and are at between 2,800m and 3,000m altitude. The walk between them is reasonably flat and accessible to people with a moderate levels of fitness, although you will be walking for much of the day. A further three community guesthouses in eastern Meket require a higher level of fitness. From these sites it is possible to trek off the Meket Escarpment and up onto the ridge running to the mountain behind Lalibela. Known as Abuna Yoseph with a peak at about 4,300m, the mountain is a refuge of the endangered Ethiopian wolf. Simple community guesthouses are located on the mountain to enable guests to climb the peak and look for the wolves.

Using native materials where possible, the Tesfa communities have constructed *tukuls* with comfortable beds, clean sheets and blankets. Each site has a dining room, simple outdoor shower, and eco-toilet.

In western Meket most treks begin or end at the town of Filakit, the administrative centre for the *woreda*, but treks on Abuna Yoseph begin or end at Lalibela. Many of the trekking routes follow the escarpment edges of the Meket Plateau, set on a lava bed associated with the formation of the Rift Valley.

Depending on your itinerary and length of stay, your first night's camp might be at any of the sites listed below:

The first guesthouse, located in Mequat Mariam, is set on a promontory of the plateau (around 2,800m), jutting out to the southwest with spectacular views across the rural landscape. The second guesthouse, at Wajela, is noted for its beautiful wood of acacia trees, and numerous stands of eucalyptus in the surrounding village. The site itself stands on a cliff above the juniper forest and church of Werketa Mariam, with its intriguing cave complex. The next guesthouse, at Aterow, is located on the edge of the escarpment near a dramatic gorge with a waterfall home to a large troop of gelada monkeys.

The fourth guesthouse, at Yadukulay, links east and west Meket treks and is set on a small twin peak below the escarpment, providing excellent views of the steep cliff face. Next is Boya, 3,200m high on a bluff of the escarpment facing west with impressive views over the river gorges flowing into the Tekeze. Further west at about 3,300m is Aina Amba, with lovely views across the Tekeze River to Abuna

to stop for a short while – we saw the endemic white-winged and Rüppell's black chat here, as well as Ortolon and cinereous buntings, paradise flycatcher, northern wryneck and ten types of raptor along the way. When you reach a little village on the left side of the road, you must follow a clearly signposted track for about 500m to reach the monastery. Entrance costs US$6. If you don't feel like the walk, you can arrange to see the monastery *en route* to or from the airport, or you can organise to go by mule, which costs US$9 for mule and muleteer, plus a guide fee.

Yoseph. Further west, the increasingly rugged highlands takes you out of Meket district into Gidan and to the new guesthouse at Kurtain Washa (about 3,450m).

Treks between sites generally take about six hours, and give participants a chance to see local farming techniques and other elements of local culture. With luck, visitors should also see some of the local wildlife (gelada monkeys, birds of prey, rock hyrax, klipspringer). For those interested in spending more time with the communities, this can easily be arranged. Donkeys are used to carry your baggage, so you don't have to carry much with you.

More recently opened are the guesthouses on Abuna Yoseph. Tesfa now operates treks onto the mountain, which peaks at 4,300m, set among giant lobelia and large troops of gelada monkeys. There is even a small pack of Ethiopian wolves on this Afro-alpine mountain. This trek is not for the faint-hearted. There are some steep paths and long walks. The nearest guesthouse to Lalibela, Ad Medhane Alem (3,500m), takes about five hours' walk to reach from Lalibela, while the other end of the trail is at Geneta Mariam, home to a beautiful rock church. A new guesthouse is being completed below the peak – Agaw Beret (at 4,000m built by Frankfurt Zoological Society), and a third guesthouse is situated between the peak and Geneta Mariam at Tadios Amba (3,400m) with spectacular views back down the ridge to Geneta Mariam. There is also a built-up church in a cave halfway between Tadios Amba and Geneta Mariam called Mekina Medhane Alem. Back down at 2,500m there's a guesthouse in the village of Geneta Mariam about 20km from Lalibela. This is the link between the Meket trek, with the possibility of walking to or from here to Aina Amba or Kurtain Washa.

Upon your arrival at each camp, you will be greeted by your hosts and served a tasty snack. Coffee and tea are provided at no additional charge, while bottled drinks including beer, water and soda are available for a small fee. In addition, three substantial meals are served each day – all locally inspired dishes.

Booking for these treks must be made in advance. The price per person per day is US$55 inclusive of food, accommodation, guide and pack animals but excludes bottled drinks, transport and church entry.

Tesfa can arrange your transport to or from the trail head from/to Lalibela, Bahir Dar and Gondar. It is US$83 for a vehicle one-way between Lalibela and Filakit (less to the closer points) and US$165 from Meket to Bahir Dar, and US$212 to or from Gondar. Alternatively, local buses can be taken. Buses from Lalibela, Bahir Dar, Gondar, Woldia or Dessie can drop you at the crossroads 'town' of Gashena or at Filakit. At either place you can meet your guide. (Guides are based in Lalibela, but for a small charge they will come to meet you.)

Please note most treks are closed during the rainy season – mid July to late September – although a few accessible guesthouses remain open all year round. For additional information, check out the Tesfa website.

ASHETON MARYAM AND MOUNT ABUNA YOSEPH Another monastery that's quite often visited by travellers is Asheton Maryam, which lies at an altitude of almost 4,000m on Abuna Yoseph, the high mountain overlooking Lalibela. This monastery also is associated with King Nakuta La'ab, who most probably founded it, and who may even be buried in the chapel. The church is carved out of a cleft into a cliff face, and the execution is rougher than at most other churches in and around Lalibela. Asheton Maryam houses some interesting crosses and other church treasures, but the excursion is just as remarkable for the church's setting and the views on the way up. Entrance costs the same as Nakuta La'ab, as does the hire of a mule and muleteer. Most people go up by mule, but it's only two hours' walk from Lalibela, albeit along a rather steep path strewn in parts with loose stones. Even if you do not plan to visit the monastery, Abuna Yoseph is worth further exploration. The fact that you can see Ethiopian wolves and large troops of gelada baboons (a few hundred in a spot) so close to Lalibela makes this mountain very attractive for anyone who wants to see the Afro-alpine environment, and at 4,300m it makes for a fun yet challenging climb. Wolves are normally seen before 08.00 and after 16.30, which limits day-trip possibilities, but if you plan to summit the peak then you are already looking at a minimum two-day excursion. Tesfa now has an Abuna Yoseph base camp set up, about a five-hour walk from Lalibela. For details, contact Tesfa – see box, page 338, for contact information.

GENATA MARYAM AND BEYOND One of the most interesting outlying churches is Genata Maryam, a large monolith carved into a pink-tinged outcrop near the source of the Tekeze River. Supported by pillars, the church is very different from any of the excavations in Lalibela in that it is not hidden within a trench, but carved openly on a rocky hilltop – though the cover of scaffolding rather detracts from the impact of seeing it from afar. According to tradition, Genata Maryam was excavated during the reign of Yakuno Amlak, the king who 'restored' the Solomonic line in the early 13th century. A notable feature of the interior is the elaborate paintings said to date to the 13th century. Genata Maryam is about four hours' walk or mule ride from Lalibela, or 45 minutes' drive. You reach it by following the airport road for 9km out of town, and then taking a clearly signposted left turn onto the old Woldia road. About 13km past this junction (rather than the 17km indicated on the signpost) you will reach a small village, also known as Genata Maryam, where a left turn leads to the church after 700m. You can drive to within 50m of the church, which is reached by a short but steep footpath. An entrance fee of US$6 is charged.

Inaccessible by road, **Mekina Medhane Alem** is a built-up cave church similar in style to Yemrehanna Kristos in its characteristically Axumite use of layered wood and stone. Although there is little historical evidence to back it up, tradition holds that the church dates to the 6th century AD. The decorated interior boasts intricate geometric patterns as well as many old paintings – notably one of roosters fighting next to the sun and the moon above the door. The monastic church lies on a spur of Mount Abuna Yosef, about three hours from Genata Maryam by foot or mule.

Hikes or mule treks to the above churches can be extended to form a four- to five-day circuit culminating with the ascent to the 4,190m peak of Mount Abuna Yosef. Several obscure churches can be visited on this circuit. The cliffs around Abuna Yosef are favoured by gelada troops and recent anecdotal evidence in the form of complaints from local shepherds suggests that the small Ethiopian wolf population associated with the mountain is on the increase. Although currently accessible only on foot or by mule, Abuna Yosef should eventually be connected to Lalibela by a road currently under construction.

VAST ETHIOPIA TOURS
"The Ultimate Travel Experience"

Do you want to see VAST natural wonders?
Do you want to experience VAST culture?
Do you want to see VAST amounts of endemic species?
Do you want to be part of a VAST history?

When you travel with VET, the Vastness of Ethiopia is at your fingertips!
Since 2005, VET has offered all types of tours including:

Popular Routes: North, South, Danakil, Trekking, Bird Watching, City Tours
Unique Tours: Mekdela, Abune Yosef, Western Ethiopia

Custom Tours: Holidays

VET offers travelers top-quality service for a reasonable price for all group sizes through a multilingual staff that will make your trip an unforgettable experience.

Contact Information

Tel +251-116 62 49 97
Mobile +251-912 0716 95
Fax +251-11-662 12 93

E-mail info@vastethiopiatours.com
habtu@vastethiopiatours.com
P.O.Box 23881 Code 1000 Addis Ababa Ethiopia
www.vastethiopiatours.com

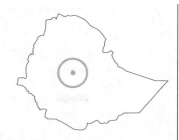

14

Dessie and Surrounds

Situated in the northeastern highlands some 400km from Addis Ababa by road, Dessie is the former capital of the defunct Wolo region, and serves today as capital of the South Wolo zone of the Amhara Nations region. **Dessie**, though probably the least interesting of Ethiopia's major cities, is nevertheless of significance to travellers dependent on public transport as a logical point to break the long trip between Woldia (at the junction to Lalibela) or Mekele and Addis Ababa. Situated only 25km east of Dessie, and linked to it by a zippy asphalt road and regular minibuses, the smaller but by no means insubstantial town of **Kombolcha** is the site of Dessie's airport. Viewed purely as an overnight stop, there is not much to choose between the two: Dessie boasts a few smarter hotels, while Kombolcha has the better selection of budget options. The decisive factor should probably be which way you'll be headed the next day, with Dessie lying closer to Woldia and Mekele, and Kombolcha closer to Addis Ababa.

Although infrequently explored by tourists, the Dessie area boasts several interesting possibilities for excursions. The most accessible of these, certainly on public transport, is the scenic **Lake Hayk**, noted for its prolific birdlife and the historic male-only monastery of **Hayk Istafanos**, and situated practically alongside the Woldia road less than 30km north of Dessie. Of interest to the history-minded traveller is the renowned monastery at **Gishen Maryam** and Emperor Tewodros's former capital at **Makdala Hill**, both of which lie along side roads west of Dessie and are something of an expedition to reach, even with private transport. More accessible from the Kombolcha side is the vibrant mixed **Afar and Oromo market** held every Monday at **Bati** (on the road towards Mille and Assaita), and the ancient and mysterious lion carved into a rock at **Geta**.

DESSIE

Large, modern and notably deficient in character, Dessie has few admirers, and its utilitarian aura is only partially offset by an attractive setting at an altitude of 2,600m near the base of Mount Tossa. The city was founded by Emperor Yohannis IV, who was struck by the apparition of 'a star with fringes of light' while encamped nearby in 1882. That an impressive comet was visible from the eastern highlands of Ethiopia in late 1882 is well documented, but the emperor, whether consciously or unconsciously echoing the actions of a distant predecessor at Debre Birhan centuries before, perceived the apparition to be a miracle. He immediately set about building a church on the site, which he christened Dessie ('My Joy'), a name whose misplaced ebullience has instigated a skyward arch in the eyebrows of more than one subsequent visitor!

In 1888, Dessie became the capital of Ras Mikael Ali of Wolo, an Oromo chief who had converted to Christianity under Yohannis IV ten years earlier. Ras Mikael

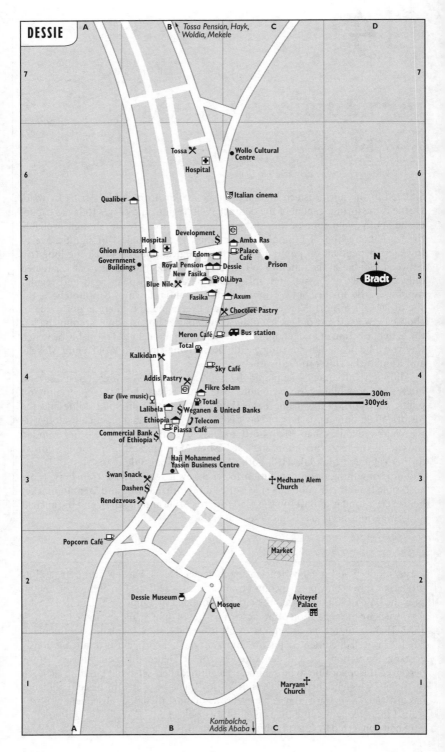

DESSIE

*Tossa Pension, Hayk,
Woldia, Mekele*

Tossa ✕

Wollo Cultural
Centre

Hospital ✚

Italian cinema

Qualiber

Development
$

Hospital ✚
Ghion Ambassel
Government
Buildings

Amba Ras
Palace
Café
Dessie
OiLibya

Prison

Edom
Royal Pension
New Fasika
Blue Nile ✕
Fasika
Axum

Chocolet Pastry

Meron Café 🚌 Bus station
Total

Kalkidan ✕

Sky Café

Addis Pastry ✕
Fikre Selam
Bar (live music)
Lalibela $
Ethiopia
Total
Weganen & United Banks
Telecom
Commercial Bank
of Ethiopia $
Piassa Café

N

Bradt

0 _____ 300m
0 _____ 300yds

Haji Mohammed
Yassin Business Centre

Swan Snack ✕
Dashen $
Rendezvous ✕

Medhane Alem
Church

Popcorn Café

Market

Dessie Museum

Mosque

Ayiteyef
Palace

Maryam
Church

*Kombolcha,
Addis Ababa* ▼

was one of the major political players in late 19th-century Ethiopia, even before he integrated himself into the Showan imperial family by marrying Emperor Menelik II's daughter in 1893. The son of this union, Iyasu, was selected by Menelik II as his successor, and became Emperor of Ethiopia in 1913, only to be toppled three years later in an imperial coup masterminded by Ras Tefari (later Haile Selassie). Ras Mikael responded to this insult by leading 120,000 troops against the Showan monarchy in the Battle of Segale, probably the largest battle fought on Ethiopian soil between Adwa and Maichew. Mikael was defeated, and taken captive. He died two years later.

Ras Mikael oversaw Dessie's emergence as a trading centre of note. With its strategic location on the trade routes between Ankober and Tigrai, Mikael's young capital served a crucial role in the war with Italy in 1896. By the outbreak of World War I, the town had become the largest market centre in Wolo. As with Gondar to its west, Dessie's pleasant climate, fertile surrounds and convenient location ensured it became an important administrative centre under the Italian occupation. Much of the modern town centre dates to the occupation and subsequent decades, the period over which Dessie outgrew its rustic roots to become the capital of Wolo region and one of the largest cities in Ethiopia. In 1970, a population of 80,000 made it the third-largest city in the empire after Addis Ababa and Asmara, the latter now part of Eritrea. Dessie lost out to Bahir Dar when the regional capital of Amhara was chosen in 1994, but due to a recent spurt of redevelopment it has gained several places to stand fifth on the national population list, with an estimated 185,000 residents.

Described in previous editions as a substantial town but with a somewhat decrepit air, only the substantial part of that description holds true today thanks to an ongoing building boom and major road construction. Dessie sprawls for more than 5km along the old main road, where many of the old one-storey buildings have been replaced by three-storey places with shops and restaurants on all levels. The town has also widened as new construction flanks a superior new asphalt road. Nevertheless, for most travellers, Dessie amounts to little more than a convenient overnight stopover point between Addis Ababa and Lalibela, or a base from which to explore Hayk or Makdala Hill.

GETTING THERE AND AWAY Ethiopian Airlines used to offer flights between Addis Ababa and Dessie, but this route has been suspended. (The service was never of much interest to tourists, as there are no flights between Dessie and Lalibela.) Should flights resume, the airport is about 25km from Dessie on the outskirts of Kombolcha.

Dessie is 400km from Addis Ababa along a (mostly) well-maintained, surfaced road, and 120km south of Woldia. The drive from Addis Ababa normally takes five to six hours in a **private vehicle**, not allowing for breaks, while the drive to Woldia takes about two hours. From Woldia, it takes around four hours of solid driving to get to either Lalibela or Mekele, which means that either town takes the best part of 12 hours' non-stop driving to reach from Addis Ababa, for which reason an overnight stop at Dessie (or somewhere close by) is recommended.

Dessie is an important **public transport** hub. Buses to and from Mekele via Woldia leave every morning at around 06.00 and take at least seven hours. Buses between Addis Ababa and Dessie also leave in the early morning and take about eight hours. There is regular local transport from Dessie to Hayk and Kombolcha, and at least one bus runs daily in either direction between Dessie and Mille (on the Assaita road) via Kombolcha and Bati. There is also a regular daily bus service between Dessie and Lalibela (US$6; 9–10 hours).

WHERE TO STAY

🏠 **WHERE TO STAY** Whilst there are plenty of options of places to stay in Dessie, on the whole they come across as run-down and over-priced. Fortunately, a new four-star hotel – the Lacomelza International – was under construction during our most recent visit and should be completed during the life of this book.

Moderate

🏠 **New Fasika Guest House** [344 B5] (24 rooms) ☏ 033 111 7705. This relatively upmarket annexe of the Fasika Hotel has increased its prices in recent years making the en-suite rooms not such the great deal as they once were. *US$18/21 sgl/dbl.*

🏠 **Fasika Hotel** [344 B5] (35 rooms) ☏ 033 111 2930. As with the above guesthouse, this long-time budget favourite has responded to its popularity by hiking up its *faranji* prices since the last edition. The large en-suite rooms with hot shower, while clean & neat, now seem more than a tad over-priced. *US$15/18 sgl/dbl.*

🏠 **Lalibela Hotel** [344 B4] (19 rooms) ☏ 033 111 3093/6908. A bit dingy by comparison with some of the places listed in this category, this comfortable hotel is still reasonably priced. The bar/restaurant is refreshingly cool, & internet is available next door. *US$14/21 dbl/twin with hot-water en suite.*

🏠 **Qualiber Hotel** [344 B6] (18 rooms) ☏ 033 111 1548. This rather oddly named hotel, set on a quiet back road a short distance northwest of the city centre, is one of the more commodious options in a city less than amply endowed with tourist-orientated lodgings. The clean, cosy & brightly decorated rooms with en-suite hot shower & TV are good value. A good ground-floor bar & restaurant is attached with meals costing around US$2–4. *US$13/15 sgl/dbl.*

Budget

🏠 **Amba Ras Hotel** [344 C5] (24 rooms) ☏ 033 111 9118. Conveniently situated on the main road through Dessie, this is another decent set-up, albeit a bit run-down, but still good budget option. The ground-floor restaurant & bar serves acceptable meals in the US$2–5 range. *US$10.50/11.50/15 sgl/dbl/suite with hot-water en suite.*

🏠 **Ghion Ambassel Hotel** [344 B5] (30 rooms) ☏ 033 111 1115. There's nothing wrong with this long-serving government hotel, which has a quiet location in green grounds just 4mins' walk from the main road, but it comes across as rather gloomy & over-priced by comparison with its competitors. *US$10/11.50 sgl/dbl with hot-water en suite.*

🏠 **Tossa Pension** [off map 344 B7] (17 rooms) ☏ 033 111 9225. Located at the north end of town, this homely pension offers the best-value rooms in town. All rooms are clean & neat with hot water & TV. Secure parking is available, but there is no restaurant. *US$9/11 sgl/dbl.*

🏠 **Ethiopia Hotel** [344 B4] (49 rooms) ☏ 033 119 0928/111 7056. With a convenient mid-town location, this hotel on the main roundabout offers decent rooms with en-suite hot shower. A bar & restaurant are attached, but the location could be noisy. *US$7.50/8.50 sgl/dbl.*

Shoestring

🏠 **Royal Pension** [344 B5] (16 rooms) ☏ 033 111 4939. Savoury shoestring options are thin on the ground in Dessie, but this small lodging, around the corner from the Fasika, is a welcome exception. If it is full, the nearby Fikre Selam & Axum hotels, though seriously inferior, are about the best of the rest. *US$3.50 using common shower, US$4/5 with real dbl bed hot-shower en suite.*

🍴 **WHERE TO EAT** With the exception of the New Fasika, the hotels listed above in the moderate category all have good restaurants serving Western and local dishes in the US$2–4 range – the **Qualiber** [344 B6] and **Lalibela** [344 B4] hotels are particularly recommended.

🍴 **Kalkidan Restaurant** [344 B4] ☏ 033 111 8834; ⏱ 07.00–20.00 daily. This extremely popular hotel is famous for its roast lamb & also has good fish cutlets & *kitfo* – actually, everything here is pretty good. Located near the Lalibela Hotel,

the Kalkidan's atmospheric dining area is best described as log-cabinesque – basic lodging is also available. *US$3–6.*

🍴 **Palace Café** [344 C5] **m** 0914 601 606; ⏱ 06.00–21.00 daily. Of the patisseries that line the main road, this café next to the Amba Ras Hotel is probably the pick serving an excellent selection of cakes & pastries for around US$1, as well as fresh orange juice, mini pizzas & local meals. *US$2–3.*

✕ **Tossa Restaurant** [344 B6] m 0914 710 894; ⏲ 06.00–21.00 daily. Not to be confused with the namesake pension above, this lively restaurant tucked in a side alley off the main road comes highly recommended for Ethiopian dishes. *US$2–4.*

Also worth trying are **Sky Café** [344 B4] and **Piassa Café** [344 B4] located above the Awash International Bank.

ENTERTAINMENT AND NIGHTLIFE John Graham wrote in one of his columns for the *Addis Tribune* that: 'The nightclubs and Asmari bars at the western end of Dessie are renowned. Asmari singers, with their one-stringed instruments, are incredibly clever at creating lyrics. Once they know your name, you will be treated to an Amharigna praise song about your generosity, intelligence, sexual appetite or whatever other compliments they can think of. You are expected to give a generous tip.'

OTHER PRACTICALITIES
Internet and email Dessie is well endowed when it comes to internet facilities, remarkably so when you arrive there from further north. One of the largest **internet cafés** [344 B4] stands on the main road opposite the Fikre Selam Hotel, but there are several others dotted around town, charging less than US$1 per half-hour to browse.

WHAT TO SEE Of minor interest are a few fading occupation-era buildings, notably **Bahil Amba** [344 C6], a once grand cinema built entirely with materials imported from Italy. Of slightly greater architectural value and antiquity is a large hilltop banquet hall known as **Ayiteyef Palace** [344 C2], constructed by Ras Mikael in 1915. Nearby, and older still, is the **Church of Enda Medhane Alem** [344 C3], which is situated on a juniper-covered hill on the eastern outskirts of town, and was built by Ras Mikael on the site of a church reputedly destroyed centuries earlier by Ahmed Gragn. More ambitiously, you could walk to the peak of Mount Tossa, which offers views in all four directions almost as far as the Afar Depression. To get there, head to the west end of the town, drive part of the way up, and you can walk the remainder in about one hour.

These minor pickings aside, the list of tourist attractions within Dessie starts and ends with the regional **museum** [344 B2] (⏲ *08.30–12.30 & 14.00–17.00 Mon–Fri, 08.30–12.30 Sat; entrance US$1.50*), which opened in 1980 in the former residence of Dejasmach Josef. In addition to some interesting ethnographic displays and traditional musical instruments, the museum houses a cannon made in 1890 and used by Menelik II at the Battle of Adwa, a few 19th-century religious tracts, and some of the most lifeless stuffed animals you'll ever see. Nothing is labelled in English, but the guide is quite knowledgeable. The hill on which the museum stands – above the junction for the Kombolcha road – offers a good view over the city centre.

KOMBOLCHA

Overshadowed by the nearby metropolis of Dessie, from which it is divided by just 25km of scenic asphalt road, Kombolcha is the site of the main airport serving South Wolo and an industrial and commercial centre of some substance in its own right – indeed, with a population estimated at around 70,000, it comfortably stands

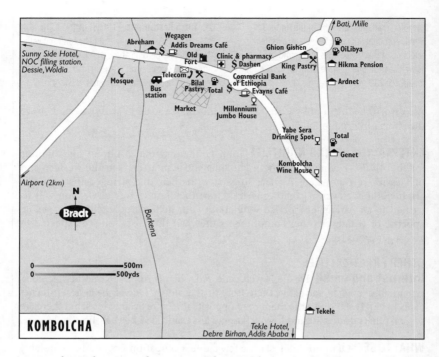

KOMBOLCHA

among the 20 largest settlements in Ethiopia. The town centre, set at an altitude of 1,850m, is likeable enough and noticeably warmer than nearby Dessie, but otherwise unremarkable.

The Yegof Forest on the ridge overlooking Kombolcha still supports relic populations of Menelik's bushbuck, vervet monkey, leopard and various smaller mammals. In a short 1996 study, 62 bird species were recorded in this forest, including the endemic Abyssinian woodpecker and Abyssinian catbird, and tropical boubou, olive pigeon and blue-headed coucal.

There is no overwhelming reason to stay in Kombolcha over Dessie, but then nor is there any real reason not to. I thought Kombolcha the more attractive of the two towns, and it is also well placed for day trips to Bati and the Geta Lion. Both towns have good facilities and public transport connections – the better hotels in Dessie are far smarter than their counterparts in Kombolcha, but Dessie fares less well when it comes to decent budget accommodation. Assuming that you're just passing through, it probably makes sense to stay in the town closest to your next destination.

GETTING THERE AND AWAY Details are much the same as for Dessie (see page 343), though it is worth noting that many long-distance buses (for instance between Dessie and Addis Ababa) generally stop to drop or pick up passengers outside the Hikma Pension, not at the bus station. Minibuses run between Kombolcha and Dessie throughout the day on a fill-up-and-go basis; the trip takes around 45 minutes. There is also at least one bus daily through to Mille (on the Assaita road), passing through Bati and sometimes continuing as far as the junction to Assaita itself.

It's a long steep walk from the bus station into the town centre, where most of the hotels are – a horse-drawn *gari* is the answer.

Should flights resume to Dessie, the airport – more accurately, the airstrip and customs shack – actually lies just 2km from Kombolcha. There are not normally any taxis to meet flights to Kombolcha, so you may have to hitch or walk into the town centre to pick up transport into Dessie.

WHERE TO STAY
Moderate
🏠 **Sunny Side Hotel** (71 rooms) 📞 033 551 2869/3016; f 033 551 5243; www.sunnyside-hotel.com. This new sprawling hotel, opposite the NOC filling station on the main road to Dessie, is far & away the best accommodation offering in Kombolcha (or Dessie for that matter!). The clean, comfortably furnished rooms all have tiled floors, TV, phone & hot-water en suite. There's an excellent bar & restaurant & the hotel accepts Visa & MasterCard & rates include breakfast. The only downside is the discriminatory pricing – *faranjis* pay double – which makes the rooms feel expensive. And the mattresses were also too firm for this updater's liking! *US$29/33/37/43 sgl/dbl/twin/suite inc b/fast.*

Budget
🏠 **Hikma Pension** (23 rooms) 📞 033 551 0015. Situated on the main traffic roundabout on the road to Bati, this place has been a favourite with travellers for some years. It's best to pay extra for the comfortable en-suite rooms in the new annex, as their gloomier counterparts in the main building are noisier & the dirty en suites are less than appealing. The attached restaurant & café with its large open-air veranda shaded by a bird-filled grape arbour is a popular local breakfast spot.

The food here is fairly priced & the menu features a wide selection of terrific juices & pastries. It's also a good place to pick up lifts on to Addis, & to take advantage of the clean public toilets. *US$7.50 old dbl, US$10.50/15 new dbl/twin.*
🏠 **Tekele Hotel** (10 rooms) 📞 033 551 0056. Located at the south end of town, this low-key hotel offers good-value accommodation in simple but bright rooms, all with hot-shower en suites. The restaurant is good, but pricey in comparison with other offerings in town – a full 3-course meal will set you back US$7.50. *US$9/10.50 sgl/dbl.*

Shoestring
🏠 **Abreham Hotel** (18 rooms) 📞 033 551 0068. Conveniently located 100m from the bus station, this place offers adequate but unexceptional rooms with hot-water en suite. The restaurant is worth a try: a substantial plate of roast lamb with bread & salad costs US$2. Fair value. *US$4.50/5.50 sgl/dbl.*
🏠 **Ghion Gishen Hotel** (34 rooms) 📞 033 551 0013. This tired, old hotel offers equally tired old rooms with clean common hot-water showers. The restaurant is recommended for roast lamb, which costs less than US$2. *US$3/4.50 dbl/twin.*

WHERE TO EAT In addition to the places mentioned above, the **Addis Dreams Café** above the Wegagen Bank looks good, while the **Yabe Sera Bar** across from the Genet Hotel and the **Kombolcha Wine House** are good places for grog.

EXCURSIONS FROM DESSIE AND KOMBOLCHA

LAKE HAYK The small town of Hayk – which straddles the main road north towards Woldia about 20km from Dessie – is surely a contender for the most underrated and under-utilised accessible stopover anywhere along the northern circuit. True, the town itself is nothing to shout about, despite its pretty setting among rolling green hills, but – although you wouldn't know it approaching from Dessie – there is a beautiful 23km² lake situated only 2km from the town. Lying at an altitude of 2,030m, the lake is of great interest both for its birdlife and for the historical monastery that stands on its western shore (see box, *Hayk Istafanos*, page 352).

Curiously, the lake is generally referred to as Lake Hayk – Hayk being the Amharigna word for lake – and less frequently but with equal redundancy as Lake Lago. There are several bodies of water in Africa whose modern name derives from a local word meaning lake, generally as a result of an excited explorer mistakenly assuming that a bemused local muttering 'lake' was doing more than stating the

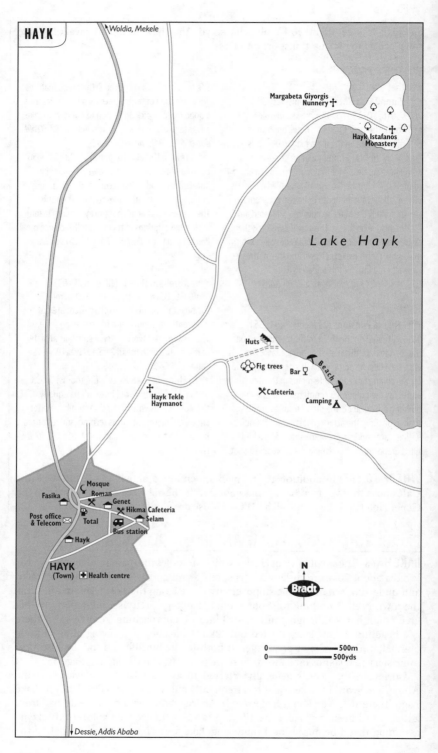

HAYK

↑ *Woldia, Mekele*

Margabeta Giyorgis
Nunnery ✝

Hayk Istafanos
Monastery ✝

Lake Hayk

Huts 🏚

🌳🌳 Fig trees   Bar 🍷   *Beach*

✝ **Hayk Tekle
Haymanot**

✕ Cafeteria

Camping ⛺

🕌 Mosque
Roman
Fasika 🏠   ✕ Genet
Post office   Total   ✕ Hikma Cafeteria
& Telecom ✉   🏠   🚌   Selam
🏠 Hayk   Bus station

HAYK
(Town) ✚ Health centre

N

Bradt

0 ——————— 500m
0 ——————— 500yds

↓ *Dessie, Addis Ababa*

obvious. It is more likely in this case, however, that Hayk's original name was forgotten centuries ago and it has come to be called after the monastery of Hayk Istafanos, which simply means 'Istafanos on the lake'.

Call it what you want – Hayk, Lake or Lago – this is a lovely, atmospheric spot. The deep turquoise water, ringed by verdant hills and fringed by lush reed beds, is still plied by traditional fishermen on papyrus *tankwas*. Birders will be in their element: not only does the lake support a profusion of waterbirds (including large numbers of pink-backed pelican), but the shore and the surrounding fields and forest patches host a rich variety of colourful barbets, woodpeckers, kingfishers, bee-eaters, sunbirds and weavers. An early morning stroll along the road between the lake and the wooded peninsula on which the monastery stands could easily yield between 50 and 100 species, with the monastery grounds in particular a good spot for flocks of the endemic black-headed lovebird and the lovely paradise flycatcher.

Getting there and away Minibuses between Hayk and Dessie run throughout the day, and take less than an hour in either direction. It would also be easy enough to disembark at Hayk from any bus running between Woldia and Dessie, or – in a private vehicle – to stop off at the lake *en route*. Whether you are in a vehicle or on foot, you can get to the lake from the main roundabout in town by following the side road that runs almost parallel to the main road (with a mosque to your right). On the outskirts of town, the road forks: the right fork will bring you to a lakeshore cafeteria next to a trio of large, gnarled fig trees (seasonally laden with breeding cormorants and pelicans), while the left fork runs uphill and parallel to the western shore of the lake for about 2km before descending to Hayk Istafanos.

Where to stay and eat

🏠 **Fasika Hotel** (38 rooms) 📞033 222 0390; e fasikahotel@gmail.com. Situated on the west side of the main road directly opposite the old Roman Hotel, this high-rise hotel is not as swanky as its exterior might suggest, but fair value given that all rooms cost less than US$5. Be warned: rooms are tiny & dark & common showers filthy. There is a ground-floor restaurant, & the rooftop *tukul* bar offers a good view. *US$2 using common shower, US$3 with cold-shower en suite.*

Å **Logo Haike Lodge** (6 rooms) 📞033 119 1279; m 0911 021 504. This quiet campsite by the lakeshore is a much better option than any of the hotels in town. Accommodation is provided in 6 very nice thatch huts, with a new 6-room lodge under construction at the time of writing. It's also possible to pitch a tent near the lakeside. There is a good bar with cold drinks, & food is available. Other amenities include a roped-off swimming area & a dock with several boats. The only toilet is a poorly constructed outhouse, but as long as the floor holds you should be fine! *Camping US$6 per tent, huts US$9/12 sgl/dbl.*

GISHEN DEBRE KERBE The monastery of Gishen Debre Kerbe – also often called Gishen Maryam after the oldest of its four churches – is one of the most revered in Ethiopia. It lies northwest of Dessie off the road to Wegel Tena, and is situated on a massive cross-shaped rock *amba* (flat-topped mountain). Gishen is one of the oldest monasteries in the country, reputedly founded in the 5th century by King Kaleb. Its greater significance to Orthodox Christians, however, is the legend that it possesses the piece of the True Cross (the cross on which Jesus was crucified) that was brought to Ethiopia during the 14th-century reign of Emperor Dawit. Gishen Amba, with its cruciform shape, was chosen by Emperor Zara Yaqob as the best place to store this holy treasure. The True Cross is reputedly stashed Russian doll-style within four boxes (respectively made of iron, bronze, silver and gold), which are suspended by chains within a closed subterranean chamber at the end of

Hayk Istafanos, set on a thickly wooded peninsula within easy walking distance of the town of Hayk, is one of the most historically important and influential monasteries in Ethiopia. According to the local priests, the church's founder was one St Kala'e Selama, a monk from Jerusalem who arrived there in AD862. The story goes that Hayk formerly supported a pagan cult of python worshippers, who were converted to Christianity when the saint made the python disappear with his cross. Shortly after, Kala'e Selama persuaded Emperor D'il Nead to visit Hayk, and together they founded a church. While they were deciding which saint to dedicate the church to, a large animal descended from the sky with two *tabots*, one for Istafanos and one for Giyorgis. The church was named for Istafanos, and the second *tabot* was stored within it for several centuries before a second church – today the nunnery of Margebeta Giyorgis – was established alongside Hayk Istafanos.

Although one tradition states that a monastic community called Debre Egziabher (Mountain of God) existed on the shores of Lake Hayk as early as AD627, it is probable that Hayk Istafanos remained an ordinary church for the first 400 years of its existence. Then, in the middle of the 13th century, during the reign of Nakuta La'ab, the Gondar-born monk Abba Iyasus Moa, having completed a seven-year apprenticeship at Debre Damo, was led to Hayk Istafanos by the Archangel Gabriel to found a monastery there. Iyasus Moa presided over the monastery for 52 years; he died in 1293 at the age of 89 and is buried within the church. Legend has it that he slept in a sitting position throughout his tenure, and that his waking hours were spent lugging around a heavy stone cross and kissing the ground – 10,000 times every day!

Hayk Istafanos was the most powerful monastery in Ethiopia from the late 13th to the early 15th century, largely as a result of the role played by Iyasus Moa in the 'restoration' of the Solomonic line c1270. It is said that the rightful Solomonic heir Tesfai Iyasus visited Iyasus Moa to ask for his help in usurping the throne from the

a tunnel 20m below the ground. In common with the Ark of the Covenant at Axum, it is off-limits to all but a select few. Whether or not there is any truth in the legend of the True Cross, the cruciform plateau and its four churches are very beautiful and sacred, and Gishen routinely attracts many thousands of pilgrims over Meskel (the Festival of the True Cross).

Gishen Amba has a second, more verifiable claim to fame, as the source of Dr Johnson's morality tale of Rasselas, the prince who was imprisoned in a valley encircled by mountains by the King of Abyssinia. During several periods in Ethiopian history, it has been customary for the emperor to protect his throne by imprisoning his potential successors – sons, brothers, uncles and other princes – on a near-impregnable mountaintop. The Portuguese priest Alvarez described this practice in his account of his lengthy sojourn in Ethiopia, providing the inspiration for Johnson's tale, as well – somewhat bizarrely – as the vision of an earthly paradise described in Milton's *Paradise Lost*. The tale of Rasselas in turn formed the driving obsession behind Thomas Pakenham's travels in Ethiopia in 1955, documented in his compulsively readable book *The Mountains of Rasselas* (see Appendix 2, *Further information*, page 615). According to Pakenham, Gishen Amba is one of three mountains that have been used to imprison princes at different points in Ethiopia's history; it was preceded in this role by the monastery at Debre Damo, and succeeded

Zagwe rulers. The monk prophesied that his noble visitor would one day have a son who would grow up to become king – and so the as-yet-unborn Yakuno Amlak did, after having first trained for several years at Hayk Istafanos. Ancient tradition claims that Yekuno Amlak transferred a third of the realm's property to Hayk Istafanos. During the 15th century, Hayk Istafanos faded in political significance due to the rise of Debre Libanos, the monastery founded in western Showa by Tekle Haymanot (who trained under Iyasus Moa), but it remained sufficiently important that Francisco Alvarez was taken to see it in the 1520s. A few years later, Ahmed Gragn destroyed the original church.

In Alvarez's day, Hayk Istafanos was set 'on a small island' which the monks went 'to and from … with a boat of reeds'. A more recent visitor, the German missionary Johan Krapf, who visited in 1841, was paddled to the monastery across a deep channel. Today, however, Hayk Istafanos lies on a peninsula and can be reached on foot – it is not clear whether this is because the water level has retreated, or the channel has simply been filled in. Either way, Hayk Istafanos is a fascinating and peaceful spot, set in lovely wooded grounds teeming with birds. The church itself appears to be quite modern, but the superb treasury houses several unusual artefacts, ranging from the heavy stone cross that belonged to Iyasus Moa, to a set of hollowed-out sacrificial stones formerly used by the pagans he converted. Women are not permitted to enter the monastery grounds, but may visit the adjacent nunnery of Margebeta Giyorgis, which was reputedly founded about 800 years ago.

Several of the most valuable treasures held at Hayk Istafanos were hidden from public view when I visited the monastery in 2001, but I was told they would be displayed in a new museum as of September that year. Most notable among these is an illustrated biography of Iyasus Moa written during his lifetime, making it one of the oldest books in Ethiopia. According to tour operator Yared Belete, the museum at Hayk Istafanos is now open and charges an admission fee of US$6.

by Mount Wehni near Gondar. Gishen first served as a royal prison in 1295, when Emperor Yakuno Amlak sent his five sons there, and it held a solid stream of similar captives until it was virtually razed by Ahmed Gragn in the 16th century.

In Pakenham's day, Gishen was accessible only by foot or by mule. Today, the monastery can be reached by road as a long day trip from Dessie, or as an overnight trip in conjunction with Makdala Hill (see below). In a private vehicle, you need to drive out of Dessie towards Wegel Tena, following a good gravel road that passes a 50m-high waterfall on the Kaskasa (literally 'Cold') River a few kilometres out of town, then runs through the small town of Kutaber. The turn-off to Gishen, signposted in Amharigna only, is roughly 70km out of Dessie, and entails a 17km ascent along a road that deteriorates badly over the last 5km. The final ascent to the top of the mountain must be done on foot and takes about 30 minutes. Reasonably regular buses run between Dessie and Wegel Tena, but there is no public transport to Gishen itself except over Meskel, when hundreds of buses head out there.

MAKDALA HILL It was to Makdala that an embattled and embittered Emperor Tewodros retreated in 1867, as his dream of a unified Ethiopia crumbled under the strain of internal and external pressures, most significantly his own growing unpopularity among his subjects. His once all-conquering army reduced through desertion and rebellion to a tenth of its former size, and his pleas for British alliance unanswered, the emperor was forced to abandon his capital at Debre Tabor and to barricade himself in the hilltop castle at Makdala. In a final and rather desperate attempt to lever Britain into giving him military support, Tewodros took with him a group of European prisoners. In 1868, after Britain's attempt to negotiate for the release of the prisoners ended in the negotiator himself being jailed, a force of 32,000 troops was sent to Makdala, under the command of Lord Napier and with the support of the future emperor Yohannis IV. Tewodros, rather than face capture, took his own life. He was buried in the church at Makdala at the request of his wife.

Makdala Hill lies about 100km northwest of Dessie as the crow flies, and about 18km cross-country from the remote town of Tenta, the usual starting point for hikes. Before heading out, you'll need to arrange an obligatory police escort at the station in Tenta at a daily charge of around US$6. (The idea, as explained to Barry Austin, is to protect travellers against various real or imaginary dangers – 'lions'? – but the escort 'turned out to be a most worthwhile investment, as he knew all the short-cuts, where we could get *tella*, and where the famous guns are located'.)

From Ajbar, you have to head back to Tenta, where mules or donkeys can be hired at US$2.50–3 per day and porters at US$3 per day. From Tenta, the trek to Makdala takes half a day using a combination of mules and walking. The path initially drops

AWLIYAW: THE LARGEST AND OLDEST TREE IN ETHIOPIA?

Edited from an article by Dr Alula Pankhurst (www.addistribune.com)

The protected Anabe Forest, one of the few areas of indigenous yellowwood forest to remain in southern Wolo, was 'discovered' as recently as 1978 by a forester looking for a nursery site. It is situated some 30km west of Gerba on the road from Kombolcha to Bati. Until recently, the rough road from Gerba to the forest was passable only as far as the market town of Adame, from where one had to walk for three hours. However, following the construction of a new road by local people through an employment generation scheme organised by Concern with EU funding, the forest is now easily accessible by 4x4.

Tucked away near steep cliffs and surrounded by cultivated fields, Anabe Forest is practically invisible until you arrive within a couple of kilometres of its edge. It currently covers an area of about 50ha, but used to be considerably larger. In *An Illustrated Guide to the Trees and Shrubs in the Red Cross Project Areas in Wolo*, Professor Mesfin Tadesse mentions an Amharigna saying which translates as 'Anabe is said to be growing old and greying, a solitary individual could now cross it without fear'.

Sadly, exotic trees, notably pines, have been planted in peripheral parts of the forest. The heart of the forest is, however, still dominated by the indigenous yellowwood *Podocarpus falcatus*, known as *zegba* in Amharigna. This gigantic tree, one of the most beautiful in Ethiopia, is an evergreen with a dense crown. It provides cool shade and nourishment for birds and small mammals, and shelter to guereza monkeys, which also eat its fruit. Indeed, we saw a few troops of this beautiful monkey, now rare in so much of the country, since its black-and-white coat is illegally sought for making carpets. Because yellowwood is classified as a 'high-class softwood', it is a prime source of timber, used for cupboards, shelves, panels, matchsticks, etc. In the middle of the past century, it was the number-one commercial species in Ethiopia, accounting for 60% of production. Less than 1% of Ethiopia's original *Podocarpus* forest is thought to survive intact today.

some 700m in altitude before ascending to the top of the mountain, which lies at an altitude of around 3,000m. The scenery is wonderful, and the fortifications erected by Tewodros are still in place. So, too, is Sebastopol, Tewodros's pet name for the unmarked (and unfireable) bronze cannon built by the missionaries he took hostage at Gafat. You could, at a push, trek to Makdala and back as a long day trip out of Tenta, but most visitors carry a tent and camp on the hill, where local people can arrange firewood and water, but not food.

Tenta itself is a rather dreary place, lacking electricity or running water, and notable mostly for the surrounding scenery, and a central square with a statue of Negus Mikael. Worth a look, and situated only a couple of kilometres north of Tenta, is the circular stone church of Tash Tenta Mikael, built by Ras Mikael of Dessie at the turn of the 20th century. A three-tiered construction enclosed by a high wall supporting majestic towers and turrets, the roadside church contains the domed tomb of Ras Mikael. It also offers stunning views of the Tukur Abay (Black Nile) Gorge and Makdala Hill. Tenta boasts a couple of grotty local hotels. Slightly better accommodation is available at Ajbar.

Coming from Dessie, the recommended route to Tenta, about 130km in all, is to follow the Wegel Tena road, passing the junction to Gishen Amba, then after about 95km turn left onto the Tenta road shortly before you reach Wegel Tena. Tenta can

The most special tree in Anabe is known locally as *Awliyaw*, a term suggestive of its revered status (*Weliy* means prophet in the Islamic tradition and *Awliya* often refers to a Zar possession cult). Legend has it that it existed before all the other trees, when the land was barren and that it gave rise to all the other trees. There is a story that a man attempted to climb the tree to catch a queen bee, but retreated when a snake confronted him. The man is said to have died within three days, for having disrespected the sanctuary.

This sacred tree is estimated by Professor Mesfin to be about 12.5m in circumference and about 4m in diameter. True enough, when we measured the tree, we found it to be 12.7m in circumference. Is this the largest tree in Ethiopia? The tree is said to be 63m high. Is this figure correct? Has anyone seen a taller tree in this country? Forestry reports from the 1940s suggest a maximum height of 50m for *zegba* trees, whereas reports in the 1990s suggest a maximum of 35m.

Awliyaw is said to be more than 700 years old, which may seem incredible, but studies of old trees in other parts of the world mention exceptional cases of trees that have surpassed a millennium and even cases of trees, notably yews, that may be up to 1,400 years old. In his beautiful book *Meetings with Remarkable Trees*, Thomas Pakenham depicts an oak that was standing at the time of William the Conqueror in 1066. If *Awliyaw* is as old as it is said to be, then it must have been planted before the restoration of the Solomonic dynasty in 1270!

It is sad that a tree as venerable as *Awliyaw* is so little known. I have only ever come across one photograph of it (showing a 'human chain' around its trunk, and published by Professor Mesfin), and it isn't described in any tourist guides. Is this because Anabe Forest has been fairly inaccessible in the past? If so, then perhaps the new road will generate greater interest in it. In a country where deforestation is such a pressing concern, this exceptional example of natural beauty surely deserves more celebration!

also be reached by following the road south to Guguftu then turning northeast through Amba Maryam. The condition of both these routes is variable, so if you are driving yourself, you may want to ask the tourist office in Dessie for current advice. If you are dependent on public transport, you will probably have to use the route through Wegel Tena. Either way, you are looking at a four–six-hour drive, depending to some extent on the state of the road.

In a private vehicle, two worthwhile onward options are possible from Tenta. The first would be return to Wegel Tena and then head northward to Gashena and on to Lalibela. The other is to continue west to Mekane Salem, site of the new Borena Sayint National Park, and an even newer bridge across the Blue Nile to Dejen, on the main road between Adds Ababa and Bahir Dar. Both these routes are covered in the *Chapter 12* section *Exploring the South Wolo heartland* on page 319.

BATI The small town of Bati is situated roughly 40km east of Kombolcha between the central highlands and the low-lying Rift Valley, where it forms an important cultural crossroads for the Amhara, Oromo and semi-nomadic desert-dwelling Afar people. For more than two centuries, Bati has hosted Ethiopia's largest cattle and camel market, attracting up to 20,000 people every Monday. If you're in the area at the right time of the week, the **market** is well worth the relatively minor diversion, not only for the sheer scale of the phenomenon, but also for the glimpse into a facet of Ethiopia very different from anything you'll encounter in the highlands. Coming from the highlands, the Afar seem to belong to another Africa altogether: the bare-breasted women with their wild plaited hairstyles and elaborate ornate jewellery, the tall, proud men strutting around with Kalashnikovs slung over their shoulder, and lethal traditional dagger tucked away in a prominent hide sheath. Note that there appear to be two separate markets now, one for livestock and another larger one for everything else – both are relatively hassle-free and worth checking out.

So far as travel practicalities go, a fair surfaced road connects Bati to Kombolcha, and several buses run between the two towns daily, with traffic being heaviest on a Monday. The trip takes about 60 minutes in a private vehicle and 90 minutes by bus, so it is possible to visit as a day trip out of Kombolcha or Dessie. It is worth noting that the road from Kombolcha to Bati continues on to Mille on the asphalt highway between Awash and Assaita/Assab. Off the road between Kombolcha and Bati lies the Anabe Forest (see box, *Awliyaw: the largest and oldest tree in Ethiopia?*, page 354).

Where to stay and eat   On market days hotels in Bati tend to fill quickly, so book your room early, or better yet, call ahead.

Vasco Tourist Hotel (18 rooms) ☎033 553 0548/0534. This is Bati's top offering: large clean rooms with king beds & mosquito nets. A restaurant & bar is attached. *US$7.50/9.50 with common shower/hot-shower en suite.*

Ghion Kersa Hotel (7 rooms) ☎033 553 0007. The Ghion Kersa lies in scenic grounds about 2km out of town on the northern verge of the Kombolcha road. Accommodation is offered in small, run-down rooms using a common shower. An acceptable restaurant & bar is attached. *US$6.*

Fasika Hotel (6 rooms) ☎033 553 0323. Another in-town option, the Fasika offers basic rooms with common shower. *US$6/7.50 sgl/dbl.*

A cluster of good restaurants surrounds these places, including the **Djibouti Café** and the **Ameha Bar and Restaurant**, which serves excellent local fare as well as the usual spaghetti with bolognaise and tomato sauce *faranji* favourite. Another good food choice is the bamboo-covered **Asser Bar and Restaurant**.

THE GETA LION One of the more intriguing of Ethiopia's lesser-known monuments is the monolithic sculpture of a lion at Geta, to the southeast of Kombolcha. Suspended about 1m from the edge of a small hill studded with euphorbia shrubs, the carving depicts the front part of a male lion, with bulging oriental-looking eyes, lines representing the mane, ferociously bared teeth, and feet stretched forwards. When the lion was sculpted, and by whom, is a matter of pure conjecture. Given the Ethiopian gift for manufacturing legend, the absence of a local tradition linking the lion to the Queen of Sheba, or Abreha and Atsbeha, or any other historical figure, is quite remarkable. The furthest that locals are prepared to commit themselves is that the sculpture has been there for as long as anybody can remember. In all probability, the Geta Lion dates to Axumite times or earlier. A Maltese cross carved into the basal rock might be seen to indicate that the lion was sculpted after Christianity was introduced to Ethiopia. It could also be that, like the cruciform carving alongside the (otherwise very different) engraving of a lion a few kilometres outside Axum, this cross was added centuries after the original lion was sculpted. The enigmatic origin of the Geta Lion is compounded when one recognises that it exists in apparent isolation – no similar monument is known within a radius of hundreds of kilometres!

The Geta Lion can be reached by following the Addis Ababa road south of Kombolcha for 12km to Chekorti, from where one must turn onto an eastbound side road signposted for Geta Mosque. From the mosque, which lies less than 5km along the side road, it's roughly a 30-minute walk to the lion sculpture. Geta Mosque, founded in the mid 19th century by the renowned Islamic scholar Haji Bushra Mohammed, is also of some interest as a pilgrimage site attracting thousands of worshippers on Muslim holidays.

HARBU HOT SPRINGS About 15km from Kombolcha along the road to Addis Ababa, the small town of Harbu is noted for its hot springs, which lie about 3km west of the main road. The springs are believed to have curative properties, and have been used by locals for bathing and drinking for longer than five centuries. They feed a short stream that flows into the larger Borkena River.

Galaxy Express Services PLC Tour Operations & Air Travel

Ethiopia offers a unique experience that is different from anywhere else you will have visited. Its 3,000-year-long history is interwoven with timeless legends, ancient religious practices and colorful festivals evoking Biblical times. Its fascinating monuments, art, culture and landscapes have captured the imagination of visitors throughout the ages.

Galaxy Express Services PLC, established in 1991, is one of the best-equipped tour operators in Ethiopia. Galaxy will plan your journeys and provide the very best service available, from car rental and ticketing to customized tours, with efficient and responsive management, a large new fleet of well-maintained vehicles, and a staff made up of articulate, friendly, energetic and flexible tour operators, multilingual guides and expert drivers. We tailor trips to fit your specific interest, at very competitive rates. We offer a range of over 15 carefully designed package tours countrywide, covering nature, history, culture and wildlife, as well as land transport around the country.

Special characteristics of Galaxy
The only tour operator with branch offices in all of Ethiopia's four main northern historical sites, **Bahirdar**, **Gondar**, **Lalibela** and **Axum**, where permanently stationed vehicles and professional guides are available at all time.

Galaxy Express is the exclusive agent for *AVIS* car rental and for Europe Assistance.

Galaxy Express Services offers you the opportunity to drive the newest models of car or enjoy the luxury of chauffeur-driven services, ideal for both leisure and business.

Contact us for all your tour and travel requirements in Africa's most fascinating country, **Ethiopia**.

P.O. Box 8309, Addis Ababa, Ethiopia
Tel: +251 115 510355/517646/517678
Fax: +251 115 551236
Email: galaxyexpress@ethionet.et
www.galaxyexpress-ethiopia.com
www.galaxyexpresstourethiopia.com
Rent a Car

IATA
Accredited

358

15

Kombolcha to Addis Ababa

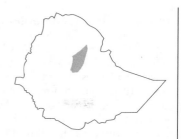

The 400km asphalt road that connects Dessie to Addis Ababa is one of many in Ethiopia that can as easily be whizzed along in a day as it can be explored more slowly over several. If you are looking at the former option, all you need really know is that it's roughly a six-hour drive in a private vehicle, and takes about eight hours on one of the many buses that depart in either direction between Dessie and Addis Ababa at around 06.00 daily.

Aside from Kombolcha, just 25km from Dessie, the largest town along this stretch of road is **Debre Birhan**, which lies about 130km (two hours' drive) northeast of Addis Ababa, but there are several smaller towns along the way, notably **Debre Sina** at the base of the spectacular **Mezezo Escarpment**.

Should exploration be on your agenda, the most popular excursion – a scenic hour's drive east of Debre Birhan – is to **Ankober**, a small town that is of interest to historians as the site of the former Showan capital, and to naturalists for its endemic birds and gelada monkeys. Even more worthwhile in terms of wildlife is the little-known Guassa Plateau near Mehal Meda, where large numbers of gelada can be observed about 90 minutes' drive east of Tarmabir, alongside the second-largest remaining population of the rare Ethiopian wolf. There are also several atmospheric but little-visited monasteries in the vicinity of Debre Sina, Tarmabir and Mehal Meda.

FROM KOMBOLCHA TO DEBRE BIRHAN

As with many such trips in northern Ethiopia, the roughly 250km run between Kombolcha (or Dessie) and Debre Birhan can be covered either as a straightforward non-stop drive or bus trip, or else broken up by hopping between towns. And, once again, which way you decide to go is largely dependent on time and temperament: a direct bus will be much quicker, but hopping between towns adds the element of chance that some travellers prefer. With an early start, you should easily get between Dessie and Debre Birhan in a day using local transport.

KOMBOLCHA TO DEBRE SINA/TARMABIR There is plenty of transport between Dessie and Kombolcha. At Kombolcha, you could wait near the Hikma Hotel, the best place to pick up long-distance buses or to try for a lift southwards in a private vehicle. Alternatively, head to the bus station and hop on one of the small buses that leave every couple of hours for Kemise, 50km south of Kombolcha. **Kemise** is a busy little Oromo town and, apparently, a popular truck stop, so there are plenty of hotels and restaurants. The likelihood of spending a night here by chance is very small, as buses run on to Senbete and Ataye until as late as 16.00. If you do stay, there are several cheap hotels along the main road. The relatively smart multi-storey **Chefa Hotel** (*19 rooms;* \ *033 554 1089*) offers clean, modern en-suite singles/doubles for

US$15/18 and the new **Abenether Hotel** (*44 rooms;* \ *033 554 0342;* m *0911 934 759*) set in large green grounds next to the NOC filling station on the southern outskirts with neat, well-priced singles/doubles with en suite for US$7.50/9 and rooms with common cold shower for US$6. The Abenether also serves the best meals in town.

With an interest in birds, you may actually choose to spend the night in Kemise. About 10km south of town, the road skirts the **Borkana Wetlands** immediately after crossing the bridge over the eponymous river. Here, stretching along the western fringe of the road for about 2km, you'll find a combination of open water, mudflats, river, marsh and reed beds, seasonally affected by the river's input, but perennially wet due to several hot springs which bubble out in the area. At the end of the rainy season, the ample birdlife may disperse to a smaller but wetter seasonal swamp about 3km north of Kemise. Either way, without leaving the road you stand a good chance of seeing marabou and saddle-billed stork, the endemic blue-winged goose, pelicans, ibises and much more.

There's not a lot to be said about **Ataye** (marked on some maps as **Efeson**), but if you do get stuck, the **Waliya Hotel** (*65 rooms;* m *0912 801 640*) near the Commercial Bank of Ethiopia is a superior cheapie, with large rooms with communal cold shower for US$3 as well as decent cold-water en-suite singles/doubles for US$6/7.50. For eating, a couple of restaurants serve indifferent *yefigel wat* and fried eggs, and the snack bar with yellow umbrellas on the Dessie side of town does juice, coffee, eggs, bread and cakes. Definitely worth checking out, should you be around at the right time, is the **market** held every Sunday at **Senbete**, only 9km south of Ataye. This is the best market in the area after Bati's famous Monday market, attracting villagers for miles around, predominantly Oromo people, but also Afar, Amhara and Argeba. Should you want to spend the night, there are a couple of indifferent small hotels in Senbete.

South of Ataye, the next town of real substance is **Robit**, on the banks of the wide but normally dry Robit River. Except perhaps on Wednesdays, when the town is the site of a colourful market, there's no overwhelming reason why you'd want to stop in Robit, but equally there is no shortage of low-rent accommodation should you decide to. Best bet is the **Weynye Hotel** (*16 rooms;* \ *033 664 0308*), which has cold-water en-suite rooms for US$6/9 per single/double and a decent but slow restaurant.

About halfway along the 32km road between Robit and Debre Sina, the small town of **Armaniya** is the base from which one can visit **Mercurios Monastery**, which is renowned for housing a very old painting of Saint Mercurios on horseback. The reason for this painting's fame, according to two local eyewitnesses, is that the horse miraculously starts to move on procession days, which are normally held on 5 August and 4 December. Frankly, your guess is as good as mine, but should you happen to be in the area at the right time, and be inspired to check it out, I'd be fascinated to hear more. The monastery stands one to two hours' walk from Armaniya. Should you need a room, the bright green Armaniya Anbassa Hotel looks adequate.

DEBRE SINA Situated along the main Addis Ababa road at the northern foot of the immense Mezezo Escarpment, Debre Sina is a significant – and significantly chilly – town boasting several hotels and restaurants. A scenic location and a bustling Monday and Thursday market aside, Debre Sina (Amharigna for 'Mount Sinai') holds little of inherent interest to travellers, but it does make a good springboard for visits to a number of little-known monasteries that lie along roads branching northwest from **Tarmabir**, a smaller – and even colder – town set at an altitude of around 3,250m on the escarpment 10km south of Debre Sina. The road between Debre Sina and Tarmabir passes through an impressive 587m-long, 8m-wide and 6.5m-high Italian-built tunnel.

Debre Sina straddles the main road between Dessie and Addis Ababa about 60km north of Debre Birhan. There is plenty of public transport along this road. Tarmabir is separated from Debre Sina by a stunning 10km road of surfaced switchbacks, passing through the Mussolini Tunnel. The cliffs here are reputedly a good place to see the endemic gelada monkey (I've yet to have the pleasure), while a site along the main road about 4km before Tarmabir is one of two established areas where the localised Ankober serin (see *Ankober*, page 366) is regular. Reasonably regular local transport connects Debre Sina and Tarmabir.

Where to stay and eat

🏠 **Tinsae Hotel** (32 rooms) m 0911 364 041. This double-storey building on the Addis Ababa side of town about 100m from the bus stop is excellent value with small but well-maintained rooms with ¾ bed & en-suite hot shower (very welcome in this climate). The ground-floor restaurant serves reasonable Ethiopian food, coffee & draught or bottled beer. *US$4.50 using common shower, US$5/6 sgl/dbl en suite.*

🏠 **Addis Metraf Hotel** (18 rooms) ☎ 011 680 0076. A similar distance from the bus station, but in the opposite direction, this double-storey hotel also has en-suite rooms – it's not bad, but there is no hot water & rooms are a bit scruffy. *US$3/4 with common shower/private en suite.*

🏠 **Degasmuch Teseme Hotel** (22 rooms) m 0911 116 124. Situated right next to the bus station, this place is as quiet & clean as you could reasonably expect for the price. *US$4 with common shower, US$4.50/5 sgl/dbl en suite.*

ADKANU MARYAM AND ADJANA MIKAEL (*entrance US$3 for each monastery*) These two monasteries both lie to the west of the main Addis Ababa road close to the small town of Sela Dingay. The more accessible of the two is Adkanu Maryam. This is an attractive and atmospheric partly hewn cave church, said to date to the 15th-century rule of Zara Yaqob, and is built up along a juniper-covered cliff face. It is open to lay worshippers, but also serves as a monastery, with several hermit cells carved into the rocks alongside the main courtyard, and a few nuns in and around the outbuildings. During Lent, large numbers of pilgrims from Addis Ababa and elsewhere congregate around the church. A nearby spring produces holy water. Church treasures include a large silver cross of unspecified date. Nearby Adjana Mikael, another cave church but reputedly much older than Adkanu Maryam, is set at the base of a cliff, and known for the holy water produced by a spring.

Neither monastery receives tourists regularly. Their very remoteness is a big part of the churches' charm, but it also means that one should be especially conscious of the sensibilities of the priest and his congregation. Women should wear a skirt that reaches below their knees and cover their head in a scarf, cloth or even a towel, and all visitors should ask permission before pointing a camera at anything.

Getting there and away To reach either monastery from Debre Sina, you first need to head to Tarmabir, 10km further south along the Addis Ababa road, then follow a side road west for 20km to Sela Dingay. The drive from Debre Sina to Sela Dingay takes about 45 minutes one-way in a private vehicle. Using public transport, there's a fair amount of traffic between Debre Sina and Tarmabir, while a daily bus and the odd light vehicle link Tarmabir to Sela Dingay; if you don't intend spending the night in Sela Dingay, the earliest possible start is recommended. Be aware that a modern church also called Adkanu Maryam lies unspectacularly alongside this road, about 3km before you enter Sela Dingay.

Once in Sela Dingay, the walk to the Adkanu Maryam Monastery, which takes 20–30 minutes, is easy though a bit steep in parts, offering some great views across the Kaskasa river gorge on the way – anybody will show you the footpath for a small tip. The monastery of Adjana Mikael is about three hours from Sela Dingay on foot, though a rough road there should be passable by 4x4 during the dry season only – either way, you will need a local guide. Note that some maps erroneously show the road towards Sela Dingay branching west from Debre Sina rather than Tarmabir.

Where to stay and eat
It would be easy enough to visit these monasteries as a day trip from Debre Sina or *en route* between Debre Sina and Debre Birhan, especially if you have a private vehicle. Should you elect to stay in Tarmabir, however, there is one acceptable shoestring hotel on the junction with the road to Sela Dingay. Alternatively, the **Addis Hotel** in Sela Dingay charges US$2 for a very simple room with a three-quarter bed; cold bucket showers are provided on request (not a request you're likely to make with any conviction at this altitude) and a restaurant serves local dishes, beers, sodas and coffee.

MENZ
Situated to the northwest of Debre Sina, the chilly highland region known as Menz was one of the few parts of Showa to survive the Muslim and Oromo incursions of the 16th and 17th centuries, and it is regarded as the ancestral home of the Showan monarchy. Practically unknown to tourists, the region boasts two significant and very different attractions, namely the spooky monastery of Arbara Medhane Alem and the fantastically underrated and wildlife-rich Guassa Plateau, the latter being the most accessible site for Ethiopian wolf anywhere north of Bale National Park. Seldom visited as they are, both sites are readily accessible from the 100km road that links Mehal Meda, the rather low-key traditional capital of Menz, to Tarmabir on the asphalt road between Debre Birhan and Debre Sina.

Getting around
In a private vehicle, the road to Mehal Meda, which bisects the Guassa Plateau, can be covered in about two hours, not allowing for stops. It is thus perfectly possible to visit both Guassa and Arbara Medhane Alem as a day trip out of Debre Sina or Debre Birhan, or *en route* between the two towns. If you are driving yourself, a potentially confusing quirk of the road running northwest to Menz is that, contrary to expectations, it initially branches eastward from Tarmabir, more or less opposite the junction for the road to Sela Dingay, only to cut back in a westerly direction above the Italian-built tunnel that encloses (and renders invisible) the main road to Debre Sina!

After about 8km, the road from Tarmabir to Mehal Meda offers some amazing views over the escarpment to the Sharobe River, before passing through the small village of Mezezo at the 14km mark. Another 15km further, the road bisects a patch of eucalyptus forest whose dense undergrowth is frequented by Bohor reedbuck, Menelik's bushbuck and the very localised Erckell's francolin. The small town of Bash flanks the road some 50km from Tarmabir, then 10km further, at Malaya, there is a junction where you need to turn right. Another 7km past this is Yegam, the closest village to Arbara Medhane Alem. The road ascends to the Guassa Plateau 8km out of Yegam and bisects it for about 10km before descending slightly for the last 15km stretch to Mehal Meda.

For those dependent on public transport, two buses daily connect Addis Ababa to Mehal Meda via Debre Birhan, leaving at 06.00 and taking the best part of a full day in either direction. It would be easy enough to hop off the bus at Yegam or on the plateau, but there isn't too much other transport along this road, so you do risk being stranded overnight. If I were to take this risk, I would first bus all the way through to Mehal Meda, spend the night there, then use the bus towards Addis the next morning to get to Guassa, which would at least mean that I'd have the best part of a day to find transport out. Outside of Mehal Meda, the only accommodation I'm aware of in Menz is one small local hotel in Mezezo.

Arbara Medhane Alem

This small cave church and monastery has a magnificent cliff setting at an altitude of around 3,000m northeast of the Mehal Meda road near the village of Yegam, 67km from Tarmabir. It can be reached in ten to 15 minutes along a very steep footpath leading downhill from Yegam into a grove of eucalyptus trees. Initially, the church might seem anticlimactic – the modern building is just 20 years old – but for a small donation the priests will lead you downhill into the patch of indigenous bush that hides the old church. The most remarkable feature of the church is an ancient mausoleum piled high with mummified corpses, some of whose limbs stick out of the wrapping in macabre contortions. Oddly, nobody in Yegam seems to have a coherent theory about how old the mummies are, or how they got there – my local informant reckoned they belonged to a tribe of angel-like beings who descended from the sky at least 100 years ago!

Guassa Community Conservation Area (www.guassaarea.org; entrance US$4.50)

The Guassa area has been upgraded to a community conservation area – the first in Ethiopia – and is now formally known as the Guassa Community Conservation Area (GCCA). Set at a mean altitude ranging between 3,200m and 3,700m, the area's main feature, the Guassa Plateau, extends over 110km², making it one of the largest extant Afro-alpine ecosystems in Ethiopia (or elsewhere in Africa for that matter). It is the highest plateau in Ethiopia's central highlands, and it forms an important catchment area, feeding some 26 streams that eventually flow into the Blue Nile and Awash rivers. Uniquely in Ethiopia, where centralised conservation efforts have met with limited success in recent years, the local community adjacent to the Guassa area has been managing its natural resources in a sustainable way for at least 400 years.

Some local ambivalence to the Guassa Plateau is revealed by a local legend concerning a monk called Atche Yohannis. A pregnant woman accused the highly respected monk, who was sworn to celibacy, of being the father of her soon-to-be-born child. The local people asked the woman to repeat this shocking claim in front of the disgraced Atche Yohannis, and so she did, stating: 'Let me turn into stone if I tell a lie.' As she spoke, the woman was transformed into stone, and the betrayed monk abandoned the area with a curse: 'Let this land turn cold and bleak for evermore, and the rich agricultural land become scrub.' As the monk spoke, the plateau, formerly known for its fine *tef*, was transformed into a bleak and non-cultivatable landscape of windswept heather tussocks and grassy swamps. Many years after the curse had reduced the area to poverty, the elders decided to beg for mercy and forgiveness. They searched far and wide for the monk, but heard that he had long since died. It was then decided to search for his body and re-bury it in the area, in the hope that the monk's spirit would take pity on them. The bones were re-buried near Firkuta Kidan Mihret, but the land has still remained under the curse. A commemorative day for Atche Yohannis is observed throughout Menz on 26 January.

The GCCA harbours seven of Ethiopia's endemic mammals (22.6% of the endemic mammalian fauna), including what ranks as one of the largest surviving populations of Ethiopian wolf, and several troops of the grass-eating gelada monkey. In addition, a total of 114 bird species have been recorded, including 14 endemics, among them an important population of the globally threatened Ankober serin (first recorded here in 1998) and spot-breasted plover, wattled ibis, thick-billed raven, blue-winged goose, Rouget's rail, Rüppell's black chat and Abyssinian long-claw. Good places to look for endemic birds (and the Ethiopian wolf) are the marshy area that lies to the right of the Mehal Meda road 80km from Tarmabir, and the moist valley fed by the Teter River to the left of the road about 1km further.

Estimates of the plateau's Ethiopian wolf population vary from 20 to 35 individuals, with the lower figure probably closer to the mark. The general consensus among local communities is that the population has decreased over the last few years due to a combination of habitat destruction, civil war, drought, disease and poisoning. Wolf densities on Guassa are strongly linked to densities of the four rodent species that account for almost 90% of their prey locally, and these were known to decline during a recent drought that also coincided with the death of at least six undernourished wolves on Guassa.

Practically speaking, Guassa is by far the easiest place to see the Ethiopian wolf after Bale Mountains National Park, and is the most accessible habitat north of Addis Ababa. The wolves are regularly sighted from the main road across the plateau, and they are not shy of human observers. They are most active in the early morning and late afternoon, but might be seen at any time of the day – I recently had two excellent wolf sightings crossing the plateau at midday, as well as seeing three gelada troops totalling some 200 individuals. Another carnivore likely to be seen on the plateau is the smaller, browner and less distinctly marked Eurasian jackal.

A newly built community-managed **lodge** here accommodates up to 12 people in basic dorm-style rooms, costing US$9 per person, and has a self-catering kitchen. Self-sufficient travellers (that means with tent, warm clothing and food) can also camp on the grounds around the lodge for US$4.50 per tent. The area close to the lodge is good for gelada and Ethiopian wolf. Local community guides can be hired for US$4.50 per day and will happily interpret the natural surroundings as well as the history and local conservation efforts. Mule rental costs US$3 per day as does a pack donkey, while a mule handler also costs US$3.

Mehal Meda The informal capital of Menz is an odd little place, far removed from the recognised tourist circuit, and very friendly – indeed the rare arrival of a *faranji* seems to induce an infectious communal mood of the giggles. That aside, it is of limited interest except as a base from which to explore the Guassa Plateau 15km to its east. As for accommodation, the best bet is the **Nyala Hotel** (✆ *011 681 3360*), 200m from the bus station, which charges US$3 for a clean room using a common shower, or US$5 for one with en-suite facilities. It's all rapidly downhill from there, but the best of the remaining half-dozen or so places (and proud possessor of what seems to be the town's only coffee machine) is the **National Hotel**, where a basic room costs US$2.50. Both hotels serve a limited selection of local dishes.

DEBRE BIRHAN

This friendly highland town of 70,000 souls, set 130km northeast of Addis Ababa, though of some historical note is nothing out of the ordinary today. It is of logistical significance, particularly to birdwatching tours, as the closest large town to Ankober (described later in this chapter), and would make a good first stop on a relaxed itinerary northwards from the capital. Debre Birhan firmly fits into the sprawling category of Ethiopian towns. A church and open fields separate the old town centre, which lies towards Addis Ababa, from the bus station and the newer buildings on the Dessie road. During our last visit the town was thoroughly torn up by road construction and basically a muddy mess. Until this situation changes, Debre Sina may be a better stopping point if you are heading north. If heading east, you may want to continue on to Ankober.

Debre Birhan – which translates as 'Mountain of Light' – was almost certainly founded in 1456 by Emperor Zara Yaqob. Legend has it that a miraculous nocturnal light (quite probably Halley's Comet) greeted the emperor when he was encamped here, prompting him to erect a church and use the site as his permanent capital until his death in 1468. The adolescent town was abandoned by Zara Yaqob's successor Ba'eda Maryam, only to rise to prominence again 50 years later when the imperial troops based at Debre Birhan were routed by the Muslim army of Ahmed Gragn. After capturing Debre Birhan, Gragn declared that 'Abyssinia is conquered' – presumptuous, as it transpired, but in the case of Debre Birhan not entirely incorrect. The area around Debre Birhan was Oromo territory for the next two centuries, to be reclaimed by the Showan monarchy only in the early 18th century. Long abandoned but never forgotten, Debre Birhan was soon rebuilt and it served as a kind of secondary capital for four successive Showan emperors throughout the 19th century.

Little indication of Debre Birhan's former importance survives today. The original church built by Zara Yaqob presumably fell victim to Gragn, and no obvious 19th-century relics remain. The church built by Emperor Menelik II in 1906, on the site first selected by Zara Yaqob, is nevertheless one of the most beautiful and spiritually affecting modern churches in the country. The inner walls are decorated with some marvellous paintings – including one of Zara Yaqob looking at a celestial body, reportedly modelled on Halley's Comet when it passed over at the beginning of the 20th century. Curio hunters might take note that the woollen carpets and blankets for which Debre Birhan is famous within Ethiopia can be bought directly from the co-operative that manufactures them at a shop close to the Telecommunications building.

GETTING THERE AND AWAY There are buses throughout the morning between Debre Birhan and Addis Ababa, and a few buses every day between Debre Birhan and Ankober. Early morning buses leave Debre Birhan for Robit and Efeson, where

DEBRE BIRHAN

you can pick up further transport to Dessie or Kombolcha. Direct buses from Addis to Dessie pass through Debre Birhan in the mid morning.

🏠 WHERE TO STAY
Budget
🏠 **Eva Hotel** (19 rooms) 📞 011 681 3607; 📧 getaneht@hotmail.com. Situated on the left side of the main road as you enter town from Addis Ababa, this slick hotel co-owned by Olympic gold medallist Gete Wami & her running partner/ husband Getaneh Tessema is easily the best in Debre Birhan. Accommodation is in spacious comfortable rooms with double or twin beds, DSTV & hot-shower en suite. A modern restaurant serving a good selection of Ethiopian & European dishes is attached. As a result of its popularity with tour groups & foreign aid workers, a monstrous new 80-room annex was under construction on our most recent visit. Prices are likely to increase once it's complete. *US$15 sgl or dbl.*

🏠 **Orental Hotel** (22 rooms) 📱 0910 791 466/0911 710 642. This new multi-storey hotel next to the OiLibya filling station at the southern end of town fails to impress with its en-suite rooms already showing signs of neglect. On the plus side the ground-floor restaurant serves chicken & beef dishes as well as burgers priced between US$2 & US$4. *US$11/12 sgl/dbl.*

🏠 **Girma Hotel** (17 rooms) 📱 0920 633 911. This likeable hotel is the pick of a cluster of decent cheapies on the Debre Sina side of town offering clean rooms with genuine double bed & hot-water en suite. There is a bar with DSTV but no restaurant. *US$7.50/12 sgl/dbl.*

Shoestring
🏠 **Akalu Hotel** (11 rooms) 📞 011 681 1115. The established favourite with most tour operators who take ornithological tours to Ankober, this pleasant small hotel, set on a quiet back road, is looking a little faded these days, but is still good value. The attached restaurant has meat dishes even during fasting seasons. *US$4.50/6 with common shower/private en suite.*

🏠 **Helen Hotel** (29 rooms) 📞 011 681 1204. Situated opposite the Girma, this is another good hotel with decent en-suite rooms with hot shower & smaller basic rooms sharing a common cold shower. *US$2/4 with common shower/en suite.*

🏠 **Etagegnehu Hotel** (22 rooms) 📱 0911 777 058. This double-storey hotel near the main traffic roundabout offers basic accommodation using common hot-water showers. *US$2/3 sgl/dbl.*

✕ WHERE TO EAT
There are plenty of decent restaurants dotted around town, but the only ones that cater towards *faranji* palates are those at the **Eva**, **Orental** and **Akalu** hotels, which charge US$2–5 for a main course. The most 'happening' place in Debre Birhan is undoubtedly the **Dibora Café**, which lies on the main road roughly opposite the Eva Hotel, and doubles as a pastry shop and restaurant, with the option of sitting indoors or out on the lively rooftop balcony.

ANKOBER

This remote small town, situated at an altitude of around 3,000m on the escarpment that falls to the Afar Depression, forms an excellent goal for a day or overnight trip out of Debre Birhan. Both the town and the road there are fantastically scenic, passing through rolling green meadows with views over the escarpment and lush Wof Wusha Forest that clings to its sheer slopes. The area is also good for endemic birds such as wattled ibis, blue-winged goose and Ankober serin (more of which below), while gelada monkeys are regularly seen along the road close to the escarpment, and Ethiopian wolves still occur, probably as vagrants from the Menz area.

Ankober, like nearby Debre Birhan, is a settlement of some antiquity, though almost certainly not – as has been suggested based on phonetic similarities – the site of the mysterious 10th-century capital of Kubar mentioned in Arab writings. In medieval times, Ankober acted as a tollgate along the trade route between the

Afar Depression and the highlands. The town's name literally translates as the 'Gate of Anko', which, according to local tradition, was the name of a wife of an Oromo chief who ruled the town at some point. In the early 18th century, Ankober fell to King Abiye of Showa, and soon after it became the capital of Abiye's son and successor Amha Iyesus, who is regarded as the founder of the modern town. From then onwards, Ankober served as the capital or joint capital of Showa, up until 1878 when Emperor Menelik II relocated his capital to the Entoto Hills.

A steep road from the centre of Ankober leads downhill for about 2km to the site of the ruined palace of Menelik II, set atop a small, steep, juniper-covered hillock some ten minutes from the road on foot. All that's left of the palace is one long stone-and-mortar wall measuring some 1.5m high; it's difficult to say why this one wall should have survived virtually intact when the rest of the palace crumbled to virtual oblivion. Locals claim that Menelik built the palace on the site formerly used by his grandfather Sahle Selassie (who ruled from 1813 to 1847), the Showan king whose regular military campaigns co-opted modern-day Addis Ababa and Arsi into Showa, and laid the political and economic foundation for Menelik's eventual domination over Ethiopia. Three 19th-century churches are dotted around the base of this hill, the oldest of which is Kidus Mikael, built by Sahle Selassie. None of these churches is of any great architectural or aesthetic merit.

Ankober's historical importance is today overshadowed by its status among ornithologists as the type locality of the Ankober serin (*Serinus ankoberensis*). First described in 1979, this rather nondescript seedeater was long thought to be restricted to a 20km stretch of escarpment running north from Ankober. In 1996, however, a flock was observed and photographed in the Simien Mountains, a vast extension to the serin's known range, and several other localities have subsequently been identified. Birders heading up this way will reliably observe seedeaters in abundance – streaky serin, brown-rumped serin and the endemic black-headed siskin are all common. But you will need to work the escarpment running immediately north of the road to stand any chance of locating the Ankober serin, which is brown with a pale streaked crown,

KOREMASH

Based on information in an article by John Graham (www.addistribune.com)

There are several places where you can drive off the road between Debre Birhan and Addis Ababa for viewpoints over the Awash Valley. One of the best is Koremash, which lies 12.5km along a 4x4, dry-season-only track from the main road, illegibly signposted 64km northwest of the Megenagna junction on Haile Gebrselassie Road. Koremash is a small Amhara village perched above a cliff offering fantastic views over the Afar lowlands and the Awash river valley. Negus Haile Melakot, the father of Menelik II, chose this site for his stronghold and ammunition dump, and Menelik used it as his armoury until the turn of the 20th century. A dozen stone buildings, about 15m long, 5m wide and 3m high, date from about 150 years ago, but undergo regular renovation, so are in good shape. In some of the buildings there are impressive juniper ceilings, on top of which the ammunition was reputedly stored. An active government centre today, the compound was used by the Italians as an administrative and military centre. In one building there is an Italian stone plaque inscribed Forttino Botteco, the name they gave Koremash, with the details of the Italian military brigade.

and most easily identified by what appears to be a pale chin in flight. Non-birders, on sighting this rather nondescript seedeater, could be forgiven for wondering what all the fuss is about! Other interesting birds to look out for along this road include the endemic blue-winged goose and Abyssinian longclaw, as well as lammergeyer, moorland and Erckell's francolin, blue rock thrush and the rare Somali chestnut-winged starling.

Dedicated birders are certain to want to follow the steep but fairly well-maintained road that descends from Ankober for 15km to the small town of Aliyu Amba. Set at an altitude of about 1,500m near the base of the escarpment, Aliyu Amba is in itself remarkable only for boasting a venerable mosque. Of interest to birders, however, is the Melka Jebdu River, 3km out of town along the Dulecha road, and recently identified as a reliable site for the yellow-throated serin (*Serinus flavigula*). This distinctively marked bird is one of the most localised of Ethiopia's endemic birds – it is only otherwise recorded with any regularity on Fantelle Volcano in Awash National Park – but is quite easy to tick in the vestigial acacia woodland lining the Melka Jebdu River where it crosses the road.

GETTING THERE AND AWAY Ankober is situated 40km east of Debre Birhan along an unsurfaced but reasonably well-maintained road that branches right from the main Debre Sina road roughly 500m after you exit the outskirts of Debre Birhan. The drive from Debre Birhan takes about 45–60 minutes without stops. If you intend visiting Ankober as a day trip from Debre Birhan using public transport, then an early start is advisable, as the few buses that cover this road daily leave at 05.00 (in either direction).

Those with a private vehicle – preferably 4x4 – should probably expect to take 45 minutes to cover the steep road from Ankober east to Aliyu Amba. From Aliyu Amba, it is possible to continue southeast along a rough road to Dulecha (23km) and then to the main road near Awash National Park (90km). There is not, so far as I can establish, any public transport through to Aliyu Amba, but you should have no trouble finding a lift on Thursday, when the main market is held.

WHERE TO STAY AND EAT There are a couple of very basic hotels in Ankober. The **Bizunesh Bekele Hotel** (*5 rooms; m 0912 027 644*), on the left-hand side of the road as you enter from Debre Birhan by the large Pepsi sign, is marginally the nicer with acceptably clean rooms using common shower (US$3). The **Getachew Tekle Selassie Hotel** (*10 rooms*) closer to the centre, located opposite the primary school, offers common shower rooms for US$2. A couple of restaurants serve local food. Ankober Palace Lodge lies on Ankober Hill.

Ankober Palace Lodge (7 rooms) 011 623 0012/662 6292; m 0911 653 643; f 011 551 5506; e ankoberlodge@yahoo.com; www.ankoberlodge.com.et. This peaceful tourist lodge, a little more than 3hrs from Addis in a private vehicle, makes for an excellent weekend getaway or could serve as a base for exploring the Guassa Plateau. The lodge has a commanding & historic location on top of Ankober Hill with sweeping views over the Rift Escarpment. Excursions include guided hikes around the property & to local villages as well as organised mule treks further afield (see the website for itineraries). The lodge's gigantic dining hall, rebuilt in the style of Emperor Menelik, is an impressive sight in itself & serves a variety of European & national dishes. Available cultural activities include hands-on opportunities to learn how to grind grain, spin cotton & bake *injera*. Accommodation is provided in traditionally styled en-suite rooms each with twin single beds & hot showers. Be warned: the rooms are a steep 470-step hike uphill (cars are left in a secure park at the bottom of the hill). It also gets very chilly here at night, so bring warm clothing. While the setting is indeed fantastic, you can't help feel that the price is steeper than the hike to the lodge. *Camping US$25, US$65/85/105 sgl/dbl/family room mid week, US$85/95/125 w/ends.*

Part Four

EASTERN ETHIOPIA

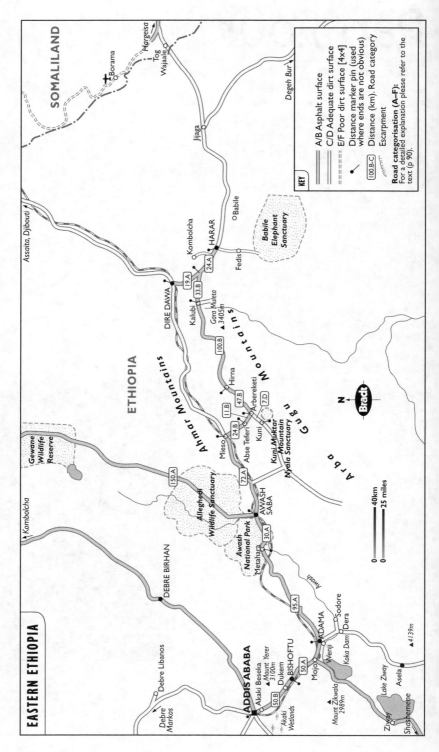

EASTERN ETHIOPIA

OVERVIEW

This three-chapter section covers parts of Ethiopia lying to the east of the capital. The first of the chapters ambles along the surfaced road between Addis Ababa and the large but rather bland town of Adama (Nazret). This 100km stretch of asphalt can be covered in a couple of hours or over several days, with obvious highlights including the **wetlands** around the Akaki River, the air-force town of **Bishoftu** (Debre Zeyit) and its attendant crater lakes and the atmospheric mountaintop **monastery** at Zikwala. All these places can easily form the goal of a self-standing day or overnight trip out of the capital. They can also be visited *en route* to southern Ethiopia – the junction for the main road south lies at Mojo, 75km from Addis Ababa, while Adama itself is the starting point for an important route south to the highlands of Arsi and Bale zones.

The second chapter in this section covers **Awash National Park**, which is the closest thing Ethiopia has to the savanna reserves of east Africa, and an excellent overnight trip from Addis Ababa. It also covers the arid section of the Rift Valley that follows the course of the Awash River north of Awash National Park to its delta in a series of desert lakes near the Djibouti border. Although little visited by travellers, this is a fascinating and very different part of Ethiopia, home to the pastoralist Afar people, and – somewhat unexpectedly – bisected by what is arguably the best surfaced road in the country.

The final chapter in this section concentrates on the alluring walled city of **Harar**, the spiritual home of Ethiopia's large Muslim community, as well as its altogether less inspiring modern twin city of **Dire Dawa**. Lying more than 500km east of Addis Ababa, Dire Dawa and Harar are accessible from the capital not only by road, but also by daily Ethiopian Airlines flights – not to mention the country's only passenger train service! The base from which Ahmed Gragn waged his 16th-century jihad against the Christian highlands, Harar formed the most important trade centre in Ethiopia for much of the 19th century – when it was visited by the explorer Richard Burton and home to the French poet Arthur Rimbaud – and it is also the birthplace of the late Emperor Haile Selassie. Today, the old town is one of the most popular tourist sites in Ethiopia. Not only does its labyrinth of alleys and Muslim shrines provide a striking contrast to the Christian pre-eminence in northern Ethiopia, but it is also home to the renowned hyena men of Harar.

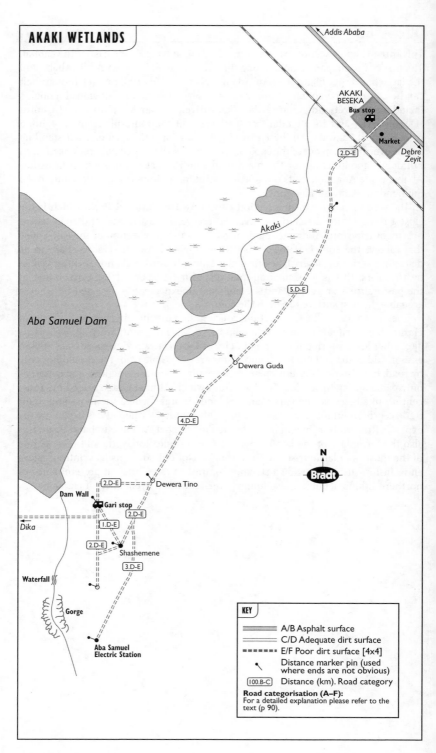

16

Addis Ababa to Adama by Road

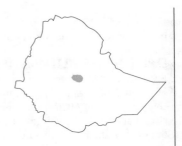

The 100km of surfaced road that runs southeast from Addis Ababa towards the bustling town of Adama (Nazret) will be traversed by most travellers heading to any parts of Ethiopia that lie south or east of the capital. Adama itself has excellent facilities for visitors, but since it is of little inherent interest to travellers, and can be reached by bus or in a private vehicle in a couple of hours from Addis Ababa, few visitors to Ethiopia spend long in the town. The road between Addis Ababa and Adama does, however, provide access to several notable natural attractions including the **Akaki Wetlands**, **Mount Zikwala** and the crater lakes of **Bishoftu** (Debre Zeyit), any of which makes for an easy goal for a day trip out of the capital.

Public transport is plentiful along the road covered in this chapter, with regular buses from the capital to Adama and other towns further east and south supplemented by light vehicles ferrying local passengers between small towns such as Akaki, Dukem, Bishoftu (Debre Zeyit) and Mojo. For self-drive travellers, or those hopping between towns in light vehicles, it's worth mentioning that Mojo, halfway between Bishoftu and Adama, forms the junction of the asphalt road that runs south through the Rift Valley to Moyale (Kenyan border) and Arba Minch (gateway to the Lower Omo Valley). Adama itself is also an important route focus, lying at the junction of the main road east towards Awash National Park, Harar and Assaita, and a dirt road heading south through the town of Asela towards Bale National Park.

AKAKI WETLANDS

The wetland complex fed by the Akaki River about 20km southeast of Addis is among the best in the country and of particular interest to birdwatchers. Its mix of habitats includes the open river, reedy marshes, a string of small natural lakes, the larger artificial Abba Samuel Dam and a very attractive waterfall. The wetlands stretch for about 12km from the small town of Akaki Beseka on the Bishoftu road, and can readily be explored as a day trip from Addis Ababa. Bear in mind that, like any seasonal wetland, it may dry out completely in the dry season or in years of drought.

GETTING THERE AND AWAY Minibuses from Addis to Akaki Beseka leave regularly from in front of the railway station and take about half an hour. They can also be picked up at the Saris minibus stop, which lies about 5km from the city centre on the Bishoftu road. When you want to move on from Akaki Beseka, it is easy to find transport back to Addis or on to Bishoftu.

WHERE TO STAY The obvious way to visit the Akaki Wetlands is as a day trip from Addis, but there are also several cheap hotels in Akaki Beseka. Best of the bunch is the **Beamlak Hotel** (*8 rooms*), clearly signposted on the main road opposite the

High Court, which has cramped musty rooms with en-suite rooms for US$3 and basic rooms using smelly communal showers for US$2.

EXPLORING THE WETLANDS The only form of public transport between Akaki Beseka and the villages around the wetlands is the horse-drawn *gari*. A *gari* out of Akaki Beseka can be picked up at the marketplace. *Garis* back to Akaki Beseka congregate about 500m from Abba Samuel Dam Wall, near a footbridge over the river that leads to the village of Dika. If you want to explore the wetlands reasonably thoroughly, the best plan would be to walk one way (about 13km and reasonably flat) and use a *gari* the other way. My feeling is that you would be best walking out provided you get an early start (you could set off at 06.00 if you spent the previous night in Akaki Beseka), as the area is very exposed and it becomes hot after around 10.00. You could then return by *gari* later in the day. With a later start, it might make more sense to take a *gari* out to get a feel for the terrain, and then to return by foot.

The interesting part of the wetlands starts about 3km out of town, where the river supports several small lakes, all of them visible from the road. During the rainy season, this whole area becomes a large, marshy floodplain. When I visited, towards the end of the rains, the marsh had receded, but I was still impressed by the numbers of greater flamingo and ducks on the open water and the variety of waders to be seen on the mudflats. This area is also noted for interesting European migrants such as European stork, yellow and grey wagtails, and a variety of wheatears. The most common terrestrial bird is the red-chested wheatear, a species that is virtually confined to Ethiopia, while the reeds and grass support large numbers of red bishop and various widows. Wattled ibis are common and vociferous.

About 7km out of town, you arrive at the nondescript hilltop village of Dewera Guda. Four kilometres further, at Dewera Tino, you come to a fork in the road. Take the right turn towards a village called Shashemene. The first sign of Shashemene is a small kiosk, where you might want to break for a soda and packet of dry biscuits. From the shop, a footpath leads for about 500m across boulder-strewn ground to the village proper and, a bit further on, the bank of the river. About 100m downstream from where you reach the river, it tumbles attractively over a cliff into a small gorge. Follow the edge of the gorge for 200m or so and there's an easy descent to the bottom, from where you can walk back over rocks to the base of the falls. The waterfall must be around 20m high and it is split into nine separate streams – it's very pretty, particularly after the rains when the water is high and the surrounding countryside is strewn with wild flowers. In the gorge, look out for the localised black duck and mountain wagtail, and the endemic white-winged cliff-chat.

From the waterfall, you can either return to the shop outside Shashemene, from where a clear footpath leads across a field to Abba Samuel Dam Wall, or else follow the river upstream to the same destination. The Italians built the dam in 1939 for the country's first hydro-electric plant, but this is no longer operative because of silt. Scenically, Abba Samuel is something of a disappointment as it is choked with water hyacinth, but the nearby bridge is the best place to pick up a *gari* back to Akaki Beseka.

Note that if you ask around in Akaki Beseka for transport to Shashemene, people are likely to think you mean the town of the same name in the Rift Valley.

BISHOFTU (DEBRE ZEYIT) AND SURROUNDS

Set at an altitude of 1,900m some 45 minutes' drive from Addis Ababa, Bishoftu is a substantial town – indeed, with a population exceeding 144,000, it is the ninth-largest in the country – that sprawls rather untidily for several kilometres along the main Adama road. The surrounding area is remembered as the site of Ahmed Gragn's famous victory over Emperor Lebna Dengal in 1529, which resulted in the destruction of several towns and the looting of some important churches, and which also cleared the way for the region to be occupied by the Oromo who still inhabit it today. The town is also known as Debre Zeyit (Mountain of Olives), the official 'Christian' name imposed on it by Haile Selassie in the early 1960s, and is still marked as such on many maps and road signs despite having officially reverted to its more historically valid Oromo name of Bishoftu in the late 1990s.

Bishoftu has since 1945 been the site of the country's main air-force base and training centre (don't photograph anything from the air-force base gate on the Adama road or about 3km further east), and it is also the site of the veterinary medicine facilities of Addis Ababa University, but otherwise it might easily be dismissed by visitors as a thoroughly uninteresting and scruffy little place on casual inspection. From the main road through town, there is not a hint of the fact that it lies at the epicentre of what is perhaps the most accessible crater-lake field in Africa. At least six such lakes are dotted around Bishoftu, two of which – Bishoftu and Hora – lie practically within the town centre – making it an excellent goal for a day trip out of the capital, or first stop before heading further east or south.

GETTING THERE AND AWAY Bishoftu straddles the surfaced Adama road roughly 50km east of Addis Ababa and can be reached from the capital in less than an hour in a private vehicle, bearing in mind that the traffic is probably the densest to be found along any open road in Ethiopia. Regular buses for Bishoftu leave from the new suburban Kaliti bus station located on the main road to Bishoftu/Debre Zeyit (US$1). The trip takes around one hour by bus, assuming the traffic out of Addis Ababa isn't too heavy. From Bishoftu, there is also plenty of transport on to Adama (US$1; 1 hour).

Bishoftu's bus station [376 A3] is located about 1km from the town centre along the Addis Ababa road. A steady stream of minibuses runs between the town centre and bus station, charging a fare of less than US$0.40.

WHERE TO STAY
Luxury
🏠 **Kuriftu Resort & Spa** [376 D6] (37 rooms) 📞011 433 5656/6860 or 011 662 3605; e kurifturesort@ethionet.et; www. kurifturesortspa.com. Located on the rustic northern shore of Lake Kiroftu, this upscale resort offers first-class rooms & amenities that rival the top hotels in Addis, but in a much more pleasant setting. All of the bungalow rooms feature locally inspired furnishings, 27" plasma screens with DSTV, modern bathrooms with 'rain' showers, minibar with wine, & private patio with fireplace & a fire prepared every night. Standard rooms lack a view, but have an enclosed private backyard that can cater for BBQs. Garden View & Lake View rooms are available at a premium – ask to see each type of room. The only downside is, because of the thatched interconnecting roof you can hear what's happening in the room next door, which, as we discovered, makes for a very restless night's sleep, especially if your neighbours' idea of a relaxing weekend away is watching movies all night – a good reason why TVs should be banned in places like this! There is no shortage of activities here, & all room prices include breakfast, kayaking, mountain biking, table tennis, billiards, movie theatre, swimming pool & steam room/sauna/jacuzzi. Additional spa services include massage, facials, manicure/ pedicure & full hair salon. The grounds & garden are meticulously maintained, & you can rent quad bikes to explore further afield. The restaurant & bar are both a bit pricey, with entrées running at US$5–7.50. Rates also include 1 complimentary massage & a mani-pedi per room. Discounts are available midweek. *US$160/170/308 standard dbl/twin/family room, US$154/165 garden view dbl/twin, US$170/181 dbl/twin lake view.*

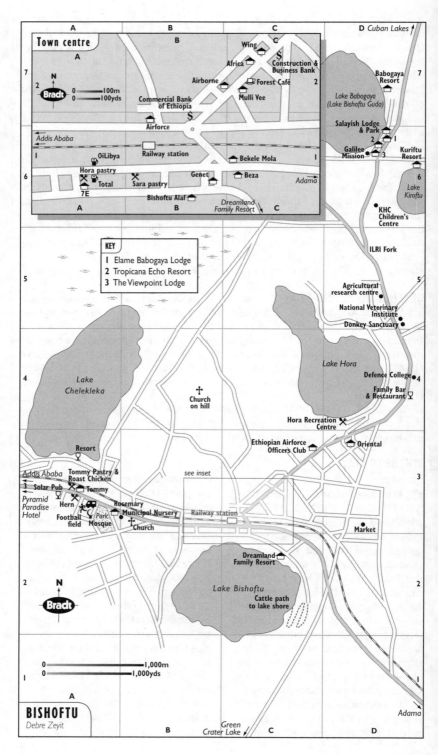

Town centre

Bradt

N

0 ——— 100m
0 ——— 100yds

A B C

7 7

Wing

Africa
Construction &
Business Bank

Airborne
Forest Café

Commercial Bank
of Ethiopia
Mulli Vee

Airforce

Addis Ababa

Railway station

OiLibya
Bekele Mola

6 6

Hora pastry
Total
Sara pastry
Genet
Beza

Adama

7E

Bishoftu Alaf

Dreamland
Family Resort

A B C

KEY
1 Elame Babogaya Lodge
2 Tropicana Echo Resort
3 The Viewpoint Lodge

Cuban Lakes

D

Babogaya
Resort

Lake Babogaya
(Lake Bishoftu Guda)

7

Salayish Lodge
& Park

Galilee
Mission

Kuriftu
Resort

6

Lake
Kiroftu

KHC
Children's
Centre

ILRI Fork

5 5

Agricultural
research centre

National Veterinary
Institute
Donkey Sanctuary

Lake
Chelekleka

Lake Hora

Defence College 4

Family Bar
& Restaurant

4

Church
on hill

Hora Recreation
Centre

Resort

Ethiopian Airforce
Officers Club
Oriental

Addis Ababa

see inset

3

Solar Pub

Tommy Pastry &
Roast Chicken

Pyramid
Paradise
Hotel

Tommy

Hern

Rosemary

Railway station

3

Football
field

Park
Mosque

Municipal Nursery

Market

Church

2

N

Bradt

Dreamland
Family Resort

2

Lake Bishoftu
Cattle path
to lake shore

0 ——— 1,000m
0 ——— 1,000yds

1 1

A

BISHOFTU
Debre Zeyit

Green
Crater Lake

Adama

B C D

376

⌂ Babogaya Resort [376 D7] (50 rooms) ☏ 011 433 7676/7; e babogayaresort@yahoo. com; www.babogayaresort.com. This sprawling new resort overlooking Lake Babogaya lacks the ambience & unique styling of the Kuriftu (see page 375). The cookie-cutter hotel rooms are comfortable but unexceptional – those in the main building all have hot-shower en suite & private balcony (suites have a jacuzzi as an extra), while cottages have a queen-sized bed, hot-shower en suite, balcony & large French windows to take in the views. Facilities include 2 dining rooms, huge patio with outside dining area, mini golf course, tennis, sauna & spa as well as a boutique art gallery located by reception. Fishing, canoeing & boat rides are also available. Rates include breakfast & free Wi-Fi. *US$119 standard dbl room, US$137 cottage, US$159 standard suite, US$750 Presidential Suite.*

Moderate

⌂ Dreamland Hotel & Resort [376 C2] (18 rooms) ☏ 011 437 1520–2; e info@ ethiodreamland.com; www.ethiodreamland. com. Not such a dreamland to look at, but from its position perched on the crater-rim above Lake Bishoftu, this hotel takes top honours with regards to the view (a crowded category with tough competition). Well-appointed rooms with private balconies facing the lake are similar in standard & styling to the luxury establishments. Rates include breakfast & internet access with weekend prices slightly higher. Even if you do not stay here, the romantic terrace restaurant is worth a visit, if only for the epic overlook. *US$40/43 dbl/twin, US$60/69/82 standard/luxury/family suite.*

⌂ The Viewpoint Lodge [376 D7] (8 rooms) m 0911 465 693; e lakebabogaya@live. com; http://sites.google.com/site/viewpointlodge/. This relaxing new Belgian–Ethiopian-run lodge tumbles in 4 sedate terraces down to Lake Babogaya. While the lodge has spectacular views, a chilled vibe, personalised service & resident free-roaming tortoises, & won a Tripadvisor Award of Excellence in 2012, it seems pricey in comparison with neighbouring resorts. The rooms are basic but comfortable with simple furnishings & hot-shower en suite; some back onto the road, so could be noisy, as could those that circle the main common area. The 2 rustic lakeside rooms built on stilts overlooking the water are certainly for the adventurous – they don't seem too sturdy considering you can see

through the wooden floorboards, bathroom facilities are shared & you have to climb down/up 120 steps to reach them or return to the main area. It's also possible to pitch a tent on one of the lower terraces. There is no restaurant as such, but well-cooked meals are available on request costing from US$4 for lunch to US$7.50 for a 3-course meal. Rates include a delicious continental breakfast & kayaks are available free. *Camping US$12 pp, US$41.50/53 sgl/ dbl, US$76.50/94.50 for a 3-/4-person family room.*

⌂ Elame Babogaya Lodge [376 D7] (8 rooms) ☏ 011 437 1584; m 0920 243 434; e zemedkunmgr@elamelodge.com; www. elamelodge.com. There may be no stunning lake views or water access here, but the lush tropical garden setting is very relaxing & the stone *tukul*-style bungalows are beautifully built & designed. The well-priced rooms all have traditional furnishings, multi-channel satellite TV & private hot-shower en suite. There's a good restaurant serving both Ethiopian & European dishes, a bar, a cultural room for coffee ceremonies & a small library. Rates include breakfast & free internet as well as afternoon tea & coffee. The lodge is situated opposite the Maritime Training Institute at the southeastern end of Lake Babogaya. *US$28/35.50 dbl/twin.*

⌂ Tropicana Echo Resort [376 D7] (10 rooms) m 0911 216 817; e tropicanaecho55resort@gmail.com. Located next door to The Viewpoint, this new place overlooking Lake Babogaya offers the same spectacular views as its neighbour for a more reasonable price – not to mention better-quality rooms & facilities. That said, it doesn't have the same homely atmosphere of The Viewpoint. Accommodation is in 10 stone bungalows built in 2 neat terraced rows, all with traditional raised double beds with stone bases, DSTV, hot-shower en suite & small balcony. The 6 bungalows on the lower terrace are more spacious with a unique split-level design, additional sitting area & have better views. A restaurant & bar are attached & a fishing & boat-hire service is available. *US$27/32.50 dbl with back/lake view.*

⌂ Hotel Tommy International [376 A3] (44 rooms) ☏ 011 433 9999/5699; m 0911 915 681; e info@tommyinternationalhotel.com; www. tommyinternationalhotel.com. With a central location in town, the Tommy International cannot be compared with the luxury resorts, but it would probably get top billing anywhere in the north.

The clean bright rooms have a European feel, with over-sized mahogany furniture, embossed plaster ceilings & flat-panel TVs. Large en-suite bathrooms feature enclosed showers, some with side jets. The Tommy is also excellent value with room rates including breakfast & free Wi-Fi. Other amenities include an open-air wine bar & elegant rooftop restaurant with dishes in the US$2.50–6 range. They also have secure parking, internet access & an elevator. *US$20/27 sgl/dbl, US$36 suite*.

Budget

🏠 **Salayish Lodge & Park** [376 D6] (6 rooms) ☎ 011 433 6878; **m** 0911 215 540; **e** salayishlodge@yahoo.com; www.ethiolodge. net. This ranks as one of the most peculiar spots in all of Ethiopia. Whereas the Kuriftu Resort (see page 375), is perfectly manicured, this place is just the opposite – very rustic & natural with simple thatch huts engulfed by a charming but overgrown garden teeming with birds. Don't let the rough-hewn exteriors throw you – inside, the huts are clean yet basic & have full-size beds & en-suite baths with hot shower & all very reasonably priced. The Sidamo-style restaurant is completely constructed from bamboo thatch, including the floors, & the food is very inexpensive. The staff are relaxed & friendly, & let's not forget the billy-goat mascot, or the zoo which contains donkeys, cows, rabbits, turkeys & deer. Horseback riding is also available. At the time of writing the owner was building a row of small rock bungalows (expect to pay upwards of US$50 per night) as well as an open restaurant, kitchen & bar all perched at the top of the hill overlooking the lake. The lodge is signed on the left side of the road about 100m past the junction for the Kuriftu Resort. *US$20–25 inc b/fast depending on the room*.

🏠 **Pyramid Paradise Hotel** [off map 376 A3] (13 rooms) ☎ 011 433 1406/1956; **e** danielas@ ethionet.et. This smart but unpretentious place is located about 2km out of town on the Addis side. The clean well-furnished rooms come in 3 classes: first-class rooms are built around a central garden & have private balconies with a cosy fireplace, second-class rooms are on the top floor of the adjoining annex, while third-class rooms are on the ground floor. All rooms have king bed, en-suite hot shower, DSTV & fridge. The pleasant courtyard with lawn area & tables under individual tents is a great place to try some of the delicious well-priced

food, juice & pastries. There is a small playground for children, an indoor restaurant with extensive menu, & a sauna & steam bath to boot. Fantastic value! *US$18/23/25 3rd-/2nd-/1st-class room*.

🏠 **Ethiopian Airforce Officers Club** [376 C3] ☎ 011 433 8035/0729. Lying along the road between town centre & Lake Hora, & formerly one of the best hotels in town, this place still deserves consideration if only for its gigantic swimming pool (with a 10m-high dive) & clay tennis courts. The massive rooms with en-suite hot shower & DSTV are acceptable, though not so smart as to entirely justify inflated *faranji* rates. The club also serves good Western & Ethiopian food, the bar has DSTV & the pretty palm-lined grounds have a play area for kids. *US$22.50*.

🏠 **Rosemary Hotel** [376 A3] (36 rooms) ☎ 011 848 0344; **m** 0911 400 152/0922 394 670; **e** rosemary7@yahoo.com. Located on the main road above the Commercial Bank of Ethiopia near the new bus station, this swish-looking hotel is the newer sibling to the long-serving 7E listed opposite. The well-priced rooms have tiled floors, nets, hot-shower en suites & DSTV. Third-class rooms are more compact with a ¾ bed & small TV, second-class rooms are marginally bigger with a full-size bed & large TV, while first-class rooms are generously sized with a full-size bed & large flat-screen TV. There's also a huge outdoor garden bar & restaurant. If your budget is tight & you don't care about a lake view, then this is the spot. *US$13/15.50/20 3rd-/2nd-/1st-class dbl*.

🏠 **Bishoftu Afaf Hotel** [inset 376 B1] (16 rooms) ☎ 011 433 8299; **m** 0923 693 630. The pick in this category for some years now, this well-run hotel overlooks Lake Bishoftu signposted from the main road and is still a great budget pick in spite of recent competition from the above. (If the Dreamland is out of your budget, but you still want access to the epic view, then this is the place!) The freshly painted rooms are clean & pleasant with en-suite hot showers. Rooms with a full-size double bed & TV are larger & cost slightly more than the rooms with ¾ bed & no TV. A pleasant & sensibly priced restaurant/bar is attached. *US$12/14 without/with TV*.

Shoestring

🏠 **Bekele Mola Hotel** [inset 376 C1] (8 rooms) ☎ 011 433 8005. Located near the main roundabout, the Bishoftu branch of the Bekele

Mola isn't the smartest in the chain – & that's saying something considering how much these hotels have deteriorated in recent years. Still its small doubles with en-suite hot water while basic are decent value & it wins points for its one-price-for-all policy. *US$6*.

🏠 **Airforce Hotel**   [inset 376 B1] (17 rooms) ☏011 433 0620. Situated on the opposite side of the railway tracks to the Bekele Mola, this place has a variety of equally uninspiring rooms, some with ¾-bed cold-shower en suites, some with hot

water & larger rooms with full-size bed, carpet & hot-water bath. *US$4.50/5.50 with ¾ bed cold/hot shower, US$6 with full-size bed.*

🏠 **7E Hotel**   [inset 376 A1] (7 rooms) ☏011 433 9888. Located near the old bus station this place, under the same ownership as the far superior & newer Rosemary Hotel, has fraying but decent rooms, ¾ beds & cold-shower en suite. The attached restaurant serves cheap & filling meals. *US$5.*

✦ **WHERE TO EAT**   In the town centre, the obvious place to eat is the **Dreamland Restaurant** [376 C2], which serves a wide selection of local dishes, alongside burgers, sandwiches, pasta and grills in green terraced grounds with a view over Lake Bishoftu. (There are now two restaurants here – the one in the Dreamland Hotel next door is smarter but the original has the atmosphere.) Also very good, close by, but less attractive overall, is the restaurant at the **Bishoftu Afaf Hotel** [inset 376 B1], which serves a reasonable variety of local and *faranji* dishes in the US$2–4 range, and has a view over the lake. Pastry shops are thin on the ground in the town centre, but the long-standing **Tommy Pastry and Roast Chicken** [376 A3] located on the Addis Ababa road across from the namesake hotel remains the top pick, serving a delicious variety of sweet treats as well as excellent chicken and a few European favourites in the attached restaurant. Service though is painfully slow.

Heading along the road towards Lake Hora, the **Hora Recreation Centre** [376 D4], situated on the lakeside, is a peaceful spot for a drink or snack with coffee, soft drinks and beer as well as a small menu of burgers, sandwiches and pasta available. But you'll need to pay a small fee for the pleasure. Further along the same road, the trendy **Family Bar and Restaurant** [376 D4] next to the Defence Engineering College is the best stand-alone restaurant in the area – the décor alone complete with vintage car makes it worth the visit! Open daily it serves a Tex Mex-inspired menu including tacos, cheeseburgers, melts, barbecue chicken, barbecue beef rib chops (rated by one reader as the best cuts of meat you will find in Ethiopia) and chicken *fajitas*. Meals are in the US$3–4.50 range.

WHAT TO SEE
Crater lakes close to town
Any of the crater lakes around town can be visited as a short foot excursion or by *gari*. It is equally possible to visit the lot of them by foot over the course of a day. The most central goal is the alkaline **Lake Bishoftu** [376 C2], which can be reached from the main road by turning uphill at the Shell petrol station and walking for about 100m. The best view over the lake is from the Dreamland Hotel & Resort on the eastern rim. On the opposite side of the crater to the Hotel Bishoftu Afaf, a small waterfall plunges into the lake. A steep cattle path leads to the shore of the lake, which measures up to 90m in depth, and supports some interesting birds, notably a wintering population of ferruginous duck and breeding pairs of Rüppell's griffin vulture.

Far more visually appealing is **Lake Hora** [376 D4], immediately north of town. This saline body of water, almost 40m deep, is the largest crater lake in the Bishoftu area, extending over 1.03km², and its thickly wooded slopes teem with birds. A footpath leads to the lakeshore, where a recreation resort sells drinks and basic meals, and has a few boats for rental. The footpath that circumnavigates most of the crater rim takes a few hours to walk – theft is a real risk, so leave your valuables behind or take a local guide. According to local tradition, an important and very colourful Oromo thanksgiving festival called the Irrecha has taken place on the shore of Lake Hora annually for more than 1,000 years. The Irrecha Festival takes place on 1 October, and celebrates the traditional Oromo notion of Waka (One God). Some believers carry a sheaf of leaves or yellow flowers to the water's edge to praise Waka for the bounty of nature, while others dance traditionally in circles, or walk around the lake in small groups. It's a fascinating affair, well worth seeing if you're in the area at the right time – outsiders are made to feel very welcome.

If you are keen to see more lakes after Hora, continue along the main road out of town towards the agricultural college until the fork in the road where a small black-and-white signpost reads 'ILRI'. Take the right fork, past the KHC Children's Centre till you reach the Catholic Galilee Mission. To your right, a side road leads to **Lake Kiroftu** [376 D6], notable more perhaps for its excellent fishing than for any scenic qualities. Alternatively, continue straight on past the Galilee Centre for about 500m, where a road to your left leads down to the shore of **Lake Babogaya** [376 D7] (also known as Lake Bishoftu Guda), a large and very attractive lake with lushly vegetated shores.

Especially if you have an interest in birds, you can walk back from here to the ILRI fork, but instead of returning to town take the fork you bypassed on the way out. Follow this road for about 1km and you come to the floodplain of **Lake Chelekleka** [376 A4], not a crater lake, but a shallow pan that shows marked seasonal fluctuations in water level and often dries up entirely towards the end of the dry season. You can follow the same road back to town with the floodplain and finally the lake to your left the whole way. Chelekleka is very pretty with Mount Yerer in the background, and also offers the best birdwatching in the area. The open water supports a variety of waterfowl. Knob-billed duck, pygmy goose and spur-winged goose might be present at any time of year, while migrants such as garganey, pintail, northern shoveler, ferruginous duck and European crane are likely during the European winter. The lake sometimes hosts large concentrations of lesser flamingo, and the shore is often dense with waders. You might want to stop in for a drink at the small resort on the southern shore – entry costs less than US$0.50 and no food other than popcorn is available.

You can walk the above circuit in its entirety – you'll cover about 10–12km in all, most of it reasonably flat – but you might also think about hiring a *gari*, at least for part of the circuit. I would be inclined to get a *gari* as far as Kiroftu, then to meander back to town on foot via Chelekleka. With a private vehicle, you could also seek out the pair of Cuban-built dams known rather imaginatively as the **Cuban Lakes** – they lie about 15km north of Lake Babogaya and are of great interest to birdwatchers.

Green Crater Lake

If the above circuit doesn't quench your lake-viewing appetite, you could think about heading out to the Green Crater Lake (also known as Aranguade Bahir or Hora Hado), which lies about 10km south of town along a road that branches from the main Adama road near the air-force base. Measuring about 30m deep, the Green Crater Lake lies at the base of a very steep crater. The unusually alkaline water supports a high concentration of the algae *Spirulina*, which creates a green cast in the right light. The algae consumes all the oxygen it produces by day during the night, so that the water becomes anaerobic in the early hours of morning, for which reason fish – and birds that survive mainly by fishing – are entirely absent. The lake does, however, support a good variety of waders, and concentrations of more than 20,000 lesser flamingo gather in its shallows from time to time. Without private transport, the best way to reach the lake is by *gari*; expect to pay around US$2.50 for the round trip.

Mount Zikwala This 2,989m-high extinct volcano, relatively recent in geological origin, rises to more than 600m above the surrounding countryside some 30km south of Bishoftu, and dominates the skyline for miles around. The juniper forest on the crater rim supports a smattering of large mammals, most visibly troops of guereza monkey, but also common duiker and klipspringer. It is also rich in forest birds, including the endemic black-winged lovebird, Abyssinian catbird, Abyssinian woodpecker and a variety of forest starlings. The beautiful lake in the middle of the 2km-wide crater is sacred to Orthodox Ethiopians, who claim that it glows at night, and it often hosts a variety of unusual migrant ducks during the European winter. Zikwala is almost certainly the source of the Abyssinian mountain marked as 'Xiquala' on Fra Mauro's world map of 1459.

The main attraction of Zikwala is the **Church and Monastery of Zikwala Maryam**, which according to one legend were founded in the 4th century by a pair of Egyptian monks. A more plausible tradition links the monastery's foundation to Gebre Manfus Kidus, also known as Abbo, an Egyptian priest who arrived in Ethiopia in the time of King Lalibela. The older of the two extant churches – constructed in the early 20th century – is covered in frescoes of its patron saint, whose St Francis-like reputation for befriending animals extended to living with lions and hyenas. The monks will show you a crack between two rocks of which it is said only the pure of conscience will squeeze through, as well as the sacred

THE DONKEY HEALTH AND WELFARE PROJECT

A little-known fact is that at 5.2 million individuals, Ethiopia has the second-largest donkey population in the world – only China has more. Another disturbing statistic is that while the average donkey has a lifespan of 35–40 years in the wild, the average Ethiopian donkey only lives between nine and 13 years! Fortunately the UK-based Donkey Sanctuary has teamed up with the veterinary department of Addis Ababa University to offer free education and treatment to owners of livestock. One of the greatest threats to donkeys is parasites of the digestive system, which usually leads to immune disorders and early death. Since this project started, over one million donkeys have been treated for parasites, along with 30,000 mules and over 10,000 horses. Another problem is poor animal care and back sores from uneven loads. Through owner training and the free distribution of padded saddles and humane hobbles, this group is making huge strides to decrease animal cruelty.

While not a tourist attraction per se, a visit to the Donkey Project [376 D5] can be a rewarding experience. (There is also a joint Horse Health and Welfare Project, in conjunction with SPANA, the Society for the Protection of Animals Abroad.) Both projects are located at the veterinary medicine facilities of Addis Ababa University, which is signposted just before the National Veterinary Institute. It is best to come on treatment days, which are Mondays and Thursdays for horses, and Wednesdays and Fridays for donkeys. Donations are greatly appreciated – it only costs birr 1 to treat an animal for parasites, so even a small gift can have a big impact. For additional information contact the office on ☏ 011 433 0304.

stone that is said to mark Abbo's grave. Note, however, that another tradition has it that the saint's body was taken to Jerusalem by angels and buried next to the tomb of Jesus, while a third claims that he is buried at Gurage zone at the ancient Abbo Medrikabd Monastery near Bui on the road between Tiya and Butajira.

It is especially worth visiting Zikwala on 5 Tekemt and 5 Megabit (normally 15 October and 14 March), when the monastery forms the scene of a large religious festival dedicated to Gebre Manfus Kidus. There is a mass pilgrimage to the mountain from Addis Ababa and other parts of Showa province on these days.

Zikwala is an easy target for a day trip from Addis or Bishoftu, provided you have your own vehicle. The turn-off to the mountain is on the Addis Ababa road, next to the juice bar just outside Bishoftu. From there it is about 30km to the base of the mountain, where there is a small village called Wember Maryam. The steep 10km road that climbs from the base to the top of the mountain is normally motorable in a 4x4, but when the road hasn't been maintained for a while it becomes impassable.

Without a vehicle, you'll be dependent on the occasional 4x4s that run between Bishoftu and Wember Maryam at the base of the mountain. These normally leave from Bishoftu at around 06.00 and take two hours. You will almost certainly have to walk the 10km up the mountain. There is no formal accommodation in the area, but you should be allowed to pitch a tent on the crater rim. If you are in the area at the right time of year, there is plenty of transport from Addis Ababa directly to Zikwala Maryam on the festival days mentioned above.

Mount Yerer The 3,100m-high Mount Yerer is a four-million-year-old extinct volcano set on the western Rift Valley wall, to the north of the village of Dukem on the Addis–Bishoftu road. The deep semi-collapsed caldera has a towering rock in its centre. The crater rim offers excellent views across to the crater lakes around Bishoftu, and is also notable for supporting large numbers of breeding raptors. Also of interest is an elusive hermit's cave, where the mummified body of a hermit can be seen in a glass coffin.

The caldera is about 10km from Dukem. You can get part way there via a motorable forestry track, which peters out at around the 2,500m mark. From the roadhead, you will have to find your own way to the summit, so it might be useful to ask around in Dukem for a guide. The Mapping Authority's 1:50,000 sheet number 0838 B2 shows Mount Yerer and Dukem. A huge selection of hotels catering to all sub-Sheraton tastes and budgets line the main road through Dukem.

ADAMA (NAZRET)

The third-largest town in Ethiopia, with a population of 250,000, Adama lies at an altitude of 1,600m on the fertile plateau that divides the narrowest stretch of the Ethiopian Rift Valley from the central highlands. It forms an important urban focal point for local cattle farmers, as well as the nearby Wenji Sugar Plantation (the oldest agricultural concern of its sort in the country) and several fruit and vegetable farms.

Popular with Addis weekenders for the nearby Sodore Spa, it is also blessed with an above-par range of tourist facilities, but otherwise it's a rather nondescript town.

As with nearby Bishoftu, Adama was renamed during the last years of the Imperial era in accordance with a policy to replace secular Oromo place names with something a touch more ecclesiastical, in this instance Nazret, a corruption of Nazareth (Haile Selassie's birthplace of Ejerso Gworo near Harer was reputedly earmarked to be renamed Bethlehem to reinforce the traditional belief in the royal

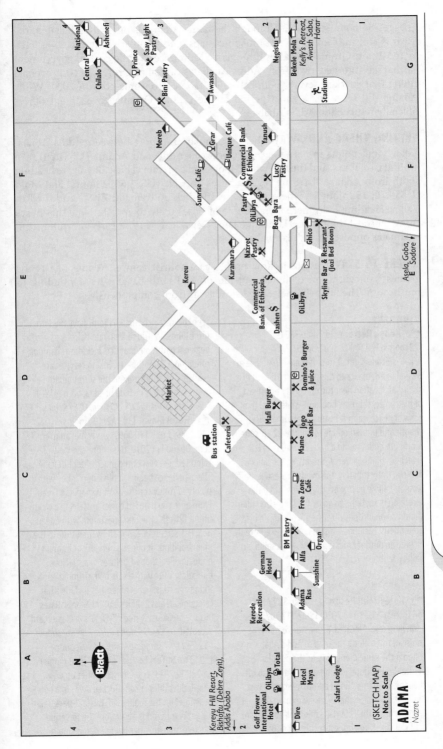

G

4

National

Central

Chilalo

Ashenefi

Prince

Saay Light
Pastry

3

Bini Pastry

e

Awassa

2

Negistu

Bekele Mola

Kelly's Retreat,
Awash Saba,
Harar

1

Stadium

Mereb

Grar

Unique Café

Yanush

Lucy
Pastry

F

Sunrise Café

Pastry
OiLibya

Commercial Bank
of Ethiopia

Beza Bara

e

Ghito

Skyline Bar & Resaurant
(Jozi Bed Room)

Asela, Goba,
Sodore

E

Kereu

Karamara

Nazret
Pastry

Commercial
Bank of Ethiopia

Dashen

OiLibya

D

Market

Mafi Burger

Domino's Burger
& Juice

e

C

Bus station

Cafeteria

Free Zone
Café

Mame

Jogo
Snack Bar

B

Kerode
Recreation

German
Hotel

BM Pastry

Alfa

Organ

Adama
Ras

Sunshine

A

N

Bradt

Kereyu Hill Resort,
Bishoftu (Debre Zeyit),
Addis Ababa

Golf Flower
International OiLibya
Hotel

Total

Dire

Hotel
Maya

Safari Lodge

(SKETCH MAP)
Not to Scale

ADAMA
Nazret

16

383

lineage's Solomonic roots). Although the name Adama is officially reinstated, the town is still marked as Nazret on some maps, and popularly referred to as such by most non-Oromo-speaking Ethiopians. More recently, the central government earmarked it to take over from Addis Ababa as capital of Oromia, a controversial ruling that sparked several political rallies (some pro, some con) in 2000. While Adama did serve for a short period as the capital, Oromia government offices officially returned to Addis Ababa in 2005.

GETTING THERE AND AWAY There is regular transport between Addis Ababa, Adama and points in between. Buses between Addis and Adama (US$1.50) take around two hours, and the trip is a bit shorter in a private vehicle. If you are heading south from Adama, there are regular buses to Asela (US$1.50; 2 hours) and Mojo (US$0.70; 15 minutes), where you can easily pick up traffic to Ziway and the Rift Valley. Heading east, there are a couple of buses daily to Awash. Note that buses from central Ethiopia to Harar and Dire Dawa leave in the early morning from Adama as opposed to Addis Ababa.

 WHERE TO STAY Despite its low profile as a tourist centre, Adama boasts the greatest concentration of hotels outside of Addis Ababa and it's continuing to mushroom. The following selective listing is far from comprehensive.

Upmarket

Kelly's Retreat [off map 383 G2] (22 rooms) 022 112 3001/3035−7; e kellysretreat@gmail.com. If there is paradise to be had in Adama, then this place is it. Hidden in a suburban location near the university northeast of the centre, this new boutique-style hotel is an oasis of peace, calm & beauty in an otherwise chaotic and unmemorable town. The 22 en-suite rooms are built around a huge central pool & sweet-smelling garden which attracts a variety of birds. Unfortunately, the overly protective staff wouldn't allow us to view the rooms, but if the reception is anything to go by the king-sized rooms should be beautifully furnished & possibly a bit pretentious. Facilities − again unseen − reportedly include an outdoor massage area, a tea salon, art gallery & library. *US$60−130.*

Moderate

Kereyu Hill Resort [off map 383 A2] (66 rooms) 022 112 7090; f 022 112 7075. The sprawling resort located 15mins' drive from the centre of town along the road to Addis Ababa is under the same ownership as the popular Central Jimma Hotel in Jimma. The latest cab off the rank in Adama's hotel boom, it boasts a vast dining room, an Olympic-size swimming pool, tennis & basketball courts, a mini golf course, an artificial lake & the hugest secure car park we've

seen this research trip. All rooms have modern furnishings, TV, fridge & private balcony as well as personal bathroom products including shampoo, conditioner & toothpaste. Hiking services are available for short treks in the surrounding mountains. Rates include breakfast & free Wi-Fi. *US$23 standard dbl, US$30 twin, US$75 suite.*

Hotel Maya [383 A2] (94 rooms) 022 112 4949; f 022 110 0699; www.mayanazret. com. Opened in 2010, this impressive new place is located just east of the much older Rift Valley. The experience begins in the smart lobby with plenty of comfy couches & newspapers to read. From here you'll be led either upstairs to a clean, bright & fresh-smelling guestroom with queen bed, flat-screen TV & hot-shower en suite in the main building, or under a network of fragrant bougainvillea-draped trellises to a spacious bungalow suite with a sofa bed, sitting room & fridge as extras. Other amenities include a bar & lounge area, a 24hr restaurant & pool. Rates include breakfast & free Wi-Fi. Visa & MasterCard accepted. *US$24/35 standard/deluxe guestroom, US$35/41/47 standard/family/deluxe suite.*

The Safari Lodge [383 A1] (18 rooms) 022 112 2013; e saf.log@ethionet.et; www. safarilodgeethiopia.com. Tucked away in a quiet backstreet off the main road, the laid-back Safari Lodge seems worlds away from the towering concrete monstrosities lining Adama's main road. The bungalows, although dated & a little dark, are cool & well maintained with queen bed, small TV, en-suite bath & sitting area. While the standard rooms are unexceptional, there is 1 special room called 'the tower' which is wacky enough to be worth the high price for a night's stay. A phallic monstrosity with 2 levels, the tower features a large sitting room & bar with 40" TV & VCR, a bathroom with separate shower & tub, & a netted king bed on the upper level. From here a tight spiral staircase leads further up to a private glassed-in observation deck with 360° views of nothing in particular. The restaurant/bar has a pool table & serves pasta, sandwiches & ice cream in addition to the standard fare. Rates include breakfast & the use of a very clean swimming pool. *US$24 standard dbl, US$29 corner suite, US$35.50 tower.*

🏠 **Dire International Hotel** [383 A2] (60 rooms) ☎022 110 0378/79/83–85; e direinth@ ethionet.et; www.direinthotel.com. This multi-storey hotel on the Addis end of town is easily the best value in this class. Compact standard doubles come complete with full-size bed, en-suite bath & TV, while a marginally bigger first-class room has a queen bed. Suites have a larger TV, fridge & bathtub. Rates include breakfast & free Wi-Fi, & the restaurant has a good menu with dishes in the US$2–4 range. Visa is accepted & underground parking is available. A new, more upmarket annex at the back of the property was under construction at the time of writing. *US$17/19 standard-/1st-class dbl, US$21 twin, US$30 family suite.*

Budget In Adama, the distinction between the hotels in the budget & the moderate categories begin to blur, especially when higher weekend pricing comes into play.

🏠 **Bekele Mola Hotel** [383 G2] (36 rooms) ☎022 111 2312. This very likeable representative of the Bekele Mola chain is set in wooded, flowering grounds about 5mins' walk from the main roundabout along the Awash road. The well-maintained rooms are all clean with balcony, hot-shower en suite & DSTV. The large carpeted bungalows are spacious, while the rooms in the double-storey building out the back are slightly smarter. The grounds are teeming with birds, & dotted with chairs & tables. An outdoor bar serves snacks & drinks near the entrance. *Bungalows US$12.50/14 w/day/w/end, standard rooms US$14/15.50 w/day/w/end.*

🏠 **Adama Ras Hotel** [383 B2] (68 rooms) ☎022 111 1993. This stalwart hotel, formerly government owned now privatised, looks tired by comparison with the competition, but the wooded grounds do lend it considerably more character & aesthetic appeal than almost anything else on offer in Adama. The en-suite double rooms are pretty good value though vary in price & cleanliness so make sure you check them out before you decide, while the suites, with 2 bedrooms sleeping 4 people as well as a lounge, might appeal to families or small groups. The restaurant & rooms form a quadrangle around a swimming pool, which was actually empty on our most recent visit in 2011. *US$7–12 en-suite dbl, US$24 suite.*

Shoestring

🏠 **Ghico Hotel** [383 E2] (28 rooms) ☎022 111 0155. This centrally located hotel offers dingy rooms with cold-shower en suite (but common toilet), or larger & equally dreary en-suite doubles with hot shower. *US$4.50/5 with cold-/hot-water shower.*

🍴 **WHERE TO EAT** As with accommodation, travellers are spoilt for choice. Most of the hotels listed above serve a good range of local and *faranji* dishes at reasonable prices with the **Safari Lodge** [383 A1] a standout, serving a varied menu of local and European favourites including vegetarian dishes and filling stir-fries in the US$2.50–4 range in a lush tropical garden setting.

Another good spot for a meal or snack is the **Kerode Recreation** [383 B2], which serves a lengthy menu of pizzas, pastas and local dishes in the US$2–4 range – the roast mutton apparently is the house speciality – as well as pastries and ice cream. The **BM Pastry** [383 B2] is another good spot for sweet cakes and treats.

If you have a hankering for a burger, try **Mafi Burger** [383 D2], not far from the bus station, or **Domino's Burger & Juice** [383 D2] located on the opposite side of the road; both charge between US$2 and US$4. For Ethiopian dishes you can't beat

The largest and most populous of the federal states defined when the central government redrew the regional map of Ethiopia in 1994, Oromia covers an area of 367,000km² – more than 30% of Ethiopia's total area – and its population has risen from 18 to 21 million over the last decade. The irregular shape of the region has been compared to a lopsided and distended bow tie, with the self-governing city-state of Addis Ababa lying roughly where the knot would be. Nine of the 20 largest urban settlements in Ethiopia lie within Oromia (12 if you include the self-governing cities of Addis Ababa, Dire Dawa and Harar), the largest being Adama (Nazret), followed by Jimma, Hawassa, Bishoftu (Debre Zeyit), Shashemene, Nekemte, Asela, Hosaina and Sodo, and another 15 towns within the region each support a population of 20,000 or more.

Divided into 12 zones and 180 districts, Oromia is a region of vast geographic and climatic diversity. It encompasses not only the highland crags and meadows around Addis Ababa, but also the lush rainforest around Jimma and Nekemte in the west, much of the southern Rift Valley, and the arid acacia scrub towards the Kenyan border. The common factor throughout the region is cultural: Oromia, as its name implies, is the home of the Oromo people, Ethiopia's largest ethnic group. Until recently more frequently referred to as the Galla, a name that was used by their neighbours rather than by themselves, the Oromo originally came from the Kenyan border area currently occupied by the Borena, a subgroup of the Oromo. They migrated north from this homeland in the early 16th century, a movement which, whether by chance or design, coincided with Ahmed Gragn's jihad against the Christian empire. It could be argued that the Oromo migration effectively put an end to the war, as both Christian and Muslim Ethiopians found their territory under siege from a third source. Certainly, the Oromo were the main beneficiaries of the holy war, taking advantage of the weakened state of both parties to occupy much of what is now southern Ethiopia, including vast tracts of land that had formerly been part of, or paid tribute to, the Christian empire.

Today, the Oromo are divided into six main groups and hundreds of subgroups, which share a rigid male age-set system, called *Geda*. At the beginning of every eight-year cycle, marked by a spate of initiations and circumcisions, the age-sets all move up one rung. The dominant age-set consists of 16–24-year-olds, who elect from within their ranks an administrative leader known as the Abagada, who serves until the next eight-year cycle begins. This is an unusually democratic social structure, because no hereditary element is involved in political leadership, and because it creates a built-in sell-by date not unlike the limit of two presidential terms written into many modern national constitutions. Once an age-set enters its sixth cycle, its members are regarded as elders, and play an advisory role in governance.

The Oromo believe in one god, known as Waka: traditionalists hold that theirs is the oldest monotheistic religion in the world, and that Moses borrowed his ideas from them. Central to Oromo belief is the sacred staff or *Boku*, which symbolises the inviolable Law of God, and is handled only by the incumbent Abagada. The most important traditional festival in the Oromo calendar is the Irrecha, held on 1 October at several sites throughout the region – notably Lake Hora outside Bishoftu. These days, however, traditional Oromo beliefs are increasingly subservient to Christianity and Islam.

Mame [383 C2], a small local restaurant tucked away in a quiet courtyard with traditional décor and meals for around US$1–3. The **Skyline Restaurant & Bar** [383 E1] just south of the Ghico Hotel rates higher on the novelty factor rather than menu with its funky airline seats.

WHAT TO SEE

Sodore The hot springs resort of Sodore, situated at an altitude of 1,700m, stretches for about 1km on the banks of the Awash River about 25km south of Adama. The large, 3m-deep swimming pool, usually dry during the week, is a popular draw for Addis weekenders. For most tourists, however, the Awash River and fringing riparian forest will probably be of greater interest. Vervet monkeys and crocodiles are often encountered in the grounds, and the odd hippo still makes an appearance. The riverine forest also offers excellent birding. The resort is riddled with footpaths and makes for a diverting day or overnight trip from Adama.

Sodore lies 7km off the Adama–Asela road; the turn-off is clearly signposted. There are regular minibuses between Adama and the resort gates. A nominal entrance fee of US$1.50/2 per weekday/weekend is charged on arrival.

Where to stay The only proper accommodation, at the newly privatised and renamed **Sodore Resort Hotel** (*136 rooms;* \ *011 111 3400;* f *022 112 0384*), is emphatically not for the budget-conscious, and is rather run-down for the outrageous *faranji* asking price of US$30 for a tiny two-person *tukul* or US$41.50/47.50 for a twin/double en-suite room. There is, however, an attractively rambling **campsite**, where you can pitch your own tent for a pocket-pinching US$15 or rent a standing tent for US$18. The campsite isn't guarded and we wouldn't recommend you leave anything valuable in your tent; lockers are available for hire in the pool enclosure. Renovations are apparently on the cards, so you can expect prices to rise during the life of this edition.

Dera Delfekar Regional Park This 25km² sanctuary protects a pair of wooded hills on the eastern bounds of the small town of Dera, which lies roughly 27km from Adama (9km past the Sodore junction) along the main Asela road. Unfenced, and lacking any formal facilities, the park nevertheless supports more than 20 mammal species – notably greater and lesser kudu, klipspringer, common duiker, hippo, striped hyena and various small predators. More than 100 birds, predominantly acacia-associated species, have been recorded. Access is straightforward, since any vehicle heading from Adama in the direction of Asela can drop you in Dera. The footpath into the reserve is signposted from the main road through town, and there are no fees or restrictions on walking, though it might be advisable to take a local guide to show you the way. Should you choose to spend the night in Dera – early morning and late afternoon being when wildlife and birds are most active – the Hotel Dodota and Yohannis Hotel look about the best of a dozen or so cheapies running along the main road.

Koka Dam and hippo pool Damming the Awash River about 15km west of Adama as the crow flies, Koka was constructed in the late 1950s with war reparation payments from Italy. Since opening in 1960, it has been one of Ethiopia's most important sources of hydro-electric power. The lake formed behind the dam – called Koka or Gelila – is to the best of my knowledge the most expansive artificial body of water in Ethiopia, with a surface area of 180km². Situated close to the dam wall is the plush Gelila Palace, which Haile Selassie donated to charity in the 1960s.

For several years after that, the Gelila Hotel had the reputation of being one of the plushest hotels in Ethiopia, managed by the Ghion Group, with all profits diverted to charity. Sadly, it is no longer functional.

Although it is an important site for waterbirds, Koka is of interest to tourists primarily for a hippo pool in the Awash River a short distance downstream from the dam, at the confluence with the river that rises from the nearby Garagadi Hot Springs. The pools here are a reliable place to see hippos, various birds and – with increasing frequency – crocodiles. The turn-off south towards the dam lies on the main Addis Ababa road about 15km west of Adama and 10km east of Mojo, at a big blue sign. Follow this road for 12km to a construction site, where you can park. A guide is bound to offer his services, but it's easy enough to make your own way to the river. The best time to visit is early morning or late afternoon, when it's still cool, and the birds and animals are most active. It's an easy side trip in a private vehicle, but public transport is limited.

Garagadi Hot Springs This collection of 16 hot springs bubbles from a large field about 15km from Adama near the village of Wenji and the eponymous sugar plantation. The steaming pools formed by the hot springs are bathed in by local villagers, as well as by pilgrims from elsewhere in the country. Further away from the springs crocodiles are still resident in the river – which eventually leads to the hippo pool at the confluence with the Awash described above.

In theory, Garagadi could be visited in conjunction with Koka Dam, as the two sites are only 6km apart along a rough 4x4 track, but this would require crossing the dam wall (which doubles as a bridge) and this is not permitted without written permission! As a result, it's debatable whether the springs are worth the effort of visiting. But if you want to, you need to backtrack almost 30km from Koka to Adama, and then turn right immediately before the Awash Hotel as you enter town. Follow this gravel road for 10km, then turn right as you enter Wenji village, following the signpost for Wenji Feeding Lot. The track is rather indistinct from here, so keep asking directions, and you should reach the river after about 3km, below cliffs inhabited by baboons. Turn left at the river and you will get to the springs after another 2km. Occasional public transport connects Adama to Wenji, where you can walk or take a *gari* to the springs.

17

Awash National Park and the Assab Road

This chapter follows the Rift Valley northwest from Adama through to Assaita, former capital of the Federal State of Afar, and on to the border post for western Djibouti and the port of Assab in the far south of Eritrea. The region in question is generally low-lying and arid, though it is also studded with several imposing free-standing massifs associated with geologically recent volcanic activity.

The only established tourist attraction in this part of Ethiopia is **Awash National Park**, which is arguably the most rewarding savanna reserve in Ethiopia, and – bisected by the surfaced road to Dire Dawa some 200km east of Addis Ababa – certainly the most accessible. The wider stretch of the Rift Valley running northward from the national park – essentially an above-sea-level southerly extension of the Danakil – offers few readily accessible tourist attractions but is notable for its austere desert landscapes and nomadic Afar inhabitants.

The dominant aquatic feature of the region is the 1,200km Awash River, which rises at Fougnan Bote (The Nostrils) in the Ethiopian Highlands about 50km west of Addis Ababa, then arcs southward past Melka Kunture and Mount Zikwala before changing direction to flow in a broad northeasterly direction through the artificial Lake Koka, past Nazret, and along the southern border of Awash National Park, eventually emptying into a series of saline lakes between Assaita and the Djibouti border. Ironically, the name Awash reputedly translates from Oromifa as 'the beast that consumes everything in its path'. Given that it flows through desert or semi-desert for most of its length, 'the river that sustains everything alongside its path' might be a little fairer!

Aside from Awash National Park, part of which falls within Oromia region, the region covered in this chapter all falls within the boundaries of the vast but thinly populated Federal State of **Afar**. Unexpectedly, perhaps, an excellent surfaced road runs right through the region, branching from the Dire Dawa road a few kilometres east of the town of Awash Saba, from where it heads north through the small towns of Awash Arba, Gewane and Mille to the Djibouti and Eritrean borders. The only other approach route is a good unsurfaced road that connects Kombolcha (near Dessie) to Mille via Bati, thereby allowing you to explore the region as an extension of the northern historical circuit. Public transport runs daily along both these major routes.

AWASH NATIONAL PARK

(*Entrance US$5.50 pp/day; US$1.50/3 per car/minibus; camping US$3 per tent; required scout US$9*) This scenic 756km² national park, established in 1966 and gazetted three years later, is situated in the dry acacia savanna of the Rift Valley some 200km east of Addis Ababa. The park is bisected by the Dire Dawa road for a distance of almost 20km between the small towns of Metahara and Awash Saba. A magnificent

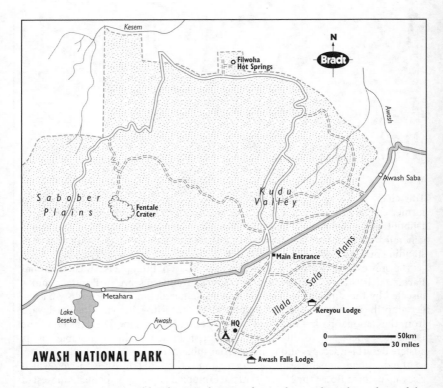

150m-deep gorge, carved by the Awash River, forms the southern boundary of the park, and there is a substantial waterfall where the river spills into the gorge. To the north of the Dire Dawa road, the skyline is dominated by the ragged edges of the 2,007m-high Mount Fantelle, a dormant volcano whose 350m-deep crater towers imperiously above the surrounding bush. Mount Fantelle is responsible for the bleak 200-year-old lava flows that cross the road immediately west of Metahara, and its steam vents can sometimes be seen displaying from the surrounding plains at night. The Filwoha Hot Springs, which feed a series of beautiful translucent blue pools, are situated in a grove of tall doum palms on the northern boundary of the park. Also of interest is the 40km² Lake Beseka, which lies just outside the park along the main road west of Metahara, nestled in a strange landscape of chunky black lava blocks where its area has increased twentyfold since 1964.

Although 80 mammal species have been recorded in Awash – the majority being bats, rodents and elusive small predators – the game viewing is arguably less of an attraction than the scenery and birdlife. The dense acacia scrub that characterises much of the park makes it difficult to spot game, populations of which are in any case rather low and skittish due to ongoing poaching. The most visible large mammals are beisa oryx, Soemmerring's gazelle and Salt's dik-dik, all of which are as likely to be seen from the surfaced public road to Dire Dawa as they are along roads within the park. Elsewhere, the thick bush and low animal densities around the Awash River harbour lesser and greater kudu, Defassa waterbuck and warthog, while more developed riverine forest may hide parties of vervet monkeys and, less commonly, guereza. The most common primate, however, is the baboon: the national park lies at a point where the ranges of the hamadryas and anubis baboons converge, and hybrids are frequently observed along the river east of the waterfall. Klipspringer and mountain reedbuck are found on the slopes of Fantelle Volcano. Predators are seen only infrequently, but a good variety is present including lion, leopard, cheetah, spotted and striped hyena, and black-backed and golden jackal. Lions are most likely to be seen in the vicinity of Filwoha Hot Springs; their nocturnal roars are regularly heard at the nearby campsite. The endemic Swayne's hartebeest was introduced to Awash in 1974, and the localised Grevy's zebra used to be resident, but neither species has been observed for some years.

Whatever the national park's limitations when it comes to big game, it has to be regarded as one of Ethiopia's premier birding destinations, with a checklist of 450 species and growing. For dedicated tickers, the primary attraction is the presence of the endemic yellow-throated serin and near-endemic sombre rock chat on the slopes of Fantelle Volcano, as well as the endemic Ethiopian cliff swallow in the Awash Gorge. Raptors are generally well represented; many species breed in the gorge and on the slopes of the volcano. Waterbirds are abundant on Lake Beseka, and to a lesser extent around Filwoha, while the riparian forest around the park headquarters harbours species. The acacia-scattered plains support an excellent range of dry-country birds such as Abyssinian roller, various sandgrouse, larks, hornbills and waxbills, and seven species of bustard – notably the localised and uncommon Arabian bustard. The gorgeous carmine bee-eater, which breeds in sandbanks in the Awash Gorge, is very common.

GETTING THERE AND AWAY If you are driving yourself, simply head out of Addis along the surfaced Dire Dawa road for about three hours, passing through Adama halfway. The road from Adama to Awash passes through a striking landscape of crumbling black lava flows and small volcanic hills, with the Rift Valley wall a haze in the background. The entrance gate lies on the main road about halfway between the towns of Metahara and Awash Saba. Without your own vehicle, the most straightforward way to visit Awash is through an Addis-based tour operator (see *Tour operators* in *Chapter 3*, page 77).

Hitching into Awash isn't really on. It's not so much that the rangers at the gate would be likely to object as that the low tourist traffic would make it most unlikely you'd find a lift. If time isn't a factor, however, you can soak up much of the park's atmosphere by spending a night in Awash Saba or Metahara, both of which are easily reached from Adama (buses take around three hours and there appears to be a reasonably regular trundle of other traffic too).

WHERE TO STAY Accommodation within the national park includes two lodges, as well as campsites.

Awash Falls Lodge (25 rooms) 022 119 1182–3 (lodge), 011 653 0245 (Addis Ababa); e info@awashfallslodge.com; www. awashfallslodge.com. This fantastic new lodge, located 11km from the park gate on the southwestern limit of an adjacent conservation area overlooking Awash Falls, is by far the best accommodation around. Accommodation is offered in a range of different-sized bungalows – all constructed from local materials including stone & bamboo. The rooms are charmingly rustic in styling with concrete floors, traditional furnishings, thatched roofs & screens on windows. The large central restaurant & bar overlooks the falls – you can actually watch crocodiles swim under the falls while eating! – & serves a good variety of local & European dishes in the US$3–5.50 range. A variety of local treks & day trips can be organised including to the hot springs & hyena caves as well as overnight camping expeditions to Mount Fantelle. *Camping US$7.50/15 with own/lodge tent exc b/fast, US$50/60/70 sgl/dbl/twin inc b/fast, US$90–140 family rooms.*

(011 550 8869/ 850 4592/515 7486; f 011 555 1275; e village.ethiopia@ ethionet.et; www.village-ethiopia.net) This eco-friendly lodge, built under consultation with local Afar communities, is situated 12km off the main Addis Ababa–Djibouti road, following a junction signposted to the left some 36km past Awash Arba. The lodge consists of 15 en-suite chalets designed in the style of Afar houses and covered in reed mats, as well as a restaurant and bar. It overlooks the Bilen Hot Spring, where Thesiger stopped on his Awash expedition in the 1930s (there are photos of the area in his *Danakil Diaries*). The springs are big enough to swim in, so long as you don't mind sharing the water with camels, which are brought here to drink by Afar herders, and enjoy a hot soak. Cultural activities on offer include organised village visits and camel treks with local Afar herders.

The area around the lodge has a similar combination of habitats to the national park, including riverine forest, acacia woodland, savanna and wetlands, and it harbours a similar variety of birds. More than 460 bird species have been recorded in this area: particularly prominent around camp are Nile Valley and shining sunbirds, golden-breasted starling, white-headed sparrow weaver, Abyssinian roller, carmine bee-eater, yellow-throated spurfowl and Liechtenstein's sandgrouse. Wildlife seen in the vicinity of the lodge includes beisa oryx, lesser kudu, Salt's dik-dik, warthog, spotted hyena, crocodile, hippo and hamadryas and anubis baboon. Lions are heard more often than they are seen, but they do pass through camp from time to time. Meals are available for US$23 per person per meal. *Room rates are US$138 double/twin and US$92 single on half board basis.*

Kereyou Lodge (23 caravans) m 0910 266 409; www.ras-hotels.com. This once thriving lodge was on the brink of dereliction on our most recent visit in Nov 2011. Part of the Ras Hotel chain, & bookable through the head office in Addis Ababa or any tour operator (not that it's often overrun with clients!), the best thing about the lodge is the location above a spectacular stretch of the Awash Gorge. Accommodation consists of 23 run-down & stuffy self-contained caravans clustered in an untidy garden behind the main lodge building. Meals & drinks are available & running water is a hit-&-miss affair. *US$9/12 sgl/dbl.*

Campsites There are 2 campsites, 1 near the park HQ (a short walk from the waterfall) & the other at the hot springs. The campsites both have great locations, but lack any facilities worth talking about, & are only suitable for those self-sufficient in food & drinking water. *Camping US$3/4 for a 4–6-person tent.*

It is also possible to stay outside the park, at the nearby towns of Awash Saba or Metahara, or at the new Bilen Lodge (see box above).

GAME DRIVES AND WALKS The main game-viewing circuit runs south from the main Amareti entrance gate to the park headquarters, which lies less than 500m from the Awash Falls, then follows a rough road east through dense scrub to Kereyou Lodge. From Kereyou, a road crosses back to the main gate via the open Ilala Sala Plain, which is reliably studded with small herds of oryx and a good place to see bustards. It's definitely worth stopping at the waterfall, which consists of several muddy streams frothing over a drop of perhaps 10m into the black volcanic rock of the gorge – a short footpath leads to the base, and the fringing woodland is good for birds. The small museum at the headquarters displays useful checklists of all the birds, mammals and reptiles recorded in the park, as well as the predictable selection of stuffed animals. This circuit, which covers about 30km in total, can normally be driven in any vehicle with reasonable clearance, and should take two to three hours allowing for game viewing, a stop at the waterfall and the lodge (cold drinks and superb viewpoint), longer if you are birding. Maps depict a road circuit east of Kereyou, but this is out of service. Visitors are not normally required to take a game scout along the roads running to the south of the main gate.

The 30km road to the hot springs leaves from the main Dire Dawa road roughly opposite the main gate, passing through the dense scrub of Kudu Valley along the way. Don't expect to see much game on this road – warthog and hamadryas baboon are both quite common, greater and lesser kudu less so – but the springs are worth the effort. The road is 4x4 only, but it's in fair condition and only takes about an hour in either direction. There is also a road to the top of Mount Fantelle, but it is in poor condition, and most visitors end up walking the last stretch – this is a steep two-hour hike on exposed slopes, and best done in the cool of the morning. For security reasons, it is mandatory to take an armed game scout on any excursion to areas north of the main Dire Dawa road. This costs US$9 per excursion.

Aside from the trek up to Fantelle, and the short footpaths to the hot springs and waterfall, walking is not permitted within the national park. It is, however, possible to walk around Lake Beseka from Metahara, and to hike around the part of the Awash Gorge that lies east of the park boundary near Awash Saba.

METAHARA

The small, scruffy town of Metahara, situated less than 5km from the national park as the crow flies, is known throughout Ethiopia for the large sugar plantation on its outskirts. Metahara is of interest to travellers for its attractive location near the base of Fantelle and proximity to the expanding Lake Beseka, which is five minutes from town on the Addis Ababa road. It is also a good place to spot Kereyu people. Pastoralist like the Afar, Kereyu men are noted for their hairstyle of short on the top, and huge Afro on the sides. (Resist the urge to take a photograph without permission – these are some of the fiercest warriors around!) Any bus heading between Adama and Awash Saba will stop here on request.

There is good access to Lake Beseka from the main Adama road, which crosses over it via a causeway that is divided into two sections by what amounts to an island of black chunky lava rocks. The birdlife on this shallow lake is profuse and the patches of acacia scrub on the far bank should also repay exploration. The scenery, too, is rather special, with the ragged edges of Fantelle Volcano looming a few kilometres to the north – the Metahara night sky is often lit with fireworks from the crater's vents.

A few words of warning: crocodiles are present in the lake and, although it's unlikely that any crocodile large enough to attack a person would survive so close to town, you should be cautious. We've been told that hippos are also present, but are inclined to think this is nonsense. Secondly, the lakeshore is hot and exposed, so it's best visited in the cool of the morning, and you should protect yourself from the sun at all times. Finally, Lake Beseka may not lie within the national park but Fantelle does – it would be illegal to try to walk there.

WHERE TO STAY

Hotel Hiwot (12 rooms) ✆022 226 0015.
This new top-pick offers a range of accommodation

from older common shower rooms in the outside courtyard to compact en-suite doubles with cold-shower en suites & tiled floors in the new multi-storey building. A good restaurant & bar is attached. *US$3–6 with common shower, US$9 en suite.*

🏠 **Makombo Hotel** (29 rooms) m 0914 093 178. This centrally located, brightly painted hotel is hard to miss. While extended since our previous visit, rooms remain bland & unexceptional. On the plus side, the price appears to be negotiable. *US$4 using common shower, US$6 en suite.*

✘ **Kassaye Hotel** Across the street from the Makombo, this has the best food in town (roasted chicken is the house special) but the lively garden bar is more fun to drink in than to sleep next to!

AWASH SABA

This scruffy and nondescript little town, which appears to have mushroomed around Awash railway station, lies about 30km past Metahara and a short distance outside the park boundary. Arrive here with a pale skin, and conversation will be limited mainly to humourless variations on the words 'you', 'money' and 'give', an unwelcome reminder of how things used to be throughout much of Ethiopia a few years ago. As for the sights – aside from the railway station, there's a church, a neat mosque, and an odd pointy stone column thing next to the station, which serves no apparent purpose other than to provide the local goats with a sliver of afternoon shade. The Monday market attracts plenty of traditional Afar people from the surrounding plains.

Awash Saba is typical small-town Ethiopia, but with one substantial redeeming feature. About 500m behind the station the dusty plain is cut into by the precipitous Awash Gorge, the drama of which is accentuated by a row of low volcanic hills above the opposite cliff. There's some good raptor-scanning here – auger buzzard, vultures, kestrels and falcons – and a chance of seeing the elusive Ethiopian cliff swallow. A footpath leads to the base of the gorge and the Awash River and, although the immediate surrounds have suffered from vigorous goat chomping, there's some interesting-looking riverine woodland a kilometre or so back towards the park boundary. Be cautioned, however, that the park begins about 3km from Awash Saba, and there's no telling what official attitudes would be if you inadvertently crossed the line.

Often referred to simply as Awash and more occasionally Awash Station, Awash Saba (Awash Seven) is so named to distinguish it from Awash Arba (Awash Forty), a town situated some 20km away on the Assab road. Nobody has ever been able to explain these numeric designations to me, and I can think of no obvious significance to them myself. All the same, it seems sensible to use the full names for these towns given that they share their first word not only with each other, but also with a nearby river, gorge and national park.

GETTING THERE AND AWAY In a private vehicle, Awash Saba can be reached in about three hours east from Addis Ababa, and five to six hours from Dire Dawa. The junction for the surfaced road northwest through Afar lies about 5km east of town along the Dire Dawa road. Awash Saba is an important transport hub, and you're unlikely to wait long for a lift east or west. Plenty of buses pass through town *en route* between Addis Ababa and Dire Dawa, and local minibuses cover the road to Adama. Public transport along the road to Afar is less frequent, but at least one bus daily heads out to Gewane, where you should easily find transport on to Mille or Logiya. If public transport fails you, you could try for a lift with a truck – dozens daily head on through from Awash Saba to Djibouti.

🏠 **WHERE TO STAY AND EAT**

🏠 **Genet Hotel** (49 rooms) ☎ 022 224 0040; m 0921 230 229. Popular with tour operators, this commendable hotel lies alongside the main Addis Ababa road on the western outskirts of

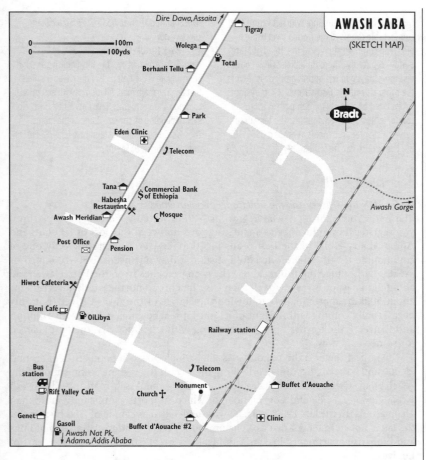

town. The hotel offers a variety of accommodation to suit most budgets. All rooms are clean & have cold-water showers, fans & nets. Older more budget-friendly rooms are built around a secure central car park, while the fresh new rooms in the adjoining multi-storey annex have a TV & offer the choice of AC or fan. The restaurant is pretty good too – roast chicken is the house speciality. *Older rooms US$7.50–13 depending on bed size, new rooms US$17/24 sgl/dbl with fan, US$24/27.50 sgl/dbl with AC.*

🏠 **Awash Meridian Hotel** (48 rooms) 📞 022 224 0051. The recently expanded Awash Meridian is set in a large compound on the main road & offers 3 standards of rooms: first-class rooms in the new multi-storey building are spacious & clean with queen-size bed, mosquito netting, fan & en-suite hot shower (only some have AC & TV, but the price remains the same); second-class

rooms have TV, fan & cold-shower en suite; while third-class rooms are similarly outfitted but are older & scruffier. A good rooftop bar is attached & a conference hall & new reception were still under construction. *3rd-class rooms US$8, 2nd-class rooms US$11/12 sgl/dbl, 1st-class rooms US$21/24 sgl/dbl.*

🏠 **Buffet D'Aouache** (aka Madame Kiki's) (20 rooms) 📞 022 224 0008. Built by the French to service the Djibouti railway ('Aouache' being the French spelling of Awash) & now under Greek management, this is an unexpected gem, with its whitewashed colonial architecture draped in flowering creepers. Your first reaction might well be to wonder how this place has stumbled viably into the 21st century, a mystery that might be explained the moment the train chugs into the adjoining station & the courtyard fills with hungry, thirsty passengers – that is if the train was currently running, which it is not! The comfortable rooms range from a twin using a big clean common shower to the 'Head of State' Suite – reputedly where Haile Selassie & Charles de Gaulle stayed in the hotel's glory days! Across the other side of the tracks a new 2-storey annex surrounded by a lovely garden houses more comfortably appointed doubles. The restaurant serves well-prepared meals at around US$2.50, but the service can be unbearably slow. *US$4.50*

with common shower, US$8.50/9.50 old/new en-suite dbl.

🏠 **Park Hotel** (19 rooms) ☎ 022 224 0015. This central place owned by a friendly English-speaking Ethio-Italian is the best pick of the cheaper hotels that line the main road. All rooms (with exception of common shower rooms) have fans & nets, but prices vary depending on the size & age of the rooms. There's secure parking, restaurant & bar. *US$4 using common shower, US$6–14 en suite.*

THE ASSAB ROAD

Updated by Tony Hickey and the staff from Ethiopian Quadrants

The main route through Afar region, is – unexpectedly, perhaps, at least until you register its significance as a trucking route between the port of Djibouti and Addis Ababa – one of the best roads in Ethiopia. Certainly it's the only one of comparable length where one could sustain a driving speed of 80–100km/h or greater without feeling too reckless. The road branches from the Dire Dawa road about 5km east of Awash Saba. It then runs in a broad northeasterly direction for about 500km, approximately following the course of the Awash River (but only occasionally coming within sight of it) until it reaches the borders with Djibouti and Eritrea – the former open and bustling with truck activity, the latter closed for some years now.

The largest town in the region is Assaita, which boasts a population of around 25,000 and a scenic location overlooking the Awash River some 50km south of the Assab road. Other relatively sizeable towns along the Assab road include Awash Arba, Gewane, Mille and Logiya, none of which supports significantly more than 10,000 souls. In the late 1990s, Assaita was superseded as capital of Afar by Semera, the latter not so much a town as a custom-built cluster of administrative buildings and high-rise apartment blocks set in bleakly surreal isolation just 7.5km east of Logiya.

Most of the region's Afar inhabitants remain semi-nomadic pastoralists, though some make a living from excavating or transporting salt blocks from the vast saline pans north of the Assab road – relics of a time not too distant when large parts of Afar region were submerged by a southern extension of the Red Sea. While the region receives little rainfall a new US$600 million dam built by the Indian government in Tendaho has assured ongoing irrigation for a massive new sugar plantation as well as a range of other crops including onions, broomcorn and cotton grown along the Awash River.

TRAVEL WARNING

In early 2012 five foreign tourists were killed in the northern region of Afar near Erta Ale (see *The Danakil Depression*, page 301). Two other tourists were seriously wounded and four people including two tourists, a driver and a police escort were kidnapped. This region is a high-risk area and has been the subject of Foreign Office warnings for a number of years. Before making a visit, we urge you to contact your embassy for up-to-date information or make enquires with the tourist office in Addis Ababa.

Afar has not always been as arid – or as low-lying – as it is today. Five million years ago, this land lay at an altitude of greater than 1,000m above sea level, and its moist climate supported a lush cover of grassland and forest – not to mention a variety of early hominids. Several of the world's most significant hominid fossils have been unearthed in Afar. The best known of these is 'Lucy', which was discovered and nicknamed by Donald Johanson at Hadar in 1974 (see box, *A Visit to Hadar*, page 400). More recently, an Ethiopian graduate student Yohannis Haile Selassie found 5.8-million-year-old fossils of a bipedal creature whose combination of ape-like and hominid features suggests it might well represent the so-called 'missing link' in the divergent evolutionary paths of modern chimpanzees and humans.

The surfaced road through Afar is an important trucking route, since it provides access to the seaports of Assab (Eritrea) and Djibouti. Passenger transport is relatively thin on the ground, however, and more or less confined to the main road, the side road to Assaita and the road between Mille and Kombolcha (near Dessie). To see the region properly, you really need a private vehicle. It is not advisable to head seriously off-road without a back-up vehicle and knowledgeable guide or GPS. No organised tours head into this remote part of Ethiopia. For tailored itineraries, a useful contact with considerable experience in Afar region is Ethiopian Quadrants (⟋ *011 515 7990;* e *ethiopianquadrants@gmail.com; www.ethiopianquadrants.com*).

The information below roughly follows the Assab road in a northerly direction from the junction 5km west of Awash Saba.

AWASH SABA TO GEWANE A few pot-holes notwithstanding, the 150km stretch of road connecting Awash Saba to Gewane is in tiptop condition. At least one bus daily runs between the two towns, taking about four hours in either direction. Coming from Awash Saba in a private vehicle, you must first head along the Dire Dawa road, then after about 5km turn left at a prominent and clearly signposted junction, passing through the not insubstantial town of Awash Arba after another 14km. The road can be covered easily in two hours in a private vehicle, though there are a few places where you might want to stop or divert from the main road.

First up, roughly 36km past Awash Arba, a road to the left leads to Bilen Lodge, 10km from the main road (see box, *Bilen Lodge*, page 392), and a good base from which to explore southern Afar. The road then passes through the austere and rather featureless Alleghedi Plain, which is afforded nominal protection in the eponymous wildlife reserve, and still harbours thin (and seldom observed) populations of game, notably beisa oryx and Grevy's zebra.

The small town of Meteka, about 30km south of Gewane, is inherently unremarkable, but it does mark the beginning of the Meteka Wetlands. This marshy part of the Awash floodplain runs close to the western verge of the main road and offers excellent birding all year through. It is particularly rewarding in the European winter. The Awash River forms part of a flyway used by thousands of Palaearctic migrants; all sorts of unusual passage migrants have been recorded around Meteka in September/October and March/April. In a private vehicle, it is possible to leave the main road at Meteka and cut west for about 10km to Lake Erta Ale (also known as Hertali).

A somewhat unremarkable urban sprawl, **Gewane** is distinguished only by the imposing presence of Mount Ayelu, an isolated peak of volcanic origin which rises above the surrounding plains to an altitude of 2,145m on the east of the town. Facilities include three filling stations, a couple of bars with chilled drinks (welcome in this climate) and a few basic hotels. If you need to spend a night, the hotel behind the Shell garage looks about the best bet, charging US$4 for a clean room with a common shower. Should you be thinking of exploring Yangudi Rassa National Park beyond the main road, the park office is in Gewane.

THE AFAR

The Afar (or Danakil) regard themselves as the oldest of Ethiopia's ethnic groups, having occupied their inhospitably arid homeland to the east of the Ethiopian Highlands for at least 2,000 years. The Afar have a history of trade with the highlanders that stretches back to the early Axumite period, and possibly before that. Until modern times, Afar country effectively served as Ethiopia's mint, producing the *amoles* (salt bars) that served as currency in the highlands – the Portuguese priest Alvarez recorded that in the early 16th century three or four *amoles* was enough to buy a good slave! Extracted from a number of salt pans scattered around the Afar Depression, the salt bars still form a major item of trade for the Afar people, who transport them on camelback to Tigrai along the ancient caravan routes.

Arabic sources indicate that, despite Afar's ancient trade links with the Christian highlands, Islam was widely practised in the region as early as the 13th century. In 1577, the Sultan of Harar relocated his capital to a town called Hawassa, which was situated more or less where Assaita stands today. This move initially sparked some resistance among the surrounding Afar nomads, though it did much to consolidate the Islamic influence in the area, especially as the sultan's army and the Afar were frequently united in battle against the invading Oromo. In the late 17th century, Hawassa fell under the rule of an Afar sultan called Kedafu, who founded a dynasty that survived into the late 20th century. The Sultan of Afar was forced into exile under the Derg, but he is still regarded as the King of Afar by his people, and his residence – about 5km outside Assaita – was restored in early 2001 in anticipation of his permanent return home.

Traditionally, the ·Afar are nomadic pastoralists, living in light, flimsy houses made of palm fronds and matting, which they transport from one location to the next on camelback. Recent decades have seen a trend towards urbanisation in Afar, as well as an increased dependence on agriculture in the fertile and well-watered area around Assaita. Nevertheless, the nomadic lifestyle is still widely practised away from the towns, and visitors to the region will often see Afar men driving their precious camel herds along the roadside. The Afar men have a reputation for ferocity and xenophobia – as recently as the 1930s, it was still customary to kill male intruders to the area, and lop off their testicles as a trophy.

By comparison with the highlanders, Afar people tend to be very tall and dark. The women have intricate frizzed and braided hairstyles, and wear long brown skirts, brightly coloured bead necklaces, heavy earrings and brass anklets. The men often wear their hair in a thick Afro style similar to that described in an account by a 14th-century visitor from the highlands. They dress in a light cotton toga, which is draped over one shoulder. Traditionally, Afar men rarely venture far without the curved 40cm-long dagger they sling around their waist in a long, thin leather pouch. These days, the traditional knife may be supplemented or replaced by a rifle slung casually over the shoulder. Both weapons are frequently put to fatal use in disputes between rival clans.

YANGUDI RASSA NATIONAL PARK Proposed in 1977, but never officially gazetted, this 5,000km² national park consists of a dormant 1,383m-high volcano called Mount Yangudi together with the surrounding Rassa Plains. It harbours a small population of shy African wild ass, a critically endangered species ancestral to the domestic donkey, and is bisected by the Assab road for a distance of roughly 50km. However, the odds of actually seeing a wild ass in transit are extremely slim, especially as feral populations of domestic donkeys are also found in the area, and the two are difficult to tell apart. You'll improve your chances slightly – but not greatly – if you pick up a guide at the park office in Gewane, and leave the main road.

Several other large mammal species survive in Yangudi Rassa, notably beisa oryx, Soemmerring's and dorcas gazelle, gerenuk and possibly Grevy's zebra, but – like the ass – they are thinly distributed and unlikely to be observed by casual visitors. A good selection of dry-country birds is resident – the Arabian bustard is a 'special' and ostriches are frequently observed – and the park lies along an important migration passage.

MILLE This small town, set on the banks of the Mille River roughly 150km north of Gewane, is of note primarily as a minor route focus. About 10km south of town lies the junction of the main Assab road and the side road that runs west towards Bati, Kombolcha and Dessie, forming the only reliable road and public transport link between Afar and the northern historical circuit. At least one bus daily connects Mille to Dessie (via Bati and Kombolcha) and to Assaita. There is not currently any public transport between Mille and Gewane, but it's easy enough to pick up a lift with a truck. Direct buses between Addis Ababa and Assaita follow the route through Dessie rather than passing through Gewane.

In a private vehicle, you're unlikely to spend longer in Mille than is required to refuel the car and grab a cold drink. Using public transport, you may well have to spend a night here between bus trips. At least half-a-dozen local guesthouses, charging around US$3.50 for a basic room, are dotted around the small town – recommend would be too strong a word, but the Central Hotel looks about the best of the bunch.

LOGIYA AND SEMERA North of Mille, the road passes through a hauntingly bleak landscape of bare volcanic boulders piled high between valleys of gravel and stunted grass, to emerge after roughly 50km at Logiya, one of the few places where the Assab road and Awash River briefly converge. Logiya feels larger and busier than either Gewane or Mille, with a good (or should that be bad?) dozen basic hotels and restaurants lining the main road. If you need a bed, the best bet is the National Hotel, which lies on the Assaita side of town and charges US$2 for a cramped but adequate room (single bed only) and a few coins for use of the shower. Opposite the National Hotel, Redwam Snacks is about the only restaurant to serve anything other than *ye fiyal tibs* – fried eggs, fresh bread, tuna sandwiches and fruit juice!

Exactly 7.5km east of Logiya, the Assab road cuts through Semera, the regional capital of Afar. More of a concept than a town, Semera comes across as the brainchild of some vindictive soul who held a serious grudge against regional government officials and their families – basically it consists of a depressing cluster of modern offices and tall apartment blocks standing in the middle of the desert, in mad isolation from any existing settlement! So far as facilities go, there is one active filling station (complete with fridge) and one decent hotel – the **Erta Ale Hotel** (℡ *022 666 0324;* m *0912 213 352*) which is the best place if you are looking for a meal or need a place to crash, with en-suite rooms costing a pricey US$22.50/30 for a single/double or twin – but that's about it. If you are travelling on north to

The formerly obscure and otherwise unremarkable patch of Ethiopian soil known as Hadar leapt to prominence in 1974 when Donald Johanson unearthed what was then the oldest hominid fossil ever discovered: the three–four-million-year-old remains of a female, nicknamed Lucy, and assigned to a new species *Australopithecus afarensis*. Hadar is the most famous of several similarly significant palaeontological sites in this part of Ethiopia, but – while the regional council does appear to have vague plans for future development – none is currently geared up for tourists. With a private vehicle, a guide and a letter of authority, however, it is perfectly possible to visit Hadar, as the following edited extract from a letter by Iain Jackson demonstrates:

> To fulfil my ambition of seeing Hadar, I first had to get a permit from the office of the Afar Regional Council in Assaita. I stayed in Assaita for three nights, and eventually got my permit. I discovered there is some confusion about the location of Hadar, arising from a map published and given wide circulation in Ethiopia, which shows a representation of Lucy covering hundreds of square kilometres to the north of Serdo. In fact, the site lies 25–30km south of Eloha, a small village on the Kombolcha–Mille road.
>
> I went to Kombolcha, hired a 4x4 land vehicle for the day, and drove to Eloha. There, two men, one of whom claimed to have worked – for eight years – with the American team that discovered Lucy, offered themselves as guide and shotgun rider. We set off in a generally southerly direction over stony scrub, through sand gullies, and eventually into more open countryside, where we saw a group of eight ostriches at fairly close quarters, an Abyssinian hare and many diverse birds. After something like an hour, we halted in a small, dusty and barren valley and walked a few hundred metres to several small hills covered in thousands of fossilised bone fragments. It was here, declared our guide, that Lucy was found.
>
> I had been told in Addis Ababa that the site had no interpretative centre and no marker, but here, aside from the fossils, there was nothing! If the Americans had been here for eight years, surely they would have left behind a fence, and a few excavation pits and spoil heaps, but the ground looked absolutely undisturbed. It crossed my mind that I was the victim of a hoax, but the site did look like it does in the few pictures I've seen, so I guess I give it the benefit of the doubt. In any event, I enjoyed the excursion.

The village Iain refers to as Eloha is actually called Eli Wuha, which I'm told translates as Tortoise Water, and straddles the Kombolcha–Mille road exactly 50km east of Bati and 40km west of the junction with the Assab road. The village isn't much to look at architecturally, but it hosts a busy traditional Afar market daily, and has a few bars selling chilled drinks. Ask around, and you should have no difficulty locating a guide to take you to Hadar, which lies off the road towards Mille about an hour's drive away and remains totally undeveloped for tourism. It is not clear whether a permit is actually required to visit Hadar – either way, it is unlikely that there would be anybody present at the site to check.

the Danakil (see *Chapter 11*, page 301), then Semera is where you need to sort out your permits before continuing on to **Serdo**, a small town all but destroyed by a magnitude 6 earthquake in 1969, which lies 40km further northeast at the junction for the track heading north to Lake Afrera. There is also a small airstrip near Semera which is open to private charters should you be short on time.

ASSAITA The former administrative capital of Afar and largest town in the region, Assaita is situated some 50km south of the Assab road on a rise overlooking a stretch of the Awash River lined with palms and cultivation. First impressions as you drive into this fantastically hot and rather dusty backwater, passing through a jumble of run-down administrative buildings and offices, are less than promising. Once you're settled in, however, Assaita is not without interest: overwhelmingly Muslim and defiantly rustic, the town centre has an atmosphere and architectural mood quite unlike any other town in Ethiopia, and it is an excellent place for contacts with Afar people. Ideally, try to be in town on Tuesday, when the main market is held.

For travellers dependent on public transport, Assaita is pretty much the end of the road, with limited possibilities for exploration, though the tourist office can arrange for you to visit an Afar village within walking distance of the town for around US$10.50 per group. With a vehicle, Assaita forms a useful base from which to explore a number of nearby attractions, many of which can only be visited with written authority from the tourist office in Semera (see box, *Lakes around Assaita*, on page 402).

The turn-off to Assaita is no more than 10km east of Semera along the Assab road. It isn't overtly signposted, and could easily be missed – look out for the blue signpost with Amharic script and 'PO Box 50' written underneath at the junction. A more enduring landmark is a small lake, fringed by acacia trees and often surrounded by Afar camel herders, on the northern side of the Assab road a few kilometres east of the junction – if you pass this lake coming from Semera, then you know you've missed the junction. Immediately after the junction, the 50km dirt road to Assaita passes through a scrubby area dotted with several apparently permanent pools (plenty of birds and occasional troops of hamadryas baboon), before opening out into a flat, thinly vegetated floodplain surrounded by large dunes. Three buses daily run between Assaita and Logiya.

There are two decent local hotels in Assaita, both situated within 200m of the bus station, and used to catering for travellers. The **Lem Hotel** (☏ *033 555 0050*),

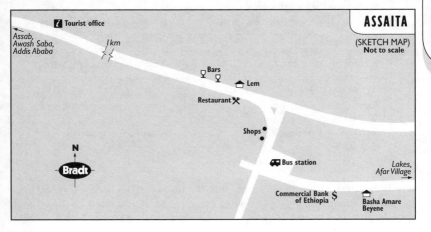

LAKES AROUND ASSAITA

With thanks to Peile Thompson, who in 2001 trekked the length of the Awash River north of Awash Saba, the first person to do so unsupported since Wilfred Thesiger in 1934

South of Assaita, the Awash River terminates in a chain of about six shallow saline and freshwater lakes, of which the largest (and last) is Lake Abbe on the border with Djibouti. The deep blue lakes, fringed by lush salt-tolerant vegetation and surrounded by high mountains, support dense populations of hippos and crocodiles. The lakes form one of the most important waterbird sites in Ethiopia, and attract large numbers of Palaearctic migrants during the European winter. On the Djibouti side, Lake Abbe is a popular weekend destination. The Ethiopian side of the lakes, however, is totally undeveloped for tourism, and likely to remain so for some time. At the time of writing, the lakes are inaccessible in a vehicle, following the collapse of the bridge across a river at Ebobe, 10km south of Assaita. Until such time as this road is repaired, the only feasible way of reaching the lakes is by hiking or setting up a camel expedition.

Over May and June of 2001, Peile Thompson explored this area on foot, using routes that hadn't been walked by a *faranji* since Wilfred Thesiger in the 1930s. Peile travelled with six camels (to carry supplies and water), and many of the routes he followed would be suitable only to experienced and well-prepared adventurers carrying sufficient water to last several days. However, he has kindly passed on details of a relatively straightforward round hike between Assaita and lakes Gummare and Afambo, which could be undertaken over two (or better three) days without inordinate preparation.

To do this hike, you'd need to carry two or three days' food, depending on how long you take over it. Drinking water is available at reasonably regular intervals, but it's always advisable to carry some water (and refill whenever possible) in case the pumps aren't working. It would be inviting problems to travel through this part of Afar country without a local Afar guide, and written permission from the regional authority. A permit can easily be arranged through the tourist office in Assaita. They can also arrange a local guide for birr 60 per day. Travelling in this area without a guide is foolhardy, not only because he will interact with local Afar people on your behalf, but also because there is a genuine risk of losing your way, with potentially fatal results.

The most accessible lakes are Gummare and Afambo, which are linked by a short stretch of river about 20km south of Assaita by road. To get to the lakes, you must first follow the main road south of town for about 10km to the river at Ebobe. If you want to cut down the walking time, a local bus service does run at least once daily between Assaita and Ebobe (timings are erratic), and there is plenty of transport along this road on Tuesdays (market day). You can normally cross the river on foot, but the banks are too steep for a vehicle, which is why the bus and all other transport terminates here. Shortly past the crossing is a police post, where you will be turned back if you don't have written authority. South of this, the track runs through fertile land dotted with rural Afar settlements and small papyrus-fringed lakes – the birdlife is incredible.

which lies on the main road coming into the town centre, charges US$3.50 for a large clean room with a proper double bed and fan. It also has a good common shower. The hotel often fills up early, so it's worth ringing ahead to book a room.

Another 10km or so along the track, you reach a deep 15m-wide river. Here, the local Afar people have made a raft out of fallen reeds and will pull you and your kit across to the other side for birr 5 each. You could swim it, but there are a lot of crocodiles around! About 500m beyond this crossing, you reach the river linking Lake Afambo to Lake Gummare. There used to be a bridge over this 150m crossing, but it collapsed some time ago. This crossing has to be done with a raft as there are many crocs and hippos around in the lake. The border traders are all queuing up to get on the rafts, with camels laden with salt and goods. The animals swim across, but the goods are placed on the papyrus raft and ferried to the other side. The people who operate the rafts will charge you ridiculous sums to get across, knowing you have no option … but don't be tempted to swim it as we did, we nearly got scoffed, and the locals went crazy! This is real smuggler's country, so be a little careful, as things get heated and everyone is armed. For the few that make it here, the view of Lake Gummare is magnificent with the rich birdlife, the Afar hustle and bustle, and the high surrounding escarpment that drops down to the opposite lakeshore.

Having crossed the river, you pick up the track again as it winds up the high escarpment towards the Djibouti border. After about 3km, this climb of several hundred metres in elevation leads towards a point marked on several maps as Afambo. We expected there to be some form of settlement here … wrong, unless you count a derelict bunch of buildings and an observation post, remnants of the old Derg border post! From the abandoned camp, the views over the lakes and back west towards Assaita are awesome. Note, however, that the surrounding area is mined, so you should always stick to the path, and that no safe route other than the track you have climbed connects the camp to the lakes. The hike up from the crossing to Afambo takes about 90 minutes, but it's really worth the effort for the views.

There is no accommodation around the lakes, nor are there formal campsites. Travellers can camp rough anywhere they like, ideally slightly away from the villages to avoid masses of people (and ticks!). The area is very hot, even at night, so it's not necessary to carry a lot of camping gear – but you will need some protection from the prolific mosquitoes. Expect to be investigated by young Afar warriors asking questions (and sometimes a fee). This is when you need a local guide and piece of paper with the Afar Tourism Board stamp on it. I should stress that federal stamps and pieces of paper count for nothing in Afar; you must have something with an Afar government stamp or people will turn you back.

From the crossing point described above, Peile notes that it's possible to continue south along a little-used track that follows the eastern shore of Lake Afambo to Lake Abbe, where you can cross into Djibouti. The hike from the crossing point to Lake Abbe takes four days. Peile stresses that *no* drinking water is available until you reach Lake Abbe, where there are some freshwater springs. Lake Afambo's water was potable in Thesiger's day, but it's now very saline due to the various irrigation schemes along the Awash River. In this hot and exposed terrain, you would need to carry at least ten litres of water each per day – that's a total of 40 litres of drinking water each for the full hike, which would have to be carried on camelback.

The **Basha Amare Beyene Hotel**, which lies just past the bus station next to the Commercial Bank of Ethiopia, has small rooms for US$3, but it's far more pleasant to sleep outdoors (US$2 per bed in the courtyard, US$2.70 per bed on the breezy balcony overlooking the river). The food at the Basha Amare Beyene Hotel is the best in town – don't miss the local speciality called *hagabi*, a firm, spicy type of *wat* made from powdered peas. There are a few more basic hotels dotted around the town, but in this stinking-hot climate you really want to sleep securely outdoors, or to have a fan in your room.

DICHIOTO Heading east from the junction to Assaita, the Assab road passes through some genuinely fascinating scenery, dominated by ancient lava flows and bizarre volcanic outcrops, before reaching the small town of Dichioto. Based on our experience, this is the one stretch of the Assab road where you're likely to see much wildlife – we encountered Soemmerring's gazelle, hamadryas baboon and ostrich – and it also passes a few small lakes where Afar pastoralists bring their camels to water. Dichioto is a rather odd settlement of brightly painted corrugated-iron buildings with large balconies. As the last Ethiopian town before the Djibouti border, it is a popular stopover with truck drivers, and has consequently acquired an unexpectedly shiftless, seedy atmosphere. Hotels there are in abundance, all charging US$2–3 per bed whether you sleep in a small sweaty room or follow the local custom of kipping outdoors – for what it's worth, the Andinet Hotel looks more savoury than most.

ELI DAR DEPRESSION East of Dichioto, the Assab road descends to the Eli Dar Depression, the most accessible of several salt lakes in Afar. The descent itself is pretty spectacular, passing over evocatively barren rocky slopes with the lake shimmering off-white below. You may also see salt caravans travelling up the pass. At the base of the depression lies Dobi – marked prominently on maps at the junction of the roads to Assab and Djibouti, but in reality little more than a collection of a dozen or so rickety shacks that provide shelter from the searing heat and sell lukewarm sodas and beers. In a private vehicle, Eli Dar makes for an easy and worthwhile diversion coming to or from Assaita. For backpackers, any bus or truck heading to Djibouti can drop you at Dobi. An early start is recommended – it shouldn't be too difficult to find a lift back out, but there is no formal accommodation should you get stuck in Dobi overnight.

18

Harar and Dire Dawa

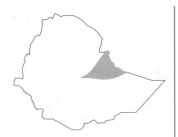

East of Awash Saba, the southern Rift Valley Escarpment rises to the Arba Gugu and Chercher mountain ranges to form a long narrow eastern extension of the southern highlands which points towards the Djibouti border like a crooked finger. Moist and fertile, the far eastern highlands are no less scenic than their northern counterparts, but culturally the area is strikingly different. The dominant ethnic group here (as in much of the Rift Valley) is the Oromo, who speak a Nilotic language, are generally less Semitic in appearance than the northern highlanders, and are relatively recent converts to Judaic religions.

Historically, the most significant settlement in the far east is the walled city of **Harar**, which more or less took its present shape in the 15th century, and subsequently served as the launch pad for Ahmed Gragn's destructive assault on the Christian empire of the central and northern highlands. Famed, too, as the birthplace of Ras Tefari Mekonnen (later Emperor Haile Selassie) and the base for the French poet Rimbaud's African adventures, Harar is regarded as the spiritual home of Ethiopia's large and ancient Muslim community. For travellers, the walled city forms a fascinating and refreshing contrast to the ubiquitous Christian monuments of northern Ethiopia. It is also renowned for its hyena men, who earn their keep by feeding wild hyenas nightly on the city's fringes.

For all its historical importance, Harar is today overshadowed as an economic force by **Dire Dawa**, which was founded 55km from Harar at the turn of the 20th century to service the Addis Ababa–Djibouti railway line, and has subsequently prospered to become Ethiopia's second-largest city. Situated at the base of the Rift Valley Escarpment, Dire Dawa is lower, hotter and drier than Harar, and of relatively little interest – though as it's the main regional transport hub and the site of the airport servicing Harar, most travellers will pass through the city at some point.

Most travellers who visit this area restrict their exploration to Harar itself and (by default) Dire Dawa, either flying in directly from Addis Ababa, or else coming overland by express bus. There is, however, some interesting sightseeing outside of the two main towns. The road to Dire Dawa from Awash Saba, passing through the Chercher and Arba Gugu mountains, is splendidly scenic and worth taking slowly. Also of interest, situated within day-tripping distance of Harar, are the **Babile Elephant Sanctuary**, the **Valley of Marvels**, the Somali regional capital of **Jijiga** and the mysterious **rock paintings** near Kombolcha.

TO HARAR AND DIRE DAWA BY ROAD

Harar and Dire Dawa are both situated about 525km from Addis Ababa and 300km from Awash National Park along a good asphalt road. In a private vehicle, one can drive from Addis Ababa to either city over the course of a longish day, while those using public transport can bus directly to Dire Dawa or Harar from Adama (Nazret) or Awash Saba. Alternatively, the journey can be done in stages, using local buses, with potential stops *en route* including Asbe Teferi, Kuni, Hirna and Kulubi.

AWASH SABA TO ASBE TEFERI Immediately east of Awash Saba, a bridge crosses the Awash River and the rocky, dusty land around town gives way to a bleakly monotonous cover of dry acacia scrub. Parties of colourfully dressed Oromo women appear from nowhere to board the bus in an excited gossipy clatter, the odd camel or donkey wanders blithely along the verge, and you may see the occasional Salt's dik-dik make a startled dash into the scrub. The most notable point of interest off this stretch of road is the **Monastery of Asabot Selassie**, which stands on the prominent peak of Asabot Mountain (2,539m) and houses several ancient Ge'ez manuscripts describing the miracles performed by Abuna Samuel, the church's founder. The monastery lies 20km northeast of Asabot town, and can be reached by a rough track which branches off the main road about 60km from Awash Saba.

About 12km past Asabot, turn right at **Mieso**, at the junction of the new road and the (practically disused) old road to Dire Dawa. It's something of a relief to break the dusty tedium when, 24km past Mieso, you pull into **Asbe Teferi**, the largest town along this stretch of road, with a population of around 29,000. Asbe Teferi is rescued from visual anonymity by the presence of a few balconied double-storey legacies of the Italian occupation and an attractive setting in the Chercher and Arba Gugu foothills, despite which it possesses a hot dusty feel more of the plains than of the highlands.

There's plenty of public transport heading out in all directions from Asbe Teferi, and little reason to linger there. But if you're in need of nourishment or a bed for the night, a few options exist.

Where to stay and eat In the centre of town, the top choice is the **Burka Hotel** (*37 rooms;* ☏ *025 551 0208*) above the Awash International Bank, which charges US$6 for a compact en-suite room with three-quarter bed, cold shower and tiled floors. There are some better options on the bypass road that skips the town centre. The current number one is the new **Kebesh International Lodge** (*18 rooms;* ☏ *025 551 0935*), located at the eastern end of the town limits, which offers a range of clean hot-shower en-suite doubles for US$7.50–12 depending the size of the room and if it has DSTV. The attached restaurant/bar has local and European meals in the US$2–3 range. On the opposite side of the road heading further east, **Agape Lodge** (*14 rooms;* ☏ *025 551 0817–18;* e *abubu@ethionet.et*) is a good second choice. This place charges US$9 for a clean, quiet en-suite room with hot water and DSTV. The outdoor beer garden here is also very pleasant. Many small taxis pass by both lodges should you need to get to town.

An ambitious excursion from Asbe Teferi would be to the **Dindin Forest** and **Achare and Aynage Caves** near Machara, roughly 100km further east. The little-studied but extensive Dindin Forest is an Afro-montane assemblage set on the steep eastern slopes of the 3,574m-high Mount Arba Gugu. The Achare and Aynage complex of caves, which lies about 6km from Machara, is thought to be the most extensive subterranean network in Ethiopia after Sof Omar, yet it remained unexplored until 1995, when it was visited by a caving expedition from Britain's Huddersfield University.

KUNI MUKTAR MOUNTAIN NYALA SANCTUARY A particularly worthwhile diversion for wildlife enthusiasts who won't have the opportunity to visit the Bale

Mountains is this defunct sanctuary flanking the village of Kuni 25km southeast of Asbe Teferi. Kuni Muktar was set aside in 1990 to protect the mountain nyala herds and other wildlife residents on the forested slopes of mounts Jallo and Muktar, which rise to altitudes of above 3,000m immediately west and east of Kuni respectively. By the mid 1990s, the sanctuary had lost any formal protection it might once have enjoyed, following an intensive bout of poaching, and it was thought for some years after this that no wildlife remained there. But recent reports suggest that the mountain nyala population on Muktar is now largely recovered: one reputable researcher counted more than 30 in a day in 2002, while local information indicates that at least 100 individuals are present, including a high proportion of youngsters. There are also large numbers of Menelik's bushbuck on Jallo, while the juniper and podocarpus forest on both mountains harbours Abyssinian catbird and other suitable endemic bird species.

The best time to seek out mountain nyala is in the early morning or late afternoon (ideally at around 07.00 or 17.00), when small herds leave the forest to drink at a stream situated about 30–45 minutes' walk along a rough track leading left from the central marketplace in Kuni. To get there from Asbe Teferi, follow the Dire Dawa road for 18km as far as Arbereketi, where a right turn leads to Kuni after 7km. You can reach Kuni on public transport (regular minibuses leave from the junction at Arbereketi) but there is no formal accommodation, which means you would need a really early start out of Asbe Teferi to be at the sanctuary in good time. There is no sanctuary office in Kuni, but it is easy enough to find a local guide to help you locate the mountain nyala.

ASBE TEFERI TO DIRE DAWA/HARAR

East of Asbe Teferi, the Dire Dawa road climbs into the cool, moist **Chercher Mountains**, a literal breath of fresh air after the hot, dusty plains. The views from the road, over row after row of verdant peaks, are fantastic; even better, perhaps, if you join the bus driver, conductor and passengers in their frenzied consumption of *chat*. The hills are densely cultivated, mostly with sorghum, but patches of juniper and eucalyptus forest can still be seen, as well as impressive stands of euphorbia candelabra in the rockier areas.

After about 60km of this gorgeous scenery, you'll pull into **Hirna**, a cheerful and colourful small town set among glistening green hills and fertile valleys. This is the sort of bountiful, beautiful setting that cannot help but bring a lightness to your step – simply strolling out of town along the main road is visual bliss, and footpaths lead from the town in all directions. This could be fantastic walking country, that is if you manage to shake off the annoying children who will follow you just about everywhere!

Where to stay and eat

As for lodging, the pick of a few unpretentious local places is the **Roza Lago Hotel** (*14 rooms;* 025 441 0441) which has decent rooms with cold-shower en suite for US$4, and basic rooms using common shower for US$2.50. It's also the spot for food and drink, with good *shakila tibs*, cold beer and a generator.

When you are ready to move on, buses for Dire Dawa or Harar leave Hirna throughout the day and take about four hours. If you can't find a bus to the town you want to go to, then catch one to the other town and ask to be dropped at the T-junction with the road that connects Harar and Dire Dawa – there's plenty of transport from this junction in either direction.

On the way to the T-junction you pass the small town of **Kulubi**, which enjoys a degree of renown disproportionate to its size thanks to the presence of a church called **Kulubi Gebriel** on a hilltop 2.5km from the town centre. In 1896, Ras

Mekonnen, father of Haile Selassie, stopped at what was then a rather modest shrine to St Gebriel on the hill outside Kulubi to pray for his assistance in the looming military confrontation with Italy. Ethiopia duly defeated Italy at Adwa, and when Ras Mekonnen returned to Harar he ordered a magnificent church to be built at Kulubi in honour of the inspirational saint.

Aesthetically, it's debatable whether the domed sandstone church built by Ras Mekonnen is of much inherent interest to anybody other than students of modern Ethiopian architecture. But, rather oddly, given its relative modernity in a country liberally dotted with ancient churches of mysterious origin, Kulubi Gebriel has become the target of a fantastic biannual pilgrimage, one regarded by Ethiopian Christians as equivalent to the Islamic call to Mecca. On 26 July and 28 December, the days dedicated to St Gebriel, more than 100,000 Ethiopians from all over the country descend on the church, a festive occasion with few peers anywhere in Ethiopia. Aside from being a wonderful cultural spectacle, the pilgrimage can disrupt normal public transport patterns in the area for a few days, and bus seats are booked up weeks in advance.

DIRE DAWA

The modern city of Dire Dawa is the second largest in Ethiopia, with a population estimated at around 307,000. It was founded in 1902 under the name of Addis Harar (New Harar) to service the Franco-Ethiopian railway that connects Djibouti to Addis Ababa. Because of its strategic location, the upstart town soon came to outrank Harar in commercial and industrial significance, though even as recently as 1970 it supported a significantly smaller population. In recent years, Dire Dawa has experienced something of an economic boom as a result of the secession of Eritrea, which left Ethiopia without a seaport of its own. The recent border war with Eritrea has served to strengthen the importance of Dire Dawa, since it effectively made Djibouti Ethiopia's only reliable link with the Indian Ocean.

Set at an altitude of 1,150m, Dire Dawa is divided into two distinct parts by the wide arc created by the *wadi* (normally dry watercourse) carved by the Dachata River. Kezira, the French-designed city centre, lies to the west of the watercourse and consists of a neat grid of avenues which emanate from the central square in front of the railway station, and which are flanked by shady trees and staid colonial-style buildings. The old Muslim quarter of Megala, by contrast, is more organic in shape and mood, with all alleys apparently leading to the colourful bustle of its vast and excellent central market. The two parts of town are connected by a bridge in the north and by a seasonal causeway in the south.

In the first edition of this guide I described Dire Dawa as 'hot, sweaty and charmless', to the ire of several readers. Subsequent visits to Dire Dawa have given me little cause to revise my original assessment (though the addition of air-conditioned hotels definitely helps), so rather than plead a cause to which I don't subscribe, let me instead refer you to Arthur Gerfers's passionate comments in the box *In defence of Dire Dawa*, opposite. Whatever else, the pro-Dire Dawa contingent does concede that 'there isn't much to see' in the town. The large **market** [411 D3], often attended by rural Oromo and Afar in traditional garb, is definitely worth a look, and busiest in the morning. A second **livestock market** is situated about 500m east of the main bridge across the *wadi*. The **railway station** [411 C6] building will be a must for students of colonial architecture. Also worth noting is a new **railway museum** [411 B5] currently being established with the aid of the Alliance Ethio-Française. The museum will be centred on the old turntable and engine shed southwest of the station and will

From an email from Arthur Gerfers

The description of Dire Dawa as 'hot, sweaty and charmless' (see opposite), I found to be out of touch with the reality. It doesn't take a city-planning expert to recognise that Dire Dawa represents a refreshing change from most other towns in Ethiopia or Africa, for that matter. The streets here, first of all, are paved and relatively clean. The pavements here are continuous and without holes. Street-side shopfronts and residences offer the eye a line of continuity, a pleasant sense of urban order so glaringly absent in African cities. This town is easy to negotiate on foot, with fountains and parks for rest stops. Graffiti-covered walls surrounding seemingly vacant lots are a far cry from the exposed open spaces of other towns, which usually resemble nothing more than rubbish heaps. The reckless misuse of space so prevalent in African town-building, from muddy corner lots to functionless green spaces to decaying military plazas, leads only to the concentration of unsightliness. Ultimately the visitor is left with a sense of placelessness. The opposite, however, is true of Dire Dawa; indeed here one always has the feeling of being someplace. Even oversized socialist-era eyesores are woven methodically into the human scale of the town. And most all of the streets are tree-lined, perhaps the strongest card in this town's suit. Their boughs keep the pavement shaded and the air somewhat cool, despite the dogged humidity. I know how circumstances can play into one's judgement of a town. Perhaps you were having a bad day when you visited, or maybe it was god-awful hot. But being so pleasantly surprised by Dire Dawa, a town to which I was exiled for one day, I felt obligated to counter your sweeping dismissal of it.

incorporate the station and its various other workshops. For more information visit the Railway Administration office located opposite the station, or ask at the tourist information office next to Mito Burger. The large multi-storey **palace** [411 C5], which served as Haile Selassie's residence whenever he visited Dire Dawa, might also be of interest, but casual visits are not permitted, and little of the building is visible from outside the palace grounds.

Once you've exhausted the sightseeing, one possibility would be to retire to the Ras Hotel, with its pretty green grounds and less certain **swimming pool** (it doesn't seem to have been full in years). You could also try the pool at the Samrat Hotel, which charges a fee of US$1.80. Less passively, you might want to pop into a bar or coffee shop to watch (or participate in) the locally popular game of bingo, or create total chaos by entering into a prolonged French dialogue with one of the locals who insist on greeting any passing *faranji* with their solitary francophone phrase: a loud '*Bonjour*'. Then again, assuming that you're not waiting for a flight or train, you could, as advised in the first edition, bugger off to Harar!

GETTING THERE AND AWAY Daily flights between Addis Ababa and Dire Dawa (US$48), with flights sometimes continuing on to Jijiga in the east, are operated by **Ethiopian Airlines** [411 C5] (✆ *025 111 1147;* e *diram@ethiopianairlines. com*). Onward tickets should always be confirmed a day in advance. The airport, situated about 5km from the city centre, is a large, modern, stinking-hot building with a bar (whew!) and roof fans that don't work because some unspeakable dolt erected supportive pillars in their line of rotation. A charter taxi to the city centre costs around US$5. Flights are also met by shared taxis, whose drivers routinely overcharge tourists and aren't very open to negotiation.

The Sky and Selam bus both run daily services to/from Addis Ababa to Dire Dawa (US$17.50; around 10 hours) departing between 05.00 and 06.00 in both directions. Other cheaper bus services cover this route, leaving from the new bus station [411 C3], but they are less reliable. Minibuses run back and forth to Harar every ten minutes or so throughout the day, leaving from the old bus station [411 D4] near the market, and taking about one hour in either direction.

The historic train service from Addis Ababa to Djibouti via Dire Dawa ceased operations in 2008 and is unlikely to reopen in its existing form, but a new line connecting the three cities is reputedly the top priority of a mooted countrywide rail network announced by the government in 2010. We will post any news on our update website: http://updates.bradtguides.com/ethiopia.

TOURIST INFORMATION If you plan on visiting the nearby Laga Oda Caves you'll need to stop by the new **tourist information office** (025 111 5657; m 0915 733 992; ⊕ 08.30–13.00 & 14.00–17.30 Mon–Sat) located in the centre close by Mito Burger to pay the US$3 entrance fee and arrange an official guide at US$15 per day. While here pick up a copy of the very handy *Dire Dawa Visitor's Guide* published by the Dire Dawa Administration Tourism Development and Promotion Core.

WHERE TO STAY
Upmarket

Delight Hotel [411 A1] (42 rooms) 028 111 2777; m 0920 457 862. Overlooking the stadium at the southern end of town, this new multi-storey hotel's delusions of grandeur seem somewhat misplaced in Dire Dawa. The rooms each with heavy wooden furniture, a minibar, writing desk, DSTV, private balcony & en-suite bathtub & hairdryer are pompously comfortable (cheaper queen & twin rooms are more compact & lack hairdryers). The Presidential Suite with its private entrance, spacious salon & gigantic sleigh bed with monster bathroom sporting a full-size jacuzzi, separate steam shower, twin sinks & private balcony is truly fit for a king. Though we're not sure they get many of those in these parts! As impressive as the Delight may be, it lacks the atmosphere & facilities of the less pretentious Samrat further down the road. Rates include breakfast, free internet & airport pick-up. *US$29/30 small dbl/twin, US$58 standard dbl, US$71 standard suite, US$112 trpl suite, US$188 deluxe Presidential Suite.*

Moderate

Samrat Hotel [411 A4] (58 rooms) 025 113 0600; f 025 113 0601; e samrat@ethionet. et. This smart new centrally located hotel is currently Dire Dawa's most popular upmarket offering. Standard rooms all come with AC, fan, multi-channel satellite TV & modern en suites with bathtub & rain showers. For those brave enough to take on Dire Dawa's infamous heat, non-AC rooms are available for around US$5 less. Rates include breakfast, free Wi-Fi & airport pick-up & access to the hotel's Shock Nightclub. Other facilities include a good Indian restaurant, 3 bars, a conference hall, a gym & swimming pool (available to non-guests for US$2). *US$36/38/43 sgl/dbl/twin standard room with AC, deluxe rooms US$42/48 sgl/dbl, VIP suite US$63.*

Orbit Hotel [off map 411 D7] (42 rooms) 025 112 5834; m 0911 449 440; e orbithotel@ ethionet.et; www.orbit-hotel.com. This new business-class hotel is conveniently located by the municipal offices not far from the airport. The modern rooms are spacious & sparsely furnished with tiled floors, AC, fridge & shower en suite. Suite rooms have a private balcony & a bathtub with rain shower. The central pool – while inviting – looked a little murky for our liking & the attached restaurant was a tad functional & lacked atmosphere. Rates include breakfast & free Wi-Fi. *US$22/27 dbl with queen/king bed, US$33 twin with 2 dbl beds, US$45 suite.*

Grand Triangle Hotel [off map 411 D7] (48 rooms); 025 112 2193; m 0915 321 042; www.triangle-hotel.com. Not so much a grand triangle as a large rectangle concrete block, this hotel right next door to the Orbit is of similar price & quality. Yet while the rooms at the Orbit come across as functional & businesslike, here the rooms

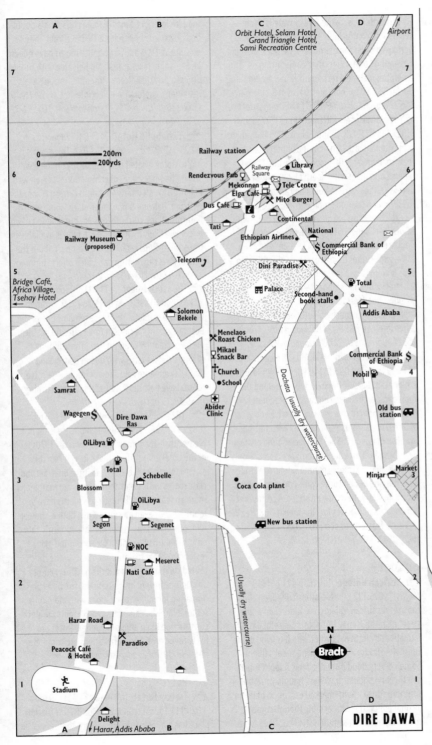

DIRE DAWA

– each with AC, satellite TV & private en suite – seem more comfortable & homely. Then again, perhaps it's just the grandma-style floral bedding screaming 'comfort inn' that's influencing us. Other amenities include a restaurant & bar, a swimming pool (US$2.50 for non-guests), gym & cinema. *US$22 dbl, US$28 suite, US$31 twin with 2 dbl beds*.

⌂ **Selam Hotel** [off map 411 C7] (27 rooms) ☏ 025 113 0219/20; e hotelselam.200846@yahoo. com. Situated just 1km from the airport along the main road towards the town centre, Dire Dawa's original upmarket hotel doesn't look as fresh as it once was. The cigarette butt-filled ashtrays guarding the reception desk do nothing to alleviate the stale air. Still, the rooms are good value & all come with AC, multi-channel DSTV & modern bathrooms. Double rooms have a fridge & in-room safe as an extra, while suites have over-sized California king beds & worn carpet & VIP suites are bigger, brighter & better value than standard suites. Other amenities include a good restaurant & a lobby bar with oversized leather couches. Rates include breakfast & free internet. *US$18/24 twin room for 1/2 people, US$21 queen dbl, US$27/30 standard/VIP suite.*

⌂ **Hotel Blossom** [411 A3] (28 rooms) ☏ 025 111 0393/0390; f 025 111 0398; e hotelblossom@ ethionet.et. Just off the roundabout behind the Total garage, this new centrally located hotel offers the added benefit of a day spa. So once you weary of Dire Dawa's sights you can relax with full-body Swedish massage (US$6) or have a sauna or steam bath. Standard rose-hued rooms are clean, simply styled & all have multi-channel satellite TV, fridge, AC & hot-shower en suite, while compact budget rooms lack AC & have tiny en suites. A restaurant & bar are attached. Rates include breakfast & free Wi-Fi. Visa & MasterCard accepted. *US$15 sgl, US$21 twin, US$24/30 2nd-/1st-class suites.*

Budget

⌂ **African Village** [off map 411 A5] (15 rooms) ☏ 025 112 6006; e africanvillage@yahoo. com; www.african-village.net. Hidden on a side street near the Tsehay Hotel, this peaceful oasis, hand built by its Swiss owner who has lived in the Horn of Africa for 20 years & who speaks fluent Somali & very good Amharic, feels & looks much like the kind popular travellers' haunts you'd find in southern Africa – with marked exception of its no alcohol policy. The comfortable though compact *tukuls* are built in traditional style but have

modern interiors. Smaller rooms boasting a double bed or 2 single beds have a TV, fan & cold-shower en suite, & TV, while larger suite rooms have queen beds – some have a small kitchen area with fridge, others a private balcony. Amenities include a restaurant, conference hall & internet. *US$9/16/19 small sgl/dbl/twin, US$24 standard suite, US$31/32 suite with balcony/kitchen.*

⌂ **Schebelle Hotel** [411 B3] (28 rooms) ☏ 025 112 6032; m 0915 751 037. This new multi-storey located near the OiLibya garage was still in the final stages of completion when viewed in late 2011. All rooms are bright & fresh & come with fan, balcony & private en suite (some with a bathtub). None currently has AC, but if added room prices will likely increase. Cheap food is available in the ground-floor café, but the best part about the Schebelle is the rooftop bar which offers stunning views over the city. *US$14/20 dbl/twin.*

⌂ **Peacock Hotel** [411 A1] (10 rooms) ☏ 025 111 3968/130 3968; m 0911 760 720. Located next to the stadium, this place remains one of the best restaurants & cafés in town offering pastries, juice, ice cream & draught beer. The addition of large, clean rooms with queen bed, ceiling fan, TV & en-suite cold shower (more expensive rooms have bathtubs) makes this a great choice. *US$9.50/15 dbl with shower/bathtub.*

⌂ **Dire Dawa Ras Hotel** [411 B3] (49 rooms) ☏ 025 111 3255. This stalwart high-rise is set in a pleasantly leafy garden. The funky retro 1970s feel of the hotel does little to make its cell-like third-class single rooms seem less institutional. Second-class rooms with small double beds are marginally more appealing, while first-class rooms have 3 rooms, 2 beds & an en suite with a bath & shower. All rooms have fans. Amenities are currently thin on the ground with only a weary ground-floor restaurant & bar to entertain guests – the much touted swimming pool out the back was empty on our most recent visit. That said, the hotel was preparing for major renovations with old rooms set for a facelift & an additional 39 rooms under construction in an adjoining annex. Prices are likely to increase once renovations are complete. *US$9/15/18 3rd-/2nd-/1st-class room.*

Shoestring

⌂ **Tsehay Hotel** [off map 411 A5] (30 rooms) ☏ 025 111 1023. Popular with locals, this friendly place has a huge garden restaurant that serves traditional food, pasta & roast meats. The basic rooms with cold-shower en suite are excellent value as are the smaller common-shower rooms. There is a rooftop disco & pub, which might get noisy. *US$4 using common shower, US$6 en suite.*

🏠 **Mekonnen Hotel** [411 C6] (8 rooms) 📞 025 111 3348. This long-serving favourite has plenty of character & a convenient location on the central square facing the railway station. The tired rooms using a common shower are spacious & clean with genuine queen bed, fan, nets & balcony. The courtyard is full of yellow weaver birds, & the house speciality appears to be spaghetti. Unfortunately, it's often full. *US$4.50.*

🏠 **Continental Hotel** [411 C6] (24 rooms) 📞 025 111 1546. One could make too much of the fact that Evelyn Waugh stayed at this central hotel in its 1930s heyday, but then again that's the most attractive thing about this place. All rooms have fans & possibly quite a bit of noise drifting in from the courtyard bar. *US$4.50 using smelly common cold showers, US$9 en suite.*

🏠 **Meseret Hotel** [411 B2] (27 rooms) 📞 025 111 3305. Set 50m from the Harar road close to the new bus station in an area liberally dotted with restaurants & bars, this quiet double-storey hotel, built around a green courtyard, is similarly over-priced. Ground-floor en-suite rooms with ¾ beds, no fan & cold shower are suffocating, but at least you might catch a breeze from rooms on the first floor. *US$4.50 using common shower, US$9 en suite.*

WHERE TO EAT Most of the higher-end hotels have restaurants serving decent Western meals; the standouts are the **Selam Hotel** [off map 411 D7] which has an extensive wine list and the **Ras Hotel** [411 B3], which wins points for its pleasant garden setting, while the food at the **Peacock** [411 A1] and **Tsehay** [off map 411 A5] hotels is also good. For something a little spicier, the **Bollywood Restaurant** at the **Samrat Hotel** [411 A4] unsurprisingly specialises in Indian dishes – the owners of the hotel are Indian, so you can be assured of a high degree of authenticity. The bar on the ground floor of the **Mekonnen Hotel** [411 C6], cool and draped with lush bougainvillea, serves beer, coffee, pastries and snacks, and is a pleasant place to hang out. But if you're looking for the perfect spot for a sundowner, then the rooftop bar at the **Schebelle Hotel** [411 B3] is the place to go.

✗ **Bridge Café** [off map 411 A5] 📞 025 112 0125. Located in Sabian near the first bridge, this restaurant-cum-pizzeria is worth a look. *US$2–4.*

✗ **Menelaos Chicken House** [411 B4] 📞 025 111 3049. This long-serving local restaurant near the palace serves whole roast chickens/good tuna salad. *US$3/US$1.*

✗ **Mito Burger** [411 C6] 📞 025 111 2206. A block back from the railway station, this popular place serves a varied & reasonably priced selection of meals, snacks, pastries, juices, hot drinks & beers. *US$1.50–3.*

✗ **Paradiso Restaurant** [411 B1] 📞 025 111 3780; 🕐 from 18.00. This excellent restaurant is set in an atmospheric old house along the Harar road, & serves a selection of Italian & Ethiopian dishes, along with various roast meats. The lasagne here may be the best on the continent. *US$2–4.*

✗ **Sami Recreation Centre** [off map 411 D7] 📞 025 112 3326. Despite its out-of-the-way location, this family-orientated centre near the municipal offices is said to have the best pizza in town, & is identifiable by the model of a blue train out front.

🍵 **Dini Paradise Café** [411 C5] This breezy garden café near the main bridge, serves a variety of snacks, pastries & juices in green surrounds. *US$1–2.*

🍵 **Elga Café** [411 C6] 📞 025 111 2468. Next door to the tourist information office, this centrally located café has a good range of gooey cakes & other sweet treats. *US$1–2.*

OTHER PRACTICALITIES

Foreign exchange The **Commercial Bank of Ethiopia** [411 D5] has a couple of branches in Dire Dawa. The best for exchanging foreign currency and travellers' cheques is the central branch located opposite the main entrance to the palace. The **Wagegen Bank** [411 A4] near the Samrat Hotel offers similar services and has an ATM.

Internet and email Most of the better hotels now offer free Wi-Fi, but if you're stuck the **Tele Centre** [411 C6] next to the post office charges around US$1 per half-hour.

EXCURSION

Laga Oda Rock Paintings

Located 35km southwest of Dire Dawa, this painted rock shelter was reputedly discovered in 1933 by Azais and Ongieu de Chapparon, and its limestone walls are decorated with about 600 paintings dating back up to 5,000 years. To visit the site you must first stop by the tourist office in Dire Dawa to pay the US$3 fee and arrange a local guide (US$15). Then head south along the Harar road for around 4km, turn right onto an unsigned rough dirt road, and follow this for another 31km. Once you reach the end, it is a ten to 20-minute walk to the shelter. The art, though very old, is too faded to convey much to the average visitor, and on our most recent visit in 2011, dozens of children followed us to the site and then threw rocks at us when we left. Reader Fiona Bluck has this to say: 'I have visited the rock art in the Acacus Mountains in southwest Libya. This overhang does not compare with that, but nevertheless it's well worth going to have a look.' For more information on the paintings and their significance see *Rock Paintings of Laga Oda* by Pavel Cervicek.

HARAR

The spiritual heart of Ethiopia's large Islamic community, Harar is considered by some Muslims to be the fourth-holiest city in the world after Mecca, Medina and Jerusalem, while travel scribe John Graham rates it as 'the most pleasant city to visit in Ethiopia'. Harar is indeed a lively, friendly and stimulating town, one whose aura of cultural integrity and lived-in antiquity is complemented by a moderate highland climate that comes as a positive relief after the festering claustrophobia of Dire Dawa.

Harar lies at the centre of a fertile agricultural area, renowned for its high-quality coffee, though this crop has been increasingly replaced by *chat* in recent years. But the main attraction of the region is Harar itself, or rather the walled city of Jugal that lies at its ancient heart. Old Harar remains strongly Muslim in character. It hosts a full 99 private and public mosques, the largest such concentration in the world, along with more than 100 *qubi* (tombs or shrines of important holy men) – hence the nickname *Gey Ada* (City of Saints). By contrast, the newer part of town, which runs along the Dire Dawa road, is predominantly Christian, though the frizzy-headed traditional Oromo are also much in evidence.

Considering the prominent role that Harar has played in Muslim–Christian–Galla conflicts, the modern town possesses a surprising mood of religious and cultural tolerance, one that is doubly refreshing in the present global political climate. Indeed, for a city of such devout pedigree, Harar has an undercurrent that is more than a little – dare I say it – hedonistic. The compulsive chewing of *chat* dominates every aspect of public life and, to paraphrase the sentiments of one (Muslim) resident, you really do need something liquid to chill you out after a good chew. Any preconceptions about fundamentalist Harar can be washed down at the bars which, I suspect, come close to matching public mosques one for one within the old city walls. Harar is the sort of easy-going, cosmopolitan town where you could settle in for a week and do nothing more exerting than just soak up the atmosphere.

GETTING THERE AND AWAY Flights from Addis Ababa terminate at Dire Dawa rather than Harar, as do most direct buses to the area, though Sky and Selam buses both run direct daily services between Addis Ababa and Harar (US$17.50; around 10 hours). Dire Dawa and Harar are connected by a good 43km asphalt road, which is covered by a regular stream of minibuses taking about one hour in either direction, and there is also plenty of minibus action along the recently surfaced road between Harar and Jijiga. The bus and minibus station is outside the city walls, close to the Harar Gate.

GETTING AROUND Of all the cities in Ethiopia, Harar is the one where having a guide is most crucial – not because of any particular hassles, but because you may miss out on many of the best sites without the assistance of a local to show you where they are. An official guide can be arranged through most of the hotels, or through the cultural centre/museum, and you will typically be asked US$18 per day for their services. We recommend Lishan Ketema (\ 025 666 4924; m 0913 451 876/0915 740 249; e lisket2006@yahoo.com) who speaks excellent English and is very professional. The young 'guides' who hang around Feres Megala and elsewhere accosting any passing *faranji* – or *faranjo* as they say locally – with an optimistic 'Remember me?' are not generally very knowledgeable and they can be irritatingly banal conversationalists.

TOURIST INFORMATION There is a **tourist information office** in the Harar Museum and Cultural Centre [419 H3] (⊕ *09.00–12.00 & 14.00–17.00 Mon–Fri*). Anybody who arrives here in search of esoteric travel tips is likely to be disappointed, but it does sell a superb fold-out colour map of Harar.

↑ WHERE TO STAY
Moderate

🏠 **Heritage Plaza Hotel** [off map 418 D1] (26 rooms) \ 025 666 5137; f 025 666 2790; e info@ plazahotelharar.com or plaza@ethionet.et; www. plazahotelharar.com. Located past the Tsadkan Tesfaye Hotel on the road to Babile, this palatial multi-storey hotel remains Harar's best. The friendly brother owners are genuinely nice & hospitable making all their guests feel at home. The rooms – all with private en suite & balcony – are spacious, clean & comfortable. Suites have 2 king beds in 1 room, as well as a bathtub & kitchen, while the luxury suite has 3 rooms & sleeps 4. More importantly, several on-site wells ensure a water supply when the rest of the city is dry. A 3rd-floor restaurant offers a US2–4 range, with hamburgers as the feature item. There is a quiet, tented café near the garden out the back, & internet is available. Highly recommended! *US$33/44/49.50 sgl/ dbl/twin, US$55/75 standard/luxury suite.*

🏠 **Harar cultural guesthouses** With the recent opening of 2 new guesthouses in the walled city – the **Rowda** [419 E2] (*4 rooms;* \ 025 666 2211; m 0915 756 439*) & the **Zubeyda** [419 E2] (*5 rooms;* \ 025 666 4692; m 0910 284 329*), it's now possible to stay in a typical Harar house. Located around the corner from each other & owned by related families, the guesthouses are impeccably clean & above all homely. The whitewashed walls are beautifully decorated in traditional style with rich carpets lining the floors & colourful baskets & plates adorning the walls. The rooms are simply furnished yet comfortable with some sharing a bathroom. A complimentary home-cooked breakfast along with freshly brewed coffee is served in the small courtyard. *Both charge US$21 per dbl bed inc b/fast.*

Budget

🏠 **Belayneh Hotel** [418 D1] (22 rooms) \ 025 666 2030. Consistently popular with both independent travellers & tour operators since it opened in 1995, this 4-storey hotel has a convenient location on the fringe of the walled city just above the Commercial Bank. The compact en-suite rooms with hot shower, private balcony & TV are among the cleanest in town, but you'd think the management could splash out on a rooftop tank to counter the regular water cuts that afflict Harar. The rooftop restaurant serves decent local & Western dishes in the US$1.50–3 range. *US$11/17/18 dbl/twin/trpl.*

🏠 **Harar Ras Hotel** [418 A2] (30 rooms) \ 025 666 0027/0288. Situated about 1km from the Harar Gate along the Dire Dawa road, this rather austere double-storey former government hotel has no garden worth talking about & isn't up to the standard of its counterpart in Dire Dawa. Nevertheless, the staff are very helpful & the en-suite rooms are pretty good value. There are 4 classes of rooms here, starting at a closet-sized twin room with 2 single beds, all the way to a first-class VIP suite with king bed, TV, sitting room & a monster bathroom you could fit a whole extra bedroom in. Bear in mind water usage is currently restricted to a couple of hours in the morning & evening.

Renovations are planned for the now-privatised hotel in 2012, so expect prices to increase. *US$9/10 twin/dbl, US$15.50/20 standard/VIP suite.*

🏠 **Rewda Hotel** [off map 418 A3] (21 rooms) 📞 025 666 9777. Out of town, slightly closer than the Abader, this hotel offers a range of blue-hued rooms with hot water & DSTV. Newer first-class rooms on the upper floors have tiled floors, while older second-class rooms on lower levels have carpet. Though cleaner & newer than the Tana (see

HARAR: A POTTED HISTORY

The early days of Harar are shrouded in legend. The city's foundation is often attributed to Emir Abu Bekr Mohammed of the Walashma dynasty, who is known to have abandoned the established Walashma capital at Dakar in favour of Harar in 1520. But, while Abu Bekr's move was instrumental in pushing the city to prominence, Harar is certainly much older than this. The town is mentioned in an early 14th-century manuscript, and its oldest mosque was reputedly founded in the 12th century. One tradition is that Harar was originally a Christian city and went by a different name until its patron saint, Sheikh Abadir Gey, led a group of 43 Arabian migrants there in the 10th century. According to this tradition, it is Sheik Abadir who renamed the city as Harar, and organised its first Islamic administrative system. Others claim that Harar became Islamic as early as the 7th century, when it was settled by an Arabic community led by a contemporary and follower of the prophet Muhammad called Sheik Hussein. Yet another legend relating to the origin of Harar is that when Muhammad ascended to heaven he saw the hill on which it stands as a shining light, and an angel told him it was the Mountain of Saints.

Harar rose to significance in an atmosphere of turmoil and bloodshed. Within five years of settling in Harar, Abu Bekr Mohammed was killed by Ahmed Gragn, a popular and highly militant imam who assumed control of the city by installing Umar Din, another member of the Walashma dynasty, as a puppet emir to be supervised by Gragn's brother. His hold on Harar secure, Gragn ordered all Muslims to stop paying tribute to the Christian emperor Lebna Dengal, who had angered him a few years earlier by sending a pillaging raid to the Islamic region of Hubut. Lebna Dengal retaliated to Gragn's subversive instructions by sending a punitive military expedition to Harar, one that was soundly defeated by Gragn's army. Inspired by this victory, Gragn then used Harar as the base from which a succession of bloody and destructive raids was launched on the Christian empire. Gragn was killed in battle in 1543, but the jihad continued with diminishing effect for several years, under the direction of Gragn's widow Bati Del Wambara and nephew Emir Nur Ibn al-Wazir. In 1559, the imperial army, led by Emperor Galawdewos, marched on Harar once again. And, once again, it was defeated – the emperor was killed and his head paraded around town on a stake.

The long years of war took their economic toll on Harar's resources. Following the battle of 1559, the jihad was more or less abandoned as the city faced a new threat in the form of the Galla (Oromo) tribes who had taken advantage of the Muslim–Christian conflict to occupy much of southern Ethiopia. It was during the 1560s that Emir Nur erected the tall protective walls that have enclosed Old Harar ever since. After Nur's death in 1567, however, Harar was ruled by two ineffective

page 418), the difference is not worth almost 3 times the price! *US$11/17.50 2nd-/1st-class room.*

🏠 **Abader Guesthouse** [off map 418 A3] (40 rooms) ✆ 025 666 0721. This hotel, which stands on the Dire Dawa road about 1km past the Ras, hasn't got the most ideal location for travellers dependent on public transport. But the large, slightly frayed-looking en-suite rooms do represent pretty good value, the common shower rooms less so – what's more it's one of the few hotels in Harar

with 24hr running hot water. *US$5.50/7 sgl/dbl using common shower, US$8/9 sgl/dbl en suite.*

🏠 **Tewodros Hotel** [418 D3] (22 rooms) ✆ 025 666 0217; m 0913 549 977. This backpackers' favourite is a short distance outside the Harar Gate, not far from the bus station, in an area frequented by hyenas after dark. The recently renovated rooms with their bright fresh new bedding are great value. Ground-floor rooms share a common cold shower, while 1st-floor rooms have

emirs in succession, and became increasingly vulnerable to attacks by the Galla. In 1575, the emir was evicted by Mansur Mohammed, who abandoned Harar in favour of a new capital at the oasis of Awsa in the Danakil Desert. For almost a century, Harar was politically subordinate to Awsa.

Harar's resurrection began in 1647, when Emir Ali ibn Daud took control of the city, and formed an autonomous ruling dynasty. Despite frequent fighting with the Galla, the walled city grew in stature over the next century to become the most populous and important trade centre in the region, issuing its own currency, and known by repute throughout the Islamic world. Only Muslims, however, were allowed to enter the city walls, and as a result its location was the source of more rumour than substance in the Christian world. The first European to visit Harar, in 1855, was the British explorer Richard Burton, who spent ten anxious days in what he referred to as 'the forbidden city', unsure whether he was a guest or prisoner of the emir (see box, *Richard Burton in Harar*, page 422). Another famous 19th-century visitor was the French poet Arthur Rimbaud, who abandoned poetry at the age of 19 and then, after seven footloose years in Europe, moved to Harar in 1880, where he set himself up as a trader and was based until his death in 1891.

Harar's almost 250-year-long era of autonomous rule came to an end in 1875, when Egypt captured the city and killed the emir. The ensuing Egyptian occupation met strong internal resistance, and it collapsed in 1885, when Emir Abdullah was installed. Two years later, however, the walled city once again lost its autonomy, this time to the Prince of Showa, the future Emperor Menelik II, who defeated Emir Abdullah's forces at the Battle of Chelenko in 1887. Menelik warded off the danger of renewed religious sectarianism by including several members of the emir's family in his new administration, which he headed with a Christian governor, Ras Mekonnen – the father of the future Emperor Haile Selassie.

Harar was regarded as the most important trading centre in Ethiopia in the late 19th century, but since 1902, when the Djibouti railway line was built, its commercial role has been secondary to that played by Dire Dawa. In some respects, modern Harar is destined always to play second fiddle to Dire Dawa, especially while Djibouti's significance as the closest Red Sea port to Addis Ababa is bolstered by the ongoing border closure with Eritrea. Nevertheless, Harar was still the third-largest town in Ethiopia in 1968, and it remained the political capital of Hararge province throughout the Haile Selassie and Derg eras. In the 1994 reshuffle of administrative regions, Harar, now the 11th-largest city in Ethiopia, was accorded a disproportionate degree of autonomy when it was recognised as one of three federal city-states countrywide.

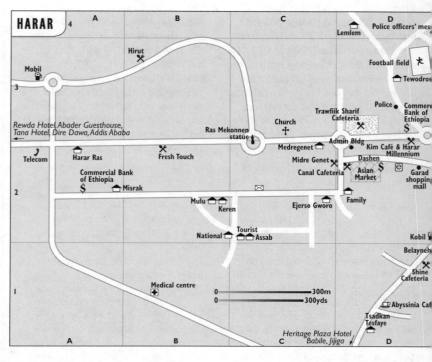

Rewda Hotel, Abader Guesthouse,
Tana Hotel, Dire Dawa, Addis Ababa

Map labels: HARAR | Lemlem | Police officers' mess | Hirut | Football field | Tewodros | Mobil | Trawfiik Sharif Cafeteria | Police | Commerc Bank of Ethiopia | Church | Ras Mekonnen statue | Admin Bldg | Kim Café & Harar Millennium | Telecom | Harar Ras | Fresh Touch | Medregenet | Midre Genet | Dashen | Commercial Bank of Ethiopia | Misrak | Canal Cafeteria | Asian Market | Garad shopping mall | Mulu | Keren | Ejerso Gworo | Family | National | Tourist | Assab | Kobil | Belayneh | Medical centre | Shine Cafeteria | Abyssinia Caf | Tsadkan Tesfaye

0 — 300m
0 — 300yds

*Heritage Plaza Hotel
Babile, Jijiga*

---

private hot-shower en suite. Ask for rooms 8, 9, 15, 16, 17 or 18 & you are likely to see hyenas crossing the football pitch below from around 21.30 onwards. A good restaurant specialising in roasted chicken is attached, & the friendly resident guide Yilma is used to arranging excursions at affordable rates. *US$4.50 with common shower, US$9 en suite.*

Shoestring

⌂ **Tana Hotel** [off map 418 A3] (40 rooms) ☎ 025 666 8482–3; m 0915 740 943. Located directly next to the Abader, this place charges less for similar quality en-suite rooms with full-size bed, hot water & DSTV. The attached restaurant serves pasta & meat dishes. *US$5.50/7.50 dbl/twin.*

⌂ **Medregenet Hotel** [418 C2] (30 rooms) ☎ 025 666 7510. This new central hotel overlooking the roundabout opposite the church is excellent value – possibly because they're yet to introduce crazy *faranji* prices. In the meantime the clean rooms are almost wrapper fresh. A restaurant is planned & DSTV is available in the basement meeting hall. *US$5/7.50 with common shower/en suite.*

✕ **WHERE TO EAT** The restaurant at the **Tewodros Hotel** [418 D3] has been one of the best in Harar for some years now, and is popular with locals and travellers alike. The house speciality is roast chicken, which comes with an impressive array of condiments, but the menu is quite extensive. The **Ras Hotel** [418 A2] dishes up the usual government-hotel food including a set three-course menu. The restaurant at the **Belayneh Hotel** [418 D1] has a long varied menu, as does the one at the **Heritage Plaza Hotel** [off map 418 D1].

✕ **Fresh Touch Bar & Restaurant** [418 B2] m 0915 740 109. Located along the main road, Fresh Touch remains the current hot spot, featuring a lengthy menu of pizzas & stir-fries as well as burgers, sandwiches & chicken & fish dishes. *US$2.50–5.*

✕ **Hirut Restaurant** [418 B3] Though not as central as the Kim and Fresh Touch, this serves good local meals at reasonable prices. It also has a decent selection of salads, pastas & burgers – the roast chicken here is also reputably very good. *US$2.50–4.*

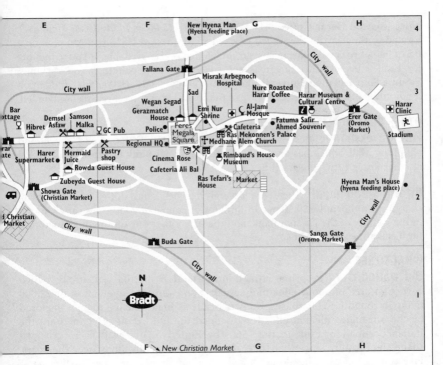

New Hyena Man
(Hyena feeding place)

Fallana Gate

Misrak Arbegnoch
Hospital

City wall

Nure Roasted
Harar Coffee

Harar Museum &
Cultural Centre

Harar
Clinic

Wegan Segad
Gerazmatch
House

Sad

Al-Jami
Mosque

Erer Gate
(Oromo
Market)

Bar
Cottage

Demsel
Hibret Asfaw

Samson
Malka

Emi Nur
Shrine

Fatuma Safir
Ahmed Souvenir

Harar
Clinic

GC Pub

Feres
Megala
Square

Cafeteria

Stadium

Police

Harer
Supermarket

Mermaid
Juice

Pastry
shop

Regional HQ

Ras Mekonnen's Palace
Medhane Alem Church

Rowda Guest House

Cinema Rose

Rimbaud's House
Museum

Zubeyda Guest House

Cafeteria Ali Bal

Showa Gate
(Christian Market)

Ras Tefari's
House

Market

Hyena Man's House
(hyena feeding place)

Christian
Market

City wall

Buda Gate

Sanga Gate
(Oromo Market)

City wall

City wall

N

Bradt

New Christian Market

✕ **Cozy Pizzeria** [418 B2] ☎ 025 666 0476.
This cosy new restaurant, located around 50m
from Fresh Touch, is equally as good & popular as
its near neighbour serving up a good selection of
pizzas, pastas, meat & fish dishes. *US$2–4.*

▢ **Kim Café** [418 D2] Of the several pastry
shops that have sprung up around Harar, this
bright café located on the Harar Millennium Corner
is the pick, serving fresh fruit juice, pastries & ice
cream & also stocks a fair range of imported sweets
& biscuits. *US$1–2.50.*

▢ **Cafeteria Ali Bal** [419 F2] Located in the
heart of the walled city, this café is a great place
to watch the passing show at Feres Megala over a
pastry or coffee. There's also an attached souvenir
shop. *US$1–2.*

▢ **Mermaid Juice** [419 E3] This quiet café is
another good spot in the walled city for pastries,
coffee & juice. *US$1–2.*

ENTERTAINMENT AND NIGHTLIFE Harar is well endowed with bars, several of
which – rather unexpectedly – lie within the walled city. The **Bar Cottage** [419 E3],
with its organic banana-leaf walls, is almost as cosy as the name suggests, and the
CD deck blares out a remarkably eclectic music selection. The bar at the **Samson
Hotel** [419 E3] is a hot spot for reggae and dancing on weekends, but be aware that
beer prices get jacked up to US$1 a bottle. Outside of the walled city, the rowdy bar
at the **Tourist Hotel** [418 C2] plays a mixture of reggae and Ethiopian music, and
hosts live music on some nights. More reliable for live music is the nearby **National
Hotel** [418 B2], where a traditional band usually cranks into action at 22.00.

SHOPPING Serious shoppers can test out their haggling skills with the fabric sellers
at the **Asian Market** [418 D2], known locally as the *cigari* market, and then watch
as one of the male tailors zips you up a traditional Harari dress (a long kaftan with
matching scarf) in a matter of minutes. The caffeine-addicted won't want to miss

Nure Roasted Harar Coffee [419 G3] (☺ *08.00–12.00 & 14.00–18.00 Mon–Sat*), located in the heart of the walled city, where for around US$4 you can pick up a 0.5kg bag of roasted coffee beans; ground coffee is also available. If you're looking for local souvenirs including baskets, silver jewellery, paintings and carvings, **Fatuma Sefir Ahemed Souvenir Shop** [419 G3] (☺ *08.00–18.00 daily*), hidden on a side street just south of the main road in the walled city, has been recommended.

OTHER PRACTICALITIES
Foreign exchange Best is the **Dashen Bank** [418 D2] out past the Grand Shopping Mall, which has an ATM. The **Commercial Bank of Ethiopia** [418 A2] also has foreign-exchange facilities.

Internet and email There are several internet cafés dotted around town, charging a uniform US$0.50 per 15 minutes. A couple of good cafés can be found in the vicinity of the Dashen Bank, and there's another one on the Jijiga road past the Tsadkan Tesfaye Hotel.

WHAT TO SEE
Old walled city The prime attraction of Harar is the old walled city, which covers an area of about 60ha and supports an estimated population of 22,000 living in roughly 5,500 houses. Known locally as **Jugal**, the old town is enclosed by the 5m-high wall that effectively defined the full extent of Harar until the Italian occupation. Built in the 1560s by Emir Nur, the wall hasn't changed shape significantly since that time, despite several renovations over the years. Five traditional gates lie along its 3.5km circumference, and two further gates were added during the rules of Menelik II and Haile Selassie, one of which was subsequently closed up during the Italian occupation.

On your first outing into the old town, it isn't a bad idea to take a guide to show you the major landmarks. The standard fee for an official guide, arranged through the Harar Guides Association office near the Awash Bank, is US$18 for a whole day and US$8 for a few hours. Once you have your bearings, it's more fun perhaps to wander around on your own and follow your nose. The old town is a fascinating place, far more than the sum of its landmarks – it boasts a rich sense of community, and every walk reveals new points of interest. You may also want to stop at the market, preferably in the afternoon when it's busiest, and perhaps look at a few of the curio shops in the area – they stock some interesting stuff and there's only the mildest pressure to do more than browse.

The normal first point of entry into the old town is the **Harar Gate** [419 E3], also known as the Duke's Gate, a motor-friendly addition dating from the rule of Haile Selassie. This gate faces west and connects the Dire Dawa road through the new town to the main road through the old town. The other gate connecting the old and new towns is the **Showa Gate** [419 E2], known in Harari as Asmaddin Beri, which adjoins the Christian Market opposite the bus station. The other four gates, running in anticlockwise order from the Showa Gate are the **Buda Gate** [419 F2] (called Bedri Beri in Harari), the **Sanga Gate** [419 H2] (Sukutat Beri), **Erer Gate** [419 H3] (Argob Beri) and **Fallana Gate** [419 F3] (Assum Beri). In addition to the Amharigna and Harari names, every gate has a different name in Oromifa, Somali and Arabic. Although it is most convenient to enter the old town via the Harar or Showa gates, neither such approach has an impact comparable to arriving at the Buda Gate, from where a labyrinth of cobbled alleys flanked by traditional whitewashed stone houses winds uphill towards Feres Megala and Gidir Megala.

The walled city is roughly oblong in shape. The most important landmark within the walls, at least for orientation purposes, is the central square known as **Feres Megala** [419 F3] (literally 'Horse Market', though these days Peugeot Megala would be a more apt description), from which radiates a quintet of main (mostly motor-width) alleys leading to each of the gates. The main commercial road in the old town, lined with shops, bars and hotels, runs between Harar Gate and Feres Megala. Strung between these main thoroughfares is a web of atmospheric cobbled alleys, which are confusing to navigate at first, though the city is too small for you to go far without encountering a main road or obvious landmark.

A walking tour Feres Megala is the obvious place to start any walking tour of Harar. The square with its curious monument commemorating the 1887 Battle of Chelenko, in which the Muslim forces lost to the Christian forces headed by Menelik II, is lined with interesting old buildings. The hotel between the police station and the corner of the road to the Fallana Gate was formerly Gerazmatch House, built by the Egyptians and used as a warehouse by Rimbaud during the first year of his stay in Harar. Also on the main square lies the **Church of Medhane Alem** [419 G3], built in 1890 on the site of a mosque constructed 15 years earlier by the unpopular Egyptian occupiers, and described by Sylvia Pankhurst as 'a charming example of Ethiopian ecclesiastical architecture of the Menelik period'. The old town's main *chat* market lies on the southern verge of Feres Megala.

The road that runs east from the square next to the church leads to Erer Gate, which is where Richard Burton entered Harar. Erer Gate is the site of a colourful Oromo *chat* market, and it is also the closest gate to the site used by the hyena men (see page 424). Outside the Erer Gate there stands an interesting Muslim cemetery comprising hundreds of graves, each of which is decorated by a unique and often very colourful painting. To get there from the gate, walk through the stadium, then after around 50m turn right where the road forks at a mosque, following an enclosed alley for about 300m until it terminates at the cemetery. One reader comments: 'This place is really amazing during sunsets and sunrises. We spent time there every evening just sitting in silence, listening to the prayers coming from the mosques and feeling this extraordinary spiritual atmosphere.'

Several points of interest lie along or off the road between the central square and Erer Gate, including the 16th-century domed **Tomb of Emir Nur**, and a Catholic mission that dates from the late 19th century. Also on this road is the **al-Jami Mosque** [419 G3], which was founded in 1216 according to local tradition. The present-day building possesses at least one minaret dating to the 1760s, but otherwise it is architecturally undistinguished and looks to be no more than 50 years old. Further out towards the Erer Gate, the **Harar Museum and Cultural Centre** [419 G3] (⊕ 09.00–12.00 & 14.00–17.00 Mon–Fri; entrance US$1.50) is worth visiting for its complete replica of an old Harari 'gey gar' (city house).

Located near Sanga Gate, the **Abdullah Sherif House** (entrance US$1.50) is a private museum that houses its enthusiastic namesake's collections of old Harari religious texts, taped recordings of traditional songs dating back to the 1940s, more than 2,000 old and other cultural artefacts relating to the city's long history. About 200m south of Sanga Gate, immediately inside the city wall, the **Tomb of Sheikh Abadir**, the religious leader who reputedly introduced Islam to Harar, is a popular substitute for Islamic Ethiopians who can't afford the pilgrimage to Mecca.

Leading east from the main square, between the Cafeteria Ali Bal and Cinema Oriental, there is a narrow lane called **Mekina Girgir** (Machine Road) in reference to the sewing machines of the (exclusively male) street tailors who work there.

18

RICHARD BURTON IN HARAR

The early European explorers of the African interior were, as a rule, prone to describing their 'discoveries' in somewhat hyperbolic terms. Perhaps the most noteworthy exception to this rule is the acerbic and unflattering description of Harar by Richard Burton, who, in 1855, became the first European to visit the most holy of Ethiopia's Islamic cities. Burton was not impressed, as the following edited extracts from his book *First Footsteps in Africa* make clear:

An irregular wall, lately repaired, but ignorant of cannon, is pierced with five large gates, and supported by oval towers of artless construction. The only large building is the Jami or Cathedral, a long barn of poverty-stricken appearance, with broken down gates and two whitewashed minarets of truncated conoid shape. The streets are narrow lanes, up hill and down dale, strewed with gigantic rubbish heaps, upon which repose packs of mangy one-eyed dogs. There are no establishments for learning, no endowments, as generally in the east, and apparently no encouragement to students: books also are rare and costly.

The Somali say of the city that it is a paradise inhabited by asses: certainly the exterior of the people is highly unprepossessing. Among the men, I did not see a handsome face: their features are coarse and debauched; many of them squint, others have lost an eye by smallpox, and they are disfigured by scrofula and other diseases.

The government of Harar is the Amir. These petty princes have a habit of killing and imprisoning all those who are suspected of aspiring to the throne. The Amir Ahmed succeeded his father about three years ago. His rule is severe if not just. Ahmed's principal occupations are spying on his many stalwart cousins, indulging in vain fears of the English, the Turks and the Hajj Sharmarkay, and amassing treasure by commerce and escheats.

He judges civil and religious causes in person. The punishments, when money forms no part of them, are mostly according to Koranic code. The murderer is placed in the market street, blindfolded, and bound hand and foot: the nearest of kin to the deceased then strikes his neck with a sharp and heavy butcher's knife, and the corpse is given over to the relations for Muslim burial. When a citizen draws dagger upon another or commits any petty offence, he is bastinadoed in a peculiar manner: two men ply their horsewhips upon his back and breast, and the prince, in whose presence the punishment is carried out, gives order to stop. Theft is punished by amputation of the hand.

Harar is essentially a commercial town: its citizens live, like those of Zayla, by systematically defrauding the Galla Badawin, and the Amir has made it a penal offence to buy by weight and scale. The citizens seem to have a more than Asiatic apathy, even in pursuit of gain. When we entered, a caravan was set out for Zayla on the morrow, after ten days, hardly half of its number had mustered.

Harar is still, as of old, the great 'halfway house' for slaves from Zangaro, Gurage and the Galla tribes. Abyssinians and Amharas, the most valued, have become rare since the King of Showa prohibited the exportation. Women vary in value from 100 to 400 Ashfaris, boys from 9 to 150: the worst are kept for domestic purposes, the best are driven by the Western Arabs or the subjects of the Imam of Muskat, in exchange for rice and dates. I need scarcely say that commerce would thrive on the decline of slavery: whilst the Falateas or manrazzias are allowed to continue, it is vain to expect industry in the land.

Follow this lane for 150m and a left turn will bring you to **Ras Mekonnen's Palace** [419 G3], said by some to date to the late 1890s and by others to 1910. Showing a clear Indian architectural influence, this house is said to be where Ras Tefari (the future Emperor Haile Selassie) spent much of his childhood, though I can find no outside confirmation of this local hearsay. Indeed, more reliable sources suggest that Ras Mekonnen built this palace for his close friend and ally Menelik II (who, as it transpired, never had occasion to visit Harar after its construction) and that Ras Tefari actually grew up in a double-storey house situated near Harar Mikael Church and the associated Tomb of Ras Mekonnen off the Jijiga road about 1.5km south of the walled town. Partially gutted during the Italian occupation, the former palace was restored as a museum and library in the early 1970s, and formally opened by Haile Selassie, but this venture evidently didn't survive the Derg – today, the house is occupied by a traditional herbal practitioner who, so the sign informs us, is able to cure anything from gastritis to cancer.

Next door to the former palace is the building referred to locally as Rambo's House – Rambo being Rimbaud – the house he is said to have rented when he lived in Harar. A vaguely oriental double-storey building constructed by an Indian merchant, **Rimbaud's House** [419 G2] (*entrance US$1.50*) is architecturally notable for its frescoed ceiling (which locals say was painted by the poet) and offers great views over the town. But it's questionable whether Rimbaud ever rented the place. So far as I can ascertain, the house was built in 1908, a full 17 years after Rimbaud's untimely death in France, caused by complications resulting from the amputation of an infected leg. Even if the timing is flawed, it is conceivable that Rimbaud did once live in an older house on the same site, but more likely the association stems from the house having been featured in a movie about the poet's life.

Restored with the help of the Italian and French embassies and various other organisations, Rimbaud's House now functions as a museum. The ground-floor displays, dedicated to the poet, are arguably of marginal interest, with the exception of a couple of photographs taken during his stay in Harar. Far more compelling is the first-floor collection of turn-of-the-20th-century photographs of Harar. Providing a fascinating perspective on the modern development of the town, this collection disproves any talk of an unchanging Harar. The plain, one-storey, flat-roofed mud dwellings of the period bear less resemblance to anything seen here today than they do to houses found in some parts of the west African Sahel (or for that matter to the Argobba houses at nearby Koremi). Likewise, the traditional 'ball' hairstyles and plain robes worn by the women of Harar a century ago have now all but vanished in favour of more generic Ethiopian braided hairstyles and bright, colourful dresses. Also of interest are photographs of Medhane Alem Church while it was under construction, and Erer and Fallana gates before they crumbled away. Excellent stuff – all the better if you're fortunate enough to be led around by the articulate and erudite curator Shakib Ahmed!

Heading back to Mekina Girgir, a short walk downhill leads you to the **Gidir Megala** [419 G2] (Grand Market), which is also sometimes referred to as the Muslim Market to distinguish it from its Christian and Oromo counterparts outside the city walls. One of the liveliest urban markets in Ethiopia, particularly on Saturdays, the market is today dominated by a rather monolithic Italian-era building. On the east side of the market, the whitewashed **Tomb of Sheik Said Ali Hamdogn**, an early leader of Harar, stands above a subterranean water source that can reputedly meet the needs of the whole town in time of drought. Immediately north of this stands the former Egyptian Bank.

Ask your guide to show you the inside of a **traditional Harari *gey gar*** (city house), about 100 of which still survive more or less intact, including one said to have been built for Emir Yusuf in the 18th century. As viewed from the outside, the houses of Harar are unremarkable rectangular blocks occasionally enlivened by an old carved door. But the design of the interiors is totally unique to the town. The ground floor has an open plan, and is dominated by a carpet-draped raised area where all social activity (ie: chewing *chat*) takes place. The walls are decorated with small niches and dangling items of crockery, including the famed Harar baskets, some of which are hundreds of years old. Above the main door are grilles from where carpets are hung to indicate there is a daughter of marriageable age in the family. When the carpets come down, newlyweds in Harar take residence in a tiny corner cell, where they spend their first week of wedlock in cramped, isolated revelry, all they might need being passed to them by relatives through a small service window.

Sprawling in a broadly westerly direction from the old city walls, the so-called **new town**, much of which dates to the Italian era, supports the majority of Harar's total population of around 100,000, but holds little of interest to tourists. The **Christian Market** [off map 419 F1] now located 500m southwest of the Belayneh Hotel (the original market located outside Showa Gate burnt down under suspicious circumstances) is worth a look, bustling as it is with mostly Oromo vendors who've come in from the villages for the day. For students of colonial architecture, the Italian-built **town hall** a block away from the Harar Gate is a rather impressive example of the genre, while art enthusiasts might want to inspect the **Statue of Ras Mekonnen** [418 C2], cast in bronze by the renowned local artist Afewerk Tekle, between the town centre and the Ras Hotel. Further out of town, about 5km along the Jijiga road and reached easily by shared taxi, the church and cemetery at Deker offer a good view over the walled city (best for photography in the afternoon).

Should the historical sightseeing start to wear you out, a worthwhile and somewhat more thirst-quenching excursion is to the **Harar Beer Factory**, which opened in 1984 and was bought out by Heineken in 2011. It can be reached in ten minutes on foot from the old Christian Market using a short cut. The best time to go is in the morning (08.00–11.00), when the general manager is in his office and can arrange a half-hour tour of the factory and possibly free souvenirs such as a T-shirt and baseball cap. After that, you can retire to the factory club, which has DSTV, the cheapest beer in town and reasonably priced hot meals.

The hyena men

One of Harar's most enduringly popular attractions is its resident hyena men. There are currently two hyena men, who make their living by feeding wild hyenas, thereby providing proof (were any needed) that Ethiopians are capable of perversity far beyond the call of duty. Exactly how and when this bizarre practice arose is an open question. One story is that it started during the great famine of the 1890s, during which, it is said, the people of Harar fed the starving hyenas in an altogether less deliberate way. Most other sources indicate that it is a more modern phenomenon, probably no more than 50 years old. So far as I'm aware, the earliest written account of the hyena man was published in a 1958 edition of the *Ethiopian Observer*. I have also recently received a letter from long-time Ethiophile Harry Atkins, who says: 'I was in Harar in 1949 and there was no hyena man; on another visit in 1959 he was there.' This dating would appear to be confirmed by one of the incumbent hyena men, Yusuf Pepe, who told me that he is the fifth in line, and that the practice was started by a man called Dozo in the 1950s.

In 1990, Ahmed Zekaria of the Institute of Ethiopian Studies wrote an essay indicating that the practice of feeding hyenas may be loosely rooted in a much older annual ceremony called Ashura, which takes place in Harar on 7 Muhharam (normally 9 July). According to the tradition related by Zekaria, the festival dates back to a famine many centuries ago, which forced the wild hyenas in the hills around Harar to attack livestock and even people. The people of Harar decided to feed the hyenas porridge to stave off their hunger, and after the famine ended they renewed their pact annually by leaving out a bowl of porridge covered in rich butter near Abobker shrine during the Ashura Festival. It is said that the hyenas' reaction to the porridge is a portent for the year ahead. If they eat more than half of the porridge, then the year ahead will be bountiful, but if they refuse to eat, or they eat the lot, then famine or pestilence is predicted. The practice of feeding meat to the hyenas on a daily basis is obviously quite a leap from an annual feeding ceremony involving porridge, but the Ashura Festival does indicate that the performance of the modern hyena man is rooted in a more ancient custom.

As something of a footnote to the above, Paul Clammer writes:

> Ashura commemorates the death of Hussein, grandson of the prophet Muhammad, at the Battle of Kerbala in AD680. This battle created an ongoing schism between the two strands of Islam – those who thought the successor to Muhammad should be elected and those who favoured the hereditary claims of Hussein. The former won the battle and went on to form the majority Sunni branch of Islam, while the losers now form the numerically smaller Shia branch, which commemorates the martyrdom of Hussein at the Ashura Festival. All well and good, but Ethiopia's Muslims are exclusively Sunni and thus don't recognise Ashura, which means that whatever link exists between Ashura and the feeding of hyenas in Harar must be obscure and interesting indeed.

However and whenever it started, a visit to the hyena man will rank as a highlight of any visit to Harar. Having seen plenty of hyenas in less contrived proximity, I must confess that I first went with a fair degree of scepticism. To my surprise, I ended up greatly enjoying the atmospheric spectacle, which starts at around 19.00, and takes place at one of two feeding sites outside the walled city: these are the shrine of Aw Anser Ahmed (between Erer and Sanga gates) and the Christian slaughterhouse (outside Fallana Gate). The ritual is that the hyena man starts calling the hyenas by name, then, after ten minutes or so, the animals appear from the shadows. Timid at first, the hyenas are soon eating bones passed to them by hand, and the hyena man teases them and even passes them bones from his mouth (visitors are invited to do the same thing).

Some reservations should be voiced regarding the wisdom of feeding hyenas. Hyenas skulk around the fringes of many African towns. Under normal circumstances they are far too timid for there to be a serious likelihood of them attacking people, but nevertheless they are Africa's second-largest predator and potentially very dangerous. Hand-feeding a hyena is, in essence, habituating it – or in plainer English, making it lose its fear of people. In *A Far Country*, a book based on a visit to Ethiopia in 1988, Philip Marsden-Smedley reports that, on the very day he was in Harar, a hyena mauled an Oromo woman close to town. The hyena was shot and Marsden-Smedley, at the time unwittingly, watched the hyena men feed its carcass to its companions.

Most people organise to see the hyena man through a guide. The rate is US$3 per person though some unscrupulous guides may tell you it costs US$6 – it doesn't! Taxi and guide fees are additional. The taxi isn't strictly necessary – the hyena man operates barely 100m outside of the city walls – but the headlights are useful for seeing the hyenas in the dark, and having seen a hyena's jaw in close-up action, you may be glad of the protection when you head back into town. Head out of the walled city through Erer Gate and turn right along the road that runs along the outside of the city wall, passing the Harar Clinic, a mosque and a small stadium to your left. After about 300m, on the left side of the road, you'll see Aw Ansar Ahmed Shrine, a whitewashed edifice intertwined with the trunk and roots of a large fig tree. Yusuf Pepe, the hyena man [419 H2], lives in the house right next to the shrine, and will set up a feeding session with a couple of hours' notice. The second hyena man [419 F4] operates outside of the Fallana Gate – if you ask around someone will find him.

EXCURSIONS FROM HARAR

AWEDAY AND ALEMAYA The small towns of Aweday and Alemaya are situated along the Dire Dawa road some 5km and 10km from Harar respectively. The former is renowned as the site of the country's largest *chat* **market**, where copious amounts of eastern Ethiopia's finest are sold for distribution to Addis Ababa and elsewhere. Alemaya, by contrast, is of interest mainly for the eponymous lake that flanks the Dire Dawa road on its northern outskirts – the most southerly and accessible of a chain of freshwater bodies that also includes lakes Adele, Hora Jutu and Finkile. When full, **Lake Alemaya** often supports considerable concentrations of greater and lesser flamingo, as well as large numbers of white pelican, avocet, black-tailed godwit and up to 10,000 red-knobbed coots. Until recent years, the lake was at its best during the European winter, when a profusion of migrant waterfowl and waders boosted the resident birds. Since the late 1990s, however, Alemaya has tended to drain completely during the dry season, the start of which more or less coincides with the arrival of Palaearctic migrants to east Africa. Any vehicle heading between Harar and Dire Dawa can drop you at Aweday or Alemaya.

EJERSO GWORO Situated high in the mountains some 25km northeast of Harar as the crow flies, the village of Ejerso Gworo is known primarily as the birthplace of Ras Tefari Mekonnen on 23 July 1892. The future emperor's parents Ras Mekonnen and his wife Yeshimebet had been unfortunate with their previous children, so they deliberately chose Ejerso Gworo for the occasion, in accordance with an ancient Ethiopian belief that the chance of a problematic birth decreases at a higher altitude. Surprisingly, perhaps, there is no obvious shrine at Ejerso Gworo to commemorate the birth of Haile Selassie – the last emperor did at one point consider renaming the village Bethlehem, but eventually he settled on constructing a church dedicated to Kidane Mihret there. *En route* to Ejerso Gworo, the road from Harar passes through the somewhat larger town of Kombolcha, which is known for its bustling daily *chat* **market**, the surrounding green countryside studded with rustic Oromo villages, and an immense cavern in the surrounding farmland. (Note that this is a different Kombolcha from the one near Dessie – apparently a third town also shares this name!)

In a private vehicle, Ejerso Gworo can easily be visited as a day trip out of Harar – expect the drive to take up to 90 minutes in either direction. There is no shortage of public transport covering the 18km road between Harar and Kombolcha, and there are a few basic lodges to choose from should you want to overnight there. Transport on to Ejerso Gworo is rather more erratic, but you shouldn't have to wait for an indecently long time, and there is at least one basic hotel there should the need arise.

KOROMI The clifftop village of Koromi, situated some 17km southeast of Harar, is reputedly one of the oldest settlements in this part of Ethiopia – indeed, some locals claim that it actually pre-dates Harar. Legend has it that Koromi's founder was a north African holy man named Emir Abu Bakr, who led his followers to Ethiopia via Yemen and Somalia circa AD1130. Known locally as the Argobba (which translates more or less as 'Arrivals'), the refugees settled briefly at Deker, 5km from present-day Harar along the Jijiga road, but were made to feel unwelcome there and eventually moved further south to what is now Koromi. According to this legend, the antecedents of the Harari people later migrated to the area from the vicinity of present-day Awash National Park and forged a good relationship with the Argobba, with whom they founded the city of Harar.

Today, the Argobba inhabit much of the hilly country immediately southeast of Harar, where they use sophisticated methods of terracing to grow cash crops such as coffee and *chat*. They share a common religion with their Harari neighbours, and they also speak the same language, albeit with an accent sufficiently different for any local to know the difference. Strongly traditional, with a general appearance similar to that of the Oromo, the Argobba are renowned for the beauty of their women, who certainly tend to be a striking apparition as they stroll through the countryside adorned by colourful robes, beaded jewellery and braided hair. They are also known for their 'double-faced' clothing, which can be worn either way around – the colourful side is reserved for weddings and other festive occasions, the black side for funerals.

Boasting an imperious clifftop setting chosen for its defensibility, Koromi is a labyrinthine conglomeration of a few dozen tightly packed stone houses, most if not all of which are many hundreds of years old. The interiors are similar to the traditional homesteads of Harar, with the main difference being that they remain unplastered and unpainted, while the rectangular stone exteriors, reminiscent of some Tigraian houses, collectively evoke what Harar itself must have looked like in Burton's day. The views from Koromi are stunning, stretching for miles across the plains to Mount Gendebure in the vicinity of Kombolcha.

Accessible only in a private vehicle or on foot, Koromi can be reached by following the Jijiga road out of Harar as far as Deker, where you need to turn right onto a rough and easily missed 4x4 track. After about 8.5km you pass through the tiny but delightfully named settlement called Hajifaj, in memory of an 18th-century holy man whose tomb stands in Harar. Hajifaj is the site of an important local market every Monday and Friday, when there may be some public transport there from Deker. Koromi lies another 4km past Hajifaj, passing a striking balancing rock formation immediately to your right about three-quarters of the way there. No formal facilities for tourism exist at Koromi, so it is advisable to take a guide from Harar to ensure all goes smoothly.

MOUNT KUNDUDO Situated about 20km northeast of Harar as the crow flies (but double that distance by road), Mount Kundudo – whose beauty was extolled by Burton when he followed its base *en route* to Harar in 1855 – is a striking 2,900m-tall *amba* (flat-topped mountain) comprising a limestone base and a basaltic cap. Undeveloped for tourism at the time of writing, it offers a wealth of natural and archaeological attractions, and is the centrepiece of a proposed conservation area being lobbied for by the Italian ecologist and professor Marco Viganó (*www.etio.webs.com*).

Kundudo is known for its beautiful scenery, including the spectacular Immis Falls, and as the site of one of only three feral horse populations in Africa. There are several old Islamic shrines in the area, including a tall stone tower dedicated to Sheikh Adem, and recent expeditions led by Viganó have discovered several rock-art sites, as well as the most important and beautiful limestone cave system in the country. It can be explored from Fugnan Bira, the reasonably substantial capital of Gursum district, which lies at an elevation of around 2,000m at the mountain's base. There are regular minibuses from Harar to Fugnan Bira, which has a few hotels.

With thanks to Yirmed Demeke of the Institute of Biodiversity Conservation

The arid country to the south of Harar supports an isolated and somewhat vulnerable elephant population afforded nominal protection in the Babile Elephant Sanctuary, which extends over roughly 7,000km² between the Gobelle River about 30km south of Harar and the Fafen River southwest of Jijiga. Some authorities assign the elephants of Babile to a unique race, *Loxodonta africana orleansi*, partially on the basis of their small tusks – though, given that reduced tusk size is a predictable feature of any elephant subpopulation that has suffered selective poaching for ivory, further molecular and morphological analysis will be required to determine the validity of this taxonomic distinction. Either way, following their probable extinction in Somalia, this is the last extant elephant population to occur in the eastern Horn of Africa, and it must thus be regarded as a high conservation priority. The sanctuary also provides refuge to the black-maned Abyssinian lion, various antelope including greater and lesser kudu, the striking hamadryas baboon, and a spectacular selection of dry-country birds, including the endemic Salvadori's serin.

Despite the establishment of the sanctuary in 1962, the range of this isolated elephant population is thought to have shrunk by about 65% in the last 20 years, with the part of the sanctuary east of the Dakata River having been abandoned some 15 years ago. Meanwhile, the population has halved from an estimated 300 individuals in the 1970s to a minimum of 148 elephants today. According to the rangers, however, the current tally does represent a significant increase on a mid-1990s estimate of around 75 individuals, a suggestion supported by the high proportion of calves (including 16 yearlings) counted in 2004–05. The elephants are sustained by seasonal movements between the Erer and Gobelle river valleys, and some travels were also noted to the west bank of the Dakata River during the transitional period of movement between these valleys. The elephants sometimes move outside the sanctuary, particularly to the western ridge of the Gobelle Valley for an average of 12km, about 17km north of the sanctuary following the Gobelle and Hamaresa valleys, and to a part of the Upper Erer Valley some 12km outside its northern boundary.

The best time of year to seek out the elephants is from mid November to early March, when they congregate in the part of the Upper Gobelle Gorge that runs through Fedis district, about an hour's drive south of Harar. To get there, from Harar town, follow the Dire Dawa road out of town for about 2km, and then turn onto the Fedis road, which branches to the left about 500m past the Abadir Guesthouse and immediately in front of a large green mosque opposite a Total garage. After about 24km, you pass through the small town of Boku, capital of Fedis district (and often just referred to as Fedis), from where you need to continue driving for another 6–22km, depending on where the elephants are currently hanging out. If you are fortunate, you might find a herd resting under the ficus sycamore trees on the close rim of the gorge. If not, you will need to trek to the valley floor. This is a steep hike that requires a fair level of agility and takes about 30 minutes in either direction, but it comes with a near certainty of spotting elephants between December and February, particularly at around 06.00–11.00 and 16.00–18.00 when the animals are most active.

The other good time of year to look for the elephants is between June and September, when they are concentrated in the Upper Erer Valley to the southeast of Harar. There are two motorable tracks to this area, one of which branches south from the Harar–Jijiga road at Bisidimo, 18km out of Harar, while the other branches south about 17km closer to Babile. Both tracks lead to the 'Menschen for Menschen' compound, from where you must drive another 6km south before you disembark. It can take up to 90 minutes to hike into the valley, but the walk is not difficult because there is no gorge. The vegetation in this area is very thick and the disturbance level by cattle herders is high, so the elephants tend to lurk in the densest acacia-cactus vegetation in the heat of the day, when they can be difficult to locate – and are prone to aggressive behaviour when surprised. The chance of seeing the elephants is highest in the evening and early morning, when they are most mobile (and it is also less likely you will startle them by stumbling on them at close quarters).

Assuming that you have access to a 4x4 (hireable through any guide in Harar), the biggest obstacle to visiting Babile Elephant Sanctuary at present is the daft bureaucratic logistics. In order to visit the sanctuary, you must first check in at the office to pick up the mandatory game scout (without whose assistance you would be unlikely to locate any elephants) and to pay the associated fee of US$5.50 per party. Unfortunately, this office is situated in Babile, 30km east of Harar in the opposite direction to the Gobelle Gorge, which enforces quite a bit of unnecessary driving on prospective visitors, especially during the dry season. Furthermore, because the office is open from 08.30 to 17.00 only, and the best time to seek out the elephants is in the early morning, you will probably need to drive out to Babile the day before you want to visit the sanctuary to pick up the scout and take him with you to sleep in Harar (which can be arranged for an extra US$5.50). The office doesn't have a phone, but another possibility would be to ask the Ethiopian Wildlife Department in Addis Ababa (☏ 011 551 4183) to radio through to arrange for a scout to meet you in Harar. Either way, the well-hidden office in Babile lies about 200m along an unsignposted side road running north from the main Harar–Jijiga road almost directly opposite the 'Bank of Abyssinia 557km' signboard – if in doubt try asking for *zihon bero* (elephant keepers' office).

The good news is that there's serious talk of relocating the sanctuary office from Babile to Harar, or at least opening a sub-office and posting some scouts in Harar. It is also possible that old tracks leading right into the elephants' territory will be repaired, so that they can be sought by vehicle rather than on foot. There is no accommodation in the reserve and it can easily be visited as a day trip out of Harar, but camping in both valleys is possible provided you are careful and take guards from the sanctuary office and possibly militia. Unless you already have a vehicle or are prepared to rent one, the sanctuary is inaccessible on public transport – the closest you could get is Boku, which has a couple of basic lodges and is passed through by elephants once in a blue moon, but the odds of that happening during a one-off visit are as good as zero.

Note *This area has recently experienced outbreaks of banditry and violence and may be unsafe. Before making a visit, ask in Harar about current safety conditions.*

BABILE AND THE VALLEY OF MARVELS The small town of Babile, which straddles the Jijiga road about 30km east of Harar, gives its name not only to a popular brand of bottled sparkling water but also to Ethiopia's only elephant sanctuary. Ironically, however, the sparkling water is now bottled at a factory in Harar, which also forms the most logical base from which to visit the eponymous sanctuary (see box, *Babile Elephant Sanctuary*, page 428). Babile does host a busy general market on Saturdays, as well as an important camel market on Mondays and Thursdays, but the main point of local interest is the so-called Valley of Marvels, which is traversed by the Jijiga road 5–10km east of town.

A desolate landscape of red earth, low acacia scrub, forbidding cacti and tall chimney-like termite mounds, the Valley of Marvels is renowned for its gravity-defying balancing rock formations, most especially Dakata Rock, which appears to be just one puff away from collapse. The rock lies close to the Jijiga road, about 7km past Babile, so the best idea is to catch a bus to Jijiga and ask to be dropped at Dakata (marked by a few stalls). A good trail starts at the telegraph pole with '36+600' written vertically down it. Inhabited by colourful Oromo pastoralists, the Dakata area also hosts a fair bit of wildlife, most visibly warthog and hamadryas baboon, but various antelope and the occasional lion and hyena are also seen. The dry-country birdlife is terrific.

Coming from Harar, it is easy enough to get to the Valley of Marvels and back in a day using public transport, since minibuses between Harar and Babile only take an hour. You could also stop at the valley *en route* between Harar and Jijiga. Alternatively, a few basic hotels can be found in Babile, none of which charges more than US$2 for a room – the Samson Hotel on the Harar side of town looks about the best.

JIJIGA

Situated 106km east of Harar along an excellent surfaced road, Jijiga is the capital of Ethiopia's Somali Federal Region and one of the country's fastest-growing towns, with a population estimated at 120,000. It is the closest Ethiopian town to the unrecognised state of Somaliland, which is still officially part of Somalia, despite having functioned as an independent state since 1991. Jijiga has close trade links with Hargeisa, the capital of Somaliland, and the vast majority of travellers who visit this otherwise rather out-of-the-way town are bound for the border post at Tog Wajaale, 75km to the east. Jijiga has existed by that name at least since 1842, when the explorer W C Barker mentioned it as a stopover along the caravan route between Zeila and Harar. By the time Captain Swayne passed through in 1893, it comprised a stockaded fort with a garrison of 25 men next to a group of wells.

On first contact, Jijiga must be classed a disappointment. Despite its antiquity and status as regional capital, it comes across as just another lowland town, one with a less perceptible Somali feel than might be expected or hoped for. That perception might change, however, when you are confronted by Jijiga's focal point: a vast sprawling market, of interest not so much for any traditional goods, but rather for secondhand and electronic goods that have fallen off the back of Somaliland. Arguably the best thing about Jijiga, however, is the drive there from Harar, which passes through the spectacular Valley of Marvels outside Babile (see above) and the impressive and well-wooded Karamara Mountains (the latter reputedly unsafe to climb due to the presence of landmines, a relic of a clash between Ethiopian and Somali forces in the 1970s).

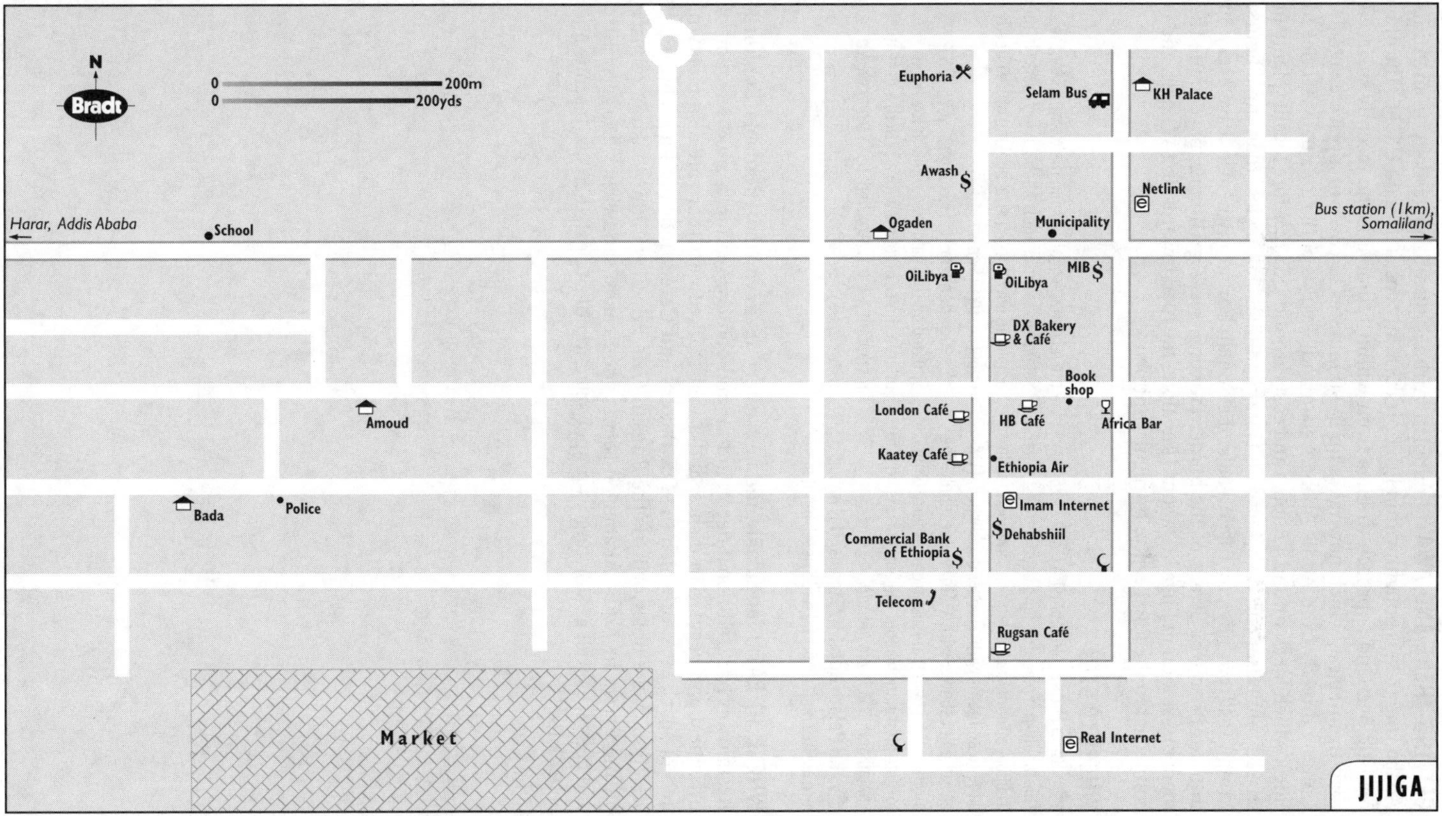

JIJIGA

Bus station (1km),
Somaliland

KH Palace

Netlink

Selam Bus

Municipality

MIB

Africa Bar

Euphoria

OiLibya

DX Bakery
& Café

Book
shop

HB Café

Ethiopia Air

Imam Internet
Dehabshiil

Awash

Ogaden

OiLibya

London Café

Kaatey Café

Commercial Bank
of Ethiopia

Telecom

Rugsan Café

Real Internet

200m
200yds

0
0

School

Harar, Addis Ababa

Amoud

Police

Bada

Market

N

Bradt

GETTING THERE AND AWAY Ethiopian Airlines flies to Jijiga daily from Addis Ababa, and tickets bought within Ethiopia currently cost a bargain US$56. The only realistic overland approach to Jijiga from within Ethiopia is the recently surfaced road from Harar, which now takes up to 90 minutes to cover in a private vehicle. Coming directly from Addis Ababa, Selam and Sky Bus both run a daily service to Jijiga, which takes around 12 hours and costs around US$22. More locally, plenty of shared minibuses run daily between Harar and Jijiga, taking less than three hours. Minibuses from Jijiga to Tog Wajaale, the Somali border town, also leave every 30 minutes or so (for details of the border crossing, see *Tog Wajaale*, page 430). The main bus station in Jijiga lies about 1km along the road towards Tog Wajaale, and is connected to the town centre by regular minibuses.

WHERE TO STAY

Bada Hotel (40 rooms) ✆025 775 2841. This family-run place has long been the best hotel in Jijiga, offering comfortable accommodation in large clean rooms with a proper double bed, TV & en-suite hot shower with a 24hr water supply. The brothers who own it are also a good source of up-to-date information about the border crossing into Somaliland. *US$15 en-suite dbl.*

KH Palace Hotel (25 rooms) This isn't as nice as the similarly priced Bada Hotel, but it has the advantage of also being the terminus for the Selam bus to/from Addis Ababa, which parks in the adjoining open lot & has its booking office directly opposite. *US$15 en-suite dbl.*

Ogaden Hotel (15 rooms) ✆025 775 4990. Situated on the main road through town, this offers a choice of rooms with a ¾ bed. A decent restaurant & bar is attached. *US$5 using shared showers, US$8 en suite.*

WHERE TO EAT

Indisputably the best eatery in town, the affordable **Euphoria Restaurant** has traditional décor, indoor and outdoor seating, a good selection of fish, meat and vegetarian dishes, and a well-stocked bar. There are also plenty of decent snack bars, of which the **DX Bakery and Café** stands out for its breakfast selection. More noteworthy is the **Rugsan Café**, which wouldn't look out of place on the Piazza in Addis Ababa – it serves good cakes, sandwiches, burgers, juice and coffee, as well as stocking a bumper selection of imported crisps, biscuits and chocolates.

Part Five

SOUTHERN ETHIOPIA

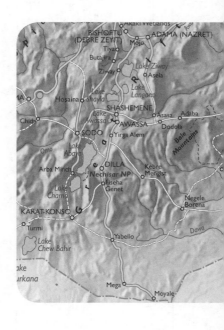

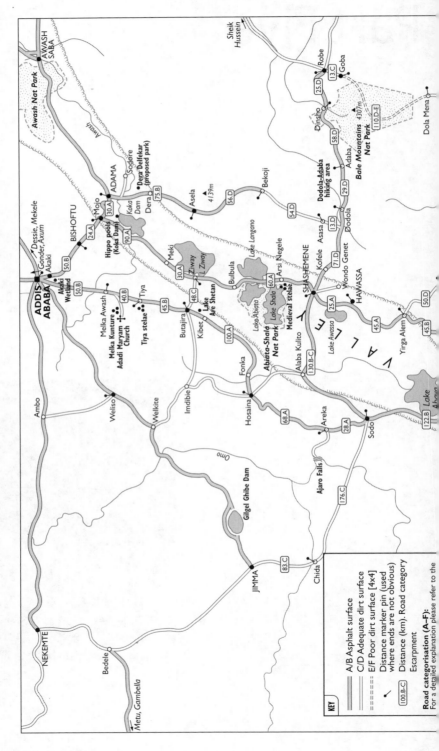

KEY

A/B Asphalt surface
C/D Adequate dirt surface
E/F Poor dirt surface [4x4]

Distance marker pin (used
where ends are not obvious)

100.B-C Distance (km). Road category

Escarpment

Road categorisation (A–F):
For a detailed explanation please refer to the

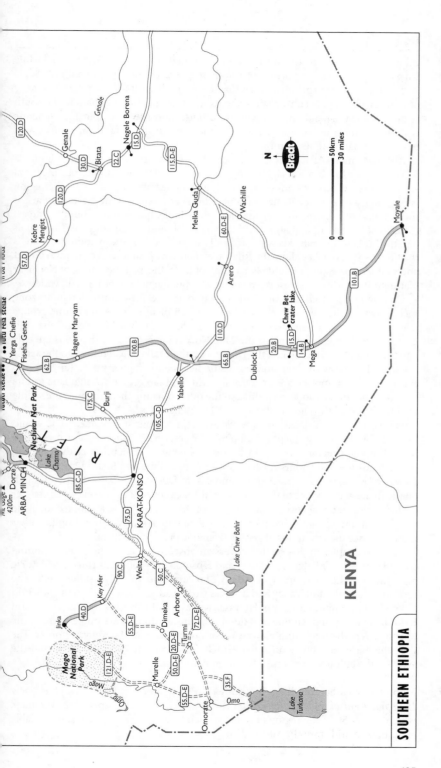

SOUTHERN ETHIOPIA

KENYA

120.D
Genale
30.D
Bitata
22.C
Negele Borena
15.D
115.D-E
120.D
Kebre
Mengist
57.D
Melka Guda
Wachille
60.D-E
Arero
Moyale
101.B
Tutu Fela stelae
Yerga Chefie
Fiseha Genet
Hagere Maryam
62.B
100.B
10.D
65.B
Dublock
20.B
Chew Bet
crater lake
15.D
14.B
Mega
Nechisar Nat Park
Burji
175.C
105.C-D
Yabello
Lake
Chamo
85.C-D
ARBA MINCH
Dorze
Mt Guge
4200m
KARAT-KONSO
75.D
Lake Chew Bahir
90.C
Weita
50.C
Key Afer
40.D
Jinka
55.D-E
Dimeka
Arbore
72.D-E
Mago
National
Park
121.D-E
20.D-E
Turmi
50.D-E
Murelle
55.D-E
Omorate
Omo
35.F
Lake
Turkana

50km
30 miles
N
0
0

Genale
Genale

OVERVIEW

Ethiopia is not one of the world's more crowded travel destinations, and while I have no idea what proportion of travellers to the country head south of Addis Ababa, I would be surprised to learn that it is more than 20%. Given the singularity of northern Ethiopia's cultural sites, the relatively scant attention paid to the south is understandable enough. And yet, were north and south to split into separate countries tomorrow, southern Ethiopia could more than stand on its feet as a tourist destination in its own right.

Although most African countries pale by comparison with southern Ethiopia when it comes to historical sightseeing – rock-hewn churches, mysterious medieval stelae and remote monasteries being among its underrated attractions – the region is of primary interest for its natural and cultural attractions. **Bale National Park** is the best part of Ethiopia for viewing endemic wildlife, home to the country's largest (though still scarce) populations of Ethiopian wolf and mountain nyala, as well as half the birds whose range is restricted to Ethiopia and Eritrea. In addition, there is the lovely string of lakes along the Rift Valley floor, the lush forests of **Wondo Genet** and southern Bale, the vast arid plains south of Dilla, the majestic setting of **Nechisar National Park**. This, in short, is a region of exceptional natural beauty and variety.

Culturally, the highlight of southern Ethiopia is **South Omo**, a remote zone tucked against the Kenyan border where a dozen or more different ethnic groups live – and decorate themselves – in a manner that scarcely acknowledges the 20th century ever happened, let alone the 21st. No less interesting are the Konso people and their walled stone villages, the Dorze with their tall conical huts, and the semi-nomadic Borena with their precious cattle herds and singing wells. Tangled into this rich cultural mosaic are the Oromo, Ethiopia's largest ethno-linguistic group, with one foot in the modern world, and the other hoisting them up onto the saddle to ride blanketed through the frosty Bale Highlands.

Southern Ethiopia lacks for any clearly defined tourist circuit, and it would be limiting rather than helpful to attempt to describe it in terms of a prescribed loop. The main regional transport hub is Shashemene, which lies at the junction of the roads north to Addis Ababa, west to Arba Minch and South Omo, south to Hawassa (Awassa), Dilla and Moyale, and east to Dodola and Bale. Passing through Shashemene, it is possible to travel between the area covered in any one given chapter in this section and that covered in another. For this reason, I have attempted to divide this section into chapters that more or less define themselves as travel units, rather than sequence them in terms of getting from one place to another.

The first chapter in this section covers an obscure but rewarding route running south from Addis Ababa to **Butajira** and **Hosaina** via **Melka Kunture Prehistoric Site**, the rock-hewn **Church of Adadi Maryam**, and the **Tiya stelae field**. The second follows the Rift Valley and its lakes from Addis Ababa south to the junction town of **Shashemene** and city of **Hawassa** (Awassa). The third covers the wonderful trekking country and wildlife of **Bale Mountains National Park** and environs. The fourth covers the road from Hawassa south to **Moyale** on the Kenyan border. The fifth chapter concentrates on **Arba Minch** and **Nechisar National Park**, and the sixth on the cultural wonders of **Konso** and **South Omo**.

Map: For anyone travelling in southern Ethiopia, *National Geographic*'s new *Ethiopia's Central and Southern Rift Valley* (2011) map is indispensable. The map, which covers 50 of the region's top natural, cultural, and historic sites, is available from BookWorld stores in Addis Ababa.

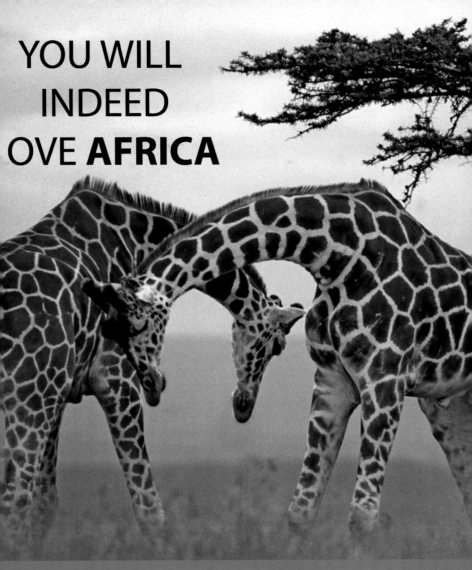

DINKNESH ETHIOPIA TOURS

dinkneshethiopiatour.com
ethiopiatravel.com

WELCOME TO ETHIOPIA

~ TOUR PACKAGES
* Historical & cultural tours
* Adventure tour
* Bird watching tour
* Personal interest tour
* Pilgrimage tour
~ LOGISTIC SUPPORT FOR DOCUMENTARY FILMS
~ CAR HIRE
~ HOTELS AND FLIGHT RESERVATION

Buska Lodge
Environmentally Friendly

Situated in the heart of Southern Ethiopia in the Omo Valley, Buska Lodge is an unpretentious eco-lodge offering travelers the best accommodation and meal service in this region.

Tel: +251-11-1567837/38 Fax: +251-11-1567840 P.O.Box 26563
E-mail: info@buskalodge.com Website: www.buskalodge.com
Addis Ababa, Ethiopia
Lodge Site: Turmi (Hammer), Southern Ethiopia

19

Addis Ababa to the Rift Valley via Butajira

The 125km road between Addis Ababa and Butajira provides access to a string of fascinating and very different archaeological and historical sites, as well as forming an attractive springboard for travel elsewhere in the southern Rift Valley. The main points of interest along this road are the archaeological site of **Melka Kunture**, the rock-hewn **Church of Adadi Maryam** and the **stelae field at Tiya**. South of Butajira, along the road towards Sodo, lie several more isolated stelae, as well as the crater lake of **Areshetan** and the remote **Ajaro Falls**. While these places are under-publicised and little visited by comparison with the more famous sites of northern Ethiopia, and admittedly less overwhelming, I would rate the time I spent exploring them as among the highlights of my Ethiopian travels.

Any of the low-key historical sites between Addis Ababa and Butajira would make for a straightforward day trip from the capital, especially since the asphalt road between Addis Ababa and Butajira opened in 2004. The same road can also be covered as part of a slower and more scenic route between the capital and Lake Ziway in the Rift Valley. With an early start and a private vehicle, you could see all the key sites along the Butajira road and still reach Ziway in one day. An extra day would be required to do the same thing on public transport.

From Butajira, the asphalt continues 100km southward to Hosaina, and reaches Sodo via Areka after another 96km. Seldom used by travellers, this road is now the quickest route between Addis Ababa and Sodo, and seems likely to gain popularity as a genuine short cut between Addis Ababa and South Omo once the terribly pot-holed stretch between Sodo and Arba Minch is repaired.

ADDIS ABABA TO BUTAJIRA

To get to any of the places covered in the following sections, you must follow the Jimma road out of Addis Ababa for 20km to Alem Gena, where the signposted road south to Butajira branches to the left. The distance from Alem Gena to Butajira is roughly 105km: the road reaches Melka Awash after 30km, passes the turn-off to Adadi Maryam after another 5km, and runs through Tiya after a further 35km. Regular public transport connects Addis Ababa to Butajira, leaving from the main Autobus Terra. There is direct transport to Melka Awash and Tiya before 09.00, but later in the day you may have to pay full fare on a bus to Butajira and ask to be dropped. Once on the Butajira road, you may sometimes have to wait a while for transport, as passing buses will often be full, but this situation is likely to improve as the volume of traffic increases following the asphalting of the road.

MELKA AWASH AND MELKA KUNTURE Also known as Awash Dilday, Melka Awash is a small town on the north bank of the Awash River, some 50km from

Addis Ababa by road. It is a good base from which to explore the nearby sites, provided that you can live with very basic accommodation. The Awash River Gorge below the bridge adjoining Melka Awash is also worth exploring. Immediately east of the bridge, at the start of the gorge, the river forms a series of three low but powerful waterfalls, the last of which has a wild, swirling pool at its base and is best viewed from the footpath along the northern rim. Also on the north of the gorge are some substantial patches of acacia woodland, which together with the raptors and swallows circling above the cliffs promise rewarding birdwatching.

The main local attraction is the **Melka Kunture Prehistoric Site** (⊕ *09.00–12.30 & 13.30–17.00 daily; entrance US$2*), which is situated on the south face of the Awash river gorge opposite Melka Awash. Regarded as one of the most important Stone Age sites in Ethiopia, Melka Kunture's potential was first recognised in 1963 by G Dekker, who realised that the layers of rock washed away by the river during the annual floods represented a fossil record covering more than a million years. The first major excavations at the site took place over the period 1965–81, and further excavations occurred over 1991–95. Until recently, the site was closed to casual visitors, but now an informative site museum spread across four *tukuls* displays a good collection of artefacts, including a particularly interesting collection of prehistoric skull replicas modelled after findings throughout Africa. There is also an open-air excavation site and a prehistoric animal butchering site a short walk away. Everything is well described on wall panels, and the curator is usually delighted to welcome a few visitors to his lonely patch!

Melka Kunture is best known for the numerous Stone Age artefacts that have been unearthed along the river, including a variety of cleavers, hand-axes and other tools made from basalt and other hard rocks. The site has also proved to be an important source of fossils of extinct mammal species, including hippo, giraffe, gelada and wildebeest, the last long absent from Ethiopia. Although the site has not yet thrown up any hominid fossils as significant as those unearthed at Hadar or Turkana, several *Homo erectus* fossils have been found, dating back between 1.5 and 1.7 million years. Cranial fragments of early *Homo sapiens*, probably more than 500,000 years old, have also been uncovered.

Situated downstream of the bridge at a bend in the river referred to in Oromifa as **Dubatu**, a vast complex of artificial caves corresponds closely with a mysterious site visited by Francisco Alvarez in 1523 but not identified again until the early 1970s, when Richard Pankhurst wrote an article about it for the *Ethiopia Observer* (vol XVI, no 1). Alvarez describes a 'very strong' town set in 'a very deep hollow … upon a great river, which made a great chasm' that consisted almost entirely of houses carved into the cliff face with an entrance the size of 'the mouth of a large vat' but 'so large inside that 20 or 30 persons could find room there with their baggage'. Alvarez was told that the caves were originally carved by the Gurage, 'a people (as they say) who are very bad, and none of them are slaves, because they say that they let themselves die, or kill themselves, rather than serve Christians.' When he visited, however, the town had been taken over by Christians who had built 'small walled and thatched houses' in the hollow, as well as 'a very good church inside'. In addition, Alvarez describes what is evidently a rock-hewn monastery on a cliff further upstream, built on a crag that 'faces the rising sun', and above which were carved 'fifteen cells for monks, all of which have windows over the water'. According to Pankhurst, the vast caves described by Alvarez, though long abandoned, can still be entered today, while the disused monastery lies nearby at a place called Wagide.

To get to Melka Kunture, follow the Butajira road southwards from Addis Ababa for about 50km until you reach Melka Awash and a large bridge over the Awash

River. About 100m after crossing the bridge towards Butajira, you'll see the signpost for Melka Kunture to your right. (Note that the turn-off is not the same as for the Adadi Maryam rock-hewn church, though it appears so on the map.) From here, it's about 1km to the fenced site, following a motorable dirt road through the fields. There are a few dollar-a-night **hotels** in Melka Awash, all of which have bucket showers. A **restaurant** serves eggs and bread.

ADADI MARYAM (*Entrance US$6; camera/video US$1/6*) The southernmost extant rock-hewn church in Ethiopia, Adadi Maryam lies to the west of the Butajira road on a small hill some five minutes' walk from the village of Adadi. Scholars date the church to sometime between the 12th and 14th centuries, while local tradition associates it with King Lalibela's visit to nearby Mount Zikwala in AD1106. Adadi Maryam is far closer in style to its counterparts at Lalibela than to any rock-hewn church in Tigrai. Although smaller and more roughly hewn, it is, like several Lalibela churches, a subterranean semi-monolith encircled by a wide tunnel containing a few disused monastic cells. It measures 19m long and 16m wide, and has 24 windows and ten doors. The tunnel that leads from the back of the church to a nearby watercourse was carved later to prevent flooding.

It has been suggested that Adadi Maryam was the site of the first meeting, in 1523, between Emperor Lebna Dengal and the Portuguese expedition led by Rodrigo de Lima and documented by the priest Francisco Alvarez. Whether or not this is true, it is known that Ahmed Gragn attacked the church a few years later. Although the excavation survived this raid more or less intact, the large cross above the entrance was severely damaged, and the priests were either killed or forced to flee. The church subsequently fell into disuse, and it remained so for several centuries while the Oromo occupied the surrounding area. Adadi Maryam was discovered by local hunters and reopened during the reign of Menelik II, and it remains in active use today, though its original name has evidently been forgotten – Adadi is the Oromifa name for a type of bush that grows in the vicinity. The Swiss Embassy funded extensive restoration work on the church over 1996–98.

Travellers with sufficient time and interest might want to seek out the disused complex of rock-hewn caves that lies in a small gorge about 2km northwest of Adadi at Laga Degaga. It is thought that these caves housed a monastic community associated with the church prior to the 16th-century attack by Ahmed Gragn.

Getting there and away The turn-off to Adadi, 5km past Melka Awash, is clearly signposted from the Butajira road. The 13km drive from the junction to the church takes less than 30 minutes in a private vehicle. The best days to visit Adadi using public transport are Thursday and Sunday (market days) when pick-up trucks head there from Melka Awash between 07.30 and 09.00 and a bus leaves from the Autobus Terra in Addis Ababa at about 06.00. Once you have viewed the church, you'll probably have to wait an hour or two for transport back to the main road. You might want to fill the time and your stomach with the excellent and inexpensive *shiro wat* served at the restaurant on the edge of the market. On non-market days, there is very little transport to Adadi. There's no sign of accommodation in Adadi, but you could probably ask to pitch a tent somewhere in the village.

TIYA (⊕ *08.00–12.00 & 13.00–17.00 daily; entrance US$3*) Tiya marks the northern limit of a belt of mysterious engraved stelae that stretches across southern Ethiopia through Dilla (on the Moyale road) to Negele Borena (see box, *The stelae of southern Ethiopia*, page 506). Remarkably little is known about the origin of these stelae, or of the meaning of the symbols that are carved upon them. Recent excavations at Tiya revealed that the stones mark the mass graves of males and females who died when they were between 18 and 30 years of age, and who were laid to rest in a foetal position about 700 years ago. The presence of several engraved swords on the stelae suggests that the people buried were soldiers, but this evidence is far from conclusive.

Listed as a UNESCO World Heritage Site, the stelae field at Tiya today comprises some 45 stones of up to 2m in height, several of which had collapsed prior to their careful re-erection in their original positions by a team of French archaeologists of the past decade. The largest stele in the field originally stood 5m high, but only the base remains *in situ* – the top part has been removed to the university in Addis Ababa. Nearly all the stones are engraved. Apart from the stylised swords, the number of which is thought to represent the number of people killed by the warrior it commemorates, two other symbols predominate: plain circles, and what looks like a pair of podgy leaves rising on a stem from a rectangular base. I noticed that where all three symbols were present on one stone, the circles were generally near the top, the swords in the middle and the twin leaves close to the base.

The plain circles appear on about one in ten stones, and seem to denote that a female is buried underneath. The pairs of leaves look like the *enset* (false banana) plantain that is still widely grown in southern Ethiopia. Recent thinking is that they represent a traditional wooden headrest, and are a sort of visual RIP note. On some stones you'll see what looks like a Greek 'E', a symbol for which no plausible interpretation has been thought up. Despite the relative simplicity of the stelae and engravings, I found them very mysterious and haunting. The repetitive intent that apparently lies behind the symbols is no less impressive than the more finely honed and grandiose stelae of Axum.

Tiya invites speculation. Even to the untrained eye, it is clear that these stelae (along with those around Butajira) don't fall neatly into the phallic or anthropomorphic schools of decoration found elsewhere in southern Ethiopia, but represent a third, more ornate style of carving. Because of this, it seems likely that they were erected more recently than their more easterly counterparts, probably between the late 12th century and the early 14th. I thought it significant that, like the stelae at Axum, the only comparable constructions that I'm aware of in sub-Saharan Africa, the Gragn Stones, appear to pre-date the arrival of Christianity to the area, and were definitely erected as grave markers. The Gragn Stone belt passes through the heart of the modern territory of the Gurage, whose language is closely affiliated to Tigrigna and who presumably moved to southern Ethiopia from Tigrai several centuries ago. Lying as it does some 30km south of the roughly contemporaneous rock-hewn church at Adadi, Tiya would appear to mark the medieval boundary between pagan and Christian Ethiopia. Could it also be that the Gragn Stones are remnants of an otherwise-forgotten offshoot of the pre-Christian stelae-building traditions of Axum?

There are vague plans to set up a cultural tourism project at Tiya, which will involve training guides, visiting other sites in the area, and upgrading the presentation of the site.

Getting there and away
Tiya straddles the Butajira road almost 40km south of Melka Awash. The stelae field lies less than 1km out of town. Coming from the direction of Addis, the turn-off to the stones is to your left, less than 100m past the Sisay Mola Hotel near the Telecommunications office. About 200m further, upon reaching a red water tank, turn right. After a minute or two's further walking, you will see the stelae enclosed in a fence on the rise ahead.

Where to stay and eat Should you need to overnight in Tiya, the recently opened **Tiya Nock Hotel** (*12 rooms*) behind the Gas Oil filling station at the Addis Ababa end of town is easily the best bet, with en-suite rooms for around US$5. Otherwise **Sisay Mola Hotel** (*30 rooms;* ☎ *046 264 009*) charges US$3 for a passably clean en-suite room with cold shower only. The attached restaurant should be operating by the time you read this. There are also three or four showerless, dollar-a-night hotels along the main road.

BUTAJIRA

Many travellers who explore the area between Melka Awash and Tiya will be likely to return directly to Addis Ababa. Should you be heading on to the Rift Valley, however, there is plenty of transport to Butajira, a pleasantly green if uninspiring small town boasting an unexpectedly good selection of affordable accommodation. The green highlands around Butajira are very attractive, and there is much to explore in the surrounding area for those with the time and inclination, as covered under the heading *From Butajira to Hosaina* on page 442.

GETTING THERE AND AWAY Regular public transport runs directly between Addis Ababa and Butajira, as well as along the 50km road between Butajira and Ziway in the Rift Valley. A third onward option, definitely worth thinking about if you intend to head directly towards Arba Minch and/or the Lower Omo Valley, would be to continue directly south via Hosaina to Sodo-Walaita. There are regular buses along this surfaced road.

GURAGE

Butajira lies at the heart of Gurage country, a mountainous area lying towards the southern end of the central highlands. The Gurage, the fifth-largest ethno-linguistic group in Ethiopia, are historically affiliated to the Amhara of the northern highlands, and have long associations with its Christian traditions as evidenced by the presence of the rock-hewn church of Adadi Maryam and numerous other abandoned troglodyte dwellings and shrines in their homeland. The Gurage evidently became isolated from Amhara during the time of Ahmed Gragn, and developed independently until they were re-integrated in the 19th century. Today, the area remains a Semitic-speaking enclave surrounded by Oromo and other unrelated peoples, and its people are split between ancient Orthodox Christians and more recent converts to Islam.

The Gurage social structure is unusual in that economic roles are not dictated by caste, class or gender. The Gurage do, however, have a strange relationship with the Watta or Fuga people, who have adopted the Gurage language and customs, and serve the triple role of artisans, hunters and spiritual mediums within Gurage society. It is the Watta who are responsible for erecting the main beams of Gurage houses, which are attractive beehive structures similar to those seen around Sodo and elsewhere in Walaita. A guiding Gurage principle is that 'idleness is a sin, work is the key to success, failure to improve one's land is bad farming and cannot be blamed on the spirits'. Perhaps related to this dictum, perhaps simply because of Gurage's proximity to Addis, there are many Gurage in the city, and they have a reputation for industry, business acumen and also academic success.

WHERE TO STAY AND EAT

Rediet Hotel (50 rooms) \046 115 0803. In spite of the 2 gaudy gold statuettes guarding the entrance, this new multi-storey hotel seems less impressive given its insalubrious location behind the NOC filling station. Failed attempts of grandeur aside, the en-suite rooms each with tiled floors, flat-screen TV & small balcony, while clean & spacious, come off as over-priced. That said, there are 2 good restaurants attached: a ground-floor restaurant serving internationally flavoured dishes & a traditional-thatched restaurant in the garden out the back. *US$40/50 2nd-/1st-class dbl, US$70 twin*.

Fikadu Assore Hotel (50 rooms) \046 115 0443. This multi-storey block is the smartest option, situated 50m from the main road behind the Telecommunications centre. All rooms have satellite TV, carpeting, balcony & clean tiled en-suite hot shower. A decent restaurant is attached. *US$10/13.50/15.50 sgl/dbl/twin*.

Butajira Bright Hotel (48 rooms) \046 115 0564. This new hotel located in the centre above the Smart Internet Café, is Butajira's best budget option. The large en-suite rooms are clean & bright. Rooms facing away from the street are quieter & marginally more expensive. There's also a lively bar & restaurant on the 1st floor overlooking main road serving dishes in the US$1.50–3 range. *US$4.50 using common shower, US$6/7.50 en-suite dbl with street/back view, US$15 family suite*.

FROM BUTAJIRA TO HOSAINA

The 100km surfaced road that runs southwest from Butajira to Hosaina via Kibet passes through some attractive highland scenery and can be covered in about 90 minutes without stops. It also offers access to a few worthwhile off-the-beaten-track sites, of which Lake Ara Shetan and the stelae of Silté are the most accessible, while the more remote Boyo Wetlands are of great ornithological significance. There's plenty of public transport between Butajira and Hosaina, whether you want to bus directly through to Sodo or prefer to explore the area more slowly.

LAKE ARA SHETAN Coming from the north, the first point of interest is Lake Ara Shetan, which stands alongside the Hosaina road at an elevation of 2,281m some 10km south of Butajira. Sometimes referred to by outsiders as Lake Butajira, this pretty emerald-green lake, nestled within the sheer 120m-high walls of an almost perfectly circular explosion crater, has a diameter of around 880m and a depth of at least 50m. It forms the most southerly link in a chain of craters, lava flows and other relics of geologically recent volcanic activity that runs for 80km northeast along the Rift Valley Escarpment as far as the Bishoftu Crater Lakes.

Scenic though it might be, Ara Shetan is viewed as a somewhat malignant presence by locals. Its name literally means 'Lake of Satan', and its creation is ascribed to an evil sorcerer who had fought the local peasants for years before finally he was mortally wounded at the site of the present-day lake. Legend has it that as the sorcerer drew his dying breath, he drove his spear hard into the ground, and bellowed out a curse 'Let this be the devil's home', whereupon the earth below him imploded, swallowed him up and filled with water. A taboo still exists on throwing any stone into the lake – legend has it that the devil would hurl it back even harder at the person who threw it, with fatal consequences.

Invisible from the Hosaina road, Ara Shetan nevertheless lies almost immediately east of it, and the rim is accessible via a 500m motorable track. Any public transport heading between Butajira and Kibet will be able to set you down at the start of this track. With a local guide, it would be possible to walk on from Ara Shetan to the nearby **Aynege Cave**, which is presided over by a Muslim holy man and supposedly connects to the Sof Omar Caves east of the Bale Mountains, as well as to a nearby lake known as Tinishu Abaya (Little Abaya).

SILTÉ Straddling the Hosaina road only 4km southwest of Lake Ara Shetan, **Kibet** is the principal town of the Silté people, whose attractive traditional homesteads with tall, domed thatched roofs can be seen dotted around the surrounding countryside. The Silté area is also known for its many medieval stelae, which are similar in shape and decoration to those found around Tiya, though generally more ornately worked. Unfortunately, archaeologists have removed many of the best stelae to Addis Ababa, and I'm not aware of any stelae field numerically comparable to the one outside Tiya.

The most worthwhile stop in this area is probably the stele known locally as **Asano Dengai**, which is the most intricately worked individual stele I've come across in southern Ethiopia, despite having been decapitated. Asano Dengai stands in isolation below a large fig tree next to a recently built mosque 500m east of the Hosaina road at Ketigora, which lies about 8km south of Kibet overlooking Lake Saida. There is also a cluster of six stelae, all of which are either decapitated or collapsed, at the village of **Wazira**, about 1km from the road between Kibet and Ketigora along a side road signposted for the Wolega Siddist Elementary School. It's worth noting, for those using public transport, that at least one basic **guesthouse** is to be found in Kibet.

BOYO WETLANDS Two sites close to Hosaina are listed in the Important Bird Area inventory published by the Ethiopian Natural History and Wildlife Society. The more interesting and accessible of these sites is the Boyo Wetlands, which consists of an extensive seasonal swamp centred upon Lake Boyo, a shallow but perennial freshwater body also sometimes known as Lake Bilate after the river that flows through its eastern tip to eventually empty into Lake Abaya near Arba Minch. There are some interesting thatched Hadiya homesteads in the lake's hinterland, many painted in geometric designs, and you may also notice modern cemeteries marked with engraved stones reminiscent of (and presumably inspired by) their more ancient counterparts around Silté.

Set at an altitude of around 1,500m near the small town of Bonosha, Lake Boyo was formerly designated a Controlled Hunting Area to protect its heaving hippo population. According to local sources, these hippos were hunted to extinction in 1994, but a couple of refugee pods from Abiata-Shala recently re-colonised the area and are quite regularly seen in the open water. For birders, the wetlands are of greatest interest during the European winter, when thousands upon thousands of migrant waders and ducks converge on the area. Resident species include black-crowned crane and a variety of ibises, egrets and herons. The wetlands are also regarded as possibly the most important northern hemisphere stronghold for the endangered wattled crane – 62 individuals were counted in a 1996 survey, while an expedition in 2004 encountered a flock of 108, the largest aggregation ever recorded in Ethiopia.

Lake Boyo is situated less than 20km east of Hosaina as the crow flies, and the wetlands extend to within 10km of town at the height of the rains. Yet by road you will need to cover 55km just to get to Bonosha, from where you still need to walk for another hour or so to reach the lakeshore. The junction for Bonosha branches east from the Butajira road 31km from Hosaina, at the police checkpoint immediately north of Achamo. From here, it is exactly 24km along a rather poor road to Bonosha, passing through Shashago after 9km, where you need to turn left at the main intersection. It should be possible to make your way to the lake unaccompanied – it lies in a depression about 4km west of town – but it would certainly simplify matters to find a local guide. If you are dependent on public transport, at least one bus daily runs between Hosaina and Bonosha, where very basic **accommodation** can be found near the market square.

The capital of Hadiya zone, Hosaina combines a bustling commercial atmosphere with a feel of dusty parochialism, possibly because it is one of the few Ethiopian towns of comparable size (population 60,000) whose hotels are so seldom troubled by the tourist trade. Set at an altitude of above 2,300m in a mountainous region, Hosaina lies at the core of an important centre of *enset* cultivation, though the region's fertile volcanic soils can grow practically any crop during the rainy season. The town must also be regarded as a route focus of sorts, now that it is connected by good asphalt to Addis Ababa and Sodo.

Hosaina (a local variation on Hosanna) is the main town of the Hadiya, culturally affiliated to the Gurage who speak a vastly different Cushitic language called Hadinya and are traditionally Muslim, though recent years have seen a strong swing towards Protestantism. Hadiya has proved to be a hotbed of anti-government feeling in the post-Derg era. In the build-up to the May 2000 election, five people were killed in the area when security forces threw a live grenade at protesters, and two more died of gun wounds in similar circumstances. Despite central government's attempts both to coerce and to cajole voters in the eventual polling, which was postponed to June in Hadiya, a full 75% of the vote went to two local opposition parties, each of which won one seat in the Council of People's Representatives.

GETTING THERE AND AWAY Although visited by very few travellers, Hosaina is a route focus of sorts, situated at the junction of a 100km road running northeast to Butajira, a 96km road south to Sodo-Walaita, and a 115km road northwest to Welkite – in all cases you are looking at around two hours' drive in a private vehicle. Hosaina is serviced by regular public transport in all directions, including a daily bus service [445 B1] running directly between Addis Ababa and Sodo.

WHERE TO STAY

Heme International Hotel [445 B5] (28 rooms) 046 555 2264. This prominent centrally located stalwart hotel is still a popular choice in spite of its shabbily faded air. The rooms each with carpet, private balcony, en-suite hot showers & TV are large but rather run-down, making it feel a little over-priced. Secure parking is available, & the restaurant is pretty good. *US$11.50/12/17 sgl/dbl/twin.*

Lemme International Hotel [445 B1] (47 rooms) 046 555 4453. This new multi-storey hotel behind the bus station has taken over the mantle from the above as the smartest hotel in town. That said, the en-suite rooms, while clean & neat, fail to match up to the pretentious shiny exterior – especially those with a view of the bus station. Frequented by aid workers & tour groups, it fills up quickly, so make sure you get in early. The ground-floor restaurant & bar also does a roaring trade. *US$8/9 small dbl without/with TV, US$11 standard dbl, US$14 twin.*

Edget Hotel [445 C4 00] (36 rooms) 046 555 2616. Located just off the main roundabout

above the Bank of Abyssinia, this new hotel is far better value than the aforementioned. The modern rooms are bright & clean, the staff are very helpful & secure parking is available. The restaurant & bar are in a separate ground-floor building, so it's pretty quiet – if you can ignore the early morning mosque call that is! *US$7.50 twin using common shower, US$6/9 en-suite dbl without/with TV.*

Canal My House Café & Pension [445 B6] (11 rooms) 046 555 2743. A strong contender for hotel with the most ridiculous name, this amiable place has very reasonably priced clean tiled rooms with queen bed, en-suite hot shower & DSTV. There's also an excellent café on the 1st floor along with a mini market; internet is available free for guests, but secure parking is not. *US$4.50–5.*

Yabsera Hotel [445 B3] (20 rooms) 046 555 2439. This friendly lodge set in a well-maintained old building next to the Millennium Café has a range of low-budget accommodation offerings. En-suite rooms have a proper double bed, hot shower & DSTV. *US$4/5/5.50 with common shower/toilet/en suite.*

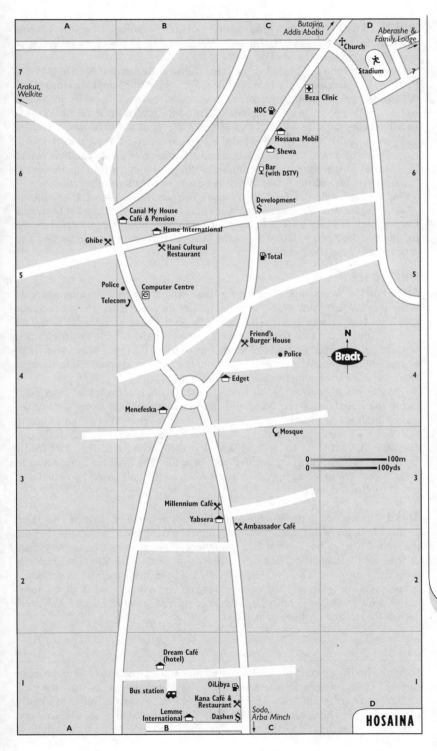

HOSAINA

✖ **WHERE TO EAT** The best – and busiest – hotel restaurant is at the **Lemme International Hotel** [445 B1], which charges around US$2.50–4 for a main course and serves a small selection of pizzas for US$3–5.

Good local food can be had at the **Hani Cultural Restaurant & Café** [445 B5] (📞 046 555 2474) opposite the Heme, while the double-storey **Canal My House Café & Pension** [445 B6] around the corner serves excellent snacks, pastries, juices and coffee. Another good spot – though definitely off the beaten track – is **Aberashe & Family Lodge** [off map 445 D7] (📞 046 555 1800; �① 08.00–20.00 daily). Hidden away in the quiet backstreets behind the stadium around 1.4km from the main road, this relaxed café offers the usual line-up of pasties, cold drinks and light snacks in a relaxed garden setting. At the time of writing the lodge was in the process of building a traditional restaurant as well as bungalow-style accommodation.

For Western-style fast food try **Friend's Burger House** [445 C4] (�① 08.00–16.00 daily) located just north of the main roundabout above Ethiopian Insurance Corporation, or **Mary Café & Restaurant** [445 C1] (�① 06.30–21.00 daily) on the top floor of the Sawo Building above the Dashen Bank, both serving burgers and sandwiches in the US$2–3 range.

WHAT TO SEE

Ajaro Falls
A worthwhile diversion for those driving between Hosaina and Sodo is the scenic Ajaro Falls, which lie to the west of the main road. The falls actually consist of two separate but parallel waterfalls on the Soke and Ajacho rivers, set perhaps 100m apart and plunging over a cliff about 100m high into the thickly wooded gorge formed by the Soke River, a tributary of the Omo. The waterfall can be reached along a 25km turn-off west from the Sodo road about 65km south of Hosaina, and a few kilometres north of the town of Areka.

The viewpoint, easily accessible from the main road, is at the top of a steep cliff facing the waterfalls. A very steep and slippery footpath runs to the base of the gorge, and is used by locals, but be warned that stories abound of people falling to their death – even the sure-footed local livestock sometimes plunge off. At the top, an easy walk leads to the forest-fringed bank of the Ajacho River. There's a friendly traditional Walaita village of beehive huts here too. The distance from Areka to Sodo is only 28km along the new asphalt road, so the falls could be visited as a round trip from there.

Arakit
Situated along the Welkite road about 55km north of Hosaina and 35km south of Imbidir, Arakit is an attractively sprawling small town characterised by the traditional Gurage homesteads and neatly fenced compounds that are so typical of these fertile highlands. Boasting a couple of small local lodgings, Arakit is potentially an excellent base for anybody wishing to immerse themselves in Gurage culture. Also of interest is the eponymous lake immediately north of the town centre, which sometimes hosts large flocks of pelican, ibis and migrant waterfowl such as the striking northern pintail.

SODO

Sodo, the bustling capital of Walaita district, lies at the crossroads where the main surfaced road between Shashemene and Arba Minch intersects with the new asphalt road north from Addis Ababa (or Welkite) via Hosaina as well as to a newly upgraded road to Jimma in western Ethiopia. Often referred to by the district name of Walaita rather than Sodo, this town of around 55,000 people lies at an altitude of around 2,100m on a green and hilly part of the Rift Valley Escarpment notable for its maize cultivation.

Most tourists pass straight through Sodo, as the town itself is a bit of a dump. But if you are travelling on public transport the town makes for a pleasant if unremarkable break *en route* between Shashemene or Hosaina and Arba Minch – if nothing else, the cool, moist highland air comes as pleasant relief after the dry heat of the Rift Valley. The mountain behind the town looks eminently climbable, and the town itself – despite having grown immeasurably since I first visited it in 1994 – is small enough that you need only walk 1km in any direction to find yourself on quiet, lush country roads with fantastic views to Lake Abaya, perhaps 30km distant and several hundred metres lower in the Rift Valley.

GETTING THERE AND AWAY Sodo stands 96km south of Hosaina along an asphalt road. The drive takes less than two hours in a private vehicle, though you need to double that if you are thinking of diverting to the Ajaro Falls. A couple of buses daily run northwards from Sodo to Hosaina, from where it is easy to pick up public transport towards Butajira (for Addis Ababa) and to a lesser extent Welkite. In

THE 'NEW' SODO–JIMMA ROAD

Completed in 1999, the reconstructed and upgraded road connecting Sodo to Jimma should, in theory, have made it far easier to cross between the Rift Valley and western Ethiopia without having to go through Addis Ababa. The road can be driven in five to six hours in a private vehicle and is very scenic throughout, especially the descent into the Omo river gorge.

If you are driving along this road yourself, head out of Sodo, past the post office for 7km, then turn left at the first junction following the signpost for Chida. Look out here for the characteristic Walaita huts, which are similar in design, although less over the top, than the famous Dorze huts of Chencha. About 50km out of Sodo, you'll cross the modern bridge that spans the Omo River. On climbing the gorge on the west side of the river, you'll notice some large stone ruins to your right, reputedly the remains of a large fort built by King Kawo Halalo of the medieval Dawaro Empire. At the 140km mark is a small bridge, where we noticed an unusual swallow overhead (I suspect it could be the undescribed cliff swallow recorded in several other parts of Ethiopia). At the 176km mark, you reach Chida, the largest town on the road (which isn't saying much), perched high on a grassy escarpment. Here, you need to turn right at a T-junction, before the final descent to Jimma.

There is no direct bus between Sodo and Jimma, but it is possible to get through in stages. First, catch a morning bus from Sodo to the small high-altitude village of Wukka (US$4.50; 89km; 4–5 hours). In Wukka, the National Hotel looks OK should you need to spend the night. But more likely you'll quickly get another bus through to Tulcha (US$1; 17km; 30 minutes), which is set in a beautiful verdant valleys. You'll probably need to spend a night here: it's a pleasant enough place to walk around, and accommodation options include the Engeda Hotel (bar, restaurant; US$6 en-suite double) on the road out of town, or the cheaper Kenean Hotel (*tukul*-style rooms, great views). The bus from to Tulcha to Jimma (US$5.50; 5–6 hours) leaves first thing in the morning, so it gets to Jimma early afternoon, all going well.

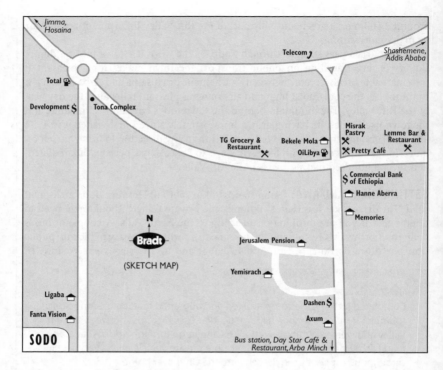

SODO

addition, one direct bus in either direction runs daily between Addis Ababa and Sodo (US$6; 7½ hours) via Hosaina and Butajira, leaving at around 06.30.

Sodo lies 120km from Arba Minch on a newly upgraded asphalt road and should take no more than two hours to drive. *En route* there is a good waterfall about 36km south of Sodo, viewable to the right as you cross the bridge that divides the Sodo and Arba Minch districts. A number of local buses ply the route between Sodo and Arba Minch (US$2.50; 2½–3 hours) throughout the day.

The 130km road to Shashemene is pot-holed, particularly towards Shashemene. Assuming you make no stops or diversions, you are looking at a two-hour drive at most. Sodo's bus station is now inconveniently located away from the centre on the road to Arba Minch. Buses between Sodo and Hawassa (US$3.50; 4½ hours) stopping via Shashemene (US$2.50; 3 hours), fill up and leave throughout the morning. There is no direct bus to Jimma or Welkite from Sodo, but if you take a bus to the small town of Waka you can continue on to Jimma from there. In a private vehicle the Sodo–Jimma drive takes at least three hours.

WHERE TO STAY

 Fanta Vision Hotel (23 rooms) ☏ 046 551 4747. Thankfully the vision of this new multi-storey hotel south of the main circle is not as orange-tinged as its odd name suggests. In fact, it's a welcoming vision of understated modernity in an otherwise nondescript town. Squarely aimed at business travellers, its simply furnished rooms are clean & neat with tiled floors & compact hot-water shower en suites. On the ground floor

there is a friendly restaurant & café & a well-stocked supermarket. Visa & MasterCard accepted. *US$15/18 sgl/dbl, US$24 suite exc b/fast.*

Bekele Mola (24 rooms) ☏ 046 551 2382–6. Once ostensibly the smartest hotel in Sodo, the Bekele Mola has aged considerably in recent years. The drab en-suite rooms are well past their prime & the pungent common showers are in dire need of a good scrubbing. Still it's a decent enough budget option & has a convenient central location in a pleasant green compound. The reasonably priced restaurant is also a justifiably popular lunchtime target for tours headed between Shashemene & Arba Minch. *US$5.50 using common shower, US$9/15 dbl/twin en suite*.

🏠 **Axum Hotel** (49 rooms) 📞 046 551 2563. This former favourite appears to have raised its game in recent years with prices for old en-suite & common-shower rooms barely increasing since the last edition. That said, it's worth paying the extra couple of dollars for one of the 10 new en-

suite rooms which are more cheerful than their older counterparts. *US$4.50 with common shower, US$6/7.50 old/new en suite*.

🏠 **Jerusalem Pension** (16 rooms) 📞 046 551 2922. The historical favourite in this price range, this pleasant multi-storey pension remains the top pick for travellers on a tight budget. Accommodation is offered in basic but clean rooms with private en suite or using a common shower. A small café serving cold drinks & coffee is attached. *US$4.50/6 with common shower/hot-water en suite*.

WHERE TO EAT For meals, the **Bekele Mola Hotel** serves fair Western food, while **T G Grocery & Restaurant** (⏰ *06.30–22.00 daily*) has been recommended as one of the best spots for traditional local dishes. Between meals, the **Misrak Pastry** opposite the OiLibya garage is excellent for pastries, coffee and juice, while the terrace at the **Tona Café** (📞 *046 551 2636;* ⏰ *06.30–20.30 daily*) in the multi-storey Tona shopping centre behind the Bekele Mola, is a pleasant place for a coffee or snack. Further afield, the impressive-looking new **Day Star Café & Restaurant** (📞 *046 551 2936;* ⏰ *08.00–21.00 daily*), located around 2km from the centre on the road to Arba Minch, offers an equally impressive menu of pastas, sandwiches and chicken and other meat dishes in the US$2–4 range. According to the signboard out the front it's also slated to become the site of a new hotel.

The Great Rift Valley is the single largest geographical feature on the African continent, and was the only such feature visible to the first astronauts to reach the moon. The process of rifting started some 20 million years ago along a 4,000km-long fault line that stretches from the Red Sea south to Mozambique's Zambezi Valley. The gradual expansion of the valley has been accompanied by a large amount of volcanic activity: the floor is studded with dormant and extinct volcanoes such as Fantelle in Ethiopia and Longonot in Kenya. Africa's two highest peaks, Mount Kilimanjaro and Mount Kenya, are also volcanic products of the rifting process, even though they lie outside of the Rift Valley. Millions of years from now, the Rift Valley will fill with ocean water, to split what is now Africa into two discrete land masses, much as happened millions of years ago when Madagascar was separated from the African mainland.

The Ethiopian portion of the Rift Valley runs from the Red Sea to Lake Turkana on the Kenyan border. In northern Ethiopia, it forms the Danakil Depression, an inaccessible and inhospitable desert that dips to an altitude of 116m below sea level, one of the lowest points on the earth's surface. South of the Danakil Depression, due east of Addis Ababa, the Rift narrows around Awash National Park to bisect the Ethiopian Highlands into the northwestern and southeastern massifs. In Ethiopia, as elsewhere along its length, the Rift Valley has formed an important barrier to animal movement and plant dispersal. For this reason, several animals are restricted to one or other side of the Rift, while populations of many animals that occur on both sides of the Great Rift, for instance Ethiopian wolves, form genetically distinct races.

The southern part of the Ethiopian Rift Valley is lower, warmer and drier than other densely populated parts of the country. Covered in acacia woodland and studded with lakes, it is also one of the few parts of Ethiopia that feels unequivocally African – in many respects the region is reminiscent of the Rift Valley lakes region of central Kenya. The six main lakes of the Ethiopian Rift formed during the last Ice Age, originally as two large lakes, one of which embraced what are now lakes Ziway, Abiata, Shala and Langano, the other lakes Abaya and Chamo.

South of Lake Chamo, the Rift Valley expands into the hot, barren scrublands of the Kenyan border region. The Rift here becomes less clearly defined, but it supports two further lakes, Chew Bahir and Turkana, both of which are practically inaccessible from the Ethiopian side (the vast bulk of Turkana's surface area lies in Kenya). The Kenyan border area is most notable for two of Ethiopia's most important national parks, Omo and Mago, which are among the most undeveloped game reserves in Africa, and noted not so much for their abundance of game (though most major plains animals are present) as for their wilderness atmosphere.

Although the Rift Valley is everywhere lower and hotter than the highlands, most of the lake region between Ziway and Arba Minch lies at an elevation of between 1,000m and 1,500m and temperatures are rarely uncomfortably hot. Rainfall figures are lower than in the highlands, but the pattern is broadly similar, with one long rainy season generally starting in April and finishing in July or August.

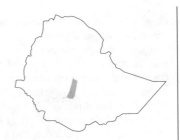

20

The Rift Valley
South to Hawassa

After the historical circuit in the north, the stretch of the Rift Valley between Addis Ababa and Hawassa via the junction town of Shashemene is probably the part of Ethiopia most regularly travelled by visitors to the country. A great many such travellers are merely passing through the region *en route* to the Omo Valley, the Kenyan border or Bale National Park, but that doesn't mean it is bereft of interest. The main attraction of the region is a string of six lakes, every one of which lies close to the main Hawassa road, and makes for a rewarding excursion.

The most northerly of these is **Lake Koka**, the only artificial body of water in the chain, and probably the least memorable. South of Koka, **Lake Ziway**, which lies alongside the eponymous town, is well worth a look for its prolific birdlife, with the possibility of exploring its ancient island monastery. Farther south again is a cluster of three lakes, **Langano**, **Abiata** and **Shala**, the first a popular swimming and watersports resort, the others protected in a national park renowned for its prolific birds and therapeutic hot springs. Finally, there is **Lake Hawassa**, situated on the outskirts of the eponymous town.

Direct access to Hawassa and the Rift Valley lakes is along a good asphalt road, which branches south from the Adama road at Mojo, 75km east of Addis Ababa, and is covered by all manner of public transport. More adventurous travellers might, however, elect to drive or bus along an asphalted road that passes through Tiya and Butajira before connecting back at Ziway (described in *Chapter 19*). This 'scenic route' offers access to a trio of very different cultural and archaeological sites: the rock-hewn church of Adadi Maryam, the ancient stelae field at Tiya, and the prehistoric diggings at Melka Kunture.

There would be a strong case for terminating this chapter at **Shashemene**, the most important junction town in southern Ethiopia. Shashemene stands at the crossroads of the asphalt road south to Moyale (see *Chapter 22*), the dirt road east via Dodola to Bale Mountains National Park (see *Chapter 21*), the asphalt road southwest towards Arba Minch (see *Chapter 23*) and the normal gateway to the Lower Omo Valley (see *Chapter 24*). It might be worth noting here that Shashemene, strategic importance notwithstanding, is one of the least appealing towns in Ethiopia. The nearby resort of **Wondo Genet** is a far more attractive place to spend a night or two.

Situated only 25km south of Shashemene along the road towards Moyale, the city of **Hawassa** is the springboard for onward travel into the arid but attractively untrammelled badlands that stretch down to the Kenyan border at Moyale. It is also a worthwhile excursion in its own right, even if you have no intention of heading further south. By refreshing contrast to the jumble that is Shashemene, Hawassa is one of the few Ethiopian cities to show clear evidence of town planning. The city's orderly, shady avenues lead down to the lushly vegetated shore of Lake Hawassa, notable for its prolific birdlife and the semi-habituated monkeys that clamber around the forested grounds.

The region covered in this chapter is readily accessible by public transport. The road between Addis Ababa and Hawassa is surfaced in its entirety, and can be covered in a private vehicle within five hours. Regular buses run directly between Addis Ababa and Shashemene, 25km from Hawassa, typically taking around six hours in either direction. For backpackers wishing to hop between various points of interest, there is also plenty of light transport connecting most towns *en route*, for instance Bishoftu, Mojo, Meki, Ziway and Arsi Negele.

ADDIS ABABA TO ZIWAY

The surfaced road to Ziway follows the Adama road (covered in *Chapter 16, Addis Ababa to Adama by road*, page 373) for about 75km as far as Mojo, passing through Akaki and Bishoftu *en route*. At Mojo a right turn to the south, at a large intersection opposite a cluster of hotels and a filling station, marks the beginning of the descent into the Rift Valley towards Ziway. In a private vehicle, this is a straightforward run, at least once you've dodged the heavy traffic for the first 20km or so out of Addis Ababa, and you can expect to reach Mojo junction in about 90 minutes and Ziway after another hour or so.

Using public transport, you can easily pick up a direct bus from Addis Ababa to Ziway, or on to Shashemene or Hawassa, but it is also possible to hop southwards using the light vehicles that connect all major towns *en route*. If you choose or need to stop over along the way, **Mojo** is an inconsequential but pretty, small town halfway, set on the banks of the Mojo River between Bishoftu and Adama. There are several decent hotels, the most popular being the **Daema Hotel** (*29 rooms;* ✆ *022 116 0022*) which charges US$4.50/6.50 for a very pleasant and clean single/twin with private hot bath, fridge and television. A good restaurant/bar is attached serving meals in the US$1.50–3 range. Visa is accepted. For details of points of interest between Addis Ababa and Mojo – including the Akaki Wetlands, Mount Zikwala and Bishoftu – see *Chapter 16*.

The first major settlement along the Moyale road is **Meki**, some 60km south of Mojo. Meki is of no great interest in itself, but it's a well-equipped little town with several restaurants, pastry shops and dollar-a-night hotels; there is a **Bekele Mola Hotel** (*18 rooms;* ✆ *022 118 0004*) behind the Kobil garage on the Ziway side of town with en-suite rooms for US$5.50, and the **Awash Hotel** (✆ *022 118 0734*) further south looks good as well. Meki is also a possible base for exploring **Lake Koka**, which fringes the main road about 20km back towards Mojo. Koka is artificial, and it is generally overlooked by tourists, but, ringed by hills and covered in flowering hyacinth, it is just as scenic as many of the natural Rift Valley lakes and it offers excellent birdwatching, particularly around the marshy area at the inlet of the Awash River. There are a couple of villages closer to Koka but neither is situated near the inlet, nor do they appear to have any accommodation, so it would be simpler to overnight in Meki and ask a minibus heading towards Mojo to drop you at the bridge over the Awash River. There are regular minibuses from Meki to Ziway when you are ready to move on.

ZIWAY

Lake Ziway, also known as Lake Dambal, is the northernmost of Ethiopia's natural Rift Valley lakes and the largest of the four covered in this chapter, with a surface area of roughly 430km². Lake Ziway lies about 160km south of the capital as the crow flies, and the well-equipped small town of the same name on its western shore lies about three hours' drive away along a good surfaced road, making it an ideal first stop on a trip through the Rift Valley. Lying at an altitude of 1,636m and ringed by steep volcanic hills, this shallow lake is fed by two major rivers, the Maki and Katar, and is drained at its southwestern tip by the Bulbula River, which in turn flows into Lake Abiata. The lake supports an abundant population of *Tilapia nilotica*, a medium-sized flat fish that can weigh up to 1.5kg and makes for fine eating (the restaurants in Ziway have a justified reputation for great *asa wat* and *kutilet*).

Although Ziway is less heralded in this respect than lakes Abiata and Shala, it arguably offers the best **birdwatching** of any Rift Valley lake, including large aggregations of water-associated species attracted to the reed-lined fringes by the thriving tilapia population. Excellent birdwatching is to be had by turning off the main road through Ziway onto the side road heading east immediately before the OiLibya garage and Bekele Mola Hotel. After about 2km, this road leads to a raised causeway and jetty fringed by papyrus marsh and teeming with birds, most visibly marabou stork and white pelican. You could easily identify 50-plus species here in a couple of hours – look out for greater and lesser jacana, white pelican, yellow-billed stork, black crake, lesser moorhen, lesser jacana, black-tailed godwit, garganey, European marsh harrier, Rüppell's griffin vulture and red-breasted pipit. This is one of the best places in Africa to see the localised black egret (also known as the black heron), whose unusual habit of fishing with its wings raised to form a canopy gives rise to its colloquial name of 'umbrella bird'.

The lake is also noted for **hippos**, which are occasionally visible from the jetty, but are more likely to be seen by hiring a boat to visit one of their more regular haunts. It is possible to extend such an excursion to visit one of Ziway's five islands, which are of ancient volcanic origin, and have supported isolated Christian communities for many centuries, as suggested by names such as Galila and Debre Sina, which are Amharigna for 'Galilee' and 'Mount Sinai' respectively. Of particular interest is the ancient **Monastery of Maryam Tsion** (see box, page 455) on the 6km² island of Tullo Guddo, whose terraced slopes ascend to a 1,889m peak 10km east of Ziway town.

GETTING THERE, AWAY AND AROUND The best access point to the lake is Ziway town, which lies on the main Moyale road about 160km from Addis and 90km from Mojo. There are two possible routes between Addis Ababa and Ziway. The first is described above, the second in meandering detail in *Chapter 19, Addis Ababa to the Rift Valley via Butajira*, page 347. If it's speed you're after, any bus leaving Addis Ababa for Shashemene can drop you at Ziway (US$3.50; 3–4 hours). Just past Ziway, Dutch greenhouses full of flowers dominate the view to the left, followed by Castel Vineyards, also on the left.

Ethiopia Community Tourism (*www.rootsofethiopia.com*) in partnership with the **Ziway Boat Owners' Association** (m *0927 340 309*; e *ziwayboatservice@gmail. com*) run a variety of boat tours to the islands on Lake Ziway including a half-day birdwatching excursion to Debre Sina (US$37/49 for one–four/five–eight people) and a full-day tour to Tullo Guddo and Maryam Tsion Monastery (US$71/89 for one–four/five–eight people).

WHERE TO STAY

Moderate

🏠 **Bethlehem Hotel** (18 rooms) ☎046 441 4084. This pleasant new hotel may be close to the lake, but in reality it's neither lakeside nor central,

so probably only worth considering if you have transport. Accommodation tops everything else on offer in Ziway: first-class rooms have a king-size bed, fridge, TV & en suite with bathtub, while second-

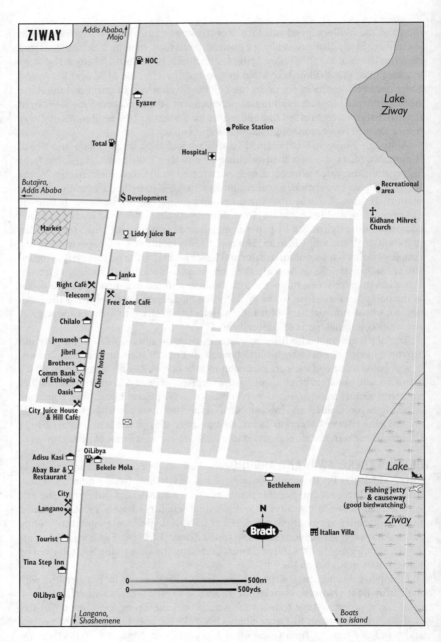

ZIWAY

Addis Ababa, Mojo

NOC

Eyazer

Lake Ziway

Police Station

Total

Hospital

Butajira, Addis Ababa

Recreational area

Development

Kidhane Mihret Church

Market

Liddy Juice Bar

Janka

Right Café
Telecom

Free Zone Café

Chilalo

Jemaneh

Jibril

Brothers

Comm Bank of Ethiopia

Oasis

City Juice House & Hill Café

Cheap hotels

Adisu Kasi

OiLibya

Abay Bar & Restaurant

Bekele Mola

City

Lake

Langano

Bethlehem

Fishing jetty & causeway (good birdwatching)

Tourist

N

Bradt

Ziway

Tina Step Inn

Italian Villa

0   500m
0   500yds

OiLibya

Langano, Shashemene

Boats to island

---

class rooms are more compact with TV & hot-shower en suite. An excellent restaurant & bar are also attached. *US$17/27.50 2nd-/1st-class en-suite dbl.*

Budget

🏠 **Tourist Hotel** (29 rooms) ☏ 046 441 4000. The aptly named Tourist Hotel is situated a few hundred metres past the town centre along the Shashemene road. The reasonably priced en-suite rooms with hot shower – though dated & a little musty – are still among the best in town. The shady garden restaurant is excellent. *US$5 using common shower, US$7.50 en-suite dbl, US$19 suite with en-suite bathtub.*

Bekele Mola Hotel (27 rooms) ☎ 046 441 2571. This pleasantly faded hotel is set in small but attractive & well-maintained flowering grounds immediately behind the OiLibya garage. Accommodation is in large chalets with either king-size or ¾ beds & en-suite hot shower. Fixtures, fittings & bedding are of variable quality & rooms have a distinct stale air, but the hotel gets high marks for its one-price-for-all policy. *US$5–5.50 en-suite dbl, US$7.50 en-suite twin.*

Shoestring
Eyazer Hotel (19 rooms) ☎ 046 441 3777. This bright new hotel located at the Addis Ababa end of town is the best-value hotel we've discovered on this research trip. The clean compact

MARYAM TSION MONASTERY

The largest of the five islands on Lake Ziway, clearly visible from the mainland, is known to the local Oromo as Tullo Guddo ('Large Mountain') and to the Amhara as Debre Tsion ('Mount Zion'). On the highest peak, the Church of Maryam Tsion is quite possibly the oldest active monastery in southern Ethiopia. A church has stood on this peak since at least the 12th century, and perhaps even earlier. Tradition has it that the Ziway area was settled by refugee priests from Axum in the 9th century, during the time of Queen Yodit, and that they brought with them the Ark of the Covenant for safe keeping. According to this legend, Tullo Guddo was the sanctuary for the Ark of the Covenant for 70 years, before it was considered safe to return it to Axum. This tradition is backed up by the fact that the Zay people of Ziway speak a Tigrigna-like tongue quite distinct from the Oromifa spoken in the surrounding area, and also by the large number of ancient Ge'ez manuscripts stored among the church's treasures, most famously a 14th-century Sinkesar containing vivid and beautiful illustrations of 19 popular saints.

During the 16th and 17th centuries, the Zay Christians led an isolated island-bound existence. They retreated to the islands in the time of Ahmed Gragn, when Christians were driven out of the Rift Valley by the Galla people, and became entirely cut off from the mainstream of Ethiopian Christianity. How the Zay survived these years of isolation with their traditions intact is something of a mystery, one most probably explained by the fact that the Galla were inept sailors and unable to build boats (indeed, the Oromo name for the Zay is Laki, which translates as rower, in reference to this distinguishing feature). As Christian–Muslim tensions eased, the islanders occasionally sailed to shore to trade, and became known to the Galla as skilful weavers, but basically they remained an isolated community, dependent on their densely terraced cultivation and on the lake's abundant fish for survival. Rumours of their isolated brethren had always filtered through to the Christians of the highlands, where it was believed, correctly, that the churches on Ziway held a wealth of ancient *tabots* and illuminated religious manuscripts. It was only in 1886 that Emperor Menelik conquered the Ziway area and the liberated islanders were able to move back to the lakeshore. Today, just three of Ziway's islands are occupied, and most Zay people visit them only for religious ceremonies. But Maryam Tsion remains an active monastery.

It's possible to take what amounts to public transport to the island, but a far easier option is to contact the **Ziway Boat Owners' Association** (see under *Ziway*, page 353), which organises full-day tours to Tullo Guddo taking in the monastery. Entrance to the monastery is US$2.

rooms have tiled floors, modern furnishing & good en-suite rooms with hot showers. Staff are very helpful & friendly. Prices like this won't last! *US$4.*

🏠 **Brothers Hotel** (54 rooms) \046 441 2609. This popular budget hotel is located on the main road near the bus station. Accommodation varies from basic rooms using common shower in the original section of the hotel to relatively smarter & cleaner en-suite rooms in the newer 3-storey annex with prices & quality rising accordingly. The attached restaurant is a long-time local favourite. *US$2/2.50 with common/en-suite cold shower, US$3–5 with hot-shower en suite.*

✗ **WHERE TO EAT** The restaurant at the **Tourist Hotel** serves excellent food indoors or in the shady courtyard. The fish cutlet, made from local tilapia, is particularly recommended at US$3.50 inclusive of a small salad, but everything is good, including the vegetarian dishes, and nothing is more expensive than US$5. Also recommended for *faranji* food are the restaurants in the **Bethlehem** and **Bekele Mola** hotels. The **City** and **Langano** restaurants next to the Tourist Hotel serve good local meals. The best place for pastries, juices and breakfast snacks is the **Right Café**.

LAKE LANGANO

Lake Langano, with a surface area of 305km² and depth of up to 45m, is more developed for tourism than any other lake in the Ethiopian Rift Valley with a number of mostly smart upscale resorts lining its western bank. A popular getaway from Addis Ababa, many of the lower end resorts take on a manic sub-Club Med atmosphere that's unlikely to appeal greatly to foreigners. During the week, the resorts all have a more restful air, and they will be far more appealing to anybody seeking a bit of natural tranquillity.

For many, the main attraction of Lake Langano is that it is safe for swimming, though frankly the murky brown water has little going for it other than a reported absence of bilharzia. The resorts all offer a variety of watersports at a price, while boat trips can be made to an island noted for its hot springs or in search of hippos and crocodiles. The wooded shore is of great interest to bird enthusiasts: not only does it support an excellent variety of water- and acacia-associated species, but two undescribed birds (a cliff swallow and a serin with a white rump) were recently reported. The resorts serve as good bases from which to explore the scenic and decidedly hiker-friendly Abiata-Shala National Park.

GETTING THERE AND AWAY Lake Langano lies to the south of Ziway, a few kilometres east of the main Moyale road. Coming from the north, you will first pass the turn-off for the 13km dirt road to the Welanesa Lodge, which is signposted out of the village of Bulbula, about 30km past Ziway. About 10km further south, the Wabe Shebelle Hotel lies about 3km east of the main road along a signposted dirt track. Another 10km or so south of this junction is the turn-off to the main entrance to Abiata-Shala National Park. The signposted turn-offs for the Africa Vacation Club and the Langano and Sabana lodges, around 3km from the main road, are between the above.

Any vehicle heading between Ziway and Shashemene will drop you at the turn-off to the hotel, though you may be asked to pay full fare to the next town (this isn't *faranji* discrimination; locals are asked to do the same).

To reach Bishangari and Wenney lodges, follow the asphalt Hawassa road south of the turn-off to the main entrance to Abiata-Shala National Park for 2km, and then turn left onto a clearly signposted dirt road and follow the signs to the lodges which are around 16km away on the lakeshore.

WHERE TO STAY

Luxury

🏠 **Africa Vacation Club** (39 rooms)
📞 046 119 1588/90, 011 515 0086 (Addis Abba);
e info@africavacationclub.com.et; www.
africavacationclub.com.et. If you have deep
pockets, this pricey new place is definitely worth
the outlay. Opening in early 2010, Ethiopia's first
time-share resort is open to travellers & anyone else
who wants to feel like they've escaped to another
world. Accommodation is in 29 spacious 3-level
tukuls – each with polished concrete floors, 2-bed
rooms, 2 bathrooms, a fully equipped kitchen & a
relaxed spherically arranged sitting room – that can
accommodate up to 6 people. Along the beachfront
there are also 10 sprawling beachside villas. Facilities
include a small spa, gift shop, gleaming pool,
breezy poolside bar & free Wi-Fi in public areas. The
attached restaurant features Western & Ethiopian
dishes as well as freshly baked pizzas from a wood-
fire oven. Plenty of activities are on offer including
table tennis, kayaking, horseriding, beach soccer
& volleyball. There is also a kids' club & children's
playground. Rates include breakfast & 2 free
massages per room. *Tukuls US$146/184 w/days/
w/end, villas US$253/316 w/days/w/ends.*

Upmarket

🏠 **Bishangari Lodge** (20 rooms) 📞 011
551 7533; m 0911 201 317; e reservations@
bishangari.com; www.bishangari.com. If your
goal is to commune with nature in a quiet,
music- & motor-free environment, & you're up for
adventures including hiking, mountain biking,
horseriding, & boat trips in search of hippos, then
Bishangari is the place! Situated on the remote
southwestern shore of Langano, this lodge,
which was originally established in 1997 to raise
funds for conservation projects in East Langano
Nature Reserve, provides accommodation in
rustic wooden *godjos*, each of which contains 2
double beds & an en-suite solar-heated shower
& toilet, as well as a private balcony. The lodge
is set in a stand of riparian ficus woodland that
attracts small mammals such as guereza &
grivet monkey, warthog, bushbuck & genet, as
well as forest birds such as the exquisite Narina
trogon, which is sometimes seen from the bar.
More than 400 bird species have been recorded
within walking distance of the camp. Among
the more conspicuous birds are the great white

& pink-backed pelican, African fish eagle, bare-
faced go-away bird, silvery-cheeked hornbill,
banded barbet, beautiful sunbird & little weaver.
Continental breakfast is included, but it costs an
extra US$32 pp for lunch & dinner. Most activities
cost extra as well, but both Visa & MasterCard
are accepted. *W/days US$78/137/145 for a sgl/
dbl/trpl godjo, US$98/162/213 for a sgl/dbl/trpl
2-room suite, US$41/73 for a sgl/dbl tukul; w/
ends US$119/205/268 for a sgl/dbl/trpl godjo,
US$149/257/336 for a sgl/dbl/trpl 2-room suite,
US$65/91 for a sgl/dbl tukul.*

🏠 **Sabana Lodge** (25 rooms) 📞 046 119 1181;
e sabana@ethionet.et; www.sabanalangano.
com. Located 7km south of the Wabe Shebelle, this
resort is owned by the same people responsible
for the popular Blue Tops & Top View restaurants
in Addis. Approached by an attractive crushed red-
lava driveway, it features smart concrete-floored
bungalows set in 2 neat rows, with simple but
tastefully furnished interiors. 'Family rooms' are
no bigger than the standard rooms – the only
additions are loft beds tacked high on the wall
that are designed for children but look easy to fall
from. The glassed-in dining *tukul* has a great view
of the brown water below. Though the setting of
the lodge is a little too formalised, the grounds
are immaculate, & internet is available. Activities
on offer include volleyball, football, kayaking &
mountain biking. Rates include breakfast & a 15%
discount applies during weekdays. *US$69/81.50
standard sgl/dbl, from US$104 family suites.*

🏠 **Wenney Lodge** (24 rooms) 📞 046 119
0603–2; e reservations@wenneylodge.com;
www.wenneyecolodge.com. Owned & operated by
Greenland Tours, this place is nearly as hard to get
to as the Bishangari, & less impressive when you
arrive. 3 types of bungalows are offered: standard
bungalows have 2 ¾ beds & en-suite hot-water
bath, 'high view' bungalows have an additional
TV & fridge, while the charm of the pricier but
musty beach bungalows is a bit spoilt by the
thin shared wall. All prices include breakfast. The
Wenney offers a similar range of activities to the
Bishangari, there is a small beach for swimming
& meals are served in a pleasant open-air dining
room/bar. *Low season US$37/43 standard sgl/dbl,
US$72/84 high view/beachside bungalow; high
season US$56/66 standard sgl/dbl, US$85/132 high
view/beachside bungalow.*

Moderate

Welanesa Lodge (15 bungalows)
\011 850 0218; m 0924 304 2850. Previously known as the Abule Bassuma Lodge, this recently reopened lodge is the most attractive of the more affordable resorts. Originally built by Mengistu as a weekend retreat for his army officers, the rather run-down feel of the lodge is compensated for by the spacious layout & pretty location on a densely vegetated peninsula on the northern lakeshore. Now under new management, the lodge consists of bungalows spread out on a hillside, each of which has 2 or 3 double bedrooms & a lounge. It's also possible to camp on a stony site, with its own toilets, amongst bungalows. There is a restaurant & bar overlooking the lake. Down the steps by the lakeside, there is a large warm-water pool (US$3 per day for non-guests) & a jetty from where boats can take you to a nearby island with hot spring & bird colony. Everyone, including guests & drivers, must pay a US$2 entrance fee. *Camping US$6 pp, US$18/36/54 bungalow for 2/4/6 people.*

Wabe Shebelle Hotel (64 rooms) \011 551 9100; m 091 658 0071. Signposted from the main road a few kilometres south of Bulbula, this beautifully situated old hotel offers a variety of accommodation options in varying states of disrepair. The shabby 2- & 3-bedroom bungalows are near falling apart with broken fixtures & fittings & useful facilities such as stoves in the self-catering kitchens missing. Older wooden chalets housing 2 & 4 people are marginally better, while newer brick chalets are hot & narrow. All rooms are en suite & include breakfast, & some have DSTV. For the more budget-minded it's possible to pitch a tent in the unkempt grounds. Though it feels a bit like a summer camp, it is very quiet during the week & arguably the best option in this price range. That said, at the time of writing the resort was set for a long overdue upgrade, with a possible name change to Spa Enterprise Langano Resort under consideration. If/when this happens, expect the prices to increase by around 20%. *US$8 pp inc b/fast, US$18/24 old/newer chalets, US$30/42 2-bedroom/3-bedroom bungalow.*

ABIATA-SHALA NATIONAL PARK

(e *abijatashallanp@yahoo.com*; entrance US$5.50 per 24hrs, vehicle entrance US$1.50/2.50 1–12 seater/12+ seater; mandatory scout US$4.50) The 887km² Abiata-Shala National Park, bordered to the east by the main Moyale road, is dominated by the two Rift Valley lakes for which it is named, and which together account for more than half of its area. Although the two lakes are separated by a mere 3km-wide sliver of hilly land, they could not be more different in character. The more southerly Lake Shala is nestled within a truly immense volcanic caldera that collapsed 3.5 million years ago, and its surface is studded with a collection of small volcanically formed islands. Despite its relatively modest surface area of 410km², Shala extends to an incredible depth of 266m, and has been calculated to hold a greater volume of water than any other Ethiopian lake, including Lake Tana, which covers an area almost ten times larger. By contrast, the northerly Lake Abiata consists of a 200km² brackish pan, nowhere more than 14m deep, and surrounded by tightly cropped grass flats exposed over the last couple of decades by a steady drop in its water level.

Little more than 1km south of Lake Shala, accessible only along a 20km track leading northwest from the Shashemene–Sodo road at Burra, a small but beautiful crater lake called Chitu Hora is nestled within a tuff ring that formed as a result of volcanic activity perhaps 10,000 years ago. The lake surface stands a full 80m below the rim, and harbours a semi-resident flock of up to 10,000 flamingoes. An Oromifa name, Chitu Hora translates as 'Broken Lake' in reference to a local tradition that it was once connected with Shala. There is no geological evidence to suggest that the two lakes have been connected at any point in the 500 years since the Galla settled this part of the Rift Valley. But oddly enough, this would have been the case up until about 1,000 years ago, when Abiata and Shala formed part of a larger body that

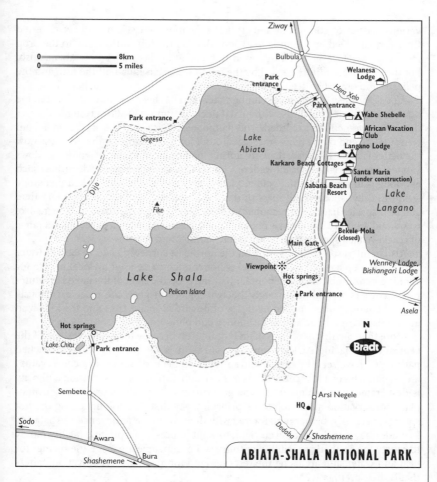

Map labels: Ziway, Bulbula, Welanesa Lodge, Park entrance, Hora Xelo, Park entrance, Wabe Shebelle, African Vacation Club, Langano Lodge, Park entrance, Gogesa, Lake Abiata, Karkaro Beach Cottages, Santa Maria (under construction), Sabana Beach Resort, Lake Langano, Dijo, Fike, Bekele Mola (closed), Main Gate, Wenney Lodge, Bishangari Lodge, Viewpoint, Hot springs, Lake Shala, Pelican Island, Park entrance, Asela, Hot springs, Lake Chitu, Park entrance, Sembete, N, Bradt, Sodo, Arsi Negele, HQ, Awara, Bura, Dedaba, Shashemene, Shashemene, ABIATA-SHALA NATIONAL PARK

0 — 8km
0 — 5 miles

also incorporated Langano and Ziway, and probably drained into the Awash River. Sometimes referred to as Lake Galla, the surface of this vast inland sea stood more than 100m above the present-day level, and the peaks along the rim of the crater nesting Lake Shala protruded from the surface as a chain of disconnected islands.

Anybody who visits this national park expecting to see large mammals is likely to be disappointed. A few Grant's gazelle live in virtual captivity at the ostrich farm next to the main entrance gate, but much of the rest of the park, which originally supported thick acacia woodland, was heavily settled and cultivated during the last years of the Derg. Wildlife has suffered badly as a consequence. Baboons are quite common, though not nearly so visible as the abundant livestock brought into the park by cattle herders. There may still be viable breeding populations of greater kudu, Grant's gazelle, Abyssinian hare, black-backed jackal and spotted hyena, but I saw no evidence of their presence. Short of being the subject of a major programme of reintroductions, Abiata-Shala can no longer be regarded as a mammal sanctuary of any note.

The main attraction of the park today is the scenic lakes, and their attendant waterbirds. Shala's main point of avian interest used to be the practically inaccessible Pelican Island, formerly an important breeding ground for white pelican as well as various species of cormorant and stork. Sadly, most of these birds have deserted their former breeding ground, an exodus that is probably attributable to the drop in Abiata's water level. The birds used to breed at Shala and feed on Abiata's fish, but the increased salinity caused by the fall in water has killed off the fish, and the pelicans and other fish-feeding birds have been forced to forage further afield.

A positive effect of Abiata's declining water level has been a marked increase in the number of algae-eating birds, with mixed flocks of almost 300,000 greater and lesser flamingoes sometimes recorded. The flamingoes typically arrive in the area from Kenya at the end of the rains and stick around for up to four months. Abiata is now the better lake for birds, particularly during the European winter when the shallows support thousands of migrant waders – large flocks of avocet alongside rarities such as Mongolian plover, Pacific golden plover, grey plover and red-necked phalarope – and the sky is a seething mass of darting European swallows. In all, more than 300 bird species have been recorded in Abiata-Shala; what survives of the park-like woodland around Lake Shala is one of the best places in Ethiopia to see a good range of acacia-related species such as hornbills, starlings and sparrow-weavers.

Also of interest is the hot spring on the northeast corner of Lake Shala. The water here throws up a cloud of steam and is hot enough to be used by local people for cooking maize cobs. It's also a popular bathing spot: the sight of the naked or white-robed bathers stumbling through the swirling steam gives the place a curiously biblical quality, rather spoiled by heaps of discarded maize cobs and the kids who accumulate around you asking for money and photographs.

More than anything, Abiata-Shala is of interest because it highlights some of the central issues facing African conservationists. It is the most heavily encroached park that I have seen in Africa, and in many respects its status as a conservation area seems a bit of a joke. But easy as it is to laugh, Ethiopia's conservation authority is desperately under-funded and the government of such a poor country cannot place conservation at the top of its priorities. My first reaction on seeing the hot springs overrun by bathers and littered with their waste was annoyance. On balance, I wonder if it is realistic, or even right, to want to preserve a pristine quality purely to satisfy the aesthetic sensibility of tourists. Local people are using the springs for heat and water, and are using the reserve's land for grazing and cultivation. Surely that is their prerogative?

Putting aside the rights and wrongs of the situation, the fact is that Abiata-Shala is not the most impressive of national parks, except perhaps to dedicated birders. If you have your own vehicle or are operating to time restrictions, it's debatable whether the park is worth visiting at all, especially when far more alluring national parks beckon further south. For backpackers, however, the park is definitely worth devoting a day to. Walking is permitted, though it is advisable to take an armed guard for security, and an excellent 12km round trip from the main entrance gate will allow you to see most places of interest, including a well-positioned viewpoint over the two lakes, the hot springs and the shore of Lake Shala.

GETTING THERE AND AWAY The main entrance gate is boldly signposted on the Moyale road directly opposite the turn-off to the now closed Langano Bekele Mola Hotel; any vehicle passing between Ziway and Shashemene can drop you there. If you plan on hiking to the lakes, it's advisable to get an early start, as the area becomes very hot around midday. The most sensible approach would be to speak to the rangers at the gate when you first arrive and organise to leave early the next day, then to head to the Bekele Mola for the night and walk back up to the gate in the morning.

WHERE TO STAY AND EAT In a private vehicle, the park can easily be visited as a day trip from any hotel in the Langano region, or for that matter *en route* between Addis Ababa and points further south. For travellers with a fairly generous budget, until the Bekele Mola Hotel reopens, one of the resorts on **Lake Langano** (see page 456) is the obvious place to stay with many also able to arrange day trips to the national park. A far cheaper option, however, would be to spend the night at **Arsi Negele** (see below). Self-sufficient travellers in a private vehicle could camp in one of the park's facility-free **campsites** for US$2.50/4 (for a tent for one to four people/more than four people) or think about staying at the little-known and inexpensive self-catering hut that lies on the southern shore of Lake Shala close to Chitu Hora, and can be reached along a 20km track from Burra or Awara on the Shashemene–Sodo road – ask at the gate or at the park headquarters in Arsi Negele for further details.

ARSI NEGELE

This small town on the Shashemene road about 30km south of the Abiata-Shala entrance gate is the site of the national park headquarters. With an early start, Arsi Negele could easily be used as a base from which to visit the national park as a day trip – there's plenty of traffic between the two. There is no shortage of cheap accommodation, with the **Awash Park Hotel** (*16 rooms;* \ *046 116 0097*) the pick.

Situated next to the Kura Evangelical Church only 2km from Arsi Negele in the direction of Addis Ababa, there is a circle of five stones, each with a ring engraved on the top and what could be a symbol of grass or wheat nearer the base. According to the tourist office in Dilla, is that they are so-called **Gragn Stones**, of similar vintage and origin to the ones at Tiya and Silté.

SHASHEMENE

Best known for the Rastafarian community called Jamaica that lies on its northern outskirts, the sprawling town of Shashemene is the major transport hub in southern Ethiopia, connecting the main road between Addis Ababa and Moyale to routes east to Dodola and Bale National Park; west towards Sodo-Walaita, Arba Minch and the Omo River; and southeast to Kebre Mengist and Negele Borena.

Unfortunately, Shashemene has little going for it other than its logistical convenience. It is the archetypal junction town: a mushrooming amorphous clutter of ugly buildings with a population that has reputedly risen by more than 2,000% to a total of 102,000 in the last decade or so. It is also the one town in Ethiopia that receives consistently negative reports from travellers, partly due to the hostility of many locals (one reader awarded Shashemene the all-Ethiopia 'Fuck You' prize in reference to a popular local manner of addressing visitors) and also due to an usually high incidence of theft, as well as con artists posing as helpful teachers or civil servants.

Unless you are visiting Jamaica or want to take in the Rasta vibes at the newly instigated **Reggae in the Rift Valley Festival** (*www.riftvalleyreggae.com*), Shashemene is probably the last place you'd want to stay the night by choice. But junction town it is, and if you spend a while in the south you may well need to bed down in Shashemene at some point. Otherwise, your first reaction on arriving there will almost certainly be to try to move on as soon as possible. If you decide to follow this impulse, it's worth knowing that there is no shortage of public transport to the infinitely more appealing town of Hawassa, or to the popular hot-springs resort at Wondo Genet, both of which are covered later in this chapter and lie around 20–25km from Shashemene.

GETTING THERE AND AWAY Shashemene lies slightly more than 250km from Addis Ababa, a roughly four-hour drive along a good asphalt road. Regular buses leave throughout the morning to and from Addis Ababa, and take about five hours in either direction. The bus station is now inconveniently located on the bypass road next to the Rani Café. Direct buses to and from Mojo or Ziway to the north leave regularly throughout the day.

Heading on from Shashemene, your options are wide open. Minibuses ply between Shashemene and Hawassa throughout the day, leaving every 15–30 minutes and taking a similar time to get to their destination. There is also reasonably regular transport throughout the day to Sodo-Walaita in the west, Dodola in the east and Dilla in the south. Direct buses to or from destinations further afield such as Yabello or Moyale (south), Arba Minch (southwest), Goba or Dinsho (east) and Kebre Mengist or Negele Borena (southeast) generally leave in the morning only. For such routings, you are advised to check departure times and book a seat the evening before you plan to travel.

🏠 WHERE TO STAY
Moderate

🏠 **Lily of the Valley Hotel** [463 F4] (28 rooms) ☎ 046 110 2732/810 0112. This multi-storey smartest place in town has the advantage of not actually being in the town, but on the bypass road just past Jamaica. The big, comfortable en-suite rooms have clean tiled floors, multi-channel DSTV & private balcony. A good restaurant & bar are attached, & there is also a rooftop nightclub with outdoor patio. Rates include breakfast. The only downside is it lacks the atmosphere of the Rift Valley below. *US$20/30 sgl/dbl, US$37 family suite.*

🏠 **Zion Train Lodge** [463 G4] (8 rooms) m 0911 887 681; e ziontrain@yahoo.fr; www.ziontrainlodge.com. From the moment you enter the brightly painted gates of this chilled new lodge, you feel as if you've boarded the peace train. Located in the heart of the Twelve Tribes community & run by a very friendly French–Ethiopian Rastafarian couple, it's an oasis of peace, greenery & unabashed feel-good Rasta vibes. Accommodation currently consists of 3 large en-suite *tukuls* (2 more are under construction) each featuring handcrafted bamboo furniture & decorated with traditional-designed bedspreads & tablecloths. There are also 3 smaller bungalow-style rooms in the central building, which share a common shower. The small restaurant serves a healthy range of dishes including rice & vegetables, banana fritters, fresh fruit & soya milk drinks. Pick-ups from Addis Ababa can be arranged as can tours to Hawassa & Lake Ziway. *Camping US$2pp, US$14 dbl using common shower, US$25/35 for 2-/4-person tukul, US$43 large 4-person tukul.*

🏠 **Rift Valley Tourist Hotel** [463 E3] (102 rooms) ☎ 046 110 5710/11. Situated north of the town centre along a side road connecting the old main road to the new bypass (it's signposted, if you look closely), this perennially popular hotel set in attractive green grounds has recently been upgraded to a smart 5-storey block & it's also one of a few places in town with a 24hr water supply. The spacious first-class rooms in the new block all have fridge, DSTV & en-suite hot shower, but the *faranji* prices are a bit annoying. Second-class rooms in the pink building are more reasonable, while third-class rooms in the old building remain fair value & also come with DSTV & en-suite hot shower. A good restaurant with a shady outdoor terrace is attached & internet is available. *US$11 3rd-class dbl, US$15/24 2nd-class dbl/twin, US$21/30 1st-class dbl/twin.*

Budget

🏠 **Dansure Pension** [463 C2] (34 rooms) ☎ 046 110 2978. Located in the town centre opposite the Total garage, this unpretentious pension is refreshingly good value. The compact modern rooms with their prettily stencilled walls each have DSTV, private balcony & hot-water en suite. A 1st-floor café/restaurant was still being fitted out at the time of inspection, but should be complete long before this book is printed. *US$9/12 dbl with en-suite shower/bathtub, US$15 twin.*

🏠 **Shalla Hotel** [463 F2] (23 rooms) ☎ 046 110 5780; m 0911 202 801. The brochure's claim that this new hotel was located in 'tha middle of most ricrational & tourist sites'& that it was

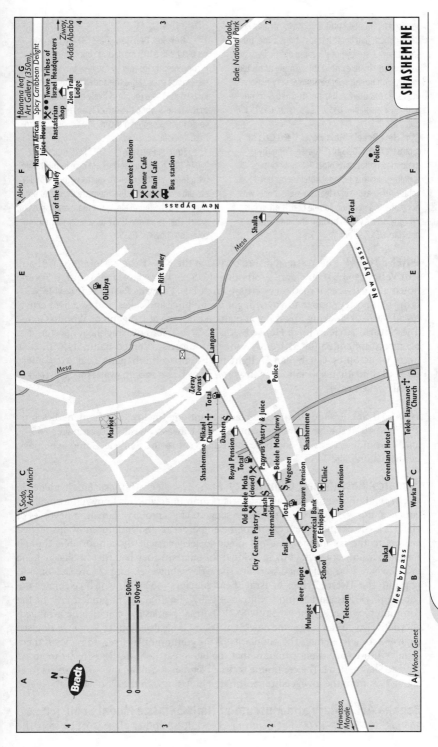

SHASHEMENE

Map labels:

Banana leaf G
Art Gallery (350m),
Spicy Caribbean Delight
Twelve Tribes of
Israel Headquarters
Ziway,
Addis Ababa
Zion Train
Lodge
Rastafarian
shop
Natural African
Juice-House

Dodola,
Bale National Park

Lily of the Valley

Alelu

Bereket Pension
Dome Café
Rani Café
Bus station

New bypass

Police

Mesa

Shalla

Rift Valley

OiLibya

New bypass

Total

Mesa

Langano

Zeray
Derass
Total

Shashemene Mikael
Church

Market

Dashen

Police

Papyris Pastry & Juice

Royal Pension
Total

Bekele Mola (new)

Shashemene

Sodo,
Arba Minch

City Centre Pastry

Old Bekele Mola
(closed)

Awash
International

Wegenen

Dansure Pension

Clinic

Tekle Haymanot
Church

Greenland Hotel

Fasil

Total

Commercial Bank
of Ethiopia

Tourist Pension

Warka

Beer Depot

School

Bakal

New bypass

Muluget

Telecom

Wondo Genet

Hawassa,
Moyale

500m
500yds

N

Braadt

serviced by trained 'stuffs and chiefs' certainly had us intrigued. Bad English translations aside, this smart new 3-storey hotel located on the bypass road, offers clean, comfortable, simply furnished rooms with hot-shower en suite at very reasonable prices. A restaurant & bar are attached & secure parking is available. *US$9/12 sgl/twin, US$15 VIP dbl.*

⌂ **New Bekele Mola Hotel** [463 C2] (36 rooms) 046 110 3344. Situated along the main road opposite its older – & now closed – namesake, this 3-storey hotel seems good value with reasonably clean en-suite rooms with hot water & a genuine double bed. It often fills up early, so it's worth ringing ahead to make a booking. *US$7.50 dbl.*

Shoestring

⌂ **Bereket Pension** [463 F3] (20 rooms) m 0912 948 810. This decent shoestring option is conveniently located by the new bus station on the bypass road. It has the added bonus of being located next to a couple of lively new cafés (packed to the rafters when the soccer is on) – though this could make sleeping difficult. *US$4/5.50 dbl with cold-/hot-shower en suite.*

⌂ **Tourist Pension** [463 C1] (10 rooms) 046 110 2056. This is the best deal in this range, with fraying but very clean rooms with a ¾ bed & en-suite cold shower. But there are dozens of other cheapies to be found along the main road, most of which charge around US$2 for a basic room using common showers. *US$3.*

✖ **WHERE TO EAT** The Western dishes served at the **New Bekele Mola** [463 C2] and **Rift Valley** [463 E3] hotels are good value at US$2–4 for a large main course. Several hotels along the main road serve Ethiopian dishes. **Papyrus Pastry & Juice** [463 C2] is the best pastry shop in town, with good fruit juice and cakes, and excellent crusty bread – worth stocking up on if you plan on camping at Langano or Wondo Genet. The **Natural African Juice House** by the Twelve Tribes of Israel headquarters has been recommended for its freshly squeezed juices sweetened naturally with cane juice, while **Spicy Caribbean Delight** next door to the Banana Leaf Art Gallery serves Trinidadian specialities such as *roti* as well as a mouth-watering selection of freshly baked cakes.

WHAT TO SEE In addition to the places mentioned below, Shashemene lies only 25km north of the far more pleasant town of Hawassa, described on pages 466–9, and it would serve as a good base for a day visit to the Senkele Game Sanctuary, described on page 466.

'Jamaica' Rastafarian Community
Many travellers who visit Shashemene do so to spend time at the nearby Rastafarian commune, which is known informally as 'Jamaica' and was formed (as the name suggests) by a group of Jamaican devotees of Haile Selassie during the later years of the emperor's reign. Until recently, unsolicited visitors to the commune were not made to feel particularly comfortable, though travellers who were invited by individual Rastafarians they had met in Shashemene or elsewhere were welcomed warmly. These days, however, tourists are welcome to pop into the **Twelve Tribes of Israel headquarters** [463 G4], which celebrates the community's Rastafarian roots. Entrance is by donation, but a guided visit of the community will cost you a hefty US$21. Formal homestays can also be arranged; alternatively you can stay at the new Zion Train Lodge listed under *Where to stay, see* page 462 for a fixed rate. The popularity of the community is likely to rocket if there is any truth to persistent rumours that the late great Bob Marley is to be reburied outside Shashemene. The commune is clearly signposted along the Addis Ababa road about 2km from the town centre, near to the junction with the Dodola road.

Banana Art Gallery and Museum of Haile Selassie Medal Shop
[off map 463 G4] (⏰ *08.30–19.00 daily; entrance US$1.50*) Another place worth a stop, the

site is signposted opposite the Twelve Tribes of Israel headquarters, about 0.5km off the main road, this place showcases the artwork and medal collection of Hailu Tefari, a very friendly Rasta immigrant with perfect English, originally from the Caribbean island of St Vincent. For a small entrance fee, Hailu will show you around and describe how he makes beautiful collages out of nothing but scraps of natural banana leaves. Artwork may be purchased at a reasonable price.

Wondo Genet
This popular hot-springs resort lies among forested hills near the village of **Wosha**, about 20km south of Shashemene. The nominal attraction is the swimming pool fed by the springs just outside the entrance of the government hotel. The springs are said to have curative properties, which encouraged Emperor Haile Selassie to build a private lodge that has subsequently been integrated into the hotel. The road up to the hotel peters out about 500m past the swimming pool, but not before you can check out the boiling, bubbling vents where the hot water rises. Beyond this, there are several footpaths up the hill, and the open view behind you means there is little danger of getting lost.

The Wondo Genet area is of great interest to hikers and nature lovers. The hotel gardens support anubis baboon, guereza and grivet monkey, as well as raucous flocks of comical silvery-cheeked hornbill and the beautiful white-cheeked turaco. The juniper-covered hills behind the hotel support a large variety of forest birds, including mountain buzzard, spotted creeper, Abyssinian woodpecker, yellow-fronted parrot, banded barbet, double-toothed barbet, Ethiopian oriole, Ethiopian slaty flycatcher, tree pipit and black saw-wing. Knowledgeable freelance bird guides can be located at the entrance to the hotel and charge US$4 to take a guided walk in the surrounding forest – they are excellent at locating the elusive Narina trogon. Regularly seen forest mammals include bushbuck. Also of interest is swampy **Lake Dabashi**, about 4km west of Wosha. The swamps are reputedly home to hippos and crocodiles, and they support a wide range of water and forest birds. There is a road between Wosha and the lake. Entrance to the resort costs US$1.30 for non-guests.

Getting there and away In a private vehicle, Wondo Genet can be reached by driving south through Shashemene to the Telecommunications Tower, from where a clearly signposted road branches east to the resort. There are a few buses daily between Shashemene and the village of Wondo Genet, but take note that the turn-off to the springs and Wabe Shebelle Hotel is 5km *before* Wondo Genet, at Wosha. From Wosha it is 3km to the hot springs and hotel; the turn-off is clearly signposted.

Where to stay

Wabe Shebelle Hotel (39 rooms) 046 119 0705; www.wabeshebellehotels.com. et. Constructed as an imperial holiday residence during the Haile Selassie era, this pleasantly faded government hotel lies in wooded grounds right next to the hot springs. The large, en-suite double rooms with TV & hot shower, while reasonably clean & neat, are exceedingly over-priced. The angular 1970s-style restaurant makes an eloquent case for the introduction of architectural crimes against humanity as a hanging offence, though this particular offender might just be spared the noose for having had the good sense to face the patio towards the spectacular sunsets over Lake Hawassa! *US$32/36 sgl/dbl.*

Abyssinia Hotel (20 rooms) 046 114 0203. The best of a few inexpensive hotels situated in Wosha, 3km from the hot springs, this popular local hotel offers clean tiled rooms with a ¾ bed & en-suite shower as well as more basic rooms using a common shower. *US$2.50/3 sgl/dbl using common shower, US$4.50/5.50 sgl/dbl with cold-shower en suite, US$7.50/9 sgl/dbl with hot-shower en suite.*

Senkele Game Sanctuary (*Entrance US$5.50, plus vehicle entrance US$1.50/2.50 1–12 seater/12+ seater*) This 58km² reserve lies to the south of the Shashemene–Arba Minch road near the small centre of Aje. The reserve was set aside to protect the country's largest concentration of the endemic Swayne's hartebeest, though the original herd of 3,000 has diminished to a few hundred because of poaching both during and after the civil war. Despite this reduction in numbers, the small size of the reserve and open terrain make it the one place in Ethiopia where Swayne's hartebeest sightings are practically guaranteed. Other mammal species to be seen in the light acacia woodland that covers the reserve include greater kudu, oribi, waterbuck, warthog and common jackal. More than 100 bird species have been recorded.

The turn-off to the sanctuary is 5km past Aje; it's a further 10km between the turn-off and the entrance gate. There are 65km of roads in the sanctuary. Walking within the reserve is permitted, but access is a problem without your own vehicle. There is no campsite or accommodation in the reserve, but you could visit Senkele as a day excursion from Shashemene or *en route* to Arba Minch. There are also a few basic hotels in Aje.

HAWASSA (AWASSA)

The lakeside city of Hawassa, situated at 1,685m in the Rift Valley 275km south of Addis Ababa and 25km south of Shashemene, was known as Awassa prior to being renamed in late 2009. It was formerly the capital of Sidamo region, and is today the capital of the snappily entitled Southern Nations, Nationalities and Peoples' Region, an ethnically and linguistically diverse region formed in 1994 when five of the Derg-era regions of Ethiopia, Sidamo included, were amalgamated into one administrative unit. Hawassa is the largest city in the Ethiopian Rift Valley, supporting a population of around 138,000, and the compact, attractively laid-out centre has an unusually bright and modern character. In addition to being a convenient staging post for journeys south towards Moyale, Hawassa – a Sidamo name meaning 'Wide plain suitable for grazing' – is an amiable and comfortable place to spend a night or two, with the added bonus of it lying on the easterly shore of the pretty Rift Valley lake also called Hawassa.

The main attraction of Hawassa is undoubtedly its lake, which is the smallest in the Ethiopian Rift Valley, extending over 9,000ha and nowhere more than 22m deep. Set in an ancient volcanic caldera, Lake Hawassa has no outlets, yet the water remains fresh, and the lake supports a rich variety of plankton and an abundance of fish. The mountainous backdrop of the lake, together with the lush fringing vegetation, matches any of the Kenyan Rift Valley lakes for scenery. The dense scrub and fig woodland along the lake's shore is well preserved and teeming with birds. Guereza and grivet monkeys are practically resident in the grounds of the Midroc Zewed Village, and very habituated to people. Hippos are also present in the lake, but generally only seen from a boat.

Built to prevent flooding when the lake rises, a dyke runs along the shore of Hawassa close to the town. It starts about 1km north of the Hotel Hawassa, and then runs southward almost to the Lewi Resort (you have to cut back to the road just before the second hotel, as a military camp prevents direct access). The dyke doubles as a good walking trail, and is of special interest to birdwatchers. Fish eagle, silvery-cheeked hornbill, grey kestrel, several types of weaver, and the endemic black-winged lovebird, yellow-fronted parrot, banded barbet and Ethiopian oriole are common in patches of forest. Blue-headed coucal, Bruce's green pigeon and white-rumped babbler are regular in the marshy scrub east of the footpath. A variety of herons, storks, terns, plovers and waders is to be seen in the water or along the shore, and there is perhaps no better place in Africa to see the colourful and localised pygmy goose.

In the city centre, there is a worthwhile open market, which draws colourful villagers from all around on the main **market** days of Monday and Thursday. For a good view over the lake, climb the small but steep Tabor Hill, located behind the Lewi Resort. The Commercial Bank of Ethiopia changes US dollars cash and travellers' cheques, as well as other major currencies.

In addition to the above, there is a daily **fish market** on the lakeshore, about 1km south of the Lewi Resort. A relaxed enough place, it is probably best for seeing a wide selection of waterbirds as well as marabou stork who are well fed with fish scraps provided by local boys. Catfish heads litter the ground, but there is a huge fig tree that provides some natural beauty. Both raw and cooked fish are available to eat. An entrance fee of US$1.50 per person is charged, plus an additional US$3/6/9 for a mandatory guide for a group of one–three/four–six/seven–nine people supplied by the newly formed **Sajato Guides Association** (m *0911 945 822*) located by the main gate. The association can also organise a **short boat trip** to see the **hippos**, taking around one hour and costing US$35.50 for a group of up to eight people plus an additional US$12 for a guide.

GETTING THERE AND AWAY Hawassa lies on the surfaced road from Addis Ababa to Moyale. The 275km drive from Addis Ababa takes four to five hours. Coming to Hawassa, note that a high proportion of public transport from destinations to the north, east and west will terminate at Shashemene. This isn't a major inconvenience, as a steady stream of minibuses covers the 25km road between Shashemene and Hawassa (around 30 minutes), so you'd be unlucky to wait more than 15 minutes for onward transport.

Buses from destinations to the south, such as Moyale and Negele Borena, will normally stop at Hawassa before continuing on to Shashemene. The bus station [469 G4] in Hawassa is 15 minutes' walk from the main road and around half an hour by foot from the lakefront hotels, so you might want to catch a horse-drawn *gari* or *bajaj* into town. Most transport coming from the direction of Shashemene does follow the lakeside road into town, before turning into the main road at the roundabout, so you can ask to be dropped somewhere more convenient before reaching the bus station.

When you're ready to move on from Hawassa, its subservience to Shashemene as a transport hub should be taken into account. There are at least two buses daily running directly from Hawassa to Addis Ababa (US$5; 6 hours) via Ziway, as well as from Hawassa to Arba Minch (US$5.50; 6½ hours) via Sodo. Buses from Shashemene to destinations along the Moyale road must pass through Hawassa, but there is no guarantee that you will get a seat if you wait for them there. For other destinations, you will generally have to catch a minibus through to Shashemene first. For relatively nearby towns, such as Sodo or Dodola, this isn't a major concern, as transport leaves from Shashemene throughout the morning. For longer hauls, for instance to Goba or Moyale, buses tend to leave Shashemene in the early morning only, so you might need to spend the night in Shashemene before heading on.

WHERE TO STAY
Upmarket

🏠 **Lewi Resort** [469 A2] (60 rooms)
📞 046 221 4143/4180; m 0916 313 131; e info@ lewihotelandresort.com; www.lewihotelandresort.

com. Known as 'the new new Lewi', this hotel has a great lakefront location. If the split-level bungalows with their steam showers, jacuzzis & circular beds with inbuilt speakers are a little too porn-star-esque for your liking, there's always the garden view or deluxe rooms each with tiled floors, DSTV & balcony or one of the many interconnecting suites. The hotel also boasts 3 restaurants, a piano bar, an 18th-century-styled wine bar & a fast-food hut. Complimentary activities include mini golf, mountain biking, steam & sauna, swimming pool, cinema (w/ends only), table tennis & badminton. Rates include breakfast & free Wi-Fi and MasterCard & Visa are accepted. *US$61.50/86.50/128.50 sgl/dbl/twin garden-view room, US$124/149 deluxe lake room without/with lake view, US$149 deluxe bungalow, US$212–312 suites.*

⌂ **Haile Resort** [off map 469 C4] (112 rooms) ☏011 661 1401/663 0155; e haileresort@gmail. com; www.haileresort.com.et. Owned by Olympic gold medallist runner Haile Gebrselassie, this impressive new hotel, located by the lakeshore a few kilometres from the centre, might look like a concrete monstrosity from the outside but inside it's very much a first-class hotel. The spacious lobby where some of Haile's trophies are prominently displayed is only the start. From here you are whisked up in the elevator to rooms that are bright & airy & very European in styling with DSTV, fridge, safe-deposit box, Wi-Fi, private balcony, the most comfortable hotel bed this updater has ever slept on & personalised extras including green tea bathroom products, bathrobes, free newspaper (w/ days only) & in-room Sidama coffee. An extensive list of facilities includes a large pool complete with waterfall, mini golf course, cinema hall, 3 restaurants, lakeside bar, spa, walking track & a state-of-the-art fitness centre said to be designed & used by Haile himself. A variety of boat trips can also be arranged & weekday discounts are available. *US$83/94 dbl garden/lake view, US$107 twin garden view, US$169–200 suites.*

Moderate

⌂ **Lewi Piazza Hotel** [469 C3] (39 rooms) ☏046 220 5554/1654; e info@lewihotelandresort. com. Commonly referred to as 'the new Lewi', this modern, multi-storey hotel boasts a central location & uncommon amenities including Wi-Fi, an elevator, a generator, smoke detectors, & in-room minibars & safes. Perhaps a bit paranoid, it also has security cameras in the hallways. Well-furnished business suites with king beds & enclosed 'massage shower' are good value. US$9

extra gets you a standard suite with the addition of a steam bath, while deluxe suites have private balcony, a 2-person jacuzzi tub & a massage chair! All rooms have multi-channel DSTV & rates include breakfast. The excellent restaurant has entrées in the US$2.50–6 range. MasterCard & Visa accepted. *US$26.50/35.50 business/standard suite, US$85.50 deluxe suite.*

⌂ **Haroni Hotel** [469 D2] (32 rooms) ☏046 220 0407. Located next to the Pinna, this new 5-storey place has double rooms with fridge, balcony, DSTV & screen shower. There's a restaurant/ bar on the ground floor, but a lack of parking. Rates include breakfast & free Wi-Fi. *US$23.50/29.50 dbl with 1/2 shower heads, US$41 suite.*

⌂ **Hotel Pinna** [469 D2] (65 rooms) ☏046 221 3356. With the opening of a second building next door, the Pinna retains a foothold in the moderate category & scores well on pretty much every account except for the uninspired location. Rooms in the new building have Wi-Fi & come with king bed or twin beds with a steam bath. A suite adds a jacuzzi & sauna. Rooms in the old building are slightly less expensive. All rooms are en suite & have DSTV. A gym & swimming pool are planned, & the restaurant is one of the best for food, service & price. *Pinna #1 US$16/17/19.50 sgl/dbl/twin; Pinna #2 US$20.50/26.50/26.50 sgl/dbl/twin, US$58.50 suite.*

⌂ **Hotel Hawassa** [469 B3] (21 rooms) ☏046 220 5395/0004. Recently bought by the United Africa Group, this site is earmarked for development as a world-class Protea resort. As things stand, however, the tiled-floor bungalows with king bed, DSTV, fridge & private bath seem a little tired. Apart from the fence that divides it from the lake, it has a superb location, A restaurant with pleasant outdoor seating is attached. *US$27 dbl or twin.*

⌂ **Oasis International Hotel** [469 A2] (38 rooms) ☏046 220 6452/25; e interoasisbr_2009@yahoo.com. Located on the road to Lewi Resort, this gleaming new multi-storey hotel is very businesslike in its approach & amenities, offering reasonably priced standard rooms with tiled floors, DSTV & hot-water shower, deluxe rooms, steam showers, while suites have a fridge, steam shower & jacuzzi. Rates include breakfast, free Wi-Fi & a complimentary massage. Visa is accepted. The restaurant serves both traditional Ethiopian & continental dishes.

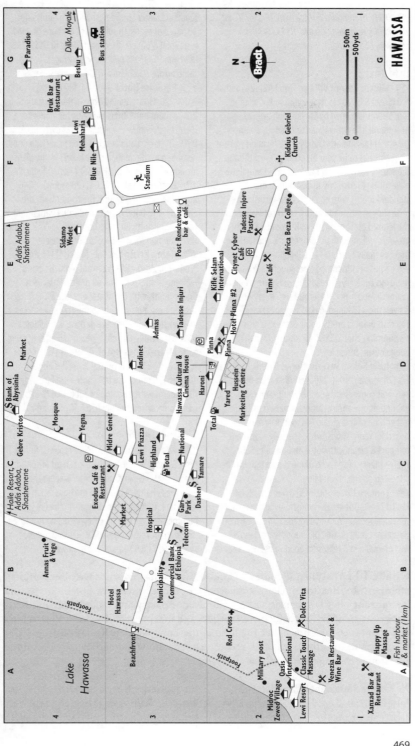

HAWASSA

N

Bradt

500m
500yds
0
0

G

F

E

D

C

B

A

4   3   2   1

G   F   E   D   C   B   A

Lake Hawassa

Footpath

Footpath

A
Annas Fruit & Vege
Hotel Hawassa
Beachfront
Midroc Zewed Village
Oasis International
Lewi Resort
Classic Touch Massage
Venezia Restaurant & Wine Bar
Xanxad Bar & Restaurant
Happy Up Massage
Fish harbour & market (1km)
Military post
Red Cross

B
Municipality
Commercial Bank of Ethiopia
Telecom
Gari Park
Dashen
Hospital
Market
Dolce Vita

C
Haile Resort, Addis Adaba, Shashemene
Gebre Kristos
Mosque
Yegna
Midre Genet
Exodus Café & Restaurant
Lewi Plazza
Highland
National
Total
Yamare

D
Bank of Abyssinia
Market
Andinet
Admas
Tadesse Injuri
Hawassa Cultural & Cinema House
Haroni
Yared
Hussein Marketing Centre
Total
Pinna

E
Addis Adaba, Shashemene
Sidamo Wodet
Post Rendezvous bar & café
Kifle Selam International
Citynet Cyber Café
Tadesse Injore Pastry
Time Café
Africa Beza College
Hotel Pinna #2
Pinna

F
Stadium
Blue Nile
Lewi Mehaharia
Kiddus Gebriel Church

G
Paradise
Bruk Bar & Restaurant
Beshu
Bus station
Dilla, Moyale

US$20/30/30 standard sgl/dbl/twin, US$35/40 dbl with king-size/queen-size bed, US$35/43 deluxe dbl/twin, US$70 suite.

Budget

🏠 **Midroc Zewed Village** [469 A2] (24 rooms) 📞046 220 5397/0415. It is common knowledge that Midroc is owned by Sheikh Mohammed Al-Amoudi, the richest man in Ethiopia & famed creator of the Sheraton Addis. If it's location you are after, this has to be your first choice, even though the scruffy rooms are not up to much. Bungalows have funky 1970s-style furnishings, while standard rooms with equally dated furnishings have showers instead of tubs. For most visitors, the relaxed atmosphere & well-wooded lakeshore grounds will more than compensate. Indeed, the hotel virtually functions as a wildlife sanctuary: fish eagles nest in the fig trees, guereza & vervet monkeys & silvery-cheeked hornbills are regular visitors, woodland & waterbirds are everywhere, & even the odd hippo makes an appearance. The restaurant is pretty good, & there is also a swimming pool. *US$17/19 standard room/ bungalow inc b/fast.*

🏠 **Kifle Selam International Hotel** [469 E2] (28 rooms) 📞046 220 2939/9927; m 0911 915 346. This conveniently central multi-storey hotel has undergone a major transformation since the last edition of this guide. Old rooms have been closed for renovations, while the new rooms are compact & clean with hot-water en suite & TV. There's plenty of secure parking & a restaurant/ bar is located on the ground floor. *US$12/18 dbl/twin.*

🏠 **Yamare Hotel** [469 C3] (69 rooms) 📞046 221 0177–8. This long-serving hotel on the main street has recently had an upgrade with a new first-class annex built on site. Older rooms are clean & well maintained & represent good value, while new

rooms are larger & have fresh modern furnishings. All have hot-water en suite, DSTV & phone. A good restaurant & bar are attached. *Old rooms US$9/13.50 dbl/twin, US$18 dbl bungalow; new rooms US$18 standard dbl, US$27 suite, US$47 family suite.*

🏠 **Paradise Hotel** [469 G4] (32 rooms) 📞046 220 4368. Situated close to the bus station, this pleasant hotel offers fair value for money for a clean, tiled room with en-suite hot shower, net & DSTV. The large patio area is a good place for a drink. According to the signboard the hotel's future plans include a swimming pool. *US$9/11 small/large dbl.*

🏠 **Beshu Hotel** [469 G4] (20 rooms) 📞046 882 4634. Situated around the corner from the Paradise, this hotel is also good value with bright tiled double with en-suite hot showers & TV. *US$5 with common shower, US$7.50 en-suite dbl.*

🏠 **Gebre Kristos Hotel** [469 D4] (45 rooms) 📞046 220 2780–1. This central high-rise has a welcome same-price-for-all policy with clean, bright rooms with hot-water en suite & TV. A 1st-floor restaurant & outdoor terrace bar serves inexpensive food, & secure parking is available. *US$7.50–12 en-suite dbl depending on size of room.*

🏠 **Midre Genet Hotel** [469 C3] (12 rooms) 📞046 220 3810. This central hotel lies about 10mins' walk from the lakeshore with large, clean tiled rooms with a genuine double bed & en-suite hot showers. Good value! *US$7.50 en-suite dbl.*

Shoestring

🏠 **Admas Hotel** [469 D3] (24 rooms) Rising head & shoulders above the usual herd of sordid cheapies, this clean & quiet hotel is set in the back roads halfway between the bus station & the lakeshore. That said, the showers in the en-suite bathrooms don't look like they've been introduced to a mop for some time. *US$2.50 using common shower, US$3 with en-suite cold shower.*

✗ WHERE TO EAT

When it comes to food, Hawassa has no shortage of exceptional offerings. In the town centre, adjacent to the eponymous hotel, the **Pinna Restaurant** [469 D2] consists of a ground-floor pastry and coffee shop and first-floor restaurant, both of which are excellent and inexpensive. The **Lewi Piazza** [469 C3] is another top choice, but the food at the **Lewi Garden Restaurant** [469 C3] is also good, with the roast lamb recommended, and you could happily spend the afternoon relaxing here before or after a meal.

✗ **Venezia Restaurant & Wine Bar** [469 A2] 📞046 220 0955; ⏰ 07.30–23.00 daily. This new Italian restaurant, run by a very friendly Italian–

Ethiopian couple, is trying hard to take the top spot from Dolce Vita. It serves 15 types of pizza daily as well as pastas & fresh fish with many of the hard-to-get ingredients imported direct from Italy. On the rooftop there is a terrace wine bar with wines from California, Argentina, Chile, South Africa, Spain & Italy. *US$3.50–6.*

✗ **Dolce Vita Restaurant** [469 A2] 046 220 5050; ⏱ 07.00–22.00 daily. This popular restaurant has some of the best Italian food in the country & features fresh pasta dishes, many with fish. On Mon & Fri nights, wood-fired pizzas are served. A small art gallery is also attached. *US$3.50–4.50.*

✗ **Exodus Café & Restaurant** [469 C3] m 0911 514 036; ⏱ 06.30–22.00 daily. This Western-style café serves a decent selection of pastries, pizza & coffee. *US$2–4.*

✗ **Xanxad Bar & Restaurant** [469 A1] m 0916 133 989; ⏱ 06.30–late daily. If you're

into literature this new restaurant is the spot to seek inspiration with its walls adorned with pictures of world-famous writers including Mark Twain. During the day it serves as a quiet café serving mostly local dishes, but by night it transforms into a lively bar. *US$2–4.*

✗ **Time Café** [469 E2] 046 220 6331; ⏱ 07.00–21.00 daily. This Starbucks wannabe café with its central location & pleasant outdoor terrace is a good spot to stop for a quick coffee or quick bite with a good range of chips, pastries, burgers & sandwiches, smoothies & juices. Just don't eat the meals during the day – we were informed the 'night chef is better than the day chef' after complaining about our inedible 'special' Time Burger, which came complete with a side order of charred fries. *US$1–3.50.*

OTHER PRACTICALITIES

Foreign exchange The **Commercial Bank of Ethiopia** [469 B3] on the main road just east of the main roundabout offers foreign currency exchange services as does the more efficient **Dashen Bank** [469 C3] by the Yamere Hotel, which also has an ATM accepting Visa and MasterCard.

The Bale and Arsi Highlands

This chapter covers the former administrative regions of Bale and Arsi, both of which still retain a distinct identity in the minds of most Ethiopians, despite having been incorporated into the Federal State of Oromia in 1995. Bale and Arsi lie in the moist green highlands southeast of the Rift Valley, and are generally quite cool by day and often very cold at night. The highlands support several substantial towns, most notably the former regional capitals of Goba (Bale) and Asela (Arsi). More easterly parts of Bale are low-lying, dry and hot, giving way to the Somali Desert. So, too, are the plains to the south of Bale, around Dola Mena and Negele Borena, an area covered at the end of this chapter.

The regional travel focus is **Bale Mountains National Park**, which protects Ethiopia's second-highest mountain range and is the best place for viewing a cross-section of the country's unique vertebrates, including Ethiopian wolf, mountain nyala, Menelik's bushbuck, giant mole rat and 16 endemic bird species. The national park offers good facilities to hikers, but can also be crossed by vehicle or on horseback. A well-organised hiking and trekking circuit outside of the national park, developed with German funding near the small town of Dodola, ranks as one of the better-organised ecotourism projects in Ethiopia.

The northern gateway town to the Arsi–Bale region is Dodola, which is situated close to the junction of the two most widely used road routes to Goba from Addis Ababa. The more direct of these routes, as followed in this chapter, runs via Adama, Asela, Bekoji and Dodola. At the time of writing only the 67km section between Bekoji and the turn-off to Dodola remained unsurfaced. Until road construction is complete, it is easier to approach Bale from the Rift Valley, using a now almost completely tarred road that connects Goba and Shashemene via Dodola (as of early 2012 the 13km stretch between Robe and Goba remained unsurfaced). Whichever way you approach Dodola, the road to Goba runs right past the park headquarters at Dinsho, so it is advisable to stop there rather than go on to Goba.

A more obscure route into or out from Bale runs south from Goba to Dola Mena and Negele Borena, from where you can cut west to the main Moyale road via Kebre Mengist (emerging north of Dilla) or via Arero (emerging at Yabello). The road south of Goba runs across the **Sanetti Plateau** – the highest point in the park and the best place to see Ethiopian wolves – and through the **Harenna Forest** before arriving at Dola Mena. This route is certainly not on if you are in a rush – it will take at least three days to complete on public transport – but if you have the time it is well worth using, both for scenery and for wildlife.

It is possible to drive from Addis Ababa to Bale National Park or Goba over one long day. The better route is via the Rift Valley, since it is surfaced all the way to Robe and (if you're not in a rush) offers access to the lovely Rift Valley lakes. The route via Asela is more scenic, so there is a strong case for heading down to Goba on one road and returning on the other. For those using public transport, direct buses run between Goba, Shashemene and Addis. Alternatively, the trip can be done in hops, using a combination of light vehicles, local buses and trucks. There is no normal public transport between Goba and Negele Borena, but light vehicles cover the route.

The area covered in this chapter is of singular interest to birdwatchers and the loop through Bale Mountains National Park to Yabello via Negele Borena is likely to form the core of any serious ornithological tour of Ethiopia. The Bale park headquarters at Dinsho is an excellent spot for montane forest endemics, while the Sanetti Plateau is the best place in Ethiopia to see highland endemics and unusual migrant raptors, and the Harenna Forest hosts an interesting selection of forest birds. Genale, on the road to Negele Borena, is the most reliable site for the eagerly sought Ruspoli's turaco, while the dry badlands around Negele Borena host two very localised endemic larks. The run from Negele Borena to Yabello offers a chance to see two species known only from southeast Ethiopia and Somalia, while Yabello itself lies at the epicentre of the small territory of the endemic Streseman's bush crow and white-tailed swallow.

ASELA

Asela is the nondescript administrative capital of Arsi zone, which, according to the Asela Ras Hotel's publicity pamphlet, is 'famous for its wild animals'. Hmmm ... while it's true that relict populations of mountain nyala do still persist in the region's more remote forests, Arsi as a whole strikes me as more notable for its decidedly domesticated hillsides, where orderly green fields of millet, maize, barley and rapeseed are bounded by neat rows of eucalyptus trees to form a series of unspectacular but eye-pleasing vistas vaguely reminiscent of the English countryside.

As for Asela itself, it's difficult to think of anything remotely interesting to say about this neat little highland town, which lies at an elevation of around 2,300m and makes for a reasonably attractive overnight stop between Addis and Bale. There's nothing much to do in Asela; the one thing it seems to have in abundance is hotel bars with draught beer and satellite television, making it a fair place to watch a football match. As for other excursions, the town is small enough that you could wander out to explore the surrounding country lanes, which on a clear day offer great views eastward towards the 4,021m peak of Mount Chilalo – a gently ascending climbable goal if you have a couple of days to spare!

GETTING THERE AND AWAY Coming from Addis Ababa, you need to take the 100km surfaced road to Adama, take a right turn at the main central junction, then follow 75km of perfect asphalt to Asela. In a private vehicle, the trip should take about three hours, with the possibility of stopping at Sodore or Dera Delfekar Reserve along the way (see *What to see*, page 387). On public transport, the most straightforward option is to hop on a bus to Adama, where you can easily pick up another bus to Asela. Transport between Asela and Dodola, to the south, generally leaves in the early morning.

 WHERE TO STAY The Olympic spirit runs deep in Asela with many of the region's famous medal-winning runners investing in new hotels in the town.

Moderate

🏠 **Derartu Hotel** (27 rooms) 📞 022 331 2828. Asela's newest, largest & nicest hotel is owned

by Derartu Tulu who made history at the 1992 Barcelona Games by becoming the first black African woman Olympic gold medallist. Located on the main road next to the OiLibya garage at the southern entrance to town, the hotel features comfortable modern rooms each with DSTV & hot-shower en suite. A good restaurant is attached & Visa & MasterCard are accepted. *US$18/21 dbl/ twin.*

🏠 **Soljam Hotel** (13 rooms) ☎ 022 331 2930. Directly opposite the Derartu, the rooms here are marginally smaller but are similarly appointed & priced. There's a bright restaurant & bar with an outside garden & small café. Visa is accepted. *US$17.50/21 sgl/dbl.*

Budget

🏠 **Kenenisa Hotel** (21 rooms) ☎ 022 331 3649. This 4-storey hotel owned by Olympic gold medallist Kenenisa Bekele has the advantage of being located across the street from the bus station. The rooms are spacious, bright & airy & the hot-shower en suites possibly the nicest, cleanest & most modern we've viewed in the budget category this research trip! There is a cheap ground-floor café-cum-restaurant & bar & an internet café on the 1st floor, but the best thing about this place is the 3rd-floor observation deck which offers excellent views. *US$7.50/10 dbl/twin.*

🏠 **Asres Abay Hotel** (30 rooms) ☎ 022 331 1089/1340. Built in the 1970s, this dated hotel is pleasant enough & fairly well maintained for a former government hotel. It offers 2 classes of en-suite rooms – second-class room with ¾ bed & hot shower, & larger first-class rooms with queen-size bed, hot shower & TV – as well as smaller budget rooms using a common shower. There's a friendly bar attached, & the cavernous restaurant serves decent meals for around US$2–4. *US$5 using common shower, US$6/9.50 2nd-/1st-class dbl.*

Shoestring

🏠 **Dara Pension** (16 rooms) ☎ 022 331 2567. This new pension overlooking the bus station offers surprising clean, neat & well-priced rooms using a common cold shower. *US$3/4 dbl/twin.*

🏠 **Tinsaaee Hotel** (10 rooms) **m** 0911 751 236. The best of the cluster of shoestring hotels opposite the bus station, this friendly place offers reasonably clean basic rooms with common showers. *US$2.50.*

🍴 **WHERE TO EAT** The best place to eat is the **Derartu Hotel**, closely followed by the **Soljam Hotel**, both serving decent Western meals in the US$2–5 range. The restaurants at the **Asres Abay** and **Kenenisa** hotels are also recommended. For fresh pastries, cakes and coffees try the **Olympic Café** on the first floor in the same building as Dara Pension.

The gateway town to the Bale region is Dodola, which lies at the junction of the Asela, Goba and Shashemene roads. If you're coming from Shashemene, you'll find no difficulty getting a bus through to Dodola, but things are less straightforward coming from Asela. There are rumoured to be direct buses, but I never located one and instead ended up hopping from town to town.

The first town to head for is **Bekoji**, which lies some 56km past Asela at a crisp altitude of 2,700m. At least one bus covers this route, leaving at 06.30, and there may sometimes be another bus later in the day. Unfortunately, the perfect new Chinese road ends just past Asela. Muddy and full of holes, the dirt road to Bekoji is at the opposite end of the spectrum – though the distance is short, it took over three hours by bus. Road quality aside, this is a lovely drive, through evocative frosty moorland covered in heath-like plants. Bird enthusiasts should keep an eye open for wattled ibis and Abyssinian longclaw. The local horsemen, swathed in warm shawls and blankets, put me in mind of the Basotho of Lesotho. Certainly if you felt like exploring the area, you'd have no difficulty finding a horse or mule to hire.

Bekoji itself is a large, sprawling country town, and the surrounding countryside has enormous walking potential. Running potential, too, come to think of it! This unassuming town and its immediate environs can lay claim to being the birthplace of a rash of top international long-distance runners, including an incredible five Olympic medallists: the legendary 5,000m and 10,000m world-record holder Haile Gebrselassie, the two-time women's gold winner Derartu Tulu, the 2004 gold and silver medallist Kenenisa Bekele, the 1996 women's marathon champion Fatuma Robe, and recent bronze medallist Tirunesh Dibala. Alas, as a visiting foreigner, you may want to take up running as well, if only to escape hordes of children yelling 'China! China!' regardless of your ethnicity. (The presence of Chinese road construction crews appears to be the source of this mania.) Should you get stuck in this skippable town, the new **Night Star Hotel** (*17 rooms;* \022 332 0838), owned by Olympic gold and silver medallist Kenenisa Bekele, is easily the best place in town. Located in a side street close to the bus station it charges a reasonable US$4.50 for an en-suite room with three-quarter bed and hot shower, while smaller rooms with common shower cost US$3.

From Bekoji, there is supposedly the odd bus on to **Asasa**, but it may be more productive to wait outside the bus station for a private truck or pick-up – you'll have to pay the same as you would for a bus but you should get away more quickly. The road here is still rough dirt, but it is in much better condition than the stretch between Asela and Bekoji. Construction of a new road is already under way, and it should be completely surfaced during the lifetime of this edition. In the vicinity of Meraro, about 30km south of Bekoji, the 2,960m Kara Pass is flanked by the 4,190m Mount Kasa to the west and the 3,806m Mount Enkolo to the east. From here on, you'll start to see the yellow and orange aloes that are so characteristic of the Bale area, and also large rural homesteads ringed by neat mud or euphorbia enclosures. Asasa itself is similar in size and feel to Bekoji, and there are several small hotels. It's only 14km on to Dodola, and the towns are connected by a regular minibus service, but arriving late in the day you may choose to stay put.

DODOLA AND ADABA

Situated a few kilometres past the junction of the roads from Asela and Shashemene, Dodola is a dusty and depressing highland town – altitude 2,400m – with little

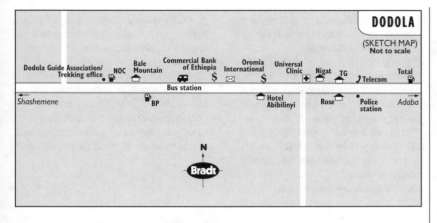

inherent appeal for tourists. You don't come to Dodola for the town though; rather it is the gateway to some of the best trekking in the country. With the support of the German non-profit group GTZ, an elaborate network of mountain huts, tented camps and trekking trails has been established through the forested mountains to the south of Dodola and **Adaba** (a small town 29km east of Dodola on the Bale road). Part of an integrated forest management project (IFMP), this professional and well-organised set-up is of considerable significance to the conservation of the fauna and flora of some of Ethiopia's most extensive remaining montane forest and moorland. It is also fantastic news for keen hikers and trekkers, who can spend anything from a couple of days to a week exploring the scenic trails and seeking out Ethiopia's endemic wildlife. For those without time to undertake extensive hikes, the attractive Lensho Waterfall, about 30 minutes' walk from Dodola town centre, forms a good goal for a short walk – the Dodola Eco-Tourism Guides Association office can supply detailed directions (see *Adaba–Dodola mountain trekking, Organisation and costs*, page 478).

GETTING THERE (DODOLA) AND AWAY Coming direct from Addis Ababa, a bus service via Asela leaves the main Autobus Terra at 06.00 and arrives in Dodola at about 15.30. Another direct bus service via Shashemene leaves Addis Ababa at 08.00. Details of travelling from Asela to Dodola are covered under the heading *Asela to Dodola*, page 476. Several buses daily run between Shashemene and Dodola (US$2), taking two hours in either direction. There is a regular bus service between Dodola and Adaba (US$0.90; 1 hour) and four buses daily to Robe (US$3.60; 4 hours).

WHERE TO STAY AND EAT

🏠 **Bale Mountain Motel** (13 rooms) 022 660 0016. Clearly signposted about 1km out of town along the Asela–Shashemene road, this motel is just a short walk from the Dodola Guides HQ. Opened in 1998 as a starting base for hikers, this hotel has great potential, but is falling into disrepair. En-suite rooms with hot shower & a ¾ bed are slightly nicer & more expensive than rooms with cold-shower en suites. The motel is set in shaded green grounds surrounded by hedges, making it a good place to pitch a tent – thankfully,

camping is permitted. The restaurant serves beers, sodas & coffee & Western & local meals are available by advance order. Portions are enormous – 1 dish might serve 2 people, & 2 dishes would easily feed 3. *US$2 using common shower, US$3/4.50 sgl/dbl with cold-shower en suite, US$6 with hot-shower en suite.*

🏠 **Rose Hotel** (12 rooms) 022 666 0520. Located at the western end of town right next door to the police station, this friendly place with its welcoming, shady outdoor beer garden was just putting the finishing touches to its 12 new en-suite double rooms. Prices hadn't been fixed, but you shouldn't pay more than *US$6*.

🏠 **Nigat Hotel** (8 rooms) ☎022 666 0121. On the opposite side of the road to the Rose Hotel, this new hotel is the best of the pocket-pleasing cheapies with the cleanest & newest rooms; all using a common cold shower. *US$4.50*.

🏠 **TG Café & Hotel** (6 rooms) ☎022 666 0232. Next door to the Nigat Hotel, this small café-cum-hotel is a step down in quality & price with adequately clean rooms – the same cannot be said about the shared bathrooms! *US$2.50*.

⚐ **Changeti Camp** (10 beds) ☎022 666 0700. If you are here for trekking, this tented camp at Changeti may be preferable to any hotel in town. The camp is a half-hour's drive from Dodola, then 20mins more by foot or horse. With a vehicle your trip to this site can begin anytime before 17.00. Without a vehicle, you must start your trek by 14.00 for this to be an option. As with the other camps, you must bring all your own food. You must also pay for a guide: US$11.50. *Camping US$3 pp.*

ADABA–DODOLA MOUNTAIN TREKKING

This circuit of guided trails and huts through the mountains south of Dodola and Adaba forms an excellent and inexpensive goal for both hikers and trekkers on horseback. Implemented by the German aid organisation GTZ, the project is part of an integrated forest management project aimed at conserving the remnants of the area's Afro-montane forest by creating employment and generating community earnings from tourism. A photographer's paradise, the trail's main attraction is the mountain scenery and high-altitude vegetation, which comprises some 50,000ha of natural forest as well as areas of Afro-alpine moorland. Birdlife is prolific and large mammals are present in small numbers. The mountains covered by the trails are effectively a western extension of the Bale range, and there are plans to link these trails and huts with two new huts that are due to be constructed in Bale's Web Valley.

The dominant tree types in the forest zone are the African juniper, the coniferous *Podocarpus falcatus* and the fragrant *Hagenia abyssinica*. Many of these trees are giants over 500 years old. Indeed, the landscapes here might be described as biblical, and are reminiscent of Dutch Golden Age paintings. Above 3,200m, forest gives way to open moorland of St John's wort and heather (*Erica*), dotted with giant Angafu thistle shrubs with ball-shaped red flowers and giant lobelias. The juniper and hagenia forests protect a similar composition of birds to that found at Dinsho. Among the more visible species are wattled ibis, Rouget's rail, black-winged lovebird, yellow-fronted parrot, banded barbet, Abyssinian woodpecker, Abyssinian longclaw, Abyssinian catbird, white-backed black tit, Ethiopian oriole, white-cheeked turaco, black kite, augur buzzard and lammergeyer. The most visible large mammals are vervet and guereza monkeys, but Ethiopian wolf, mountain nyala and Menelik's bushbuck inhabit the mountains, and although they are not as common as in Bale, they are sometimes seen by trekkers.

The circuit of trails connect one permanent tented camp (Changeti) and five simple but fully equipped mountain huts. Running from west to east, these are Wahoro (3,300m), Angafu (3,460m), Adele (3,300m), Mololicho (3,080m) and Duro (3,350m). The full circuit can be covered over five nights and six days, but any one of the huts can be reached from the trailhead within four hours, so it is possible to visit one or two huts only. The Dodola Eco-Tourism Guides Association encourages visitors to trek on horseback, for which no prior riding experience is necessary. (If you do take a horse, make sure to check his/her back for saddle sores. For the animal's well-being, you should refuse any horse who is injured or bleeding.) Hiking is also permitted, but ascending to an altitude of 3,500m can be very tiring, particularly if you are not acclimatised to high altitudes. A guide must accompany all visitors. The best time for trekking is the dry season, between November and May. During July and August, afternoon showers are an almost daily occurrence, but it is possible to do all your hiking or trekking in the morning, and the wet conditions are compensated for by the lush vegetation and abundant wild flowers. A hat and sun block are essential at all times of year, as is warm clothing and solid footwear.

TREKKING ROUTES The staff at the Dodola Guides headquarters are knowledgeable and helpful, and will be able to advise on an itinerary depending on your available time and your interests. Six days are required to cover the full circuit. Approximate trekking times are two hours from Dodola to Changeti, three hours from Changeti to Wahoro, five hours from Wahoro to Angafu, one hour from Angafu to Adele, four hours from Adele to Mololicho, six hours from Mololicho to Duro, and three hours from Duro to the eastern trailhead. Depending on your level of fitness, hiking generally takes about 50% longer. It is possible to cut a day from the circuit by trekking directly between Angafu and Mololicho.

Several shorter variations are possible, since the first three huts all lie within four hours of the western trailhead, Mololicho lies about three hours from a central trailhead near Herero village, and Duro lies about four hours from the eastern trailhead. With three nights to spare, you could loop between the three western huts; with one or two nights you could visit any one hut as a round trip. With an early start, it is even possible to visit Wahoro as a day trip. The trek from Wahoro to Angafu is nothing short of epic, while Duro is possibly the most beautiful hut for a one-night stay, offering great views of Bale's Harenna Forest. Angafu and Adele lie in the area where you are most likely to encounter wildlife. The Berenda Ridge, which can be hiked to as a day trip from Duro, is noted for its bamboo forest and as a good place for mountain nyala and Ethiopian wolf.

ORGANISATION AND COSTS Treks and hikes must be arranged through the **Dodola Eco-Tourism Guides Association** (\ *022 666 0700*; m *0913 348 375*) in Dodola, where you will be allocated an English-speaking guide to handle your requirements. Except during the peak seasons of Christmas and Easter, booking isn't really required. If you arrive in Dodola early enough, you may be able to start your trek that same day; if travelling by bus, you will likely arrive too late in the afternoon. In this case, you might be allowed to go to Changeti camp; if not, you will head out on the following day. The fees are very reasonable. At the office each person pays a US$2.50 entrance fee. A guide is required, and the fee is US$11.50 per group per day. Horse rental costs US$3 per horse per day, while the horse handler is paid US$3 per group day. Accommodation on the mountain costs US$4.50 per person per night. Warm bedding is provided, and there is no need to bring your own sleep gear. All camps also offer hot bucket showers for US$0.30. If you have a vehicle, you can leave it at the forest edge with a guard for US$2.50 per 24 hours. Apart from the entrance fee assessed at the guide headquarters, all payments are made directly to the individuals who provide the service. For this reason, it is very important that you bring plenty of small bills with you, as no change is available at the camps. Detailed receipts are provided for all transactions, making the experience virtually hassle-free.

MOUNTAIN HUTS There are five camps in the mountains, each of which consists of a hut with a communal eating area and two four-bed dormitories. Facilities

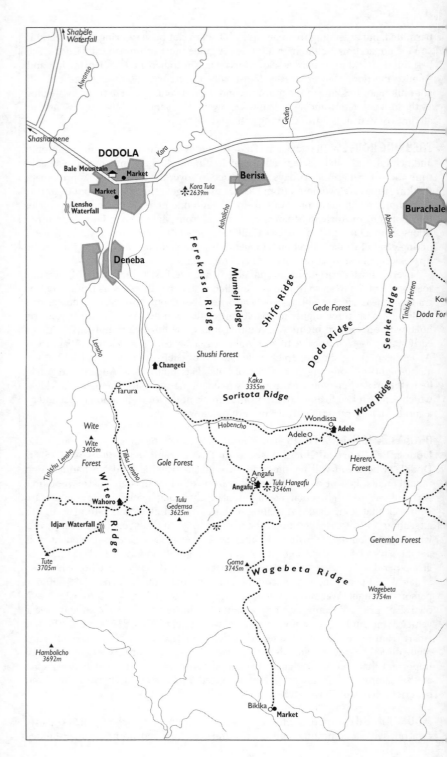

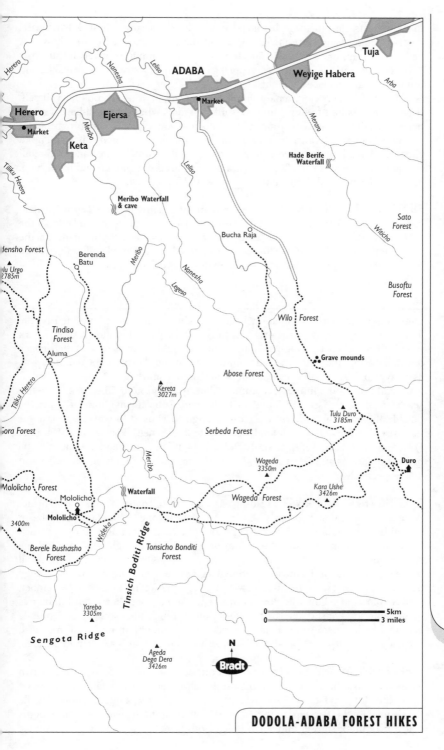

DODOLA-ADABA FOREST HIKES

include sheets, sleeping bags, blankets, towels, flip-flops, stoves, basic kitchenware, crockery, cutlery and kerosene lamps. An outside annex has a toilet and shower. A bed in the dormitory costs US$4.50 per person, while camping outside the hut costs US$3 per person. Clean water from springs or mountain streams is available, and water filters are in place at all huts.

The camp keepers can prepare simple local meals, or you can cook for yourself. If possible, it is best to buy your foodstuffs in Addis where you will have a much better selection. Otherwise your guide will show you where to buy provisions in Dodola. Pasta, rice, lentils, dried peas, tinned oat flakes, powdered coffee and milk, chocolate bars, biscuits, cheese, tomato concentrate, tinned butter and oil are all available. You can also arrange to have a goat or sheep slaughtered and barbecued. The camp keepers sell soft drinks, beer, wine and local spirit.

FURTHER INFORMATION The project has an informative website (*www.baletrek. com*), and information sheets and an excellent colour map are available at the office in Dodola. Although trekking arrangements can usually be made on the spot, queries and advance bookings can be directed to the Dodola office (↘ *022 666 0036/0103;* e *gtz.ifmp@ethionet.et or gtz-ifmp@les-raisting.de*).

DINSHO

Dinsho is an attractive montane village: chilly, wet, and recently uplifted by the arrival of electricity. With the park headquarters for Bale Mountain National Park only 2km east along the Dodola–Goba road, you could easily use one of the village's few dollar-a-night hotels as a base from where you could explore the national park as a day trip. Also worth checking out is the Tuesday **market**.

In addition to the limited accommodation in and around Dinsho, a far better selection of hotels is to be found in **Goba** and **Robe** towns, both of which lie outside the national park but are close enough to Dinsho to serve as a base for motorised visitors. If you intend heading to the Sanetti Plateau and Harenna Forest, or continuing south towards Dola Mena, it's best to spend a night in Goba beforehand. Robe and Goba are covered under separate headings on pages 491 and 493 respectively.

GETTING THERE AND AWAY Heading eastward from Adaba, it's 58km to Dinsho. At least one bus going towards Dinsho will pass through Dodola and Adaba in the mid morning, but you may struggle to find a seat. Catching a ride on a truck between Adaba and Dinsho should not be a problem (though bear in mind the regulations against truck drivers carrying foreigners). Once you've got a lift, you'll be treated to some of the most sensational landscapes in southern Ethiopia: craggy peaks interspersed with streams and waterfalls and, between August and November, fields of blue and yellow wild flowers and stands of red-hot poker. A few kilometres before entering Dinsho, the road passes briefly through the Gaysay sector of Bale National Park, where you are almost certain to see mountain nyala and may well catch a glimpse of a member of the Ethiopian wolf pack that is resident in the area.

🏠 **WHERE TO STAY AND EAT** The only accommodation in Dinsho is in one of two bare-bone basic hotels which lie opposite each other on the main road through town: the **Hoteela Tsehai** (*7 rooms*) has grim rooms using a bucket shower, while the **Genet Hotel** (*10 rooms;* m *0913 348 903*) offers similarly dismal-looking rooms using a common shower and squat toilet. Both have acceptable local restaurants.

Owned by a member of the Ethiopian Wolf Conservation Programme, the appropriately muralled **Wolf's Den Café** serves coffee, tea and breakfast staples. Around the corner by the mosque the unassuming and un-signed **Kebe's Place** has to rate as one of the best finds of this research trip. The friendly restaurant with its intimate fairy lighting serves cheap and filling dishes for less than US$2; they also sell delicious take-away samosas for US$0.30 each, perfect for taking hiking.

BALE MOUNTAINS NATIONAL PARK

(*Entrance US$5.50 per 24hrs; vehicle entrance US$1.50/2.50 1–12 seater/12+ seater; www.balemountains.org*) This scenic 2,200km² national park, set aside in the 1960s but never officially gazetted, protects the higher reaches of the Bale range, including Mount Tullo Deemtu, which at 4,377m is the second-highest peak in Ethiopia. The main attractions of the park are the wild alpine scenery, particularly on the 4,000m-high Sanetti Plateau, and the relative ease with which one can see up to a dozen endemic birds as well as Ethiopian wolves and mountain nyala. Bale is very accessible on public transport, and can be explored on foot, on horseback or by vehicle. The road across the Sanetti Plateau, built by the Derg to provide an alternative emergency access route to the south, is reportedly the highest all-weather road in Africa.

The Bale Mountains are of relatively ancient volcanic origin, having formed from solidified lava more than ten million years ago. The slopes above 3,500m supported glacial activity until as recently as 2,000 years ago, and still receive the occasional snowfall, most often in the dry season between November and February. More than 40 streams including the Web, Genale and Welmel rise in the Bale Watershed, most of which eventually flow into the mighty Juba or Wabe Shebelle rivers after they cross the border into Somalia.

The main habitats protected by Bale are juniper and hagenia woodland, Afro-montane forest and Afro-alpine moorland. The juniper–hagenia woodland lies at elevations of between 2,500m and 3,300m, and is mostly found on the northern slopes, such as around the park headquarters at Dinsho. At similar elevations on the southern slopes, the vast and little-studied Harenna Forest is the park's main stand of Afro-montane forest. Afro-alpine moorland is characteristic of altitudes above 3,500m, with the most extensive patches to be found on the Sanetti Plateau and in the Web river valley. The moorland, as well as the open vegetation below the forest zone, is characterised by wonderful wild-flower displays, particularly between August and November. One of the most common and distinctive plants throughout the Bale region is the red-hot poker, an aloe that grows to shrub height and can be identified by its orange spear-shaped flowers.

The characteristic large mammals of Bale's juniper woodland are the mountain nyala and Menelik's bushbuck (both endemic to Ethiopia), as well as warthog and bohor reedbuck. Moorland is the favoured habitat of the Ethiopian wolf. Commonly seen mammals of the extensive Harenna Forest, which lies south of the Sanetti Plateau, include guereza, vervet monkey, the localised bamboo-dwelling Bale monkey, olive baboon, Menelik's bushbuck, bushpig and the lesser known giant forest hog. Large predators such as lion, leopard and African wild dog are still resident but are seldom seen by visitors. Bale National Park region is undoubtedly the best part of Ethiopia for endemic birds.

Accessible as it is today, Bale was one of the last parts of Africa to attract serious scientific exploration, and it remains sufficiently out of the way even today that very few travellers make it there by comparison with, say, the Simiens.

The earliest-recorded visitor to the Sanetti Plateau was the German naturalist Carl van Erlanger, who traversed it in 1899, discovering the giant mole rat in the process. Bizarrely, no further expedition to the upper slopes of Bale was documented between then and the late 1950s, when the Finnish geographer Helmer Smels made several visits to the area, discovering – among other things – that the mountains hosted a previously unsuspected population of the rare Ethiopian wolf. It was the British naturalist Leslie Brown, upon visiting the mountains in 1963, who first recognised that Bale might actually be the wolf's main stronghold, and it was he who proposed that the area be set aside as a national park. Only in 1974 did James Malcolm collect the first wolf census data to confirm Brown's belief. The wolves are now recognised as being Africa's most endangered carnivore, as well as the world's rarest canid species.

FURTHER INFORMATION The *Bale Mountains National Park Official Trekking Map* (2010), produced by the Frankfurt Zoological Society and available from the park headquarters, is indispensible for anyone planning on spending some time in the mountains. Another must-have is the recently released 100-page colour *Bale Mountain Guidebook* (2012) compiled by the Frankfurt Zoological Society which contains comprehensive information on Bale National Park as well as an extensive section on four selected driving routes from Addis Ababa that pass through other southern parks including Awash National Park and Yabello Game Sanctuary. A downloadable version is hoped to be available through the park website (*www.balemountains.org*); in the meantime it can be obtained through the park headquarters along with the new *Bale Region Birding Route and Sites* booklet which has a detailed description about birding sites in Bale as well as a handy checklist. In addition the older, but still excellent, 52-page booklet *Bale Mountains: A Guidebook* written by Ethiopian wolf expert Stuart Williams and published in 2002 by the Ethiopian Wolf Conservation Programme (EWCP) in conjunction with various other international conservation bodies can be bought at a few bookshops in Addis Ababa as well as at the EWCP offices within the park headquarters at Dinsho. Another excellent source of information is the Frankfurt Zoological Society (FZS), which oversees the Bale Mountains Conservation Project (e *biniyamadmassu@fzs. org; www.fzs.org or www.balemountains.org*).

GETTING THERE The park headquarters and lodge are situated off the Dodola–Goba road, about 2km east of the village of Dinsho. The forest immediately around the headquarters is the best place to look for the park's endemic antelope and forest birds. It is also where all hikes and treks must be set up and paid for. Coming from the direction of Dodola in a private vehicle, you need to drive through Dinsho and continue uphill in the direction of Goba, then take the signposted turn-off to your right, which immediately brings you to the park entrance gate. Any bus or truck heading between Dodola and Goba will stop at Dinsho, from where it takes about 30 minutes to walk to the headquarters following the same route. This walk can be cut to ten minutes if you stay on the bus through town, and then ask to be dropped off at the turn-off. This will also limit your exposure to the unofficial, unqualified guides who hang around the town waiting to latch on to tourists. Once you pick up one of these guides they are, like leeches, hard to shake off – see the box, *Lost on the Sanetti*, page 490, for why an official guide is essential. When you decide to move on from Dinsho, note that most buses passing through Dinsho in either direction will be full. Get an early start, and ask any trucks that pass through for a lift. It's worth noting that on weekends, there may not be a fee collector present. If not you will

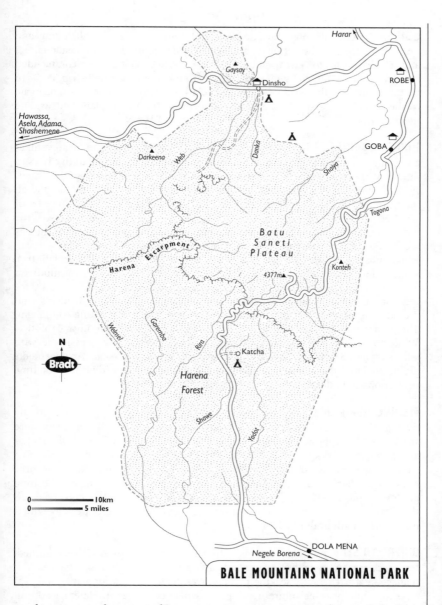

BALE MOUNTAINS NATIONAL PARK

need to return to the gate at a later stage to organise payment and get a receipt. This receipt must be shown to the gate operator at the base of the Sanetti Plateau if you choose to travel from Dinsho to Sanetti.

By road, the Sanetti Plateau lies about 60km from Dinsho, following the main road through Robe and Goba, then continuing south from Goba towards Dola Mena. The Harenna Forest lies further south along the same road. This is an all-weather road, and it can be driven along in a private 4x4, or else by using the limited public transport that runs between Goba and Dola Mena (see page 490). To visit the plateau by road, it is best to base yourself in Goba. To visit it by foot or horseback, you will have to make arrangements at Dinsho.

GUIDES Park regulations stipulate that guides are required for all hiking and horseriding treks in the national park. For walking around the park headquarters and self-drive trips to Gaysay and to the Sanetti Plateau guides are recommended but *not* required. Official guides cost US$9/10 for a day/overnight trip, and can be hired through the **Nyala Guides Association** stationed at the entrance gate to the park. Guides speak English and have been trained in plant and wildlife identification.

HIKES AND HORSE TREKS The staff at the park headquarters can arrange hikes and pony/horse treks deeper into the park. These range from one to five days in duration. The most popular option is a three-day horse or pony trek to the Sanetti Plateau, which allows you plenty of time to explore the alpine moorland and all but guarantees a sighting of Ethiopian wolf. In addition to the park entrance fee of US$5.50 per 24 hours, a camping fee of US$2.50 per person per day is assessed. The required guide costs US$9/10 for a day/overnight trip. If you take a vehicle there is a US$1.50–2.50 fee (depending on the number of seats) per 24 hours. Horse rental, which must be organised a day in advance, costs US$3/4 for a day/overnight trip, while a horse assistant costs US$5/6 for a day/overnight trip. Bear in mind you will also need to pay for load horses and for handlers as well. Apart from entrance fees for the park, all other payments are made directly to the individuals who provide the services. You must organise your own food and cooking equipment. The guides may be able to help you with this if you give them advance notice. While not required, be prepared to have to feed all guides and horse assistants with your supplies. Several day hikes to nearby peaks are also possible. Arrangements are flexible and the warden and rangers can advise you according to your time restrictions and interests.

FISHING The Bale Mountains apparently offers excellent opportunities for fly fishing. During the late 1960s, the park's Danka, Web and Shaya rivers were stocked with rainbow and brown trout from Kenya. The fish stock flourished and today the park's rivers and streams offer keen anglers one of Africa's most stunning wilderness fishing experiences. Fishing permits costing US$12 for three days are available from the Agriculture Office in Dinsho. Mandatory fishing guides costing US$12 per day can also be arranged here. Anglers must bring all their own equipment and catch is limited to five fish per angler per day with a minimum length limit of 25cm.

WHERE TO STAY Accommodations within the park are currently very limited, for which reason many visitors use Goba as a base. This might soon change. Park management is currently seeking private investors to build an upmarket lodge at Dinsho, while possible future developments include lodges in Harenna and on the Sanetti Plateau. In addition, FARM-Africa and SOS Sahel Ethiopia have long talked about establishing a traditional community-run *tukul*-style lodge on the banks of the Shaya River, though no progress had been made by early 2012. For more information, see www.balemountains.org, www.pfmp-farmsos.org and www. ethiopianwolf.org.

Plans for a network of mountain huts, in place since the last edition of the guide was researched, have not as yet eventuated. If they ever do, the first two huts should be situated within the Web river valley and at the top of the valley. Aimed towards hikers based out of Dinsho, these huts are intended to form part of an extended trail network connecting Dodola to the Sanetti Plateau.

Dinsho Lodge Tucked away in the juniper forest at the park headquarters, this rustic but comfortable self-catering lodge currently offers the only formal accommodation in the national park. A variety of rooms is available, dorm-style with bunk beds. Warm bedding is provided, so you do not need a sleeping bag unless you plan to trek. The lodge has basic facilities including a communal kitchen, toilets & cold showers, & a large lounge with a log fire. During our stay the one thing in short supply was water, which was not available in the kitchen or bathrooms, but could be obtained from a pump outside. Electricity is also unreliable, so charge all camera batteries, etc before arriving in Bale. Mountain nyala & Menelik's bushbuck often walk past the lodge gardens, as do warthog, while hyena can often be heard calling at night. If you are staying here, you may want to take advantage of the kitchen, & cook for yourself. Basic foodstuffs such as eggs, potatoes & macaroni can be bought in Dinsho, but it's advisable to bring most of what you need along with you. *US$4–12 pp, depending on how many beds are in the room.*

Nyala Guest House This new guesthouse is located in the centre of the park headquarters at Dinsho in what was once the park warden's house. It is a good spot for viewing wildlife, & the endemic mountain nyala is often seen through the large windows of the front room. This big house is encircled by juniper & hagenia trees, & consists of 2 comfortable twin rooms, a big salon with fireplace & a bathroom with hot shower & toilets. Currently guests must bring their own cooking utensils for self-catering, although kitchen utensils should be available shortly. Contact the FZS for bookings & details (e *biniyamadmassu@fzs.org; www.fzs.org*). *US$15 pp per bed.*

HQ campsite The facility-free campsite on a hill behind the lodge offers panoramic views over Dinsho village & across to several peaks, including Batu Tiko. There is a long-drop toilet at the campsite, but water must be carried from the lodge. The hill is covered in heath-like vegetation & juniper forest & there is plenty of wildlife to be seen in the area. *US$2.50/4 per tent for 1–4 people/more than 4 people.*

Other campsites The only option at present for overnight trekkers & hikers is to camp at one of these designated campsites dotted around the park. There are no facilities at these campsites, so you must bring all of your own camping equipment & firewood. Sustainable eucalyptus firewood can be arranged at the park entrance, but it is illegal to collect firewood within the park.

WHAT TO SEE AND DO
Natural History Museum (⏲ *08.00–17.00 Mon–Fri; entrance free*) The Ethiopian Wolf Conservation Programme (EWCP) (e *info@ethiopianwolf.org; www.ethiopianwolf.org*) has set up a small museum at its base about 200m from Dinsho Lodge. It displays a selection of tired-looking stuffed animals, including several endemics. At present, the museum is the only source of information on the natural history of Bale, with a focus on the endangered wolves and the programmes currently in effect to ensure their survival. It is hoped that it will eventually expand into a proper interpretation centre. In the meantime, the attached library is useful for researchers or anyone interested in Bale's flora and fauna.

Dinsho walking trail The walking trail, which leads through the juniper forest around the park headquarters, demands a few hours' exploration as it protects the main concentration of Bale's mountain nyala. This exceptionally handsome antelope is abundant in the area – estimated population is about 1,000 and it's not unusual to come across four or five herds – as is the superficially similar but much smaller and more solitary Menelik's bushbuck. Other mammals you can expect to see here are warthog, bohor reedbuck and possibly black-and-white colobus monkeys. Birdwatching around the headquarters is good (see box, *Bale's birds*, page 488), though, as is often the case, you will probably see fewer birds in the forest proper than you will in the broken woodland fringing the road that leads from the turn-off to the headquarters. The forest is characterised by light undergrowth, which allows for good game viewing, and also by the herby aroma of fallen hagenia leaves. An

Bale National Park is rightly regarded as the best place to see a good range of those birds that are endemic to Ethiopia and Eritrea. At least 16 such endemics have been recorded in the park, including the Bale parisoma, which is unique to Bale, and a casual visitor could hope to spot most of them over the course of a few hours each at Dinsho and on the Sanetti Plateau. In addition to its endemics, Bale is a good site to pick up several localised highland birds and migrant waterfowl and raptors, and the park supports isolated breeding populations of several other noteworthy species.

Even before arriving at Dinsho, it is worth stopping a few times as you pass through the Gaysay extension of the park, a reliable site for the endemic Rouget's rail and Abyssinian longclaw, as well as several other water and grassland birds. Dinsho itself is an excellent spot for endemics – Abyssinian owl, black-winged lovebird, white-backed black tit, Abyssinian catbird, Abyssinian slaty flycatcher, thick-billed raven and white-collared pigeon – while other forest birds include white-cheeked turaco, Abyssinian ground thrush, olive thrush and Cape eagle owl.

The most alluring birdwatching spot is of course the Sanetti Plateau. The ascent there from Bale is not without interest. Forest patches along this road hold similar species to Dinsho, notably the nondescript but endemic Bale parisoma. Ascending above the forest zone, the alpine chat and endemic black-headed siskin are abundant, and moorland and chestnut-naped francolin often dart across the road. A few pairs of very confiding Rouget's rail are resident along the artificial drainage stream that runs to the left of the road for about 1km.

At one or other of the tarns on the Sanetti Plateau, you can be confident of sighting the endemic blue-winged goose, wattled ibis and spot-throated plover, as well as a representative of sub-Saharan Africa's only breeding population of ruddy shelduck and, in season, a number of migrant waterfowl. An isolated population of the localised wattled crane is present seasonally, and usually easy to observe when it is around. The variety of smaller birds is somewhat limited. Red-throated pipit, Thekla lark, Abyssinian longclaw and (seasonally) yellow wagtail are the common ground birds, while the lovely tacazze sunbird is often seen feeding on flowering aloes.

The commonest raptor is the auger buzzard, sometimes seen in its localised melanistic phase. Kestrels and buzzards are quite common too: the rare saker falcon has been recorded three times on the plateau, though be aware that the more common lanner falcon here often has an unusually pale crown. Sanetti is a great place for large eagles. The tawny eagle is the most common of these, supplemented by the European imperial and steppe eagle. In 1993, it was discovered that Bale hosts sub-Saharan Africa's only recorded breeding population of golden eagle. The plateau also supports the most southerly breeding population of the crow-like red-billed chough.

The Harenna Forest, though less well known scientifically, supports a greater variety of forest birds, with new records likely as more birders explore the area. Endemics include white-backed black tit, Abyssinian catbird, Abyssinian woodpecker, Ethiopian oriole, yellow-fronted parrot and the taxonomically uncertain brown saw-wing swallow. Other specials include the African cuckoo hawk, and brown-backed honeyguide.

unusual plant of the Dinsho area is the white-flowered Abyssinian rose, the only flowering rose that is indigenous to Africa.

The Gaysay extension

This northerly extension of Bale National Park protects the 3,543m Mount Gaysay, as well as the eponymous river and small Lake Bassasso. Consistently underrated, the Gaysay may be the best place to view large concentrations of mountain nyala and Menelik's bushbuck. Moreover, it is of particular interest to travellers with limited time and without transport, since it is transected for several kilometres by the Dodola road, starting about 3km west of Dinsho. Some indigenous forest remains here, but otherwise the area is covered in moist grassland that becomes quite marshy near the lake and river. At least one pack of Ethiopian wolf has a territory centred on the Gaysay extension. Warthog are abundant, spotted hyena are often seen in the early morning or at dusk, while serval can also be seen in the evenings. The marshy areas also support birds more normally associated with the Sanetti Plateau, most visibly Rouget's rail, which is very common here. Guided walks to Gaysay can be arranged at the park headquarters about an hour away on foot. It is also possible to hike to the top of Mount Gaysay.

Web River Valley

Set at an elevation of roughly 3,500m, about 10km southwest of Dinsho, the Web Valley supports a moorland cover similar in appearance to the Sanetti Plateau, though with a markedly different floral composition, dominated by various Alchemilla species. Abundant small rodents make the valley ideal Ethiopian wolf territory. Several packs are resident, and are as easily seen as they are on the Sanetti Plateau, despite large numbers having perished as a result of a (rapidly contained) rabies outbreak in 2003. The rough 11km track between Dinsho and the Web Valley takes about an hour to drive – 4x4 only – and involves crossing a natural rock bridge over the Danka River where rock hyrax are frequently observed. There is an attractive waterfall at the confluence of the Web and Wolla rivers. With an early start, it is possible to hike or trek to the Web Valley as a day trip out of Dinsho, with a stop for lunch at Fincha Habera Waterfall. Camping is permitted in the area.

Sanetti Plateau

The Sanetti Plateau is cited as the world's largest expanse of Afro-alpine moorland, a montane habitat confined to altitudes of 3,500–4,500m on east Africa's tallest mountains. Because such habitats are isolated from similar ones on other mountains, they tend to display a very high degree of endemism, and Sanetti is no exception. Among other things, the plateau is renowned for supporting the most substantial extant population of Ethiopian wolf, which is far more numerous and more easily seen here than in the Simien Mountains. It is some measure of how little explored Bale was until recent times that this wolf population was first made known to science in 1959. Other characteristic mammals of the plateau are golden jackal and klipspringer, neither of which is seen with great frequency, and Starck's hare, the endemic giant mole rat, and a number of other endemic small burrowing rodents.

The Sanetti Plateau can be driven to from Goba town in about 45 minutes. The road starts with a 1,300m hike in altitude, through tangled thickets and woodland where francolins sprint across the road and, in summer, fields of red-hot poker point ever skywards. Look back, and the plains around Goba stretch to an indistinct horizon. About 13km past Goba, the road levels out and you are surrounded by typical Afro-alpine vegetation: clumped grey heather interspersed with lichen-covered rocks and stands of giant lobelia, strange other-worldly plants that can grow up to 3m high and whose corky bark and waxen leaves readily withstand extreme sub-zero temperatures. Drive slowly, as Ethiopian wolf are unexpectedly common

21

and are easily sighted from the road, most often seen singly or in pairs sniffing out small rodents before they can scurry to the safety of their burrows. About halfway across the plateau the road skirts a series of crystal-clear tarns, where you can expect to see several endemic birds as well as migrant waterfowl. Somewhat desolate in appearance when it is overcast, the plateau is uniquely beautiful under blue skies, particularly in the soft light of early morning and late afternoon.

In a private vehicle, a round trip to the plateau from Goba should take about four hours, depending of course on how long you choose to spend up there. Travellers without a private vehicle can visit the plateau on a three- or four-night trek out of Dinsho, or by catching a lift with one of the trucks that serve as public transport between Goba and Dola Mena. It is possible to hire a 4x4 for the day through one of the hotels in Goba, but this will cost at least US$200.

Harenna Forest At the southern end of the Sanetti Plateau, the Harenna Escarpment affords an astounding view over the forest almost 2,000m below. The

---

LOST ON THE SANETTI

With thanks to Matan Shefi, Yuval Mann and Shira Ben Ami

At an elevation of 3,500–4,500m, a large portion of the Sanetti Plateau lies above the treeline. Weather can move in quickly, and the barren plains provide little shelter should you get caught in a storm. This is not a place for casual trekking. Night-time temperatures can drop close to freezing, making a good sleeping bag, warm clothes and reliable tent and rain gear essential. Our group of four had all the requisite equipment and plenty of food as well. Nevertheless, our trip turned out to be a nightmare. Immediately upon arriving in Dinsho we were greeted by a man named 'Perdido' who said he was a guide; he even produced an identification card verifying that he was a member of BATO, the Bale Association of Tour Operators. 'Perdido' said he could arrange a four-day trek to the Sanetti Plateau, and accompanied us to the park headquarters where we paid our fees. Day one of our trek was uneventful. We followed a well-worn path and stayed at an established campsite. On day two clouds began to roll in, obscuring the mountains in the distance. Though we were unable to locate the official campsite that night, at this point none of us worried. On day three we awoke to rain and were basically clouded in. After several hours of hiking, we began to question whether our guide might be lost. Our fears were confirmed when we got out a compass. 'Perdido' ensured us that we were heading east towards the Goba road, when in reality we were heading south. To make matters worse, the rains picked up – after several hours our Gore-tex slickers were soaked through, and all of us were cold and wet. High winds made setting up a tent in the open impossible; finally we found an abandoned hut where we spent a miserable night. From this point on our guide was useless. Luckily, we had the good sense to bring a map and compass of our own. After another miserable 20km day, we eventually found the Goba road. Back at park headquarters we learned the truth – 'Perdido' was not an official guide (yet no-one said a word about this when we booked our trip five days earlier). All official guides are thoroughly trained by the Frankfurt Zoological Society and carry a card that says **Nyala Guides Association**. Don't make the mistake we did; before heading out make sure your guide is properly qualified!

road then switchbacks exhilaratingly to the base of the escarpment, where the green heather suddenly transforms to a Grimm Brothers' forest of low gnarled trees laden with moss and swathed in old man's beard. The forest clears as you hit a collection of mud huts known as Rira, where, with a bit of luck hot tea and dry biscuits are available. After Rira, the road south towards Dola Mena continues through the Harenna Forest for a further 40km or so.

Before 1983, when the road under discussion was cut, the Harenna Forest was virtually unknown to science and, although a pioneering expedition has since collected several new amphibian and reptile species, the bulk of the Harenna Forest has never been explored and there are doubtless countless species awaiting discovery. The forest is far denser than the juniper woodland around Dinsho, and it comprises a more varied selection of trees, with a similar appearance and composition to the forests found on other east African mountains. A wealth of birds is resident, while mammals likely to be seen from the main road include olive baboon, guereza monkey, bushbuck and bushpig. Leopard are still around, a small pride of lions is resident in the area around the campsite, and African wild dogs are seen from time to time – most recently in 2011. The forest is also home to the newly discovered but rarely seen Bale monkey, which is similar to a vervet.

As with the Sanetti Plateau, the Harenna Forest can be visited as a day trip out of Goba in a private vehicle. Allocate a full day to the trip, and leave as early as you can. With camping equipment and a private vehicle, you could pitch a tent at the small campsite a few kilometres from Rira. Hiking or trekking to Harenna from Dinsho isn't a realistic proposition, unless you have a lot of time to spare. All transport between Goba and Dola Mena passes through the forest.

ROBE

The town of Robe lies on the main Goba road 25km past Dinsho and 13km before Goba itself. It is a large town with adequate facilities, but strangely subdued and nondescript, straggling for a couple of kilometres along a eucalyptus-lined main road. There are few compelling reasons to stay in Robe, unless perhaps you are heading to Sof Omar (see page 493) on public transport, or else you are motorised and want to use Robe as a base to explore the region. The hectic Thursday **market** is worth a look, while the **Bale Museum** (\ *022 665 1066*), hidden in a blue tin shed at the back of the Bale Zone Justice office, might be of interest – unfortunately no-one was available to show us around or tell us about the displays.

A possible 4x4 day excursion from Robe is to **Gasera**, which offers a magnificent viewpoint over the Wabe Shebelle Gorge, home to Ethiopia's most southerly gelada population. Gasera lies about 65km out of Robe, branching northward from the Dinsho road after 6km, then turning right at the small market town of Ali after another 20km or so.

GETTING THERE AND AWAY Coming from Dinsho, any vehicle heading towards Goba can drop you at Robe. The bus station stands in isolation some distance from the town centre along the Goba road, so unless you are heading for the Bekele Mola (see page 492), ask to be dropped off more centrally. From the station there are daily services to Dinsho (US$1.50; 1 hour), Shashemene (US$6; 7–8 hours) and Addis Ababa (US$9; c12 hours). It's worth noting that buses out of Robe towards Dodola may be full by the time they reach Robe. More sensible, perhaps, is to get up early and catch a local minibus to Goba, where long-distance buses start. Regular minibuses (US$0.40) ply the 15km route between Robe and Goba.

WHERE TO STAY

🏠 **Bekele Mola Hotel** (24 rooms) 📞022 665 0065. Clearly signposted on the Goba side of town between the bus station & main traffic roundabout, this hotel – even though faded – is still far better value than anything in Goba. The semi-detached rooms, set around an overgrown grassy compound, are large & airy with freshly painted interiors. The time-worn en-suite rooms with hot showers are long overdue an update. The restaurant serves unmemorable but affordable Western dishes. *US$9/12 dbl/twin.*

🏠 **Abadama Hotel** (18 rooms) 📞022 865 0260; m 0920 202 543. This friendly new hotel located south of the centre on the road to Goba currently offers Robe's most comfortable accommodation. The clean, tiled rooms are spacious & neat with simple modern furnishings & hot-shower en suite. The only downside is there is no restaurant, but cold drinks are available. *US$9.50/10 dbl/twin, US$11 suite with TV & bathtub.*

🏠 **Hotel Matafaria Danagaa** (18 rooms) 📞022 665 0046. This simple lodge is set in large quiet grounds on the Dinsho edge of town. The rooms – all with double beds – are huge, but the cold-shower en suites don't look like they've been introduced to a mop or a scrubbing brush in a very long while. *US$6.*

✗ **WHERE TO EAT** The most promising-looking places to eat, aside from the **Bekele Mola**, is the **Choice Bar and Restaurant** next to the Hotel Matafaria Danagaa and the buzzing **Hani Café** opposite the Oromia Bank. Robe is well served with good pastry shops: the **Fountain Café** and **Wel Mall Cafeteria** are recommended, while **Zed Juice House** is the top spot for fresh juices.

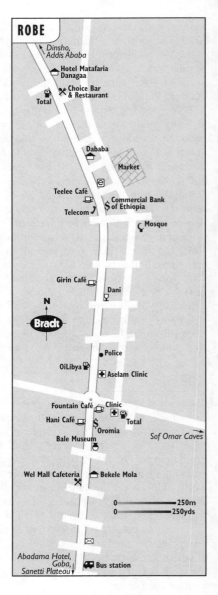

SOF OMAR CAVES

This vast network of limestone caverns, reputedly the largest in Africa, lies 100km east of the Bale range at an elevation of 1,300m. It has been carved by the Web River, which descends from the Bale Highlands to the flat, arid plains that stretch towards the Somali border. Following the course of the clear aquamarine Web River underground for some 16km, the caves are reached through a vast portal, which leads into the Chamber of Columns, a cathedral-esque hall studded with limestone pillars reaching up to 20m high. A 1.7km trail leads from the entrance through several other chambers, taking about an hour to walk and crossing the river seven times. The caves are named after Sheikh Sof Omar, a 12th-century Muslim leader who used them as a refuge, and they remain an important site of pilgrimage for Ethiopian Muslims. Their religious significance can, however, be dated back to the earliest animist religions of the area.

Sof Omar is regularly visited by birdwatchers because it is one of two sites where it's reasonably easy to see Salvadori's serin, a threatened and localised dry-country endemic with a bold yellow throat. The serin is often elusive, but even if you miss it, the area holds several other good acacia-scrub species, notably orange-bellied parrot, blue-naped mousebird, Abyssinian scimitar-bill, sulphur-breasted bush shrike, small grey flycatcher, brown-tailed chat, brown-tailed apalis, bristle-crowned and Fischer's starling, and Somali tit.

GETTING THERE AND AWAY You first need to get to **Goro**, a small town about 60km east and two hours' drive from Robe. A few small vans do this run throughout the morning. From Goro, it is roughly 40km to Sof Omar, which lies on the Ginir road. If you are restricted to public transport, the only day when you can get through to Sof Omar from Goro is Saturday, when there is a market in the village. The best plan would therefore be to head out to Goro on Friday and spend the night there – it's not much of a place and there is no electricity, but there are a few dollar-a-night hotels to choose from. On the way out to the caves, look out for greater and lesser kudu, both of which are common in the dry acacia scrub around Goro and Sof Omar, as is Salt's dik-dik.

The area around Sof Omar is prone to outbreaks of fighting between the local Oromo and Somali peoples – I suggest you enquire about **security** at the Bale National Park headquarters before heading out this way. During the rainy season you should also enquire about high water, which can render the caves impassable.

GOBA

The largest town in the vicinity of Bale, Goba lies at an altitude of 2,500m in the cool, breezy foothills below the Sanetti Plateau. It's an open, spacious and rather unfocused town – the main residential areas sprawl outwards from a disused airstrip that is gradually being built over, while the government buildings and churches are perched discretely on a nearby hill. Like Robe, Goba has a subdued, almost rural atmosphere, which makes it seem cut off from the mainstream of Ethiopian life.

For anyone interested in conservation, the **Bale Beauty Nature Club** (m *0913 470 100*; e *bbnclub@gmail.com*) has a small 2.5ha nature reserve area on the outskirts of Goba on the road to the Sanetti Plateau where they have developed a tree nursery site to raise indigenous seedlings for distribution amongst the community. Visitors are welcome and future plans include building a new lodge and creating a campsite.

GETTING THERE AND AWAY Buses coming from Addis Ababa and Shashemene terminate at Goba, and there is also a steady stream of local transport from nearby Robe. Buses [494 C2] returning to Shashemene leave Goba. Details of the route southwards to Dola Mena are on pages 495–6.

WHERE TO STAY Accommodation in Goba is appallingly over-priced. We recommend you save your money and stay in Robe. That said, a new multi-storey hotel was under construction at the time of research, so perhaps things could be looking up for Goba.

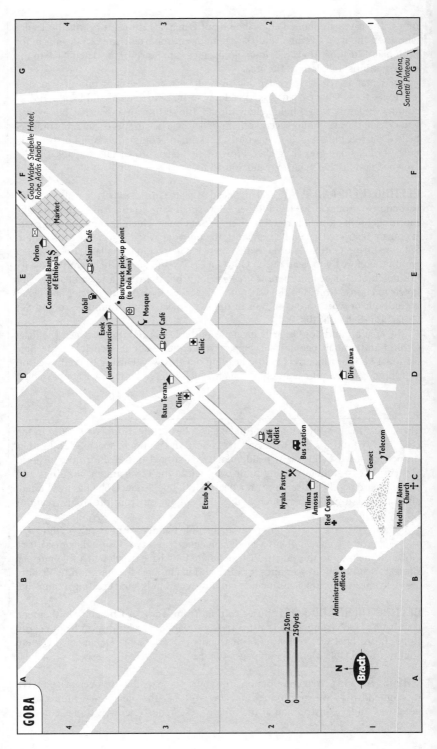

GOBA

494

🛏 **Goba Wabe Shebelle Hotel** [off map 494 F4] (51 rooms) ☎ 022 661 0041; www. wabeshebellehotels.com.et. At the top end of the range, this seriously over-priced former government hotel lies in overgrown grounds about 2km out of town along the Robe road. Foreigners pay almost 3 times the local rate for the pleasure of staying in fraying outdated en-suite rooms with hot water. If you want to stay in Goba in 'style', there is 1 additional room called the Saloon, which has a huge bedroom & bathroom, a separate sitting room & outmoded décor. Despite the gloomy atmosphere, the restaurant is still head & shoulders above anything else in Goba. It is reputedly due a full 5-star revamp, in which case expect a further rise in price. *US$24.50/27/27 sgl/dbl/twin inc b/fast.*

🛏 **Orion Hotel** [494 E4] (12 rooms) **m** 0922 508 531. This new hotel located on the 2nd floor of the Yamara Bldg, possibly offers Goba's best & most reasonably priced accommodation. Unfortunately, all the en-suite rooms were booked out when we passed through, so we weren't able to confirm our suspicions. Mind you, the music blaring from the Denver Café located on the top floor of the building was more than a little off-putting. *US$9 en-suite dbl.*

🛏 **Genet Hotel** [494 C1] (12 rooms) ☎ 022 661 0002. Facing the bus station, this is about the best shoestring option, though the rooms are small & there is no running water. On the plus side, it is quiet, the people seem friendly, the grounds are large & rustic, the double beds are quite large, & hot water by the bucket can be provided on request. *US$4.*

🛏 **Batu Terana Hotel** [494 D3] (14 rooms) ☎ 022 661 0712. This central hotel offers small passably clean en-suite rooms with full-size bed & hot shower, but before taking a room do check whether there's live music that night – or once again you're unlikely to get much sleep until the wee hours. *US$2.50 with common shower, US$4 en-suite dbl.*

WHERE TO EAT The best option, despite being some distance from the town centre, is the **Wabe Shebelle Hotel** [off map 494 F4]. In town, the **Batu Terana Hotel** [494 D3] has a butcher's shop right on the premises and serves excellent *shakila tibs*, fried meat served in a charcoal-heated clay pot. Several good pastry shops run along the main road – the **City Café** [494 D3] and **Selam Café** [494 E4] are recommended, as is the **Nyala Pastry** [494 C2] next to the Yilma Amossa Hotel. If you're heading out to Dola Mena and you fancy a breakfast or you want to stock up on eatables, the Nyala opens, with freshly baked bread on sale and coffee machine whirring, at the unusually early hour of 06.00.

GOBA TO NEGELE BORENA VIA DOLA MENA

The trip south from Goba to Negele Borena is one of the most exciting off-the-beaten-track routes in Ethiopia. Normally, it can be driven in a day in a private vehicle, or covered over two or three days using the hit-and-miss public transport. The road may be impassable in parts after heavy rain (one traveller wrote to say it took him six days to cover in the flooding of 1997). Before heading down this way in a private vehicle, you might want to check that the bridge over the Genale River has been rebuilt, or that the river itself is low enough to be fordable.

The best part of the journey is the initial 110km, where the road leads across the **Sanetti Plateau** and through the **Harenna Forest** (covered in detail under *Bale Mountains National Park* on page 483) to Dola Mena. A few buses and trucks make the journey between Goba and Dola Mena each day, the stunning scenery and surprisingly good game viewing making it one of the best public transport rides in Africa, but unfortunately recent regulation changes bar drivers from giving lifts to foreigners. Still, if you want to try your luck, vehicles headed in this direction congregate on the main road in Goba next to the OiLibya station.

After the Sanetti Plateau and Harenna Forest, dusty little **Dola Mena** could hardly fail to be an anti-climax. I suspect, though, that under any circumstances it would be a bit of a dump. Nevertheless, whether you intend to retreat to Goba or advance to Negele Borena, you will almost certainly have to spend the night here. The whole tone of Dola Mena takes some adjustment after a few days in the Bale Highlands: dusty acacia scrub replaces lush cultivated fields; camels throng the marketplace (main market on Wednesday) and their skimpily dressed Somali owners replace the blanketed horsemen of the highlands. Most of all, those cold showers you flirted with in the Goba evening chill seem suddenly the stuff of dreams. The only hotels in Dola Mena rub shoulders with each other on the Negele road, the best of which is the **Mekurya Mengestu Hotel** (*18 rooms;* ✆ *022 668 0163*) where grubby rooms using a common shower and unbearably pungent long-drop toilet (you really don't want to think about what's underneath) cost US$3. As for eating, you have the choice of *yefigel wat* or scrambled eggs, though careful perusal of the main road will reveal a restaurant with a coffee machine and fresh crusty bread. For amusement, you could wander down to the river outside town or the market, or glue yourself to the screen of the video cinema opposite the hotels.

From Dola Mena at least one vehicle runs daily to Negele Borena, supposedly departing at 06.00, though often only leaving a few hours later depending on how quickly it fills up. As with the Goba–Dola Mena run, fares are high and not particularly negotiable. When you finally hit the road, the first 20km out of Dola Mena are unpromising – dense acacia woodland and potentially good kudu country – but this is Ethiopia, and pretty soon you are climbing through broadleaved woodland with sweeping views across rugged mountains in all directions. As the journey progresses, you'll notice some wonderful termite sculptures, many of which must top 5m in height. The 178km ride through this thinly populated countryside takes six to eight hours, and is broken by meal stops at **Midre** and **Genale** (see box, *Genale and Prince Ruspoli's turaco*, page 497).

NEGELE BORENA

Negele is something of a frontier town, a cultural boiling pot that is predominantly Oromo but also has strong Somali, Borena and Muslim influences making it quite unlike anywhere else I visited in Ethiopia. Despite its size – Negele is unexpectedly substantial – there is a dusty impermanence about the place that I found quite appealing. The only really solid-looking building in the town centre is the bank, otherwise the streets are lined with shanty-like homesteads and small private businesses. Negele's distinctive character and cultural blend are personified in one of the most lively and absorbing markets in east Africa – especially on Saturdays when the camel market is held. True enough, most people wouldn't go out of their way to visit Negele – birdwatchers once again being the exception – but it is a friendly and interesting place, and after two days of bump-and-grind in pick-up trucks, you'll be more than happy to settle in for a couple of nights.

GETTING THERE AND AWAY Transport from Goba and Dola Mena is described in the preceding section, and transport on to Kebre Mengist and Shashemene is described in the one that follows. In both cases, the route can be reversed without any significant changes. It's also worth noting that the new bus station is now inconveniently located just north of the centre.

A less obvious route to or from Negele, but one of particular interest to travellers who are tying in a trip to Bale with other parts of the far south, or who are going to or coming from Kenya, would be to hop on a truck for Yabello or

While it may be of limited interest to most people, the small town of Genale is a veritable Mecca for birdwatchers. The riverine forest along this stretch of the Genale River is a prime locality for sighting one of Africa's rarest birds, the beautiful Prince Ruspoli's turaco. This large and colourful frugivore is named after the Italian explorer who first collected a specimen in 1892, but died without making a record of where the turaco had been found. For a full 50 years after this, the locality and habitat favoured by the prince's enigmatic turaco was a mystery to scientists.

In the early 1940s, the first live specimen was recorded in the Arero Forest east of Yabello. It would be another 30 years before a second population was found at Genale. A couple of other sites have subsequently been discovered, and although the nest, eggs and habitat requirements of Prince Ruspoli's turaco remain a complete mystery, it is now thought that the bird is commoner than was previously supposed. Nevertheless, its remarkable appearance – large, bright green, with red eyelids and a floppy white crest – has combined with its unusual history and endangered status on the IUCN Red List to ensure it ranks as among the most prized of Ethiopian endemics.

Prince Ruspoli's turaco is quite easy to locate in the riparian forest along the banks of the Genale River near the eponymous town, but you do need to know where to look. A local guide called Adem Dube has been recommended by several ornithologists, who would probably not have found the turaco without his expertise. It usually takes an hour or two to reach the right spot and locate the bird. There is a good chance of encountering several other interesting species along the way – black sparrowhawk, Narina trogon, Bruce's green pigeon, Levaillant's cuckoo, rufous chatterer and the highly localised white-winged dove and Juba weaver are all around. If you need to spend the night in Genale, it is a pleasant enough town, with a very attractive setting, and there are a few local restaurants and hotels to choose from. There is regular transport south to Negele Borena.

Mega. These leave from the market at around 06.00 on most days, and the 300km ride takes a full day. Mega lies on the main highway between Addis Ababa and the Moyale border, about 100km from the border post and 100km from Yabello. All transport along the Yabello–Moyale road stops at Mega. From Yabello, much transport continues north to Hawassa and there should be a pick-up truck most days heading east to Konso, from where you can get transport on to Jinka or Arba Minch. This route is covered under the heading *From Negele to Yabello* later in this chapter, page 499.

WHERE TO STAY

🏠 **Nile Hotel** (12 rooms) ☎ 046 445 1582. The best accommodation is at this new centrally located hotel. The comfortable double rooms each have hot-shower en suites & a popular local restaurant is attached. *US$8.50 en-suite dbl.*

🏠 **Green Hotel** (18 rooms) ☎ 046 445 0374. Once reputably the best hotel in town, the Green Hotel now makes a decent second choice. Rooms are reasonably clean & a good restaurant is attached. *US$5 using common shower, US$7.50 with private toilet, US$8.50 en suite.*

🏠 **Selam Pension** (24 rooms) ☎ 046 445 0375. If both the above are full, this friendly family-run pension located around the corner from the Nile Hotel has good clean rooms with ¾ beds & private cold shower. Toilets are shared. *US$4.50.*

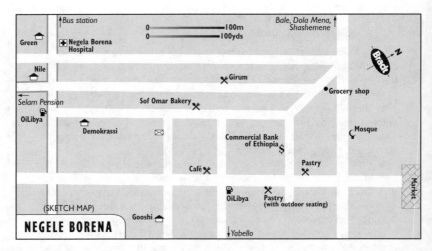

(SKETCH MAP)

NEGELE BORENA

Bus station · Green · Negela Borena Hospital · Nile · Selam Pension · OiLibya · Demokrassi · Girum · Sof Omar Bakery · Grocery shop · Mosque · Commercial Bank of Ethiopia · Café · Pastry · OiLibya · Pastry (with outdoor seating) · Gooshi · Yabello · Bale, Dola Mena, Shashemene · Beach · Market

✗ WHERE TO EAT

The best place to eat is the restaurant at the **Nile Hotel**, serving a good range of Western dishes in the US$1.50–3 range. If you don't eat at your hotel, try the **Girum Restaurant** east of the Nile Hotel, especially if they are serving *espestino*, a deliciously spicy stew of beef, potatoes and carrots that I encountered nowhere else in Ethiopia (probably a Somali dish). They also do *wat* and pasta. For breakfast and snacks, the **coffee shop** with outdoor seating around the corner from the bank does good juices, coffee, cakes, bread and light meals such as eggs and pasta.

FROM NEGELE TO SHASHEMENE

The 320km drive westward from Negele Borena to the main Moyale road takes the best part of a day. One bus to Shashemene leaves Negele Borena every morning at around 06.00, taking about ten to 12 hours to reach its destination. The trip can also be covered in hops using the local buses and light vehicles that connect the small towns along the way.

A couple of buses leave Negele Borena for **Kebre Mengist** daily before 09.00. This is a 120km ride and it takes three to four hours, gently rising from the thorny, termite-sculpted landscapes around Negele to the dense forest and pine plantations of the southern highlands. Kebre Mengist is not the most intrinsically prepossessing place – the first serious *faranji* hysteria I had hit since Dodola, though not anywhere near as bad – but the forested surrounds offer some compensation. If you are staying over, the the **Tegist Firee Hotel** (*22 rooms*) opposite the OiLibya garage is currently the most attractive option with basic rooms using common shower costing US$2.50. The attached restaurant is very popular, otherwise try **Goldenland Bar & Restaurant** across the road. At the time of writing a new multi-storey hotel was under construction next door to OiLibya.

The mushrooming mining settlement of **Shikaro** lies about 20km south of Kebre Mengist and the main road. It's an easy afternoon trip from Kebre Mengist as buses in both directions leave every half-hour or so, but the road out is a lot more interesting than the town itself. Shikaro is the quintessential mining town – ugly, loud and sprawling – and whatever charms it may have were entirely wasted on me. I was rather more interested in the forested ridge immediately south of the town, at least until I was informed it was crawling with armed policemen who are instructed to shoot suspected gold collectors on sight. A more alluring prospect than Shikaro would be to disembark from the bus at **Abake Forest Station**, halfway between Kebre Mengist and Shikaro, where the road passes through some excellent forest. There are guereza monkeys and other large mammals to be seen in the area, and the birdwatching should be excellent (this is one of the few areas where the endemic Prince Ruspoli's turaco has been recorded). The least encroached-upon patch of forest starts about 1km past the forest station towards Shikaro.

Getting out of Kebre Mengist is fairly straightforward before mid morning. Buses to Shashemene leave at around 06.00 and 08.00, depending on how quickly they fill up. You could also wait for the bus from Negele, though that runs the risk of there being no seats available. The trip from Kebre Mengist to Shashemene takes a good eight hours.

From Kebre Mengist, the road climbs through light forest into a hilly area reminiscent of western Uganda, where small wood-and-thatch huts are lit by smoky fires and surrounded by thickets of a plantain-like plant that is used to make porridge. The road then switchbacks into much denser forest, crawling with guereza monkeys and birds, and interspersed with thickly grassed meadows. This is a lovely area – if you're tempted to explore, the village of **Irba Muda**, 57km past Kebre Mengist, looks a suitable base, and there is at least one basic **hotel** (painted yellow). Irba Muda is ringed by cultivation, but it's all pristine forest and lush highland meadow beyond a radius of 1km or so.

The next town along the road, **Bore**, is about 27km past Irba Muda. Although it is just a dot on most maps, Bore seems a more substantial settlement than Kebre Mengist, and it's a popular lunch stop with bus and truck drivers. There is no forest close enough to Bore to warrant a special stop, but in hindsight it's probably a more attractive overnight option than Kebre Mengist. If you were coming from Negele and got to Kebre Mengist after all transport to Shashemene had departed, it might be worth looking for a lift as far as Bore – there's also far more onward transport from here. If you end up spending a night, the smart new – though seemingly misplaced – **Mi'i Hotel** (*29 rooms;* \ *046 667 0025*) with its clean, modern rooms is definitely the place you'll want to bed down for the night if stuck here. The en-suite rooms costing US$9.50 have clean tiled floors, hot shower and television, while the compact common shower rooms feel a little over-priced at US$7.50 but are still spick and span. The attached restaurant also serves decent Western meals and has the biggest sound system we've seen this side of Addis Ababa.

The scenery immediately after Bore, though a little dull, is enlivened in the rainy season by red-hot pokers. Then, rather suddenly, you hit the Rift Valley Escarpment, from where the road snakes downhill through eucalyptus plantations with occasional glimpses of Lake Awes in the distance. The descent is interrupted by a brief stop at the singularly ramshackle and charmless town of **Wendo**. There are a few basic hotels, but there's little reason to make use of them, especially when half an hour out of town you connect with the tarred Moyale road, from where it's a straightforward 60km cruise through the Rift Valley northwards to Shashemene via Hawassa, or southwards to Dilla.

FROM NEGELE TO YABELLO

The rough and rutted 300km road directly connecting Negele Borena to Yabello is unlikely to do any favours to anybody with a susceptible back, nor will it hold much of interest to the average tourist, but it is travelled by almost all serious birdwatching tours through Ethiopia. The primary reason for this is that the road connects two towns known as the best places to spot particular endemics, but it also passes through an area of genuine ornithological interest in its own right. The road can be covered in a day with an early start, assuming you are in a private vehicle, but there is some basic accommodation in Arero, some 180km from Negele Borena, should you want to break up the trip. Public transport is as good as non-existent, though the occasional pick-up trucks that traverse the road will take passengers for a negotiable fee.

Coming from Negele, you need to follow the Bogol Manyo road southeast of town for about 15km, where a right turn to the southwest takes you onto the Yabello road. The junction lies at the north end of the **Liben Plain** and it is the best place to look for the threatened Sidamo lark, a taxonomically controversial Ethiopian endemic first collected in 1968. Unfortunately, the junction is also a sensitive military area, so you will need to ask permission from the soldiers there before you leave your car. The lark is not uncommon within its restricted range, but it is elusive and can be quite difficult to identify because several other lark species are present.

About 10km southwest of the junction, the road to Yabello skirts the **Mankubsa-Welenso Forest**, an unusually low-lying patch of open-canopy juniper woodland where the endemic Prince Ruspoli's turaco and Salvadori's serin both occur sparsely along with several other interesting forest species. The forest and surrounds are also home to a variety of mammals, including warthog, giant forest hog, leopard, spotted hyena, guereza and vervet monkey and olive baboon.

Roughly 120km out of Negele, the road enters the small town of **Melka Guda**. Almost immediately after passing through this town, the bridge across the Dawa River is an obligatory stop for birders, since it is a reasonably reliable place to pick up white-winged turtle dove and Juba weaver, species whose ranges are restricted to southeast Ethiopia and neighbouring Somalia. Even if you miss these jackpots, a host of good birds – smaller black-bellied sunbird, golden pipit, Pringle's puffback, red-naped bush-shrike and bare-eyed thrush – are common in the area.

Another excellent place to stop, and possibly spend a night, is **Arero**, which lies about 60km past Melka Guda near to the most southerly forest in Ethiopia. Local specials are headed by two endemics, the beautiful Prince Ruspoli's turaco and rare Salvadori's seedeater, both of which are fairly common in this area. More than 160 birds have been recorded in all, as has a fair variety of large mammals, notably bushbuck, bushpig, guereza monkey – even the occasional lion and leopard. Passing through Arero, a wide variety of dry-country species includes the endemic Streseman's bush crow and white-tailed swallow (see box, *Yabello for birders*, in *Chapter 22*, page 510), along with black-capped social weaver, grey-headed silverbill, Archer's greywing and little spotted woodpecker.

22

The Moyale Road

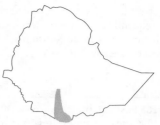

The 500km road that runs southward from Hawassa to the border town of Moyale is likely to be travelled in its entirety only by people heading to or from Kenya. Nevertheless, far from being just a feeder road, this long stretch of mostly well-maintained asphalt does boast several worthwhile and untrammelled cultural, archaeological and ornithological attractions. The largest town it passes through is **Dilla**, a relaxed agricultural hub set at the heart of an area of considerable archaeological interest for its ancient rock engravings and medieval stelae fields. Continuing south from here, green highland eventually gives way to low-lying acacia scrub, populated by colourful Borena pastoralists and their prized herds of cattle. **Yabello**, the largest town between Dilla and the border, is renowned among ornithologists for lying at the heart of the territory occupied by two of Ethiopia's most localised endemics: the white-tailed swallow and the peculiar Streseman's bush crow.

Past Yabello, the Moyale road passes through the heart of **Borena country** towards the somewhat underwhelming small town of **Mega**. Wild mammals still persist here, albeit in low concentrations. Pairs of Guenther's dik-dik are regularly sighted on the side of the main road, while ground squirrels and mongooses scamper across it – and with luck one might come across larger antelope such as Grant's gazelle, gerenuk and lesser kudu. For a better chance of encountering large mammals – Burchell's zebra, warthog and the endemic Swayne's hartebeest – a side trip to the remote Yabello Game Sanctuary Park is a possibility for motorised travellers. Interesting stops towards Mega include the Borena village of **Dublock**, known for its so-called singing wells, as well as the bizarre apparition that is **Lake Chew Bet**, a small saline body of water at the base of an immense volcanic crater.

Remote it might be, but the Moyale road is surfaced in its entirety and serviced by reliable if relatively infrequent public transport. Accommodation south of Dilla and north of Moyale tends to be rudimentary, even by Ethiopian standards, but it can be found in Yabello, Mega and even Dublock. One practicality worth noting is that foreign-exchange facilities are lacking entirely south of Hawassa, at least before Moyale itself, where there is an equipped bank. For those crossing between the two countries, visas for Kenya can be obtained upon arrival at the border, but there is no chance of crossing from Kenya into Ethiopia without a visa bought in advance in Nairobi or elsewhere.

There are a few routes by which one might connect with, or depart from, the main 500km of road between Hawassa and Moyale. Coming from Negele Borena a reasonable dirt road, covered by regular buses, leads westward via Kebre Mengist to the junction of Wendo 60km south of Hawassa (see *Chapter 21*, page 499). The far rougher road that connects Negele Borena directly to Yabello is of little interest to most travellers, but is popularly followed on ornithological tours. Two further routes connect this road to Konso, the gateway for South Omo. The first, an upgraded 105km road from Yabello, is covered by a few pick-up trucks weekly, and frequently used by travellers heading between Kenya and South Omo. A newer and better road runs to Konso from Fiseha Genet, about 30–40km south of Dilla. Both routes are covered in *Chapter 23*.

DILLA

The bustling, breezy town of Dilla, administrative capital of Gedea zone, and since 1996 site of the most important college in southern Ethiopia, lies in the fertile green mountains of the eastern Rift Valley Escarpment. It is an important agricultural business centre, known particularly for the excellent coffee grown in the vicinity, and the surrounding hills are covered in patches of indigenous forest interspersed with rustic homesteads and small *enset* plantations. Dilla is a pleasant if unremarkable town, not unattractive from whichever direction you approach it, but coming from the dusty badlands of Ethiopia's far south and the north of Kenya, it must – both literally and figuratively – come as a breath of fresh air. The town is mostly of interest to travellers as the best base from which to visit a number of important archaeological sites, including two major stelae fields and some fine prehistoric rock carvings.

GETTING THERE AND AWAY Dilla is situated roughly 90km south of Hawassa along a good surfaced road. *En route*, close to the junction for Kebre Mengist and Negele Borena (see *Chapter 21, The Bale and Arsi Highlands*, page 473), the road passes through Yirga Alem, an undistinguished semi-urban sprawl that – somewhat incredibly – served as the capital of Sidamo before this role was usurped by Hawassa. A short distance before entering Dilla, you'll see plenty of vendors selling locally grown pineapples along the roadside. The drive takes about two hours in one of the regular minibuses and buses that connect Dilla to Hawassa, but is quicker in a private vehicle.

For travellers trying to get between Addis Ababa and Moyale as quickly as possible, Dilla is the place to break up the two-day trip. A few buses daily connect Addis Ababa to Dilla, leaving Addis from the main Autobus Terra at around 06.00 and taking about ten hours, with stops at Ziway, Shashemene and Hawassa. From Dilla around four buses daily travel north to Shashemene (US$2.80; 3 hours) stopping via Hawassa (US$2.40; 2½ hours). Heading south, a daily service departing at 06.00 covers the 420km stretch of road between Dilla and Moyale (US$6; 7 hours) stopping at Yabello (US$4.50; 4 hours). See also *Dilla to Yabello by road*, page 507.

🏠 WHERE TO STAY

🏠 **Afomia Hotel** [503 B3] (17 rooms) \046 331 4444. This swish new hotel located in the main road at the western end of town is Dilla's top choice though is definitely on the pricey side. Rooms are fresh & clean & come with tiled floors, flat-screen TV & en-suite hot shower. 1 smaller budget room is available, but it's often booked & is noisy, as it is closest to the main road. A good bar & restaurant are attached. *US$14 budget room, US$18 en-suite dbl.*

🏠 **Tourist Hotel** [503 A3] (10 rooms) m 0918 696 095. Further west along the main road heading towards Hawassa, this new set-up located opposite the Abyssinia Bar & Restaurant trumps

Afomia in terms of price & atmosphere. It also offers a cross-section of rooms suiting most budgets. Accommodation is in 3 en-suite double rooms with hot shower & TV, 1 similarly appointed en-suite twin with 2 double beds accommodating up to 4 people, & 6 compact doubles using a common shower. In the central garden there's a suitably decorated traditional restaurant & bar. *US$6 using common shower, US$12/24 en-suite dbl/twin.*

🏠 **Lalibela Pension** [503 D3] (20 rooms) \046 331 2300. This popular local hotel lies a short distance from the main asphalt road through town. The double rooms are clean & airy – 10 have

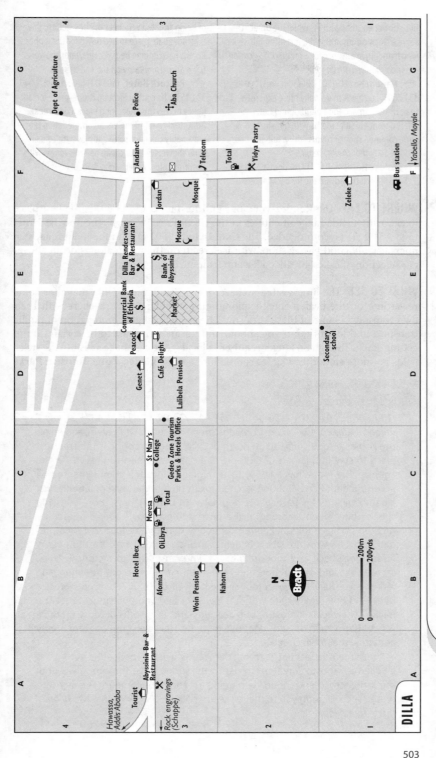

DILLA

hot-shower en suite with TV, while the other 10 share a clean common shower. It is often full, so it's worth ringing in advance for a room. *US$5/9 using common shower/with en suite.*

⌂ **Nahom Hotel** [503 B2] (30 rooms) `046 331 2841. Fresher & marginally more expensive than the Get Smart, this neighbouring hotel offers decent en-suite rooms with hot showers & large common shower rooms with a full-size bed. *US$5/8.50 without/with en suite.*

⌂ **Zeleke Hotel** [503 F1] (20 rooms) `046 331 1535. With the advantage for backpackers

of being situated very near the bus station, this is an adequate place to bed down for the night. Rooms have double beds & cold-water showers. *US$4.50/6 using common shower/en suite.*

⌂ **Peacock Hotel** [503 D3] (20 rooms) `046 331 1535. Its central location & one-price-for-all policy makes this shoestring place a good deal. Admittedly a bit rundown, accommodation is in reasonably clean en-suite doubles with cold en-suite showers & TV or cheap no-frills rooms with common cold shower. *US$2/4.50.*

✖ **WHERE TO EAT** The **Rendez-vous Bar and Restaurant** [503 E3] is the best place to eat, with a wide range of entrées in the US$1.50–2.50 range. The **Tourist Hotel** [503 A3] is also recommended. The **Café Delight** [503 D3] on the main road is an unexpectedly good pastry shop, with ice cream on the menu alongside an above-par selection of cakes, bread, coffee and fruit juice.

WHAT TO SEE The little-visited archaeological sites around Dilla make for some rewarding off-the-beaten-track exploration, particularly for travellers with their own transport. Some of these sites could be visited using a combination of public transport and legwork, but you should aim for an early start to be certain of not getting stuck. Though no longer required, a local guide can make a visit to the stelae fields go more smoothly. Guides can be hired at the **Gedeo Zone Tourism Parks**

AREGASH LODGE

(10 rooms; `046 225 1136 or 011 551 4254/82/90;* f *011 551 4221;* e *info@ aregashlodge.com; www.aregashlodge.com)* Situated in Yirga Alem, a town off the Hawassa road some 30km north of Dilla, Aregash Lodge is the smartest place to stay in this part of Ethiopia and one of the best-run resorts in the country. The lodge has a lovely rustic highland location complemented by accommodation in bamboo thatched *tukuls* built in the style of a traditional Sidamo village. It is particularly popular with birdwatchers; more than 100 species have been recorded in the nearby forest. Upon arrival, guests are greeted with a traditional coffee ceremony that can be followed by a pre-dinner hyena viewing. Other activities include guided treks to the nearby forest, horseback and mountain-bike riding, and visits to historical caves, sacred sites and natural hot- and cold-water springs. Accommodation is in ten en-suite *tukuls;* six with four single beds in each, three with queen-size beds, and one family suite with a queen-size bed and two single beds. The Italian-style meals are extra, but delicious and fairly priced. Most produce served is grown in on-site vegetable gardens. They also raise bees for honey and grow their own coffee.

Yirga Alem is located 8km off the Hawassa–Dilla road – the turn-off is labelled as Aposto Junction. To get to the lodge drive through town until the asphalt road ends, then keep going for another kilometre. The first turn on the left will bring you to the lodge after 400m. *US$60/90 one–two people/ three–four people.*

which lies just off the main road a few blocks west of the market in Dilla.

Tutu Fela stelae field (*Entrance US$3*)
This densely clustered field of roughly 300 stelae lies within a small village encircled by natural forest and subsistence plantations of *enset* and coffee. Most of the stelae here are of the anthropomorphic type, but several are (or were originally) phallic, and you can still see clear circumcision marks near the top. Like most similar sites, little excavation has taken place at Tutu Fela, but formative investigation revealed numerous artefacts – ranging from iron and copper bracelets and beads to chisels and shards of pottery – buried alongside the bodies in the graves below the stelae.

To reach Tutu Fela, follow the Moyale road south from Dilla, passing through Wenago after 15km. Continue for about 3km past this small town, then take the dirt turn-off to your right, which leads uphill across a roadside ditch with a small bridge. Continue along the dirt road for another 2km, until you reach a rough dirt track leading uphill through the forest to your left. You will probably need to walk along this track, which leads to the stelae field after about 700m. With an early start, it should be possible to bus to the junction 3km south of Wenago, walk to and from the stelae (allow two hours for this), and grab a lift back to Dilla when you reach the main road.

Our last visit was marred by the presence of particularly bold and annoying children calling 'you, you, you'. At the top of the hill near the entrance we were greeted by a swelling crowd. Taking along a guide from Dilla might mitigate some of the unwanted attention. Fortunately, the field itself is secured by a fence. Children are not allowed past the gate, so the stelae viewing itself can be done in peace.

Tututi stelae field
Lying to the south of Tutu Fela, this equally impressive but more dispersed field comprises around 1,200 stelae scattered in and around a small village called Tututi. Almost all of the stelae here are phallic, and one measuring 7.55m from base to top is probably the tallest stele ever erected in southern Ethiopia. About 90% of the stelae at Tututi have toppled over, the tallest one among them. Some stelae have been incorporated into the base of the local huts, or are used as seats or to sharpen knives (one large stele rather ignominiously props up a rustic latrine). Despite this, there are still several stelae of up to 6m high standing where they were originally erected more than 1,000 years ago. So far as I can establish, no excavation has taken place at Tututi.

To get to the Tututi field, follow the Moyale road through Wenago, past the turn-off for Tutu Fela, and then for another 6.5km to the tiny village of Chelba. At Chelba, take a right turn onto a dirt road, which will bring you to Tututi after 1.5km. It would be possible to visit this site by using public transport as far as Chelba, then walking to the stelae. After rains the dirt road can be very muddy, making it impassable for vehicles. Under such conditions, the stelae can still be reached by foot.

Manchiti rock engravings
The area around Dilla, although better known for its wealth of medieval stelae, is also rich in rock engraving sites, moving and mysterious relics of an otherwise-forgotten prehistoric society, adding yet another layer to one's perception of Ethiopia's enigmatically complex past. The most accessible and probably finest of these sites is Manchiti (also called Shappe), situated at an altitude of 1,300m roughly 8km from the town centre. The site consists of a partially collapsed frieze of at least 50 cattle, which move herd-like along the vertical rock face at the top of a narrow river gully. The individual engravings, ranging in length from 40 to 70cm, are nearly

An estimated 10,000 stelae (obelisks) are scattered across the south of Ethiopia, extending in a rough belt from Tiya southeast to the vicinity of Negele Borena. Little concrete is known about the origin of these stelae or the societies that erected them. Local tradition attributes the stelae to the 15th-century Muslim leader Ahmed Gragn, but the formative findings of Professor Roger Joussaume, the only archaeologist to have worked the sites, indicates that they were erected centuries before Gragn was born, over a 400–500-year period starting in the 9th century.

Approximately 50 stelae fields are known in Gedea zone, and two broad styles of stelae are recognised. The older of these, probably dating to the 9th century, are the phallic stelae, which are typically cylindrical in shape, and rounded at the top, with incisions that leave little room for ambiguity about what they are meant to represent. The stelae appear to have marked graves, and the bodies beneath them were buried in a foetal position. The later anthropomorphic stelae, thought to date to the 12th century, are attributed to a different society from their precursors. These stelae are generally flattened, and are marked with symbolic human features, though in several instances they have a cylindrical shape, and were clearly modified from existing phallic stelae. Although they, too, marked graves, the society which erected them evidently buried their dead lying flat rather than in a foetal position.

The two largest stelae fields in Gedea are Tutu Fela and Tututi, both of which lie within 45 minutes' drive of Dilla and are described on page 505. The Tututi field is made up almost exclusively of phallic stelae, whereas anthropomorphic stelae dominate at Tutu Fela. It is thought that the relatively well-known stelae at Tiya and Silté, which are flattened like anthropomorphic stelae, but carved with far greater sophistication and more abstract symbols, were erected and carved at a later date than those further south. It is not known to what extent these mysterious medieval stelae influenced the decorated gravestones still erected today by the Oromo, who are relatively recent arrivals to the area and might well have displaced the original stelae-erecting society. There are also some parallels between the later stelae found around Dilla and the anthropomorphic wooden grave markers of the Konso – who, interestingly, retain an oral tradition suggesting that they might have migrated to their present homeland from the eastern Rift Valley Escarpment.

identical in their highly stylised form, with unnaturally small heads, large decorated horns and grossly engorged udders. The identity of the carvers, like so much about Ethiopia's past, remains a mystery, but the engravings show affinities with those at sites in the vicinity of Harar and parts of Eritrea. It is thought that the engravings at Manchiti are at least 3,000 years old. Roger Joussaume, the first Westerner to visit the site back in 1967, noted that the triangular objects that decorate the engraved horns resemble the buffalo-hair 'acorns' hung from the horns of the cattle of present-day Ethiopian pastoralists such as the Nuer and Dinka.

Manchiti is difficult to find without local guidance. From the main roundabout in Dilla, you need to follow the Hawassa road for roughly 2km, forking left (away from Hawassa) on the outskirts of town opposite the Dilla Higher Medical Centre. Follow this road for another 2km, passing the Teacher Education and Medical University, then after another 100m turn left into a side road. After another 3km, you will cross a bridge over a stream. Having crossed the stream, the road diffuses into several indistinct but motorable tracks, one of which, after another 2–3km, will bring you to the top of the valley in which the engravings lie (if you don't have a guide, you'll need to keep asking directions). The rutted track to the bottom of the valley was impassable when we visited, but the engravings lay no more than five minutes on foot from where we parked. Travellers without private transport can grab a minibus as far as the university, but they will have to walk the last 5–6km, and should employ the services of a local guide and carry plenty of drinking water.

Three similar sites lie within 2–3km of each other to the southeast of Dilla, around the border of Bule and Wenago districts. None of these sites is as impressive as Manchiti, and access will be difficult unless a bridge that collapsed c2000 along the main road to Bule has been repaired. The most important site here is **Gelma** (or Ili Malcho Kinjo), situated in the village of Odola near Wechema. Ten stylised cows, very similar to those at Manchiti, are engraved here in two clusters. About 2km north of this, the **Soka Dibicha** site consists of two sets of three relatively roughly engraved cattle lying on facing banks of the Bulla River. At the third site, **Godena Kinjo**, 'discovered' as recently as 1993, are three engraved cows. All three sites can be reached by following the Moyale road south for about 5km from the main roundabout, then turning left onto the Bule road shortly after you pass the church of Gebriel Chichu. After about 12km, you need to turn right at the village of Kuda until you reach the collapsed bridge. A local guide would be close to essential to find the actual sites, which lie between 3km and 5km from the bridge.

Gidicho Island

The old Amhara name for Lake Abaya, whose eastern shore is situated some 30km due east of Dilla as the crow flies, is Yegidicho Hayk – the Lake of the Gidicho, a people whose territory is confined to the northern lake hinterland and islands. Their main stronghold is the remote island also known as Gidicho, which extends over about 20km² off the northeastern shore of Lake Abaya, about 30km south of the mouth of the Bilate River. The eponymous inhabitants of Gidicho, who speak a Cushitic language with affiliations to Somali, are known for the unusual two-storey houses they build, and for their impressive wooden boats, which can measure up to 8m long. The island also supports a small community of Gatami people, who are hippo hunters and potters by tradition, though most now subsist from a combination of fishing and cultivation. The water around Gidicho Island is home to a profusion of crocodiles, hippos and birds. The small settlement of Gidicho Market on the facing mainland can be reached along a rough 4x4 50km trail through the near-uninhabited plains that descend to the lakeshore, ideally in the company of a local guide. From there you will have to take a boat across the channel to the island, which lies about 1.5km offshore.

DILLA TO YABELLO BY ROAD

The 210km asphalt road from Dilla south to Yabello marks a dramatic shift in landscape from cool, fertile highlands to the barren acacia scrub of the southern Rift Valley. The drive should take about four hours in a private vehicle, while buses take around six hours. All the larger towns between Dilla and Yabello are connected by local minibus services, which backpackers can use to cover the journey in stages. The opportunities for sightseeing along this road are, to put it bluntly, somewhat limited.

The first town of substance along the way is **Yerga Chefie**, which literally means cool grass, and is famous within Ethiopia for its high-quality coffee. The only reason

Perhaps the most rigid pastoralists of all southern Ethiopia's people, the Borena occupy a vast territory of arid land stretching from the escarpment north of Dilla all the way south to the Uaso Ngiro River near the foot of Mount Kenya. Linguistically and ethnically, the Borena are regarded to be a southern branch of the Oromo nation, but their adherence to a semi-nomadic lifestyle has more in common culturally with the other desert nomads of northern Kenya than with any modern Ethiopian ethnic groups.

Characteristically tall and lean, the Borena acquired a reputation as fearsome warriors among early European visitors to their inhospitable homeland, based on their regional supremacy at the time. In later years, as the Abyssinian highlanders made inroads into the northern part of their territory, many Borena families were forced to migrate southwards, where they subsisted by cattle-raiding and attacking agriculturist settlements in northern Kenya. Within Ethiopia, however, the Borena have a reputation as a peace-loving and gracious people. Between themselves, the Borena hold strong taboos against raising one's voice in anger, and unprovoked violence.

Staunchly traditional in both custom and dress, the Borena add a definite splash of colour to the harsh, monotonous country they inhabit. The women, decorated similarly to some of the people of South Omo, drape colourful shawls and dresses from their shoulders, while the men walk around bare-chested with a sarong wrapped around their waist, and a spear or gun slung over their shoulder. In common with many other African pastoralists, Borena society is based on a rigid age-set system, with each set moving through stages of life and responsibility together. The Borena measure their wealth and worth in terms of the size of their herd. It is said that two Borena men will enquire about the state of each other's cattle long before they enquire about the health of wives, children and other such trivialities. I'm not sure whether to believe a related story, which is that a married Borena woman may sleep with any man she chooses – the man drives his spear into the ground in front of her hut, and the husband is not permitted to intrude while the spear is in place.

A remarkable feature of Borena culture is the 'singing well'. Many such wells are dotted around Borenaland, both in Ethiopia and in Kenya, each one supporting many thousands of cattle living for miles around. Water is retrieved from these wells communally, by a row of up to 50 men who sing and chant as they pass buckets from one to the other – an inspiring sight. The most accessible singing well in Ethiopia lies immediately outside Dublock, on the main road between Yabello and Mega. This well can be visited in conjunction with the crater lake Chew Bet – a major source of the salt bars that have long formed an important export item in the Borena barter economy.

In the rainy season of 1999–2000, Borenaland was denied its usual measly quota of precipitation, resulting in a serious drought with drastic consequences for the region's inhabitants. In some areas, up to 90% of the cattle died, and crops grown to supplement the staple diet of milk and meat were completely destroyed. An unfortunate result of the drought was increased tension over water and grazing areas between the Borena and their Somali neighbours to the east. This drought has subsequently ended, and the area is perfectly safe for travel.

you'd be likely to want to sleep here, or at Fiseha Genet 10km further south along the Moyale road, is if you are thinking of using the new all-weather road that connects Fiseha Genet to Karat-Konso (see *To/from Fiseha Genet* in *Chapter 23*, page 528). The **Lesiwon Hotel** (*30 rooms;* \ *046 332 0154*) in Yerga Chefie is currently the best around, with clean but expensive rooms with hot showers and television for US$18, & rooms with cold showers and no television for US$12. Several shoestring hotels can be found in Fiseha Genet.

The largest town between Dilla and Yabello, lying roughly halfway between them, is **Hagere Maryam**, where several budget hotels and restaurants are clustered around the minibus station. The **Hagere Mariam Hotel** (*37 rooms;* \ *046 443 0221*) has a nice garden and good food, and en-suite rooms with hot water are available for an optimistically inflated *faranji* price of US$10/22/24 for a single/double/twin. South of this unremarkable town, the road passes through one last patch of juniper forest with the notable feature that most trees share a distinctive (perhaps wind-induced?) lean, particularly on the west side of the road. Finally you descend to the dry plains – home to the colourful Borena people (see box opposite) and renowned by ornithologists for two highly localised endemics (see box, *Yabello for birders*, page 510).

YABELLO

Yabello can lay fair claim to being a minor route focus, since it lies at the junction of the asphalt road between Dilla and Moyale, the recently upgraded eastern route towards Konso and the Lower Omo Valley, and a rougher road running northeast to Negele Borena. Yabello is likely to form an overnight stop on any serious birding tour of Ethiopia, or for anybody who is driving from the Kenyan border directly to Konso or the Omo Valley. Unfortunately, Yabello has little other than its location and birding to recommend it, except perhaps on Saturday when it is the site of a big market attended by Borena pastoralists from miles around. But as one traveller recently wrote: 'I found Yabello to have a lot of charm. The light and the climate made it great for photos and for birdwatching and people watching. The town is peaceful, or so it seems after spending an afternoon there. It has the similar feel as Dire Dawa and Harar (without the *faranji* hassle), with lovely hills surrounding it.'

GETTING THERE AND AWAY Yabello lies roughly halfway between Dilla and Moyale, 5km west of the main asphalt road along the Konso road. In a private vehicle, the direct drive from either Dilla or Moyale should take no longer than four hours. The drive to Konso now takes about two to three hours. The 300km road between Negele Borena and Yabello takes a full day, allowing for stops at the main birding locations *en route*.

Public transport to Dilla or Moyale is reasonably reliable. In addition to local minibuses between various small towns along these roads, a daily bus service connects Yabello and Dilla (US$4.50), taking around five hours in either direction. The daily bus between Dilla and Moyale (US$4.50) stops in Yabello. No formal public transport runs along the roads following the east–west axis to Konso and Negele Borena. The occasional trucks that run along them may take paying passengers, but bear in mind they may expect a high payment given the ban on carrying passengers.

WHERE TO STAY AND EAT In the past, the only lodging options were in Yabello itself, a 5km detour from the Moyale road. Now there are a number of hotels located right at the Moyale–Yabello junction, all of a superior quality to anything you will find in the town proper.

YABELLO FOR BIRDERS

Whatever else the area may lack in terms of tourist attractions, Yabello and its immediate surrounds form an essential fixture on any birding itinerary through Ethiopia. The reason for this, quite simply, is the exclusive presence of two of the most range-restricted of African bird species. These are Streseman's bush crow and the white-tailed swallow, respectively described in 1938 and 1942, and restricted to the arid acacia scrub that lies within a radius of 100km or so of Yabello. Quite why these two birds occupy such a small territory is a mystery that has so far baffled ornithologists – the arid acacia scrub around Yabello is practically indistinguishable from that which covers much of southern Ethiopia and northern Kenya. But whatever the explanation, few self-respecting birders would visit Ethiopia and not come in search of this pair of localised endemics, both of which are common within their restricted range, and often seen along the main asphalt road.

Streseman's bush crow is by far the more interesting of the two birds. Placed in the monospecific genus *Zavattarionis*, its nearest genetic ally is thought to be the European chough, a small, lightly built crow whose range extends into the Ethiopian Highlands. However, with its white head and belly, grey back, black wings, narrow pointed beak and bare blue facemask, Streseman's bush crow bears little outward resemblance to any other African crow. Usually seen hanging about in small family parties that hop along the ground like overgrown sparrow-weavers, it is roughly the size of a roller, but holds itself like a starling. Although little-studied, this fascinating bird is totally unmistakable even at a distant glance – you'd be extraordinarily unlucky to drive along the main road north or south of Yabello and not encounter a flock.

Fortunately, Yabello's interest to birders is not limited to the two endemics. The route to Yabello from Negele is known for hosting several localised specials, while the acacia bush immediately around Yabello, arid though it may be, supports a rich proliferation of colourful birds, several of which are more or less endemic to the dry scrub of northern Kenya and southern Ethiopia. Vulturine guinea fowl, golden-bellied starling, Abyssinian ground hornbill, white-headed buffalo weaver, golden pipit, bare-faced go-away bird and the ubiquitous but aptly named superb starling are just a few of the more striking species you can expect to see in the area, along with a good selection of small raptors.

Upmarket

🏠 **Borana Lodge** (10 bungalows) m 0913 306 105; www.yabeloboranalodge.com. If you want to escape the hectic, almost border-town feel of Yabello junction, then this new lodge just off the road to Moyale & operated by Alviaggi Tour is the spot. Serenity however doesn't come cheap. Accommodation is provided in raised concrete bungalows – 6 standard & 4 superior with a living room & possibility of an extra bed – spread out around the property. Each of the bungalows has 2 queen-size beds, a fridge, writing desk, private balcony & hot-shower en suite (superior rooms

have bidets!). Facilities include a swimming pool & a central bar & restaurant with lounge area & book exchange. Rates include breakfast & dinner. To reach the lodge head south along the road to Moyale for 7km, then turn right onto a signed dirt road & follow for another 2.3km to the main gate. *US$88/96/96 standard sgl/dbl/twin, US$136 superior*.

Moderate

🏠 **Yabello Motel** (52 rooms) ☎ 046 446 0785; e mekdmazd@yahoo.com. Located at the junction next to the Total station, this ever-expanding hotel is the top offering in terms of facilities, but charges inflated *faranji* prices for both accommodation & food. A variety of accommodation is offered including clean compact en-suite doubles with tiled floors, hot showers & fresh towels as well as budget rooms sharing a common shower. **Camping** is also possible. *US$14 using common shower, US$30/45 old en-suite dbl/twin, US$35/50 new en-suite dbl/twin, camping US$5/6 for 1/2 people.*

Budget

🏠 **Hawi Hotel** (24 rooms) 📞 046 446 1114. This sand-coloured hotel, located on the Moyale road just north of the junction, is next in line after the Yabello Motel in terms of quality of rooms, but the manager's attitude leaves a lot to be desired. After viewing the property & coming away with a very good impression of the clean en-suite rooms, we returned to book a room to find that the manager had hiked the price up by an extra US$6! *US$18/24 en-suite sgl/dbl.*

🏠 **Adonay Pension** 📞 046 446 0654/0129. This bright new mauve & green pension located opposite Yabello Secondary School on the road heading back into Yabello from the main junction is an odds-on budget bet. The spacious en-suite rooms with tiled floors & hot showers are well appointed with simple modern furnishings. The only drawback is it's popular with NGOs, so is often booked out. *US$12/15 en-suite dbl/twin.*

🏠 **NOC Hotel** (12 rooms) Located behind the NOC filling station on the opposite side of the main road to the Yabello Motel, this small hotel is convenient & very reasonably priced. Management is very friendly, & the common-shower rooms each have ¾ beds & spring mattresses. *US$7.50.*

WHAT TO SEE Assuming that you have wheels, Yabello forms a useful base for a few day trips, for instance to one of the **Borena cultural sites** described in *From Yabello to Moyale,* below. Also within easy day-tripping distance of the town is the **Yabello Game Sanctuary** (*entrance US$5.50; US$1.50 per car; US$6 for a scout*), which protects 2,500km² of dry acacia savanna a short distance east of the main Moyale road. A small number of Swayne's hartebeest are supposedly present in the sanctuary, as are other savanna species such as Burchell's zebra, greater and lesser kudu, Grant's gazelle and a variety of small predators, though from our most recent experience in 2011, actual mammal sighting is scarce. The sanctuary is best known, however, for its endemic birds (see box opposite). The road from Yabello to Negele Borena via the Yabello Game Sanctuary and Arero is also of great ornithological interest (see heading *From Negele to Yabello* in *Chapter 21,* page 499). To visit the sanctuary you must first visit the tourism office in Yabello, where you'll pay the fee and organise a scout.

FROM YABELLO TO MOYALE

The 200km stretch of asphalt connecting Yabello to Moyale runs through dry, red-earth plains covered in light acacia scrub, punctuated by towering termite sculptures, and thinly populated by the Borena pastoralists whose bright traditional attire lends a welcome splash of colour to an otherwise harsh landscape. There is some game to be seen in this area, with the diminutive dik-dik and long-necked gerenuk being the most visible large mammals. Birders who have missed out on Streseman's bush crow still stand a good chance of encountering it as far south as Meta, the only town of substance along the route. Look out, too, for the proliferation of more widespread but equally colourful birds (see box opposite), which do their best to outdo the human population in the gaudiness stakes.

Not allowing for stops, the drive from Yabello to Moyale should take no longer than three hours in a private vehicle. It will take closer to five hours using the daily bus between Yabello and Moyale. If you want to head straight between Dilla and Moyale, there is at least one bus daily in either direction. A low volume of local transport runs between Yabello and Mega, and Mega and Moyale.

Crossing through to Kenya, border formalities are relaxed, though the border does close from time to time, so check the situation in advance. Visas for Kenya can be obtained on the spot (as they can these days at all Kenyan borders). Coming in the opposite direction, do note that Ethiopian visas must be bought in advance – this, among almost all borders in this part of Africa, would be about the most depressing to be turned back at. One minor note of caution: it could be a freak incident, but one reader reports that his entrance permit was accidentally stamped to expire on the day he entered Ethiopia. This error was picked up when he passed through the roadblock outside Moyale, and when he went back to the immigration office to have the error corrected, the official who stamped his passport wasn't around and he was forced to leave Ethiopia immediately! As I say, probably a one-off error, but sufficient justification to check the dates stamped in your passport on the spot.

As for finances, you may be encouraged to exchange money in the 'no-man's land' between the two countries. Issues of legality aside, I found it was just as easy to arrange for a money-changer to meet me at my hotel, where I received a comparable rate of exchange. There are also banks located on both sides of the border. On the Kenyan side of Moyale, the Hotel Sherif is about the best bet, though it really can't be recommended by comparison with what is available on the Ethiopian side (the most favourable report calls it 'tolerable') and water is often unavailable.

In the past, a couple of companies ran regular but unscheduled charter flights between the border and Nairobi at a cost of around US$100, but no flights were running at the time of research. If and when flights resume, they are highly recommended as the best way of getting to Nairobi. The road trip through northern Kenya can be described as nothing short of brutal. (A Kenyan man who made the trip with me said he would break the bank to buy a flight back from Addis rather than endure the return trip by land!)

There is no formal road transport between Moyale and Isiolo in Kenya, but truck convoys cover the route roughly three times a week. It's easy to find a lift on a truck, so the best thing is to check on the Ethiopian side of the border when the next convoy leaves or else you might be stranded on the Kenyan side of the border for a couple of days. A truck ride to Isiolo should cost in the region of US$20, and it will take two hot, dusty, bumpy days, passing through some stunning desert scenery where the occasional large mammal and traditional Samburu village break the tedium.

You'll probably stop overnight at the montane oasis of Marsabit, where the Jey Jey Centre is the best place to stay. This is a stop that you might want to prolong, since the town lies adjacent to the forested Marsabit National Park, home to many elephants, antelope and birds. An excellent campsite lies on the edge of town, close to the park entrance gate, and you can also camp at the little-used lodge, which lies about 5km into the park on the edge of a stunning crater lake. Once in Isiolo the Bomen Hotel is the current favourite and also has excellent food. The Mochoro Hotel, Silver Bells Hotel and Jabal Nur Lodge are other good options. From there, plenty of transport runs on to Nairobi along a blissfully surfaced road – buses take five to six hours, so you'll get through in a day.

The most interesting stop along the asphalt is **Dublock**, an overgrown Borena village straddling the main Moyale road about 65km south of Yabello. Two so-called **singing wells** are situated on the edge of Dublock, in a small evergreen grove no more than 500m east of the main road. The name 'singing wells' refers to the Borena tradition of forming a chanting human chain to haul buckets of water from the well to its lip roughly 50m away. This communal activity generally takes place only in the dry season, when herdsmen who live two hours' distant will congregate at the edge of Dublock between around 09.00 and 14.00 to collect water for their livestock (the water isn't considered fit for human consumption). Viewing the singing wells costs US$3 per person entrance, US$3 per vehicle and US$12 for a required guide. For travellers dependent on public transport, it might be optimistic to stop off at Dublock unless you intend staying the night, in which case the choice lies between the **Hotel Bifftun Baree** and the **Hotel Nayaayaa**, both of which are functional shoestring set-ups unlikely ever to attract superlatives.

Roughly 20km south of Dublock, a good gravel road heads eastward for 15km to come out at a small village on the rim of a **saline crater lake** known to Amharigna speakers as **Chew Bet** (Salt House) and to Orominga speakers as Ili Sod. The inky-black lake, which lies at the base of a 200m-deep crater, is at once starkly beautiful and rather menacing, and the detour is justified by the view from the rim alone. Looking, as they say, costs nothing, but not according to the over-zealous guides of the newly formed **Chew Bet Guide Association** (m *0916 178 424*). Once you arrive you'll be swarmed by hawkers, guides, would-be guides and all kinds of hangers-on. If you can elbow your way through the crowd to find an official guide you'll be asked for US$3 just for parking the car, swiftly followed by a US$3 per person village entrance fee. Should you want to take photographs you'll then have to shell out more. Should you then be tempted to follow the steep footpath leading to the crater floor – advisable only in the cool of the early morning or late afternoon – then you'll be asked an extortionate fee of US$12 per person for a guide to lead you down to the lake. For an additional US$18 your guide can even organise a staged photograph of someone diving into the water. If, like this updater, you choose to simply stand by the rim and take in the view, you're likely to have a guide (or someone posing as a guide) cosy up beside you and start droning on – unasked – about the history and facts of the lake, then, once they've finished their monologue, demand you pay them for their 'guiding' services. The lake is an important regional centre of salt extraction, worked by the villagers on a 15-days-on, 15-days-off basis so as to keep the levels sustainable. There's no accommodation in the village, but the raw salt is collected by regular pick-up trucks from Mega, which should make it easy enough for backpackers to get a lift to the lake – just make sure that the driver is willing to give you a lift back when his truck is full!

From the turn-off to the lake, the asphalt road continues south for 14km to **Mega**. Nestled in a pretty valley, this one-street town offers little in the way of sightseeing, but it has a fair selection of shoestring hotels – **Beetesebaa Hotel** (*10 rooms;* \ *046 448 0002*) looks to be the best with basic rooms using a common cold shower costing US$6. Students of Italian military history might want to check out the impressive, ruined **Mussolini-era fort** that stands on a hill alongside the Dilla road about 1km from Mega. The section of road immediately north of this fort passes through a somehow unnatural-looking plain of cropped grass hemmed in by barren hills – barren and remarkably even, it looks almost like a floodplain, but is presumably the result of a recent (in geological terms) fall of volcanic ash. The **old British Consulate** also lies on a hill outside town; you may even bump into the consul's ex-chauffeur!

MOYALE

Lying 100km south of Mega, **Moyale** is in effect two different but economically interdependent towns that share a name but are divided by an international border. The Ethiopian town is marginally larger than its Kenyan namesake, but it offers much better facilities with regard to food, lodging and just about everything else. (The one advantage of the Kenyan side is the presence of an ATM at the **Kenya Commercial Bank**, which allows currency withdrawals from a Visa card.)

GETTING THERE AND AWAY Buses to Yabello (US$4.50; 3½ hours) depart between 05.00 and 06.00 daily. If you are heading south to Kenya, see the *Moyale to Nairobi* box, page 412.

WHERE TO STAY

Koket Borena Moyale Hotel (37 rooms) \046 444 1161. This hotel is the best place in town, with clean & neat motel-style rooms with private shower, hot water & TV. There are also 10 traditional *tukuls* with private shower & hot water dotted around the grounds (priced the same as the rooms) & **camping** is also available. Camping prices may be high, but Koket's location near the top of the hill has the key advantage of a slight breeze; downhill hotels may be cheaper, but even at night heat can be insufferable without good airflow. At the time of research the ever-expanding hotel was in the process of building a new multi-storey annex. *US$11/24.50/32.50 sgl/twin/trpl, camping US$6 pp.*

Ghion Hotel (21 rooms) \046 444 0065. If budget is your concern, this place is an OK choice for the night. In general, as you head down the hill the quality of the accommodations tends to go downhill as well, with those at the bottom being noisy disco bars best suited for activities other than sleep. *US$4 using common shower, US$4.50 private en suite.*

WHERE TO EAT
Finding good food is not a problem in Ethiopian Moyale. The **Koket** is your best bet for Western dishes; **Fast Pastry** and **Smart Juice** are also recommended. Upon enquiring about where to eat on the Kenyan side, the repeated response was 'Head over to Ethiopia'.

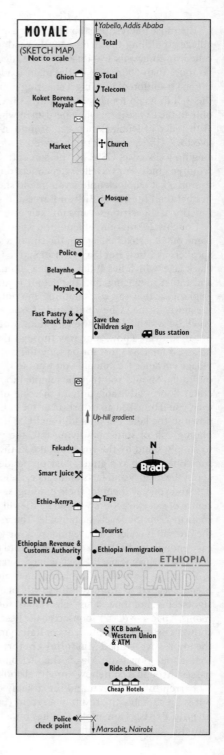

23

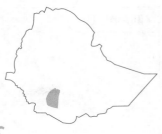

Arba Minch and the Konso Highlands

The principal town of southwest Ethiopia, Arba Minch is seldom visited by travellers in its own right, but it does see quite a bit of tourist traffic as a result of forming the most convenient overnight stop between Addis Ababa and South Omo. It is nevertheless a rather attractive town, situated about 500km south of Addis Ababa among green hills that offer grand views over the Rift Valley lakes of Chamo and Abaya. It also serves as the base for several worthwhile day or overnight trips, most notably to the underrated Nechisar National Park, and the forest-fringed hot springs for which Arba Minch is named.

Also within easy striking distance of Arba Minch is the highland village of Dorze, noted for its unusual traditional architecture. Of further cultural interest, situated on a southerly extension of the Ethiopian Highlands some 90km along the route to South Omo, is the small town of Karat, capital of Konso, a district named after its skilled agriculturist inhabitants, who are noted for their fortified hilltop villages and eerie grave statues.

ARBA MINCH

Arba Minch, the former capital of the defunct Gamo-Gofa province, consists of two discrete settlements separated by 4km of tar road and an altitude climb of almost 200m. Downtown Sikela is the larger, more bustling commercial and residential centre, while uptown Shecha is a vaguely posher settlement of unimposing government buildings, hotels and the homes of government employees. Despite its former status as provincial capital and a population estimated at around 75,000, Arba Minch retains a small-town character – perhaps because it really is two small towns as opposed to one large one.

If Arba Minch is inherently just another humdrum medium-sized Ethiopian town, it does boast a setting that is far from the ordinary. The town lies at an elevation of approximately 1,300m in the foothills of the Rift Valley wall, above a cliff overlooking the mountainous sliver that separates the lakes of Chamo and Abaya. With mountains rising to almost 4,000m to the west, it is really quite difficult to think of a more perfectly sited town anywhere in east Africa. Moshi, on the footslopes of Kilimanjaro, comes close – the difference being that in Arba Minch, wherever you walk, and at whatever time of day, there are absolutely stunning views in all directions, and the longer you spend in the town the more impressive it all becomes.

Once you have tired of the town itself, there is plenty to do in the vicinity. Immediately east of town lies Nechisar National Park, which protects large parts of lakes Chamo and Abaya, as well as fair-sized herds of game. Even without a vehicle, parts of the park and the lakes' shores can be explored either on foot or by

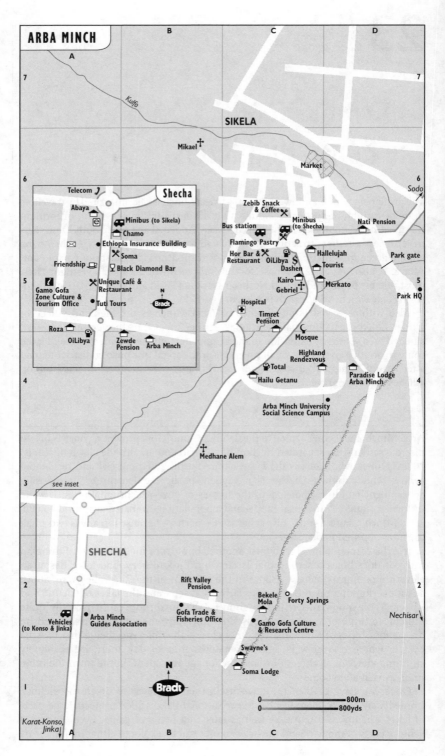

ARBA MINCH

SIKELA

Kulfo

Mikael ✝

Market

Sodo

Shecha (inset)

Telecom ♪

Abaya

Minibus (to Sikela)

Chamo

Ethiopia Insurance Building

Soma

Friendship

Black Diamond Bar

Unique Café & Restaurant

Gamo Gofa Zone Culture & Tourism Office

Tuti Tours

N

Roza

OiLibya

Zewde Pension

Arba Minch

Zebib Snack & Coffee

Bus station

Minibus (to Shecha)

Nati Pension

Flamingo Pastry

Hor Bar & Restaurant

OiLibya

Hallelujah

Dashen

Tourist

Park gate

Kairo

Gebriel

Merkato

Park HQ

Hospital

Timret Pension

Mosque

Highland Rendezvous

Paradise Lodge Arba Minch

Total

Hailu Getanu

Arba Minch University Social Science Campus

Medhane Alem ✝

see inset

SHECHA

Rift Valley Pension

Bekele Mola

Forty Springs

Nechisar

Vehicles (to Konso & Jinka)

Arba Minch Guides Association

Gofa Trade & Fisheries Office

Gamo Gofa Culture & Research Centre

Swayne's

Soma Lodge

N

Bradt

0   800m
0   800yds

Karat-Konso, Jinka

boat. Also of interest is the highland village of Dorze, an easy day trip using public transport from Arba Minch.

GETTING THERE AND AWAY

By air Flights direct to Arba Minch from Addis Ababa are operated by **Ethiopian Airlines** (✆ 046 881 0649) three times weekly (US$60). The airport lies about 7km from Sikela, off the Sodo road. A charter taxi to the airport from the centre should cost no more than US$6.

By road The most popular access route from the north or east is via the surfaced 250km road that branches westward from the Moyale road at Shashemene. Coming from Addis Ababa, it is easy to cover this route in one day, whether by bus or in a private vehicle, though most people choose to break the journey with an overnight stop at Langano, Hawassa or Wondo Genet (see *Chapter 20*). An alternative route via Butajira and Hosaina, connecting with the main road at Sodo, is actually shorter than the road through Shashemene and has grown in popularity since it was surfaced (see *Chapter 19*). From the west, Arba Minch can be reached in a day along a good gravel road connecting Sodo to Jimma, while the best route from the south is via Yabello and Karat-Konso.

There are plenty of buses between Arba Minch and Shashemene (US$5; 5½ hours), and at least one daily to Hawassa (US$5.50; 6½ hours), and Addis Ababa (US$9; 11–12 hours). These leave from the main bus station [516 C5] in Sikela, but morning buses normally stop in Shecha, outside the Abaya Hotel, to pick up passengers before they head to the bus station. Heading south there are daily bus services to Konso (US$2; 3½ hours), Weita (US$4; 5 hours) and Jinka (US$6; 8 hours). If you don't connect with the bus you want, then you'll be reliant on lifts with the pick-up trucks that cluster in front of the OiLibya garage in Shecha at around 06.00. Bear in mind that drivers may not be willing to risk a fine to take you. More locally, there is a twice-daily service to Chencha (US$1.50; 2 hours), stopping at Dorze (US$1; 1½ hours).

GETTING AROUND Regular minibuses ply between Sikela [516 C7] and Shecha [516 A2], starting up at around 06.30 and costing around US$0.25.

Boat hire Most hotels including Paradise Lodge can arrange boat hire and tours to the crocodile market and Nechisar National Park for their guests. Alternatively, **Tuti Tours** [516 A5] (m 0911 805 971; e tutiman_utd@yahoo.com) has a small fleet of 7m boats: four with a 40hp engine, 12 with a 25hp engine, and four with a 15hp engine. Prices for 2–2½-hour trips to the crocodile market and islands with birds start at US$30 for one to five people, while a group of six to ten people costs US$59. Longer trips crossing the lake to the national park cost US$89/118 for one to five people/six to ten people and take around seven hours. Another resource is the **Salayish Lake Guide Association** (✆ 046 885 0070; m 0913 974 738).

TOURIST INFORMATION The **Gamo Gofa Zone Culture & Tourism Office** [516 A5] (✆ 046 881 2046; m 0916 830 961; ⊕ 07.00–17.30 Mon–Fri), located a block west of Unique Café in Shecha, is worth visiting for current advice before you head out to the places described later. The newly formed **Arba Minch Guides Association** [516 A2] (✆ 046 881 0117; m 0912 119 515; ⊕ 07.00–17.30 daily) lies around 300m south of the roundabout in Shecha on the main road to Konso. The helpful staff can arrange guided 4x4 trips to South Omo and Nechisar.

WHERE TO STAY
Sikela

Upmarket

Paradise Lodge Arba Minch [516 D4] (51 rooms) ✆046 881 2398/011 661 2191; e info@paradiselodgeethiopia.com; www. paradiselodgeethiopia.com. With a high bluff location between the 2 towns, this sprawling lodge, which opened in late 2008, takes the title for best view. Not long after it opened however, the main resort was quickly taken over by the US air force & disgruntled guests were forced into smaller, cheaper accommodation in what looked like a construction site, & were even made to enter via a service entrance. On our most recent visit in late 2011, we were assured that guests would soon be moved back into the main section of the lodge & would have full access to all facilities. If so, accommodation will be in small but well-built individual stone *tukuls* each with king bed, net, fridge, DSTV & private balcony with a rocking chair from which to enjoy the scenery, with an additional 13 bungalow-style budget rooms also available. The attached restaurant specialises in fish, while the outdoor terrace is a great place for a drink, & an elevated bar under a tree is in the works. Other services include horse, motorcycle & boat rentals, Wi-Fi, spa services & beauty salon. Future plans include an additional 69 rooms, a conference hall, gym, swimming pool, small clinic & souvenir shop. *US$40 budget rooms, US$59/70/85 sgl/dbl/twin inc b/fast.*

Budget

Tourist Hotel [516 C5] (36 rooms) ✆046 881 2171/3662. Centrally located in the heart of Sikela, this friendly place lacks the views of the Highland below & is subject to both church & mosque noise. Foreigners also pay double the local rate for rooms – all with fridge, DSTV & en-suite bath – that are clean, but nothing special. That said, the shady central garden restaurant & bar with draught beer is very popular. *US$15/19/21.50 sgl/dbl/twin.*

Merkato Hotel [516 C5] (35 rooms) ✆046 881 0245. This sparkling new multi-storey hotel was set to open within days of our visit in late 2011. The yet-to-be-unveiled rooms each will have tiled floors, DSTV, hot-water shower en suite & small balcony. A ground-floor restaurant & café was also in the works. *US$18/21 dbl/twin.*

Nati Pension [516 D5] (10 rooms) ✆046 881 3269. Located opposite the entrance gate to Nechisar, this new place, like others in this price range, charges double *faranji* rates. The rooms have tiled floors, clean private bathroom, DSTV & nets, but come off as poor value. A restaurant is forthcoming as are 28 new rooms, all of which will be housed in a new multi-storey building under construction in the middle of the complex. *US$17/20 dbl/twin.*

Highland Rendezvous Hotel [516 C4] (30 rooms) ✆046 881 1721. With a view over Sikela town, this motel-style place has large, spotless rooms with hot-water en suites (make sure you check, as 3 rooms have cold water only). The 3 major drawbacks are the discriminatory pricing (*faranjis* pay almost double), it does not serve food & the hotel is far from everywhere save the Paradise above (which is not a problem if you have a vehicle). Cold drinks are available. *US$12/18/18 sgl/dbl/twin.*

Timret Pension [516 C5] (19 rooms) ✆046 885 0125. This new pension situated in a large green compound along the main road between Sikela & Shecha just before the turn-off to the hospital currently offers the best budget-friendly accommodation in Sikela. The en-suite rooms with tiled floors & hot-water showers are on the small side, especially the bathrooms, but they're bright & clean & very well priced. (Management here has yet to catch on to the 2-tier price system flaunted to the extreme by the hotels above.) The only real downsides are that it's located opposite the mosque – so it could be noisy – & there's no restaurant. *US$9 en-suite dbl.*

Shoestring

Kairo Hotel [516 C5] (22 rooms) ✆046 881 0323. Situated next to the OiLibya garage, this is probably the pick of the numerous cheap dives in Sikela. But the small rooms – 12 with private cold-water en suite & 10 using common cold-water showers & all with ¾ beds – feel over-priced, especially considering you'd be staying in a virtual construction site. At the time of writing the hotel was undergoing a major expansion adding 28 new en-suite rooms with DSTV & internet, set to be priced in the moderate range as well as a restaurant, cafe & bar. *US$4.50 using common shower, US$6 en suite.*

Hailu Getanu Hotel [516 C4] (5 rooms) 046 881 0320. Situated next to the Total garage along the main road between Sikela & Shecha, this congenial place offers acceptably clean rooms with ¾ bed & common showers. The location is relatively quiet, perhaps inconvenient if you are on foot, but the attached late-night restaurant & bar (serving draught beer) could make sleeping difficult. *US$3*.

Shecha

Upmarket

Swayne's Hotel [516 C1] (72 rooms) 046 881 1895 or 011 629 9260; e reservations@ swayneshotel.com/swayneshotel@yahoo.com; www.swayneshotel.com. Owned & managed by Greenland Tours, this clifftop hotel, which lies about 2km outside Shecha, is perched on the edge of a rocky scarp inhabited by semi-tame olive baboons. The restaurant has a spectacular view over lakes Chamo & Abaya to the eastern Rift Valley wall & offers over-priced drinks along with reasonably priced mains for around US$4. Unfortunately, only the first row of rooms shares this view, while the rest have a poor view of another room directly in front of them! All rooms sport similar traditional décor common to all Greenland properties & have 2 ¾ beds with nets & private hot bath with tub though in general feel over-priced. *US$50/60/60 sgl/dbl/twin without view, US$60/70/70 sgl/dbl/twin with view*.

Moderate

Soma Lodge [516 C1] (4 *tukuls*) 046 884 0395–6. Located near Swayne's, this small quiet lodge was developed by the same owner of the popular Soma Restaurant in Shecha. Accommodation is in very well-priced 2-bedroom beehive-style *tukuls* each with 4 twin beds & 2 bathrooms. A large central *tukul* acts as a reception & eating area that opens up to a breezy outside terrace with fabulous views. A full restaurant is planned, but in the meantime only breakfast & cold drinks are available. *US$36 for the 4-bed tukul inc b/fast*.

Budget

Bekele Mola Hotel [516 C2] (32 rooms) 046 881 0046. Situated close to Swayne's Hotel & offering a similarly spectacular view, the Bekele Mola has sadly suffered from neglect in recent years. That said, the hotel is set for an upgrade, which may increase the prices along with the standard of the rooms. Until that time, the time-worn rooms each with private en suite & hot shower are clean if a little musty. Decent meals are available at US$2.50–4, with the choice of eating in the rather moribund dining room or on the pretty veranda overlooking both lakes (if you do eat outdoors, keep an eye open for the semi-tame olive baboons that come past most days). *US$14 dbl or twin*.

Rift Valley Pension [516 B2] (10 rooms) 046 881 2531. Located *en route* to the Bekele Mola, this unpretentious place is relatively new & very quiet. The modest rooms with en-suite hot water & DSTV are adequately clean & priced fairly. A small restaurant & bar are attached. *US$9/12 sgl/dbl*.

Shoestring

Arba Minch Hotel [516 B4] (13 rooms) 046 881 0206. Situated a couple of hundred metres along the road towards the Bekele Mola, this place offers spacious single/twin beds with en-suite cold shower & long-drop toilet. *US$6/9 dbl/twin*.

Abaya Hotel [516 A6] (10 rooms) Set in attractive grounds on the main road through Shecha, this place is good value, offering decently clean en-suite rooms with a ¾ bed & cold-water shower, with the bonus that most long-haul buses stop immediately outside to pick up passengers before heading down to the main bus station in Sikela. Be warned, however, that the bus drivers who crash here are partial to revving their engines at antisocial hours, the noisy bar stays open very late, & the resident bevy of bar girls has a reputation for hassling male travellers & making female travellers feel unwelcome. *US$5 en-suite dbl*.

Zewde Pension [516 B4] (6 rooms) 046 881 6403. Located just down from the Arba Minch Hotel, this small pension is the current pick of the clutch of shoestring places in Shecha. Quiet & clean, it offers well-priced compact en-suite rooms with cold shower & long-drop toilet. *US$4 en-suite dbl*.

Roza Hotel [516 A5] (12 rooms) m 0910 999 611. Although better known for its food, this unpretentious hotel also offers basic rooms using a common shower. The young Italian-

Ethiopian owner is very friendly, but the rooms are frightfully dirty & it's right next to a mosque. New improvements including a pizza oven & 6 more rooms with new shower facilities, however, were well under way on our most recent visit. The attached restaurant naturally has a strong leaning towards Italy with favourites such as lasagne, pasta & pizza dominating the menu. *US$2*.

✕ WHERE TO EAT The local speciality in Arba Minch is *asa kutilet* (fish cutlet), which consists of a mound of fried battered tilapia, a spicy green dip called *dataa*, a couple of crusty bread rolls and a plate of salad, and costs around US$3 at most places. The **Soma Restaurant** (see listing below) takes top honours, but a good fish cutlet is to be had at many of the hotels. The restaurant at the **Paradise Lodge** [516 D4] serves fish cutlets at twice the price (arguably worth it just for the view). If you want something other than fish, the **Tourist Hotel** [516 C5] serves a decent menu of European and Ethiopian dishes for around US$3 as well as a good selection of freshly squeezed juices in a relaxed garden setting. The **Bekele Mola Hotel** [516 C2] offers a similarly priced menu of Ethiopian/European fare along with some stunning views from the outside terrace, while the restaurant at the **Roza Hotel** [516 A5] is best known for its strong Italian flavours including delicious traditional wood-fired pizzas.

✕ Kibiye View Café & Restaurant [516 C5] `046 881 3711`; ⊕ 07.00–22.00 daily. Located in Sikela above the Dashen Bank this bright & airy café/restaurant offers a surprisingly good selection of vegetarian dishes as well as the usual mix of Ethiopian/European favourites. *US$2.50–4.50*.

✕ Hor Bar & Restaurant [516 C5] `046 881 1384`; ⊕ 06.00–22.00 daily. Hidden away down an alleyway behind the OiLibya garage in central Sikela, this friendly local beer garden-cum-restaurant shaded by large jacaranda trees buzzing with weaver birds is a cool oasis. Traditional dishes such as *kitfo* are the staples here. *US$3*.

✕ Soma Restaurant [516 A5] m 0911 737 712; ⊕ 07.00–22.00 daily. This long-serving restaurant located next to the Diamond Bar in Shecha is *the* place to try *asa kutilet* (fish cutlet). *US$4–9*.

⊡ Flamingo Pastry [516 C5] `046 881 2050`; ⊕ 07.00–21.00 daily. A haven for the sweet-toothed, this patisserie just off the main roundabout in Sikela serves a yummy selection of cakes, inexpensive snacks & coffee. *US$1–2*.

⊡ Friendship Café [516 A5] `046 881 2841`; ⊕ 06.30–20.30 daily. Located opposite Soma Restaurant in Shecha, this convivial café is another great spot for pastries, coffee & other breakfast staples. *US$1–2*.

⊡ Unique Café & Restaurant [516 A5] `046 881 3282`; ⊕ 06.30–20.00 daily. Previously known as Chocolet Pastry, this place located near Friendship Café in Shecha is still a good spot for snacks, cold drinks & pastries. *US$1–2*.

OTHER PRACTICALITIES

Internet There are several internet places in Shecha charging around US$0.10 per minute.

Foreign exchange The best place to change foreign currency is at the **Dashen Bank** [516 C5] located opposite the Tourist Hotel in Sikela. It's open 08.00–12.00 and 13.00–16.30 Monday to Friday.

Swimming pool A tempting goal on a hot day is the swimming pool at the university on the road to Shashemene. You can take a bus to the campus, also known as the Institute of Water Technology, which is run-down and laid out with lots of gaping empty green spaces. The pool, located at the rear of the campus, is big and refreshing, though over-chlorinated. A half-hearted lifeguard will charge you a nominal fee to leap in. Beverages are available at the small cafeteria in the next block of buildings.

NECHISAR NATIONAL PARK

(*Entrance US$5 valid for 24hrs; US$1.50/2.50 for a 6-/12-seat vehicle; US$6 obligatory scout*) Designated and demarcated in 1974 but never formally gazetted, the 514km² Nechisar National Park protects an untrammelled landscape of mountains and lakes as thrillingly beautiful as that of any African game reserve. Set in the Rift Valley at an altitude of 1,100–1,650m, within walking distance of Arba Minch, the park protects not only the easterly Nechisar ('White Grass') Plains for which it is named, but also significant portions of lakes Chamo and Abaya, and the mountainous Egzer Dilday ('Bridge of God') that divides the two lakes. Habitats range from the knotted acacia scrub of Egzer Dilday to the wide-open grasslands of the Nechisar Plain, or from the open water of lakes Abaya and Chamo to the dense groundwater forest that divides the lakes from Arba Minch.

This high level of habitat diversity is reflected in a checklist of 70 mammal and 342 bird species, though many of the larger mammals on that list have been exterminated. Scientific exploration of the park is far from complete: a 1991 Cambridge expedition to Nechisar discovered 15 endemic butterflies and eight endemic dragonfly species. The same expedition also returned home with the wing of a previously undescribed bird, which was described and named the Nechisar nightjar, *Caprimulgus solala*, in 1995. Thought to be endemic to Ethiopia, this nightjar might well be regarded as the most elusive of all African birds – a live individual has yet to be identified. Nechisar is also the only known Ethiopian locality for the white-tailed lark and it also protects an exceptionally isolated population of white-fronted black chat.

The practically uninhabited plains of Nechisar fared reasonably well as a sanctuary until 1991, but its conservation infrastructure collapsed along with the Derg, leading to an influx of settlement by the agriculturist Kori and the pastoralist Guji Oromo, as well as over-grazing, over-fishing, high levels of poaching and illegal firewood collection. By the late 1990s, it was estimated that 1,800 Kori had settled in the Sermille Valley in the southeast of the park, while the Nechisar Plains sustained some 3,000 Guji cattle. In addition, at least a dozen large mammal species resident when the park was designated had been exterminated, including elephant, buffalo, black rhinoceros, cheetah, African wild dog, Rothschild's giraffe, Grevy's zebra, Beisa oryx, eland, lesser kudu and gerenuk.

After long years of neglect, Nechisar received two welcome shots in the arm in 2004. The first was the negotiated relocation of all the resident Kori to a new settlement with boreholes, a clinic and a school at Abulo Alfecho, 15km south of the park. A similar agreement with the Guji Oromo was far advanced in early 2005, but both efforts seem to have failed; the Guji Oromo remain, with some Kori returning to the park as well. The second shot was the signing of a management contract with the African Parks Foundation, a non-profit organisation that has played a significant role in rehabilitating similarly down-at-heel game reserves elsewhere in Africa. Unfortunately, after only three years, this effort has failed as well. Citing a lack of confidence in future sustainability due to non-compliance on the part of the Guji Oromo, African Parks completely pulled out in June 2008.

Discouraging news aside, for the time being, Nechisar remains a low-key wildlife destination, most notable for its wild scenery. It has an untrammelled atmosphere, in part because of the rough roads, which force its closure after rain, and in part because of the low tourist volume (the park attracts an average of around 1,500 foreign tourists annually, so in all probability you'll have it to yourself). The road across the Egzer Dilday is particularly exhilarating as it twists and bumps around the curves of the hills offering splendid views across Lake Chamo and its volcanically formed islands. Once across the bridge, there are sweeping views over the plains to the majestic volcanic hills on the eastern boundary.

A great part of the park's appeal derives from its two scenic lakes. Set at an altitude of 1,268m, Lake Abaya is the second-largest water body in Ethiopia (after Lake Tana, with a total area of 1,160km²). The more southerly Lake Chamo is the third largest in the country, despite covering slightly less than half of Abaya's surface area, and it supports substantial numbers of hippo and crocodile. Both lakes are rather shallow, reaching a maximum depth of 13m and 10m respectively, but they are very different in coloration: also known as Kai Hayk ('Red Lake') Abaya has an unusual rusty appearance resulting from a suspension of ferrous hydroxide in its water, whereas the more saline Chamo is a more conventional blue.

The first European visitor to this area, Arthur Donaldson-Smith, passed through *en route* to northeast Turkana in 1895, with the hope of confirming the rumoured existence of one 'Lake Aballa'. He discovered that the locals actually called it Abaya, and was led not to the lake we know today as Abaya but rather to the one we now know as Chamo. A year later, the Italian explorer Vittorio Bottego became the first European to reach the shores of the larger lake, which he christened Regina Margherita, the name by which it was most widely known through the remainder of the Imperial era. Unlike the name Chamo, which was used by the Burji people on its southern shore, the name Abaya has little historical validity. This lake is traditionally known by at least half-a-dozen names locally, among them Gumaraki, Yegidicho, Begade, Beki, Kai and Dambala, but not Abaya, which literally means 'Big Water' and was applied generically to any substantial freshwater body (part of the reason for Donaldson-Smith's apparent misidentification).

The best area for game viewing is the open Nechisar Plain. The most common large mammal here is Burchell's zebra, which is regularly seen in herds of 100 or more. You should also see Grant's gazelle and, with a bit of luck, one of the 100-odd resident Swayne's hartebeest. Cheetah and African wild dog are probably extinct, and lions are heard more often than they are seen – though a large maned male was reported lounging around on Egzer Dilday in early 2005. The acacia and combretum woodland of Egzer Dilday is home to Guenther's dik-dik and greater kudu, while crocodile, hippo and waterbuck are frequently seen from the viewpoint over Lake Chamo. Acacia birds such as rollers, sparrow-weavers and starlings are well represented, and Nechisar seems to be particularly good for raptors.

Entirely different in its faunal composition is the lush groundwater forest close to the park entrance, which is dominated by sycamore figs reaching up to 30m high. Guereza and vervet monkeys are common here, as are troops of olive baboon. Other forest animals include bushbuck, bushpig and warthog. The forest is a very rewarding area for birds, but it is also predictably frustrating in the dense cover – you can at least be certain of encountering the large and raucous silvery-cheeked hornbill. Also on the Arba Minch side of the park is the famous and misleadingly named crocodile market, where hundreds of these large reptiles accumulate to sun themselves on the shore of Lake Chamo.

GETTING THERE AND AWAY The park headquarters [516 D5] lie about 2km from Arba Minch. To reach them, follow the Sodo road out of Sikela for about 1km, and then turn right into the side road next to the training college. You need a 4x4 vehicle to enter the park itself, but you can walk to the headquarters or to the hot springs and surrounding forest below the Bekele Mola Hotel.

The crocodile market is only accessible by boat. (There is a rough 9km track to the crocodile market about 3km past the park headquarters and immediately after the bridge across the Kulfo River, but visitors are not allowed to use it.) For boat hire see page 517.

WHERE TO STAY Most people visit Nechisar as a day trip from Arba Minch. There are, however, four little-used **campsites** – Forty Springs and Bridge of Kulfo campsites are both less than 5km from the headquarters on the forested banks of the Kulfo River, while Viewpoint is roughly 26km from the main gate and Viewpoint Hot Springs 35km – costing US$2.50 per person. None of these sites has anything in the way of facilities, but if you're properly equipped they are blissfully peaceful and wonderfully sited for seeing forest animals. Watch out for crocodiles in the river.

It is permitted to camp elsewhere in the park, provided that you are self-sufficient when it comes to food and water, and remove all your rubbish when you leave.

THE HOT SPRINGS Arba Minch translates as 'Forty Springs' [516 C2], and the field of springs after which the town is named lies within Nechisar National Park at the base of the cliff below the Bekele Mola Hotel. Previously, visitors were allowed to visit the springs without paying the US$5.50 Nechisar Park entrance fee, but this is no longer the case. In the past you could also access the springs by walking down a steep path from the Bekele Mola, but this is also now forbidden. Given these new rules, the springs are probably worth a visit only if you have already paid the US$5 fee to see Nechisar.

The area around the springs is covered in dense forest, which gives you an excellent opportunity to explore this habitat on foot, and you can swim in a pool at the springs. Even if the springs are closed to the public, as seems to have been the case recently, the walk out is arguably of greater interest than the destination.

If you don't have a vehicle or don't want to pay the US$1.50–2.50 vehicle fee, the springs can be reached on foot. From park headquarters, it is about a 4km walk along a road that offers excellent birdwatching. Vervet and guereza monkeys and olive baboons are abundant, and the odd dik-dik and bushbuck might be heard or seen crashing into the undergrowth. You will know that you have reached the springs when you come to a blue gate. Past the gate is a pump house and a fenced-off pool where local children swim. To reach the springs, cross a small footbridge and the springs are immediately on your right. To the left there are openings in the fence should you choose to join the locals for a swim. Note that the springs are not hot, but tepid at best.

ARBA MINCH CROCODILE FARM (⊕ *08.30–17.30 daily; guided tour US$3 pp*) The Arba Minch Crocodile Farm, run by the Department of National Resources, lies about 6km out of town near Lake Abaya. About 8,000 animals are kept on the farm, with an age range of one to six years. The crocodiles are hatched from eggs taken from the lake but a number have been reintroduced to keep the natural population in balance. The farm consists of a dozen or so cages, each of which contains several hundred bored-looking crocodiles of a similar age.

To get to the farm, follow the Sodo road out of Sikela for about 4km till you reach the clearly signposted turn-off. On the way you will cross a bridge over a river and later detour round the town's airstrip to your right. If you don't feel like the walk, vehicles heading towards the lakeside town of Lante will be able to drop you at the turn-off. The 2km of road between the turn-off and the farm passes through forest and thick scrub, excellent for birds and monkeys, and worth exploring in its own

23

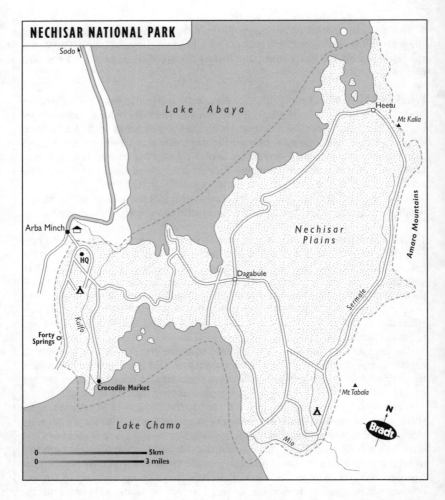

NECHISAR NATIONAL PARK

right even if you are not particularly interested in visiting the crocodile farm. The road continues past the farm for about 500m to a landing stage on the shore of Lake Abaya, where there is good birdwatching and a chance of seeing hippos and crocodiles in their natural state.

For anyone wanting to stay nearby, it's possible to pitch a tent under a shady tree at the **Salaysh Lake Guide Association Campsite** (◊ *046 885 0070*) located directly opposite the entrance to the crocodile farm. At the time of writing there were no facilities, but cold drinks and coffee were available. Camping costs US$2.50/4 for a two-person/four-person tent.

CHENCHA AND DORZE

Mention the small highland town of Chencha to anybody in Arba Minch and they give an involuntary shiver. Set at an altitude of 2,900m in the Guge hills, 37km north of Arba Minch by road, Chencha is best known locally for its cold, misty weather and year-round moist climate culminating in an average monthly precipitation of 200mm in each of March, April, May and October. Chencha today is something of a backwater – the dramatic series of switchbacks that climbs 1,600m to the town over a mere 22km is often impassable after heavy rain – but incredibly it once served as the capital of Gamo-Gofa before it was usurped by Arba Minch.

Aside from the dramatic views back to the Rift Valley lakes near Arba Minch, the mountainous region is of interest to travellers as the home of the Dorze people, renowned cotton weavers whose tall beehive-shaped dwellings are among the most distinctive traditional structures to be seen anywhere in Africa. The Dorze speak an Omotic tongue, similar to several languages of the Lower Omo Valley, and are thought to have occupied their present highland enclave of less than 30km² for at least 500 years. The main occupations of the region are subsistence farming and weaving; every Dorze compound is surrounded by a smallholding of tobacco, *enset* and other crops, and contains at least one loom which is constantly worked by one or other member of the family. The *shama* cloth produced here is regarded to be the finest in Ethiopia; plain white *gabbi* robes and brightly coloured scarf-like *netalas* are sold along the roadside.

It is, above all, the unique Dorze houses that make this such a worthwhile diversion, though. These remarkable extended domes measure up to 6m tall (roughly the height of a two-storey building) and are constructed entirely from organic material. A scaffold of bamboo sticks is first set in place, and then a combination of grass and *enset* (false banana) leaves is woven around the scaffold to create solid insulating walls and a roof. Most Dorze houses also have a low frontal extension, used as a reception area. The spacious interior of the huts is centred on a large fireplace, used for cooking and to generate heat, and different areas are set apart for sleeping and for smaller livestock. Dorze dwellings are enduring structures, and one hut will generally serve a married couple for a lifetime – when the base of a hut becomes infested by termites or starts to rot, the entire structure can be lifted up and relocated to a close-by site.

Coming from Arba Minch, the main concentration of traditional houses is reached before you arrive in Chencha, at the small town known as **Dorze**. Within Dorze town, it appears to be normal for only one hut to be enclosed within a compound. Along the road between Dorze and Chencha, there are several compounds containing two or more huts. It is possible to stop at any compound and ask to look around, but you will be expected to pay a standard fee of US$3 to go inside or to take photographs. In recent years a couple of new ecotourism projects, including the **Besa Dorze Hayzo Weavers** and **Potters Co-ops**, both established by Irish NGO Vita (*www.vita.ie*), as well as two new tourist lodges have opened, making visiting and staying in Dorze village a very appealing prospect for anyone wanting to experience the traditional lifestyle of the Dorze people. The local **market** at Dorze, held on Monday and Thursday, is renowned for being very colourful. Also of interest is the impressive 30m-high **Toro Waterfall**, which can be reached from the village along a pretty 30-minute walking path – any local will be able to guide you. And if you are in the area at the right time, the Dorze celebration of Meskel (1 October) is reputedly very colourful.

GETTING THERE The drive from Arba Minch to Chencha takes about an hour in a private vehicle. The route involves following the surfaced Addis Ababa road back for 14km, then turning left onto a dirt road which reaches Dorze after 15km and Chencha after another 8km. By bus there is a twice-daily service from Arba Minch to Chencha (US$1.50; 2 hours) that stops at Dorze (US$1; 1½ hours), departing the bus station in Sikela at 06.30 and 13.30. The trip takes around two hours in each direction, so a day trip is perfectly feasible, especially on the market days of

Monday and Saturday. Along the route you will undoubtedly encounter numerous children lining the road calling 'you, you, you!' and dancing for the passing tourist traffic. Many of the dancing children we encountered actually lined-up across the road blocking oncoming traffic which was hurtling down the mountain and a few even managed to do the full splits right there in the middle of the road in front of our car. While their antics may be somewhat entertaining we urge you *not* to encourage them by giving them sweets, money or water. Not only are the children skipping school, but also what they are doing is dangerous!

WHERE TO STAY AND EAT

Dorze Lodge (7 bungalows) \046 881 1278; e tsehab@yahoo.com; www.dorzelodge. com. This fantastic new community-run lodge is set on the edge of the mountain range with stunning views stretching back to Arba Minch. Designed to emulate a traditional compound, accommodation is provided in dome-shaped huts all constructed entirely from locally sourced material. 2 of the huts have a small double bed while the remaining 5 are twins; all share a common hot-water shower. There's a large thatched-roof restaurant & lounge area serving a small menu of European/Ethiopian favourites (breakfast costs US$3, lunch or dinner US$5) as well as a bar located high up on a hilltop viewpoint overlooking the valley below. The friendly staff can arrange local guides & village walks, as well as hiking & horseriding treks. The only downside is there's no electricity, though a generator is on hand when needed. *US$12/18 dbl/twin.*

Dorze Hayzo Lodge (28 huts) m 0916 880 720; e tezeradorze@gmail.com. Helped to set up by Irish NGO Vita, this new lodge located 2km from the centre of Dorze on the way to Chencha allows travellers the opportunity to spend the night in a traditional-style hut in the middle of a real family compound – though tourists have the added benefit of electricity & hot water. Accommodation is in simply furnished huts – some double, some twin – all using common hot showers. **Camping** is also permitted on the grassy knoll opposite the compound. There is a small central restaurant & bar where you can order simple European dishes as well as local fare (breakfast costs US$2, lunch or dinner US$3). A variety of local tours can be arranged such as guided village walks, visits to the weaving & potters co-ops, hikes to the waterfall & there's traditional dancing & music most nights. Pick-ups from Arba Minch are also available for groups of 6 or more. *Traditional hut US$4.50 pp, camping US$3 per tent.*

Chencha Hotel (9 rooms) Should you wish to spend a night in Chencha, this basic but friendly hotel on the main road through the town is the best bet with rooms with a double bed & common cold shower (not a madly tempting prospect at this altitude!). *US$3.*

KARAT-KONSO

Situated on the banks of the seasonal Segen River at an altitude of 1,650m, Karat-Konso is the capital town of Konso Special Woreda, and the junction town through which passes all road traffic into South Omo. Physically dominated by that road junction, this town of roughly 5,000 inhabitants might prosaically be described as a traffic roundabout of comically vast dimensions surrounded by a solitary petrol station, a scattering of local hotels, and a sprawl of dusty lanes lined with scruffy, low-rise buildings. Certainly, Karat-Konso could hardly offer a less auspicious first impression of what is actually a fascinating part of Ethiopia.

First impressions of Karat-Konso can be deceptive. It is undeniably the case that the town boasts little to distinguish it from a hundred other small Ethiopian settlements of its ilk. Equally true, however, is that the Konso people of the surrounding hills adhere to a unique and complex culture every bit as absorbing as that of the more renowned lowland peoples of the Omo region. Highlighting the significance of the Konso people's living traditions, in mid 2011 the Konso cultural landscape, which features stone-walled terraces and fortified settlements dating back 400 years, was officially listed as a UNESCO World Heritage Site. On most days, you'll see few signs of this in the town itself, the exception being Mondays and Thursdays, when a large traditional market is held about 2km from the town centre along the Jinka road. Also worth a look, especially if you will not be heading out to one of the traditional villages, is the **Konso Museum** (⊕ *08.00–17.00 daily; entrance US$1.50 payable at the tourist office*) (see page 528) funded by the French government and located across from the Kanta Lodge, which houses a collection of wooden totems known as *wagas*. The newly opened **Konso Cultural Centre** (◟*046 773 0419*; ⊕ *09.00–12.30 & 14.00–17.30 daily*), set up by an Italian corporation with the support of the European Union to provide a visual archive of the Konso people, screens films and hosts revolving exhibitions highlighting Konso culture. It also has a good library, internet café and a few shops selling local handicrafts.

Karat-Konso forms an excellent base from which to explore the surrounding hills, and the traditional villages that dot them. For travellers dependent on public transport or on their own two feet, the obvious first point of call is **Dekatu**, a walled Konso village situated close to the market and only 3km from the centre of Karat-Konso. Further afield, and with access to a vehicle, the magnificent hilltop settlement of Mecheke, the region's established 'tourist village', can be reached though several other similar villages can be visited in the company of a good local guide. Other local points of interest include the **sculpted sand formation** outside Gesergiyo village, and the house of the traditional chief **Walda Dawit Kalla**.

Note that the town of Karat-Konso is generally referred to as Konso, but its official (and more correct) name is Karat. In order to preclude confusion between the Konso people, the region of Konso and the town that governs them both, I have referred to the town throughout as Karat-Konso, and reserved the use of the term Konso for the people and their territory.

GETTING THERE AND AWAY Karat-Konso is the gateway town to South Omo, and all travellers who visit the region by road will have to pass through it. Whether you travel in a rented or private vehicle, or use public transport, the road trip from Addis Ababa to Karat-Konso takes at least two days in either direction. Although many travellers visit the region covered in this chapter as a self-standing trip out of Addis Ababa, it is equally possible to tag it onto broader travels in southern Ethiopia, or *en route* between Kenya and central Ethiopia. Details of reaching the various springboards for Karat-Konso – Arba Minch, Yabello and Fiseha Genet – are given in the relevant sections elsewhere in this guide.

The most popular access road to Karat-Konso goes via Arba Minch, which is where most people break up the trip for a night or two. A second established access road, one that has seen great recent improvements, cuts across eastwards from the main Dilla–Moyale road at Yabello. A third and newer road to Karat-Konso leads southwest from the small town of Fiseha Genet on the Dilla–Moyale road.

To/from Arba Minch The 85km asphalt and gravel road between Karat-Konso and Arba Minch is regularly graded, and is currently the best of the access roads. The drive generally takes up to three hours in a private vehicle, with little to distract you along the way. The one exception is the Monday cattle market by the Gato River, about 26km outside of Karat-Konso. A bus runs daily from Arba Minch to Konso (US$2; 3½ hours), continuing on to Jinka (US$6; 8 hours), throughout the year, though the service may be suspended after unusually heavy rain, in which case you can assume that roads from Konso into South Omo will be firmly out of commission. Various light vehicles also cover the road between Arba Minch and Jinka – all going well, the run shouldn't take longer than four hours.

To/from Yabello The 105km road between Yabello and Karat-Konso now takes about three hours to drive in a private vehicle, ideally a 4x4. (Some 95% of the road is good gravel, but the presence of several unimproved river crossings necessitates a vehicle with high clearance.) Leaving from Yabello, the road is in fair condition, passing through the small Borena town of Leloi after 26km, and it remains so until **Brindal** 40km further. Brindal is a lovely and unaffected Borena village, dominated by circular reed-and-grass houses with flat or rounded roofs. It's a rewarding place for photography – assuming that you're prepared to pay the going rate of US$0.15 per person – and a small roadside bar serves tea, coffee, beer and biscuits. There is no accommodation here, but **camping** is safe, provided that you ask permission before pitching a tent.

Upon leaving Brindal, you need to turn right at the first junction (the southerly fork leads to Tenta). You will know that you are on the correct road when you cross a rickety wooden bridge a few minutes later, which marks the dividing line between Borena and Konso territory. The hilly semi-desert scenery from here on in is fantastic, with further compensation in the form of remote settlements, and a surprising amount of wildlife – olive baboon, Guenther's dik-dik, and flocks of vulturine guinea fowl, iridescent cobalt chests to the fore as they scurry dementedly across the track. After 35km, the road connects with the new Fiseha Genet road about 5km out of Karat-Konso.

There is no public transport along the road between Yabello and Karat-Konso, but occasional trucks will take passengers for a fee. It's easy enough to find out about suitable transport; in theory the best days to travel by truck are Saturday (market day in Yabello) and to a lesser extent Monday or Thursday (market day in Karat-Konso). In practice, it's all rather hit-and-miss.

To/from Fiseha Genet The 175km all-weather dirt road connecting Fiseha Genet to Karat-Konso opened in 2002. The significance of this new route for locals, as well as for travellers heading to or from Kenya, is that it allows for direct access between the Dilla–Moyale road and Karat-Konso all year through. For travellers coming from Addis Ababa, it forms an easy alternative to the Arba Minch route, allowing one to visit South Omo as a loop, coming along one route and returning via the other. Unfortunately, there have been reports that the road fails to live up to its all-weather billing, and may be impassable at times when crossings are washed away; better to check on current conditions rather than have to backtrack!

Fiseha Genet straddles the surfaced Moyale road about 55km south of Dilla. Several local hotels are dotted around the small town, though better **accommodation** is available at nearby Yerga Chefie on the Dilla road (see *Dilla to Yabello by road* in *Chapter 22*, page 507). In a private vehicle, the drive from Fiseha Genet to Karat-Konso takes about five hours, which means that it would be possible to cover this route in a day starting at Dilla or Hawassa. There is no public transport along this road, nor is it in regular use by trucks.

TOURIST INFORMATION A stop at the relocated **tourist information office** (\ *046 773 0073/0196*; ⏰ *07.00–17.00 daily*) is necessary if you want to visit any of the major sights within the region as it is here where you need to pay entrance fees and organise a local guide. The tourist office also doubles as the base for the local **Karat-Konso Guides Association**.

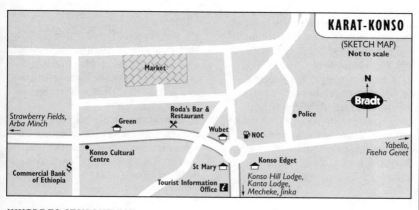

Strawberry Fields,
Arba Minch

Market

Green

Roda's Bar &
Restaurant

Wubet

NOC

Police

N

Yabello,
Fiseha Genet

Konso Cultural
Centre

Commercial Bank
of Ethiopia

St Mary

Tourist Information
Office

Konso Edget

Konso Hill Lodge,
Kanta Lodge,
Mecheke, Jinka

WHERE TO STAY AND EAT
Upmarket

Kanta Lodge (29 bungalows, 30 rooms) 046 773 0092, 011 618 2224–6 (Addis Ababa); e hesstravel@ethionet.et. Located a few kilometres out of town on the road to Omo, & built & operated by Hess Travel, this is currently the best place to stay in Karat-Konso. Accommodation consists of spacious *tukul*-style stone bungalows with modern furnishings & fittings including hot-shower en suite, which are clustered closely together & terraced down the hillside. There's a good restaurant attached with dining offered indoors or out on a shaded stone-paved terrace with views over the valley. Future facilities include a camping area with shower block, toilets & cooking area, tent hire, internet & a swimming pool as well as 30 additional budget rooms to mostly serve drivers & guides. *US$46/58/58 standard sgl/dbl/twin exc b/fast, US$6 to pitch a tent.*

Konso Hill Lodge (40 rooms) 011 555 09475 (Addis Ababa); e hadar.tours@ethionet.et; www.ouroriginhadar.com. Kanta Lodge will soon receive stiff competition from this lodge currently being built by the owner of Hadar Tours further up the escarpment, almost guaranteeing the views here will be even more spectacular. The 20 *tukuls* will each house 2 separate bungalows with private en suites. A restaurant, bar, sauna & spa are also planned. Expect to pay around *US$45/60/65 sgl/ dbl/twin.*

Budget

Strawberry Fields Eco-Lodge (9 *tukuls*, 1 dorm) 046 884 0755/773 0489; m 0912 214 687; e info@permalodge.org; www.permalodge.

org. Located about 200m past the Green Hotel on the road towards Arba Minch, this has to be one of the most interesting ventures in the entire country. In addition to providing lodging, this place functions as a permaculture training centre & offers 2-week courses on sustainable living & organic farming at an all-inclusive price of US$650. 'Cultural Immersion Adventures' are also available, as is WWOOFing (WWOOF = World Wide Opportunities on Organic Farms). The place has a true sense of community, attracting visitors from around the world as well as locals who want to improve their farming techniques. The owner is extremely knowledgeable about sustainable living, making this worth a stop even if you are just passing through. Facilities include eco-friendly composting toilets, solar showers, & gardens for growing fruits & vegetables. There is free camping for WWOOFers, & a small organic restaurant serving soups, salads, juices & burgers using fresh produce harvested from the garden. *Tukuls US$9/17.50/19 sgl/dbl/trpl, dorm US$4 pp, camping US$2.50 per tent.*

Saint Mary Hotel (30 rooms) 046 773 0006. Situated on the main traffic roundabout, this 3-storey hotel has decidedly un-saintly like single rooms with ¾ bed & cold-water shower en suites. Double rooms have 2 ¾ beds & can accommodate up to 4 people. The attached restaurant is said to be better than the one at the Konso Edget, but the subtlety was wasted on us – both have a *faranji* surcharge on food, but at least the Edget does not charge *faranji* prices for beer. *US$9/18 sgl/dbl.*

Green Hotel (18 rooms) 046 773 0151. Similar in standard to the Edget, this quiet hotel on the Arba Minch road has en-suite rooms with cold-water shower & ¾ bed. Food is available with advanced order. *US$7.50/9.50 sgl/dbl*.

🏠 **Konso Edget Hotel** (29 rooms) 📞046 773 0300; e konso_edget2000@yahoo.com. Set in large but rather barren gardens on the main traffic roundabout, this pleasant hotel offers accommodation in clean, bright rooms with cramped cold-water shower en suites. A restaurant-cum-bar serves refrigerated drinks, fruit juice & decent local meals. Internet is available. *US$5/9.50 sgl/twin*.

Shoestring

🏠 **Wubet Hotel** (11 rooms) 📞046 773 0151. This friendly place across from the Edget has basic rooms with ¾ bed, clean bedding & net using a common cold-water shower. There's no restaurant, but if you order ahead simple meals can be prepared. *US$3*.

✕ **Komya Campsite** The local guide association, based at the tourist information office, is planning to build a new campsite 6km from town on the road to Jinka. Prices were unknown at the time of writing. Contact the tourist information office (see page 528) for more details.

WHAT TO SEE The main attractions of the Konso region are the traditional Konso villages described in the box *The Konso* on page 532. Several such villages, notably Dekatu and Mecheke, can be visited using Karat-Konso as a base. Before visiting any villages, it is mandatory to pop into the tourist information office where you pay a US$3 per-person fee, plus US$4 per vehicle. This allows you to visit as many villages as you like, but you must collect a receipt and permit for each village you intend to visit. It is also required that you pick up an official guide from the tourist office at a cost of US$9. The official guides are very knowledgeable and helpful, but will expect a fair tip.

Aside from Dekatu, none of the following attractions listed is easily visited without a private vehicle. If you arrive in Karat-Konso using public transport, the tourist office can arrange rental of a 4x4 vehicle for half a day – sufficient time to visit at least two villages. This will cost around US$48, but do make sure that the driver, the guide and yourself are clear about which places you will be visiting. Although the blanket fee covers entry to any village of your choice, and in theory photography, you should expect to tip any individual you specifically photograph. The going rate in the Konso area is US$0.15.

Every village in Konso has a caretaker whose job it is to collect and keep your permit for that specific village, and also to check that a receipt was issued by the tourist office in Karat-Konso. The caretaker will most likely refuse entry to any traveller who doesn't have this paperwork in their possession. Be warned that the tourist office in Karat-Konso may be unable to issue a receipt on a Sunday or a public holiday, but with luck you might find a guide and pick up permits at the Konso Edget.

Dekatu Although it practically borders on Karat-Konso, the town of Dekatu is rightly regarded as a separate entity, since it still functions as a self-standing traditional community. Contained within Dekatu's town walls are 21 sub-communities, each of which has its own *mora* (community house), making this one of the largest traditional towns anywhere in Konso. Dekatu is known for hosting one of the region's best *waga* makers; should you want to meet him, or to have a statue commissioned, you will need to go with a guide. Otherwise, assuming that you have the requisite paperwork from the tourist office, Dekatu is easy enough to reach independently on foot. Follow the Jinka road out of Karat-Konso for about 2km until you reach the large Monday and Thursday market on the left side of the road. From here, Dekatu is visible to your right, a walled town perched on a hill below and about 1km from the market. It is easily reached by a number of footpaths. At the time of writing, Ethiopia Community Tourism in conjunction with US-based NGO Aid to Artisans was in the process of establishing the **Komaya Heart of Konso Cultural Handcraft Market** in Dekatu. When completed, the market will offer visitors an interactive experience, with a craft demonstration area, craft shop, and small café overlooking the surrounding landscape. For more information visit www.rootsofethiopia.com.

Mecheke The best known and most regularly visited of the traditional Konso towns (among other things, this is where Angela Fisher did much of her exquisite Konso photography; see *Appendix 5, Further information*, page 613), Mecheke lies on a tall hill some 13km from Karat-Konso. Judging by the number of generation poles, the town is at least 400 years old, and today it supports about 3,000 people split into about ten sub-communities. People here are very used to tourists – your presence is likely to be greeted by youngsters playing the *kehaita* (a local musical instrument) and weaving, in the hope of being photographed – but the atmosphere is pretty relaxed and friendly. There are four groups of *waga* statues left in Mecheke, some of them estimated to be more than 150 years old.

To reach Mecheke from the main roundabout in Karat-Konso, follow the Jinka road for 5.5km, turn left onto a side road which you need to follow for 5km, then turn left again onto a motorable track and follow it for 3km to a parking spot below the town walls. No public transport runs along this road. Should you be interested in spending the night a new community **campsite** was under construction at the time of writing and should cost no more than US$3.

Gesergiyo Smaller and less atmospheric than the two towns listed previously, Gesergiyo is of interest primarily for the adjacent formation of sand pinnacles sculpted by occasional water flow in a normally dry gorge. It is a magnificent and very unusual natural phenomenon – I've seen similar rock formations, but nothing comparable made entirely of sand. The superficial resemblance to a row of 'skyscrapers' led some local wag to christen the formation 'New York', a nickname that has stuck.

Oral tradition has it that 'New York' is of supernatural origin. The story is that a local chief awoke one day to find his ceremonial drums had been stolen during the night. He enlisted the help of God, who swept away the earth from where the thieves had buried the drums, creating the sand formation in the process. It is said that the thieves, realising that God knows all, immediately confessed to their sins – their fate goes unrecorded! To this day, light-fingered Konso youngsters are taken to Gesergiyo as a reminder that God doesn't like thieves, and will see what they get up to.

Gesergiyo lies 17km from Karat-Konso by road, and is easily visited in combination with Mecheke. Coming from Mecheke, drive back 3km to the last intersection, where – instead of heading right towards Karat-Konso – you need to turn left. After 2.5km, the road passes through **Fasha**, known for holding what is regarded to be one of the four most important Konso markets every Saturday, and as the site of a century-old Orthodox church that is reputedly the oldest in the Konso territory. Driving on through Fasha, the road reaches Gesergiyo after another 4km.

Chief Gezahegne Woldu's Compound Isolated on a hill and surrounded by juniper forest, the compound of Chief Gezahegne Woldu is situated some 7km from Karat-Konso off the road towards Mecheke. It's a fascinating and atmospheric

With thanks to Dinote Kusia Shenkere of the Konso Tourist Information Office

Although less celebrated than the colourful ethnic groups of South Omo, Konso must rank as among the most singular of African nations. Now governed as a Special Woreda within the Southern Nations, Nationalities and Peoples' Region, the people of Konso had little contact with the rest of Ethiopia until recent times, and the area remains staunchly traditionalist in character.

The Konso inhabit an isolated region of basalt hills – essentially an extension of the southern highlands – lying at an altitude range of roughly 1,500–2,000m, and flanked to the east by the semi-desert Borena lowlands and to the west by the equally harsh Lower Omo Valley. Oddly, the Konso have no strong tradition relating to their origins, other than that they came to their present homeland from somewhere further east 500–1,000 years ago. They speak an east Cushitic language, and have few apparent cultural links with the people of the surrounding lowlands or the Ethiopian Highlands.

Mixed agriculturists, the Konso make the most of the hard, rocky slopes that characterise their relatively dry and infertile homeland through a combination of extensive rock terracing, the use of animal dung as fertiliser, crop rotation and hard work. The most important crop in the region is sorghum, which is harvested twice annually: after the short rains in June and July, and after the long rains in February and March. Sorghum is used to make a thick local beer, while the finely ground flour forms the base of the Konso staple dish of *korkorfa* or *dama*, a sort of doughball that is cooked like a dumpling in a stew or soup. Other important crops include maize, beans and coffee. Oddly, the Konso shun coffee beans in favour of the leaves, which are sun-dried, ground to a fine powder, and mixed with sunflower seeds and various spices, to form an easily stored local equivalent to instant coffee!

The most outwardly distinctive feature of Konso country is the aesthetically pleasing towns and villages, which in some respects bear an unexpected (though purely coincidental) resemblance to the Dogon villages of Mali. Unusually for this part of Africa, the Konso traditionally live in congested centralised settlements, typically situated on the top of a hill and enclosed by stone walls measuring up to 2m high. These walled hilltop settlements usually have no more than three or four entrance gates, and can be reached only via a limited number of steep footpaths. This made the villages easily defensible, an important consideration for an isolated people whose territory was, in the past, under constant threat of cattle raids and military attacks from the flanking lowlands.

Within the defensive town walls, low stick-and-stone walls and leafy *Moringa stenopetelai* (shiferaw) trees enclose every individual compound, to create a labyrinth of narrow, shady alleys. Each family compound typically consists of between three and five circular thatched stone huts, as well as an elevated granary or *kosa* used to store sorghum and maize, and a taller but smaller platform where freshly cooked food is stowed away too high for children to reach it. The compounds are entered via gateways, which are supported and covered by thick wooden struts, a defensive design that forces any aspirant attackers to crawl into the compound one by one.

Every village consists of a number of sub-communities, each of which is centred upon a *mora* or communal house. This is a tall building with an open-sided ground floor supported by juniper trunks, and a sharply angled thatched roof covering a wooden ceiling. The ground floor serves as a shaded place where villagers – men, boys and girls, but not grown women – can relax, gossip, play and make important communal decisions. Customarily, all boys from the age of 12 upwards are required to sleep in the ceiling of the mora until they get married, and even married men are expected to spend part of the night there. This custom, though still enforced, derives from more beleaguered days, when the older boys and men often needed to be mobilised quickly when a village was attacked. The mora also serves as a guesthouse for male visitors from other villages. Girls and women are not generally allowed to sleep in the mora, though these days some villages will make an exception for *faranji* tourists!

Konso society is structured around the Kata generation-set, a system not dissimilar to the Gada of the neighbouring Borena people, or that practised by the Maasai and Samburu of east Africa. Although the exact cycle differs from one village to the next, any given village will initiate a new generation – consisting of boys of between eight and 25 years old – every 18 years. Traditionally, young men who had not yet been initiated into a generation were usually permitted to marry, but any offspring that their wives produced would be killed at birth – a custom that is no longer practised. Should you happen to be in Konso country during December, January or September, this is when Kata induction ceremonies take place, so it's worth asking about them locally. The highlight of the ceremony is the erection of an Olahita (generation pole) in the village's ceremonial square – it is easy to tell roughly how old any given village is by counting the number of poles and multiplying the total by 18!

The erection of poles and stones forms an important part of Konso ritual. In any village square, you'll see a number of so-called Victory Stones standing to mark important events – generally victories over attempted raiders or conquerors – in the village's history. More famous are the Konso *waga*, carved wooden grave markers that are often (and rather misleadingly) referred to as totems. Traditionally, a waga will be erected above the grave of any important Konso man or warrior, surrounded by smaller statues of his wives and defeated foes. The sombre facial features of the dead warrior are carved onto the waga, complete with enlarged and bucked teeth made from animal bones – creating a rather leery impression that is only reinforced by the impressively proportioned penis the deceased typically has clasped in his hand! Intriguingly, these grave markers and victory stones have an obvious precursor in the stelae that mark medieval graves around modern-day Dilla, and oral tradition indicates that the proto-Konso migrated from about the right place at about the right time for there to be some link between these customs.

The practice of erecting engraved grave markers has largely disappeared in recent decades, and many of the finest remaining examples were recently collected by the regional tourist office before they could be damaged or sold to foreign collectors.

Although the Konso are animists by custom, the last 50 years have seen many youngsters convert to Protestant denominations. Traditional attire is gradually giving way to the ubiquitous trousers or skirt and T-shirt – one could actually be forgiven for thinking that the traditional Konso costume consists of blue T-shirts with an angled white stripe, a huge consignment of which must have been imported from China a few years back! In most other senses, however, modern Konso society remains strikingly informed by, and in touch with, a unique and ancient cultural heritage. The area is well worth exploring.

place, cluttered with venerable chiefly artefacts ranging from beer vats to furniture, and the chief himself speaks good English and makes for a gracious and welcoming host – provided that visitors arrive in the company of an official guide. In the forest outside the compound stand several *waga* statues, marking the graves of earlier chiefs and their wives. By arrangement with the tourist office, it is permitted to **camp** outside the compound, or to sleep within it, for US$4.50 per tent.

Chief Gezahegne is the paramount leader of the Kertita clan. The clan is an important patrilineal unit of Konso society – members of the same clan, for instance, are forbidden from marrying – and each of the nine clans is represented by its own elected local headman in any given Konso village. The paramount chief of any given clan acts as a spiritual guru as well as in a judicial role; he and his immediate family live in total isolation, in order that he has no involvement in the day-to-day life of a community. The idea is that this will ensure his impartiality when settling intra-clan disputes and crimes, which are still often dealt with by the chief rather than national government. The title of clan chief is strictly hereditary, and Gezahegne is 20th in a line that has lived in the same compound for about 500 years. Sadly, the Kertita lineage is one of only three of the original nine chieftaincies to survive into the present day.

It is customary in Konso for the death of a paramount clan chief to be denied after the event. An official embalmer tends (for which read mummifies) the chief, and word is given out that he is very ill. Only after nine years and nine months is it finally announced that the chief is dead, with full blame falling on the embalmer, who – poor sod – is heavily fined for his predetermined failure. How and why this unusual custom arose is unknown. It has been suggested that a delayed announcement will allow time for a relative of the chief to remedy the problem should he have died without male issue. A more plausible explanation, given that it is tacitly realised that any chief being attended by an embalmer is unlikely to make a full recovery, is that the charade softens the blow of the departure of a popular and respected leader.

This custom was followed in 1990, when Kalla Koyote, Gezahegne's grandfather, died at an age of more than 100 years. The chief was duly embalmed, and confined to his compound with influenza. This, however, was a difficult time in Konso, due to a severe local drought and the ongoing civil war, and it was felt that a living chief was better equipped to navigate any crises than a terminally ill one. Kalla's death was announced seven months after he had died, his embalmed body was buried in a ceremony that lasted for eight days, and his son (and Gezahegne's father) Walda Dawit Kalla was installed as chief. The events surrounding Chief Kalla Koyote's death form the subject of a fascinating article in an old issue of the *Social Ethnology Bulletin of Addis Ababa University*, a copy of which is kept in the chief's compound. Sadly, the amiable Chief Walda Dawit Kalla passed away in 2004 – his body was held in state for just nine days before it was buried and his son Gezahegne was made the new chief.

24

South Omo

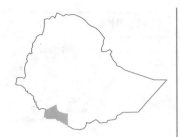

Nothing in highland Ethiopia prepares one for South Omo. Nor, for that matter, does much else in modern Africa. It's apocryphal, perhaps, but easy enough to believe when confronted by the region's extraordinary cultural integrity, that there is more than a smattering of truth in the assertion that as recently as 50 years ago the people of South Omo were scarcely aware that such an entity as Ethiopia existed.

South Omo is literally fantastic. Descending from the green, urbane highlands into the low-lying plains of South Omo feels like a journey not merely through space, but also through time, as one enters the vast and thinly populated badlands that divide the mountainous centre of Ethiopia from its counterpart in Kenya. Like much of neighbouring northern Kenya, South Omo is as close as one can come to an Africa untouched by outside influences. The culturally diverse, immaculately colourful and defiantly traditionalist agro-pastoralists who inhabit the region seem to occupy a physical and psychic landscape little different from that of their nomadic ancestors. This is Africa as it once was, or as some might still imagine it to be, and its mere existence is at once wonderful and scarcely credible. That this surreal oasis of Afro-traditionalism lies within the boundaries of Ethiopia – the least stereotypically African of the continent's sub-Saharan nations – borders on the outrageous.

It seems facile to label South Omo as a living museum. Yet in many senses, that is exactly what it is. Four of Africa's major linguistic groups are represented in the region, including the so-called Omotic-speakers, a language group as endemic to South Omo as the Ethiopian wolf is to the Abyssinian Highlands. All in all, depending on where one draws the lines, as many as two-dozen different tribes occupy South Omo, some numbering tens of thousands, others no more than 500, each one of them culturally unique. The most renowned of the Omotic-speakers are the Mursi, known for their practice of inserting large clay plates behind the lower lips of their women. Other important groups of South Omo include the Hamer-Bena, the Karo and the Ari, whose cultures and quirks of adornment – body scarring, body painting and the like – are treated more fully in textboxes scattered throughout this chapter.

South Omo is often portrayed as some sort of cultural Garden of Eden. This notion is unduly romantic. The Mursi disfigure their women monstrously. Ritualised wife beating is an integral part of Hamer society. Every year without fail, outbreaks of inter-tribal fighting – usually provoked by cattle disputes – result in numerous fatalities. In South Omo, such killers are not normally apprehended; on the contrary, they wear whatever mark of Cain is customary within their specific tribe with a warrior's pride. But, while one cannot gloss over the harsh realities of life in South Omo, there is much that is genuinely uplifting about the sheer tenacity of this incredibly rich cultural mosaic, comprising some 30 distinct ethno-linguistic

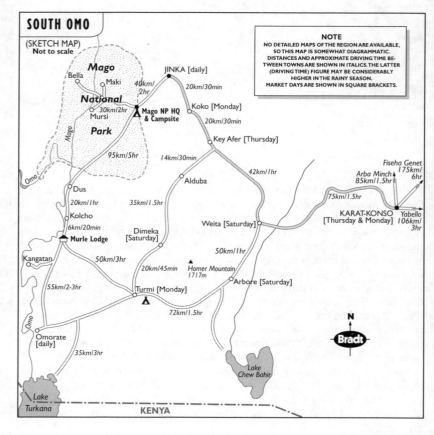

groupings, several of which number fewer than 1,000 people. Romanticise or condemn it, South Omo is there, it is fascinating, and it is utterly unique.

Tourism to South Omo, while hardly large scale, is catching on in a substantial way, and it does seem to have stimulated a vociferous and often grasping spirit of commercialism that can seriously detract from what would otherwise be a fascinating experience – indeed, as one traveller pointed out, South Omo may be an interesting place to visit, but it is not much fun to travel there. In the fourth edition a visit to South Omo was described as 'a once-in-a-lifetime experience'. At the time this was meant to convey the uniqueness of the experience, but upon returning in 2008 and 2011 for the fifth and sixth editions, both updaters felt it took on a different meaning – if you have seen this place once, the hassles may not be worth a return!

A related, and more serious, concern is the extent to which tourism could undermine the area's traditional cultures. There are a variety of factors – the increasing influence of central government, the infiltration of exotic religions, the steady population growth – that will conspire to make it difficult for South Omo to remain as it is today indefinitely. Tourism, doubtless, is also one such factor, though possibly as reinforcing of traditional culture as it is destructive.

Of greater concern to the people of the Omo Valley is the threat posed by the construction of a €1.55 billion dam on the Omo River 300km southwest of Addis Ababa. As local tour guide Dehina Hunu points out: 'Ironically tourism is protecting the tribes. All tribes from the Omo Valley will disappear soon, because of the construction of the electricity dam on the northern part of the Omo River. So they will have to leave the area because the river will just bring little water. Most of the tribes don't even know it.' Due to be completed in 2012, the new Gibe III hydro-electric dam, the government claims, will not only eliminate annual flooding, but will also give pastoralists a 'sustainable income and modern life'. However, many like Dehina Hunu fear that the dam will have a devastating impact on more than half a million people, in both Ethiopia and Kenya, who depend on the Omo flood for their livelihoods. For more information about the impact of the dam on the region's people visit www.mursi.org.

PLANNING YOUR TRIP

In keeping with its traditionalist mood, South Omo does not lend itself to efficient casual exploration. Jinka, the administrative centre, is accessible enough on public transport. Elsewhere, one must explore the region on what amounts to a private safari, using a car and driver hired in Addis Ababa. Though never an easy place to visit as an independent tourist, this is now all but impossible as local trucks are forbidden from taking *faranji* passengers.

WHEN TO VISIT Unlike other tourist areas in Ethiopia, travel in South Omo is strongly limited by seasonal factors. C J Carr describes the region as 'highly unstable … in terms of precipitation and winds throughout the year, with great fluctuations often erratic in occurrence'. Add to this the poor roads that characterise the region, and the black cotton soil around Mago National Park (treacherously sticky and often impassable after any significant rainfall), and it will be evident that travelling through South Omo during the rainy season is a serious no-no!

The rainy season in the far southwest is significantly different from that in the rest of Ethiopia, and although rainfall figures are low – typically no more than 400mm per annum – the unpredictable timing and quantity of rain regularly lead to local flooding or drought. Bearing this in mind, Ethiopian Rift Valley Safaris, which owns Murelle Lodge and has 20 years' experience in the region to its credit, advises strongly against travelling during April and May, when the big rains usually fall. If the rains are early or late, or unusually heavy, March or June might be just as bad. The rest of the year is normally fine, though the short rains, which generally fall in October, sometimes put a temporary stop on travel.

The above warnings apply mainly to places south of the main Konso–Jinka road. Karat-Konso itself is normally accessible throughout the year, as are villages along the main road towards Jinka. Depending on how heavy the rains have been, it may also be possible to reach Turmi and Omorate during the rainy season.

ACCESS AND PLANNING The normal – and best – way to explore the region covered by this chapter is on a road safari out of Addis Ababa. A minimum of eight days, but ideally longer, should be allocated for such a journey (see *Itineraries*, page 538). Because there are few organised tours to the region, the normal procedure is to pre-book a vehicle with a recognised tour operator in Addis Ababa (see *Tour operators* in *Chapter 3*, page 77). This will generally work out at around US$200–250 per day, inclusive of camping gear, guide and cook. The advantage of dealing with an acknowledged tour operator is that the vehicle will generally be in good shape, and the guide will have experience of the region, both of which are important considerations in this remote and unpredictable area. It is possible to arrange a private vehicle more cheaply upon arrival in Addis Ababa with some hotels offering rates as low as US$150 per day, but this will depend on season and your negotiating skills. Be warned, however, that while privately arranged safaris generally run smoothly, there are no guarantees about the state of the vehicle or experience of the guide, and there will be little accountability should things go wrong.

Your other option is an organised fly-in safari. This will generally be more costly than driving down, since you'll have to pay for a charter flight and the vehicle will need to drive from Addis Ababa whether or not you are on board. The main advantage of flying down, aside from the added comfort, is that it cuts two days of travel either side off exploring South Omo. Once again any recognised tour operator can arrange a package of this sort. It should be noted that, even if you fly into Jinka and work with the best operator, the rough roads that characterise the region cannot be avoided and are a great equaliser – streamlined, air-conditioned luxury is not an option.

A final option, and by far the cheapest, would be a DIY approach, but unfortunately the government rules prohibiting the transport of foreigners in Isuzu trucks puts a huge damper on this! This is not to say that catching a ride is impossible, but you will likely be asked to pay US$20 or more – ten times the normal rate, so that the driver is covered should he be stopped and fined by the authorities. And should you get caught, you could find yourself on a bus back to Arba Minch!

In the unlikely event that these restrictions are lifted, the DIY approach would involve bussing down to Karat-Konso, and exploring the region using a limited network of internal public transport. The villages along the Jinka road, such as Key Afer, are readily accessible on public transport, while Turmi and several other more remote villages can be reached on the sporadic trickle of passenger-carrying trucks. Realistically, Mago National Park and its Mursi inhabitants can be visited only in a private vehicle. In Jinka, it is possible to hire a 4x4 at a similar daily rate to those offered in Addis Ababa, with the obvious financial advantage that you'll be paying this rate for one or two days only, as opposed to longer than a week. If you intend travelling independently in South Omo, be warned that this is as tough as it gets in Ethiopia – erratic and bumpy transport, lousy accommodation and indifferent food are to be expected. Assuming that this doesn't put you off, a realistic minimum of eight days should be allocated to explore the region as a round trip out of Addis Ababa on public transport, though this would entail spending a high proportion of your waking hours on buses and trucks. Ten days or two weeks, inclusive of a few stops *en route*, would be far more relaxed.

ITINERARIES This section is best studied in conjunction with the map on page 536, which shows all roads through the region, as well as distances, approximate dry-season driving times, and important market days. Essentially, the road network through the region consists of the 205km trunk route running northwest from Karat-Konso to Jinka, and three rougher roads that run south from this trunk road to connect at the town of Turmi. The most easterly of the southbound roads – in other words, the one closest to Karat-Konso – runs directly south from Weita through Arbore to Turmi. The central road leaves the main road a few kilometres east of Key Afer, and runs through Alduna and Dimeka to Turmi. The most westerly road runs from Jinka south through Mago National Park and Murelle, from where two roads lead to Turmi, one direct, the other via Omorate.

The relatively limited number of halfway-decent roads through South Omo means that the tourist circuit is fairly well defined. Assuming that you have a private vehicle, and sufficient time – realistically, an absolute minimum of four days (three nights) to get between Karat-Konso and Jinka – there is little reason to deviate from the established circuit. This circuit entails driving from Karat-Konso to Turmi via Weita on the first day, from Turmi to Murelle (with a possible side trip to Omorate or Dimeka) on the second day, from Murelle to Mago National Park on the third day, then heading up to Jinka on the fourth day. For those travelling out of Addis Ababa, this loop will form the core of a trip of at least eight days' (seven nights) duration, allowing for overnight stops at Arba Minch and Karat-Konso on the way down, and at Jinka and Arba Minch on the way up. An additional two days would allow you to explore Nechisar National Park outside Arba Minch, and to stop over for a full day somewhere in South Omo – Turmi, Mago National Park or Murelle are the obvious contenders. Two full weeks would make for a very relaxed trip, with little need to pre-plan your itinerary in detail, and plenty of opportunity to explore places of interest on the way to or from Addis Ababa.

For travellers without private transport, the above circuit is unrealistic because of a lack of public transport through Murelle and Mago National Park. A more realistic circuit, malleable dependent on market days, would be to spend a day exploring the villages outside Jinka, then head southwards to Turmi on a truck (*if permitted*), and after a night or two there return back to the main Jinka–Karat-Konso road, to stop over at Weita or Key Afer. Short of catching an extraordinarily lucky hitch, the only way to get to Mago National Park and the Mursi villages is in a private vehicle rented in Jinka.

One factor that will come into play with any itinerary through South Omo is market days, which are generally held to be the best days to arrive in any given town. I must confess that I think the importance of markets is sometimes overstated – I found it far more rewarding to visit smaller villages on non-market days – but certainly you should aim to tailor your itinerary to coincide with at least one big market. The best markets are probably the Saturday market at Dimeka, the Monday market at Turmi and the Thursday market at Key Afer. Other market days are given under individual town entries, and on the map on page 536.

WHERE TO STAY
Full details of accommodation are given here under individual town and village entries, but the following overview might help in planning your trip.

The only remotely upmarket bases from which one can explore the region are Murelle Lodge, which is owned by Ethiopia Rift Valley Safaris and overlooks the Omo River at Murelle; Greenland Tours' Evangadi Lodge; Splendor Ethiopia Tours' Turmi Lodge and Buska Lodge in Turmi; or the newly opened Eco-omo Lodge in Jinka. Basing yourself at any of these lodges is somewhat restrictive insofar as all other villages and towns must be visited as a day trip, but there is no alternative that doesn't entail staying in very basic lodges or camping.

Reasonable local hotels with en-suite rooms are available in Jinka. Otherwise, the only settlements in the region to offer any form of accommodation are Turmi, Dimeka, Omorate and Key Afer. On a scale that admittedly runs from the truly sordid to the merely basic, the hotels in Omorate plumb depths of awfulness rarely equalled even in Ethiopia. The hotels in Turmi and Dimeka are only marginally better, and there is a comparatively good hotel in Key Afer.

A more appealing option, assuming that you have a tent, is to camp. Proper campsites exist at Jinka, Turmi, Key Afer, Arbore and Murelle Lodge, while in Weita and Omorate it is established practice to camp at the police station for a small fee.

WHERE TO EAT AND DRINK
Culinary delights are few and far between in South Omo. The hotel restaurants in Jinka serve reasonable Ethiopian fare and a very limited selection of Western meals. Elsewhere, you'll always find at least one local

restaurant that serves the standard Ethiopian diet of *injera* and *wat*, occasionally supplemented by (normally cold) spaghetti. If you are camping, it's probably preferable to cook for yourself – speak to your tour operator about this, or (if travelling independently) try to stock up on dry food before you reach South Omo. Jinka has a few decent supermarkets, but the selections available in Arba Minch, Shashemene, Hawassa and Addis Ababa are infinitely better.

The usual bottled soft drinks and beer are widely available, along with tea and fizzy Ambo mineral water. Bottled still mineral water is thin on the ground, and generally vastly over-priced where it is available, so it's worth bringing a stash with you, assuming that you are in a private vehicle. The water in South Omo is generally not safe to drink without purification.

South Omo is the one part of Ethiopia where the practice of charging inflated *faranji* prices now extends to food and drink as well as hotel rooms.

OTHER PRACTICALITIES

Permits All private vehicles are now stopped at the Weita Bridge, and will be turned back if a written letter of authority is not produced. If you are on an organised tour, the company should already have this letter in their possession. If you are not part of a tour, you will need to pick up a letter at the tourist office in Addis Ababa, Jinka or Karat-Konso. All travellers are asked by the police to produce their passport and a letter of authority in Omorate and more occasionally in Turmi. Without such a letter, you could hit quite serious problems – the protocol in Omorate is that you will be 'jailed' in a hotel and shoved onto the next vehicle out of town. Things are unlikely to come to that in Turmi, but a letter will save you a lot of hassle. I've not heard of written authority being asked for elsewhere in the region, but that doesn't mean it couldn't happen.

Village fees Apart from major towns, most villages now charge a fee just to visit. This is typically US$15 per vehicle and an additional US$6 per person, but the Karo now demand US$21 per vehicle. It is also a requirement that you have a local guide with you who will cost between US$6 and US$12 per day.

Road improvement fee All private vehicles are charged a US$9 road improvement fee just outside of Jinka and Dimeka. You should be given a receipt, which you need to keep during your visit.

Photography You can assume that anybody you want to photograph in South Omo will expect to be paid. The going rate varies from one person and one village to the next. For straight portraits, a fee of US$0.20 is pretty standard, though the Mursi in particular will generally expect more (US$0.30 in 2011), and it is increasingly the case that the subject will count how many times you click the shutter and increment the fee accordingly – in other words, somebody who asks for US$0.20 will demand US$1 if you click the shutter five times. If you really want to spend some time photographing one particular person, it's best to explain this and agree a higher rate in advance. Once the finances have been agreed, people are generally relaxed about being photographed, though it is also not uncommon for arguments to break out.

Unfortunately, the 'pay to snap' mentality in South Omo has recently mutated into the rather presumptuous expectation that tourists should be willing to photograph (and pay) any local who wants them to. This can sometimes create an unpleasant atmosphere: every person you walk past seems to yell *'faranji'*, 'photo', 'birr' or a variation thereof, and some become quite hostile if you don't accede to their demand. Certainly, photography has come to dominate relations between travellers and the people of South Omo to the extent that any less voyeuristic form of interaction seems to be all but impossible. One way around this is to simply pack away your camera while you are in South Omo, and buy a few postcards instead.

THE KONSO–JINKA ROAD: WEITA, KEY AFER AND KOKO

The scenic road between Karat-Konso and Jinka covers 205km and is in the process of being upgraded to asphalt with the sections between Konso and Weita and Key Afer and Jinka completed on our most recent visit. Depending on the number of detours, it takes about four hours to drive, longer on public transport. At 28km past Karat-Konso you will cross the Delbina River. Once past here, the villages of Weita, Key Afer and Koko all lie along this road, and any one of them is worth stopping at, particularly on the local market days of Saturday in Weita, Monday in Koko and Thursday in Key Afer.

Heading west from Karat-Konso, it should take about 90 minutes to cover the 75km road westward to Weita in a private vehicle. Note that private vehicles may be stopped at the Weita bridge, and refused permission to continue unless you have a letter of permission as described previously. From Weita it takes another two hours to reach Jinka or 2½ hours to Turmi. The only formal public transport heading westward is the daily bus from Arba Minch to Jinka (US$6; 8 hours), which may or may not have seats available by the time it passes through Karat-Konso.

Most locals depend on pick-up trucks and other transport that informally carries paying passengers; *should travel restrictions be lifted*, one of the hotels in Karat-Konso would be able to put you in touch with truck drivers heading west. As a rule, it is easy enough to find transport on any given day to Jinka, or to

THE TSEMAI

The Tsemai, the dominant people of Weita village on the Konso–Jinka road, are among the least-known ethnic groups of Ethiopia. Estimated to total some 5,000 people, their territory extends along the western bank of the Weita River, known in Tsemai as the Dulaika River. They are mixed subsistence farmers who practise flood cultivation, with the major crops being sorghum and maize. They also rear livestock, especially cattle, and keep beehives for honey. The Tsemai speak an east Cushitic language that is closely related to the one spoken in Konso, which, according to oral tradition, is from where their founding chief, Asasa, originated. The present chief, who lives at the long-standing Tsemai capital of Ganda Bogolkila, is claimed to be the ninth in line after Asasa, suggesting that this migration might have happened between 150 and 250 years ago.

Although their appearance and dress style is similar to that of the Omotic Ari people, the Tsemai share closer political and spiritual affiliations with the Arbore, who speak a similar language, and whose territory lies adjacent to the Tsemai chief's village. The Tsemai also frequently and openly intermarry with the Hamer, whose territory lies immediately west of theirs. In common with many other people of southern Ethiopia, society is structured around an age-set system. Four fixed age-sets are recognised, with every set graduating in seniority once a decade, when a new generation of boys between the ages of about 11 and 22 is initiated.

Edited from a letter from Arthur Gerfers

At last, my first real live pagan African market. The lovely Bena woman with red clay braids who was seated before me has moved on over into the main marketplace. Her husband has stayed behind and keeps watch over ornately bound gourds containing butter and vegetables. Many of the men have shaven heads from the forehead to the middle of the skull, lending them a proud, regal appearance. Their earlobes are pierced three, sometimes four times, with large rings and strings of beads hanging down. They are usually bare-chested and wear a tight cloth wrap around the waist reaching about mid thigh; the calves are large and muscular. They wear jewellery round the neck consisting of red and blue or black and orange beads. I can only guess at the significance. The gold or silver bands and bracelets they wear may have some meaning too. The bright colours and lustrous metals against black skin are striking. These people smell intensely of wood smoke. Their variety and exotic appearance defies written description. Photography has also proven disappointing, as the beautiful or striking views of these people cannot be captured by the tourist's camera, before which their exquisitely handsome features seem to turn to stone.

villages along the main road between Karat-Konso and Jinka. Trucks heading southwest to Turmi or Omorate are rather less frequent, but run as far as Turmi on most days.

WEITA Situated some 75km from Karat-Konso along the Jinka road, about 5km west of the bridge across the Weita River, the tiny settlement of Weita lies within Tsemai territory (see box, page 541), though the busy Saturday market is also attended by Ari and Bana people. Weita has a rather impermanent feel, one that suggests it probably owes its existence to its location at the junction of the side road to Turmi via Arbore. Market day excepted, Weita isn't a terribly interesting place, dominated as it is by a large outdoor cafeteria and restaurant complex that attracts more passing truck traffic than it does colourful locals. There are basic rooms available at the **Meheret Hotel** (*15 rooms;* m *0910 874 739*) for US$4/9 for a single/double, which also has food at jacked-up *faranji* prices. It is also permitted to camp in the police compound.

KEY AFER The relatively large and cosmopolitan town of Key Afer is situated at a refreshing altitude of around 1,800m on the Konso–Jinka road, 42km northwest of Weita, and a few kilometres west of the junction with the side road south to Turmi via Dimeka. For travellers dependent on public transport, Key Afer is by far the most accessible town of interest in the Omo region – any vehicle heading between Karat-Konso and Jinka can drop you there – and well worth dedicating a night to.

The dominant people of Key Afer are the Ari (see box, page 544), but Bana and Hamer people also live in and around town. The best day to visit is Thursday, when the town hosts a multi-cultural market that is as colourful as any in the region. On other days, the town centre is relatively modern in feel, but the backstreets east of the market square are lined with traditional homes. Local boys will offer to take you to a small traditional village about 15 minutes' walk from town.

Where to stay and eat The new **Zarsi Hotel** (*10 rooms;* ☎ *046 271 0056*), at the Jinka end of town, is a cut above most village hotels in the region. Very clean en-suite rooms with cold shower, three-quarter bed, mosquito net and squat toilet cost US$9. Camping is also permitted for US$3 per tent and there's a shady garden restaurant serving decent local dishes for around US$2–3 as well as cold beers and soft drinks. The next best option is the more centrally located **Nasa Hotel** (*12 rooms;* ☎ *046 271 0021*) with clean en-suite rooms with cold shower, three-quarter bed and a net costing US$9, and US$6 using a common shower. Camping is permitted in the police compound, though pitching a tent in the grassy compound of the Zarsi Hotel is a more appealing prospect.

KOKO Lying roughly halfway along the 40km stretch of road between Key Afer and Jinka, and sharing these towns' temperate highland climate, Koko is a small but attractive Ari village noted for its busy Monday market. For independent travellers, this market would make for a straightforward day excursion out of Jinka, as a fair number of vehicles trot back and forth from Jinka to the market. On other days of the week, Koko is of marginal interest. Basic **rooms** are available, but no place looks particularly appealing.

WEITA TO TURMI VIA ARBORE AND LAKE CHEW BAHIR

The 120km road running southwest from Weita to Turmi passes, for the most part, through flat arid acacia scrub populated by the Tsemai in the north and the closely related Arbore people in the south. This harsh landscape, thinly populated by pairs of Guenther's dik-dik and home to a variety of colourful dry-country birds, is dominated by the austere Hamer Mountains, which rise to a height of 1,707m on the western horizon. The full drive takes the best part of three hours without stops.

The only urban punctuation *en route*, and well worth the minor diversion, is the small town of Arbore, which lies a few hundred metres east of the road, close to the boundary of Tsemai and Arbore territory some 50km south of Weita. A kilometre or two south of Arbore, a rough and little-used track veers southeast from the main road to reach the alluringly remote Lake Chew Bahir after three or four hours of virtual bushwhacking – a side trip best undertaken in the company of a police escort from Arbore town. Perhaps 40km south of Arbore, the road veers westward to climb into the Hamer Mountains, offering sweeping views back to the open Arbore Plains, before descending again into the wild expanses of Hamer country, covered under the next heading.

ARBORE Although relatively large, Arbore is far more rustic and unaffected than many similarly sized towns in South Omo, with the police station on its outskirts more or less the only building that isn't constructed along traditional lines. In common with their linguistically and culturally affiliated Tsemai neighbours, the Arbore migrated to their present homeland from Konso perhaps two centuries ago. Because they have ancestral and cultural links to Konso and the pastoralists of the surrounding lowlands, the Arbore traditionally played an important role as middlemen in trade between the Omo River and the Konso Highlands. The town of Arbore lies in an area where several tribal boundaries converge, and because the Arbore people routinely intermarry with other ethnic groups, it is also inhabited by a substantial number of Hamer and even Borena women – adding a cosmopolitan feel to the worthwhile Saturday market. There is no accommodation in Arbore, but it is possible to camp in the new **community campsite** for US$3 per tent, plus an additional US$3 for a guard.

LAKE CHEW BAHIR The territory of the Arbore people runs as far south as Lake Chew Bahir, a vast but little-visited expanse of salt water abutting the Kenyan border. It comes as no surprise to learn that this saline sump, still remote and inhospitable today, was perhaps the last African lake of comparable size to remain unknown to Europeans: its existence was little more than a rumour until Count Teleki arrived on its shore, fresh from having been the first European to set eyes on Lake Turkana, in April 1888. Teleki christened the lake in honour of Princess Stefanie, the consort of his Hungarian sponsor Prince Rudolf. The name Lake Stefanie is still sometimes used today, but the older local name of Chew Bahir – literally 'Ocean of Salt' – seems more apt.

Lying at an altitude of 520m, Lake Chew Bahir is a curious body of water, noted for its substantial fluctuations in water level and expanse. In the 1960s, the lake consisted of some 2,000km² of open water, nowhere more than 8m deep, but for much of the rest of the 20th century it was reduced to a rank swamp in an otherwise dry basin. The key to Chew Bahir's fluctuating water level is thought to be the level of Lake Chamo, which feeds it via the Segen and Gelana Delai rivers. Lake Chew Bahir has no outlet – it lies in an area where evaporation outstrips rainfall fourfold – and as a consequence it quickly shrinks in area without sufficient inflow, and the water is too saline to be drunk by man or beast.

Nominally protected within the vast **Chew Bahir Wildlife Reserve**, the lake and its hinterland of dry acacia woodland still support low volumes of ungulates such as Grevy's zebra, greater and lesser kudu, gerenuk and Grant's gazelle, as well as lion, spotted hyena and various small carnivores. More reliable is the birdlife in the permanent swamp that lies at the mouth of the Gelana Delai River, the closest part of the lake basin to Arbore. Lesser flamingoes are usually present in concentrations ranging from a couple of thousand to hundreds of thousands, along with a variety of storks, waterfowl and waders. The surrounding acacia woodland is an important site for dry-country birds characteristic of the badlands that separate the highlands of central Kenya from those of southern Ethiopia: vulturine guinea fowl, Shelley's and golden-bellied starling, pink-breasted lark, scaly chatterer and grey-headed silverbill are just a few of the more interesting species present.

Lake Chew Bahir can be reached in three or four hours from Arbore, following a track that heads southeast from the Turmi road immediately south of town. The track is difficult to follow unless you know the way, and the lake's location on the

THE ARI

The Ari occupy perhaps the largest territory of any of the ethno-linguistic groups of South Omo, extending from the northern border of Mago National Park into the highlands around Jinka and Key Afer, and further north. The Ari numbered 100,000 souls according to the 1984 census, and the population is considerably larger today. In common with the Hamer, the Ari speak a south Omotic language, which is divided into ten distinct regional dialects. The Ari of the highlands and lowlands have quite different subsistence economies, but both are mixed farmers who grow various grains (as well as coffee and *enset* at higher altitudes), keep livestock and produce excellent honey. In urban centres such as Jinka and Key Afer, the Ari now mostly wear Western costumes. In more rural areas, you will still see Ari women draped in the traditional *gori* (a dress made with leaves from the *enset* and *koisha* plants), and decorated around the waist and arms with colourful beads and bracelets.

sporadically sensitive Kenyan border makes it inadvisable to visit without an armed escort. This can be arranged at the police station in Arbore, where you can also ensure that somebody in authority knows to send out a search party in the event of a breakdown or any other mishap – weeks may pass without a vehicle heading down this way! A full day must be allocated to the excursion – better still, take camping gear and spend the night at the lake – and it would be advisable to carry sufficient water and food to last a couple of days longer than you intend to spend at the lake.

HAMER COUNTRY: TURMI AND DIMEKA

The Hamer, with their characteristic high cheekbones, elaborate costumes of beads, cowries and leather, and thick copper necklaces, are among the most readily identifiable of the South Omo peoples (see box, *The Hamer*, page 548). The main towns of the Hamer are Turmi and Dimeka, both of which host compelling and colourful weekly markets – on Monday and Saturday respectively – and will reward anybody who settles into them for a few days. Turmi and Dimeka alike boast a fair selection of (admittedly somewhat unwholesome) hotels and restaurants, and can be reached with relative ease either in a private vehicle or, *if permitted*, on the back of a truck. Turmi in particular will form an undoubted highlight of any trip through South Omo, and it is particularly accessible, since all roads lead there eventually.

TURMI Despite its small size, Turmi is an important transport hub, lying at the pivot of the three main roads that run southward from the Konso–Jinka road. Best known for its Monday market, possibly the most important in Hamer country, Turmi is a strikingly traditional small town, and well worth a couple of days whether or not they happen to coincide with the market. A couple of small traditional Hamer villages lie within a 2km radius of Turmi town; you can arrange a local guide through the newly formed **Turmi Evangadi Guide Association** (m *0916 825 037*) for US$12 a day. At the time of writing the association didn't have a permanent office and were instead using the Tourist Hotel as their base.

Reaching Turmi is reasonably straightforward. If you are driving through the region, you could scarcely avoid the place, since all roads pretty much lead to it. On most days, at least one passenger truck will travel to Turmi from Karat-Konso via Weita and Arbore, as will one truck from Key Afer via Dimeka. This is not, however, written in stone – it is perfectly possible that you'll have to wait around for a day before finding transport to or from Turmi.

Where to stay and eat With very little competition, especially in the form of moderately priced hotels, and due to the remoteness of the region the rates and facilities of the upmarket hotels listed below are way out of line when viewed in comparison to similarly priced hotels elsewhere in Ethiopia.

Upmarket

Buska Lodge (20 rooms) ✆ 011 156 7837–8; e info@buskalodge.com; www.buskalodge.com. This friendly new lodge on the banks of the normally dry Little Kaske River about 3km out of town along the Karat-Konso road is spaciously laid out within a well-maintained green compound featuring some 120 species of plants & offers views over the plains to the Buska Mountains.

Accommodation consists of rooms in large thatched-roof *tukuls* each with hot-shower en suite & private balcony with an additional 10 roofed island **camping** sites for those who'd rather rough it. Other facilities include 2 restaurants, a mini spa offering massages, pedicures & manicures, a BBQ area, & secure covered parking. The birdlife around the lodge can be prolific & colobus monkeys make regular appearances. *US$65/85/90/120 sgl/dbl/*

twin/trpl inc b/fast, camping US$15/35 with own tent/tent supplied pp.

🏠 **Turmi Lodge** (24 rooms) 📞 011 663 1480–1; e info@turmilodge.com or reserve@turnilodge.com; www.turmilodge.com. Owned & operated by Splendor Ethiopia Tours, this new lodge just out of town on the Dimeka road by St Michael's Church feels more like a bland institutional camp rather than as claimed 'the desert rose of Hamer Village', with accommodation provided in a series of long pink concrete blocks. The rooms however are spacious, neat & clean with tiled floors, bamboo furniture & good modern en suites with hot-water shower. It's just a shame that the rooms are located a long hike from the restaurant & bar. **Camping** is also permitted & rates are seasonably negotiable. *US$65/75/95 sgl/dbl/trpl inc b/fast.*

🏠 **Evangadi Lodge** (20 rooms) 📞 011 663 2595/7/8; e reservations@evangadilodge.com; www.evangadilodge.com. Owned & managed by Greenland Tours, this lodge verges the normally dry Little Kaske River, about 1km out of town along the Karat-Konso road. Accommodations consist of comfortable rooms with tiled floors, ¾ beds, nets & en-suite cold shower & fan. There is also a separate **campsite** with shower & toilet facilities. The large thatched-roof restaurant & seating area offers a cool place to retreat in the heat of the day. In addition to the stock-standard Ethiopian/European menu of dishes, cold drinks, salads & freshly baked wood-fired pizzas (US$5.50) are available. *US$50/60/75 sgl/dbl/trpl inc b/fast.*

Budget

🏠 **Green Hotel** (19 rooms) Located next to the more popular Tourist Hotel, this unsurprisingly green-painted hotel offers slightly dirtier (& more expensive) rooms using common shower. Pluses include a Western toilet & proper screens on the windows. *US$6/9.50 dbl/twin using common shower.*

🏠 **Tourist Hotel** (17 rooms) Situated along the Weita road, on the outskirts of town about 500m from the main junction, this friendly favourite is without a doubt the top budget choice offering 5 reasonably clean rooms with no-so-private open en-suite showers as well as basic rooms using common shower. It also has an acceptable local restaurant, serving some of the best *shiro tegabino* anywhere (expect to pay around US$2–4 per dish), but some say the Kaske Bar & Restaurant next door is better. *US$4.50 using common shower, US$9 en suite.*

🏠 **Arba Minch Hotel** (8 rooms) Located directly in front of the market, it offers good-sized & reasonably pleasant singles with net, using common shower, & a restaurant. Given the location, it could be noisy. *US$6 with common shower.*

Camping

🏠 **Kaske River Campsite (aka Mango Camp)** More appealing than the hotels in Turmi is this attractively situated community-run campsite, which lies about 3km out of town along the Weita road. The campsite has an unexpectedly lush & shady setting in the riparian fig woodland along the western bank of the normally dry Kaske River, & is passed through most days by guereza monkeys & baboons. It is also rattling with birdlife, with Bruce's green pigeon, black-headed oriole & grey-headed bush shrike among the more prominent & colourful species. The dry acacia scrub behind the site is a good place to seek out dry-country birds such as the gorgeous golden-bellied starling. Alongside the campsite is a water pump that produces potable water & attracts a steady stream of local Hamer villagers. Facilities include 2 toilets, 2 showers, a cooking hut, generator & fridge. There are also 2 very basic – & very hot – en-suite *tukuls* available with 4 bungalow-style rooms planned. *Camping US$4.50 per tent, tukuls US$15.*

DIMEKA The principal town of Hamer country, Dimeka is larger and more built-up than Turmi, and correspondingly less traditional in overall mood. Assuming that you've already spent some time in and around Turmi, however, my feeling is that making a specific side trip to Dimeka is worth the effort only on Saturdays, when the market positively vibrates with Hamer villagers who have walked into town from miles around. Dimeka lies on the southern verge of Bena territory, and its market also attracts a fair number of Bena people, agriculturists who are similar in appearance to the Hamer, with whom they share strong cultural affinities and freely intermarry.

Dimeka lies about 20km north of Turmi and 55km south of Key Afer along the road connecting these two towns. You will therefore pass through Dimeka – with the option of stopping over – if you travel directly between Key Afer and Turmi, a drive of roughly four hours in a private vehicle. At least one passenger-carrying truck runs along this road on most days, though this cannot be relied upon fully. There is normally regular transport between Turmi and Dimeka on market days in either town.

The pick of the accommodation in Dimeka – all things being relative – is probably the **Buska Bar** (*7 rooms*), where a simple room with a single bed using a proper common shower costs US$6. The rooms at the **Tourist Hotel** (*7 rooms*) are the same price though have bucket showers, while the **Ham Hotel** next door charges US$5 for a small cell-like room with bucket shower. The first two places above have a fridge for cold drinks, and the best place to eat, if you go by the steady stream of tourist vehicles and the number of local diners, is the **Abyssinia Hotel**. Should you need a guide, a boy named Aike speaks excellent English.

OMORATE

Marked on some maps as Kalem, Omorate lies on the sweltering eastern bank of the Omo River at the terminus of a 72km road running west from Turmi. The town itself is the archetypal tropical backwater: unexpectedly large, not at all traditional in mood, yet almost totally isolated from the rest of Ethiopia. There is, it has to be said, something rather depressing about Omorate, epitomised by the relics of the agricultural scheme that was initiated with North Korean funds in the Mengistu era and faltered to a standstill more than a decade back. The entrenched victims of this aborted master plan still haunt the bars of Omorate, willing to talk the ear off any stranger about their misfortune. The seedy, end-of-the-road atmosphere that hovers over Omorate isn't helped by its climatic shortfalls – temperatures upwards of 40°C combine with fine clay dust and a paucity of shade to make life pretty uncomfortable.

In its favour, Omorate is a very friendly place, and relatively free of *faranji* hysteria. It is also – bizarrely – the only place in South Omo where travellers without a private vehicle can actually *see* the river for which the region is named. And, with only one simple shower in town, the Omo River, muddy though it may be, provides nigh irresistible, if not necessarily bilharzia-free, relief from the merciless heat. The river aside, the main attraction of Omorate is the Dasanech villages that lie outside of the town; see *What to see*, page 550.

Omorate, though it lies some distance from Kenya, functions by default as a minor border town. Improbable as it might sound, pick-up trucks from goodness knows where in Kenya regularly appear on the opposite bank of the river to unload mysterious parcels of goods onto the local boats. The police, for reasons best known to themselves, insist that all *faranjis* arrive with a letter of authority from the tourist office in Addis Ababa, Jinka or Karat-Konso – when pressed for an explanation, they knowingly explain 'we are close to Kenya'. For expeditions across the river to the Dasanech village on the facing bank, you'll need to take a local guide, arranged through the **Omorate Guide Association** (m *0926 295 557*), costing US$6.

GETTING THERE AND AWAY The 72km road from Turmi to Omorate has been upgraded and passes through flat and relatively open grassy savanna country. Pairs of Guenther's dik-dik are to be seen in relative profusion, and we also encountered a few gerenuk, a lovely long-necked antelope related to gazelles. On the avian front, flocks of white-throated and northern carmine bee-eaters hog the limelight, dazzlingly colourful and acrobatic as they swoop and hawk from their roadside perches. The road is usually in pretty good shape except after rain, and the drive should take well under two hours. Coming from Turmi there is no public transport (ask around in Turmi and you might be able to gain a lift on one of the trucks heading to Omorate), but a twice-weekly bus service runs from Jinka to Omorate on Sunday and Wednesday. Precisely 59km from the central junction, you pass a junction south towards Lake Turkana, a little-used route that should emphatically not be attempted except with a local escort who knows the way. Four kilometres further towards Omorate lies the junction with the road north towards Murelle and Mago National Park (covered under *Murelle and surrounds* on page 550).

 WHERE TO STAY AND EAT The highly coveted accolade of 'best hotel in Omorate' goes to the newly built – and oddly named – **Hulu Beersu Hone Hotel** (*10 rooms*; m *0916 856 920*), located on a spacious compound 1km from the centre on the left-

THE HAMER

The Hamer, who number about 35,000 and occupy a large territory that stretches east from the Omo River to Lake Chew Bahir, stand out as perhaps the archetypal people of South Omo. Not only do they speak one of the Omotic tongues unique to this small area of southern Ethiopia, but they also display an elaborate and eclectic selection of body decorations that embraces the full gamut of Omo specialities, with the notable exception of lip plates.

The women are particularly striking, adorned with thick plaits of ochre-coloured hair hanging down in a heavy fringe, leather skirts decorated with cowries, a dozen or more copper bracelets fixed tightly around their arms, thick welts on their body created by cutting themselves and treating the wound with ash and charcoal, and colourful beaded bands hanging from around their waists. Married women wear one or more thick copper necklaces, often with a circular wedge perhaps 10cm long projecting out of the front. The men, though also given to body scarring, are more plainly adorned except when they paint themselves with white chalk paste before a dance or ceremony. The clay hair buns fashioned on some men's heads indicate that they have killed a person or a dangerous animal within the last year.

In common with most other people of South Omo, the Hamer are pastoralists by custom, and take great pride in the size of their cattle herd, though in reality agriculture now plays a far greater role in their subsistence. They are closely allied to the Bena people, whose territory lies to the north of theirs, and who speak a similar language and freely intermarry with the Hamer. The well-documented cultural links between ancient Egypt and highland Ethiopia may also extend to the Hamer and other people of South Omo. Professor Ivo Strecker, who has studied Hamer culture for three decades, and lived among them for long periods, notes that the environment and agro-pastoralist lifestyle of the Hamer are close to those of the early period of Egyptian civilisation. Furthermore, he has documented striking similarities between current-day utensils and decorations of the Hamer and identical items depicted on early Egyptian paintings, notably the *woko*, a type of hooked, forked herding stick, and the headrests used by Hamer men.

Although most visitors to South Omo visit a Hamer market, it is also very rewarding to visit one of the smaller villages that lie outside the Hamer towns of

hand side of the road as you approach from Turmi, which has clean rooms using a common cold shower for US$6 and offers camping for US$3/6 with your own tent/ with tent supplied. An attached restaurant is planned and cold drinks are available.

In the centre the top choice is the **Dagmawi Hotel** (*8 rooms;* m *0911 915 828*), mostly because it is new, which means the rooms – all using a common cold shower and costing US$5 – are fresher and cleaner than its competitors (well, at least at the time of writing!). Of the three other contending hotels, all clustered iniquitously opposite the police station, the lamentably mistitled **Tourist Hotel** (*6 rooms*) seems to be the least off-putting with its basic rooms costing US$3 sharing a proper common cold shower, while the **National Hotel** (*6 rooms*) charges US$5/6 for single/double rooms which, although somewhat clean, have dirt floors and a bucket shower. Whether the marginally cheaper and even more sordid **Park Hotel** (*10 rooms*) represents better value for money is the sort of burning question that will help see you through the night should counting cockroaches fail to cure any insomnia brought on by the heat and dirt! All of these hotels have bars, and restaurants of a sort.

Turmi and Dimeka. Incredibly neat, and constructed entirely from mud, wood and thatch, one of the most striking aspects of these small villages – which typically consist of a few extended families across perhaps ten to 15 huts – is the total absence of non-organic or Western artefacts. It might seem banal when put into words, but it is nevertheless rather sobering to encounter such simplicity and evident lack of material want, and to contrast it against our own restless need for distraction and accumulation of useless paraphernalia.

The most important event in Hamer society is the **bull jumping ceremony**, the culmination of a three-day-long initiation rite that is normally held before the long rains, between late February and early April. The third day begins with the women getting drunk in preparation to be beaten ritualistically with sticks. These beatings are by choice, and show devotion to the boy who is jumping. The women rarely scream, but rather taunt the men to hit them harder, resulting in huge bleeding gashes and honorific scars. In the late afternoon, up to 30 bulls are lined up in a row, but these days six to eight bulls is more common. The initiate, stark naked and sporting a demented unkempt Afro hairstyle, has to leap onto the back of the first bull, then from one bull to the next, until he reaches the end of the row. He must then turn around and repeat the performance in the opposite direction, then a third and fourth time, before he has proved his worth to everybody's satisfaction. Should he succeed then he may take a wife (not necessarily immediately; some boys as young as ten are initiated), but if he fails he will have to wait a year and try again.

Much has been made about the authenticity and perceived devaluing of the bull jumping ceremony with some travellers claiming it has now been reduced to a staged 'show' put on for tourists. As one traveller recently wrote on the Bradt update forum, 'It felt very much like a circus put on for the *faranji*.' But as another reader quickly replied, 'The Hamer people are cashing in on the tourists. It is normal. They have the right to do so. South Omo tourism is a big business these days; while it may seem "circus like", we cannot stop them from taking advantage of the tourist interest.' Should you wish to see the ceremony for yourself, expect to pay at least US$18 per person.

WHAT TO SEE

Dasanech villages The Dasanech, alternatively known as the Galeb or Reshiat, range across a large territory following the western banks of the Omo River south to Lake Turkana. Local oral tradition, reinforced by that of the Turkana, recounts that the Dasanech migrated to their current homeland from a region called Nyupe, to the west of Turkana, after being forced out by the expansionist wars of the Turkana in the late 18th century. Like the Turkana, Samburu and Gabbra of northern Kenya, the Dasanech were originally pure pastoralists, living an almost totally nomadic lifestyle. The abundant water frontage and fertile soil of their present territory has subsequently pushed them towards a more diverse subsistence economy, based around fishing and agriculture as well as herding livestock.

The nomadic roots of the Dasanech are most clearly seen today in their traditional villages, comprising small, flimsy, domed huts strongly reminiscent of the impermanent structures built by other African desert pastoralists, from the Tuareg of the Sahara to the Nama of the Kalahari. One such village lies on the west bank of the Omo, practically opposite Omorate, and can be reached for US$3 and in a few minutes by utilising the flat-bottomed boat that serves as a ferry across the river. Another similar village lies about 20 minutes' walk south of the town centre on the east bank of the river. Taking a local guide – arranged through the Omorate Guide Association for US$6 – is mandatory, as is the US$6 per person village entrance fee, while taking any pictures will cost you a further US$0.25 per snap.

MURELLE AND SURROUNDS

Situated on the eastern bank of the Omo River, some 55km north of Omorate and a similar distance northwest of Turmi, Murelle Lodge is the one set-up in South Omo to which the term upmarket could conceivably be applied. It thus forms the normal base for fly-in tours of the region, and for any other visitors who don't fancy camping or sampling the rustic delights of South Omo's local hostelries. The lodge is conveniently situated along the road from Turmi or Omorate to Mago National Park and Jinka, for which reason the adjoining campsite is a popular overnight stop with camping trips. For visitors on an extended tour of South Omo, the main local attractions are the Karo villages of Kolcho and Dus, and the Bumi village of Kangatan, all of which lie within an hour's drive of Murelle. For visitors basing themselves out of Murelle, the towns of Turmi, Dimeka and Omorate form feasible day trips, while Mago National Park and its Mursi villages can be visited as an overnight camping trip from the lodge, or *en route* to/from Jinka.

GETTING THERE AND AWAY Coming from the south, two routes can be used to reach Murelle. The direct road from Turmi is about 70km long and generally takes two to three hours, with a fair amount of game to be seen along the way.

We travelled along the 55km road that branches northward from the Turmi–Omorate road about 9km east of Omorate. The dry, red-earth savanna this road passes through offers some of the best game viewing in the region. Guenther's dik-dik is as common as ever, and there is a good chance of seeing gerenuk, Grant's gazelle and the localised tiang (a race of topi associated with the most easterly extent of its range). With an early start, you might well encounter the delightful bat-eared fox, easily distinguished by its over-sized ears and black 'bank-robber' eye-mask as it trots through the grass or dozes under a shady shrub. As for birds, colourful swooping bee-eaters do their best to steal the show, but look out too for raptors – we saw at least a dozen species including the handsome black-breasted snake eagle

– and colourful red-and-yellow barbets performing their risible clockwork duets from the top of the prolific termite hills.

The road north from Murelle to Mago National Park is covered under the section on that park, see page 580. No public transport runs close to Murelle from any direction, nor do trucks head there with any regularity – a private vehicle, or lucky hitch, are the only options.

WHERE TO STAY AND EAT

🏠 **Murelle Omo Explorer's Lodge** (10 bungalows) Bookings through Ethiopian Rift Valley Safaris (ERVS), PO Box 3658, Addis Ababa; 📞011 155 2128/8591/1127; f 011 155 0298; e ervs@ethionet.et; www. ethiopianriftvalleysafaris.com. Set in a shady riverine grove fringing the Omo River, this lodge consists of rather run-down bungalows with shady verandas & en-suite showers & toilet. The lodge lies in the heart of the Murelle Hunting Concession, an area where wildlife, though hardly prolific, is far more visible than in any other unprotected part of South Omo. The grounds are a delight: guereza monkeys swing by on a daily basis, & birds are everywhere – notably the colourful & vociferous black-headed bush-shrike. Originally built as a hunting camp, Murelle Lodge now primarily caters to the ecotourism market, & is used by ERVS as the base for a variety of all-inclusive, exclusive & costly packages, ranging from fly-in charters that land right at the nearby airstrip, to drive-down trips out of Addis Ababa. Activities include game drives & nature walks with a tracker, seasonal boat trips on the Omo River & of course visits to nearby & more remote traditional villages. The food is good, with a strong Italian flavour, & refrigerated soft drinks & beers are available to lodge guests. Accommodation is available to visitors who are not on an ERVS package, but it *must* be pre-booked in Addis Ababa. *US$135/225 FB (inc b/fast, lunch & dinner)*.

▲ **Murelle Campsite** A leafy campsite, also owned by ERVS, lies right alongside the lodge. It is by far the nicest place to camp in South Omo, & well worth the asking price. Unlike the lodge, no advance booking is necessary, but it is important that campers are self-sufficient in terms of food & drinks. Due to the difficult logistics of obtaining food & drink supplies in this remote corner of Ethiopia, meals & drinks are not for sale to campers. *US$14 pp per night*.

WHAT TO SEE

Kangatan Kangatan is the only accessible habitation of the Bumi, a tribe of some 6,000 pastoralists who live on the western side of the Omo River. They normally inhabit the land south of Omo National Park, but will move into the park's southern plains when water or grazing is scarce. The Bumi speak an eastern Nilotic language, and share close affiliations with the Turkana people of northern Kenya, immediately evident in the tentacle-like tangle of leather necklaces and side-cropped hairstyles worn by the women. Like the Turkana, the Bumi are semi-nomadic hunters and cattle herders by custom, measuring their wealth in terms of the size of their herd, though flood agriculture now plays an increasingly important role in their subsistence. They also share with the Turkana a reputation for aggression and ferocity in battle: even today, they are often involved in fatal altercations related to cattle raiding and inter-tribal rivalry with their Surma, Karo and Hamer neighbours.

Kangatan lies above the western bank of the Omo, perhaps 10km southwest of Murelle as the crow flies. The drive from Murelle takes 30–45 minutes, following the Omorate road south for about 10km, then turning right onto a track leading to a police compound on the eastern bank of the river facing Kangatan. You can park safely in the compound, from where a small local boat will take you across the river for a small fee. It is advisable to visit in the company of a guide from Murelle, who will know the villagers and ensure you are welcomed.

The origin of the name Murelle – also transliterated as Murle and pronounced with a rolling 'r' – is somewhat enigmatic. It has always been a place where wild and domesticated animals come to drink, because of the gentle decline of the land towards the river. Aside from the modern lodge, however, Murelle has not supported a settlement in living memory, yet Murle is depicted on several maps, dating right back to the one produced by Count Teleki based on his pioneering 1888 Turkana expedition. Stranger still, there actually is a Murle tribe living in this part of Ethiopia, mentioned in several accounts of European explorers, but based for as long as anybody can remember to the west of the Omo River near the Sudanese border.

Why the Karo now refer to this part of the riverbank as Murelle, or Murle, is anybody's guess: it could be that some Murle people settled in the area at some point, or that it was the site of a fight between the Karo and Murle, or something equally significant. Call me a sceptic, but given the inaccuracies that exist on most maps of South Omo, I would not be surprised to learn that the name stems from generations of cartographers having copied a misunderstanding on the part of Teleki regarding the placement of the Murle territory!

Kolcho and Dus Murelle Lodge lies within the territory of the Karo, a small tribe – some estimates place the population as no more than 1,000 – who speak an Omotic language close to that of the neighbouring Hamer. Pastoralists by tradition, their cattle herds were exterminated by disease some years back, and they now subsist primarily by growing sorghum, maize and other crops along the river. In common with the Hamer, scarification plays an important role in Karo body decoration, and the men plaster their hair into tight buns after killing a human enemy or a dangerous animal. The hairstyle favoured by Karo women is rather striking: tightly cropped at the side, and tied into bulbous knots and dyed ochre on top, it makes them look as if they have rushed out of the bathroom without removing their shower cap.

The Karo are best known for the elaborate body painting they indulge in before important ceremonies. They dab their torsos with white chalk paint, reputedly in imitation of the plumage of a guinea fowl. Colourful face masks are painstakingly prepared with a combination of pastes made by mixing water with chalk, charcoal, powdered yellow rock and iron ore. You'd have to be unusually lucky to arrive at Murelle when a genuine celebration is about to take place, but colourful dances can be arranged through the lodge (or directly) at one of the nearby Karo villages for around US$35 per party.

Discounting the staff village, the closest Karo settlement to Murelle is Kolcho, a compact settlement of perhaps 30 simple huts set on a magnificent sand cliff overlooking a large sweep in the Omo River. Kolcho is about 6km – no more than 20 minutes' drive – from Murelle. Further afield, about 20km from Murelle and a good hour by road, the Karo village of Dus is much larger and has a less spectacular setting, but is worth a visit if you are heading on north towards Omo National Park.

MAGO NATIONAL PARK

(*Entrance US$6 pp/48hrs, US$1.50 per vehicle & US$1 for parking; mandatory armed scout US$5 per day; camping US$2 per tent*) Proclaimed in the 1960s, the 2,162km² Mago National Park is bisected by the Mago River, which flows into the Omo on the park's southern boundary. Although Mago National Park shares some 5km of its southwestern boundary with Omo National Park, and the protected areas form one ecological unit, crossing between the two was never easy, and it has become practically impossible since the region's bridges were swept away in the flooding of 1997.

Along with Omo National Park, Mago is the closest thing in Ethiopia to the renowned savanna reserves of east Africa, and its potential as a tourist attraction – marketed in combination with the cultures of South Omo – is immense. For the time being, however, the access roads to the park are poor (and sometimes impassable after rain), internal roads are little better, and tourist development is limited to a few basic camping sites along the Mago River. Despite the financial impetus that tourism might give to preserving what wildlife remains in this beleaguered sanctuary, it seems that this situation is unlikely to change in the foreseeable future.

Mago National Park is dominated by dense acacia woodland, which is interspersed with small areas of open savanna, the pristine riparian forest that lines the Mago River, and the extensive Neri Swamp. Most of the park lies on the Rift Valley floor at an altitude below 500m, and is correspondingly hot and sweaty, but the northern sector rises sharply to the Rift Escarpment and the 2,528m-high Mount Mago.

The extensive checklist mentions close to 100 mammal species, though populations of many large mammals are now severely depleted through years of poaching and inadequate conservation measures. According to the park rangers, the thousand-strong buffalo herds for which the park was once renowned are today reduced to about 400 head. Only 200 elephants remain, generally concentrating in the area around the park headquarters and campsites during the dry season, particularly in August. As for other large herbivores, the density of the bush makes it difficult to get much of a feel for numbers, especially as the wildlife here is generally quite skittish. Based on our observations, however, Defassa waterbuck is by far the most visible antelope, though gerenuk, tiang, bushbuck, Lelwel hartebeest, greater and lesser kudu and the ubiquitous Guenther's dik-dik are also present in significant numbers.

Most tourists who visit the park do so not for the wildlife, but to see the Mursi villages along the Mago River (see box, *The Mursi*, page 554), and Mago is emphatically not suited to a first-time safari-goer hoping for a few quick snaps of lions and elephants. On the other hand, should you be seeking a more holistic picture of the African wilderness as it was before mass tourism, Mago is pretty much that – tsetse flies and mosquitoes included! With that frame of mind, whatever animals you do come across will be a bonus. And you never know your luck – the only predator we encountered was a solitary black-backed jackal, but leopard are around (though secretive as ever), cheetah may be seen in more open areas, and the lion population is estimated at a healthy 200. You might also look out for two unusually marked dry-country variations on more familiar creatures: the beautiful and highly photogenic reticulated giraffe, and the striking Grevy's zebra, which is larger and has much narrower stripes than the more widespread plains zebra (also found in Mago). Olive baboon are frequently seen, while the common savanna-dwelling patas and vervet monkeys are supplemented along the river by guereza, blue and De Brazza's monkey – the last an isolated population of a species associated with the west African rainforest. More than 300 bird species have been recorded, with typical dry-country specials boosted by more localised birds such as the Egyptian plover, Pel's fishing owl, black-rumped waxbill and dusky babbler.

GETTING THERE AND AWAY

Mago National Park headquarters can be approached by road from Murelle in the south or from Jinka in the north. The 115km drive from Murelle takes about six hours, and there is a genuine risk of getting lost without a

THE MURSI

The most celebrated residents of South Omo are undoubtedly the Mursi, a distinctive group of pastoralists who number about 5,000, and whose territory is more or less bounded by the Omo River to the west and the Mago River to the east. The subject of several television documentaries, as well as Leslie Woodhead's book *A Box Full of Spirits* (Heinemann), the Mursi are best known for one admittedly very quirky item of decoration: the famous lip plates.

The custom is that when a Mursi woman reaches the age of about 20, a slit is cut beneath her lower lip, creating a small hole between the lip and the tissue below. Over the next year, this gap is progressively stretched, forming a 'lip loop' large enough for a small circular clay plate, indented like a pulley, to be inserted between the lip and the mouth. As the lip stretches, so the plate is replaced with a larger one, a process that is repeated until eventually the gap is large enough to hold a clay plate of perhaps 15cm (6 inches) in diameter, and the woman can ideally pull her distended lip loop over her head. The larger the lip plate a woman can wear, the greater her value when she is married – a real whopper might fetch a price of 50 head of cattle.

An alternative and probably false explanation – that the idea is to make a married woman as unattractive as possible to potential adulterers and slave raiders – does take on a grim ring of truth when you actually visit a Mursi village. Contrary to what the publicity shots might have you believe, Mursi women don't actually wear their lip plate all that much – it's far too heavy and uncomfortable. Instead, the wretched ladies wander about in what appears to be a monumental sulk, with their distended lip hanging limply below the jaws. Call me culture-bound, but a Mursi woman sans lip plate is not, by any standards, a pretty sight – one can't help but feel for the teenage girls who will soon be mutilated in a similar fashion.

Mind you, the path to matrimony is no smoother for Mursi men. Traditionally, no Mursi man can marry unless he has won a *donga*, a stick fight in which two contestants painted in white chalk paste pummel each other violently with heavy 2m-long poles. In past times, fights to the death were commonplace, but these days it is more normal for one fighter to submit before things go that far. The victorious fighter is carried off by a group of eligible girls, who then decide which one of them will marry him.

The easiest village to visit, some two hours' drive from the park headquarters, is Bella, which can be reached by following the Jinka road north for 8km, then turning left onto a track that leads to a ranger outpost some 15km further, then continuing straight ahead for another 17km, ignoring the track for Maki to your right, and climbing the escarpment as you approach the village itself.

Bella is situated just outside the northwestern park boundary, on a beautiful plateau that is encircled by mountains and lies near the source of the Usno River. A fee of US$15 per vehicle and a US$6 per person entrance fee must now be paid to the elders. A further fee must be paid to any person you photograph. The going rate is now an outrageous US$0.30 per picture, and they count every click of the shutter. Lip plates can be bought from the girls and women, should you fancy a souvenir. Further relevant details are included under the heading *Mago National Park* (see page 552). Also see the website (*www.mursi.org*), which has an excellent map of the area.

driver or guide who knows the route. The road is in reasonable shape as far as Dus, 20km north of the lodge, but after that it deteriorates to a very rough and frequently indiscernible track. It is impassable after rain.

The steep dirt road between Jinka and Mago National Park headquarters is only 40km long, but it generally takes two hours to cover in the dry season. After light rain, the black cotton soil becomes very slippery, and the drive might take three to four hours. After heavy rain, this road is also impassable.

Mago National Park can be reached only in a private vehicle. If you are travelling independently on public transport, the only realistic way to visit Mago is as a day or overnight trip out of Jinka. The NTO office in Jinka, 2.5km from the town centre along the Karat-Konso road, rents out 4x4 vehicles at a daily rate of around US$224. Cheaper rates are generally offered by private individuals through the various hotels in Jinka – just ask around. It will obviously cut the individual cost if you can hook up with like-minded travellers in Jinka to form a group.

WHERE TO STAY AND EAT There is no accommodation in or near Mago National Park. Unless you intend to visit the park on a day trip out of Jinka, which is perfectly possible, you will have to camp at one of the sites that line the Mago River a few kilometres from the park headquarters. Although basic – facilities are more or less limited to a water pump – the sites are very beautiful, tucked away in the riverine fig forest. Forest birds and monkeys are likely to be seen from the campsite, and elephant occasionally come through during the dry season. All food and drinks should be brought with you, as nothing is available in the park. The camping fee is US$2 per tent, and you must also pay US$9 to have an armed scout stay with you overnight.

JINKA

As the administrative capital of South Omo zone, Jinka is often perceived to be the obvious gateway into the region. In reality, while Jinka is serviced by the only scheduled flights to South Omo, and is the best place for independent travellers to rent a vehicle into Mago National Park, it is pretty much the end of the line insofar as road travel is concerned. Backpackers could easily explore the more accessible villages of South Omo without ever coming within spitting distance of Jinka, while those travelling in a private vehicle are likely to pass through Jinka only because it happens to lie along the main road in or out of Mago National Park. A 'road tax' of US$9 per vehicle is levied upon entering town from the Karat-Konso side.

Existing in virtual isolation from the rest of Ethiopia, Jinka has a rather quaint atmosphere that combines urban and rural attributes in equal proportion. Which of these comes to the fore will depend largely on whether you've bussed or flown in directly from Addis Ababa or Arba Minch, or bumped and skidded uphill from the sultry backwaters of South Omo. Either way, the town seems to straddle two worlds. High, cool and damp, Jinka stands far apart from the rest of South Omo, with such typical small-town facilities as petrol stations, a bank and a clutch of acceptable hotels. Equally, elements such as the grassy airstrip at the centre of town undermine any pretensions Jinka might have to be much more than a small, half-forgotten administrative centre in the back of beyond. Whatever else, this is a likeable enough town, and the large Saturday market is certainly worth a look, attracting traders from all over South Omo, in particular Ari, Bana, Besheda and Besketo people.

The one formal tourist attraction in Jinka is the **South Omo Research Centre & Museum** (⟋ *046 775 0332;* e *croc@ethionet.et; museum* ⏱ *08.00–18.00 daily; entrance US$2*), which is perched on a hill overlooking the town centre and offers

24

an attractive view over it. The excellent anthropological museum provides a useful overview of the various cultures of South Omo, and is well worth the entrance fee. Film programmes and anthropological lectures can be set up for groups with advance notice. At US$1 per person, film offerings include ethnographic movies on the people of South Omo, ie: *The Leap across the Cattle* by Ivo Strecker or *Two Girls Go Hunting* by Jean Lydall. On Wednesdays there are guided tours of the Aari Mountains behind the museum. Souvenirs can be purchased at the museum gift shop, and a small local house next to the museum sells paintings and postcards, with the proceeds supporting a water-pump project for the Aari village of Girsh.

GETTING THERE AND AWAY Jinka is situated 205km northwest of Karat-Konso, and can be reached in about four hours via a good dirt road that is being upgraded to asphalt. A daily bus connects Arba Minch and Jinka (US$6; 8 hours) via Karat-Konso, as do various light vehicles and trucks. For details of driving between Jinka and Mago National Park, see the section on *Mago National Park*, page 552.

GETTING AROUND
Car rental The **NTO office**, located 2.5km from the centre of town along the Karat-Konso road, can arrange 4x4 hire for expeditions into Mago National Park costing US$224 per day including fuel, tax and driver. Contact Temesgen Belay (m *0916 853 515*) for more information.

WHERE TO STAY As with Turmi, most hotels in Jinka charge foreigners up to double the local rate, making even budget options feel decidedly over-priced.

Upmarket
Eco-Omo Safari Lodge (20 safari tents) 046 775 1500, 011 861 2040 (Addis Ababa); e villaggioglobale@ethionet.et. Located on the western outskirts of Jinka on the bank of the Neri River, this pleasant new Italian-owned lodge is reminiscent of the archetypal bush lodges found throughout much of southern & east Africa. Accommodation is provided in a series of safari tents raised on wooden platforms each with a small but adequate hot-shower en suite. In spite of its large compound, the tents are tightly lined up down one side of the property which means you can hear everything in the neighbouring tent. A very good restaurant is attached serving delicious Italian-flavoured dishes in the US$4.50–6 range & rates include a delicious continental breakfast served on the deck overlooking the river. **Camping** is also permitted & trekking, horseriding & birdwatching trips can be arranged. Future plans include a massage room & a swimming pool. *US$30/50 sgl/twin using common shower, US$50/80 en-suite sgl/twin.*

Moderate
Jinka Resort (18 rooms) 046 775 0143–4, 011 618 9240 (Addis Ababa). This long-serving lodge lies in large green grounds a short distance from the town centre next to a Total garage on the Karat-Konso road. The comfortable rooms each have tiled floors, en-suite hot shower & nets. There is also a pleasant **campsite** with clean toilets & showers & a good restaurant is attached. *US$14/27.50/27.50 sgl/dbl/twin.*

Budget
Goh Hotel (25 rooms) 046 775 0033. The pick of the second stringers is this modern hotel centred on a pleasant courtyard bar & restaurant on the edge of the central airstrip. It's a nice enough place, with a good range of decent, reasonably clean – if a little weary – en-suite rooms. The restaurant located in the adjoining property is also very reasonable. *US$14/18.50/18.50 sgl/dbl/twin.*

Orit Hotel (10 rooms) 046 775 1045. Set in flowering green gardens no more than 200m from the Goh, this long-serving & reliable hotel is shabbier than the Goh, but charges similarly high *faranji* rates. The en-suite rooms all have cold-water showers, while 12 new en-suite doubles, each with hot-water en-suite shower & TV, should be completed by the time this book

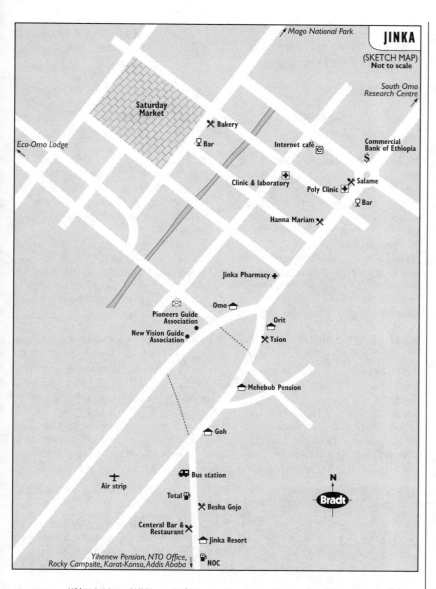

JINKA

(SKETCH MAP)
Not to scale

Mago National Park

South Omo
Research Centre

Saturday
Market

Eco-Omo Lodge

Bakery

Bar

Internet café

Commercial
Bank of Ethiopia

Clinic & laboratory

Poly Clinic

Salame

Bar

Hanna Mariam

Jinka Pharmacy

Omo

Pioneers Guide
Association

Orit

New Vision Guide
Association

Tsion

Mehebub Pension

Goh

Air strip

Bus station

N

Total

Bradt

Besha Gojo

Central Bar &
Restaurant

Jinka Resort

Yihenew Pension, NTO Office,
Rocky Campsite, Karat-Konso, Addis Ababa

NOC

goes to press. *US$12/15/15 sgl/dbl/twin, US$24
new en-suite dbls*.

Shoestring

⌂ **Yihenew Pension** (12 rooms) ✆046 775
5080. The friendly new pension with quiet, clean
rooms using common cold shower is a far more
appealing option than both the hotels listed
below. The only downside is its out-of-the-way
location. It's signposted 40m off the main road to
Karat-Konso around 1.5km south of the centre.

There's no restaurant, but cold beer & soft drinks
are served. *US$5*.

⌂ **Omo Hotel** (10 rooms) ✆056 775
1130/0067. Shabbier than the above, but cheaper &
more central, the Omo Hotel is a favourite haunt for
truck drivers. Basic rooms with en-suite cold-water
shower using a common toilet are loud. *US$4.50*.

Camping

⋏ **Rocky Campsite** m 0916 856 530. This
beautiful green site, set some 3km along the Karat-

Konso road, combines an attractive setting with good facilities, including clean toilets & showers, 3 kitchen houses, & a bar selling cold beers & sodas. You must bring your own food, but a cook is available if you don't feel like preparing it yourself, & they have a generator. *US$3 pp.*

✕ WHERE TO EAT The best place to eat is the restaurant at **Eco-Omo Safari Lodge**, but it's a little off the beaten track for anyone without transport. Of the centrally located hotels, **Jinka Resort** is the top pick, serving a good selection of Western and local dishes. Adequate restaurants can also be found at the **Goh** and **Orit** hotels.

✕ Besha Gojo Restaurant `046 775 0568;` e besha.gojo@gmail.com; ⏱ 06.30–22.00 daily. This friendly little restaurant is the current top spot, with dining either inside or at a small outdoor eating area with covered bench tables. The beer is ice cold! Western & local dishes. *US$2–3.*

✕ Hanna Mariam Restaurant `046 775 1343;` ⏱ 06.00–23.30 daily. Their refreshing one-price-for-all policy backed by good food makes this local restaurant a good choice. The astute owner also has plans to open a second restaurant & lodge just out of town on the road to Karat-Konso. *US$1.50.*

✕ Pioneers `046 775 1728;` ⏱ 06.00–22.00 daily. This small shady garden restaurant run by the local guide association is a great place to meet other travellers, arrange your tours, check your email or even have a shower. The food is filling & cheap too. *US$1.50.*

✕ Tsion Restaurant `046 775 0600;` ⏱ 06.30–22.00 daily. Located opposite Nasa Supermarket, this is another popular local choice with a one-price-for-all policy. There's no menu as such but they serve the usual staples as well as good coffee. *US$1.50.*

WHAT TO SEE AND DO The helpful staff at the **Pioneers Guide Association** (`046 775 1728;` m *0916 856 681;* e *andualem1039@yahoo.com;* ⏱ *06.30–22.00 daily*), opposite the airstrip just south of the Omo Hotel, provide the necessary guides for trips to nearby Mursi villages (US$12 per day). They also arrange multi-day treks in Mago National Park. On site there's a good restaurant (see *Pioneers* in the listing above), a reliable, but slow, internet café (US$1.80 per half-hour), a small grocery store and even a basic cold-water shower where you can freshen up after the long drive to Jinka (for a small fee, of course). Next door, the newly opened **New Vision Guide Association** (m *0916 712 096;* ⏱ *07.00–20.00 daily*) can also arrange official guides, treks, horseriding and guided city tours for similar prices.

RAFTING THE OMO

The most adventurous way to reach South Omo (and now the only way to see the area as it once was) is along the river for which the region is named which, during September and October, is high enough to be navigable for most of its length. Rafting trips of 14, 17 and 25 days on the Omo River have been run by Remote River Expeditions during these months almost yearly since 1984. The trips start near Weliso, passing through the 1,500m-deep Serenity Canyon, as well as otherwise inaccessible Walaita villages, waterfalls, swimming holes and hot springs. Hippos, crocodiles, monkeys and various antelope – sometimes even lions – are often encountered on the way. The 17-day trip ends at the bridge on the Sodo–Jimma road, while the 25-day version continues into South Omo, offering contacts with the Bumi, Bodi and Mursi peoples. (The 14-day trip covers only the second half.) Although most of the journey is on flat water, and no experience is required, both sections include challenging rapids. For more information contact Remote River Expeditions, USA (`+26 1 20 955 2347;` e *gary@remoterivers.com; www.remoterivers.com*).

Part Six

WESTERN ETHIOPIA

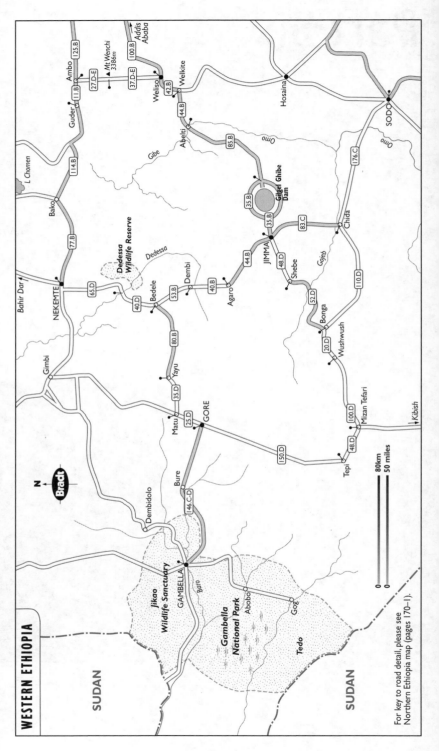

WESTERN ETHIOPIA

SUDAN

SUDAN

For key to road detail, please see
Northern Ethiopia map (pages 170–1).

560

OVERVIEW

More than any other part of the country it's the lush western highlands, all rolling hills, neat cultivation and dense montane forest, that subvert preconceptions about Ethiopia being a land of desert and famine. Despite its natural beauty, the western highlands lacks for a well-defined sightseeing route and boasts few organised tourist attractions, meaning the region is largely ignored by travellers. This, really, is half of the charm of western Ethiopia: the chapters that follow describe one of Africa's great off-the-beaten-track loops, an area of intimate and lush green scenery broken into convenient day-sized travel bites by a series of well-equipped towns.

The ultimate goal for any traveller heading west of Addis Ababa is the steamy riverport of **Gambella**, reached via a dramatic descent from the breezy highlands into the sweltering Sudanese border region. Set on the northern bank of the Baro River, part of the Nile drainage system, Gambella is both an atmospheric and fascinating destination in its own right, and more or less the end of the road insofar as public transport is concerned. The region can be explored as a loop between Addis Ababa and Gambella, which entails heading out to Gambella via Ambo and Nekemte, and returning to Addis Ababa via Jimma and Weliso, but it could as easily be done in reverse. Equally, those with limited time could restrict themselves to a short overnight loop through Ambo and Weliso via Lake Wenchi, as described in *Chapter 25*, or travel more extensively in the highlands described in *Chapter 26* without actually going as far as Gambella.

There is regular public transport connecting the towns on both legs of the loop. During the wet season, the direct road between Nekemte and Gambella on the northern leg may be out of service; when this happens, you can get there via a road connecting Nekemte to Bedele on the southern leg which is tarred in its entirety with the exception of the 105km stretch between Nekemte and Bedele and the 25km section between Matu and Gore. The loop described in the following chapters is all but self-contained, in that there are few decent roads connecting it to other parts of Ethiopia. An exception is the upgraded road between Sodo and Jimma, which would allow travellers to cross between the Rift Valley and western Ethiopia without returning to Addis Ababa.

Most of the places described in this section lie at an elevation of 2,000m or greater, and are thus relatively cool and moist. Gambella, which lies below the escarpment, has a hot, humid climate reminiscent of the east African coast and Lake Victoria hinterland.

An inviting taster for the western highlands and worthwhile excursion out of Addis Ababa is provided by the road loop that runs west for 125km from the capital to the bustling town of **Ambo**, then cuts southward for about 65km to the resort town of Weliso, 100km from Addis Ababa on the Jimma road. The focal point of this loop is the spectacular **Wenchi Crater Lake**, which lies to the east of the road connecting Ambo to Wenchi, and also offers some worthwhile indigenous forest reserves, a trio of attractive waterfalls in the vicinity of Ambo, and a hot-springs resort at Weliso. In a private vehicle, you could complete this loop in one long day, though this wouldn't leave a great deal of time for sightseeing. A more realistic approach would be to take two or three days, planning on overnight stops at Ambo, Weliso or Menegasha State Forest depending on your budget and interests. There is plenty of public transport along the main roads connecting Addis Ababa to Ambo or to Weliso, the respective springboards for travel on to Nekemte/Gambella or Jimma/ Mizan Tefari, but transport between Ambo and Weliso is more limited.

25

The Wenchi Loop

FROM ADDIS ABABA TO AMBO

The hot-springs resort of Ambo makes an obvious goal for a first overnight stop on any trip to western Ethiopia, but there are a few interesting diversions along the way, all of which – like Ambo itself – can easily be visited as a day trip from the capital. Of interest solely to birdwatchers is the **Gefersa Reservoir**, while further west the road to Ambo cuts through the historical small town of **Addis Alem**. Another point of interest is the **Chilimo Gaji Forest** near Ginchi, the site of a newly established community tourism project.

GEFERSA RESERVOIR This large reservoir, set at an altitude of 2,600m in the Akaki catchment area some 18km west of Addis Ababa, was dammed in 1938 as a source of water for the expanding capital, and its carrying capacity was boosted by a second dam built further upstream in 1966. The lack of fringing vegetation makes the reservoir rather bland visually, but it is popular with birdwatchers, as much as anything for its proximity to the capital. Gefersa probably can't be recommended to travellers who will be heading to the prime birdwatching spots of southern Ethiopia, but it is a good place to observe some endemic species not easily seen at the main stops along the northern historical circuit. The ubiquitous wattled ibis and more localised blue-winged goose are virtually guaranteed at Gefersa, while Abyssinian longclaw, Rouget's rail and black-headed siskin are also regular, along with a few interesting non-endemics such as red-breasted sparrowhawk and (during the European winter) a variety of migrant waterfowl.

ADDIS ALEM Situated roughly halfway between Addis Ababa and Ambo, the small town of Addis Alem was founded in 1900 as the projected capital of Menelik II, who gave it its name, which means 'New World'. Addis Alem would probably be the capital of Ethiopia today were it not for the introduction of the fast-growing Australian eucalyptus tree at a time when Addis Ababa's wood resources were looking decidedly finite. The hilltop palace constructed for Menelik under the supervision of American and Indian engineers prior to 1902, when the planned relocation to Addis Alem was abandoned, became the **Church of Ejare Debre Tsion Maryam** (*entrance US$3*) which today pokes above the forest 1km from the main road to dominate the town's skyline. The circular church, decorated with paintings of lions and cheetahs, is of interest primarily for the Menelik-era treasures it keeps in its adjacent **museum** (⏱ *08.30–15.00 Mon–Thu, 09.00–16.00 Sat & Sun; entrance included with church*). These historical connections aside, Addis Alem is a rather dull little town. If you need to spend the night, the newly expanded **Alemu Selassie Hotel** (*31 rooms;* ☏ *011 283 0024*) at the Mobil garage has spotlessly clean en-suite rooms for US$7.50 as well as four passable older rooms with common shower for US$2.

CHILIMO GAJI FOREST (*entrance US$3*) Chilimo Gaji Forest is a small area of indigenous forest extending over about 50km² some 7km north of the town of Ginchi, which lies 87km west of Addis Ababa on the Ambo road. An isolated relic of the dry evergreen montane forest that once covered much of this part of Ethiopia, it offers the opportunity to experience Ethiopia's natural environment relatively close to the capital. Chilimo also offers numerous natural features, from stunning views to dense closed-canopy forest teeming with monkeys, birds and other forest creatures. The Royal Lodge in the centre of the forest was a gift from Haile Selassie to the Empress Menen to celebrate the birth of their son.

Community-based management groups in various local villages have been assigned to control adjacent forest patches under signed forest-management plans and agreements. These communities will currently offer informal hospitality to self-sufficient campers (at their own risk) and will also act as local forest guides. Fees for all services are negotiable. It is hoped in the near future that the communities will be providing formal camping services, as well as guided walks, rides and local activities. For news of progress, contact the **Oromia Forest and Wildlife Enterprise** (*Finnine Branch;* \ *011 646 1150;* m *0911 842 893*) or Chilimo Gaji Forest Union Chairman, Abera Tefeshu (m *0920 585 286*).

AMBO

This scruffy small town of around 50,000 inhabitants stands at an altitude of around 2,100m on the Huluka River some 125km west of Addis Ababa by road. It was temporarily renamed Hagare Hiwot ('Healthy Country'), and is still referred to as such on some maps. Haile Selassie was rather partial to bathing in the therapeutic **hot springs** that lie in the town centre and which still form the centrepiece of a low-key resort and accompanying swimming pool. Entrance to the hot-springs complex costs less than US$2, and is worthwhile whether you want to take a dip in the pool (which despite the dirty appearance of the mineral-rich water is refilled regularly) or just enjoy the birdlife attracted to the surrounding fig trees. Ambo is also the home of Ethiopia's most popular brand of mineral water, and visits to the **bottling factory**, about 5km out of town on the Nekemte road, are possible if you call ahead (\ *011 371 6242;* e *info@ambowater.com; www.ambowater.com*).

GETTING THERE AND AWAY The 125km drive from Addis Ababa takes about two hours along an asphalt road, passing through a pretty but less than dramatic highland area of green cultivated fields set below distant mountains. Public transport to Ambo leaves the new Asco Bus Station located several kilometres from the centre of Addis Ababa on the main road to Ambo throughout the day. Direct buses between Addis Ababa and Nekemte, the next main town along the western loop, pass through Ambo but are usually full. There is no direct transport between Nekemte and Ambo; you will probably need to change buses at Bako (see *Getting there and away* under *Nekemte* in *Chapter 26*, page 586).

 WHERE TO STAY AND EAT
Budget
Abebech Matafaria Hotel (50 rooms) \011 236 2365–6. This smart 5-storey hotel lies in compact but shady grounds close to the bus station on the Addis Ababa side of town. The clean & unusually modern rooms are fair value & the

attached restaurant serves a wide range of local & international dishes in the US$3–4.50 range. Standard en-suite rooms all have king-size bed, hot shower, DSTV & balcony, while budget rooms on the ground floor have 2 single beds, a compact hot shower & no TV. Suites have a king bed, sitting room, DSTV, balcony, & en suite with bathtub. *US$9.50 budget twin, US$15.50/16 standard sgl/ twin, US$21 suite.*

🏠 **Ambo Ethiopia Hotel** (46 rooms) ✆ 011 236 2002/7; e amboethiopiahotel@gmail.com. Built as an elementary school in 1949 & converted to a hotel 6 years later, this former government hotel, set in a leafy riverfront garden opposite the hot-springs resort, had become rather run-down prior to being privatised in 2003. An attractive stone building with wooden floors & high ceilings, it remains a tempting prospect. The rooms don't match the standard set by the Abebech Matafaria, but the place has character & ranks as fair value. The restaurant serves good food indoors or al fresco at US$2–3 for a main course & entrance into the hot springs is free for guests. Camping is also permitted (US$6 in hotel-provided tent). *US$5 twin with common shower, US$8/8.50 ¾ bed en suite without/with DSTV, US$12 dbl en suite & DSTV, US$18 suite with king bed & DSTV.*

Shoestring

🏠 **Jibat Mecha Hotel** (36 rooms) ✆ 011 236 2253. Not the bargain it once was, this place is nonetheless a popular shoestring choice offering clean, spacious en-suite rooms with cold shower. The flowering grounds boast a bar & restaurant, but the rooms are set far enough away that noise isn't a discouraging factor. At the time of research 38 new rooms were yet to be completed. *US$5.50 en-suite dbl.*

🏠 **Derara Hotel** (28 rooms) ✆ 011 236 2311. The pick of several cheap hotels studded around town, this friendly local lodging has quiet rooms set back from the street & a good restaurant/bar. *US$3.50 using common shower, US$4.50 en-suite dbl.*

🏠 **Robe Hotel** (14 rooms) m 0911 650 055. Previously known as Ambo Africa Hotel, this place offers adequately clean rooms with hot shower – a rare find in this price range. *US$2.50 using common shower, US$3.50 en-suite dbl.*

WHAT TO SEE
Abareba Park at Teltele Valley
This small park, once affiliated with the Ambo Ethiopia Hotel, no longer

AMBO

Addis Ababa

OiLibya

Qana'a

Abebech Matafaria

Kitani Café & Bedroom

Welega

Nightclub ☆

Bus station

Hot Springs Resort & Sibona Bar & Café

Ambo Ethiopia

Royal Juice

Tekeste

Ambo Mini

Wenchi

Police

Gimbe

Commercial Bank of Ethiopia

Telecom

Jibat Mecha

N ← Bradt

Nekemte Café & Restaurant

Administration buildings

Hospital

Marata Café

Yordanis

Poly Clinic

Robe

OiLibya

Bakery

Derara

0 ——— 100m
0 ——— 100yds

College of Agriculture

Nekemte, Gambella

officially operates, and a new government hospital now blocks its main access, making it pretty missable unless you really like waterfalls. It lies below the 2,200m Senkele Mountain and consists of a steep wooded gorge carved by the Teltele and Huluka rivers prior to their confluence about 4km west of Ambo. There are three waterfalls, the tallest of which measures 25m in height, while a range of low-key wildlife includes Anubis baboon, guereza, bushbuck, porcupine, monitor lizard and a great many birds – there are camels and pigs too. To get there follow the Guder road for 2km then turn right onto a rough dirt track (marked by a Renewable Energy Power Station sign) and drive to the top of the hill from where you can hike down around the hospital to the ravine. The guards will allow you to view the falls from a rickety wooden platform for a US$2–3 fee.

Guder Falls (*Entrance US$2; US$2 for video*) This waterfall, which lies on the Nekemte road about 1km past the small town of Guder, really doesn't warrant the prominent posting it receives on most maps of Ethiopia, but it does carry an impressive volume of water in the rainy season, and the surrounding riverine forest is rattling with monkeys and birds. It's supposed to be best on Sundays, when the sluice gates are opened for Ethiopian weekenders. To get to the waterfall from Ambo, catch one of the regular minibuses that cover the 13km road to Guder, and then walk out of Guder along the Nekemte road. The road crosses a large bridge, and then climbs a gentle rise, at the top of which there is a gate to your left. You may have to bang at the gate for a while to get somebody to open it, but once you are in the enclosure there is a clear footpath to the base of the waterfall.

Given that public transport to Nekemte starts in Ambo rather than Guder, Ambo is the more attractive place to overnight for westbound travellers. There is, however, plenty of inexpensive accommodation in Guder as well as a new, more upmarket hotel under construction next to the Commercial Bank of Ethiopia. Best bet is the **Guder Falls Hotel** (*22 rooms;* \ *011 282 0137*), which lies above the waterfall in green grounds inhabited by guereza and a variety of birds, charges US$3 for an adequate single room in a chalet, US$2.50 per tent for camping, and serves acceptable meals and drinks.

MOUNT WENCHI

This massive extinct volcano, which reaches an elevation of 3,386m, is situated to the south of Ambo along the dirt road that connects to Weliso on the Jimma road. The main attraction is the picturesque caldera, which is settled and quite densely cultivated, and also encloses a 4km² crater lake dotted with small islands. On one of these islands stands the venerable **Monastery of Wenchi Chirkos**, the foundation of which is attributed by some to the 15th-century Emperor Zara Yaqob and by others to the 13th-century St Tekle Haymanot. An extensive plateau covered in Afro-alpine heather and moorland surrounds the crater, and a few relic patches of natural forest remain in the area. Although the lake is currently accessible only as a day trip (whether out of Ambo or Weliso, or *en route* between the two), the owners of Abebech Matafaria Hotel in Ambo have built a small lodge with eight thatched huts on the crater rim, but it was closed at the time of research, and it is unclear if or when it will reopen.

In a private vehicle, the 27km drive from Ambo to the market village of Wenchi takes about one hour. Wenchi can also be approached from Weliso on the Addis Ababa–Jimma road, by turning onto the dirt road that heads roughly northward from opposite the Reffeera Hotel. After 24km, this road passes through the small town of Daryun, from where it is another 13km to Wenchi village. Whichever way you come, you might want to ask about the condition of the road in advance, particularly if you are not in a 4x4 vehicle. It was excellent in the dry season of 2011, with the exception of a 2km stretch north of Wenchi village, which was split by rivulets but still passable slowly in any vehicle.

Now administered by **Wenchi Eco-Tourism Association** (WETA) (✆ *011 356 0009; www.wenchi-crater-lake.com*) and funded by GTZ, the same German non-profit organisation that started the trekking programme in Dodola, you must pay a nominal entrance fee of US$2 per person at the signposted park headquarters to visit Wenchi Crater as well as an additional US$1.50 for parking. It's also possible to hire a horse for a trek down to the crater. Rates vary from US$6 to US$9 per horse including a horse handler, while a guide costs between US$9 and US$15 depending on your itinerary. The full circuit takes up to seven hours – see their website for details. Boat trips to the Hudad Church cost US$2 per person round trip, or you can add a stop at Emogili Harbour for an extra US$2.50 per person. A good map is available at the park office, and additional information can be found on the WETA website.

If you are just driving through, a second viewpoint over the crater is situated 2km from Wenchi, practically alongside the Ambo road. From this viewpoint, you can also see the freshwater **Dendi Crater Lake** in the distance. According to one very excited local we encountered, the people who dwell near Lake Dendi live in mortal fear of a solitary but gigantic man-eating crocodile, for which reason they refuse to take boats onto the water. True or not, you could check this out for yourself by hiring a horse in Wenchi for around US$9 plus US$15 for a guide – the trip reportedly takes about three hours in each direction on horseback.

Without private transport, reaching Wenchi is problematic. The occasional 4x4 vehicle does serve as public transport between Ambo and Weliso. These reportedly run most mornings in the dry season and will drop passengers at Wenchi village, from where it is easy enough to walk to the crater. So far, so good – the problem is how to get back; until the **lodge** is opened, no accommodation is to be found in Wenchi, and what little transport there is in the afternoon is likely to be fully loaded by the time it passes through Wenchi. One way to get around this would be to visit on a Sunday: this is the main market day in Wenchi, and plenty of trucks head to and from the village throughout the day. On other days, one possibility would be to use public transport from Weliso as far as Daryun, where the basic, clean and inexpensive Hotel Beeteli serves as a fallback. Finally, it is possible to **camp** near the lake for US$5 per tent, plus an additional US$27 for an obligatory scout.

WELISO

This small town on the Jimma road about 100km southwest of Addis Ababa is sometimes referred as Ghion in reference to its hot spring, the water of which is regarded to be holy by Ethiopian Christians. The holy water flows into the church of Weliso Maryam, 15 minutes' walk from the main road, which attracts many sick and disabled pilgrims. It is customary for those cured by the water to leave behind artefacts associated with their illness. A museum-cum-barn in the church grounds holds dozens of crutches and walking sticks, as well as chains left behind by the mentally ill, and charms and talismans by those possessed by evil spirits. No fee is charged to visit the church, but a donation is expected.

WHERE TO STAY

Moderate

Negash Lodge (35 rooms) 011 341 0002/0147; e pabomi@ethionet.et; www. negashlodge.com. The best place to stay in Weliso, indeed one of Ethiopia's most underrated hostelries, the excellent Negash Lodge is a recently privatised & renovated former government hostel situated about 1km south of the main street past the church via an unexpectedly rough road. The hotel is centred on an excellent hot-spring-fed outdoor pool (full Fri–Mon) & it also contains Ethiopia's only indoor pool. The main building hosts beautifully decorated double rooms, while the grounds are also dotted with a number of modern *tukuls*, each modelled after a different style of traditional Ethiopian house. (To tell you the truth, they all look pretty similar, except for the Addis Ababa block, which is 'condominium style'!) An excellent base for visiting Wenchi, this hotel also hosts plenty of monkeys in the garden, not to mention prolific birdlife. A tree bar constructed under a gracious old ficus tree provides the perfect spot for wildlife viewing. The restaurant is excellent with a European menu featuring chicken, beef & fish entrées in the US$2.50–5 range. The wood-fired pizzas are fantastic & rates include breakfast. *US$45 en-suite dbl, US$52.50–60/86 twin/family suite tukul, US$45 twin bungalow.*

Budget

Belay Hotel (39 rooms) 011 341 0639. The Negash Lodge is definitely the top choice in town, & there are cheaper options as well, but the Belay's convenient location near the bus station & excellent food make it worth mentioning. Rooms with full-size bed, en-suite hot shower & TV are also exceptionally clean. (Doubles are a bit cramped – 2 singles might be preferable.) The large central bar is surrounded by a huge dining room with local & international dishes in the US$2–3 range. *US$6 using common shower, US$12/18 en-suite sgl/dbl.*

Ebenezer Hotel (28 rooms) 011 341 0374/0053; f 011 341 0374. Located at the eastern end of town by the Total station, this new hotel is the smartest & most attractive in this price range. Rooms are all well sized, comfortably furnished with TV & hot water. The attached restaurant/café serves decent meals & internet is available for a small charge (around US$0.05 per min). *Dbls US$6–9 depending on bed size.*

Refera Hotel (77 rooms) 011 341 0294. Next door to the Ebenezer Hotel (don't confuse it with a lesser hotel of the same name), this recently expanded place offers a wide range of accommodation options. Rooms with hot-shower en suite & TV in the older section of the hotel behind the Total station are well priced but faded, & the bar here can get noisy, making the new tiled rooms with hot-shower en suite, TV & balcony in the multi-storey extension above the Oromia International Bank a more appealing option. The restaurant has a basic menu plus sandwiches. *US$4.50/6 old en-suite sgl/dbl, US$7.50–9 new en-suite dbl.*

Shoestring

Kerazhi Hotel (28 rooms) 011 341 1026. *En route* to the Negash Lodge, this hotel lacks food or a bar, but this makes for a quiet place & a good night's sleep. *US$2.50 using common shower, US$6 en-suite sgl with hot water & TV.*

WHAT TO SEE There is plenty of transport out of Weliso in either direction throughout the day. Heading to or from Addis Ababa, the foremost attraction is the underrated and under-utilised Menegasha National Forest, where a network of foot trails and excellent budget accommodation can be found in one of the largest remaining montane forests in Ethiopia. You could also take a break at the small town of Debre Genet, where a church dedicated to St Gebriel is notable for its large golden dome and some excellent paintings inside. The wooded grounds have been known to throw up interesting birds, such as white-cheeked turaco and Gambaga flycatcher. A short distance from the church, there are some hot springs in a small valley.

Menegasha National Forest (*Entrance US$3, US$2 vehicle, US$6 video camera*) The magnificent Menegasha National Forest incorporates some 2,500ha of natural forest along with 1,300ha of exotic plantation forest, at altitudes ranging from 2,300m to 3,000m on the southern and western slopes of Mount Wechecha. Dominated by tall juniper, hagenia and podocarpus trees, Menegasha protects the most substantial remaining patch of indigenous forest in the Addis Ababa region. Above the forest line, the 3,385m-high Mount Wechecha, an extinct volcano, supports a cover of Afro-alpine moorland dominated by *Erica* and *Helichrysum* species. The forest is inhabited by various large mammals, and offers birders with limited time in Ethiopia the opportunity to see several key species more often associated with the forests around Wondo Genet and at Dinsho in Bale National Park. It is worth noting that a mountain called Menegasha lies between Addis Ababa and Mount Wechecha.

Menegasha Forest has an unusual place in east African history, providing the earliest-known instance anywhere in the region of an official conservation policy being adopted. In the mid 15th century, Emperor Zara Yaqob became concerned at the high level of deforestation on Mount Wechecha, and he arranged for a large tract of juniper forest to be replanted with seedlings from the Ankober area. The forest was protected by imperial decree over the subsequent centuries, until eventually Emperor Menelik II set it aside as the Menegasha State Forest in the late 1890s.

Menegasha is well organised for day visits and for extended stays. Emanating from the forestry headquarters are five colour-coded walking trails ranging in length from 0.3km to 9km and variously taking in a lovely waterfall as well as the 3,385m Damocha Peak. While intended for trekkers, most of these trails are accessible by 4x4 as well, which is great news if you only have one day and want to cover a lot of ground. The most frequently seen large mammals along these trails are the guereza monkey and endemic Menelik's bushbuck, but baboon and common duiker are also encountered on occasion, and leopard and serval are both present. The forest birding is superb. The endemic Ethiopian oriole and yellow-fronted parrot are regular around the headquarters. Several other endemics are likely to be encountered – black-winged lovebird, banded barbet, Abyssinian woodpecker and Abyssinian catbird among them – alongside other good forest birds such as crowned eagle, Narina trogon, white-cheeked turaco and Abyssinian ground thrush.

The forest is currently only accessible from the Addis–Jimma road. Coming from Addis, turn right along the road just past the Meta Brewery (roughly 30km from Addis Ababa, right after you pass through the small town of Sebeta). The approach road from Sebeta is 16km long and is generally in a fair state of repair and, except after heavy rain, it should be passable in a saloon car. There is no public transport to the park headquarters, though you might be able to hire a horse cart. Hitching might involve a very long wait at the junction; should you fail to find a lift, Sebeta does boast a few basic hotels.

In the past, the forest was also accessible from the Ambo road using a turn-off near the Ethiodreams flower plantation. This rough side road was not well maintained and required a 4x4 during the rainy season, but after 16km it led you to a small bridge and then to the town of Suba. From Suba the park headquarters is only 2km further. Unfortunately, that small bridge has been washed away, and there are apparently no plans to repair it anytime soon.

Where to stay Accommodation at the forestry headquarters consists of a large homely cottage containing one double room, two twin rooms, a lounge, a toilet and shower, and a kitchen with a fridge and gas cooker. The bedrooms are rented out individually at US$12 per person. There is also an eight-bed dormitory, with common shower and kitchen attached, at a charge of US$2 per person. Camping is permitted at the headquarters for US$2–4 per tent (depending on the tent size), as well as at designated spots along the walking trails. Tents are available for rent if you do not have one, but visitors should bring all their own food and drink. Booking is not normally necessary, though the cottage does occasionally fill up over weekends, so you might want to ring the forest manager (\ *011 515 4975*) in advance to be on the safe side. Guides are available on weekends only by appointment; contact Ato Haile (m *0911 389 389*) to arrange one.

26

The Western Highlands

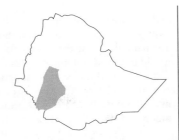

Disadvantaged when it comes to both prescribed sightseeing and tourist amenities of any merit, the undulating highlands of Ethiopia's 'Wild West' do nevertheless boast a distinct sense of place, one that stands in bountiful contrast to the stark landscapes associated with the dry eastern borderlands. Indeed, this little-visited highland region, with its rich loamy soils and plentiful year-through rainfall nourishing an uninterrupted swathe of lush cultivation, dank natural forest and feral coffee, could easily deceive the unprepared visitor into thinking they had taken a wrong turn and ended up somewhere on the verdant slopes that characterise the Ugandan–Congolese border.

Despite this natural abundance, the region is difficult to recommend wholeheartedly to first-time visitors to Ethiopia, at least not unless they have plenty of time on their hands or nurse a penchant for wilful off-the-beaten-track exploration. The towns of the southwestern highlands, with the arguable exception of **Jimma**, are uniformly unmemorable, while road conditions and public transport tend to be ropey even by Ethiopian standards. Acceptable accommodation and restaurant options are few and far between, and the range of tourist attractions is as limited as it is low-key. All things considered, the most likely reason why you'd choose to travel through the western highlands is by way of transit to the dormant riverboat terminus of Gambella, a travel cul-de-sac that might well be resuscitated as an international trade route following moves towards renewed political stability in southern Sudan.

JIMMA

Jimma is comfortably the largest settlement in western Ethiopia, with a population estimated at around 175,000. Until 1994, it served as the administrative capital of Kaffa, a region whose Oromo and non-Oromo components were subsequently split between the new administrative regions of Oromia (of which Jimma is a part) and the Southern Nations, Nationalities and Peoples' Region. The fertile hills of what was formerly Kaffa are probably where the coffee plant was first cultivated, and the area remains one of Ethiopia's main coffee-growing centres, with cultivated strains often growing metres away from their wild counterparts in the forest undergrowth. Essentially a 20th-century creation, Jimma saw a great deal of development during the Italian occupation, but its name derives from that of a much older kingdom whose former capital Jiren lies on the outskirts of the modern city.

Although Jimma lacks for any major tourist attractions, there is some interesting sightseeing to be had around town, and you couldn't hope for a friendlier, greener or better-equipped place to rest up between bus trips. In fact, after you've spent a couple of weeks travelling in the west, Jimma – with its cropped green lawns and neat well-tended grid of roads – comes across as quite shockingly modern and cosmopolitan, a reminder of just how poky most western Ethiopian towns really are. The park alongside the river wouldn't look out of place in a European village, nor would the hand-holding couples you see walking through it. There are even public baths, for goodness' sake – though the absence of water helps to bring perceptions crashing back to earth! Also, be on the lookout for the 'corrugated mosques' located in and around Jimma of which the entire building, including the minaret and the moon and star on top, are all made out of shiny zinc sheeting.

The only organised tourist attraction within the city centre is the **Jimma Museum** (047 111 5881; ⊕ 09.30–17.30 daily; entrance US$2; tours every hr on ½hr), close to the public baths, where a selection of the personal effects of Abba Jiffar, the last independent king of Jimma, are housed alongside some worthwhile ethnographic displays relating to the Oromo and other local cultures. Also worth a look is the patch of riverine woodland behind the museum, which appears to support a resident troop of guereza monkeys as well as the outlandish silvery-cheeked hornbill. At the other side of the city centre, the bustling **market** is worth a look, particularly if you are eager to buy some of the excellent local basketwork. Of interest to wealthier curio hunters (and evidence of Jimma's relative prosperity) are the numerous **jewellery shops** that line the main road, selling locally crafted silver and gold products. Somewhat more bizarrely, this road also houses what might well be the world's largest concentration of **barber's shops**. Also worth a mention is the excellent **Read Books** next to Daily Bread, which stocks a good selection of English-language fiction and non-fiction.

GETTING THERE AND AWAY Flights between Addis Ababa and Jimma are operated four times weekly (US$45) by **Ethiopian Airlines** (047 111 0030; e jimtsm@ ethiopiaairlines.com). Jimma's airport lies about 3km from the town centre. There are daily local buses in both directions between Jimma and Nekemte, and Jimma and Matu, all of which leave at around 06.00 and stop in Bedele between 10.00 and midday. Both Selam and Sky Bus both run twice-weekly services directly from Addis Ababa (US$12; 5½ hours). For details of the road connecting Jimma to Sodo, see box, The 'new' Sodo–Jimma road in Chapter 19, page 447.

WHERE TO STAY
Moderate

Honeyland Hotel (34 rooms) 047 114 1515/8383 e honeylandh@yahoo.com; www. honeylandhotel.com. Overlooking the coffee pot roundabout at the turn-off to Jimma, this new business-class hotel seems strangely misnamed. Then again, first dibs on the name Coffee Land Hotel might have already been taken by the hotel below. In any case, in spite of its less than central location Honeyland is by far the best hotel on offer in Jimma. Rooms are clean & spacious with DSTV & hot-shower en suite. 1st-floor rooms are near to the kitchen & restaurant so could get noisy. Rates include breakfast & free Wi-Fi. US$24/28/34 sgl/ dbl/twin, US$56 suite.

Central Jimma Hotel (91 rooms) 047 111 8282/3. This multi-storey hotel, situated opposite the bus station, is the first choice with tour groups – hence the over-inflated faranji prices. That said, rooms are spacious & clean (especially the rooms in the new section) & all have balconies & hot water. It's also the most atmospheric hotel in Jimma, with a popular coffee bar & restaurant on the ground floor & a full-size swimming pool out the back. US$6 with common shower, US$15/16/16 sgl/dbl/twin, US$18.50/29 2nd-/1st-class suite.

Coffee Land Hotel (30 rooms) 047 111 9464; m 0911 206 607. With a great location opposite the bus station & good-quality rooms on offer, this place would deserve top honours if it weren't for the 2-tiered pricing. As it stands, foreigners pay double the price for large clean rooms with DSTV, private balcony & hot-shower en

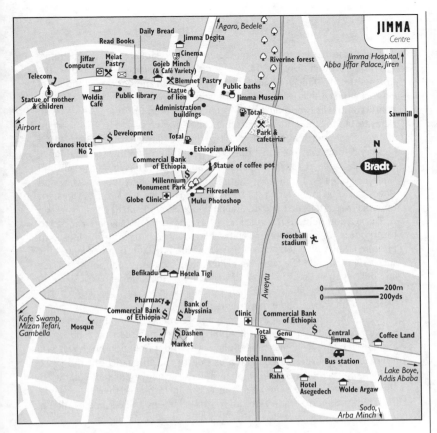

Agaro, Bedele

Daily Bread
Jimma Degita
Read Books
Cinema
Jiffar Melat
Computer Pastry Gojeb Minch
(& Café Variety)
Telecom Blemnet Pastry
Public baths
Statue
of lion
Statue of mother Woldia Jimma Museum
& children Café Public library
Administration
Airport buildings Total

Development Total
Yordanos Hotel Ethiopian Airlines
No 2
Commercial Bank Statue of coffee pot
of Ethiopia
Millennium
Monument Park Fikreselam
Globe Clinic Mulu Photoshop

Riverine forest

Jimma Hospital,
Abba Jiffar Palace, Jiren

Sawmill

Park &
cafeteria

N

Bradt

Football
stadium

Befikadu Hotela Tigi

Pharmacy Bank of
Commercial Bank Abyssinia Clinic Commercial Bank
of Ethiopia of Ethiopia
Kofe Swamp, Total Genu Central Coffee Land
Mizan Tefari, Mosque Dashen Jimma
Gambella Telecom Market
Hoteela Innanu Bus station
Raha Lake Boye,
Hotel Addis Ababa
Asegedech Wolde Argaw
Sodo,
Arba Minch

Aweytu

0 200m
0 200yds

suite. There's a small ground-floor restaurant, but it lacks atmosphere & feels a little disjointed from the hotel. *US$13.50 en-suite sgl, US$15.50–22.50 en-suite dbl depending on room size, US$26 suite.*

Budget

Jimma Degita Hotel (33 rooms) 047 111 0646. Now under new management, this former government hotel is much brighter than the Gibe, & the best deal in town in this price range. The recently upgraded rooms are clean & spacious with hot-shower en suite (the exception being the matchbox-sized eco-room which has an even smaller en suite where you shower over a squat toilet!). The restaurant offers a good selection of local & Western dishes (US$2–4), there are 2 new bars including a rooftop bar & funky Euro-style wine bar-cum-café & draught beer is served on the outdoor patio. Future plans include an additional 65 new rooms. *US$4.50 eco-room, US$6/9 sgl/dbl, US$18–24 suites.*

Wolde Argaw Hotel (57 rooms) 047 111 2731/2; f 047 111 6434. Although the rooms are starting to look in need of a little TLC by comparison with their counterparts at the Central Jimma Hotel, this 3-storey hotel, situated on the opposite side of the bus station, remains one of Jimma's more popular choices despite charging *faranjis* double the price. *US$6.50 common shower, US$11/13 en-suite dbl without/with TV, US$17 en-suite twin, US$18 suite.*

Yordanos Hotel No 2 (57 rooms) 047 111 9295. Under the same ownership as Yordanos No 1, this fresh new hotel next door to the Development Bank offers well-priced rooms in a great quiet location. There are 5 classes of rooms starting from a basic bed-only room using a common shower to a first-class double with king-size bed, wardrobe & flat-screen TV. All rooms are nicely furnished & have tiled floors. *US$8.50 common shower, US$12/13 small en-suite dbl without/with TV, US$14/15.50 2nd-/1st-class dbl.*

Although the modern town of Jimma served as the capital of an administrative region called Kaffa until 1994, it is – rather confusingly – situated to the northeast of the ancient kingdom of Kaffa, within the discrete kingdom of Jimma, which unlike Kaffa had its roots in the Oromo incursion of the 16th century and was predominantly Muslim rather than Christian. Blessed with richly fertile soils and noted for its fine coffee, Jimma served as an important centre of commerce at the convergence of several trade routes. By the 19th century, Jimma was the most powerful political entity in western Ethiopia, covering an area of 13,000km², and with an economy based on the sale and trade of coffee and other agricultural produce, precious metals, ivory and slaves captured in the far west. The market at Hirmata, the largest in western Ethiopia, was attended by up to 30,000 people every Thursday.

The last autonomous ruler of Jimma was King Abba Jiffar, who ascended to the throne in 1878 and made his capital at Jiren, only 7km from the modern town of Jimma. Abba Jiffar took power at a time when the autonomy of kingdoms such as Jimma and Kaffa was severely threatened by the expansionist policies and military prowess of Showa under the future Emperor Menelik II. Six years into his reign, Abba Jiffar, rather than resisting the inevitable, decided to throw his lot in with Showa, and to pay tribute to Menelik.

After that, Jimma effectively became a semi-autonomous vassal state to Showa, still under the rule of Abba Jiffar, but overseen by a governor appointed by Menelik. Alexander Bulatovich, who travelled through western Ethiopia in 1897, described Jimma as one of the three 'richest and most industrial settlements' in the region and 'very densely populated'. Bulatovich also wrote that: 'The best iron items and cloth are fashioned there. Merchants from Jimma conduct trade with the southern regions and with Kaffa. All the residents of Jimma, as well as King Abba Jiffar, are Mohammedan.'

Shoestring

🏠 **Gojeb Minch Hotel** (18 rooms) m 0911 103 519. Built in the 1930s by the Italians, this time-warped hotel was undergoing major renovations on our most recent inspection, with a new reception & dining room not far off completion & all rooms set for a makeover. Prices are bound to go up once complete, but in the meantime the deceptively pleasant rooms remain a good deal. There's also an excellent café & hot-bread shop on the ground floor. *US$5–6 with common shower depending on room size, US$7.50 en suite with cold water.*

🏠 **Aramaic Hotel** (12 rooms) ☎ 047 111 4359. Situated along the Addis Ababa road about 1km past the turn-off to Jiren, this friendly hotel must rank as the overall best value in Jimma,

though its location is less than ideal for travellers using public transport. Accommodation is currently in spacious double rooms with clean, tiled floors & hot-water en suite, with 8 new rooms under construction. The restaurant serves a selection of local & international dishes in the US$1.50–4 range, & there is also a pleasant garden bar, which closes at around 22.30, early enough so as not to interfere with one's sleep. Internet is available at US$0.60/half-hr. *US$5 en-suite dbl.*

🏠 **Yordanos Hotel No 1** (15 rooms) ☎ 047 111 7392. This place has a similar out-of-town location to the above, & its one-price-for-all policy is very refreshing. The restaurant serves cheap local food. *US$5 using common shower, US$7.50 cold-shower en suite with squat toilet.*

✗ **WHERE TO EAT** The restaurant on the ground floor of the **Central Jimma Hotel** is excellent, charging US$2.50–5 for a varied selection of local and exotic dishes –

pastries, juice, coffee and cheap draught beer are all available too. The restaurant at **Honeyland Hotel** is also similarly priced, while both the **Gibe** and **Jimma Degita** hotels serve good Western and local meals for around US$2–4. Several juice and pastry shops and local restaurants line the main roads through the town centre: **Café Variety** on the ground level of the Gojeb Minch Hotel gets special mention, the **Woldia Café**, while not as smart, is equally popular, and the **Melat Café** has good *ful*. For delicious, hot, freshly baked bread though don't miss **Daily Bread** located next door to Café Variety. If you have transport the **Sports Café** opposite the university *en route* to Abba Jiffar's Palace is the liveliest place around.

EXCURSIONS FROM JIMMA

Abba Jiffar's Palace
(⏰ *09.00–12.30 Mon–Fri & 14.00–17.30 daily; entrance US$2 pp inc guided tour; US$1 camera*) Abba Jiffar was the charismatic, powerful – and exceptionally tall – king who ruled over Jimma from 1878 until his death in 1932. He is remembered today for his canny decision in 1884 to pay tribute to Menelik's then-expanding empire of Showa in exchange for a degree of autonomy not conceded to fiefdoms that were co-opted into Showa by force. The impressive palace built by Abba Jiffar during the early years of his rule still stands on a low hill at the former royal compound of Jiren, 8km from the city centre by road. Constructed at a cost of 400kg of gold and 65,000 Maria Theresa dollars – money gained largely through the ruler's active involvement in the slave trade – the palace is a fine example of an admittedly no more than diverting style of early colonial architecture. The largest of the four buildings in the palace compound, which served as the king's residence, spans two storeys, and its wide veranda and shady overhangs are reminiscent of early missionary buildings in parts of west Africa. The whitewashed interior, restored with partial funding from UNESCO, is somewhat austere at present, but it is expected that it will eventually be furnished with the authentic property of the king, currently on display at the Jimma Museum in town. The centrepiece of the building is a ground-floor auditorium enclosed by first-floor balconies (the inspiration perhaps for the similar public area of the Gojeb Minch Hotel in the city centre?), from where the king and his guests would watch musicians, gladiators and entertainers at play. Alongside the palace, the public mosque built by Abba Jiffar is still in active use today.

To reach the palace in a private vehicle, take the road to the Jimma Hospital. Continue until the pavement ends, then turn left (north) along a signposted dirt road that leads past Jiren University to the palace. The palace lies 5km from this junction, after you've climbed first through suburbia then cultivated slopes. Roughly 1.5km before reaching the palace, the Tomb of Abba Jiffar (signposted for Qabrii Mootii Abbaa Jifaar) lies on the left side of the road. No public transport heads up to the palace: travellers without a vehicle can either catch a minibus to the junction at Jiren and walk the last 5km, or else take a taxi from the city centre or hire a bicycle from one of the stalls around the market.

Lake Boye
This small marsh-fringed lake, situated no more than 200m south of the Addis Ababa road a few minutes' drive from Jimma, is a reliable and accessible spot to see hippos, and it also supports an interesting selection of waterbirds and woodland birds. To reach Boye, follow the Addis Ababa road out of Jimma for about 8km. As you approach the turn-off, you'll notice a pine and eucalyptus plantation to your left, as well as two white signposts, one of which reads 'Bon Voyage'. Almost immediately after the second signpost, a rough dirt track leads through eucalyptus trees to within 50m of the lake. Lake Boye can easily be visited as a half-day trip from Jimma using public transport, or by hiring a taxi or bicycle.

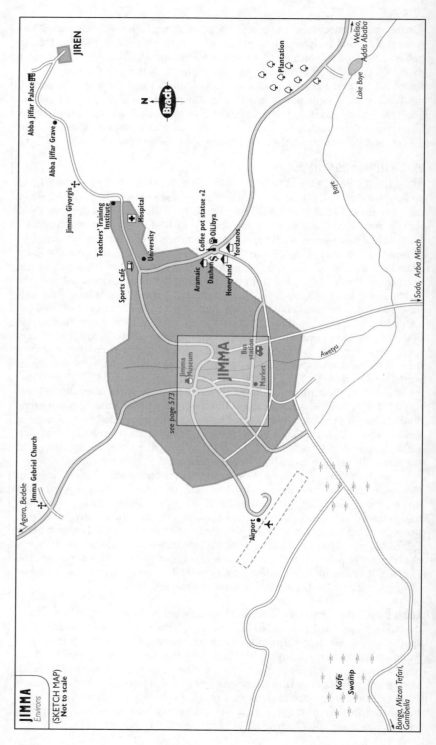

JIMMA
Environs

(SKETCH MAP)
Not to scale

JIREN

Abba Jiffar Palace

Abba Jiffar Grave

Jimma Giyorgis

Teachers' Training Institute

Hospital

University

Sports Café

Aramaic

Dashen

Honeyland

Coffee pot statue 2

OiLibya

Yordanos

Jimma Gebriel Church

Agaro, Bedele

see page 573

Jimma Museum

JIMMA

Bus station

Market

Awetu

Airport

Boye

Lake Boye

Plantation

Weliso, Addis Ababa

Sodo, Arba Minch

Kofe Swamp

Bonga, Mizan Tefari, Gambella

N

Bradt

The resident pod of hippos seems to favour the shallow western part of the lake, the end furthest from the main road – this can be reached by following a rough footpath alongside the eucalyptus trees for about 500m. The birdlife on the lake and its marshy fringes includes the little grebe, white pelican, endemic blue-winged goose and wattled ibis, as well as a variety of herons, ducks and waders, of which painted snipe was our most notable sighting. Silvery-cheeked hornbills can be seen – and heard – in the patch of indigenous woodland on the far shore.

Kofe Swamp   Also of interest to birders are the perennial swamps that lie about 3km southwest of Jimma close to the airport and at Kofe 4km further along the same road. These swamps are best known as a regular breeding site for the highly endangered and impressive wattled crane and the elusive red-chested flufftail. A good range of other water-associated bird species is also present, particularly during the European winter, as is a substantial population of the endemic Abyssinian longclaw. No hippos are present, but small herds of Bohor reedbuck are sometimes encountered. As with the sites listed previously, Kofe can easily be visited as a day trip in a private vehicle, by bicycle or taxi.

FROM JIMMA TO ADDIS

The 350km road between Jimma and Addis Ababa is now surfaced in its entirety, including a 34km new detour road around the southern end of Agelgil Ghibe Dam, which opened in 2004 as a fresh source of hydro-electric power for Addis Ababa, Gondar and Mekele. The drive generally takes around six to seven hours in a private vehicle, while the early morning buses that cover the route typically arrive at their destination up to ten hours later, and buses that leave later in the day may stop overnight at either Welkite or Weliso.

The main point of scenic interest *en route* is the Omo river gorge between Jimma and Welkite. The descent to the base of the gorge follows a spectacular stretch of road with wild granite outcrops in the distance and dense acacia woodland clinging to the hills. At the bottom of the gorge, the small village of Gibe (marked on some maps as Abelti) straddles the Omo River. There is nothing that is obviously a hotel in Gibe, but the women who run the coffee shop claim that rooms are available – with plenty of dense riverine scrub to explore, and wild scenery in every direction, you may well be tempted. The 'real' Abelti, incidentally, lies on a tall mountain which you pass a bit further north – you can walk up to the hilltop town, which boasts stunning panoramic views, a couple of OK cheap hotels, and great roast chicken at the Zeray Deres Restaurant!

You're more likely to spend a night at the busy little roadside town of Welkite by accident rather than design, since buses between Jimma and Addis Ababa sometimes stop there overnight, as mentioned above. Welkite isn't somewhere you'd make an effort to visit, but if you are stranded it's a friendly little place with plenty of shoestring hotels and bars lining the main strip. The newly opened **Soresa Hotel** (*33 rooms*) has clean, modern double rooms from US$12 and the restaurant serves a selection of Ethiopian and Western dishes in the US$2–4 range. From Welkite, unless you arrive too late in the day, there is plenty of local transport on to Addis Ababa, passing through the resort town of Weliso, covered as part of the Wenchi loop in *Chapter 25*.

Beletegera Forest About 40km west of Jimma, this forest features densely packed pines and many sub-canopy species. A few kilometres further on you will pass some of the tallest and spindliest eucalyptus trees in Ethiopia. Locals in the town of Shebe say you can find many species of monkeys and even lions here. A restriction on bringing locally made wood products back to Addis serves as a conservation effort.

BONGA

The medieval Kingdom of Kaffa, whose name is immortalised as the derivative of the words 'coffee' and 'café' (see box opposite), lay to the southwest of Jimma in what is now the Kaffa-Sheka zone of the Southern Nations, Nationalities and Peoples' Region. The people of Kaffa are part of the Ghibe ethno-linguistic group, and speak their own Kaficho language. A credible oral tradition states that Kaffa was founded in the late 14th century by the Minjo dynasty, and was originally ruled from a town called Shada, of which little is known except for its name. In the early 16th-century reign of King Bonkatato, the royal capital shifted to the extant town of Bonga, which retained its importance into the 1880s, when Paul Soleillet, the first European visitor to Kaffa, regarded it to be the largest settlement in the region, and reported that a palace was still maintained there.

Kaffa, though it lay outside the Christian empire of the highlands, appears to have fallen under its sporadic influence. Oral traditions indicating that Emperor Sarsa Dengal's 16th-century expedition to western Ethiopia resulted in the limited introduction of Christianity to Kaffa are backed up by the presence of a monastery dating to around 1550 only 12km from Bonga town. Kaffa was too remote to be affected by the jihad of Ahmed Gragn, and it withstood the subsequent Oromo incursion into the western highlands by digging deep protective trenches around the major settlements. Kaffa remained an autonomous state from its inception until Emperor Menelik II conquered it in the late 19th century, and imprisoned its last king at Ankober.

Although Bonga remains the administrative centre of Kaffa-Sheka zone, there is little about Bonga today that hints at any great antiquity or former significance. Situated some 3km south of the Mizan Tefari road, it's an attractive enough town, sprawling along a high ridge that offers some stirring views over the surrounding forested slopes, and studded with a few buildings that must date to before the Italian occupation.

Perhaps unsurprisingly, the town will soon boast a small **coffee museum**, which is expected to open before this edition is published.

A more convincing reason to visit Bonga perhaps is the opportunity to explore the **Kafa Biosphere Reserve** (*www.kafa-biosphere.com*), officially designated by UNSECO in 2011, which sprawls over some 760,000ha of the surrounding hillsides and incorporates the former Bonga, Gesha and Gewata-Yeba forests. These are among the last remaining subtropical moist forests of any significant size to be found in Ethiopia, and are renowned for their abundance of sustainable non-timber forest products – coffee, forest cardamom, forest pepper and honey. Relatively unexplored by outsiders, and managed by community-based committees, these closed-canopy forests also host large numbers of monkey, a rich and largely undocumented avifauna, and numerous interesting natural features including hot springs and waterfalls. It is hoped that in the near future the communities will be providing formal camping services, horseback excursions and other activities. In the meantime, guided walks ranging from a few hours to

Kaffa is generally regarded to be the region where the Arabica strain of coffee originated, and it is also where this plant was first cultivated. A popular legend, said variously to date to between the 3rd and 10th centuries, claims that a young herdsman called Kaldi first observed the stimulating properties of wild coffee. When his goats became hyperactive after eating the leaves and berries, Kaldi swallowed some of the berries himself, found that he too became abnormally excited, and ran to a nearby monastery to share his discovery.

Initially, the monks didn't share the young goatherd's enthusiasm, but instead chastised him for bringing evil stimulants to their monastery and threw the offending berries into a fire. But then, seduced by the aromatic smell of the roasting berries, the monks decided to give them a go and found that they were unusually alert during their nocturnal prayers. Soon, it became accepted practice throughout Christian Ethiopia to chew coffee beans before lengthy prayer sessions, a custom that still persists in some parts of the country today. Later, it was discovered that the roasted berry could be ground to powder to produce a tasty and energising hot drink – one that still goes by a name derived from the Kaffa region in most places where it is drunk.

The drink of coffee probably remained an Ethiopian secret until the 16th century, when it was traded along the Indian Ocean spice route and cultivated in Yemen and other hilly parts of Arabia. The bean first arrived in Europe via Turkey in the 17th century, and it rapidly took off – more than 200 coffee shops reputedly traded in Venice alone by the early 18th century. Today, coffee exports typically account for up to 70% of Ethiopia's annual foreign revenue. Of Ethiopia's annual coffee crop of four million bags, 90% or more is grown on subsistence farms and smallholdings, and about 40% remains within this coffee-mad country.

multi-day treks can be arranged through the Office of Culture and Tourism in Bonga (✆ *047 331 0842*).

There's plenty of public transport connecting Jimma to Bonga, and a fair selection of accommodation to choose from once you are there. The best bet is the new **Coffee Land Hotel** (*34 rooms;* ✆ *047 331 0010*), which lies alongside the 3km feeder road to the town centre from the main road between Jimma and Mizan Tefari. The pastel-painted rooms, all with tiled floors and nets, cost US$6 for a common cold shower, US$11/12 without/with television for a double with three-quarter bed and hot water, or US$18 for a queen-size double. The restaurant serves delicious, well-priced Ethiopian and Western dishes (the oven-cooked goat is highly recommended). Alternatively, the multi-storey **Makira Hotel** (*54 rooms;* ✆*047 331 0647*), located near the Telecom tower, offers similarly priced rooms.

MIZAN TEFARI AND SOUTHWEST OMO

Whether you drive there from Jimma in the east or Matu in the north, the road to the muddy, misty highland town of Mizan Tefari traverses some of the most lush of Ethiopian landscapes, climbing hill after verdant hill swathed in indigenous montane forest. Unlike the surrounding scenery, however, the town

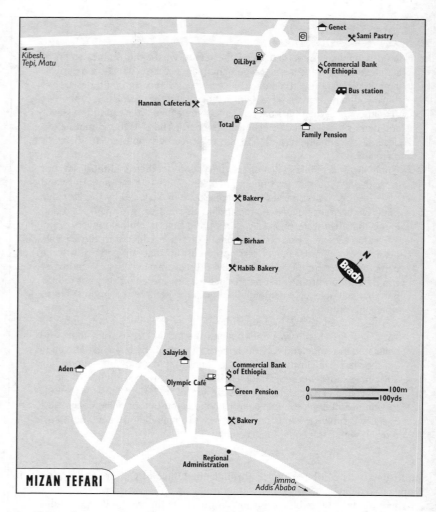

MIZAN TEFARI

Map labels:
Kibesh, Tepi, Matu
Genet
Sami Pastry
OiLibya
Commercial Bank of Ethiopia
Hannan Cafeteria
Bus station
Total
Family Pension
Bakery
Birhan
Habib Bakery
Salayish
Aden
Commercial Bank of Ethiopia
Olympic Café
Green Pension
Bakery
Regional Administration
Jimma, Addis Ababa

0 — 100m
0 — 100yds

itself doesn't impress greatly. True enough, it's a friendly little place, set below an attractive backdrop of forested hills, but it is primarily of interest to travellers as a springboard for visits to the nearby Bebeka and Tepi coffee plantations, or the descent to the small Surma village of Kibish on the southwestern frontier of southwest Omo.

GETTING THERE AND AWAY Most visitors to **Mizan Tefari** approach from the northeast, along a relatively rough 250km road passing through Shebe, Bonga and Wushwush, home of the huge tea plantation which lends its name to Ethiopia's most popular brand. While at the time of writing the road was being upgraded (the 52km stretch between Shebe and Bonga is now tarred), the drive still takes around six hours in a private vehicle, not allowing for stops, and the best part of a day by bus. A worthwhile stop a few kilometres east of Wushwush, at least for aficionados of *tej*, is at Arat Silsa (literally 460, after a prominent signpost showing the distance from Addis Ababa in kilometres), where an isolated roadside shop sells a high-quality brew for a less than US$0.50 per litre.

Mizan Tefari can also be approached in a southerly direction from Matu. This drive takes at least six hours in a private vehicle and a full day using public transport, most probably swapping vehicles at Gore (25km south of Matu at the junction with the Gambella road; the Tewodros Hotel has rooms for US$3 should you get stuck there overnight) and at Tepi (50km before Mizan Tefari).

WHERE TO STAY AND EAT

Hotel Salayish (28 rooms) 047 335 0865. This smart place is the clear choice in Mizan Tefari; it often fills up quickly, so call ahead. Rooms are compact & clean with private balconies & en-suite hot showers. 2 restaurants are attached, 1 traditional & 1 modern; the food is inexpensive & the bar is popular. *US$11/13.50/18 sgl/dbl/twin.*

Birhan Hotel (42 rooms) 047 335 1330. This newly opened hotel provides a good alternative if the above is full. All rooms have hot-water en suites, though TVs are a hit-or-miss affair. There's also a pleasant terrace bar & restaurant serving meals in the US$2–4 range. *US$8.50/16 dbl/twin.*

Green Pension (15 rooms) 047 335 0538. This adequate hotel is cleaner & quieter than the Fitsum, but poor value by comparison with the Birhan, given that the rooms are not en suite. That

said, around 12 new en-suite rooms are currently under construction above the Commercial Bank of Ethiopia (conveniently located next door) & should be complete by the time this book goes to press. *US$6 with common shower.*

Edene Hotel (20 rooms) 047 335 0542. Situated in a green compound on the southeastern outskirts of town, this small hotel once popular with tour groups is looking more than a little worse for wear these days. In the 3 years since the last edition was researched prices for the rooms haven't increased. However, this has more to do with their grim state than affordability. The restaurant is decent, & a bar with DSTV is attached, but it is advisable to check out food & drink prices before you order – the billing system seems to be rather elastic! *US$2.50 with common shower, US$3 en suite.*

AROUND MIZAN TEFARI To the west of Mizan Tefari you enter an area of particularly lush jungle. On a cool morning you may see steam rising from thatch huts as you pass through low clouds blanketing the roadway. While men in the north of the country carry a walking stick called a *dula*, out west a machete is in every hand. Raining and no umbrella? No problem, a huge *enset* (false banana) leaf will suffice – some leaves are over 3m long! The dirt road here is supposedly all-weather, but there are some sections that are not; extremely slippery mud can sneak up on you and is a true hazard worthy of caution.

Tepi The main attraction of this small town 50km northwest of Mizan Tefari, and the only reason you'd be likely to overnight there (unless you misjudged your public transport timings), is the eponymous coffee estate that lies on its immediate outskirts. Extending over some 6,000ha, the **Tepi Coffee Estate** is the second largest in the country, and of as much interest to travellers for the varied birdlife that rustles through the forest undergrowth – accessible by several walking trails that lead from the plantation guesthouse – as for the opportunity to investigate the production of western Ethiopia's finest export. There is no fee to tour the plantation, but you must first get permission from the 'Tepi Council' office in town.

The best place to stay is the **Tepi Coffee Plantation Guesthouse** (*10 rooms;* 047 556 0062), which lies about 1km from the town centre, charges US$6/7.50 per single/twin for a tiled en-suite chalet, and also boasts a restaurant/bar. (Traditional food and pasta are always available, and Western dishes can be ordered in advance.) The coffee here is expectedly excellent, and at 30 cents a cup it is by far the cheapest anywhere. Unfortunately, other than drinks, the plantation does not sell coffee, but it can be purchased from private growers in the area. Should you fail to secure a

26

room here, the best option is the new **Genet Pension** (*21 rooms;* ⟍ *047 556 2145*) on the road to Jimma about 200m past the turn-off to the plantation. Rooms with common cold shower cost US$5, while en-suite doubles with cold water cost US$6. In the centre, the pick is the **Tegist Hotel** (*26 rooms;* ⟍ *047 556 0227*), which charges US$6/9.50 for a tiled en-suite single/twin, net and cold water only and US$4.50 with common shower.

Just past Tepi, pockets of giant ferns abound. With a little imagination you might think you have been transported back to the Jurassic period, that is until a roadside group of baboons reminds you that you are firmly in the age of mammals. About 60km past Tepi the road forks and then forks again – not to worry, they all soon reconnect. You then ascend into the Highland Bamboo Conservation Area, the browner colour of the bamboo providing contrast to the many surrounding shades of green. About 87km past Tepi you will come to the town of Masha, which is a good stop for lunch if you are headed to Gore and beyond.

Bebeka Coffee Estate
Ethiopia's largest coffee estate sprawls across some 6,500ha of lushly forested hillside 30km south – 45 minutes' drive – of Mizan Tefari along the road towards Kibish. As with the estate outside Tepi, Bebeka is of great interest to birdwatchers, and it offers clean accommodation in a small guesthouse run by the plantation. The hills to the west of Bebeka reputedly still harbour some larger wildlife, including a little-known population of small reddish buffaloes that presumably has closer genetic affinities to the west African forest race than the more widespread savanna.

Kibish and southwest Omo
Set in the semi-arid southwestern lowlands roughly 180km south of Mizan Tefari, the unassuming village of Kibish is the conventional springboard for excursions into the western half of South Omo, an area divided from its better-known eastern counterpart by the long, bridgeless stretch of the Omo River that runs southward from the Sodo–Jimma road to Lake Turkana. Southwest Omo is home to the Surma, a group of some 25,000 Nilotic-speakers divided into three main subgroups – the Mursi, Chai and Tirma – all of which still adhere to a traditional pastoralist lifestyle. Best known for the lip plates worn by their women (see box, *The Mursi*, in *Chapter 24*, page 554), the various Surma subgroups all participate in a rigid but egalitarian political system based around age-sets similar to those of the related Maasai of the Kenyan–Tanzanian border area.

Individual travellers seldom visit southwest Omo due to the paucity of public transport in the region. Some specialist tour operators do offer trips to the region, however, catering to hardy walkers who want to explore a part of South Omo as yet largely unaffected by tourism. A popular option is to spend five or six days hiking from Kibish to the Omo River, overnighting at various traditional villages on the way, then crossing by boat and having a support vehicle to meet you on the other side.

Kibish may be a good starting point for treks, but the village itself highlights the ugly side of cultural tourism, with its Surma residents affecting all manner of quirks associated with the region's other tribes to come across as a sort of South Omo one-stop shop. When I visited, the absence of any market or other focal point other than me meant that I was trailed around by a mob of several dozen adults and children pleading for razors, sweets, pens and medical care and trying to sell everything from lip plates to spears – all uncomfortably inauthentic and voyeuristic, even if it is difficult to say whether I or the villagers were guilty of voyeurism!

There is no public transport to Kibish and the drive from Mizan Tefari takes a good five to six hours in a private 4x4. The first semi-urban punctuation comes 30km south of Mizan Tefari in the form of Bebeka and its fantastically verdant coffee plantation. From here the road descends into more open savanna, studded with tall acacias and bands of riparian woodland that support a rich birdlife. After 70km of this rough road and thinly inhabited countryside the road emerges at Dima, a small market town set on the north bank of the Akabu River. Dima offers the choice of a few hotels, the best of which is the Mahari Hotel, which offers basic rooms, local meals and cold drinks to passing travellers.

After crossing the Akabu, the road runs southeast for another 67km to Tulgit, a small traditional village centred on an American missionary outpost. On the way, you should see the occasional Surma cattle-herder wandering stark naked through the empty countryside, generally armed with a spear or gun as protection. It's another 15km to Kibish, a giddy descent that will probably take at least 45 minutes – hopefully you'll have better luck than I did trying to convince the driver to drop down to first gear rather than sticking in second and relying solely on an overheating brake to control his speed!

The first thing you need to do upon arriving in Kibish is pop into the police station to part with as much money as the officers on duty can extract from you. Simply to visit the marketplace 100m down the road you may be asked to hand over US$6 per person for the village entrance fee, US$12 for a local guide and US$0.30 for every photograph you take. An additional fee is charged to camp in the police station – no other accommodation options exist.

MATU

This attractive highland town, the former capital of the defunct Illubador province, is of interest to travellers primarily as the springboard for the descent into the steamy tropical lowlands that flank the Baro River and the port of Gambella. Despite its well-wooded hilly surrounds, it is an unremarkable sort of place: a typically sprawling highland town, founded in 1913, at an altitude of 1,600m near the western escarpment of the Ethiopian Highlands, and today dotted with a few smart but rather unconvincing administrative buildings. The central market is lively and welcoming, or you could stretch your legs by taking a short walk to the forest-fringed Sor River, which crosses the Bedele road some 2km northeast of the town centre (a good spot for guereza monkeys). Further afield, an excellent goal for a day trip is the impressive Sor Waterfall (see box, *Sor Waterfall*, page 585).

GETTING THERE AND AWAY Coming from Mizan Tefari, a reasonably maintained 220km dirt road runs northward to Matu via Tepi and Gore, a journey that should take up to six hours in a private vehicle and the best part of a full day by bus. Heading west from Matu, a daily bus service to Gambella leaves in either direction at around 06.00; with the road now newly tarred the 170km journey takes around four hours.

Coming from Jimma or Nekemte, Matu lies about 115km from Bedele along an eclectically surfaced road – at least 60% is good asphalt or all-weather dirt, some sections are smooth gravel, some rough gravel, and worst of all are several stretches of severely pot-holed asphalt. The drive between Bedele and Matu takes about two to three hours in a private vehicle or four to five hours by bus. Direct buses run between Jimma and Matu but coming from Nekemte you will probably have to change buses (and possibly spend the night) at Bedele.

WHERE TO STAY AND EAT

Sena Hotel (44 rooms) 047 441 4286. Situated on the right side of the main road as you enter town from Bedele, this long-serving establishment has recently been extended with the addition of 16 new rooms. While it remains a popular choice, the 30% *faranji* surcharge can be a little hard to swallow. It has an excellent restaurant with very quick service, & a busy bar with a veranda. The only drawback, at least if you need an early start to catch a bus, is that it is a 10min walk from the bus station. *US$4 with common shower, US$9 en suite.*

Anteneh Hotel (19 rooms) 047 441 1002. With a convenient location across from the bus station, this is easily the most appealing hotel in town; it escapes top honours only for its lack of a restaurant or nearby food options. The rooms too, though spacious & well priced, are starting to fray & there's no hot water. Cold drinks are available. *US$6 with common shower, US$7.50 ¾ bed en suite.*

Lucy Tensae Hotel (29 rooms) 047 441 1557. This hotel next to the Sena is similar in standard & better value, given the one-price-for-all policy. Rooms are clean & hot water is available. The restaurant is adequate, & the bar can be quite lively. *US$2.50 with common shower, US$7.50 en suite.*

Boggalach Wayaa Baruu Hotel (37 rooms) 047 441 1184. One of the better basic hotels closer to the bus station, this hotel offers a range of rooms varying in price depending on the size of the room & quality of mattress (some rooms have spring mattresses, others foam). All share a common shower. Traditional food is always available, but Western dishes must be ordered in advance. *US$2.5–4.*

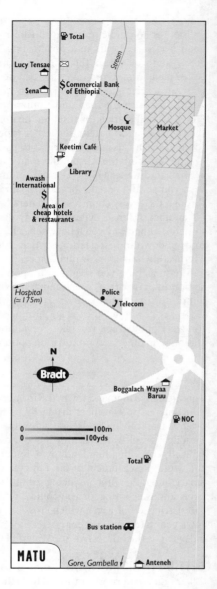

MATU

Gore, Gambella Anteneh

BEDELE

This small, nondescript town is something of a route focus, lying at the junction of the roads to Matu, Jimma and Nekemte. Bedele's main claim to fame is that it is the home of Ethiopia's newest and best beer factory, the **Bedele Brewery**, which lies about 2km out of town and is owned by Heineken. Tourists are welcome to stop by for a taste test (US$0.20/0.40 for a standard/jumbo draught beer) or take a free factory tour on Wednesdays and Fridays provided they have a passport to hand. Also worth a look might be the forested hill a kilometre or so past the market, known locally as Mutay Mountain. According to a local kid, this hill is crawling with lions and tigers; the odd yeti too, no doubt, had I asked. Guereza monkeys and forest birds seem more likely. To get there, follow the Nekemte road out of town until you get to a gated police checkpoint. Just past this there is a 'water treatment' sign on the left and a path that leads to the base of the hill.

The road west from Bedele towards Matu is among the most densely forested in western Ethiopia, crossing several large rivers and bypassing some attractive waterfalls. The forest here has a great diversity of tree species; olive baboons are abundant, vervet monkeys and guereza monkeys are reasonably common, and birdwatching should be excellent. A good base would be the village of **Yayu**, about 40km from Matu along the Bedele road, which boasts a couple of very basic **hotels** serving reasonable food. The area immediately around Yayu is quite cultivated, but there are some lovely forested hills about 2km along the main road to Bedele.

GETTING THERE AND AWAY Bedele is situated at a crossroads roughly 105km south of Nekemte, 115km east of Matu and 135km north of Jimma. In all cases, expect the drive there to take around two hours in a private vehicle and three to four hours by bus. There are direct buses between Jimma and Nekemte and between Jimma and Matu, so on either of these routes you will pass straight through Bedele. There is, however, no direct transport between Matu and Nekemte; on this route you will have to take a Jimma-bound bus as far as Bedele, then try to find a bus coming *from* Jimma to take you where you want to go. This shouldn't normally be a problem, but you may have to overnight in Bedele. If you do stay over in Bedele, you can skip the 06.00 start for once and enjoy a bit of a lie-in and breakfast. Buses pass through Bedele between 10.00 and midday.

SOR WATERFALL

The main attraction in the vicinity of Matu is the Sor Waterfall, which can be reached by following the Gore road west out of town for 7km, then turning left at the sign for the Gore Water Treatment Plant to follow a rough and muddy track that passes the water treatment plant after 7.5km and arrives at the village of Becho after another 5.5km. From Becho, you can drive or walk along an even rougher track for about 4km, before heading onto an indistinct and slippery footpath through a patch of dense jungle alive with creepers, butterflies, baboons, guereza monkeys and birds – most visibly silvery-cheeked hornbill, Heuglin's robin-chat and Ethiopian oriole. More than likely you'll attract an entourage of enthusiastic children to lead you in the right direction, but if not, anybody will point you the right way – *fafuati* is the local word for waterfall!

After about 30 minutes of slipping and tripping through the forest, you'll hear the waterfall, the signal for a steep ten-minute descent – watch out for the vicious nettles – to a viewpoint near the top of a gorge. It is an impressive sight even in the dry season, plunging about 20m over a sheer rock amphitheatre surrounded by tall tree ferns and mist forest, and must be thoroughly spectacular after heavy rain. It is possible to walk to the bottom of the gorge and swim in the chilly pool at the waterfall's base.

The excursion is straightforward if you have a 4x4 vehicle, and you should be able to do the round trip in three to four hours. There is limited public transport from Matu to Becho in the form of 4x4 'taxis', but it all leaves in the morning and turns back almost immediately, so you'll either have to charter a vehicle or plan on staying in one of the very basic, US$1.50 rooms attached to the *buna bet* (coffee shop) in Bechu.

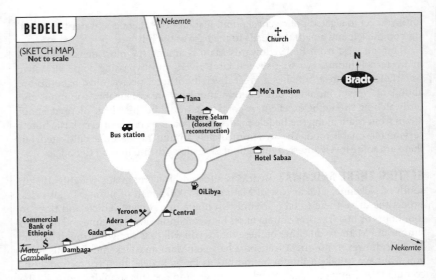

WHERE TO STAY AND EAT

 Hotel Hagere Selam (39 rooms) ℡047 445 0123/59. By far the best lodging in Bedele, this long-standing favourite was being completely rebuilt on our most recent visit in late 2011. Going by the signboard it should be quite impressive when complete. Watch this space.

Mo'a Pension (30 rooms) ℡047 445 0141. Until the Selam reopens, this newly expanded pension is currently the best accommodation offering in Bedele. Rooms come in 3 classes, varying from basic rooms with common shower to smart en-suite tiled doubles with hot water & TV. The downside however is it lacks a main road entrance (access is via a very rough side dirt road

or through the pension's original – & somewhat seedy – bar) & the central courtyard restaurant with its movie screen projector is a popular local hangout, meaning it can be noisy especially when the football is on. *US$2.50/5.50 old/new rooms with common shower, US$9 en-suite dbl.*

Tana Hotel (40 rooms) ℡047 445 0169. Located near the bus station, this hotel is the pick of the cheapies & a passable choice for the night should Mo'a be full & the Selam not reopened. The older rooms have ¾ beds & common shower, while the newer but still scruffy rooms have private en suite with cold shower. *US$2.50 common shower, US$4 en suite.*

NEKEMTE

Formerly known as Lekemti, Nekemte, which lies about 200km west of Ambo by road, was until 1994 the capital of Wolega region, and today it serves as the administrative centre for the East Wolega zone of Oromia region. The lushly forested area around Nekemte is one of the most agriculturally productive in Ethiopia, and it boasts considerable mineral wealth in the form of gold, platinum, copper, iron and lead. Nekemte itself is a leafy, pretty and (during the rainy season) very muddy small town, centred on a pair of traffic roundabouts set some 200m apart. Its likeable tropical ambience is undermined by an unusually poor selection of hotels and the inordinate degree of pointing, yelling and giggling directed at any passing *faranji* – nothing hostile, but rather exhausting.

High on the list of Nekemte's redeeming features is the excellent **Wolega Museum** (⏲ *09.00–12.30 & 14.30–17.30 Tue–Sun; entrance US$2*), which was established in 1989 on the northern traffic roundabout, and is definitely one of the best ethnographic museums in the country. Displays include a vast collection of Oromo artefacts such as leatherware, basketwork, woodcarvings and musical instruments, as well as the first Bible translated into the local Oromo dialect. The guide speaks little English but his imaginatively mimed demonstrations of how the various artefacts are made or used are almost as entertaining as the exhibits themselves. Also worth a look if you have time is **Kumsa Moroda Palace** (*⌚ 09.00–12.30 & 14.30–17.30 Tue–Sun; www.hambisfoundation.org; entrance US$2*), located around 1km from Nekemte on the road to Bure, noted for its authentic Oromo architectural style and for its political significance, having served as a military camp for much of the 20th century.

GETTING THERE AND AWAY The roughly 325km drive from Addis Ababa to Nekemte via Ambo takes around five to six hours in a private vehicle, not allowing for stops. The scenery between Ambo and Nekemte is wonderful. Past Guder, the road climbs into a highland area with panoramic views across the surrounding valleys and mountains. The whole area is well watered: the road crosses several fast-flowing streams and, after Bako, the cultivation and moorland give way to thick woodland and patches of forest. Vervet monkeys and a variety of widow birds can be seen from the road.

There are direct buses between Addis Ababa and Nekemte. If you are leaving from Ambo, you may be better off catching a bus from Ambo to Bako, where you can pick up another bus to Nekemte. With a reasonably early start – 09.00 at the latest – you should make it through to Nekemte in a day, but transport out of Bako peters out at around 13.00. There are several **hotels in Bako** if you do get stuck; the food at the Gibe Hotel is recommended.

A little-used but reasonably good 250km dirt road also connects Nekemte to Bure on the surfaced road between Addis Ababa and Bahir Dar. Using private transport, it is perfectly possible to travel between Nekemte and Bahir Dar in one (long) day

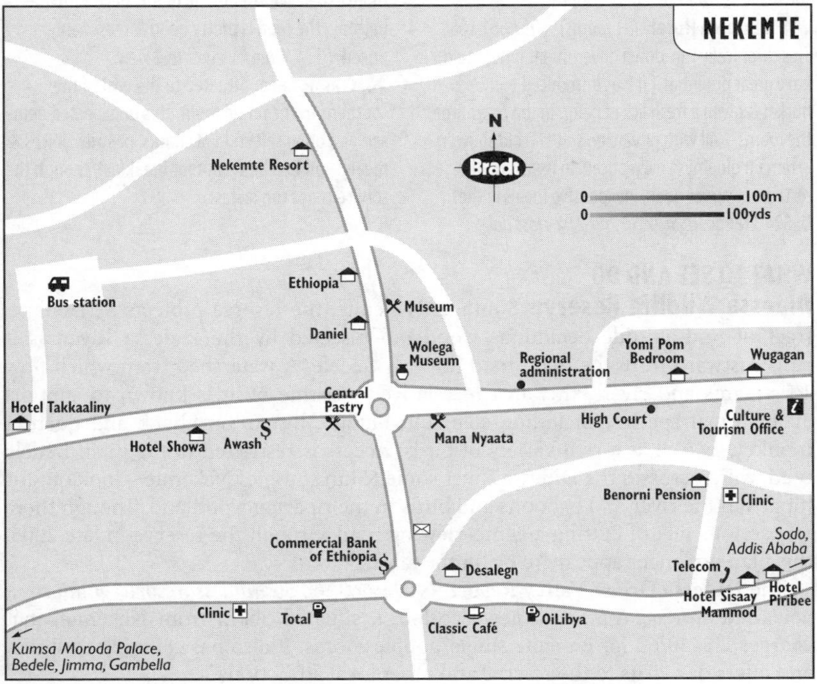

using this road, but travellers dependent on public transport will probably need to break up the trip at Kosober, which straddles the road between Bure and Bahir Dar.

For details of travelling on to Gambella via Dembidolo, see the *Getting there and away* section under *Gambella* in *Chapter 27*, page 597. If you are doing your own navigating, note that there are two towns called Arjo in this area – one is on the road to Gimbi and the other on the road to Bedele.

WHERE TO STAY AND EAT

Benori Pension (24 rooms) ☎ 057 661 4096; e brbfjerry@yahoo.com. Nekemte's newest offering is this smart multi-storey pension tucked off the main road about a block back from the Telecom office. The slick modern rooms come with tiled floors, hot-shower en suite & free Wi-Fi, but seem a little over-priced given the compact size of the rooms & current lack of restaurant. The latter should be fixed with the expected opening of a new restaurant next door. *US$18/27 dbl/twin inc b/fast.*

Desalegen Hotel (30 rooms) ☎ 057 661 6162; f 057 661 5555; e dessalegen.hotel@ gmail.com. This smart 5-storey hotel near the roundabout comes in a close second to the Benori in terms of newness & quality, but wins points for its budget-friendly range of bright clean rooms & its good restaurant & bar. Internet is also available for less than US$0.05/min. *US$6 using common shower, US$14/19.50 en-suite dbl/twin.*

Ethiopia Hotel (31 rooms) ☎ 057 661 1088. This chronically run-down government hotel could have great potential if it was introduced to mop & bucket & given a fresh lick of paint. In the meantime, the rooms – all with private en suite & cold shower – remain gloomy & over-priced. In its favour, the restaurant serves good, inexpensive meals in the US$2–3 range. *US$6/7.50 2nd-/1st-class dbl.*

Nekemte Resort (17 rooms) m 0922 252 293. Previously known as the Anger Hotel, this one-time government training centre situated a couple of hundred metres north of the northern traffic roundabout is now under new management. While plans are afoot to renovate the entire property, the rooms as they stand retain a sterile dorm-like air. The grounds though are attractive & the food is pretty good & cheap at around US$1.50–3.50 per dish. *US$5 using common shower, US$6.50 en suite.*

Wugagan Hotel (42 rooms) ☎ 057 661 1508. The rooms at Nekemte's other government hotel are a little brighter & more spacious than those at the Ethiopia, but not as fresh as the newly repainted façade would have you believe. All rooms have an en suite with hot water – though water supply can be erratic – while the slightly more expensive street-side rooms have a private balcony. The food is pretty good & reasonably priced. *US$5/6 back view/street view.*

✗ **Classic Café** Situated to the east of the southern traffic roundabout, this unexpected gem serves a good selection of snacks, pastries, juices & meals – an excellent spot for breakfast, though the service is not the fastest.

WHAT TO SEE AND DO

Didessa Wildlife Reserve South of Nekemte, the reserve protects a 1,300km² tract of mid-altitude deciduous woodland bisected by the Didessa River as it runs eastward from the main road towards Bedele. A watershed from which flow 15 streams and rivers, this area of relatively pristine bush is known to support 30 mammal species, including elephant, buffalo, hippo, bushbuck and guereza monkey, as well as a rich variety of birds. Access is restricted to the main Bedele road, which crosses the Didessa River some 65km south of Nekemte – look out for hippos in the river and baboons and birds in the riparian woodland. Though there was serious talk of cutting a game-viewing road through the reserve in late 2005, this plan no longer appears to be on the table.

The **Didessa Green Valley Resort** (☎ 011 663 9575; e didessaresort@gmail.com; www.didessaresort.com) is a new eco-lodge, situated 50km from Nekemte, that charges US$40/60 for en-suite single/double rooms. It also has camping facilities, and offers day visits to the reserve and other local attractions.

27

Gambella

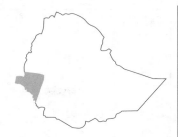

The small westerly state of Gambella, boasting a population of just over 300,000, is something of an anomaly within Ethiopia, displaying stronger historical, ethnic and climatic links to neighbouring Sudan than to the highlands to its east. Hot, humid, low-lying and swampy, Gambella is dominated geographically by the sluggish Baro River and its various tributaries, all of which eventually flow across the border into the Blue Nile – navigable from the port of Gambella on the northern bank of the Baro all the way to its confluence with the White Nile at Khartoum.

The only real tourist attraction in the region is the remote **Gambella National Park**, which hosts several rare antelope and bird species, but requires considerable effort – as well as a reliable 4x4 and experienced driver – to visit. Unless you are planning to explore the national park, when the dry season has obvious advantages, the best time to visit Gambella is during the rainy season of May to October, when the scenery is lush and green, and temperatures seldom hit the peaks of 40°C or more that are regularly recorded during February and March.

Two main ethnic groups live in Gambella. The Anuwak speak a language closely related to that of the Luo in Kenya, and are fishermen and mixed agriculturists by tradition. They are strikingly tall and very dark-skinned for Ethiopians. Their elegantly enclosed homesteads give the region much of its character, and the name Gambella derives from the Anuwak name for the *Gardenia lutea* tree that grows widely in the surrounding area. The also dark-skinned and even taller Nuer originated in Nilotic-speaking parts of Sudan. Despite being relatively recent arrivals in this area, they are now the numerically dominant group in Gambella. Nuer men were once marked with six cuts across their forehead as a rite of passage, but the practice is much less common now. Some Anuwak men have facial scarification at their temples.

There is a long history of tension between Anuwak and Nuer, fuelled in part by Sudan People's Liberation Army (SPLA) incursions from Sudan, and parts of the region have been unsafe for travel since the end of 2003, when an attack on a UN truck sparked a series of riots that left more than 150 people dead, destroyed hundreds of homes and caused several thousand villagers to flee across the border into Sudan. This tension spilt over into Gambella town itself in early 2004, when local militants led a series of fatal attacks on highlanders resident in the town, causing Ethiopian Airlines to suspend all flights to Gambella for several months. Things seemed fairly harmonious when we revisited the area in 2011, but it would certainly be advisable to seek current advice before heading this way.

GAMBELLA

Gambella is an oddity among Ethiopian towns, and a most appealing one. Lying at an altitude of 450m in the swampy, mosquito-ridden lowlands west of the Ethiopian

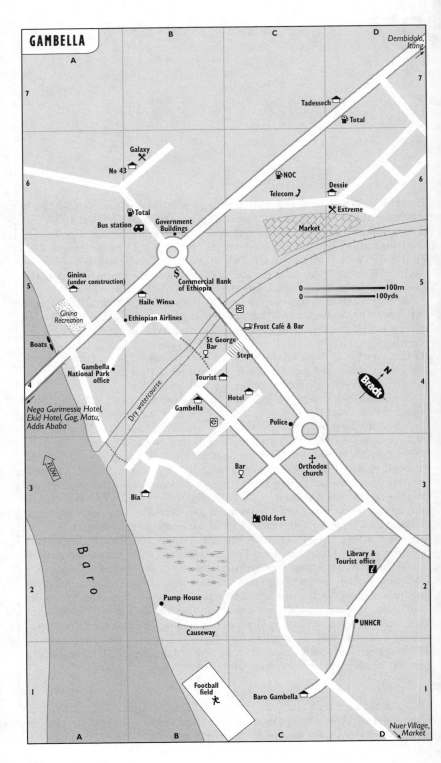

GAMBELLA

Dembidolo, Itang

Tadessech

Total

Galaxy

No 43

NOC

Telecom

Dessie

Extreme

Total

Bus station

Government Buildings

Market

Ginina (under construction)

Commercial Bank of Ethiopia

Haile Winsa

Ginina Recreation

Ethiopian Airlines

Frost Café & Bar

Boats

St George Bar

Steps

Gambella National Park office

Tourist

Nega Gurimessa Hotel, Ekid Hotel, Gog, Matu, Addis Ababa

Hotel

Gambella

Police

FLOW

Bar

Orthodox church

Bia

Dry watercourse

Old fort

Library & Tourist office

B a r o

Pump House

UNHCR

Causeway

Football field

Baro Gambella

Nuer Village, Market

0 _____ 100m
0 _____ 100yds

Bradt

N

Plateau, the port exudes an atmosphere of tropical languor, dictated as much by its lush riverine vegetation and almost unbearable humidity as by its remoteness from just about everywhere else. This powerful sense of place is underscored by the presence of the Baro River, whose brown waters roll lazily past town to create an almost absurdly accurate fulfilment of every Western archetype of a tropical riverport – particularly during the rainy season, nowhere else in Ethiopia is quite so overwhelmingly Conradian, so cinematically African!

Part of Gambella's charm lies in its spacious, amorphous layout. Years ago, when I first entered the town via the large, impressive concrete bridge over the Baro, I expected something equally grand. Instead, I found myself deposited at the nominal bus station (a bare patch of ground in front of a Total garage) with a large roundabout to my right and no obvious evidence of a town anywhere in sight. After a slightly panicky walkabout, I established that what passes for the town centre lies hidden in a well-wooded dip between the main road and the river. Gambella, as it transpired, isn't really a town, but two wide avenues spasmodically lined with government buildings, and a scattering of small village-like hut clusters kept discrete by patches of forest, swamp and streams. Today, almost all of the streets here are paved, but for little reason save the light traffic of *tuk-tuks*.

Whatever the climate between locals, as far as a *faranji* need be concerned Gambella couldn't be a friendlier town. I found it rather sad that, *en route* to Gambella, I was repeatedly warned by highlanders of the backwardness of the people ('it is not good place for you'). In my opinion, the Nuer and Anuwak could teach many highlanders a thing or two about civility to foreigners. Wherever I went I was greeted in Nuer or Anuwak ('*Mali*' and '*Derichot*' are the respective greetings); several times English-speakers came up to exchange greetings and shake hands with no hint of a motive other than friendliness; and the children were bashfully playful rather than loud and demanding. On the few occasions I was yelled at in Gambella, I invariably turned around to see the distinctive features of a highlander. Don't be put off by advance notices – Gambella is a lovely place and the people are utterly charming.

Among its other singularities, Gambella has a rather curious modern history. In the late 19th century Sudan fell under British rule, and the Baro, which is navigable as far as Khartoum, was seen by both Britain and Ethiopia as an excellent highway for exporting coffee and other produce from the fertile western highlands to Sudan and Egypt. The Ethiopian emperor granted Britain use of part of Ethiopia as a free port in 1902 and, after an unsuccessful attempt to establish a port elsewhere, Gambella was established in 1907. This tiny British territory, a few hundred hectares in size, was bounded by the Baro River to the south, the tributary which now bisects the town to the west, the patch of forest to the east of the modern town, and the small conical hill to its north. Gambella became a prosperous trade centre as ships from Khartoum sailed in regularly during the rainy season when the water was high, taking seven days downriver and 11 days upriver. The Italians captured Gambella in 1936, when the now-ruined fort near the Gambella Hotel was built, but it was returned to Britain after a bloody battle in 1941. Gambella then became part of Sudan in 1951, but it was re-incorporated into Ethiopia five years later. The port ceased functioning under the Mengistu regime and it remains closed because of ongoing tension between the SPLA and the Ethiopian government.

Gambella offers little in the way of organised sightseeing, and its remoteness hardly makes it a prime target for mass tourism. The area is, however, rich in wildlife, and the layout of the town is such that just strolling around you can see plenty of birds and monkeys. It is worth devoting some time to the bridge over the Baro, which only one vehicle is permitted to cross at a time. Photographing the bridge, or from the bridge, may or may not be forbidden, dependent most probably on the attitude of the guard on duty, so do ask permission before you pull out a camera. To the west of the bridge is a shady avenue that follows the river's course – one of Gambella's few apparent British relics, along with a group of old gravestones near the port.

Local people wash and swim here without apparent concern, but every now and again somebody is taken by a crocodile, so it would definitely be chancy to leap into the water in areas not used by locals. The people of Gambella will still caution travellers with the sad story of Bill Olsen, the Peace Corps volunteer who took a holiday in Gambella in 1966, ignored local advice about a large crocodile known to live in a certain part of the river, and was never seen alive again. On the whole, better to stick to your hotel shower than to tempt a similar fate by leaping into the muddy Baro!

Gambella's main attraction is its singular and absorbing sense of place, and wonderfully evocative atmosphere. Specific points of interest are the ruined Italian fort close to the river, the swamp between the river and the fort, the isolated hill about 1km north of the town centre, and the village of traditional homesteads running down towards the river from the small market about 100m east of the Baro Gambella Hotel. In the market, you can buy the woven baskets and bubble pipes that are characteristic of the area, while birders might want to head down to the river's edge immediately downriver of the bridge in search of the rare Egyptian plover, a regular visitor.

GETTING THERE AND AWAY Ethiopian Airlines flies from Addis Ababa to Gambella twice weekly (US$110). The airport lies about 15km out of town, and there are no taxis, so you will need to hitch a ride in with a fellow passenger or ask the people at the **Ethiopian Airlines Office** [590 B5] (✆ 047 551 0099) to help you out.

If you are looping through the west, the most obvious (though emphatically neither the best nor the shortest) route between Nekemte and Gambella runs through Gimbi and Dembidolo (see *Dembidolo*, page 595). Clashes between Oromo and Beni-Shangul people have led to incidents of violence and banditry along this route, so do check the current situation before heading this way. Even when things are calm, this route is generally impassable during the rains, in which case the alternative route using the far better road through Bedele, Matu and Bure is advised. With the road between Gore and Gambella now newly tarred, the drive from Matu to Gambella should take around three hours, but while the roads throughout the western region of Ethiopia are slowly being upgraded, still allow a full day to reach Gambella from either Nekemte or Jimma in a private vehicle. Using public transport, you will have to catch the 06.00 bus from Nekemte or Jimma to Bedele, which takes three to four hours. At Bedele, you should be able to find transport on to Matu the same day. You will, however, have to overnight in Matu before heading on to Gambella. Should you be coming from Mizan Tefari, the trip to Gambella can be made in one day in a private vehicle.

Coming from Matu or Mizan Tefari, the turn-off for Gambella is at the small town of Gore. About 10km beyond you will pass through the enormous Gumaro Tea Plantation, with neatly manicured plants covering the fields into the distance. From Gore, it takes 90 minutes or so to reach the small highland village of Bure, a popular lunch stop for bus drivers. There isn't much to see at Bure today but Alexander Bulatovich, who passed through the village in 1897, mentioned that it lay at the junction of several trade routes and formed 'an important point of barter with tribes on this side of the Baro ... and market for coffee'. Bulatovich described how people from the lowlands 'bring for sale elephant tusks and sometimes their livestock, and in exchange for that they buy ornaments, beads and cloth'. From Bure, you descend almost 1km in altitude to the Baro Valley, a spectacular switchback drive through tall elephant grass, passing several troops of olive baboon along the way.

The road follows the course of the Baro River for a while before crossing one of its tributaries on a rather rickety wooden bridge, then about 30km before Gambella there's a police roadblock, near to the substantial Sudanese refugee village of Bonga, which now grows enough maize to be self-sufficient. Approaching Gambella, the road passes through a thinly populated and primal savanna of acacias and tall clumped grass interspersed with bald granite hills – the atmosphere is such that I found myself half expecting to see an elephant cross the road at any minute, even though I know there is no longer much wildlife in the area. The 146km stretch of road between Gore and Gambella has now been tarred in its entirety. In a private vehicle the trip should take under two hours.

TOURIST INFORMATION The unsigned **Gambella Bureau of Culture & Tourism** [590 D2] (*047 551 2351;* ⏱ *07.30–12.30 & 15.00–17.30 Mon–Fri*) is located in the same building as the excellent library, on the opposite side of the road before you reach the **UNHCR headquarters** [590 D2]. Here you can get information about visiting the national park, as well as surrounding villages, lakes and waterfalls. The people at the **Gambella National Park office** [590 A4] (*047 551 0912;* ⏱ *07.30–12.30 & 15.00–17.30 Mon–Fri*, located near the Ethiopian Airlines office, are also knowledgeable and helpful when it comes to information about exploring outlying parts of Gambella state. It's also here where you must pay your park fees.

WHERE TO STAY
Budget

🏠 **Tadessech Hotel** [590 D7] (14 rooms)
047 551 0559. This new 2-storey pink hotel is located opposite the Total filling station on the road to Dembidolo. Rooms all have cold-water en suite with nets, TV & fan. Yet while the rooms are impressively clean & neat, they're over-priced especially given that *faranji* pay double, breakfast isn't included & at the time of inspection there was no restaurant, bar or other tourist facilities to speak of. *US$18 en-suite dbl.*

🏠 **Nega Gurimessa Hotel** [off map 590 A4] (10 rooms) m 0911 990 146/205 972. Similarly priced as the above, this new place situated on the right-hand side of the road immediately before the bridge as you enter Gambella feels better value given its pretty riverside location & attractively landscaped setting. The freshly finished double rooms are light & airy & come complete with tiled floors, cold-shower en suite, DSTV, fans & nets. A restaurant & bar are also attached. *US$18 en-suite dbl.*

🏠 **Baro Gambella Hotel** [590 C1] (47 rooms)
047 551 0044; e jediwondi@gmail.com. Set in potentially very attractive but poorly maintained grounds overlooking the northern bank of the Baro

River about 1km east of the town centre, this former government hotel, with its time-worn rooms in varying states of disrepair, is lousy value. The good news is that it is set for an upgrade with ambitious new plans including 24 AC rooms, a pool, a conference hall & wellness centre. In the meantime, the hotel has a steamily decrepit charm in keeping with the overall mood of Gambella. There is DSTV in the bar, plenty of monkeys & birds roam the gardens, the food is pretty good, & the staff do an impressive job of keeping ready a supply of cold beers & sodas in the face of regular power cuts & intense natural heat. *US$13/14 en-suite twin/dbl.*

Shoestring

🏠 **No 43 Hotel** [590 B6] (20 rooms) m 0911 606 423. Previously known as the Opena Hotel, this newly expanded place situated opposite the bus station seems fair value with 10 basic rooms with common shower & 10 more with private en suite, nets & fans. A decent restaurant & bar are also attached. *US$3 using common shower, US$7.50 en suite.*

🏠 **Bia Hotel** [590 B3] (10 rooms) 047 551 1611. This hotel overlooking the river, 100m upriver of the bridge, has a perfect location & attractive green grounds, but the en-suite rooms with ¾ bed are rather run-down, cramped & depressing. Still it does have fans, & it has to be classed as a tempting option given the price. The attached bar is a good place for a riverside drink but (like most other hotels in Gambella) has some potential to disrupt attempts at an early night. *US$6 sgl or dbl*.

🏠 **Tourist Hotel** [590 B4] (22 rooms) **m** 0912 765 866. The pick of a less than tempting batch of budget dives scattered around Gambella, this adequate hotel offers moderately grubby rooms with ¾ bed & access to the common hot shower. The attached bar seems more sedate than most, but on weekends it runs drink specials such as the drink-10-beers-&-get-free-popcorn-&-coffee touted on our most recent visit hoping to lure the crowds away from the St George Bar across the road. So it may get noisy! *US$6.*

✗ **WHERE TO EAT** Located across from the Dessie Hotel, the **Extreme Café** [590 D6] is extremely popular for breakfast. *Ful* is a speciality, and though no two bowls looked alike, they were all good! The **Galaxy Bar & Restaurant** [590 A6] near No 43 Hotel serves a decent line-up of local and European dishes as well as good fish when available.

WHAT TO SEE AND DO The **Gambella Library** [590 D2] comes as quite a surprise. Most of the books here are in English, including a large selection of popular novels and classic literature. Cool and quiet, it's a great place to spend a lazy afternoon. Along the Baro, just down from the riverboat port, the **Ginina Recreation** is a great place to join in a local game of fuse ball or enjoy a coffee ceremony under the shade of a tree.

On the outskirts of town past the Baro Gambella Hotel, the **Nuer Village** [off map 590 D1] is well worth a visit. The people here are very friendly, and there was zero begging, just lots of handshakes and smiles and greetings of '*Mali*'. You might see *injera* being made, milk being portioned for sale, men squatting in a circle cutting up meat, or snuff laid out to dry. You'll have to visit the tourist office first to arrange a guide (US$6), get a letter of permission and pay the US$6 per person entry fee. The tourist office can also arrange visits to nearby **Anuwak Village**.

GAMBELLA NATIONAL PARK AND SURROUNDS

(*National park office* ☎ *047 551 0912; entrance US$5.50 pp/day; US$1.50 per vehicle; US$9 for a guide; US$9 for a scout*) This remote and swampy park was established primarily to protect its populations of two endangered wetland antelope whose range is restricted to this part of Ethiopia and adjacent regions in southern Sudan: the white-eared kob and the Nile lechwe. The park has never been fully protected, and the wildlife today has to compete with cotton plantations and Sudanese refugee or resettlement camps. Nevertheless, the area does support significant – though rapidly shrinking – populations of elephant, buffalo and lion, as well as roan antelope, tiang, Lelwel hartebeest, olive baboon and guereza monkey.

Several interesting birds inhabit the Gambella National Park, notably Ethiopia's only population of the elusive and weird-looking shoebill stork, a papyrus dweller that has been recorded in the area just once since the 1960s, more likely due to a paucity of observers than any serious decline in numbers. Other interesting and unusual species found in the park include the country's only population of the localised Uelle paradise whydah, the lovely red-throated and little green bee-eaters, as well as black-faced firefinch, red-necked buzzard, Egyptian plover, African skimmer and several localised but drab cisticolas and other warblers.

According to the helpful warden, who can be contacted at the national park office in town, the best part of the park for game viewing is called Matara and lies about 185km west of Gambella town along a road running through the village of Inwany on the southern bank of the Baro. White-eared kob and Nile lechwe are both likely to seen in the Matara area, but its distance from town and the poor condition of the road means that you would need a reliable 4x4 to get there, and should plan on camping for at least one night. You'd also need to bring all your own food and drink, and arrange a game scout and possibly an armed guard through the national park office.

Less challenging would be to head south to the small towns of Abobo and Agenga, which lie on the recently redrawn eastern boundary of the national park, 42km and 105km respectively from Gambella town. Although animals might be seen anywhere in this area (or, for that matter, nowhere), one worthwhile stop just a few kilometres from Abobo is at Lake Alwara. Abobo has a few basic **lodgings**, and can be reached by public transport (currently only on Mondays and Fridays, when there is a convoy to tie in with the local market). Further south, Agenga can be reached in about three hours in a private 4x4, and has been earmarked as the site of the new national park headquarters, but is currently of limited interest in terms of wildlife-viewing possibilities. Also of interest is the very scenic Lake Tata, which lies off the road between Abobo and Gog. Occasional buses from Gambella to Gog via Abobo can drop you at the gravel junction to Lake Tata, from where it's less than an hour on foot to the shore. **Anuwak Village** lies alongside the lake. To visit the village you'll need to arrange a permission letter and a local guide at the tourist office in Gambella [590 D2] as well as pay a US$6 entrance fee.

Another possibility would be to follow the good dirt road that runs parallel to the Baro River (and the northern boundary of Gambella National Park) from Gambella to the Sudanese border at Jikawa. This takes you through an area inhabited by Anuwak fishermen and Nuer pastoralists whose lifestyles are virtually untouched by Western influences. This is best seen at the sprawling village of Itang, which stands on the northern bank of the Baro some 7km south of the Jikawa road along an unsignposted feeder road 50km from Gambella. At least one bus connects Gambella and Itang daily, taking about two hours in either direction, and a couple of shops around the busy traditional market serve tea and basic food. So far as I can ascertain there is no accommodation so you would need to ask around for a bed in a local dwelling or to arrange to camp at the police station. The area is rich in birds not easily seen elsewhere in Ethiopia, and there is some wildlife around (most visibly bushbuck, oribi and baboon). It is also potentially volatile, due to its location on the Sudanese border, so do make enquiries before heading off – especially if you intend to continue onward to the equally traditional border village of Jikawa.

DEMBIDOLO

Founded in the 19th century on the western edge of the Ethiopian Highlands, Dembidolo peaked in importance in the early 20th century, when it formed an important stop along the trade route to Sudan via Gambella and the Baro River. Dembidolo served for some decades as the major commercial centre and administrative capital of Wolega province, but has subsequently become something of a backwater, serviced by erratic public transport and inaccessible during the rainy season. However, Dembidolo does have the distinction of being the largest town along the 340km northern route between Nekemte and Gambella and is a good base for the newly designated **Dhati Walal National Park**, located near Kelem, which is known for its buffaloes. Do check the safety situation before visiting, as tribal conflict between the Oromo and the Beni-Shangul could be an issue.

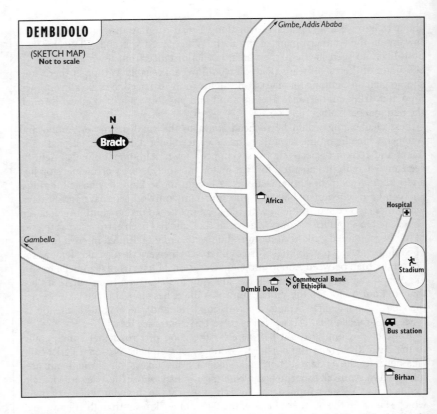

GETTING THERE AND AWAY Public transport through Dembidolo is of the hit-and-miss variety. There is, in theory, a daily bus between Nekemte and Dembidolo. This leaves in either direction at anytime between 05.30 and 07.00, costs an unusually steep US$6, and takes anything from ten to 15 hours, depending on the state of the – normally horrendous – road and the number of breakdowns. If this bus isn't running, then you'll probably have to change vehicles at Gimbi, 113km from Nekemte and 100km from Dembidolo. In the opposite direction, a daily minibus sometimes runs between Dembidolo and Gambella, leaving Gambella at 06.00, reaching Dembidolo at midday or so, before turning around back to Gambella. And sometimes it doesn't – one reader spent three days stranded in Dembidolo (during the dry season) until he found a lift with a truck on to Gambella. He also points out that if the truck had broken down, he could have been in for a long wait ('bring plenty of Ambo' is his advice. After rain, no vehicles at all run along this road.

🏠 **WHERE TO STAY** There are a few hotels in Dembidolo, of which the best is the new multi-storey **Dembi Dollo Hotel** (*14 rooms*; \ *057 555 2366*), located near the Commercial Bank of Ethiopia on the road to the hospital. Clean en-suite rooms with hot water cost between US$4.50 and US$6 depending on the size and location of room (rooms on the top floors are smaller and cheaper) and there's a good patisserie on the ground floor. Alternatively, the long-serving **Birhan Hotel** (*24 rooms*; \ *057 555 0313*) near the bus station has adequate common/private shower rooms for US$4/5.50 as well as a friendly bar with satellite television.

Appendix 1

LANGUAGE

With thanks to Yared Belete of Grant Express Travel & Tours Services (GETTS)

Amharigna (pronounced Amharinya and more often known outside the country as Amharic) is a Semitic language that derives from Ge'ez, the language of the Axumites and the Ethiopian Orthodox Church to this day. Amharigna is the first language of the Amhara people who live in north-central Ethiopia. Along with English, Amharigna is still the official language of Ethiopia and is thus the language most often used between Ethiopians of different linguistic backgrounds, performing a similar role to that of Swahili in the rest of east Africa.

In practical terms, you will find that most Ethiopians who have been to high school speak passable, if idiosyncratic, English, though in many cases they get little opportunity to use it, and so are rather rusty. Except in Tigrai and remote rural areas, almost everyone speaks some Amharigna, and – unless you stay exclusively in tourist hotels – you will find it difficult to get by without a few basic phrases. People are often very surprised and responsive if you can speak a few words of the language. If you spend a while in Tigrai, and in Oromifa-speaking parts of southern Ethiopia (which includes the Rift Valley and most points east of it), it can be helpful to know a few words of the local tongue. In Tigrai, the response to a tourist who can say even one Tigrigna phrase is less that of surprise than of total astonishment. It really is worth making the effort.

AMHARIGNA The section that follows is not meant to be a comprehensive introduction to Amharigna. A cheap and light grammar and mini dictionary, *Amharic for Foreigners* by Semere Woldegabir, is readily available in Addis Ababa and recommended to natural linguists who want to get to grips with the complex grammar and sentence construction of Amharigna, or the intricacies of pronunciation. My experience, however, suggests that most visitors will find this book more daunting than helpful and that the few basic phrases they need to know are buried beneath reams of detail that are of little use to somebody with no long-term interest in becoming fluent in the language. Better to carry Lonely Planet's *Amharic* phrasebook.

What follows is essentially the pidgin-Amharigna I picked up over four months in the country. Most of this came not from books, which invariably confused me, but from English-speaking Ethiopians with a natural sympathy for the difficulties of learning a language from scratch. It could be argued that I should be getting a fluent Amharigna-speaker to write this. I would disagree: it is not difficult to get by in Amharigna, but only if you ignore its grammatical complications. I simply don't speak enough Amharigna to be able to complicate it, and what little I do speak was learnt the hard way. It is difficult to imagine that many tourists to Ethiopia will need more Amharigna than the simplified version that follows. If, after a couple of weeks, you exhaust what I learnt in four months, it only strengthens the case for keeping things simple.

597

But I do apologise to Amharigna speakers for any liberties that I might have taken with their language; my only excuse is that whatever errors might follow stood me in good stead during my time in Ethiopia; my only rejoinder is that you do some utterly bemusing things to my home language, and I would never let 'correctness' override the will to communicate.

It is worth noting that there is often no simple and correct English transcription of Amharigna words, as evidenced by such extremes of spelling as Woldio/Weldiya, Mekele/Maqale, Zikwala/Zouqala and even Addis Ababa/Adees Abeba. Generally, I have spelt Amharigna words as they sound to me. People who are unfamiliar with African languages should be aware that Amharigna, like most other African languages, is pronounced phonetically – the town name Bore is not pronounced like boar, but *Bor-ay*.

The magic word The one word that every visitor to Ethiopia should know is *ishee*. This is the sort of word that illustrates the gap between 'proper' grammar/dictionaries and the realities of being in a new country and trying to assimilate the language quickly. *Ishee,* more or less, means OK but (not unlike the English equivalent) it can be used in a variety of circumstances: as an alternative to the myriad ways of saying hello or goodbye, to signal agreement, to reassure people, etc. This is not just a foreigner's short cut – *ishee* is the single most spoken word in Ethiopia, and I have often heard entire conversations that apparently consist of nothing more than two Ethiopians bouncing *ishee*s backwards and forwards. Of course *ishee* is a colloquial word – but most people aren't out to take offence and they understand the problems facing foreigners who can't speak the local language; a foreigner smiling and saying the word *ishee* is as acceptable a signal of goodwill or friendliness as would be a foreigner smiling and saying 'OK' in Britain. Another useful catchphrase in some situations is *chigger yellem* – no problem. And, incidentally, 'OK' is also widely used in Ethiopia.

Greetings and farewells Useful all-purpose greetings are *tadias* and *tenayistillign*, which basically mean 'hello, how are you?' These are common greetings that can be used with anyone and on all occasions. In many parts of the country, the Arabic greeting *selam* – literally 'peace' – is in common use. To ask how somebody is, ask *dehnaneh?* to a male and *dehnanesh?* to a female. The correct response, always, is *dehena*, pronounced more like '*dena*' or *dehnanegn* – I am well. There are tens of other greetings, depending on the time of day and the sex and number of people you are speaking to. There is little need for visitors to learn these greetings. If you want to anticipate them being used on you, all you need know is that they invariably start with the phrase *indemin-* and the correct response is invariably *dehena*. There are just as many ways of saying goodbye or farewell – *dehnahunu* or *chau* (adopted from and pronounced like the Italian *ciao*) is fine in most circumstances. Ethiopians often precede their *chau* with an *ishee*!

Some essentials The first barrier to be crossed when you travel in linguistically unfamiliar surroundings is to learn how to ask a few basic questions and to understand the answers. The answers first: *awo* means yes and *aydelem* means no. In casual use, these are often shortened to *aw* (pronounced like the 'ou' in our) and *ay* (pronounced like eye). Some Ethiopians replace their *aw* with a rather startling inhalation of breath.

In general travel-type queries, you'll often use and hear the words *aleh* (there is) and *yellem* (there is not). To find out if a place serves coffee (*buna*), you would ask *buna aleh?* The response should be *aleh* or *yellem*.

Once you have established that what you want is in the *aleh* state, you can ask for it by saying *ifelegalehu* (I want). More often, Ethiopians will just say what they want and how many – *and buna* (one coffee) or *hulet birra* (two beers). It is not customary to accompany your request with an *ibakih* or *ibakesh* (please, to a male and female respectively), but you should always say *ameseghinalehu* (thank you) when you get what you asked for. The response to thank you is *minimaydelem* (you're welcome).

If you don't want something – like, say, the green comb that a street hawker is thrusting in your face – then say *alfelagem* or simply shake your head. If this makes little impression, you can say *hid* (go) to children, or anyone who is obviously much younger than you, but you shouldn't really say something that overtly offish to an adult.

In Amharigna, the word *no* (pronounced like the English know) means something roughly equivalent to 'is'. In Amharigna conversations, Ethiopians often interject a *no* much as we might say 'true' or 'really'. Needless to say, this can cause a certain amount of confusion if you say 'no' to somebody who isn't familiar with English – they may well assume you are saying 'yes'.

The word for 'where' is *yet*, from which derive the questions *yetno?* (where is?), *wedetno?* (to where?) and *keyetno?* (from where?). The word for 'what' is *min*, which gives you *mindeno?* (what is it?), *lemin?* (why?), *minaleh?* (what is there?) and *indet?* (how?). *Meche?* means 'when?', which gives you *mecheno?* (when is it?); *man?* means 'who?'; and *sintno?* means 'how much?'.

Simple questions can be formed by prefixing the above phrases with a subject. Some examples:

Awtobus yemihedow?	Where is this bus going?
Migib minaleh?	What food is there?
Alga aleh?	Is there a room? (*alga* literally means bed)
Postabet yetno?	Where is the post office?
Wagaw sintno?	How much does it cost?
Sa'at sintno?	What (literally 'how much') is the time?
Simih mano?	What is your name? (male)
Simish mano?	What is your name? (female)
Hisap sintno?	How much is the bill?

Some useful Amharigna words

after/later	*behuwala*	come (female)	*ney*
afternoon	*kesa'at behuwala*	come (male)	*na*
again	*indegena*	correct	*lik*
and	*na*	cost	*waga*
at	*be*	(make a discount)	(*waga kenis*)
bad	*metfo*	country (or region)	*ager*
banana	*muz*	cow	*lam*
beautiful	*konjo*	dirty	*koshasha*
bed	*alga*	donkey	*ahiya*
beef	*yebere siga*	egg	*inkulal*
beer	*birra*	enough	*beki*
before	*befit*	(enough!)	(*beka!*)
bicycle	*bisikleet*	Ethiopian	*Habesha* or *Ityopyawi*
big	*tilik*	excuse (me)	*yikirta*
bus	*awtobus*	far	*ruk*
but	*gin*	fast	*fetan*
car (or any motor vehicle)	*mekeena*	first	*andegna* or *mejemerya*
cart	*gari*	fish	*asa*
cent (or just money)	*santeem*	food	*migib*
chicken	*doro*	foreigner	*faranji*
church	*bet kristyan*	glass	*birchiko*
clean	*nitsuh*	go	*hid*
coffee	*buna*	good	*tiru*
cold	*kezkaza*	he	*issu*

help	*irdugn*	pig	*asama*
here	*izih*	problem	*chigger*
horse	*feres*	quickly	*tolo*
hospital	*hakim bet*	region	*bota*
hour	*sa'at*	restaurant	*migib bet*
house (or any		river	*wenz*
building)	*bet*	road	*menged*
I	*ine*	room	*kifil*
in	*wust*	salt	*chew*
insect	*tebay*	sea	*bahir*
island	*desiet*	she	*iswa*
key	*kulf*	shop	*suk*
lake	*hayk*	short	*achir*
little	*tinish*	shower	*showa* or
luggage	*gwaz* or *shanta*		*metatebia bet*
me	*inay*	sleep	*inkilf*
meat	*siga*	slowly	*kes*
milk	*wotet*	small	*tinish*
money	*genzeb*	sorry	*aznallehu*
morning	*tiwat*	stop	*akum*
mountain	*terara*	sugar	*sukwar*
Mr	*Ato*	tall	*rejim*
Mrs	*Weyzero*	tea	*shai*
Miss	*Weyzerit*	thank you	*ameseghinalehu*
much	*bizu*	there	*iza*
mutton	*yebeg siga*	they	*innessu*
near	*atageb* or *kirb*	ticket	*karnee* or *ticket*
newspaper	*gazeta*	today	*zare*
nice	*tiru*	toilet	*shintbet*
night	*lelit*	tomorrow	*nege*
now	*ahun*	very	*betam*
of	*ye*	warm	*muk*
or	*weyim*	water	*wuha*
orange	*birtukan*	yesterday	*tilant*
peace	*selam*	you (female)	*anchee*
petrol	*benzeen*	you (male)	*ante*

Numbers

1	*and*	20	*haya*
2	*hulet*	25	*haya amist (hamist)*
3	*sost*	30	*selasa*
4	*arat*	40	*arba*
5	*amist*	50	*hamsa*
6	*sidist*	60	*silsa*
7	*sabat*	70	*seba*
8	*simint*	80	*semagnya*
9	*zetegn*	90	*zetena*
10	*asir*	100	*meto*
11	*asra and*	200	*hulet meto*
12	*asra hulet*	1,000	*shee*
		1,000,000	*meelyon*

Days of the week

Sunday	*Ihud*	Thursday	*Hamus*
Monday	*Segno*	Friday	*Arb*
Tuesday	*Maksegno*	Saturday	*Kidame*
Wednesday	*Irob*		

Festivals

New Year	*Inkutatash*	Easter	*Fasika*
Christmas	*Gena*		

Time

(See box, *Ethiopian time* in *Chapter 1*, page 37.)

TIGRIGNA Many people in Tigrai speak no Amharigna, so a few words of the local language – which shares many words with Amharigna as the two are both derived from Ge'ez – might be useful:

bad	*himek*	milk	*tsaba*
banana	*mu-uz*	nice	*dehan*
beautiful	*gondjo*	no	*nanai*
black	*tselim*	No	*Yechone*
border	*dob*	OK	*hirai*
bus	*shishento*	rain	*zenab*
chicken	*dorho*	red	*kaje*
coffee	*buna*	room (in hotel)	*madakasi*
come (female)	*ne'e*	sick	*houmoum*
come (male)	*na'a*	tea	*shai*
egg	*unkulale*	thank you	*yekanyelay*
excuse me	*yikerta*	The coffee tastes	*Oo-oum buna*
fine	*tsebuk*	good	
food	*migbi*	This way	*Uzi*
go	*kid*	today	*lomo anti*
good	*tsbuk*	toilet	*shintebet*
goodbye	*selamat* or *daahankun*	tomorrow	*naga*
hello	*selam*	water	*mai*
here	*hausi*	What is your name?	*Shimka men yoe?*
How are you?	*Kemayla-hee?*	where?	*lave?*
(female)		white	*tsada*
How are you? (male)	*Kemayla-ha?*	yes	*ouwa*
How much?	*Kendai?*	yesterday	*tsbah*
is there…?	*alo…?*		

Numbers

1	*hada*	6	*shidista*
2	*kilita*	7	*showata*
3	*salista*	8	*shimwunta*
4	*arbata*	9	*tishiata*
5	*hamishte*	10	*aseta*

OROMIFA Oromifa is the main language of southern Ethiopia, spoken throughout the Federal State of Oromia. Unlike Amharigna, it is transcribed using familiar Roman letters, though with little consistency in spelling. In theory, the consonants are doubled to denote a stress (with *manna*, for instance, you would stress the 'n') while doubled vowels denote that the sound of that vowel should be longer than a single vowel. In practice, the application of the doubled letter seems rather more arbitrary – one signpost in any given town might read 'hotela' (hotel), another 'hootteellaa', and others different variants thereof. There is no overwhelming need to speak any Oromifa – everybody in this area speaks some Amharigna – other than the delight that it will give Oromifa speakers to hear a *faranji* speak their language.

Some Oromifa words and phrases

again	*ammas, lammaffaa*	man	*dira*
bar	*manna buna*	market	*gabaaya/gabaa*
black	*guracha*	mineral water	*bishaan amo*
brown	*magala*	money	*qarshi*
bus	*awtobisii*	mosquito	*bookee busaa*
business	*daldala*	mother	*haadha*
buy	*bituu*	mountain	*tullu*
child	*muca*	no (I do not)	*wawu/laki*
church building	*mana kadhataa*	no problem	*rakkon hin jiru*
coffee	*buna*	now	*amma*
cost	*gati*	office	*wajira*
Did you	*Isini galeeraa?*	please	*maaloo*
understand?		police	*polisii*
Do you speak	*Afaan faranji ni*	post office	*mana posta*
English?	*beektaa?*	quantity	*baay'ina*
drink	*dhugi*	red	*dima*
early	*dafee*	restaurant	*mana nyaataa*
eat	*nyaadhu*	road	*daandii, karaa*
enter	*deenaa*	room	*kutaa*
far	*fagoo*	shop	*sukii*
father	*abba*	sister	*obboleettii*
fire	*ibidda*	tea	*shaayii*
friend	*michu*	thank you	*galatoomi/ galatoomaa*
go	*deemuu*	there	*achi*
goodbye	*nagaan turi*	today	*har'a*
green	*magarisa*	toilet	*mana fincaanii*
grey	*dalacha*	tomorrow	*booru*
hello	*ashamaa/akkam/attam*	traveller	*kara-adeemtuu*
here	*as*	village	*ganda*
hotel	*hoteela/*	water	*bishaan*
	mana keessummaa	We are visitors	*Nuyi duwwattoota*
house	*mana/manna*	What is your name?	*Maqaan kee eenyu?*
How are you?	*Attam jirta/jirtu?*	when	*yoom*
How much? (price)	*Mega?*	Where is it?	*Eessa?/Eessa dha?*
I am fine	*Nagaa/Fayyaa*	white	*adi*
lady	*gifti*	woman	*dubartii*
lake	*garba*	yellow	*kelloo*
late	*yeroo dabarsuu*	yes (I do)	*eeyyee*
light	*ibsaa*		

Days of the week

Sunday	*Dilbata*	Thursday	*Kamsa*
Monday	*Wiixata*	Friday	*Jimata*
Tuesday	*Kibxata*	Saturday	*Sanbata*
Wednesday	*Roobii*		

Numbers

1	*toko*	12	*kudha-lama*
2	*lama*	20	*digdama*
3	*sadi*	30	*sodoma*
4	*afur*	40	*afurtama*
5	*shan*	50	*shantama*
6	*jaha*	60	*jaatama*
7	*torba*	70	*torbatama*
8	*saddet*	80	*saddeettama*
9	*sagal*	90	*sagaltama*
10	*kudha*	100	*dhiba*
11	*kudha-tokko*	1,000	*kuma*

SPEAKING ENGLISH TO ETHIOPIANS As you learn to speak a bit of Amharigna, you will generally find your skill at communicating in the language is largely dependent on the imagination and empathy of the person you are speaking to. The moment some people realise you know a few words, they will speak to you as if you are fluent and make you feel thoroughly hopeless. Other people will take care to speak slowly and to stick to common words, and as a result you feel as if you're making real progress. The same principle applies in reverse and, as a result, many Ethiopians find it easier to communicate in English with native French- or Italian-speakers than they do with native English-speakers.

Communicating with Ethiopians is not just about learning Amharigna, but also about pitching your use of English to reflect Ethiopian idiosyncrasies of pronunciation, grammar and vocabulary. In other words, the English-language communication skills of any Ethiopian you meet will partly be dependent on *your* empathy and imagination.

The first and most obvious rule is to speak slowly and clearly. If you are not understood at first, don't simply repeat the same phrase but look for different, less complex ways of conveying the same idea.

A good way of getting a feel for pronunciation is to look at the English transcription of Amharigna words that were initially borrowed from English – *meelyon* (million), *giroseri* (grocery) or *keelometer* (kilometre). A common tendency is to make more emphatic vowel sounds. Another tendency, presumably because few Ethiopian words have consonants without a vowel in between, is to drop things like the 'r' in import (so it sounds like *im-pot*), or else to insert a vowel sound – often an 'ee' or 'i' – between consonants (I pointed one Ethiopian girl towards the market when she asked for a *pinipal*; it was only when she took out a pen and paper I realised it was a penpal and not a pineapple she was after).

Remember, too, that there is always a tendency to use the grammatical phrasing of your home tongue when you speak a second language. For instance, an Ethiopian might ask you 'time how much?', which is a direct translation of *sa'at sintno?* They are more likely to understand *you* if you say 'time how much?' – or at least keep your question as straightforward as possible, for instance 'what is the time?' – than if you ask something more embroidered like 'do you happen to have the time on you?' Many English-speakers are inclined to fluff straightforward queries to strangers with apologetic phrasing like 'I'm terribly sorry' or 'could you tell me'. In an Ethiopian context, this sort of thing just obstructs communication.

You will find that certain common English words are readily understood by Ethiopians, while other equally common words draw a complete blank. The Amharigna word *bet* literally means house, but it is used to describe any building or even a room, so that a *postabet* is a post office, a *buna bet* is a coffee shop, and a *shintabet* is a toilet. You will thus find that Ethiopians often use the English word 'house' in a much looser context that we would. Another example of this is the phrase 'it is possible', which for some reason has caught on almost everywhere in Africa. 'It is possible to find a bus?' is more likely to be understood than 'do you know if there is a bus?' Likewise, 'is not possible' is a more commonly used phrase than 'it is impossible'.

This sort of thing occurs on an individual level as well as a general one. One Ethiopian friend used the word 'disturb' to cover every imaginable simile of the word. If a phrase like 'I am angry about this' or 'this is really noisy' didn't click, then 'I am much disturb over this' certainly would. Another middle-aged friend kept referring to a girl in her late teens as his parent – presumably he meant cousin. One decided 'plonker' who befriended me kept talking about my family (he must have said 'I think you have good family' 50 times); it took me some time to realise that the family to which he was referring was in fact the hotel where I was staying. The point being not only to attune yourself to the nuances of English as it is spoken in Ethiopia, but also to pick up on the words favoured by individuals, and to try to stick to words you have heard them use.

Finally, you should be aware that when Ethiopians ask you to play with them, they only want to talk. This one has all sorts of potential for misunderstandings. I was thrown a little on my first night in Addis when a bar girl (local euphemism for prostitute) sat down at my table and suggested 'we play?' A woman travelling on her own might – understandably to us, but not to the enquirer – respond rather curtly to such a suggestion. This is because the Amharigna phrase used in the same situation – *techawat* (say something) – is the imperative of both *mechewawot* (talk) and *mechawot* (play)!

Appendix 2

GLOSSARY

Abba	Father (priest)
Abuna	The title of the metropolitan bishop, or head of the Ethiopian Orthodox Church
Amba	Hill or mountain with flat top, often the site of a monastery or church
Ambo	Fizzy bottled mineral water, named after the town from where it is sourced
Amharigna	Amharic, language of the Amhara people and national language of Ethiopia
Animist	Religion worshipping ancestors and/or animate objects (plants, animals)
Ato	Mister
Autobus (*terra*)	Bus (station)
Bet	Literally 'house', often used to denote a shop (eg: *buna bet* = coffee shop)
Bet Israel	see *Falasha*
Bet Kristian	Church
Buna	Coffee
Chat	Mildly narcotic leaf chewed in vast quantities in Muslim areas
Coptic Church	Alexandria-based Church affiliated to but not synonymous with Ethiopian Orthodox Church
Derg	Military socialist dictatorship 1974–91
Endemic	Bird or mammal found only in one country
Enset	Type of plantain (false banana) grown widely in southern Ethiopia
Falasha	Ethiopian group who practise an archaic form of Judaism
Ful	Popular vegetarian breakfast dish, often very garlicky
Gabbi	Plain off-white cotton cloth worn toga-like by rural Ethiopian men, particularly in the north
Galla	Obsolete term for people now known as the Oromo
Gari	Horse-drawn cart used for carrying goods and passengers
Ge'ez	Archaic language, used in Ethiopian Church, root of Amharigna
Ghebbi	Palace or large house
Injera	Vast pancake made from fermented *tef*, the staple diet of Ethiopians
Itegue	Empress/Princess
Kidus	Saint
Kitfo	Local delicacy made with minced meat, often raw or very lightly cooked
Maize	Corn

Mana/Manna	Oromifa equivalent of Amharigna 'bet' (eg: *manna buna* = coffee house/shop)
Mercato	Market
Meskel	Cross; also the name of a religious ceremony and yellow flower
Monolithic church	Rock-hewn church standing free from the surrounding rock on all four sides
Monotheistic	One god; used to describe the Judaic faiths: Christianity, Islam and Judaism
Negus	King
Netela	Cotton cloth similar to *gabbi*, but with embroidered edge, worn by women
Nine Saints	5th–6th-century saints who are largely responsible for spread of Christianity beyond Axum
Oromifa	Language spoken by the Oromo people
Ras	Prince
Selassie	Trinity
Semi-monolithic church	Rock-hewn church standing free from the rock on three sides
Shai	Tea
Shama	White cloth worn toga-like by Ethiopian women
Shifta	Bandit
Stele (pl: stelae)	A standing stone or obelisk, usually marking a grave in Ethiopia
Tabot	Replica of the Ark of the Covenant that sanctifies an Ethiopian church
Tankwa	Papyrus boat
Tef	Grain endemic to the Ethiopian Highlands
Tej	Mead-like alcoholic drink made from honey or sugar
Tella	Thick low-alcohol 'beer' made from millet or barley
Tholoh	Tigraian dish of barley balls dunked fondue-style in a spicy sauce
Tukul	Round thatched house
Wat	Sauce, often spicy, eaten with *injera*
Waziro	Mrs

Appendix 3

KEY HISTORICAL AND LEGENDARY FIGURES IN ETHIOPIA

Following the Ethiopian custom, Ethiopian figures are listed by their name, not by their father's name.

Abadir Umar Arrida	13th-century sheikh regarded to be the holiest saint of Harar
Abba Jiffar II	Powerful late 19th-century ruler of Jimma
Abreha we Atsbeha	4th-century twin emperors of Axum who adopted these names after converting to Christianity
Afewerk Tekle	Ethiopia's leading post-World War II artist with noted works in St George Cathedral and Africa Hall in Addis Ababa
Afse, Abba	5th–6th century, one of the Nine Saints, founded church in Yeha
Ahmed Gragn	16th-century Muslim leader who waged jihad against Christian empire
Alvarez, Francisco	16th-century Portuguese priest who spent a decade in Ethiopia, visiting Lalibela and other important sites
Aregawi, Abba	5th–6th century, one of the Nine Saints, founded Debre Damo Monastery
Arwe	Legendary serpent king of pre-Judaic cult of Axum area, killed by a royal ancestor of the Queen of Sheba
Aster Aweke	Popular modern Ethiopian female singer, now based in USA
Athanasius	4th-century Patriarch of Egyptian Coptic Church who baptised Frumentius and died a refugee in Ethiopia
Bani al-Hamuya	10th-century queen, led attack on Axum, often identified with Yodit, more likely from pagan Damot Empire
Basen	Important Axumite king, ruled at about the time of Christ
Bruce, James	18th-century Scottish explorer who travelled widely in Ethiopia, credited as finding source of Blue Nile
Burton, Sir Richard	19th-century explorer, first European to visit Harar
Cosmos Indicopleustes	Alexandrian merchant who visited Ethiopia in 6th century and wrote detailed account of trip
Da Gama, Christopher	Leader of 16th-century Portuguese expedition to find Prester John, died in battle in Muslim war
De Covilhão, Pero	Spanish Jesuit 'spy' sent by King John of Portugal to the Kingdom of Prester John during rule of Susneyos
Eleni	Influential wife of Zara Yaqob, whom she outlived by 50 years; regent during the early rule of Lebna Dengal
Ethiopic	Legendary great-grandson of Noah, said to have founded Ethiopia

Ezana	Pre-Christian name of Axumite emperor later known as Abreha, regarded to be greatest of Axumite rulers
Fasilidas	Emperor of Ethiopia 1632–67, son of Susneyos, restored Orthodox Church and civil order, founded Gondar
Frumentius	4th-century priest, converted Axumite rulers and became first Patriarch of Ethiopian Church
Gadarat	2nd-century Axumite king credited with expanding the empire into modern Yemen
Galawdewos	Ethiopian emperor who defeated Ahmed Gragn in battle (with Portuguese assistance) in 1543
Garima, Abba	5th–6th century, one of the Nine Saints, founded eponymous monastery south of Adwa
Gebre Meskel	6th-century Axumite king, son of Kaleb, associated with foundation of several monasteries
Gebriel	Archangel Gabriel
Giyorgis	Ethiopian name for St George
Graziani, Rudolfo	Viceroy of Ethiopia during Italian occupation
Gudit	Synonym for Yodit (Judith)
Habbuba, Emir	Legendary 10th-century founder of Harar
Haile Selassie	Last Emperor of Ethiopia, murdered 1974
Ilg, Alfred	Swiss adviser to Menelik II, played a major role in development of Ethiopia during Menelik's rule
Iskinder	Emperor of Ethiopia 1478–94, ascended to throne aged eight, died in battle aged 24
Iyasu	Emperor of Ethiopia 1682–1706, strongest of Gonderine rulers
Iyasu II	Emperor of Ethiopia 1913–16, ousted in conspiracy led by Ras Tefari
Iyasus	Ethiopian name for Jesus, several variants of spelling in use
Iyasus Moa	Eminent monk trained at Debre Damo, founded Hayk Istafanos Monastery, helped 'restore' Solomonic rule
Jafar Taleb	6th–7th-century cousin and follower of prophet Muhammad, founder of Islamic community in Ethiopia
Kaleb	6th-century Axumite king, successful military expansionist, built large palace outside modern Axum
Lalibela	12th-century emperor and saint, excavated the complex of churches in the town that is now named for him
Lebna Dengal	Emperor of Ethiopia 1508–40, name translates as 'Incense of the Virgin', died during war with Ahmed Gragn
Libanos, Abba	5th–6th century, one of the Nine Saints, eminent Monastery of Debre Libanos named for him
Lij Iyasu	see *Iyasu II*
Lucy	Name given to 3.5-million-year-old human skull found in Hadar in 1974
Makeda	Ethiopian name for Queen of Sheba
Maryam	Ethiopian name for Mary, mother of Jesus Christ
Meles Zenawi	Prime Minister of Ethiopia 1991–present
Menelik I	Legendary Axumite king, credited by tradition as founding Axum circa 1000BC
Menelik II	Emperor of Ethiopia 1889–1913, defeated Italy at Battle of Adwa; co-founded Addis Ababa with wife Taitu
Mengistu Haile Maryam	Dictatorial leader of Ethiopia 1974–91

Mentewab	Queen Consort 1730–55 after death of husband Bakafa, end of reign signalled end of Gonderine strength
Nakuta La'ab	Nephew and successor to Emperor Lalibela, founded eponymous monastery outside Lalibela town
Napier, Sir Robert	Led 1869 British military expedition that led to defeat and suicide of Tewodros II
Nur Ibn al-Wazir	Nephew and successor to Ahmed Gragn as leader of Harar, continued Gragn's jihad
Páez, Pedro	Spanish priest, first European to the Blue's Nile's source, convertor of Susneyos to Catholicism, sparking a civil war and expulsion of Portuguese
Pantaleon, Abba	5th–6th century, one of the Nine Saints, founded eponymous monastery near modern Axum
Prester John	Legendary medieval figure, ruled rich Christian empire in Indies, possibly based on emperor of Ethiopia
Queen of Sheba	Legendary queen, claimed by Ethiopians as Axumite mother of Menelik I, more probably Yemeni
Ramhai	3rd-century Axumite ruler associated with the largest stele (33m high) ever erected in ancient times
Ras Desta Demtew	Son-in-law of Haile Selassie, led unsuccessful military campaign against Italian invasion in 1936
Ras Mekonnen	Nobleman appointed as Governor of Harar by Menelik II, father of future Emperor Haile Selassie
Ras Mikael Ali	Powerful late 19th-century ruler of Wolo, ally of Menelik II, grandfather of Emperor Iyasu II
Ras Tefari	Pre-coronation name of Emperor Haile Selassie
Rimbaud, Arthur	Prodigal French poet who abandoned poetry aged 19 to end up dealing arms in Harar
Sahle Selassie	Expansionist ruler of Showa 1813–47, paved way for grandson Menelik II's eventual rise to emperor
Salama, Abba	Pseudonymous with Frumentius
Solomon	King of Israel, legendarily said to have sired Menelik I
Susneyos	Early 17th-century emperor, converted by Portuguese Jesuits causing civil war, abdicated 1632
Taitu	Wife of Menelik II, co-founder of Addis Ababa
Tekle Haymanot	Priest who spread Christianity through Showa in the 13th century, and founded Debre Libanos Monastery
Tekle Haymanot	10th-century emperor credited as founding Zagwe dynasty and effectively ending Axumite era
Tewodros II	Emperor of Ethiopia 1855–69, first emperor in a century to unify fiefdoms of various princes
Yakuno Amlak	13th-century emperor who founded (or restored) Solomonic dynasty
Yared	6th-century priest, patronised by King Gebre Meskel, credited with writing most Ethiopian church music
Yemrehanna Kristos	Medieval emperor, predecessor of Lalibela. Best known for the eponymous church he built near Bilbilla
Yodit	Legendarily militant 9th-century Falasha queen, razed Axum and many churches in northern Ethiopia
Yohannis IV	Emperor of Ethiopia 1872–89, played a major role uniting Ethiopia

| Zara Yaqob | 15th-century emperor, founded several churches and monasteries, as well as town of Debre Birhan |
| Zawditu | Empress of Ethiopia 1921–30, daughter of Menelik II |

The titles 'Emperor' and 'King' are occasionally used interchangeably in the text, in reference to particular heads of state.

Appendix 4

SOME ETHIOPIAN TRANSCRIPTIONS OF PLACE NAMES

Yared Belete of Grant Express Travel and Tours Services (GETTS)

Abi Aday	አቢአዳ	Debre Tabor	ደብረታቦር
Adadi	አዳዲ	Dembidolo	ደምቢዶሎ
Adama/Nazret	አዳማ/ናዝሬት/	Dessie	ደሴ
Addis Ababa/Finfine	አዲስ አበባ/ፍንፍኔ/	Dilla	ዲላ
Addis Alem	አዲስ አለም	Dinsho	ዲንሾ
Adi Arkay	አዲ አርቃዬ	Dire Dawa	ድሬዳዋ
Adigrat	አዲግራት	Djibouti	ጅቡቲ
Adwa	አድዋ	Dodola	ዶዶላ
Akaki Beseka	አቃቂ በሰቃ	Dola Mena	ዶሎ መና
Alem Katema	አለም ከተማ	Entoto	እንጦጦ
Aliyu Amba	አልዩ አምባ	Fiche	ፍቼ
Ambo	አምቦ	Gambella	ጋምቤላ
Ankober	አንኮበር	Gefersa	ገፈርሳ
Arba Minch	አርባ ምንጭ	Goba	ጎባ
Arero	አረሮ	Gondar	ጎንደር
Arsi Negele	አርሲ ነገሌ	Gorgora	ጎርጎራ
Asbe Teferi]	አሰበ ተፈሪ	Harar	ሐረር
Asela	አሰላ	Hawzien	ሐውዜን
Assaita	አሳይታ	Hayk	ሃይቅ
Atsbi	አጽቢ	Hosaina	ሆሳእና
Awash	አዋሽ	Inda Selassie/Shire	እንዳስላሴ/ሺሬ
Awassa	አዋሳ	Jijiga	ጅጅጋ
Axum	አክሱም	Jimma	ጅማ
Babile	ባቢሌ	Jinka	ጅንካ
Bahir Dar	ባህር ዳር	Karat/Konso	ካራት/ኮንሶ
Bati	ባቲ	Kebre Mengist	ክብረመንግሥት
Bedele	በደሌ	Kombolcha	ኮምቦልቻ
Bilbilla	ቢልቢላ	Kosober/Injibara	ኮሶበር/እንጅብራ
Bishoftu/Debre Zeyit	ቢሾፍቱ/ደብረዘይት/	Lalibela	ላሊበላ
Butajira	ቡታጅራ	Matu	ማቱ
Chencha	ጨንቻ	Maichew	ማይጨው
Debark	ደባርቅ	Mega	መሐል ሜዳ
Debre Birhan	ደብረብርሃን	Mehal Meda	መቀሌ
Debre Markos	ደብረማርቆስ	Mekele	ሜታ
Debre Sina	ደብረሲና	Metahara	መተሐራ

Mille	ሚሌ	Sodo/Walaita	ሶዶ/ወላይታ
Mizan Tefari	ሚዛን ተፈሪ	Sodore	ሶደሬ
Mojo	ሞጆ	Sof Omar	ሶፍኦመር
Nechisar	ነጭሳር	Tarmabir	ጣርማበር
Negash	ነጋሽ	Tiya	ጢያ
Negele	ነገሌ	Weliso	ወሊሶ
Nekemte	ነቀምቴ	Welkite	ወልቂጤ
Robe	ሮቢ	Woldia	ወልድያ
Sekota	ሰቆጣ	Wondo Genet	ወንዶገነት
Sela Dingay	ሰላድንጋይ	Wukro	ውቅሮ
Senkele	ሰንቀሌ	Yabello	ያቤሎ
Shashemene	ሻሽመኔ	Yeha	የሃ
Silté	ስልጤ	Zege	ዜጌ
Simien	ሰሜን	Zikwala	ዝቋላ
Sinkata	ሰንቃጣ	Ziway	ዝዋይ

Appendix 5

FURTHER INFORMATION

Books about Ethiopia aren't quite so thin on the ground as they were a few years back, though many more interesting titles remain difficult to locate or are dauntingly expensive. Within Ethiopia, the best places to buy local-interest books are **BookWorld** and the **Africans Bookshop** in Addis Ababa. The curio shop next to the ETC tourist office and shops in Bole Airport stock a good range too.

Few European or American bookshops stock much in the way of books about Ethiopia, but you can order most of the volumes listed below through online sellers such as amazon.com, amazon.co.uk or abebooks.co.uk (who are often also good sources of out-of-print books). The **Red Sea Press**, one of the most prolific publishers about Ethiopia and the Horn of Africa, has an online catalogue and ordering facilities at www.africanworld.com. **Shama Publishers**, an Ethiopian company with a tantalising and ever-expanding selection of titles, should soon have similar facilities at www.shamabooks.com.

Eastern Books (*128 Ashtonville St, London SW18 5AQ;* ✆ *020 8871 0880*) specialises in rare and out-of-print books on Ethiopia. Contact them for a full stock list with prices.

BOOKS
General and coffee-table books

Amin, M, Matheson, A and Willetts, D *Journey through Ethiopia* Camerapix, 1997. This is one of the best general coffee-table books about Ethiopia, combining strong photography and quality reproduction with readable introductory text. The publisher was founded by the late Muhammad Amin, who won an award for the documentary coverage that indirectly prompted the international response to the 1985 famine.

Batistoni, M and Chiari, P C *Old Tracks in the New Flower: A Historical Guide to Addis Ababa* Arada Books, 2004. This is a fascinating record of the early days of Ethiopia's capital, with illustrations and descriptions of about 100 of the most interesting old buildings scattered around the city.

Beckwith, C and Fisher, A *Africa Ark* Harry N Abrams, 1990. It seems almost dismissive to describe this visually superlative, lavish – and very expensive – tome as a coffee-table book. Carol Beckwith and Angela Fisher are regarded to be the finest photographic documenters of African culture in the business, and this book – ranging from South Omo to Tigrai – leaves one in no doubt as to why! Supplemented by Graham Hancock's informative text, this is simply one of the finest photographic books ever produced about Africa.

Burhardt, Majka *Vertical Ethiopia: Climbing toward Possibility in the Horn of Africa* Shama Books, 2008. A must for rock climbers, this book follows four women as they make first ascents of some of the sandstone monoliths that dot the north.

Di Salvo, Mario *Churches of Ethiopia: The Monastery of Narga Selassie* Skira, 1999. A fascinating and visually impressive photographic document of the beautiful church built

613

by the Empress Mentewab on a remote island in Lake Tana, with text that ties the specific church into a broader overview of the monastic tradition on Lake Tana – not nearly as dull as it sounds!

Gibb, Camilla *Sweetness in the Belly* Penguin, 2007. This provocative **novel** explores the issues of race and religion, looking beyond the Islamic stereotypes to follow the story of a young white British Muslim woman who struggles with cultural contradictions after moving to Harar in the 1970s and is then forced to flee back to the United Kingdom.

Golzábez, J and Cebrián, D *Touching Ethiopia* Shama Books, 2004. This sumptuous 400-page tome can't quite decide whether it wants to be a coffee-table book or something more authoritative, but it succeeds remarkably well on both counts. Probably the best overall visual introduction to Ethiopia in print, it is particularly strong on the oft-neglected south, west and east.

Hancock, Graham *The Sign and the Seal* Heinemann, 1992. This lively account of the Ark of the Covenant's alleged arrival in Ethiopia is as popular with tourists as it is reviled by academics (the respected historical writer Paul Henze describes it as 'fiction masquerading as historical research'). It is, for all that, an entertaining work, one that captures the imagination, and as the only popular book of a historical (or quasi-historical) nature published about Ethiopia in decades, it must qualify as almost essential reading.

Mengiste, Maaza *Beneath the Lion's Gaze* W W Norton & Company, 2011. Set during the 1974 Ethiopian revolution, this beautifully written first **novel** by the American-based Ethiopian author is about drought, famine, civil war and one family's struggle to survive them all.

Munro-Hay, Stuart *Ethiopia: The Unknown Land* I B Tauris, 2002. This authoritative site-by-site historical overview of Ethiopia's most popular antiquities is a superb companion to a more conventional travel guide for readers seeking more scholarly and detailed background information.

Munro-Hay, Stuart *The Quest for the Ark of the Covenant: The True Story of the Tablets of Moses* I B Tauris, 2005. Inspired by the more outlandish postulations in Hancock's *Sign and the Seal*, this readable albeit rather dry work provides a scholarly assessment of the probable fate of the Ark – inevitably concluding that it is almost certainly not (and never was) stashed away anywhere in Ethiopia.

Nomachi, Kazyoshi *Bless Ethiopia* Odyssey Publications, 1998. Photographically, this is by far the most creative document of Ethiopia I've come across, capturing typical ecclesiastical scenes from unusual and striking angles. Highly recommended.

Pankhurst, Richard and Gerard, Denis *Ethiopia Photographed* Kegan Paul, 1997. A follow-up to *Ethiopia Engraved*, this lovely and absorbing book is a must for old-photograph junkies, consisting of a wealth of photographs taken from 1867 to 1936, placed in context through accompanying text by Richard Pankhurst.

Pankhurst, Richard and Ingrams, Leila *Ethiopia Engraved* Kegan Paul, 1988. This book is a fascinating visual document of 17th- to 19th-century Ethiopia as seen through the engravings of contemporary European visitors.

Verghese, Abraham *Cutting for Stone* Vintage, 2010. This **fictional** tale of medicine and miracles that moves from Addis Ababa to New York City and back again reads almost like a memoir – perhaps because its author is also a doctor.

Travel accounts

Alvarez, Francisco *Prester John of the Indies: A True Relation of the Lands of Prester John* Cambridge: Published for the Hakluyt Society at the University Press, 1961. The oldest Ethiopian travelogue in existence, written by a Portuguese priest almost 500 years ago, remains a fascinating and often astonishingly insightful read, but it is out of print and very difficult to locate.

Avrahamís, Amhuel *Treacherous Journey* Shapolsky Books, 1986. A different type of travelogue, described by one reader as a 'tremendous adventure story' of a Falasha's escape from persecution under the Derg. It also includes a lot of information about the Bet Israel or Falasha, and the beliefs and values of the people who shelter the author along the way.

Buxton, David *Travels in Ethiopia* Praeger, 1967. Short but interesting document of Ethiopian travels in the immediate post-World War II era, has some interesting black-and-white photographs. Out of print but often available at a price at secondhand bookstalls in Addis Ababa.

Graham, John *Ethiopia off the Beaten Trail* Shama Books, 2001. John Graham is the popular travel correspondent for the *Addis Tribune*, and a contributor to the fourth edition of this Bradt Travel Guide. This first collection of his informative and occasionally irreverent travel essays reflects the author's delight in exploring Ethiopia's less travelled corners.

Henze, Paul *Ethiopian Journeys* Shama Books, 2001. Classic travel account of Ethiopia during the last years of the imperial era, out of print for two decades, is another alluring title in the new Shama Books catalogue.

Kaplan, Robert *Surrender or Starve: Travels in Ethiopia, Sudan, Somalia and Eritrea* Vintage, 2003. This excellent and often rather chilling journalistic travelogue details the political factors that hugely exacerbated drought-related famines in the Horn of Africa during the 1980s.

Marsden, Philip *The Chains of Heaven: An Ethiopian Romance* HarperCollins, 2006. A follow-up to *A Far Country* below. Marsden first visits a war-torn Ethiopia in 1982, then returns 12 years later to experience more of the country he fell in love with.

Marsden-Smedley, Philip *A Far Country* Century, 1990. This is a readable and interesting account of a 1988 trip through Mengistu-era Ethiopia. I can't say that I noticed the author exploring, as the jacket blurb suggests, 'the way that individuals – and whole races – idealise far places and how this prompts dreams of returning'. But the simple fact that he explores Ethiopia, and was the first person to write about doing so in several decades, is good enough reason to read this entertaining book.

Murphy, Dervla *In Ethiopia with a Mule* John Murray, 1969. Recommended travelogue that describes an Ethiopia way away from any tourist trail.

Pakenham, Thomas *The Mountains of Rasselas* Seven Dials, 1999. This is a vivid and well-written account of the author's failed attempt to reach the remote Ethiopian mountaintop where princes were imprisoned in the Gonderine period. Originally published in 1959, it was reissued in a glossy coffee-table format four decades later, complete with photographs taken in 1955 as well as more recent ones.

Rushby, Kevin *Eating the Flowers of Paradise* Flamingo, 1999. A fascinating book about the culture of *chat* consumption, half of which is set in Ethiopia, between Addis and Harar, before crossing the Red Sea from Djibouti to Yemen – as one reader notes 'the book reads a lot better than *chat* tastes!'

Shah, Tahir *In Search of King Solomon's Mines* Arcade Publishing, 2003. Set mainly in Ethiopia, this compulsively readable and highly entertaining book follows the misadventures of a London-based member of the Afghan aristocracy who is led a wild goose chase by – of all things – a map, bought in a Jerusalem market, that purportedly shows the route to King Solomon's mines!

Stewart, Julia *Eccentric Graces: Eritrea and Ethiopia through the Eyes of a Traveller* Red Sea Press, 1998. This modern travelogue about Ethiopia, based on travels shortly before the two countries declared war on each other, this readable book seems to fall into the 'love it or hate it' category, but is nevertheless a good introduction to travelling through Ethiopia today.

Thesiger, Wilfred *The Life of My Choice* HarperCollins, 1987. This includes childhood reminiscences of growing up in Abyssinia, Haile Selassie's coronation, the liberation campaign in 1941, treks in the south of the country, plus a vivid account of a six-month journey through the Danakil in 1933. Recommended, along with the same author's *Danakil Diaries*, particularly if you are heading into the eastern deserts.

Waugh, Evelyn *Remote People* Penguin, 1931. Witty travelogue detailing parts of Haile Selassie's coronation, plus travels in Djibouti and an account of the railway to Awash.

Waugh, Evelyn *When the Going was Good* Greenwood Press Reprint, 1976. One of several Waugh books that refer to his Abyssinian sojourn, this is recommended by Dr Ann Waters-Bayer for 'including some interesting accounts of his travels in Ethiopia'.

History and background

Beyene, T, Pankhurst, R and Bekele, S *Kasa and Kasa: Papers on the Lives, Times and Images of Tewodros II and Yohannis IV (1855–1889)* Institute of Ethiopian Studies, 1990. Exactly why Ethiopia survived into the 20th century as an independent state is a question open to some debate. It is certainly linked to the mid to late 19th-century rise of three successive emperors of unifying vision, two of whose careers are covered in this excellent collection of essays.

Bredin, Niles *The Pale Abyssinian* Flamingo, 2001. This highly readable biography of the explorer James Bruce is a good accompaniment to a trip in the north of the country.

Buxton, David *The Abyssinians* Thames & Hudson, 1970. A number of people have recommended this as a good general introduction to just about every aspect of Ethiopian history and culture. It's a bit dated, but well worth reading if you can locate a copy.

Getachew, Indrias *Beyond the Throne: The Enduring Legacy of Emperor Haile Selassie I* Shama Books, 2001. Edited by Richard Pankhurst, with a foreword by Harold Marcus, and endorsed by the royal family, this well-written and lavishly illustrated overview of Ethiopia's last emperor, with several never-before-seen photographs, is the first in a series of three related titles about Haile Selassie.

Giday, Belai *Ethiopian Civilisation* Giday, 1991. Cheap and widely available in Ethiopia, this book essentially consists of unqualified legend posing as history. I have no problem with the legendary aspect, but the author should clarify that modern historians dismiss much of it as myth. (In fact, instead of merely recounting legends dressed as fact, it would be rather nice to see an Ethiopian who apparently knows his/her stuff convince us of the truth behind the legends.)

Gill, Peter *Famine and Foreigners: Ethiopia since Live Aid* Oxford University Press, 2010. The 1986 Ethiopian famine left an indelible imprint in the minds of people the world over. Gill, who wrote the definitive account of the disaster, *A Year in the Death of Africa,* returns to Ethiopia to investigate the real story of the last 25 years.

Hailemelekot, Abebe *The Victory of Adowa* Abebe Hailemelekot, 1998. This is a workmanlike overview of the proudest moment in modern Ethiopian history, well worth the birr 30 it costs in shops in Addis Ababa.

Henze, Paul *Eritrea's War* Shama Books, 2001. Written by the former diplomat and recognised expert on Ethiopian politics, this should be of great interest to travellers wishing to get to grips with the circumstances surrounding the recently ended border war between Ethiopia and Eritrea.

Henze, Paul *Layers of Time: A History of Ethiopia* Hurst, 2000. Probably the most approachable one-volume introductory history in print, this includes a useful overview of ancient and medieval Ethiopia, but is particularly good on modern history up to the fall of the Derg. Described by the noted Axumite historian Dr Stuart Munro-Hay as offering 'a well-balanced overview of Ethiopian history from the remotest past to modern times'.

Hibbert, Christopher *Africa Explored: Europeans in the Dark Continent* Penguin, 1982. This readable and interesting overview of the age of European exploration of Africa includes good accounts of Bruce's expedition, as well as Richard Burton's trip to Harar.

Johanson, D and Edey, M *Lucy: The Beginning of Humankind* Simon & Schuster, 1990. The definitive account of the discovery of the legendary hominid fossil dubbed Lucy, as co-written by the acclaimed palaeontologist who led the digs.

Kapuscinski, Richard *The Emperor* Random House, 1983. This impressionistic and strangely compelling account of the last days of Haile Selassie is transcribed from interviews with his servants and confidants, and offers valuable insights into Ethiopia immediately before the 1974 revolution.

Lepage, Claude and Mercier, Jaques *Ethiopian Art: The Ancient Churches of Tigrai* Adpf, 2005. Boasting wonderful photographs, this book provides even more detailed information about the rock-hewn churches described in *Chapter 10* of this guide.

Marcus, Harold *A History of Ethiopia* University of California Press, 1994. In this very readable general history, Marcus summarises all the initiate needs to know over a flowing and erudite 220 pages – a recommended starting point.

Mezlekia, Nega *Notes from the Hyena's Belly: An Ethiopian Boyhood* Picador, 2002. A fascinating account of a boy's life in Jijiga and the coming of the Derg. This account delves into folklore, magic and customs as only a native could.

Moorehead, Alan *The Blue Nile*, 1962. This compulsive introduction to the exploits of James Bruce and the Napier expedition is one of the few books about that little chunk of Africa between Egypt and South Africa that sits on the shelves of most libraries.

Munro-Hay, Stuart *Aksum: An African Civilisation of Late Antiquity* Edinburgh University Press, 1991. This very readable book by a well-known authority on the subject offers a good overview of all aspects of Axumite civilisation.

Pakenham, Thomas *The Scramble for Africa* Jonathan Ball, 1991. One of the most crisp, unsentimental and informative books ever written about African history places Ethiopia's independence in a continental context. It was the winner of the W H Smith Literary Award, and is, in the words of Simon Roberts (*The Natal Witness*) 'Conrad's *Heart of Darkness* with the floodlights switched on'. Its Chapter 27 is as good an account as you'll find of the pivotal events in Ethiopia c1895–97.

Pankhurst, Richard *History of Ethiopian Towns from the Middle Ages to the early 19th Century* Wiesbaden, 1982. This is the first in a two-volume series covering the origin and history of most large towns – and many small ones – in Ethiopia (the second deals with the mid 19th century onwards). It's an invaluable resource that deserves wider circulation.

Pankhurst, Richard *Social History of Ethiopia* Institute of Ethiopian Studies, 1990. This detailed tome covers Ethiopian society between the late medieval period and the rise of Tewodros in the 19th century. Thorough and insightful, it is probably too academic and esoteric for the general reader.

Pankhurst, Richard *The Ethiopian Borderlands* Red Sea Press, 1997. Subtitled *Essays in Regional History from Ancient Times to the End of the 18th Century*, this fascinating book sees Pankhurst, the most prolific writer on Ethiopian historical matters, provide a historical overview to those parts of Ethiopia that are generally ignored in mainstream texts.

Pankhurst, Richard *The Ethiopians (People of Africa)* Blackwell, 2001. This reissued title by the doyen of modern Ethiopian historical writing provides an excellent introduction to Ethiopia's varied cultures and social history.

Phillipson, David *Archaeology at Aksum 1993–7* Society of Antiquities of London, 2001. This long-awaited two-volume work is the first to contextualise the extensive excavations around Axum that have taken place since the fall of the Derg in 1991. At more than US$150 for the two volumes, however, it is aimed at the truly dedicated rather than casual readers.

Phillipson, David *The Monuments of Aksum* Addis Ababa University Press, 1997. The book is essentially an annotated and translated transcript of the original findings of the DAE Axum Expedition of 1906. It remains an excellent introduction to Axum's archaeological wealth, and also contains some great pictures of early 20th-century Axum.

Plant, Ruth *Architecture of the Tigre* Ravens Education & Development Services, 1985. This is the most detailed available work to the remote rock-hewn churches of Tigrai. Hardback copies can be purchased from the author's granddaughter, Jasmine Petty, at a cost of £20+pp (e *jasminepetty@googlemail.com*).

Reader, John *Africa: A Biography of the Continent* Hamish Hamilton, 1997. This award-winning book, available as a Penguin paperback, provides a compulsively readable introduction to Africa's past, from the formation of the continent to post-independence politics – the ideal starting point for anybody seeking to place their Ethiopian experience in a broader African context.

Schofield, Louise *Eyesus Hintsa: An Ethiopian Journey through Landscape and Time* Scanplus, London, 2007. A small book that provides information about the Eyesus Hintsa rock-hewn church and conservation project.

Tibebu, Teshale *The Making of Modern Ethiopia 1896–1974* Red Sea Press, 1995. This book provides an excellent and original overview of modern Ethiopia and its ancient cultural roots. In a sense, it possibly provides a more meaningful and comprehensible introduction to Ethiopia than the straight general histories. Recommended.

Woodhead, Leslie *A Box Full of Spirits: Adventures of a Film-maker in Africa* Heinemann, 1987. An account of Woodhead's experiences making TV documentaries about the Mursi people.

Zewde, Bahru *A History of Modern Ethiopia 1855–1974* James Currey, 1991. Pitched at the general reader as much as the historian, this book is accurate, well written, affordable and generously illustrated – an essential purchase. It is available in most bookshops in Addis Ababa for around US$5.

Health

Wilson-Howarth, Dr Jane *Healthy Travel: Bugs, Bites and Bowels* Cadogan, 2006

Wilson-Howarth, Dr Jane, and Ellis, Dr Matthew *Your Child Abroad: A Travel Health Guide* Bradt Travel Guides, 2005

Art and music

Falceto, Francis *Abyssinie Swing: A Pictorial History of Modern Ethiopian Music* Shama Books, 2001. This monochrome document of the emergence of the (now almost forgotten) jazz-tinged music scene that blossomed in the dying years of the imperial era is utterly irresistible. The photographs, which span the years 1868 to 1973, are consistently evocative, while the text, though more concise than might be hoped for, is as authoritative as one would expect of a book compiled by the editor of the acclaimed *Ethiopiques* CD compilation series. All in all, it's an essential purchase for anybody with more than a passing interest in Ethiopia's rich musical heritage.

Gerster, Georg *Churches in Rock* Phaidon Press, 1970. Superb but long-out-of-print visual document of the Tigraian rock churches, as well as lesser-known architectural gems such as Bethlehem Gaynt, south of Lalibela.

Heldman et al, Marilyn *African Zion: The Sacred Art of Ethiopia* Yale University Press, 1994. Expensive (£40) but beautiful, and written by leading scholars of Ethiopian and Byzantine art, this lavishly illustrated book covers the art of highland Ethiopia from the 4th to the 18th century.

Natural history
Mammals

Estes, Richard *The Safari Companion* Green Books (UK), Russell Friedman Books (SA), Chelsea Green (USA), 1999. This unconventional book might succinctly be described as a field guide to mammal behaviour. It's probably a bit esoteric for most one-off visitors to Africa, but a must for anybody with a serious interest in wildlife.

Kingdon, Jonathan *The Kingdon Field Guide to African Mammals* Academic Press, 1997. The most detailed, thorough and up to date of several titles covering the mammals of the region, this superb book transcends all expectations of a standard field guide. The author, a highly respected biologist, supplements detailed descriptions and good illustrations of all the continent's large mammals with an ecological overview of each species. An essential purchase for anybody with a serious interest in mammal identification – or natural history.

Last, Jill *Endemic Mammals of Ethiopia* Ethiopian Tourist Commission, 1982. This lightweight, slightly dated and very inexpensive booklet includes detailed descriptions of appearance and behaviour for Ethiopia's seven endemic mammal species and races. A worthwhile purchase!

Sillero-Zuburi, C and Macdonald, D *The Ethiopian Wolf: Status Survey and Conservation Action Plan* IUCN, 1997. Although primarily what it claims to be, this important work of reference also includes detailed information about most aspects of Ethiopian wolf ecology.

Stuart, Chris *Mammals of Southern and East Africa* Struik, 2002. This excellent mini guide, compact enough to slip into a pocket, is remarkably thorough within its inherent space restrictions, though Ethiopia's wildlife is less well covered than that of more popular safari destinations.

Birds

Ash, J and Atkins, J *Birds of Ethiopia and Eritrea* Christopher Helm, 2009. Not a field guide but a more specialised hardcover bird atlas that maps the known distribution of a full 872 Ethiopian and Eritrean species across 132 grids, and provides more detailed background information than the field guide when it comes to individual species and to Ethiopian ornithology. Though not aimed at casual birders, it's an invaluable tool and source of data for regular visitors and residents. In addition, the highly detailed maps and text will be an invaluable research resource to anybody trying to maximise a birding itinerary in terms of ticking endemics and other localised species, as well as in assisting with the identification of tricky species.

Behrens, K, Barnes, K and Boix, C *Birding Ethiopia* Lynx, 2010. Another very useful addition to Ethiopian birding literature, this is an ideal complement to a field guide or bird atlas, coming across like a vastly extended and illustrated trip report – the perfect hands-on starting point for anybody planning a birding trip to Ethiopia.

Redman, N, Stevenson, T and Fanshawe, J *Helm Field Guide to the Birds of the Horn of Africa* Christopher Helm, 2009. This is the first dedicated field guide to a vast region dominated by Ethiopia, but that also includes Eritrea, Djibouti, Somalia and Socotra, and as such it can be recommend without reservation as the one book that all birders to Ethiopia absolutely need. Every species present in the region is illustrated across 213 colour plates accompanied by detailed descriptions and distribution maps, and the overall standard is in line with the same publisher's superb *Birds of East Africa*.

Sinclair, I and Ryan, P *Birds of Africa South of the Sahara* Struik Publishers, 2003. The first and only field guide to this vast region covers all 2,100-plus species recorded there in 700-odd pages. The accurate illustrations are supported by reliable text and good distribution maps. Obviously it is not as detailed as the field guide specific to the Horn of Africa, but it remains the second-choice field guide for Ethiopia.

Smith, Steve *Bird Calls of Ethiopia*. This self-published tape of common Ethiopian bird calls can be ordered from the author at 42 Lower Buckland Rd, Lymington, Hampshire SO41 9DL.

Spottiswoode, C, Gabremichael, M and Francis, J *Where to Watch Birds in Ethiopia* Christopher Helm, 2010. An excellent complement to the same publisher's field guide and bird atlas, as listed above, this provides detailed coverage and GPS readings for 50 key birding sites, mostly in southern Ethiopia, along with photographs and descriptions of the country's 'top 50 species'. At 180-odd pages, it is very portable, and it will be especially useful to birders travelling without a specialist local guide.

Tilahun, S, Edwards, S and Egziabher, T *Important Bird Areas of Ethiopia* Ethiopian Wildlife & Natural History Society, 1996. This detailed booklet provides a very detailed overview of Ethiopia's most important birding locales, and is of interest to ecologists and birders alike.

Urban, E and Brown, L *Checklist of the Birds of Ethiopia* Haile Sellassie I University Press, 1971. The best general survey of Ethiopia's avifauna in print until 2009, this was once a must for serious birders. However, it is no substitute for a proper field guide (there are no illustrations for a start), and it is obviously dated with respect to recently described endemics and other newly recorded birds.

Urban, E and Poole, J *Endemic Birds of Ethiopia* Ethiopian Tourist Commission, 1980. Similar to the 'endemic mammals'/Vivero title, this is a useful and inexpensive booklet describing and illustrating the 23 Ethiopian and Eritrean endemics that had been described prior to 1980.

Van Perlo, Ber *Birds of Eastern Africa* Collins, 1995, 2nd edition 2009. Van Perlo's guide was until recently the only book to illustrate and show distribution details of all Ethiopian species. It has since been superseded by two vastly superior field guides, those listed above by Sinclair & Ryan and Redman, Stevenson & Fanshawe, though it does have the advantage of being a lot lighter than either of them.

Vivero, Jose *The Endemic Birds of Ethiopia and Eritrea* Shama Books, 2001. This recently published pocketbook provides the most detailed and up-to-date coverage yet of the 30-plus bird species endemic to Ethiopia and Eritrea, making it an excellent supplement to a standard field guide – though note that several recently recognised species, such as the Ethiopian cisticola, are excluded.

Others

Kingdon, Jonathan *Island Africa* Collins, 1990. This highly readable and award-winning tome about evolution in ecological 'islands' such as deserts and montane forests is recommended to anybody who wants to place the high level of endemism noted in the Ethiopian Highlands in a broader continental context.

Nievergelt, B, Good, T and Guttinger, R *A Survey on the Flora and Fauna of the Simien Mountains National Park* Walia, 1998. This massively detailed and attractively illustrated 100-page book will be of great interest to any wildlife or plant lover visiting the Simien Mountains.

WEBSITES

www.abyssiniacybergateway.net Good search engine and plenty of historical links.

www.addisconnexion.com An informative site about what's new in the capital.

www.bestethiopia.com Information about Ethiopian tourism.

www.cyberethiopia.com News, chat lines and useful links.

www.ethioembassy.org.uk Informative not only regarding pre-visit paperwork, but also current affairs. Online articles by the likes of Paul Henze.

www.ethiopianairlines.com Booking site for Ethiopian Airlines.

www.ethiopianhotelsguide.com Ethiopian online hotel search and booking portal.

www.ethiopians.com/Books_On_Ethiopia.htm An excellent list of children's books about Ethiopia. *Fire on the Mountain* by Jane Kurtz and *The Perfect Orange* by Frank P Araujo are personal favourites.

www.ethiopica.org A Spanish-language site with a lot of useful information and essays about Ethiopia, Eritrea, Yemen and Somalia.

www.safarilink.com Safari link is an impartial African information resource which can be useful when planning holidays to Africa.

Bradt Travel Guides

Africa

Access Africa: Safaris for People with Limited Mobility	£16.99
Africa Overland	£16.99
Algeria	£15.99
Angola	£17.99
Botswana	£16.99
Burkina Faso	£17.99
Cameroon	£15.99
Cape Verde	£15.99
Congo	£16.99
Eritrea	£15.99
Ethiopia	£17.99
Ethiopia Highlights	£15.99
Ghana	£15.99
Kenya Highlights	£15.99
Madagascar	£16.99
Madagascar Highlights	£15.99
Malawi	£15.99
Mali	£14.99
Mauritius, Rodrigues & Réunion	£15.99
Mozambique	£15.99
Namibia	£15.99
Niger	£14.99
Nigeria	£17.99
North Africa: Roman Coast	£15.99
Rwanda	£15.99
São Tomé & Príncipe	£14.99
Seychelles	£16.99
Sierra Leone	£16.99
Somaliland	£15.99
South Africa Highlights	£15.99
Sudan	£15.99
Tanzania, Northern	£14.99
Tanzania	£17.99
Uganda	£16.99
Zambia	£18.99
Zanzibar	£14.99
Zimbabwe	£15.99

The Americas and the Caribbean

Alaska	£15.99
Amazon Highlights	£15.99
Argentina	£16.99
Bahia	£14.99
Cayman Islands	£14.99
Chile Highlights	£15.99
Colombia	£17.99
Dominica	£15.99
Grenada, Carriacou & Petite Martinique	£15.99
Guyana	£15.99
Nova Scotia	£14.99
Panama	£14.99
Paraguay	£15.99
Turks & Caicos Islands	£14.99
Uruguay	£15.99
USA by Rail	£15.99
Venezuela	£16.99
Yukon	£14.99

British Isles

Britain from the Rails	£14.99
Bus-Pass Britain	£15.99
Eccentric Britain	£15.99
Eccentric Cambridge	£9.99
Eccentric London	£14.99
Eccentric Oxford	£9.99
Sacred Britain	£16.99
Slow: Cornwall	£14.99
Slow: Cotswolds	£14.99
Slow: Devon & Exmoor	£14.99
Slow: Dorset	£14.99
Slow: Norfolk & Suffolk	£14.99
Slow: Northumberland	£14.99
Slow: North Yorkshire	£14.99
Slow: Sussex & South Downs National Park	£14.99

Europe

Abruzzo	£14.99
Albania	£16.99
Armenia	£16.99
Azores	£14.99
Baltic Cities	£14.99
Belarus	£15.99
Bosnia & Herzegovina	£14.99
Bratislava	£9.99
Budapest	£9.99
Croatia	£13.99
Cross-Channel France: Nord-Pas de Calais	£13.99
Cyprus see North Cyprus	
Dresden	£7.99
Estonia	£14.99
Faroe Islands	£15.99
Flanders	£15.99
Georgia	£15.99
Greece: The Peloponnese	£14.99
Helsinki	£7.99
Hungary	£15.99
Iceland	£15.99
Kosovo	£15.99
Lapland	£15.99
Lille	£9.99
Lithuania	£14.99
Luxembourg	£14.99
Macedonia	£16.99
Malta & Gozo	£12.99
Montenegro	£14.99
North Cyprus	£13.99
Serbia	£15.99
Slovakia	£14.99
Slovenia	£13.99
Spitsbergen	£16.99
Switzerland Without a Car	£14.99
Transylvania	£14.99
Ukraine	£15.99

Middle East, Asia and Australasia

Bangladesh	£17.99
Borneo	£17.99
Eastern Turkey	£16.99
Iran	£15.99
Iraq: Then & Now	£15.99
Israel	£15.99
Jordan	£16.99
Kazakhstan	£16.99
Kyrgyzstan	£16.99
Lake Baikal	£15.99
Lebanon	£15.99
Maldives	£15.99
Mongolia	£16.99
North Korea	£14.99
Oman	£15.99
Palestine	£15.99
Shangri-La: A Travel Guide to the Himalayan Dream	£14.99
Sri Lanka	£15.99
Syria	£15.99
Taiwan	£16.99
Tibet	£17.99
Yemen	£14.99

Wildlife

Antarctica: A Guide to the Wildlife	£15.99
Arctic: A Guide to Coastal Wildlife	£16.99
Australian Wildlife	£14.99
Central & Eastern European Wildlife	£15.99
Chinese Wildlife	£16.99
East African Wildlife	£19.99
Galápagos Wildlife	£16.99
Madagascar Wildlife	£16.99
New Zealand Wildlife	£14.99
North Atlantic Wildlife	£16.99
Pantanal Wildlife	£16.99
Peruvian Wildlife	£15.99
Southern African Wildlife	£19.99
Sri Lankan Wildlife	£15.99

Pictorials and other guides

100 Alien Invaders	£16.99
100 Animals to See Before They Die	£16.99
100 Bizarre Animals	£16.99
Eccentric Australia	£12.99
Northern Lights	£6.99
Swimming with Dolphins, Tracking Gorillas	£15.99
Through the Northwest Passage	£17.99
Tips on Tipping	£6.99
Total Solar Eclipse 2012 & 2013	£6.99
Wildlife and Conservation Volunteering: The Complete Guide	£13.99
Your Child Abroad	£10.95

Travel literature

Fakirs, Feluccas and Femmes Fatales	£9.99
The Marsh Lions	£9.99
Two Year Mountain	£9.99
Up the Creek	£9.99

Index

Entries in **bold** indicate main entries; those in *italics* indicate maps

INDEX OF ADVERTISERS